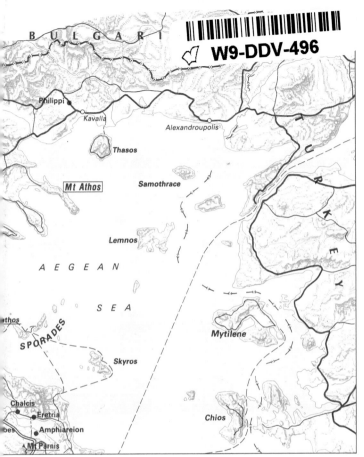

B U L G A R I

W9-DDV-496

Philippi
Kavalla
Alexandroupolis
Thasos
Mt Athos
Samothrace
Lemnos
A E G E A N
S E A
thos
SPORADES
Skyros
Mytilene
Chalcis
Eretria
bes
Amphiareion
Mt Parnis
Chios

see Key under map 2 (back endpaper)

Metsovon
Mytilene (Island of)
Nekromanteion
Nikopolis
Pella
Philippi
Samothrace (Island of)
Skyros (Island of)
Thasos (Island of)
Tempe (Vale of)
Thebes
Vergina

Greece

Guide Bleu

Greece

PRENTICE HALL

NEW YORK

Published by Prentice Hall Trade Division
A division of Simon & Schuster Inc.
1 Gulf + Western Plaza
New York, New York 10023

Originally published in France by Hachette Guides Bleus 1984
Copyright © 1984 by Hachette Guides Bleus

Maps © Hachette and ITC 1989

English translation copyright © Harrap 1989

Published in Great Britain by Harrap 1989

First American Edition 1989

U.S. Editorial Consultant: Maxwell Vos

Production by Book Production Consultants Ltd, Cambridge, UK

Phototypeset by Witwell Ltd, Southport, UK

Printed and bound in UK by Richard Clay & Co., Bungay, Suffolk.

While every care has been taken in the compilation of this guide, the
publishers cannot be held responsible for any changes to the
information listed.

Library of Congress Cataloguing-in-Publication Data

Boulanger, Robert, 1926-
  Greece.

  (Les Guides bleus)
  Translation of: Grèce.
  Bibliography: p. 976
  Includes index.
    1. Greece—Description and travel—1981— —
Guide-books. I. Title. II. Series.
DF716.B.6813   1989   914.95′0476   86–542
ISBN 0-13-364985-7

Preface

Greece officially joined the Common Market on 1 January 1981. This association, so eagerly awaited by the Greek people, could be seen as a new symbol of the spiritual, cultural and emotional bonds linking Europe and a land where civilization was born. Towards the end of 1981 a major political change, which had a marked effect on the daily lives of the Greek people, showed that democracy was still alive in the country where it originated. Both these events go to prove that Greece, the outpost of Europe at the gateway to the East, is today a dynamic country which is constantly developing and changing.

Travel to Greece, for many generations the seat of classical culture and pinnacle of the humanities, is now also changing. Greek history and art are still popular, increasingly so as more becomes known about the past. But a growing number of visitors are drawn nowadays to Greece by the abundance of sun and sea, the unspoilt countryside and friendly people.

Apart from those obvious tourist attractions, there is within most Westerners a natural affinity for Greece. In addition to membership within the European Community, evidence of these links can be seen in the international effort for the preservation of the Acropolis against depredation.

The *Guide Bleu* would like you to get to know the living Greece, the country confronted by today's realities and displaying great skill in handling them, as well as the Greece faithful to her past, her history and especially to her traditions of hospitality. To that end, this new edition has been brought up to date with archaeological and travel information, organized for ease of use. You will find a section on Useful Information, including hotel guidance, at the back of the book, in alphabetical order according to place name. Practical information for your journey is at the beginning of this book, followed by introductory essays on different aspects of Greece's history, geography and culture. This Guide aims to be of practical help and a convenient companion throughout your discovery of Greece.

Contents

Preface   5
Maps and Plans   10
How to use this guide   12
Key to symbols   14
Abbreviations   15

Travel in Greece

Your Journey   19
When to go?   19

How to get there   19

Some formalities (19). Travel by air (20). Travel by ship (21).
Travel by train (21). Travel by car (22). Travel by bus (22).
Organized travel (22).

Travelling in Greece   23
Greece by plane (23). Greece by boat (24).Greece by train
(24). Greece by bus or coach (24). Greece by car (25).

Your Stay   27
Accommodation   27
Hotels. Youth hostels. Camping. Private houses. Beaches
and coastal resorts. Thermal spas.

Dining out   28
Restaurants. Greek cuisine. Drinks. Greek coffee.

Daily life in Greece 29
  Your budget. Newspapers. Theatre, festivals, concerts (29).
  Religious festivals. Sport and leisure. Night-clubs and
  discotheques. Photography (30). Guides. Opening hours
  for museums and archaeological sites. Life according to
  Greek time (31). Shopping. Postal and telephone services
  (32).

  Further information 32

Some Notes on Language and Vocabulary 33

Some Useful Words and Phrases 37

Tourist Greece 49

What to see? 49
The islands 49

Suggested tours 52

  Some standard tours. Supplementary journey in Crete.
  Island cruises.

Route Maps 57

  1. BITOLA-LARISA-LAMIA 58
  2. EVZONI-LARISA-LAMIA 60
  3. LAMIA-ATHENS 62
  4. ANDIRRHION-DELPHI-THEBES 64
  5. PATRAS-CORINTH-ATHENS 66
  6. CORINTH-SPARTA-AREOPOLIS 68
  7. PYRGOS-TRIPOLIS-NAUPLIA 70
  8. TRIPOLIS-KALAMATA-PYLOS 72
  9. PATRAS-PYRGOS-PYLOS 74
10. IGOUMENITSA-ANDIRRHION 76
11. IGOUMENITSA-VOLOS 78
12. THESSALONIKI-KALAMBAKA 80
13. KASTORIA-THESSALONIKI 82
14. THESSALONIKI-ALEXANDROUPOLIS 84
15. FLORINA-IOANNINA-ARTA 86
16. KHANIA-HERAKLEION-SITA 88

Table of Distances between the Main Towns 90

Understanding Greece 91
The Geography of Greece 93

A Glance at History, by *P. Lévêque*   100
Aspects of Ancient Greece   122
Byzantine Greece, by *A. Ducellier*   135
Art in Ancient Greece, by *P. Lévêque*   149
The Archaeological Adventure, by *R. Ginouvès*   164
Some Notes on Architecture   174

Discover Greece   179
Alphabetical Guide   181
A Guide to Greek Mythology   877
Glossary   885

Useful Information Index   891
Tourist and hotel symbols   892

Maps and Plans

(*see also Route Maps pp 58–89*)

Maps

Attica	327
Chios	362
Corfu	374–5
Crete (Western part)	416
Crete (Eastern part)	418
Meteora (Monasteries of the)	639
Mykonos	662
Mytilene	664
Rhodes	757
Mount Athos	346
Thera (Santorini)	826
Thermopylae (Pass of the)	829
What to see in Greece	50–1

Plans

Aegina: Temple of Aphaia	180
Amphiaraos (Sanctuary of)	338
Argos	203
Heraion of Argos	209
Asclepius (Sanctuary of)	560–1
Athens I: general plan	222–3
Athens II: Syndagma	224–5
Athens III: Omonia	226–7
Athens IV: Acropolis	242–3
Athens: Agora	284–5
Athens: Kerameikos Cemetery and Dipylon Gate	298
Athens: National Museum	306
Corfu	368
Corinth: Agora	384–5
Cos: Asclepieion	404

Daphni (Church of) 489
Delos 496-7
Delphi: general plan 518
Delphi: Temenos of Apollo 522-3
Eleusis (Sanctuary of) 548-9
Epidaurus: Sanctuary of Asclepius 560-1
Gortyn 467
Gournia 481
Hagia Triada (Palace of) 476
Herakleion (Candia) 428
Hosios Loukas (Church of) 580
Kato Zakros (Palace of) 483
Knossos (Palace of, ground floor) 454-5
Knossos (Palace of, west wing) 459
Lerna 614
Mallia (Palace of) 450
Messene 636
Mistra 648-9
Mount Athos 346
Mycenae: Acropolis 655
Olympia 690-1
Phaestos (Palace of) 470-1
Philippi 720
Piraeus 726
Pylos (Palace of Nestor) 736
Rhodes I: general plan 742-3
Rhodes II: Walled city and Collachium 748-9
Saint Demetrius (Church of) 837
Samothrace: Sanctuary of the Great Gods 777
Sparta 793
Thasos I: general plan 804
Thasos II: Agora 806
Thessaloniki 838-9
Tiryns 854
Tylissos (Villa of) 444

Illustrations

Athens: Reconstruction of the Acropolis 248
Olympia: Pediments of Olympia 704
The Three Classical Orders 175

Colour maps and plans

Northern Greece   Inside front cover
Southern Greece   Inside back cover

How to use this guide

The guide is divided into four parts:
Travel in Greece

All general practical information to prepare for and plan your trip. The section is divided up into several chapters:

YOUR JOURNEY - the best times to go to Greece, the formalities involved, how to get there, what packages are available, travel in Greece (pp. 19-26);

YOUR STAY IN GREECE - everything you need to know about accommodation, restaurants, Greek food, everyday life in Greece (currency, shopping, opening times, etc.) as well as a glossary of useful Greek phrases (pp. 27-48);

THE TOURIST'S GREECE - will help you plan your holiday with the help of a map 'What to See in Greece', suggested tours and 16 route maps with descriptions (pp. 49-90).

Understanding Greece

You will find on pp. 91 to 178 a series of introductions to various aspects of Greek civilization, both ancient and modern: Greece's history, geography, art, archaeology.

Discover Greece

This alphabetical section, from pp. 179 to 876, describes towns, sites and monuments. In addition, a helpful Glossary of specialized terms can be found on p.885-9 and a guide to Greek Mythology on p.877-84.

Useful Information Index

To locate a place name, choose a hotel or restaurant, obtain the address or telephone number of a tourist agency or discover the main events and festivities where you are staying, turn to this alphabetical list of places referred to in the guide section (pp. 891-973).

Classification of places and items of interest:
Sites, buildings, museums, works of art, documents.

These are classified according to two criteria:

– Their place in a 'hierarchy of merit', drawn up as objectively as possible:

*noteworthy	***of exceptional interest
**of great interest	☆remarkable, unusual, of special interest

– The location, by means of symbols, of the most important places and items of interest along each route.

Symbols

A list of the symbols to be found in the margin of the text follows. The same ones are used in all the *Guides Bleus*, though they do not all necessarily appear in this particular book.

They are extremely simple in design and are mostly commonly understood symbols. They will enable the reader to locate at a glance the places and items of interest along any route or in any district. They can also help in planning stops or excursions to the places or buildings of the greatest interest.

14 KEY TO SYMBOLS

⟨ Panorama, viewpoint

☼ Site or building in exceptional setting

👁 Unusual sight or feature

▮ Place of great historic interest

🏰 Castle, fortification, ramparts

∴ Ruin, archaeological site

▢ Civic building of interest

▣ Museum

◯ Work of art or document of such exceptional interest that it alone makes the museum or building worth visiting

🖊 Literary information or anecdote

♪ Musical information or anecdote

✝ Church, abbey

⊥ Wayside cross

☿ Islamic mosque or monument

🜨 Hindu monuments and shrines

◉ Buddhist monuments and shrines

🈁 Shinto monuments and shrines

👪 Periodic gatherings, e.g. markets, religious and folk events

🔬 Arts and crafts

⛲ Thermal spring

≋ Seaside resort, beach

🌲 Forest, park, wooded area

👢 Walk

🏔 Recommended mountain excursion

🎿 Winter sports resort

🦢 Zoological gardens, nature reserve

🐟 Fishing

🐆 Hunting

🌴 Palm grove, oasis

Abbreviations

alt.	altitude	**km**	kilometre
approx.	approximately	**kWh**	kilowatt-hour
arch.	architect	**l.**	left
Ave	avenue	**m**	metre/s
Bd	boulevard	**mls**	miles
bldg	building	**mm**	millimetres
c.	circa/century	**mins**	minutes
cm	centimetre	**Mt**	Mount
cuis.	cuisine	**N**	north
d.	died	**p./pp.**	page/s
E	east	**Pl.**	place
ELPA	Automobile Touring	**pop.**	population
	Club of Greece	**r.**	right
ft	feet	**rm/s**	room/s
GNTO	Greek National Tourist	**S**	south
	Office	**sq. (ml/ft)**	square (mile/foot)
h.	hour/s	**t**	ton
ha	hectare/s	**Tel.**	telephone
hab.	inhabitants	**V**	see
HNTO	Hellenic National	**vol.**	volume
	Tourist Office	**W**	west
in	inch/es	**yd/s**	yards/s
it.	itinerary		
kg	kilograms		

Travel in Greece

Your Journey

When to go?

May or June are definitely the best months to go to Greece; if you are tempted by sea bathing, we suggest September. At those times you will not be overwhelmed by the heat, especially not in May, and you will not have any problems with accommodation, except in Athens where the shortage is almost permanent (for those imprudent souls who have not booked!).

Alternatively, travel in summer: Greece's tourist season is at its height as the dry atmosphere makes the heat tolerable; sea breezes relieve the heat along the coasts and may even call for slightly warmer clothes.

Are you looking for culture, theatre or music as well as the pleasures of travel? In that case, consider going to the Athens Festival, the Festival of Epidaurus, or some of the many other summer events. The Hellenic National Tourist Office (HNTO) will supply program information and a calendar of events.

Consider also the possibility of winter travel: Athens, Corfu and Rhodes especially can escape the rigors of winter, but beware of cold spells which sometimes strike even the eastern Mediterranean and Aegean regions. Worth knowing: you can get considerable reductions on the usual hotel charges in some establishments (20 to 30% depending on the month and the hotel) at that time of year.

How to get there
Some formalities

TRAVEL DOCUMENTS. You will need a passport; for British nationals, a British Visitor's Passport will suffice. Visas are unnecessary for a stay of less than two months in the case of US nationals or less than three months in the case of European or British travellers. For longer stays, contact the Tourist Information office at 9 Chalcocondili Street, Athens (Tel. 362-83-01) 2 Amerikis Street, Athens (Tel. 322-31-11), or 37 Vas. Konstantinou Street, Piraeus (Tel. 417-40-23).

INTERNATIONAL DRIVING PERMIT. This is essential if you plan to drive to Greece via any of the Common Market countries. You will be able to obtain this in your own country or on arrival at the Greek frontier from the Automobile Touring Club of Greece (ELPA) — you will need a passport photo and around 500 drachmas. If you are travelling in your own car, you will need a 'green card' — make sure the insurance is valid in Greece.

INOCULATIONS. None is currently required by law for entry into Greece, but regulations may change.

CUSTOMS. Regulations are not too strict, unless you attempt to export a second Venus de Milo or some lesser antiquity; if, however, that is your intention, you should expect fairly stringent restrictions on the export of works of art (for information, contact the antiques dealers' section of the Archaeology Service at 13 Polygnotou Street, Athens; they will fix an export tax of up to 50% of the declared value).

Customs Information Office: 53–55 Hagiou Konstantinou Street, Athens (Tel. 5249–338).

DUTY FREE ALLOWANCES for personal effects, alcohol, cigarettes, movie-cameras, photographic equipment, etc., for travellers arriving from an EEC country are the same as for most of Western Europe; slightly less if you are coming from other countries.

CARS, CARAVANS AND TRAILERS are admitted for four months by simply having a description entered on the owner's or the driver's passport.

A GREEN CARD is essential if you drive to Greece (otherwise you are liable to insurance coverage when you enter the country).

CURRENCY. Check at your bank on your country's restrictions for currency export, whether in the form of travellers' cheques, letters of credit or bank notes, at least one week before departure (especially during the summer season). You are allowed to import into or export out of Greece, only 1,500 drachmas in cash. There is no restriction on travellers' cheques. Credit cards are becoming generally accepted in Greece, especially VISA.

PETS. Your dog or cat will require a rabies inoculation certificate issued by a veterinary authority testifying that inoculation took place less than a year prior to arrival in Greece. You pet will not be greatly appreciated in Greece! If you're a resident of the UK, it will be quarantined for 6 months on your return.

Travel by air

From the United States – Olympic Airways (the Greek national carrier) operate a daily direct service between New York and Athens (about 9hrs flight). TWA also operate this route but with one stop on the way.

You may save a lot by looking into the possibilities of choosing a package fare or even of travelling to London and booking further from there.

From the United Kingdom – Services to Athens, Thessaloniki and Corfu are operated by Olympic Airways and British Airways (3hrs to 3½hrs flights).

APEX and charter flights as well as many package tours are available at economic rates. Enquire at your local travel agency.

In Athens you will land at Hellenikon airport (West Hellenikon if you travel by Olympic Airways; East, for other companies and charter flights).

Travel by ship

From Italy – Numerous services operate from Adriatic ports, allowing for seasonal variations:

– from Venice, to Piraeus and Rhodes by the Adriatica Line;

– from Ancona, to Corfu (Karageorgis Lines, Med Sun Lines), to Igoumenitsa (Strintzis Lines, Minoan Lines), Patras (DFDS, Karageorgis, Strintzis and Minoan Lines), Piraeus (Med Sun Lines, Turkish Maritime), Herakleion (DFDS) and Rhodes (Med Sun Lines);

– from Bari, to Corfu and Igoumenitsa (Prekookeanska), Patras (Rotability Line);

– from Brindisi, to Corfu and Igoumenitsa (Adriatica, Hellenic Med., Fragoudakis, Libra Maritime, Strintzis Lines), Corfu and Patras (Adriatica, Ionian Lines, Hellenic Med., Fragoudakis, Libra Maritime and Strintzis), Piraeus (Stability Lines, Sol Maritime) and Herakleion (Stability Lines);

– from Otranto, to Corfu and Igoumenitsa (Rotability Lines).

From France – Cruises starting from Toulon (Paquet), from Nice or Cannes (Chandris) will take you as far as Greece.

From the United States – A fly/sail combination (fly in one direction, sail in the other) can be arranged through *Freighter Travel*, 201 East 77 Street, New York, NY 10021 or *Pearl's Freighter Trips*, 175 Great Neck Rd, New York 487-8351.

Cunard's QE2 still offers first- and tourist-class accommodation on regular crossings to Europe.

For travel around the Mediterranean there are also sea links between Greece and Israel (Stability Lines, Lesvos Maritime, Sol Maritime) or Libya (GNMTC), Syria (Sol Maritime, GNMTC), or Turkey (Turkish Maritime).

Anyone wishing to enter Greece by yacht or other pleasure boat should find out from the HNTO what formalities are necessary and which ports can be used.

Travel by train

The main train connections to Greece are from Germany and Italy, by the Hellas Express (Dortmund to Thessaloniki and Athens), Akropolis Express (Munich to Thessaloniki and Athens), Venezia Express (Venice to Athens).

Athens and Thessaloniki can also be reached by a daily service from Paris (Gare de Lyon). Twice a week there is a direct train with sleeping cars for 1st-class passengers.

Travel by car

Athens is 1,915mls (3064km) from Paris via the Italian route; Mâcon, Annemasse, Mont-Blanc tunnel, Milan, Trieste, Ljubljana, Zagreb, Belgrade, Skopje. This is the fastest route, as well as the easiest, with excellent motorways and main roads through Italy and Yugoslavia.

If you take the route through Germany and Austria, you will reach Athens (1,901mls/3,060km from Paris) via Strasbourg, Munich, Salzburg, Badgastein, Villach, Ljubljana, Zagreb, Belgrade and Skopje, most of the way on motorways.

Travel by bus

This is the cheapest, but also the longest way to get to Athens.

From London, during the summer months, there are several direct services to Athens: Europabus, weekly from Victoria Coach Station, travelling via Austria; Euroways, travelling via Italy.

Organized travel

You will find that travel agents offer holidays of all types in Greece, ranging from those devoted mainly to gaining a suntan to highly specialized cultural tours. The best arrangement giving you both security and freedom is one which provides the travel arrangements and accommodation (plane + car + hotel); this guarantees, for an all-inclusive price which is considerably lower than the sum total of the individual prices, travel to Greece, hotel accommodation and the rental of a car, usually with unlimited mileage, and you pay only for your petrol. Under an 'à la carte' system you choose your hotel category (with half-board) and decide on your excursions, or else you choose to be completely independent with no pre-paid hotel expenses. Even under this arrangement you will still have the option of spending some time at a seaside resort, or in a town or holiday village, etc.

On a package tour, you can either choose to stay in one place, or follow an organized itinerary or combine the two.

In addition to the cultural holidays and lecture tours you will find that most travel agents offer package holidays. If you need advice on a reputable tour operator, contact the American Society of Travel Agents, 711 Fifth Avenue, New York, NY 10022, or the Association of British Travel Agents, 55 Newman Street, London W1.

For further information, write to the Greek National Tourist Organization (GNTO): **in the United States**: Olympic Tower, 645 Fifth Avenue, New York, NY 10022; 611 W. Sixth St, Los Angeles, Calif. 90017; 168 N. Michigan Avenue, Chicago, Ill. 60601; **in Great Britain**: 195 Regent St, London W1R 8DR.

Travelling in Greece

A comprehensive network of bus routes enables you to go almost anywhere; some railway routes will be useful to you, particularly those between Athens and Thessaloniki, and Athens and Patras. There is a relatively cheap air service which is invaluable for reaching the islands, and numerous boats, both large and small, can take you to almost all the islands. These methods of travel will likely be of most interest to you in Greece, particularly since the prices for boat and bus travel are so reasonable. You can travel between some towns and especially between certain villages and towns by shared taxis identified by the word ΑΓΟΡΑΙΟΝ (i.e. *Agoraion*) – reasonably priced. Personal taxis are obtainable at fairly reasonable rates within towns.

Greece by plane

INTERNAL AIR LINKS. The network of air routes has as its central point the Olympic Airways West Hellenikon airport at Athens, but this situation is changing gradually with the development of tourism. Cross-routes are still quite rare, and it is regrettable that there are not more flights linking the islands, especially those in the NE Aegean (Lemnos, Mytilene, Chios, Samos). The national air company, Olympic Airways, holds the monopoly of internal air traffic. For information write to the main office at 96 Syngrou Avenue, Athens (Tel. 929-22-51), 6 Othonos Street (Tel. 929-24-44) or call the Hilton Hotel (Tel. 929-24-45).

From Athens you can take a plane to the following towns and islands (some routes are reliable only in summer): Aktion (Preveza), Alexandroupolis, Khania, Chios, Corfu, Cos, Herakleion, Ioannina, Kalamata, Kastoria, Kavalla, Karlovassi (via Samos), Komotini, Kozani, Larisa, Lemnos, Mykonos, Mytilene, Zakinthos (Zante), Rhodes, Samos, Skiathos, Thera (Santorini), Thessaloniki.

Destinations from Rhodes: Cos, Herakleion, Karpathos.

From Thessaloniki: Lemnos.

In Athens the Olympic Airways buses run every 30 mins from the terminal at 96 Syngrou Avenue to Hellenikon airport (West airport, Olympic Airways only).

PLANE HIRE. With or without a pilot (on certain types of plane only), from Olympic Air Taxi, a branch of Olympic Airways; information from Hellenikon airport (Tel. 981-35-65).

Greece by boat

SEA LINKS. Numerous companies down to the very smallest offer sea transport; their only asset might be a single caïque which plies between a couple of islands not otherwise served, providing a regular and reliable service. The port of Piraeus is the centre of a vast amount of Greek sea traffic. Timetables are generally adhered to, but can vary from one year to the next and from season to season. You can obtain information on sailings from travel agents, shipping companies or from the Port of Piraeus (Tel. 451-13-11); but if you want a more complete overall picture of the possibilities open to you, you can buy the *Key Travel Guide* (from 6 Kriezotou Street, Athens), containing all the shipping information you may require. There is a car ferry service between many of the islands. Warning: advance bookings cannot be made and tickets are issued by different offices depending on boats and destinations.

CROSSINGS. We do not intend to cover in detail here sea crossings from Greece to other countries, but from May to October there are many possibilities using Piraeus as your starting point: whole-day crossings to the islands in the Saronic Gulf (leaving from the smaller Zea harbor), three- or four-day tours of the Cycladic islands or whole-week trips in the Eastern Mediterranean. Wherever you wish to go it is advisable to make reservations before you leave your own country.

BOAT HIRE. Yachts or any other type of boat with or without crew are normally chartered privately or through Greek charter companies.

The National Hellenic Tourist Office will send you a list of these companies and the terms under which they operate, as will the Association of Agents for the Hire of Boats and Yachts, 62 Akti Koumoundourou, Mikrolimano, Piraeus (Tel. 412-36-74).

Greece by train

RAIL CONNECTIONS. The railway system has been reorganized to remain competitive with the roads, and certain routes are worth using. The rail networks are now combined in the Greek Railway Organization (OSE), 1-3 Karolou Street, Athens (Tel. 522-24-91). Second-class fares are slightly lower than those on the inter-city buses. You can buy a travel voucher for 10, 20 or 30 days, valid for an unlimited number of journeys or miles. There are two stations in Athens: Larisa station (Tel. 821-38-82) for the northern routes, and the Peloponnese station (Tel. 513-16-01). Note that return tickets are 20% cheaper than two single tickets.

Greece by bus or coach

INTER-CITY BUSES. Most towns of any size have a bus station (there are several in Athens — see Useful Information on Athens). The bus network is particularly comprehensive compared to the railways. if only because the railways do not extend to certain regions. One of the advantages of taking buses is that it enables you to enter into the everyday life of the Greek people, who use them a great deal. Fares are very reasonable.

EXCURSIONS FROM ATHENS. Some Athenian travel agents such as *CHAT Tours, Key Tours, ABC, Hellenic Express*, etc., offer excursions (one to three days) from the capital, in air-conditioned coaches, to the main sites in Attica, to Corinth, Nauplia and Mycenae, and Delphi. Some even offer fast plane trips to Crete, Rhodes, or Corfu (one to seven days) as well as mini-cruises to the islands.

Greece by car

CAR HIRE. There are many car-hire firms and a wide range of cars available. Prices vary according to the season and the place of rental — they have a definite tendency to be higher in the islands. The main car-hire firms operating in Greece usually have a counter at Hellenikon and other airports. If you wish to use the international firms, such as Avis or Hertz, you can make arrangements in your own country.

PETROL. Petrol is sold by the litre and there are two qualities available: standard and super. By using your own or a rented car you can escape the restrictions on consumption that are imposed on Greek motorists to conserve energy.

ROADS. The improvement and extension of the road system have produced some excellent results, but roadworks on a large scale can take you by surprise. Beware of unguarded level-crossings and also of the many donkeys and mules which have not yet adapted to the ways of modern traffic. There are some 'motorways' on which a toll is payable. The transliteration of Greek place-names, on road signs can vary and the same name can appear in several forms (Pireefs, Piraias, Pireus, for example).

REGULATIONS. Make sure you have an industrial insurance 'green card'. In case of emergency, the Motor Insurance Bureau of the Association of Insurance Companies in Greece, 10 Xenofontos Street, Athens (Tel. 323-67-33), will give you the name of your insurance company's representative, and will help you to insure yourself if you are not already covered in Greece. The speed limit is usually 80 or 90km/hr (50–60mls/hr).

PARKING. There are paying parking zones (parking meters) in some towns and Athens reserves certain special parking spaces for you if your car has a foreign registration-plate. There are serious penalties for illegal parking.

AUTOMOBILE CLUB. The Automobile Club of Greece (ELPA) will be of great help to you if you get into difficulties. The headquarters is in Athens (see Useful Information on Athens) and there are branches in Chania, Herakleion, Larisa, Patras, Thessaloniki, Volos, Corfu, Rhodes, Kavalla and Tripolis. A motorway assistance scheme (OVELPA), with yellow cars, operates in Athens and Thessaloniki

(Tel. 104) and on the main routes. This service is free for members, even temporary ones (you can obtain information from the frontier posts), and also for members of foreign automobile clubs.

Your Stay

Accommodation

HOTELS. Over the last few years considerable progress has been made, although the tourist boom has been responsible for a certain degree of negligence in the upkeep or the services of hotels in the medium range. Reservations should be made as far in advance as possible in Athens (where it is almost impossible to find a room at the last moment), Nauplia, Olympia, Delphi, Corfu, Thessaloniki, Mykonos, etc., and in the motels or hotels Xenia, run by the Government; most of which are very attractively situated. A 10% supplement is charged for all stays of less than three days. You may often find that you are charged half-board. A supplement may sometimes be charged during the peak season or at the time of special festivals. On the other hand, reductions are available for a twin-bedded room occupied by a single guest and for the period November to March.

In summer non-residents may use the swimming pools of the large hotels in Athens, although an entrance fee is charged. If you wish to make a reservation anywhere in Greece you should write to the Greek Hotels Department, 6 Aristidou Street, Athens, or you should apply in person to 2 Karageorgi Servias Street, Athens (Syntagma Square, inside the National Bank of Greece; Tel. 323-71-93); reservations may also be made at the Hellenikon airport (Tel. 900-23-95). The Hellenic National Tourist Office (HNTO) has recently opened rooms or apartments in restored old houses in desirable spots (Santorini [Thera], Chios, Psara, Cephalonia, Pelion). Information concerning the conditions for renting may be obtained from the HNTO ticket offices.

YOUTH HOSTELS. Holders of an International Federation of Youth Hostels card are generally admitted to the Greek youth hostels. A list of these may be obtained either from your federation or, in Athens, from 4 Dragatsaniou Street (Tel. 323-41-07). YMCA (Young Men's Christian Association) hostels and YWCA (Young Women's Christian Association) hostels are open in Athens, Thessaloniki and, during the summer, Rethymnon. You will need an international card for these organizations (see Useful Information for addresses).

CAMPING. Unauthorized camping is now forbidden throughout Greece; there are, however, well equipped camping sites, often besides the sea, in all parts of the country: they are listed in the Useful Information section.

ACCOMMODATION IN PRIVATE HOUSES. This type of accommodation is widely available, especially on the islands, and while it is scarcely palatial, does give you the opportunity to discover more about the Greek way of life and enjoy the traditional hospitality of the inhabitants. You can obtain a list of rentals (three categories) from the Tourist Services who will also help you to make a reservation (see alphabetic guide; the prices are fixed each year by the HNTO).

BEACHES AND COASTAL RESORTS. There are a great many beaches and even more small, secluded inlets, while the number of well-planned coastal resorts is increasing. Those of the Apollo coast, from the environs of Athens to Cape Sounion, Rhodes and Corfu are among the most pleasant. Mykonos, Hydra and Skiathos are popular, although they may not be for long, as fashions change so quickly in this field. Other resorts are currently being developed, for example along the coast facing Hydra and Spetsae. Chalcidice has experienced a rapid expansion of tourism, while little-frequented islands are becoming fewer and fewer.

THERMAL SPAS. The rich geology of Greece is reflected in the number of springs with waters that are often of an exceptionally high quality. Rapid development of the services and amenities of these areas is likely, since at present, in many cases, facilities are very modest (see Useful Information).

Dining out

RESTAURANTS. The choice of restaurants is as wide as the choice of hotels. There are, at one end of the scale, luxury restaurants and, at the other end, very simple restaurants or tavernas, where the quality of the dishes is scarcely below restaurants of the highest class. The opening times are generally as follows: from 12.00 to 15.00 (and even 16.00 in the small restaurants of the coastal resorts) and from 20.00 to around 23.00 or midnight. Many of the tavernas open only in the evening. Service is automatically included in the bill, but it is customary to leave a few drachmas for the waiter. Prices are now relatively high, even in the tavernas.

GREEK CUISINE. Fresh fish (it is often frozen) and shellfish (in Athens, Piraeus, Corfu and Skyros especially) are among the delicacies of Greek cuisine. There are other appetizing dishes, especially roast lamb (which is best in the tavernas or steakhouses where it is spit-roasted), kokretsi, mutton andouillette, stuffed vine leaves (*dolmadakia*), eggplant salad (*melitzano salata*), taramasalata (purée of fish roe with oil, breadcrumbs and lemon), *souvlakia* (meat kebabs, unfortunately most often veal, which is drier than lamb), *moussaka* (minced meat and eggplant), and Eastern cakes (*baklava, kataifi,* etc.).

DRINKS. Each region has its own wine. Some of these, especially the white wines, are very pleasant. Among the higher quality of red wines worth sampling are Monte Nero, Naoussa Boutari, Athos, Cava Boutari, Caviros or Pella, mostly from Macedonia; among the white wines, Cava Cambas, Arcadia, Santa Elena and Verdea; and among the rosé wines, Cimarosa and Bella Rosa. White or red, the Château Carras is excellent. The resinous wine, with its unique taste, also has its connoisseurs. Beer, especially that produced in Greece under licence (for example Amstel), is of good quality. Ouzo, anisette drunk with or without water, is the national drink (if you are tempted to take a bottle home with you, the best is Sans Rival Number 12 or Tsandalis). Imported alcoholic drinks are expensive, so we advise you to enjoy the Greek cognac (Cambas or Metaxa range from one to five stars, or Votris, five years old) or the liqueurs (kumquat, banana, rose or lemon liqueurs from Panayiotakis or Kolinounis, who also distill an excellent mint liqueur).

GREEK COFFEE. This is drunk at all times of the day and is always accompanied by a glass of water. Never refer to it as Turkish coffee, even if it is prepared in the same way on both sides of the Aegean Sea. Order it *sketo*, without sugar; *metrio*, weak and with little sugar; *gliko*, with a lot of sugar; or *gliko vrasto*, sugared and boiling. Do not stir it since the grounds will be in the bottom of your cup.

Daily life in Greece

YOUR BUDGET. The drachma is the main unit of currency; it is divided into 100 leptas. The coins currently in circulation are of 50 leptas and of 1, 2, 5, 10, 20 and 50 drachmas. Bank notes are of 50, 100, 500 and 1,000 drachmas (blue, pink, green and brown respectively). Obtain the leaflet(s) concerning hotel prices from an HNTO office.

NEWSPAPERS. You will have no difficulty in getting hold of foreign newspapers in Athens (at kiosks in Syntagma Square) or Thessaloniki. Those available include *Athens News*, a weekly published in English, *The Week in Athens*, a weekly bilingual guide that you can obtain free from the offices of the HNTO, and *Time-In* and *The Athenian*, two monthly publications which include many useful addresses and carry details of events taking place in Athens and in the principal Greek cities.

THEATRE, FESTIVALS, CONCERTS. During the winter the National Theatre produces works by ancient and modern Greek authors, as well as works by foreign authors (in Greek). From July to September, during the Festival of Athens, the National Theatre also presents works in the Odeon of Herodes Atticus. Concerts and ballets are featured here as well, including the National Orchestra of Athens and foreign orchestras and soloists (see also Useful Information for Athens).

Among the most important festivals in the provinces are those in Dodona and, above all, Epidaurus, as well as Philippi, Thasos, etc.

The HNTO Festivals Office, 2 Gallery Spyrou Miliou, Athens (Tel.

322-14-59) will provide you with a yearly list of the programmes of these events.

RELIGIOUS FESTIVALS. During religious festivals you will also see interesting displays of folklore, especially at the time of the Orthodox Easter. There are the Good Friday processions around Athens and other parts of Greece, the Saturday procession in Corfu, the Saturday midnight mass in most of the country's churches and the popular celebrations with dancing and feasts in the public squares on Easter Sunday. In Megara, on the Tuesday after the Orthodox Easter, an interesting local festival takes place in which the country women dress in their traditional costumes. The Feast of the Assumption, 15 August, is also celebrated in Greece.

On the last two Sundays before Orthodox Lent, Patras is enlivened by a boisterous carnival, while on the first day of Lent (called Monday of Abstinence) in Thebes you can watch an amusing satire parodying a peasant marriage.

Also deserving of mention are festivals in Corfu, celebrated on 6 August (procession by boat to Pondikonissi) and 11 August (festival of Saint Spyridon); in Tinos, which, at the time of the Assumption of the Virgin (15 August), is the most popular place of pilgrimage among Greek Catholics; and in Thessaloniki on 26 October (festival of Saint Demetrios). The majority of the islands in fact have festivals for their patron saints. In certain places (see Useful Information) festivals with pagan origins survive. These have in many cases been Christianized. Examples of these pagan festivals are the curious walk on fire at Langada, near Thessaloniki (the end of May) and the festival of the bull in Mytilene (end of May).

SPORT AND LEISURE. If you are interested in sports, the sea will provide a great arena. Swimming and underwater fishing are both available. Skin diving and aqualung diving are officially forbidden except in restricted zones; you can obtain a list of these zones from the HNTO. Be careful if you come across amphoras and other antiquities; these are protected and you may not interfere with them. (Hellenic Federation of Underwater Activities, Haghios Kosmas, Hellenikon, Tel. 981-99-61.) You can also go water-skiing (Apollo Coast, Corfu, Rhodes, etc.). The Athens region has golf courses (Glifadha, Varibobi, Kalamaki for beginners, Corfu and Rhodes). There are many tennis courts: the best hotels in the coastal resorts often have their own.

NIGHT-CLUBS AND DISCOTHEQUES. Many nightspots are located in the tourist areas along the Apollo coast. Entrance is generally forbidden to unaccompanied individuals except in the large international hotels.

PHOTOGRAPHY. Amateur photographers and film-makers will be delighted with the sun and light of Greece, as well as with the countryside and monuments. You will, however, need filters and a lens hood. You should also beware of the moisture content of the sea air, and it would be sensible to have some film in reserve. You are allowed to take 'a reasonable quantity' of film through customs. You may take pictures at the archaeological sites and in the museums if you pay a supplementary entrance fee; if you wish to use a tripod or artificial lighting you will have to pay extra charges, which vary.

GUIDES. In the important cities and towns and at archaeological sites you can hire a guide, bilingual or trilingual and usually a university graduate. You can obtain information about guides on the spot, in travel agencies or from the Association of Greek Guides, 7 Karageorgi Servias Street, Athens (Tel. 322-97-05).

OPENING HOURS FOR MUSEUMS AND ARCHAEOLOGICAL SITES. Although the Greek tourist services have attempted to simplify and standardize them, the opening times of the different museums and sites can be confusing. The majority of the museums are closed on Tuesdays. Official instructions are often ignored and the times advertised locally may be different from those advertised officially. The opening hours may depend on the warden's whim or the length of his siesta. The tendency, especially for sites of secondary importance, is to be open for a continuous period from 0.800 to 15.00, or from 09.00 to 16.00, and to be closed for the rest of the day. In the more important sites and museums timetables are supposed to be altered four times a year, on 1 April, 15 May, 1 September and 15 October. You should obtain as much information as possible from the HNTO or the Tourist Services (see the Useful Information on the places concerned). Closing times are always earlier in winter.

LIFE ACCORDING TO GREEK TIME. Punctuality in Greece is often treated with a Mediterranean flexibility. The Greeks have words that refer to different periods of the day, and it is as well to know these in case you arrange any meetings, etc. The word *messimeri* (midday) designates a period from 13.00 to approximately 15.00; *apoghemataki* (early afternoon) is the period following the siesta, while *apoghevma* (afternoon) lasts until dinner time, 20.00 at the earliest. Then *vradaki* (early evening) begins before evening itself, and *vradi* may last far into the night. The night, as far as the Greeks are concerned, is only the period that you are actually asleep.

In the towns and cities shops are generally open from 08.00 to 15.00 on Mondays, Wednesdays and Saturdays and from 08.00 to 13.30 and 16.30 to 20.00 on the remaining days. Banks are open from 08.00 to 13.30 and certain branches are also open in the afternoons. They are all closed on Sundays and on public holidays. The National Bank of Greece, in Syndagma Square in Athens, is open until 20.00 every day.

Official public holidays are: 1 January; Epiphany or Day of the Kings (6 January); the national holiday (25 March); Shrove Monday; Good Friday; Sunday of Holy Week (Orthodox Easter), as well as Easter Monday; 15 August (the Assumption); and 28 October (the day of refusal to capitulate in the face of the Italian ultimatum on 28 October 1940). Shops will be closed on local festival days.

As an energy-saving measure, night-life now stops at two in the morning.

SHOPPING. Athens, Corfu, Rhodes, Thessaloniki, Mykonos are the best places to spend your drachmas. But what should you expect to buy? Icons, certainly, genuine or imitation; objects in bronze and silverplated metal, for example ancient filigree jewellery, vases and goblets, which you will find in abundance in the antique shops in Pandrossou Street in Athens; deep-pile wool carpets (Flokati) that you can buy by the kilo; embroidery and weaving from Mykonos; wooden sculptures from Vytina, Metsovon and Skyros (wonderful!). Then there are furs and modern jewellery from Lalaounis or from Zolotas; these will not be cheap, although the furs are priced reasonably.

POSTAL AND TELEPHONE SERVICES. Your letters can be addressed to the hotel or to the *poste restante* (in Athens, either to the Central Post Office or to the annex branch in Syndagma Square: specify which in the address), where they can be picked up between 08.30 and 13.00 and between 15.00 and 18.00, except Sundays. If you wish to send letters you can obtain stamps from the reception desks in your hotel, in certain kiosks (which sometimes sell everything) or, as a last resort, from a post office.

In order to make a telephone call or send a cable, whatever the destination, do not go to the nearest post office but to the OTE (Telecommunications Office); there are several OTE offices in Athens, and at least one in each city, town or large village, generally open until late (often 22.00 in summer). You can also make internal calls, and even some overseas calls, from certain kiosks that are equipped with meters.

To make direct-dial overseas calls, dial 00 and then the code of the country you wish to call, the code of the city and finally the number of the person you are calling. International information (given in English, French and German): 162.

Note that the updating of the Greek telephone system now taking place may mean that some numbers have changed since the publication of this Guide, especially in Athens.

Further information

Further information may be obtained from the Hellenic National Tourist Office (HNTO). Information is given on the spot in Greece at 2, Karageorgi Servias Street, Athens (Tel. 322-25-45); Hellenikon airport (Tel. 979-95-00) and in many cities and towns in the provinces (see Useful Information); in writing, from 2 Amerikis Street, Athens.

Remember that throughout Greece the Tourist Services will give you information or receive your complaints and, where necessary, help you; they are listed in the Useful Information sections for each particular city or town, at the back of the Guide (central Athens, Tel. code: 171).

Some Notes on Language and Vocabulary

The Greek language
by André Mirambel

A LONG EVOLUTION. Modern Greek is the result of an uninterrupted evolution which began with the *Koiné* (common language) in the 4th century BC. During the Middle Ages different dialects appeared in the spoken language, but a common language has become established in modern times, rather different in sound and form from that spoken in antiquity. The vocabulary has expanded and, as a result, of contact with other languages, acquired Latin, Arabic, Slavic, Albanian, Italian (especially the Venetian dialect), Turkish, English and French words; generally the Greek base has resisted and then assimilated these foreign contributions.

In comparison with the spoken or demotic language, a scholarly tradition has been trying to preserve the historic written language, *Katharevousa*, officially used in the country's principal institutions. In 1976, however, the demotic language was finally recognized as the official language. The sometimes bitter conflict between purism and 'vulgarism' has perpetuated a 'language question' which increases some of the difficulties of Greek and which cannot be ignored.

SOME BASIC NOTIONS OF GRAMMAR. Modern Greek has retained a declension with four cases (nominative, vocative, accusative and genitive), three genders (masculine, feminine and neuter), and two numbers (singular and plural).
The definite article (ό, ή, τό) is widely used. A singular indefinite article is used (ἕνας, μία or μιά, ἕνα).

Verbs, split into two groups of conjugations depending on whether the accent falls on the inflection or not, have two voices, three principal moods to which are added derived moods (Modern Greek has, however, lost the infinitive and reduced the participles), three tenses (only in the indicative), and, naturally, three persons and two numbers. The verb is normally constructed on two stems, one of which expresses continuous action (present), the other momentary action (*aorist*).

Except for certain accessory words, all Greek words have an accent, the position of which varies (it always falls on one of the last three syllables). This accent is important for comprehension and cannot be omitted. The accent is written according to the ancient written form (acute, grave, circumflex: ά, ὰ, ᾶ). The mark showing whether an initial vowel was aspirate or not is still used, but is only a convention of spelling (ἁ, ἀ).

Modern Greek has retained the ancient alphabet, although certain letters and groups of letters have developed different values over the centuries.

Capitals	Small letters	Pronunciation
A	α	*a* (open)
B	β (initial) ϐ (internal)	v
Γ	γ	*g* (fricative before a, o, u and consonants, cf German *g*, or Arabic *gh*) *y* (before i and e)
Δ	δ	(hard English *th*)
E	ε	*è* (open)
Z	ζ	z
H	η	*i*
Θ	θ	*th* (soft English)
I	ι	*i*
K	κ	*k*
Λ	λ	*l*
M	μ	*m*
N	ν	*n*
Ξ	ξ	*ks* (gz after n)
O	ο	*o* (open)
Π	π	*p*
P	ϱ	*r (rolled)*
Σ	σ/ς (final)	*s* (z before voiced consonants)
T	τ	*t*
Y	υ	*i*
Φ	φ	*f*
X	χ	(hard German *ch* before consonants and a, o, u) (soft German *ch* or guttural *h* before i and e)
Ψ	ψ	*ps (bz after n, m)*
Ω	ω	*o* (open)

All the vowels are short, except when accented.
The following vowel groups are pronounced:
αι = *è* (open)
ει = *i*

οι = *i*
υι = *i*
ου = *ou* (German u)
αυ = *av* (but af before voiceless consonants)
ευ = *ev* (but ef before voiceless consonants)
ηυ = *iv* (never if)

A diaeresis on the second letter of a vowel group indicates that each vowel is pronounced separately: αϊ = *a + i*, εϋ = *e + i*, etc. Vowels are articulated separately before nasals: αν = *an* (not a nasal a).

Double consonants are pronounced as single consonants:
λλ = *l* μμ = *m*, etc.

The following consonant groups are pronounced:
γγ (always within word) = *ng*
γκ = *g* (hard) at the beginning, *ng* within, occasionally *nt* (some loan-words)
ντ = *d* at the beginning, *nd* within, occasionally *nt* (some loan-words)
μπ = *b* at the beginning, *mb* within, occasionally *mp* (some loan-words)
τζ = *dz*
τσ = *ts* (but after n = *dz*).
ω (pronounced *m* before π, μπ, and *ng* befor κ, γκ).

The subscript ι (written after capitals) is still sometimes marked but it is not pronounced: (ᾳ = a, ῃ = i, ῳ = o, Αι = a, Ηι = i, Ωι = o).

The following letters are used in transcription, providing a compromise between phonetic pronounciation and conventional spelling:

Vowels: *a* = α, ᾳ
         è = ε, αι
         i = η, ῃ, ι, υ, ει, οι, υι
         o = ο, ω, ῳ
         ou = ου
Consonants: *p* = π, ππ within only
           t = τ, ττ within only
           k = κ, κκ within only
           b = μπ initial
           d = ντ initial
           g = γκ initial
           mb (possibly mp) = μπ within
           nd (possibly nt) = ντ within
           ng (possibly ntc) = γκ within
           ng = γγ within
           v = β, 6, 66 only within
           gh = γ
           dh = δ
           ch = χ
           h = θ

f (but academic words ph) = φ
s = σ, σσ within only, ς final
ts = τσ
dz = τζ

The stress will be marked by heavy type: *kalos* = καλός (good), *pino* = πίνω (I drink), *chorus* = χῶρος (space).

Be careful to distinguish between words that are homophones but have a different stress, for example: pèrno (παίρνω, I take) and pernò (περνῶ, I pass), fora (φορά, time) and fora (φόρα, vigour), mila (μήλα, apples) and mila (μιλᾶ, he speaks), etc.

Some Useful Words and Phrases[1]

The Months

Month	μήνας m.	*minas*
January	ἰανουάριος m.	*ianouarios*
February	φεβρουάριος m.	*fevrouarios*
March	μάρτιος m.	*martios*
April	ἀπρίλιος m.	*aprilios*
May	μάϊος m.	*maios*
June	ἰούνιος m.	*iounios*
July	ἰούλιος m.	*ioulios*
August	αὔγουστος m.	*avghoustos*
September	σεπτέμβριος m.	*septemvrios*
October	ὀκτώβριος m.	*octovrios*
November	νοέμβριος m.	*noemvrios*
December	δεκέμβριος m.	*dhekemvrios*

The week

Week	(ἐ)βδομάδα f.	*(e)vdhomadha*
Monday	Δευτέρα f.	*dheftera*
Tuesday	Τρίτη f.	*triti*
Wednesday	Τετάρτη f.	*tetarti*
Thursday	Πέμπτη f.	*pempti*
Friday	Παρασκευή f.	*paraskevi*
Saturday	Σάββατο n.	*savato*
Sunday	Κυριακή f.	*kiriaki*

The day

Day	(ἡ)μέρα f.	*(i)mera*
Today	σήμερα	*simera*
Yesterday	χτὲς and χθὲς	*chtes (chthes)*
Day before yesterday	προχτὲς (προχθὲς)	*prochtes (prochthes)*
Tomorrow	αὔριο	*avrio*
Day after tomorrow	μεθαύριο	*methavrio*
This morning	τὸ πρωΐ	*to proï*
This evening	ἀπόψε	*apopse*

[1] In Greek punctuation the semi-colon serves as an interrogation mark; the stop which we indicate with a semi-colon is marked by a single point written above the line in the position of the upper point of a semi-colon.

The time

Morning	πρωΐ n.	proi
Midday	μεσημέρι n.	mesimeri
Afternoon	ἀπόγευμα n.	apoghevma
Evening	βράδυ n.	vradhi
Midnight	μεσάνυχτα n. pl.	mesanichta
Hour	ὥρα f.	ora
Quarter of an hour	τέταρτο n. (τῆς ὥρας)	tetarto tis oras
One minute, a minute	ἕνα λεπτό n.	ena lepto
One second	ἕνα δευτερόλεπτο	ena dhefterolepto
Watch	} ρολόϊ n.	roloï
Clock		
What time is it?	τί ὥρα εἶναι;	ti ora ine?
What time do you open?	τί ὥρα ἀνοίγετε;	ti ora anighete?
It is one o'clock	εἶναι μία (μιά)	ine mia (mia)
It is midday	εἶναι μεσημέρι	ine mesimeri
It is midnight	εἶναι μεσάνυχτα	ine mesanichta
At two o'clock precisely	στὶς δύο (δυὸ) ἀκριβῶς	stis dhio (dhio) akrivos
At five minutes to three	στὶς τρεῖς παρὰ πέντε	stis tris para pende
At ten minutes past four	στὶς τέσσερεις καὶ δέκα	stis tesseris ke dheka

Numbers

One	ἕνας, μία (μιὰ), ἕνα	enas, mia (mia), ena
Two	δύο (δυὸ)	dhio (dhio)
Three	τρεῖς, τρία	tris, tria
Four	τέσσερεις, τέσερα n.	tesseris, tessera
Five	πέντε	pende
Six	ἕξι	eksi
Seven	ἑφτα (ἑπτὰ)	efta (epta)
Eight	ὀχτὼ (ὀκτὼ)	ochto (okto)
Nine	ἐννια (ἐννέα)	enia (enea)
Ten	δέκα	dheka
Eleven	ἕντεκα (ἕνδεκα)	endeka (endheka)
Twelve	δώδεκα	dhodeka
Thirteen	δεκατρεῖς, δεκατρία n.	dhekatris, dhekatria
Fourteen	δεκατέσσερεις, δεκατέσσερα n.	dhekateseris, dhekatesera
Fifteen	δεκαπέντε	dhekapende
Sixteen	δεκάξι (δεκαέξι)	dhekaksi (dhekaeksi)
Seventeen	δεκαεφτά (δεκαεπτά)	dhekaefta (dhekaeepta)
Eighteen	δεκαοχτὼ, (δεκαοκτὼ)	dhekaochto (dhekaokto)
Nineteen	δεκαεννιὰ (δεκαεννέα)	dhekaenia (dhekaenea)
Twenty	εἴκοσι	ikosi
Twenty-one	εἴκοσι ἕνας (μιὰ, ἕνα)	ikosi enas (mia, ena)
Thirty	τριάντα	trianda
Forty	σαράντα	saranda
Fifty	πενήντα	peninda
Sixty	ἑξήντα	eksinda
Seventy	ἑβδομήντα	evdominda
Eighty	ὀγδόντα	oghdhonda

Ninety	ἐνενήντα	eneninda
One hundred	ἑκατὸ	ekato
Two hundred	διακόσιοι, -σιες, -σια	dhiakosii, -sies, -sia
A thousand	χίλιοι, -ιες, -ια	chillii, -ies, -ia

Ordinal numbers

First	πρῶτος, -τη, -το	protos, -ti, -to
Second	δεύτερος, -οη, -ρο	dhefteros, -ri, -ro
Third	τρίτος, -τη, -το	tritos, -ti-, -to
Fourth	τέταρτος, τ-η, το	tetartos, -ti, -to
Fifth	πέμπτος, -τη, -το	pemptos, -ti, -to
Sixth	ἕκτος, -τη, -το)	ektos, -ti, -to
Seventh	ἕβδομος, -μη, -μο	evdhomos, -mi, -mo
Eighth	ὄγδοος, -οη, -οο	oghdoos, -oi, -oo
Ninth	ἔνατος, -τη, -το	enatos, -ti, -to
Tenth	δέκατος, -τη, -το	dhekatos, -ti, -to
Eleventh	ἐνδέκατος, -τη, το (ἐντέ-κατος, -τη, -το)	endhekatos, -ti, -to (endeekatos, -ti, -to
Twelfth	δωδέκατος, -τη, -το	dhodhekatos, -ti, -to
Thirteenth	δέκατος τρίτος, -τη, -το	dhekatos tritos
Fourteenth	δέκατος τέταρτος	dhekatos tetartos
Fifteenth	δέκατος πέμπτος	dhekatos pemptos
Sixteenth	δέκατος ἕκτος	dhekatos ektos
Seventeenth	δέκατος ἕβδομος	dhekatos evdhomos
Eighteenth	δέκατος ὄγδοος	dhekatos oghdhoos
Nineteenth	δέκατος ἔνατος	dhekatos enatos
Twentieth	εἰκοστὸς, -τὴ, -τὸ	ikostos enatos
Twenty-first	εἰκοστός πρῶτος, -τη, -το	ikostos protos, -ti, -to
Thirtieth	τριακοστός, -τὴ, -τὸ	triakostos, -ti, -to
Fortieth	τεσσεϱακοστός, -τή, -τό	tessarakostos -ti, -to
Fiftieth	πεντηκοστός, -τή, -τό	pendikostos
Sixtieth	ἑξηκοστός, -τή, -τό	eksikostos
Seventieth	ἑβδομηκοστός	evdhomikostos
Eightieth	ὀγδοηκοστός	oghdhoïkostos
Ninetieth	ἐνενηκοστός, -τή, -τό	enenikostos
Hundredth	ἑκατοστός, -τὴ, -τὸ	ekatostos, -ti, -to
Two-hundredth	διακοσιοστός, -τὴ, -τὸ	dhiakosiostos, -ti, -to
Thousandth	χιλιοστός, -τὴ, -τὸ	chiliostos, -ti, -to

Common words and expressions

I	ἐγώ,	egho
You	ἐσύ	esi
He, she, it	αὐτός, -τὴ, -τὸ	aftos, -ti, -to
We	ἐμεῖς	emis
You (pl.)	ἐσεῖς	esis
They (m., f. and n.)	αὐτοί, -τὲς, -τὰ	afti, -tes, -ta
The (m. and n.) (sing.)	ὁ (m.), τὸ (n.)	o, to
The (m. f., and n.) (pl.)	οἱ (m.) αἱ (f.) τὰ (n.)	i, i, ta
My (m. f., and n.) (sing.)	δικός, -κή, -κό μου	dhikos, -ki, -ko- mou
My (m., f., and n.) (pl.)	δικοί, -κές, -κά μου	dhiki -kes, -ka mou
Our (sing.)	δικός μας	dikos mas
Our (pl.)	δικοί μας	dhiki mas
Yes, certainly	ναὶ, μάλιστα	ne, malista
No	ὄχι	ochi

I am	εἶμαι	*ime*
You are	εἶσαι	*ise*
He, she, it is	εἶναι	*ine*
We are	εἶμαστε	*imaste*
You (pl.) are	εἶστε	*iste*
They are	εἶναι	*ine*
Not (used before verb)	δὲν	*dhen*
Thank you	εὐχαριστῶ	*efcharisto*
Please	παρακαλῶ	*parakalo*
Good day! (in greeting)	καλὴ μέρα	*kali mera*
Good evening!	καλὴ σπέρα	*kali spera*
Good night	καλὴ νύχτα	*kali nichta*
Have a good trip	καλὸ ταξίδι	*kalo taksidi*
Goodbye (the first is very formal)	{ καλὴ ἀντάμωση	*kali antamosi*
	χαῖρε	*chere*
	χαίρετε pl.	*cherete*
Until tomorrow	ὡς αὔριο	*os avrio*
Here	ἐδῶ	*edho*
There	ἐκεῖ	*eki*
Up there	ἀπάνω	*apano*
Below, down, down there	κάτω	*kato*
Before	πρην, μπροστά	*prin, brosta*
After	μετά, ὕστερα	*istera*
where?	ποῦ;	*pou?*
On	ἀπάνω σὲ (ἀπὸ)	*apano se (apo)*
Under	κάτω σὲ (ἀπὸ)	*kato se (apo)*
Why?	γιατί;	*ghiati?*
Because	γιατὶ	*ghiati*
Often	συχνά	*sichna*
Sometimes	κάποτε	*kapote*
Never	ποτέ	*pote*
A little	λίγο	*ligho*
A lot, much	πολὺ	*poli*
Nothing	τίποτα	*tipota*
Something	κάτι	*kati*
All	ὅλο	*olos*
Very much, too much	πάρα πολὺ	*para poli*
Very little, too little	πάρα πολὺ λίγο	*para poli ligho*
More	περισσότερο	*perisotero*
Less	λιγότερο	*lighotero*
Enough	ἀρκετὰ	*arketa*
Far, a long distance	μακριὰ	*makria*
close, near	κοντὰ	*konda*
Quickly, hurry!	γρήγορα	*ghrighora*
Slowly, be calm, quietly	σιγά	*sigha*
Ahead, come in!	ἐμπρὸς	*embros*
Behind	πίσω	*piso*
Good	καλὸς, -λὴ, -λὸ	*kalos, -li, -lo*
Bad	κακὸς, -κὴ, -κὸ	*kakos, -ki, -lo*
Big	μεγαλος, -λη, -λο	*meghalos, -li, -lo*
Small	μικρὸς, -ρὴ, -ρὸ	*mikros, -ri, -ro*
Broad	φαρδὺς, -διὰ, -δὺ	*fardis, -dhia, -dhi*
Narrow	στενὸς, -νὴ, -νὸ	*stenos, -ni, -no*

Hot	ζεστὸς, -τὴ, -τὸ	zestos, -ti, -to
Cold	κρύος, -ύα, -ύο	krios, -ia, -io
I have	ἔχω	echo
You have	ἔχεις	echis
He, she, it has (& there is)	ἔχει	echi
We have	ἔχουμε (ἔχομε)	echoume (echome)
You (pl.) have	ἔχετε	echete
They have	ἔχουν(ε)	echoun(e)
I want	θέλω	thelo
I wish, would like	ἐπιθυμῶ	epithimo
Is there?	ἔχει; ὑπάρχει;	echi? iparchi?
Do you speak English?	μιλᾶτε ἀγγλικά;	milate agglika?
I say	λέω	leo
Do you understand?	καταλαβαίνετε;	katalavenete?
Speak slowly	μιλήσετε σιγὰ	milisete sigha

Status, titles, etc.

Mr	{ ὁ κύριος m. / κύριε	ὁ kirios / vocative: kirie
Mrs	{ ἡ κυρία f. / κυρία	i kiria / vocative: kiria
Miss	{ ἡ δεσποινὶς f. / δεσποινὶς	i dhespinis / vocative: dhespinis
Father	πατέρας m.	pateras
Mother	μητέρα f.	mitera
Brother	ἀδερφός m.	adherfos
Sister	ἀδερφὴ f.	adherfi
Man	ἄντρας m.	andras
Woman	γυναίκα f.	ghineka
Child	παιδὶ n.	pedhi
Boy	ἀγώρι n.	aghori
Girl	κορίτσι n.	koritsi
Age	ἡλικία f.	ilikia
Young	νέος, -έα, -έο	neos, -ea, -eo
Old (person)	γέρος, γριὰ	gheros, ghria
Height	μπόϊ n.	boï
Name	ὄνομα n.	onoma
Last name	ἐπώνυμο n.	eponimo
First name	(μικρὸ) ὄνομα m.	(mikro) onoma
Nationality	ἐθνικότης f. (ἐθνικότητα)	ethnikotis (ethinkotita)
Date of birth	{ χρονολογία, ἔτος / γεννήσεως	chronologhia, etos / gheniseos
Married	παντρεμένος	pandremenos
Unmarried man, bachelor	ἀνύπαντρος	anipandros
Widower, widow	χῆρος, χῆρα	chiros, chira
Passport	διαβατήριο n.	dhiavatirio
Policeman	ἀστυφύλακας m.	astifilakas
Consul	πρόξενος m.	proksenos

The weather

Good weather, nice day	καλοκαιριὰ f.	kalokeria
Bad weather	κακοκαιριὰ f.	kakokeria
Sun	ἥλιος m.	ilios
Rain	βροχὴ f.	vrochi

Hail	χαλάζι n.	*chalazi*
Snow	χιόνι n.	*chioni*
Cold (noun)	κρύο n.	*krio*
Cold wind	μελτέμι n.	*meltemi*
Heat	ζέστη f.	*zesti*
Cool	δροσερός, -ρὴ, -ρὸ	*dhroseros, -ri, -ro*
Damp, wet	ὑγρός, -ρὴ, -ρὸ	*dhroseros, -ri, ro*

In the street

Street	{ δρόμος m.	*dhromos*
	ὁδὸς f.	*odhos*
Avenue, boulevard	λεωφόρος f.	*leoforos*
Highway	ἀρτηρία f.	*artiria*
Turn, furning	στροφή f.	*strofi*
The first street	ὁ πρῶτος δρόμος m.	*o protos dhromos*
The second street	ὁ δεύτερος δρόμος m.	*o dhefteros dhromos*
To the right	δεξιά	*dheksia*
To the left	ἀριστερά	*aristera*
Can you tell me?	μπορεῖτε νὰ μοῦ πεῖτε;	*borite na mou pite?*
Policeman	ἀστυνομικός	*astinomikos*
Bus	λεωφορεῖο n.	*leoforio*
Tram	τραμβάι n. (τράμ)	*tramvai (tram)*
Taxi	ταξί n.	*taksi*
I walk, go	περπατῶ	*perpato*
I run	τρέχω	*trecho*
Bank	τράπεζα f.	*trapeza*
Post office	ταχυδρομεῖο n.	*tachidhromio*
Church	ἐκκλησιὰ f.	*eklisia*
Theatre	θέατρο n.	*theatro*
Castle, palace,	{ κάστρο n.	*kastro*
great house	πάλάτι n.	*palati*
Store, shop	{ μαγαζί n.	*maghazi*
	κατάστημα n.	*katastima*
Home, house	{ σπίτι n.	*spiti*
	οἶκος m.	*ikos*

On a journey

(The) airplane	τὸ ἀεροπλάνο	*to aeroplano*
(The) airport	τὸ ἀεροδρόμιο	*to aerodhromio*
Ship	βαπόρι n.	*vapori*
Where is the station the stop?	ποῦ εἶναι ὁ σταθμός;	*pou ine o stathmos?*
(The) train	τὸ τραῖνο	*to treno*
(The) window (for tickets)	ἡ θυρίδα	*i thirida*
One ticket for...	ἕνα εἰσιτήριο γιά...	*ena isitirio ghia...*
First, second class	πρώτη, δεύτερη (δευτέρα) θέση f.	*proti, dhefteri (dheftera) thesi*
Return ticket, round-trip	ἐπιστροφή f.	*epistrofi*
One way	ἁπλὴ μετάβαση f.	*apli metavasi*
Supplement	συμπλήρωμα n.	*simpliroma*
Half-fare	μισὸ εἰσιτήριο n.	*miso isitirio*
I change (trains)	ἀλλάζω	*alazo*
How much does... cost?	πόσο κοστίζει...;	*poso kostizi..?*

Would you keep this seat for me?	μπορεῖτε νὰ μοῦ κρατήσετε αὐτὴ τὴ θέση;	borite na mou kratisete afti ti thesi?
I should like to stop at...	Θὰ ἤθελα νὰ σταματήσω στὸ...	tha ithela na stamatiso sto...
When does the train leave?	τί ὥρα φεύγει τὸ τραῖνο;	ti ora fevghi to treno?
When does it arrive?	τί ὥρα φτάνει;	ti ora ftani?
Stop	στάση f.	stasi
Baggage	{ ἀποσκευές f. pl.	aposkeves
	πράματα n. pl.	pramata
Left luggage/Check room for baggage	{ μπαγάζια n. pl.	baghazia
	ἀποθήκη f.	apothiki
Suitcase, valise	βαλίτσα f.	valitsa
Trunk	μπαοῦλο n.	baoulo
Dining car	βαγόνι φαγητοῦ n.	vaghoni faghitou
Platform	ἀποβάθρα f.	apovathra
Compartment	διαμέρισμα n.	dhiamèrizma
Waiting room	αἴθουσα ἀναμονῆς	ethousa anamonis
Exit	ἔξοδος f.	eksodhos
Entrance	εἴσοδος f.	isodhos
Porter	{ χαμάλης m.	chamalis
	βαστάζος m.	vastazos
Conductor, ticket-inspector	ἐλεγκτής m.	elengtis

At the customs

Passport	διαβατήριο n.	dhiavatirio
Identification	ταυτότητα f.	taftotita
Triptych (automobile pass)	τρίπτυχο n.	tripticho
Customs officer	τελώνης m.	telonis
Currency exchange	{ συνάλλαγμα n.	sinalaghma
	ξένα χρήματα n. pl.	ksena chrimata
Have you anything to declare? } Nothing to declare?	τίποτα νὰ δηλώσετε;	tipota na dhilosete?
Open your baggage	ἀνοίξτε τὰ μπαοῦλα	aniksete ta baoula
Here are the keys	νὰ τὰ κλειδιὰ	na ta klidhia
Used (not new) possessions	μεταχειρισμένα πράματα	metachirizmena pramata
Personal possessions	προσωπικά πράματα	prosopika pramata

At the hotel

Can you recommend a hotel?	μπορεῖτε νὰ μοῦ συστήσετε ἕνα ξενοδοχεῖο;	borite na mou sistisete ena ksenodhochio?
A moderate price	λογική τιμή f.	loghiki timi
Clean	καθαρὸς, -ρὴ, -ρὸ	katharos, -ri, -ro
Pension	πανσιὸν (α) f.	pansion (a)
Reservation	ἐνοικίαση f.	enikiasi
Do you have any rooms?	ἔχετε δωμάτια;	echete dhomatia?
I should like a room.	θὰ ἤθελα ἕνα δωμάτιο	tha ithela ena dhomatio
A room with one bed.	ἕνα δωμάτιο μὲ ἕνα κρεββάτι	ena dhomatio me ena krevati
With two beds	μὲ δυὸ κρεββάτια	me dhio krevatia
A private bath	ἰδιαίτερο μπάνιο	idhietero banio

What is the price?	ποιά εἶναι ἡ τιμὴ;	pia ine i timi
Service charge included	μαζὶ μὲ τὴν ὑπηρεσία	mazi me tin ipiresia
Breakfast	πρωϊνὸ n.	proino
When is dinner served?	τί ὥρα τρῶνε;	ti ora trone?
Wake me at eight o'clock.	θὰ μὲ ξυπνήσετε στὶς ὀχτὼ (ὀκτὼ)	tha me ksipnisete stis ochto (okto)
Give me the bill/ check.	δῶστε μου τὸ λογαριασμὸ	dhoste mou to loghariazmo

In the restaurant

Where will find a restaurant?	ποῦ θα βρῶ ἕνα ἑστιατόριο	pou tha vro ena estiatorio
Taverna (serving meals)	ταβέρνα f.	taverna
Waiter	γκαρσόν(ι) n.	garson(i)
Waitress	δεσποινίς f.	dhespinis
Inexpensive	φτηνὸ	ftino
Expensive	ἀκριβὸ	akrivo
With service charge	μαζὶ μὲ τὴν ὑπηρεσία	mazi me tin ipiresia
Good	καλὸ	kalo
Bad	κακὸ	kako
I eat	τρώω	troo
I drink	πίνω	pino
I am hungry	πεινῶ	pino
I am thirsty	διψῶ	dhipso
Food	φαγητὸ n.	faghito
Drink	ποτὸ n.	poto
Alcoholic drink	οἰνοπνευματώδες n. / οἰνόπνευμα n.	inopnevmatodhes / inopnevma
Breakfast	πρωϊνὸ n.	proino
Lunch	μεσημεριανὸ n.	mesimeriano
Dinner	δεῖπνο n.	dhipno
Menu	λίστα f.	lista
Plate	πιάτο n.	piato
Glass	ποτήρι n.	potiri
Knife	μαχαῖρι n.	macheri
Spoon	κουτάλι n.	koutali
Fork	πηρούνι n.	pirouni
Napkin	πετσέτα f.	petseta
Cup	φλυτζάνι n.	flitzani
Salt	ἁλάτι n.	alati
Pepper	πιπέρι n.	piperi
Mustard	μουστάρδα f.	moustardha
Oil	λάδι n.	ladhi
Vinegar	ξύδι n.	ksidhi
Sugar	ζάχαρη f.	zachari
Butter	βούτυρο n.	voutiro
Bread	ψωμὶ n.	psomi
Wine	κρασί n.	krasi
Bottle	μποτίλια f.	botilia
Water	νερὸ n.	nero
Beer	μπύρα f.	bira
Cider	μηλίτης m.	militis
Egg	αὐγὸ n.	avgho

Meat	κρέας n.	*kreas*
Mutton	ἀρνί n.	*arni*
Lamb	ἀρνάκι n.	*arnaki*
Pork	χοιρινό n.	*chirino*
Chicken	κοτόπουλο n.	*kotopoulo*
Roast (a)	ψητὸ n.	*psito*
Casserole (a)	ὀραστὸ n.	*vrasto*
Fillet	φιλέτο n.	*fileto*
Chop	μπριζόλα f.	*brizola*
Fish	ψάρι n.	*psari*
Fish soup	ψαρόσουπα f.	*psarossoupa*
Fish stew	κακαβιά f.	*kakavia*
Shrimps	γαρίδες f. pl.	*gharidhès*
Crab	καβούρι n.	*kavouri*
Mussels	μύδια f.	*midhia*
Octopi	χταπόδι n.	*khtapodhi*
Vegetables	{ χόρτα n.pl.	*chorta*
	χορταρικά n. pl.	*vhortarika*
Fried potatoes	τηγανιτὲς πατάτες f. pl.	*tighanites patates*
Salad	σαλάτα f.	*salata*
Dessert	γλυκὸ n.	*ghliko*
Cheese	τυρὶ n.	*tiri*
Yogurt	γιαούρτι n.	*ghiaourti*
Fruit	φροῦτα n. pl.	*frouta*
Custard	κρέμα f.	*kreema*

Greek dishes

Kebab; lamb or beef, roasted on a skewer	σουβλάκια n. pl.	*souvlakia*
Squid	καλαμαράκια n. pl.	*kalamarakia*
Crayfish, small lobster	γαρίδες f. pl.	*gharidhes*
Egg soup of sauce, flavoured with lemon	αὐγολέμονο	*avgholemono*
Stew of mutton or liver and kidneys	πατσᾶς m.	*patsas*
Liver and kidneys, roasted on a spit	κοκορέτσια n. pl.	*kokoretsia*
Smoked meat	παστουρμᾶς m.	*pastourmas*
Macaroni, cheese and minced meat, baked	παστίτσιο n.	*pastitsio*
Meat, potatoes, egg, plants, cheese, baked together	μουσακᾶς m.	*mousakas*
Squash (stuffed)	κολοκυθάκια n.pl. (γεμιστὰ)	*kolokithakia (ghemista)*
Okra	μπάμιες f. pl.	*bamies*
Botargo (fish roe relish)	αὐγοτάραχο n. pl.	*avghotaracho*
Meat balls in tomato sauce	σουτζουκάκια n. pl.	*soudzoukakia*
Stew	στιφάδο n.	*stifadho*
Meat balls	κεφτέδες m. pl.	*kefthedhes*
Vine leaves stuffed with rice	ντολμάδες m. pl.	*dolmadhes*
Salt tuna	λακέρδα f.	*lakerdha*

Mille feuille pastry	μπουρέκι n.	*boureki*
Baklava (pastry of honey and almonds)	μπακλαβᾶς m.	*baklavas*
Rice pudding	ριζόγαλο n.	*rizoghalo*
Halvah (semolina)	χαλβᾶς m.	*chalvas*
Kadaïf (shredded wheat pastry with honey)	καταΐφι n. (κανταΐφι)	*kataïfi*

By car

Accelerator	ἀκσελερατὲρ n.	*akselerater*
Ignition	ἀνάφλεξη f.	*anafleksi*
Automobile	αὐτοκίνητο n.	*aftokinito*
The battery is dead.	ἄδειασε ἡ μπαταρία	*adhiase i bataria*
Gear box	γρενάζι n.	*ghrenazi*
Spark plug	μπουζὶ n.	*buzi*
Hood, bonnet	καπάκι n.	*kapaki*
Trunk, boot	πορτ-μπαγκάζ n.	*port-bagaz*
Gear shift	ἀλλαγή ταχύτητος f.	*alaghi tachititos*
Key	κλειδὶ n.	*klidhi*
Ignition key	ἔνωση f.	*enosi*
Wrench, spanner	γαλλικὸ κλειδὶ n.	*ghaliko klidhi*
Nail	καρφὶ n.	*karfi*
I've got a puncture.	ἔπιασε τὸ λάστιχο	*epiase to lasticho*
The gears slip	ντεμπραγιάρω	*debraghiaro*
Starter	μίζα f.	*miza*
Steering unit	τιμόνι n.	*timoni*
I get into gear.	ἀμπραγιάρω	*ambraghiaro*
Gasoline, petrol	{ βενζίνη f.	*venzini*
	μπεντζίνα f.	*bendzina*
Windshield wiper	σφουγγιστήρι n.	*sfoungistiri*
Heater	πισινὸ φῶς n.	*pisino fos*
I brake	φρενάρω	*frenaro*
Oil	λάδι	*ladhi*
Crank	μαναβέλα f.	*manavela*
Motor	μοτὲρ n.	*moter*
Tool	ἐργαλεῖο n.	*erghalio*
Windshield, wind screen	μπροστινὸ-τζάμι n.	*brostino dzami*
License, driving permit	ἄδεια f. ὁδηγοῦ	*adhia odhighou*
Headlight, lamp	{ φῶς n.	*fos*
	φανάρι n.	*fanari*
Bumper	ταμπὸν n.	*tampon*
License plate	μητρῶο n.	*mitroo*
Tire, tyre	λάστιχο n.	*lasticho*
Fuel tank	ντεπόζιτο n.	*depozito*
Spring	σοῦστα f.	*sousta*
Muffler	σιγαστήρας m.	*sighastiras*
Oil drainage	τιμόνι n.	*timoni*

Sightseeing

Village	χωριὸ n.	*chorio*
Island	νησὶ n.	*nisi*
Mountain	βουνὸ n.	*vouno*
River	ποτάμι n.	*potami*
Sea	θάλασσα f.	*thalasa*

Temple	ναός m.	*naos*
Antiquities, ruins	ἀρχαῖα n.pl.	*archea*
Museum	μουσεῖο n.	*mousio*

The post office

Where is the post office?	ποῦ εἶναι τὸ ταχυδρομεῖο;	*pou ine to tachidhromio?*
Letter box, post box	γραμματοκιβώτιο n.	*ghramatokivotio*
Collection	ἄδειασμα n.	*adhiazma*
Letter	{ γράμμα n.	*ghrama*
	ἐπιστολή f.	*epistoli*
Postcard	{ κάρτα f.	*karta*
	δελτάριο n.	*dheltario*
Printed matter	ἔντυπο n.	*endipo*
Registered	συστημένο n.	*sistimeno*
Air mail, par avion	ἀεροπορικῶς	*aeroporikos*
Package	δέμα n.	*dhema*
Stamp	γραμματόσημο n.	*ghramatosimo*
Telegram, wire	τηλεγράφημα n.	*tileghrafima*
Telephone call	τηλεφώνημα n.	*tilefonima*
Telephone	τηλέφωνο n.	*tilefono*
Address	διεύθυνση f.	*dhiefthinsi*

Health

Doctor, physician	γιατρὸς m.	*ghiatros*
Chemist, drugstore	φαρμακεῖο n.	*farmakio*
Ill, sick	ἄρρωστος, -τη, -το	*arostos, -ti, -to*
Head	κεφάλι n.	*kefali*
It (this, that) hurts	πονᾶ	*pona*
Heart	καρδιὰ f.	*kardhia*
Hand, arm	χέρι n.	*cheri*
Foot, leg	πόδι n.	*podhi*
Tooth	δόντι n.	*dhondi*
Back	ράχη f.	*rachi*
Stomach	στομάχι	*stomachi*
Throat	λαιμὸς m.	*lemos*
Chest	στῆθος n.	*stithos*
Eye	μάτι n.	*mati*
Ear	αὐτί n.	*afti*
Nose	μύτη f.	*miti*
Mouth	στόμα n.	*stoma*
Bone	κόκκαλο n.	*kokalo*
Nail	νύχι n.	*nichi*
Lips	χείλια n.	*chilia*
Tongue	γλῶσσα f.	*ghlosa*
Face	πρόσωπο n.	*prosopo*
Forehead	μέτωπο n.	*metopo*
Cheek	μάγουλο n.	*maghoulo*
Finger	δάχτυλο	*dhachtilo*
Blood	αἷμα	*ema*
Vein	φλέβα f.	*fleva*
Nerve	νεῦρο n.	*nevro*
Fever	πυρετὸς m.	*piretos*
Alcohol	οἰνόπνευμα n.	*inopnevma*
Aspirin	ἀσπιρίνη f.	*aspirini*
Cotton wool balls	βαμπάκι n.	*vambaki*
Poultice, compress	κατάπλασμα n.	*kataplazma*

Thermometer	θερμόμετρον n.	*thermometron*
Salve	ἀλοιφὴ f.	*alifi*
Pill	χάπι n.	*chapi*
Tonic	τονωτικὸ n.	*tonotiko*
Clinic	κλινικὴ f.	*kliniki*
Hospital	ωοσοκομεῖο n.	*nosokomio*
Virus	ἰός m.	*ios*
Knee	γόνατο n.	*ghonato*

Tourist Greece

It has long been said that a visit to Greece is essential to a person's general education. It offers a tangible picture of the masterpieces of antiquity as they are uncovered from day to day by archaeologists. If you have a sense of curiosity, however, you will not restrict yourself to antiquity, whether Minoan, Mycenaean or Classical; you will keep in mind the merits of Byzantine, Frankish or Venetian monuments as well. Moreover, do not forget that Greece is a living country. There are places and monuments to be savoured, some of which occur by chance; on arrival at Piraeus in the early morning, a bazaar in a Cretan village, a wedding at Metsovon, a bouzouki player at an inn in Piraeus... As for the countryside, serene or fantastic but always beguiling, it alone is reason enough to visit Greece.

What to see?

WHAT TO SEE IN GREECE. The map on pp. 50-1 shows you where to find the many attractions of Greece, whether archaeological sites, monuments, works of art, scenery or folklore. Different symbols are used to grade the various places, corresponding to the use of asterisks in the text: *noteworthy; **very interesting; *** exceptional.

THE ISLANDS. Because of its jagged shoreline, and above all because of its islands, Greece is a country of the sea, a country of sailors, fishermen and shipbuilders. Today, the islands are the major asset in the tourist development of Greece. Corfu, Mykonos and Rhodes will attract those drawn by the liveliness of their summer resorts. Some islands, however, still escape the flood of visitors in the tourist season, especially the Cyclades. It may sometimes be possible to reach them from Piraeus, but you can usually get to them only from the large neighbouring islands: Melos for Kimolos; Siphnos for Folegandros; Ios for Sikinos; Naxos for Iraklia, Schinoussa, Koufonissa, Donoussa or Amorgos; Thera (Santorini) for Anafi. If you go to small islands, be prepared to stay in a villager's house and to travel by donkey... The Greek islands are also full of history: Minoan discoveries on Thera (Santorini), the famous ancient city of Delos, the temple of Aphaia on

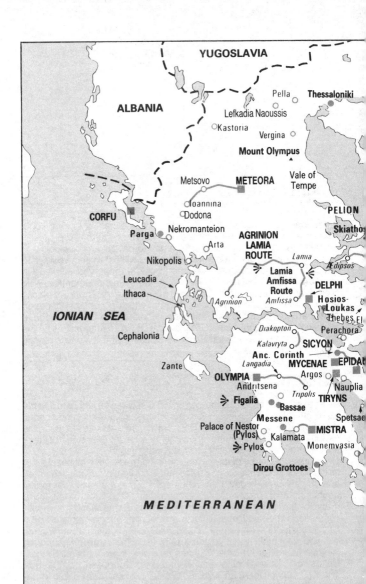

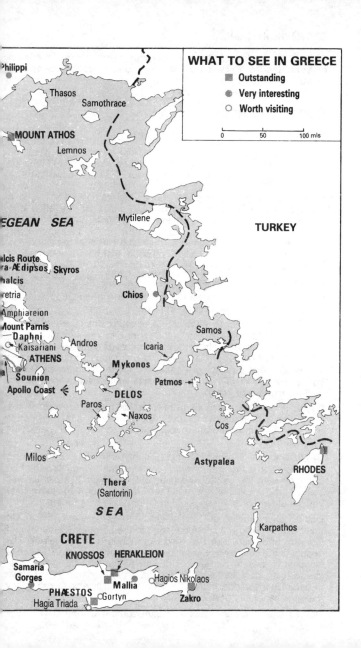

Philippi

Thasos
Samothrace

MOUNT ATHOS
Lemnos

EGEAN SEA

Mytilene

TURKEY

lcis Route
ra-Ædipsos **Skyros**
halcis
retria
Amphiareion
Mount Parnis
Daphni
Kaisariani
ATHENS
Sounion
Apollo Coast

Chios

Samos

Icaria

Mykonos

Patmos

Andros

DELOS

Paros
Naxos

Cos

Milos

Astypalea

RHODES

Thera
(Santorini)

SEA

Karpathos

CRETE
KNOSSOS **HERAKLEION**
Samaria
Gorges
Hagios Nikolaos
PHÆSTOS Mallia
Hagia Triada Gortyn **Zakro**

WHAT TO SEE IN GREECE
- ■ Outstanding
- ● Very interesting
- ○ Worth visiting

0   50   100 mls

Aegina, the shadow of St John on Patmos or reminders of medieval times on Rhodes. You will obviously need to visit these places by boat or, in some cases, by air.

Suggested tours

SOME STANDARD TOURS. The map showing the principal sites of interest will allow you to work out your own programme. To help you choose, we have suggested four tours lasting from one to three weeks in mainland Greece (with the exception of a brief excursion to Mykonos and Delos) as well as a supplementary tour of Crete and two tours on the Aegean Sea. These last are simple suggestions for those who have a yacht at their disposal. All these programmes are arranged in accordance with the probable opening times of the sites and museums, which tend to be from the morning until 15.00. Because of the many and unforeseen variations in these opening hours over the last several years, you will have to consult the Tourist Service or the personnel of the individual site or museum just before your visit for more specific information.

1 PROGRAMME FOR ONE WEEK STARTING FROM ATHENS (665mls/1,055km)

Days 1 and 2. Visit Athens and take an excursion to Cape Sounion (82mls/132km); see the plan of Athens.

Day 3. Athens–Nauplia (99mls/160km; route maps 5 and 6). After visiting the Byzantine monastery at Daphni, discover ancient Corinth, then lunch in a taverna along the road that leads to Mycenae. You will relive a little of the history of the Atreids when you visit the tombs and the remains of the palace of Agamemnon and Clytemnestra. Before you arrive at Nauplia, if you still have time, have a look at the cyclopean walls of Tiryns.

Day 4. Excursion to Argolis from Nauplia Tiryns and Argos in the morning and then return to Nauplia and have lunch in the harbour or on Tolon beach; in the afternoon visit the sanctuary of Asclepius in Epidaurus.

Day 5. Nauplia–Olympia (126mls/203km; route map 7). Enjoy a long drive across the Peloponnesian mountains, the savage Arcadia that contrasts with the gentle landscape of the site of Olympia, so well suited to the reconciliations of the ancient Hellenes. If you leave early you should arrive at the banks of the Alpheus in time for lunch.

Day 6. Olympia-Delphi (165mls/266km; route maps 4, 7, and 9). On this busy day you will cross the strait to the entrance of the Gulf of Corinth, and then take the road from Andirrhion to Delphi. The beauty of the countryside will make the journey seem short. Lunch at Naupaktos, beside the sea, or, if you prefer a rustic setting that suggests the past, in the mountain village of Lidorikion. If you arrive in Delphi in the middle of the afternoon, you will be able to visit briefly the great sanctuary of Apollo.

Day 7. Delphi-Athens (130mls/210km; route maps 3 and 4). In the early part of the morning finish the visit to the sanctuary and then return to Athens, visiting the monastery of Hosios Loukas on the way.

2 PROGRAMME FOR TWO WEEKS STARTING FROM ATHENS (830mls/1,335km)

Days 1, 2 and 3. Visit Athens and take an excursion to Cape Sounion (82mls/132km); see the plan of Athens.

Day 4. Athens (Piraeus) - Mykonos; by boat, of course, since this is the only way to get to know the Greeks while traveling.

Day 5. Excursion to Delos, leaving from Mykonos.

Day 6. Mykonos–Athens.

Day 7. Athens–Nauplia (99mls/160km; route maps 5 and 6); see programme 1, day 3.

Day 8. Excursion in Argolis from Nauplia (52mls/84km); see programme 1, day 4.

Day 9. Nauplia–Sparta (90mls/146km; route map 6). If you leave early you will arrive in Sparta in time for lunch, although you may prefer to lunch in a taverna in Mistra 3mls (5km) further on. This way you will be ready to visit the Byzantine city that is the reason for making this detour to Sparta. This city is strikingly located and evokes the medieval past of Greece.

Day 10. Sparta-Andritsena by the Mani (133mls/214km; route 7 and 8). This is a long day; you will visit the grottoes of Diros, beyond Areopolis, where you will travel by boat through one of the greatest natural curiosities of the country; at lunchtime you should arrive at Kalamata (you may prefer to lunch in one of the tavernas beside the sea before reaching Kalamata). In the afternoon, you will journey to Messenia and then, at the end of the day, from Andritsena, you will visit the temple of Bassae.

Day 11. Andritsena–Olympia (52mls/85km; route map 7). A fairly quick journey along the deep valley of the Alpheus brings you to the famous site of Olympia by lunchtime.

Day 12. Olympia-Delphi (165mls/266km; route maps 4, 7 and 9); see programme 1, day 6 (but take your time as you will stay in Delphi the next day).

Day 13. Delphi: excursion to Itea (23mls/38km).

Day 14. Delphi-Athens (130mls/210km; route maps 3 and 4); see programme 1, day 7.

3 PROGRAMME FOR THREE WEEKS STARTING FROM CORFU (1,440mls/2,317km).

Day 1. Corfu; visit the city and enjoy excursions 1 and 5 in the vicinity.

Day 2. Corfu-Igoumenitsa-Arta (74mls/120km; route map 10). Take the early morning ferry to Igoumenitsa (reserve room for your car the evening before), and then take the Arta road. On the way make three detours: one to Parga, the pleasantest spot to lunch, the second to

Nekromanteion and the third to Nikopolis.

Day 3. Arta-Olympia (170mls/275km; route maps 9 and 10). This portion of the trip, until you arrive at Olympia, is of little interest unless you are an archaeological enthusiast (Stratos, museum of Patras).

Day 4. Olympia.

Day 5. Olympia–Pylos (86mls/139km; route map 9). Visit in passing the famous palace of Nestor, then Pylos (Navarin), where the natural harbour is worth a boat trip, unless you prefer to visit the Venetian fortress at Methoni (12mls/20km extra, there and back).

Day 6. Pylos-Sparta by the Mani (140mls/226km; route maps 6 and 8). Beyond Areopolis visit the grottoes of Diros, one of the greatest natural curiosities of Greece, where you will lunch. You will arrive in Sparta early enough to make the trip to Mistra, a strikingly situated Byzantine town.

Day 7. Sparta-Andritsena (139mls/224km; route maps 7 and 8); see programme 2, day 10. You will, however, take the most direct road to Kalamata.

Day 8. Andritsena–Nauplia (110mls/117km; route map 7). En route, stop at the ruins of the Great City, Megalopolis. You will probably arrive in Nauplia fairly early, in which case you will be able to visit Tiryns and Argos in the afternoon.

Day 9. Excursion in Argolis from Nauplia (37mls/60km), to the sanctuary of Asclepius in Epidaurus.

Day 10. Nauplia-Athens (99mls/160km; route maps 5 and 6); see programme 1, day 3.

Days 11, 12 and 13. Athens and excursion to Cape Sounion (82mls/132km); see the plan of Athens.

Days 14, 15 and 16. Athens (Piraeus)-Mykonos and back; see programme 2, days 4, 5 and 6.

Day 17. Athens–Delphi (130mls/210km; route maps 3 and 4); see programme 1, day 7.

Day 18. Delphi-Volos (128mls/206km; route maps 2, 3 and 4). You reach Lamia, where you can have lunch, by making a detour towards Thermopylae,then Volos.

Day 19. Excursion on the Pelion from Volos (127mls/205km); see vicinity of Volos, 7.

Day 20. Volos-Kalambaka (97mls/157km; route map 11). You do not have to leave very early to reach Kalambaka in time for lunch; the afternoon will be free for a visit to the famous monasteries of Meteora.

Day 21. Kalambaka–Igoumenitsa (148mls/238km; route map 11). This is a journey through the mountains, full of twists and turns. You will be able to relax, however, when you visit Metsovon, a village that has retained all the simple nobility of the villages in the Pindos mountain chain, and Ioannina, where you can have lunch beside the lake. An early start from Kalambaka should give you time to visit the site of the ancient city of Dodona (26mls/42km extra, there and back).

4 PROGRAMME FOR THREE WEEKS STARTING FROM THESSALONIKI (1,668mls/2,684km).

Day 1. Thessaloniki, the most interesting Byzantine city in Greece.

Day 2. Thessaloniki-Kalambaka (128mls/206km; route map 12); see programme 3, day 20.

Day 3. Kalambaka-Arta (171mls/275km; route maps 10 and 11); see programme 3, day 21, but do not forget that you must take the Arta road from Ioannina.

Day 4 to day 20. See programme 3, from day 3 to day 19.

Day 21. Volos-Thessaloniki (209mls/337km; route maps 2, 12 and 13). After Larisa stop for a few moments in the cool vale of Tempe; after Katerini follow the ancient Thessaloniki road to Aighinion; from there make a detour to Veria, passing Palatitsa (a Macedonian palace). Then return to Thessaloniki via Lefkadia Naoussis (a Roman underground chamber decorated with paintings) and Pella (the ancient Macedonian capital).

5 SUPPLEMENTARY JOURNEY IN CRETE (5 days; 317mls/510km).

Day 1. Khania: if, as we advise, you take the boat from Piraeus the night before, you will be ready to begin exploring Crete on the morning of the first day; start by visiting Khania and its vicinity.

Day 2. Khania-Herakleion (85mls/138km; route map 15). An early start will bring you to Herakleion and give you time to spend in the town's important archaeological museum and, in the afternoon, in Knossos, the most famous Minoan capital.

Day 3. Excursion to Mesara, leaving from Herakleion (112mls/180km); see Crete, section 4.

Day 4. Herakleion-Hagios Nikolaos (77mls/125km; route map 15). In order to avoid returning by the same route, go to Hagios Nikolaos via the high plain of Lassithi, from Chersonissos. Visit Kritsa and Lato in the vicinity of Hagios Nikolaos.

Day 5. Hagios Nikolaos-Herakleion (41mls/67km; route map 15). Visit Mallia, but make sure you arrive in Herakleion with enough time to catch an evening boat to Piraeus, where you will arrive very early the next morning.

6 CRUISE IN THE SARONIC GULF AND TO THE CYCLADES (about two weeks and 530 nautical miles)

The itineraries offered for this and the following cruise are merely suggestions; there are an almost infinite number of cruises available in the Greek seas. There are more than a thousand islands and islets, and a multitude of harbours on the mainland coasts, some of which are as isolated as the most inaccessible islands. From this enormous range of possibilities we seek only to provide you with a selection from which you may make your own choice. The information we have given concerning the duration of the two chosen cruises is naturally relative: everything depends on your boat and on other factors, such as the wind, the swell and your own wishes. For this reason, rather than provide a day-to-day programme, we have preferred to indicate briefly possible excursions from various ports.

Saronic Gulf. Aegina: excursion to the temple of Aphaia, 7mls (12km) from Aegina (taxis and bus) or 5mls (8km) from the bay of Hagia Marina, one of the pleasantest of the islands. Poros (convent of the Panaghia and sanctuary of Poseidon, 3mls/5km). Hydra.

Cyclades. Melos (kastro of Plaka, 2½mls/4km from Adamas, beside one of the most beautiful natural harbours in the Mediterranean). Thera (excavations of the Minoan city of Akrotiri, 8mls/13km from Phira, and the Kaïmenes). Paros (the vale of Pelatoudes). Delos, an island 'Pompeii'. Mykonos, one of Greece's leading tourist attractions. Tinos, the very holy Tinos where you will visit the church of the Panaghia Evanghelistria (Annunciation) and where you will see the sanctuary of Poseidon and of Amphitrite. Syros, where you will visit the Ermoupolis quarter and visit the small tavernas along the Poseidonia beach.

7 CRUISE TO CRETE, THE DODECANESE AND THE CYCLADES (about four weeks and 800 nautical miles).

The Gulf of Argolis. Hydra. Nauplia (excursions to Tiryns, Mycenae and Epidaurus). Monemvasia.

Cyclades. Melos (see 6 above). Thera (see 6 above).

Crete. Herakleion (visit the museum and Knossos, 3mls/5km; and hire a car to make the excursion of 112mls/180km in Mesara, to Phaestos and Hagia Triada). Hagios Nikolaos (you will find excellent mooring in the gulf of Mirabello, in the shelter of the Spinalonga peninsula; excursions to Kritsa and Lato, 7mls/11km and 9mls/15km respectively; and to Mallia, 17mls/28km).

Dodecanese. Karpathos. Lindos, on the E coast of the island of Rhodes (acropolis and medieval village). Rhodes, where you will moor in the port of Mandraki (excursions to Camiros and to Mt Philerimos). Cos (sanctuary of Asclepius, 3mls/5km). Kalymnos. Patmos, the island of St John (visit the monastery).

Cyclades. Mykonos (see 6 above). Delos (see 6 above). Tinos (see 6 above). Syros (see 6 above).

Route Maps

You will find sixteen suggested route maps on the following pages, in each case showing the best way to get from one region of Greece to another, and to the most interesting cities, towns and sites in both mainland Greece and in Crete. An Index to Route Maps is on the inside front cover.

The left-hand page gives a diagram of the route which lists the distance from place to place in both directions. Together with this map are a brief description of the area you will travel through; useful information concerning the distances and the road conditions; and suggestions regarding the principal places you may wish to visit.

The right-hand page lists the principal places and points of interest for each route, including a short description with the basic facts. Tourist sites not covered by the route map are indicated by an arrow (pointing in their direction and relative to your route) and the distance from the route is given. For information concerning hotel accommodation, consult the Useful Information section at the back of this Guide.

BITOLA-LARISA-LAMIA

This route is certainly not recommended for anyone wishing to cover the distance from Yugoslavia to Athens quickly. You will be delayed by crossing the rough mountainous massifs of Macedonia and Thessaly. You may expect the stretch from Niki to Kozani to take about one and a half hours, three hours from Kozani to Larisa and two hours from Larisa to Lamia. Along this route the beauty of the countryside will prevail over archaeological interest, unless you feel inclined to make long detours, to *Kastoria and the ***Meteora for example. If you make these detours you will appreciate the wealth of Byzantine art, especially painting, influenced by the school of Mount Athos, that originated in the N of Greece.

220mls (345km) of a very winding road. From Larisa or Lamia you have the option of taking a very quick toll road; this, however, means travelling an extra 18½mls (30km).

Because of the rough nature of this part of Greece, do not expect to find first-class accommodation. The hotels in Larisa are of average quality. Florina and Loutra Ypati, off the main route near Lamia, do at least offer a hotel in a pleasant setting.

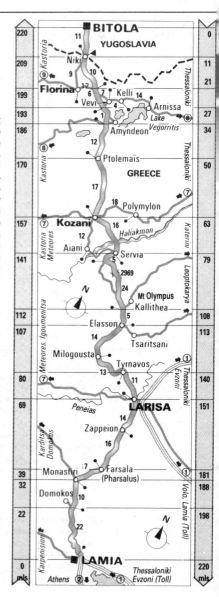

BITOLA

Niki. Greek frontier post (open day and night).

← 9/7mls (15/12km). Florina, small typically Balkan city in a pleasant wooded setting.

← 45mls (73km). *Kastoria (off the map). Set beside a romantic lake, this town features Byzantine art and churches decorated with frescoes.

PTOLEMAÏS

Kozani. A crossroads; Aiani, nearby, has several churches decorated with frescoes.

Servia, reached after crossing the lake of Haliakmon (see vicinity of Kozani). Originally a Serbian town that guarded a gorge, as can be seen from the ruins of a Byzantine fortress built in the 13th c.

→ 38½mls (62km). Katerini (off the map), reached by a mountain road (partly asphalted) that climbs the N slope of **Mount Olympus (9,570ft/2,917m), the highest mountain in Greece (3mls/5km from the fork; a road to the r. along the S slope leads to Leoptokarya and to Litochoron, 34½mls/56km).

Elasson (see vicinity of Katerini).

Tyrnavos, 2mls (3km) from the ruins of the ancient Phalanna. In the town there are churches from the 17th century.

Larisa. A place to break your journey at an important crossroads. Interesting archaeological museum. One of the roads that crosses the town leads to the ***Meteora (see route map 11), a natural curiosity, and also a group of monasteries.

Farsala (Pharsalus), a historical site, the place where Julius Caesar defeated Pompey in 48 BC.

← 22mls (36km). Karditsa.

LAMIA

A place to break your journey (Loutra Ypati, 11mls/18km to the W, is pleasanter).

← 118mls (190km), Agrinion (off the map), via Karpenision and a superb ***mountain road across the wild massif of Tymphrestos (vicinity of Lamia, 3).

← 41½mls (67km). Amfissa (off the map) and ***Delphi (61½mls/99km) towards the gulf of Corinth. From the **slopes of Mt Oeta (7,060ft/2,152m) you will see the plain of Lamia.

EVZONI-LARISA-LAMIA

You can cover the distance between Evzoni and Lamia in little more than four hours, crossing Macedonia and Thessaly. Do not forget that you will be near Thessaloniki, an excellent introduction to Byzantine Greece. There are also sites of archaeological interest: *Pella, *Palitsia (vicinity of Veria, 1,) Dion (vicinity of Katerini) and the sites in the vicinity of Volos. As you approach from the N you reach the Mediterranean world on the shore of the Pagasetic Gulf. Before this you skirt the magnificent **Olympus. Do not miss the verdant region of the ***Pelion (vicinity of Volos, 7).

210mls (339km) by a fast (toll) road; the lanes are not separated. (By the free roads, 265mls/424km.)

On the way you may like to lunch beside the sea, at Platamon for example (192mls/149km – 118mls/190km), where the restaurants serve fresh fish (which can be rare in Greece). Near Volos seek the cool of Portaria (vicinity of Volos, 6) for dinner. Or you may prefer one of the tavernas beside the sea, along the Pelion road (vicinity of Volos, 7).

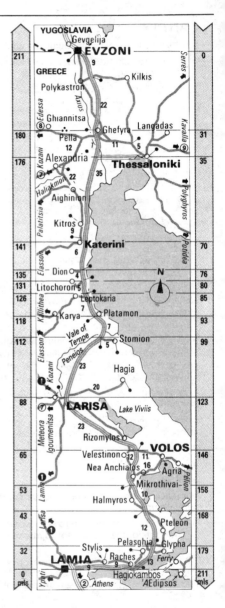

EVZONI

Frontier post open day and night.

→ 15½mls (25km) **Thessaloniki, a city full of Byzantine art that almost rivals Constantinople and Ravenna. From there you can tour Chalcidice (vicinity of Thessaloniki, 2), or you can head for ***Mt Athos.

← 9mls (15km). *Pella, one of the principal archaeological sites of Macedonia. Here you can see some remarkable mosaics.

← 17mls (28km). *Palatitsia (off the map, vicinity of Veria, 1) a site from the Hellenistic period; of special interest is the magnificent Macedonian tomb.

Kitros, near the site of Pydna, where in 168 BC the Romans defeated the army of Perseus, preventing him from conquering Greece.

Katerini, from where a road leads to Elasson (43mls/70km; see route map 1) across the N slope of **Mt Olympus. A second road leads to Dion (8mls/13km).

← 2mls (3km). Litochoron, the point from which you can begin your visit to the massif of **Olympus.

Leptokaria. Coastal resort near a medieval fortress.

Platamon. Coastal resort near a medieval fortress.

*Vale of Tempe, one of the gateways to Greece and an ancient place of pilgrimage consecrated to Delphian Apollo.

Larisa, a place to break your journey at a very important crossroads; interesting archaeological museum. One of the roads that crosses the town leads to the ***Meteora (see route map 11).

← 11mls (18km). Volos, in a region rich in archaeological sites; from here you may visit the ***Pelion (vicinity of Volos, 7).

→ 3½mls (6km). Nea Anchialos (vicinity of Volos, 6), a palaeo-Christian site.

Halmyros. Small museum housing prehistoric and Mycenaean collections and Hellenistic funeral stelae.

→ 11mls (18km). Glifa: ferry to Euboea.

LAMIA

A place to break your journey (Loutra Ypati, 11mls/18km to the W, is more attractive).

← 118mls (190km). Agrinion (off the map), via Karpenision and a superb ***mountain road, across the wild massif of Tymphrestos (vicinity of Lamia, 3).

← 41½mls (67km). Amfissa (off the map) and ***Delphi (61½mls/99km) towards the gulf of Corinth. From the **slopes of Mt Oeta (7,060ft/2,152m) you will have a view over the plain of Lamia.

LAMIA-ATHENS

Scarcely two and a half hours' drive across the austere areas of Boeotia and Attica. In your haste to reach Athens do not disregard points of great interest in the areas through which you will travel. There are sites of great historical interest such as Thermopylae, Thebes and Tanagra (39½mls/64km – 98mls/158km). Bear in mind also that you will pass within 13½mls (22km) of the *Amphiareion (vicinity of Athens, 7) and that by varying your route from Thebes you will reach Athens by the historical route.

139mls (222km) by an excellent fast (toll) road (127mls/205km by the free road via Livadia and Thebes by the direct road, or 145mls/234km if you go along the coast to Arkitsa).

Visit charming Kamena Vourla (beach and small restaurants). Better still, if you feel able to make a 12-ml (20-km) detour, go to *Chalcis (see Euboea) and visit one of the small restaurants near the beach, opposite the old city, in a pleasant setting at the mouth of the Euripos channel which is continually crisscrossed by brightly coloured caïques (small boats).

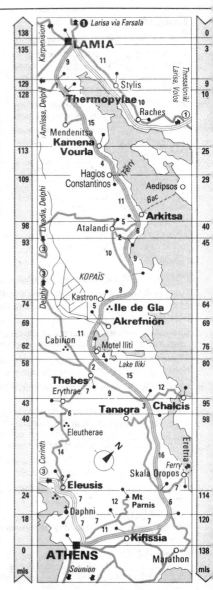

LAMIA

A place to break your journey (Loutra Ypati, 11mls/18km to the W, is pleasanter).

← 118mls (190km). Agrinion (off the map), via Karpenision and a superb ***mountain road across the wild massif of Tymphrestos (vicinity of Lamia, 3).

← 41½mls (67km). Amfissa (off the map) and ***Delphi (61½mls/99km) towards the Gulf of Corinth. From the **slopes of Mt Oeta (7,060ft/2,152m) you will have a view of the plain of Lamia.

Thermopylae. A historic site.

Kamena Vouria. Thermal spa and coastal resort on the edge of the gulf of Lamia.

Hagios Constantinos. Beach on the gulf of Lamia (boats to Volos and the northern Sporades).

Arkitsa. Ferry to Loutra Aedipsos (see Euboea) that travels nine times daily between 07.00 and 21.30.

→ 1ml (2km). Island of Gla. One of the five principal sites from the Mycenaean period, on what used to be an island but is now part of the mainland.

2½mls (4km). Akrefnion (vicinity of Thebes, 4). Site from the Archaic period of the Ptoön, consecrated to Apollo.

YLIKI

← 2½mls-9mls (4-15km). Thebes, whose history reflects the essence of tragedy, was once a prestigious city. It was completely ruined, as its museum testifies.

A secondary road leads to ***Athens (43mls/69km) via Eleutheres (9mls/15km; road to the r. to Porto Ghermeno), *Eleusis and Daphni (mosaics on a gold background).

→ 12mls (20km). Chalcis, on the island of Euboea. If you are attracted by the 'Archaic smile', visit the museum and see the sculpted group of *Theseus and Antiope. If you like nature, follow the Loutra Aedipsos road through magnificent forest countryside.

← 2½mls (4km). Tanagra. The name refers to a place, but also indicates (sometimes wrongly) many terracotta objects, Greek or otherwise.

→ 7mls (12km); Scala Oropos (off the map; ferry for Eretria, in Euboea, between 04.00 and 23.00) and the *Amphiareion (13½mls/22km; vicinity of Athens, 7).

← 3mls (5km). Kifissia (vicinity of Athens, 7) among the pines.

***ATHENS

Athens alone justifies a journey to Greece and an extended stay in Attica.

(4)

ANDIRRHION-
DELPHI-THEBES

Near Naupaktos or Itea take the modern road that follows the coast, since the mountain road is interrupted by a dam near Lidorikion, which makes a long detour by a very poor road necessary. By the main route ***Delphi is two hours from Naupaktos across Aetolia and W Locris, and less than two hours from Thebes across Phocis and Boeotia. The Gulf of Corinth served as a divider between the Peloponnesian cities, some of which were advanced, such as Sicyon and Corinth, and the quasi-barbarity of the inhabitants of the harsh mountains to the N of the Gulf. Delphi is an exception which explains the absence of interesting archaeological sites outside the Delphic sanctuary. The beauty of the countryside and of the villages, Lidorikion and Arachova for example, as well as the magnificence of the mosaics of **Hosios Loukas, make up for the absence of such sites.

134mls (216km) by a good road.

Tourism has made life a little less harsh, especially near the beaches, in Naupaktos and above all in Itea, where the beach and the restaurants in the port provide an excellent opportunity to relax.

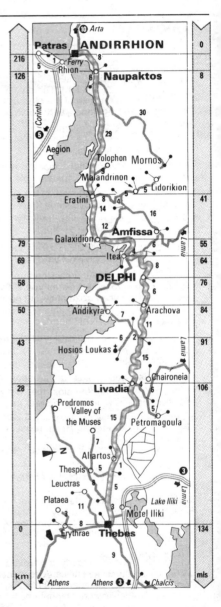

ANDIRRHION

Ferry (day and night) to Rhion.

Naupaktos, a pleasant coastal resort on the gulf of Corinth.

Shortly after Naupaktos a secondary road to the l. leads to Mornos (30mls/49km; see Lidorikion). The only way for you to continue your journey is to skirt the lake of the Mornos dam, which involves driving about 12mls (20km) along a very poor road.

Eratini. Near Tolophon (5½mls/9km), an ancient fortress which has been fairly well preserved. The fortress is a thirty-minute walk away, in a place called Marmara.

→ 13mls (21km). Malandrinon, near the ruins of the ancient Physkeis, and Lidorikion (34mls/55km), a simple mountain town that is full of character.

Galaxidion, the ancient Olanthea (traces of an ancient boundary wall, small museum, ruins of the monastery of the Holy Saviour, 2mls (3km) away, with a 13th c. church).

Itea, a quiet resting-place near Delphi.

→ 5½mls (9km). Amfissa, below a Frankish castle.

→ 47mls (76km). Lamia. After passing through the villages of Gravia and Bralos, you approach Lamia as you descend the steep **slopes of Oeta by a magnificent road of recent construction that provides you with a *View over the gulf of Lamia. This road rejoins the main Athens-Lamia road 1m (2km) N of Thermopylae (i.e. 9mls/15km from Lamia).

***Delphi, one of the glories of ancient Greece (sanctuary of Apollo) at the foot of Mt Parnassus.

Arachova, one of the main attractions of Greek tourism.

Triodos (the Three Roads). According to Sophocles it was here that Oedipus killed his father Laïos (they did not know each other) who had struck him with his whip in order to make him stand aside.

← 8mls (13km). **Hosios Loukas, splendid mosaics on a gold background and Andikyra (10½mls/17km).

Livadia, the site of the springs of Memory (Mnemosyne) and Forgetfulness (Lethe).

← 19mls (31km). Thespis and the valley of the Muses (see vicinity of Thebes).

→ 53mls (86km). Lamia (off the map) by a road leading to Petromagoula (8mls/13km) and overlooked by the Mycenaean site of Orchomenos, and Cheroneos (8½mls/14km; vicinity of Livadia).

THEBES

At the heart of Greek tragedy, a prestigious city that was completely ruined, as its museum testifies. A secondary road leads to ***Athens (43mls/69km), via Eleutheres (9mls/15km; road to the r. to Porto Ghermeno), *Eleusis and *Daphni (mosaics on a gold background).

PATRAS - CORINTH - ATHENS

***Athens is one hour from Corinth and three hours from Patras by the fast road. These journeys take twice as long by the old road. The route through the sacred region of Eleusis, in Attica, and the Megarid on the way to the Peloponnese that is cut off from the mainland by the Corinth Canal (a noteworthy sight) should satisfy your taste for archaeology, with *Eleusis, *Sicyon and, above all, **Ancient Corinth. The archaeological sites are complemented by the colourful Byzantine mosaics of *Daphni with their gold background. You will also see golden countryside around the gulf of Corinth if you take the **road which leads from Diakopton to Megaspilaion.

136mls (219km) by a fast (toll) road (there is also a free road).

There are numerous attractive beaches; the pleasantest are those around Corinth, on the coast of the Saronic gulf. Lunch half-way through your journey, with mutton roasted on a spit, in one of the small tavernas along the Argos road, about 12mls (20km) from Corinth.

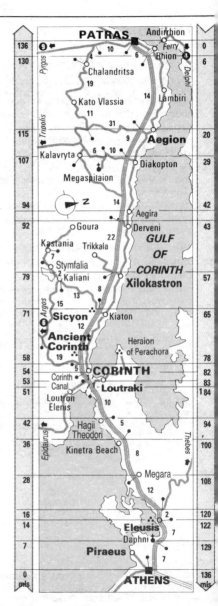

PATRAS

Deep-water port, from which you can take a boat to *Cephalonia and *Ithaca.

→ 1ml (2km). Rhion (ferry day and night to Andirrhion), near the castle of Morea, built by the Turks at the end of the 15th century.

Aegion, capital of Achaea in the 4th century BC, and the home of the federal sanctuary (Homarion) of the Achaean League.

Diakopton, terminal of the cog railway and of the road which lead to the monastery of the Megaspilaion and to Kalavryta. If you make this detour you will have extremely beautiful *views over the Gulf of Corinth and the mountains of Phocis, if the weather is good.

Aegira, where excavations of an ancient theatre and acropolis are in progress.

Xilokastron, coastal resort on the Gulf of Corinth.

← 21mls (34km). Stymfalia (Stymphalia), a village renowned in mythology, and Kastania (28½mls/46km).

← 3½mls (6km). *Sicyon (Sikion) with the ruins of an ancient city.

← 2mls (4km). **ancient Corinth, one of the most evocative of ancient sites, at the foot of Acrocorinth.

Corinth, near the sanctuary of the Isthmus (vicinity of Corinth, 2) and the Corinth Canal.

← 41mls (66km). ***Epidaurus (off the map; via Loutra Elenis), by a *road that borders the Saronic gulf.

→ 3½mls (6km). Loutraki, coastal resort and thermal spa with hotels of varying standard near the *Heraion of Perachora.

Hagii Theodori and Kineta Beach, along a vast beach near the Scyronian Rocks (see Hagii Theodori).

Megara, opposite the Island of Salamis.

*Eleusis (Elefsis), a great religious centre, site of the famous Eleusinian Mysteries in a sanctuary which is now in ruins.

*Daphni. Byzantine church with magnificent mosaics.

***ATHENS

Athens in itself justifies a journey to Greece and an extended stay in Attica.

CORINTH - SPARTA - AREOPOLIS

This journey across the Peloponnese takes in some of the most important archaeological sites. From **Ancient Corinth you will reach Mycenae in an hour. A further fifteen minutes brings you to Argos, an hour and a half more to Tripolis, another hour to Sparta and finally a further hour brings you to Areopolis. From Argos, however, a 52-ml (84-km) detour takes you to ***Epidaurus via ***Tiryns. For variety, take the *Epidaurus road via Loutra Elenis and stay at Nauplia. Sparta deserves more than a brief visit, not for itself, but for its vicinity: above all but also *Monemvasia and the strange region of Mani.

151mls (244km) by a good road, often very winding.

The art of living is much better understood in the Argolid than in Sparta. Near Nauplia there are beaches (the most attractive face Hydra and Spetsae; vicinity of Nauplia, 4) and tavernas (visit those of Tolon, near Nauplia) while there are many attractive country walks around Epidaurus.

CORINTH

Near **Ancient Corinth the sanctuary of the Isthmus (see vicinity of Corinth, 3) and the Corinth Canal.

← 3mls (5km). Nemea, the scene of one of the labours of Hercules (Heracles) with the remains of a temple consecrated to Zeus and the ruins of a stadium.

→ 2mls (4km). ***Mycenae, where the cyclopean wall around the palace of the Atreids, the Lion Gate and the Treasury of Atreus count among the marvels of Greece.

*Argos, another city with a fabulous past, a museum, vicinity rich in archaeological sites such as **Tiryns (4mls/7km), the Heraion (5½mls/9km; vicinity of Argos, 1) and ***Epidaurus (26mls/42km), in the vicinity of a coastal resort; *Nauplia (Nafplion) (7mls/12km).

Lerna, once haunted by the Hydra.

→ 44½mls (72km). Leonidion (off the map), a harbour in the middle of nowhere linked to the outside world by a **road that borders the gulf of Argolis (see vicinity of Lerna).

Tripolis, a place to break your journey in the heart of the Peloponnese.

→ 3½mls (6km). Tegea (Teghea) (vicinity of Tripolis, 1), with the ruins of one of the most famous Arcadian sanctuaries (museum).

→ 5½mls (9km). Karyos (vicinity of Tripolis, 4), monastery decorated with frescoes.

Sellasia. Ruins of an acropolis and of a perimeter wall on Mt Hagios Constantinos. It was here, in 221 BC, that the Archaeans and the Macedonians defeated a Spartan army.

Sparta, a modern city near the site of one of the most famous cities of ancient Greece and ***Mistra (3mls/5km), a ghost town with a remarkable collection of medieval churches, many decorated with frescoes.

→ 45mls (73km). *Monemvasia (off the map), a medieval city at the foot of an imposing fortress beside the gulf of Argolis.

Gythion, a peaceful port on the gulf of Laconia.

AREOPOLIS

The gateway to the Mani, one of the most curious areas of Greece (vicinity of Areopolis, 2). The **caves of Diros are to be found here (vicinity of Areopolis, 1).

← 48mls (78km). Kalamata (off the map), reached by a *road that passes the foot of Taygetos (vicinity of Areopolis, 3).

→ 15½mls (25km). Yerolimín (off the map), in the Mani, from where you may take a trip to Cape Matapan (vicinity of Yerolimín).

PYRGOS-TRIPOLIS-NAUPLIA (NAFPLION)

This route brings you into contact with the geographical and historical diversity of the Peloponnese. One and a half hours after leaving the gentle countryside of Elis, where Pyrgos is thirty minutes from ***Olympia, you will arrive at Andritsaina, where a thirty minutes' climb takes you to the **temple of Bassae. After nearly two hours' drive you will reach Tripolis. Otherwise, allow between four and a half and five hours of almost incessant twists and turns by the direct road from Olympia to Tripolis. Another hour and a half will bring you to Nauplia, which you can use as a base to visit the Argolid, including ***Tiryns, *Argos and ***Epidaurus.

135mls (218km). A good road; winding throughout but less so than the direct road from Olympia to Tripolis (80½mls/130km).

If you take the direct road, you will appreciate the peace and authentic character of *Langadia, just as you will enjoy Andritsaina if you take the other route. Both towns have a comfortable hotel, as does Vytina (on the direct Olympia–Tripolis road), in a wooded region, very pleasant for lunch al fresco in the summer.

PYRGOS

→ 12mls (20km). ***Olympia: here, in a calm and peaceful setting, you can visit one of the most famous holy places of ancient Greece. Beyond Olympia the *road to Tripolis (80½mls/130km), which is narrow and winding, passes through picturesque villages, such as Langadia (36mls/58km) and Vytina (53mls/85km). After 43mls (70km) a road to the r. leads to Dimitsana (5mls/8km) and Karytaina (18½mls/30km).

*Andritsaina, an old Arcadian town that clings to the side of a deep valley running down to the bed of the Alpheus far below, at the foot of Mt Lycea (vicinity of Andritsaina, 3).

← 9mls (15km). **Temple of Bassae, wonderfully well-preserved, in a magnificent setting in the heart of the Arcadian mountains.

Karytaina, a village hidden away at the foot of a castle. From here a *scenic mountain road leads to Dimitsana (18½mls/30km).

Megalopolis, a modern town very close to the ruins of the old 'Great City'. From here you should visit the ancient **Messene at the foot of Mt. Ithomi (see route map 8).

Tripolis, a place to break your journey in the heart of the Peloponnese. From here a narrow winding road leads to ***Olympia (80½mls/130km; see above).

← 6mls (10km). Tegea (vicinity of Tripolis, 1), with the ruins of one of the most famous Arcadian sanctuaries (museum).

← 44½mls (72km). Leonidion (off the map), a port well off the beaten path linked to the outside world by a **road that borders the gulf of Argolis (see vicinity of Lerna).

Lerna, once haunted by the Hydra. A direct road bordering the gulf bypasses Argos.

*Argos, a city great in history and legend, with a museum and a vicinity rich in archaeological sites, such as the Heraion (5½mls/9km; vicinity of Argos, 1) and ***Mycenae (8mls/13km).

**Tiryns, a Mycenaean city and palace once defended by an imposing wall of cyclopean stonework.

NAUPLIA (NAFPLION)

A charming coastal resort from where you can visit ***Epidaurus (18½mls/30km) with its sanctuary of Asclepius.

TRIPOLIS - KALAMATA - PYLOS

The greater part of this route is in Messenia, in the SW of the Peloponnese, and takes you away from the beaten track. Nevertheless, the site of the ancient city of Messene, an hour and forty minutes from Tripolis and forty-five minutes from Kalamata, is an interesting and impressive spot, as is the bay of *Pylos (Navarino), an hour from Kalamata. It is a pleasanter place to stay than Kalamata and provides an opportunity to visit *Nestor's palace at Pylos, or the Venetian citadel at Methoni.

85mls (137km) along a road which is moderately winding (although not during the ascent to Mavromati, the village that now occupies the site of Messene).

We recommend that you lunch beside the sea at Kalamata, in one of the small tavernas along the Areopolis road, or at Methoni, or even in the shade of the plane trees on the main square in Pylos (Navarino). From Pylos, hire a boat and explore one of the most beautiful natural harbours in the country, the scene of the naval battle that brought about Greek independence.

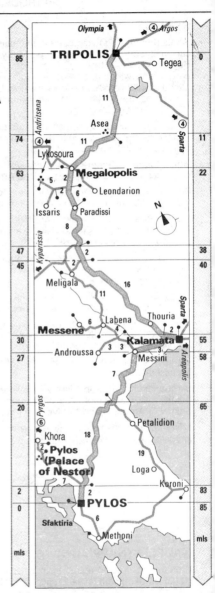

TRIPOLIS

A place to break your journey in the heart of the Peloponnese.

← 28mls (45km). Vytina (off the map, 44½mls/72km) and Langadia (80½mls/130km), ***Olympia, by a narrow winding *road.

→ 6mls (10km). Tegea (vicinity of Tripolis, 1), with the ruins of one of the most famous Arcadian sanctuaries (museum).

Megalopolis, a modern town near the ruins of the ancient 'Great City'.

← 5mls (8km). Lykosoura (vicinity of Megalopolis, 2). Here, in a secluded and pastoral spot, can be seen the ruins of an old Arcadian sanctuary.

← 25mls (40km). Kyparissia, after passing the foot of the prehistoric acropolis of Malthi (9mls/15km), the ancient Dorion (?), abandoned around 1200 BC. A Swedish team has uncovered the scanty remains of a palace surrounded by houses here.

← 2mls (4km). Meligala, capital of the first Dorian dynasty in Messenia, that of Cresphonte (12th century BC), near the ancient triple bridge of Mavrozoumenos (20-min walk), and **Messene (19mls/31km), an ancient site at the foot of Mt. Ithomi, where there is a rampart said to be the masterpiece of the complicated military engineering of the 4th century BC.

→ 2mls (4km). Kalamata, principal port of Messenia, at the foot of a Frankish castle.

48mls (78km). Areopolis (off the map) by a *road (vicinity of Areopolis, 3) that passes the foot of Mt Taygetos.

12mls (20km). **Messene (see above).

→ 19mls (31km). Koroni (vicinity of Kalamata, 1), small port at the foot of an imposing Venetian and Turkish citadel.

← 7mls (11km). *Pylos (Nestor's palace), one of the three great Mycenaean sites of the Peloponnese (objects of interest in the museum of Khora; 2mls/3km).

PYLOS (NAVARINO)*

Charming little seaside town by one of the most beautiful natural harbours in Greece.

↓ 6mls (10km). Methoni, with an immense Venetian fortress where the Lion of St Mark guarded the entrance to the Adriatic.

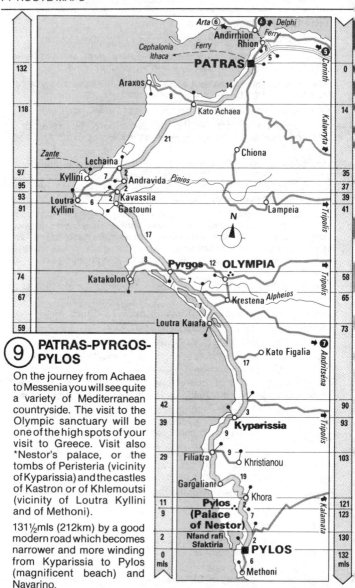

Arta ⑥ ④ Delphi
Andirrhion Ferry
Cephalonia Ferry Rhion
Ithaca ← ↙ ②⑦⑤
PATRAS ■ Corinth

132 0

Araxos ○ 14 Kalavryta

118 Kato Achaea 14

21

○ Chiona

Zante ← Lechaina
97 2 35
Kyllini ○ 7 2
95 Andravida Pinios 37
93 2 39
Loutra ○ 6 Kavassila Lampeia Tripolis
91 Gastouni 41

17

N

8 **Pyrgos** 12 **OLYMPIA**
74 7 → Tripolis
Katakolon ○ 58
67 ○ Krestena Alpheios 65
7
59 Loutra Kaiafa 73

○ Kato Figalia ⑦ Andritsena

⑨ PATRAS-PYRGOS-PYLOS

On the journey from Achaea to Messenia you will see quite a variety of Mediterranean countryside. The visit to the Olympic sanctuary will be one of the high spots of your visit to Greece. Visit also *Nestor's palace, or the tombs of Peristeria (vicinity of Kyparissia) and the castles of Kastron or of Khlemoutsi (vicinity of Loutra Kyllini and of Methoni).

131½mls (212km) by a good modern road which becomes narrower and more winding from Kyparissia to Pylos (magnificent beach) and Navarino.

17

42 3 90
39 **Kyparissia** Tripolis 93
9
29 Filiatra 9 103
○ Khristianou
19
Gargaliani ○
11 Khora 121
Pylos 2
9 **(Palace** 7 123
2 **of Nestor)** Kalamata
Nfand rafi
2 Sfaktiria 2 130
0 ■ **PYLOS** 132
mls 6 mls
○ Methoni

Loutra Kyllini is a thermal spa, but also an ideal place to stay (due to its magnificent beach) and to use as a base for touring Elia and Achaea, as far as Patras. There are also excellent hotels in Olympia (although you are strongly advised to book in advance).

In the vicinity you may like to visit the Miramare Olympia beach, in Skafidia (see Pyrgos), or to seek a little tranquility at Katakolon beach or at Loutra Kaïafa.

Pylos (Navarino) or Methoni are the best places to stay in W Messenia. In Pylos you can lunch under the cool shade of plane trees in the main square.

PATRAS

Maritime gateway to Greece, where you can take a boat to *Cephalonia and *Ithaca.

— 8mls (13km). Araxos (vicinity of Patras, 2), near a prehistoric acropolis (Dimean wall).

— 7mls (12km). Kyllini (ferries to *Zante) and *Loutra Kyllini (12mls/20km), thermal spa and seaside resort with one of the most beautiful beaches of the Peloponnese.

Andravida, ancient capital of the Frankish princes of the Morea.

Gastouni, near ancient Elis (vicinity of Gastouni).

PYRGOS

→ 12mls (20km). ***Olympia. Here, in a calm and peaceful setting, you can visit one of the most famous of pan-Hellenic sanctuaries.

Loutra Kaïafa, a modest thermal spa near the acropolis of Samikon (vicinity of Loutra Kaïafa).

— 41mls (66km). Megalopolis (off the map) and Tripolis (62½mls/101km) passing the foot of the prehistoric acropolis of Malthi (15½mls/25km; see route map 8).

Kyparissia, in the heart of a region rich in Mycenaean sites, such as that of Peristeria (vicinity of Kyparissia) a little way from the road between the Kyparissia and Tripolis roads.

→ 8½mls (14km). Khristianou, with Byzantine church.

Khora, where a museum brings together the finds made in W Messenia, especially in Nestor's palace.

*Pylos (Nestor's palace), one of the three great Mycenaean sites on the Peloponnese.

PYLOS (Navarino)*

A charming little seaside resort beside one of the most beautiful natural harbours in Greece.

↓ 6mls (10km). Methoni, where you can visit an immense Venetian fortress where the Lion of St Mark guarded the entrance to the Adriatic.

IGOUMENITSA-ANDIRRHION

As you travel from Igoumen-itsa to Andirrhion, from Epi-rus to Adarnania and Aetolia, you will see varying types of countryside. The savage beauty of the mountains of Epirus gives way to a Mediter-ranean landscape from *Arta onwards, two and a half hours from Igoumenitsa. Richly wooded groves, hills covered in scrub, fertile orchards, shimmering lakes and impres-sive cliffs appear in turn, until you reach Andirrhion, two and a quarter hours after leav-ing Arta. The journey is also of archaeological interest with the *Nekromanteion, *Nikopolis, Stratos and the Byzantine art of Arta.

171mls (276km). A good road, paralleled between Parga and Preveza by a new coast road, part of which is open.

Your journey will take you close to a small paradise: **Parga, on a remote part of the coast of Epirus, which is well worth visiting for lunch. Another pleasant place for a midday break is Amphilokhia (beaches). The Hotel Xenia in Arta deserves special men-tion for its excellent situation within the walls of the citadel.

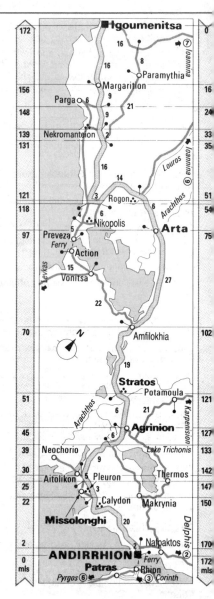

IGOUMENITSA

One of the maritime gateways to Greece (regular services to the Italian ports of the Adriatic and ferries for ***Corfu, that leave ten times a day; the journey takes around one and a half hours).

← 6mls (10km). **Parga, a fishing village on a wild stretch of coast with beautiful beaches.

← 3½mls (6km). *Nekromanteion, a strange place of worship supposed to be at the entrance to Hades.

→ 3½mls (6km). Zalongon, the ancient Kassope (vicinity of Nikopolis, 2), with the ruins of a small theatre and buildings from the 4th century BC.

→ 3½/6mls (6/10km). *Nikopolis (ruins of several palaeo-Christian basilicas; mosaics) and Preveza (8½–11mls/14–18km).

Rogon (or Roguns), on a hill partially surrounded by a loop of the Louros. Ruins of a church and a medieval citadel with a polygonal surrounding wall. You reach Rogon by a road that climbs the *gorges of Louros.

← 38mls (61km). *Ioannina.

*Arta, a town rich in Byzantine art.

Amfilokhia, a charming little town with an oriental flavour, at the heart of the gulf of Arta.

← 23mls (37km). Vonitsa (off the map), a small port at the foot of a Turkish castle, and *Lefkas (36½mls/59km), an island linked to the mainland, especially remarkable for its countryside.

Stratos, an ancient city which has its walls (5th-century BC) almost intact and the remains of a fine temple of Zeus.

AGRINION

→ 118mls (190km). Lamia (off the map), via Karpenision and a superb **mountain road across the wild massif of Tymfrestos (vicinity of Lamia, 3).

Aitolikon, a village just above sea-level, from which amateur archaeologists may visit the site of Oeniadae.

Missolonghi, where Lord Byron gave his life for the cause of Greek independence. In the vicinity amateur archaeologists should visit Calydon and Pleuron.

→ 6mls (10km). Nafpaktos, a pleasant coastal resort on the Gulf of Corinth.

ANDIRRHION

Ferry (day and night) for Rhion.

IGOUMENITSA-VOLOS

This journey in Epirus and Thessaly will take you through a Balkan region to a Mediterranean region. The countryside is superb. In Epirus both *Ioannina and *Metsovon, two hours and three and a half hours respectively from Igoumenitsa, have retained their Balkan character. In Thessaly you can admire the ***cliff monasteries overlooking Kalambaka, one hour from Metsovon. The journey across the plain of Thessaly to Larisa, one hour from Kalambaka, and Volos, one hour from Larisa, may seem tedious although the ***Pelion (vicinity of Volos) will prove of interest. There are points of archeological interest including Dodona and various examples of Byzantine architecture: the convents at Ioannina, the Meteora and the church of Porta Panaghia (vicinity of Trikkala).

229mls (369km) by a road that winds continually until Kalambaka.

In Epirus there are well-situated hotels along the road (Xenia in Igoumenitsa, Ioannina; Metsovon). In Ioannina you may like to lunch beside the lake beneath the plane trees. You may also like to lunch or dine in the cool of the Pelion, or even in one of the tavernas at the water's edge, as you leave Volos in the direction of Tsamgarada.

IGOUMENITSA

One of the maritime gateways to Greece (regular services to the Italian ports of the Adriatic and ferries to ***Corfu ten times a day, a journey of about one and a half hours).

← 2mls (4km). Paganion monastery; 3mls (5km) after the Preveza fork in the direction of Ioannina; a road that is not asphalted, but is suitable for vehicles, leads to this monastery, whose church, dating from 1652, contains frescoes.

→ 3½mls (6km). Zitsa, famous for its sparkling red wine, near the Hagios Ilias monastery, founded in the 14th century.

← 2mls (4km). Konitsa (off the map) in the heart of a region containing some beautiful churches.

← 2mls (4km). *Ioannina, an oriental and Balkan city beside a romantic lake (island monasteries). From here you can visit the **grottoes of Perama (2mls/4km; vicinity of Ioannina, 1) and *Dodona (13mls/21km), ancient sanctuary and oracle in a harsh mountain setting.

← 1ml (2km). *Metsovon, a simple mountain town that is trying to retain its authentic character despite tourist development.

Kalambaka, a small city at the foot of the Meteora, enormous rocks that make up a surrealistic landscape in the style of Hieronymus Bosch and which, with their monasteries, resemble a present-day Thebaid.

Trikala, seat of the demi-god and healer Asclepius.

← 13mls (21km). Porta Panaghia (vicinity of Trikala), basilica decorated with 13th-century mosaics and 14th-century mural paintings.

Larisa. A place to break your journey at a very important crossroads; interesting archaeological museum. From here you can visit the *vale of Tempe and the **Olympus massif.

VOLOS

In a region rich in archaeological sites from the prehistoric period (Sesklo, Dimini, Iolkos) and the Hellenistic period (Pheres, Pagasae, Demetrias). Do not fail to drive along the roads of ***Pelion (vicinity of Volos, 7), an imposing wooded massif between the Aegean Sea and the gulf of Pagasae.

THESSALONIKI - KALAMBAKA

This journey in Macedonia and Thessaly connects **Thessaloniki, the city of Byzantine art, to the ***Meteora, a unique mass of rock which seems about to crush the small city of Kalambaka with its weight. The Meteora are five and a half hours from Thessaloniki and are also a monastic centre where mural paintings provide some examples of the art of ***Mt Athos. Those with a liking for archaeology will be interested by Macedonia, especially if you follow our suggestions about visiting *Pella, *Lefkadia Naoussis (vicinity of Veria, 2) and Palatitsia (vicinity of Veria, 1).

161mls (259km) by a road that is very busy between Thessaloniki and Ghefyra and becomes winding, especially between Veria and Kozani. To save time you may prefer Veria which shortens the journey by 7mls (11km).

Thessaloniki is a large, lively, cosmopolitan maritime city, with beaches on the Thermaïc Gulf and, further away, on the Gulf of Chalcidice. We advise you to make the most of all these amenities, since you will not find them along the journey.

**THESSALONIKI

A city whose Byzantine art almost rivals that of Constantinople and Ravenna. From here you can visit Chalcidice (vicinity of Thessaloniki, 2) from where you may reach ***Mt Athos.

→ 5mls (8km). *Pella, one of the principal archaeological sites in Macedonia. Here you will see some remarkable mosaics.

From Pella go on 37mls (60km) to Veria (see above on the main route) by means of a detour along the Edessa road, turning l. to Veria after 21½mls (35km). In this way you will also be able to visit *Lefkadia Naoussis (26mls/42km; vicinity of Veria, 2), a Macedonian tomb from the Hellenistic period decorated with exceptionally well preserved paintings.

Veria, a small city where there are still reminders of the Turkish occupation and where you may visit small churches, often decorated with frescoes. In the vicinity do not miss the trips to *Verghina (9mls/15km; vicinity of Veria, 1) and *Lefkadia Naoussis (11mls/18km; vicinity of Veria, 2) especially if you are interested in archaeology.

Kozani. A crossroads. Aiani, in the vicinity, possesses several churches decorated with frescoes.

— 3mls (5km). Siatista, a large town founded in the 14th century which flourished from the 16th century to the 18th century, as can be seen from its stately old houses decorated with naive paintings, houses which are today in a poor condition. Notice in particular the Manoussos, Nerandzopoulos and Poulko houses.

— 41mls (66km). *Kastoria (off the map). Beside a romantic lake, a city rich in Byzantine art where the churches are decorated with murals.

KALAMBAKA

A small city at the foot of the Meteora, enormous rocks that make up a surrealistic landscape in the style of Hieronymus Bosch and which, with their monasteries, resemble a present-day Thebaid.

KASTORIA - THESSALONIKI

This journey in W Macedonia links two important centres of Byzantine civilization, *Kastoria and **Thessaloniki, the most interesting centre of Byzantine art in Greece, four and a half hours from Kastoria. Between the two you will pass through two ancient Macedonian capitals, Edessa and *Pella, which are of archaeological interest. We suggest that you make an archaeological detour to *Lefkadia Naoussis (vicinity of Veria, 2) and *Vergina (vicinity of Veria, 1), in order to enliven an otherwise rather uninteresting journey.

133mls (214km) by a road that is winding until it reaches Edessa, then straight but very busy, especially near Thessaloniki.

In Kastoria there is the Hotel Xenia in a fine setting overlooking the lake. At more or less the halfway point you will reach Edessa, which is relatively cool at the height of summer. This is an ideal spot to stop for lunch, although it is in Thessaloniki that you will find real comfort.

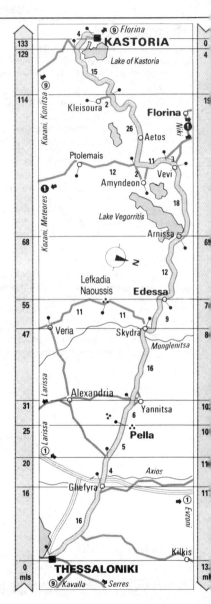

*KASTORIA

Besides a romantic lake, a city full of Byzantine art with churches decorated with frescoes. Near the Albanian frontier, the direct road from Florina (44mls/71km), which also serves Vronderon (49½mls/80km; Byzantine churches), near lake Mikri Prespa, is subject to special regulation, but you can follow it for 7mls (12km), and enjoy a remarkable view over the lake of Kastoria.

← 2mls (3km). Kleisoura, a small mountain village 3,937ft (1,200m) above sea-level, which has a church consecrated to Saint Demetrios (fine 15th-c. iconostasis in sculpted wood).

← 13½mls (22km). Florina, a small, typically Balkan city in a very pleasant wooded setting.

Arnissa, a village on the edge of Lake Vegorritis. The lake is full of fish and rises and falls perceptibly. There is an island, a long way from the present shoreline, on which there are the remains of a small mosque; this, according to the inhabitants, was once the centre of the village, a large part of which must have been submerged.

Edessa, ancient capital of Macedonia, seems a cool oasis at the height of summer.

→ 10½mls (17km). *Lefkadia Naoussis (off the map; vicinity of Veria, 2) where you will see a Macedonian tomb from the Hellenistic period decorated with well preserved paintings, and Veria (21½mls/35km). If you are interested in archaeological sites, go on from Veria to *Vergina (9mls/15km; vicinity of Veria, 1), then to Kypseli (21½mls/35km), 3½mls (6km) N of Aiginion (see route map 2) from where, by the old Thessaloniki road, you can reach Pella (46½mls/75km; see above) from the fork at mile 20/113 (km 32/182) of route map 13.

*Pella, one of the principal archaeological sites of Macedonia. The local museum contains some remarkable mosaics.

**THESSALONIKI

A city whose Byzantine art rivals that of Constantinople and Ravenna. From here you can visit Chalcidice (vicinity of Thessaloniki, 2) from where you can reach ***Mt Athos.

THESSALONIKI-ALEXANDROUPOLIS

From **Thessaloniki to the border between Greece and Turkey and to Istanbul follow the Via Egnatia across E Macedonia and Thrace. This was one of the main arteries of the Roman empire that linked Dyrrachium (modern name Durres, in Albania) to Byzantium (Constantinople). Kavalla is three hours from Thessaloniki and Alexandroupoulis two hours and forty-five minutes from Kavalla. You will not, however, wish to make the journey in a single day as your interest will be aroused first by **Philippi, then by *Thasos and finally by *Samothrace.

210mls (338km) by a good road, winding most of the way, except between Xanthi and Komotini.

You will find Kavalla and Thasos the pleasantest places to stay; Kavalla because it is one of the liveliest and most picturesque ports, and Thasos because this island offers a peaceful refuge and attractive countryside. On the way you may prefer to lunch at Kavalla, in one of the small restaurants along the harbour where you will be offered fresh fish and shellfish.

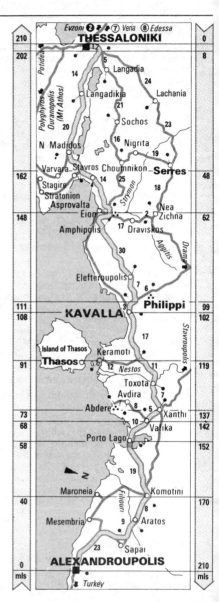

THESSALONIKI

A city whose Byzantine art rivals that of Constantinople and Ravenna. From here you can visit Chalcidice (vicinity of Thessaloniki, 2) from where you can reach ***Mt Athos.

A secondary road links Thessaloniki to Kavalla (128mls/206km; see above) and passes Serres (60mls/97km), Drama (105½mls/170km) and Philippi (118mls/190km).

Amphipolis, once an important city, will attract your attention with a colossal marble lion; on the other side of the Strymon, opposite the road leading to the modern village near the ancient site, another road leads to its ancient port Eion, with the remains of a Byzantine castle and a boundary wall, perhaps formerly Caesaropolis, a city founded in 837 by the Byzantines.

→ 6mls (10km). **Philippi, an abandoned city on the ancient Via Egnatia, and Drama (18½mls/30km).

Kavalla, a very lively city that represents the beginning of the Orient. The city is laid out in the shape of an amphitheatre and the very busy port is the stage (regular services to Thasos, Mytilene, Turkey and Rhodes).

← 12mls (19km). Keramoti; ferry service (seven times a day between 07.30 and 19.30) to *Thasos, a green island with an archaeological site that bears witness to the fact that this was an outpost of Greek civilization.

XANTHI

← 12mls (19km). Abdere (vicinity of Xanthi, 1), another dead city, overgrown by vegetation which in the 5th century BC was the site of a school of philosophy made famous by Democritus.

Porto Lago (vicinity of Xanthi, 2), countryside just above sea-level, between the sea and a lagoon.

Komotini, a foretaste of Turkey with its minarets. Between Komotini and Alexandroupolis the modern road follows, sometimes fairly closely, the line of the Via Egnatia (signs) and leaves to the r., 31½mls (51km) from Komotini, the site of the ancient Mesembria (founded very early by settlers from Samothrace). At this site a group of houses, of which only the foundations remain, was recently uncovered. These houses are bordered on three sides by a boundary wall with towers (4th century BC). Nearby there is a necropolis with a cist burial chamber.

ALEXANDROUPOLIS

A port that provides a link with the island of *Samothrace, another centre of a mystery cult.

← 27mls (44km). Kipi and Istanbul.

(15)

FLORINA-IOANNINA-ARTA

This long journey across the steep and wooded massif of Pindos, where the road has only recently partially been opened (check on current conditions at Florina, Kastoria or Ioannina), takes you from a typically Balkan world into Mediterranean countryside on the edge of the Ionian Sea. The journey takes about one and a half hours from Florina to Kastoria, then about six hours to Ioannina, and finally an hour and a quarter to Arta, passing the picturesque gorge of Louros.

220mls (354km) by a good mountain road which is often very tortuous.

Four Xenia hotels, in Florina, Kastoria, Ioannina and Arta, offer an agreeable stay in this region. In Ioannina, enjoy lunch beside the lake, beneath the plane trees.

FLORINA

A small, typically Balkan city in a very pleasant wooded setting.

↑ 9mls (15km). Niki, Greek border post (open day and night).

*Kastoria. Beside a romantic lake, a town full of Byzantine art where the churches are decorated with frescoes.

→ 12mls (20km). Siatitsa (off the map), near the road from Thessaloniki to Kalambaka (see route map 12), is a large town founded in the 14th century that flourished from the 16th century to the 18th century, as can be seen from its stately old houses decorated with naive paintings, houses which have today lost their former glory. Notice in particular the Manoussos, Nerandzopoulos and Poulko houses.

Konitsa, in the heart of a region that has some beautful churches.

← 17mls (28km). Molyvdoskepastos, a modest village that was once the seat of an archbishop. Worth visiting are the church of an abandoned convent and the Hagii Apostoli church, both decorated with medieval murals.

→ 12mls (19km). *Monodendri, an old village that has retained all its original character.

*Ioannina, an oriental, Balkan city beside a romantic lake (island monasteries), near the **grottoes of Perama (vicinity of Ioannina, 1).

← 8½mls (14km). *Dodona, ancient sanctuary and oracle in a rugged mountain setting.

→ 6mls (10km). Ammotopos, ruins of a city from the 4th century BC (vicinity of Arta, 5).

← 20½mls (33km). Nikopolis (ruins of several palaeo-Christian basilicas; mosaics) and Preveza (25mls/41km).

*ARTA

A city of Byzantine art.

(16)

KHANIA-HERAKLEION-SITIA

This route (see section on Crete) along the N coast of the island takes you by a fast road from Khania (see Crete, 1) to ***Herakleion (see Crete, 3) in about two hours, and then to Sitia (see Crete, 6 - vicinity 4) in another two hours. You will find it necessary to leave the main route at several points in order to visit archaeological sites such as ***Knossos (see Crete, 4), ***Phaistos (see Crete, 5), *Hagia Triada (see Crete, 6) and **Mallia (see Crete, 3 - vicinity 7) which are probably the reason for your visit to this island. Do not forget that Crete had one of the most prolific schools of Byzantine painting. You will appreciate the exceptional talents of the island's artists in Kastelli, Avdou (see Crete, 3 - vicinity 6) and Kritsa (see Crete, 6 - vicinity 2), etc. and in the monasteries of Vrondisi and Varsamonero (see Crete, 5).

171mls (275km) by an excellent modern road.

The most attractive coastal resort is that of Hagios Nikolaos (see Crete, 5). Near Herakleion you will find hotels that are for the most part on the beach, as well as a good number of small restaurants.

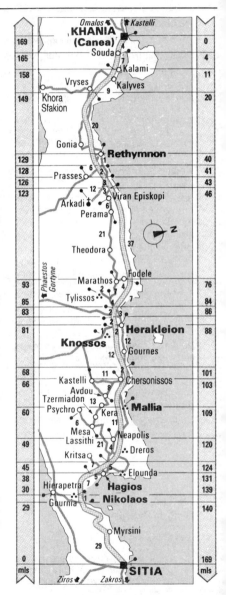

KHANIA

(See Crete, 1). Khania is the capital of Crete, a city on which Venice and the Turks have left their mark; if you are interested in natural curiosities, do not miss the trip to the **gorges of Samaria (vicinity of Khania, 3).

← 25mls (40km). Khora Sfakion, a peaceful fishing port on the S coast of the island which is the easiest place from which to reach the *** gorges of Samaria.

→ 1ml (2km). Rethymnon, a small city with an oriental atmosphere, a reminder of the Turkish occupation. It was here that the University of Crete was established some years ago.

← 12mls (19km). Monastery of Arkadi, one of the important places in the Cretan resistance and a convent of moving simplicity.

2mls (3km). Fodele, the village where Domenikos Theotokopoulos (El Greco) was born, probably around 1541.

← 5½mls (9km). Tylissos (vicinity of Herakleion, 1) a Minoan site on the Ida road.

***Herakleion (Iraklion) (section 3), a city-bazaar, enclosed by an imposing Venetian wall. Of particular interest is a museum, the collections of which trace the evolution of Minoan civilization. Especially, do not miss the excursions to ***Knossos (4) and Mesara (5) where you will visit *Gortyne, ***Phaistos and *Hagia Triada.

Chersonissos. From here you can reach Hagios Nikolaos (47mls/76km) by the high plain of Lassithi on which you will see many windmills.

**Mallia, one of the four Minoan sites not to be missed. The others are Knossos, Phaistos and Hagia Triada.

Neapolis, a small town with little character where archaeological enthusiasts will leave the main route for their visit to Dreros.

→ 5mls (8km). Hagios Nikolaos, the most attractive coastal resort in Crete.

Gournia, with the ruins of a small Minoan city.

← 8½mls (14km). Hierapetra, an easy trip to the S coast.

SITIA

A peaceful little port from where you can visit the E part of the island, towards the Minoan site of Kato Zakros (at the eastern end of Crete), and the only palm grove in Greece, at Vaï.

Table of Distances between the Main Towns (in miles)

	ATHENS	CHALCIS	DELPHI	EVZONI	IGOUMENITSA	IOANNINA	KALAMATA	KALAMBAKA	KAVALLA	LARISA	OLYMPIA	PATRAS	THESSALONIKI	TRIPOLI	VOLOS
ATHENS		55	100	341	301	295	177	211	416	206	201	136	330	121	196
ALEXANDROUPOLIS	526	494	451	252	485	432	668	378	110	306	562	515	211	613	345
ARTA	226	243	163	284	71	45	235	113	368	174	173	100	268	206	236
CHALCIS	55		83	309	314	278	213	197	384	188	238	169	283	157	164
DELPHI	100	83		264	292	228	285	146	347	131	170	82	246	244	142
EVZONI	341	309	264		291	237	483	180	142	121	507	327	42	428	159
IGOUMENITSA	301	314	292	291		62	306	146	374	185	298	171	275	277	223
IOANNINA	295	278	228	237	62		281	81	321	127	234	146	221	252	164
KALAMATA	177	213	285	483	306	281		369	558	342	115	135	438	56	339
KALAMBAKA	211	197	146	180	146	81	369		257	52	315	241	167	340	89
KAVALLA	416	384	347	142	374	321	558	257		194	590	404	101	503	234
LAMIA	133	101	57	212	131	161	252	84	287	87	189	117	186	220	68
LARISA	206	188	131	121	185	127	342	52	194		374	207	95	308	38
NAUPLIA	91	128	205	397	277	252	92	285	472	277	121	114	372	37	253
OLYMPIA	201	238	170	507	298	234	115	315	590	374		74	489	81	404
PATRAS	136	169	82	327	171	146	135	241	404	207	74		303	106	185
SPARTA	158	195	244	465	314	290	37	360	540	345	109	143	439	37	320
THESSALONIKI	330	283	246	42	275	221	438	167	101	95	489	303		402	133
TRIPOLI	121	157	244	428	277	252	56	340	503	308	81	106	402		283
VOLOS	196	164	142	159	223	164	339	89	234	38	404	185	133	283	

Understanding Greece

The Geography of Greece

Situated at the extreme edge of the Balkans, Greece is the most southern and eastern region of Mediterranean Europe. The main elements in its landscapes are sea and mountain. Indented shores, the interpenetration of sea and land, is a true image of this country which is made unique by certain distinctive characteristics: the luminous atmosphere, the dry and infertile land, the torrential throbbing of the rivers, the scrubland and the olive groves – all set side by side, complementing and contrasting with one another.

The geographical framework

THE GREEK SEA. The life of Greece has always been directed towards the Aegean Sea. The Greek sea is a blue sea, scattered with islands that the sun cloaks with a reddish patina; these islands are like the supports of a bridge thrown down between Europe and Asia Minor; the navigator can use them both as so many ports of call to shelter him and as seamarks to guide him. The underwater plateau divides the Aegean Sea into basins. In the north, the Sporades extend the Thessalian ranges towards Lesbos and Chios. In the south, the arc of islands made up of Cytherea, Crete, Karpathos and Rhodes links Asia to the Peloponnesian ranges; between the two, the Cyclades are the outcrop of a former insular shelf.

A TREACHEROUS SEA. The sea, which seems easy to navigate, is nevertheless treacherous. The bad season lasts from November to March, with sudden violent gusts of wind and storms that break up the sea into small angry waves. In summer, for four months, from May to September, atmospheric currents called Etesian winds blow from the north-east in cycles of remarkable steadiness and disrupt sailing conditions; this famous *meltem* dies down in the evening: the sky is clear but the horizon is slightly hazy and the clouds capping the mountains proclaim that the wind will persist for several days. In September the weather can be fickle and the autumn equinox is marked by storms.

OMNIPRESENT MOUNTAINS. Eighty per cent of the Greek land-surface is mountainous, leaving little room for plains; only in Thessaly and Macedonia are there some fairly extensive open stretches of country; elsewhere ranges and massifs wall off the different regions. Although mountainous, Greece is not a country of high mountains; only a few summits exceed 6,500ft (2,000m) (Olympus, Pindos, Parnassus, Taygetos). These mountains rising near the sea or the narrow plains, stand proudly exposing on their steep slopes patches of bare rock or masses of fallen stone.

A THREEFOLD RELIEF SYSTEM. In Greece the mountains form a complicated system in which three groups stand out.

In the west, ranges of mountain folds with predominantly limestone rocks link two units: the Pindos range, indented with sharp and tortuous crests, and the Ionian ranges which are associated with the islands of Corfu, Cephalonia (Kefallinia) and Zante.

In the east, low-lying massifs (Olympus, Ossa, Pelion, Othrys) are separated or bordered by broad depressions (the plains of Macedonia and Thessaly); the island of Euboea, Citheron, Parnassus as well as the Gulf of Corinth belong to this physical system. In the south, the Peloponnese is formed by a group of crests and mountainous blocks (Olonos, Taygetos, Parnon) separated by depressions (the basins of Arcadia, Megalopolis, Messenia and Laconia).

A THREEFOLD GEOLOGICAL ORIGIN. This complexity reflects geological vicissitudes. Three structural elements may be distinguished.

In the north-east in Thessaly and in Macedonia, as well as in Euboea, the extremity of Attica and the Cyclades, mountains such as Olympus belong to a group of primary massifs of which the Cyclades are an insular extension.

In the centre, the axis of the Hellenic peninsula and Crete form a heterogeneous group of overthrust nappes, horsts and rift basins which have in turn shaped the secondary and tertiary formations.

In the west, the Ionian ranges are fold mountains. These three groups have been formed or taken up by the Alpine folds; therefore; the Hellenic mountain structure reflects recent movements of the earth's crust, still liable to changes, as volcanic activity and earth tremors show. For example the island of Santorini (Thera) is a volcano whose crater, damaged by an eruption in the 16th century BC, was flooded by the sea.

THE CLIMATE AND THE SEA. Bathed on all sides by the sea (no part of the country is further than 60mls/90km from the coast) and including a great number of islands, Greece has a predominantly maritime climate. But the mountainous skeleton runs counter to this influence and gives a certain ruggedness to the regions of the interior. Rain is rare and more abundant in the west (Corfu: 50in/122cm) than in the east (Athens 16in/41cm); it is distributed over a small number of days (98 days in Athens). It falls mainly in winter and in the form of sudden showers. Sometimes it is so violently torrential that it is as unpleasant and damaging as a hail storm.

THE RHYTHM OF THE SEASONS. Winter begins towards the middle of December; usually it is not harsh and is of limited length. The number of days when the thermometer is at zero (32°F) is small. But this is only true in the regions adjacent to the sea or at a low altitude, such as Attica, a part of the Peloponnese, and the islands. Western Macedonia, a large part of Epirus, and the central Peloponnese suffer from harsher winters (-54°F/-12°C and even -68°F/-20°C), with heavy snowfalls.

The spring is brief: it causes a swift and brilliant flowering, violets and narcissi display their velvety finery under a hard blue sky against which are outlined the blossoming trees. Summer arrives abruptly, as early as May, and burns everything; during the hottest months (June and July) certain regions of Greece endure temperatures of 98°F, 102°F, 106°F (36°C, 38°C, 40°C). Frequently, there is no rain at all in July and August; across the overheated country the air vibrates and powders the trees with dust. The pale foliage of the olive trees becomes lustreless.

The autumn is an extension of the summer season because of the winds blowing from the south. Then come the rains (maximum rainfall in November) announcing winter.

A THREEFOLD CLIMATIC ZONE. Following the pattern of the seasons, Greece divides up into three climatic areas.

The continental zone, which includes the interior of Epirus, Macedonia, Thrace and Thessaly, offers a kind of transition between the Mediterranean climate and that of Central Europe, with a dry summer season and marked differences in temperature. Frosts occur often, atmospheric precipitations are infrequent, rains are not violent as in the Mediterranean zone, but fine and long-lasting; there are no olive trees in this region.

The Ionian region, which includes the western coasts and the Ionian islands, has a typically Mediterranean climate, with a mild winter, light cloud cover, and hot dry summers. Rain is abundant and the vegetation luxuriant, while the streams rarely lack for water.

The eastern region, with Attica, the coasts and the islands of the Aegean Sea, well known for the dryness of the air, and the clarity of the atmosphere, is considered to offer the classic type of Hellenic climate.

A FEW MAJOR RIVERS AND MANY LESSER ONES. The small rivers reflect the climate. Only the rivers of the west (Epirus, Aetolia, Acarnania) and those of Thessaly flow abundantly and have proved suitable for harnessing to hydro-electric installations. The other regions feed only scanty rivers. These small, impetuous rivers render little service to man, with their narrow gorges, their irregular flow, and their muddy, undrinkable water. On the other hand, underground the circulation of water never stops; in the limestone, grottoes, chasms or fissures, *katavothres*, open up to absorb the water and to re-emerge as springs, from whence originated towns such as Mycenae, Thebes and Athens.

A MEDITERRANEAN VEGETATION, BUT WITH VARIATIONS. In the main part of the country, the flora is characterized by perennial flowers and evergreen trees; bushy formations, the *garrigue* and scrub, are the dominant elements of the botanical landscape, with a pre-eminence of species with indeciduous, leathery, glossy leaves; a few trees (evergreen oaks or cork-oaks) stand alone or in clusters, below which the shrubs crowd round, myrtles, arbutus, laurels, lentisks, bush heather, wild olive trees; here and there clearings covered with flowers stand out (narcissi, asphodels, hyacinths, crocuses) or sweet-smelling herbs (mint thyme, wild thyme). But the climatic modifications caused by the terrain also transform the vegetation: the plains of northern Greece have a steppe-like aspect, while forests remain on the mountains of the interior, where the olive disappears, and is replaced by deciduous trees: oaks in Epirus or Macedonia, chestnuts in Chalcidice or Pelion, firs from Taygetos to Parnassus, beeches in Pindos.

SPECIFIC REGIONS. Within the overall Mediterranean landscape, geographical divisions are noticeable.

In the north people are leaving the mountains, and the plains of Thessaly, Macedonia and Thrace, which, despite a severe and extreme climate but with the help of large irrigation schemes, now produce cotton, maize, rice and sugar-beet. Tobacco remains the traditional crop.

The west, from Epirus to the Peloponnese, is characterized by a good rainfall, with numerous and constantly-flowing rivers (hence hydro-electric installations). But Epirus, isolated, wild and depopulated, is the poorest region of Greece. On the other hand, the coastal plains (Arta, Agrinion) lend themselves to rich agricultural use (tobacco, fruit).

Central Greece seems to epitomize in its landscapes the whole country, but its own features are becoming increasingly obliterated by the attractions of the capital. As for the Peloponnese, it is fascinating because of its hillsides, where vines and olives are grown as well as vegetables and citrus fruits; there again the uplands isolate the plains of the interior, which nevertheless remain pleasant (regions of Sparta, Megalopolis).

The islands retain their own individuality. Corfu, luxuriant, rich and fertile like the other Ionian islands, contrasts with the harsh and desolate Cyclades while in the Sporades and the Dodecanese is seen the entire range of Mediterranean vegetation (scrub, pine forests, olives). As for Crete, it is almost a small continent in its diversity: desolate coasts like those between Herakleion and Mallia, the summits of the White Mountains or of Psiloriti (8,186ft/2,456m), the fertile plain of Messara ...

Human geography

A REMARKABLY HOMOGENEOUS PEOPLE. If you consider the vicissitudes to which the Greek people have been subjected and the geographical boundaries of Greece, the persistence of national unity is surprising: 98% of the population of this country are Hellenes, consider themselves as such, speak Greek and practise the Orthodox religion. This unity is explained by the links with the past and by the very qualities of the Greek people. Greece has a spirit of independence that has allowed it to retain the same peninsular and insular detachment over the centuries in spite of the upheavals in its history.

SOME FIGURES. Because of the birth rate, one of the highest in Europe, and the influx of Greeks forced to leave Turkey, Bulgaria, Egypt, etc., the population has more than doubled since 1913. Today it has reached ten million, but large Greek communities are still established outside national soil, in Cyprus, Germany, the United States, South America, etc.

For a surface area of 51,698sq. mls (132,560km^2) (of which 18,968 sq. mls/48,635km^2 are islands), the density is 193 inhabitants per sq. ml (75 per km^2). But over most of the country this average is far from being reached; the population is concentrated in Attica, round Athens and Piraeus, in Macedonia, from Thessaloniki to Kavalla and over the western area of the Peloponnese.

RELIGION, FERMENT OF UNITY. The popular faith is a mixture of pagan and Christian traditions, but the Orthodox Church weaves a much deeper weft across social and cultural life than in many other Christian countries. Under Turkish domination it has been the strongest defender of language, customs and national consciousness.

THE GREEK ORTHODOX CHURCH. Orthodoxy was, until 1982, the official religion of the Greek State and that of the great majority of the population, although the Constitution guarantees freedom of worship (there are about 100,000 Muslims, 50,000 Catholics and a few hundred Jews). The coming of the Socialists to power in October 1982 brought about the separation of the Church and the State. The national Greek Church is autocephalous although recognizing the supremacy of the patriarch of Constantinople, and is placed under the direction of an archbishop chosen by a synod (in 1982, Archbishop Serafim).

The history of the Orthodox Church dates back to the establishment of the capital of the Roman Empire in Constantinople in 313 AD, which gave prime importance to the patriarchal seat of this city (there were five originally), all the more so as Rome soon fell into the hands of the barbarians, and Jerusalem, Alexandria and Antioch took advantage of the arrival of the Muslims during the 7th century to set up as independent churches. The break between Rome and Constantinople was for the most part political (struggles for influence, problems of supremacy, the role of the emperors of Germany and Byzantium, etc.) though it involved some points of theology. This breach was consummated in 1054, when Michael Cerularius, patriarch of Constantinople, excommunicated Pope Leo IX who hastened to do the same to him.

Far more important for the history of this Church was the taking of Constantinople by the Turks in 1453. Under Koranic law, Christians recognized as 'People of the Book' were protected by the caliph-sultans in exchange for a 'protection tax'. This was the Milliyet system which guaranteed them a wide administrative autonomy and total freedom of religion, language and education. On the other hand, the notion of nationality did not exist in the Turkish Empire, where differentiation between peoples was by religion alone. The patriarch of Constantinople thus became the representative vis-à-vis the secular power of the Orthodox peoples of the Ottoman Empire. His role was therefore much more important than in the Byzantine period: administrative and political functions were added to his religious ones. The confusion between Greek and Orthodox dates from this period as well, the two being considered as one regardless of ethnic group (which led to numerous problems during the struggles for independence of the Slavic people of the Balkans).

At the time of the struggle for independence, at the beginning of the 19th century, the Greek Church played a leading part and the banner of faith became that of revolt. It was then that the Greek Church nominally parted company from Constantinople, judging it impossible to be governed by a patriarch subjected to the Turks from whom the Greeks had just obtained their freedom (1833).

On the other hand, at the time of the enlargement of the national territory the Orthodox Christians of the new provinces remained faithful to the patriarch of Constantinople. This was the case for Crete (1913) and for the Dodecanese (1947), while Thrace (1913), though continuing to give allegiance to Constantinople, sent representatives to the Athens synod. There are no determining differences between the Orthodox and the Catholic Church on the theological level, other than the complex problem of the *filioque* (the Catholics consider that the Holy Ghost proceeds 'from the Father and the Son' while Orthodox Christians think, following Saint John, that the Holy Ghost proceeds only from the Father) and, more recently, the question of papal infallibility (1870).

The two Churches stand on the same foundations, that is to say the seven ecumenical councils, and it is ritual and discipline, born of a different history, that mainly separate the two principal branches of Christianity (autocephalous churches, systems of election of bishops, married priests, etc.).

Although, from the time of the patriarchate of Athenagoras (1948–1972) there was a reconciliation with the Vatican (a meeting between Athenagoras and Pope Paul VI, and then between Demetrios and Pope John Paul II), the Greek Church remained for its part slightly withdrawn; not until June 1980 did it cease to oppose the setting up of diplomatic relations between the Government of Athens and the Vatican.

The Greek Church still plays a major role in the country, whether on the level of daily life or that of the State (the archbishop is present at all State occasions); only the Orthodox Church has the right to proselytize.

THE GREEK VILLAGE. The typical rural habitat is the hill-top. This preference for defensible positions on the heights is attributable no doubt to long periods of insecurity, but it also reflects the need to cultivate the slopes in terraces. The village houses are tall, sometimes cube-shaped with a terraced roof, sometimes topped with red tiles. Life is concentrated on the square near the church, in the shadow of the plane trees; from there narrow cobbled alleys climb up, made dark by balconies and overhanging roofs. In the islands, the buildings are more clustered, a huddle of white shapes grouped around the port as if set between sea and sky.

THE URBAN SETTING. The urban population is larger than the rural population. Numerous small towns are established in the comparatively few suitable sites here and there across the country, towns on inland plains, acropolis-towns, towns on islands, all with their chapels, their market stalls opening wide onto the street, and the innumerable little donkeys who hasten to market in the mornings. The only important towns are the ports: Piraeus, Patras, Kavalla, Volos, Corinth.

The towns are animated and lively; the streets with their many cafés seem full of idlers, or rather of small commission agents: garrulous travelling salesmen, sellers of titbits and watermelons. The narrow streets lined with shops give to these towns a very special atmosphere.

ATHENS AND THESSALONIKI. Two large towns stand out against the whole urban network: Athens and Thessaloniki. The latter occupies a remarkable commercial position at the opening of the Morava and Vardar valleys, but its role is atrophied by the frontier, which is a politico-economic barrier. Athens, the population of which fell to 2,000 at the end of the War of Independence, is the leaven for all Greek life. It forms, with Piraeus and the peripheral areas, a huge agglomeration with a population of more than 2,500,000, a quarter of the population of the country. The modern town has developed vastly, first between the hills of the Acropolis and Lycabettos, then overflowing on each side to the slopes of Hymettos and Parnassus, fusing with Piraeus and running along the Apollo coast bathed by the waters of the Saronic gulf, to Varkiza, 17mls (27km) from the centre of the capital.

A Glance at History

by **Pierre Lévêque**

Former President of the University of Besançon

Ancient Greece

Ancient Greek civilisation has left its stamp on the Mediterranean world and, in a more general way, the Western world, because of the extraordinary creative power that it displayed, during the Classical period (5th and 4th centuries BC). For a long time only this classicism merited attention, and not until the nineteenth century was much interest taken in the earlier part of Greek history (although only through it can we truly understand the climactic 'century of Pericles') or the unfolding of Hellenistic history up to the Roman conquest. It is, however, worthwhile to follow the development of Greek history, which in the course of around two millenia shows an astonishing continuity.

But it should also be noted how arbitrary it is to limit this history to the Balkan peninsula that we call Greece. One of the most outstanding characteristics of Hellenism has been its conquering dynamism that led the Greeks to take root in Asia Minor and to colonize widely around the shores of the Mediterranean and the Black Sea. Plato's image that shows them on these coasts 'like frogs around a pond' is justly famous. We shall therefore not forget that we are taking a view of Hellenism that is inevitably incomplete when we restrict it to the geographical limits of present-day Greece.

1 Greece until the end of the 2nd millennium BC

GREECE BEFORE THE GREEKS. The development of human societies on Greek soil was slow if one compares it to the brilliant and precocious successes of protohistory in Egypt or Mesopotamia. The Palaeolithic Age had little part in it. In the two stages of the Neolithic Age (Neolithic I: 4500–3000; Neolithic II: 3000–2600 BC) settlements increased substantially, in particular in Thessaly (Dimini), but the civilization was still primarily agricultural and pastoral.

Towards the year 2600 BC, Greece entered the Bronze Age; the period until 2000 BC is conventionally called Ancient Helladic. It was ushered in by the arrival by sea of invaders from Anatolia, overwhelming the ancient Neolithic populations. Undeniable progress was evident in all spheres: the introduction of new crops and of the plough (that is the modest swing-plough), the advent of bronze metallurgy and of a new, wonderfully glazed pottery (style of the *Urfirnis*), the development of maritime trade. True cities grew up, of which the best known is Lerna, on the gulf of Nauplia, where a place has been discovered (the House of Tiles) which clearly bears witness to the power of a monarchic institution. Religious life was intense and, as in the whole of the eastern Mediterranean, it was principally the Earth-Mothers who were worshipped, the mistresses of fertility, fecundity and eternal life of which many corpulent statues remain.

THE ARRIVAL OF THE GREEKS AND THE MIDDLE HELLADIC PERIOD (2000-1580 BC). Towards 2000 BC new invaders occupied Greek soil, coming from the north; these were the first Greeks. Their invasion was part of a much vaster movement: in the middle of the third millennium, Indo-Europeans, until then gathered in a common habitat that can be placed in the steppes of southern Russia and in the Carpatho-Danubian region, began to separate; their migrations were slowly to bring about the populating of Europe and of a part of Asia; the first among them to reach Mediterranean shores were, more or less simultaneously, the Hittites and the Luites in Asia Minor and the Greeks in Greece.

Towards 2000 BC archaeology on nearly all sites shows a very clear division that corresponds to the arrival of the Greeks and their seizure of the country. These first Greeks, who perhaps bore the name of Ionians, were still fairly primitive. However, little by little they learned from their predecessors how to grow vines, olives, figs, the art of navigation, and doubtless there were already many popular and religious traditions as well. Certain of their settlements are well known, such as Dorion-Malthe in Messenia; the fortification, where a rudimentary palace is to be found, is in the centre of a massive surrounding wall that encloses houses, booths, shops and open spaces no doubt intended for cattle at moments of attack.

The period between 2000 BC and 1580 BC is called Middle Helladic. It corresponds to the arrival of the Greeks and their settlement on Greek soil. Towards 1580 BC a new period began called Recent Helladic or, after the name of the most famous site, the Mycenaean period. Between the two there is no break-point, no violent invasion as in 2000 BC. Rather, there was an internal development that may be explained by new factors: a marked gain in productivity; the arrival of a second round of Greek invaders, the Achaeans (referred to by Homer as well as in the Hittite texts), who reinforced with new blood the Greek population of Hellas, and particularly the influence of the Cretan world on Greece.

THE MYCENAEAN PERIOD (1580-1100 BC). Rich and powerfully fortified palaces (Mycenae, Tiryns, the island of Gla, Athens) now took the place of the relatively meagre settlements of the preceding period, each of them the centre of an independent kingdom. Society was strongly structured around a king, the *wanax*, assisted by a general-in-chief or grand vizier (*lawagetas*) and numerous officers, officials and scribes (at Pylos royal archives have been discovered, written in the script known as linear B, which has recently been deciphered and has its origin in Minoan linear A). Below them came the freemen, the craftsmen and especially the peasants, forming the people (*demos*), and the slaves, generally the product of fruitful raids. The organization of this centralized and bureaucratic monarchy that animated and controlled economic activity recalls that of the Middle Eastern and Cretan despotisms.

Among all these kingdoms, that of Mycenae incontestably enjoyed moral supremacy, as the *Iliad* tells us, by making Agamemnon the leader of the Achaeans in their expedition against Troy. It is this cohesion of the Achaean world that explains its expansion over the whole of the eastern Mediterranean: the Achaeans took possession of Crete (15th century), Rhodes (where the Hittite texts mention a powerful kingdom of Akhkhi jawa, i.e. Achaeans), of Cyprus (where the fortified enclosure of Enkomi recalls the fortified castles of Argolis). But the best known enterprise of conquest is, of course, the siege of Troy because of its survival in the famous epic. Towards 1180 BC, according to the most common ancient tradition, or more probably towards 1230 BC according to the moderns, all the Achaeans took part in a common expedition against the opulent Asiatic city of Troy; after a siege of ten years they took it, ransacked it, and returned home. The pretext given later for the undertaking was the abduction of the beautiful Helen by a Trojan prince, but it may be supposed that the wish to take possession of the enormous riches accumulated over the centuries in Priam's palace was the underlying reason for an expedition that was the swan-song of Achaean expansion.

Economic life was flourishing. The principal wealth was the land. We know from old tablets about the complicated regime of land allocation: setting aside the great estates reserved for the *wanax*, the *lawagetas* and the officers, a part of the land belonged collectively to the people, who shared it among the heads of families, perhaps by periodically drawing lots; another part was subject to private ownership. Craftsmanship flourished, particularly in pottery and the luxury industries. The inscriptions prove that there was already very extensive specialization by craftsmen. As for trade, it affected nearly all the Mediterranean coasts from Syro-Phoenicia, where Achaean objects are numerous in Ongarit and in Al Mina, to Sicily and Italy and as far as Egypt and Libya. Not satisified with occupying the large islands in the eastern Mediterranean (Crete, Rhodes, Cyprus) the Achaeans set up commercial settlements everywhere, foreshadowing the *emporia* of the Archaic Era.

The outburst of creativity is to be seen not only in its great artistic creations: an epic literature appeared of which unfortunately no trace remains, except for that which survives in Homer's later re-elaboration. New religious forms were created, by a synthesis of Nordic and Mediterranean elements, that is Greek and Cretan. Thus Zeus was the Indo-European god of the luminous vault of the sky or of rain and snow, father of the gods and of men, but he was also a young Cretan god, son and lover of the Earth-Mother. The deities mentioned on the tablets are on the whole those that were to make up the classical Greek pantheon: Zeus, Poseidon, Hermes, Dionysus, Hephaestus, Hera, Athena, Artemis...; but Apollo and Aphrodite are not there. The gods were honoured in consecrated places (grottoes, woods, springs, etc.), in small decorated shrines, or in temples. The cult of the dead was highly developed as is testified by the numerous offerings found in the tombs. The princely dead were the object of special honours, which made them heroes. It can be seen that all the main features of subsequent religion in Greece were laid down as long ago as the Mycenaean period.

THE DORIAN INVASIONS (from 1200 BC). Towards the end of the second millennium, a new wave of Greek invaders, the Dorians, submerged Hellas. Coming from the north and down the two sides of the Pindos, they occupied a part of central Greece, almost the whole of the Peloponnese (except Arcadia), Crete and the southern Cyclades and the Sporades. The Greeks had retained a memory of this great movement in the myth of the return of the Heraclids. The result of these invasions has been much discussed. Fundamentally, they had a destructive aspect, causing the disappearance of all the marvels accumulated in the Achaean palaces and spreading ruin everywhere. Throughout the history of Greece there is no more frightful cataclysm, not even the Roman conquest. However, the definitive populating of Greece was ensured: after the Ionians came the Achaeans, then the Aeolians, who settled during the 2nd millennium, and finally the Dorians formed the last wave of Greek, that is to say Indo-European, invaders. All these ethnic groups differ on the one hand through their dialect (and it was their successive arrivals that explain the dialectal groups that could be distinguished in Greece until the very end of Hellenism), and on the other hand by their degree of civilization, the last comers being by far the most barbaric. But they bear a resemblance to each other because of their common origins which meant that soon, when the tumult of the invasions had subsided, they were to feel as if they belonged to the same race. It is no longer customary to attribute to the Dorians the responsibility for two innovations that appeared in Greece simultaneously with them, but without direct relationship to them: iron metallurgy, which little by little was substituted for bronze, and geometric pottery. On the other hand, there certainly was a Dorian society, a military society, founded on a virile comradeship in arms, that continued to exist in part in Sparta. And there were certain religious forms or usages that were specifically Dorian: the predominance of gods over goddesses (in the great sanctuaries masculine deities were substituted for the Earth-Mothers of the preceding period, at Delphi, Olympia and Delos for example), and cremation of the dead which replaced burial.

2 The Geometric era and the Archaic era 11th–6th centuries BC)

THE GEOMETRIC ERA (1100–750 BC). The era that followed the invasions is called, according to conventional ceramic terminology, the Geometric era. It is divided into proto-Geometric (1100–900 BC) and Geometric proper (900–750 BC). It witnessed the new, slow and timid beginnings of civilization. Attica in particular, spared by the Dorians, made great progress, which is attested by the rich funerary furniture of the new cemetery of Kerameikos in Athens.

A new art appeared that was not totally separated from the past. Homer also made the transition with the Mycenaean period (the two epics attributed to him rework fragments of the earlier epos, but the society they depict is in the main that of the 10th and 9th centuries BC). Hesiod sang the genealogies of the gods, and (in *Works and Days*) Boeotian peasant life. Religious life revived, a new rationalism organized the pantheon, as can be seen in the *Theogony* of Hesiod. New gods originating from the Anatolian or Semitic East, such as Apollo and Aphrodite, were assimilated by the Greeks. Towards 900 BC an alphabetic writing was created, imitating Phoenician writing, with a creative subtlety peculiarly Greek. Finally, from around 800 BC, a form of political organization was seen to develop which for centuries dominated the Greek world: the *polis* (or city-state) where, under the hegemony of the aristocrats, the population of small peasants was assimilated into the civic community. In short, towards 750 BC the 'dark ages' resulting from the invasions were over. All this progress was possible only with the resumption of trade throughout the Mediterranean, which generated fruitful exchanges. This movement was to expand during the following period, Archaism, that began towards 750 BC.

THE DEVELOPMENT OF CITIES DURING THE ARCHAIC ERA (750–500 BC). From the 7th century a new name appeared for all the Greeks: Hellenes. In point of fact the unity of Hellenism first showed clearly in the political sphere, since the rate of evolution was appreciably the same in all the cities. The first form of government everywhere was monarchy, but the power of the kings was strictly limited by the aristocracy, who held all the good land, and whose insolent pride and rapacity had already been exposed by Hesiod. Little by little the nobles seized power, usually without violence. Authority was then exercised by magistrates who replaced the king and by a council which emanated from the land-owning aristocracy. In the 7th century an economic revolution altered the Hellenic world profoundly: the introduction of money, invented a short time before in Lydia. Crafts and commerce were greatly stimulated and for the first time in the Mediterranean basin a commercial economy appeared. The social consequences were no less important: the advent of wealth based on movable assets side by side with the land-owning wealth of the nobles. Thus the nobles' power was gradually eroded. It was also shaken by the violent changes that stirred the people, whose economic situation worsened little by little as the division of inherited land decreased the size of properties below subsistence level for a family. A social crisis of extraordinary intensity then shattered the stability of the aristocratic regime. Sometimes efforts were made to resolve it by resorting to legislators, who for the first time set down laws in writing. But often it was only violence that put an end to it and the seizure of power by a tyrant.

Tyranny was a phenomenon fairly limited in area: in Greece proper it mainly affected the neighbouring towns of the isthmus (Corinth, Sicyon, Megara), but Athens also underwent it belatedly. The tyrant made use of the mass of the small peasants crushed by the nobles and upon those who lived from crafts and trade, against the aristocracy, which he decimated, exiled and deprived of its lands. He conducted a policy of prestige, multiplied public works (aqueducts, fountains, etc.), erected sumptuous temples, liked to surround himself with a court of artists and poets ...

In several cities tyranny tended to became hereditary: thus in Sicyon the Orthagorid ruling family was a real dynasty which remained in power for a century; in Corinth the Cypselids reigned with remarkable brilliance for more than 70 years. But gradually the tyrannies collapsed. In fact, they carried within themselves their own ruin, in so far as the reforms that they made contributed to the solution of the social crisis from which they were born. Most of the time the aristocracy, sometimes made wiser by its recent misfortunes, regained hegemony — for example in Corinth. In Athens, on the contrary, it was democracy that quite quickly succeeded tyranny.

ECONOMIC TRANSFORMATIONS AND COLONIZATION. During the centuries of Archaism, fundamental economic changes came about. Cultivation of vines, olive and fig trees, which grow remarkably well on the generally arid Greek soil, increased considerably in comparison with cereals, especially in Attica. The result was at one and the same time overproduction of wine and oil and a scarcity of grain, an imbalance for which the only solution was colonization.

So, from 775 BC to about 550 BC, a vast movement of expansion took place which resulted in the establishment of Greek colonies on the shores of the Mediterranean and of the Black Sea. Those who left their country were generally prompted by the sternest necessity: political differences in the cities, and above all the extreme poverty that generates despair. But the results of this movement were especially favourable to Hellenism: at the same time as Greece, unable to feed its population from its own land, recovered its stability and developed the ability to import cereals and ores, new cities were born, especially in the west (Sicily, Magna Graecia, southern Gaul, eastern Spain), but also on the shores of the Propontis and the Black Sea. It was a whole 'New World' that quickly appeared, as demonstrated by the brilliance of Selinus, Agrigentum or Paestum.

The new cities thus created were independent of their parent states with which, however, they maintained religious and, especially, economic links. From then on vast economic currents crossed the

Mediterranean and the Black Sea. The Greeks obtained, from distant places, cereals, salted fish, precious or base metals, wood. In exchange, they disposed of their semi-luxury agricultural products (wine, oil) and products manufactured by their incomparable craftsmen (gold plate, cloth, pottery, perfumes and unguents). All the elements of a great Mediterranean trade were brought together at that time, and Greece expanded widely in every direction.

SPARTA AND ATHENS. Two cities are worthy of of special mention, the more so as they formed a living antithesis. Sparta offers the example of a city where all the citizens devoted themselves to the exclusive service of the State. Brought up from childhood with a view to serving at arms, its inhabitants were uniquely soldiers. They lived by the harsh exploitation of a class of subjugated peasants, the Helots, descendants of the Achaean peoples conquered at the time of the Dorian invasions. For the most part the citizens, or Spartiates, were small landholders, although this did not exclude the existence of an aristocracy. Civilization, which for a long time was brilliant, was abruptly stopped in its progress in the 6th century by a deliberate decision of the leaders, anxious to preserve the ancestral traditions and to avoid the supposedly dangerous contagion of other cities.

In contrast to Sparta, frozen in opposition to progress, Athens developed with prodigious rapidity. Politically, it moved towards democracy during the whole of the 6th century, from Solon to Cleisthenes, and even the intermediary episode of the tyranny of the Pisistratids did not impede this march towards the government of the people by the people. On the economic level, Athens developed its crafts (especially pottery) and its trade, to the point of gradually ousting from the markets the towns that were formerly more illustrious than itself, such as Corinth, Aegina, Chalcis. And already it had begun to adorn itself with temples, particularly on the Acropolis.

ARCHAIC CIVILIZATION. After the long painful striving for renewal of the Geometric period, Greek civilization experienced a rapid development during Archaism, helped by the close contacts which trade established with the Eastern world. Literary life was marked above all by the advent and development of lyricism (that is to say poetry accompanied by music).

Religious life attained a new stability. Eastern religions, already introduced, were completely assimilated into the Greek pantheon, while new Asiatic deities (for example Hecate and Cybele) made their appearance. Dionysus, a god who had been well established since the 2nd millennium, experienced prodigious success by his special function: to protect the vine, its growers and the drinkers of wine. Cults of mystery inherited from the Aegean world pursued their long career and were assimilated by the State: thus the Mysteries of Eleusis, near Athens. In Athens new festivals were established, for example the Panathenaea and the Great Dionysia.

Around 500 BC, maturing Archaism changed radically. It is difficult to explain this sudden change, but it is certain that the great growth crisis which at that time crossed the Greek world and which found its climax in the Persian Wars must have played a determining role in this development.

3 Classical Greece (5th–4th centuries BC)

THE PERSIAN WARS. The end of the 6th century was marked in Asia by the rise of the Persians who built an immense empire from the plateaux of Iran to Egypt. The conquest of the Greek towns of Asia Minor, followed by their rebellion, brought about the first collision between Greeks and Persians and provided at least the pretext for two Persian interventions in Greece, which we call the Persian wars. In 490 BC the Athenians repelled the soldiers of Darius at Marathon but ten years later Xerxes wished to avenge the defeat of his father and tried to submerge Greece under the weight of a huge army and fleet: the victories of Salamis (480 BC) and of Plataea (479 BC) allowed the Greeks to repulse the invader, whom they then pursued into Asia. The danger of conquest by the barbarians was definitively averted. It is astonishing that only a few thousand men could resist the Persian hordes, but their passion for freedom inspired them with the courage and desperation imbued them with energy.

The consequences of this victory, so painfully won at the price of incredible sacrifices, were vast: for example, the Athenians had to abandon their town, which the Persians entirely destroyed. A balance of power was established between Greece and Persia and the Greek cities of Asia Minor were liberated from the Persian yoke; the exaltation of victory gave a new impetus to Hellenism, which at the same time triumphed in Sicily over the Carthaginians at the battle of Himera in 480 BC. But one city benefited more than all the others from a triumph to which it had contributed more than all the others —Athens.

THE POLITICAL APOGEE OF ATHENIAN DEMOCRACY. Athens gained in status from the voluntary withdrawal of Sparta, which was little concerned with distant adventures that could put it at the mercy of a revolt by its Helots, and it took the lead in the Greek world. The Delian League was a league of cities on the islands or in Asia that placed themselves voluntarily under its hegemony in order to secure themselves against a renewed offensive from Persia. But quite quickly this free association changed into an empire, in which Athens alone directed matters and the allied towns became subject towns. The common treasury was symbolically transferred from Delos to the Acropolis in 454 BC and from then on it was used not only to ensure the defence of the confederation but also to cover Athens' own expenses. This empire, closely supervised by military settlements, gave Athens great resources, considerable strength and incomparable prestige. But once the power of Athens was broken, the empire was to disintegrate entirely.

Internally, democratic progress was rapid from the end of the Persian wars, due in part to the role that the least privileged classes played in the victory. It became more marked towards the middle of the century, in the time of Ephialtes and especially of Pericles, an aristocrat who embraced the cause of the people and whose genius inspired Athenian policy for about 30 years. His most important political reform was *misthophoria,* the allocation of a wage to jurymen, which allowed all, even the most humble, to participate effectively in public affairs and the administration of justice. At the same time he undertook great public works, rebuilt the sanctuaries destroyed by the barbarians and with the aid of Phidias gave the Acropolis its ornamentation of marble that has withstood the centuries: a way both of procuring work for innumerable labourers, craftsmen and artists and of ensuring for Athens the supremacy that beauty confers. Literary life was no less scintillating. The form most in evidence was drama: tragedy and comedy were in fact intended to appeal to all the people and contributed to the raising of their intellectual level. Tragedy in particular, represented by three illustrious names (Aeschylus, Sophocles, Euripides), aroused terror and pity and taught great lessons through the old myths which, constantly reworked and altered, often allowed the expression of very new religious, moral or political ideas. History was really born with Herodotus, that Greek from Asia who had settled in Athens and told the story of the Persian Wars. Little by little, thinkers, artists, men of letters, sophists flocked to Athens from all over the Greek world. Pericles, supported by his mistress Aspasia, liked to converse with them: he was the friend of Herodotus, of Protagoras, of Hippodamus, and it is with justice that his name is used to describe the whole of this period of the ephemeral grandeur of Athens. In fact, this century scarcely spanned the 'fifty years' that separated the Persian wars from the war of the Peloponnese.

The age of enlightenment had already started, but it also represented the economic apogee of Athens. The port of Piraeus, created by Themistocles, quickly became the centre of all Mediterranean communications. Goods from all over the world poured into it, in particular luxury goods from the East and corn. Resident foreigners, aliens who enjoyed a far more liberal regime there than anywhere else, contributed to a great extent to this extraordinary rise.

THE PELOPONNESIAN WAR AND THE FALL OF ATHENS (431–404 BC). This prosperity did nor survive the 30-year conflict that raged between Athens and her Peloponnesian rivals led by Sparta. The loss of Pericles at the very beginning of the war deprived Athens of an irreplaceable leader, and his successors, brilliant though some of them were, like the handsome Alcibiades, put their own ambitions before the State's interests. Athens misguidedly embarked on a campaign too far away in Sicily, where almost all of the expeditionary force was annihilated. She was finally defeated at Aegospotamoi (goat rivers) in 405 BC, despite her earlier incontestable maritime supremacy, and in the following year Athens was captured by the coalitionists. It was the destruction of a century's steadfast efforts to secure her hegemony over the Greek world.

The arts continued to flourish, despite the great turmoil of the period—it was at this time that the principal structures of the Acropolis were completed. The literary field was equally productive: comedy finally acquired a first-rate author in Aristophanes, who satirized the changes in customs introduced by the long war; Thucydides laid the foundations of history in the modern sense, with his lucid analysis of the causes and the progression of the war. New religious ideals took shape, with the advent of individualism at the expense of official cults and the development of mysticism.

THE STRUGGLE FOR HEGEMONY (404-361 BC). The end of Athenian hegemony did not, however, guarantee the autonomy of the Greek cities. In fact, Sparta held Greece under as heavy a yoke as had Athens in the past. To prevent any challenge to her authority, Sparta did not shrink from forming an alliance with the Persian Great King, nor from signing the shameful Treaty of Antalcidas with him (386), and the price of Persian assistance was Greek withdrawal from Asia. But Sparta was being undermined from within by oligarchic tendencies and struggles between the excessively rich and the excessively poor, and her dominion collapsed under the blows dealt by Thebes, the rising power that crushed Sparta at Leuctra in 371 BC.

It was now Thebes' turn to try to establish her hegemony over Greece. Bearing in mind her rather uneventful past, Thebes' sudden rise to power is astonishing. The explanation lies in the vigorous action of two men, Epaminondas and Pelopidas, who reorganised the Boeotian Confederation around Thebes. Thebes was confronted, however, by a coalition of Athenians and Peloponnesians, and although she was still able to defeat them at Mantinea (362), Epaminondas' death on the battlefield marked the beginning of an irreversible decline in Thebes' fortunes.

Athens, on the other hand, regained some of her former power. A number of her former allies rallied round her again in the Second Athenian Confederation, which took great precautions to avoid past mistakes and to ensure that the cities were really autonomous, despite the pre-eminence of Athens. Athens was to play a prominent role when a new threat, the Macedonians, loomed over a divided Greece, ruined by several decades of internal wars.

PHILIP II AND THE CONQUEST OF GREECE. The arrival of Philip II of Macedon in 359 profoundly altered the balance of power in the Greek world. Until then, Macedonia had played only a secondary role, but this was to change completely when this vigorous, tenacious, astute man came to power. He extended and reorganized his kingdom, and made full use of his infantry (the famous phalanx) to overpower the divided Greek cities. The only resistance he encountered was from Athens, whose economic interests, especially those in Chalcidice and Thrace, were severely damaged by Philip's advance. The Athenian nationalist party was ardently championed by Demosthenes, who succeeded in remustering the entire strength of a city slumbering in luxury and undermined by strife. But in 338 the Macedonians were victorious at Chaeroneea which marked the end of Greece's freedom.

To be sure, when Philip united most of the cities in the Corinthian League, he guaranteed their autonomy in theory; but in practice, they came under the strict control of the Macedonian king. Thus, the price paid for Greece's first unification was the enforced renunciation of what for centuries the Greeks had considered to be their most sacred possession.

HELLENISM IN THE 4TH CENTURY BC. If Greece was unable to resist Macedonia as she had resisted Persia, it was because her inner resilience had been broken. Collective dedication to the common weal, the essence of the polis (city state) system, was gradually eclipsed by individualism and unrestrained personal ambition. And this was true not only of Athens, but even of Sparta.

Nevertheless, creative excellence was still achieved in all the arts. Socrates, the victim of both his fidelity to his principles and the struggles between political factions in Athens, drank his fatal dose of hemlock in 399. Following Socrates, Plato founded a prodigious philosophical system which has never ceased to inspire Western thought, and his disciple Aristotle, the universal thinker, brought together all aspects of human knowledge. Eloquence reigned supreme in Athens: Lysias won acclaim in the oratory of the Law Courts, Isocrates in state oratory, and Demosthenes still symbolizes the effect which an ardently patriotic speech can produce on a crowd. Xenophon, another of Socrates' followers, continued Thucydides' historical work. Even Middle Comedy developed a more acute scrutiny of the manners of the time. As in the previous century, Athens was unquestionably the spiritual and cultural capital of the Greek world.

Religion took a noticeable turn towards mysticism, continuing in the direction it had begun to take at the end of the 5th century. The oriental gods, from Egypt, Syria and Asia Minor, daily gained more adherents who found hope of personal well-being in them. There was also great enthusiasm for Dionysus, celebrated in orgiastic ceremonies, as well as for Asclepius, the compassionate god and healer of the sick. On the other hand, the traditional city gods were forsaken, during the slow demise of the cities they used to protect.

ALEXANDER THE GREAT AND THE CONQUEST OF THE EAST (336–323 BC). Alexander, Philip II's son and successor, led the expedition into Asia which his father had been unable to lead. With the combined Macedonian and Greek armies under his command, he won an impressive series of victories over Darius III and his generals which, in the space of about ten years, secured his hold over an immense empire stretching from Egypt to India. It was as if he were avenging the Persian invasion of Greece during the Persian Wars, and the century of lamentable negotiations during which certain Greek cities had begged for the Great King's assistance.

This famous conqueror, who was recognized by the oracle of Ammon at Siwa as the god's own son, showed great breadth of outlook in the organization of his enormous empire. He endeavoured to produce a harmonious fusion of the Greek and Persian elements, despite the contempt felt by the Greeks for the barbarians. He founded several Alexandrias, even as far away as the Indian border, in order to promote Hellenism, and with it, urbanization, Commerce did not suffer under Alexander; on the contrary, it was aided by the unification of so many territories under strong control. But part of this titanic achievement would eventually collapse, and this became plain when the 33-year-old Alexander died in 323 BC. His empire soon fragmented into several kingdoms, but one fundamental remained: Alexander's oriental subjects were to be administered by Greeks right up to the Roman conquest. Who would have dreamt that Hellenism would expand to such an extent? The year 323 BC thus marks the beginning of a new era; it is no coincidence that Demosthenes, the champion of the bygone age of independent cities, took his own life at Kalauria in the following year.

4 Hellenistic and Roman Greece (323 BC–AD 395)

THE DECLINE OF GREECE DURING THE HELLENISTIC PERIOD (late 4th century-late 3rd century BC). The Hellenistic period is characterized by two correlated facts: Greece herself was waning, whereas the Greek kingdoms in the east resulting from the dissolution of Alexander's empire (Ptolemies in Egypt, Seleucids in Syria, Attalids at Pergamon) were enjoying extraordinary growth. Alexandria, Antioch, Seleucia and Pergamum were becoming veritable capitals of Hellenism, whereas the great cities of classical Greece were resting on past laurels, when they were not tearing each other apart in pointless struggles. We shall leave aside the Greek states in the east, which were so lively in economic terms, and where Hellenism and the old Asian or Egyptian civilizations combined to produce fruitful and curious syntheses. Only Greece proper is under consideration here.

The most important political fact is the prominence of the Macedonian sovereigns, the Antigonids, who were descended from Antigonus the One-Eyed, one of Alexander's former companions. Even those towns which had retained their autonomy in law were, in reality, subject to the will of the Antigonids. Thus, Athens was forced to accept Macedonian garrisons at Piraeus and Munychia. Her prosperity was seriously eroded by the shift of trade routes, and she was now hardly more than the intellectual capital of the Greek world. Sparta was increasingly weakened by oligarchy and troubled by violent social disturbances which reforming monarchs like Agis IV and Cleomenes III were unable to curb. Even Sparta came to suffer tyranny under Nabis. However, peoples that had long been the poorest of the peninsula now enjoyed a more exalted lot by forming quite extensive confederations, such as the Aetolian and Achaean Leagues. The city, in the classical sense, was by now well and truly dead, although more often than not the institutions of the past still survived superficially; the only elements of Greece with any vitality were the confederations, and they were to play a major role at the time of the Roman intervention.

Economic activity dwindled considerably. Smallholders had to sell their land and huge estates were created. These, however, were under-exploited, due to competition from the agricultural produce of the oriental Hellenic kingdoms. From the same source, the crafts were hit by substantial unemployment and extremely low wages, which provoked a grave social crisis. Commercial acitivity had clearly moved elsewhere. Piraeus no longer served as the warehouse for the whole world's goods — Delos or Rhodes now played that part.

Decline in spiritual and cultural life is much less evident. Religious vitality had never been more intense, and there were now no limits to the development of mysticism, begun at the end of the 5th century. Conquest had established constant contact with the other coasts of the Mediterranean, and as a result, more and more people placed their faith in the compassionate or ecstatic gods of the East. Large numbers of religious brotherhoods (e.g. *thiaseis* or *eranoi*) were formed, allowing followers of the same deity to come together in a new spirit of fraternity. Worship of the city gods was abandoned in favour of new, state-organized cults which worshipped the sovereign in person. Philosophy flourished anew in Athens at the end of the 4th century with Epicurus and Zeno of Citium, the founders of Epicureanism and Stoicism respectively; both systems had as their goal wisdom gained by detachment from the contingencies of a troubled existence. But literature and the arts were withering away in Greece, and it was now the great creative centres of Alexandria, Pergamum and Antioch that were achieving literary, scientific and artistic renewal.

ROMAN INTERVENTION IN GREECE (214–116 BC). From the end of the 3rd century the Romans felt it necessary to intervene against the Antigonids, resulting in the three Macedonian wars. The first was merely a series of skirmishes with Philip V, but the second saw him roundly defeated at Cynoscephalae (197 BC) by Flamininus, who proclaimed the freedom of Greece at the Isthmian Games in 196 BC. At Pydna (168 BC) Aemilius Paulus triumphed over Philip V's son Perseus. The kingdom of Macedonia was then annexed and soon became a new Roman province.

With the strength of success, the Romans administered harsh treatment to Greek trouble-makers and rebels, particularly the Achaean Confederation. Corinth was besieged and destroyed by Mummius in 146 BC, the same year as the destruction of Carthage, and a phenomenal number of art works, pillaged from this city of riches, made their way to Italy. Greece provisionally came under the control of the Macedonian proconsul.

Of course, Greece had already lost her independence under Philip II, but the Macedonians who had dominated her then were Greeks too; now Greece was experiencing foreign occupation for the first time. How can this irremediable defeat be explained? First, by the Romans' strength and military power, and the dogged imperialism of senatorial policies. But it can also be explained by the discord among the Greeks, an endemic ill that the confusion of the times only aggravated. And we must not forget that Alexander's conquest and organization of the oriental kingdoms meant that many of the most dynamic Greeks had emigrated, bleeding Greece dry of her most vital spirits.

GREECE AS A ROMAN PROVINCE. Henceforth, Greece remained attached to the ever-expanding body of the Roman Empire. Her history was now merely the history of one province among many. She stood out, however, for her role in the civilization's development: because of her plundered works of art, and Greek slaves and merchants, Rome gained a wider knowledge of the subtleties of Hellenism. A profound truth lies in the often quoted words of Horace: 'When Greece had been enslaved she made a slave of her rough conqueror'. Rome's Hellenization was an immensely far-reaching phenomenon, because Rome became the intermediary for transmission of Greece's message throughout the Western world.

In the 1st century BC, Greece was closely involved with Rome's struggles against Mithridates (Athens was captured by Sulla in 86 BC) and with the emperors' rivalry for supreme power (48 BC: the Battle of Pharsala between Caesar and Pompey; 42 BC: the Battle of Philippi between Antony and Octavian on one side and Caesar's assassins on the other; 31 BC: Octavian defeated Antony and Cleopatra at Actium). But from the time of Augustus onwards, Greece was at peace with Rome, and there was a noticeable revival even under the Antonines in the 2nd century AD. Hadrian, whose enthusiasm for Hellenism earned him the sobriquet 'Graeculus' (the 'little Greek'), covered Greece with sumptuous buildings. Shortly after, Herodes Atticus, a rich Athenian sophist, spent a large part of his huge fortune on the embellishment of the major sanctuaries. At the same time, literature and philosophy shone forth again, ending a long period of obscurity caused by the conquest and the resulting hopeless languor of the vanquished. After his exile from Rome, Epictetus set up a world-famous school of stoic philosophy at Nicopolis. Plutarch's parallel lives extolled the virtues of the great men of the past. Pausanias, the Greek geographer, left an important source for the history and topography of ancient Greece in his *Descriptions of Greece*. Traditional religion still lived on and several emperors, including Hadrian, came to be initiated at Eleusis.

But this revival was unreal. Greece was now nothing more than a gallery, a museum. Athens, in particular, was still famous for her schools, but the town was quite lifeless. This was because economic activity had barely resumed and because there was nothing to support the efforts of those who wanted to regenerate a past which they so loved and longed for.

In the 3rd century AD, the Goths crossed the Danube and devastated Greece. This was the first barbarian invasion of Greek territory, where peace had reigned for centuries under the Romans. Security was regained during the Later Empire, but the decline became ever more apparent, especially as Christianity prevailed from the time of Constantine onwards. Emperors became increasingly suspicious of

Hellenism — the name then given to traditional thought and religion — until it was proscribed once and for all by Theodosius I the Great in AD 381. Antique civilization really came to an end in AD 395, when Greece was totally devastated by another Gothic invasion, and when the Roman Empire was divided into two parts following the death of Theodosius I the Great.

Medieval and Modern Greece

1 Byzantine Greece[1]

GREECE OPEN TO INVASION. Greece naturally became part of the Byzantine Empire after the division of 395. She did not escape barbarian invasion any more than other regions and was regularly raided by the Huns after Attila's incursion in 447. Besides being devastated by the Huns, Greece was also threatened by the Slavs, who had designs on Thessaloniki in particular. Although they failed to capture Thessaloniki, their Peloponnesian expedition was more successful, and resulted in the permanent settlement of some Slavs. It is this factor which lies behind Fallremayer's theory of the total 'Slavonization' of Greece from the early 7th century.

GREECE AND THE SLAVS (7th century-9th century). Whole tribes of Slavs invaded and failed to reach Thessaloniki (617–619); they settled in Greece, forming 'ghettos' scattered from Macedonia and Epirus to central and southern Greece, and even reaching as far as the Greek islands, which were accessible to the Slavs because of their boats, *monoxiles*. The profoundly disturbing effect of these massive settlements was the renewal and transformation of the Hellenic population.

From the political point of view, regions like Macedonia, which had become practically entirely Slavonic, remained under a more or less effective Byzantine suzerainty, whereas the newcomers adopted the Greek way of life and gradually became integrated in the regions where their numbers were few.

This worrying presence of the enemies of Byzantium at the very centre of the Empire explains the creation of the *theme*[1] of Hellas, in the Empire's defence system inaugurated by Heraklius. The theme was intended to restrain the continual infiltration of the Slavs at the same time as the theme of Thrace put up opposition to the Bulgars.

Thus began a period of defence which continued throughout the Isaurian and Amorian dynasties, until the Iconoclast (8th century to first half of 9th century) movement brought a new Greek offensive against the barbarians to which the departure of Cyril and Methodius in 863 to evangelize Greater Moravia, namely the Slavs, bears witness.

THE FAILURE OF THE BULGARIANS IN GREECE AND THE HELLENIC REBIRTH

[1] From the 7th century the *theme* was an administrative subdivision of the Byzantine Empire, governed by a military chief, the *Strategos* (General).

UNDER THE MACEDONIAN EMPERORS (10th century–11th century). The danger presented by the Bulgarians was not new but it became more significant with the Bulgarian tsar, Simeon I, whose ambition was increased by a Byzantine education. Having conquered the Greeks and forced Leo VI to pay homage to him, he was seduced by the vision of Thessaloniki and Constantinople which, after the conquest of Macedonia and Thrace, led him to incessant conflicts on Greek soil.

The Bulgarian threat was renewed with Tsar Samuel, whose empire had extended to Thessaly, until the victory of Basil II Bulgaroctonus (1014) returned control of the Balkan peninsula to the Byzantines.

The Hellenic rebirth, at first marked throughout a large part of the empire by a general infatuation on the part of artists and writers for everything that was Greek, culminated in Greece itself with the admirable mosaics of Daphni which remain its most prestigious testimony.

THE FRANKS IN GREECE

The Norman threat. From the 11th century, throughout the Byzantine Empire and in Greece as elsewhere, Italian cities, notably Venice, came forward with growing demands and secured important commercial privileges, especially when the Emperor had to ask the Venetians for help against the first Frankish incursion made by the Norman king, Roger II of Sicily, into Corfu and as far as Attica.

The Latin states in Greece. In 1204, at the end of the fourth crusade, Greece was included in the spoils of the victors: Venice and the Frankish princes.

Venice, the merchant city, chose centres of commerce, especially islands: the Ionian islands, most of the Aegean towns, Rhodes, Crete, (Euboea, and those well-situated in the Peloponnese, the Hellespont (Dardanelles), and in Thrace.

The Frankish feudal system imposed in Greece sought to create a new France there. There were the vassal Frankish principalities of the Latin Empire of Constantinople: the kingdom of Thessaloniki went to the Montferrats, the duchy of Athens to Otho de la Roche (this later passed from the French to the Catalans), the principality of Achaea (or Morea) to the Champlittes and the Villehardouins. Only the despotate of Epirus under the Comnenus (1057–9 and 1081–1185, dynasty of six emperors of Constantinople) bore witness to the past grandeur of Byzantium in its ambitions to reconquer Thessaloniki and Constantinople, at least until John Vatatzes staked a claim on Epirus (mid-12th century) and Michael Paeologus defeated the despot of Epirus and Guillaume de Villehardouin; but even this did not mean that Epirus and Morea returned immediately to the Empire.

Spiritual vitality. Greece which was in turmoil, nevertheless displayed a remarkable cultural vitality. Proof of this are the decorations in the 'Macedonian style' of the oldest churches in Athos and the museum-city of Mistra. There, in the heart of the Peloponnese, the living strengths of the Empire in its decline, political, spiritual and religious, take refuge. The brilliance of the court at Mistra after the Byzantine reconquest (notably with the Platonic philosopher Gemistos Plethon) eclipsed that of the capital, thereby regenerating the kingdom of Greece. It was this world, undergoing complete renewal, which was to be destroyed by the Turkish conquest.

2 Greece under Turkish domination

THE CONQUESTS (14th century-17th century). It was well before the fall of Constantinople that the Ottoman Turks began their conquest of Greece, first with Thrace, Macedonia, Thessaly and Epirus, and then Ioannina and Salonika. Finally, between 1458 and 1460, they abolished the duchy of Athens and the Greek despotate, marking a new stage in their advance which, in the 16th century, reached out to Rhodes, Chios, Cyprus, Naxos and the Cyclades, despite the efforts of Cardinal Bessarion and the Turco-Venetian wars.

Their expansion was halted only by the Treaty of Karlowitz (1699), and they then relinquished the Peloponnese and Aegina to the Venetians. The Church and intellectuals (such as Cardinal Bessarion and John Lascaris) led the resistance movement in Europe and in Greece proper, giving their support to European interventions (the most important of which led to the victory of Lepanto in 1571) and to Greek uprisings (late 16th century and 17th century).

THE VILAYET OF ROUMELIA. It was in this administrative unit that Greece and the conquered Balkan countries were organized. If they had offered no resistance, the Christian populations were given a regime of relative freedom as permitted by the tenets of Islamic law (although this freedom was greatly restricted by the Islamization of children and their compulsory enrolment in the Corps of Janissaries). Otherwise, they were subjected to the authority of the Turkish military feudal system throughout the fertile regions, and Greek peasants now became sharecroppers or serfs where they had once been landlords.

Thus, all that was left in Greek possession after the conquest were the poor, mountainous regions and land belonging to the orthodox monasteries. These came to play a dominant role in economic and spiritual matters, especially when massacres, Islamization, slave-taking and emigration were on the increase.

GREEK RESISTANCE. This was organized on two fronts. First, from outside the country, thanks to Greece's relations with the West (the role of Greek immigrants in Italian trading towns was of prime importance to these relations), and secondly, from within Greece. Resistance was as much the concern of the middle classes working for the Turkish administration (the Armatolian militia, churchmen and the Phanariots), as of the people, who were voluntarily arming themselves against the occupiers. This was the case especially in mountain areas, where the Klephts were already building up their strength for the war of Independence. The same duality can be seen on the intellectual level, with a formal, fundamentally orthodox, scholarly tendency on the one hand, and on the other, a popular tendency (expressed in *threnes*, songs of lamentation about the conquest) which was much more open to Western influence.

THE REVIVAL OF NATIONAL AWARENESS (18th century-early 19th century). Paradoxically, Greek national awareness revived only when the Turks had completed their conquest of Greece with the capture of the Peloponnese and had restored peace. This resulted in a lasting economic boom (of which Thessaloniki was the principal beneficiary) which explains both the development of the Greek navy (e.g. the Hydra fleet) and the rise of a bourgeoisie, evidence of Greece's links with the 'enlightened' West. Thus, Greece's vitality stands out from a Turkish Empire that was increasingly beset by anarchy and fragmentation from within (cf. the epic *Ali of Tebelen*, Pasha of Ioannina), and by the threat of the great powers from without (Russia, France and England). Thenceforth, the 'oriental question' was raised, and with it, the question of Greece's independence — witness the meetings of the Society of Friends of Greek Independence (founded in Odessa in 1815), chaired by Ypsilanti, and the development of the 'philhellenic' movement in Europe.

THE STRUGGLE FOR INDEPENDENCE (1812–1831). The weak forces of Ypsilanti (abandoned by the tsar) and of the Greek uprising succeeded in shaking the Turks (cf. the victory at Kolokotronis) whose appeal to Mohammed Ali, Pasha of Egypt, triggered the intervention of the European powers (Russia, France and England). Following the victory at Navarino (1827), the Treaty of Adrianople (1829) and the Second Treaty of London (3 February 1830), Greece became an independent state under the protection of the three powers. But as an independent state, Greece was quite wretched, with only 600,000 inhabitants, most of whom were confined to poor and mountainous areas. The Klephts therefore remained as powerful as ever. And it was they who, in 1831, assassinated Count Capodistria (foreign minister, and Greek president for three years). From then on, the terms of the Treaty of London were applied and Greece became a monarchy under Otto of Bavaria. And from the following year, the Sublime Porte recognized Otto I and Hellenic independence.

3 Independent Greece after 1832

THE GREEK KINGDOM'S EARLY STAGES AND THE EVOLUTION OF THE OTTONIAN MONARCHY (1832–1862). The new kingdom's capital was at first Nauplia (Nafplion), then Athens, and it covered only the Peloponnese, the Cyclades and mainland Greece as far as the Arta-Volos line. Its territorial and economic base was therefore limited, and its political foundations barely seemed stable. In fact, the Bavarian dynasty removed all real power from Greek hands, and Greek troops were replaced by contingents from Bavaria.

Independent Greece therefore remained prone to foreign interference. Bavarian influence was particularly direct ('xenocracy' was spoken of), but that of the European powers, who even gave their names to the various political parties in Greece, was far more serious. Quite soon, these political parties produced certain liberal demands (for a constitution especially) and nationalistic claims for 'pro-Orthodox' religious policies, the religion of the royal family, and for the expulsion of the Bavarians).

The problems facing Otto's authoritarian monarchy were worsened by chronic bankruptcy, and further aggravated by the Oriental crisis of 1839–40. But from then onwards, the 'Grand Plan' to resurrect Hellenism, and with it the Empire of Constantinople, gave encouragement to Greek aspirations to reconquer Thessaly, Epirus, Macedonia and the Islands. These aspirations were supported by the Russians and, less forcefully, by the English who were anxious to maintain good commercial relations with the Ottomans. Anarchy, disorder and constant intervention in Greek politics by the great powers worked to the advantage of the conspirators who successfully brought off the *coup d'état* of September 1843. A National Assembly, in office for about six months, drafted and ratified the Constitution (a rather conservative one in fact), which was promulgated in March 1844.

The constitutional monarchy resulting from the *coup d'état* remained purely theoretical, to such an extent as to spark off a series of uprisings in defence of constitutional freedom. At the same time, successive administrations tried to direct public attention towards territorial expansion, which they saw as the only possible cure for all the kingdom's ills. From this stems the pro-orthodox, pro-Russian attitude of the Greeks at the time of the Crimean war, and also during the Turkish reprisals and the Anglo-French occupation of 1854–57. Greece remained central to the problems relating to the thorny question of the East, the focal point of European greed.

All of these factors partly explain the fact that, from then on, all that was economically important to Hellenism was more often than not to be found outside Greece, among the Greeks of Constantinople or of the *diaspora*. It was their capital which controlled Greece's economic evolution. The Greeks of the Ionian islands also played their part, and it was as a result of their intense activity that the 'Seven Islands' were returned to the kingdom in 1864. Thus, all that survived in Greece proper were the cultural forces, sustained by Athens University. But liberal opposition, which the war had temporarily restrained, started up again with even greater strength and violence in the 1860s: an uprising was quelled in the spring of 1862; there were mutinies in the garrisons of Acarnania, Patras, Corinth and finally, a decisive one in Athens which brought about Otto's deposition and exile (October 1862).

THE DANISH DYNASTY AND THE DEMOCRATIC MONARCHY (1862–1909). A year later, it was the English who found Greece a new king; Prince William of Denmark became George I, King of Greece. From then onwards, Greece's domestic evolution took a new direction, with the democratic constitution of 1864 and the introduction of a parliamentary system in 1875. This evolution bears witness to certain important social changes, namely the rise of the bourgeoisie and extensive economic development. In fact, the Greek economy gained from governmental stability, and a large-scale construction policy is evidence of an upswing (witness the building of the Corinth Canal in 1882-93).

Of course, the national question remained as pressing as ever. And so the Russo-Turkish war of 1877-78 seemed an excellent opportunity for the Greeks to round off their territorial frontiers. But government action and the uprisings in Thessaly, Epirus and Crete came too late, and once she had signed the armistice, Turkey was again able to threaten Greece. War was narrowly avoided. Thanks to Greek efforts in the 1890s, Thessaly was at last returned, but not Crete; declared independent in 1897, Crete was to be effectively united with Greece in 1908, and officially only in 1913. These events brought forward a young Cretan named Eleutherios Venizelos, who used the growing political, economic and social dissatisfaction with the court and government to restore the international position of Greece. The military league which carried out the *coup d'état* in 1909 called for his assistance.

PROBLEMS AT HOME AND STRUGGLES ABROAD: MODERN GREECE AND VENIZELOS. As premier, the 'wily Cretan' adopted a revisionist domestic policy and displayed skilful, active diplomacy in the Balkans, resulting in the Balkan League of 1912 (Greece, Serbia and Bulgaria). A liberal state was created, very gradually given the extreme difficulty of harmonizing divergent political tendencies. But the 1911 Constitution brought considerable political and social improvements. Public services were reorganized, the economy was given support (with technical aid), but above all, a first attempt at social reform was made: tax was levied on all income, agricultural cooperatives were set up, with available loans from the National Bank (1914), and lastly, the foundations of trades unions were laid. Greece's neutrality during World War I allowed these reforms to continue, despite the fighting in the Balkans.

The Balkan League defeated the Ottomans on all sides. The Greeks occupied Thessaloniki, Ioannina and the Aegean Islands (Chios, Samos and Mytilene), while their allies were in Macedonia and Thrace. From these victories and then the Treaties of London and Bucharest (1913), Greece gained Thessaloniki, Chalcidice, Kavalla, Ionnina, southern Epirus and the Aegean islands.

During the same year, King George was assassinated in Thessaloniki, and thereafter, his son Constantine adopted policies that were sympathetic to Germany, which set him in violent opposition to the liberals — that is, Venizelos, who supported the Triple Entente.

Forced by the king to resign, Venizelos established an insurrectional military government at Thessaloniki (1916) and, aided by the Allies (especially the French, present in Greece at that time), he overthrew Constantine, who was replaced by his son Alexander (1917). From then onwards Greece's national policies were as one with those of the Allies, and thereby involved in the world conflict. But the peace treaties of 1919–20 granted Greece only minor territorial gains (eastern Thrace, Imbros and Tenedos, and the administration of the Smyrna region), while the policies of Mustapha Kemal, later known as Ataturk, crushed Greece's long-cherished hopes of reconquering Constantinople, now Istanbul (with the Graeco-Turkish war in 1922 and resultant exchanges of population). Furthermore, the Greeks were tired of constant war, and from the 1920s they were receptive to pacifist and royalist opposition to Venizelos' excesses. King Alexander's death in 1920 and the ensuing train of events (with power repeatedly passing from Venizelos to King Constantine and back again until the latter's death in 1923, the year of George II's accession) had brought the country's uncertainty and chronic disorder to a peak.

The political sickness spread into economic and social areas, and was considerably aggravated by the influx of refugees from Turkey. New reformist parties with republican and distinctly socialist tendencies came into being (the Greek TUC was formed in 1918 and the Communist Party of Greece in 1924). The general situation was one of degeneration. George II abdicated in December 1923 but the Republicans did not gain their final victory until three months later, with the departure of Venizelos.

REPUBLICAN GREECE (1924–36). From the start, the regimes following *coups d'état* allowed the domestic deterioration and the problems broad to continue unchecked. The only exception to all this instability was the government led by Venizelos from 1928 to 1932.

Republican Greece came up against traditional problems. At home, reform was needed. To begin with, economic measures were taken, in the form of major construction projects, aid to refugees, drainage (in Macedonia) to increase the cultivable acreage, stabilization of the currency, and the establishment of the Bank of Greece. But, important though they were, these changes were still insufficient, as there was growing unemployment and increasing numbers of strikes. Abroad, Greek nationalistic claims were now focused on the problem of Cyprus, which was the root cause of Venizelos' resignation.

THE RESTORATION AND WORLD WAR II. Following a further period of military rule, George II's restoration in 1935 succeeded (and sustained) the military dictatorship of General Metaxas, established by the *coup d'état* of 4 August 1932.

The Italian attack on 28 October 1940 brought Greece into World War II. The defense mounted by the Greek army was at first successful (especially in the mountains of Epirus, spring 1941). But shortly after, when the Germans swarmed into the country, Greece was forced to surrender, and the king left for England, while the government went to Egypt. During the three-year occupation by the Axis powers (Italy, Germany and Bulgaria), secret resistance groups multiplied in this devastated country, decimated by famine.

The solidarity which had united most of Greece's forces did not, however, outlast the victory. Political rivalry resumed even more violently than before, and the king's restoration (September 1946) after a plebiscite was followed by harsh purges of the left wing. A brutal civil war raged for three years, culminating in victory for the right wing. The situation was made even more dramatic by the extent of human loss and the destruction suffered (agricultural production was ruined, communications were practically non-existent, villages had been destroyed, etc.). More than ever before, despite the potentially decisive outburst of national feeling, Greece's very existence was wholly dependent on foreign aid (from Britain until 1947, and then from the United States).

CONTEMPORARY GREECE. Greece gained some consolation from the return of the Dodecanese after the Treaty of Paris (1947). The Cyprus question became increasingly critical until the grant of autonomy in 1959. But national issues were relegated to the background and precedence given to political, economic and social problems. During the reign of King Paul I (1947–64) and after King Constantine's accession (7 March 1964), the popular vote brought mainly right-wing governments to power, and their stability was quite remarkable (Karamanlis was in office from 1953–63). But this stability merely masked the strength of left-wing forces, despite the government's repressive policy towards them (the Communist party was proscribed, a certificate of good citizenship was required for state employment, and the leading activists were sent into exile. Greece then underwent a remarkable economic boom due to an active and productive tourist policy, and also to efforts made to industrialize a country which had hitherto imported almost all manufactured goods (these efforts included electrification, construction of oil refineries, the opening of new mines, etc.). Trade was boosted by both the development of shipping (the Greek fleet was among the largest in the world) and the return to Greece of capital which had previously been taken abroad for security. But it was chiefly the middle classes that profited from this economic achievement, and there was little social progress to accompany it.

The huge success which the left wing would have achieved in the 1967 elections was thwarted by the intervention of a *coup d'état* which set up a military dictatorship under Papadopoulos (and then Ioannidis). The government of the Colonels, supported by the United States, was among the most repressive in Greek history, with the constant use of torture, deportation and political trials. King Constantine went into exile in 1967, and in 1969 the regime was condemned by the Council of Europe. From 1972, the number of demonstrations by workers and students increased, and each time they were brutally suppressed (the Polytechnic Institute was occupied in November 1973). Corruption and inefficiency were destroying the country. It was the Colonels' inability to react during the Cyprus crisis, always an issue on which Greek opinion was sensitive, that finally brought about their downfall (23 July 1974). Recalled from exile, Karamanlis organized the transition and prepared the elections which confirmed its success. The Republic was founded and democratic freedom was restored.

Aspects of Ancient Greece

Greek civilization is always spoken of as if it existed: that is, as if it were an unchangeable thing, like an Idea, a fixed star in Plato's metaphysical sky. In fact, the open-minded observer is at once struck by the diversity of Greece, its history, its genius, its many and often contradictory aspects in which unity, if it exists, can be grasped only after long research, beyond the outward appearances which seem to deny it.

Diversity or harmony? Diversity first in space. In spite of the smallness of Hellas, each of the many independent states within it had its own, original stamp. In the Classical era, democratic Athens and aristocratic Sparta shared neither the same ideal nor the same lifestyle. Corinth, Argos, Thebes and fifty other cities each had its own individual character. Even the Pan-Hellenic sanctuaries, where a certain 'common spirit' of Greece did form, were not interchangeable: the traditions of Delphi and Olympus had little in common.

Diversity, next, in time. Greek civilization differs as much between the Minoan and the Mycenaean as an elegant lady of Tanagra from a priestess of Knossos, her breasts bare above a pulled-in waist, from which falls a bell-like skirt in pleated frills. The civilization of Archaic Greece is separated from the Mycenaean era by a deep gulf like a Dark Age, between Antiquity and the Renaissance of the 6th century BC.

As to Hellenistic civilization, it prolonged the Classical period, but with numerous radical changes. The city, that essential setting of Greek life for centuries, had collapsed. Aristotle had just defined man as 'a being who lives in a city', and already his pupil, Alexander, was making this definition void by widening the world and completing the breaking-down of past political forms.

Note, in social history, in literature and art, some of these disparities and contrasts which make up the infinite richness and variety of Ancient Greece, then try to find the central theme, the subtle and hidden melody which runs through it from Mycenae to Alexandria in Egypt, and from Homer to Plotinus.

THE BRONZE AGE. The first contrast: civil and political liberty was assuredly the invention of the Greeks, yet Marxist historians do not err in pointing out that Ancient Greek society was based on slavery. A long, laborious invention, Greek democracy was a progressive achievement which required several centuries for its fulfilment.

At the time of Homer and even of Hesiod, in the 9th and 8th centuries BC, only kings and chiefs, at the same time great landowners and the judges of the people, were important; only these lords were truly free, for good as for evil. Hesiod complains bitterly of their extortions and unjust sentences. Everything was subject to them, in war as in peace. In the Achaean army laying siege to Troy, Thersites, a common soldier, had only to grumble for an instant about Agamemnon to be punished by Odysseus; the balance of things was restored by the 'Homeric' burst of laughter which acclaimed the unlucky man's punishment.

The Iron Age peasant, like Hesiod, groaned under the weight of the labour and poverty that made life so hard for him. The poet of Ascra sighs:

> Ah! truly, what misery for me to belong to the Fifth Age: this age of iron! I should have been born earlier or later.

THE SMALL FLAME OF DEMOCRACY. But in Greece the poor and oppressed were, more so than elsewhere, intelligent and courageous. They quickly realized that they had to form groups, especially in the towns and surrounding villages, and after many setbacks they succeeded in gaining ground against the nobles and the powerful. In Athens, at the beginning of the 6th century, Solon forbade the arresting of insolvent debtors and also freed the land; this legislator was also a poet and proclaimed proudly in his verses:

> I have torn up the boundary-stones of the black earth: hitherto in bondage, now it is free. I have also freed many Athenians... All that have I done by the force of the law, equal for all.

THE FLOWERING OF ATHENIAN DEMOCRACY. The evolution thus begun was to continue after the fairly gentle tyranny of Peisistratos and his sons, through the revolutionary work of Cleisthenes, the true founder of Athenian democracy, in the 6th century. It was to culminate at last with Pericles, who was to institute the allowance paid to magistrates: thereafter the poorest Athenians were to be able to occupy the great offices of state. Athens was a direct, not a parliamentary, democracy. The assembly of the people, which all citizens could attend, was the sole source of legislative, executive and judiciary power. Never has democracy been so complete, so *absolute*, in the sense in which one speaks of absolute monarchy. Thucydides gives these words to Pericles in his *Funeral Oration*:

> Our constitution serves as a model for neighbouring cities. Its name is Democracy, because it stands for the interests of the whole people. All, subject only to the law, enjoy

equality; consideration is given only to merit; the honours conferred by the state are obtained by excellence, not by any sort of privilege. The most obscure and the poorest are called to take part in public affairs. We all freely give our opinions on the government of the city.

SLAVERY, OR THE OTHER SIDE OF THE COIN. In Athens, as throughout Greece, and, more generally, the rest of the Ancient world, there was a multitude of slaves, many more than there were free men. Their condition could be bearable if they were fortunate enough to have a humane master — 'philanthropist' — which in Athens was not rare. But they possessed no rights, no form of protection against despotism and violence; they owed increasing obedience to their 'owner' until death or emancipation. The hardest of manual labour was often their lot. In judicial proceedings their evidence was obtained by torture. They were commonly considered less as men than as beasts with a human voice, instruments in the form of man, objects to be bought and sold.

At the time of the ancient civilization, when techniques were rudimentary and productivity low, a small group of citizens needed a large pool of slave labour, if they were to have time to attend to their intellectual and political affairs. This is why Plato and Aristotle, describing the organization of the city, only rarely and weakly protested against this cruel but necessary institution. However, Euripides, a pupil of the Sophists, had already declared: 'Many slaves have souls which are more free than those of free men'. Aristotle, in his *Politics*, speaks of people who affirm that 'only the law establishes the difference between the free man and the slave and nature has nothing to do with it', and that this difference is unjust, since it is violence (especially the violence of war) which produced it. Aristotle himself refrained from sharing this opinion, but the very fact that he mentioned it proved that the more liberal of the Greeks were beginning to have qualms of conscience about it.

From the Hellenistic period onwards, the emancipation of slaves escalated, as did the protests of philosophers against an unjust institution. The Stoic philosopher Epictetus, under the Roman Empire, was himself a freed slave. Only Christianity was to bring about the gradual disappearance of slavery.

WOMAN OR GODDESS? The second contrast, not unconnected to the first: the ancient Greeks were the first to recognise, in free men at least, the eminent dignity of the human being, and yet for a long time their daughters and wives were kept in an inferior and humiliating condition.

It was not always thus in Greece: in the Minoan and Mycenaean periods, women enjoyed real consideration and relative freedom of movement. In the Homeric poems, which reflect the civilization of Crete and Mycenae, Helen, Andromache, Hecuba, Penelope, Arete, wife of the king of the Phaeacians and Nausicaa, their daughter, do not appear as simple servants of men.

PHAINOMERIDES OR KEPT IN PURDAH. The Dorian invaders, who spread through Greece in about the 9th century, after the Trojan War, seem to have brought with them a military ideal of 'complete virility', the corollary of which was misogyny. However, things were perhaps not so simple, for in Sparta, a Dorian city, the 'second sex' was freer and less persecuted than in Athens. Did not Spartan girls show their thighs (*phainomerides*) in the course of their physical exercises? In Aeolis, on Lesbos, the curious case of the great poetess Sappho, who directed a boarding-school for daughters of the nobility at the time of Solon, proves that women there had a much higher standing that that of Athenian women during the same period.

In spite of some amusing paradoxes, it appears probable that from the 7th century to the middle of the 5th, most Athenian girls and women spent the greater part of their lives as recluses in the gynaeceum. They were held there, not by locks and bars, but by the constraining force of manners and public opinion. In Athens as well as in other Greek cities, the cult of homosexuality, so characteristic of Greek culture, flourished.

A HEROINE BECAUSE SHE COULD NO LONGER SPEAK? In the 6th century the act of the Tyrannicides, Harmodius and Aristogiton, further heightened the esteem (in public opinion if not in law) in which male lovers were held, and related it to the passion for liberty and hatred of Tyrants. It must not be forgotten, however, that at least one woman, a courtesan, shared their glory, if Plutarch is to be believed (*On Gossip*: Book 8):

> Leaiana (a name meaning 'lioness'), through her self-mastery, obtained a fine distinction. A courtesan linked to the group of Harmodius and Aristogiton, she was told of the plot against the tyrants and, so far as a woman could, shared the hopes of the conspirators: she had been filled with enthusiasm by drinking from the famous and beautiful krater of Eros and, through the intervention of this god, was initiated into the secrets. Her friends failed and were executed. Interrogated in her turn and called upon to give the names of those conspirators who had not yet been discovered, she refused to speak and held firm. She bit out her own tongue. She showed thus that these men, in loving a woman such as herself, had remained worthy of themselves. The Athenians made a statue of a lioness without a tongue, the proud courage of this animal symbolizing the invincible steadfastness of Leaiana and the absence of the tongue her silence and discretion.

Aeschylus, who belonged to the tough generation of *Marathono-machoi* (those who fought at Marathon), 'had nothing of Aphrodite in him', as Aristophanes was to remark, but he did not disdain to celebrate, on stage, the masculine Eros; his lost tragedy of the *Myrmidons* made the friendship of Achilles and Patroclus, which in Homer had no overt sexual component, a physical relationship in the style of the time.

Art reflected customs as clearly as did literature. Greek sculptors, and also vase-painters, took a serious interest in the female body only from the 4th century on. Until then, statues of goddesses or women were almost always clothed, while male nudity, familiar to the Greeks through the games of the palaestra and the stadium, spread everywhere. The large bronze, the Great Kouros of Apollo, discovered in Piraeus in 1959, which seems to date from around 490 BC, the year of the Battle of Marathon, is one among many proofs.

TOWARDS THE EQUALITY OF THE SEXES. The period of the sophists, which was that of the Greek Enlightenment, marks a turning-point in this, as in attitudes to slavery. Sophocles was already moved to pity for the plight of his heroines, but it was Euripides (whom tradition, by a strange paradox, presents as a misogynist), who makes heard in his *Medea* the most vehement protests against the unjust humiliation of women. A foreigner, Aspasia of Miletus, who was the mistress of Pericles, certainly played an important role in the feminist movement which apparently began during the Peloponnesian War, and Socrates, who admired Aspasia, maintained the then paradoxical view that the two sexes are naturally equal. While Plato and Aristophanes followed him only tentatively down this path, other, less famous, disciples — Aeschines the Socratic and Antisthenes — associated themselves with these protests, notably in their dialogues entitled *Aspasia*.

Artists of the 4th and succeeding centuries vied with one another to celebrate the grace of the uncovered female body. The new comedy of Menander, the poetry of Callimachus and Theocritus in the 'Alexandrian' style and later the Greek romances (prose novels) gave pride of place to love, requited or not, between man and woman. Even under the Roman Empire, the Platonist Plutarch went so far as to affirm that conjugal union could have the strictly philosophical virtues which Plato attributed only to love between men.

Nevertheless, this evolution could not totally change traditional customs. Menander created numerous female characters who attract and retain the love of their fiancés, husbands or lovers, but in a play of his youth, *Dyskolos* (*The Misanthrope*), restored to us by a recently discovered papyrus, the Athenian Sostratus obtains a girl in marriage without her having been consulted either by her father or brother; at least he fell in love with her on sight, but later he gives her sister in marriage to his brother-in-law Gorgias, who accepts her without the two young people having even seen one another!

Most Greeks, even after the 4th century, continued to think that marriage was, as Montaigne was to say, a 'wise bargain' and if, to experience the sentiment presided over by Eros, they concerned themselves less often with boys, they willingly frequented the *hetaerae* (high-class prostitutes).

THE PEOPLE WHO SAW THE SPLENDID LIGHT OF HELIOS. A third contrast: the Greeks loved life and sang its praises with fervour, yet their greatest writers were, at bottom, pessimistic and, like the Hellenizing author of *Ecclesiastes*, deplored the sadness of the human condition.

Certainly the numerous modern authors who have pointed to the contrast between the *joie de vivre* of the Greeks and the sombre tints with which certain of their religions and philosophies colour the world are not altogether wrong. The Greeks especially loved the light of the sun, the diaphanous clarity of their almost always untroubled sky, which is so hard to quit for the shadows of the Underworld. For them, 'to live' and 'to see the splendid light of Helios [the Sun]' are synonymous expressions. And they were enraptured above all by the beauty of the human body, first the male, then the female, but also by the beauty of rivers, forests, mountains and plains, incarnate in all the deities of the countryside: Pan, the Satyrs and the Naiads.

If one looks hard enough one can find even in Greek literature some resolutely optimistic declarations. Euripides, in *Suppliant Women*, gives these words to Theseus, the king of Athens:

> I have already defended against others the following theme. Someone was just saying that human existence is richer in unhappiness than in happiness. Now, I am of an opposing view. The sum of our blessings, to my mind, exceeds the sum of our ills. It it were not so, humanity would not live on this earth. And I give thanks to the god who ordered the existence of mortals which was formerly so confused and bestial, who gave us first reason, then the tongue, the messenger of the word, and made our voice clear; who gave men wheat for food, and with wheat the heavenly dew to make their earth fertile and refresh their bodies… That which still remains obscure and is hidden from human knowledge, the soothsayers reveal to us, consulting fire, entrails and the flight of birds. When a god thus arranges our existence, ah, is it not the madness of spoilt children to wish for more? But human reason claims to be stronger than divine reason and, arrogance in their hearts, certain men think themselves truly more sensible than the gods!

THOSE WHOM THE GODS LOVE DIE YOUNG. However, the contrary argument, that 'human existence is richer in unhappiness than in happiness' is the one most often expressed by Greek writers, and by Euripides himself, who is not above the occasional inconsistency.

In Homer, in Book XXIV of the *Iliad*, Achilles says to Priam:

> What good are your sobs, since such is the fate which the gods have spun for mortals, to live in suffering, while they alone are free of all care. For Zeus has two jars which lie in the earth: one contains the evils, the other the blessings which he intends for mortals. The man to whom Zeus the Thunderer makes gifts lives now in pain, now in joy. He who receives from him only misery is the object of scorn.

The possibility that Zeus might give only blessings to a man is not even envisaged, so unreal does it appear to the poet. Theognis proclaims: 'The most enviable of all earthly blessings is not to have been born, never to have seen the rays of the sun or else, once born, to pass as soon as possible through the gates of Hades and to sleep beneath a thick covering of earth'.

Menander thinks that 'those whom the gods love die young' and, as Croesus puts it in summing up the message of Solon, 'no living being is happy'.

The choruses of Greek tragedies advise several times: 'call no man happy before he is dead, for do you know what the gods have in store for him?'. Euripides himself, when he is not in an optimistic vein, as in *Suppliant Women*, echoes Theognis and says 'that it would be proper to weep over him who comes into the world and who is thus promised so many misfortunes, and to accompany with songs of joy him who is dead and who has therefore ceased to suffer'. It thus seems that the Greeks, even if they enjoyed life, were clear-headed about the reality of the human condition.

A MIDDLE-CLASS MORALITY. This short and mostly unhappy life, for what should it be used? Philosophers propose a lofty ideal, attainable only with difficulty, and how many true disciples did those masters of high wisdom, like Pythagoras, Socrates, Plato and the Stoics have?

The 'average Greek' admires the heroism of Achilles, who could choose, as Racine says:

> Either many years without glory
> Or few days followed by a long memory

and who preferred fame to life. The Greek loves glory; he is avid for reputation and honour (*philotimia*), but is not always particular about the means to the end. Homer's other hero, the astute Odysseus, was an exemplar of the power of intelligence, but also of the ruse and the lie. The Delphic maxims which sum up contemporary morality do not lead the men of Plutarch's race to heroism. They are somewhat down to earth. 'Know thyself' means: know your human condition and do not seek to raise yourself too high, which would bring down divine vengeance (Nemesis). 'Nothing too much' and 'if you commit yourself, there is misfortune': these precepts advise moderation in all things, and to caution above all against excessive zeal on behalf of others, or what we call charity. Lessons of wisdom, no doubt, but of a prudent and middle-class wisdom!

IDEAL OF VIRTUE. The noblest virtue preached to the Greeks by Aristotle and the Stoics was magnanimity: greatness and firmness of spirit in the face of adverse fate. This virtue was based on disenchantment and pessimism; it is an invitation to suffer patiently, like Odysseus, the worst ordeals, and lucidly to command one's destiny. 'The man stronger than his destiny', R.P. Festugière has written, 'this is perhaps the last word of Greek wisdom.'

REASON AND MAGIC. A fourth contrast: the Greeks were the founders of rationalism, yet they believed in oracles, the Mysteries, magic and, all in all, showed themselves as superstitious as any other people in Antiquity.

If 'man is the measure of all things', as Protagoras said, he is so first by the exercise of his intelligence, his reason (*logos*), with which he examines and explores the universe. Not even the most ancient and venerated of religious traditions escape the penetrating criticism of the philosopher, who reflects upon them and rejects as pure fable all that seems to him to lack propriety, verisimilitude or reason. Paul Decharme's *La Critique des traditions religieuses chez les Grecs* retains, after more than a half-century, almost all its interest and all its value. Such a rationalism tends to exclude the notion of the miracle. Saint Paul (Corinthians 1:22) said 'Jews call for miracles, Greeks look for wisdom'. When the apostle declares in Athens, on the Areopagus (Acts 17.33), before an audience of Stoic and Epicurean philosophers, that Jesus is risen from the dead, they interrupt him with scorn and mockery: 'We will hear you on this subject some other time'.

THE MOST RELIGIOUS OF MEN? However, at the beginning of this same speech, Paul said (Acts 17.22): 'Men of Athens, I see that in everything that concerns religion you are uncommonly scrupulous'. Was this only flattery, *captatio benevolentiae*, in imitation of the rhetoricians? No, the Athenians, and all Greeks with them, were indeed, as were all the peoples of Antiquity, very religious. It is true that from the 5th century onwards there were many sceptics among the élite, such as Pericles and Thucydides, but it would be wrong to say that only the mass of people remained believers: many Athenians of the ruling class, military commanders and writers like Nicias and Xenophon, though they lived after the age of intellectual emancipation, remained deeply religious and even superstitious.

The Greek philosophers, for the most part, were not at all atheist. The Epicureans, unbelievers and rationalists though they were, accepted the existence of the gods — distant gods, it is true, and detached from human affairs. Even more so, the other philosophical schools allowed of the existence of the supernatural, in one form or another, without renouncing the full and normal exercise of reason.

The word 'mystery' and its slightly disquieting derivatives, like 'mystic' and 'mysticism', are of Greek origin. It is doubtless because *muo* means 'to close or keep closed the eyes or the mouth' that the verb *muéo* has taken on the meaning of 'to initiate into a secret cult'; hence: *mystes*, the initiate, *mystikos*: 'pertaining to initiation' (*myesis*), and finally *mysterion*: a secret religious ceremony, for the initiated alone as, for example, are the rites of the 'Mysteries' of Demeter and Kore at Eleusis.

DIVINE ANGUISH AND REASON. Just as they created democracy, the Greeks invented philosophy. The primary attitude in philosophy is inquiry, the search for knowledge that gives rise to a curiosity perpetually alert. In spite of the attempts of the Ionian and Eleatic philosophers to explain the cosmos by a simple principle (fire or water, friendship or hatred, the One, the dual, the multiple), too many realities on Earth remain obscure and mysterious.

Leaving aside questions of theology, how to explain the profoundly transforming love engendered by the physical and moral beauty (for the Greeks it is all one) of a human being, a love which can 'be born in an instant and lastingly invade the whole field of consciousness'? And where did Homer, the great poet who delighted and instructed every generation of Greeks, find the fount of ideas, images and words from which sprang the *Iliad* and the *Odyssey*? He himself speaks to his muse: 'Goddess, sing to us of the anger of Achilles'. Did he not have the feeling that a divinity, present in his heart and in his very voice, inspired him to his songs? How could certain gods, notably Apollo, communicate knowledge of their will and of future events to their prophets?

How also can the gods of the Mysteries, Demeter and Kore in Eleusis, Dionysus and his prophet Orpheus elsewhere, bring to men the revelation of their destiny and lead them, by secret rites, to eternal beatitude?

Mysteries of love, of poetic creation, of inspired deification, the secret religions pose difficult problems for the inquiring intelligence. However firmly one may believe in the power of reason, however firmly one rejects on principle the unintelligible and irrational, one cannot fail to recognize the multiple, disquieting, agonizing existence around us and within ourselves, of mystery. The emotion evoked in man by the approach of these forces, or these mysterious beings who are gods and 'demons', good or bad, is *thambos*, a word of pre-Hellenic origin whose proper meaning is 'fear before the sacred'.

ENTHUSIASM OR DIVINE POSSESSION. Plato, in his *Phaedo* group, distinguishes between two kinds of madness: that of the insane, which is a sickness of the mind, and that of the genius and of the authentically inspired, which is a divine Fate (*theia moira*). He discerns four forms of salutary frenzy sent to men by the gods for their good: prophetic frenzy, the frenzy of initiation, poetic frenzy, and the frenzy of love. Then he compares the soul to a chariot drawn by two winged horses, which is able, thanks to love, to lift itself to the supra-celestial place where the 'beatific vision' (*makaria opsis*) appears. The principal means to knowledge, for Plato, at least in the matter of gaining access to the eternal Ideas, of the supreme Good, that is to say to God, is no longer reason — which, while always necessary, cannot suffice — but love.

Nietzsche distinguished, by comparing them, between the Apollonian and Dionysian sides of Greek religion. Wherever the Greco-Roman world offers examples of maenadism, that is of individual or collective frenzy, religious in origin, Dionysus-Bacchus is found, the god of nature and wildlife, of the beasts, the mountain and the forest, the tree, the ivy and the vine, whose fruit produces drunkenness. Even at Delphi, where the calm and luminous Apollo reigns, the base of the oracle contains the grave of Dionysus, the god who died and was reborn, like Osiris of Egypt, and the frenzy of the Pythia is a Dionysiac, not an Apollonian phenomenon, even if poets have slightly exaggerated the violence of this 'enthusiasm', as Paul Valéry writes in *Charmes*:

> 'The Pythia breathes out the flame
> From nostrils hardend by incense
> Panting, intoxicated, screaming! ... the soul
> Dreadful, and the flanks howling!'

BACCHANALIA. At Eleusis, the cry of *Iacchos* uttered by the great procession on the Sacred Way differs from the name Bacchus only in its first letter. Bacchus had a strong influence on the cult of Demeter, mother of Bromios-Dionysus.

Dionysus is also the god of male and female Bacchantes, of Maenads and Thyiads, the god of orgiastic rites, in which men, and especially women lost their reason, possessed through mystical frenzy by the god who ruled them, tearing apart every living animal they caught and devouring the warm, raw flesh (the rite of *omophagia*).

ORPHIC ASCETICISM. Orpheus, devotee of Dionysus, is the Thracian singer and musician who, by the glorious power of his music, so entranced Cerberus that he was moved to let Orpheus pass to find his wife Eurydice. This descent into the Underworld must be linked with the Orphic beliefs about the afterlife. According to the Orphic poems, the cycle of birth and death is endless for the uninitiated, but Orpheus' revelation offers the only way of salvation to his disciples. The Orphic leads an ascetic life of abstinence and renunciation; he is vegetarian and rejects everything that could reinforce the corporeal element, the source of impurity, within him, because his body is the tomb of his soul, and the latter must be free to reach the true life. Thus, the initiate could say to the Queen of the Underworld:

> 'I come from a community of pure ones, Oh pure sovereign of the Underworld and you other immortal gods! I am sure I belong to your blessed race. But destiny has overthrown me. At last I have leapt beyond the cycle of pain and grief, and with a hasty step I press on towards the desired crown. I find shelter beneath your breast, Lady of the Underworld.' Persephone (Kore) replies: 'Oh fortunate, oh blest! Thou hast become god from the man that thou wast.' And, in his turn, the Orphic: 'Yes, I have fallen as a kid into milk.'

Such beliefs, which had a great influence on Plato and on all the currents of thought which derived from him, contained an element of revelation, superior to reason.

The first Christians, on the walls of their catacombs, represented Orpheus as though he had been a prophet of the True God.

THE NINE STAGES OF HUMAN DIGNITY. A fifth contrast: the Greeks despised manual labour as fit only for slaves and the lower classes, but their mathematical discoveries are the origin of the amazing progress of modern science and technology.

Euripides, in his lost tragedy *Antiope*, makes the twins Amphion and Zethus discuss the comparative merits of the active life embodied by Zethus, the athlete and hunter, and the contemplative life personified by Amphion the musician. Amphion had the better of it, becoming king of Thebes and building its ramparts by making the stones move to the music of his lyre.

Plato and Aristotle, in contrast with Socrates, who talked so readily with artisans, were aristocrats. For them *poïesis*, that is, the 'making' of any object, a bed, a house, or even a work of art (sculptural, poetic or musical), was an activity of a secondary order, unworthy of the philosopher, who should involve himself only in *praxis* or in *theoria*, that is, either the practice of political affairs or study and the philosophical life. In his *Phaedo* group Plato classifies the different kinds of life according to their status, into nine castes: that of the worker and the artisan is the seventh, just above the demagogue and the tyrant who are the most despicable of men.

This attitude probably retarded the development of Greek science, which was so remarkable in respect of abstract mathematical speculation, because physical experimentation, which involves some manual work, scarcely appeared before the time of Archimedes, in the 3rd century BC.

SOURCES OF MODERN SCIENCE. The names of Thales, Pythagoras and Euclid are sufficient reminder that the Greeks created mathematics. The inscription at the door of the Academy read: 'None enter here who are not geometers.'

But Alexandrian science went much further. The great scientific names of the 3rd and 4th centuries BC were: Euclid, who codified the geometry of the Classical era; Eratosthenes of Cyrene, head of the library in Alexandria, founder of historical chronology and of scientific geography, who calculated the circumference of the Earth with amazing accuracy; Archimedes of Syracuse, geometer, engineer and the creator of modern physics; Aristarchus of Samos, whose intuition and astronomical knowledge anticipated Copernicus in the affirmation that the Earth went round the sun and not the opposite; Hipparchus of Nicaea, who discovered the precession of the equinoxes and was, in the words of Bigourdan, 'the greatest astronomer of Antiquity, and perhaps of all time'; Herophilus of Chalcedon and Eristrates of Ioulis who, through vivisection practised on animals and also on men condemned to death as criminals, discovered the circulation of the blood twenty centuries before Harvey. Greek science did not stop with Pythagoras and Hippocrates; the Hellenistic era, long (and erroneously) considered as a period of decadence, belonged no less than the Classical era to the history of Greece.

As early as the 5th century BC, Democritus, whose physics heralded those of Epicurus, evolved his theory of atoms. Of course the atom, which he thought indivisible, has since been split, but his deterministic and mechanistic conception of the world foreshadows some of the hypotheses which have permitted the prodigious development of modern science. Democritus truly opened the way to scientific research, so that, as M. Solovine has written: 'the image of the universe is for us today the same as it was for Democritus: an inconceivable number of small bodies scattered through a space without limits and eternally in movement'.

Besides this, the Greeks dreamed of yet more triumphs of technology: aviation, with the legend of Icarus; robot machines, with the metal servants of Hephaestus, in Book XVIII of the *Iliad*; interplanetary journeys in Lucian's *Icaromenippus*.

MAN THE PRINCIPLE OF UNITY. What is the underlying principle of unity which binds together the different Greek civilizations: the civilizations of Knossos and of Mycenae, of archaism, of classical Athens, of the Alexandrian era? In a word: man. Man was always at the centre of Greek thought, literature and art.

We know that in most ancient literatures the earliest poems are devoted to the divinity and to the origin of the world. In Greece, certainly there is Hesiod's *Theogony*, but first there is the *Iliad* and the *Odyssey*; Homer did not ignore Olympus, but he gave the forefront of the stage to men, and when these are called Achilles, Hector or Ulysses they are more admirable than the gods. The Athenian vase-painters, from their first clumsy experiments in the 8th century BC, made a place for the human figure in the Geometric design of their pottery. Thereafter, all Greek art — Archaic, Classical, then Hellenistic — was to exalt the beauty of the body, male and female. In vases and bas-reliefs the depiction of man eclipsed everything else; only in the Alexandrian era did country and city landscapes make their appearance. As to statues, from the kouros of Piraeus to the Venus of Melos, they speak for themselves.

In Ionia, the first philosophers turned their eyes to the world but, in the 5th century, the Socratic and sophist 'revolution' concentrated attention on man. The maxim 'know thyself', borrowed by Socrates from Delphic wisdom, and the adage of Protagoras: 'man is the measure of all things', converge and meet. Each in his own way, the Athenian and the Abderite were humanists. In this 5th century the thinking of poets turned away somewhat from the gods and was secularized or humanized. Aeschylus, in *Prometheus,* attributed the beginning of human civilization to Prometheus, and Euripides, in *Suppliant Women*, gave similar words to Theseus.

Sophocles, though not a pupil of the sophists, had the chorus of *Antigone* intone:

> There are many marvels in this world; none is greater than
> man ... The word, thought as fast as the wind, aspirations
> from which cities are born, all that, he has taught himself.

All the contradictions — more or less apparent — that we have indicated do not alter the fact that Greece has always been concerned first with men.

In politics, the Greeks founded civic liberty, that ideal whose most eloquent spokesman was Demosthenes. When the classical city had had its day, the Stoics proclaimed man *cosmopolitan*, that is to say a citizen of the world. For Aristotle's definition, Chrysippus substituted this one: 'Man is a being who lives in a universal society (koinonikon)'. The Greeks had succeeded in breaking out of political particularism into citizenship of the world.

Most of them were also able to profess a rationalism, not restricted like that of Lucian, but open to mystery and the inexpressible. If they also believed man to be an incomplete, unfinished being, and thought that in the universe there are realities other than visible things, this viewpoint, shared by Plato, Plutarch and Plotinus, will not appear in any way alien to humanism.

THE CULT OF THE BEAUTIFUL. But what best defines Greek humanism, what confers upon it its particular tone, its own nuance, is the cult of the beautiful. The admiration, but above all the beauty, physical and moral — inextricably linked — of the human being, is a constant theme in Greek literature from Homer to Plotinus and well beyond. Beauty inspired love naturally, but while elsewhere love is reputed to be blind, with Plato it becomes the primary condition of the highest knowledge and of supreme illumination.

Homer, in Book III of the *Iliad*, made Paris say:

> Do not reproach me the charming gifts of the Golden Aphrodite: the shining gifts of the gods are not to be scorned, those which they alone give us, and which no one would acquire by himself.

More than a thousand years later Plotinus, the ascetic and mystic philosopher, echoes the poet:

> The beauty of the human body derives from its participation in a rational principle come from the gods.

Even Fathers of the Greek Church were to consider as an apologetic argument not only the heavens 'which recount the glory of god', but also the moral and physical beauty of man, created by the Lord in his own image.

If the religion of Ancient Greece is anthropomorphic that is because the Greeks, seeking a pattern for the divine, found nothing more beautiful than the human form. Let us end therefore with André Bonnard:

> The most important of the conquests which, taken together, define Greek civilization, all have the same aim: to increase the power of man over nature, to increase his very humanity. That is why we call Greek civilization a humanism. It was man and human life that the Greek people strove to make better.

Byzantine Greece

by Alain Ducellier
Professor of Medieval History
at the University of Toulouse-Le-Mirail

The time has now fortunately passed when even the educated tourist would go into raptures over a shapeless ruin from classical antiquity, only a few yards from a magnificent Byzantine church at which he might cast only a fleeting glance. The superlative quality of Greece's numerous medieval monuments has finally prevailed over the indifference, even scorn, which anything Byzantine used to receive. This 'return to Byzantium' may perhaps be due to the recent efforts of specialists to explicate the thousand-year history of Greek Christendom — a period which is as long as Hellenic and Roman Antiquity put together. It is not just the historian who will take delight in this new interest in the Byzantine, because it also helps us really to understand the Greek people of today, who are profoundly aware that they have inherited more from Byzantium than from Athens. For anyone who sees Greece as more than a museum, be it the finest museum in the world, it is well worth coming to know and love the civilization which managed to endow Greece with the strength to endure four centuries of Turkish occupation, which sustained Greece's traditions, literature and even language, and the Greek people's deep sensitivity.

From Rome to Byzantium

RESISTANCE TO INVASION. The rift between East and West in the Roman Empire became more and more marked during the 4th century, especially after the foundation of Constantinople in 330; but this had absolutely no effect on Greece's status, which remained that of one among many imperial provinces. The remote province of Greece was an integral part of the prefecture of Illyricum and harboured its capital, Thessaloniki, whose pre-eminent position underlines the northward shift of the Hellenic peninsula's administrative, economic and religious centre of gravity. Justinian's attempt in 535 (a failure, as it happens) to transfer the capital of the prefecture to Justiniana Prima, near Niš (now in Yugoslavia), is undoubtedly the most striking indication that Greece constituted merely an element with no special privileges in the mosaic of peoples that made up Illyricum. It would be wrong, however, to think of Greece as being fundamentally decadent in the 4th and 5th centuries; quite the contrary: archaeological discoveries prove that this was a period of remarkable prosperity, even though the country had long been affected by a slow process of depopulation, like the rest of the Balkans. The same discoveries also enable us to affirm that, contrary to what is normally believed, Greece suffered very little before the 6th century from the invasions which were then laying waste the rest of the Empire. There were, of course, many often terrifying raids: after the death of Valens on the battlefield at Adrianople in 378, the Goths pillaged Thrace and Macedonia, and then did the same to Greece; but it was much further north, between the Danube and the Balkans (Haemus) that they settled under Theodosius the Great in 382. Following the emperor's death in 395, Alaric's conquest of Thessaly and Attica was merely an inconsequential episode, and the same can be said, despite the atrocious pillaging, of the Huns' incursion under Attila in 447, which reached Thermopylae. The final episode in the invasions of Greece was a series of expeditions under the Gothic chiefs Theodoric Strabo and Theodoric the Amal between 743 and 473, but these did not pose a real threat and only northern Greece was affected: Larisa was captured and the outskirts of Philippi were burned down, but Thessaloniki withstood the barbarian assault. All in all, these invasions, brutal though they often were, never resulted in barbarian settlement in Greece, and they do not seem to have seriously affected the existing population. The same Greece, slightly depopulated but still remarkably prosperous, can be seen both before and after the period of invasions.

In the 4th and 5th centuries, Greece, at the heart of the Empire, certainly did not enjoy her former cultural prestige: the schools at Alexandria, Antioch, Berytos and now Constantinople were in strong competition. The School of Athens, however, which was the centre of both a pagan neo-platonist cult of the arts and of serious study of Platonic philosophy, underwent a great revival in the 5th century: students flocked there from Egypt, Syria and Asia Minor, and Proclus, the greatest Neoplatonist philosopher of the time, taught there. With the growth of Christianity in Greece, however, the School became increasingly inward looking, and in 529 Justinian had no difficulty in removing its temporal power and prohibiting the instruction of pagans. When the last of the philosophers had been dispersed all that was taught in Athens until the 7th century was a modest amount of grammar and rhetoric.

THE ARTS. This last burst of creativity in philosophy coincided with a real flowering of the arts: even though in this area the Greeks merely borrowed forms which originated elsewhere, Greece was clearly a remarkable melting-pot producing some very worthwhile syntheses.

From the 4th century, the Hellenistic, or 'Constantinian' style of basilica which was common throughout the Empire, made its appearance in Greece; but the fact that it barely reached the Argolic Plain is further proof that only the north was thriving. The basilicas at Nea Ankhialos near Volos, at Nicopolis, Corinth and Epidaurus are all of this type. Nevertheless, certain Macedonian buildings already show signs of innovation: 'Basilica A' at Philippi has a proper transept and that of St Demetrius at Thessaloniki, which had been a true Hellenistic basilica in the 5th century, underwent the same transformation in the 6th century. But a more important innovation was the introduction of the cupola; the centrally-planned church, which originated in Asia and of which the finest examples are San Vitale, Ravenna, and Saints Sergius and Bacchus at Constantinople, has certainly never been found in Greece, but it would seem that the Greeks were the first to combine the cupola with the old style of basilical plan. During the 6th century, cupolas were placed over the sanctuaries at Athens (the basilica of Illissos) and at Philippi ('Basilica B'). Despite certain important technical developments, however (the dome at Philippi is supported on the north and south sides by two barrel vaults), this type of church was not to be perfected in Greece: perfection was achieved, although it was short-lived, at Hagia Sophia in Constantinople, with the idea of placing the cupola above the nave.

In sculpture and mosaic it would be difficult to find specifically Greek characteristics; the most one can say is that compared with those of Ravenna or Parenzo, the few mosaics which escaped the fire at St Demetrios at Thessaloniki in 1917 have a more mystical, oriental flavour, and a more 'Hellenic' discretion in the colours.

The Slav invasions and the Dark Ages

A SERIES OF ASSAULTS PENETRATE GREECE. The 4th to 5th centuries mark a time of change in the rest of Europe, but it was at the beginning of the 6th century that the change occurred in Greece, following the Slavonic invasions — events which were of the utmost significance to the history of Greece. Instigated by the Bulgarian Turks, a huge horde of Southern Slavs, Antae and Slavonians, descended on the borders of the Empire from the end of the 5th century; in 517, they raided Macedonia and Thessaly, and swept on as far as Thermopylae. In 540, one horde of Bulgaro-Slavs laid waste Macedonia from Chalcidice to Thessaloniki, before going on to threaten Constantinople, while another ransacked Greece as far as the Corinthian isthmus. If contemporary sources are to be believed, the barbarians took 100,000 prisoners at that time. Of course, Byzantium managed more or less to protect the Danube border, but splinter groups of invaders concentrated their attacks on Thrace, Macedonia and what is now Bulgaria, and Greece proper did not always escape. In 559 the country was raided again as far as Thermopylae and the situation deteriorated after 560 when the Slavonians fell under the power of the Avars. In 582, the Avars gained control over the Empire's main defensive point on the Danube, Sirmium (Mitrovica, 50mls/80km west of present-day Belgrade).

At that time, Emperor Maurice's bitter struggles against the Persians prevented him from making any effective intervention in the Balkans, and the Slavs were thus able to spread across them without much hindrance; in 597, Thessaloniki was besieged for the first time. A peace treaty was undoubtedly signed with the Avars in 599, but while this may have kept the Avars at bay across the Danube, it certainly did not prevent a disorganized and uncontrollable horde of Slavonians from steadily making its way towards the Aegean coast and Greece. The Greek plains began to suffer the same fate as the northern Balkans, with the gradual but lasting settlement of Slavs. From the early 7th century, Thessaloniki stood out alone in a country that was extensively 'Slavonized' and constantly had to withstand the unsuccessful assaults of the barbarians, who were still unskilled in siege warfare. But the Slavs began to make progress technically: the *Miraculi Sancti Demetrii* show for certain that by 620 the Slavs had ships, allowing them to reach Achaea and Epirus as well as Macedonia, and to raid the islands as far as the Cyclades; but they still failed to take Thessaloniki, which they had attacked from both land and sea. An important fact is that the Slavonians were now free of the domination of the Avars, who had been considerably weakened by their unsuccessful attempt on Constantinople in 626. The Sclavenes gradually infiltrated all of the Greek countries, and the fact that we are told that in 658 Constans II Pogonatus went to war against the 'Slav countries' (*sclaviniai*) and that he 'subjected' them, proves above all that there were now Greek regions with predominantly Slavonic populations, and that through their 'subjection' these Slavs had actually acquired official rights of residence.

Unfortunately, it is difficult to determine the exact geographic locations occupied by the Slavs. But it is known for certain that Macedonia, and the Thessaloniki region especially, were by far the most affected areas. In 667 and then in 687-688 Thessaloniki came under attack again, which was the reason behind two victorious expeditions, one led by Constans IV and the other by Justinian II, both of whom are referred to by the chronicles as 'the conquerors of the Slavs'. But it is significant that Greece proper is not under consideration in the accounts of these campaigns; the strategic requirement was to defend Thessaloniki, but meanwhile the Slavs were relentlessly occupying the Greek province except perhaps for the coastal fringes, especially in the south-east. Still, this invasion should certainly not be thought of as a brutal catastrophe; the Slavs' advance into Greece was more of a slow, spreading movement which might on occasion have been accompanied by violence, but which must be credited with bringing new blood to a dwindling population. The large number of Slavonic place-names, a particularly striking feature in the Peloponnese, emphasizes the importance of this colonization and suggests that the newcomers were responsible for establishing settlements where none had previously existed. In general, however, the Slavs must have settled alongside the indigenous populations, some groups of which undoubtedly remained undisturbed; only the Taygetos massif seems to have been occupied by a homogenous Slavonic population, with the Melinges and Lezerite tribes, who continued to inhabit the area until the Ottoman invasion. At any rate, certain 8th-century sources still considered Greece as a Slavonic country: in the biography of St Willibald of Eichstätt (723–728), we are told that the saint disembarked at Monemvasia, *in Slavinica terra*, and the writings of Constantine VII Porphyrogenitus, concerning the mid-8th century, show us a glimpse of a country which was 'entirely Slavonic and became Barbarian'. It is not surprising, therefore, to note the disappearance of all traces of normal administration in Greece until the end of the 8th century.

THE EMPIRE'S REACTION. It was at this time that the Imperial government began to react: in 783, the Imperial commander Stavrakios attacked the Slavs in the Thessaloniki area, and then in Greece as far as the Peloponnese. Although the Slavs waged a counter-attack, and swooped down on Patras in 805, the Empire had regained control of the situation. New administrative sectors were created: until then Greece had only constituted a single province, the *theme* of Hellas, created no doubt between 690 and 695, whose jurisdiction was limited to central Greece, and which formed a kind of border march where the Empire's authority only existed, at best, in theory. But in the late 8th century, the Macedonian and Peloponnesian *themes* came into being, followed by the *theme* of Cephalonia (the Ionian Islands) at the beginning of the 9th century, and those of Thessaloniki and Dyrrachion at some time before 850. Although the Slavonic element remained strong in Greece, Byzantium was once again able to exert a consistent influence on administrative, economic, and above all cultural matters. Culturally, it must be said that the Slavonic invasions had made a waste land of Greece, but not without sowing the seeds for future growth: the church of St Sophia at Thessaloniki, constructed in the 8th century, is the first example of the transition between the basilical plan and the future Byzantine cruciform church. The Slavs had infused new life into Greece, but not to the point of destroying her identity, and her 'return to Byzantium' will show that Greece would once again be able to lead the rest of the Empire in many ways.

Byzantine Greece from the 9th to the 13th century

ECONOMIC AND ARTISTIC RENEWAL. History, however, paints a rather dull picture of Greece in the 9th and 10th centuries. Towns were few in number and small in size: Athens, Corinth, Monemvasia, Sparta and Patras were not much more than large villages. The Greek language, having withstood the Slavs, became fragmented into mutually incomprehensible dialects: even in the 12th century, Michael Choniates, Archbishop of Athens, could not make himself understood by his congregation when he undertook a sermon in the vernacular of the capital. Moreover, Greece had not been fully converted to Christianity in the 6th century, and superstition, magic and unorthodox rites were not rife; in some areas, such as Crete, which was occupied by the Arabs from 827 to 961, Christianity was even in danger of disappearing: around 965, St Nikon Metanoites shouldered the double task of reconverting the Cretans and converting the Peloponnesian Slavs, many of whom were still pagan. Nevertheless, Greece was experiencing a remarkable economic boom at that time: Thebes, Corinth and Sparta were the trade capitals of oil and silk which were exported to the rest of the Empire, and of which the Venetians came in search from the late 11th century. From Dyrrachion where they landed, the Italians forged their way across northern Greece, through Macedonia and Thessaloniki, to reach Constantinople, and at the same time made their way through Kastoria and Ioannina to reach Almyros (south of present-day Volos), and, above all, Thebes and Corinth. They were also making increasing contact with the various ports of the peninsula. This economic upswing is all the more remarkable given that Greece was not free from foreign aggression: in 918, the Bulgars under Symeon invaded as far as Corinth, and then again in 997 under Samuel; and even the Hungarians carried out raids; for their part, the Arabs returned to capture and loot Thessaloniki in 904. The most important threat, however, came from the West; the Norman expeditions led by Robert Guiscard in 1081-4 and by his son Bohemund I in 1108, only reached Albania and the borders of Epirus, but in 1147 Roger II of Sicily took possession of Corfu; then captured the Corinthian and Theban silk workers to relocate them in his own kingdom, thus delivering a fatal blow to Greece's principal industry. Then in 1185, William II of Sicily (builder of Monreale and its mosaics) seized the Ionian Islands and Thessaloniki, subjecting them to atrocious looting. Although forced to retreat, William still kept his hold on Cephalonia and Zante, which Byzantium would never recover.

PROSPERITY IN THE ARTS. While it is not the only explanation for Greece's artistic prosperity at that time, the economic boom is an important factor. Along with Constantinople, Greece was then one of the two main sources of Byzantine architecture. As early as 874, the unpretentious church of Skripou in Boeotia already stood as a model of the classical edifice with a Greek cross plan, even though the dome was supported by the corners of the walls rather than by columns, as would later become the norm. The technique of placing the dome on columns and supporting it with four equal barrel vaults was certainly perfected in Constantinople, but once the Greeks had adopted the technique they wer enot content to make mere slavish copies. Whereas the dome was generally placed on four columns in the capital's churches, the Greeks preferred what seemed to be their own 'simple plan', with the dome supported by only two columns and the walls of the apse; examples of this can be seen in the Taxiarkhon (church of the Archangels) in Athens, and the churches at Samari and Gastouni in the Peloponnese. Furthermore, apart from the monastery of Nea Moni on Chios, the only examples of the large-scale octabonal edifice in which the dome is supported by four squinches and covers the width of the three apses, are to be found in mainland Greece: the finest of these is the church of Hosios Loukas (St. Luke) (9th century), but other examples of this type can be seen at Daphni (late 9th century), at Christianou near Kiparissia, at the Panayia Likodimou in Athens (1144), and finally at St Sophia at Monemvasia (early 13th century).

We should not imagine, however, that Greece escaped the influence of Constantinople: the prototypes of these domed churches with supporting squinches are surely to be sought in Constantinople, in particular at the now ruined Peribleptos, built by Romanus III between 1028 and 1034. Equally, many churches of the Constantinian type, with four columns (the 'complex' plan), were built in Greece: a number of churches in Athens are of this type (the Small Metropolis, or Panayia Gorgonepikoos, the Kapnikarea, the Kaisarianis on Mt Hymettos), as are most of the sanctuaries in the Argolic plain (Khonika, Merbaka, Hagia Moni near Nauplia), and some Peloponnesian churches (the small church of Hosios Loukas, and certain churches in the Mani, like Karouda). All in all, there is abundant proof that between the 9th and 13th centuries Greece was able to adapt and at the same time to exercise as undeniable inventiveness.

Greek individuality may be more difficult to detect in other areas of the arts: from the 9th century, the Greeks, like the rest of the Empire, used the same iconographic programme in the decoration of their churches (Christ Pantocrator in the cupola, Theotokos, the Mother of God, and Eucharistic scenes in the central apse, Biblical themes in the subsidiary apses, liturgical calendar in the naves, and the life of the Theotokos in the narthex). Nevertheless, regional tendencies do come across in the techniques used and the general feeling of the works: the mosaics of Nea Moni on Chios display a certain 'orientalism', but those of Daphni, which are undoubtedly the more beautiful, manage to combine a truly Byzantine religious fervour with a revival of the classical relief, which most probably started in Greece.

Frankish Greece

THE DEVELOPMENT OF FEUDALISM. This economic and cultural prosperity should not obscure the longstanding, disturbing social evolution that was taking place in Greece and the rest of the Empire. From the 10th century especially, powerful men (dynatoi) were creating vast estates for themselves at the expense of the small and medium-sized properties, the essence of Byzantine social structure, which were thus being gradually whittled away, despite constant legal protection provided by the great sovereigns of Macedonian dynasty (867–1056). As Greece was a remote province, the Empire had difficulty in exerting its authority, and this trend possibly developed faster and more substantially than elsewhere, with the result that, just prior to the Frankish invasion, certain men had become veritable lords, who saw themselves as the absolute masters of their lands. Among these were the Cantacuzene family in Messenia, and the Sgouroi between

Corinth and Nauplia. It is no coincidence, therefore, that the invaders returning from the fourth Crusade chose Greece, and especially the Peloponnese (thenceforth called the Morea), as the stock on to which to graft their own feudal system. The crisis resulted in the tripartite division of Greece: the kingdom of Thessaloniki in the north was given to Boniface of Monferrat; great fiefs in the centre, the most important of which was the Duchy of Athens, were granted to Otho de la Roche; and lastly, the Morea fell into the hands of the Villehardouin family in 1209. In 1224, the Greeks of Epirus recaptured Thessaloniki, but Athens and Frankish Morea (the principality of Achaea) were not liberated until shortly before the Turkish invasion.

While the Franks were never really accepted by the Greek population, the Principality of Achaea was nevertheless the most brilliant and viable of all the Latin states in the east: once they had completed the laborious process of suppressing resistance from the Greek lords (archontes), the first three Villehardouins maintained friendly relations with them; and, since their privileges were generally recognized, these Greek lords came to tolerate the installation of the barons and their vassals in Greece. This colonization was detrimental to the smaller landlords and, even more so, to the Church's estates. As for the common people, who were probably no more oppressed by their new rulers than they had been by the former Byzantine administration, they often gained from princes' protective policies intended to prevent the traditional injustices they suffered. The Franks' desire for friendly relations is best expressed in the case-books of the Romanian Assizes, for they are much more lenient than those of the Jerusalem Assizes which governed the other Latin states. The Jerusalem casebooks, moreover, show that feudal law had been somewhat contaminated by Byzantine legal elements. At the same time, the feudal mentality was taking root in the Greek upper classes, a phenomenon which was not without its consequences later on, when Greece was restored to Byzantine control. All of these factors, however, did not reconcile the Greeks to foreign yoke, and the Church, now dispossessed and theoretically subject to Rome, provided the focal point for resistance and for a sense of endangered cultural community.

THE BYZANTINE RECONQUEST. This, then, was the setting for the Byzantine reconquest, which was the work of the great Nicaean emperors John III Vatatzes, Theodore II Lascaris and Michael VIII Palaeologus. Macedonia became Byzantine again with the re-conquest of Thessaloniki from the Greeks of Epirus in 1246, and in 1258 Michael VII defeated the Epirotes and Franks who confronted him at the battle of Pelagonia. The prince of Achaea was taken prisoner and, in 1261, forced to yield four fortresses in the Morea to the emperor, including Mistra and Monemvasia, marking the beginning of a painstaking reconquest which lasted for almost two centuries. Byzantium had not only the Franks to contend with: there were also the Venetians, who had holdings in Messenia (Koron and Modon especially), as well as the Neapolitan Angevins, who had been allied to the Villehardouins since 1267; the Principality even came under Neapolitan rule following the death of the last Prince in 1278. All things considered, however, the disappearance of the Ville-hardouin family was quite useful to the Byzantines: their work of reconquest was greatly facilitated by feudal anarchy and by the general dissatisfaction caused by a ruling power which was both remote and yet meddlesome, and which, moreover, was considerably weakened after 1282 by the 'Sicilian Vespers' affair. Even in Crete which the Venetians had ruled since 1210, the great uprising led by Alexis Kalergis lasted for twenty years and was not suppressed until 1229; and even then, the Venetians, who had hitherto set up a colonial power in Crete which left the Greeks with almost no rights, were forced to devise a more liberal policy towards them, eventually culminating, in the 14th century, in something increasingly similar to the upper classes of Hellenic society. With this policy Venice also ran the risk of angering her own vassals, who went so far as to rebel against her in 1368. In central Greece, however, the Duchy of Athens was under attack and in 1311 fell to the Almugavars, Catalan mercenaries, who had been ploughing their way across the Empire for ten years; they founded their own Duchy of Athens which lasted until 1388.

Frankish Greece was by no means a cultural desert. The *Chronicle* of *Morea*, which unfortunately gives only a very incomplete account of the history of Frankish Greece, has come down to us in four different languages, French, Greek, Catalan and Italian, and it bears witness to an incipient synthesis, of languages as well as mentalities. In fine art, the Byzantine canons were still faithfully followed: the beautiful 13th-century churches which can be seen in the Mani, at Platsa for instance, come to mind as examples of this. In those regions which escaped Frankish domination, especially Epirus and Acarnania, there were even some remarkable new developments in art, as is shown by the Panayia Parigoritissa at Arta. In addition, there was imported Latin art, the remains of which, like the cathedral at Andréville (Andravidha) or the cloister at Daphni, moving though they are, should not obscure the fact that they had hardly any influence on artistic evolution. The same cannot be said of the Frankish fortresses, such as Mistra, Caritaine (Karitaina), Clairmont (Chlemoutsi) and Arkadi, since their construction techniques undoubtedly inspired Byzantine architects before and after the reconquest.

THE GREEK DESPOTATE OF THE MOREA. At the beginning of the 14th century, Byzantium regained control of Epirus and Thessaly, and the local Greek dynasties, who had held power there since the disintegration of the Empire, became extinct. Most important, however, was that after 1308 the Emperor liberally delegated power to the governors of the Morea, members of the ruling dynasty, who were kept in office for many years, with two fundamental consequences: greater strength and extra means for the work of reconquest, and a progressive evolution towards autonomy without breaking the links with Constantinople. Thus, the Greek Despotate of Morea came into being, and its structure was more or less established under the reign of John VI Cantacuzene (1341–55) who usurped the throne of John V;

his sons, the Despots Manuel and Matthew, who ruled the country until 1382 and who lived at Mistra, adopted a policy of redevelopment, consisting of the recolonization of deserted areas by bringing in Albanian nomads who had begun to appear in Epirus and Thessaly at the beginning of the 14th century; at the same time, they actively pursued the war against the Franks, and repelled the first Turkish onslaughts. In 1382, this task was taken up again by Theodosius I, the first of the Palaeologi Despots and son of Emperor John V, but there were increasing difficulties. Frankish domination was, of course, almost nonexistent by now: Athens had passed from the Catalans to the Florentine Acciauoli and the tattered remnants of the principality of Achaea fell into the hands of a company of mercenaries from Navarre. But the Ottomans, who already controlled almost all of Asia Minor, gained a foothold at Gallipoli in 1354, and beset the Greek borders from then on; Theodosius had scarcely been invested as Despot when he had to accept the suzerainty of Sultan Murad I, in return for his assistance against the Latins. Such assistance was dangerous, for the Turks did not hesitate to switch from one alliance to another, according to what best suited their interests: in 1394, when Theodosius looked as if he would lay hold of Athens following the death of Prince Nerio Acciauoli, Sultan Baazid I turned to the Navarrese instead, who helped him to invade the Morea, where the Turks would, from then on, control several strongholds. For their part, the Venetians took advantage of the crisis to take possession of Corfu in 1386, Argos and Nauplia in 1388, and finally Athens in 1395. As for the other Ionian islands, these were held from 1357 by the Neapolitan Tocco family, the counts palatine of Cephalonia. In 1397, it seemed as though the Despotate's fate was sealed when the Turks, who had temporarily seized Athens, made forays as far as the southern Peloponnese. However, Timur's resounding victory over Bayazid at the battle of Ankara in 1402 was to give the Greeks a last respite.

A blueprint of Greece?

BETWEEN THE VENETIANS AND THE TURKS. In 1415, Emperor Manuel II Palaeologus came to aid of his son, the Despot Theodosius II, in an ambitious attempt to restore order at home: it was a question of subduing the restless archons of the Morea, who had become too accustomed to an independence which was fostered by the relaxing of central authority and by the ever available support of the Latins, and even the Turks. Furthermore, to avert the foreseeable return of the Turks, Manuel took the opportunity to construct the Hexamilion wall on the Corinthian isthmus and in the shadow of the mighty citadel of Acrocorinth. The restoration of order enabled the despot, during the years that followed, to dispossess almost totally the last prince of Achaea, Centurione Zaccaria, who was only saved from utter ruin by the Venetians. However, when Sultan Mehmed I died in 1421, the Ottoman Empire, which had long been beset by fratricidal struggles, fell under the iron rule of Murad II, whom Byzantium had offended by showing favour to his brothers. After the terrible siege of

Constantinople in 1422, the Turkish invaders wreaked havoc on the Morea, once the Hexamilion wall had been dismantled; during the same year, the governor of Thessaloniki, the Despot Andronicus Palaeologus, was forced to yield the town to the Venetians, who in turn had to give it up to the Turks in 1430. Notwithstanding, the Greek reconquest continued: in 1428 the Tocco family yielded their properties in the Morea to the despots, in 1430 Constantine Dragatses took possession of Patras, and finally in 1432 what was left of Frankish Achaea fell into Greek hands. Apart from the towns belonging to the Venetians, Koron, Modon, Argos and Nauplia, the whole of the Morea now recognized the authority of the Greek sovereigns, for the first time since 1204. But the advance of the Turks was irreversible: in 1446, Murad II crossed the Hexamilion again and made a terrible raid on the Morea, taking 60,000 prisoners and forcing Mistra to pay tribute to him. The situation deteriorated even further when, in 1449, Constantine Dragatses left Greece to become the last emperor of Byzantium: the Morea's history then amounted to sterile struggles between his two brothers, the Despots Demetrius and Thomas, under the interested eyes of their Turkish overlords and judges. In 1453, the year of the fall of Constantinople, the Morea was also the scene of a great uprising against the despots, which was carried out mainly by Albanians but led by Greek archons who were prepared to solicit Turkish aid in ridding themselves of the recently restored Byzantine control. Such domestic disruption naturally assisted the latest advance of the Turks, who were in control of Athens as early as 1456; in 1458, on the pretext of a delay in the tribute payment, they annexed a third of the Morea, and it was during a final war between the two despots that Mohammed the Conqueror decided to take the rest: Mistra fell on 30 May 1460 and the following year, despite the often heroic resistance which unified the Greeks and the Albanians, the whole country was turned into an Ottoman pashalik, apart from Monemvasia, which would remain Venetian until 1540. Thomas fled to Italy, while Demetrius died in captivity.

FAILURE. The brilliance of some aspects of the Greek reconquest under the great Despots Theodosius I, Theodosius II and Constantine, should not blind us to the fact that this was an enterprise which was doomed to failure. The country had been economically ruined by two centuries of war and the population was now so small that some regions were almost deserted. Calling in the Albanians, who were pastoral people and farmers, helped to redevelop a number of areas, especially in Arcadia, Messenia, the Argolic Plain, Achaea, Elis, and even Attica and Euboea; but the Albanian immigrants, who also significantly swelled the ranks of the army, could not fill all the gaps, even if we estimate the Albanian element to be about a third of the total population in the mid-15th century, which seems to be an exaggeration. Also, the Albanians were unruly and not interested in Mistra's political ambitions, and, as we have seen, they played no small part in the 'feudal' uprisings which so undermined the work of the despots. The philosopher George Gemistus Pletho had rightly seen that the Morea's future health could only be obtained by carrying out radical economic reform and by bringing into line the archons, who were always capable of treachery. He had also been aware of the need for a real change of mentality, even if his idea of returning to ancient paganism as a means of re-establishing 'Greek patriotism' must be seen as pure fantasy. Perhaps the Despots and intellectuals really did have a vision of a Greek nation rising out of the ashes of the Empire; there is no doubt that the masses, unified as they were by their religion and its ministers, were, whether they were aware of it or not, the embodiment of what may be called the orthodox Greek community, more than they had ever been before. But there is no denying the fact that medieval Morea was never a nation and could scarcely be called a state, having no social and economic framework capable of reflecting the wishes of the masters or of transmitting the aspirations of the people. On the strength of this, it would be unwise to think off the Morea as a blueprint for the future Greece, which, in any case, would come into being north of the Corinthian isthmus.

The final Byzantine renaissance in Greece

MISTRA: CULTURAL AND ARTISTIC CAPITAL. Throughout this deluge of invasions, uprisings and disorder, Greece in the 14th and 15th centuries was the main centre of the last cultural and artistic renaissance of the Byzantine Middle Ages. Under the Palaeologi Despots, Mistra became the rallying point of the greatest intellectuals of the time, who found more security there, as well as the support of a cultured government, chiefly personified by Constantine Dragatses. Thus, the historians Laonikos Chalkokondylis and George Sphrantzes, and, above all, Gemistus Pletho, the greatest and perhaps the only real Byzantine philosopher, all thrived in Mistra. Pletho was curious about everything, from economics and politics to religion, and he was in a good position to bring Plato's ideal of universal competence back to life; well aware of the philosopher's civic role, he was such a free thinker that he was prepared to abandon even his Christianity, once he was convinced of its subversive effect on the body social. The fact that Pletho, who came too late and was often quite unrealistic, was able to work and teach in peace in Mistra, is nevertheless a good indication of the liberal, innovative spirit which reigned in the Despotate's capital, whereas the most arid Aristotelianism reigned supreme in Constantinople, under Pletho's old enemy George Scholarios.

ARCHITECTURE. Despite the adverse circumstances, Byzantine art in Greece can be seen to have undergone an astonishing revival in the 14th and 15th centuries, without ever abandoning its traditions. As in Constantinople, the classic Greek cruciform church tended increasingly towards the perpendicular and had more and more domes, which were themselves increasingly tall and slender. Meanwhile, the very plain, even austere style of exterior decoration which had hitherto been the norm, gave way to polychrome paintwork and a baroque tendency in sculpture; this was already the case with the church of the Holy Apostles in Thessaloniki, in 1312–15. After 1350, however, and before being totally overwhelmed by the Turks, the Morea, and Mistra in particular, was the cradle of the last school of Greek architecture, which is characterized by a recovered freedom of choice in form and style. Further churches of the classical type were constructed, like the Peribleptos (c. 1350), but following a course already taken for the Parigoritissa at Arta. St Demetrios, reconstructed around 1310, is a traditional basilica at ground level, with a cruciform building superimposed at gallery level. The same plan in the shape of a Greek cross prevails in the Vrontokhion monastery's Aphentiko church, as well as in the Pantanassa, rebuilt in 1428, whose most striking feature is the bell-tower which bears Gothic, and perhaps even Islamic, influences. This taste for the complex plan, moreover, was not restricted to the Morea: many churches on the relatively sheltered island of Mt Athos combine the Greek cross with basilical features; but the three-apse church, which was so common in the orthodox Slav countries, was also quite widespread: it is no coincidence that the most remarkable building of this type is the church of the Serbian Chilandari monastery.

PAINTING. It is perhaps this which is most representative of Byzantine art in its final phase. Soon after the completion of the masterpieces in the Kariye Camii at Constantinople at the beginning of the 14th century, mosaic died out, partly for economic reasons, and partly because the fresco was more flexible and better suited to the expressionism of troubled times. Henceforth the fresco predominated, but not without a clash of different trends. On the whole, it may be said that 14th- and 15th-century wall painting was dominated by two schools, not that it is easy, or even desirable, to draw a rigorous distinction between them. The 'Macedonian' school predominated at Mt Athos and was in evidence as far away as Mistra, in the oldest paintings of the Metropolitan Church, from the early 14th century; the former individual panels were substituted by this school's long narrative cycles which, in a fresh but somewhat naive manner, illustrated the main episodes from the Scriptures. But at Mistra, it was a so-called 'Cretan' school which prevailed; their style was expressionistic and full of pathos, with emphasis on realistic, touching details and on the representation of movement; they liberally used, and over-used, chiaroscuro, as is the case in the Peribleptos and, especially, in the Pantanassa. From Mistra, this tendency was to become established in Crete, Mt Athos and the Slavonic countries as far as Russia, both in wall painting and in icons. Such incontestable supremacy, moreover, carried within itself the potential for its own sterility: having become an untouchable model, the inventive 'Cretan' school was to go on tirelessly reproducing itself right through the Turkish period. But we cannot overlook the fact that it was this style which inspired two very great painters whose work has a universal value: the Russian Andrei Rublov and the Cretan Domenikos Theotokopoulos, later known as El Greco.

The Turkish conquest plunged Greece into an apparent torpor which lasted for four centuries: throughout this long period, there was little real creativity, but most of the Byzantine traditions were still preserved, betokening a passionate desire for orthodoxy. Having gradually shed their imperial character (already a thing of the past by the 15th century), these traditions were to play an important part in the Greek revival which would later take place; also, they explain why all things Byzantine are felt by the Greek people to be part of their common historical inheritance.

Art in Ancient Greece

by **Pierre Lévêque**
Former President of the University of Besançon

In the course of a millennium of creative activity the Greeks opened a new era in human civilization with the establishment of democracy, literary genres of all types (epic and lyric poetry, tragedy, comedy, rhetoric, history, etc.) and two new rational disciplines unknown to the older civilizations of the East: philosophy and natural science, which sought to explain the workings of the universe. But to the modern traveller in Greece the most manifestly successful achievement of all was in art, and this study will now attempt to trace briefly the birth and development of Greek art.

1 Art in Greece in the 2nd millennium BC

Many traces of the earliest periods are still to be seen in Greece. the Neolithic settlement of Dimini in Thessaly with its multiple rampart, and the early Helladic palace of Lerna in the Argolid, called the 'House of the Tiles', are interesting examples. The vases and images of the 3rd millennium BC likewise already showed considerable artistic refinement.

However, it was the arrival of the Greeks and the development of creative skills that contributed most to the sudden outbursts of artistic creativity. Its beginnings were relatively slow: the Middle Helladic period saw the appearance of fortified palaces (e.g. at Dorion-Malthe in Messenia) and of a new type of pottery commonly known as Minyan. This was made of fine, highly refined micaceous clay and its matt finish contrasted sharply with the glazed pottery of the previous period (the Urfirnis style). The vases were grey until the superior yellow type appeared, but it was not until the late Helladic period (also known as the Mycenaean period) that artistic creativity in Greece reached its full flowering.

MYCENAEAN FORTIFIED CASTLES AND TOMBS. The most tangible remains of the Achaean kingdoms are the fortified castles where the leaders centred their power and collected their treasures. The most impressive of these castles is Mycenae, perched like an eagle's nest on a triangular acropolis and surrounded by such massive walls that the Greeks attributed them to the Cyclopes, not believing they could have been built by men. Inside the walls there were storerooms, houses and above all the palace, built on the top of the hill and enclosing a throne room, sanctuary and megaron comprising three rooms: an outer vestibule or aithousa, an inner vestibule or prodromos and a main room (the megaron proper) with a central hearth surrounded by four columns supporting a skylight. This palace, with essentially the same plan as those of Tiryns and Pylos, represents a completely different architectural style from that of Crete: the Minoan labyrinth is replaced by a clearly ordered arrangement: the terraced roof by a ridged one; the central colonnade dividing the façade into two by a double colonnade forming a triple division; the one large living area, open to the air and sun, by a narrow one with a single entrance on the shorter face; and the movable brazier by a fixed central hearth. On the one hand we have a specifically Mediterranean manor and on the other a fortified castle, more typical of the cold, damp northern countries where it undoubtedly originated.

The dead were not forgotten: the tombs (*tholoi*) at Mycenae are among the most impressive remains of the period. Three types can be distinguished: shaft graves (the most notable examples being the two royal grave circles, one in the plain and the other on the acropolis); chamber tombs carved into the rock; and beehive tombs (masterpieces of engineering) which could have an access corridor (dromos) leading to a circular chamber corbelled vault, the finest example being the Treasury of Atreus.

MYCENAEAN PAINTING AND SCULPTURE. In both painting and sculpture the Cretan influence was very strong. The Achaeans borrowed Cretan styles and techniques for the decoration of their manors and the utensils of their daily lives. Great paintings were as important as they were in Crete. The walls of palaces were covered with frescoes in the Minoan tradition, but designs tended to be simpler and colours less naturalistic, to an extent that suggests an art-form in decline. Some subjects are definitely Cretan in inspiration: one of the great paintings of the period, the fresco of the procession at the palace of Tiryns, depicts on the walls of the megaron two lines of women in brilliant ceremonial costumes advancing to meet one another. Other subjects, while treated in the Minoan style, were more in accordance with mainland Greek taste, and at Mycenae horses and warriors are depicted together on the same frieze.

The Mycenaeans produced little sculpture in the round, but some remarkable specimens have been found, notably the beautifully carved head with curious tattoo marks discovered at Mycenae. However, stone relief carving was developed to a degree unknown in Crete and heralded the decorative sculpture of later periods in Greece. At the entrance to the citadel of Mycenae, the tympanum above the lintel of the gateway is carved in relief so deep as to be almost detached, with two lionesses facing each other, their forefeet resting on two altars. This is the oldest confronted monumental sculpture in Greece, and is full of life and power; they have no equal. The huge beasts are carved with an amazing attention to detail, showing a distinct Oriental influence. There is no superfluous ornamentation but the carving has a certain noble simplicity in complete accord with the austere character of the fortified bastion which stands in front of the entrance.

MINOR ARTS OF THE MYCENAEAN PERIOD. In the pottery of the period, quantity has a tendency to replace quality. Vases were still carefully executed in a whole range of different styles, of which the most famous are the 'stirrup jar' kylix, the 'pilgrim's bottle' and the 'false-necked jar'. The decoration, which had originally taken its inspiration from Cretan pottery, became exaggeratedly stylized and by the end of the Mycenaean period consisted of no more than horizontal stripes or trivial floral motifs.

This forms a sharp contrast with the work produced in gold and silver and embossed and inlaid metal; here the brilliance of the Mycenaean craftsmen was employed to produce incomparable works of art which are often difficult to distinguish from the Cretan masterpieces on which they were modelled. All the splendour of 'Mycenae rich in gold' is dazzlingly displayed in the great Mycenaean Room in the National Museum in Athens. The strange gold masks found in the graves of the Upper Circle, which were long held to be crude barbarian embossings, are now considered to be evidence of Egyptian influence. But the most important pieces, found at Mycenae, Midea and Vaphio, are of Cretan-Mycenaean inspiration. The silver rhytons discovered at Mycenae are the originals of those described in Homer's epics, and a gold cup with doves ready to drink perched on the handles prefigures the magnificence of old Nestor's cup in the *Iliad*. A gold cup from Midea (Argos) is decorated with a typically Minoan underwater scene, while ducks fly up from medallions embossed on a goblet. But the Vaphio cups are perhaps the finest examples we have of Mycenaean relief work, with their sure sense of composition and logical clarity, in which may be discerned the first signs of the new Greek spirit: one of them depicts a wild bull against a mountain landscape, while on the other are seen tame bulls on a plain.

The funerary weapons buried with the Achaean princes are no less beautiful. Some experts think they are Minoan. Here again Cretan craftsmen led the way in forging, chasing and inlaying precious metals. A most remarkable piece is a bronze dagger from Mycenae, its sheath inlaid with gold and silver, depicting Oriental-inspired scenes such as a lion hunt and a hunting lion. There are many small masterpieces of seals on carved gemstones, also directly inspired by Cretan art. Scenes from everyday life are common, showing the lively Achaean taste for hunting and war. The subjects are often religious and impossible to distinguish from the equivalent Cretan subjects, since they usually portray the great Mother Goddess, alone or surrounded by her divine *paredrae* (attendants).

Mycenaean art was thus very versatile and varied, no less capable of building massive structures such as the fortresses of the Argolid or the relief of the Lion Gate, than of producing beautifully decorative masterpieces like the vases, swords and seals. This variety is attributable partly to the hybrid nature of an art which gained its techniques and most of its inspiration from Crete while also drawing on some Northern traditions, and partly to the spirit of the Greeks which clarified and adapted the Minoan heritage. All these early attempts were not to be wasted, in spite of the disastrous Dorian invasions which engulfed all the works of one of the most creative arts Greece has ever known.

2 Art in Greece in the first millennium BC

THE ARTISTIC REVIVAL: PROTO-GEOMETRIC AND GEOMETRIC. After the long period of crisis brought about by the Dorian invasions, pottery was the first art form to show signs of recovery. The proto-Geometric style which developed at the beginning of the 10th century BC, was once believed to have been brought by the invaders, but modern scholarship draws attention to its links with the Mycenaean tradition and the obvious Oriental influences. Vases were covered with a dull glaze and decorated with simple geometric patterns (circles, arcs, traingles). The best examples of this style come from the Kerameikos Cemetery at Athens. The full Geometric style appeared around 900 BC. Decoration became more varied, and meanders, swastikas and then animals and human figures were added to the geometric patterns already used. The human figures were always naked and very stylized: the head was a circle, the body a triangle and the legs straight lines. On the bigger vases complex scenes were depicted, such as funerals, chariot processions, dance choruses and boats; in these larger compositions a taste for narrative painting was fused with an intellectual and formalized approach to beauty.

The first Greek temples were built between 850 and 750 BC, their design possibly based on that of the Mycenaean megaron. These early attempts were rudimentary, but the layout was already developing which was to become the set pattern for Greek temples: a rectangular building with a double sloping roof and a portico in front.

Early sculpture also had very humble beginnings: in Crete, the home of the mythical Athenian craftsman Daedalus and his followers, the first Greek creators of plastic sculpture, a series of 'shields' (but in fact dulcimers used in religious ceremonies) have been discovered in the caves of Ida, representing bronzework of the 9th or 8th century BC. In the 8th century small bronze works were produced (animals, warriors, a very few female figures) with the same Geometric style of decoration as contemporary pottery. Finally, in the 7th century, ivory carvings began, as found at the temples of Artemis at Ephesus and Sparta.

All this amounted to very little. Art in the Geometric period, with the exception perhaps of pottery, was in its infancy. It was not until the

Archaic period (750–500 BC) that Greek art began to make rapid progress which was to culminate, in less than three centuries, in the supreme achievements of the Classical period. This progress was due partly to the stabilizing of society (the growth of cities ruled by powerful aristocracies), and partly to the close links which were established with the Orient. We shall now go on to trace the development of the main art forms from the High Archaic period to the end of the Hellenistic Age.

Art in Greece: Archaism, Classicism, the Hellenistic period

1 - **ARCHITECTURE**. One of the striking characteristics of Greek architecture is the quality of the materials used; at first limestone but, gradually, whitish marbles. There are no facings hung, Roman-fashion, on to poor-quality bricks; on the contrary, fine stone, carefully cut and dressed, was used, and metal clamps and dowels held the blocks together so efficiently that no mortar was used.

We shall concentrate first on the main types of structure found in Greece and note that, at least until the Hellenistic period, religious buildings were by far the most important. We shall then briefly outline the development of architecture.

TYPES OF RELIGIOUS BUILDING. Monumental architecture as it developed in Greece was essentially connected with religion. The most important building was the temple, the sole purpose of which was to house the god, believed to be present (in every possible sense) in the cult statue. The earliest temples consisted of only one room, the naos, which held the statue, but they soon became more complex and in their most common form consisted of three parts: the pronaos or entrance hall in front of the naos, the naos and the opisthodomos (or rear room, symmetrical with the pronaos but with no means of access to the naos). It is probable that this layout derives in part from the Mycenaean megaron, although there are many objections to this theory and it is by no means as widely accepted as it was at the beginning of the century.

But the Greeks would never have allowed their art to become stereotyped, and in practice almost every temple had its own special characteristics resulting from the site, the requirements of the cult or simply a desire for variation. Thus in temples used for secret rites there was a fourth room, the adytum (sacred place), a kind of holy of holies situated at the back of the naos or inner cell (e.g. the temple of Apollo at Delphi). In the temple of Apollo at Corinth and at the Parthenon, the opisthodomos has been doubled in size to increase the space available for religious objects and for the city's treasure. Even the one normally inviolable rule, the orientation of the building towards the East, which derived no doubt from Asia, could on occasion be broken, as at the temple of Apollo at Figalia (Phigaleia). There were some temples without colonnades but these were very rare. Even in the simplest type of temple, the pronaos was usually supported by two columns between the antae. Later temples had one or more façades embellished with columns, or else the whole temple was supported by a colonnade on all four sides (peripteral). The various styles are distinguished according to the number of façade columns: tetrastyle, hexastyle, octostyle, etc.

Local variations were always important in Greece because of the lack of political cohesion. From the High Archaic period onward two great types of temple can be distinguished: the Doric and the Ionic. The first originated in the Peloponnese and took hold where Peloponnesian influence was strongest, particularly in Sicily and Magna Graecia. Its characteristic feature was a massive column with no base. The capital had a convex moulding supporting a square abacus. The architrave was smooth and the frieze consisted of alternating triglyphs (stone blocks with two central flutings and semi-flutings at the sides) and metopes which were often carved. On the underside of the cornice overhang were mutules carved with a pattern of small roundels in relief. In the Doric order elements borrowed from primitive techniques (construction in wood) are important: thus the triglyphs are the equivalent in stone architecture of the ends of wooden beams, and the metopes represent the blocks covering the space between the beams.

The Ionic order originated in Greek Asia and in the islands. Here a much slimmer column rested on a base. The capital was more complex and ornate and was characterized mainly by its scrolls. The architrave consisted of three bands (fasciae) placed one above the other. The frieze, where there was one, was a continuous moulding eminently suitable for a long pictorial narration. The cornice overhang (corona) was often decorated underneath with denticles. A strong Asian influence may be detected in some of these elements, and the continuous frieze in particular clearly derives its inspiration from Oriental temples. On the other hand the profuse decoration so characteristic of the Ionic style is completely in accord with the luxurious refinement of Ionian civilization. These two orders reflected the basically different aesthetic tastes of the Dorians and the Ionians. The Greeks considered them as respectively 'masculine' and 'feminine' architecture. Later on both these styles were reduced to the sum of their decorative elements and thus could both be used in the construction of a single temple, in which case the Doric elements would be outside and the Ionic inside, or else, in the internal colonnade, the Ionic order would be superimposed on the Doric. Both styles were also blended with the Corinthian style which in fact was not an order of its own but evolved from the Ionic, distinguished by the acanthus leaves on its capitals. The Corinthian style was pioneered by Callimachus in the late 5th century (first known example: temple of Apollo at Figalia), but it spread rapidly in the 4th century and further still in the Hellenistic period because of its rich decorative appeal.

In front of the temple was the altar on which the sacrifice was offered. There were two distinct types: a rectangular altar or bomos, facing east, which was a table for offerings to the Uranian (heavenly) gods;

and a round altar or bothros, which was a ditch where the blood of the victims was offered to the Chthonian or Earth gods. A sanctuary of importance would also have a treasury; there were small buildings, usually just one room and an entrance porch, where offerings too valuable to be left outside could be stored and where cities could display their piety and wealth.

PUBLIC BUILDINGS. Theatres played an important part in the cult of Dionysus in whose honour tragedies, satyr plays, and comedies where performed. The earliest theatres were basic constructions of wood, and stone was rarely used until the 4th century. There were many gymnasia because of the great importance placed by the Greeks on physical exercise. The stadium was a narrow track surrounded on three sides by tiers of seats. The gymnasium, which was often attached to a wrestling ground, was used for training athletes. The hippodrome or race course was larger than the stadium but built to the same plan. In the Hellenistic period these buildings, particularly the gymnasia, became popular meeting places for the youth of the city or their elders, and were the real centres of intellectual and religious life. Other important meeting places, in a society in which men spent very little time at home, were the porticos, especially those around the agora (marketplace) at the centre of the city. The very word 'stoicism', which derives from the Greek word *stoa* (portico), shows that the porticos were used not only by merchants and idle gossipers but also by philosophers teaching their pupils.

The Assembly (the legislature, which usually included all free male citizens) met in the open air and thus only very rudimentary arrangements needed to be made, in the manner of those at the Pnyx in Athens for example. The Thersillion at Megalopolis, however, is a remarkable attempt at building a very large meeting place. There were many council meeting rooms (bouleuterions and prytaneums) but they were simple and of no great architectural interest.

THE DEVELOPMENT OF ARCHITECTURE. The greatest new developments in Greek architecture took place during the Archaic period. In the Doric order the most famous temples were: the Heraion at Olympia (7th century BC in its final form), of which the original wooden columns were replaced with stone in the 6th century; and the temple of Apollo at Delphi, rebuilt at the end of the 6th century by a noble Athenian family, the Alcmaeonids. In the Ionic order the Heraion of Samos (c. 575 BC) was a sumptuous two-winged building with a forest of columns, where the Oriental influence of hypostyle (many-pillared) halls is evident. The sanctuaries became filled with treasures: thus at Delphi we find the Doric treasury of Sicyon and the delightful Ionic treasuries of Cnidus (545 BC) and Siphnos (525 BC) where the façade columns are replaced by female figures later known as caryatids.

In the 5th century architectural development reached its zenith. In 468 a Doric temple was begun in the Altis at Olympia in honour of Zeus, who had previously been worshipped in the open air. It was an austere, majestic building, suited to the nature of the god. The destruction caused by the Persian Wars necessitated much new building work, particularly in Athens where the people wisely waited a generation before building any new temples. The inspiration of Pericles, with the assistance of the brilliant decorative artist Phidias and a team of architects, crowned the Acropolis with an array of fine marble buildings: the Parthenon, a Doric temple to which an Ionic frieze (almost invisible) had been added as if to synthesize the finest of all architectural creations, was a glorious symbol of Greek achievement; the Propylaea, the monumental entrance at the west of the acropolis; the amphiprostyle Ionic temple of Athena Nike; the Erechtheum, the temple in honour of both Athena and Poseidon, which might have been massive but is perhaps the crowning achievement of the restrained golden age of Ionic art. At Eleusis Pericles built a new telesterion (hall of initiation) to celebrate the Mysteries of the 'two goddesses', which was to be the first great meeting hall built in Greece.

At the end of the 5th century new tendencies appeared and could already be seen in the temple of Apollo at Figalia (Phygaleia) which was, however, the work of Ictinus, one of the architects of the Parthenon. These new developments became even more marked in the 4th century: at Delphi, where the temple of Apollo was entirely rebuilt after the catastrophe of 373, the treasury of Cyrene resolved in its design some of the geometric problems which were currently being discussed, notably by disciples of Theodore, the great mathematician of Cyrene. At Epidaurus the argive, Polyclitus the Younger, built the most beautiful of Greek theatres and a lavish tholos, using for the foundations the remains of a vaulted archaic building. Scopas was summoned to Tegea for the temple of Athene Alea and to Gortys for the temple of Asclepius; gradually the Corinthian style gained acceptance alongside the two more traditional orders.

The Hellenistic period is less well represented in Greece, since it was in the kingdoms newly won for Hellenism, or in Asia Minor under the Attalids, that architecture was most successful. Magnificent new cities such as Alexandria and Pergamum were built, showing for the first time a real attempt at town-planning. Nothing on such a grand scale took place in Greece, but decorative elements were added to the towns, particularly Athens, where Attalus II built a vast stoa in the Agora.

Artistic life in Greece suffered a decline in the Roman period, except perhaps in the 2nd century AD when Hadrian's philhellenism and the self-glorifying generosity of the sophist Herodes Atticus together produced many new buildings in the cities and sanctuaries: thus in Athens, where a whole new town of beautiful villas was built close to the classical city, as much building went on as in the time of Pericles. But this scholarly enthusiasm, directed as it was towards the past, was powerless in the face of the inexorable decline of Greece resulting from changing political and economic conditions.

2 - SCULPTURE. It was in the field of sculpture that Greece produced her most outstanding works of art. Techniques and treatment varied over

the thousand of more years of the history of Greek sculpture but of one subject, the human form, the sculptors never seemed to tire. This may at first appear paradoxical since for centuries the object of sculptors and architects alike was principally to glorify the gods. But from the very beginning the gods themselves had been anthropomorphized. Down the ages representations of the gods made them even closer to common humanity, whose feelings and passions they shared. Only a few lesser supernatural beings (centaurs, satyrs, chimaerae or the Sphinx) retained their animal characteristics. 'What is more wonderful than man?' asks Sophocles in a famous chorus; and in the view of Protagoras, 'Man is the measure of all things.' Long before the 5th century it would seem that this was the maxim for all Greek sculptors.

SCULPTURE OF THE ARCHAIC PERIOD. While Greek sculpture, like Greek architecture, has roots going as far back as the second millennium BC, the (mid-7th c.) lion relief at Mycenae with its perfect proportions, equilibrium and attention to detail is, in spite of many Minoan and Oriental influences, the first Greek masterpiece. But the first real works of sculpture are to be found in the High Archaic period, after the dark era of the invasions and the tentative beginnings of the Geometric style.

(a) Statuary. Great works of plastic art now make their appearance. Unfortunately the first works in wood have disappeared: these were the crudely shaped poles, *xoana*, often mentioned in texts of later periods; they were cult figures. Some very primitive works in marble, such as the Artemis dedicated at Delos by Nicander which looks like a billet of wood, bear a resemblance to them. But from the second quarter of the 7th century onward stoneworking came to the fore, with the appearance of two new forms, the masculine *kouros* and the feminine *kore*.

The kouros represents a young man, standing naked, his arms at his sides, his left leg slightly advanced in a manner which recalls Egyptian models. The kore is a young girl in cloak and tunic, usually holding an offering in her right hand while with her left she clutches her clothing to her thigh. There has been much speculation about the meaning of these figures, many of which have been found in the sanctuaries, particularly on the Acropolis at Athens, at the Ptoion and in Delos. They were once taken for representations of gods (the kouroi were called 'Archaic Apollos', but the modern view is that they were young people in the flower of their youth dedicated to serving the god. The few statues of divinities which have been found, such as the fine head of Hera at Olympia, which may well have belonged to the cult statue of the Heraion (7th century), have a more severe appearance and fewer personal characteristics.

There are as many different schools of sculpture as of architecture. In Doric areas statues are frequently massive, precisely defined, even severe, like the *Twins* of Delphi, Cleobis and Bitoc, which were the work of an Argive sculptor. In the islands where the influence of nearby Anatolia is strong an Ionian art developed which was far more delicate and serene and favoured compound curves rather than straight lines. It is not surprising that this graceful style should find its best expression in the feminine form. The young women of Delos are a charming subject with their fine linen *chitons*, the delicate folds setting off the heavy mass of the woollen *himation* with its bulky folds. There is an emphasis on decorative effect, especially in the manner in which the girl's hand grasps the material bunched up on her thigh. In Athens a mixed art finally developed which sought to combine the severity of the Doric style with the delicacy of the Ionic. Some mutilated pieces of the statues of the period, destroyed by the Persians, have been rediscovered and provide excellent examples of this measured and balanced style; among them are the *Sulky Girl* and her 'brother', the blond ephebe.

(b) Monumental sculpture. The Greeks now began to decorate the topmost parts of their temples, especially the friezes and pediments. A monumental sculpture developed, generally enriched by painting, which was to be one of the most outstanding achievements of Hellenic art. The pediment presented special problems because the triangular shape required that the figures be of different sizes. At the early 6th-century temple of Artemis in Corfu small figures surrounded the central motif (Gorgon flanked by panthers); on the stone pediments of the Acropolis the corners are decorated with monsters, especially dragons; and at the treasury of Siphnos at Delphi the decoration consisted of crouching or lying figures, a solution to the problem which was to be widely adopted. The frieze offered varying opportunities for decoration depending on whether it was Doric or Ionic. The metopes divided the Doric frieze into squares, imposing certain restrictions, and these were often used for the depiction of successive scenes from the same story; the labours of Hercules for example soon became one of the most popular themes. But the Ionic frieze offered a continuous surface which could be used for the portrayal of larger continuous scenes of more complex composition: the best example is at the treasury of Siphnos at Delphi, around which four separate themes are developed: the judgment of Paris, the seizing of Hippodamia, the battle before Troy and the battle of the Giants.

From the end of the 6th century BC there were considerable developments in Archaic sculpture: great efforts were made to portray the human body more naturally, faces became more expressive and lost that fixed smile common to all, even the wounded or dying. The Persian Wars, however, provided the real stimulus necessary to bring about a rapid, appreciable transformation in sculpture.

CLASSICAL SCULPTURE

(a) The 5th century. The first generation after the Persian Wars produced a style of sculpture which has, with some justification, been called severe. It was radically opposed in style to the later works of the Archaic period: muscles were precisely defined, expressions were serious and statues were realistically three-dimensional. The finest works which have been found are two bronzes: the noble figure of Poseidon from Cape Artemision, brandishing his trident, and the *Charioteer* of Delphi, the only remaining part of a quadriga dedicated by the Deinomenids after a Pythian victory. A good example of monumental sculpture of the period is the decoration on the temple of Zeus at Olympia. The labours of (Heracles) Hercules are depicted on the metopes, no longer in the narrative pictorial style of the Archaic period, but now with a didactic purpose similar to that of Pindar. On the pediments the sculptor superbly develops the theme of the preparations for the race between Pelops and Oenomaüs and of the battle between the Centaurs and the Lapiths, offering one static scene and one dynamic one.

It was not until the next generation that Classical artists gained perfect mastery over their materials. Three great names represent this period: Myron, Polyclitus and Phidias. The first two portray athletic subjects superbly. Myron excelled at showing rapid movement, so that in the exceptional *Discus thrower* (*Discobolus*, surviving in copies), a fleeting moment is caught for eternity; he was also a good animal sculptor. Polyclitus of Argos was more abstract and sought to portray the 'canon' of the human form in perfect mathematical proportions. This was an old dream dear to the Greeks and was to be perpetuated in the following century by Lysippus. But Phidias of Athens was more important still. A friend of Pericles, he helped him to plan the buildings of the Acropolis. He sculpted the cult statue for the Parthenon, the Athena Parthenos, and later the majestic Zeus at Olympia. His greatest work was in designing and supervising the construction of the Parthenon frieze. The four Doric friezes show the battle of the Giants, the capture of Troy, the battle of the Amazons and the struggle of the Centaurs, four symbolic subjects exalting the triumph of reason over chaos. On the two pediments the birth of Athena and her dispute with Poseidon over possession of Attica glorify the divine patroness of Athens. The Ionic frieze shows the whole city taking part in the Panathenaic procession and going to pay homage to the gods represented on the principal façade. It was Phidias again who created, this time for the 'two goddesses of Eleusis', the relief of Demeter and Kore (Persephone) giving the young Triptolemus the ear of wheat, the source of all human nourishment and the promise of life hereafter. Phidias was famous for the supple, gracious dignity of his style, giving the gods the 'Olympian' air of serenity so typical of Athens in the age of Pericles, who was himself called 'the Olympian'.

Contemporary with Phidias and immediately after him new techniques were seen. Alcamenes, the sculptor of *Aphrodite of the gardens*, sometimes also sought inspiration in works of the Archaic period (viz. his Hermes Propylaeus); Cresilas, whose standards rivalled those of Phidias and Polyclitus in the *Wounded Amazon of Ephesus*, sculpted a wonderful bust of Pericles, a unique mixture of idealization and individual characteristics. Callimachus, the inventor of the Corinthian capital, introduced 'wet drapery' and Paionios

(Paeonius) of Mende carved a great winged Victory (Nike) for Olympia. The anonymous reliefs on the temple of Athena Nike illustrate the new, gracious style which can also be seen in the pottery of the period.

(b) The 4th century BC. These tendencies are further developed in the 4th century when sculpture becomes less serene, more restless and more mystical than in the 5th century. Almost all the contradictory trends of the period are represented in the work of three great sculptors. The Athenian Praxiteles expressed the beauty of the human form in young, often effeminate, slim-hipped adolescent boys. Even his gods languished (e.g. *the Sauroctonus* [Phoebus killing a lizard] and *Hermes carrying the infant Dionysus*). He was also an incomparable sculptor of feminine beauty and created the first important nude, Aphrodite naked. He favoured very low reliefs full of exquisite tenderness where individual features blended together, and he was famous, too, for his portrayal of beautiful heads of hair. But it would be incorrect to regard the lover of the courtesan Phryne as an aesthete solely concerned with beauty, for he was greatly influenced by Plato, and his work has a mystical quality, not conveyed by copies.

Human disquiet is even more apparent in the work of Scopas of Paros. His fame brought him numerous commissions, both in Asia Minor where he worked on the decoration of the mausoleum (tomb of King Mausolus at Halicarnassus) and in Greece (temple of Athena Alea at Tegea). His faces, with deepset eyes gazing towards heaven, express a desperate pathos. Unlike Praxiteles he loved to portray violent physical movement signifying deep passions of the soul, as in the case of the Maenad tearing apart a kid-goat in a Dionysiac trance.

The prolific sculptor Lysippus of Sicyon was predominantly a worker in bronze. He concentrated, as Polyclitus had done, on the proportions of the human body, and modified the canons of his predecessor in several respects, especially in the elongation of the silhouette. His masterpiece is without doubt the *Apoxyomenos* (athlete cleaning himself) in which is embodied all his skill in creating lifelike and supple human forms; but in the Farnese Hercules his power seems to have got out of control and he has exaggerated the muscles of the subject. His portraits were excellent and he had the honour of being chosen by Alexander to immortalize his likeness in bronze. The copies of these portraits show the almost divine nature of the young conqueror, his head on one side, his gaze directed towards the sky.

HELLENISTIC SCULPTURE. All this early work culminated in the amazingly fertile Hellenistic age. But here again, the most innovative schools of sculpture were outside Greece itself: for example, in Alexandria, where the influence of Praxiteles was seen in numerous statues of Aphrodite, while at the same time a taste for the ornamental was developing, particularly in the so-called picturesque reliefs and genre scenes, perhaps in imitation of the local Egyptian tradition. At Pergamum the Attalids attracted many great artists and a true romantic style developed full of pathos and violent, unrestrained passions, directly influenced by Scopas, which was at its most beautiful in the decoration of the great altar of Zeus. In Syria art tended to be more warm and sensual, as in the heavy Levantine Aphrodite forming a group with Pan and Eros, found on Delos in the excavations of the buildings of the Poseidon-worshippers of Berytos. Greek sculpture spread a long way into Asia where it continued for several centuries and contributed to the development of mixed arts which were Greek in technique and Asian in inspiration (e.g. the Graeco-Buddhist art of Gandhara).

In Greece itself inspiration began to dry up at the same time as the economy was becoming dangerously insecure. However, the most active centres maintained a high level of artistic production. In Delos numerous works of art were produced in the Hellenistic age; in Rhodes especially a great school of sculpture appeared beginning with Chares of Lindos (1st century AD; a disciple of Lysippus), creator of the famous Colossus of Rhodes, one of the wonders of the ancient world (the climax of his work was the Laocoon group of the 1st century, now in the Vatican museum).

But the main body of production continued to be in the traditional style. There were sculptures of groups of young lovers, Aphrodites after the style of Praxiteles and 'dying Alexanders' after the style of Scopas. Some pieces were more adventurous: the Winged Victory of Samothrace (erected *c.* 305 BC to mark a naval victory of Demetrius I Poliorcetes) with its disordered drapery revealing the majesty of the female form below, and the Venus de Milo whose perfection contrasts with the affectation or eroticism of so many contemporary works.

The sculptural tradition was not destroyed by the Roman conquest; it could even be said that Hellenistic sculpture itself expanded still further to conquer Rome. Its influence was seen until well into the 2nd century AD, in works like the Antinous, perhaps one of the last products of Greek genius.

3 – PAINTING AND POTTERY. It is very difficult to trace the development of painting in Greece as all the pictures have disappeared. A few great names are known, such as Polygnotus of Thasos (first half of the 5th century BC) who painted vast compositions such as the murals decorating the Cnidian Lesche at Delphi, and who paid particular attention to facial expressions. Zeuxis (4th to 5th century) perfected Apollodorus's use of shading; he also used a kind of grisaille; Apelles (4th century) was court painter to Philip and Alexander of Macedon. In Antiquity he was believed to be the greatest of Greek painters, but none of his work survives.

It is much easier to follow the development of vase painting which followed fairly closely in the traditions of contemporary fine-art painting, especially in the 5th century. Many different shapes of vase were produced to suit varied purposes, whether religious or utilitarian (note for example the loutrophoros for use at weddings and the lekythos for funerary use).

ARCHAIC POTTERY. Eastern influence was of great importance in the production of early pottery of the Archaic period. The Orientalizing style appeared in the late 8th century at Corinth. The Geometric style was replaced, new subjects appeared: real or imaginary animals (lions, birds, sphinxes, goats, griffins), lotus flowers, palmettes, stars. All these new subjects were borrowed from the Orient. The works produced in some areas were quite remarkable: in Rhodes a concern for decoration resulted in the production of beautiful vases with exclusively animal or plant motifs; Corinth was famous for its perfume flasks (aryballoi) with their paintings of fauns and monsters, often in heraldic designs. In Athens human figures were particularly popular, as on the amphora of Hercules and Nessus at the National Museum in Athens. In the 6th century a new style known as 'black-figure' appeared. Human representations became more important than the animals and plants of the Orientalizing period. Athenian vase painters produced fine works, notably the François vase (named after its finder) of the second quarter of the 6th century, now in Florence. It depicts heroic themes in separate friezes, one above the other, representing in all more than 200 figures. Among the famous vase painters of the period was Exechias who produced mythological scenes in miniature. Corinth imitated the figure painting of the Athenian school but after 550 was eliminated from the market by its rival. At Sparta beautiful cups were produced (e.g. the Archesilas cup).

'RED-FIGURE' VASES. Around 530 BC a new style was invented which changed the whole appearance of vase painting: red-figure took over from black-figure so that now the background was painted black while the figures remained unpainted and appeared in the red colour of the clay. While previously artists had been able to do little more than outline a silhouette, now they portrayed with fine brush strokes details of anatomy, drapery and even facial expressions.

From 530–460 BC the Severe style was in vogue. Epictetus led a reaction against the preference for mythological subjects and painted above all genre scenes, particularly drinking scenes. Euphronius returned to mythological themes, especially Hercules, but with a new sense of composition and balance. Brygos, the greatest vase painter of the Severe style, gave his paintings a dramatic quality which rivalled that of his contemporary Aeschylus. In about 460 the severe style gave way to a greater freedom of expression. Vase painting was strongly influenced by the great painting of the period, notably the work of Polygnotus: it sought to convey facial expressions and tended to paint human subjects in friezes above one another (the Orvieto krater in the Louvre). Later figures became more harmonious and serene, reminiscent of the work of Phidias. Finally, after 420, an ornate style developed, represented by the work of Meidias, whose graceful figures with their light draperies appeared a little too mannered and precious.

In the 4th century production continued at Athens, but mainly for export to the Crimea, and for this reason vases of this period came to be known as 'kerch'. The vases were mainly intended for use in women's toilette and commonly portrayed scenes from the gynaeceum. The painting was now hastily and poorly executed, and the use of many colours did not compensate for this irrevocable degeneration of style. Moreover Athens suffered from the competition of Greek vases produced in southern Italy. The last decades of the 4th century saw the definitive end of red-figure pottery which had been one of the styles most characteristic of the Classical period.

HELLENISTIC POTTERY. In the Hellenistic period the production of painted vases declined without altogether ceasing, but human figures were usually replaced with floral decoration. Popular taste favoured relief vases, inaccurately called 'Megarian bowls', which were cheap copies of the great works of contemporary gold- and silver-smiths, or even moulded vases aimed at an effect of surprise rather than of beauty.

4 - THE MINOR ARTS. We can make only a brief reference here to the minor plastic arts which followed the development of great sculpture but produced many remarkable works—in general with more freedom of expression and imagination. Craftsmen of Tanagra in Boeotia were particularly famous for their delightful figurines of young women, strolling or chatting, wearing elaborate hats or carrying sunshades; these were particularly common in the 4th century.

Gold and silver objects and embossed metalwork were produced in great numbers both in Magna Graecia (especially in Tarentum) and in Athens. These works often travelled far afield to become the possessions of Thracian or Scythian princes in whose graves wonderful jewels and engraved plate have been found.

Coins followed the development of sculpture, and at their best, particularly in Sicily, were miniature masterpieces. They were produced in large quantities (each city minted its own and the different types changed rapidly) and are an indispensable source of evidence of the political and religious life of Greece from the time when coinage was introduced in the 7th century until well into the Imperial period.

Neither the Roman conquest nor even the barbarian invasions succeeded in destroying Greek art altogether. It survived in Byzantine Constantinople, then reappeared in the West during the Renaissance: via the intermediary of Roman art, which was itself often an extension of Hellenistic art; it inspired the birth of the European Classical movement.

The Archaeological Adventure

by **René Ginouvès**

Professor of Classical Archaeology at the University of Paris

Everywhere in Greece, the tourist finds evidence of archaeological activity. Archaeology goes back a long way here; in a country with such an ancient history, it is not surprising that the Greeks should feel an interest in it. Later, particularly after the Renaissance, travellers became interested in the 'antiquities' which they could link with their own classical culture. However, it was only after Greece became independent that serious excavations began throughout the country. Since World War II archaeological activity in Greece has expanded considerably, while radically improved conditions have opened up new opportunities.

ANCIENT ARCHAEOLOGY. The ancient Greeks had plenty of opportunity to encounter their own antecedents, for example at Tiryns or Mycenae, whose massive walls they attributed to those mythical giants, the Cyclopes, but which we now know date from the 14th or 13th century BC. Hesiod also refers to the same myth when he puts his theoretical Bronze Age before the Iron Age in his *Works and Days*, but in fact the Mycenaean period made little use of bronze, and the use of iron did not become widespread until much later. Hesiod puts the Gold Age and the Silver Age even earlier in time, to evoke the memory of the fabulous riches of this same Mycenaean world to which the Homeric poems also refer. Greek education is based on this Homeric epic cycle which conjures up an archaeological vision of a very different civilization. And since the Greeks were passionately interested in the origins and development of man, and also had contacts with many 'barbarian' peoples (that is, those who did not speak Greek or share their life-style) this interest in the past was inevitably awakened very early. Herodotus was certainly not the only historian to apply a comparative approach to barbarian cultures. It is also remarkable that Thucydides, discussing the origins of the Greek people in the introduction to his history of the Peloponnesian War (Book I is characteristically referred to as his 'archaeology'), cites as evidence the forms of the weapons found in the tombs on Delos at the time of the purification in 426, and the burial methods used, to conclude that the tombs were Carian and that consequently there had been a Carian occupation. Like a modern archaeologist he draws a historical conclusion from his observation of artefacts and practices. It does not appear, however, that the ancient Greeks ever carried out excavations in order to understand their historical origins, nor were they, for a long time, interested in making collections of archaeological finds, though that is what the treasures amassed in the sanctuaries over the centuries were in effect.

But in the Hellenistic period the houses of the well-to-do (in Delos for example) were decorated with original works, as well as copies and imitations; kings bought the most famous works of art for their collections, and it was at this time that the 'Museum' at Alexandria was set up; though today we would consider this to be more a research centre. This passion for collecting treasures continued to thrive after the Roman conquest: the discovery of burial grounds near Corinth, where Caesar was founding a colony, led to some real excavations, and the resulting finds, particularly the bronze vases, were sold for a high price; a considerable trade in *objets d'art* developed to provide ornaments for public buildings in Rome and the villas of rich art lovers. Certainly this vogue for archaeology was linked at first to aesthetic requirements, as in the case of the Emperor Hadrian who had replicas built of his favourite Greek buildings and landscapes in the grounds of his villa in Tiroli: the Academy, the Lyceum, the Stoa Poikile and the Vale of Tempe. However, there are some indications of a more historical approach to archaeology: Vitruvius and Pliny the Elder give technical and historical details of the buildings and works of art to which they refer; and in the following century Pausanias, who belonged to a long tradition of erudite travellers, the *periegetai*, wrote the first guide to Greece which has come down to us. It was very incomplete since it covered only the Peloponnese, Attica, Boeotia and Phocis and it often proves inadequate for the modern archaeologist who is misled by the digressions and omissions, but at least Pausanias puts the monuments and works of art he describes in their historical context or sometimes, interestingly, links them to their legends.

TRAVELLERS AND ARCHAEOLOGY. We now have to wait for many centuries before we again find travellers making journeys for scholarly purposes, and such travels were henceforth to bring Greece and the West closer together. During the Renaissance humanism extols the values and forms of classical antiquity; but already in the 15th century the merchant Cyriacus of Ancona was taking advantage of his travels in the Peloponnese, around the Aegean and in Athens, to collect notes and drawings which have been partly preserved, and several volumes of commentaries which have unfortunately been lost since the 16th century. Such documents are of major importance for modern archaeology: a Flemish artist made sketches of the sculptures on the Parthenon in 1674 while accompanying the Marquis de Nointel, Louis XIV's ambassador, on a visit to the Sultan.

In 1687 when the Venetian Morosini was laying siege to the Parthenon on the Acropolis, the central part, which housed a Turkish powder store, blew up, and the following year, while he was attempting to remove the sculptures from the west side to carry them off to Venice, they fell to the ground and were shattered. In the 18th century another French ambassador to Constantinople, the Comte de Choiseul-Gouffier, published a *Picturesque Journey through Greece*, containing much valuable information, and he also made a collection of antiquities which eventually found its way to the Louvre. In the 19th century a French consul named Fauvel sent one of the most beautiful panels from the Parthenon frieze to the Louvre.

In 1816 the British Museum put on display most of the remaining sculptures from the Acropolis which Lord Elgin had purchased, while the last great example of this type of activity, explained if not excused by the circumstances of the time, was the purchase of the Venus de Milo by the French ambassador's secretary, Vicomte de Marcellus. But soon, the antiquarianism of these travellers, most of whom were diplomats and noblemen, was to be replaced by the work of the archaeologists.

ARCHAEOLOGY FROM INDEPENDENCE TO THE BEGINNING OF THE 20TH CENTURY. From the beginning of the 19th century full-scale archaeological digs were carried out on Greek soil, in the manner of those of 18th-century Italy. But the finds they yielded still found their way to the West. Thus the clearing of the temple of Aegina in 1811 led to the discovery of the two carved pediments, whose statues were restored by Thorwaldsen in Rome and later acquired by Ludwig I of Bavaria: they can be seen at the Munich Glyptothek, now relieved of their disfiguring restorations. The excavations in 1912 at the temple of Bassae near Figalia (Phigaleia) procured for the British Museum a long series of friezes; and the archaeological mission attached to the French expeditionary force which travelled through the Peloponnese in 1829, and was to publish *The Scientific Expedition to the Morea*, also sent back some metopes from the temple of Zeus at Olympia for the Louvre.

The situation was to change gradually with the coming of national independence and the setting up of permanent archaeological missions to which certain sites were entrusted. In 1846 the French School of Athens was founded, the first of the institutions of this type which were to multiply in Greece and which today number about ten. Work on the sites became steadily more systematic. In 1858–59 an official of the British Museum carried out a thorough survey at Cnidus, a site on the Asia Minor coast, and was able to establish the ground plan of the whole of the old city; this was to be the first detailed study of an ancient city. The excavations on Samothrace in 1873 and 1875 produced what may be considered as the first modern 'excavation report' with plans, and, for the first time, photographic illustrations. But it was perhaps the German excavations at Olympia between 1875 and 1881 which were most innovative: this site had already been explored in 1723 by a Frenchman, Montfaucon, and the

Morea expedition had discovered the temple of Zeus there. Henceforth both the objects found the architectural context were to receive equal attention; the excavation was carried out stratigraphically, that is, the layers of earth were removed one at a time to reveal different periods of occupation, destruction and so on, and thus archaeologists were able to establish the history of the site. It became illegal to export any of the articles discovered so that the excavators received no reward other than the advancement of learning and the first rights to research and publication. All the items uncovered are displayed in a museum which became the first site museum.

Thus the 'great excavations' began; such undertakings employed large numbers of workers and often used special narrow-gauge railways to cart away the earth. Gradually they were extended to take in the most famous sites. In 1872 the French excavations began on Delos; in 1881 Greeks were working at Eleusis, Epidaurus and on the Athens Acropolis; and 1882 saw the beginning of the 'great excavation' at Delphi — there had been earlier surveys here by the French from 1838 on, but as the site was covered by the little village of Kastri, a special grant had to be made by the French Assembly to enable all the inhabitants to have their houses rebuilt about one and a half miles (2km) further to the west. The excavation immediately produced substantial finds: it was said that at times the epigraphers received a hundred inscriptions a day, and a first museum was opened there in 1902. In 1895 the Americans began excavating at Corinth, and in 1907 the British at Sparta. One of the most recent of these large-scale excavations is the Agora in Athens. This site, one of the most historic in the whole of Greece, attracted scholars very early: the 'Giants' Porch' had already been mentioned and drawn in the 15th century, and Greek, and to a lesser extent German, archaeologists were working there from the second half of the 19th century. With the steep increase in the population of Athens after World War I and the subsequent exchange of populations with Turkey, the problem of land ownership in the city itself became more acute, until in 1930 the passage of a law, and financing from the Rockefeller Foundation which enabled the land to be bought and work to be started on a grand scale, with the dramatic results with which we are familiar. After some preliminary explorations in Thasos in 1914 and then again between 1921 and 1923, a large excavation was begun by the French in 1939 – only to be halted by the war. In addition to classical archaeology proper, excavations of proto-historic sites developed with equal success: the exploration of Mycenae and Tiryns had begun in 1874 and of Knossos in 1900. Also in 1900 the Italians had begun excavating the palace of Phaestus; in 1921 the French started work at the palace of Mallia, and just before the outbreak of war in 1939 the amazing palace of Nestor was discovered at Pylos. Palaeo-Christian and Byzantine sites were also excavated, and the ruins of one of these, Philippi, had already been described in the middle of the 16th century by a Frenchman, Pierre Belon. The French School played an important part in the excavation of this site.

Sites grew in size and number and excavation techniques and data-recording methods became more efficient (with the gradual predominance of the stratigraphic method). The display and conservation of finds improved in the museums, and considerable efforts were made by Greek archaeologists, and to a lesser extent by foreign schools, to manage the sites properly and to restore the ancient buildings. In 1834, the year after the Turks had left Athens, the Greeks symbolically marked their repossession of the Acropolis by solemnly restoring a drum to its place on one of the columns of the north colonnade of the Parthenon. Between 1835 and 1837 the little temple of Athena Nike was rebuilt, from its fallen stone blocks which had been incorporated into later fortifications. This somewhat premature reconstruction was itself demolished between 1935 and 1939, and a new restoration produced the delightful building we know today. Meanwhile, considerable work was done on the Parthenon (beginning in 1898; the north colonnade restoration dates from the years 1922–30), the Erechtheum (from 1902) and the Propylaea (from 1909). Similar reconstruction work was transforming the landscape at sites such as Delphi where the Treasury of the Athenians was rebuilt in 1905–06, while several columns were replaced at the Tholos of Marmaria and the great temple of Apollo between 1939 and 1941.

By the end of this period archaeology had become established in Greece as a considerable corpus of scholarship and research, all under the control of an efficient, well-developed Greek Archaeological Service, organised into a number of sections to administer the various archaeological regions, delegating responsibility for a certain number of sites to foreign schools. It gradually became the rule for each of these schools to concentrate its efforts on only three sites a year, even though they might hold responsibility for many more. This sensible rule compels archaeologists to alternate between different sites, thus leaving time for the finds to be properly studied and for relevant material to be prepared for publication. This approach contrasts with that of the first forty years of the 20th century, which were marked by many publications of monographs devoted to a single collection, to documents of certain types, or to a specific problem; there were also whole series of works attempting to cover all the finds from one site.

ARCHAEOLOGY AFTER WORLD WAR II. As one would imagine, archaeological activity, if not completely halted, was at least very sharply reduced by the violent events that overtook Greece in 1940. Although in 1945 work was resumed on repairing damage caused by the fighting, reopening museums and cleaning and conservation, it was not until 1949 that excavation work was able to return to normal. But the archaeologists soon found they were encountering new situations, sometimes favourable, sometimes difficult, leading them into uncharted territory.

At first sight continuity is evident in their activities. Existing sites were developed and new ones were opened, at an even faster rate than before. Thus in 1948 Greek archaeologists began clearing the sanctuary of Artemis at Brauron in Attica, and in 1952 excavations began at the isthmus of Corinth. The same year, 1952, saw the beginning of American excavations at Lerna, the resumption of work on the palace at Pylos, discovered just before the war, and also the opening of a new French excavation at Argos, one of the major ancient Greek sites. In 1957 the excavation of Messene was resumed, and work was begun at Pella, the ancient capital of Macedonia. In 1958 the exploration began of the famous Nekromanteion of Ephyros where divination was practised with help from the dead; 1961 saw the start of a Graeco-French excavation at Dikili-Tasch, and at Kato Zakros in Crete where the remains of a Minoan palace were found. In 1962 the University of Pennsylvania opened an excavation at Porto Kheli and a new Franco-Greek excavation began at Medeon, a Phocian site on the bay of Andikyra. In 1963 Belgian and Greek archaeologists were working at Thorikos; there were Americans at Kenchreai and Greeks and Austrians at Elis. In 1964 British excavations were in progress at Lefkandi on Euboea (Evia), and Graeco-Swiss excavations at Eretria, also on Euboea. In 1967 the University of Syndey was excavating at Zagora on the islands of Andros and a new Greek excavation began at Akrotiri on Thera (Santorini) which was to lead to the discovery of a Minoan villa buried by volcanic ash. In 1970 there was digging by Greek archaeologists at Marathon and in 1971 by Greeks and Swedes at Khania in Crete; in 1973 the French School resumed the exploration of the sanctuary of Poseidon and Amphitrite on Tinos, first begun early in the century. This list of the principal most recently opened sites, though very incomplete, gives an idea of the extent of archaeological activity. It also shows that work now tends to be conducted on less important, though that is not to say less interesting, sites, but now new approaches are often used: instead of digging over a wide area, archaeologists examine a small area in depth to establish the chronology of the site. Documentation from the growing number of sites of all these types becomes even richer, producing a growing problem in museum storerooms and a 'data explosion' with the ever-increasing volume of publications, the consequences which are beginning to be felt.

This slow research was enlivened from time to time by spectacular finds, such as the discovery of the second circle of graves at Mycenae in 1951, and in 1959 of four big bronzes, one of which was a kouros dating from the end of the 6th century, and one a mid-4th century Athena, found when a sewer was being dug at Piraeus. Other such finds were: in 1961 a beautifully decorated bronze krater found at Derveni near Thessaloniki; in 1963 two hoards discovered at Thebes, among the contents of which were, in particular, seals carved with Mycenaean subjects but also with orientalized scenes, sometimes surrounded by cuneiform inscriptions; in 1964 at Kenchreai a whole collection of glass mosaic panels, still in the packing from which they were waiting to be removed when disaster struck and buried them; in 1966 more than 4,000 potsherds used as ballots for ostracism at the Kerameikos in Athens; in 1972 a kouros and a marble kore at

Markopoulo in Attica, remarkably preserved and still with their original colours, lying less than 13½ins (35cm) below the present-day soil level; and in the same year in Corinth a marble sphinx from the second quarter of the 6th century, which is one of the most remarkable examples of archaic sculpture. In 1977–78 an excavation of the royal tombs beneath the tumulus at Palatitsa-Verghina uncovered exquisitely beautiful paintings and gold and silver treasures. But these sensational finds, whether the result of shrewd intuition on the part of the archaeologists or of pure luck, certainly contribute less to the overall progress of archaeology than methodical, patient, even tedious work month after month on hundreds of sites and in museum storerooms and libraries, which enables archaeologists, by painstaking labour, to piece together the history of ancient Greece in all its aspects. At the same time restoration projects were proceeding; between 1953 and 1956 the stoa of Attalos on the Athens agora was reconstructed and turned into a museum where the finds from the site are displayed to great advantage. From 1955 work was carried out at the temples of Sounion and Aegina, and from 1959 on the odeon at Patras, and at the same time restorations continued on the Acropolis and on the other main sites.

These restorations, and particularly those of the theatres, are obviously linked to the needs of the tourist trade and especially to the growing number of festivals. They are justified from an archaeological viewpoint because only thus is it possible fully to appreciate the beauty of the dimensions, the qualities of light and shade and the other effects which architecture sets out to create. Moreover, restoration is often the best way of preventing ruins from crumbling away completely, and since it cannot be carried out without first making a thorough study of the building, leading to publication of the relevant details, much important information would otherwise be lost. It can be said that the restoration of the odeon of Herodes Atticus on the south side of the Athens Acropolis has saved the theatre of Dionysus, though the problems of the latter are still far from being solved. There are dangers, for obvious reasons, of tourism hindering the archaeologist, for example on Delos where it is increasingly difficult to find qualified workers, as labourers from Mykonos prefer the obvious advantages of work in the tourist trade. There are other more serious constraints: the approach roads to Delphi have had to be widened, a new access road to the Athens Acropolis has been built, and more generally site presentation and museum organization now need to take into account the crowds of people which will be moving about in them. But archaeologists are well aware of the public's right of access to monuments of the past, and they are also conscious of the benefits of tourism, which in a country like Greece is one of the incentives behind archaeological activity. Tourism can sometimes be responsible for the resumption of work on abandoned sites: in 1967 for example the French School resumed work at Lato in Crete, largely because the Port of Hagios Nikolaos, which had become a seaside resort, needed the additional attraction of an archaeological site. In Rhodes a series of hasty rescue digs enabled the Hippodamian grid plan of the old city to be established. To meet the needs of tourists archaeologists have to produce guides to their sites which are both readable and accurate. However, there can be no doubt that the daily influx of thousands of people in places which would rarely have been visited in ancient times is a serious threat to conservation; some decisions have to be taken which, while inconvenient, will be readily understood and welcomed by the informed tourist. Thus for example access to certain parts of the Athens Acropolis is now prohibited as a necessary precaution for their preservation.

But in themselves such precautions are inadequate since the archaeologist now has to face another phenomenon, industrial development, which is also a result of the development of tourism. For a long time no more than aesthetic or sentimental objections were raised to the locating of factories close to ancient sites, for example at Eleusis and on the Rharian plain where legend says the first grain of wheat was sown. It is now realized that there are many ancient monuments which are being threatened by atmospheric pollution, the most notable example being that of the Acropolis in Athens where smoke, carbon dioxide, sulphuric acid blown from the industrial area by west winds, the fuel oil used by heating systems and fumes from road vehicles have all damaged the marble of the Porch of the Caryatids of the Erechtheum for example, to an average depth of 1/10in (4mm). Even if pollution could be rapidly brought under control in this very exposed area, the sculptures would still be doomed if they were left any longer in the open air. This is why they have been taken down and replaced with copies. The originals will now be exhibited in a new museum with a controlled atmosphere, this being the only means of preserving what can still be saved. Other sites need the same treatment.

Industrial and urban development create an increasing number of problems for archaeologists. Vast changes in the landscape are taking place as the towns spread further out into the countryside, foundations are dug deeper for high buildings, new airports and motorways are constructed, more and more quarries excavated and with more intensive farming methods hillsides are being cut into so that machines can maneouvre upon them. All these factors contribute, in a country richer than any other in evidence of the past, to destroy a structure which had remained relatively unchanged since ancient times, by effacing much of the evidence of its previous occupation by man. What can the archaeologist do to prevent this legally permitted destruction? Fortunately in most cases rescue digs at least make it possible to ascertain what is being lost forever and to protect exceptional finds. But the continual need to survey threatened sites brings fresh difficulties: in spite of their industry and dedication and the help provided by foreign schools, Greek archaeologists frequently find their time wasted by work which later proves to be useless: objects found in the course of these surveys may only be fragments, insignificant in themselves, which add further to the storage problems of the museums and may never be properly studied. The archaeologist feels increasingly that he is losing control of the situation.

THE FUTURE OF ARCHAEOLOGY IN GREECE. However, the archaeologist may well find that progress in his own field offers a means of resolving these problems. As regards pollution there are the solutions already mentioned in connection with the Acropolis and others resulting from a scientific study of building materials; perhaps, also, it will soon be realized that what is disastrous for marble cannot be good for human health. The answer to the problems of urban development could be cooperation between archaeologists, economists and town planners, so that plans for further development could take account of the major needs of archaeology. Fortunately today there is a greater awareness that the remains of the past are a valuable cultural possession, not just a tourist attraction, which must be given due weight in the development of our societies. The identification of these 'archaeological reserves', which would thus be protected, then excavated and suitably arranged, could be facilitated by new techniques such as aerial photography or scientific methods of surveying on the ground. The most urgent cases should be dealt with by appealing for international collaboration.

Such collaboration seems to be necessary, and specific research programmes need to be proposed if the increase in the number of sites and investigations is not to end in pointless duplication of effort and harmful scattering of the results. Thus a certain balance could be maintained between archaeology of the Classical period and that of earlier and later periods. Prehistoric archaeology in particular has shown promising results in the last few years: in 1958 proof was at last found of the existence of a paleolithic culture in Greece, and in 1960 a Neanderthal-type skull was discovered, the first in the whole of the southern Balkans. Within classical archaeology itself, monuments dating from the Roman period, which have hitherto been treated with undeserved scorn, are beginning to occasion new research, as in the case of the great baths at Argos or on Samos.

In all these spheres archaeology appears to be taking an equal interest both in outstanding works of art and in finds that shed light on humble everyday lives, with the excavation of many rural and urban dwellings, industrial complexes (such as those for the extraction and processing of silver ore currently being studied by Belgian archaeologists in the region of Thorikos), and indeed in everything which enables us to improve our understanding of economic and social history. This research is further assisted by aerial surveys which show, for example, near Thessaloniki, traces of several different field divisions, one on another, and by underwater research, first undertaken in Greece in 1950, which produces so much evidence of commercial activity. And now archaeological teams include specialists in the fields of paleoethnology and paleobotany as well as geographers: since 1957 a geomorphological study of the region of Delphi has been carried out, and a soil study of the coastal region near Mallia. All this research gives us a better understanding of the ancients' way of life and the manner in which they adapted to their environment.

For this type of research the old method of one institution jealously guarding its own site is no longer the best: it has now become necessary to obtain international cooperation to define the problems and organize the means of solving them. Just such a cooperation was arrived at in Greece in 1967 when excavation of land, due to be inundated by the artificial lake created on the river Peneios, was entrusted to five archaeological schools. All this work increasingly benefits from constant technological development; reference to such development has already been made in connection with surveying, but scientific methods of locating and dating finds, standardization of terms, the use of modern data-processing equipment to deal with the welter of information — all should contribute to the development of archaeology as a science, complementary to, and not a replacement of, traditional archaeology in which flair or intuition were of great importance. The combination of all these factors, and others as yet unforeseeable, could help archaeology in Greece to retain the freshness of its approach by a constant renewal of its methods and, possibly, of some of its objectives.

Some Notes on Architecture

THE CITY, PRIVILEGED SECTOR OF ANCIENT SOCIETY. Towns were divided into two parts: the acropolis or high town, usually the nucleus of the primitive city which had become a citadel, and which often contained, as in Athens, the most ancient sanctuaries; and the lower town, surrounded by fortifications which often joined those of the acropolis.

At the centre of the town was the agora, a public square surrounded by porticoes marking the ends of all the main streets. Public buildings included the theatre (ekklesia), which was also used for public assemblies, the odeon (*odeum* or concert hall), the gymnasium, the stadium and the bouleuterion (council chamber), seat of the Senate (Boule); there were also stoas (*stoai*), fountains, public benches, etc.

THE NECROPOLIS. Burial grounds were usually situated outside the city walls, alongside the most important roads. There were many different types of graves: Mycenean beehive tombs, simple trenches with or without sarcophagi, and tumuli. All contained funerary items: vases, figurines, jewels and weapons. Graves in the burial ground were marked by large terracotta or marble funerary urns, gravestones (stelae), columns, pillars or real monuments of varying degrees of ostentation.

FORTIFICATIONS. The building style of the ramparts varied according to the period of construction. The walls were reinforced by rectangular or round towers (the latter for the defence of sallyports or gateways) set at irregular intervals: theoretically about half the distance of a javelin throw, that is about 80–100ft (25–30m). Gates were often built in such a way as to force the attacker to present his right side, unprotected by a shield. The enceinte (surrounding walls) would also be pierced by postern gates, sometimes very close together, to enable the fighting units to regroup at the foot of the walls before rallying to the attack.

Masonry of the cyclopean type consisting of huge rough stone blocks with smaller stones packed into the interstices, and of the pelasgic type, that is, irregular stone blocks, are found in ruins of the Mycenaean period. Other types of masonry were: polygonal —

THE THREE CLASSICAL ORDERS

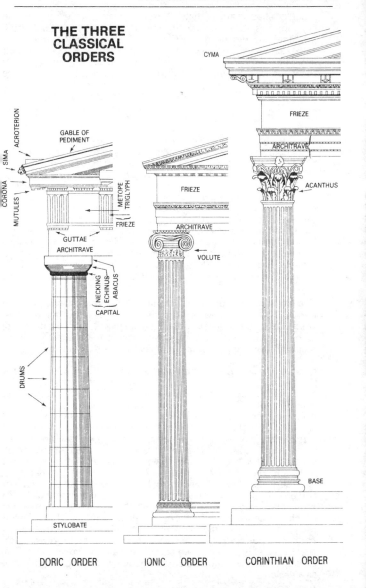

DORIC ORDER

IONIC ORDER

CORINTHIAN ORDER

irregular shaped stones hewn in such a way that they fit perfectly together; this style is characteristic of the Archaic period but was in use until the 4th century BC for ramparts, retaining walls, etc. Trapezoidal — masonry with regular or irregular courses of stones, in use from the 6th to the 4th century BC: Hellenic — rectangular stones laid in regular courses. This was the style most typical of the Classical period; it is also known as isodomic when the vertical joints fall regularly in the centre of the stone below, as for example in carefully constructed temple walls. The stones protruded outwards in the centre and were chamfered around the joints.

SANCTUARIES. The sanctuary or hieron was a plot of sacred ground (temenos) surrounded by an enclosure wall or peribolos, or by a line of marker stones. There was not necessarily a temple; there could be only one or more open-air altars, a sacred grove or tree, niches hollowed out of the rock, statues, etc. The great sanctuaries where games were held were true sacred cities sometimes containing several enclosures with their temples, altars, portico for the pilgrims, a theatre, a stadium, treasuries or votive chapels belonging to different cities, and outside the peribolos there were priests' houses, lodging houses for the pilgrims, baths, council meeting rooms, etc. The main entrances to the sanctuaries were through monumental gates o propylaea, and the route taken by the processions was called the Sacred Way (*hiera hodos*), lined with votive slabs, statues, stelae seats, etc.

The focal point of worship was the altar (bomos) where sacrifices and offerings were received, always outside the temple. The sacrifices were killed at the foot of the altar, cut into pieces, then laid on the top to be roasted over a fire of logs. Many of these altars, however received only offerings of cakes or libations of milk or wine.

TEMPLES. The temple or naos was the home of the god, a tabernacle for the cult figure, accessible only to priests and a few other authorized faithful. There were even temples which were too holy to enter (abaton). The Classical type of Greek temple was divided into the inner sacred enclosure (sekos) which was the house of the god and the outer colonnade or peristyle which served as a shelter for the suppliants. Temples which were surrounded by these colonnades were called peripteral. The sekos, which was often all the temple consisted off, was divided into three parts: (1) the entrance pronaos or porch, generally facing east; (2) in the centre the naos, the sanctuary chamber containing a cult statue; and (3) at the back and completely cut off from the naos, the opisthodomos which was sometimes used as a treasury or place for storing the offerings Primitive temples such as those at Selinunte (Sicily) and Paestum (Italy), the old temple of Athena at Athens (replaced by the Parthenon), or the temple at Delphi, also had a fourth division, the adytum or holy of holies which only the priests could enter. This chamber contained the statue of the god or was the seat of an oracle as at Delphi.

Temples are classified according to the number of their façade columns: a temple with four columns is called tetrastyle, with six columns hexastyle, with ten columns decastyle and with twelve columns dodecastyle. Temples are also classified according to their layout: a temple with two porch columns standing between the pillars of a doorway is called *in antis*, with a portico at one end consisting of a row of free-standing columns it is prostyle; with a colonnaded portico at both ends it is amphiprostyle and with one continuous row of columns all round it is peripteral. A round temple or tholos encircled by a colonnade is monopteral.

The temple stood on a platform of ordinary stone, the stereobate, which compensated for any differences in the ground level. The uppermost course of this base, the euthynteria, established the horizontal line or the curves necessary to produce an illusion of horizontality, as at the Parthenon. Above this was the foundation proper, or krepis, consisting of three steps of marble or fine stone; the topmost step, on which the colonnade rested, was called the stylobate.

The horizontal ceiling of the colonnade was made of coffered marble panels which rested on marble crossbeams (soffits); that of the naos was often of wood with crossbeams and coffers, or there was no roof at all (hypaethral temples) when the width of the naos exceeded the span of an ordinary ceiling beam (32ft/10m). In order to reduce the roof span, interior colonnades consisting of two stages could be added for the beams to rest on.

The interior of the temple, often decorated with paintings and tapestries, was lit only from the door. Temple roofs were made of marble or terracotta tiles, or bronze sheets, resting on rafters. Acroteria were placed at the lower angles and on the apex of the pediment, bearing a statue or a carved finial.

Polychrome decoration, perhaps surprising to our preconceived ideas of ancient Greek aesthetics, enriched the capitals, triglyphs, cymas, metopes and other parts of the temple.

BYZANTINE CHURCHES. The basic type of Byzantine church made of flat bricks and covered with domes springing from square bases is still in use in Greece. This Byzantine architecture which appeared under Justinian I in the 6th century but which has Hellenistic and Near-Eastern antecedents, is above all an oriental form, as much in building technique as in decoration. From the time of the Macedonian dynasty (AD 867–1057) Byzantine architecture was enriched by Arab influences (for example the church of Hagii Theodori in Athens), then by Armenian and Georgian influences (cross-in-square plan). The style was diversified under the dynasty of the Paleologi (AD 1258–1460), of which Mistra provides the best known examples.

LAYOUT OF A BYZANTINE CHURCH. The church of the monastery at Daphni near Athens is an example of one of the most accomplished types of Byzantine church in Greece (see plan p. 50). These churches were divided into several parts: (1) an open poreth (exonarthex); (2) the porch (narthex): these were the outer parts of the church; (3) the naos or nave to which the faithful were admitted and (4) the sanctuary behind the iconostasis or screen, reserved for the clergy and where the altar stood. On either side of this were the northern apse (prothesis) and the southern apse (diaconicon).

The Greek liturgy re-enacts the drama of the Passion: the victim, in the form of sacrificial bread and wine, is sacrificed in the prothesis; then, while the 'cheroubikon' is chanted in the sanctuary, it is carried in solemn funeral procession across the church and placed on the altar which represents the Holy Sepulchre, from whence, after the descent of the Holy Spirit, it is resurrected to give life to the faithful.

Discover Greece

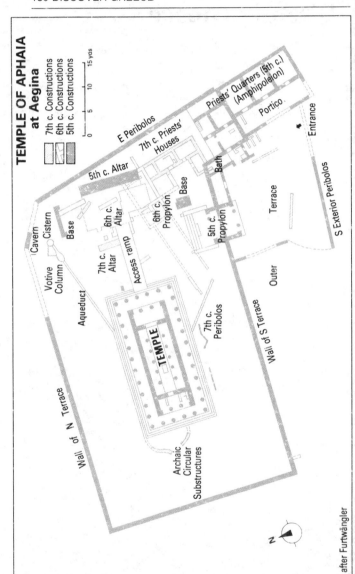

TEMPLE OF APHAIA at Aegina

7th c. Constructions
6th c. Constructions
5th c. Constructions

0 5 10 15 yds

E Peribolos

Priests' Quarters (5th c.) (Amphipoleion)

7th c. Priests' Houses

Portico

5th c. Altar

Bath

Entrance

6th c. Altar

Base

6th c. Propylon

Cavern

Cistern

Base

5th c. Propylon

7th c. Altar

Access ramp

Terrace

S Exterior Peribolos

Votive Column

Aqueduct

7th c. Peribolos

Outer

TEMPLE

Wall of N Terrace

Wall of S Terrace

Archaic Circular Substructures

N

after Furtwängler

■ Acarnania

Route map 10.

Acarnania, lying between the Gulfs of Patras and Arta, is a province of ancient Greece which occupies a wide strip of the coastal area and has a Mediterranean climate. It is irrigated by the Acheloös (Achelous) river which flows down from the Pindos mountains. The river is named after a god who gave Alcmaeon his daughter Callirhoe. She gave birth to Acarnan, the eponymous hero of the Acarnanians. The rugged coastline is dominated by the Xeromeros massif (5,246ft/1,599m) with its oak and chestnut forests. There are several lakes in the central enclosed low-lying area.

Aegina [Island of] (Aighina)**

32sq. mls (85km²) – Pop: 15,000 approx.

All the delights of the Greek islands little more than an hour away from Athens, must be the reason for this island's popularity. In the Saronic Gulf it is much visited by those living in the capital. 'Pistachio island', as it is called, provides a change of scene, with its colourful little harbour (a long-standing maritime rival of Athens), its beaches and its ever less peaceful countryside; but the island is of archaeological interest too, and you should visit the temple of Aphaia in its lovely setting.

LEGEND AND ARCHAEOLOGY. According to legend the hero Aeacus originally ruled over the island; he was the son of Zeus and Aegina, the father of Peleus and Telamon, and the grandfather of Achilles, Ajax and Teucer. Along with Minos and Rhadamanthus he became one of the three judges of the nether world. The island was then called Oenone. According to archaeologists, however, the island must have been inhabited from the 5th millennium BC by tribes which had crossed over from the Peloponnese. In the 3rd millennium BC the Cretans might have established a trading post there. Probably from the beginning of the 2nd millennium BC Aegina was occupied by Achaeans and then by Ionians. But its expansion was restricted by

Minoan power over the seas. At the time of the Dorian invasion the island is thought to have been occupied by Myrmidons from Thessaly.

A PINT-SIZED STATE. c. 950 BC Aegina was conquered by Dorians from Epidaurus and was part of the Amphictyony of the Heptapolis (Seven Towns) centred on the sanctuary of Poseidon of Calauria, on the island of Poros. Shipowners and traders lived there, and in the 6th century BC, after freeing itself from Argive domination, the island grew rich through trading and the manufacture of metal goods, perfumes and earthenware. The first Greek currency is thought to have been struck on Aegina. The Aeginetan navy extended its influence as far afield as Italy, Egypt and the Black Sea, and it founded far-flung colonies.

A BEAM IN THE EYE OF PIRAEUS. The rise of Athens as a maritime power was dependent on the disappearance of Aegina. Though Pindar might call it the 'nurse of heroes', it was referred to by Pericles as a beam blinding Piraeus. The struggle between the two was long and bitter, starting before the Persian invasions, which brought about a truce. But in 458 BC the duel between Aegina and Athens resumed, with two big naval battles in which the Athenian fleet defeated the combined fleet of Aegina, Epidaurus and Corinth. The Athenians laid siege to the town which surrendered in 455, on severe terms: it destroyed its own fortifications, handed over its ships, and paid a tribute. In 431 BC at the beginning of the Peloponnesian war Athens expelled the Aeginetans and installed Athenians on the island. The Aeginetans were repatriated by Lysander in 404 BC, but their role in history was over.

HOW TO SPEND YOUR TIME ON AEGINA. If you intend to return to Athens the same day, it would be best to go straight to the temple of Aphaia either by taking the Hagia Marina bus from the quayside or by taxi. It takes 1hr to look round the temple, and then if you have come by bus you can walk (in 30 mins.) to the pretty little bay of Hagia Marina, where the blue water is very inviting to swimmers. The other pleasant beaches are on the E and S shores. Have lunch there before setting out on the return journey; if you are a very good walker, you can go back via the site of Paleochora (Palaiokhora) which was the main town on the island in the Middle Ages. While you wait for the evening boat you can walk around the main town built on the site of the ancient town. If you want a longer visit including excursions to Paleochora and Oros, the highest mountain on the island, you could very happily spend at least two days on Aegina.

THE TOWN OF AEGINA. You go into the harbour past the white chapel of Hagios Nikolaos and disembark on a quay which is lined with the traditional café terraces which are the heart of the small town's life. Here ouzo will be served with pistachios, which are one of the island's main crops, along with almonds, figs, grapes and olives.

■ Near the cathedral at the end of the quay is the little museum which covers the island's history from the Neolithic to the Roman period.

Open: summer, 09.00–18.00; winter, 09.00–15.00; Sun 10.00–17.00 in summer, 10.00–15.00 in winter; entrance fee (Tel. 0297 226–37).

The first items on display are Mycenaean figurines and pottery articles and the inscription found at the temple of Aphaia enabling it to be identified; then there are prehistoric objects and some Geometric earthenware. Among the sculpture there are the sphinx of Aegina and fragments from the temple of Aphaia.

To retrace the outlines of the ancient town, partly covered over by modern buildings, go back to the harbour and carry on past the stop for buses going to Kolona. You can see remains of the Kryptos Limin, the concealed harbour which was the Aeginetans' military harbour (submerged remains of moles and shelters for triremes), and in 10 mins. you reach the site of the sanctuary of Apollo (long thought to be a sanctuary to Aphrodite), on a partly artificial mound known as Kolona.

All that remains of the early 5th-century BC temple is the shaft of a column, with no capital. These buildings were themselves on top of an early 7th-century BC sanctuary; from this a stone-built sacrificial pit and a square house with three rooms have been uncovered, but worship goes back to the Geometric period as various finds have proved. Nearer the shore you can see the remains of two little temples and circular foundations which may be those of the tomb of Phocus, and the foundations of the bouleuterion. The outlines of the Attaleion, built during the Hellenistic period, can be discerned near the coast.

In 1981 a museum was built on the Kolona site for finds made in the sanctuary of Apollo to be exhibited.

VICINITY OF AEGINA (TOWN)

1 OMORPHI EKKLISIA (1.6mls/2.5km along Hagia Marina road, then l. and 1.2mls/2km further). The 'beautiful church', dedicated to both the saints Theodore in 1282, has inside it frescoes some of which are quite well preserved. You can recognize a Nativity, a Crucifixion and a Resurrection. They are of a later date than the church itself.

2 HAGIOS NEKTARIOS AND PALEOCHORA (4.7mls/7.5km along Hagia Marina road). 3.7mls (6km): Monastery of Hagios Nektarios 19th century; Archbishop Nektarios (d. 1920) 'who was canonized in 1961' lived here. Since 1961 the monastery has been renowned as a place of pilgrimage.

4.7mls (7.5km): Paleochora. The abandoned town of Paleochora which from the Middle Ages until the 19th century was the main town of the island, lies on the slopes of a mountain topped by the remains of a medieval fortress; its white chapels, houses and monasteries are now in ruins.

A PIRATES' DEN. In the 9th century the people of the island fleeing from their homes on the coast which were being ravaged by the Saracens founded Paleochora. When Aeginetans in turn became pirates they retired to this eagle's nest if danger threatened, unless they preferred to take refuge in the cave of Poursospilia. It was first destroyed by the Turks in 1537 under the command of the renowned Kair-ed-Din Barbarossa, then rebuilt, only to be destroyed again by the Venetians who captured it in 1654. Nothing daunted, the Aeginetans set about raising it from its ruins and 18th-century travellers testify that Paleochora still had more than 400 houses and many churches. It was occupied until c. 1800, then the inhabitants left and went to live near the coast.

About twenty churches, some tumbledown, some restored, but all coloured white, give the appearance of being perched on the rock of the steep slopes. They date from the 13th century. Some have vaulting with tierce-point arches. The earliest follow the plan of a Greek cross, with domes. Almost all the churches have stone-built iconostases, decorated with frescoes.

At the bottom of the hill the little Stavros basilica lies on the l., surrounded by a fence. A stone-paved path climbs up from this enclosure, and if you follow it you will see on your l. some ruined chapels; one with a small paved yard in front of it is called Hagios Georgios Katholikos (St George, the Catholic) because the Roman Catholic Venetians used it for worship. The path becomes steeper as it leads up to Episcopi (Episkopi), the former cathedral of Aegina, where St Dionysus of Zante lived in a still extant cell at the end of the courtyard. On the iconostasis a 16th- or 17th-century icon of the Panagia is worth seeing.

Above the saint's cell a winding, stony path passing by the Hagios Nikolaos chapel, which is decorated with sculpture, leads up to the fortified castle. It was built in 1654 by the Venetians and is becoming very dilapidated. On the r. a rough path passes near three small churches with poorly-preserved frescoes and on to the monastery of Hagia Kyriaki (St Dominica) which was not deconsecrated until 1830. The church stands alongside that of the Zoödokhos Pighi (life-giving spring), and both are covered with quite well-preserved frescoes which predate the 17th century.

From the monastery a winding path goes steeply downhill to the metalled road that weaves round the side of the hill among ten or so churches that rise amidst heaps of rubble that were houses. The first church you come to is Hagios Ioannis Theologos, built during Catalan occupation (14th century); the wall paintings, however, are later. Then there is Hagios Nikolaos, thought to be the oldest church in Paleochora.

The frescoes in the fifth church are in fairly poor condition and are primitive, almost crude, in style. In Hagios Efthymios, the seventh church, the frescoes are Peloponnesian in character. The ninth church is dedicated to Hagios Georgios, who is depicted on the frescoes alongside St Dominica dressed as a Byzantine princess. When you reach the last church, dedicated to Hagios Stephanos (St Stephen), you are back at your starting point.

Souvala, 3mls (5km) N of Paleochora, is a very unpretentious little port and watering place with some direct services from Piraeus.

3 **TEMPLE OF APHAIA AND HAGIA MARINA** (6.2mls/10km and 7.5mls/12km). The temple, which is strikingly situated on top of a high pine-covered hill, was built at the beginning of the 5th century BC on the site of an earlier temple. I was dedicated to Aphaia, a very old indigenous deity, credited by Pindar with being the patron of Aegina, and must have been abandoned in 431 BC when the Aeginetans were driven off the island.

Open: daily, 09.00–15.00; Sun. 10.00–17.00; entrance fee.

THANKSGIVING AFTER THE PERSIAN INVASIONS. The identification of this temple famed for its position, its well-preserved condition, and its sculpture, has long been the subject of debate, but in 1901 German archaeologists recovered a 6th-century dedication to Aphaia, who is related to the Cretan goddess Britomartis (Artemis). Work carried out in 1969 by D. Ohly of the Glyptothek in Munich has shown that the original temple, a huge peripteral building, must have been built c. 570 BC and destroyed c. 515–510 BC. The temple that can be seen today was also dedicated to Aphaia, but as she was not well known outside Aegina, Athena was chosen to appear as the protectress of the Greeks in their battles against the Trojans, depicted on the pediments, especially the eastern pediment which is slightly later (c. 490–480 BC); these battles are shown as symbols of the Persian invasions. The sculpture that was found from 1811 on is in the Glyptothek in Munich. Recent excavations have brought to light more fragments which are in the collection of the Aegina and Athens museums.

As you climb up towards the temple from the road, you come first to the remains of a perimeter wall (the outer peribolos), then to a 5th century BC building used by the priests. Next you reach an artificial terrace, enclosed by a wall, the inner peribolos, and the temple stands on the terrace. The Sacred Way led into the enclosed area through a propylon or monumental entrance and extended as far as the altar.

The **temple which was built of local limestone follows the Doric order, and is peripteral (an unbroken colonnade going round all four sides). The vestibule leads into the holy place (naos or cella), the side walls of which have been partly re-erected. An inner double colonnade of five columns on which a second order rested divided the cella into three naves, like the Parthenon, and held up the roof. The cella, which was the room belonging to the deity, contained a statue of Aphaia. Behind the cella you can see the back part of the temple, the opisthodomos. Just beside the foundations of the temple in a pit you can see the substructure of the Archaic temple.

Beyond the temple of Aphaia the road carries on to the Hagia Marina beach, which some shipping lines choose as a port of call; the town lies at the foot of verdant hills.

4 **OROS** (3.7mls/6km to Marathon, then approx 2hrs walk). This large hill or mount, Hagios lias (the Holy Prophet Elias), which rises to a

height of 1,745ft (532m) is the conical peak which makes Aegina stand out wherever you are in the Saronic Gulf. When it is covered with clouds, rain is on the way. This must be the origin of the fable according to which Aeacus after a long drought successfully persuaded his father Zeus to send rain. There was an early sanctuary to Zeus Hellanios at the summit, later changed to Zeus Panhellenion. When excavations were carried out the remains of a group of dwellings were found, belonging to the Thessalian tribes who introduced the cult of Zeus Hellanios which had come from Thessaly and Dodona. A sanctuary was built during the Geometric period with an altar dedicated to Zeus Panhellenion, and its foundations have been discovered. When the kings of Pergamum were its overlords (2nd century BC) the whole mountain was dedicated to the Father of the Gods and of the Hellenes.

You can go back to Aegina (town) by following the path that leads down past the convent of Panagia Chrysoleontissa (the Virgin of the golden lioness), one of the earliest in Greece, which lies in a remote valley. With its sturdy, squat architecture and its keep, it is reminiscent of the fortified monasteries on Mt Athos. It dates back to 1600, but its church was enlarged in 1806. It has a remarkable iconostasis made of carved wood, depicting scenes from the Old Testament. The icon of the Panagia, the origin of the convent's name Chrysoleontissa, which is attributed to St Luke, is displayed on a separate iconostasis. The feast-day of the convent is 15 August (the Assumption, or Dormition).

It will take you three-quarters of an hour along a hilly road to reach the metalled road going from Ageina to the temple of Aphaia.

5 ISLANDS OF MONI AND ANGISTIRI. The first of these really very tiny islands, SW of Aegina, is no more than a place where people camp in the summer, with no amenities provided, while the second more westerly island has a delightful little port, Milo, and a holiday club.

■ Aegion

Route map 5.

Patras, 20.6mls (33km) – Corinth, 62mls (99km) – Athens, 116mls (186km) – Pop: 18,910.

Aegion was one of the 12 cities of the Achaean League, and it was here that Agamemnon assembled the Greek chiefs before setting off for the Trojan war. As the 4th-century capital of Achaea, the town became the federal sanctuary (Homarion) where meetings of the Achaean League were held.

Today Aegion is a commercial port. Remains still to be seen are parts of the old city wall overlooking the port, and a network of underground galleries cut out of the rock and containing grain silos and cisterns.

■ Aegira

Route map 5.

Aegion, 21.2mls (34km) – Corinth, 36.2mls (58km) – Patras, 43mls (67km).

The Austrian School has recently been excavating a theatre and the ancient acropolis of Aegira on the summit of Mt Evrostira. The theatre, of which the horseshoe-shaped orchestra (dancing space) has been completely cleared, must have been constructed in the 3rd century BC, certainly after the reforming of the Achaean League (281–280 BC), and then altered in the Roman period, probably in the reign of Hadrian (117–138). The back of the stage was divided by an axial colonnade as at Epidaurus. On the acropolis Austrian archaeologists have uncovered painted architectural fragments from the Archaic and Classical periods, perhaps originating from the temple of Artemis Iphigenia mentioned by Pausanias. The remains of two megaron-type buildings are evidence that the site was inhabited during the Mycenaean period.

■ Aetolia

Route map 10.

Lying between Acarnania and the entrance to the Gulf of Corinth, Aetolia is a typically Mediterranean region on the coast. But pressing down on the coastal fringe is a range of fair-sized mountains, rising to an altitude of over 6,562ft (2,000m) in the E, with Mt Tymphrestos (7,611ft/2,320m) which lies in a continuation of the Pindos mountains, while Mt Vardousia (7,995ft/2,437m) and Mt Giona (8,235ft/2,510m) separate Aetolia from Phocis and Boeotia. This mountain area is quite green, with its forests of oak, pine and chestnut, but the spurs jutting out towards the entrance of the Gulf of Corinth are mainly bare of trees as a result of over-grazing. In the Agrinion basin where there are still lakes and in the plain surrounding Missolonghi the drained areas are fertile and covered with a variety of crops: olive trees, vines (producing currants — the word is derived from Corinth), and especially tobacco.

■ Agrinion

Route map 10.

Arta, 52.5mls (84km) – Athens, 176mls (281km) (via Corinth) – Missolonghi, 22.5mls (36km) – Pop: 32,650 – tobacco manufacturing – chief town of the admin. region of Aetolia and Acarnania.

Agrinion is a sizeable town 1.9mls (3km) to the SW of the ancient town of the same name, of no further interest beyond its situation at one end of this fantastic mountain route, which links it to Karpenision and Lamia over the Panaitolikon and Vardousia mountains, which are an extension of the Pindos chain. There is, however, a small archaeological museum containing the finds of the region. This building also houses the public library.

The road from Agrinion to Lamia is difficult though it has been partially asphalted, and is not suitable for high speeds (allow at least 6 hrs to Lamia). Those intrepid enough to take this route will be rewarded (25mls/40km from Agrinion) with the wonderful ***view of the lake formed by the Acheloös river dam; the scene is set in a frame of crystalline mountains.

VICINITY

THERMON (20.6mls/33km; leave by the Lamia road), along the shore of the beautiful lake Trichonis. Thermon is a small village close to the site of ancient Thermos, the seat of the wealthy federal sanctuary of the Aetolian League. In 218 BC this sanctuary was attacked by Philip V of Macedon, although it was protected by a small wall, fortified with towers of the 3rd century BC. The temple of Apollo Thermios, of which the axial colonnade can still be seen, is one of the earliest known examples of the peripteral style, dating from the first half of the 7th century BC. This was built on top of an older edifice, believed to date from the Geometric period, and joins another very long apsidal building, the walls of which can be seen to the NE of the temple and which is believed to date from the late Helladic period. Close to the temple is a small museum, particularly well stocked with architectural terracottas of the Archaic period. Further south are a fountain and remains of the agora with porches and stone seats.

■ Aitolikon

Route map 10.

Agrinion, 17.5mls (28km) – Missolonghi, 6.2mls (10km) – Athens, 167 (267km).

This curious place of refuge with its houses at sea level was built in the Middle Ages on an islet in a lagoon.

VICINITY

OENIADAE (9.4mls/15km). Passing straight through Aitolikon you come to Katochi (6mls/9.5km, 8.7mls/14km in all): the road runs along the 3rd century BC.

Oeniadae was a seaport often fought over. In 455 it was taken by the Messenians of Naupaktos, and attacked by Pericles in 453, but the attack he right. Continue on foot with the channel on your right.

9.4mls (15km): Ruins of the ancient port of Oeniadae (to the left at the foot of the acropolis), reconstructed by Philip V of Macedon. In 424 BC Demosthenes, the general, handed it over to the Athenian League.

The area around the port is now rather overgrown but part of the quay still exists with traces of the berths and slips where ships moored.

The remainder of the site was surrounded by a city wall 4.4mls (7km) in circumference, which widens out at the top of the hill. The American School has uncovered some houses and a theatre which were difficult to locate. At the highest point of the acropolis stands a great gate, its arch made with wedge-shaped stones (voussoirs) from the 4th century BC in a keystone style of building influenced by Italy.

■ Alexandroupolis

Route map 14.

Istanbul, 184mls (295km) – Kavalla, 109mls (175km) – Komotini, 41.2mls (66km) – Thessaloniki 213mls (341km) – Pop:23,995 – district capital of the admin. region of Evros.

According to Plutarch, this town was founded by Alexander the Great in 340 BC. There is hardly anything of interest here except for the wine festival from 1 to 15 August. From here you take the boat to the island of Samothrace (at least one per day in summer).

The town hall has a small collection of archaeological finds from the region.

VICINITY

1 FERAI. Taking the road towards Turkey you come first (9.4mls/15km) to the ruins of the Roman and Byzantine city of Trajanoupolis which was important from the 4th to the 8th century AD; all that remains of it now is a small part of the fortifications and a 14th- or 15th-century building close to the road) called Chana (the Khan or caravanserai).

At (16.2mls/26km) Ferai: enter the town to see the church of the Virgin Kosmosoteira (Saviour of the World) built around 1152 by workers from Constantinople inside a monastery founded by the Sebastocrator Isaac Angelus Comnenus. The inside of the church is decorated with frescoes of the same period painted by artists from and Constantinople.

2 DIDIMOTIKHON. A good road runs from the fork (20mls/32km) to Ipsala, a frontier post with Turkey, and (162mls/260km) Istanbul, and follows the course of the Evros towards Edirne, the ancient Adrianople. The road passes through the old city of Didimotikhon with its Balkan-style houses, Byzantine churches, ancient mosques and bazaar clustered about the foot of a medieval citadel. The Cantacuzene family, one of whose members, John VI, became a Byzantine emperor, originated from the town. It was built in the 8th and 9th centuries AD on a rocky hill encircled by the Erythropotamos river. Didimotikhon replaced Plotinoupolis, the ruins of which stand on the hill of Hagia Petra where the gold bust of the Roman Emperor Marcus Aurelius was found which is now in the museum at Komotini.

10mls (16km) to the NE of Didimotikhon is the citadel of Pithion, built on a spur of the eastern Rhodope mountains at the edge of the Evros valley. The town is a masterpiece of Byzantine military architecture. Around 1340 John VI Cantacuzene turned it into an impregnable refuge. The two central towers are still almost intact; the square tower, three storeys high, was for living while the other, smaller in size but four storeys high, was used mainly for defence. Between the two towers the great vaulted gateway led from the outer to the inner walls.

■ Alonissos [Island of]

Pop: 1,500 – 259sq. mls (130km²).

Alonissos is a mountainous and wooded island in the northern Sporades with some small cultivated plains (olive and almond trees). It is usually approached in a caïque and can be recommended to those in search of a quiet holiday; there is also good underwater fishing. There are good beaches (Palavomylos, Steni, Vala, Kalamaki) and several rocky caves by the sea, notably the Cave of the Cyclops on the little island of Gioura. Most of the population now lives in the port of Patitiri having abandoned the town of Alonissos after an earthquake in 1965. It has some small tavernas. The old town is being gradually rebuilt but its undistinguished architecture does little to enhance the beauty of the island.

➡ To discover the rest of the island use a caïque which will take you to the site of Kokkino Kastro (good beach), which has been identified with ancient Ikos where the remains of the ramparts can still be seen. From there there is a fine view over the neighbouring island of Peristera. The islet of Psathoura has some partly submerged remains of an ancient city, while the wreck of a Byzantine ship still lies in the sea off Hagios Petros. Caves and deserted beaches abound on all the islets near Alonissos. Some seals – the last in the Mediterranean — have chosen to live on one of them and some wild cats on another. Underwater swimming is permitted (snorkelling only) in the caves of the islet of Skantzouras.

To the NE lies the islet of Kyra Panagia or Pelagonissos (9.7sq. mls/25km²), with the remains of a Byzantine monastery.

■ Amfissa

Route map 4.

Andirrhion, 74.4mls (119km) (via Itea) or 75.6mls (121km) (via Lidorikon) – Delphi (Delfi), 13.7mls (22km) – Lamia, 41.9mls (67km) – Pop: 6,000 – district capital of the admin. region of Phocis (Fokis).

Amfissa has a strange appearance when glimpsed from the Andhirrhion road, dominated by an old castle remaining from the Frankish occupation.

AN ENCHANTING SACRED PLAIN. Amfissa was renowned in antiquity for its disputes with the Amphictyony (a religious association) of Delphi over possession of the sacred plain of Krissa. This most fertile plain, today covered with olive trees, could have been an important source of wealth for the inhabitants of Amfissa and several other areas had cultivation not been forbidden. The Locrains, restricted to the permitted area but tempted by this untapped resource, violated the law several times, thus provoking the Sacred Wars. The denunciation of the Amphissans by the Athenian orator Aeschines in 339 BC led to the fourth Sacred War.

AN IMPORTED FEUDAL SYSTEM. The taking of Constantinople in 1204 by the fourth Crusade led to the occupation of several Greek provinces by the Franks. Amfissa, known as Salona (or *La Sole*), was given as a fief to a knight from Picardy, Thomas d'Autremencourt, and the Franks, and later the Catalans, retained control of the town until it fell to the Turks in 1394. Of this feudal period only the empty shell of the castle remains, accessible by road. It was built on the site of the ancient fortress and some of the original building blocks were re-used in the lower courses.

VICINITY

KRISSA (5.6mls/9km to the SE on the Delphi road) is surrounded by magnificent olive groves and was inhabited from the Middle Helladic period, as excavations by the French School have revealed. The town was rebuilt at the beginning of the Mycenaean period, then fortified with a rampart, which is still visible in parts, in the Late Helladic Period III when it was particularly flourishing.

■ Amorgos [Island of]

Pop: 1,300 – 47.5sq. mls (123km²).

This little island, whether it is considered the most easterly of the Cyclades or the most westerly of the Dodecanese, will surely be the last outpost in the Aegean of authentic 'Greekness', as long as it is not engulfed by the tide of tourism: already the young people of Athens like to gather there and one wonders how long the two monks at the monastery of the Panagia Khosoviotissa will be able to go on offering coffee and cakes to their visitors.

You land at Katapola (Porto Vathi) at the end of a small well-protected bay about 2.5mls (4km) from Khora (or Amorgos; by taxi or bus), the chief town of the island, which happily has no modern buildings, or at the little port of Aigiali. About 30 mins' walk from Khora is the white monastery of the Panaghia Khosoviotissa (11th–12th century), founded in 1088 by the Emperor Alexius Comnenus, containing several icons, manuscripts and old liturgical objects.

At the southern tip of the island, about 7.5mls (12km) from Khora is Arkesini and, above it, the remains of a medieval castle. This site was one of the three principal cities of the island in antiquity; the others were: Aigiali (N of Khora) and Minoa (above Katapola), some remains of which can still be seen at the top of Mt Moundoulia. In its isolated position on the NE coast, Aigiali is today a quiet little port with several good beaches nearby.

■ Amfilokhia

Route map 10.

Agrinion, 25mls (40km) – Arta, 27.5mls (44km) – Levkas, 23.1mls (59km) – Pop: 5,114.

This beautiful little town was founded at the beginning of the 19th century by Ali of Tebelen, Pasha of Jannina (Ioannina) in a commanding position at the head of the Gulf of Arta. It is overlooked by the remains of the castle from which there is a fine view over the Gulf (vehicular access possible by dirt road turning left off the Agrinion road shortly after leaving the town).

■ Amphipolis

Route map 14.

Kavalla, 40mls (63km) – Thessaloniki, 62.5mls (100km).

To the left of the road coming from the direction of Thessaloniki is a huge marble statue of a lion, from the Hellenistic period, reminding the passer-by of the existence of a city which in earlier times owed its prosperity to its location and the gold mines on Mt Pangaeos.

AMPHIPOLIS AND ATHENIAN IMPERIALISM. The site, which had been inhabited since prehistoric times, occupied a position of great strategic importance, at the mouth of the Strymon (now called the Struma), which proved a temptation first to Miletus, and then to Athens. The city was founded in 436 BC by Hagnon, son of Nicias, to secure for Athens a supply of wood and the revenue from the gold mines of Mt Pangaeos. For this reason the city was one of Sparta's prime objectives during the Peloponnesian War. It was captured in 423 BC, although Sparta failed in its attempt to gain control of the city's port Elion, which was defended by the general and historian Thucydides. Amphipolis won its independence from Athens and resisted the latter's attempts to regain control of it in 360 BC, through its alliance with Olynthus. It could not however avoid being annexed to Macedonia by Philip II in 348 BC. Under the Romans, Amphipolis became the capital of one of the four provinces established in Macedonia.

The ancient city is situated beyond the bridge over the Struma as you approach from the direction of Thessaloniki, on the heights to the left of and overlooking the main road. It was encircled by a 'long wall' (nearly 5mls/7.5km), mentioned by Thucydides (IV, 102, 4), which is currently being excavated in both the upper and lower parts of the site, where it was covered by thick deposits of alluvial soil. The excavations began in 1972.

About 220yds (200m) to the left of the road, 0.6mls (1km) after the lion and 865yds (800m) after the bridge as you approach from the direction of Thessaloniki, the first thing you will notice is a section of that part of the wall which protected the city on the seaward side. At this spot the remaining section is over 13ft (4m) high and constructed, as is the entire site, from large, regular-shaped blocks of local limestone. The wall is intersected by a street (well-preserved Hellenistic paving) which passes through a fortified gateway. This, which is certainly the main gate of the city on this side, is provided with a double defence system: an outer and an inner gate were separated by a courtyard which constituted an enclosed defensive area.

That this entrance is at the Roman level is shown by two bases bearing inscriptions, found in their original position in front of the outer gate. Each of them, preserved *in situ*, bore a bronze statue, but these have unfortunately disappeared. The one on the left, as you look towards the city, was of Augustus, described by the inscription as 'the founder of the city'. The statue on the right was of a distinguished member of the Senate, Lucius Calpurnius Piso, described as 'Patron and benefactor of the city'. It is possible to establish the date of the two inscriptions, which are contemporary, as 29 BC, by means of the inscription on the emperor's statue. To the W of the gate emerged a sewer, the pipes of which were equipped with gratings for purposes of defence.

To reach the very centre of the ancient city, situated near the modern village of Amphipolis, continue along the Kavalla road for about 880yds (800m) and about a mile from the bridge over the Strymon (Struma) take the Serrai road to the left. About 0.6mls (1km) after the fork, on the right, there is a Macedonian tomb carved into the rock; 400m (¼ml) further on a track on the r. leads, after 500m (550yds) to the remains of a gymnasium. This was a vast building constructed from local limestone uncovered in 1982 and identified by means of several inscriptions (one of which is dedicated to Hermes, god of the gymnasium). The main access was from the E (a large stairway of ten steps). The fact that several pieces of the stonework were re-used in the building (for example, triglyphs and metopes from a Doric building) shows that the state in which the monument has been preserved dates at the earliest from the Hellenistic period. The remains of a bath house have been uncovered in the northern part of the ruins. Return to the paved road, follow it for about 100m (110yds) to the fork (going l. towards Amphipolis) leading to the modern village. Follow it and you will reach a section of the wall which encircled the upper part of the city. On the right you will see the building which is intended to house the museum.

After walking up to the left for a few minutes, along the line of the wall, you will reach a section of the fortifications uncovered in 1980; a large round tower acting as an advance bastion towards the N. This is connected to the main body of the wall by a second wall of identical construction. Continuing eastwards you reach another recently uncovered section on either side of an opening which, without doubt, was originally a gate. Return to the museum and continue along the road towards the village. After about 220yds (200m) turn left along a track, suitable for motor vehicles, towards a church. Approximately 1 mile (1.6km) further on, and a steep climb, you come to a plateau where cars may be parked. The first path to the left leads to various excavation sites. Here are the remains of several palaeo-Christian basilicas; their tiled floors, however, will doubtless be covered by sand. You will also see traces of a colonnade belonging to a stoa of the Hellenic period, as well as some remains of the wall. A second path leads you (towards the SW) to a building of the Roman period partly protected by a modern roof under which there are some mosaic pavements decorated with masks.

Take a track, which begins several dozen yards before the building containing the mosaics, down towards the SE (that is, in the direction of the sea, which is visible in the distance) and after walking for 330yds (300m) you will reach, on the left, traces of a house from the Hellenistic period (3rd century BC?) at least one piece of which, excavated in 1982, included polychrome murals. The north wall, which is well preserved (about 6ft 6ins/2m high) is divided into three rectangular panels bearing geometric patterns (yellow rectangles and diamonds on a red background, with a green frame) separated by two white-painted colonnades. Above an entablature, also painted, there was a stuccoed cornice decorated with reliefs, of which only a few fragments have been found. Another room decorated in monochrome was uncovered in 1983.

Return to your vehicle and take the Serrai road to the left. About 0.5mls (0.8km) further on (that is 1.5mls/2.3km from the Thessaloniki-Kavalla road) at the bottom of a steep hill, turn left again to reach the most interesting part of the new excavations which are being carried out with a view to uncovering the lower part of the northern wall on the Struma side.

0.3mls (0.5km) from the fork, before you reach a large medieval tower, you will find, to the left of the road, a section where excavations have uncovered over 165yds (150m) of the wall from the Classical and Hellenistic periods. This whole section is preserved to a height of 24ft (7.25m) in places, but with later modification in the upper sections. Two gates, one from the Classical period, the other, at a higher level, from the Hellenistic, are included in this section. The most interesting and unusual feature consists of a fine drainage system found at two points, the more impressive being on the eastern side. Six piers, equal in length to the width of the wall (i.e. 6ft 6in/2m), are positioned on the foundations of the wall. The piers are triangular in shape and rounded at one end (on the side towards the city). They form seven channels which become gradually narrower towards the outer side of the wall allowing the water to drain away. Further to the W, between this system and the gate, one of the access stairways to the covered way has been found, adjoining the inner part of the wall and consisting of 16 steps. In the immediate vicinity of the wall there are traces of several buildings, one of which is a large house from the Hellenistic period, bordered by a row of pillars.

Continuing towards the W, beyond and to the right of the medieval tower, along the Struma, you will soon reach two new areas where the Classical fortifications, altered during the Hellenistic period, have been extensively uncovered. In the first area, just beyond the tower, the wall includes two gates, one of which gives access to a paved street. 330yds (300m) further along, the wall has been uncovered for more than 220yds (200m). Although this section of the wall is less well preserved as regards height than the first part, it is equally interesting, running within only a few dozen yards of the bank of the Struma. You will see first, on the outside of the wall, three large tanks and traces of a house that antedates the fortifications. About 27yds (25m) to the west there was a fortified gate, 10ft 10½ins (3.30m) wide, of two discernible styles, Classical and Hellenistic (with paving on the ground). 76yds (70m) to the west of the gate, a round tower, partly rebuilt to a square design in the Hellenistic period, flanks the wall at a point where it begins to curve to the S. Between the gate and the tower three triangular-shaped sewer outlets can be discerned, as well as several storm-drains of the Hellenistic period. There are remains of some, as yet unidentified, buildings inside and outside the walls.

Another gate has been discovered 65yds (60m) west of the round tower; this is both the biggest (43ft 11½ins/13.40m high and 29ft 6½ins/9m wide) and the stoutest (walls 6ft 6in/2m thick) since it undoubtedly controlled access to the bridge over the Struma. This bridge is mentioned by Thucydides (IV, 103 and 108). Its position to the north of the gate has been confirmed by the discovery, less than 50ft (15m) from the present river bank, of a series of wooden posts with metal-reinforced tips, apparently belonging to the infrastructure of the bridge. To combat the effects of flood water from the river, the sandy soil on which the walls between the gate and the round tower were built was also stabilized by numerous wooden posts sunk deep in the ground, which the excavators have found almost intact. You can see a large number of these which have been treated and left *in situ*. Such a device in so good a state of preservation is still unique in Greece. The posts between the gate and the river are now protected by a transparent roof supported by a wooden frame.

Returning to the Thessaloniki-Kavalla road one can see on the right, on the site of the port of Eion, the ruins of a Byzantine castle and of a vast will fortified with towers which must once have defended the town of Caesaropolis, founded in 837 in the reign of the Emperor Theophilus.

VICINITY

1 **ASPROVALTA** (10mls/16km on the Thessaloniki road), good beach at the head of the gulf of the Struma enclosed by Mt Pangaeos to the N and Mt Athos to the S.

2 **RODOLIVOS** (13.7mls/22km NE) on the slopes of Mt Pangaeos, from where one can reach the village of Kormitsa; from Kormitsa it would take fit walkers 2hrs to reach the Kousynitzo monastery, founded in 518 (modern frescoes, 14th-century gospel book). Then begins the ascent of Pangaeos (6,417ft/1,956m) passing the cave of Askitotrypa on the way.

■ Andikyra

Route map 4.

Delphi, 28mls (45km) – Livadia, 26.9mls (43km) – Itea, 18.7mls (30km).

Coming down from Distomon towards the sea you will come upon the vast bay of Andikyra with its impressive ring of mountains. We know from historical sources that this natural anchorage was much sought after in antiquity.

The huge industrial complex built by Aluminium of Greece to process bauxite from Mt Parnassus has turned this into a very busy region. The new town of Aspra Spitia ('White Houses'; pop. 4,500), built beside the sea, houses some of the factory employees. A road to the right leads to the developing town of Andikyra on the site of ancient Antikyra (a few remains), while to the left there is a road leading to the factory which is built on a narrow coastal plain. It is called Hagios Nikolaos and is the only one in Europe to produce both alumina and aluminium.

To the right of the road and above the factory is the acropolis of ancient Medeon which is mentioned by Pausanias and was inhabited from the Middle Bronze Age (beehive tomb on the northern side); some exceptionally well-preserved sections of the fine classical walls survive. The site continued to be occupied over an unusually long period and for this reason its necropolis, excavated jointly by Greek and French archaeologists, has yielded finds of considerable archaeological interest (jewels, vases, coins).

A road through wild country returns to Desfina and then to Itea, after a steep and dangerous descent. From here a visit to Delphi is essential.

■ Andravida

Route map 9.

Patras, 40mls (64km) – Pyrgos, 27.2mls (34km).

This large Achaean village would hardly be worth mentioning were it not for the fact that the Frankish princes, who called it Andréville, took up residence there at the time when the Morea was under Frankish rule. Nothing remains of this period except the gothic apse of the church of Hagia Sophia.

■ Andritsena

Route map 7.

Vassai (Temple of Vassae) 9.4mls (15km) – Pyrgos, 38.1mls (61km) – Tripolis, 50mls (80km) – Pop: 1,077 – alt. 2,493ft (760m).

☼ This is a picturesque, tranquil village with old wooden houses and the atmosphere of a bygone age. It is beautifully situated *at the foot of Mt Lykaion overlooking the Alpheios gorge.

VICINITY

1 **TEMPLE OF VASSAE** (9.4mls/15km); see under Vassae.

2 PHIGALEIA (Figalia) (12.5mls/20km); mountain roads, dangerous after rain, bad sign-posting. Take the road from Pyrgos, then turn left towards the temple of Vassae.

1.9mls (3km): turn right on to an asphalt road towards Lynistain in the direction of Archaia Figalia, or else continue to the temple of Bassae and follow a dirt road to:

12.5mls (20km): Phigaleia (Figalia or Phiala) which occupies a majestic **mountain site and was originally the westernmost market-town in Arcadia. It was taken by the Spartans in 659 BC but regained its independence with the help of the neighbouring town of Oresthasion. The city wall dating from the 4th century BC enclosed an extensive area and is quite well preserved.

The site is overgrown but is notable for its fine views over the austere Arcadian mountains, and in clear weather of the western coast of the Peloponnese. The agora, the temple of Dionysus Akratophoros (the Bearer of Pure Wine) and the tomb of the Oresthasians are still to be excavated on a terraced plateau overlooking the modern village of Figalia. The sanctuary of Eurynome, the marine equivalent of Artemis with the body of a woman and the tail of a fish, was outside the walls on a terrace planted with cypresses and overlooking the meeting of the Lymax and the Neda.

A 3hr walk from Phigaleia, with a guide, will bring you to the *waterfalls (Aspra Nera) and to the chasm (Stomion) of the Neda between cliffs 656ft (200m) high where in ancient times there was believed to be an entrance to Hades.

If you continue along the unasphalted road, you can go down to the sea (about 9.4mls/15km) to Tholon, passing through the hamlet of Petralouna and the village of Kato Figalia where you rejoin a narrow asphalted road.

3 MT LYKAION (3hrs 15min climb; take a guide), with its legends of bloody sacrifices, was one of the strangest high places in ancient Greece, and it is still a most awe-inspiring sight.

WAS ARCADIA SUCH A HAPPY PLACE? The mountain owes its name to Lycaon, the legendary king of Arcadia, who either sacrificed a child on an altar, or served human flesh at a banquet offered to Zeus. The god was angry and he killed all but one of the king's fifty sons by striking them with lightning. The king was turned into a wolf. This punishment was ineffectual because human sacrifices to Zeus continued until historic times (apparently into the time of Pausanias in the 2nd century AD). The sacrificial killing was followed by a ritual banquet at which each participant would 'communicate' by eating a piece of the raw flesh of the victim.

The altar cut in the rock, which Pausanias mentions, has been discovered, as well as the stadium and the hippodrome where the Lycaean Games were held. However, it is the magnificent **view from the summit rather than archaeology which makes this excursion so rewarding.

■ Andros [Island of]*

117.4sq.mls (304km²) – Pop: 11,000, of whom 2,200 live in the capital, Andros.

Andros the largest of the Cyclades, is mountainous and wooded, fertile, and rich in mineral springs (Sarisa, Zenio, Zanaki). Dovecotes are a familiar feature of the landscape, as are the stone walls marking out the fields. It has not yet been overtaken by the tourist boom, despite the fine beaches, especially at Batsi, and the attractive little capital. The island produces figs, citrus fruits and wine.

Approaching from Rafina you land at Gavrion, the ancient Gaureion, a little fishing port on the NW coast (beach to the NW). From here you take the road to Andros (20mls/32km), the principal town, at the end of a narrow road along the E coast, passing on the way through Batsi (5mls/8km) and Palaiopolis (10mls/16km), two villages on the W coast (see below).

*Andros has all the charm of an Aegean seaside town with white houses, often neo-Classical in style, terraced above the port with steps intersecting the little streets, and the ruins of a Venetian fortress.

In the central square you can visit the picture gallery (interesting modern works by contemporary Greek painters) and an archaeological museum opened in 1981; the arrangement of exhibits applies the latest ideas in museum science including audio-visual equipment.

Upstairs are displayed finds from excavations carried out 1967–74 by the Archaeological Society of Athens and the University of Sydney on the Geometric site at Zagora (8th century BC). Among the items downstairs are inscriptions, sculptures and fragments of architecture of all periods found in various parts of the island and in particular on the site of the ancient capital Palaiopolis. Amongst these items you will note the *Hermes (the so-called Andros Hermes) and the *'Matron of Herculaneum'. These two marble statues are copies of the 4th-century BC originals and date from the end of the Hellenistic period. The statues were found at Palaiopolis and returned recently to their place of origin by the National Museum of Athens where they had been kept. Near the central square you can visit a small maritime museum and, more particularly, the chapel of the Zoödochos Pigi ('Fountain of Life') with the atmosphere, at once subdued and sparkling, so characteristic of Orthodox churches. There is an iconostasis dating from 1717.

VICINITY

1 KORTHION (5.5mls/9km) is an anchorage at the foot of the Paliokastro

where the medieval town nestled around a Venetian fortress, now in ruins. Good beach at the end of the bay.

2 PALAIOPOLIS (10mls/16km by the Batsi road). After crossing the plain of Messaria (Byzantine church dating from 1158 in the village of Messaria), dotted with the characteristic dovecotes built as square towers, you reach this village on the W coast near the ancient capital of the island: scattered remains of the old wall, submerged moles in the harbour and remains of a portico in the agora.

If you turn left about 1.2mls (2km) before Palaiopolis, alon a road in the direction of Korthion, about 1.6mls (2.5km) S of the fork you can reach the Zagora promontory where traces of a fortified village dating from the Geometric period have been uncovered and also the remains of a 6th-century BC temple.

3 BATSI (15mls/24km) is a seaside resort (good beach) from where one can climb on foot (about 1hr.) to the Hagia convent, and in two hours reach the village of Hagios Petros. Near the village there is a round Hellenic tower of five floors, 65ft (20m) high, its curious round chamber covered with a corbelled dome.

■ Arachova

Route map 4.

Delphi, 7.5mls (12km) – Livadia, 22.5mls (36km) – Pop: 2,828 – alt. 5,250ft (960m).

This large village, identified with ancient Anemoreia, clings picturesquely to the mountainside and could perhaps be a typical view for a Greek tourist poster. Seen close up, however, the effect is a little spoilt; most of the houses have the commercialized air you find in popular tourist centres. However, this could be the opportunity to buy woollen rugs (flokatia) or colourful bags. The Orthodox Easter processions, especially the night-time processions on Good Friday, give the village a special character.

A few miles along the Polydrosos road, on the slopes of Mt Parnassus, you come upon a vast, open landscape which is quite unexpected when you are in the village. At 6.6mls (10.5km) to the left of the road, you meet the track to the Corycian cave (see vicinity of Delphi, 5).

At 12.5mls (20km) the asphalted road reaches Eptalofon and from there one can go down to the Kephisos valley, enclosed to the N by the Kallidromos chain, passing below the ancient Phocian city of Lilaia, its ramparts climbing the foothills of Mt Parnassus.

■ Areopolis

Route map 6.

Gerolimin, 15.6mls (25km) – Kalamata, 48.7mls (78km) – Sparta,

44.4mls (71km) – Pop: 774.

This town, standing at the edge of the world, buffeted by the winds, marks the entrance to that strange region, the Mani, where the few scattered villages perch in almost inaccessible places and the pathetic crops grown on terraces can scarcely support life, yet the towers still stand as witnesses to the wild, proud spirit of the inhabitants. The Mani is one of the most singular parts of Greece, remarkable as much for its strange, primitive landscapes as for the customs of its people. You will also see many little churches and Byzantine chapels.

INDOMITABLE FOLK. The Mainotes or Maniotes are the descendants of the Laconians who took refuge in the Taygetos mountains after the Slav invasion, and have always been renowned for their bravery and independent spirit towards the rulers of the Morea, whether Byzantine, Frankish, Venetian or Turkish. Until recently they lived in clans headed by chieftains and beys, in the high towers which make the Mani villages so distinctive. The people were not converted to Christianity until the 9th century; they clung to their pagan customs for a long time and even in the 19th century resented seeing their land absorbed into the new Kingdom of Greece.

VICINITY

1 **··DIROS CAVES** (7.5mls/12km along the Gerolimin road, then right to Pyrgos); there are three caves: Glyfada, Alepotrypa and Katafiyi. The first two are open to the public.

Open: daily 08.00–20.00 – in summer, 08.00–18.30 in winter; time taken 35mins; entrance fee.

In the Glyfada cave you follow an underground river for 1.2mls (2km) by boat. Alepotrypa has two lakes, and a considerable amount of Palaeolithic and Neolithic material has been found in the cave.

2 **FROM AREOPOLIS TO GEROLIMIN** (15.6mls/25km). Beyond Pyrgos (Diros caves, see above) you cross the most characteristic part of the Mani with its scattering of square towers and dignified old churches.

6.2mls (10km): on the right: Karouda, church of the Taxiarchs (11th century) decorated with frescoes of a later date.

6.9mls (11km): on the left: Dryalos, dominated by its towers.

9.4mls (15km): on the left: Vamvaka; church of Hagios Theodoros, 1075.

11mls (17.5km): road to the right to (0.6mls/1km) Gardenitsa; church of Hagios Sotir, 11th or 12th century.

13.4mls (21.5km): Kitta; 0.6mls (1km) to the N of the village, church of Hagios Georgios, end of 11th century.

15.6mls (25km): Gerolimin (see under this name).

3 **FROM AREOPOLIS TO KALAMATA** (48.7mls/78km). The scenery along this route is constantly changing; at times the road is very narrow,

winding across the heights dominated by the impressive Taygetos mountains and linking a series of villages, built on slopes that plunge down to the sea, and attractive little creeks.

7.2mls (11.5km): Itylo, the ancient Oetylos, overlooked by the Turkish fortress of Kelepha; Dekoulos convent (18th century) with frescoes dating from 1765. Wine produced.

 16.2mls (26km): Thalame; church of Hagia Sophia (13th century).

18.1mls (29km): Platsa; churches of Hagios Nikolaos and Hagia Paraskevi (13th century), Hagios Ioannis (15th or 16th century), and Hagios Demetrius (13th century).

28.7mls (46km): Kardamyli: medieval castle with 18th-century church; the church of Hagios Spyridon at Ano Kardamyli has an unusual clock tower decorated with reliefs.

38mls (61km): Kambos is a village at the foot of the Zarnata fortress, built on an ancient site identified with the Alagonia mentioned by Pausanias. The castle, built by the Franks and altered by the Turks, rests on ancient foundations: in the curtain part of the rampart some vestiges of a polygonal wall of the Hellenistic period may be distinguished.

49.4mls (79km): Kalamata (see under this name).

A | Argos

Route map 6.
Athens, 82mls (132km) – Corinth, 30mls (48km) – Epidaurus, 25mls (41km) – Mycenae, 8mls (13km) – Nauplia, 7.5mls (12km) – Tiryns 5 mls (8km) – Tripolis, 38mls (61km) – Pop: 18,900 – admin. region of Argolides.

The town lies on the site of the ancient city at the foot of two hills one of which, Kastro, is crowned by a medieval fortress. This town is considered to be one of the oldest in Greece; its origins are in fact lost in the mists of time and Argos is associated with marvellous legends in which heroes with such evocative names as Perseus and his mother Danae appear, and with the tale of the expedition of the Seven against Thebes.

FROM PREHISTORY TO THE EPIC. The site where Argos stands (the Plain) has been inhabited from about the year 2000 BC, evidence of which has been discovered in a prehistoric city on the hill Aspis (the Buckler), a hummock at the foot of the Kastro hill. Originally, its name referred to all the flat country from Mycenae to the Gulf of Nauplia which was occupied by the Achaeans towards the beginning of the second millennium before the present era. The Argives took part in the expedition of the Seven against Thebes in the 13th century with

Adrastos and Amphiaraos, then in the Trojan war under the orders of Diomedes and Agamemnon the Aetolian, their feudal overlord and king of Mycenae.

THE LEGENDARY RETURN OF THE CHILDREN OF HERCULES. Towards the end of the 7th century BC, Argos and the major part of the Peloponnese were occupied by the Dorians, a people from the north, who came from the region of the Danube through the valleys of the Morava and Vardar rivers. Greek legend portrays them as the children of Heracles (Hercules), who had long ago been exiled. Having established leadership over the other Dorian cities of the Argolid the town soon became the rival of Sparta. Under the brilliant tyranny of Phedon (7th century) who introduced a kind of coinage into Greece (iron spits or *obeloi*) Argos' dominion spread over the whole of the Peloponnese.

WHAT IS BAD FOR SPARTA IS GOOD FOR ARGOS. Towards the end of the 6th century the Spartan Cleomenes I broke the leadership of Argos, which owed its salvation to the heroism of the poetess Telesilla. Consequently, Argos avoided participating in wars which could have weakened it (it did not take part in the Persian Wars) or, still out of jealousy of Sparta, it entered into most of the coalitions formed against its most hated neighbour. In fact, it played only a secondary role in Greece after the end of the 6th century BC. Around 460 BC it gave itself a democratic constitution and drew nearer to Athens in order to fight against the Lacedaemonians. In 421 it formed a league with Athens, Mantinea, Corinth and Elis which was crushed in the first Battle of Mantinea in 418 BC. It renewed its endeavours, without success, opposed by the aristocratic party (civil unrest) and fought on the side of the Thebans in the second Battle of Mantinea against Sparta in 362. Pyrrhus attacked it and perished at the city walls in 272 BC.

THE PHOENIX TOWN. Reduced to ashes at the time of the Gothic invasions in AD 267 and 395, Argos never ceased to be inhabited. In the Middle Ages its destiny was linked with that of the Morea which likewise suffered Slav, Frank and Turkish invasions. In 1822, Demetrios Ypsilanti successfully defended the citadel against the Ottomans, but the town was completely burnt down in 1828 by the Egyptian army led by Ibrahim Pasha.

THE DORYPHORUS, THE DIADUMENUS AND THE THOLOS. Three famous works of art produced by artists who won more fame for the name of Argos. Polyclitus (c.480–c.420), born in Argos or Sicyon but trained by the Argive bronze sculptors, is the creator of the *Doryphorus* (the *Spear Bearer*), a principal work in bronze, known to us from a replica in the Naples museum, and of the *Diadumenus* (an athlete wreathing a band around his head). The sculptor and architect of the same name, Polyclitus the Younger (c.435–c.360) who was born in Argos, apparently drew up the plans for the famous Tholos (rotunda) of Epidaurus as well as those for the town's theatre which is considered the most perfect in Greece. Polyclitus the Younger's sculptures are known only through the descriptions of Pausanias. Argos was also

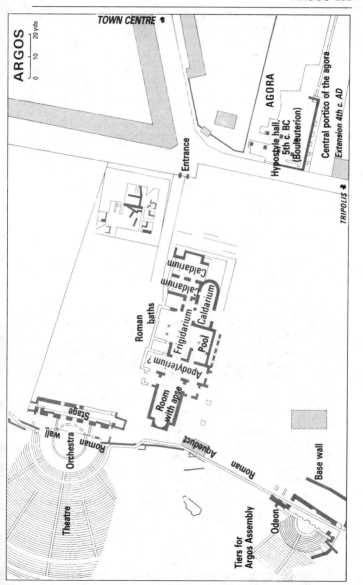

ARGOS

0   10   20 yds

TOWN CENTRE

Entrance

AGORA

Hypostyle hall
5th c. BC
(Bouleuterion)

Central portico of the agora

Extension 4th c. AD

TRIPOLIS

Roman
baths

Caldarium

Caldarium

Caldarium

Frigidarium

Pool

Apodyterium ?

Room
with apse

Stage

Roman wall

Orchestra

Theatre

Roman Aqueduct

Tiers for
Argos Assembly

Odeon

Base wall

the home of the sculptor Ageladas (c.515–460) all of whose works have disappeared.

Visiting the town

THE TOWN ON FOOT. Argos is not a town to wander around in: it is hot in summer and always dusty; it is a modern city, Eastern European in style without much character. The only places of interest to the visitor are the museum and the area around the theatre, opposite the market place (about 1hr in all). The first is 110yds (100m) from the main square beyond the church, the second as you leave the town on the Tripolis road. But one should not neglect the surrounding area which will be of interest to lovers of archaeology (the Larisa acropolis, the hill of Aspis, the Heraion of Argos, etc.) and some Byzantine architecture (Khonika, Merbaka).

IF YOU LIKE... Details of the daily life of past civilizations, visit the museum in Argos which houses vases decorated with scenes from Greek mythology.

Roman monuments, see the excavation site in the vicinity of the theatre where the ruins of the Roman baths will enable you to imagine the splendour of the public buildings at the time of Hadrian.

THE 'ARGOS MUSEUM. While it cannot rival those of Olympus and Delphi, its collections, brought together mainly by the French School of Athens, throw light on certain aspects of everyday life in Greece from the 8th to the 6th century BC, in a very attractive way.

Open: daily, summer 08.30–12.30 and 16.00–18.00, Sun. 09.00– 15.00; winter 09.00–13.30 and 16.00–18.00, Sun. 10.00–16.00; closed Tues.; entrance fee.

The Vestibule. Here you can admire the largest and most beautiful vase in Argos: a jar (middle of the 7th century BC) 39ins (1m) high, richly decorated with geometric shapes and, on the handles where, unusually, painters allowed themselves to experiment with new designs, the truly exceptional representation of two warriors fighting. One could imagine it to be the fight between Odysseus and Ajax during the famous funeral games in honour of Patroclus (*Iliad*, XXIII, 712 ff). Another large vase of the Argive Geometric period (2nd half of the 8th century) depicts horses being broken in, and a Roman mosaic shows a woman with fruit in her lap.

Small Ground-Floor Room. Assembled here are antiques of the Middle Helladic times (c.2000–1580 BC), a period whose beginning was marked by the arrival of the Achaeans in Greece, antiques from Mycenae (c.1580–1100 BC) and proto-Geometrics (c.1100–900 BC), that is dating from the first two centuries after the Dorian invasion.

The Great Hall. Grouped here are antiques from the Middle Helladic period (c.2000–1580), marked by the arrival of the Achaeans in Greece; and Mycenean antiques (1580–1100); and proto-Geometric (c.1100–900) objects, that is dating from the first two centuries after the Dorian invasion; and antiques from the Geometric (c.900–750 BC) and Archaic periods (c.750–500 BC) which mainly correspond to the time of Argos' leadership of the Peloponnese. You will see huge funerary *pithoi* (wine jars) from the 2nd millennium BC. The glass cases contain an abundance of painted vases, including several from the Mycenean period, with terracotta figurines, and, particularly, objects decorated in the Geometric and Archaic styles (Argive, Attic and Corinthian). One brick has a relief of a *pothia theron* (animal mistress).

Particularly noticeable is the Argive bronze armour (end of 8th century BC), a unique specimen consisting of a breast-plate and a back-plate and, most importantly, the only complete example ever found of a 'homeric' helmet which bears a curved crest, on top of which is attached a golden horse's tail.

The remaining funeral furniture coming from the same tomb as the Argos armour is displayed in the nearest high glass case (no. 8): take special note of two iron fire-dogs in the form of battle ships from the Geometric period, with their rams and their prow-horns and curved sterns. These fire-dogs enabled meat to be cooked on iron spits. Also in the Great Hall, the last high glass case (no. 9) on the left contains among other things six iron spits. These roasting spits, identical to those seen today, were the first form of coinage used in Greece (apparently from 7th century BC) and were quickly replaced by pieces of metal, except in Sparta where they remained in use for longer. These spits bore the name *obelos* from which comes the word *obol*. The six of these which a normal-sized man could hold in his hand formed a handful of *drachma* — then, and still, the standard Greek unit of currency.

At the end of the Great Hall in a glass case (no. 12) is one of the most beautiful examples of ancient Greek painting: Polyphemus blinded by means of a long, very pointed stake or a spit (*obol*) by Odysseus and his companions, on a potsherd from a large bowl of the 7th century BC, a very clear drawing with delicate polychromy.

In the following case (no. 13) is an example of an ancient lyre made from the shell of a tortoise; on the underneath a piece of ox skin has been stretched over four pins fixed into the shell. While describing this modest little instrument it is perhaps time to stress the importance of music in the lives of the ancient Greeks; it is primordial, essential even, as it was likened to something sacred, intangible. The Greeks believed the learning of music to be of the utmost importance in their education, and Plutarch in his *Life of Themistocles* tells how Themistocles regretted not having learned how to play the lyre in his youth; similarly, Plato agrees with Damon when he declares 'that one cannot touch the mood of music without touching the most important laws of the city'. The word law itself had musical connotations.

In the last case (no. 14) at the back of the Great Hall, the only known bowl of the ancient painter Hermonax illustrates Theseus killing the Minotaur in front of Ariadne who is holding out a crown to him.

First-floor room. A collection of sculptures discovered during the excavations of Argos and the surrounding area, mainly from the Hellenistic and Roman eras.

The Kallergion room (lower ground floor). Objects from the prehistoric period, mainly ceramic, originating for the most part in Lerna; Neolithic terracotta statue, pottery from the Bronze Age (Early Middle and Late Helladic), several Cycladic vases. The porch at the end of the museum garden shelters the mosaic pavings brought to light in a Roman house in Argos: six panels allegorically represent the 12 months of the year, grouped two-by-two. January is a person throwing stones to welcome the new year. February a peasant holding two ducks; March an armed warrior; April a shepherd carrying a lamb; May by people offering roses; June by a reaper; July by a person with a winnowing-fan and a casket; August by a lightly-clothed person holding a fan and a water-melon; September by a grape-harvester, November by a ploughman; December by a warmly clothed old man. The other panels show various scenes: hunting, dancing, allegories of the four seasons (from N to S: winter, spring, summer, autumn).

THE VICINITY OF THE THEATRE. Before entering the vicinity of the theatre itself archaeological enthusiasts are urged to visit the excavation site of the Argive agora or market place, where one can see, according to Pausanias, Greek geographer and historian of the 2nd century AD, 18 temples along the four sides of the square.

The agora appears to have been used from the 5th century BC until the Byzantine period and extends at least in part above a necropolis of the Geometric period. Important changes took place when, in the 2nd century AD, a spa was established to the S of the porch.

Among the rare vestiges of what was the heart of the ancient city you will notice (below the Tripolis road) the ruins of a great hall with an interior colonnade (a hypostyle) probably built in the last quarter of the 5th century BC on a sort of wide base. It was perhaps the senate house of Argos. Beyond this hall to the E there is a porch, shaped like this Greek letter π, built in the second half of the 5th century BC, but altered in Roman times when it was extended to the W as far as the hypostyle room, and the architraves were replaced by brick arches. This porch was to occupy a central position in the agora and to assure the linking up of several spaces or areas of rather irregular design. To the S of this porch the existence of another porch has been discovered, one which was demolished at the end of the Hellenistic period to make room for a palaestra (for exercises) which, in turn, was used as a courtyard in a spa set up in the agora towards the end of the 3rd century AD.

To the E of the π shaped porch the only exploration that has so far been carried out has been on a drainage system dating from the end of the Classical period which remained in use until the 6th-7th century AD. Perhaps it is here that 'the place called delta' should be sited, without doubt because of its shape as mentioned by Pausanias (11.21.2). The Greek capital letter 'delta' is an equilateral triangle.

The heart of the agora, where the most important monuments are to be found, must be situated to the N of the porch. Immediately next to the long side a running track was set up at the end of the Classical period (as was done on the agoras of Athens and Corinth), of which traces of the starting line have been found.

The most representative vestiges so far uncovered are the remains of a square grotto of the 2nd century AD and further E those of a round monument of the same period which without doubt was also a grotto. To the W of this can be found the ruins of a rectangular building also of the Roman period, standing on foundations made of re-used blocks; underneath this even older foundations measuring 157 × 78ins (4 × 2m) have been found. To the N of these monuments on the side of the present road is the site of the Lycian Apollo's sanctuary; according to Pausanias this is the most remarkable of all Argos' sanctuaries.

The archaeological site in the vicinity of the theatre between the Tripolis road and the Larisa acropolis consists of various monuments, notably the baths which justify a stop in Argos. The ruins of the *Roman baths, now completely uncovered, lie practically opposite the entrance and are bordered to the N by a road leading to the theatre.

In their original state in the 1st century AD the buildings consisted of a hall with an apse and three transversal rooms opening on to a four-sided porch. During the 2nd century they were converted into baths which were restored in the 4th century after the invasion of the Goths.

While surveying the spaciousness of these baths, it is easy to see that their function was not only one of hygiene; they were very social places and therefore dependent on the life of the agora. Situated as these baths are between the agora and the theatre there can be no doubt as to their social function.

A large transverse passage or changing room (apodyterium) leads on the l. to a vast apsidal room which must be a reception room. From the changing room one passes through the frigidarium or cold room, a huge room which housed three swimming pools, then into one of the two caldaria or warm rooms, where the floor was held up by round fragments of brick above the hypocaust or underground furnaces (in this way the warm air could circulate under the floor and, by means of special apparatus, along the walls). The warm rooms likewise housed one or several pools. At the end nearest the entrance to the site there is a third caldarium equipped with three marble baths.

The theatre of Argos, carved in the side of the hill of Larisa, is one of the largest in Greece and can hold 20,000 spectators; it is therefore larger than those in Athens and Epidaurus but matches neither in interest or charm.

Built towards the end of the 4th century BC or perhaps at the beginning of the 3rd century BC, this theatre was twice altered during the Imperial Roman period, in the 2nd century and again at the end of the 4th century when the orchestra or dancing space was changed into a pool and used for naumachy (water fighting). The Greek stage, of which the foundations remain, was partly destroyed during an alteration in the 2nd century and replaced by another stage covered in marble which has since been destroyed in order to uncover the orchestra.

ART AS A SERVICE TO THE CITY. Pausanias informs us that in the theatre in Argos one could see a sculpture representing an Argive warrior named Perilaos killing a Spartan named Othanadas: 'it symbolizes the rights of the people of Argos over the Thyreatid, the border country over which they have fought the Lacedaemonians throughout their history' (W. Vollgraff).

About 110yds (100m) from the theatre (pass between the theatre and the Roman baths) a semi-circular odeon (odeum), probably covered by a roof, was built during the Roman period, perhaps in the 1st century AD, then altered in the 3rd century. It stands on the site of a tiered theatre, carved in the rock, of which some tiers are still visible; this must date from before the 4th century AD and served as the meeting place for the Argive parliament.

Immediately to the S of the odeon lie the ruins of the Aphrodision, a sanctuary with a temple erected around 430–420 BC on an ancient site of worship, which was destroyed at the time of the invasion of the Goths at the end of the 4th century AD. To the E of this temple are the remains of an ancient stoa.

THE HILLS OF LARISA AND ASPIS. Both can be reached by car from the centre of the modern city; a small road, recently surfaced, bears l. at the pass which separates Aspis from Larisa and continues to the foot of the fortress which crowns Larisa.

The Kastro was built by the Byzantines, continued by the Franks, then altered and enlarged by the Turks. It covers the double surrounding wall of the ancient acropolis; the first which is polygonal dates from the 6th century and the second which is Hellenic from the 5th century BC. Here stood the temples of Zeus Larissaios and Athene Polias, of which some evidence has been found.

 From the summit (948ft/289m) there is a beautiful view over the plain of Argos and the gulf of Nauplia (Nafplion). From the Kastro you can descend by means of steps carved in the rock which end at a path traced in the side of the hill of Larisa where a left turn would take one to the Aspis (and a right turn to the theatre).

While walking notice a rock carving featuring a hero on horseback and a snake. After a terrace along which runs a polygonal wall, go down to the level of the ancient convent of the Panagia tou Vrachou (the Virgin of the Rock), whose white buildings overhang a cliff. It rises up over the site of the temple of Hera Akraia (Hera of the Cliff).

The Hagios Ilias mound, beyond a valley which separates it from Larisa, corresponds to the ancient Aspis (the Shield) where the

French School in Athens uncovered some remains of dwellings of the Middle Helladic (2000–1580 BC) as well as several Mycenaean tombs. The sanctuary of Apollo and Athene was here, occupying four terraces with a manteion or seat of an oracle. Beyond, another terrace supported a tholos or round temple. On a terrace higher up the temple of Athene Oxyderkes (the clear-seeing) was situated near a great water tank.

At the top of the hill, crowned by a chapel dedicated to Hagios Ilias, is a Hellenic fortress, polygonal in structure, dating probably from the 4th century BC and resting in places on the remains of a prehistoric enclosure, cyclopean in structure, which protected this, the most ancient habitat of the Argolid, after that of Lerna (Early Helladic).

VICINITY OF ARGOS

1 KHONIKA AND HERAION OF ARGOS (4mls and 5.5mls/7 and 9km). From the central square in Argos follow the signs to Nauplio for 500yds/450m then turn l. towards Corinth, then r. (no signs, poor roads) 180yds/150m further on into Papaoikonomou road (2nd on r.) – 0.75mls (1.7km). Continue in the direction of Ira (on the l.).

4mls (7km): Khonika, church of the Kimissis, mid 12th century.

5.5mls (9km): Heraion of Argos (other route arrowed from Tiryns), national sanctuary of the Argives, dedicated to Hera, situated on three terraces from where you can see right over the plain of Argos. This view will be the main attraction of the excursion for those not seriously interested in archaeology.

THE GODDESS WHO BROUGHT MISFORTUNE TO TROY. It is in Hera's sanctuary (the goddess who pursued the unhappy Trojans with her wrath) that the Achaean leaders made an oath to Agamemnon, the

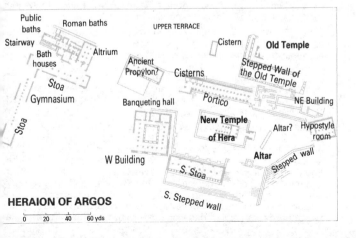

HERAION OF ARGOS

0   20   40   60 yds

King of Mycenae, before their memorable expedition. Hera, who was originally worshipped in the Peloponnese, could be a merciful goddess, at least to her own people. She therefore granted eternal sleep (which to her constituted the greatest human happiness) to Cleobis and Bito, the two sons of Cydippe, a priestess at the Heraion, who had pulled their mother's chariot from Argos.

The primitive temple of the 8th century was destroyed by a fire in 423, but it was rebuilt a little lower down by the Argive architect, Eupolemos. Beyond a powerful sustaining wall (mid 5th century) whose courses are stepped back, lie the ruins of the S porch, built it seems before the new temple around the middle of the 5th century.

On the next terrace lie the remains of the temple of Hera built a little after 420 by Eupolemus. The cella continued the chryselephantine statue of Hera, the work of Polyclitus, and a xoanon of the goddess in pear wood, discovered in Tiryns by the Argives in 468. The excavations have produced some beautiful bits of pediments in the Polyclitean style (the birth of Zeus and the battle between Gods and Giants (Gigantomachy on one side and the taking of Troy on the other), some metopes (warriors and Amazons) and part of a cornice. To the I. of the temple, below the terrace, are the ruins of a square building with a central courtyard surrounded by a peristyle (one of the oldest known examples) dating back to the last quarter of the 6th century BC, and three chambers which have been identified as dining halls.

The upper terrace is occupied by the ruins of the old temple (8th century). The remains are now reduced to the stump of a column which, here, rests on the flattened rock. You can also get to Khonika and Heraion via Mycenae (7km via Monastiraki) or by Tiryns (10km via Argolikon, Hagia Triada and Anifron).

2 MIDEA (9mls/15km). As you go into Khonika (see **1** above) take the road to Anifion and then to Manessis.

8mls (13km): Dendra, a hamlet from where you can climb up to the acropolis of Midea (30 mins.), founded by Perseus and home of Alcmene, the mother of Hercules. The surrounding wall, cyclopean in structure of the same type as in Tiryns, forms part of a circle on the side of the village. 218yds (200m) from Dendra is a Mycenaean necropolis with a large tomb where the oldest known cuirass was found (15th century BC); it is made of bronze and has been presented to the Nauplia (Nafplion) museum.

3 MERBAKA OR HAGIA TRIADA (7.5mls/12km). From Anifion (see **2** above) take the road to Platanition (0.5mls/1km) (very pretty Byzantine church) then to Hagia Triada, the other name for the village of Merbaka (after Guillaume de Merbeke, archbishop at the time of the Frankish rule in Morea in the 13th c.) whose church, one of the most beautiful of Argolis, is dedicated to the Panagia (mid 12th century altered in the 15th or 16th century); the walls, made partly from reused ancient stones, are decorated on the outside with the original sculpture. From Hagia Triada one can return to either Tiryns by a metalled road (a few mls S) or Mycenae (via Khonika and Monastiraki, about 6mls/10km NE).

4 THE PYRAMID OF KENKHREAI (6.5mls/10.5km along the Tripolis road). 3mls (5km) from Argos turn r. to Kefalari (5mls/8km), a village at the foot of Mt Chaon, riddled with grottoes dedicated to Pan and Dionysos where the feast of Tyrbe (Disorder) was celebrated, which has been succeeded by a panegyria (feast) on 18 April. From here you can walk to the great spring (Kefalari) of the Erasinos (1.5mls/2.5km) on the side of Mount Khaon, to the ruins of the pyramid of Kenkhreai (Helleniko) which, according to Pausanias, was the polyandreion (collective tomb) of the Argive victors over the Spartans in a battle fought when Peisistratos was archon of Athens, in 669 BC. This pyramid, built rather roughly, but solidly, in local limestone and polygonal in structure (around the end of the 4th century BC), appears originally to have been a commemorative monument, perhaps later changed into a small fort.

Arta

Route maps 10 and 15.

Arginion, 52mls (84km) – Athens, 227mls (365km) (via Corinth) – Ioannina, 45mls (73km) – Levkas, 55mls (89km) – Nicopolis, 26mls (42km) – Preveza, 32mls (51km) – Pop: 20,538 – capital of admin. region of Arta – archbishopric.

In spite of its past, this small, lively, typically eastern European town, with its windy, dusty streets will not reveal any ancient monuments to the visitor; on the other hand, it will not fail to arouse the curiosity of lovers of Byzantine art with its metropolis and several 13th-century churches.

A CORINTHIAN COLONY. Arta, the ancient Ambracia, a town founded by Corinth in the 7th century BC, fought alongside its mother city against Corcyra (Corfu, Kerkyra) in 435 and 433, then during the Peloponnesian war proved the faithful ally of Sparta against Athens by supplying several ships.

THE CAPITAL OF THE CONQUEROR PASSES TO PYRRHUS. Around 295 BC the king of Epirus, Pyrrhos II (in Latin, Pyrrhus), the same who in 280 won the disastrous victory of Heraclea, joined Ambracia to his kingdom and made it his capital. As it passed under Roman domination (189 BC) it suffered from the defeat that Octavius inflicted on Mark Antony in the naval battle of Actium at the mouth of the Gulf of Arta (31 BC): the victor, the future Augustus (27 BC), wanting to commemorate his success, founded a town, Nicopolis, to the detriment of Ambracia which was depopulated.

From 1205 it again became the capital of an independent state, the despotic state of Epirus, founded by Michael I Angelus Comnenus, which disappeared in 1318 after a division between Serbia and Albania. For almost four and a half centuries it was occupied by the Turks (from 1449–1881).

Visiting the town

AN AFTERNOON IN ARTA. In 1½hrs you can visit the citadel and the three most interesting Byzantine churches in the town. If you are fond of Byzantine architecture take the road that leads to the Hagios Dimitrios Katsouris church. In the late afternoon wander down Skoufa Street, the liveliest in this populous city.

WHERE TO PARK? In the citadel enclosure (Hotel Xenia) or near the old cathedral.

THE TOWN ON FOOT. From the citadel which you will reach easily by following the signs for the Hotel Xenia, go down a little road almost opposite the castle hill, then turn r. 22yds (20m) further on; you will arrive at a small square which you should cross to come out into Vassiliou Street, which in 22yds (20m) leads to Hagios Vassilios church (get the key at no. 14 or no. 16). Return to the square and turn right into Vassileos Pyrrhou (King Pyrrhus) Street. About 218yds (200m) on your right, before the Palas cinema you will see the church of Hagia Theodora; 437yds (400m) further on, still on the r. of Pyrrhou Street, those interested in archaeology can examine the foundations of a temple. Another 22yds (20m) and you will come out on Garoufalia Square; continue straight on and after 55yds (50m) on your l. go up on to the esplanade of the old cathedral.

From Garoufalia Square, Skoufa Street is reserved for pedestrians in the evening; wander down the street to enjoy the lively atmosphere found there, for at this time of the day the street will be crowded. Allow yourself to be tempted by the specialities of the psistaria (roast meat shops) which emit enticing smells and try, for example, some kokoresti (mutton chitterlings) or arni psito (lamb roasted on a spit) even if the tavernas appear modest.

IF YOU LIKE… unusual architecture, go and examine the cupola of the old cathedral where, at the end of the 13th century, an architect found ingenious ways of using remains from antiquity.

…the elegance of Byzantine architecture, visit the churches of Hagios Vassilios and Hagia Theodora as well as the old cathedral.

THE CITADEL. Near the r. bank of the River Arakhthas. It was built in the 13th century by the despot of Epirus, Michael III, on the site of an ancient fortress (numerous blocks have been re-used).

CHURCH OF HAGIOS VASSILIOS. This charming little 14th-century church is decorated on the outside with glazed earthenware tiles and with bricks laid in a zig-zag pattern. On the r. of the apse window notice a brightly painted terracotta plaque depicting St Gregory, St Basil (the church is dedicated to him) and St John. Inside, look at the paintings – those in the apse are in the best condition; notice also the old icons on the iconostasis.

† **CHURCH OF HAGIA THEODORA.** It was built on a basilican plan with three naves and a narthex or vestibule. The capitals of the four sanctuary columns come from palaeo-Christian buildings of the 5th or 6th century. Notice also the frescoes which adorn the walls and the apse and in the narthex a carved sarcophagus of the 13th century of Theodora, wife of the Despot of Epirus, Michael II.

• **THEATRE.** The remains of the theatre of ancient Ambracia were discovered at no. 13 Hagiou Constantinou Street in 1976. There exist a small orchestra and four rows of tiered seating which probably date from the end of the 4th century BC, in addition to remains which possibly belong to the Classical theatre of the end of the 5th century BC.

THE TEMPLE IN PYRRHOU STREET. Today reduced to its foundations, which are particularly interesting and well preserved, this great temple, surrounded by columns in the Doric style was constructed at the end of the Archaic period.

† **THE OLD CATHEDRAL.** Dedicated to the Panagia Parigoritissa (Virgin of Consolation) it was built around 1295 by Anna Paleologus, daughter-in-law of a Despot, and her husband Nicephorus.

Open: weekdays 09.00–13.00 and 16.00–18.00; Sun. 10.00–13.00 and 16.00–18.00; entrance fee.

Notice the system, the only one of its kind, of the pendentives, held up by Byzantine columns from Nicopolis, driven into the walls horizontally like consoles. The purely Italian style of the sculptures is explained by the connections between the despots of Epirus and the Angevin princes of Naples. The roof of the cupola carries a mosaic depicting Christ Pantocrator. Several paintings will hold your attention: on the iconostasis note the icon of the Virgin Parigoritissa (15th century) on the r. and the large icon of the Virgin and Child (16th century) on the l.; in the apse (15th century) the Last Supper dates back to the 18th century. The frescoes (a frieze of the saints) in the nave were painted in the 16th century; above the door, the Dormition (Assumption) of the Virgin.

VICINITY OF ARTA

1 THE CONVENT OF KATO PANAGIA (2mls/3km). Take a road, suitable for vehicles, on the r. coming from Ioannina, before the old cathedral. On the front of the narthex and inside the church of this convent, founded in the 13th century by Michael Ducas, you will see some frescoes.

2 THE MONASTERY OF PETA (3mls/5km along the Athens road, then l. for 1ml/2km). In the church of this monastery is a painting of the Holy Shroud from the 17th century.

3 HAGIOS DIMITRIUS KATSOURIS (3mls/5km). Leave the town on the Ioannina road, cross the Arakhthos (on the r. look out for a hump-backed bridge) and turn l., continue for 2.5mls (4km): turn r. and follow the road for 0.5mls (1km). 2 or 3 mins. walk from the end of the road you will find the church of Hagios Dimitrius Katsouris, founded in the 10th century (?) and restored in the 13th century.

4 THE BLACHERNAE MONASTERY (on the hills to the NE of the town; an excursion of several hours). This 12th-century monastery houses the tomb of the despot, Michael II. The church, basilican in plan, is decorated with sculptures. In the narthex, opposite the present entrance to the church you will notice a mural from the end of the 13th century depicting the procession of the image of 'the most holy Theotokos Hodigetria (Mother of God who points out the way) of Constantinople'. This composition, unique of its kind, includes many interesting details of the crowd of faithful, especially the women, of the traders who walked with the procession and of the architecture of this sanctuary which sheltered the famous icon of the Virgin Hodigetria, blessed, it is said, by St Luke. It disappeared in 1453 when the Turks took Constantinople. In the three naves of the church and the two lateral apses, are other remarkably well-preserved frescoes from the 13th century depicting scenes from the Life of the Virgin, from the Passion, the Resurrection and perhaps Pentecost with the saints portrayed in full-length portraits, in busts and on medals.

5 AMMOTOPOS (14mls/23km along the Ioannina road, turn r. after 8mls/13km). On Kastri hill, which has to be climbed on foot (about 30mins), three large ancient buildings, rectangular and regular in structure, are extremely well preserved to a height of 16–25ft (5–7.50m) retaining an upper storey, windows and dormer windows. Doubtless they formed part of a town built during the first half of the 4th century BC which was defended by a surrounding stepped wall 11ft (3.5m) thick, reinforced by eight rectangular towers built at the time of Pyrrhus II (beg. 3rd century BC). This town was very probably destroyed by the Roman general Aemilius Paulus Macedonicus in 167 and was deserted.

■ Astypalea [Island of]

36sq. mls (93km²) – Pop: 1,100.

Small, isolated, barren, badly served by the regular ferries from Piraeus, this island which belongs to the Dodecanese archipelago offers a real haven from the modern world to anyone wanting to stay there. The wonderful coves which form its coastline make the island a paradise for those who love the sea and under-water fishing. Volcanic in origin, it is formed by two mountain ranges linked by a narrow isthmus.

Ovid tells us that the island was conquered by Minos, King of Crete. Later it became a colony of Epidaurus and then autonomous at the time of the Romans when its bays sheltered the fleets of ships fighting the pirates. After this, it shared the fortunes of the other islands in the archipelago.

The capital Astypalea, on the site of the ancient city of the same name, is very small and its festivities are much more frugal than the nickname of the island in antiquity would lead one to suppose: it meant Table of the Gods because it was so fertile.

The port, where there are still old houses with wooden balconies, is dominated by a fortress of Venetian construction (13th century) which has recently been restored. Above the port entrance is the church of the Evangelist. The road which links Astypalea and Vathy on the N of the island provides wonderful views over the gulfs separating the island's two mountain ranges; the coast at Livadi to the south of Astypalea is equally beautiful. You can also visit the convent of the Panagia Portaitissa (icons), where, during the feast of 15th August, the traditional costumes still worn by the women can be admired.

Athens***

Route maps 3 and 5.

Corinth, 52.5ml (84km) – Delphi (via Eleusis) 101.2mls (162km) – Delphi (on the toll-motorway), 110.6mls (177km) – Epidaurus (via Loutra Elenis), 91mls (146km) – Epidaurus (via Nauplia), 108.7mls (174km) – Evzoni, 360mls (575km) – Igoumenitsa, 303mls (485km) – Mycenae, 79.4mls (127km) – Olympus (via Tripolis and Andritsera), 223mls (357km) – Patras, 137mls (219km) – Sparta, 160mls (256km) – Thessaloniki, 339mls (542km) – Pop: 2,540,241 (including Piraeus and the suburbs) – capital of Greece and of the admin. district of Attica – archbishopric, university.

Athens alone justifies a trip to Greece to see its Acropolis and Parthenon, shrouded in the majesty of bygone centuries; its National Museum where some of the most sublime examples of the genius of Greek artists are to be found — artists who from the 5th century BC sought to use sculpture, not only to portray divinities but to depict the lot of mankind. Its Byzantine works of art are fascinating and, at the same time, you can experience the life of this exciting modern town which, although typically Mediterranean, is inimitably Hellenic in its attraction and even oriental in certain aspects.

The Athens of today, with a population of more than two and a half million, taking into account the whole widespread urban fabric which runs along the Apollo coast towards Cape Sounion, surrounds the Acropolis, a superb relic set in the heart of an extremely built-up and rather disorganized area. This sea of houses has grown to such an extent that it reaches the foot of Mt Parnassus, the slopes of Mt Hymettos and even covers the foothills of Mt Pentelikon.

Alongside the luxury of wealthy districts (Kolonaki, between the Lycabettos and the National Park or along the Kifissia road) near the business capital of Syntagma Square, there are still thousands of homes in the suburbs without any modern conveniences where people huddle, attracted to the capital as if by a mirage. Piraeus, at the same time a port and a suburb of the capital, is not only a great Mediterranean emporium but also the crossroads of the Greek diaspora, enlivened by the people from the islands, fishermen, sailors from one of the greatest merchant fleets in the world, sailing under either the national flag or flags of convenience, and by workers from the shipyards and factories. City life is concentrated in the triangle made by Syntagma, Omonia and Monastiraki Squares, to the edge of the old districts of Plaka and Anaphiotika, whose original authentic folkways have now been adulterated for the tourist. Somewhat aristocratic in the neighbourhood of Syntagma Square, life remains essentially working class around Omonia Square; there is an agreeably old-fashioned commercial life in the district around Monastiraki Square.

The town's place in history

THE INVASION THAT MADE ANCIENT GREECE. During the great Indo-European migration at the beginning of the 2nd millennium BC, Attica was brutally invaded by a barbaric people who still carried out ritual murders and human sacrifices. These newcomers called themselves Ionians, after the name of their mythical ancestor Ion, while the Achaeans, who also formed part of the Indo-European migration, flocked to the Peloponnese. The pre-Hellenic inhabitants of Greece, referred to for convenience as Pelasges by the Hellenes (in fact the Pelasges only seem to have inhabited one part of Thessaly), initiated the Greeks into the cultivation of the olive tree and the vine which were to play such an important role in the economy and even the civilization of the country.

THE 12 IONIAN TRIBES. One cannot imagine what these great invasions were like, involving not only warriors but whole populations, men, women and children, with their gods, their herds of animals, gathered together in clans and tribes, searching for a homeland. Tribal solidarity dwindled when the goal had been reached; with danger no longer present, circumstances favoured the setting up of a feudal system, reflected in history by the coalition of the Achaeans under the direction of Agamemnon at the time of the Trojan war. Attica was divided into 12 states or tribes. The most important were those of Cecropia, the future Athens, Eleusis and the tetrapolis (union of four towns) of Marathon, etc., often at war with one another.

THE MYTH OF THE SERPENT KING. Cecropia owed its name to Cecrops, a snake-man; the second mythical king of Attica, this serpent king (or serpent god) was therefore the symbolic father of the Ionians of Attica, who could consequently declare themselves to be the legitimate masters of that land. The discovery of richly furnished princely tombs on the side of the hill of the Areopagus, dating from the 14th century BC, shows the great antiquity of the monarchy in Athens. Cecrops' role was that of a hero bringing civilization: the suppression of human sacrifices has been attributed to him. A priest and king, Erechtheus, succeeded him and built a temple on the Acropolis dedicated to Athena, the goddess of the olive tree who began the ancient cult of the awl, to Poseidon and Cecrops, in fact to all the deities who had presided over the history of the city.

THE TRAGIC RETURN OF THE HERACLIDAE. Using their iron weaponry to full advantage, the Dorians, who came from the regions of the Danube, brutally put an end to the Achaean civilization of the 12th century BC, destroying Mycenae, Tiryns and Argos. Attica, undoubtedly too poor to tempt the Dorian warriors, was not invaded immediately and became the refuge of the hunted. In the 11th century (?) Attica was invaded and its king, Codrus, was killed in battle. Attica and Greece were to enter a long period of lethargy which has sometimes been called the Greek Dark Ages, during which time, more than three centuries, new values developed.

THESEUS THE UNIFIER. Between the 10th and 13th centuries, during which period the Hellenes had practically to relearn all the Creto-Mycenaean heritage which had been lost with the Dorian invasion, Athens brought about, for its own benefit, the unification (synoecism) of Attica. The Athenians attributed to the mythical king Theseus, son of Aegeus, the honour of having succeeded in reuniting the city states which shared Attica. Communal celebrations (Panathenaic games) preserved the memory of this union. The population was divided into four tribes and the body of citizens into three classes: the eupatrids, noblemen and large property owners; georgoi, small farmers; and lastly, demiurges or artisans.

THE LONG MARCH TO DEMOCRACY. Towards the beginning of the 8th century BC royal power devolved on the eupatrids, while the king had charge only of official sacrifices. Military command was entrusted to a polemarch, appointed for life, and executive power to a life-long archon, but these became annual appointments in 686-685 BC when a college of six thesmothetes was appointed to legislate and bring about justice. The development of agriculture, commerce and industry throughout the 7th century was conducive to the creation of new social classes. The Athenian oligarchy, under threat, looked for allies among the tyrants of Megara, Corinth and Sicyon, who were related to the most powerful families in Athens, such as the Alcmeonidae. With the people demanding a written constitution, the task undertaken by the thesmothetes was resumed and in 621, one of them, Draco, set up a reformed code of law and judicial procedure whose severity, exaggerated by legend, has become a byword.

THE DECISIVE TURN TOWARDS DEMOCRACY. In 594-593 BC or 592-591 BC, under the archon Solon, one of the Seven Sages of Greece, new legislation was promulgated which brought about the decisive turn towards democracy in Athens. To clear up any ambiguities it is necessary to define the exact meaning of the word democracy in the Greek city. The limited size of the states of ancient Greece certainly favoured direct participation of the citizens in public affairs, in the framework of a people's Assembly, but it is important to stress that the body of citizens did not include all the adult men of the city. Those excluded were slaves, metics (foreigners who had settled in the city) and even those who had only one parent enjoying the status of citizen.

TYRANNY, OR THE STUMBLING BLOCK OF DEMOCRACY. After the death of Solon (or shortly before) the polemarch (war minister) Peisistratos set himself up as a champion of the peasants, recruited a bodyguard and took possession of the Acropolis in 561 BC. He instigated a new tyranny which, despite two periods of interruption through exile, was continued by his two sons Hippias and Hipparchus after his death in 528. Hipparchus was assassinated in 514 and Hippias overthrown in 510 by the intervention of the Spartans. Under the tyranny of Peisistratos and his sons, Athens blossomed as an intellectual centre which welcomed scholars, poets and artists fleeing from the Persian suppression in Ionia. It was at this time that Thespis invented Tragedy.

OSTRACISM OR THE DEFENCE OF DEMOCRACY. With Cleisthenes, who in 507 BC decreed a new constitution, democracy was renewed. Attica was divided into ten tribes; each took the name of a hero (Erechtheus, Aegeus, etc.). The Senate (the Boule), answerable to the people's Assembly, was increased to 500 members chosen by lot for one year (50 per tribe). The prytany, which was in charge of day-to-day administration, was assigned to the tribes in rotation, for one month apiece. Executive power was still restricted to the nine archons chosen by lot from a list of candidates presented by each tribe. The eponymous archon gave his name to the official year of 365 days which began on the summer solstice (21 June). A board of ten strategoi commanded the army of the ten tribes. As a final safeguard for democracy against the ambitious, the practice of ostracism was instituted, whereby anyone thought to be dangerous to the state could be banished by popular vote for 5–10 years.

THE PERSIAN WARS: MARATHON AND SALAMIS. To avenge the affront he suffered when the Athenians (in 499) sent an expeditionary fleet and army to support the Ionian colonies in revolt, the king of Persia, Darius, resolved to bring the war to Greece. The Athenian and Plataean victory at Marathon in 490 rudely shattered the reputation for invincibility held by the king of kings, whilst at the same time assuring the triumph of Athens. Despite party rivalries Athens reinforced its fleet to resist the Persians, having anticipated their counter-offensive. The silver mines of Laurion enabled Themistocles to build 200 triremes (ships with three rows of oars) which proved very useful at the Battle of Salamis in 480. Defeated, the Persians under Xerxes abandoned Attica and were beaten the following year, this time on land, at Plataea in Boeotia, whilst a second naval defeat at Mycale assured the total and definitive failure of the Persians' attempts at expansion in Europe.

ATHENS, IMPERIALIST POWER. These successes made Athens a powerful maritime rival to Sparta which still ruled over much of the mainland. It profited from this by imposing protectorates on the Greek cities of

Asia Minor and the islands for a contractual tribute of 460 talents, assuring, in return, their protection. The victories of Cimon (the campaigns in Byzantium and Thrace in 476 BC, victory at the battle of the Eur in 466 BC, the taking of Thasos in 464 BC) ensured hegemony over the Aegean Sea for Athens. Themistocles, shortly before his banishment (472-471 BC) ordered the construction of a surrounding wall enclosing Athens and its Port Piraeus (478 BC). All this took place at the time when Aeschylus was writing *Persians* (471 BC), when people were attending the first staged plays of Sophocles (469 BC), when Pindar composed his odes and Bacchylides sang his poems, and Polygnotus was decorating the Stoa Poikile (painted portico).

THE GOVERNMENT OF PERICLES. After the assassination (457 BC) of the orator Ephialtes, leader of the democratic party, by the oligarchic party, Pericles became head of government. Having been a strategos (army commander) several times, he actively furthered anti-Spartan colonial policies, democratic reforms and the embellishment of Athens, which he made the ideal Greek city. Until 436 BC Athenian fleets and armies were operating in all directions, even as far as Egypt (456-450 BC). Athens founded more colonies: the Chersonese (Crimea), Lemnos, Imbros, Euboea, Naxos, Samos (441-439 BC), Amphipolis (436 BC). But the break with Sparta in 462 BC brought about the first war between the two nations and divided Greece into two camps, alternately victorious one over the other.

THE CENTURY OF PERICLES. During the period from 460 BC to the end of the 5th century and even during the first half of the 4th century, a marvellous flowering of genius made Athens the home of philosophy and the Greek arts. It was preponderant in all spheres, economic, intellectual and artistic. Posterity has named this period the Golden Age or the Age of Pericles, thereby recognizing the influence of the great statesman who surrounded himself with the most distinguished Greek scholars and artists of the time, among whom can be found the names of the sculptors Phidias and Myron, the tragedian Sophocles, the philosopher Socrates and the historian Herodotus.

THE PELOPONNESIAN WAR. The war (431-404 BC), which was to settle the struggle for supremacy over the Greek world between Sparta and Athens, saw the collapse of the great Athenian illusions. After an interminable series of successes and setbacks the fate of Athens was played out at sea in the last decade of the 5th century, but Pericles was already long dead, a victim of an epidemic of the plague which had marked the beginning of the hostilities. The worst disaster for Athens was to take place in August 405 BC, when its fleet was destroyed by the Spartan admiral Lysander at Aegospotami. In November of the same year the Spartan commander besieged Athens which was forced to surrender in April 404 BC. Lysander immediately had the ramparts of Piraeus and the Long Walls demolished to the sound of flutes. For a while Athens fell under the authority of the Thirty Tyrants, but democracy was restored in 403 BC by Thrasybulus. A new era, although sullied by the unjust condemnation of Socrates (399 BC), seemed to begin for Athens.

THE LAST OF ATHENIAN SPLENDOUR. The 4th century marks a period of political decline for Athens. Its civilization became less original and less creative than in the 5th century, but more refined. Language became more flexible and was enriched with dialect. It was the century of Plato and his Academy, of Aristotle, Xenophon, Menander, and of the constellation of orators, true artists of eloquence (Isocrates, Lysias, Isaeus, Aeschines, Hyperides) and of sculptors (Cephisodotus and Praxiteles, who is thought to be his son).

THE UPHEAVAL. For some time Athenian democracy was vigorous enough to shake off Spartan suppression and build up its marine hegemony again, helped by the Theban alliance (second marine confederation in 390 BC). It fought alongside Boeotia and Epaminondas on land to crush Sparta and Agesilaus (Battle of Mantinea 362 BC), but its unreasonable demands soon lost it allies and subjects (war within the alliance in 357-355 BC).

THE END. Profiting from the setbacks of the Athenians, Philip of Macedon befriended the former allies of Athens and won over its outposts in northern Greece (Amphipolis in 357 BC, Potidaea in 356 and Methone in 353 BC). For a while the eloquence of Demosthenes rekindled the patriotism of the Athenians who became the champions of Hellenic freedom against Philip (first Philippic by Demosthenes in 351 BC, formation of the Anti Macedonian League in 340 BC). Despite its defeat of Chaeronea (338 BC) Athens once more became a military and naval power, thanks to Lycurgus, and continued its program of beautiful public works. This was the time when Aristotle was teaching at the Lyceum (335-322 BC). After the death of Alexander the Great Athens defended the freedom of the Greeks against Antipater (Lamian war from 323-322 BC), but Demetrius Poliorcetes took Athens in 307 BC, set himself up in the Parthenon and was awarded divine honours. From that time, Athens alternated between independence and servitude, multiplied its alliances and even sought protection from the kings of Pergamum and Ptolemaic Egypt. The sovereigns of these countries acknowledged Athens as a venerable Hellenic city, used it as a foundation for their own culture and greatly enriched it, but in a spirit which was not that of Greek Athens.

ROMAN DOMINATION. In 168 BC Roman domination took over from the Macedonian. From this time Athens owed the respect it received from the Roman elite only to the brilliance of its arts and of its past. Involved in the war between the Romans and Mithridates (88 BC) it was roughly handled by Sulla in 86 BC, but the kings of Pergamum, Cappadocia, Seleucia and afterwards Pompey, Agrippa, Augustus and especially Hadrian, as well as rich individuals such as Herodes Atticus, overwhelmed it with generosity and monuments in imitation of Greek prototypes.

Between AD 143 and 160 under Antoninus, Pausanias visited Athens and wrote a description of the city. There was a rapid decline in paganism and growth of Christianity as preached in Athens by St

Paul in AD 49. The fall of Rome in the 3rd century left Athens open to pillage by the Heruli in AD 267 and by the Goths under Alaric in AD 396.

THE BYZANTINE MIDDLE AGES. Time was running out for the gods of Olympus whom the schools of philosophy, notably the neo-Platonits, were striving to abolish. Greece, which was part of the diocese of Illyria, was exempted from the edict of Theodosius II (435) ordering the destruction of pagan temples, but the schools were closed and the temples converted into churches or stripped and the monuments taken to Constantinople. From the 11th century numerous monasteries were found in the vicinity of Athens.

LATIN DOMINATION. Following the capture of Constantinople in the 4th crusade in 1204, Athens was assigned to a Burgundian lord, Otho de la Roche, who established his capital in Thebes, but a Latin archbishop was placed in the Acropolis, which had been converted into a fortified castle (1225-1308). The duchy of Athens, founded by St Louis, was offered to the crown of Aragon after the Catalan victory under Roger de Flor in 1311, then passed to the Acciaioli family of Florence who intrigued with both Venice and the Turks.

UNDER THE SIGN OF THE CRESCENT. Following the capture of Constantinople by Mohammed II in 1453, Greece came under the authority of the Patriarch of Constantinople; the duke (at that time Nerio III) placed Athens under the suzerainty of the sultan. But three years later the new duke again put his state under the protection of Venice; the people protested and called on the Turks for help. The Acropolis, occupied by the Christians, was to resist for two years before becoming the seat of the Turkish government. A mosque was then built in the Parthenon. In the 16th and 17th centuries Athens had been reduced to a town of 8-9,000 inhabitants confined to a small area at the foot of the Acropolis which the Turks used as a stronghold when besieged by Francesco Morosini. From 1750, writers and artists began to travel to Athens where the monuments were further damaged in the fighting for the liberation of Greece in 1821-27.

INDEPENDENCE. In April 1833, a French colonel officially took possession of Athens in the name of King Otto and from the following year it became the capital of liberated Greece. The Greek defeat in Asia Minor at the time of the Greco-Turkish war in 1921-22 resulted in an influx of refugees which considerably increased the size of the population. Occupied by German troops on 25 April 1941, Athens was recaptured in October 1944, but the job of liberation was marred by the fighting in December 1944 between the royalists and left-wing parties.

Tours of the city and its vicinity

FIVE DAYS IN ATHENS. This is the minimum stay for those who really wish to see the remarkable sights Athens and its vicinity have to offer. This programme includes a variety of pleasures and the afternoons will often be taken up by excursions to the surrounding areas.

ATHENS (I)

0   200   400 yds

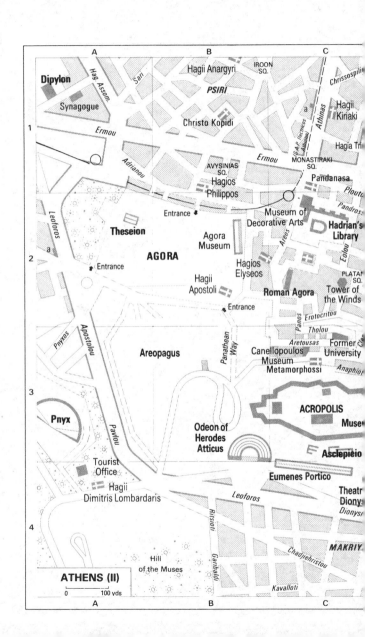

ATHENS (II)

0   100 yds

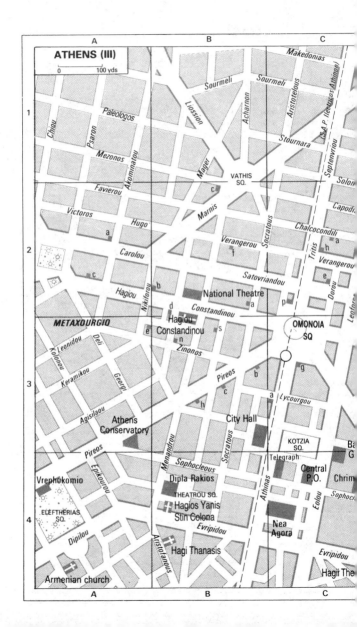

ATHENS (III)

0   100 yds

A

Chiou
Paleologos
Psaron
Mezonos
Akominatou
Favierou
Victoros
Hugo
a
Carolou
c
Hagiou
METAXOURGIO
Nikiforou
b
Leonidou
Kolonou
Deli
Keramikou
Georgi
Agisilaou
Athens
Conservatory
Pireos
Epikourou
Vrephokomio
ELEFTHERIAS SQ.
Dipilou
Armenian church

B

Sourmeli
Liossion
Mayer
Sourmeli
Acharnon
VATHIS SQ.
c
Marnis
Verangerou
f
Satovriandou
National Theatre
a
Constandinou
d
Hagiou
e Constandinou
s
n
Zinonos
Pireos
b
c
h
City Hall
Menandrou
Socratous
Sophocleous
Dipla Rakios
THEATROU SQ.
Hagios Yanis
Stin Colona
Evripidou
Aristofanous
Hagi Thanasis

C

Makedonias
Aristotelous
I.S.A.P. Ilectricos Athinon
Stournara
Septemvriou
Soloi
Chalcocondili
Capodi.
a
h
Tritis
Verangerou
e
Durou
Lenforos
p
OMONIA SQ.
g
Lycourgou
a
KOTZIA SQ.
Telegraph
Ba
G
Central P.O.
Chrim
Eolou
Sophocle
Nea
Agora
Athinas
Evripidou
Hagii The

A   **B**   **C**

1

2

3

4

Socratous

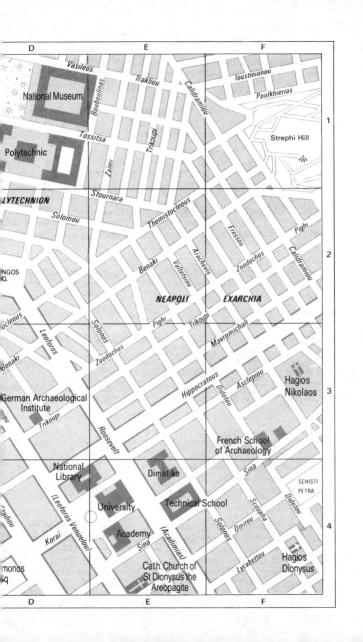

Day 1. Discover Athens from the hill of Lycabettus (Lykabettos) which is easily ascended by cable-car, then reach the Acropolis (V) via the Olympieum (II) and the southern slope of the Acropolis (IV). In the afternoon you could go on an excursion to Rhamnous or even Amphiareion (see Vicinity of Athens, 7).

Day 2. Go to the National Museum (VIII), then in the afternoon visit the Agora (VI) and the Kerameikos cemetery (VII). In the evening, experience the freshness of the Attic countryside by dining at Kifissia or Varibobi.

Day 3. Explore Plaka (III) then leave the city on the Cape Sounion road (Vicinity of Athens, 6); you will reach Vouliagmeni in time to swim before lunch. Return to Athens via Mesogeia. Take time to visit Thorikos and Brauron.

Day 4. Devote the morning to visiting the Benaki (IX) and Byzantine Museums (X) then wander through the city centre, through Syntagma and Omonia Squares (I) using the opportunity to do some shopping. Spend the afternoon in Daphni and Eleusis.

Day 5. Leave early for Piraeus which you can visit before going on to Aegina. Here you can visit the temple of Aphaea. In the evening when you are back in Piraeus dine at Microlimano, then spend the rest of the evening listening to the bouzouki.

TWO DAYS IN ATHENS. The shortest time possible if you are to see anything of the Greek capital.

On the first day go up Lycabettus, then visit the Benaki Museum (IX), the Olympieum (II) and wander through Plaka (III). In the afternoon go up the southern slope of the Acropolis (IV) and then link up with the visit to the Agora (IV) and the Kerameikos (VII).

The second day should be spent in the National Museum (VIII) and on a trip to Cape Sounion (see Vicinity of Athens, 6).

Please note: subject to frequent unforeseen changes, the opening and closing times of the museums and archaeological sites are given here with reservations. Certain rooms in the National Museum may be closed in rotation. Enquire on arrival or at the tourist office.

WHERE TO PARK?

Theoretically there is at your disposal a certain number of reserved parking places for cars registered abroad. Between Syntagma and Omonia Squares you can try to park in Kolokotroni Place, opposite the National Historical Museum (plan II, E–1), Klafthmonos Place (plan III, D–4), Kotzia Square (plan III, C–3), Sina Street (plan III, E–4). In the neighbourhood of the Acropolis, park near the Areopagus (plan II, B–3) or, failing this, at the foot of the hill of the Muses (plan II, B–4). Near the Agora there is reserved parking in Areos Street (plan II,

C-2) and in Plaka in front of the cathedral (plan II, D-2). When visiting the Olympieum, reserved parking can be found on Olgas Avenue (plan II, E/F-4).

SEEING THE CITY ON FOOT. You will have recourse to public transport, taxis (cheap) or you can use your car as much as possible to save yourself long journeys on foot in the exhausting summer heat. Of course you will do some walking, if only through Plaka (III) or to reach the Olympieum across the National Gardens (II: we will give precise details at the head of these chapters), or to get a good impression of modern Athens and do some shopping, notably between Syntagma and Omonia Squares. From Syntagma you will reach Omonia by following Venizelou Avenue where the University (Panepistimiou) is. From Omonia Square return along Stadiou Street passing through Kafthmonos Place, the Place of Tears, a name given humorously by well-educated officials who came to protest under the windows of King Otto.

IF YOU ENJOY ...

Mycenaean gold: You will no doubt wish to visit the treasuries of the royal tombs in the Mycenaean room of the National Museum, but do not miss, in the same room, an amazing signet ring (No. 6208 – Case 15) which comes from Tiryns.

The purity of line in ancient art: take time to linger over the impressive collection of korai in the Acropolis Museum.

Noble art from the Classical period: then the discovery of the Ionic frieze in the Parthenon, the paving slabs of the parapet in the temple of the Wingless Victory (Nike Apteros) in the Acropolis Museum, and the bronze statue of Poseidon attributed to Calamis in the National Museum will be among the great moments of your trip to Greece.

Details of everyday life in Ancient Greece: some objects in the Agora Museum will amuse you or will bring to mind some pages of history, such as potsherds on which the name of Themistocles, the victor of Salamis, was inscribed when a vote for ostracism was taken.

Byzantine art: you will, of course, want to visit the Byzantine Museum, but exceptional collections are also to be found in the Benaki and Kanellopulos Museums.

China and in particular T'ang pottery and Sung ceramics: in the Benaki Museum you can see the collection of a wealthy Egyptian, of Greek origin, which was bequeathed to the State.

Second-hand dealers: in Avysinias Square (plan II, B-1), and in neighbouring streets you will find an incredible collection of bric-à-brac, but don't hope for too many bargains. In this area, one of the most popular in ancient Athens, you can still see craftsmen practising occupations (such as decorative metalwork) which prospered here in the Ancient World.

High places: make sure you climb to the top of the hill of Lycabettus and the hill of the Muses; here you will find the two most beautiful panoramas of the town and the Acropolis; and the view is even more vast from the tops of Mts Parnassus and Hymettus which can both be ascended by car.

I – The centre of Athens

This is a long walk with the sole aim of discovering the Greek capital as a modern, active, lively commerical city, where you will see that Athens is not merely a museum-town.

SYNTAGMA OR CONSTITUTION SQUARE. (plan II, F-2). One of the centres of Athenian life – the other being Omonia Square – this will be one of your regular haunts during your stay in the capital. It is pleasant to stop at one of the café terraces in the centre of the square before going to explore Plaka or the Olympieum. You will find you return here often, either to use the banks or travel agencies or buy postcards at one of its kiosks – a Greek institution. Perhaps you will be lucky enough to be there for the changing of the guard in front of the monument to the unknown soldier at the foot of the terrace of the Old Palace (plan II, F-2) of 1834–38.

If for a moment you can turn your attention away from the *evzones* (these popular soldiers 'with beautiful belts' – literal translation of *evzone* – dressed like young ladies with their chechia (headdress), their black, embroidered red-collared short jackets, their leg-of-mutton sleeves and white kilts), you might like to muse over the two phrases which frame the monument to the unknown soldier, taken from the funeral oration of Pericles: 'Famous men have the whole world as their tomb', 'An empty bed is prepared for the humble'.

Greek independence in 1829 was born of Greek heroism. Poets such as Lord Byron, and even a nephew of Napoleon, Paul-Marie Bonaparte, became passionately involved in this sacred cause (and died as a result).

If you wish to go back to this romantic period, visit the National Historical Museum, very close to Syntagma Square down Stadiou Street (Tel. 323-7617; open every day except Monday 09.00–13.00), located in the palace of the former Chamber of Deputies (plan II, E-1), built by the French architect Boulanger (1871). Here you will see a collection of weapons and historical souvenirs and portraits of the heroes of the War of Independence. Continuing down Stadiou Street you will soon have Klafthmonos Square on your l., where a section of the city walls of Classical times was unearthed during the excavation of an underground car park. On the square, the old palace of King Otto houses the new Museum of the Town of Athens (open Mondays, Wednesdays, Fridays and Sundays, 09.00–13.30) where the history of the city has been traced through various documents, notably a large sketch of the city in 1842. On the r., Korai Street, which leads to the neo-Classical quarter of the Academy. Here the National Library (plan III, D-4) (open weekdays, except in summer,

09.00–13.00 and 17.00–20.00) opens its doors to scholars and non-scholars alike. Be careful not to get lost; there are over three million volumes, but make sure you see the most important ones, in particular two richly illuminated collections of the Tessera Evangelia (four gospels) from the 10th and 11th centuries.

Not far from these monuments, on the l. as you return to Syntagma Square, is the late 19th-century Catholic Church of St Denis the Areopagite.

Following Panepistimious Avenue to the l. you will enter the most popular part of the city, Omonoia Square.

OMONOIA SQUARE (plan III, C-3). There are fewer tourists here but more Greeks, in unceasing crowds, especially at the end of the day. In the neighbouring streets the cafés, grocer's shops displaying oriental produce, and the department stores share their animation. Not far to the S, right in the heart of this commercial quarter, the town hall and post office border Kotzia Square and you will see the flower market a short distance from the central market (open until 15.00). Down Eolou Street, then l. into Evripidou Street will take you back to Kaftminos Square passing Hagii Theodori church.

For lovers of Byzantine art it must be pointed out that this church Hagii Theodori (plan III, C-4) or the Two Saints Theodore, in its present state, could be the result of a reconstruction dating from around 1070, on the site of a sanctuary probably founded in the 9th century. The outside walls are decorated with pseudo-Kufic letters, whose origins lie in the arrival in Greece of Arabs banished from Crete after the island was recaptured by Nicephorus Phocas in 971.

Stadiou Street or Venizelou Avenue will bring you back to Syntagma Square: the expensive shops are a sign of its proximity.

LYCABETTUS. (plan I, E-2). The funicular railway, signposted from Avenue Vasilsis Sophias, a wide modern track which goes to the area of the Hilton Hotel and then to Kifissia, enables you to reach quite effortlessly the summit of the hill of Wolves, the rock (909ft/277m) which Athena abandoned at the time of her migration from Pentelicon to the Acropolis.

It is said that the goddess heard the raucous cry of an owl, which she considered to be a bad omen, or that she had been irritated by the disobedience of the three daughters of Cecrops, Aglaurus, Herse and Pandrosus. In any case, the gods are dead and Athena is no longer there to repent of her actions. According to popular tradition the goddess is supposed to have hidden her illegitimate child there, something hardly compatible with her reputation. In an atmosphere of serenity, therefore, you will be able to discover Athens in its immensity, the Acropolis and in the distance Piraeus and the sea. Unfortunately, industrialization has left its mark and the pure, serene skies of Attica, once so praised, are in danger of becoming only a memory.

On Holy Saturday a great gathering takes place on Lycabettus, when processions lit by candles, torches and Bengal lights, with songs and peals of bells blend in a joyful, colourful celebration.

On descending Lycabettus you will cross the pleasant Kolonaki Square (plan, I, D–3) in the centre of the residential quarter in which the Benaki Museum can be found (plan, 1, C–3).

II – The Olympieum

As the first important stage in your trip around ancient Athens the Olympieum has the advantage of being situated, in beautiful gardens, close to the stadium which, although modern, is an example of the continuity of the Greek contribution to civilization.

THE NATIONAL GARDEN (plan II, F–2/3), situated on the other side of Avenue Vasilisis Sofias and a hundred yards from Syntagma Square, offers, in the sultry heat of the Athenian summer, two very rare things in this city: refreshing shade and coolness.

Those obsessed by ancient relics will find here mosaic pavings, remains of Roman baths behind the Old Palace, some remains of Hadrian's wall and the Peisistratos aqueduct (near a rock forming a belvedere in the angle S–E) which crossed the present site of the garden.

To the S of the National Garden amid flowery lawns, stands the Zappeion, a small semi-circular palace of neo-Ancient style, holding exhibitions (1874–78). In the SW corner of the garden there is a monument to Byron by Chapu and Falguière.

HADRIAN'S GATE (plan II, E–4). The modesty of this monument, erected in the 2nd century AD on the site, apparently, of a gate of the 6th century BC, leads one to suppose that it was not erected by the emperor Hadrian, a fervent admirer of Athens. Perhaps it was built by the Athenians to gratify the founder of the New Athens. Among the Greek inscriptions engraved on this marble gate can be read, on the side of Acropolis: 'Here is Athens, the ancient town of Theseus', and on the side of the Olympieum: 'Here is the town of Hadrian, no longer that of Theseus'.

OLYMPIEUM (plan II, E–4). This venerable sanctuary of the Olympian Zeus was a colossal temple of which fifteen columns still stand, their impressive height giving an idea of the former size of the building.

Open: daily 09.00–15.30; Sun. 10.00–15.00 (summer); in winter closes 30min. later; entrance fee, in fact often closed.

AFTER THE DELUGE. Legend attributes the consecration of the first temple of Zeus and Ge, or Gaia, goddess of the Earth, to Deucalion, son of Prometheus, in the place where the flood waters subsided near the river Ilissos.

THE MEGALOMANIAC WORK OF THE TYRANNY OF THE PEISISTRATIDS. Around 515 BC the Peisistratids undertook the construction of an enormous Olympieum, of the Ionic order. The tufa columns, unfluted sections of which have been found, are evidence of the colossal nature of the work, having a diameter of 7ft 10in (2.38m), greater than that of the columns of the temple of Zeus in Olympus and of the present columns (5ft 7in/1.7m at the lowest part). At the time of the fall of the Tyrants (510 BC) the temple was far from completion.

THE HOMAGE OF FOREIGN SOVEREIGNS TO HELLENISM. After several centuries of interruption, work began again in 175 BC on the impulse of a Seleucid king of Syria, Antiochus IV Epiphanes, whose architect, a Roman named Cossutius, enlarged the initial plan, modified its position and adopted the Corinthian style. The death of Antiochus (164 BC) again interrupted the work. Finally, Hadrian resumed completion of the sanctuary which he had the honour of opening in AD 131–132, at the time of the opening ceremony of the pan-Hellenic celebrations. During the Middle Ages the temple was used as a quarry.

When following at a distance the long side beyond Hadrian's Gate note the ruined houses of the 4th century BC and the remains of a large Roman spa of the 2nd century AD. Nearby, in a part of the ditch (4th century BC) which antedates the wall of Themistocles, rest the column sections of the temple founded by the Peisistratids.

The Propylaea or monument at the entrance to the Olympieum, on the E side (opposite the entrance to the site), has been partly rebuilt. In front of the propylaea the remains of a gate to the enclosure of Themistocles are evident (beginning of the 5th century) and have been likened to the gate of Aegeus (Plutarch, *Life of Theseus*, 12). The Olympieum was dipteral (2 rows of 20 columns on either side), octastyle (3 rows of 8 columns on the façades, the corner columns being counted twice), comprising in all 104 Corinthian columns with 20 vertical channels. Vitruvius points out that the cella was hypaethral, that is, open to the sky, but at that time the building was unfinished, and it is unlikely that Hadrian would have left the chryselephantine statue of the god uncovered. From its dimensions this temple can only be compared to the sanctuaries of Ephesus (Artemision), Samos (Heraion), Selinunte and Agrigento.

In the vicinity of the Olympieum the remains of three temples have been discovered, one of which, from the Classical period, was of the Doric order; a second from the Roman period was probably dedicated to Cronos and Rhea, while the Pythion or sanctuary of Pythian Apollo was identified by its dedications to this god, in particular those on an altar consecrated by Peisistratos the Younger and quoted by Thucydides (VI. 54).

THE IMPOSSIBLE MIRAGE. Beyond the Olympieum, to the S on the banks of the Ilissus, stretched an area of gardens and hills redolent of pastoral poetry, a probable site of the Callirrhoe, the fountain of 'fair flowing' water where sacred water was drawn for religious ceremonies, in particular for the lustral bath of the bride before her marriage. According to Lucian, Socrates liked to teach philosophy here in the shade of a plane tree. Nowadays, especially since major roadworks have resulted in the disappearance from view of the course of the Ilissus, there is no point in recommending, even to those who love detail, a visit to this area which once inspired Plato's description of the countryside at the beginning of *Phaedrus*.

Hagia Fotini church, of the Byzantine period, now stands on the site of the sanctuary of Hecate, the evil divinity of the underworld; and the Metroön of Agras, where in spring the Lesser Mysteries were celebrated in honour of Demeter, Persephone and Dionysus, has been located 130yds (120m) to the NE. The Ilissus, which was deified, also had a temple in these gardens.

STADIUM (plan I, D–4). Built in 1895 in a natural ravine, or rather rebuilt by Averoff as the setting for the first modern Olympic Games, nearly 1,500 years after the last ancient games, on the initiative of Baron Pierre de Coubertin. It occupies the site on which the Panathenaic gymnastic competitions took place, which explains the strange shape – for a modern stadium – of its track.

The stadium consists of a flat track running between two long slopes joined at one end by a curve (the sphendone or catapult). The track is 670ft (204m) long and only 110ft (33m) wide. The length used for the races was the ancient Greek unit of measurement. The course was marked by double-faced herms, four of which have been found. The runners took up the whole width of the track and in the double races, instead of running a circuit they turned around at the last pillar.

Plaka and Psiri, the Roman Agora

Plaka (Flat Land), probably so named in contrast to the Acropolis by which it is dominated, is the oldest part of the capital. Although it has become a tourist trap, a morning walk away from the busy streets, a pause before an old house, a detour into a side street from which the Parthenon can be seen – all this still has great charm. The rehabilitation of the district is in progress, restoring the beauty of the 19th-century houses. Plaka and Psiri remain typically Athenian. At night it is the most lively district in the city.

From Syntagma Square (plan II, F–2) follow Philhellinon Street (plan II, E–2). You will soon see on your l. the Church of Hagios Nikodemos, called *Soteira tou Likodimou*, which was founded in the 11th century but rebuilt in 1847. It has become the Russian Orthodox church of Athens. Beyond this church, take the first road on your r. (Kidathineon Street) which leads deep into the old Plaka.

■ MUSEUM OF POPULAR GREEK ART. At 17 Kidathineon Street (plan II, E-3, Tel. 321–3018) this museum exhibits collections of traditional art and the most important pieces from the old Museum of Decorative Arts.

Open. daily 09.00–13.00 (summer); 10.00–14.00 (winter); closed Mon; admission free Sun. and Wed.

The museum displays mainly objects of the post-Byzantine period, especially of the 18th and 19th centuries. On the ground floor you will see chests, embroidered materials from the Dodecanese, copper objects. On the mezzanine: distaffs, needles, and other objects carved from wood and decorated by shepherds; a beautiful embroidered bed curtain from Kos; plates from Rhodes. First floor: embroidery (Epirus, Skyros, Mytilene); naïve murals by Theophilos Hadjimichael (1868–1934). Second floor: embroidered clothing, jewellery, weapons, amulets. Third floor: traditional clothing (kilts, bouffant trousers called vraka, etc.)

On the r. of the museum is Soteira tou Kotaki church (plan II, E-3), built in the 13th century, transformed into a three-naved basilica with pillars decorated with icons from Pelekassis. You will now arrive at Philomousou Etaireias Square, which is cool and pleasant with cafés on all sides, the most agreeable being on the corner of Farmaki Street (Ouzeri O Kouklis). Farmaki Street leads you to Hagia Ekaterini church (plan II, D/E-3) of the 13th century, another of the charming little chapels built in the Middle Ages under the Byzantines or the Franks. Further down the road notice two columns supporting a fragment of architrave: these are the remains of a temple dedicated to Artemis or, perhaps, of a spa.

By taking Lysicratous Street you will arrive at the choregic monument of Lysicrates (plan II, D-3), an elegant little marble rotunda made in the second half of the 4th century BC; on a high pedestal it supports a bronze tripod, the prize of the choregos Lysicrates in 335–334 BC.

PATRONAGE IN ANCIENT GREECE. The Choregi (chorus leaders) were citizens designated by each of the ten Attic tribes to bear the cost of recruitment, upkeep and equipment of a chorus which would take part in the dramatic or musical productions of the Dionysia (celebrations in honour of Dionysus, very popular in Attica in the 5th and 6th centuries BC), the Thargelies (celebrations in honour of Apollo and Artemis), and panathenaic games, etc. Citizens who had a net worth of less than three talents were not subjected to this duty. A tripod was awarded to the winning chorus, chosen by a jury. As the inscription on this monument reveals, the choregus Lysicrates, from the region of Kikynna, of the Akamantid tribe, received first prize in a Dionysiac competition in 335–334 BC under the archon, Euaenetus, Theon being the flautist and Lysides of Athens the Choirmaster (chorodidascalus). It is known that the present-day street of the Tripods (Odhos Tripodon) has been identified with the ancient street of the same name which ended at the theatre of Dionysus. It was bordered with choregic monuments displaying other tripods, symbols of victory.

Above the inscription is a frieze depicting Dionysus sitting on a rock caressing a panther, surrounded by young satyrs who are offering him bowls of wine. Other satyrs, armed with thyrsi, torches and clubs, inflict punishment on Tyrrhenian pirates who are hurrying towards the sea, already metamorphosed into dolphins. The subject taken from the Homeric hymn to Dionysus, was perhaps also the theme of the cantata which won the prize for Lysicrates. On the same square as this monument can be seen one of the rare shadow theatres still functioning in Athens.

KARAGHIOZE, INCARNATION OF THE GREEK SPIRIT. An old popular tradition, the Greek shadow theatre is far from being entertainment just for children. Long considered vulgar by the upper classes, it satirizes the critical and ironic mind of the people through stock characters who have become classics, such as Sior Dionysius, the pretentious snob; Morphonios, the intellectual; Hadziavtis, a timorous rascal and stooge of the real hero, Karaghioze, with whom the spectator always identifies and who sometimes runs through the whole of Greek history and introduces its most famous figures.

From the monument of Lysicrates, follow Shelley Street which is an extension of Tripods Street (Odhos Tripodon), then turn l. into Epikarmou Street, which is interrupted by steps.

The church of Hagios Nikolaos tou Rengava (plan II, D-3), founded in the 11th century, was part of the palace of the Rangabe family, some members of which were emperors and patriarchs in Byzantium.

As you go down the first flight of steps in Erechtheos Street notice on the l. the entrance to the monastery tou Panagiou Tafou, a sister to the Holy Sepulchre in Jerusalem. The monastery church dedicated to the 'holy moneyless ones' SS. Cosmas and Damian said to have been physicians who took no fees (Hagii Anargyri, plan II, D-3), dates from the 17th century. The reredos, the throne and the iconostasis are in finely sculptured gilded wood, in oriental Baroque style.

At the corner of Erechtheos Street and Erotocritou Street notice the charming little church, Hagios Ioanis Theologos, 13th century. Follow Erotocritou Street, then cross a small square. Then go up Clepsydras Street (Odhos Clepsidras; first road after the square) which rises gradually on to the slope of the Acropolis. After crossing the part of the city which still recalls old Athens with houses from the beginning of the 19th century, you will come to the enchanting little 14th-century church Metamorphossi (church of the Transfiguration).

Inside on the r. of the church you can see a grotto transformed into a chapel dedicated to Hagia Paraskevi, where the tiny altar is made from a beautiful early Christian column. In the nave there are some traces of paintings and, on a small iconostatis, an icon of the Panagla Tricheroussa (the Most Holy Virgin of the Three Hands).

Following the path on the side of the hill, which affords good views over Plaka and the rest of the town, you will reach the northern slope of the Acropolis at the foot of the Long Rock cliffs.

■ **THE PAUL AND ALEXANDRA KANELLOPOULOS MUSEUM** (plan II, C-3). This palatial house ideally situated at the foot of the Acropolis houses many objects from the Neolithic age to Coptic Egypt and, on the ground floor, a rich display of icons. These collections are well presented even if somewhat overcrowded; they faithfully reflect the taste of enlightened amateurs.

Open daily 09.00-13.00 and 16.00-18.00; Sun 10.00-15.00; closed Mon.; Tel. 321-2313; admission fee except Sun.

The ground floor, entirely devoted to Byzantine antiques, displays as well as numerous icons, some fragments of frescoes, jewels, vases, fabrics, various utensils (particularly lamps), coins and especially liturgical objects of the period; cases 6, 8, 10 and 12 contain an important collection of bronze crosses, and cases 13 and 16, two very beautiful chalices.

In the hall at the foot of the staircase, notice two marble heads (one of which is of the Emperor Galerius, from the beginning of the 4th century AD), and three magnificent funerary portraits painted on wooden panels from sarcophagi from Fayoum in Egypt, dating from the late Roman period (wall case 20).

Going upstairs you will first notice two adjoining rooms reserved especially for antiques of the 2nd and 1st half millennium BC: small vases, necklaces and bracelets in coloured glass (case 45). Cypriot vases and figurines (case 46), small bronzes from the Geometric period (case 48), Mycenaean vases (case 49), prehistoric pottery, Cycladic figurines and vases (case 50).

At the top of the staircase, cases 54 and 55 contain golden jewelry, in particular from the Achaemenid period (5th century BC). A small room on the l. contains ancient Corinthian vases (case 56), several fragments from Cretan vases with decoration in relief, from the 7th century BC (case 58), urns and bronze weaponry (cases 59 and 60). In the large room which occupies most of the first floor the exhibits are mainly vases and terracottas; on the l. are Ancient and Classical black-figure and red-figure vases, mostly Athenian. Among other interesting vases you will notice a beautiful black-figure hydria representing women at the fountain (no. 71), two black-figure amphorae signed by the potter, Nicosthenes (nos. 75 and 76), and a red-figure cup (no. 81) from the last quarter of the 6th century BC, as well as a red-figure bowl in the form of a chalice (no. 80) which could be the work of an artist of the third quarter of the 5th century called the Painter of the Deinos. It depicts a very rare scene: Meleager and his son Parthenopaeus. Among the Boeotian black-figure vases of the second half of the 6th century there is a skyphos (no. 64) decorated with scenes from everyday life (women pounding grain, weaving, washing their hair, each one named by an inscription) and a cantharus (no. 66) representing a battle between Heracles and an Amazon. Case 77 contains beautiful gold and silver jewellery and silver coins of the 6th and 5th centuries BC. In cases 91 and 92, there are some remarkable polychrome grave-lekythoi (perfume-filled vases offered to the dead) from Athens. On the r. of the room are the collections of bronzes, vases, terracottas, jewels, coins and marbles, dating from the 4th century BC and the Hellenistic period.

Once back on the ground floor you can glance at the lekythoi and marble funeral stelae which are kept in the courtyard. Then, if time permits, go down to the rooms exhibiting Byzantine and post-Byzantine works of art: icons, jewels, utensils, cloth, wooden coffins (sculptured and painted), liturgical objects, old books, texts on parchment. The decoration of certain ceilings in the house will also hold your attention.

Continuing along the same path you can reach the Propylaea and the Acropolis (V) more easily than by car; you can also cross the Hellenic Agora (VI) on the way to the temple of Hephaestus. But in order to continue your tour of Plaka, walk down Pan Street and you will soon come across the Roman Agora.

•˙• **THE ROMAN AGORA** (plan II, C–2) which should not be confused with the Hellenic Agora, whose evocative power it does not share.

Open daily 09.00–15.00 (summer); 09.00–13.30 (winter); Sun. 09.00–14.00.

The most remarkable building in this Agora is the Tower of the Winds (plan II, C–2), identified by the hydraulic clock of Andronikos, built in the 1st century BC probably under Julius Caesar. Made of white marble it housed a mechanism which regulated the flow of water into a cylinder. The successive levels of water therein would indicate the time.

This building, changed to a tekke or convent by the Turks, was called the School or the Tomb of Socrates in the Dark Ages. Identified by the hydraulic clock mentioned by Varro (*Rerum rusticarum libri* III, 5, 17) and described by Vitruvius, this tower was built by the Syrian architect Andronicus Cyrrhestes (from Cyrrhus, in N Syria).

Each of its faces is oriented towards one of the eight points of the Athenian compass which corresponded to the winds, whose names are engraved with symbolic figures sculpted on the frieze. Notice on the N face between the two sides where the gates have been made, Boreas, the god of the north wind, depicted as a bearded, sullen-looking man, covered with heavy clothing, about to blow into a conch. On the other faces, going clockwise, you will see Kaikias (to the NE), bearded, emptying his shield of hail-stones; Apeliotes (E), a young man laden with fruit and ears of grain; Eurus (SE), bearded, wrapped in a coat, Notus (S) the rain wind, personified by a beardless man emptying an urn; Lips (SW) holding an aplustre (ornament from the stern of a ship) in his hand; Zephyrus (W) portrayed as a handsome young man in flowing garments from which spring flowers fall; Sciron (NW) holding a vase. Sun dials were later engraved under the eight figures.

The small round tower backing the S face served as a reservoir for the hydraulic clock which was fed with water through an aqueduct. The interior partitions regulated the flow of water into the octagonal tower which housed the mechanism. As demonstrated by Graindor, this tower represents the most ancient known example of the use of the octagonal plan to increase the thickness of the walls supporting the roof.

From the esplanade of the clock tower go down in stages into the grand courtyard of the Roman Agora, which still retains in places the original marble flagstones and its drainage gutter at the foot of the gates.

It appears that this Agora was begun towards the end of the

Hellenistic era or at the beginning of the Roman period. During the second half of the 1st century BC a monumental propylaea was built to the W. Later, during the first half of the 2nd century AD, perhaps in Hadrian's time, the central courtyard was surrounded by porticoes with smooth Ionic columns of Hymettos marble. A second propylaea built on the E gives Access to the courtyard.

At the point in the Agora opposite this propylaea, examine the remains of the W gate called the gate of Athena Archegetes (Who Governs), built in 11-10 or 10-9 BC under the archon Nicias, which bears an inscription (on the northern part of the main gate) fixing the amount of olive oil which producers had to reserve for the State. Outside the gate itself stand four Doric columns surmounted by a Doric entablature with a pediment. The whole forms a monumental propylaea opposite the library of Pantainus.

Just inside the excavation site of the Agora is a small Turkish mosque, the Dzami tou Staropazarou (mosque of the corn market) of the Athenians.

Leaving the Agora to the N follow Eolou Street opposite the Tower of the Winds. On the r., facing the tower, notice the sculptured door of an old school of Koranic theology (1721).

To the l. of Elou Street extends the excavation site of Hadrian's library (plan II, C-2); the most interesting remains are to be found on the side of Pandrossou and Areos Street. From the street you will be able to see two exedras which decorated two of the porticoes surrounding the vast central courtyard, undoubtedly a garden with an immense pool (190ft/58m long, 43ft/13m wide) which disappeared under various structures, notably a church built by the Byzantines.

Retracing your steps, take the first road on the l. (Odhos Adrianou); about 55yds (50m) down here (opposite no. 52), hidden behind some trees are the ruins of an imposing Roman building, the sumptuous pantheon which Hadrian built in Athens to receive his mortal remains (they were in fact placed in Rome in a mausoleum which is the present-day Castello Sant'Angelo).

Go back up Adrianou Street as far as Areos Street on your r. You will skirt the southern side of Hadrian's library and arrive in front of the imposing façade of the library which from this, the main side, is preceded by a colonnade of the Corinthian order. Under a little shelter built against the wall, there are some traces of frescoes (16th century) from a 10th or 11th century Byzantine church which has since disappeared.

DZAMI TOU PARAZOU MOSQUE. At the corner of Areos and Pandrossou Street, this ancient market-place mosque of 1759 used to house the Museum of Decorative Arts (plan II, C-2). Nowadays all you will see here are Byzantine ceramics of the 12th and 13th centuries (*open 09.00-13.00, except Tuesdays*), the other collections having been transferred to the Museum of Greek Popular Art.

All along Pandrossou Street, also called Tsarouchadika, there are street stalls selling *tsarouchia*, red or black leather clogs, richly pomponned, leather belts, unusual double-wallets, etc. The way back to Syntagma Square is lined with little shops, especially along Hermes Street (Odhos Ermou). During opening hours it is very crowded and picturesque, for this part of the city has retained the charm of an oriental souk.

Right in the middle of Hermes Street, Kapnikarea church (plan II, D–1), which belongs to the University of Athens and is used for its official religious celebrations, is one of the most interesting in the city. Built in the 11th century, extended in the 12th century by a narthex (note the graceful two-columned porch and the finely sculptured marble door). Time has covered it with an ochre patina.

A sharp r. turn from Hermes Street will lead you to the cathedral (plan II, D–2) built in 1840–55, which you can ignore unless the pomp of orthodox ceremony is of interest to you. This road also leads to the Little Metropolis (the old, or little, cathedral) (plan II, D–2), a wonderful little church which receives much attention to the detriment of its imposing neighbour, the cathedral. This sanctuary, dedicated to the Panaghia Gorgoepikoös ('the Most Sacred One Who is Swift to Answer Prayers') and to St Eleutherios (Hagios Eleftherios), is the most beautiful of these tiny 12th-century churches whose dimensions are in keeping with the modest scale of Byzantine Athens.

Outside on the walls, which have a patina like old ivory, notice the numerous marble sculptures, classical or Byzantine, reused in its construction. On the façade an ancient frieze originally from a 4th-century BC monument is particularly interesting: it illustrates a religious calendar on which the months are depicted by their signs of the zodiac, starting with *pyanepsion*, the fourth month of the ancient year (October–November).

The scenes illustrate the principal festivals of each month: grape harvest, dances, cock fights, a Dionysiac procession, naked athletes, the sacrifice of a bull and the Greater Panathenaea with the prow of a ship mounted on wheels (the Byzantine crosses engraved on this frieze are obviously later additions). Lastly, note the coats of arms of two families of the time of the Latin occupation: La Roche and Villehardouin.

IV – The S slope of the Acropolis

On the S slope of the Acropolis you can visit one of the most venerable Athenian sites, where some of the most famous playwrights in history have presented their dramas and comedies to the public: the theatre of Dionysus. Other monuments, mainly ruins, line the pleasant hillside walk to the odeon of Herodes Atticus, which is at the foot of the entrance to the Acropolis. Visiting these two monuments is most pleasant between 8am and 1pm, and will serve as an introduction to the discovery of the most famous high place of Ancient Greece.

WHERE TO PARK?

In the adjacent streets as far as Dionysiou Areopaghitou Avenue.

• **THE THEATRE OF DIONYSUS** (plan II, C–4; plan IV D/E–3/4). The coexistence in the sacred enclosure (temenos) of Dionysus Eleutherius of a theatre, two temples and an altar, confirms the sacred origins of the Greek theatre and its important role in the feasts given in honour of the god of wine and drunkenness, notably on the occasion of the Dionysia.

Open: weekdays 08.00–13.45; Sun. 08.00–12.45; entrance fee.

THE BIRTH OF ANCIENT DRAMA. Because it was part of the temenos of Dionysus Eleutherius, who was first worshipped in Athens in the 6th century BC, the theatre took the name of Dionysus. The feast of the god, organized by Peisistratos under the name of urban Dionysia or great Dionysia (from 8th – 14th of the month of Elaphebolion; March – April), was accompanied by dances performed by choric dancers dressed as satyrs, led by a coryphaeus with a chorus that spoke and mimed scenes, from which ancient drama was born.

The first play was presented in the second half of the 6th century by Thespis, originally from the deme of Marathon, and from that time drama competitions (tragedies, comedies, satyr plays) and dithyrambic competitions became a regular feature. These first performances took place on the Agora of the Kerameikos.

THE THEATRE OF THE CLASSICAL PERIOD: FROM AESCHYLUS TO ARISTOPHANES. The first theatre in the temenos of Dionysus Eleutherius must have been hastily set up shortly after 490 BC, with a bank of earth supporting the wooden seats. The stage was nothing more than a wooden platform and the only accessories were an altar and a tomb. A little later on, perhaps around 460 BC, it is probable that more representational background scenery was introduced, notably of wood and canvas depicting a palace or a temple. During this period painted scenery became very popular. Agatharous of Samos was noted for stage scenery and even experiments in perspective. He painted the scenery for the production of *Seven Against Thebes* by Aeschylus. The great plays of the Classical theatre of the 5th century BC were performed in this theatre: plays by Aeschylus (525–456 BC), Sophocles (496–406 BC), Euripides (480–406 BC) and Aristophanes (445–385 BC).

Towards the end of the 5th century, perhaps under Cleophon (410–404 BC) the theatre of Dionysus was rebuilt in stone and extended, but work was not completed before the time of the government of Lycurgus, around 330 BC, when a permanent stage was fitted which was raised during the Hellenistic period towards the end of the first half of the 2nd century BC.

FROM NERO TO CIRCUS GAMES. Important modifications took place under the reign of Nero, notably in the structure of the stage (the wall decorated with a relief landscape dates from this period), then under the archonship of Phaedrus (AD 224–5). The rail around the orchestra

ACROPOLIS OF ATHENS (IV)

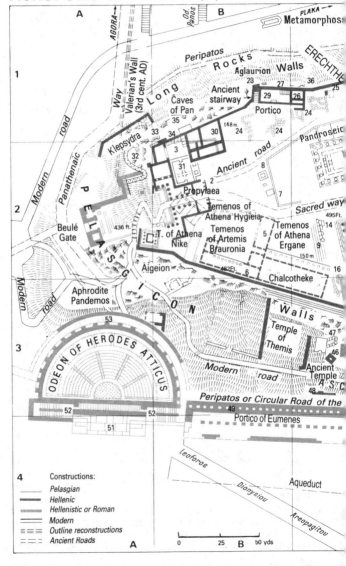

A — AGORA — **B** — PLAKA — Metamorphos

Sounio Pd — Panas Pd — ERECHTH

1
Peripatos
Rocks
Long — Aglaurion — Walls
Valerian's Wall — 28 — 27 — 36 — 25
(3rd cent. AD) — Caves — Ancient — 29 — 26
of Pan — stairway — Portico — 24
Way — 35 — 148 m. — 30 — 24 — Pandroseic
33 — 34 — 3 — 24 — 8
Klepsydra — 32 — 31 — Ancient — road — 7
Panathenaic — 2 — Propylaea

2
PELASGICON
Temenos of
436 ft. — Athena Hygieia — Sacred way — 495 Ft.
Beulé — T. of Athena — Temenos — Temenos of — 14
Gate — Nike — of Artemis — Athena Ergane
Brauronia — 5 — 9 — 150 m — 16
Aigeion — 482 Ft. — 6 — Chalcotheke

Modern — road
PELASGICON

3
Aphrodite
Pandemos — Walls
53 — Temple — 47
of
ODEON OF HERODES ATTICUS — Themis — 46
Modern — road — Ancient — Temple
52 — 52 — A'S'C — 48
Peripatos or Circular Road of the
51 — 49 — Portico of Eumenes

Leoforos
Dionysiou — Aqueduct
Areopagitou

4 — Constructions:
— Pelasgian
— Hellenic
— Hellenistic or Roman
— Modern
≡≡≡ Outline reconstructions
--- Ancient Roads

0 — 25 — **B** — 50 yds

A

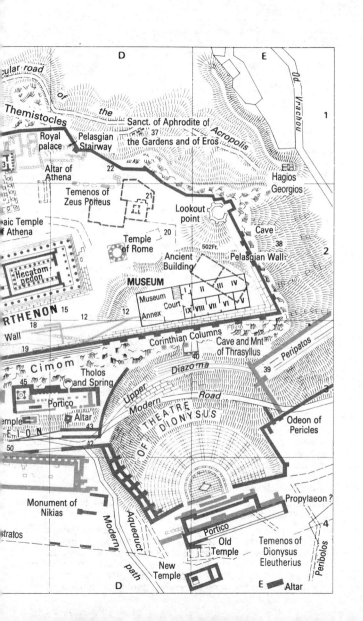

D **E**

cular road

Themistocles

of the

Sanct. of Aphrodite of
the Gardens and of Eros 37

Royal
palace

Pelasgian
Stairway

Altar of
Athena

Temenos of
Zeus Polieus

22

21

Hagios
Georgios

aic Temple
f Athena

Temple
of Rome

20

Lookout
point

Cave

38

502 Ft.

Pelasgian Wall

Ancient
Building

MUSEUM

Hecatom
pedon

Museum
Court

I

II

III

IV

V

RTHENON 15

12

12

Annex

IX

VIII

VII

VI

18

Wall

19

Corinthian Columns

Cave and Mnt
of Thrasyllus

Peripatos

Cimom

Tholos
and Spring

Diazoma

39

45

Upper

Portico

Altar

Modern

Road

THEATRE

DIONYSUS

40

Odeon of
Pericles

emple

ΕΙΟΝ

43

OF

50

42

Monument of
Nikias

Propylaeon ?

stratos

Modern

Aqueduct

Portico

Old
Temple

Temenos of
Dionysus
Eleutherius

4

Peribolos

path

New
Temple

D

E

Altar

(dancing space) was erected during the Roman period, while, as a sign of the times, gladiators fought one another in the orchestra which was previously reserved for danced religious or dramatic productions. Then came the time when the orchestra was changed into a pool for spectacles depicting sea fights (naumachy).

Just by the entrance you will notice the ruins of the new temple of Dionysus Eleutherius (plan IV, D/E--4) (end of the 4th century BC) of which only the foundations remain.

On the r. there is a beautiful round Dionysiac marble altar (2nd century AD) adorned with satyr masks, garlands and rosettes. Further on are the remains of the old temple (plan IV, E-4) of the 6th century, its foundations made from the blue limestone of the Acropolis. Smaller than the new temple, it contained the xoanon (wooden statue) of the god brought by Eleutherius from Boeotia, which was paraded during the Dionysia. The stage buildings (4th century BC) next to the old temple, included a portico which offered the spectators a covered walk, sheltered from the sun and rain, in addition to a stage of the same period. Against the back wall of the stage, set against the portico, a block of masonry no doubt served as foundation for the machinery used to hoist up the baskets in which characters who were to appear in the air were raised. On the projecting wings on either side of the stage itself, two triangular prisms were installed on a pivot (periactes); a different scene was painted on each face of the prism thus allowing the scene appropriate to the action to be presented to the spectators.

The stage underwent numerous alterations after the 4th century BC, the most spectacular vestiges of which are the sculptures on the front of the stage, carried out under Nero in the 1st century AD. The subjects of the sculptures are taken from the legend of Dionysus.

As you leave the staircase, notice:

The Birth of Dionysus. Zeus is seated in the centre and Hermes is standing in front of him holding the new-born child; at either end two curetes are performing a Pyrrhic (war) dance.

A scene of sacrifice in honour of Dionysus: on the l. Icarus, a peasant initiated in grape cultivation and wine-making by Dionysus, is approaching the altar leading a goat, accompanied by the dog Maera, and his daughter Erigone who is carrying cakes on a platter. On the right, Dionysus offers the vine, followed by a young satyr. This scene symbolized the rural Dionysia.

Silenus crouching in the posture of Atlas (there are two other similar ones in the recesses).

Homage paid by the gods and the city of Athens to Dionysus. The god of wine and drunkenness is on the r. seated on a throne, probably in his theatre, as the relief portrays the upper part of an eight-columned Doric building, without doubt the Parthenon as seen from the S slope of the Acropolis. Among the characters walking towards him the following have been identified: on the right Hestia,

Theseus, Eirene (peace) with a cornucopia, and on the l. other person-ifications of the city. This subject symbolized the urban Dionysia.

The orchestra where the choruses originally stood (there being no stage at that time) acquired the pavings visible today in the reign of Nero or Hadrian. A large diamond-shaped stone marks the place where Dionysus' altar, or thymele, stood.

The auditorium, almost circular in shape, is composed of 78 tiers divided into three zones. The total number of seats is estimated at between 14,000 and 17,000 but in fact it could hold more. Plato cites an improbable figure of 30,000 seats. In the 4th century the first row was reserved for the fifty senators, archons and priests. Most of the 67 official seats of honour in this row date back to Roman times, but are perhaps copies of the seats of the 5th century BC. The most honoured place, in the middle, belonged to the priest of Dionysus, Eleutherius; this seat, marble like the others, is distinguished by the delicacy of its bas-relief which, although classical in style, displays oriental inspiration, recalling the Asian origins of Dionysus.

On the front band the inscribed dedication to the priest can be made out; on the frieze above are two heraldic lions back to back, and on either side two Arimaspians (legendary one-eyed inhabitants of Scythia, they disputed with the griffons over the possession of the gold dust in the river Arimaspis); on the back, two satyrs are carrying an enormous bunch of grapes; on the outer sides of the arms cupids are setting fighting cocks against each other. The names of the dignitaries for whom the other seats were reserved are inscribed upon them. These are mainly priests of various divinities (sacrificers, interpreters of the holy word or heralds), magistrates (archons, thesmothetes, strategoi, polemarchs) or benefactors.

Up the second staircase, to the r. of the central pillar, some wider, lower steps led to an imperial lodge built for Hadrian.

The imperial statues, whose bases have partly survived, of great tragic and comic poets, musicians, statesmen, orators and benefactors of Athens, were scattered throughout the theatre. (The base of the statue of Menander, signed by Praxiteles, is situated on a corner of the stage, on the r. as you view it.)

The odeon of Pericles (plan IV, E-3) completed in 443 and considered the most beautiful concert hall of the Greek world, was burnt down in 86 BC by Sulla but rebuilt twenty years later by a king of Cappadocia. Here the dramas destined to be played in the theatre of Dionysus were re-enacted. Having almost completely disappeared, it can now only be mentioned for historical interest.

Above the theatre there is a cave (plan IV, 40 in E-3) where the *ex-voto* of victory were displayed and which, today, houses the chapel of the Panagila Chrysospiliotissa (Our Lady of the Golden Caves), the walls of which are covered with Byzantine frescoes, now darkened by the smoke of many candles. The choregic monument of Thrasyllus, erected in 320 BC, stands at the entrance to the cave.

Higher up, on the r., on the slope of the Acropolis, you can see an ancient, marble sundial.

THE ASCLEPIEION (plan IV, C-3). The sanctuary of Asclepius, the Aesculapius of the Romans, who was first worshipped in Athens after the peace of Nicias at the time of the Greater Mysteries of 420 BC, occupies a vast terrace at the foot of the steep slope of the Acropolis. There were two sanctuaries, the first of which was built after 420 by a rich Athenian and doubled in size by a second sanctuary in the mid-4th century AD when the worship of the healer-god was made official. Each one contained a temple with an altar, a portico, a dormitory where worshippers lay down while awaiting the nocturnal appearance of the god, a holy spring where the sick purified themselves by washing before entering the portico dormitories (see Aristophanes, *Plutus*, V. 621–747). First of all you must cross the site of the Asclepieion (6th century), now in ruins, the most remarkable part of which was a long portico built between a grotto with a natural spring, and a small elevated terrace with a hollow altar covered by a little temple (plan IV, 46 in C-3): this altar or bothros, for chthonian (earth) rites, is the simplest example in a series of structures of which the most perfect is the tholos at Epidaurus.

The Asclepieion of the 5th century, with its temple (plan IV, 46 in C-3) and its spring (plan IV, 47 in C-3) is more in ruins than its predecessor.

To the W of the Asclepieion, the sanctuaries listed by the Pausanias are no more: they disappeared at the time of the building of the Venetian or Turkish fortifications. Pausanias mentions a temple of Themis, a tomb of Hippolytus, sanctuaries of Ge Courotrophos and Demeter Chloe (plan IV, A-3) to which must be added the sanctuary of Aphrodite Pandemos (plan IV, B-2); following the tradition mentioned by Diodorus, this last temple was founded by Phaedrus on a site from which one could see Troezen.

THE PORTICO OF EUMENES (plan IV, B-4). All that remains of this vast portico built by Eumenes II, king of Pergamum (197–195) as a covered walk for the spectators from the theatre of Dionysus, are the foundations, below the Asclepieion.

•˙• THE ODEON OF HERODES ATTICUS (plan IV, A-3). This little theatre with 5,000 seats is one of the most impressive monuments in Athens, especially because of its excellent state of preservation and its situation at the foot of the Acropolis. It was built in AD 161 as a concert hall and theatre for use all year round.

The interior of the odeon of Herodes Atticus is in the style of the Roman theatre, with a stage structure rather ostentatiously decorated with columns, and recesses containing statues. According to the Greek sophist Philostratus, the odeon would have had a cedar wood ceiling but perhaps only above the stage. Generally, odeons were covered buildings, but in this case the absence of any evidence of roof support makes it doubtful that there was any kind of cover over the auditorium.

V – The Acropolis and the Aeropagus

The **Acropolis (plan II, C-3), the crowning glory of Athens and of the whole of Greek civilization, is a natural fortress forming a plateau that towers 512ft (156m) above sea-level and about 330ft (100m) above the lower city. This, the most remarkable collection of monuments that ancient Greek civilization ever produced, covers an area of a little less than 7 acres (3ha) and is enclosed by walls beyond the entrance to the Propylaea. It includes the Parthenon, the Erechtheum, the Propylaea, the temple of Athena Nike and several other places of worship, monuments that were formerly adorned with sculptures that were the work of the most famous artists. Certain of these works, which have so far escaped the ravages of time and of man, have been brought together in a noble museum within the Acropolis itself. This alone, however, has been insufficient and several drastic measures are now urgently required to combat the latest enemy to assail the Acropolis: pollution. Already, scaffolding can be seen springing up as the restoration of the monuments is undertaken; the interiors of the Parthenon, the Propylaea, the temple of Athena Nike and the Erechtheum are inaccessible to the public. The famous caryatids of the Erechtheum have been placed for safekeeping in the museum of the Acropolis, and from now on only copies will be seen in the Erechtheum (the installation of these began in October 1980). Moreover, a new museum of the Acropolis is planned and a joint French and Greek team have won the architectural competition for the right to construct the building.

THE MYCENAEAN ACROPOLIS. It seems that the Mycenaean Acropolis was inhabited from the end of the Neolithic age (the middle of the 3rd milennium BC). In the Mycenaean period, perhaps in the 15th century BC, a wall was built around the Acropolis when it was used as the residence of the Athenian kings. The main gate was certainly to the W as in the time of Pericles, but there was a secondary entrance in the N façade in a tower, some traces of which have been found near the temple of Aphrodite of the Gardens. From this gate, an access ramp with a stairway (plan IV, Pelasgic stairway, in D-1) led to the royal palace, some remains of which have been uncovered near the Erechtheum. From this period there was certainly a postern installed in the NW wall, with steps cut into the rock leading to the Clepsydra spring (plan IV, A-2). A little after the Doric invasion, perhaps towards the end of the 13th century, the old wall, which was now considered to be too weak, was replaced by a wall of cyclopean design, of which several fragments have been found to the S of the Parthenon. To the W the principal access was defended by an advance bastion, the remains of which were found in the upper crepidoma (base) of the temple of Athena Nike. This new wall did not have a secondary gate, but an underground stairway was built near the N side (plan IV, ancient stairway, B-1) to provide access to a grotto that was continually supplied with water, even in summer. This cyclopean wall, known as the Pelasgikon or Pelargikon, was mentioned by the ancient writers from Hecataeus, quoted by Herodotus, to Pausanias.

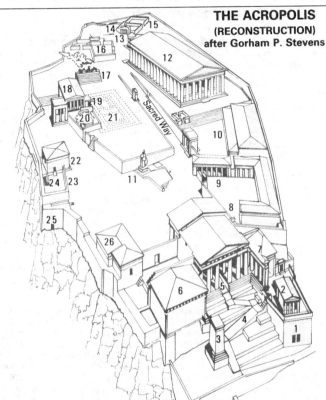

**THE ACROPOLIS
(RECONSTRUCTION)
after Gorham P. Stevens**

Sacred Way

1 Pirgos (bastion) of the temple of Athena Nike
2 Temple of Athena Nike
3 Pedestal of the Agrippa monument
4 Access ramp to the Propylaea
5 Propylaea
6 Propylaea (N. wing)
7 Propylaea (S. wing)
8 Temenos of Artemis Brauronia
9 Temenos of Athena Ergane
10 Chaltotheke
11 Athena Promachos
12 Parthenon
13 Temple of Rome and Augustus
14 Heroön of Pandion
15 Storage shed (?)
16 Altar of Zeus
17 Altar of Athena
18 Erechtheum
19 Cecropion
20 Pandroseion
21 Ancient temple of Athena
22 House of the Arrephoroi
23 Court for ball games
24 Mycenaean stairway (leading to a pool of water)
25 Stairway leading to the circular way (peripatos)
26 Accommodation, administrative offices, etc.

Later, the fortress of the Acropolis was called the Enneapylon (the wall with nine gates, a sacred number).

THE ACROPOLIS OF THE PEISISTRATIDS. Peisistratos and his sons planned the main entrance as a propylaea or monumental gate. After the fall of the Tyrants, in 510 BC, the Pelasgikon was demolished, except to the W, and declared accursed by a Delphic oracle. In 480 BC the Persians breached the defences of the Acropolis by scaling the steep slopes near the grotto of Aglaurus, on the N side. The sanctuary was sacked and set on fire. Fragments of the ancient temple of Athena, that of the Pisistratids, and of the old Parthenon, were reused in the wall that Themistocles had built after the Persians left. Later, Cimon, chief-statesman of Athens, continuing Themistocles' work, widened the plateau occupied by the Acropolis by moving the course of the wall further to the S. After 468 BC, he had the E and S walls built, on fine stepped courses of limestone.

Open: weekdays 08.00–19.30 between 1 April and 30 Sept.; 09.00–17.00 between 1 Oct. and 31 March; Sun 08.00–16.45 (16.30 in winter); these times cannot be guaranteed; entrance fee (Tel. 321–0219).

The Acropolis' highly complex collection of monuments has been divided into ten sections. You are advised to follow the route indicated, the N side and the Areopagus are treated as an eleventh section; visitors who have only an hour and a half to devote to the Acropolis should follow itineraries 1, 2, 3, 5, 7 and 9.

1 – FROM THE BEULÉ GATE TO THE PROPYLAEA. The modern access road to the plateau of the Acropolis follows the line of the last section of the Panathenaic Way.

The Beulé gate (plan IV, A–2), named after the archaeologist Ernest Beulé, who discovered it in 1853 below a Turkish bastion, is to the l. of the path. It was built by the Byzantines below a great Roman stairway dating from the end of the 2nd century or the beginning of the 3rd century AD. Among the fragments of sculptures lying near the towers of the Byzantine gate you will see three Venetian lions.

To the r. of the rocky level at the foot of the winding ramp leading to the entrance to the Propylaea, the crepidoma (stepped base) of the temple of Athena Nike (plan IV, B–2) with its two niches housing votive monuments, contains the remains of an Archaic temple, from the 6th century BC, and of a Mycenaean bastion built towards the end of the 13th century (?) to defend the main entrance to the Acropolis.

To the l. the pedestal of the monument of Agrippa, constructed from Hymettus marble, was without doubt built in the 2nd century BC to support the statue of a patron of Athens, perhaps a king of Pergamum (Asia Minor); later, this statue was replaced by that of another patron, Vipsanius Agrippa, the son-in-law of Augustus (63 BC–AD 14).

Near the rocky level, you may still see several steps of the monumental stairway built under Caligula or Claudius (1st century AD), later completed by the stairway referred to above between the Beulé gate and the rocky level. This stairway is vertically intersected in the centre by a paved and grooved track, 11ft (3.5m) wide, which formed an extension of the Sacred Way and allowed the sacrificial beasts and horsemen to reach the Propylaea. It is in this part of the Acropolis that the scene from *Lysistrata*, where Aristophanes shows the old men marching on the Acropolis, would have taken place.

A VICTORY OFFERING. At the level of the second bend of the winding ramp, a small stairway gives access to the platform of the bastion of the temple of Athena Nike. One of the two pilasters flanking this stairway is surmounted by a block of Hymettus stone, the upper surface of which bears traces of the hoofs of a bronze horse, smaller than life-size; on one surface there is a legible inscription, in letters from the 5th century BC, to three Athenian horsemen, Lacedaemonius, Xenophon and Pronapes, who consecrated this offering with the plunder taken from the enemy. This monument, commemorating the Euboean campaign, was signed by the sculptor Lycias, son of Myron. On the opposite side of this same block, a second inscription probably alludes to Germanicus (1st century AD).

2 - THE °PROPYLAEA (plan IV, B–2). Constructed from Pentelic marble from the crepidoma upwards (although blue Eleusinian marble was used to highlight certain architectural features) the Propylaea form a monumental entrance consisting of a central body and two wings. This entrance, which aroused the admiration of the ancients, was built by Mnesicles, under the government of Pericles, on the site of the Propylaea of Peisistratos (6th century BC) which itself occupied the site of the main entrance to the Mycenaean Acropolis.

AN ARCHITECTURAL FEAT. The Greeks called a simple vestibule before a sanctuary, a palace, a forum, etc., a propylaeum (propyle). The plural, propylaea, was applied to the more complex, monumental entrances as in Epidaurus, Corinth, Eleusis, etc. Designed to replace Peisistratos' entrance, the Propylaea of Pericles could only have been begun in 437 BC, after the Parthenon had been finished. This was because the building of the Parthenon occupied the best workers and the heavy materials used in its construction required free passage by the W ramp. The work lasted for five years; it was interrupted shortly before the Peloponnesian War, in 432 BC, and was never completed. The difficulty of Mnesicles' task lay in the differences in level in the central part, and in harmonizing this part of the monument with the wings, which were asymmetric, the S wing being much smaller than the N. The Propylaea cost 2,012 talents, more than 12 million gold sovereigns.

USED AS A POWDER STORE. Having been used as a bishop's palace in the 12th century AD, the building remained almost intact until the 13th century. It was then that the dukes of Athens installed their offices in the N wing, which was raised. In the 14th century, the Florentine, Nerio Acciaioli, set up his palace in the other parts of the monument and had a high square tower built above the S wing. Disaster struck, however, when the Turks converted the central vestibule into an arms depot and powder store. Lightning caused it to blow up in October

1656. After being restored, from 1909 onwards, the Propylaea became once more one of the jewels of the Acropolis.

The central part of the Propylaea forms a rectangle of sizeable proportions preceded to the W (on the outside) and followed to the E (on the inside) by a Doric portico. It is divided by a transverse wall including five gates. The central gate led to the Sacred Way and was used by the processions of the Panathenaea and the sacrificial beasts. The five gates had heavy wooden doors mentioned by Aristophanes. In the S part (to the r.) of the external portico, below the crepidoma, several blocks of poros (the alignment of which is different from that of the Propylaea of Mnesicles) have been identified by G.P. Stevens as belonging to the remains of the base of the quadriga (four-horse chariot) which Herodotus tells us stood before the entrance of the Acropolis, but which Pausanias saw near the famous statue of Athena Promachos. Between the antae of this same portico, the paving was carefully polished, doubtless to accommodate the bases of statues, among which G.P. Stevens thinks the statues of Hermes and of the Graces may be recognized, while C. Picard identifies those of the Dioscuri or 'twin sons of Zeus'.

IN PAUSANIAS' FOOTSTEPS. Following a study in which he traced Pausanias' footsteps, the American archaeologist G.P. Stevens is of the opinion that he has been able to locate in the inner portico the palace occupied by the tongueless lioness, sculpted by Amphicrates in honour of the courtesan Leaena (despite being tortured, she remained silent and refused to betray the killers of the Tyrant, Harmodius and Aristogeiton). Near this spot stood the statue of Aphrodite Calamis and perhaps that of Diotrephes, the work of Cresilas.

THE N WING OF THE PROPYLAEA. To the l. is the better preserved of the two wings. It housed the art gallery which contained a collection of pictures that must have been fixed to the wall of blue Eleusinian marble, still visible, or perhaps placed on easels.

The S wing of the Propylaea is much smaller, and in practice consists only of one room opening towards the Sacred Way and the temple of Athena Nike. Its design is highly original and is based principally on religious considerations: in particular, it was agreed that the sanctuary of Athena Nike should be protected. By various artifices Mnesicles succeeded in giving an appearance of symmetry to the Propylaea as it is first seen from the ramp.

To prevent the thousands of visitors from causing progressive wear to the marble, a wooden protective stairway has recently been installed on which one crosses the Propylaea. One has to be satisfied with admiring the Athena Nike temple from here, since access through the S wing of the Propylaea is now prohibited.

3-**ATHENA NIKE TEMPLE** (plan IV, B-2). This small monument, a triumph of the elegance of Hellenic architecture, still called the temple of Nike Apteros (wingless victory), was built by the architect Callicrates in the second half of the 5th century BC to replace the modest structures which had succeeded the sanctuary destroyed by the Persians in 480 BC. Built entirely from Pentelic marble, elevated at the top of a bastion, or pyrgos, it is one of the most remarkable features of the view of the Acropolis, calling attention to its main entrance with incomparable grace.

ATHENE, GODDESS OF VICTORY. The history of the site begins towards the end of the 13th century (?) with the construction of a strong Mycenaean bastion. Under the Pisistratids, around 550 BC, a place of worship was founded on the Mycenaean bastion and consecrated to Athene goddess of victory – an aspect of the goddess attested to by inscriptions. This was destroyed by the Persians in 480 BC. The repairs began in 478 BC with the construction of a second altar, later enlarged, but which originally must have been very modest.

THE TEMPLE OF CALLICRATES. In 448 BC, the Mycenaean bastion was covered in limestone coffering, this constituting the pyrgos which may be seen today. From this time on the construction of a marble temple was planned and was entrusted to Callicrates. The work, delayed by the construction of the Parthenon and of the Propylaea, only progressed after 432 BC. Once the Propylaea was constructed problems soon arose between Mnesicles and Callicrates, the latter being supported by priests of Athena Nike, regarding the installation of the S wing of the Propylaea on the temenos of the temple. A compromise was reached by the two architects and the platform of the pyrgos was lowered to the level of the Propylaea. The inauguration took place only after the peace of Nicias (421 BC). Between 421 and 415, according to G. Welter, or between 411 and 407, according to C. Picard, the splendid reliefs on the parapet surrounding the pyrgos were executed.

The temple (access prohibited) is made up of a single room (cella) housing the cult statue, a reproduction of an old wooden statue (xoanon) probably destroyed by the Persians when they sacked the Acropolis. Perhaps derived from a primitive trophy, the statue did not have the wings characteristic of Victories, which Athena Nike originally had. One explanation that has been offered is that the Athenians removed the wings of the Victory so that the goddess could not leave them. On the entablature, above the Ionic columns of the main façade and on the other three sides, there is a continuous frieze of reliefs; only the reliefs of the main front (E) and of the left-hand side (S) are originals. The others, the originals of which were taken to London by Lord Elgin, are, except for a few damaged fragments of poor quality, cement casts. All have deteriorated and the heads have disappeared, along with much else.

The Olympian Assembly may be seen on the E façade, with Zeus and Poseidon flanking Athena. The S and N sides (to the l. and r.) show combats between the Greeks and the Persians, while the W side shows a battle between Greeks and Boeotians, allies of the Persians at Plataea.

Pallas Athena occupies the place of honour on the best façade, above the entrance. She is represented as standing, shield in hand, between Zeus (to the r.) seated on his throne and Poseidon (to the l.) seated on a rock. To the l. may be seen a group comprising Peitho and Aphrodite, who is holding Eros with her right hand. Athena is present before the gods to plead the cause of the Greeks who are engaged in merciless combat, the events of which are sculpted on the other sides. To the r. Demeter (seated) and her daughter Persephone (standing) seem to have taken their places in the assembly. Before them a winged messenger, Iris, has come to tell them of the bitter combat represented on the N front. To the N and S the Greeks may be seen fighting against Orientals who can be identified by their quivers, small crescent-shaped shields and fine bow cases as in the bas-reliefs at Persepolis, or by their narrower tunics which have the sleeves drawn tight at the wrist. These battle scenes would have symbolized the victory of the Greeks over the Persians, a victory in which the sons of Pallas played a major part. The scenes give a historical character, highly unusual in Greek sculpture, to the reliefs. The W side shows another episode from the wars against the Persians, in which Greek warriors fought each other in a fratricidal struggle. Boeotians, Locrians, Malians and Thessalians came to reinforce the Persian army on the eve of the Battle of Plataea (479 BC) and fought at their side against the Greek alliance. The marble cornice that crowns the edge of the pyrgos of the temple of Athena Nike is surmounted by a marble parapet, the outer face of which was decorated with reliefs representing the winged Victories preparing to sacrifice a heifer in Athena's honour (some sections are in the museum of the Acropolis).

A TRAGIC ERROR. It was from the top of the bastion above the pyrgos that, according to legend, Aegeus, watching for the return of his son Theseus, glimpsed, by accident, a black sail rather than the white sail which was to proclaim his son's victory over the Minotaur. He threw himself on to the rocks below, thus fulfilling a primitive rite (*katakremnismos,* self-destruction by leaping from a high place), in the same way as Cecrops' daughters.

4 – FROM THE PROPYLAEA TO THE PARTHENON. Once you have crossed the Propylaea, you will see the majestic colonnade of the Parthenon, set firmly on its massive socle, and to the l. the elegant outlines of the Erechtheum.

The colossal statue of Athena Promachos previously stood between these two temples and to the r. there were several sanctuaries and the innumerable stelae and votive monuments listed by Pausanias. Their traces and the holes where they were embedded, as well as the grooves cut into the rock to make the path easier, follow the course of the Sacred Way (plan IV, B/C-2) which led from the Propylaea to the E façade of the Parthenon. This way has recently been given a cement covering on which visitors will walk from now on. This is yet another measure that has been taken to preserve the marble of the Acropolis. You will find it difficult to tear your eyes away from the Parthenon, especially as the sanctuaries that bordered the Sacred Way to the r. as far as the famous monument are now no more than a confusion of foundations and grooves in the rock. The details given below, then, may be of interest only to students of history and archaeology.

Immediately beyond the Propylaea was the temple of Athena Hygieia (plan IV, B-2) or Athena goddess of health, which once housed a group of several monuments. One of these was the bronze statue of the goddess, undoubtedly erected by the Athenians at the time of the plague in 429 BC. The semi-circular marble base of this statue remains, situated against the corner column of the Propylaea.

THE TEMENOS OF ARTEMIS BRAURONIA (plan IV, B-2) or Brauronion (who, imported from the deme of Brauron, was especially worshipped by women and young girls) was built in the first place by Cimon, and then modified at the time Mnesicles' Propylaea was built. Near the entrance, perhaps in the temple itself, stood the Trojan horse, a bronze offering mentioned by Aristophanes in his play *The Birds*, which was first performed in 414 BC, and later by Pausanias.

Opposite the entrance to the Brauronion stood a bronze quadriga (plan IV, B-2), consecrated by the Athenians after their victory in 506 BC over the Boeotians and the Chalcidians, and the famous statue of Athena Promachos (see page 248) which measured more than 29ft (9m). Set up around 454 BC, this vigilant guardian of Athens was the work of Phidias, the master craftsman of the Parthenon. Today the memory of these two monuments is preserved only by two foundations partly cut from the rock.

A QUADRIGA'S TRIBULATIONS. The bronze quadriga, erected with the tithe of the plunder taken during the course of the campaign of 506 BC in Euboea, was probably carried off or destroyed by the Persians in 480. The quadriga that the historian Herodotus saw after 450 BC near the Propylaea of Peisistratos was certainly a copy. It must have been moved to the Acropolis, where Pausanias saw it, when the Propylaea of Mnesicles was built.

ATHENA IN ARMS. The statue of Athena Promachos was, according to Demosthenes, constructed with the tithe of the plunder from the wars against the Medes (or, according to a second tradition, with the plunder from Marathon). It was taken to Constantinople, probably during the reign of Justinian. In 1203 the superstitious inhabitants of Constantinople smashed the statue because, as Nicetas Choniates reports, the goddess's extended hands were beckoning to the invaders from the West (the Franks).

The temple of Athena Ergane (that is, Athena the worker) (plan IV, B/C-2) received offerings dedicated by the workers and the women which they selected from the produce of their work, just as the peasants offered the first fruits of their harvest. We know, for example, that a potter called Bacchius offered the goddess the work that had earned him first prize in a competition. To the side of the temple was the Chalcotheke (plan IV, B/C-2) or bronze store which contained weapons and ship rams, products of the manufacturing industry of which Athena Ergane was the protector. The gallery of the

Chalcotheke, probably built around 450 BC, was enlarged after 432 by a portico, one end of which rests on rock steps cut opposite the Parthenon.

IN PAUSANIAS' FOOTSTEPS. In this area there were two important groups of sculptures mentioned by Pausanias. The first, attributed to Myron, represented Athena and Marsyas; the second, Theseus and the Minotaur. Athena was slapping the plump, elderly Marsyas for picking up the pipes that she had thrown down since, when she played, they spoiled the shape of her cheeks. In this part of the Acropolis, the base of a statue consecrated by Hermolycus, son of Diotrephes, and signed by Cresilas, was discovered. This socle has been identified as belonging to the statue, mentioned by Pausanias, of Diotrephes, the Athenian strategist referred to by Thucydides (especially VII, 29). The sculptor would have presented him as a warrior pierced with arrows.

Beyond the wall of Athena Ergane, the Sacred Way, traced on the rock, passes at the level of the seventh column of the Parthenon; to the r. is an inscription in the rock (plan IV, 3 in C–2) which is protected by a grille. This spot was consecrated to Ge Carpophoros (the fruit-bearing Earth); nearby stood a statue imploring Zeus to end the drought.

5 - ⋯THE PARTHENON. The Parthenon, the jewel in the crown of the Acropolis, bathed in Athena's glory, 'clothed in the majesty of centuries', today seems even more alive, 'with a living incorruptible breath, a never-ageing soul' (Plutarch). It was built between 447 and 432 BC. To its name is indissolubly linked that of Pericles, the brilliant spirit who dedicated the greatness of Athens to eternity, and that of Phidias, recognized by the ancients as one of the greatest sculptors of the 5th century, along with Myron and Polyclitus. The architect Ictinos, and the most famous artists of Athens, worked in association with Phidias.

Inscriptions refer to it as the great temple, or simply as the temple. The name 'Parthenon' (Virgins' chamber) originally referred to only part of the building. This name, which has been consecrated by common usage, was applied to the whole building only in the 4th century. The first record of the wider usage may be found in a speech made by Demosthenes in 355 BC. The name was understood to mean the temple of the Virgin or of Athena Parthenos, although this epithet was not really ritual, but rather poetic and popular. Those who built the Parthenon intended it to be an enlargement of the Hecatompedon, that is, a temple essentially dedicated to Athena Polias, and designed to house the statue of the goddess and her ever-increasing treasures. The new temple never supplanted the Erechtheum in the Athenians' veneration and was honoured above all as an architectural masterpiece. The precise role of the Parthenon in the celebration of the Panathenaea is not known.

THE HUNDRED-FOOT TEMPLE. Between 570 and 566 BC the first temple built on the present site of the Parthenon was constructed beside the ancient temple of Athena dating from the Geometric period. This temple was called the Hecatompedon, the building one hundred feet long. Important remains of the temple's decorations were found in the banks of the terrace constructed to the S of the Parthenon. The Hecatompedon must have been destroyed around 488 to make way for the old Parthenon. This sanctuary, however, had not been completed when the Persian invasion took place.

THE TEMPLE OF PERICLES. Shortly after coming to power, Pericles suggested that a temple of Pentelic marble be erected. Work began in 447 BC and continued until 432 BC. When the great Panathenaea took place in 438, Phidias' statue, Athena Parthenos, had been consecrated. Pericles directed and supervised the progress of the work as administrator, helped by Phidias, who acted as foreman. Under Phidias' orders were the architect Ictinus, the contractor Callicrates who built the Central Long Wall, and the most famous sculptors in Athens – some the rivals of Phidias, others his students.

A TEMPLE'S FORTUNES AND MISFORTUNES. The Parthenon survived intact until the decline of the Roman Empire. It was constantly enriched with new gifts: Alexander the Great presented gold-plated bronze shields after his victory at Granicus (334). In 304–303 Demetrius Poliorcetes committed the first desecration when he installed courtesans in the W part of the building, where the Athenian treasury was kept. In 298 he returned to besiege Athens. The city was defended by Lachares who fled with the temple's golden ornaments and the jewels from the statue. Respected by the Romans, the Parthenon was converted to a church in the 6th century. However, Theodosius II had already ordered that Phidias' statue of Athena Parthenos be taken to Constantinople. The crusaders reconsecrated the church in the Roman Catholic faith in 1208. The Turks transformed it into a mosque in 1460.

REMOVAL OF SEVERAL STONES WITH INSCRIPTIONS AND FIGURES. In 1687, during the siege conducted by Koenigsmark (fighting in the pay of Morosini), a mortar shell blew up the monument, which had been turned into a powder store by the Turks. The pillaging of the sculptures began. Lord Elgin, bearing an official permit to 'remove several blocks of stone with inscriptions and figures' took a dozen statues, 56 stones from the frieze and 15 metopes, during a mission on behalf of the Sublime Porte, probably saving them for posterity.

The Parthenon, the masterpiece of Greek architecture, was built entirely from Pentelic marble. The technique used shows it to be a peripteral Doric temple, i.e. octastyle (eight columns forming a façade), with two pediments. It measures, at the level of the stylobate, 230ft (69.51m) by 125ft (30.86m). The interior layout is very simple: two rooms, the naos or cella and the Parthenon itself, open to the E and W on a portico of six Doric columns. The naos was the sanctuary of the goddess, while the Parthenon, which was not used for worship, housed Athena's treasure. The columns of the external galleries supported an entablature consisting of an architrave, a Doric frieze and a cornice. The frieze, as in all such Doric temples, was decorated with triglyphs (ornaments with three incised vertical grooves) and sculpted metopes (square spaces with figures in relief alternating with the triglyphs). These elements were highlighted by the use of colour, something that seems scarcely imaginable since the lines of the majority of Greek temples, softly glowing with a warm patina, are so perfect that such treatment seems unworthy of them.

The moulding of the frieze was decorated with a brown Greek key pattern and alternating white and red leaves picked out with gold lines. Traces of blue paint have been identified in the grooves of the triglyphs and of the mutules, and red on the guttae. The bottoms of the metopes were probably red, and those of the pediments blue. The drapery and other details of the metopes were also painted. Although no trace of colour have been found on the columns and capitals, they were certainly painted. The interior walls of the naos must have been deep red, while the coffering of the ceilings was decorated with rosettes and leaves. Finally, gold-plated metal accessories were used, for example for the acroteria, and there were also offerings such as the 22 gold-plated bronze shields hung on the façade by Alexander the Great to commemorate his victory over the Persians at the battle of Granicus.

A close look at the pediment reveals a curious detail with regard to the construction: the marble adjustment course, above the last course of the limestone foundations, is not exactly horizontal but slightly parabolic. Greek marbles were suitable for the most delicate precision cutting, so that it was possible for the long horizontals of the stylobate and entablature to be subtly curved throughout their length, as in the pediment above. Each column leans very slightly towards the axis of the building, those at the corner being doubly canted and set in towards their neighbours so that they do not seem weaker as the light falls on them. The whole pediment has a slight tilt forward to redress the backward tilt of the columns. These artifices create the impression of beauty and equilibrium.

SCULPTURES OF THE DORIC FRIEZE. Of the 92 metopes very few remain in place and the majority have been defaced and are hardly recognizable. Those of the main façade, to the E facing the museum, depict the Battle of Gods and Giants, those on the S the struggle between the Lapiths and the Centaurs, those on the W facing the Propylaea, show an amazonomachy, or struggle between the Greeks and Amazons, and finally those on the N depict scenes from the Trojan War.

SCULPTURES ON THE PEDIMENTS. Athena, who sprang fully-armed from the head of her father Zeus, was glorified in marble sculptures on the pediments, works to which Phidias must have contributed. Unfortunately only disappointing fragments are now to be seen either at the original site or in the museum.

The birth of Athena, depicted on the E pediment, represented a measure of reassurance for the Athenians. Having inherited wisdom and reason from her divine father, the goddess, carrying a spear and her famous shield painted with the Gorgon's head, was the personification of rational courage, a guarantee of safety for the city.

Only a few heads remain in place at the two ends: two of the four horses of Helios (the Sun), whose chariot marked the appearance of day (to the l.), one of the horses of Selene's (the Moon's) chariot, which was disappearing in the far corner. The other horses from these groups have been defaced but their necks are still preserved. A horse's head, well preserved, and the reclining figure (Dionysus?) are only copies of originals now in the British Museum, together with the majority of the remaining pieces of this pediment.

The W pediment stressed Athena's pacific and civilizing vocation, depicting the famous dispute with Poseidon for the possession of Attica, ending in the triumph of Zeus' daughter, who presented the olive tree as a symbol of peace and also of wealth, to the city of Athens.

Only two figures remain in place on the l.: they possibly represent Cecrops and his daughter Aglaurus (this is the finest and most complete fragment remaining in Athens). In the opposite corner there is the elongated figure of a woman (allegorical representation of the spring Callirrhoe?).

SCULPTURES OF THE IONIC FRIEZE. This frieze, one of the most famous works of art in the world, is today 'shared' between the museum of the Acropolis (Room XIII) and the British Museum, apart from the W band, which is still in place. It lay under the external gallery. The composition began in the SW corner (the right-hand corner of the façade as seen from the Propylaea). From here two files of figures were depicted parading along each of the four sides of the building and converging towards the middle of the E side. The W frieze shows preparations for the procession's departure, with the gathering of the horsemen. To the l. a magistrate or a priest begins to organize the procession.

Then follows the cavalcade in well-ordered ranks along the N side (13 sections in the museum of the Acropolis), and the S (five sections in Athens), consisting of horsemen riding in a troop, chariots, thallophori (bearers of olive branches), those leading heifers to sacrifice, magistrates, musicians, basket bearers, etc. Little by little the movement subsides, although reappearing vigorously in places, as the procession approaches the E side. The procession terminates on the E side (two sections of which are in Athens) in a scene of apotheosis depicting the gods and divinities divided into two groups appearing to welcome the two branches of the procession.

INTERIOR OF THE TEMPLE. A temple without worshippers (tourists no longer have access to it and the figures of the great Panathenaea are now housed in the museum, if they are not in exile in London), the Parthenon is also a sanctuary without a divinity. The statue, Phidias' famous Athena Parthenos, is now no more than a memory poorly evoked by the very modest statue of Athena of Varvakeion, which you will perhaps see in the National Museum. The spot she 'inhabited' is, however, still there, painfully bare, calling for a great effort of the imagination.

The naos, or temple itself, opens to the E under a portico. It was known as the Hecatompedos naos, a sanctuary 100ft (30m) long, recalling the name of an Archaic temple, on the site of the present Parthenon, which was indeed 100ft (30m) long.

Two rows of Doric columns joined to the W end by a transverse colonnade, on which was superimposed a smaller colonnade – the imprints of the bases are still visible on the ground – divided the naos into three naves. The central nave formed a sort of chapel, lit only by the door. There, in the shadows, stood the statue of Athena Parthenos, on a spot marked on the ground. Consecrated in 438 BC, in the presence of Pericles, this statue of gold and ivory, sculpted or perhaps constructed by Phidias, stood 26 cubits high – 39ft (12m), or 49ft (15m) including the base.

A GODDESS WITH A DELICATE COMPLEXION. Pausanias tells us (V, II, 5) how the level of humidity in the cella was kept artificially high when necessary in order to protect the ivory of the great statue. Apparently a broad, shallow basin was installed in the cella, and evaporation from it maintained the humidity of the ambient atmosphere. The care of this fragile chryselephantine statue was entrusted to an Athenian priest's family.

IN SEARCH OF A LOST STATUE. The intrinsic value of the statue of Athena Parthenos was too high to allow it any chance of surviving, even as fragments, to our time. The statue may however be described with a high degree of accuracy thanks to the descriptions left by ancient travellers, and with the help of several copies. The most interesting copy seems to be that called Athena of Varvakeion (kept in the National Museum) despite the inferior workmanship (it should be noted that this copy is 500 years later than the original).

PORTRAIT OF A GODDESS. Phidias' Athena Parthenos stood clothed in an Attic peplos that fell to her feet. On her breast was an ivory Medusa's head. In her right hand, supported by a small column, she held a Victory, about six feet high. In the other hand she held a spear. At her feet, leaning against her left knee, was a shield decorated on both the inside and outside with reliefs. One side showed an amazonomachy in which Pericles and Phidias would, according to Dio Chrysostom, have been represented. The other side depicted, according to Pliny, a gigantomachy. Even the edge of the thick soles of the goddess' shoes had been decorated with a centauromachy and the base of the statue, about 5ft (1.5m) high, was decorated with reliefs depicting the birth of Pandora. The goddess wore a helmet, the crest of which bore a sphinx, while the sides were decorated with two griffins as well as winged horses.

A SACRILEGIOUS AUTOPSY. A rectangular hollow in the block of tufa on which the marble base of the statue originally stood held a vertical wooden post which provided the framework on which the various parts of the statue were assembled. Such artifices bring to mind the sarcastic comments of Lucian when he mocked the statues of some of the divinities: 'On the outside it is Poseidon, trident in hand; it is Zeus, shining in gold and ivory; but take a look inside; levers, wedges, iron bars, nails passing through the structure at various points, pegs, pitch, dust and many other unattractive things; that is what you will find'. Humour apart, it would be difficult to find a text that more accurately describes the internal construction of these colossal chryselephantine statues.

You must reconstruct in your mind's eye the wall that separated the goddess' chamber from the Parthenon itself, that is to say from the Virgin's chamber, a rectangular room at the rear of the building in which four Ionic columns supported the ceiling. The purpose of this room was unclear for a long time but it is now recognized that it must have been used to house the sacred treasure, before being used as the treasury of the state.

MARBLE VIRGINS. According to P. Graindor, the name of this room was essentially traditional, and referred to the design of primitive temples where a chamber was often reserved for temple servants who, like the Vestal Virgins in Rome, concerned themselves with divine service and had to be lodged in the chamber next to the divinity. According to the same author there came a time when these servants were replaced by marble effigies assembled near the temple in honour of the ancient tradition. This would explain the large number of korai (statues of young women) to be found in the vicinity of certain large temples, especially near the Parthenon. The famous korai exhibited in the museum of the Acropolis would have stood around the Hecatompedon. The custom of building, near the temple's cella, the lodgings of these servants who traditionally formed part of the sanctuary, would also have been retained.

6 - FROM THE PARTHENON TO THE MUSEUM OF THE ACROPOLIS. The short stretch between the Parthenon and the museum of the Acropolis is a kind of caesura between two powerful movements. You should therefore take advantage of it to admire the panoramic view over the S slope of the Acropolis, where the theatre of Dionysus stands, coiled, at your feet.

From the W façade of the Parthenon onwards you will notice blocks of Hymettus stone (plan IV, 14 in C-2) from the peristyle of the ancient temple of Athena and from the drums of the columns of the Archaic Parthenon. Following this you will see, in a ditch (plan IV, 17 in C-3), a fragment of the second supporting wall, of Hellenic design, of the old Parthenon. Further along, in a second ditch (plan IV, 19 in C-3) are the remains of the first supporting wall, of polygonal design. A few yards from here were found the traces of a 5th-century building (plan IV, 18 in C-3) which Phidias may have used as a workshop (he would have set his model up there and made several assembly trials for the statue of Athena Parthenos). In front of the museum, notice the drums of the unfinished columns of the old Parthenon lying on the ground.

7 - THE MUSEUM OF THE ACROPOLIS plan IV, D-2). The collections, all of which have come from the Acropolis, bring together all that archaeologists and centuries of violence have left to Greece and make this one of the great museums of Hellenic art.

Open: weekdays (summer) 08.00–19.15; Sun. 08.00–16.45; weekdays (winter) 09.00–17.00; Sun, 10.00–16.30; closed Tues.; entrance fee (the ticket to the Acropolis does not entitle you to visit the museum). (Tel. 323–6665).

The museum of the Acropolis provides a very clear summary of the history of Attic art from the Archaic period to its full Classical flowering, in the 5th century BC. One name and one work dominate: Phidias and the Ionic frieze of the Parthenon (Room VIII). Several other fine works are, however, included: a statue of a horseman (Room IV), attributed to a certain Phaedimus, one of the greatest sculptors of the Archaic period; a fine collection of korai (statues of young women), the finest collection of Attic sculpture from the 6th century BC; and a superb pediment from the ancient temple of Athena (Room V), another work from the Archaic period, which is exceptionally well represented in this museum.

OUR ROUTE. This is very simple: begin the visit with the room that opens to the left of the entrance hall. The rooms then follow in logical order.

Room I – Two groups of sculptures in particular draw the attention; one of them, against the left wall, is the most ancient pediment (1) of the Acropolis, in painted tufa, it dates from the beginning of the 6th century BC. It comes from a small temple or from a treasure-house. In the centre Heracles can be seen seizing a head of the Lernaean hydra to crush it with his club. The hydra's body stretches out in tortuous folds. To the l. Iolaus, the hero's charioteer, with one foot on the chariot, watches the combat. In the l. corner can be seen a crab, sent by Hera to help the hydra by pinching Heracles' heel. Traces of the original colouring may still be seen. The second group (4) depicts a lioness bringing down a bull. This is a fragment of a pediment of a temple from the beginning of the 6th century BC. Especially worth noticing among the other sculptures is a Gorgon's head (701), in Pentelic marble, which was from one of the acroteria of the ancient temple of Athena (second quarter of the 6th century). Traces of red paint may still be distinguished on the tongue, lips and mane.

In the passage between Rooms 1 and 2 you will see a serpent's head on the r. (41) and on the l. an owl, the bird of Athena and the emblem of Athens.

Room II – To the l. of the entrance, the central group (9) of an Archaic pediment dating from around 580 BC draws the attention; it represents the apotheosis of Heracles (recognizable on the r. by his headgear made from the hide of the Nemean lion); the gods of Olympus are welcoming the hero, who is escorted by Hermes. The king of the gods, Zeus, is seated on the throne. The fragment (55) placed to the r. of the entrance belongs to this pediment.

The highlight of this room is, without doubt, the Moschophorus (Calf Carrier) (624), an Archaic statue (around 570 BC) in Hymettus marble, depicting a sacrificer whose name, according to the inscription engraved on the base, is '(Rh)ombus'. This offering, which depicts the dedicant in a conventional fashion, is a work of admirable serenity.

Against the right-hand wall is the *pediment (35) decorated with a sculpted group, from the Archaic period (around 580–570 BC), depicting Heracles fighting Triton under the eyes of Nereus, the old man of the sea, a hybrid being with three human torsos ending in a dragon's tail. Notice the striking expressions on the faces and the numerous traces of colour.

Just to the r. of the pediment is a small votive column (dedicated to Athena) bearing a vertically engraved inscription in Archaic characters, giving the names of the artist who made the offering (Pythis epoiesen – Pythis made me), the dedicant (Epistelis anetheken – Epistelis set me here) and the goddess to whom it is dedicated (Athenaiai – to Athena). On either side of the pediment are the remains of Doric and Archaic Ionic architecture.

On the l. wall are also the remains of two other Archaic pediments in limestone from the Acropolis: two serpents (37 and 40), the struggle between Heracles and Triton (2), and in front of this last group a large votive sphinx in marble (630) dating from the middle of the 6th century. On either side of the pediments there are display cabinets containing Archaic terracotta figurines and plaques depicting offerings made to Athena in her sanctuary of the Acropolis. Be sure to look at the olive branch pediment (52), on the l. of the exit door, so called because of the olive branches carved on the l. The central structure was at one time identified as belonging to the primitive Erechtheum, but it is in fact a fountain, with a figure called a hydrophoros (water carrier). It thus serves as a backcloth to the myth of Troilus, a Trojan prince treacherously killed by Achilles, whose story inspired numerous paintings and vases, as well as a play by Sophocles (around 570–560).

Opposite the exit there is a kore (593 – from the beginning of the second quarter of the 6th century). This is the oldest of the Attic korai and is unfortunately headless. In her r. hand she holds a crown and in the l. a pomegranate, the sacred fruit of Demeter and Athena Nike, clasped to her breast. To the r. of the door are the remains of a votive quadriga (575–around 570).

Room III – Of special interest, in the left-hand part of the room, is an imposing group in tufa (3) showing a bull brought down and devoured by lions, of which only the feet remain. This work, which dates from 570–560 BC, decorated the pediment of an Archaic temple.

To the r. of the entrance there is a votive sphinx (632) with 'the tender expression of a young girl and a charming smile' (M. Brouskoi), dating from 540–530. Beyond the sphinx, on the r., are primitive types of korai (first half of the 6th century) of Ionian origin (from Samos or Naxos; 619 and 677) and a matching piece, the lower part of two statues of seated women (618 and 620, c.520); above, fragments of Doric architecture.

Room IV – In the entrance there is a goddess, probably Athena, depicted in bas-relief (581) in the style of the Ionian korai. She wears a smile for the tourist as well as for the two worshippers who, with their children, are bringing her an offering of a piglet.

To the l. is a small votive column (124) bearing a long inscription in Archaic characters, vertically engraved on three of the grooves (to the r. as you look at the column). Above is an Ionic column with traces of paint on the volutes. On the capital was a statue dedicated to the daugher of Zeus, that is Athena, by Alcimachus (information provided by the inscription).

In the first part of the room are four admirable works attributed by certain critics to a single Athenian sculptor, one of the greatest artists of the Archaic period, Phaidimus. The **horseman (590) in the corner to the r. of the entrance is the first known work of this artist. It dates from around 560 BC. The head is only a cast, the original, known as the Rampin head, being in the Louvre in Paris. This horseman formed part of a group of two equestrian portraits (the sons of Pisistratus?) placed opposite each other.

The *Peplos kore (679), next to the horseman, is the second work attributed to Phaidimus. Dating from around 530, it also shows great sensitivity in the execution of the face, framed by long, supple tresses. The eyes seem to reflect a deep inner mystery. The lines of the body, moulded by the folds of an austere Doric peplos, are also very delicate.

In the centre of this half of the room are two other sculptures attributed to the same hand; a remarkable running dog (143), executed around 520 BC, and a gargoyle in the shape of a lion's head (69), which decorated the cymatium of the temple of Athena in the time of the Pisistratids.

This part of the room also contains the upper part of the bust and head of an unusual kore (669) which has both ancient features (tiered wig, wide smile) and more recent ones (undulating folds of drapery that fall freely); it must date from around 500.

Also of interest: two other Archaic heads of women (617 and 654); the lower part of a statue of Athena (136 – around 500 BC), barefoot and very delicate, which stood on a column with a capital in the form of a chalice (very clear traces of paint; a Greek-key pattern on the upper band or abacus, small palm leaves on the echinus); a small, highly-coloured relief (702 – end of the 6th century) depicting a lively dance in which three women (perhaps the Three Graces) preceded by a piper, lead a young boy to the rhythm of the music; a magnificent Scythian or Persian horseman (606 – around 520 BC), unfortunately badly defaced but with the rich colour of the costume perfectly preserved (red, black and green) on the legs and reins; a relief (1343) that retains the torso and fine head of a bearded man wearing a petasus or broad-brimmed hat (probably the god Hermes; end of the 6th century); a kore (269 – around 550-540 BC) the upper part of which is only a cast, the original being in the museum of Lyon in France.

The second part of the room houses a fine ***collection of korai grouped according to style, which were discovered on the Acropolis, in a ditch, a true sacred cemetery where they had been buried after being desecrated by the Persians in 480 BC. These magnificent and beautiful works were executed, between 550 and 480, by sculptors highly influenced by Ionian art, which enjoyed a great vogue under the Pisistratids.

The nuances of construction, costume and style give each of the korai an individual personality. It is interesting to study the details of their dress, the colouring that warms the marble and the expressions on their faces. The lively eyes, the coloured lips smiling in either welcome or mockery, and the complexions, give such an intriguing illusion of life that it is fascinating to try to divine the reflection of an inner character in the faces. These figures are not portraits, however, and the expression that we attribute to them is often caused by a detail of execution in which the artist had no express intention. They are not specified as goddesses, or priestesses, nor as the effigies of pious donors. They are simply offerings consecrated in the form of young maidens (korai), and as impersonal and anonymous as the korai of the Erechtheum.

HELLENIC DIVERSITY REFLECTED. They are divided into several groups, which included primitive korai, works that imitated the ancient statues of worship (xoana), costumed in a sheath (as with the figures of the ancient xoana), with straight, tight-fitting drapery, or in the form of columns. At the exit of the second room there is a statue of the first type (593), and in the third room two korai formed like columns, called Samian (from Samos or Naxos; 619 and 677). The group of Ionian korai stands out for the remarkable refinement of the costumes and the faces, with their very oblique eyes and curved lips (682, 594, 673, 670 and 675). The group of pseudo-Ionian korai (672, 674, 683, 685), in which the Ionic style is no longer original, but reflected in the style of the Attic disciples of the Ionians, is followed by the group of Attic korai, which show Attic art regaining its independence and returning to its traditions of gravity and sobriety. The queen of the group, if not for beauty then for her ample proportions and her state of preservation, is kore 681, a work executed around 510 BC by the Athenian sculptor Antenor, who also produced the first group of the Tyrannicides.

The costume generally consists of a long tunic of linen, or a chiton, drawn tight at the waist. The upper part forms a bodice, puffed-out to varying degrees and pleated (671, 683). The lower part, gathered up in one hand, is held to the side of, or in front of, the body. The borders and the middle of the skirt are decorated with coloured embroidery, and the entire costume is sprinkled with embroidered motifs. The costume also includes the himation, or embroidered woollen outer garment flying over the left shoulder (594). The majority of the korai are holding in one hand an offering, fruit or a vase. In most cases the forearm was detachable, allowing the offerings to be changed as the dedicator wished.

At the back and in the middle of the central row, there is an extremely interesting *head of a kore (643), perhaps the finest in the collection. Her smile shrouds her face in mystery (*circa* 510 BC).

Kore 675 (same date), on the r., draws attention by the richness of her costume and the stylishness of her hair, which falls to her breast in long braids. Kore 682, at the back of this row, is of interest: of the Ionian series (end of the 6th century), she adds a particularly sophisticated costume to her slender contours. Kore 684, of the Attic type, sculpted between 500 and 480, concludes the Archaic series. The serenity of her expression offers a marked contrast to the affable appearance of the Ionian korai. The style of kore 670, in the apse, is a little affected, and betrays an oriental influence from Ionia (around 510 BC). Beside this kore, there is a statue of a marble seated Athena (625), the work of the Athenian sculptor Endoeus. This charming work dates from the last quarter of the 6th century.

Kore 680 (530-520), against the r. wall of the apse, appears, by the rich detail of her costume, to be quite exceptional in this series and offers a clear contrast with the relative sobriety of her neighbour's costume (on the other side of the passage leading to Room V), kore 671. This sobriety is a certain indication of the Attic style, as is the discreet smile that animates the face (around 520 BC).

Among the other pieces exhibited in Room IV is one of the finest equestrian statues (700) from the end of the 6th century, which stands in the second row. It is constructed from Pentelic marble. There are also three male figures which are unfortunately headless: a scribe seated in a life-like pose (629 - last quarter of the 6th century), a kouros (665 - third quarter of the 6th century) - the only one in the museum of the Acropolis - and a young man, perhaps Theseus (145 - around 520), full of movement. In the third row, the head of kore 696, behind 643, with headdress and wearing an expression at once gentle and sad, brings the Archaic series to an end (around 500 BC). Relief 1342, on the wall facing the entrance to Room V, depicts a person (man or woman?) mounting a chariot.

Room V - On either side of the steps leading to this room you will see two small fragmented marble reliefs from the end of the 6th century; to the l. an Athena Promachos (121), and to the r. a man and a horse (3706). But your attention will immediately be drawn by the impressive sculpted group from the ***E pediment of the ancient temple of Athena from the time of the Pisistratids (around 525 BC). The theme of this group is a gigantomachy or the Battle of Gods and Giants on Olympus, symbolizing the triumph of reason over brute force. Athena, in the centre, is a figure full of authority, brandishing her famous aegis, a superb shield (occasionally a breastplate) fringed with serpents, with which she inspired terror. The rest of the composition has been reduced to fragments, except for a wounded giant and some giants stretched out at each of the tips of the pediment.

To the r. of the entrance door as you approach from Room IV, you will see six fragments of Archaic pithoi (large wine jars – 68) attached to a stone support. The stamped reliefs with which these are decorated depict either rows of chariots with warriors and charioteers, or a scene from Komos (a sort of dance). Next the impressive marble **kore 681 may be the work of the Athenian sculptor Antenor (his signature is in the third line of the text, on the base exhibited to the l. of the statue). This work is very large (over 6ft/2m) but also very delicately executed (late 6th century BC). To the l. of the door there is a charming little statue of Nike, Victory (691), an Ionic work from the end of the 6th century. Kore 1360 follows, as large as that of Antenor, but in a very different style. This is certainly Doric, but its brilliance is marred by severe damage to the marble (late 6th century). In the left-hand part of the room, a raised alcove contains several pieces of sculpture and several cases displaying marbles and ceramics. The two large terrcotta Victories (6476 and 6476A) positioned on either side of the entrance may very probably date from the imperial Roman period, but their execution is based on an Attic prototype from the 5th century BC. The small kore 683, in the entrance to the alcove, is probably, with its large head supported by a squat and clumsy body, a Peloponnesian work of around 510.

The seven display cases at the back of the alcove contain an interesting selection of vases from different periods, principally Attic (Geometric, Archaic black-figure and Classical red-figure), but also Corinthian (recognizable by their lighter clay). The majority of these vases are from the sanctuary of the Nymph, on the S slope of the Acropolis, as well as a few votive plaques which are painted (pinakes) and a few terracotta figurines. Particularly interesting among the vases is, in case 6, a magnificent **lekythos 6471. This is an Attic work (found in a tomb some distance from the Acropolis) which depicts a scene in a gynaeceum with young women, a young man and Eros, the small winged cupid. The decoration of this vase is attributed to an Athenian painter, Aison, and is a characteristic example of the 'florid' style of the end of the 5th century BC.

In cases 3, 4 and 5 numerous fragments of Archaic sculpture found on the Acropolis are displayed. These are less famous than the preceding works, but are often fine and attractive in their own right. They include such works as the torso of a horseman (623), from around 520–510 BC, the head of a bearded man (621), the small fragmented kore (668) circa 500 BC, and the kore's head (641), which belongs to the Severe style, around 490 BC.

To the l. and r. of the passage to Room VI are exhibited two fine Archaic heads of korai (616 and 660) which are the last examples of this great period of Greek art on show in the museum of the Acropolis.

Room VI – The end of the tyranny of the Pisistratids (510) freed Athenian democracy from the yoke under which it had been kept for decades. This event marked the conclusion of the final phase of the Archaic period (750–500 approx.), a period of gestation which saw Athenian society change from a patriarchal structure to a fairly direct form of government. Art, after a slight delay of about a decade, also began to bear witness to this upheaval. The Archaic aesthetic, its canon, its conventions and its purely decorative conceptions were abandoned in favour of a freer form of art, marked by its gravity. It is from this gravity that the name 'Severe' comes, which was given to this art that presages the splendours of Classicism. This room, in fact, includes some of the finest examples of the Severe style, which covers the period from approximately 500 to 450 BC. This was the time of the wars against the Medes. To the l. of the entrance the **relief of the so-called pensive Athena (695) which depicts the goddess, her head inclined and resting on her lance, apparently contemplating a stele, or rather the milestone of a stadium, is an excellent example of the Severe style (around 460 BC).

This is followed by the *head of a young man (689), called the fair-haired Ephebe, the origin of which, Peloponnesian or Attic, is the subject of controversy, but which must have been sculpted around 485 BC and, from the same period, a *statue of a young boy (698) called the Ephebe of Critius (it is attributed to the workshop of this sculptor who, with Nesiotes, executed the group of the Tyrannicides which replaced that removed by the Persians in 480 BC).

Animal art also reflects the new aesthetic. An extraordinary marble *horse (697), the hindquarters of which are unfortunately damaged, bears witness to this.

Next to the horse stands the headless statue of a young man, which reveals a strong Ionian influence (around 490 BC). The relief displayed in the corner of the room (1332), depicts the figure, still extremely beautiful despite the damage, of a potter from the end of the 6th century, holding two goblets in his l. hand, about to offer them to Athena Ergane. To the l. may be read the end of the dedication, vertically inscribed, '*ios anethekenius erected me',* which was highlighted in red. It has been thought, not without reason, that this could be a statue of the great painter and potter Euphronius.

On the other side of the room you will see in succession: the head of a young man (699) which may be attributed to an artist of Phidias' workshop (around 450–440 BC); a small headless statue of Athena (140 – around 480–470 BC), recognizable by her aegis; a relief from the beginning of the 5th century depicting Athena struggling with a giant (120); the torso of a headless archer (599); an Attic work of 470–460, kore 688, called the kore of the Propylaea (after the place where she was found); the last of the series of the korai of the Acropolis (around 480); and her sister of about ten years older, kore 686, known as the sullen kore, consecrated to the goddess by a certain Euthydicus, son of Thaliarchus (this information is taken from the dedication engraved and painted on the base into which was fitted what is thought to be the lower part of the statue). The costume and the attitude of this kore are still influenced by Archaic sculpture, as is the subject, but it differs in some respects, most noticeably in the severity of the face. Notice also a painted terrracotta plaque (67) which must have formed part of a polyptych, or frieze, depicting a hoplite carrying a shield decorated with a satyr, the tail of which is still visible (end of the 6th century). Finally, there are two fragments of a Nike (690), perhaps dedicated to the memory of the Athenian polemarch Callimachus, killed in the battle of Marathon in 490 BC.

Room VII – It is a saddening experience to visit this room which mainly contains atrociously damaged, sometimes burnt, fragments of figures from the pediments of the Parthenon: decapitated torsos, severed heads, arms and legs are scattered around.

A *Metope (705) from the Doric frieze of the Parthenon, where a centaur is carrying off a Lapith woman, is the only work really worthy of note. The small-scale reproductions of the pediments are of little anecdotal interest, since the arrangement of the figures as well as their identification is extremely controversial.

Room VIII – In this room you will see some of the greatest masterpieces of sculpture of any period. They come from the Ionic frieze of the Parthenon and from the parapet of the temple of Athena Nike, majestic works of the Classical period. The ***Ionic frieze of the Parthenon, 525ft (160m) long in all, represented in the museum by only 20 plaques, shows the procession of the great Panathenaea, which took place every four years. The citizens of Athens, accompanied by the metics (resident aliens), with a procession of magistrates, sacrificers, musicians and young girls bearing offerings, with an escort of mounted ephebes, went to deliver to Athena the new sacred clothing (peplos) woven by the Arrephoroi, and a golden crown.

Begin the examination of the plaques of the Ionic frieze with the N band, the best represented, following the direction of the procession across the room to the far end, and return clockwise. On the other side of the entrance door you will see plaques from the E and S bands. A wall plan of the Parthenon shows clearly the positions of the different elements of the frieze. Finish the visit to this room with the sculptures of the Erechtheum and of the temple of Athena Nike.

The first four plaques (862, 861, 863 and 872) depict mounted ephebes hastening to rejoin the procession. On plaque 863 an official personage, turning backwards – a very striking break in the rhythm – seems to be exhorting them to regain their places quickly. Plaque 859, one of the finest in the museum, shows an apobate, i.e. an athlete who had to jump from a moving chariot and then remount.

After plaque 871, fragmentary, which depicts a chariot with its charioteer, plaque 874 shows an official standing in front of the team of a chariot which appears to be going in the wrong direction (an interesting variation of perspectives) and plaque 865 shows a group of six thallophoroi (former magistrates), the second of whom is wearing a crown.

The fragmentary plaque 876 is followed by plaque 875 which shows lyre players, admirably draped in their flowing robes, while plaque 864 depicts young men carrying hydria perhaps filled with wine to be used during the sacrificial rites. The beasts of sacrifice are the rams led by four youths on plaque 860 or the two heifers led by three men, on plaque 857. This plaque is one of the finest of the series and has been attributed to Phidias by some critics.

The two plaques of the E band, the most important, since it depicted the assembly of the gods of Olympus and the deified heroes, shows from l. to r. on plaque 856, Poseidon, Apollo and Artemis, and on plaque 877 three young girls, possibly Arrephoroi. The third plaque, the first in the series on this façade, is only a cast of the original, which may now be seen in the British Museum. The first, one of the finest of the frieze, is notable for the elegance of the draperies. This plaque was probably the work of Alcamenes, a student of Phidias.

The five following plaques (873, 869, 868, 867 and 866), belonging to the S band, depict actors in the second file of the procession of the Panathenaea.

On the upper part of the wall that has been placed across the room a fragment of the entablature of the Erechtheum has been set, and on this various elements of the frieze that decorated the monument have been reconstructed in blue Eleusinian Marble. Installed around 408–407 BC, this depicted the myth of the birth of Erichthonius. The decoration does not, however, seem to have been centred on a single subject, as in the Parthenon. The 15 or so small statues presented here are, unfortunately, badly damaged.

Below this there is a quotation from Plutarch's *Lives (Pericles*, 13, 6) to the glory of Phidias. You will find the inscribed stele (6509) of especial interest; it bears the text of a treaty or alliance between the Athenians and the Chalcidians of Euboea, concluded around 446–445 BC. The simple form of the letter, arranged stoichedon, i.e. in the form of columns that are regular in both the vertical and horizontal planes, produces a beautiful aesthetic effect.

The ***sculptures of the parapet of the temple of Athena Nike, only part of which are to be seen in the Acropolis Museum, were certainly the work of several artists – some critics think that the work of six artists can be identified – and were executed between 421 and 415, or more likely, between 411 and 407 BC.

In the centre of the W face of the temple, which was most highlighted due to the layout of the site, Athena was shown seated (989), receiving two converging groups of winged Victories, devoted to her worship, preparing trophies (994) and the sacrifice of a heifer (972). A Victory, the most famous of all, is removing her sandal (973) with an exquisitely natural movement: the contours of the breasts and of her thighs and the treatment of the costume are magnificent.

Room IX – This room now contains the four authentic, complete caryatids from the S portico of the Erechtheum. It is generally accepted that there were originally six; one taken at the beginning of the 19th century by Lord Elgin is to be found in the British Museum, the second is very badly damaged and extremely unlikely to be exhibited. For a description of these beautiful statues of young girls, without doubt produced in the workshop of the great Athenian sculptor Alcamenes, refer to the pages below concerning the Erechtheum.

A relief showing a trireme (1339), with nine naked rowers pulling on their oars with all their strength (end of 5th century BC), a colossal mask of Dionysus from the Imperial Roman period (6461) and two antefixae of Pentelic marble are exhibited on the wall opposite the caryatids. In this room you will also see a fragmentary relief from the 4th century (1334) and a marble stele (1335) from the end of the 5th century that bears a decree in honour of the Samians. Below this are effigies in relief of the protecting goddesses of Athens (Athena) and Samos (Hera).

Vestibule – This has inherited a number of pieces previously exhibited in Room IX. In the centre is the group, almost fragmentary, of Procne and Itys. Pausanias, who saw this near the Parthenon, attributed it to Alcamenes. In one hand Procne is holding the sword which she used to kill her son, an act of vengeance against her husband, who had raped her sister Philomela. This work must date from around 425 BC.

To the l. is the *portrait of Alexander the Great (1331), in Pentelic (1338) marble, which may be an original work by the sculptor Leochares, decorated with two groups of armed men performing a war dance. To the r. is the head of a philosopher (1313), very expressive; the possibility that it is an antique copy cannot be discounted. A base from the second half of the 4th century BC the most recent work exhibited in the museum, probably dates from the first half of the 5th century BC.

Finally, before leaving the museum, you will see a marble base (1326) from the end of the 4th or the beginning of the 3rd century BC. This bears a relief depicting an apobate, a subject already represented on the N frieze of the Parthenon. As you go through the exit, you will get the impression of being greeted by a marble owl (1347) from the beginning of the 5th century BC (Athena's bird and the symbol of the city of Athens).

8 – FROM THE ACROPOLIS MUSEUM TO THE ERECHTHEUM. Before turning towards the entrance of the Acropolis, visit the belvedere (plan IV, E–2), from where you have a superb view of Athens. The old quarter of Plaka lies at your feet in the shadow of the Acropolis, and you can look down on its narrow streets.

Between the museum and the Erechtheum is the site of the primitive city. The first inhabitants of Athens lived here around the palace and a sanctuary, in the Mycenaean period. Once the Acropolis was dedicated exclusively to the gods, the dwellings disappeared, giving way to places of worship.

Beyond a square area excavated in the rock can be seen a line of holes (plan IV, 8 in D-2) into which were fitted blocks of limestone, remains that have been identified as belonging to the foundations of a platform supporting the ceremonial table around which assembled those involved in the religious rites of cutting up the flesh of the sacrificial animals.

At the highest point of the Acropolis are foundation lines (plan IV, 9 in D-2) of polygonal design on walls of tufa. This was the temple of Zeus Polieus which consisted of an altar and a shed in which the bullocks for sacrifice were kept.

Pausanias tells us that two statues of Zeus Polieus stood near the altar. According to other authors, several sacrificial bullocks could wander freely around the altar. A sacrifice known as *bouphonia* – killing of the bullock – took place each year, at harvest time, in honour of Zeus Polieus. After an offering of grains or cakes of corn had been laid on a bronze altar-table, the bullocks were brought near, and the first animal to eat the corn was sacrificed. The beast was killed on the spot, skinned and its flesh probably cut up on the table, the foundations of which are referred to above. The animal's skin was then stuffed with straw and sewn up and the stuffed bullock was attached to a plough.

This scene signified the Athenians' gratitude towards the god who granted harvests.

THE ETERNAL SCAPEGOAT. According to a tradition that is doubtless as old as Demeter herself, in times when the slaughtering of domestic animals was strictly forbidden, those making sacrifices, and others who had taken part in the sacrifice, were judged guilty of murder and sacrilege. Obviously the humans were pardoned and, finally, only the instruments of sacrifice were condemned. They were thrown ceremoniously into the sea. This process was repeated annually. Aristophanes scoffed at these sacrificial celebrations, the mystical sense of which had been lost by his time.

About 40ft (12m) towards the Parthenon lie the remains of a large rectangular base which supported a small round temple, built after 27 BC by the Athenians and consecrated to Rome and Augustus (plan IV, D-2) deified. In the wall that encircled the Acropolis, the Pelasgic stairway, in actual fact from the Mycenaean period, served the original palace (plan IV, C/D-1). The foundations of this building, of pre-Archaic design in limestone from the Acropolis, have been discovered near the Erechtheum. Here, or under the Erechtheum itself, stood the house of Erechtheus mentioned in the *Iliad* (II, 546-551) and in the *Odyssey* (VII, 80-81) which housed the ancient sanctuary of Athena.

9 - ¨THE ERECHTHEUM (plan IV, C-1). The Erechtheum, temple, tomb and place where the Mysteries were celebrated, is a curious assembly of sanctuaries which, however, displays an apparent architectural unity. It seduces the visitor at first sight with the grace of its porticoes and its delicacy of decoration.

The monument has recently been restored. The original caryatids from the S portico, some of which are now in the museum of the Acropolis, have been replaced with casts (see above).

A PLACE OF WORSHIP WHERE ATHENS' PAST IS RELIVED. The Erechtheum was intimately bound up with the birth and growth of Athenian power. It was here that Athena and Poseidon disputed the title to the possession of Attica, Athena offering an olive tree, Poseidon causing a pool of salt water to spring forth with a stroke from his trident. This divine combat symbolized the more real struggle between Athens and Eleusis for supremacy in Attica. The Erechtheum was also the place where the heroes, usually legendary, who founded the city and confirmed its authority were venerated; Cecrops, Erechtheus, Pandrosus and Butes. The reminders of their existence and their legendary roles were still visible: Athena's olive tree, the traces left by Poseidon's trident stroke, sometimes considered to be the spot where Erechtheus was mortally wounded, Cecrops' tomb, Athena's ancient place of worship, etc., were all piously preserved and amalgamated in the present building. In 480 BC the temple was burnt down by the Persians. However, according to Pausanias, a new growth, one cubit high, sprang from the ashes of the sacred olive tree the very next day. The sanctuary was provisionally restored but after 421, during the peace of Nicias, its reconstruction in marble, part of Pericles' programme, was undertaken. The work was completed in 406, the same year that the temple of Athena, which had been provisionally rebuilt after the Persians left, was destroyed by fire.

THE TEMPLE THAT HOUSES THE OLD STATUE. Called 'the temple of Athena Polias', or 'the temple that houses the old statue', the guides in the Roman period knew it by the name of one of its parts, the Erechtheum, to distinguish it from the Parthenon. Converted to a church in the 7th century, and to a harem by the Turks in 1463, it was then to be subjected to the depredations of Lord Elgin and the sieges of the Acropolis during the War of Independence.

The reconstruction of the layout of this very complex building, constructed between 421 and 406 BC, is a difficult task. The main building is a complicated rectangle with three projecting porches. This irregular layout is rendered even more complex by a difference in levels both lengthways and breadthways which led to the division of the main construction into two chapels, one to the E (cella of Athena Polias; plan IV, 22 in C-1) and a second to the W (cella of Poseidon Erechtheus; plan IV, 23 in C-1).

 THE ···PORTICO OF THE KORAI, on the other hand, is a major work of Hellenic art. Sometimes also called the portico of the caryatids, it constitutes the most original motif of the Erechtheum and provides a sort of funeral canopy over the tomb of Cecrops, the serpent-king, one of the mythical founders of Athens. The six statues of young girls gracefully perform their function of supporting the canopy. Upright and clothed in long, white Ionian tunics they are crowned with a circular capital decorated with egg and dart moulding.

The figures are designed in such a way that the external lines remain vertical, while the inflected lines are thrown back towards the interior. The result is a rhythmic composition of alternating rigid and supple lines symbolic of the stability of the inert column and the fluidity of the figure. From the shaft, the load is transferred to the neck, which is reinforced by the mass of hair thrown backwards, and to the chest arched without apparent effort; from there it is diffused into the legs, which are straight or bent. This motif, of Ionian origin, is reminiscent of a characteristic feature of the architectural treasures of Cnidos and Siphnos, in Delphi. The six caryatids to be seen *in situ* are only casts: the originals are in Room IX of the Acropolis Museum.

This portico may have served as a tribune from which certain official personages (priestesses, Arrephoroi) could watch the procession and ceremonies of the Panathenaea, as well as masking the stairway that joined the Erechtheum to the terrace of the Acropolis.

The layout of the cella of Athena Polias was drastically altered when, in the 7th century, a Byzantine chapel was constructed. A transverse wall cut in two the huge chamber, which did not have the present floor. The first room was the chapel of Athena Polias containing an ancient idol in olive wood, said to have fallen from the sky, which, according to tradition, had been consecrated by Cecrops. Each year, with increasing splendour at the time of the great Panathenaea (every four years), the statue was clothed, in the primitive manner, in a new peplos woven by the Arrephoroi and the priestess of Athena.

The *N portico (facing that of the korai), consisting of an elegant Ionic colonnade, is one of the masterpieces of Attic art, with its architrave, its frieze of blue Eleusinian marble, its ceiling decorated with coffering and the rich ornamentation of its doorway. Its function was not, however, merely decorative, since it contained the piece of rock on which Zeus' thunderbolt had left traces. This imprint could be viewed through an opening in the stonework, enclosed in a small crypt. It is also certain that the N portico contained at least one altar, that of Zeus Hypatos, and, without doubt, that of Thyechous (he who makes the sacrifice).

The altar of Zeus Hypatos would have been situated near the opening in the stonework, while the altar of Thyechous, mentioned in the inscriptions, would have been placed near a second small hole. This hole would have been near the wall of the temple and through it would have been scattered the blood of the beasts sacrificed in honour of Erechtheus who, it was said, had been killed and buried in this spot. It is possible that this hero may at one time have acted as a soothsayer, like Amphiaraus, who had also been struck down by Zeus and buried in a crevice whence he spoke the oracles. This would explain the passage made in the foundations of the N wall of the temple, just wide enough to allow a man to reach the small crypt where the pipe used for the libations ended; hidden in this way, he could give the oracles to the people, who thought they were hearing the voice of Erechtheus.

In the immediate proximity of the portico was an unusual place of worship, enclosed by walls with tiered seating, reserved for ceremonies in which only certain privileged Athenian families could participate, along with the city's magistrates. The investiture of city officials consisted in their taking part in the cult of the Founding Heroes, or laying hands on the holy objects. At the back of the N portico were two doors, one of which, the lower, led to the Pandroseium and Athena's olive tree. The other, larger door served as an entrance to the cella of Erechtheus. This door is framed by an Ionic decoration famous for its beauty. The decoration is not, however, unmixed in style, a broken lintel having made restoration necessary around 27 BC.

THE SANCTUARY OF ERECHTHEUS (which probably housed the altars of Hephaestus and the hero Butes, as well as a crypt consisting of several compartments the use of which is unknown) was called the Hall of the Well. It owed its name to the fact that it housed, in the SW corner (at the back, to the r.) a hole, surrounded by a coping, constituting a well believed to contain the sea of Erechtheus, which sprang up under Poseidon's trident. According to Pausanias, the sound of waves could be heard in the well when the wind blew from the S. This was doubtless the work of priests hidden in the neighbouring crypt, or the effect of a current of air rushing in through the portico of the Korai. It has been suggested that the sea of Erechtheus, called 'Thalassa' in the earliest inscriptions, had a role to play relating to the worship of Aphrodite of the Gardens whose sanctuary was located on the N slope of the Acropolis. The Hall of the well gives access to the Pandroseium (plan IV, C-1), or sanctuary of Pandrosus, consisting of a courtyard containing Athena's olive tree (the present one is still somewhat small), an altar of Zeus Herkeios and possibly a chapel of Pandrosus, daughter of Cecrops. Little was in fact known about this sanctuary, which must have been a subdivision of the Erechtheum.

In the angle formed by the front wall of the Erechtheum and the crepidoma of the ancient temple of Athena stood the Cecropion, the funeral sanctuary of Cecrops, mythical king of Athens, often depicted in the form of a serpent.

10 – FROM THE ERECHTHEUM TO THE PROPYLAEA. The visit to the Erechtheum marks the end of the most spectacular section of the Acropolis. The path to the Propylaea through which you must pass before crossing the Propylaea to reach the hill of the Areopagus is marked out by a jumbled confusion of remains. The portico of the korai rests partly on the foundations of the ancient temple of Athena (plan IV, C-2), the ruins of which occupy a vast terrace between the Erechtheum and the Parthenon.

THE OLD TEMPLE. The first temple of Athena must have been built during the Geometric period on the site of the Mycenaean palace. In the last years of the tyranny of Peisistratos, it was replaced with a new sanctuary but around 570–566 BC a new temple, the famous Hecatompedon, was consecrated to Athena on the site now occupied by the Parthenon. From then on the Geometric sanctuary was given the name Archaios naos, to distinguish it from this second sanctuary. This name (Old Temple) was traditionally accepted, so that the temple built by Peisistratos, destroyed by the Persians in 480, inherited the name despite the fact that the Hecatompedon was half a century older. Partly rebuilt after Athens was sacked in 480, to house the relics and the statue from the old sanctuary, it became redundant when the Erechtheum was built. It was destroyed by fire in 406 BC and no longer marred the beauty of the Erechtheum, which now stood in glory opposite Pericles' Parthenon.

Among the ruins you will notice, protected by railings, two bases in limestone designed for wooden columns, as in the palaces at Mycenae and Tiryns, which belonged to the sanctuary-palace of Erechtheus.

Near the wall surrounding the Acropolis lie the ruins (plan IV, 26 in C–1) of a square building from the 5th century BC, which was possibly the living quarters of the Arrephoroi. The Arrephoroi were young girls of noble birth who were responsible, together with Athena's priestess, for weaving the sacred costume (peplos) which was solemnly carried each year to the sanctuary of the goddess. Near this house the Arrephoroi had a courtyard where, according to Plutarch, they could play games with a ball.

THE SECRET OF THE GARDENS OF APHRODITE. The night before the procession of the Panathenaea took place, two Arrephoroi performed a mysterious rite. Athena's priestess gave each of them a packet which they carried, on their heads, into the sanctuary of Aphrodite of the Gardens, situated on the N slope of the Acropolis, by way of a hidden stairway. After laying down their packets, they were given other, carefully wrapped, objects, which were to carry to the Acropolis. Many guesses have been made as to the nature of these objects. Perhaps they were phallic symbols and salted loaves to be thrown into the 'sea' of Poseidon or Erechtheus, to commemorate the birth of Aphrodite and to bring about her rebirth, bound up with the idea of the seasonal rebirth of nature and the harvests.

Two stairways are to be seen near the house of the Arrephoroi. One, situated towards the E (plan IV, 27 in B–1) allowed them to leave the Acropolis and reach an underground grotto that was continuously supplied with water. It must have been used from as early as the Mycenanean period. The second (plan IV, 23 in B–1) led perhaps to the circular path halfway up the slope of the Acropolis which gave access to the sanctuary of Aphrodite of the Gardens.

11 – THE AREOPAGUS AND THE N FLANK OF THE ACROPOLIS (plan II, B–3, C–3). The Areopagus, that is, the hill of Ares, provides a marvellous observation point from which to view the Propylaea of the Acropolis and the vast area of excavations of the Hellenic Agora. It is an elevated site, previously consecrated to Ares, the god of war (equated with Mars) and to the Furies, female spirits of justice and vengeance. The hill of Ares gave its name to the criminal court called the senate of the Areopagus, or the high council, where for a time murderers and arsonists were judged.

THE STONE OF OFFENCE AND THE STONE OF COMPLAINT. Gods and heroes, convicted of murder, appeared before this court. The Furies were given the name 'Eumenides' (the Kindly Ones) after the trial of the hero Orestes took place on the Areopagus in Aeschylus' tragedy of the same name. The high council, whose members were originally recruited from among the eupatrids (nobles), then, from the time of Solon, from among the archons who became members upon quitting office, was stripped of its political powers by Ephialtes and Pericles in 461 BC. However, it retained control over the constitution and morals. The courtesan Phryne, model for the sculptor Praxiteles, and the orator Demosthenes (324 BC) sat on the Stone of Offence, which served as a seat for the accused, the stone of Complaint being reserved for the plaintiff.

Only the rocky tiers and an isolated cube of rock, which may have been the altar of Athena Areia or one of the stones mentioned above, remain of the installations of the high council.

A SERMON IN THE DESERT. A modern bronze stele, set up at the S foot of the hill, recalls that it was on the Areopagus that the apostle Paul, in the middle of the 1st century AD, addressed the Athenians and invited them to be converted to the faith whose good news he was proclaiming (Acts 17:2-32). Prudently St Paul began by capturing his audience's attention, flattering them and saying that he was doing no more than bearing witness for a God whom they already honoured without knowing it. He introduced his sermon as follows: 'Ye men of Athens, I perceive that in all things ye are too superstitious. For as I passed by, and beheld your devotions, I found an altar with this inscription; "To the unknown God". Whom therefore ye ignorantly worship, him declare I unto you.' When he spoke of Christ returning from the dead, however, the rationalist spirit of the Athenians filled them with scepticism; some began to laugh while others declared they would hear more another time. When the apostle left Athens for Corinth, he had made few converts. Among them, however, was Dionysius, called 'the Areopagite' (the first Athenian convert to Christianity), still venerated today as the patron saint of the city of Athens.

Visitors with a thirst for detail will discover at the foot of the Areopagus the foundations of a basilica with three naves from the 16th century, consecrated to St Dionysius the Areopagite. There is no longer any trace, however, of the sanctuary of the goddesses of the Curse. To the NE a luxurious house from the 5th or 6th century AD has just been uncovered, laid out around a courtyard with an Ionic peristyle.

We recommend, even after a long and no doubt tiring visit, that you go down to the Agora by the Panathenaic Way. Along this path you will see, after the Acropolis, this other great symbol of Greek civilization. Agile visitors may like to wander along the N slope of the Acropolis, not to relive the exploits of those Persian warriors who scaled this slope, but to became acquainted with a part of the legendary and religious past of the Athenians. You will need special authorization for this, which is not always easy to obtain.

The path leading towards the Clepsydra spring and the N slope of the Acropolis begins below the Beulé gate. A rock stairway, no longer usable, gave access to the Clepsydra spring (plan IV, A-1/2), mentioned by Aristophanes (*Lysistrata*, 911), which was used from the Neolithic period onward. The oldest defences of this water supply, which was of paramount importance, and the structure enclosing the spring, date only from the 5th century BC, after the Persians had left. Further along two small grottoes open on a terrace which may be reached by means of badly damaged rock steps. The smaller (plan IV, 33 in B-1) was consecrated to Apollo Hypacraos (votive bas-reliefs) and the larger (plan IV, 34 in B-1) was undoubtedly the main place of worship of the sanctuary of Pan, introduced to Athens after the Battle of Marathon (490 BC), in gratitude for his assistance.

In front of the entrance a cylindrical fissure with a diameter of almost 6ft 6in (2m) corresponds to what is traditionally believed to be the tomb of Erechtheus, father of Creusa, who was killed by Zeus or Poseidon (Euripides, *Ion*, 291); the unfortunate Creusa, raped by Apollo, exposed her son Ion there. Ion was then taken by Hermes to Delphi. It is also in this retreat that Aristophanes (*Lysistrata*, 911) has Myrrhine, imprisoned on the Acropolis, grant her husband Cinesias a secret rendezvous.

From here you can reach a gate and a stairway (plan IV, 23 in B-1), which led to the Acropolis or to an underground gallery below a protruding section of the wall, which led to a grotto (plan IV, 36 in C-1) possibly part of the sanctuary of Aglaurus. Aglaurus was the daughter of Cecrops and priestess of Athena who threw herself down to this spot from the heights of the Acropolis. The sanctuary itself, the Aglaurium, where the ephebes came to take the oath, must have been an open-air place of worship.

The E part of the N slope of the Acropolis, in which numerous niches have been hollowed out, was mainly dedicated to Eros and Aphrodite. Their sanctuary is situated near the middle of the slope, not far from the traces of a Mycenaean entrance gate. Pausanias mentions the existence of a temple of Aphrodite of the Gardens, not the one where Alcamenes' famous statue, situated near the Ilissos, was found.

VI – The hill of the Muses, the Pnyx and the Agora

Walking along the hill of the Muses becomes, thanks to the Pnyx, a pilgrimage to the heart of Greek democracy, as well as providing a marvellous view of the two other privileged places in ancient Athenian life, the Acropolis and the Agora. As you walk around the latter, you can imagine the animation in the centre of the city, where political, commercial and religious life were mixed together.

WHERE TO PARK?

There is no problem at the foot of the hill of the Muses (plan II, B-4) where there is a large car park. The best place for the Agora is the entrance to the Avenue (Leoforos) Apostolou Pavlou (plan II, A-2/3); park in a side street; or leave your car at the foot of the hill of the Muses and walk to the Agora along the Panathenaic Way (plan II, B-3).

THE HILL OF THE MUSES (plan II, B-4). A small, shady road brings you on foot to the top of the hill, once called Mouseion and consecrated to the Muses.

THE MONUMENT OF PHILOPAPPUS (plan I, B-4), built by the Athenians between AD 114 and 116 in honour of a prince of the Commagene dynasty (Asia Minor) who was a benefactor of Athens, is in fact a tomb, occupying what is without doubt one of the most remarkable sites in the world. Caius Julius Antiochus Philopappus, whose statue is placed in the central niche, and was previously flanked by the effigies of two kings of Commagene, seems to be enjoying an intimate **view of the beauty of the Acropolis.

On the slopes of the gully between the hill of the Mouseion and that of the Pnyx, towards the hill of the Nymphs (plan I, A-3) and the Areopagus, lay a city of rock consisting of the quarters of Koile and Melite, enclosed in the 5th century BC by Themistocles' wall and the Long Walls. Over-populated during the Peloponnesian war, they were deserted the following century. Among the excavations in the rock is alleged to be the tomb of Cimon, near the church of Hagios Dimitris Lombardaris (plan II, A-4), and 55yds (50m) from this spot in the direction of the monument of Philopappus there is a house of rock which is called, according to a fanciful tradition, Socrates prison.

THE PNYX (plan II, A-3). This was the meeting place for the Assembly of the People, where the great orators from the 6th century to the first half of the 4th century BC spoke: Aristides, Themistocles, Pericles, Demosthenes, etc. This spot is of sentimental interest only for most visitors, especially as the beauty and exceptional position of the site, facing the Acropolis and the Agora, have led to its being chosen as the theatre for a 'son et lumière', the stage for which is the Acropolis.

The word *pnyx* means a place where one is cramped, squeezed one against another, and few images so forcefully convey the Athenians' passionate vocation for democracy. Towards the end of the 6th century BC, after the long tyranny of the Pisistratids, Cleisthenes created what was without doubt the most important legacy of Greek civilization: the government of the People. The Pnyx was altered at various times. It was enlarged towards the end of the 5th century, and then again in the second half of the 4th century, possibly towards the end of Lycurgus' active career (the period between 330 and 326 BC).

WEAKENING OF THE CIVIC SPIRIT. There came a time when a procedure similar to a roundup had to be used to bring together 5,000 citizens, the legal quorum for certain meetings. The citizens were literally pushed towards the Pnyx by Scythian archers who stretched red dyed string across the Agora and neighbouring streets. Those who bore traces of red dye were not granted the stipend accorded to participants in the assembly (at first two, then three obols and finally a drachma at the end of the 4th century).

From the large semi-circular terrace, at the foot of a small cliff where the meetings were held, you will enjoy a marvellous **view of the Acropolis. A projecting rocky cube at the foot of the cliff represents the tribune used by the orators from the 4th century onwards. Behind this tribune another rocky cube represents the altar of Zeus Agoraios, although this is not certain (cf. below), where the archons came to take the oath before entering office. A large niche and several smaller ones on the cliff-face belong to a sanctuary of the Roman period, dedicated to Zeus Hypistos (The Highest). The vast esplanade that you reach by climbing up behind the tribune has some ancient foundations or carvings in the rock, notably those of the altar of Zeus Agoraios, according to the American archaeologist H.A. Thompson, about 15ft (4 or 5m) from the tribune, and the base of the sundial placed there by the astronomer Meton in 433 or 432 BC (second base to the r. as you face away from the Pnyx). Finally, on the crest of the hill, are two porticoes of which only the grooves cut into the rock remain: the construction of these galleries began around 325 BC and was not finished, as can be seen by the fact that their foundations were covered by fortifications dating from the last quarter of the 4th century BC.

THE **AGORA (plan I, B--3 and plan II, A/B-2). The excavation site that you now reach is one of the most famous spots in Athens. Despite the fairly recent myrtle, cypress and olive plantations, the site may appear a little unprepossessing with its confusion of walls, too often no more than foundations. Do not be discouraged. Thanks to the remarkable excavations carried out by the American School of Archaeology and the erudite interpretations provided by archaeologists of all nationalities, these ruins will reveal their history to you. It is a fascinating one, providing as it does the framework of the life of the greatest city of Hellenic antiquity. There are two particular points of interest in the visit to the Agora: the temple of Hephaestus, incorrectly called the Theseum, and the museum installed in a portico of the Hellenistic period, which has been faithfully reconstructed.

Open: weekdays, 09.00–15.00; Sun. and holidays, 09.00–13.45 (these times cannot be guaranteed); entrance fee.

SUGGESTED ROUTE: Depending on when you make your visit, it is advisable to visit the museum during the hottest part of the day; about 1.30 p.m. After visiting the temple of Hephaestus, walk around the

Agora in a clockwise direction, beginning with the Tholos (see the plan of the Agora) in the SW corner.

THE **TEMPLE OF HEPHAESTUS** (plan A-2). This temple, built between 449 and 444 BC, is certainly the best preserved Greek sanctuary. It is however, obviously not as interesting as the Parthenon, or even the temple of Bassae, perhaps simply because of its situation. This Doric temple was consecrated to Hephaestus (the Roman god Vulcan), the god of metals, and not to Theseus. In accordance with ancient Greek tradition, Theseus, despite his illustrious forbears and his merits, would not have had the temple dedicated to him because, although a local hero, he had not had the good fortune to be admitted to Olympus as had Heracles, his famous rival in glory. The temple owes its traditional name of Theseum to the fact that most of the sculptures decorating it represented Theseus' exploits.

THE BIRTHPLACE OF THE ATHENIAN METAL INDUSTRY. Early on, the mound of the Agora (Kolonos Agoraios) was occupied by metal-workers, especially bronze-founders. It was thus natural that the creator of metallurgy, Hephaestus, should be honoured at this spot. After a great deal of debate, archaeologists now agree that this building corresponds to the Hephaesteum mentioned by Pausanias. Hephaestus, god of industrial workers and ceramic craftsmen, was soon associated in Athenian worship with Athena, called Hephaesta, as protector of armourers and the industrial arts in general.

Built, according to the American archaeologist W.B. Dinsmoor, by the same unknown architect who built the temple of Ares, (or by Coroebus according to others) and discovered on the Agora, it was converted into a church dedicated to St George, undoubtedly at the beginning of the 5th century, and subsequently escaped destruction during the occupations by the Franks and the Turks.

A curious feature of the Hephaesteum was its surrounding garden in which probably grew pomegranate and myrtle trees, as well as vines, placed in the earthen pots, numerous examples of which have been discovered in holes hollowed out in the rock. The modern plantations that now encircle the temple thus form a link with the past.

The main façade, with six columns, was to the E, that is, on the side facing the Agora. The sculptures of the pediment are no longer to be seen, having been lost, as have those of the rear pediment with the exception of a few fragments now in the museum. You should not, however, miss the reliefs of the Doric frieze, which have, for the most part, been preserved.

As a result of the unusual design, only the metopes of the main façade, ten in number, and the first four metopes of the long sides, have been sculpted. The scenes are divided into two cycles: the works of Heracles on the metopes of the façade, and the exploits of Theseus, Heracles' Athenian emulator, on the metopes of the lateral wall.

THE METOPES OF THE FAÇADE. You will see, in succession, from l. to r., Heracles triumphing over the Nemean lion (1), Lerna's hydra (2), the hind of Mt Ceryneus (3), the wild boar of Erymanthus (4); then the hero is shown carrying off the tame mares of Diomedes, king of Thrace (5), subduing Cerberus, the fearsome guardian of Hades (6), in the company of Hippolyta, queen of the Amazons (7), competing at archery with Eurytus(?) (8), killing Geryon in order to steal his red oxen (9) and, finally, receiving the apples from the Hesperides (10).

N metopes (to the r.). From l. to r., the exploits of Theseus: vanquishing Procrustes (1), Cercyon (2) and Sciron (3), and killing the wild sow of Crommyon (4).

S metopes (to the l.). From r. to l., Theseus triumphing over the Minotaur (1), the bull of Marathon (2), the brigand Sinis (3) and the outlaw Periphetes (4).

You will then enter the place of worship (naos or cella) through a vestibule or pronaos. In this part of the temple a badly damaged frieze depicts a combat taking place before six seated divinities. The divinities are divided into two groups and occupy the centre of the composition. This is possibly the combat of Theseus and the Athenians against the Pallantids, giants who inhabited Mt Hymettos.

The probable location of bronze statues of Hephaestus and Athena, executed by Alcamenes between 421 and 415, at the back of the naos, is suggested by two piles of stone blocks. Other blocks, laid out along the sides, help the visitor to reconstruct the interior Doric colonnade, in two superimposed orders, which encircled the cella, except on the side opening to the vestibule, imitating the interior colonnade of the Parthenon. The vault was added when the temple was converted to a church.

Through a gate made in the back of the cella when the Christian sanctuary was constructed, you can reach the opisthodomos (enclosed section at the rear) where you will see a sculpted frieze of Parian marble. It depicts the combat of the Lapiths, aided by the Athenians, against the centaurs during the marriage festivities of Pirithous, a friend of Theseus. Theseus can be seen, in the middle of the group to the r., as a warrior armed with a large round shield, while Pirithous appears in the left-hand group, coming to the aid of Kaineus, who is threatened by two centaurs each brandishing a piece of rock.

From the terrace in front of the main façade of the temple of Hephaestus, there is a fine view of the whole Agora. This is an ideal place from which, with the aid of the plan, to identify the principal monuments, or to familiarize yourself a little with the history of this public place.

THE SACRED CENTRE OF CIVIC LIFE. The ancient Greeks thought that only a barbarian city could be without an agora. As a result all the Hellenic cities had one, but that of Athens was the largest and most famous. It was at the heart of the city's public life, the centre of the State's services, a place for business and the social, artistic and intellectual meeting place. It was even used for meetings of the Assembly of the People until the end of the 6th century. It was here that the first athletic competitions were held and, on the central orchestra, dramatic games took place with literary and dance competitions.

FROM SOLON TO CLEISTHENES. While the original Agora seems to have been situated just in front of the Acropolis, the area stretching out before your eyes as you look from the temple of Hephaestus was considered the city's most important zone around the beginning of the 6th century, in the time of Solon. The first public buildings and the first sanctuaries to be discovered date from this period. In the time of Cleisthenes, towards the end of the 6th century, after the fall of the tyrants, these were replaced by other, larger buildings.

AFTER THE PERSIANS. The destruction caused by the Persians, 480–479 BC, necessitated a vast programme of reconstruction, which entirely altered the appearance of the Agora. The work, attributed to Cimon and Pericles, was, however, long and costly. This was the Agora of Pericles' century, arbitrarily fixed as dating from 450 to about 350 BC. The period may, however, be extended until Lycurgus' financial administration (338–326 BC).

THE HELLENISTIC AND ROMAN AGORA. Great changes occurred during the Hellenistic period, in the course of which the Agora acquired the usual appearance of the great public squares of the Greek cities of Asia Minor. Several sovereigns of this region, such as Attalus II, king of Pergamum, showed their interest in and concern for the most illustrious Hellenic city, by participating in this rebuilding. During the Roman period, after the sacking of Athens by Sulla, in 86 BC, the Agora once again changed its appearance. It now became fairly crowded, considering that the central area, formerly free of any sizeable building, was now occupied by an immense odeon and a temple of Ares which was transferred stone by stone from the Roman Agora (plan II, C-2) or from the deme (administrative region) of Acharnae.

BURIAL AND ARCHAEOLOGICAL RESURRECTION. The Gothic invasion in AD 267, which led to the sacking of the city, marks the beginning of the end of the Agora, which was not even included within the city of Valerian. The Agora remained devastated for more than a century, but in 400 the ancient line of fortifications was re-established and various buildings rebuilt. From this period a gymnasium dates, possibly the University of Athens, of which there survives the portico of the Giants. The closing of all schools of philosophy, on the orders of Justinian in AD 529, plunged Athens once more into inertia. Subsequently, this became no more than an oriental-style residential quarter; further construction caused it to disappear when in 1931 the American School of Classical Studies undertook a vast programme of excavations, which is still unfinished.

THE THOLOS (plan B-3). This was a circular building, constructed around 470 BC on the site of a building destroyed by the Persians.

This acted as a centre for the presiding magistrates, or prytanis, 500 in number, who by rotating a third of their strength assured themselves of a permanent base and took their meals at the State's expense.

A SHORT-LIVED MAGISTRACY. The suspicious Athenian democracy had devised a system of government complex enough to protect itself against the over-ambitious. The institution of the body of prytaneis testifies to this preoccupation. Fifty prytaneis were drawn from each tribe or deme and for about a tenth of the year were responsible for carrying out the day-to-day affairs of the city, receiving ambassadors, etc., under the presidency of an epistates, appointed by drawing lots, who was the guardian of the seal and keys of the state treasury. The epistates' function was more ephemeral than the life of a rose since it lasted no more than one day.

THE SHADE OF THE CITY'S CENTRE. The Tholos had the attractive nickname of parasol (Skias). This name was given by the lexicographers of the 2nd century BC, no doubt because of the pyramidal shape of its roof. It played a role in the city's religious life, as shown by inscriptions. It housed the city's sacred treasury and seems to have been consecrated to Artemis Boulaia and to the Phosphoroi, feminine divinities mentioned in an inscription from the Imperial period, probably associated with Artemis in a common sanctuary.

HISTORY OF A GUARDROOM. Excavations have revealed that the Archaic prytaneum was built around the middle of the 6th century. It consisted principally of a place of worship and a collection of small rooms, including a kitchen, ovens, etc., around a central courtyard with porticoes. When, after the Persian invasion, the prytaneum was rebuilt in the form of a rotunda (tholos), the annex rooms, the kitchen, ovens, etc., were rebuilt, as well as the place of worship, right on top of the former prytaneum, which was marked by a monument consisting of two cylindrical stones. This tholos was destroyed in 86 BC by Sulla, then rebuilt and remained in use until the middle of the 5th century.

BOULEUTERION AND METROÖN (plan B-2). The bouleuterion, or senate house, and the Metroön, or sanctuary of the Mother of the Gods, are a group of almost totally ruined buildings that will be of interest only to enthusiastic archaeologists. The Bouleuterion was the meeting place of the Boule (the Senate), created by Solon and endowed with legislative, executive and occasionally judicial powers. Its members, of whom there were 500 from the time of Cleisthenes (508 BC), were selected by drawing lots, 50 from each tribe, from among the candidates put forward by each of the Attic demes. The senate, in its original form, dates from the end of the 5th century BC. The Metroön from the 2nd century BC was used to house the state archives, doubtless recorded on papyrus, parchment or wooden tablets, as well as public documents. A public slave was entrusted with the safe-keeping of these archives.

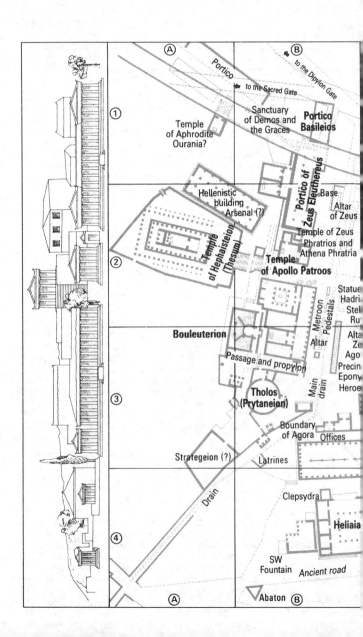

Portico

to the Dipylon Gate

to the Sacred Gate

Portico Basileios

① Temple of Aphrodite Ourania?

Sanctuary of Demos and the Graces

Portico of Zeus Eleutherius

Base

Altar of Zeus

Hellenistic building Arsenal (?)

Temple of Zeus Phratrios and Athena Phratria

② **Temple of Hephaisteion (Theseum)**

Temple of Apollo Patroos

Statue Hadri Stel Ru

Metroon Pedestals

Bouleuterion

Alta Ze Ago

Altar

Passage and propylon

Precin Epony Heroe

Main drain

Tholos (Prytaneion)

③

Boundary of Agora

Offices

Strategeion (?)

Latrines

Drain

Clepsydra

Heliaia

④

SW Fountain Ancient road

▽ Abaton Ⓑ

Ⓐ

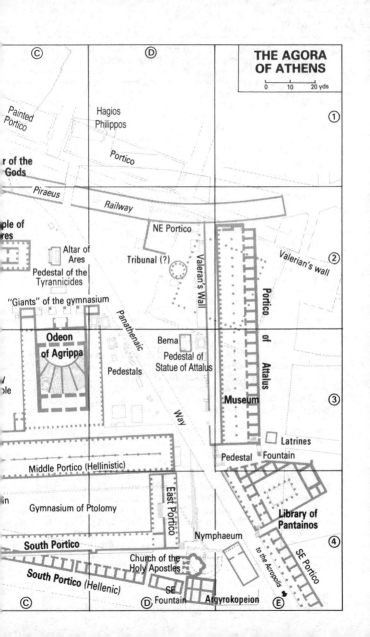

THE AGORA OF ATHENS

0   10   20 yds

① Painted Portico

Hagios Philippos

Portico

r of the Gods

Piraeus

Railway

NE Portico

Valerian's wall ②

ple of res

Altar of Ares

Pedestal of the Tyrannicides

Tribunal (?)

Valerian's Wall

Portico

"Giants" of the gymnasium

Odeon of Agrippa

Panathenaic

Bema

Pedestal of Statue of Attalus

of

Pedestals

Attalus

W ple

Way

Museum ③

Latrines

Pedestal   Fountain

Middle Portico (Hellenic)

Gymnasium of Ptolomy

East Portico

Library of Pantainos ④

in

Nymphaeum

SE Portico

South Portico

to the Acropolis

Church of the Holy Apostles

South Portico (Hellenic)

SE Fountain

Argyrokopeion

Ⓒ   Ⓓ   Ⓔ

THE PRICE OF BLOOD. The cult of the Mother of the Gods was introduced to Athens after a priest of this divinity was put to death in 430 BC. The Delphic oracle demanded, in reparation, that a sanctuary be consecrated to Cybele in the Bouleuterion. The present ruins lie on top of a first building, of primitive polygonal design, from the end of the 7th century, or the beginning of the 6th century. The modesty of this first building is a fairly accurate reflection of the difficulties experienced by Athenian democracy in the time of Solon. A second building also lies below the present ruins, dating from the time of the Pisistratids, of a more refined polygonal design. This also was certainly a bouleuterion.

A third senate house, called the old bouleuterion, was built around the end of the 6th century, without doubt at the time of Cleisthenes' reform, on the site of part of the Metroön. The building was destroyed before the temple of the Mother of the Gods was constructed in the 2nd century BC. The fourth senate, however, whose foundations may be distinguished at the foot of the mound of the Agora, was built after the end of the 5th century. The Metroön and the Bouleuterion were devastated during the sacking of Athens by Sulla, and then subsequently by the Heruli in AD 267, and then restored towards the end of the 4th century or at the beginning of the 5th century.

ENCLOSURE OF THE EPONYMOUS HEROES (plan B-3). Beyond a large sewer, dating from the end of the 5th century BC, is the enclosure of the Eponymous Heroes, built here around the middle of the 4th century BC. It was here that the Athenians honoured the protector of the ten tribes of Attica, legendary figures represented here by their statues. These protectors constituted to some degree the link that the traditionalist Athenian democracy had sought to establish between its ancestors and its political practices. This monument also served as an information centre. Laws, regulations, notices, eulogies, lists of new ephebes and conscription lists, etc. were attached to it, engraved on tablets, so that this information would reach the people.

THE TRIBAL HEROES. When Cleisthenes implemented his administrative reform in 508 BC, he gave to each of the ten tribes that together made up the population of Attica, the name of a hero (called eponymous from that time: he who gives his name). These heroes were recognized as the patron-protectors of the respective tribes. Before the construction of the enclosure, the remains of which may be seen today (traces of the limestone posts that encircled the pedestal on which the statues were placed in a row), the protecting heroes of Attica were venerated, probably from about 430 BC onwards, in the SW corner of the Agora. In this place recent excavations have revealed under the W end of the portico called the Centre portico, the foundations of a large building which encroached upon a street leading to the Pnyx by the N slope of the Areopagus.

THE ALTAR OF ZEUS AGORAIOS (plan B/C-3) was originally situated on the Pnyx, then transferred to the Agora when the Assembly of the People met in the theatre of Dionysus, the altar of Zeus Agoraios providing a solemn setting for the ceremony in which the archons took the oath before entering office. This oath had been imposed by Solon in the first half of the 6th century BC and perpetuated by tradition. The steps of the altar, of Pentelic marble, remain and have been returned to their original position. The crepidoma, in blocks of limestone, and a few remnants of the superstructures, decorated with casts, also remain.

THE STELE OF RUFUS (plan B/C-2). This stele, of which only the base remains, was erected in honour of Quintus Trebellius Rufus, of Toulouse, who was an archon and benefactor of Athens in about AD 90. A letter from the city of Toulouse and the province of Gallia Narbonensis was also engraved, expressing gratitude for the tribute paid to their compatriot. Beside this, the statue of Hadrian in Pentelic marble (2nd century AD) is found near the Metroön.

THE TEMPLE OF APOLLO PATROUS (plan B-2). Separated from the Metroön by a wide passage that connects the Agora to the monumental stairway leading to the Kolonon Agoraios, this sanctuary of Apollo (called Patrous because he was recognized as father of Ion, mythical ancestor of the Ionians, whose descendants the Athenians were considered to be) was built, in its final version, towards the end of the 4th century BC. Only the foundations remain. The sanctuary would have contained a statue of Apollo, presumed to be the work of Euphranor of Corinth, now in the museum of the Agora.

There were two temples on this site. The first, called Archaic, must have been built around the end of the first quarter of the 6th century BC. Destroyed by the Persians in 480-479 BC, it was situated beneath the S part of the temple built at the end of the 4th century and may have been consecrated to Apollo. The second temple was built towards the end of the 4th century above the Archaic temple. The portico leading to the E cella, on the side facing the Agora, was added in the 2nd century, in order to align the temple with the newly built Metroön.

THE TEMPLE OF ZEUS PHRATRIOS AND OF ATHENA PHRATRIA (plan B-2). Dating from the middle of the 4th century BC, this temple consisted of a simple, small chapel, or naos, where these protective divinities were worshipped. The names Phratrios and Phratria recalled the phratries, or ancestral subdivisions of the tribes, and the civic and fraternal character of the worship that took place in this sanctuary.

PORTICO OF ZEUS ELEUTHERIOS (plan B-1/2). The site is now indicated merely by an area of raised earth. The portico was built around 430 or after the peace of Nicias (421 BC). There was an annex behind, from the Roman period. In front lie the foundations of several monuments, notably an altar of Zeus Eleutherios.

STOA BASILEIOS (plan B-1). There remains practically nothing to be seen of what was one of the most famous buildings of the Agora. Adjacent to the portico of Zeus, the N end of which has been removed to make way for a section of the Athens-Piraeus railway, it is in fact situated on the far side of the railway lines in a sector recently excavated by the American School.

The Stoa Basileios, or royal portico, was the home of one of the three (annually) elected archons, the one holding the title archon-king, and housed the stelae on which the laws were engraved, amongst them those of Solon and of Draco. It was here that the archon-king publicly announced criminal accusations that came under his jurisdiction, especially trials involving impiety and homicide, judged by the court of the Areopagus. Socrates was summoned here by the archon-king, who accused him of impiety and of corrupting youth. The trial ended tragically for the philosopher, condemned to drink hemlock in 399 BC.

From this office the archon-king also prepared religious festivities, the celebration of the Mysteries of Eleusis and all the sacrifices recorded in the state calendar. The Stoa Basileios was in the Doric order, with a façade of eight columns, and was separated from the portico of Zeus Eleutherios by a narrow passage scarcely a yard wide. It was built around 530 BC, but underwent repairs and restoration on several occasions, notably after the Persian invasion and at the end of the 5th century. It was used as a public building until 267 when it was destroyed by the Heruli. The principal remains consist of the stylobate and the main façade. The slots in the façade must have held large marble stelae doubtless bearing inscriptions relating to particularly important regulations.

The royal portico stood, in the NE corner of the Agora, at the point where the Panathenaic Way entered the great public square of Athens, in the area containing the herms (see section on the Panathenaic Way). The remains of a double portico, in the Doric order, have been discovered, dating probably from the time of Augustus and mentioned by Pausanias. This portico sheltered pedestrians walking along a section of the Panathenaic Way from the Dipylon as well as those walking along another street running parallel to, and to the S of, this great artery.

Along the N side of the Agora, between the crossroads of the Panathenaic Way and the N end of the stoa of Attalus, on the other side of the railway line, lie the foundations of two enormous buildings from the time of Hadrian (2nd century AD), one of which, with an interior peristyle, was decorated with a profusion of marble.

ALTAR OF THE 12 GODS (plan C–1). Nothing of great interest remains of this famous altar, consecrated towards the end of the 6th century BC by the Pisistratids. This altar disappeared almost completely when the site of the Agora was broken up by the engineers who innocently but unfortunately laid the lines of the Piraeus railway across this venerable collection of ruins. This altar, used as a point from which to calculate distances from the capital, was known during the Roman period as the altar of Piety since it was a sacred place of refuge. The needy, supplicants, and foreigners requesting the right of refuge came here, among others. Only a corner of the peribolos, or fenced enclosure, remains. After the Pisistratids were overthrown, the Athenians enlarged the altar in order to make the tyrants' dedicatory inscription invisible.

THE TEMPLE OF ARES (plan C-2). The site of this temple is now marked only by an area of raised earth, but it is known to have been built around 435-420 BC in Achaea or on the site later occupied by the Roman Agora and to have been moved to the Hellenic Agora, stone by stone, towards the end of the 1st century BC.

The temple of Ares, of the Doric order, presents such similarities with the temple of Hephaestus that it was attributed to the same architect. At the time it was discovered there were too few remains to give a precise idea of its design. The appearance of the blocks that have been uncovered, and the style of such pieces of the superstructure as remain, only show that it was built in the second half of the 5th century BC. Destroyed in 267, its ruins were used in the Valerian wall, ten years later.

THE SOCLE OF THE TYRANNICIDES (plan C-2). The identification of this is open to debate and is certainly not the socle of the famous sculpted group which symbolized Liberty for the Athenians. The Tyrannicides were two Athenians, Harmodius and Aristogeiton, who in 514 BC assassinated the tyrant Hipparchus, one of Peisistratos' two sons.

THE TRIBULATIONS OF A SYMBOL. A first group in bronze, executed by Antenor about 506 BC, was erected on the Agora on the original orchestra. It was carried off by the Persians during the pillaging of Athens in 480-479 BC. A second group in bronze, the work of Critius and his partner Nesiotes, known through a replica in the museum of Naples, was erected in 477 after the Persians had left. Later Alexander the Great, when he subjugated Persia, discovered the first group in one of the many treasure houses of the Achaemenids. Finally, this group was restored to the Athenians who placed it near the monument of Critius and Nesiotes. The Agora thus had two works on the same subject. According to Pausanias, these statues were moved from the centre of the Agora to a site near the temple of Ares when the odeon of Agrippa was built. Two fragments of the epigram inscribed on the base of a statue have been found near the temple of Ares.

THE ODEON OF AGRIPPA. (l. C-3). The entrance to this enormous ruin is marked by three colossal statues representing two tritons and a giant, on a massive pedestal. These three sculptures later formed the propylon of a gymnasium, built around AD 400, without doubt the most important building of the University of Athens.

This late Roman gymnasium succeeeded another very large one constructed at the end of the Hellenistic period, between 175 and 125 BC approx. It was built on the site of a sanctuary erected in celebration by the Athenians, of the repatriation of Theseus' remains after Cimon had conquered the island of Skyros in 475-474 BC. The foundation in the SE corner (D-4) was annexed to this Hellenistic gymnasium, after first being converted into a swimming pool. Later the building was further enlarged, around 15 BC, when Agrippa's odeon was built. This was a large conference hall built by Agrippa, one of Augustus' ministers. The library of Pantainos was also added (plan E-4), around AD 100. The three colossal statues were sculpted in the 2nd century AD to adorn the main façade of the odeon. Philostratus, who refers to the odeon as the Agrippeion, tells us that in the 2nd century it was used to hold the sophists' rhetoric classes. The entire gymnasium was devastated by the Heruli in AD 267 and was abandoned for a long period before being restored around AD 400. Justinian's edict, ordering all Athenian schools to close, was a blow from which the gymnasium did not recover.

Despite the general dilapidation of the odeon, the scale of the auditorium is striking. It consists of a single square chamber. The walls were 82ft (25m) high free from any kind of support on the interior, capable of holding about 1,000 students. Repairs carried out following the collapse of the roof, in the 2nd century, reduced the width to 57ft (17.5m).

Behind the odeon lie the foundation, in red conglomerate, of the central portico from the 2nd century BC which was also part of the Hellenistic gymnasium, as well as of the Roman. Its W end covered a street that was used from the Archaic period until the 2nd century BC. There was a building, the rectangular foundations of which may still be seen, encroaching on the street at the point where it reached the Agora. This was certainly an importantant building, probably the first enclosure of the Eponymous Heroes, built around 430 and systematically demolished towards the beginning of the 4th century BC (it was replaced by a second enclosure, opposite the Metroön).

As you walk along the portico towards the W (in the direction of the Theseum), you will notice on the r. a heap of blocks suggesting the layout of a temple called the SW temple, possibly Roman. At the end of the portico you will see, besides the foundations of what was certainly the first enclosure of the Eponymous Heroes (see above), the ruins of a building identified as offices. Two marble slabs were discovered there, doubtless used as standard measures for terracotta tiles of the Laconian type. One of them may still be seen *in situ*.

Among the workshops and stalls was one that possibly belonged to the cobbler Simon, with whom Socrates loved to talk at length.

Near the 'offices' you will see the spot where a secondary channel branches off from a large sewer and passes under the central portico. Notice also a milestone from the 6th century BC bearing the inscription 'I am the milestone of the Agora'.

HELIAI (plan B/C-4). This ruined building was where the People's Court deliberated. This was an institution which may be traced back to the 6th century BC, to the time of Solon. It dealt with virtually all cases, but not murder. The building was extremely large as, during the course of a trial, a court (of which there were several) could include up to 2,001 jurors or heliasts, drawn at random (see the kleroterion – machine for drawing lots – in the museum of the Agora): 600 from each tribe.

Originally the court met in the open air at sunrise (helios) from which it took its name. The building of the Heliaia, founded in the second quarter of the 6th century BC, originally consisted of a set of four stone benches. Around 490 BC, an enclosure with a propylon was erected, while an annex, on the site later to be occupied by the SW fountain (plan B–4), housed offices. These buildings disappeared at the end of the 5th century when the fountain was installed. Certain pieces of the S portico (plan C–4) originally formed an annex. In the second half of the 4th century BC, a peristyle courtyard was constructed in the interior of the Heliaia. The construction of the Hellenistic gymnasium drastically altered this whole section of the Agora. However, the Heliaia retained a certain degree of importance until its destruction in 86 BC by Sulla.

EXCAVATIONS ON THE W SLOPE OF THE ACROPOLIS. Beyond the Heliaia, the excavations on the W slope of the Acropolis will be of interest to the archaeological enthusiast. These excavations are a confusion of ruins uncovered by the German archaeologist Dörpfeld at the beginning of the 20th century and, more recently, by the German School in 1963 and 1964.

In this spot, tucked between the hill of the Acropolis and Apostolou Pavlou Avenue, lie the remains of a whole district of the ancient deme of Melite, served by a main road from the Agora. From the point where the old road seems to emerge from beneath the modern one you will see, to the l. at the foot of the Aeropagus, traces of a temple identified by Dörpfeld as the Dionysion in Limnai (in the marshes), the oldest temple consecrated to this god of Athens. Dionysus awoke once a year, on the 12th Anthesterion (end of February), at the time of the flower festivals and the mystical marriage of Dionysus to the wife of the archon-king; it housed a sacred wine press and the vat invented by Dionysus.

A little further from the old road, behind the temple, the Dionysian brotherhood of Iobacchoi (from the mystical call of the Bacchantes) erected their premises or Baccheion in the 2nd century AD.

S STOA (plan C–4). This is so ruined that it scarcely serves as a landmark to lead you back to the road, i.e. the Panathenaic Way. The final version was built before the middle of the 2nd century BC, and also formed part of the Hellenistic gymnasium. It was built with materials originally used in the construction of the Parabyston law court and replaced a portico from the last quarter of the 5th century BC. The Hellenic portico, facing in a different direction (see plan), would have served as a public refectory, each of the rooms being provided with a certain number of banqueting couches where the guests ate. The presence of such an establishment in this area was justified by the proximity of the Heliaia. On the other side of the road which ran along the rear of the Hellenic portico an abaton (holy place) has been found (plan B–4), dedicated to an unknown divinity and built towards the end of the 5th century BC. A small structure from the Archaic period (7th century BC) was incorporated, possibly the tomb of an Athenian hero:

CHURCH OF THE HOLY APOSTLES (plan D-4). This was built after the 11th century on the ruins of a Roman sanctuary of a nymph from the 2nd century AD, and contains remarkable Byzantine paintings. Behind the church notice the fountain to the SE, of which only the foundations remain. This was installed during the second half of the 6th century under the Pisistratids, and then altered in the 5th century.

ARGYROKOPEION (plan E-4). It was in this building, the mint of Athens, built towards the end of the 5th century BC, that the 'Owls of Laurium', the beautiful Athenian coins, were struck. These were masterpieces of ancient coinage, made with metal from the mines of Laurion, that 'source of money, a treasure held by the earth' (Aeschylus, *Persians*).

THE MONETARY SYSTEM. Imagine you are a foreigner recently arrived in Athens, towards the end of the 5th century BC, and not yet a metic, a resident alien (literally, 'he who lives with') – this term was not too pejorative when used by an Athenian. Having just come ashore at Piraeus, you are not yet aware of how the Athenian monetary system operates, but you are eager to visit the Agora, with its tradesmen's wooden stalls. Do not ask about the news, as most Athenians do, but try to remember that six obols make one drachma, i.e. 4.36g of silver of a good alloy (98.3 per cent fine silver), or that there are one obol, two obol (diobol) and three obol (triobol) coins as well as coins of one drachma, two (didrachma), four (tetradrachma) and ten drachmae (decadrachma). You will probably have no need to reckon in minas (100 drachma) and much less in talents (60 minas), unless you are eager to ransom one of your relatives, a prisoner of war, on sale at the slave auctions held on the Agora each new moon.

THE SE TEMPLE. This temple from the 1st century AD is of only limited interest. According to the American archaeologist M.H. Thompson it was partly built with materials taken from an unfinished Doric temple of Thoricus. On the other side of the Panathenaic Way a long suite of small rooms, only the ground-plan of which remains, indicates that this was a commercial arcade, with a portico, in line with the main façade of the library of Pantaenus (plan E-4), later addition to the gymnasium of Ptolemy. This was built around AD 100 by a certain Flavius Pantaenus, destroyed by the Heruli in 267 and partly covered by the 'Valerian' wall.

THE PANATHENAIC WAY (plan D/E-2/4). Still paved with large blocks laid in the Roman period, 2nd century AD, this is the most spectacular section of the Panathenaic Way, not because of the condition in which the buildings that border it have been preserved, but rather because of the presence of the Acropolis which forms the backdrop to which it leads.

SUGGESTIONS FOR A PANATHENAIC FRIEZE. As it led from the Kerameikos, the Panathenaic Way entered the Agora by the NW, between the royal portico and another. According to Harpocrates, a scholar from the 2nd century AD, the space between these two porticoes was chosen as the spot on which to erect herms (fragments of 19 of these pillars were discovered in 1970 opposite the royal portico). These herms were closely linked to the cavalry processions that took place during the Panathenaia between the Pompeion (the store for the equipment used in the processions) and the Acropolis, passing the Agora. It was near the herms that the phylarchs released the ephebes in the processions. Xenophon, the philosopher and writer who was one of the generals involved in the retreat of the Ten Thousand, while discussing the role of the cavalry in the processions suggested that the riders effect a complete circle of the Agora, starting from the herms, rendering homage to the divinities, before returning to the herms, whence they would continue towards the Eleusineum.

THE ASCENT TO THE ACROPOLIS. After crossing the sector of the herms, the Panathenaic Way passed near the altar of the twelve gods and the orchestra, a flat space for dancing, where the religious festivities, and in particular the Great Dionysia, were held. The Dionysia were later transferred to the sanctuary of Dionysus. The Way must have been situated to the N of Agrippa's odeon. After crossing the Agora diagonally, the Way climbed the Areopagus in a straight line to reach the entrance of the Acropolis. This section is bordered on the l. by the remains of the 'Valerian' wall, built ten years after Athens had been sacked by the Heruli (AD 267). On the r. lie the ruins of the Eleusineum, a temple consecrated to Demeter and Kore (Persephone), which was built during the first quarter of the 5th century BC.

THE MUSEUM OF THE AGORA (plan E–3). This is installed in the Stoa of Attalus, reconstructed by the American School of Archeology, on the same site as the stoa erected by Attalus II, king of Pergamum (Asia Minor), doubtless in memory of the time when he was a student in the New Academy of Athens, founded by the philosopher Carneades, who was his teacher.

Open: weekdays the same hours as the site; closed on Tues.; (Tel. 321-0185).

The museum houses sculptures and various antiquities discovered during excavations of the Hellenic Agora. It does not include any works of the highest quality, but some of its collections do cast light on certain aspects of Athenian public and private life which are both interesting and entertaining.

OUR ROUTE. Starting from the r. (S) end of the ground floor gallery, examine the sculptures displayed along the walls then, retracing your steps, those displayed in the spaces between the central columns. Then visit the museum's main room, which opens almost in the centre of the portico. Finally, if it is open, the upper gallery will prove of interest to lovers of detail.

Ground floor gallery – Of special interest: a statue of Apollo Patrous (S 2514), from the sacred part (cella or naos) of the temple of this name on the Agora; executed in the third quarter of the 4th century BC, it is attributed to Euphranor, a Corinthian painter and sculptor, but also author of a treatise on symmetry (now lost), who worked mainly in Athens; an Ionic capital (A 2973) bearing traces of paint (end of the 5th century BC); the base of the statue of the Iliad (I 6628) bearing the inscription 'I am the Iliad, who existed before and after Homer. I stand next to him who created me in his youth.' It may thus be deduced that on this base stood a female statue, the personification of the *Iliad*, next to another statue representing Homer. The fact that the inscription states that Homer composed the *Iliad* during his youth implies that the *Odyssey*, generally considered to have been composed by Homer during the last years of his life, must also have been placed next to the statue of the famous bard. Further on in fact you will see two statues, one identified as the Iliad, the other as the Odyssey (S 2038 and S 2039). This group must have stood in the principal room of the library of Pantaenus (2nd century AD).

To the l. of this statue there is a small room where you can learn about the amphorae and the production of, and trade in, wine in antiquity, between the 6th century BC and the 6th century AD. Many complete amphorae are exhibited and there is a display case devoted to the stamps often displayed on the handles (in particular in Rhodes and in Thasos: these were symbols or names of magistrates, or producers).

There is also a hermaic pillar (S 33) supporting Hermes holding the child Dionysus. This is a Roman copy, possibly of a group sculpted by Cephisodotus, a Greek artist of the 4th century BC, perhaps the father of Praxiteles. A statue, certainly of Aphrodite (S 1882), from the end of the 5th century BC, is similar in style to works assigned to Callimachus, a sculptor with a refined, detailed style, possibly owing to his work as an engraver, thought to have invented the Corinthian capital.

*Statue of a Nereid (S 182), in Parian marble, possibly sculpted (around 400 BC) by Timotheus, who worked in the temple of Asclepius in Epidaurus and participated, along with three other well-known sculptors, in the decoration of the tomb of the satrap of Caria, Mausolus, in Halicarnassus, one of the Seven Wonders of the World.

On the other side of the entrance door to the museum's main room there is a statue of a goddess (S 37) perhaps Aphrodite, in Pentelic marble, from the beginning of the 4th century BC. There is also a votive relief dedicated to Pan and to the nymphs (I 7154), from around 330 BC.

There are also fragments of sculptures from the temple of Hephaestus, notably a group of two statues (S 249; the Hesperides?) which without doubt decorated the top of the E pediment (around 420 BC), as well as fragments of reliefs probably from the frieze of the temple of Ares (around 430–420) and a relief with horsemen (I 7167) from the beginning of the 4th century BC. There is also the bust of a colossal female statue (S 2370) from the second half of the 4th century BC.

At the N end of the gallery there is a *winged Victory (S 312), a work from the beginning of the 4th century BC which constituted one of the acroteria of the portico of Zeus Eleutherios.

From the N end of the ground floor gallery return towards the entrance door to the main room, examining the sculptures displayed in the spaces between the central columns, paying particular attention to the following items:

Portrait of Herodotus (S 270) – Herodotus (484?–425? B.C.) was a Greek historian, a native of Halicarnassus in Asia Minor, whose work is of great importance for those studying the wars against the Persians. His work covered Greek society in the 5th century BC and the Achaemenid Persian empire; this statue is a Roman copy of a Hellenic original.

Statue of a nymph (S 1654), an adaptation of a model of Aphrodite created in the 5th century BC. It decorated a Roman sanctuary of the nymph from the 2nd century AD.

Head of Victory (S 2354), from the 2nd century AD, based on an original by Paeonius (5th century BC).

Main room – Of particular interest, following a series of display cases containing examples of ceramics from the Neolithic period, are the offerings from a rich Mycenaean tomb (case 5), which were discovered on the N slope of the Areopagus (14th century BC).

Case 12 – The firing test pieces found in an oven among the ruins of a potter's workshop from the beginning of the Proto-Geometric period (around 1000 BC) are among the museum's most interesting exhibits. These test pieces were used to calculate the ideal firing time. In an unnumbered case on the l., after cases 11 and 12, notice the ceramics from the Geometric period, in particular a scale model of a grain silo.

Case 18 – Ceramics from the Geometric period (900-700 BC). Notice a vase (P 4885), or more accurately an oenochoe, from the end of the 8th century. The body of the vase is decorated with scenes depicting a combat and the neck with a frieze of warriors. There are four holes in the body, into which were inserted two terracotta tubes. This was to allow the wine contained in the vase to cool more rapidly when it was placed in a container of cold water which then passed through the two tubes.

In an unnumbered case on the r. there is a clay mould (S 741) used to cast a bronze statue, probably an Apollo (6th century BC). The mould comprised three layers of clay applied over a wax model, which melted and ran out as the metal was cast. These fragments were found near the temple of Apollo.

Also on the r., on the shelf display, a kore's head (S 1071) in marble from the islands (beginning of the 5th century BC, the end of the Archaic period) and the head of a second kore (S 2476) in Parian marble and a head of Heracles (S 1259) in Pentelic marble, from the same period.

Case 27 – Notice here seven bronze ballot tablets, used at the time of the sessions of the Court of the Eleven (the parabyston), a court located on the site now occupied by the museum. The parabyston must have been built towards the end of the 5th century BC and rebuilt under Lycurgus when he was in charge of the public finances of Athens (338–326). This court dealt in particular with thieves taken *in flagrante delicto*. Notice a curious water clock, or clepsydra, of terracotta from the 5th century BC, of the type used in the Athenian courts of justice. These clocks were used to measure the time each party might plead before the court. Aristotle tells us that the flow of water was interrupted during the reading of the laws and the introduction of witnesses.

 After Case 27 there is a kleroterion (I 3697), a machine used in the allocation of public duties that were drawn by lots. Each candidate who fulfilled the conditions required by the law inserted a plaque bearing his name into one of the many numbered slots. To each slot corresponded a ball, also numbered. The public officials were thus designated according to the order in which the balls emerged. The machine displayed in this museum seems to have been used by the senate in the 3rd or 2nd century BC during the period of the Twelve Tribes.

In a small unnumbered case in the centre of the room there is a moulded *terracotta vase (P 1231) depicting a victorious athlete, which was probably consecrated to a divinity by the winner of an athletics competition. Executed without doubt in Attica, it dates from around 540 BC.

Case 30 – Collection of red-figure and black-figure pottery (6th and 5th centuries BC). This collection includes a fine perfume vase (alabaster; P 12628) attributed to the painter of Amasis, one of the best known artists of the middle of the 6th century BC. Notice also, two goblets (P 24114 and P 24110) attributed to the painter Epictetus, in addition to four goblets (P 23165, P 24102, P 24116, P 24115) which were certainly the work of an artist called the painter of Charias, around 500 BC. The second goblet shows a naked woman before an altar, throwing a crown into the flames in homage to Aphrodite or another divinity.

Case 32 – *Collection of painted vases. This collection includes a shallow drinking cup (P 24113) or kylix signed by the potter Gorgias from around 510–500 BC. The medallion depicts a young man, holding a hare and on one side of the exterior, Dionysus, a bacchante and two satyrs are depicted, and on the other, the combat between Achilles and Memnon.

A HOMERIC COMBAT. Memnon has transfixed Achilles' shield but his lance is stuck. Achilles is about to deliver the fatal blow to his antagonist with his lance. Behind Achilles stands Thetis, his mother, while behind the Ethiopian king is his mother Aurora, who has come to the Trojan's aid.

A goblet (P 24131) attributed to Epictetus bears a painting that depicts a woman leaving the bath and holding a pair of boots of supple leather (around 520-510 BC).

Beside this, in an unnumbered case, there is a vase (crater) executed by Exekias around 530 BC. The paintings depict, on one side, Heracles being admitted to Olympus, and on the other, the fight between the Greeks and the Trojans for the possession of Patroclus' body. The inscriptions provide the names of the characters.

In an unnumbered case on the l. there is an amphora in black-figure (P 1247) dating from the beginning of the period around 620-610 BC, which must have been turned and decorated by the painter of the Nessus vase which is exhibited in the National Museum in Athens. Notice also, in another unnumbered case to the l., a curious terracotta chair designed for a child.

In the centre of the room is a bronze Victory's head (around 430 BC) which was covered with gold leaf. The edges of the metal plates were disguised in the grooves (hollowed out at two separate times) as can be seen at certain points, especially on the neck, the nape of the neck, the forehead etc. The small metal protuberance that you will see at the top of the head was designed to hold locks of hair, separately cast, that formed a ponytail.

Case 37 – *Attic ceramics from the 6th to the 4th century BC, simply coated with a black slip that gives them a metallic appearance.

 Case 38 – The collection of fragments of glass is worth examining. They bear the names of several people who appeared, shortly before the second war against the Persians, before the Assemblies of Ostracism. This name was derived from the word *ostraka* (singular *ostrakon*) meaning 'potsherds'. Each of the members of these assemblies engraved on a fragment the name of the person he wanted to condemn to banishment during the sessions. The majority of the ostrakon exhibited here concerned the ostracisms of Aristides the Just, Themistocles, Callixenos, etc., which occurred in 482 BC.

A SUSPICIOUS DEMOCRACY. Ostracism was instituted in Athens by Cleisthenes after the end of the Tyranny of the Peisistratids and was in some measure designed to prevent the return of tyranny. It was a means of protection against those citizens judged by the city to be dangerous. Those whose influence was feared were sent away, as a rule for ten years. The ostracized person could choose his place of exile and his possessions were not confiscated. Ostracism, which doubtless was abused many times, was abandoned during the Peloponnesian war, Hyperbolus being the last victim in 417.

Case 42 – Coins, (gold, silver and bronze) of various periods. Cases 44 and 45: various ceramics from the Hellenistic period. Case 52: lamps from different periods.

In a display case in the centre of the room there is a *statuette of Apollo (BI 236). This is a small ivory replica of Praxiteles' Apollo Lykeios, probably dating from the 2nd century AD. The work in its present state is a miracle of reconstruction.

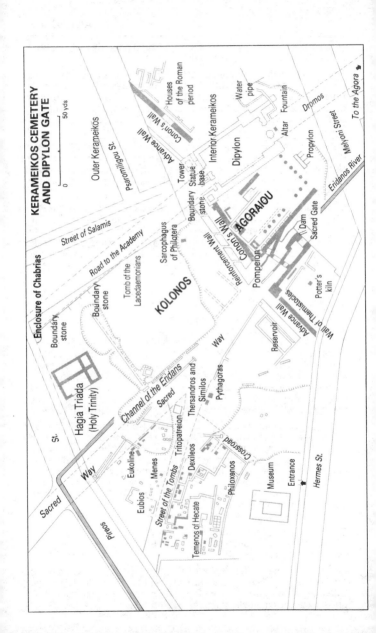

KERAMEIKOS CEMETERY AND DIPYLON GATE

0   50 yds

Outer Kerameikos

Psaromiligou St.

Houses of the Roman period

Advance Wall

Conon's Wall

Tower

Statue base

Interior Kerameikos

Boundary stone

Dipylon

Water pipe

Altar   Fountain

Propylon

Dromos

To the Agora

Melyoni Street

Eridanos River

AGORAIOU

Street of Salamis

Road to the Academy

Sarcophagus of Philotera

Boundary stone

Tomb of the Lacedaemonians

KOLONOS

Conon's Wall

Reinforcement Wall

Dam

Sacred Gate

Pompeion

Potter's kiln

Advance Wall

Wall of Themistocles

Enclosure of Chabrias

Boundary stone

Boundary stone

Hagia Triada (Holy Trinity)

St.

Channel of the Eridanos

Sacred

Way

Thersandros and Similos

Pythagoras

Way

Reservoir

Pireos

Sacred

Way

Eukoline

Menes

Tritopatreion

Dexileos

Philoxenos

Eubios

Street of the Tombs

Temenos of Hecate

Crossroad

Museum

Entrance

Hermes St.

At the back of the room to the r., there is a statue of a satyr (S 221) holding a syrinx (panpipe), executed in the 2nd century AD and based on a Hellenistic model.

First floor gallery – Besides the models of the Agora and the Acropolis, those who love detail may enjoy the stelae bearing inscriptions and some sculptures, dating in the main from the 2nd and 3rd centuries AD. Notice in particular the portraits of emperors.

VII – The Kerameikos cemetery (plan I, A–3)

About 44yds from the Agora, the traveller leaving Athens by the road that passes the Academy (where Plato became famous) crosses the city's principal cemetery, after passing through the Dipylon (double gate). Rich citizens and metics, famous men, and those the State wished to honour for their service and to hold up as an example, were all buried here; many had died at war.

One of the major preoccupations of the more fortunate, throughout all Greece, was that of providing an example for others, of being shown to passers-by and being present after death. This was true to such an extent that a sumptuary law had to be promulgated in 317 BC which imposed simplicity; cemeteries were being used to extend vanity even beyond death. Still, this attitude has filled Greek museums with stelae, highly elaborate funeral monuments, expressions of art which are often stereotypical, are sometimes remarkable. While some monuments have remained *in situ*, those that have been moved have been replaced with casts. The setting retains, with its new cypress plantation, an atmosphere of meditation.

Open: weekdays 09.00–15.00 (summer), 09.00–15.30 (winter); Sun. and public holidays 10.00–16.00; these times cannot be guaranteed; entrance fee.

Leave your visit to the museum as late as possible and head directly for the Dipylon gate, where the cemetery began, by descending the path to the r. after the entrance, that leads to the bottom of the basin in which the ruins are to be found.

∴ The first thing to notice is traces of the wall, built by Themistocles (479–478), then altered by Conon (394) and doubled by a wall built under Lycurgus (338–326). These fortifications extend along a 600ft (200m) front and are intersected by the Sacred gate on the r. and by the Dipylon gate on the l.

SACRED GATE. Situated at the exit of the Sacred Way this gate offers a mixture of stonework from various periods. Built by Themistocles, it consists of a long passage enclosed between two long walls and two corner towers (the one on the l. is partly Roman). It was divided into two by a longitudinal wall. The left-hand part served as an exit for a stream, the Eridanos, which descended from Lycabettus and was carried along an aqueduct. A transverse wall with a double gate defended the passage in Themistocles' time. This defence was doubled when a second wall was built 12yds (11m) further back by

Conon. As you head towards the Dipylon you will walk along a section of the wall built in polygonal design, erected in Conon's time. This was defended by two projecting square towers. On the city side the space between the two gates is taken up in the main by the foundations of the Pompeion.

DIPYLON. This double gate led to the road to the Academy which led to the Academos park at a distance of six stades (1,200yds/1,100m). The Dipylon included two identical doors, one on the side facing the country, and one on the city side. Built under Lycurgus at the same time as the doubling wall, it included an outer doorway divided into two openings by a pillar against which stands the marble base of a votive monument.

Go through the outer doorway and you will enter a courtyard enclosed between two thick walls from where the besieged defenders rained arrows down upon the assailants who had forced the first gate, as happened to the soldiers of Philip V of Macedon in 200 BC. The inner doorway, flanked as above by large square towers, also had two entrances; each was wide enough to allow two carriages to pass at the same time (the axle width of Greek chariots was 4ft 9ins/1.45m). On the city side you will see, before the central pillar, a round altar dedicated to Zeus Herkeios, Hermes and Acamas; and on the l. the remains of a fountain.

The Dipylon, which replaced the ancient gate of Thria, in the wall of Themistocles and Conon, opened on the city side on to a wide road (128ft/39m in the time of Sulla) which led towards the Agora and was bordered by porticoes. This avenue, called Dromos (street), crossed the Inner Kerameikos quarter and led to the great Athenian public square between the portico of Hermes and the royal portico.

POMPEION. To the r. after the inner gate there is a propylon (or monumental entrance) in ruins which led to the Pompeion, which was used to store the equipment required for the processions and was the point from which the processions of the Panathenaia left. Notice the traces left by chariot wheels. The building itself (only the foundations remain today) dates partly from the time of Hadrian (2nd century AD), but was built on the site of the Greek Pompeion from the 4th century BC. This place was in fact occupied from the 5th century BC by a building in which the chariots and other equipment used in the processions (*pompes* in Greek) were stored.

ROAD OF THE ACADEMY. Retrace your steps and follow the ancient road of the Academy, 131ft (40m) wide at this spot. You are now in the cemetery of the great Kerameikos, once celebrated for the beauty of its tombs and public monuments. Among those buried in this cemetery were Solon the Wise, Thrasybulus (who restored democracy after the Thirty Tyrants had been overthrown), and Pericles (the brilliant orator, fiery strategist and statesman, who wished to establish Athenian ascendancy through the grandeur of his achievements, such as the Parthenon, etc.). Famous orators such as Pericles, Lysias, Demosthenes and Hyperides pronounced funeral orations there during the ceremony of the Epitaphia, the national funeral rites bestowed upon warriors who died in battle.

This cemetery occupied the suburban territory called Outer Kerameikos, which itself owed its name to the potters and tilers who had their workshops in this quarter. From the 7th century BC the rule was established that the dead were to be buried outside the city walls, along the roads close to the gates. Thus the tombs were easily accessible and the worship of ancestors was facilitated. The most luxurious of these tombs, by attracting the attention of passers-by, perpetuated the memory of the famous, or of those who had been favoured by fortune while living. The installation of a cemetery in this region may be traced back to the 12th century BC. The tombs of this date belonged to the transition period called pre-Mycenaean. Around 1100 a new burial ritual, cremation, appeared. This reflected the arrival of the Doric peoples. The ceramics discovered in this cemetery dating from this period to the 8th century show the evolution of the Geometric style, illustrated by the famous vases of the Dipylon, a remarkable example of which is displayed in the National Museum.

Among the funeral monuments identified along the road of the Academy is one on the l. in which several Spartan officers who lent their assistance in overthrowing the Thirty Tyrants in 403 BC are buried. They included two generals, Chairon and Thibrachus, and a former champion in the Olympic Games, Lacrates.

'AVENUE OF THE TOMBS. Retrace your steps and follow the Sacred Way for 110yds (100m) before entering the avenue of the Tombs. In the corner formed by two roads was a sanctuary of the Tritopatreis, or remote Ancestors, which may date from the 5th century BC. In this avenue, pieces of land were granted to rich Athenian families and metics, from around 394. Enclosures on either side contain several monuments of various types; small chapels (naiskoi) with pediments, decorated with sculptures; stelae with palm-leaf ornamentation; painted brick sarcophagi; lekythoi or loutrophoroi; vases that were placed on the tombs of the unmarried; very simple cippi (monumental pots) on the tombs of slaves who were buried near their masters. The most luxurious monuments were of course erected before the decree of Demetrius of Phaleron which in 317 BC imposed simplicity. On the r. of the avenue, after the enclosure of the Ancestors, you will see some paving stones and stelae, one of which bears the name Hipparetas, granddaughter of Alcibiades (the funeral stone, in the form of an altar, must have been installed about the year 350).

About 22yds/20m to the r., the tomb of Eukolinus is decorated with a relief depicting the deceased holding a bird, with a dog at his feet, surrounded by two women and a man. Another 22yds/20m further on, as you continue to the l. in a direction parallel to the avenue, the monument of Aristion is decorated with a relief depicting the dead man also holding a bird, accompanied by his servant who is holding a strigil (a blade used by athletes to scrape oil off the body) and, above them, a weeping siren.

The most interesting funeral monuments on the r. are to be found in the plot belonging to Coroebus of Melitus (loutrophoroi, stelae, one of which is a facsimile of the stele of Hegeso in the National Museum).

As you return along the other side notice especially, in the plot of the Lysimachids, from the deme Acharnae (second half of the 4th century), the bas-relief in Hymettus marble of Charon, the ferryman who carried the souls of the dead across the river Styx or infernal river, a votive offering that depicted the funeral banquet of two couples in Hades (a Roman addition), a bitch and a lion (damaged), which formed the acroteria.

In the plot of Dionysus, from the deme Collytus, there is a small building (naiskos) that stands against a pillar bearing a magnificent bull in Pentelic marble.

The plot of the metic brothers Agathon and Sosicrates (around 350 BC) from Heraclea Pontica includes the small chapel of Agathon, the palm-leaf stelae of Agathon and Sosicrates and the touching bas-relief of Korallion who, in a farewell scene, is clinging to her husband's arm and holding out her hand to him.

Next comes the plot of Lysanias, from the deme of Thoricus, with a heroön in a circular arch that forms the memorial of Dexileos, the most famous of Lysanias' sons, who was killed in 394 at the age of twenty in the Corinthian wars. His name can be read on the public monument (where he was buried) erected in the Kerameikos in honour of the mounted soldiers killed in action at Corinth and Coronaea.

To the r. of the side street that ascends towards the museum is the plot of Macareus, poet or tragic actor, after the plot of Demetria and Pamphile (around 350 BC), with the fine bas-relief of Pamphile, which depicts the deceased seated near Demetria. It also includes the loutrophoros (a purely decorative vase here) of Hegetor, who died a bachelor.

 THE KERAMEIKOS MUSEUM. This houses the most interesting finds from the Kerameikos cemetery, except for a few to be found in the National Museum.

Open: weekdays 09.00–15.00 (summer); 09.00–15.30 (winter); Sun. and public holidays 10.00–16.30; closed Tues.; entrance fee. These times cannot be guaranteed. (Tel. 346–3552).

Ceramic works abound and the collections exhibited cover the whole period when the cemetery was in use. The Geometric period is very well represented, notably by a large terracotta amphora, in the style of the Dipylon. Notice especially the bas-relief of Dexileos, from the plot of Lysanias (avenue of the Tombs); a large relief of a priestess from the temple of Hecate holding a lustral hydria (water jar); a sphinx of the Archaic period that surmounted a funeral column and a marble lion (580 BC).

VIII-***The National Museum

Despite the wealth of ancient Greek art in the British Museum and the Louvre, to mention only two, the National Museum houses the richest collection in the world of sculptures and ceramics of Archaic, Classical and Hellenistic Greece. These are complemented by works from the Roman period and Neolithic, Cycladic and Mycenaean antiquities. An intelligent policy of decentralization has left the majority of the finds made on the most important archaeological sites in museums near where they were found. Thus a visit to the museums of Delphi and Olympus is essential. Crete, the cradle of a civilization that was unique until it was invaded, by the Achaeans first then by the Dorians, is not represented in the National Museum; in order to complete your study of the arts that flourished over the whole of present Greek territory you must visit Herakleion.

Address: 1, Tositsa Street, by 44, Patission Street (plan III, C-1; Tel. 821-7717).

Open: weekdays 08.00-18.00; Sun. 09.00-17.00; closed Tuesdays. Certain rooms are opened only in rotation; those housing the collection of ceramics (1st floor) are open 08.00 or 09.00-14.00 or 15.00. An extra charge must be paid to visit the rooms devoted to the discoveries of Thera (Santorini). Entrance is free on Sundays.

Photographs may be taken on payment of a fee which is higher if you use a tripod.

Guided tours: in French, English, German, Italian etc. (information available in the museum foyer).

THESEUS, THE PROTECTOR OF THE FIRST ATHENIAN MUSEUM. The first Greek museum was created in Aegina following independence in 1829, but its collections, the majority of which came from the temple of Aphaia, were transferred to Athens in 1837. The temple of Theseus (called more accurately, the temple of Hephaestus, although this was not known at the time) seemed a fitting place to bring together finds made in Greece and to install in 1834 the collections provisionally deposited in an Athenian church. The stream of discoveries continued and new premises had urgently to be found. In this way the library of Hadrian, the tower of the Winds, the Propylaea of the Acropolis, the University and a building called the Varvakeion became annexes of the main museum. This period of improvisation ended in 1874 when the collections were installed in a wing of the present buildings, neo-Hellenic in style, which were completed in 1869 (they were enlarged between 1935 and 1939, and again after the war). This work became urgent due to the extraordinary discoveries made by Greek archaeologists and foreign schools, the first of which was the French School of Athens, founded in 1846.

THE MUSEUM'S PRESENTATION. This is inconsistent: the Neolithic, Cycladic and Mycenaean rooms are remarkable and the arrangement of the collections of sculptures, where certain very important works are intelligently highlighted, is very satisfactory. The presentation of the majority of the rooms on the first floor (collections of vases) is old-fashioned, and there is clearly an excessive number of exhibits.

SUGGESTED ROUTE. Although this involves breaking the chronological order, we suggest that you visit the Mycenaean room first, then examine the Neolithic collections, followed by the Cycladic. You can then examine the sculptures from the Archaic to the Hellenistic period. In the rear of the museum you will see bronzes from the Archaic and Classical periods and Roman sculptures. Finally go up to the first floor and examine the collections of ceramics in chronological order, as well as the murals recently discovered in Thera (a temporary exhibition which may last some time). No inventory of the collections in the National Museum is given below, since we have preferred to indicate only the most interesting and significant works.

****Mycenaean room (4)** – Here you will see antiquities dating from the 16th to the 11th century BC from the palaces, houses and, above all, the tombs discovered in Mycenae, which has produced almost half the objects exhibited here. There are also exhibits from other areas and sites of the Peloponnese, such as Tiryns, Argos, Pylos (Nestor's palace), etc., and even Attica (Athens, Salamis, Thorikos, etc.). There are golden jewellery, bronze arms (swords, daggers), bronze, ivory and terracotta figurines, large bronze containers (dishes, cauldrons), some fragments of frescoes, sculptures, etc.

Beginning at the entrance door the cases are numbered in a clockwise direction around the room followed by the central cases. Among the exhibits there are some that deserve explanation or a special mention.

Case 2 – Notice especially the boar's tusks (6568) used to reinforce a helmet of the type described by Homer.

Case 26 (to the r. of the entrance door) contains three ivory heads (2468–2470) showing a helmeted warrior of the type described above.

In cases 3, 4 and 27 there is a splendid collection of three *daggers (394, 395 and 765) fashioned in bronze inlaid with gold, silver, electrum (alloy ¾ gold and ¼ silver) and niello (black metal inlaid in incised designs) from royal tombs of the Mycenaean acropolis (16th century BC). The famous golden funeral masks are from the same site and date. The most beautiful (624 in case 3) has been given the imaginative name of **Agamemnon's mask.

Case 27 contains a golden goblet (412) decorated on the rim with doves, called Nestor's goblet, and a magnificent silver rhyton (384) in the form of a bull's head with golden horns and a golden rose leaf on the forehead (16th century BC). The quantity of gold discovered in the tombs of Mycenae fully justifies the Homeric epithet 'polychrysos' (rich in gold).

Case 5 – Notice especially the perfume vase (8638) of rock crystal, in the shape of a duck (Mycenae; end of the 17th or beginning of the 16th century).

Case 8 contains two more beautiful bronze daggers damascened with gold, silver and niello inlay, found in Pylos (8339, depicting a seascape, and 8340, depicting bushes and running cats). There are also ten small male heads of gold leaf inlaid with niello (7842) which decorated a silver phial, similar to phial 2489 from Mycenae (case 26).

Opposite and in the centre, case 31 contains a group of ivory figures sculpted in the round, depicting two women (goddesses?) and a child (acropolis of Mycenae; beginning of the 13th century BC) and an ivory figurine (5897) of a woman seated on a rock (same date).

Case 9 contains tablets of terracotta from Pylos, inscribed in linear B (the name conventionally given to a hieroglyphic script of late Minoan Crete which M. Ventris deciphered in 1953. It was written in characters both syllabic and ideographic).

Opposite and in the centre, case 31 contains small-scale ivory models of shields, bilobate in the form of a figure '8' (7402–7405), which decorated furniture, boxes, etc., as well as earthenware vases from the Syrian or Phoenician coast, the same source as the ivory of the shields, which probably came from the valley of the Orontes. This case also contains other tablets with inscriptions in linear B.

Fragmentary frescoes from Tiryns precede cases 10 and 11, which contain vases.

Opposite and in the centre of the room, case 32 deserves special attention. It contains the two **golden goblets (1758–1759) from the domed tomb of Vaphio, near Sparta, which are masterpieces of Creto-Mycenaean toreutics (chased metalwork) and are decorated with scenes depicting the capturing and taming of the bull (15th century BC).

Case 14 (at the back of the room) contains fragments of **frescoes from Mycenae, in which two Geometric motifs flank the bust of a woman.

Case 15 contains finds from Tiryns, one of which is a golden **seal ring (6208) on which four spirits with lions' heads hold libation vases before a seated goddess (this work shows extraordinary delicacy; 15th century BC).

As you retrace your steps you will see, to the l. of case 20, the famous warriors' vase (1426), a large krater found in a house on the acropolis of Mycenae (around 1200 BC) showing seven armed men marching probably to war, saluted by a woman standing on the l.

To the r. of case 20 is a remarkable **head in painted limestone (4575) found on the acropolis of Mycenae and belonging to a sphinx. This is one of the rare examples of the great Mycenaean plastic art (13th century BC). Next to this head and to the l. of the passage leading to the room of the Cyclades is a sandstone funeral stele (3256) first engraved in the 16th century and then painted in the 13th century.

Case 21 contains a miniature fresco (2665) found in Mycenae and depicting what is doubtless a ritual procession with people wearing asses' heads; 14th century BC.

National Museum (ground floor)
1 Main entrance–2-3 Entrance hall (tickets, catalogues souvenirs, etc.)–4 Mycenaean Room–5 Neolithic Room–6 Art of the Cyclades–7-13 Archaic sculpture–14-15 Sculpture from beginning 5th c. BC–16-20 Classical sculpture, 5th c. BC–Garden: sarcophagi, giant statues, etc.–21 Hall of the Diadumenos (Roman copies of Classical works)–22 Epidaurus Room (sculptures, 4th c. BC)–23-4 Funeral monuments, 4th c. BC–25-7 Votive reliefs, 4th c. BC–28 Last funeral monuments and sculptures, 4th c. BC–29-30 Hellenistic sculpture–31 temporary exhibitions–32 Stathatos Collection–34 Temenos (votive reliefs)–36 Karapanos Collection–37 Small bronzes–38-9 Roman sculpture–40 Large bronzes–41-3 Roman sculpture 1st c. BC-3rd c. AD.

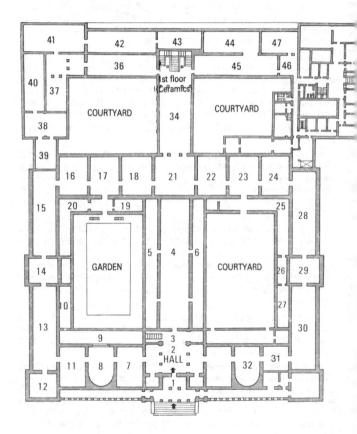

Neolithic room (5) – This contains stone and above all ceramic objects from the Neolithic (3500–2500 BC) and Chalcolithic (stone and bronze age; 2500–2000 BC) periods found in mainland Greece, especially in Thessalia (Sesklo, Dimini) and the islands in the north of the Aegean sea (Lemnos).

Room of the Cyclades (6) – Here are examples of prehistoric Cycladic art, i.e. of the Neolithic and Chalcolithic cultures of the Cyclades islands: idols from Naxos, Amorgos, Paros, etc. stylized in the form of 'violins' or rough-hewn silhouettes, representing especially the mother-goddess of the Cyclades. There is a *lyre player (3908) and a flute player (3910) in Parian marble (2400–2200 BC) from Amorgos, as well as the large idol (3978), which is of exceptional size, exhibited at the back of the room to the r. of the entrance.

Curious circular tools called *poeloi*, the purposes of which is not certain, were discovered on Syros and on Naxos (cases 56–58). The ceramics testify to the skill of the potters of the Cyclades in the 3rd and 2nd millennia BC: vases with a simple and varied incised linear decoration and later, ceramics decorated with dark geometric motifs painted on light grounds (Melos, Syros) or a beautiful ceramic piece decorated with human figures (Melos), or animal or vegetable forms (Melos), testifying to a clear Cretan influence.

In the section opposite the entrance you will see fragments of frescoes from Phylakopi, on Melos (fish).

Return to the entrance hall and enter on the r. the first room (7) of Archaic sculpture.

ARCHAIC SCULPTURE. The seven rooms that house the exhibition of Archaic Greek sculpture contain works of the highest quality, such as the colossal kouros from Sounion (Sunium-Room 8) and that from Anavissos (Room 13) which show the progress made in a little less than a century (between 600 and around 520 BC). There are also less important sculptures which will help to give you a wider view of these first examples of true Greek sculpture. This appeared only in the 7th century BC in various parts of the territories occupied by the Hellenic peoples. The original art, called daedalic, flourished above all in Crete (museum of Herakleion). Essentially religious in feeling, it is marked by the progress from the sacred stone, or betylos, to the anthropomorphization of the gods, often very unadventurously in wood. Observation of the material world resulted in kouroi and korai (statues of young men and maidens), particularly in Boeotia in the Peloponnese. Attica, Ionia and the islands (especially Chios and Samos) deserve a place apart, as does Magna Graecia (the Greek cities of Sicily and southern Italy). Each school has its own distinctive character: lyricism in Ionia, discreet gaiety in Attica, gravity in Boeotia and the Peloponnese. Towards the end of the Archaic period (around 500 BC), a great step forward was taken when vast compositions began to appear; despite the fact that these were sometimes a little clumsy, they were full of promise (treasure of Siphnos in Delphi).

Room 7 (vases from the Geometric period of the 8th century BC and sculptures of the 7th century BC). Ivory statuette (776) of a goddess found in a tomb of the Dipylon (this is the only sculpture of the Geometric period in this room; middle of the 8th century BC). Statue of Artemis (1), of the xoanon (wooden) type, consecrated by a certain Nicandrus of Naxos, sculpted by an artist of Naxos influenced by the daedalic style and found in Delos (around 650 BC). Among the vases there is a magnificent funerary amphora with geometric decoration (804) from around 750 BC, found in the cemetery of the Kerameikos and representing the laying out of the deceased, as well as a pithos (large wine jar) from the 7th century decorated with a relief (large mother-goddess flanked by animals).

Room 8 (sculptures from the end of the 7th century and the beginning of the 6th century BC). Statuette of a flute player (Br. 16513) in bronze (around 540 BC). *Colossal kouros (2720) which once stood before the most ancient temple of Poseidon, on Cape Sounion (around 600 BC). Head of a kouros (3372) called 'head of Dipylon' (same date). Head of a kouros (15) from Ptoön (sanctuary of Apollo in Boeotia) whose angular features possibly correspond to a tradition inherited from the wooden sculptures (around 580 BC). Large funerary amphora (353) from Attica decorated in black-figure, called the amphora of Piraeus and decorated with a procession of chariots (around 600 BC).

Room 9 (sculptures from the 6th century BC). Statue of a winged Victory (21), the work of an island artist, found on Delos (around 550 BC). *Funerary kouros (1558), a work from the islands (Melos; around 550 BC). Headless kore (22), found in Delos, of the Cycladic style (last quarter of the 6th century). Magnificent **kore (4889), intact, discovered in 1972 in Markopoulo in Attica, the base of which bears the signature of Aristion, a sculptor from Paros (around 550 BC). The young girl was called Phrasicleia (the name is given in the inscription); her costume, with incised decoration, shows very clear traces of colour.

Room 10 (sculptures from the 6th century BC). Stelae and funerary reliefs, including the upper part of a *stele (unnumbered) depicting a young man holding a lance and (behind this exhibit) the top of another *stele (38) with a young man holding a discus, an Attic work sometimes attributed to Phaidimos, around 560 BC. Various sphinxes which surmounted Attic funerary stelae (see the suggested reconstruction to the r. of the entrance door) illustrate the stages of development of this theme in the first half of the 6th century BC; around 550 the sphinx was replaced by an anthemion (honeysuckle pattern). *Kouros from Markopoulo (4890) found beside kore (4889) and possibly the work of the same sculptor (around 550 BC).

In the second part of the room there is a *funerary kouros (1906), an Attic work discovered in Volomandra to the SE of Athens (around 560 BC). Cinerary hydria in bronze (18232), the vertical handle of which is in the form of a kneeling kouros.

Return to Room 8, which provides access to Room 11. Room 11

(sculptures from the middle and the second half of the 6th century BC). *Funerary stele (29), in Pentelic marble representing the warrior Aristion in the classical Greek armour of a hoplite, the work of the sculptor Aristocles (around 510 BC); this exceptionally delicate sculpted stele was painted, as can be seen by several traces of paint. *Funerary kouros (3686), the work of an island artist (from Paros?) discovered on Keos (around 530 BC). *Funerary stele (3071) of hoplite resembling that of Aristion; an Attic work (around 525 BC). Kore (24) and *kore's head (27) that resemble those in the museum of the Acropolis. A very expressive head of a young man (61) found in Eleusis (around 560 BC). Next to this, socle of a funerary statue (81) bearing the signature of the sculptor Phaedimus (around 550 BC).

Room 13 (sculptures from the end of the 6th century BC). Kouros (12) from the sanctuary of Apollo in Ptoön, the work of a Boeotian artist (around 510 BC). Similarly kouros 20 which bears engraved on the hip and thigh an inscription stating that it was consecrated to Apollo of the silver bow by Pytheas of Akraiphion (in Boeotia) and Eschrion. *Funerary statue of Aristodicus (3938), of the kouros type in Parian marble; this is a work of great delicacy and to some extent marks the culmination of the development of this type of statue. It is an Attic work from around 500 BC. **Funerary kouros (3851) of a certain Croesus, one of the finest examples of an Archaic statue, found in Anavissos in the Mesogeia; this is an example of Attic art (around 525 BC). **The base of a statue of a kouros (3476) decorated with bas-reliefs depicting gymnastic competitions and a fight between a dog and a cat (Attic work from around 510 BC). **Base of a statue (3477) with more gymnastic scenes of a sport similar to hockey) and an apobate (soldier) mounting a chariot (Attic work from around 490 BC). Very fine head and bust (unnumbered) in painted high relief.

Room 12 (sculptures from the end of the 6th century and the beginning of the 5th century BC). Warriors' heads (1933-1938) from the temple of Aphaia in Aegina (around 500 BC). Bas-relief of a running hoplite (1959), an Attic work (around 500 BC). In the corner of the room there is a base of a votive statue (4797) in the form of a primitive Ionic capital, resembling the Aeolian type (middle of the 6th century BC).

CLASSICAL SCULPTURE. The decisive victory (480 BC) of the Greeks at Salamis, over the Persians, marked a turning point in Greek political life and also in the evolution of Greek art. In sculpture there is a great contrast between the cheerful and mannered rigidity of the last stages of Archaism and the rigour and nobility of this important stage leading towards pure Classicism, the style of Phidias, called the Severe style (480-450 BC). This was the time of the first portraits, when the greatest artists began strongly to assert their individuality in sculpted works with a high intellectual content, and in studies, executed in marble, of the body's movements, which are sometimes violent, sometimes supple. The famous statue of Poseidon from Cape Artemisium, the pride of the National Museum, is the crowning glory of the Severe style, which during the century in which Pericles lived (from 450) and until the end of the 4th century, was to become supple, gracious and aristocratic with Phidias, balanced with the elder Polyclitus, vigorous with Paeonius of Mende, indolently sensuous with Praxiteles, worked with inner passion by Scopas, before reaching the baroque mannerism of Hellenistic art which began in the 3rd century BC. Rooms 14 to 28 represent the history of these exciting developments.

Room 14 (sculptures from the first half of the 5th century BC). *Votive relief (3990), displaying the famous 'Greek profile' in all its splendour. This is a woman's profile (perhaps that of Aphrodite or Selene?); it is a work from the islands, possibly by an artist from Paros, found on Melos (around 470–460 BC). Ephebe placing a crown on his head (3344), an Attic relief found on Cape Sounion (around 460 BC). Bronze statue (unnumbered) from the beginning of the 5th century.

Room 15 (sculptures from the 5th century BC). ***Relief of the Initiation (126) a work of a style that is already classical depicting Demeter and Kore (Persephone), the two Eleusinian goddesses, and Triptolemus, possibly the son of King Celeus of Eleusis (around 440–430 BC). The meaning of this relief, probably placed in the Telesterion of Eleusis, where the Athenians were admitted to the secret of the Mysteries, is clear: by giving Triptolemus the first grains of corn, Demeter confers on the young man the task of initiating humans into the techniques of agriculture; he travelled over the world in a magic chariot drawn by winged serpents to scatter the grain. *Stele of a horseman (828) depicted as galloping, chlamys flying in the wind; this is the work of a Boeotian artist (around 430 BC). Funeral stele of a young man (742), the work of a Boeotian artist influenced by Ionian art (around 440 BC). ***Bronze statue very probably of Poseidon (Br. 15161), 6ft 10in (2.09m) high, recovered from the sea off Cape Artemisium, possibly the work of Calamis (around 460 BC). The god is portrayed as about to hurl his javelin and was certainly holding a trident. The muscles of the body, remarkable for their contours, are those of a man in his prime. The expression of the face, at once severe and detached, as befits an Olympian god, is very delicately portrayed. The hair, very elaborate, is in the archaic style and contrasts with the general technique of construction which is resolutely classical. The patina that coated the statue has been preserved to a large degree. Only the ivory of the eye-sockets, the inlay of the eyebrows and the mouth, as well as the attribute (the trident) are missing. Head of a bearded god, Zeus or Hermes (332), discovered in Piraeus and belonging to a hermaïc stele (around 440 BC). *Omphalos Apollo (45), a copy from the 2nd century AD, based on a bronze original attributed to Calamis. The statue has been given this name because of the omphalos (stone) (46) found nearby (in the theatre of Dionysus in Athens); the two are certainly unrelated. Group of Theseus (1664) and the Minotaur (1664A), a Roman replica of a Classical original.

Room 16 (funerary reliefs from the Classical period). Fragments of a marble funerary stele (37); a Cycladic work (around 420 BC).

Funerary stele of a young man (715), holding a bird and accompanied by his small servant (an Attic work found on Salamis, around 430 BC). *Large lekythos (4485) in marble, the relief of which depicts Hermes Psychopompos (guide of souls) leading a young woman, Myrrhine, by the hand to the ferryman Charon, who will take her across the Styx to Hades (around 420 BC).

The funerary monuments of the 5th and 4th centuries BC, commercial works that were mass-produced, depict scenes of farewell or of life in a conventional manner. Sometimes the deceased is shown giving a last clasp of the hand to his family (symbol of the union that continues after death), sometimes he is depicted surrounded by his family and relations, listening to them with a dreamy expression. Finally, the deceased may be seen adorning herself, if it is a woman, or in the case of a man, with his dog or the insignia of an athlete. Certain stelae were simply painted (stele 2611, dedicated to the memory of a Scythian archer); but in many cases the paint has largely disappeared.

Room 17 (sculptures of the Classical period from the second half of the 5th century BC). Fragment of a sculpted group (2348) by Agoracritus of Paros, a student of Phidias, for the temple of Nemesis at Rhamnous (around 420 BC). Sculptures from the Heraion, including a head of Hera (1571) attributed to the school of the Argive sculptor Polyclitus (end of the 5th century BC). Votive stele (226) of a priestess of Apollo, found at Mantinea; this is probably the famous Diotima of the *Symposium* of Plato (the work of an Argive sculptor, around 410 BC). Votive relief (1783) dedicated, according to the inscription on the epistyle, to Hermes and to the nymphs; it has sculpted decoration on both surfaces; on one side there are divinities with Cephissus, the horned river god, standing in the centre; the other side shows a quadriga (chariot) preceded by Hermes Nymphagogos (conductor of nymphs) (around 420–410 BC). Votive relief (1500) dedicated to Dionysus, the patron of Athens' two great dramatic festivals, the Lenaea and the City Dionysia, by a group of actors shown with their masks and tambourines (around 410 BC).

Rooms 19 and 20 (sculptures – or copies – from the 5th century). Fragmentary votive relief (3572) depicting Demeter and Kore (Persephone) seated (an Attic work, around 420 BC). Statue of the Lenormant Athena (128), a copy of Phidias' Athena Parthenos. Statue of Athena of the Varvakeion (129), another mediocre copy of Phidias' famous statue, one tenth of the original size (2nd century AD).

GARDEN GALLERIES. In this haven of peace, which is relatively cool in summer (the ideal spot to take a short rest), you will see sarcophagi, statues, Attic funerary stelae from the 5th and 4th centuries BC, etc. You cannot miss the horses covered with marine deposits due to a long period in the sea following a shipwreck off Anticythera, probably in the 1st century BC. Opposite there is a colossal statue of Heracles of the same type as the Farnese Hercules (Roman copy of a Classical original from the middle of the 4th century BC).

Room 18 (funerary reliefs from the Classical period; end of the 5th century and beginning of the 4th century BC). Fragments of the monument (754 and 2744) erected by the city of Athens in honour of the cavalry who fell in 394 at Corinth. Funerary stele (726) of a woman; an Attic work (around 380–370). Stele of Ktesileos and Theano (3472); an Attic work from the end of the 5th century. Stele of Hegeso (3624), in the form of a chapel (naïskos); the deceased Hegeso, is receiving a jewel case, that was hers during her lifetime, from the hands of her servant. This is an Attic work, found in the cemetery of the Kerameikos (around 400 BC). *Funerary stele (717) of a young woman, depicting a farewell scene; an Attic work, found in the Kerameikos cemetery (beginning of the 4th century).

Room 21 (hall of the Diadumenos). This room mostly contains Roman copies of Classical works, including the *Diadumenos of Delos (1826), a young man wrapping the victory cloth around his forehead. This is an excellent copy of a famous bronze executed by the elder Polyclitus around 420 BC. **Racehorse and rider of Artemision (15177), original in bronze from the 2nd century BC, recovered off Cape Artemision, a work of remarkable liveliness and tension.

Recent investigations (B. Callipolitis) have shown that the horse, until recently dated from the 5th century, in fact belonged, as does the race-rider, to the Hellenistic period. The two belong to a single group from the middle of the 2nd century, and should, if the displays were to be strictly chronological, be placed in another room.

Room 22 (sculptures from Epidaurus, from the 4th century BC). *Collection of sculptures (and fragments of architecture) from monuments from the sanctuary of Asclepius in Epidaurus: tholos built by the younger Polyclitus; temple of Artemis; and, in particular, the temple of Asclepius, built by the architect Theodotus, and decorated, around 380, by several sculptors, including Timotheus and Hectoridas (inscription). The pediments of this temple depict to the E the Iliupersis (the sacking of Troy by the Greek conquerors), to the W the amazonomachia (combat between the Greeks and the Amazons). Their current presentation owes a great deal to research by N. Yalouris. The figures on the acroteria (155, 156 and 157) were of young women: in the centre a Victory holding a bird (possibly a cock); in the corners of the pediment, wind and sea nymphs or heavenly deities on horseback. A votive relief (173) depicts the god Asclepius himself (around 380). *Statue of a young athlete (254), an Attic work based on a Polyclitean model (beginning of the 4th century).

Rooms 23 and 24 (funeral monuments from the 4th century). *Large relief (869) called the relief of Illissos is from a funerary monument in the form of a naïskos. This work may possibly be attributed to Scopas (around 340).

Rooms 25 to 27. Votive reliefs from the 4th century BC.

Room 28 (the last of the Attic funeral monuments and sculptures from the 4th century BC). *Funerary stele (820) depicting a farewell scene (Attic work from around 330). *Funerary stele (833), originally in the form of a naïskos, from Rhamnous (around 320). **Large relief (4464), in two sections: a horse and a young black armour-bearer, a work of transition between the Classical and Hellenistic styles which must have decorated an officer's tomb (end of the 4th century or beginning of the 3rd century). **Ephebe of Anticythera (13396), in bronze. It is not certain who the person depicted is (god, hero, athlete?) This work was recovered from the sea off Anticythera; it may be Paris offering a golden apple to Aphrodite, or Heracles picking the fruit from the tree in the garden of the Hesperides. It is probably the work of a Peloponnesian artist, possibly Euphranor of Sicyon (around 340). *Base of a tripod (1463) decorated with reliefs depicting Dionysus, holding his thyrsus (staff) and cantharis (drinking-cup), and two winged Victories, one bearing a phial, the other holding an oenochoe (wine jar). This is an Attic work from the school of Praxiteles (middle of the 4th century). **Head of the Goddess Hygeia (3602), found in Tegea and very probably the work of Scopas; the expression, full of a meditative gentleness testifying to a very intense inner life, and the elegant, refined style are, according to the ancient authorities, perfectly compatible with the Paros master (around 360).

HELLENISTIC SCULPTURE. The Hellenistic period, from Alexander the Great to the arrival of the Romans, was a period of rapid growth, in the physical sense, with the prodigious expansion of Greek territory in Egypt and even in Central Asia, as well as in social and religious life, following these conquests. Hellenistic art reflects these upheavals; Pergamum and Alexandria were extremely active centres, rivalling the Athenian school and Rhodes; they were much closer to Ptolemaic Egypt than to Greece itself. Under the influence of eastern religions, the sculptures testify to different spiritual preoccupations reflected by a wider repertoire in which, for example, Dionysiac scenes are common, and by the creation of new styles; baroque, expressionist (ugliness was no longer considered undesirable), sensual. This explosion led to a return to the past with a subtle and gracious neo-Attic style, before the arrival of Roman art.

Room 29 (Hellenistic sculptures). Bust of a divinity of the underworld (181), from the beginning of the Hellenistic period (beginning of the 3rd century). Flute competition (215, 216 and 217), three sections from a base of a group sculpted by Praxiteles (according to Pausanias). The group has disappeared; the base is decorated with reliefs depicting the musical contest between Apollo and the satyr Marsyas in the presence of the six Muses (around 320 BC). Large statue of Themis (231) from Rhamnous and sculpted by Chaerestratus (beginning of the 3rd century). Colossal heads of Demeter, Artemis and the giant Anytos (1734, 1735 and 1736 respectively), from the sanctuary of Despoina, in Lycosura (Arcadia). The bodies are still in the local museum. These are the work of the sculptor Damophon from Messene (2nd century BC). Next to these you will see fragments that decorated the thrones of the great goddesses. Statue of a warrior from Galatia (247), an example of the heroic style peculiar to Pergamum (end of the 3rd century BC).

Room 30 (Hellenistic sculptures), *Portrait of a philosopher (Br. 13400), a bronze recovered off Anticythera, possibly a portrait of the Cynic philosopher (Br. 13400), a bronze recovered off Anticythera, possibly a portrait of the Cynic philosopher Bion the Borysthenite, a freed slave (3rd century BC). **Portrait (3266) of a beardless man, possibly a poet of the 'New Comedy' (middle of the 2nd to 1st century BC). *Portrait of an Olympic victor (Br. 6439), boxer (bronze from the 4th century BC). *Colossal statue of Poseidon (235), from the 2nd century. *Portrait (Br. 14612), in bronze, of a beardless man (end of the 2nd or beginning of the 1st century). *Portrait of a foreign priest, doubtless from Thrace (351), an Attic work from the beginning of the 1st century BC. *Group of Aphrodite, Eros and Pan (3335), found in Delos; a work from the beginning of the 1st century BC. *Dancers (259 and 260); two sculpted plaques from the theatre of Dionysus in Athens, which possibly depict two Horae (Hours), from the end of the 1st century BC.

Room 31. This room is reserved for temporary exhibitions.

Room 32. (Stathatos collection). Remarkable above all for its bronzes and for its ancient and Byzantine *jewellery.

Now retrace your steps to room 21 from where you may enter a large room called the Temenos.

Room 34 (Temenos). Votive reliefs, many of which are consecrated to Pan and to the nymphs, sculptures relating to the worship of Pan, of the nymphs, of Aphrodite, of Eros, etc., and, in the middle, an altar (1495) dedicated by the Athenian senate to Aphrodite Hegemon and to the nymphs (around 200 BC).

Room 36 (Karapanos collection). Remarkable series of *small bronzes, dating from the Archaic period to the Hellenistic and Roman periods, principally from Dodona. Case 5: large figurines in terracotta from Corfu, mainly representing the goddess Artemis, with her bow and her favourite animal, the hind. In the second part of the room are some heads and funeral stelae in marble.

 Room 37 (room of bronzes). Rich **collection of figurines and bronze objects from various sources dating from the Geometric, Archaic and Classical periods. Notice in particular a warrior's head (6466) from the end of the Archaic period, found on the Athenian Acropolis (around 490 BC); a head of Zeus (6440), dating from approximately the same period, from Olympia, and a flute player (16513) from Samos (around 540 BC). There is a case devoted to an explanation of casting large bronzes by the lost-wax process.

Room 40. This room formerly contained four large bronze statues discovered by chance at Piraeus in 1959. These statues are now in the museum at Piraeus, having been transferred in October 1982. Notice another large bronze found in the sea: this is the Ephebe of Marathon

(15118). The graceful and supple posture and contours of this statue suggest that it belongs to the school of Praxiteles (third quarter of the 4th century BC). It is, without doubt, the young Hermes looking at a tortoise that has been placed on his left hand, raising his right hand, snapping his fingers with pleasure at the idea of making a sounding-board for a lyre from the animal's shell.

Two cases contain small bronze statues, discovered in 1964 in Athens, in the Ambelokipoi quarter of the city which, may be dated from the 2nd century AD. These are, however, copies of Classical originals executed by the great masters of the 5th and 4th centuries. There is a statue (16774) of the Heracles-Alexander type, a statue of Dionysus (16773) inspired by the famous Doryphorus (spear bearer) by Polyclitus, a statue of a shepherd (possibly the god Hermes) carrying a lamb (16789), a statue of a dancer (16787), a Poseidon of the Lateran type (16772), etc.

Rooms 41, 42 and 43 are devoted to Roman sculptures. These rooms contain some fine portraits of poets, philosophers, emperors and unknown men and women, together with stelae and reliefs. Especially noticeable is a large statue of a nude man (1828) found in Delos and representing, not an athlete, but a well-known Roman (around 50 BC). A bust of the philosopher Metrodorus (2nd–3rd century AD), a head of a bearded man (372) that possibly belonged to a funeral statue (2nd century AD), three heads (3085–3087) from a funeral monument (end of the 1st century AD), a bust (249) and a head (3729) of the emperor Hadrian, as well as a bust of his favourite, Antinous (second quarter of the 2nd century AD; 417), a bust of Herodes Atticus (4810), the wealthy benefactor of Athens and Greece (middle of the 2nd century AD), and, finally, the portrait of a philosopher (419; around 200 AD).

Return to the hall and climb the stairs to visit the frescoes from Thera and the collection of ceramics on the first floor.

THE DISCOVERIES OF THERA. The excavations of the Minoan site of Akrotiri in the S of the island of Thera (modern Santorini), undertaken in 1962 and carried on until his death in 1974 by Professor S. Marinatus, have uncovered exceptionally rich material, a small part of which is on display – a temporary exhibition that has lasted several years – on the first floor of the National Museum (Room 48). Most remarkable is a collection of admirable frescoes full of grace and fresh colour.

In the first room, opposite the stairway, a wooden bed, reconstructed from the imprint it left, together with several pieces of bronze or earthenware pottery with painted decoration, illustrates daily life around 1500 BC. At the back is the room in which **frescoes found in several houses are exhibited. Notice, among the other scenes depicted, two children boxing, an antelope, a fisherman and the 'Spring' fresco developing its floral motifs over the three walls of a reconstructed room. Notice especially the **frieze of a naval combat, exceptional for its accurate detail and its documentary interest.

THE CERAMICS OF THE NATIONAL MUSEUM. A visit to the ceramics section is a must: it contains exhibitions of pottery from the Bronze Age (c. 2300–1100 BC) to the Hellenistic period (c. 323–27 BC). The collections will give you a more accurate idea of the social, religious, aesthetic, professional, commercial and domestic preoccupations and activities of the ancient inhabitants of mainland Greece and the Islands. The pre-Hellenic period is dominated by the brilliant Minoan civilization that flourished in Crete from the beginning of the 2nd millennium BC. The ceramics from this period are not represented in the National Museum but in the place where they were discovered and produced, in Crete, in the museum of Heraklion. The objects displayed in the Mycenaean room, on the ground floor, and in the ceramics section on the first floor, reflect the Minoan style, as do those from Thera. This Minoan ceramic art, which produced so many masterpieces, exerted an influence on the mainland, particularly Attica and Argolis, and on the Cyclades. Its influence was particularly felt in the first period of the Late Minoan culture (1580–1400 BC). In the rest of mainland Greece the ceramic art, in the pre-Hellenic period, shows tendencies that place it outside the Cretan sphere of influence. During the Early Minoan period, when Crete had already entered the Bronze Age, the civilization of the centre and north of Greece was of a Chalcolithic character which nevertheless produced some remarkable pottery.

Room 49 (ceramics from the Bronze Age to the Geometric period). In the first part of the room there are several examples of Bronze Age pottery (3rd and 2nd millennia BC), and of ceramics from the Mycenaean period, including pithoi (large jars) the decoration of which drew its inspiration from the vegetable kingdom (grasses, flowers, clumps of papyrus, etc.), very characteristic of the Mycenaean period. The pottery of Argolis and Attic perpetuated the artistic traditions of the Late Minoan civilization. The larger part of the room contains ceramics from the Geometric period (late 11th to late 8th c. BC), as well as, in case 12, some examples of sculpture (bronze and terracotta) from the same period.

After the disappearance of the Mycenaean civilization, around the 12th or 11th century BC, Greece entered a period which has often been called the Greek Dark Ages, and which lasted for four or five centuries. Ceramic art underwent profound changes evident in the use of geometric figures, which gave rise to the term Geometric period. Sculpture modelled in the round produced figures of people, and especially of animals, that were also geometric in appearance.

At the beginning of the actual Geometric period (c. 10th century), vases were decorated with a few, simple motifs – especially circles and semi-circles – drawn on the clay with compasses.

Then the motifs were arranged in horizontal bands, the surfaces of which accentuated the curve of the vase. On amphorae 769 and 17935, for example, you can see the tendency to cover the surface with a collection of lightly hatched geometric figures arranged in belts around the pots.

The Geometric style of ceramic art spread through the whole Greek world. Nevertheless, there was a new mode in Attica, which was to become absolute during the Classical period: the paintings were no longer merely an abstract decoration, but became a representation in which social activities of the period might be depicted. The funeral representations were the first to appear, while this use of ceramics occasionally produced vases, amphorae or kraters of great size. Athens was then the most important artistic centre in Greece, where the potters of the Dipylon, near the Kerameikos cemetery, showed the greatest skill in their ingenious compositions (see, for example, on the large funeral amphora 803 and on the large krater 900 – in room 50 – which date from the middle of the 7th century BC).

Room 50. Ceramic art in the Geometric style, from various workshops and early examples of pottery of the Orientalizing style (7th century BC). You will notice particularly the large Attic funeral krater (990) from the Dipylon cemetery, at the W exit from Athens, representing the ritual scene of the laying out and mourning of the deceased, and below a procession of chariots (middle of the 8th century BC); as well as the hydria (313) from Analatos, in Attica, on which floral decoration is mixed with the purely Geometric patterns and where the human figures on the neck of the vase are not merely juxtaposed, but are involved in a collective action, a sort of round dance (beginning of the 7th century BC).

Case 19 contains charming little perfume vases from Corinth (7th century). On a base there is a large Boeotian amphora (220) depicting the Potnia Theron, the goddess who reigns over animals, birds and creatures of the sea (first half of the 7th century BC).

Room 51. Pottery of the Orientalizing style (7th century BC).

The 7th century was for Greece a period of great economic and political expansion. Greek cities established distant colonies that were to last for centuries. Miletus, in Ionia, and Corinth made the most of these opportunities: Corinth became the centre for the diffusion of a ceramic art in which appeared, growing gradually deeper, the trends born from the aesthetic conceptions of the potters of the Geometric period. The majority of the vases produced in the best Corinthian workshops testify to the oriental influence (Asia Minor) adapted to the decorative conceptions of the Greek potters. This influence shows itself in the wider iconographic repertoire, especially lotus flowers and fighting animals, in the heraldic devices. However, the decoration was already anecdotal and found an inexhaustible source of inspiration in mythology.

This rooms contains a number of examples of large vases from this period (amphorae, kraters, pitchers) produced in various workshops, principally on the islands: Euboea (particularly Eretria), the Cyclades (possibly Melos, more probably Paros), Rhodes and even Cyprus (vases in case 27). The best known are the 'Melian' kraters, made with showy clumsiness, in particular krater 911, the most ancient in the series. This work depicts the epiphany of Apollo, standing on his winged chariot in the company of two young women (possibly the Hyperborean Virgins, whom Apollo was to take to Delos), opposite his sister Artemis (around 640 BC); and number 354, which depicts Heracles departing in his chariot, accompanied by a young woman (around 610 BC). The Eretrian krater (12129), brightly coloured, is also worthy of note, with a sphinx on the side and a procession of women on the neck (last quarter of the 7th century); as well as two oinochoae (wine pitchers) from Rhodes (12717 and 12718) decorated with rows of animals drawn in a refined style (second half of the 7th century).

At the exit from this room you will notice the *Nessus amphora (1002), an Attic work from the end of the 7th century BC, on which the decorations are arranged in horizontal bands and which displays a certain hieratic character in the attitudes of the painted figures on the body (the Gorgons fleeing from Perseus) and on the neck (Heracles killing the Nessus centaur). This decorative style evokes Orientalizing ceramic art.

Rooms 52 and 53. Black-figure ceramics from the 7th and 6th centuries BC.

The black-figure vases (end of the 7th–6th centuries), and especially the red-figure pieces (end of the 6th to the 4th century), represent the beginning of the great period of Greek, and especially Attic, pottery. To meet the demands of a wide market during this period, a specific type of vase existed for each particular use, whether for the storage or carrying of liquids, decanting or drinking, or for other special purposes whether ritual, funerary or for washing, etc.

Ceramics, then, formed part of the basic furnishings of all homes and sometimes, because of their rich ornamentation, were a highly sought-after luxury. The trade in vases proved of great economic value to Corinth in the 7th and 6th centuries, and above all to Athens in the 6th century and during the Classical period.

Both in the black-figure vases (6th century), and, during the Classical period (end of the 6th century to the 4th century), in the red-figure vases, the essential part of the ornamentation was the representation of human figures. The motifs taken from the animal and vegetable kingdoms played a secondary decorative role. One of the most interesting points of the ceramics from these two periods is that they help us to visualize the intimate life of the Greeks. Indeed, the vases were not only decorated with motifs with a mythical, legendary or, more rarely, historical inspiration, but also with scenes from everyday life (in the workshop, in the fields, at a banquet, in the gymnasium or on the running track, domestic chores or a woman's toilette in the gynaeceum, children's games in the street, etc.); scenes sometimes focused on a paticular moment, comic or tragic, solemn or relaxed, funeral or religious processions, religious rites, scenes domestic or ceremonial . . .

These are the scenes that you will see as you examine the majority of the display cases in Rooms 52 and 53. A few vases or Attic fragments bear a signature: that of Sophilus occurs several times, in particular on a *lebes (a sort of terracotta cauldron) which is fragmentary (case 46; 15499). This lebes represents an episode inspired by canto XXIII of Homer's *Iliad*: the funeral games in honour of Patroclus, Achilles' friend, who died fighting the Trojans. The scene may be identified with certainty thanks to an inscription (around 580 BC). Case 47 contains a *krater (12587) on which is depicted the combat between Heracles and Nereus, the old man of the sea. This vase is attributed to Sophilus (around 570 BC).

Do not miss, at the back of Room 52, the terracotta metopes from the Archaic temple of Apollo at Thermon, in Aetolia. On the r. metope, to the l. of the door, is depicted the myth of the metamorphosis into birds of the daughters of Pandion, king of Athens, Procne and Philomela, following a gruesome family tragedy. Here, they are shown in their human form, but the artist has inscribed the names of the birds (Procne, Philomela, a nightingale; whose tongue had been cut out, a swallow). Below, terracotta antefixes from the same temple: heads of satyrs and nymphs.

In the centre of Room 52 (cases 43 and 44), are bronzes found in the sanctuary of Hera at Perachora, near Corinth and on the Spartan acropolis, in the ruins of the sanctuary of Athena Chalcioecus. These are worthy of note, as are the small ivory figurines from the temple of Artemis Orthia (7th and 6th centuries; see case 50 in particular).

Case 45 contains copies of paintings on wood executed by Corinthian or Argive artists around 520–500 BC.

Cases 35–39 contain a collection of vases, broken fragments and small bronzes in the Heraion in Argos. The small terracotta model of a temple or house, exhibited beside the cases (15471), is from the same source (around 700 BC). To the r. of case 41 there is a magnificent head, very expressive, of a sphinx in painted terracotta (17870), which served as the corner acroterion in a temple at Calydon in Aetolia (beginning of the 6th century).

Room 53 houses a rich collection of black-figure vases from the 6th century, the majority of which are Attic. To the l. after the entrance door there is an interesting terracotta group representing a funeral procession, with the coffin placed on a chariot surrounded by mourners and escorted by a horseman (second half of the 8th century). To the r. at the back of the room two sarcophagi of Clazomenae (13939 and 13427), the upper rims of which are decorated in black-figure (6th century); nearby, in case 54, there are some Etruscan vases in Bucchero (clay). To the l. at the back of the room are fragments of terracotta plaques depicting funeral scenes, including some (2414–2417) painted by the great artist Exekias (around 540–530).

Room 54 (collections of black-figure and red-figure ceramics). In the middle of the room you will see the red-figure krater (Acr. 735; Theseus and the Minotaur), the work of the painter of Syriscus (around 400). Cases 70 and 76 contain numerous fragments of vases from the Athenian Acropolis, very badly damaged but decorated by the great vase-painters.

Room 55 (white lekythoi). Notice to the r. several lekythoi, some of which, with a cream-coloured background, are the precursors of the lekythoi with a white background. These vases with a cream background depict a wide range of themes which make no allusion to death, in contrast to the great majority of the lekythoi with a white background. Notice, in case 80, the beauty of the design of the goblet attributed to the painter of Pistoxenes (around 470–460 BC), which depicts Orpheus being killed by the Thracian Maenads. Case 84 contains beautiful white background lekythoi, the theme of which is Hermes helping a dead soul climb into Charon's boat (17916) and an offering being made on a tomb (1935). Case 85 contains lekythoi with very refined designs by the painter of Achilles and the painter of Thanatos.

Room 56 (red-figure pottery, from the end of the 5th and the 4th century BC). The works are mainly Attic, together with some Boeotian or Corinthian works. Notice in particular, in case 106, several works attributed to an Athenian artist from the beginning of the last third of the 5th century called the painter of Eretria, including a famous *epinetron (used by women to protect the knee and thigh while spinning wool) decorated with scenes from the gynaeceum (1629; around 425 BC).

On the table facing case 107 there are several Panathenaic amphorae (vases offered as prizes to victors in the games held in Athens at the time of the great Panathenaia) from the 4th century, still decorated in black-figure through religious conservatism; on one side is the goddess Athena, on the other, athletes.

On the wall next to the exit door is a terracotta *plaque (11035) painted in the Attic red-figure style and dedicated by a certain Ninnion to the goddesses of Eleusis, Demeter and Kore. The plaque is in the form of a naïskos, with a pediment and central acroterium; the main theme is taken from a stage in the ritual of initiation into the Mysteries of Eleusis (second half of the 4th century BC).

In the wing of the museum on the Tositsa road side, visitors with a love of detail may visit two annexes to the National Museum: the Epigraphic Museum and, especially, the Numismatic Museum (Greek, Roman, Byzantine coins, ancient cameos, etc.)

Open: weekdays 08.00–13.00; Sun. 09.00–14.00; closed Mon.; entrance free.

IX **Benaki Museum (plan I, D–3)

Installed in a town house, a building of the aristocratic Athenian type of the last century, this is not a large museum. Its collections, however, are rich, varied and interesting. It is one of the museums not to be missed, however short your visit to Athens.

THE CONCERN OF GREEKS LIVING ABROAD FOR THEIR HOME COUNTRY. For 35 years Anthony Benaki, a wealthy man from the Greek colony in Cairo, brought collections of Byzantine, Arabic, Persian and Chinese art in Egypt and Europe. He offered them to the State and assumed all the costs of installation and maintenance of the museum. To these first collections were added jewellery, fabrics and Greek costumes, donations that have made the museum the most important in Athens as regards the decorative arts.

THE MUSEUM'S PRESENTATION. This was for a long time romantic and lavish, reflecting the tastes of an aesthete and patron at the beginning of the century. The presentation of the collections has gradually become more modern and uncluttered. We will not attempt a definitive description of the rooms, but indicate only the most interesting objects displayed.

Address: 1, Kounbari Street, on the corner of the Avenue Vasilissis Sofias (Tel. 361-1617).

Open: weekdays 08.00-14.00; closed Tues.; entrance fee; these times cannot be guaranteed.

Ground floor. While the collection of icons cannot be compared to that of the Byzantine Museum, it is still extremely interesting. You will notice in particular, divided among the various rooms, of the Philoxenia (Hospitality) of Abraham (2973; 14th century), symbol of the Holy Trinity; the Descent into Limbo (155; 16th century) signed by Michael Damaskinos, of the Cretan school; St Anne (126; 17th century), signed by Emmanuel Tzanes. The important collection of jewellery, bronzes and Greek vases provides a retrospective view, since it begins with the Neolithic period: two golden goblets from the N of Euboea (3000-2800 BC; case 1); a beautiful amphora in the late Geometric style (second half of the 8th century BC); golden goblet from the Mycenaean period (15th century BC, case 3); Hellenistic gold jewellery from the 3rd, 2nd and 1st centuries BC (case 12); polychrome Byzantine vases (case 10); fine pendant in rock crystal from the Byzantine period (2113) with Christ Pantocrator (11th century).

At this point you will also see the reconstruction of a Muslim reception room, combining objects from various sources (tiles of enamelled earthenware from Nicaea or Rhodes, 17th century, marble tiling from Cairo, 18th century), pottery from Asia Minor, said to be from Isnik (16th and 17th centuries), collections of priest's clothing (17th and 18th centuries), numerous vases and objects of worship in precious metals, sculpted wooden crosses, Byzantine illuminated manuscripts on parchment (case 44), various pieces of glasswork, especially Egyptian (8th–15th centuries). Two of the earliest paintings of El Greco (Domenikos Theotokopoulos) are also on display: St Luke the Evangelist (1542), in pure Byzantine style, and an Adoration of the Magi (1543) recall the time when El Greco was a disciple of Titian.

First floor. Here you will see a collection of precious fabrics, velvet from Bursa (16th and 17th centuries), silks and brocades from Venice (17th and 18th centuries), as well as a very rich collection of Chinese ceramics, the most important of its kind in Greece, particularly remarkable for its marvellous T'ang figurines (618–907). Visitors with a romantic leaning will not want to miss the collections on this floor that relate to the beginnings of modern Greek history (19th century and beginning of the 20th century). The poetic prints and lithographs, several paintings including a Delacroix, autographs of Lord Byron, and weapons, will all bring to life the old-fashioned charm of that time.

Basement. All the Greek provinces are represented in a magnificent collection of costumes and jewellery from the 18th and 19th centuries, while the reception room of a house from Kozani (18th century) is reconstructed, the walls covered with panelling (donated by Eleni Stathatos).

X **Byzantine Museum** (plan I, D–3)

A visit to this museum is not to be missed by anyone interested in Byzantine art and in particular Byzantine painting. The museum in fact houses one of the most important collections of icons in the world. It provides an opportunity to appreciate the brilliant art, inspired by classicism, that flourished in Constantinople under the Palaeologi (1258–1453) from the time of the reconquest of the Latin Empire (1261) to their fall (1453) before the Ottoman army, and which spread in Greece to Mistra, to the despotate of Morea, to Athos and to the Slavonic kingdoms of Serbia, Bulgaria and Russia, and which was to influence Gothic painting in Italy and France.

A MUSEUM EXCLUSIVELY DEDICATED TO BYZANTINE ART. Established by the State in 1920, the Byzantine museum inherited collections aseembled at the end of the 19th century by the Christian Archaeological Society and various collections previously scattered throughout other museums of the province. The defeat of the Greek army during the war between Greece and Turkey in 1921–22 led to many Greek communities of Asia Minor returning to their homeland, bringing with them their cult objects etc., many of which found their way into the collections of the Byzantine Museum. These collections were subsequently increased by purchases, excavations and the depositing for safe-keeping of mural paintings from churches that were too prone to pillage or dilapidation.

PRESENTATION OF THE MUSEUM. This is careful, sometimes elegant, sometimes a little overabundant. The museum is housed in a villa built in the Florentine style for the Duchesse de Plaisance, and in various subsidiary buildings.

Address: 22, Avenue Vasilissis Sophias (Tel. 71-10-27).

Open: weekdays (except Mon.) 09.00 to 15.00; Sun. 09.00 to 16.00; entrance fee.

On the ground floor of the villa three rooms have been converted into churches from three different periods: palaeo-Christian, Byzantine and post-Byzantine. Attempts have been made to collect all the furnishings corresponding to each of the three churches and exhibit them here.

To the r. of the entrance the palaeo-Christian church (5th and 6th centuries) with its altar and its episcopal seat, the cathedral has been reconstructed from elements from various excavation sites. The objects and architectural fragments are also from several sites. The following room contains Byzantine sculptures. You then enter a cruciform church, domed, of a type favoured by Byzantine architects from the 10th century onwards. The sculpted slab depicting an eagle with spread wings represented the omphalos, the symbolic centre of the church. The fourth room has been converted into a post-Byzantine church from the time of the Turkish occupation (notice in particular the beautiful iconostasis with elements from the 17th and 18th centuries, from Cephalonia and Ithaca). Frescoes from the 18th century complete this collection.

The most interesting section on the first floor is the exhibition of icons. This includes works ranging from the 9th to the 17th centuries. Note in particular in the first room a *crucifixion (169) from the 14th century, a second *crucifixion (246) from the Venetian school of the 14th century and a *virgin and child (145), a work of great tenderness probably executed in Constantinople in the 13th or 14th century. This room also contains manuscripts and liturgical scrolls.

The next room contains mural paintings from various Greek churches including *frescoes from the church of St George at Lathrinon (island of Naxos). An X-ray performed on an icon from the 17th century has shown that it was painted on top of an older one, dating from the 12th century, a practice which was unfortunately widespread. Liturgical objects, ceramics and silver icons are exhibited in the third room. A last room houses priests' vestments and fabrics, patriarchal croziers (rhabdi) and Byzantine crosses. A case contains a *gold-braided corporal or cloth from the early 14th century, from Thessaloniki.

In the subsidiary buildings around the garden are other *collections of icons, from the 14th to the 19th century, the most interesting of which date from around 1600, with a room devoted to works of popular inspiration.

Next to the Byzantine museum is the Military Museum. (*Tel. 73-95-60, open weekdays (except Mon.) 09.00–14.00; Sun. 09.30–14.00.*) Through reconstructions this museum conjures up the ancient and modern weapons, the uniforms and the military history of Greece from antiquity until World War II.

Beyond the Hilton Hotel the Avenue Vasilissis Sofias crosses a modern quarter of the city where (about 880yd/800m further on, to the l.) you will see the American Embassy building, designed by Walter Gropius. Still further along the outline of the tower of Athens may be seen above the district of Ambelokipi.

In this area art lovers may like to visit the *National Gallery (plan I, E-3), Avenue Vasileos Constantinou *(Tel. 721-10-10; open weekdays – except Mon. – 08.30–12.30 and 16.00–18.00; Sun. 09.00–15.00; entrance fee, except on Sun. and Wed.)* The gallery contains several works attributed to El Greco, works by Rubens, Caravaggio and Tiepolo, but above all canvasses by modern Greek artists (Lytras, Ghiziz, Volonakis) and by the great contemporary artists: Picasso, Modigliani, Magritte, etc. Two works in particular stand out; the *Greek on Horseback* by Delacroix, and the *Prodigal Son*, a bronze by Rodin. Temporary exhibitions.

VICINITY OF ATHENS (ATTICA)

Attica is the small triangular peninsula which gave birth to the most briliant Greek civilization, that of the Athenians. Anyone who wishes to understand fully the miracle of Athens must, in addition to seeing the highlights of the metropolis, visit at least some of the ancient demes, if not all. Although Athens eclipses these demes with her glory, without them she would never have flourished as she did.

You will find archaeological sites (Cape Sounion [Sunium], Amphiareion [the Amphiaraeum], Rhamnous, Eleusis, etc.), Byzantine monuments (Kaisariani, Daphni, etc.), a typically Mediterranean port (Piraeus), beaches (Glyfada, Vouliagmeni, Schinias, etc.), holiday resorts and rest centres (Vouliagmeni, Kifissia, Ekali, etc.), a large health resort (Mt Parnes), in countryside which, despite the urban spread of Athens, still retains its Mediterranean beauty (Hymettus, the Apollo coastline towards Cape Sounion, Parnes, etc.).

1 – Academy of Plato

Route: 2mls (3.5km)

Leave the centre of the city by Platanos Street (plan I, A-2).

2mls (3.5km) Excavation sites, of interest only to archaeologists, in which lie the remains of ancient buildings, on the site of the Academy, where Plato founded a famous school of philosophy.

AN ANCIENT PLACE OF WORSHIP. The academy owed its name to Akademos, possibly a local hero, in whose honour a heroön was built (a rustic sanctuary). Greek archaeologists have discovered there traces of a building dating to the ancient Helladic period (2300–2000 BC), called the 'house of Akademos', also traces of a building similar to the 'sacred house' of Eleusis, from the Geometric period.

A PROPERTY CONSECRATED TO THE MUSES. The spot was also dedicated to Athena, whose temple was here surrounded by a sacred wall inside which grew 12 sacred olive trees originally from a cutting of the famous tree planted by the goddess on the Acropolis; oil was extracted from these and offered to the victors in the Panathenaic games. A sanctuary was also consecrated in this spot to Prometheus, and the pilgrims from the Panathenaia came here to light their torches. There were also three gymnasia for the ephebes. Their covered tracks were used both for the exercises of the young, and the sophists' conversations. It was here that, towards the end of his life (around 388-387) Plato founded his school of philosophy where he gathered together his disciples. He owned a property in the neighbourhood, dedicated to the Muses, and it was there that he taught and was buried.

Near the Academy, on the other side of the Lenormant road (plan I, A-1), a limestone hillock indicates the position of the ancient district of Kolonos, called Kolonos Hippios to distinguish it from the Kolonos Agoraios near the Agora. Sophocles was born in this deme and immortalized it in his *Oedipus Coloneus*. It was in this place consecrated to Athena Hippia and Poseidon Hippios (protectors of horses), close by a sanctuary of the Eumenides, that Oedipus, blind, banished from Thebes and led by Antigone, found exile in Attica, where he died, only Theseus knowing the site of his tomb.

2 - **Daphni and *Eleusis

Route: 6½mls (11km) and 14mls (23km) (see route maps 3 or 5).

Leave by the Corinth road (plan I, A-2). The modern road leaves the ancient Sacred Way from Athens to Eleusis to the l. The ancient way, used by the processions that went to celebrate the Mysteries, was bordered by altars, chapels and tombs, all of which have long since disappeared.

6½mls (11km): Daphni (see section on Daphni).

8mls (13km): Near the milestone a piece of rock, to the r., marks the site of a sanctuary of Aphrodite with its votive niches for statuettes and offerings. Here you may still see a small section of the Sacred Way.

9mls (14.5km): The road to the l. leads to Skaramangas, 1ml (1.5km), where the multi-millionaire shipowner Niarchos has established the very large Hellenic Naval Shipyards with the largest dry dock in the Mediterranean. National Naval College.

14mls (23km): Eleusis, which you reach after leaving the Corinth road.

3 - *Piraeus (see section on Piraeus)

Route: 6mls (10km) by the Piraeus road (plan I A-3) or 6½ (11km) by Syngrou Avenue (plan I, B/C-4). The new road is much quicker and reaches almost to the coast, to the New Phaleron, near the Karaïskos stadium.

4 - *Kaisariani and *Mt Hymettus

During this three-hour trip you will visit, in a pleasantly cool site, one of the most beautiful Byzantine churches in the vicinity of Athens.

You will also have magnificent views over Athens, Attica and the Saronic Gulf as you ascend the bare slopes of Mt Hymettus.

Route: 4mls (7km) and 11mls (17.5km) by a good asphalt road.

Leave the centre by Ymittou road (plan I, E–4).

4mls (7km): *Kaisariani convent, at the bottom of a small shaded valley which was once famous for a spring said to have healing powers. Only a spout in the form of a ram's head remains of this fountain, but it has been immortalized in some of Ovid's verses, in the *Art of Loving* (*Ars amatoria*, 3. 111, 687), as has the bucolic charm of its setting, at the foot of Hymettus, among the pines, cypresses and plane trees.

Open daily 08.30–13.30 (12.00 in winter) and 16.00–18.00.

The charming little 10th-century church was consecrated to the Presentation of the Virgin. The narthex and the annex, or pareoclesum, to the r. of the church, are from the 17th century, as are the paintings that decorate the narthex. The paintings in the church, however, date from the 16th century, with a Christ Pantocrator on the dome and, on the N wall, the tree of Jesse and the figures of the apostles. A cycle depicting the life of Christ begins in the apse and continues around the transept.

6½mls (10.5km): To the l. of the road, in a small valley, you will see yet another religious building, the Asteriou convent, with an 11th-century church, the frescoes of which date from the 16th century.

You reach the top of Mt Hymettus by a short, winding road, very narrow in places (3,366ft/1,026m; military zone, access prohibited). A statue of Zeus once stood on the summit. The mountain used to be covered with aromatic plants, thyme, terebinth, mint, lavender, sage, etc. from which the bees gathered nectar and produced a highly perfumed honey. Nowadays heather predominates and the bees have migrated to Pentelicon and Tourkovouni, although several apiaries still exist at Pigrati, near Paiania. Hymettus marble was extracted, in ancient times, from the W slope; modern quarries have been dug to the N of the mountain. In the grotto at the summit of the mount some ancient traces have been discovered indicating the existence of a sacred cult from the Geometric period to the 6th century BC. Above were the remains of an altar, possibly consecrated to Zeus Ombrios, mentioned by Pausanias (1, 32 2)

5 – Phyle and **Mt Parnis

We suggest that you spend half a day here: you will discover, in the gorges of Phyle, the hidden enchantment of the Attic countryside and enjoy, on the slopes of Mt Parnis, a coolness at the height of summer that is difficult to imagine on the over-heated streets of the capital.

Route: 69mls (111km) there and back.

Leave Athens by the Liossion road (plan I, B–1).

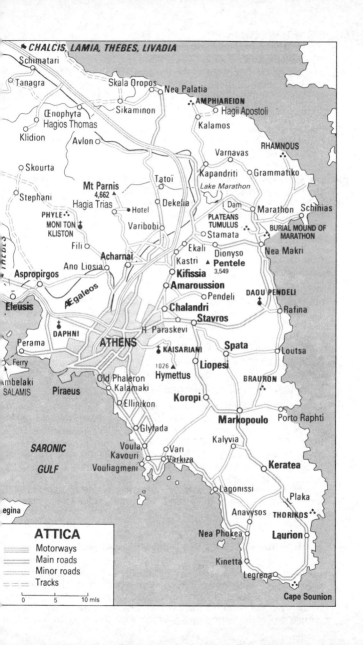

CHALCIS, LAMIA, THEBES, LIVADIA

Schimatari
Tanagra
Skala Oropos
Nea Palatia
AMPHIAREION
Hagii Apostoli
Œnophyta
Hagios Thomas
Sikaminon
Kalamos
Klidion
Avlon
Varnavas
RHAMNOUS
Skourta
Tatoï
Kapandriti
Grammatiko
Lake Marathon
Stephani
Mt Parnis
4,662 ▲
Dekelia
Marathon
Schinias
Hagia Trias
• Hotel
L Dam
PLATEANS
TUMULUS
Stamata
BURIAL MOUND OF
MARATHON
PHYLE
MONI TON
KLISTON
Varibobi
Dionyso
Nea Makri
Fili
Ekali
Ano Liosia
Kastri
Pentele
3,549 ▲
Acharnai
Kifissia
Aspropirgos
Amaroussion
Ægaleos
Pendeli
DAOU PENDELI
Eleusis
Chalandri
Rafina
DAPHNI
Stavros
Perama
ATHENS
H. Paraskevi
KAISARIANI
Spata
Ferry
1026 ▲
Liopesi
Loutsa
mbelaki
SALAMIS
Old Phaleron
Hymettus
BRAURON
Piraeus
Kalamaki
Ellinikon
Koropi
Glyfada
Markopoulo
Porto Raphti
SARONIC
Voula
Kalyvia
GULF
Kavouri
Varkiza
Keratea
Vari
Vouliagmeni
Lagonissi
Plaka
egina
Anavsos
THORIKOS
Nea Phokea
Laurion
ATTICA
Kinetta
——— Motorways
——— Main roads
Legrena
–––– Minor roads
= = Tracks
Cape Sounion
0   5   10 mls

6mls (10km): Ano Liosa. 11mls (18km): Fili.

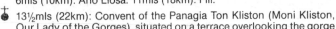

13½mls (22km): Convent of the Panagia Ton Kliston (Moni Kliston, Our Lady of the Gorges), situated on a terrace overlooking the gorge of Potami Gouras. This place is well worth a visit. Then continue along the recently asphalted road for several miles: this will bring you to the fortress of Phyle which you will see to your l. and which you reach by a path scented with shrubs, through wild, overgrown countryside that seems far removed from today's world. Several sections of the 4th-century rampart remain, built to a fine quadrangular design.

THE FORTRESS OF PHYLE, today known as the Kastro, controlled the most direct road from Athens to Thebes over Mt Parnis massif. It was built in the 4th century BC to replace another fortress, the remains of which are to be found on another summit at a distance of approximately 1,600yds (1,500m) as the crow flies, to the NE. It was, without doubt, this latter fortress that Thrasybulus occupied in 404 as he returned from Thebes to Athens with seventy supporters, determined to overthrow the Thirty Tyrants.

28½mls (46km): Return to Ano Liosa, from where you can take the Akharnai road.

30½mls (49km): Akharnai (Acharnae), once one of the most important rural demes of Attica, provided 500 hoplites at the beginning of the Peloponnesian War. Aristophanes, in his *Acharnians* (425 BC) depicted the peasants of the deme, the majority of whom were charcoal-burners from Parnis. They were forced to shelter in Athens while the Spartans laid waste to Attica.

32½mls (52.5km): The road begins to climb the slopes Mt Parnis

41mls (66km): Secluded hotel (hotel management school).

43mls (69km): Crossroads. The road to the l. (1½mls/3km) leads to the Mt Parnis refuge, at 3,821ft (1,165m) above sea-level, the road to the r. (1ml/2km) leads to a hotel and casino, which you can also reach from the plain by means of a cable-car.

47mls (76km): Summit of Mt Parnis, 4,662ft (1,411m) above sea-level above a thickly wooded base. The finest **views are from the cliff road on which the hotel-casino stands. Several forest tracks suitable for vehicles cross the slopes of Mt Parnis; it is by one of these that you may descend towards the N and rejoin the Lamia-Athens road at Skala Oropos.

6 – Apollo coast and the plain of Mesogeia

From Old Phaleron to Cape Sounion (Sunium), the shore bordering the Saronic gulf is fringed with small inlets nestling between wooded promontories; or it unfolds in long carpets of sand which make it the most beautiful coast of Attica. This is doubtless why it has recently been given the name of the Apollo coast, although it ends at the temple of Poseidon, on Cape Sounion. The construction, since the mid 1970s, of many hotels, villas and housing estates, has transformed this coast into a sea-side and residential suburb of Athens, one of the finest developments being the seashore resort of Vouliagmeni. Bear in mind, however, that the international airport of Hellenikon is a source of considerable noise. The area affected stretches from Kalamaki to Voula, and unfortunately includes Glyfada, a pleasant and lively, but very noisy, resort. The presence of nearly two and a half million inhabitants in the immense urban area of Athens, along with factories of all kinds, calls into question the purity of the water of the beaches between Eleusis and Glyfada, especially when the sea is rough. We recommend that you choose, for your own welfare, a hotel or a beach beyond Voula, from Kavouri onwards, which still leaves a wide selection.

As you return to Athens you will cross the most fertile plain in Attica, the Mesogeia, rich in ancient cemeteries. Near here you can visit the sanctuary of Artemis at Brauron.

Route: a circular route of 80mls (130km) (90mls; 146km including the visit to Brauron) along good roads. The trip will take half a day if you strictly limit the duration of your visits. If you have a whole day to spare you will find the trip much more enjoyable.

You are advised to leave Athens by Syngrou Avenue (plan I, E-4); this, although not the quickest route to Sounion, is the most attractive; you may also take the Vouliagmeni road (plan C-4), a quicker road leading to the international airport at Hellenikon (foreign airlines). In this case you will rejoin the route described below at Voula (see below, 11mls/18km).

3½mls (6km): After the Hippodrome turn l. towards Glyfada, arriving at the bay of Phaleron. Turning to the r. you will reach (3mls/5km) Piraeus, passing New Phaleron (1½mls/3km). New Phaleron (Neon Faliron), suburb of the great centre of Athens, one of the areas famous for the bouzouki.

5mls (8km): Old Phaleron (Paleo Faliron). A coastal resort and water sports centre, on a very jagged shoreline. Cemeteries containing the bodies of British soldiers who died 1941–45.

6mls (9.5km): Kalamaki, pleasure port.

6mls (10km): Alimos, birthplace of Thucydides (471 BC).

7mls (11.5km) Hellenikon airport (Olympic Airways); main building designed by Eero Saarinen. US airforce base.

7½mls (12km): Hagios Kosmas: Hellenic sports centre. Excavations have revealed the presence of an ancient cemetery along the shore and a Mycenaean settlement. Practically nothing remains of the sanctuary of Aphrodite mentioned by Pausanias.

10mls (16km): Glyfada, coastal resort; golf course (18 holes). The ruins, near the Antonopoulos restaurant and the Astir hotel, belong to a palaeo-Christian basilica which must have been built to commemorate St Paul's first landing in Greece.

FORBIDDEN TO MEN, ON PAIN OF DEATH. At the foot of Hymettus, on the edge of Glyfada, was the deme of Aixone, where for five days towards the end of October, the thesmophoria were celebrated in the sanctuary of Demeter. These were ceremonies which took place after the autumn sowing in honour of the goddess who had initiated humans in the cultivation of the earth. Only women were allowed to participate. Any men who attempted to do so risked the death penalty. This festival inspired Aristophanes to write his play *Thesmophoriazousai* (*Women at the Thesmophoria*).

11mls (18km). Voula, coastal resort (HNTO – Hellenic National Tourist Organization – beach).

12½mls (20.5km): To the r. among the pines, the resort of Kavouri.

 14mls (23km): Vouliagmeni, thermal spa and the pleasantest of the coastal resorts in the environs of Athens, in particular on the peninsula, where winding roads lead from the marina to secluded inlets, hotels sheltered by pines, including the Astir Palace, one of the best situated hotels in Greece.

 The Fallen (translation of the Greek place name for this coastal resort) owes its name to a small natural basin, deeply embanked, from which spring at a temperature of more than 68° F (20° C) the chlorosulphurous waters that are used to treat rheumatism and gynaecological problems. To reach this spot, turn l. off the Sounion road after having left the access road to the peninsula.

On the isthmus that joins Cape Zoster to the mainland a sanctuary has been found, consecrated to Apollo Zoster, comprising a small temple dating from the 6th century, together with several buildings including those reserved for the priests and pilgrims. The temple's ruins may be seen near the Akti Astir beach. In 1936 M. Stravropoulos uncovered the remains of a 6th-century building enlarged in the 4th or 3rd century, identified as being the priests' accommodation or a hostel for pilgrims.

16½mls (27km): Varkiza, a resort that stretches round a sandy bay (HNTO beach).

17mls (28km): Road straight ahead for Vari (1ml/2km). A cemetery has been excavated on the site of Anagyrous, dating from the 8th, 7th and 5th centuries BC. The tombs contain fragments of ceramics decorated with Geometric motifs or figures.

Forty-five min. walk from Vari, to the N, is the grotto of Pan, or grotto of Archidamus, in Hymettus. Archidamus was responsible for the inscriptions and sculptures. The grotto, which is difficult to reach, consists of two stalactite rooms consecrated to the nymphs, to Pan and to Apollo.

25mls (40km): Lagosini, small resort currently being developed. It is still fairly quiet, lying beside a long beach of fine sand.

27mls (44km): Saronis, recently established resort.

32mls (52km); Anavissos, resort.

39½mls (64km): Legrena.

41½mls (67km): Cape Sounion beach, with a small secluded inlet which provides a view of the famous columns of Poseidon's temple in the distance. Turn r. a little beyond the road that gives access to the beach for Poseidon's temple.

42mls (68km): **Cape Sounion, well known by sailors, once consecrated to Poseidon, the god of the sea, and Athena, providing the splendid setting for the temple of Poseidon, which includes possibly the most beautiful marble columns in Greece.

Open: weekdays 09.00–sunset (summer); 10.00–sunset (winter); opens one hour later on Sun.; entrance fee.

Before reaching the temple you will see the remains of the wall of the acropolis, which was fortified by the Athenians during the Peloponnesian War in 409, to serve as a position from which to keep watch over the coast. This wall began in the bay of Sounion, where the water sports were held at the time of the lesser Panathenaia and where there was a military port with a mooring for triremes (war galleys). The wall was separate from that encircling the temple. Only a few traces of the foundations remain, together with the propylaea, or monumental entrance, from the 6th century, built in limestone and rebuilt in marble in the 5th century. To the l. you will see under cover several fragments that decorated the architrave of the temple's vestibule.

The **temple of Poseidon, which stands at the edge of a headland falling sheer to the sea, must have been built between 444 and 440 by the same architect who built the temples of Hephaestus (Theseum) and Ares, in Athens, and the temple of Nemesis in Rhamnous (of these only the Theseum survives). As for the temple at Sounion, 15 Doric columns remain in place. The fact that these are without entasis (not curved) gives them a somewhat rigid and narrow appearance designed to compensate for their lack of height by giving them an impression of thrusting upwards. Another peculiarity is that there are only 16 flutes instead of the usual 20. This was to make the edges more resistant to the action of salt water and to give greater substance to the shaft. The temple, for a long time supposed to be dedicated to Athena Sounias, was finally restored to Poseidon following the discovery in 1898 of an inscription. It stood on the site of an ancient sanctuary in tufa, part of the substructures of which may be seen underneath the 5th-century building. The 5th-century temple was peripteral with six columns in the façade and 13 to the sides; it consisted of a central naos or cella, a pronaos or vestibule and an enclosed section at the back with two columns *in antis*. A sculpted frieze decorated the architrave of the pronaos and depicted the exploits of Theseus, combats between the Centaurs and Lapiths and the battle of the Gods and the Giants, several fragments of which you will have been able to see before reaching the temple.

550yds (500m) away, on the low hill to the N that overlooks the isthmus, lie the remains of the temple of Athena Sounias, from the 6th century, and of the surrounding wall.

43mls (69km): Return to the fork in the road which brought you to the temple of Poseidon.

48mls (78km): Laurion (Laurium, Lavrion), a small industrial town with an unusual background of slag heaps and vegetation burnt by the sulphurous waste produced by the treatment of silver-bearing lead which was mined in this area. (Port: weekly link with Keos and Kythnos).

Laurion is possibly the oldest example of what may today be called industrial pollution. The Athenians can have had few complaints, however, as the discovery, in 484 BC, of the deep and rich deposit in Maroneia (Kamariza) came just in time for Themistocles to order the construction of a fleet of 200 triremes (war galleys) with the revenue from this mine. Without this fleet the Greeks might not have defeated the Persians at Salamis in 480. Finally, under Pericles, the silver from Laurion contributed substantially to the founding of the Athenian maritime empire.

Laurion, source of silver and of the earth's treasure. The outcrops of silver-bearing lead of the Laurion hills, the Athenians' principal source of wealth, described by Aeschylus as 'a treasure granted them by the earth' in *Persians*, seem to have been exploited from very early times (around the year 1000 according to geologists). At the time when Themistocles assigned the revenue to the construction of the fleet, the mines paid 100 talents to the State. Some Athenians made great fortunes from them. The State, which owned the mines, leased them out for three or ten years, at a rent of 4.16% of the yield. Up to ten, or even twenty thousand slaves worked there, bought by the industrialists on the Athens Agora, where auctions took place each full moon. Harshly treated, they were not allowed to have any members of their family to live with them, so as to reduce labour costs. The incursions of the Spartans and the occupation of Dekelia in 413 provided them with the opportunity to escape. Towards the beginning of the 2nd century BC, the competition from the gold mines at Pangaeon in Thrace dealt a severe blow to the Laurion mines, as the costs of exploiting them had become too high.

The ancients collected only silver, lead and some secondary products such as cinnabar and ochre. Today calamine (zinc) and manganese in particular are extracted, but modern processes also allow lead and silver to be extracted from ore which the ancients ignored as too poor, and even from their tailings.

Off Laurion is the island of Makronissos, which was used as a detention centre after the civil war of 1946.

51mls (82km): Thorikos, one of the most ancient places in Attica, was probably a naval base belonging to the kingdom of Crete, and was certainly an important centre in antiquity, where the ores from Laurion were treated.

From the road you will see an ancient theatre, in a very ruined condition, which, together with the recently uncovered 'industrial quarter' constitutes the principal building still worthy of attention. Excavations carried out at the end of the 19th century, and in recent years by a Belgian team, have shown that the site was occupied from the pre-Achaean period (2000–1800), and then in the Mycenaean period, since a cemetery with two royal tholoi has been found here. One of these tombs was built shortly after 1500 BC. A boundary wall has also been found. The Athenians fortified the site (peninsula of Hagios Nicolaos), since it formed part of the ring of defences of the mines of Laurion and itself possessed two ports and industrial establishments, including ore-washing facilities. Below the theatre the Belgian team has uncovered a cemetery, the tombs of which, either for cremation or burial, date in the main from the Archaic and Classical periods. As for the mining installations, with their washeries and cisterns, these are to be found to the W of the theatre, where you will also find the entrance to a gallery belonging to the ancient mine (protected by a modern grille).

61½mls (99km): 1ml (2km) to the l. Kalyvia, with the Taxiarchis, Soteria and the Evangelismos churches are decorated with frescoes from the school of Georgios Markos, of Argos.

64mls (103km): Markopoulo, a large agricultural town with several churches decorated with frescoes that can be attributed to Georgios Markos. Do not fail to make the trip (5mls/8km) to Brauron.

2mls (3km) SE of Markopoulo the Antiquities Department has excavated a large cemetery which lay not far from an old well in a place called Merenda, near the ancient site of Myrrhonte. The tombs uncovered range from the 8th century (Geometric period) to the 4th century BC and the finds are exhibited in the Brauron museum. A section of an ancient road, just over 3yds (3m) wide, has also been uncovered. It was in this area that the Greek archaeologist E. Mastrokostas discovered in 1972 a kore and a kouros, masterpieces of Archaic art (National Museum in Athens).

5mls (8km) from Markopoulo by the direct road (5½mls/9km from Brauron), Porto Rafti is a fishing village in a bay full of rocky inlets and strewn with islets; on one of these there is a Roman statue, in marble, 9½ft (3m) high (a figure from the tomb of Erysichton), depicting a seated person, popularly known as the tailor (Raftis).

On the Koroni headland, which encloses the bay of Porto Rafti to the S, a hastily built fortress has been uncovered, possibly constructed by the admiral Patroclus, sent to help the Athenians by Ptolemy II at the time of the Chremonidean war (265–261) which ranged Athens, Sparta and Ptolemaic Egypt against Macedonia.

64½mls (104km): To the l. at a distance of 3mls (5km) is Koropi, in the heart of the highly fertile clay area of the Mesogeia (resinous wines are produced here). In the church of the Metamorphossi (church of the Transfiguration) are Byzantine frescoes from the 10th century.

The village has several other churches containing paintings attributed to Georgios Markos.

69½mls (112km): Paiania (ex-Liopesi). The name of this village comes from the ancient deme of Paiania which was the birthplace of the orator Demosthenes (384–322); the churches of Zoödochos Pigi, Hagi Thanasis, Hagios Dimitrios and Hagios Spyridon are decorated with frescoes attributed to Georgios Markos and his school.

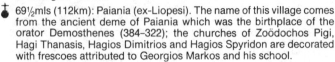

2½mls (4km) from the town along a new road towards the E, on the slope of Hymettos, is the grotto of Koutouki which will attract those with an interest in natural curiosities. This grotto (also called Païna) is one of the most beautiful in all Greece. It covers an area of 4,545yds² (3,800m²) and its rich mineral growths are set off to good effect by the intelligent use of indirect lighting.

Open: weekdays 09.00–19.00 (summer); 10.00–18.00 (winter).

3mls (5km) to the W is Spata, a large wine-growing village on the edge of which the construction of a new airport serving Athens has been proposed.

73mls (118km): Stavros. Gargetos, the birthplace of Epicurus, the Athenian atomist philosopher (341 BC), is not far from here.

74mls (120km): Hagia Paraskevi: National Centre for Nuclear Research. A road to the l. after the little church of Hagia Paraskevi leads to the monastery of Hagios Ioannis Kynigos (St John the Hunter), half-way up the slope at the N end of Hymettus. The church, cruciform and domed, dates from the 12th century. The narthex, also domed, was built in the 17th century. The frescoes, which were for the most part done with lime plaster, also date from this period.

76mls (123km): Cholargos, a residential suburb of Athens, on the site of the ancient deme of the family of the Akamantides, Pericles' native land. The headquarters of the Greek Armed Forces is situated here.

80½mls (130km): Athens.

7 — *Excursion to Marathon and the Amphiareion

The attraction of this visit lies not so much in the vision of the armies fighting at Marathon, nor in the whispers of the soothsayer Amphiaraus, as in the beauty of the countryside in this part of Attica. There are also some very beautiful beaches, such as those at Schinias or Haghi Apostoli, opposite the island of Euboea. This half-day excursion is full of the beauties of nature (although you will need a day if you decide to visit Rhamnous and pay an extensive visit to the Amphiareion). On the edge of Athens you will pass through an extremely pleasant residential suburb, especially from Kifissia onwards, cooled by the pines and the winds that come down from Pentelicon in summer more than by the sea breezes from the Apollo coast.

Route: 106mls (171km) – 115mls/185km including the visit to Rhamnous – along good roads, generally wide but quite winding.

Leave Athens by the Kifissia road. (plan I, F–1).

4mls (7km): Chalandri, 1ml (2km) to the r., is a residential suburb between Hymettus and Pentelicon.

7mls (11.5km): Amaroussion (Maroussi), the ancient deme of Athmonon, once famous for its sanctuary of Artemis Amarysia, is now renowned for its workshops that produce glazed ceramics (there are numerous shops along the road).

7½mls (12km): A road to the r. leads to Melissia and the monastery of Pendeli (3½mls/6km see below). After 1ml (1.5km) you reach the entrance to Melissia (film studios); continue along the same road. After 2mls (3km) turn l. in the direction of Nea Pendeli then left again after 550yds (500m) and continue towards Palea Pendeli.

After 3½mls (6km) you will reach the monastery of Pendeli, founded in 1578 (the buildings you will see are of recent construction), situated in a beautiful shaded flower garden; the narthex of the church contains several old paintings and icons. To the S of the monastery (Stavros road) is the Rododaphni palace, built in the 19th century in the neo-Gothic style for the Duchesse de Plaisance.

The monastery is situated on a spur of Mt Pentelikon (Pentelicon) 3,638ft/1,109m), where marble has been extracted from quarries since the 6th century BC. The Pentelicon is today unprepossessing, especially in the centre, since it has been totally disfigured by the quarries, the slag heaps and the antennae of the sound wave relay. The N slope, which the road to Marathon crosses, is still covered by fine pine forests.

PENTELIC MARBLE. The exploitation of the quarries, which began in 570 BC, was at its height under Pericles, and consequently the Hymettus marble was neglected. Previously, in tufa constructions, marble was used only for the decoration. In the 5th century entire buildings of Pentelic marble began to be built, Parian marble being reserved for sculptures, since it had a coarser grain, was less compact and easier to cut with a chisel. Pentelic marble, however, with its compact, close grain, was especially well suited to architectural use because of its suitability to take a smooth, polished surface.

The processes of extraction used in this period can be reconstructed. First, the surface of the rock would be levelled with a chisel. Then the blocks were marked out with deep rectangular grooves using a saw and finally removed with moistened wooden wedges, pushed in from above. The blocks were rough-hewn on site and then lowered along the paved track on wooden sleds that were braked by cables coiled around strong posts placed in holes that had been dug at various points on either side of the track.

8½mls (14km): Kifissia, at the foot of Pentelicon, 905ft (276m) above sea-level, surrounded by pines and plane trees, is one of the most popular summer spots among the Greek upper middle classes, especially around Kefalari, where most of the hotels are situated. The Piraeus and Athens railway line also makes it a very popular area with a less well-to-do clientèle, who come to spend an evening enjoying the cool and the taverns around the station.

A Natural History Museum is situated in Kifissia, centre for the study of the flora and fauna of Greece (13, Levidou Street; Tel. 801–5870; open daily 10.00–17.00 (winter); closed Fri.)

9½mls (15.5km): At this point a road to the l. leads to Dekelia, a town also known as Tatoï, which commanded a depression of considerable strategic importance to Athens. The supply route from Euboea passed through here (remains of a fortified camp, or paleo kastro, probably established during the Spartan occupation at the time of the Peloponnesian war). Tatoï (fine park) was the summer residence of the Greek sovereigns and contains the mausoleum of the Greek kings. There is also an important Greek air base. The road passes through Varibobi, a very popular holiday resort in summer situated on the lower slopes of Mt. Parnes.

11mls (17.5km): Kastri. Secluded hotel among the pines.

12mls (20km): Ekali. Holiday resort among the pines.

13mls (21.5km): Turn r. towards Nea Makri.

15½mls (25km): Dionyso, a village situated in a high wooded valley at the foot of the Pentelicon, which takes its name from the ancient sanctuary of Dionysus in the deme of Icaria, the native land of Thespis.

16mls (26km): ½ml (1km) to the l. are a few remains of the sanctuary of Dionysus, uncovered during the excavations carried out by the American school in 1888. Important festivals were celebrated here in honour of the god who had revealed the vine to the local hero Ivarios.

 19½mls (31.5km): Hagios Petros, a church and a café-restaurant which provides a magnificent *view over the plain of Marathon, the Euboea channel (or Euripos) and the S of the island of Euboea itself, a very mountainous area.

24½mls (39.5km): Nea Makri, a very popular beach on the bay of Marathon.

24½mls (39.5km): The road divides and the r. fork leads to Rafina (7mls/11.5km), the ancient deme of Araphen, a charming little marina situated around an inlet. The treeless area around, however, is not very attractive, except towards the Hagios Andreas beach.

VICINITY

Monastery of Daou Pendeli (3mls/5km). The monastery has been turned into a sanatorium. The monastery's church, founded in the 12th or 13th century and rebuilt in the 17th century, testifies to various influences: Byzantine, Armeno-Georgian and Anatolian. The gothic narthex dates from the time of the Franks. In the wood not far from the monastery there is a military cemetery (German; from the campaign of 1941–44).

4mls (7km) to the SW of Rafina lies Pikermi, a hamlet famous among palaeontologists for its rich deposits of neo-tertiary fossils investigated by A. Gaudry. These have shown species of animals related to the primitive fauna of E Africa (monkey, rhinoceros, giraffe, hipparion, helladotherium, mastodon, antelope, and dinotherium, the largest known fossil).

Where the road divides at 24½ mls (39.5km) turn l. towards Marathon, where you can visit the site of the famous battle, the cemeteries and the new museum.

26mls (42.5km): A road to the r. leads to the Marathon Tumulus (½ml/1km).

29mls (46.5km): A road to the l. leads to the tumulus of the Plataeans and the Museum of Marathon. (Refer to text on the museum).

38mls (53km): To return to the Schinias beach and Rhamnous, turn r. If you wish to go directly to Marathon continue straight on. (See below, 45mls/73km onwards.)

34½mls (56km): Take the first road to the r. for Schinias; for Rhamnous continue straight on.

37mls (59.5km): Second road to the r. for Schinias and road to the l. for Rhamnous (4mls/7km).

RHAMNOUS. This 'land of the buckthorn', the birthplace of the orator Antiphon, is famous for its acropolis that overlooks the entrance to Euripus and for its sanctuary of Nemesis.

Open: weekdays (summer) 08.30–15.30; Sun. 09.00–15.00; (winter) 09.00–13.30; 16.00–18.00; entrance fee.

On this secluded and romantic site, from which there are superb views over the Euripus channel and Euboea, you will see the remains of the sanctuary of Nemesis, which lay on a terrace partly tiered by a massive supporting wall (from the middle of the 5th century BC); ruins of the temple of Themis (or Small Temple; from the beginning of the 5th century); and of the temple of Nemesis (or Great Temple) in marble, of the Doric order with 6 columns in the façade and 12 on the long sides, which must have been built between 436 and 432 as a replacement for an older temple destroyed by the Persians in 479. Fragments of the cult statue and of its sculpted base, in marble, probably the work of Agoracritus, a pupil of Phidias, have been discovered in the cella.

The lower part of the site, towards the shore, is no longer open to the public. Amateur archaeologists and students who wish to visit this part of the site may, however, apply to the chief warden who will usually give special authorization. If you apply for and obtain this authorization you will descend to the fortress by a path that follows the line of the ancient Sacred Way and passes between traces of large funerary monuments from the 4th century BC (for example, that of Diogeiton, which has been restored). The fortress was built in the 4th century BC with the ramparts in isodomus arrangement. Here you will see the remains of various public buildings, including a small

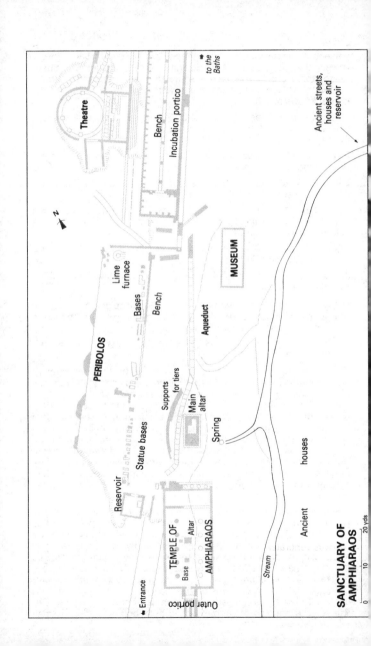

SANCTUARY OF AMPHIARAOS

Entrance

Outer portico

TEMPLE OF AMPHIARAOS

Base
Altar

Reservoir

Statue bases

PERIBOLOS

Supports for tiers

Main altar

Spring

Bases

Lime furnace

Bench

Bench

Aqueduct

MUSEUM

Theatre

Incubation portico

to the Baths

Ancient streets, houses and reservoir

Ancient

houses

Stream

N

0   10   20 yds

temple of Dionysus Lenaios, a gymnasium, a small theatre (of which some fine seats remain), fortifications (the ruins of the upper terrace represent those of the original acropolis), etc. To the NW of the fortress, on the slope of the hill, lie the ruins of a small sanctuary of the seer Amphiaraus who foresaw the failure of the Seven against Thebes, which was in use from the 6th century BC until the 3rd century AD.

The lower town occupies the small triangular area by the sea.

A large storehouse was constructed in the upper part of the site (to the SE of the sanctuary of Nemesis) for several fine funeral monuments from the 4th century BC (naskoï with human figures sculpted in the round, stelae and large urns in marble decorated with reliefs), as well as numerous elements from the temple of Nemesis (entablature, base of the cult statue) together with explanatory plaques. You cannot visit this store without special authorization.

≋ 39mls (62.5km): Schinias beach, a long ribbon of clear sand, bordered by a pine wood, popular with Greeks and foreigners alike.

44½mls (72km): Return to the fork at mile 33 (km 53) and turn r.

46mls (74km): Marathon (the 'fennel field') modern town on the territory of one of the most ancient demes of Attica. Continue towards Kapandriti.

50mls (81km): Grammatiko.

58mls (94km): Kapandriti, from here take the Kalamos road.

66mls (107km): Kalamos, a road to the r. leads to the beach of Hagii Apostoli.

To reach the Amphiareion from Kalamos turn l. after the church. As you make the descent you will have a remarkable *view over the channel of Euboea.

69mls (111km): *Amphiareion or sanctuary of Amphiaraus, at the bottom of a small valley, among the pines. Most of the buildings that you will see date from the 4th century BC; they are very dilapidated, except for the theatre which is relatively well preserved; the site, however, is one of the most charming in the whole of Attica. As you reach the excavation site you will notice on the r., below the road, the ruins of the temple of Amphiaraus, in the Doric order, built in the 4th century.

A hero and a soothsayer, Amphiaraus was one of the Seven Argive champions who besieged Thebes. According to legend Zeus caused him and his chariot to be swallowed by the earth near Thebes, where he was venerated. His place of worship then passed to the region of Cropos and became established in this deep ravine, near a spring famous for its healing properties. Thus the Amphiareion was founded, and here the hero was invoked as oracle and the god of healing.

Open: weekdays 09.00–15.30; Sun. 10.00–15.00; entrance fee.

The table for offerings was in the middle of the cella, while at the back stood the base of the statue. 33ft (10m) beyond the temple to the N lie the foundations of a monumental altar on which sacrifices were made to various gods and heroes. To the l. you can still see a complete line of steps and to the r. the circular orifice of the sacred spring through which Amphiaraus, transformed into a god, is supposed to have reappeared on earth. Those who were cured after taking the oracle's advice threw a gold or silver coin into the spring. The water was not used for sacrifices or for ritual purification, but was drunk from shells, a great number of which have been found.

At the foot of the hill to the l. lay a terrace with a line of more than thirty pedestals for statues covered with inscriptions, and a bench. Beyond this bench was a long portico (from the beginning of the 4th century BC) where those who came to consult the oracle lay to await the dream in which the remedy that would cure them would be revealed. A marble bench that rested on feet also of marble (53 have been found) ran along the walls.

The theatre, behind the portico, was large enough to hold three thousand people; its acoustics were excellent. Besides several tiers of seats, you can still see five marble seats with reliefs and inscriptions bearing the name of the priest of Amphiaraus, and the ruins of the stage. The façade of the stage, in the Doric order, has been restored (eight columns flanked by two pilasters support the entablature). Beyond the portico were the thermae, supplied by an aqueduct only a few ruins of which remain.

In the small local museum you will see several fragments of sculpture, some funeral stelae, a statue of Amphilochus (a famous doctor), Byzantine reliefs discovered in the vicinity, a ceramic bath-tub and numerous architectural fragments. If you cross the stream, you will visit the ruins on the right-hand bank. Here you will see the remains of a collection of houses, porticoes and small altars, all of which are very dilapidated.

75mls (121km): Skala Oropos, beautifully situated on the channel of Euboea. Ferries cross the channel every half hour for Eretria (see section on Euboea). Inland, lignite mines. From here head for Malakassa and Athens.

83mls (133km): Lamia-Athens road 6 (see route map 3).

106mls (171km): Athens.

 # Athos [Mount]***

Route map 14.

Kavalla, 98mls (156km) (from Ouranopolis) – Thessaloniki, 85mls (138km) (from Ouranopolis); admin. region of Mt Athos.

Athos, which has given its name to the 'Holy Mountain' (Hagios Oros) is the principal summit of a 28mls (45km) long peninsula joined to Chalcidice by a narrow spit of land 1ml (2km) wide through which Xerxes had a canal built so that the Persian fleet would not have to round a cape feared for its tempests. To the N it consists of wooded hills, where the Mediterranean forest is in evidence, to the S of austere and virtually deserted landscape. But if nature in general is preserved, it is because Athos is also, indeed first of all, a sanctuary where the contemplative tradition of orthodoxy is still very much alive in a curious theocratic republic populated exclusively by monks and anchorites in this 'Garden of the Virgin' – the only thing feminine there. Admission is for men only; and you will often find the treasures stored in the monasteries – the frescoes, icons, mansucripts and reliquaries – only after long tiring walks, although the exceptional character and beauty of the place makes these worthwhile.

Athos in history

MYTH AND HISTORY. According to legend Mt Athos was the stone thrown at Poseidon by the giant Athos; according to another tradition Poseidon separated it from the peninsula of Pallene during his fight with the giant. It was known in ancient literature: Homer mentions it and Aeschylus (*Agamemnon*, 285) calls it the place 'where Zeus reigns'.

It was occupied by a certain number of towns which paid tribute to the Athenians. It is famous for the attempt by Xerxes to dig a canal there in 480, so that his fleet could sail through it and escape the disaster of Mardonius, who lost 3,000 ships and 20,000 men in 491 when trying to round the cape. But the canal turned out to be too shallow. We do not know when monastic life took root there, but the first foundations apparently go back to the 10th century. Athanasius the Athonite (d. c.1000), friend and adviser of the Emperor Nicephorus II Phocas, organized the communities of hermits living on Athos. He founded the monastery of Hagia Lavra (963) and from then onwards pious foundations multiplied, protected by the emperor, who granted them privileges.

SPIRITUAL CENTRE OF ORTHODOXY. About 1300, Gregory the Sinaite reanimated Athos's contemplative tradition by encouraging inward, private prayer, but monastic life did not reach its apogee until the 15th century. After the conquest of Constantinople by the Turks, the monks kept on good terms with the sultans, one of whom, Selim I, was ceremonially received. Thanks to these skilful politics, Mt Athos remained the centre of Orthodoxy. It possessed schools for its monks and one of them, called Vatopedi, had an illustrious master, Eugene Bulgaris, from 1753–59. Mt Athos remained under the Turkish yoke until 1830, although recruitment benefited from the surge in Russian monasticism which lasted until 1917. Today, in spite of an appreciable increase in coenobite life in the monasteries of Gregoriou, Dionysiou and St Paul, and the intellectual renaissance of the monastery of

Stavronikita, there are only about 1,000 monks left (15,000 in the 16th century) and several monasteries are virtually abandoned.

A THEOCRATIC REPUBLIC. Although its inhabitants have withdrawn from the world, Athos has always attracted the attention of outside powers. Venice tried to exercise its influence, but never succeeded. Russia, on the other hand, was more fortunate and Pan-Russian politics dominated Athos from 1830 to 1890. In 1912, the mountain was occupied by the Greek army; in 1913 the Treaty of London confirmed its independence and neutrality. Since then, its situation has been clearly defined. A decree of 16 September 1926, confirmed by the constitution of 1927, laid down its organization. The peninsula forms part of the Greek state, which is represented there by a governor with the rank of prefect, coming under the Ministry of Foreign Affairs, although Athos enjoys some degree of autonomy. It is administered by the Holy Council, resident at Kariyes. It is composed of 20 representatives or antiprosopoi, (one per convent), elected in January, four of whom, the epistates, share executive power under the presidency of one of them, the protepistatis, elected for five years. The Council also has financial and legal responsibilities.

COENOBITES AND IDIORRHYTHMICS. The convents are divided into two groups: the coenobites (who live communally, leading an austere life throughout the year), and the idiorrhythmics ('living as they please') who can eat as they wish, have a milder regime and live by their own resources. This relaxation was introduced around the 17th century. The monks pray for eight hours a day: litourgia (Mass), hesperinon (vespers), apodipnon (compline), nycterinon (nocturnal office which may last all night), agrypnia (vigils), panygiris (solemn meeting); in addition they must make a certain number of genuflexions every day.

HERMITS AND VAGABONDS. Apart from these main categories, you will also find anchorites (hermits who live apart in sometimes inaccessible cells), sarabites (groups of two or three hermits living in isolated houses – kellies or kalyves – with a private chapel), and gyrovagi (poor mendicant and vagabond monks).

FORBIDDEN TO EVERY SMOOTH-FACED PERSON. Among the oldest and most strictly observed rules is the abaton of Constantine Monomachus, who issued a bull in 1060 forbidding access to the mountain 'to every woman, every female animal, every child, eunuch and smooth-faced person'. In spite of the disputes it aroused under Turkish domination and recent efforts by Greek feminists, it has stayed in force.

What you should know

THE ATHONITE MONASTERY. The monastery is usually surrounded by a solid wall flanked by towers. The wall protects a space called the peribolos, in the centre of which is the communal cruciform church or catholicon with several domes and a double narthex. It is the main feature of the convent. Around it are the subsidiary buildings: the phiale, a kind of rectangular shelter above the holy water; the tower-shaped belfry, the trapeza or apsidal refectory, with several rows of tables and an ambo from which a monk reads an edifying discourse during meals: near the seat of the hegoumenos (superior) is a dish for the consecrated bread (panagirion). Lastly, the monk's cells are arranged along the walls. The katholikon and the trapezium are frequently the oldest part of the monastery. The archontaria is the guest room. We should also mention the hermitages by the sea, reached by ladders, occupied by seafaring or fishing monks. The sketes are small monasteries attached to larger ones, all with many chapels or hermitages of their own.

ART ON ATHOS. You will not find any very old works, apart from the famous Vatopedi mosaics. Discoloured frescoes have been touched up (especially in the late 17th or early 19th century), a fact which might deceive the unwary visitor. There were two rival schools, one of which succeeded the other. The first, or Macedonian, school skilfully adapts wall painting to the architectural framework. It is represented by the painter Manuel Panselinos, whose works are hard to identify (chapel of St John the Baptist), and his pupils (monasteries of Vatopedi and Chilandari). The second is the Cretan school, which took its inspiration from icon painting. A celebrated member was Theophanes, who painted between 1535 (Katholikon of Lavra) and 1558, and later Frangos Castellanos of Thebes, who worked c. 1548–60. Many of the monasteries house treasures, reliquaries, portable icons and liturgical objects, but the monks are reluctant to show them. They regard them as sacred objects, not works of art.

PAINTING IN THE SERVICE OF DOCTRINE. Painted décor is so stylized that it can be codified. The Katholikon of Dochiariou is the perfect example. Generally, the centre of the dome is occupied by the Pantocrator (Christ in Glory), surrounded by the Virgin and the Ioannes Prodromos (John the Baptist), prophets and angels. In the three apses and behind the iconostasis are paintings dealing with the life of the church's patron saint. In the dome of the apse the Virgin and Child; above, Christ. In the apse of the prothesis, to the l., the death and resurrection of Our Lord with figures from the Old Testament. To the r. the same figures with Christ and the Trinity in the centre. Above the altar, the Son of God outside the tomb and crowned with thorns. In the nave and the choirs, the main holy days are depicted in four parallel zones. The same arrangement holds good for the narthex: the domes glorify Christ and the walls represent Church councils, the lives of the martyrs and the Last Judgment. Frescoes in the refectory relate to food. However, these traditional principles are sometimes modified by picturesque variations in detail.

Useful information

ADMISSION FORMALITIES. For a time conditions of entry were relaxed and gave rise to some abuses. Now Mt Athos is very difficult to get into. So you must prove your respectability to obtain a permit. As mentioned before, women and children (under 21) are strictly forbidden and males must have 'well cut' (i.e. short) hair, or they risk being forbidden to stay in the monasteries by the Holy Epistasia (an Athonite authority).

Visitors wishing to enter Mt Athos – no more than eight foreigners a day – should obtain a letter of introduction from their embassy in Athens or their consulate in Thessaloniki (see addresses under Useful Information for those towns). This document should be presented to the Ministry of Foreign Affairs, Directorate of Churches, Zalokosta and Vasilissis Sofias Streets (Tel. 362–6894) in Athens, or to the office of Political Affairs of the Ministry of Northern Greece, Dikitiriou Square (Tel. 260–427) in Thessaloniki. Once they have received the approval of the ministry, visitors should go to the police (foreign department) who will issue a permit valid for a maximum of three days.

FORMALITIES DURING YOUR STAY. You embark at Ouranopolis (see Vicinity of Thessaloniki). On landing at Daphni, present your permit to the police, then go to Karyes for your residence permit (diamonitirion) from the Holy Epistasia on payment of approximately $3.00. You can stay either at Daphni in small rather primitive inns, or, on presentation of your diamonitirion, at the hotel at Karyes run by monks, or in the actual monasteries (not more than three days). If you wish to spend the night in a monastery, you should arrive before sunset, otherwise you will find the doors shut. Hospitality is dispensed when you show your diamonitirion, but you should always make a small donation on leaving.

We recommend taking some extra provisions, as the monks' daily fare is extremely frugal.

You can travel from one monastery to another on foot or by caique, but the services are very irregular. We can say that in recent years there has been a regular twice-daily summer service between Ouranopolis and Daphni, every two days between Daphni and Hagia Anna; every two days between Hierissos and the Grand Lavra.

A bus runs between Daphni and Karyes.

Please note that smoking is forbidden in the main street in Karyes and that shooting films and taking photographs with a flash or tripod are banned throughout the Mt Athos complex. The calendar on Mt Athos is 13 days behind our own.

Tourists without entry permits for Mt Athos can view it from the sea by taking a boat from Hierossos or Ouranopolis, but they are not allowed to land. They may stay in the ports just mentioned (see Vicinity of Thessaloniki).

Visiting Athos

From the port of Daphni, Karyes can be reached by bus or a two-hour walk. On the way you pass the monastery of Xeropotamous (idiorrhythmic) which, according to tradition, was founded before the 10th century by St Irene or the Empress Pulcheria. The paintings in the katholikon date from 1783. Ask to see the 13th-century Paten of St Pulcheria.

Also on route to Karyes, the (coenobite) monastery of Koutloumoussiou, on a hillside in a verdant setting, is dedicated to the Transfiguration of Our Saviour. It was donated in the late 13th century by a Turkish prince. The frescoes in the katholikon date from 1540.

Karyes, capital of the community, is a little village grouped around the monastery with a few shops run by monks. You can visit the Church of the Protaton, presumed to date from the 10th century (the frescoes were executed in 1540 by the painter Panselinos) and the Chapel of Ioannes Prodromos (John the Baptist) with frescoes also attributed to Manuel Panselinos (1526). Other, more recent ones, are notable for their freshness and delicacy.

About 1 hr from Karyes, the skete of Hagios Andreas, the most recent monastery on Athos, was founded through the generosity of the Tsars of Russia. You will recognize it from afar, by its bulbous green belfries crowning vast white buildings.

About 1½hrs from Karyes, the idiorrhythmic* monastery of Vatopedi looks like a veritable city encircled by battlements; it occupies a beautiful site overlooking a lovely bay. It is believed to have been founded in the late 10th century by three monks from Adrianople.

THE RASPBERRY-BUSH AND THE CHILD. The following legend is told about its origins. The sons of the Empress Theodora, Arcadius and Honorius, were travelling from Naples to Constantinople with their mother when they were assailed by a tempest. Arcadius fell into the sea and was later found under a raspberry bush by monks who took him to Constantinople. When he succeeded his brother, he had a convent which he called Vatopaidon (from *vatos*, raspberry bush, and *paidion*, child), built on the spot where he was cast ashore by the sea.

The blood-red 11th-century church is a domed basilica flanked by two more churches, the external vestibule (exonarthex) being common to the three sanctuaries. You will note the 15th-century bronze doors which come from the Church of St Sophia at Thessaloniki, as well as the 11th-century mosaic of Intercession (Deesis) above the door of the katholikon. The katholikon was decorated with frescoes by painters of the Macedonian school in 1312 (they have been restored). In the chapel of Hagios Dimitrios, you may see the icons of St Peter and St Paul, the icon of the Panagia Hodigitria, in a 12th- or 13th-century frame with reliefs depicting Christian festivals, and the iconostasis, etc. In the *treasury, you can admire some beautiful pieces of goldsmith's work, some of them dating from the 10th century, and in particular the Cup of Michael Palaeologus (early 15th century), a solid piece of jasper 10ins (25cm) in diameter on a silver base decorated with enamel and with engraved handles in the shape of dragons. You should ask to see some very beautiful crosses, a portrait of the Virgin attributed to St Luke, etc.

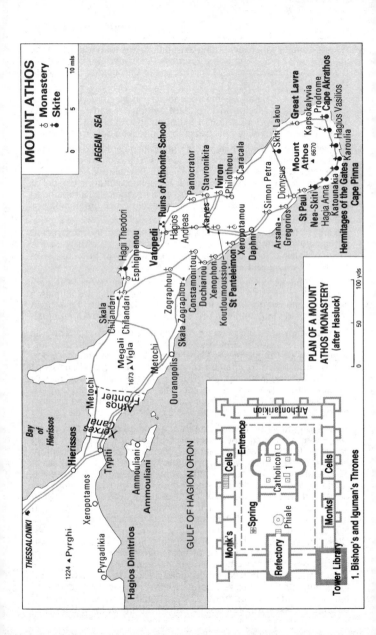

MOUNT ATHOS

⊕ Monastery
✝ Skite

0   5   10 mls

AEGEAN SEA

Great Lavra
Cape Akrathos
Kapsokalyvia
Prodrome
Skiti Lakou
Mount Athos ▲6670
Hagios Vasilios
Karoulia
Hermitages of the Gates
Katounakia
Hagia Anna
Nea-Skiti
Cape Pinna
St Paul
Dionysus
Arsana-Gregoriou
Simon Petra
Caracala
Philotheou
Iviron
Stavronikita
Pantocrator
Ruins of Athonite School
Vatopedi
Hagios Andreas
Karyes
Xeropotamou
Daphni
Koutloumoussiou
St Panteleimon
Xenophon
Dochiariou
Constamonitou
Zographou
Skala Zographou
Ouranopolis
Metochi
Megali Vigla ▲1673
Chiliandari
Skala Chiliandari
Esphigmenou
Hagii Theodori

Athos Frontier

Xerxes Canal
Trypiti
Ammouliani
Ammouliani
Bay of Hierissos
Hierissos
Metochi

GULF OF HAGION ORON

THESSALONIKI
Pyrghi ▲1224
Xeropotamos
Pyrgadikia
Hagios Dimitrios

PLAN OF A MOUNT ATHOS MONASTERY (after Hasluck)

0   50   100 yds

Archontarikion

Cells
Entrance
Cells

Catholicon
1

Cells

Spring
Phiale

Monk's
Monks

Refectory

Tower Library

1. Bishop's and Iguman's Thrones

Nor should you fail to visit the library, with its precious volumes, notably an 11th-century octateuch (a collection of the first eight books of the Old Testament), adorned with 162 minatures.

✝ The monastery of Esphigmenou, about 2½hrs from Vatopedi, is situated on a picturesque gulf. It was founded in the early 11th century and has a fortress-like aspect intended as a protection against pirates. St Gregory Palamas, was its higoumenos (abbot) in the 14th century. You will be able to see a 12th-century portable mosaic icon of Our Lord and, in the library, a menologion (a calendar of Greek Christian Saints' days), on purple parchment ornamented with 60 miniatures (12th century).

✝ The (idiorrhythmic) monastery of Chilandari, in a wooded valley 40 mins from the preceding one, was founded, according to Brehier, in 1197 by the Serbian prince Stefan Nemanija and rebuilt in 1299 by Stefan Milutin, a Serbian prince who retired to Vatopedi after his abdication. The term 'idiorrhythmic' (self-regulating) means that the monks lead their own lives.

The katholikon contains frescoes from the late 13th or early 14th century; the cycle of the baptism has admirably executed details. Don't forget a visit to the treasury, with precious icons, and to the library with Serbian and Russian icons from the 12th to the 17th century, illuminated manuscripts from the 13th to the 18th century, and an Italian diptych adorned with miniatures overlaid with crystal plaques (late 13th or early 14th century).

Retrace your steps to Vatopedi to visit the S part of Athos.

✝ The (idiorrhythmic) monastery of the Pantocrator, 2hrs from Vatopedi, was founded by Alexis Stratigopoulos, a general of Michael Palaeologus, in 1270. It has a rather curious location on top of a rock dominating the coast. In the library, you can examine various manuscripts, including a late 11th-century psalter with a miniature of the Annunciation.

✝ The (coenobite or strict-rule) monastery of Stavronika, 1hr walk, was founded in 1542 by the patriarch Jeremiah of Constantinople. It crowns a precipitous rock adjoining the sea and its architecture is massive and beautiful. In 1546 the monk Theophanes, who worked in the Meteora, and his son Simon, painted the frescoes in the katholikon. For some years now, this monastery has been the centre of a spiritual and intellectual revival on Mt Athos.

The (idiorrhythmic) monastery of Iviron, 1hr walk, was founded in 979 by a general, John Tornikios, and two monks, in honour of St John the Baptist. Its massive tower and the domes of its churches contrast sharply with other parts of the convent built of wood and stone and painted in many colours.

The 11th-century katholikon is decorated with frescoes from 1592.

In a small neighbouring chapel, ask to see the miraculous icon of the Panagia Portaitissa (much worn; 10th century?) which the monk Gabriel took from the sea. It is supposed to have enabled him to walk on the waters. The library contains a rich collection of illuminated manuscripts. We should mention especially manuscript no. 1 (11th century Gospel), manuscript no. 5 (a Tetra-Gospel from the 13th-14th century) and manuscript no. 453 (*Romance of Barlaam and Jehosophat*, early 13th century). Near the library is the convent's treasury. It is worth asking the monks to open it; it houses precious fabrics (homophorion of Galaction, of the Patriarch Dionysius 1672), a beautiful cross carved in 1607, a 17th-century carved cross (raising of Lazarus), etc.

Near the convent is a hospice where the monks looked after lunatics and lepers. From it, you can descend to the little harbour (arsana) where the fishermen-monks, who provide the convent with fresh fish, reside.

The (coenobite) monastery of Philotheou, 2hrs walk from Iviron, less imposing than the others, will attract you by the charm of its site. Founded before the 12th century, it was entirely rebuilt after a fire which destroyed it in 1871, except for the katholikon with its frescoes from 1572.

The (coenobite) monastery of Caracala, slightly inland and 30mins walk from Philotheou, was founded around the 12th century by a Turk and dedicated to the Apostles Peter and Paul.

The **Great Lavra (idiorrhythmic), 4hrs walk, is possibly the most beautiful of the monasteries on Athos. It was founded in 963 by St Athanasius, under Nicephorus and John Tzimsces. With its triple gates, its alleyways and squares it looks like a large fortified village.

The *katholikon, completed in 1004, has a peculiar shape, its proportions and heavy vaults being explained by the dimensions of the dome (20ft/6.25m in diameter). It served as a model for the katholikon of Iviron and Vatopedi. Its frescoes were painted in 1535 by the Cretan painter Theophanes.

Opposite the katholikon you can visit the refectory. Its **frescoes by Frangos Castellanos (1560) are considered among the most beautiful on Mt Athos. On the rear wall, you will notice the Last Supper and on the side walls three friezes in which are depicted, below, images of the saints Athanasius, Euthymus and Gregory Palamas, in the centre, scenes of martyrdom and lastly, in the upper frieze an illustration of the hymn Akathistos (literally, not seated) sung standing in honour of the Virgin. The l. side wall shows the life of St Athanasius of Athos, the Council of Nicaea and episodes from the Life of the Virgin. On the r. side wall, a depiction of the Last Judgement (in the centre, the second coming of Our Lord; to the l. the Chosen and Paradise, to the r., Hell).

Next you should visit the chapel of St Nicholas, with frescoes painted by Frangos Castellanos in 1560, and the Chapel of the Trinity (Hagia Trias), with its iconostasis door dating to the 15th-16th century. You will also see the icon of Koukouzelis (c. 12th century), a reliquary of Nicephorus Phocas (12th century at the earliest), and an enamelled icon said to be that of John Tzimsces, but actually dating from the 12th century. The library is also very rich, with its 5,000 volumes and more than 2,000 manuscripts, especially 11th- and 12th-century evangeliaries. Visit the little museum in the hall, containing archives.

From the Grand Lavra, the ascent of Mt Athos is about 15mls (24km) on foot. From the summit (6,680ft/2,033m), crowned by the Chapel of the Transfiguration, you will have a magnificent panorama of the singularly beautiful summit of orthodox asceticism which is Mt Athos.

1½hrs walk from the Grand Lavra, you will come to the Romanian Skite of Prodromos, founded by the monks, princes and the Metropolitan of Moldavia, then you will round the tip of Athos passing various retreats of pious anchorites; the hermitage of Kapsokalyvia, 1hr walk from the last-named, the hermitage of Hagios Vassilios (St. Basil), 30mins away, the hermitage of Katounakia, at 40yds (36m) distance, not far from the hermitages of Portes, clinging to the side of the cliff above the sea, most of which are difficult of access. From the hermitage of Katounakia, the track leads towards the port of Daphni, passing the hermitage of Hagia Anna, 30mins away, a place of ascetic retreat where the desiccated foot of St Anne is preserved in a silver reliquary and then to Nea Skite (fine portable icon of the Annunciation carved in wood).

The (coenobite) monastery of St Paul, founded in the 11th century by Serbian and Bulgarian monks and considerably enlarged in the 19th century clings to the mountain in a lovely location.

The ancient katholikon, built in 1447 by the Serbian prince George Bankovitch and decorated by painters of the Macedonian school, is now destroyed. In the chapel of St George, there are frescoes in the Cretan manner surely dating to the 16th century and not to 1423 as the inscription (probably apocryphal) would have you believe.

The (coenobite) monastery of Dionysou accessible by a mountainous path, is about 30mins from St Paul. It was founded in 1375 by the Emperor of Trebizond, Alexis III, and his wife Theodora (the founding charter is still in the convent). The site is remarkable, on top of a high rock dominating the sea and terraced gardens, with an extensive view of the coast.

In the katholikon are frescoes executed by the Cretan painter Zorzis in 1547. In the refectory, do not fail to look at the frescoes with scenes of martyrdom, the Apocalypse, and the Last Judgement, as well as the carved wooden ambo. In the library you can ask to see an exquisite evangeliary from the 12th century and the founding charter of the monastery, a veritable masterpiece of calligraphy.

The (coenobite) monastery of Gregoriou, 1½hrs walk from Dionysou, is also situated on a rock dominating the sea, near a small port. It was founded in the 14th century. In the katholikon note the murals dating from 1779.

The (coenobite) *monastery of Simon Petra was created in the 14th century by a hermit called Simon on the top of a vertiginous rock which is reached by a curious bridge of three superimposed arches. This exceptional site has made the monastery famous. You will admire the architectural audacity of its galleries supported by wooden beams overhanging a dizzy void of more than 650ft (200m). From Simon Petra, you can return to Daphni in about 1½hrs.

The (coenobite) monastery of St Panteleimon, still known by its name of Roussicon, founded in 1814, is Mt Athos' Russian monastery.

Built between the sea and a wooded hill, it forms an impressive complex with a marked Slavic aspect. It could once house 2,500 monks (the refectory can hold a thousand guests). In 1968, a fire destroyed a large part of it, but you can still see one curiosity: one of the largest bells in the world, weighing 13 tons and measuring 28ft (8.70m) in diameter. Moreover, you will appreciate the touching beauty of its chimes when the offices are sung.

The (coenobite) monastery of Xenophon, 1½hrs away, was founded in the 11th century near the sea. In the chapel of St George note the frescoes of the school of Theophanes of Crete, in the ancient katholikon, the paintings by Antonios (those in the narthex or vestibule dated to 1545 are anonymous), and in the refectory a painting of the Last Judgement.

The (idiorrhythmic) monastery of Dochiariou, 45min away, founded in the 11th century, has paintings by an anonymous artist of the Cretan school (1568) in the narthex of its church.

The (coenobite) monastery of Constamonitou, 1½hrs walk away, on a rock, dates from the 11th century if we are to believe a golden bull of 1037, but more probably to the 14th century. Frescoes from 1443–47 in the katholikon.

The (coenobite) monastery of Zographou, 1hr walk, dates from the 13th century, but was rebuilt in the 19th century. For a long time the monks were mostly Bulgarian. Ask to see the miraculous icon of St George.

■ Attica

Route maps 3 and 5.

This ancient territory of the city of Athens forms a peninsula of 1,023sq. mls (2,650km²) (including the region of Oropos on the channel of Euboea and the islands of Salamis and Aegina, with mountains occupying more than 386sq. mls (1,000km²). Their slopes are steep and desolate, their summits covered with conifers, for example in the ranges of Citheron and Parnes which separate Attica from Boeotia, or on Mt Pentelikon, a major source of marble for building, or Hymettus, supplier of honey, which dominates Athens. Attica, ancient Pedion, the cereal granary of the Athenians, with scenery sometimes reminiscent of the islands, has only a small proportion of land available for agriculture. Among trees the olive reigned supreme. It was considered as a gift from Athena to the town of Athens at the time of her memorable dispute with Poseidon on the Acropolis. But the vine, a gift from Dionysus, was and still is a major agricultural resource, especially on the inland plain of the Mesogeia. Today, agriculture is retreating before the drive of Athenian urbanization, but one still finds sheep and cereal crops, which are tending to become industrialized. Minerals, another natural resource, have also been exploited from antiquity. The production of minerals is still quite large, but the quality is poor, except perhaps for the marble of Pentelikon which supplies a purely local industry. Nevertheless the silver-bearing lead mines of Laurion, that 'treasure of the earth' (Aeschylus), from which other minerals are extracted today, enabled the Athenians to arm the fleet which secured their victory over the Persians at Salamis, and partially to finance their building programmes and political expansion.

Industry, however, is the main resource of Attica, based on large-scale immigration which reanimates villages abandoned by farmers (Markopoulo, Aspropirgos). Unfortunately, this does not happen without spoiling them and the much lauded purity of the Attic skies is now only a memory, at least above the Athenian region. The industrial triangle Athens-Piraeus-Eleusis contains two thirds of Greece's industrial activities, with refineries, mechanical constructions, metal and chemical works, textile and clothing industries, flour mills and other factories for food products, oil refineries, soap works, etc. There is a textile industry at Megara, while foundries and chemical factories add a new dimension to the mines at Laurion. Lastly, one cannot describe Attica without mentioning the enormous commercial activity generated by the traffic at the port of Piraeus.

B

Bassae [Temple of]**

Route map 7.

Andritsena, 8.5mls (14km) – Pyrgos, 49mls (79km) – Tripolis, 58mls (94km) – admin. region of Arcadia.

Any impatience aroused by the poor road from Andritsena will be completely forgotten when you reach this **remarkable site of high, rocky mountains, dotted with oak trees, in the very heart of Arcadia. At an alt. of 3,707ft (1,130m), in splendid isolation, you will find one of the best preserved Classical temples in Greece, reputedly built by Ictinus, one of the architects of the Parthenon, in 420–417 BC. Unfortunately you may find some scaffolding there, because the monument frequently has to undergo essential restoration work.

AN EX VOTO MONUMENT. The temple of Bassae was consecrated to the god Apollo Epikourios by the inhabitants of the neighbouring town of Phigaleia (see Vicinity of Andritsena) in gratitude for delivering them from the plague during the Peloponnesian war, probably that of 420 BC, and protecting them in this place, which was their refuge. Bronzes found near the temple show us that Apollo Epikourios was a warrior god. Discovered in 1765 by the Frenchman Bocher, it was explored in 1811–12 by the Society of Dilettanti, who took away sculptures (23 slabs of the internal frieze, very well preserved and some badly mutilated metopes) now in the British Museum in London.

•.• Built of local limestone and showing the warm patina of centuries, marble being reserved for sculptures, the temple of Bassae is a strange mixture of the three orders, Doric, Ionic and Corinthian. Its construction on a narrow platform explains its orientation and the peculiarities resulting from this. Restoration work is continuous. Six Doric columns on the façade and 15 on the side surround the vestibule (pronaos) and the sanctuary (naos). The interior of the latter is decorated with pilasters forming buttresses, the last two arranged obliquely, bounding the adyton, the heart of the sanctuary, which is also separated from the naos by an isolated Corinthian column, undoubtedly the oldest example of that order. Around the naos (inside court) ran a frieze (in the British Museum) depicting battles between the Greeks and the Amazons and between Lapiths and Centaurs. There is a door in the E wall of the adyton, an unusual feature perhaps intended to re-establish the E-W orientation of the sanctuary, so that the light would fall on the statue of the god placed opposite.

Some 77yds (70m) to the W of the temple, the foundations of some Archaic and Classical buildings have been found. One of them may have been the workshop used by the sculptors working on the temple.

Boeotia

Route maps 3 and 4.

Set between the Gulf of Corinth and the Atalandi Canal (which also washes the island of Euboea) Boeotia and the neighbouring regions of Locris and Phocis link northern Greece with Attica, and are being increasingly marked by the economic and industrial expansion of the latter. The orographical structure of this territory is simple, with mountains and plateaus intersected by depressions expanding into plains. To the N the wooded mountains of Locris rise above the Gulf of Lamia, with Mt Callidromos dominating the famous pass of Thermopylae from its 4,501ft (1,372m). In the centre, the plains, exchange and transit zones, were ideal sites for major battles: Plataea, Leuctra, Elateia and Chaeronea. Lastly, to the S, are Mt Helicon (5,735ft/1,748m), which sheltered the Valley of the Muses in one of its folds, and Mt Parnassus (8,061ft/2,457m), on whose slopes the Panhellenic sanctuary of Apollo was founded at Delphi; their villages, which lived by agriculture and stock breeding, were de-populated by moves to the plains.

The Boeotian plains (Elateia, Chaeronea, Thebes, the ancient basin of Lake Copais) and Phocian plains (Sacred Plain of Itea at Amfissa), basically devoted to agriculture in spite of a very dry climate (cereals, olive trees) and, at one time, to horse breeding (region of Thebes), were and are still the source of wealth for these regions. That is why Boeotia was able to retain – only briefly to be sure – its hegemony over Greece and to hold in check the Athenians' aspiration to expand into northern Greece. Today irrigation and mechanization have improved the crops, which are more varied and increasingly orientated towards provisioning the capital. Cotton is also grown. Two harvests a year are common in the basin of Livadia or ancient Lake Copais.

Some small industries are scattered around Thebes, the population of which has increased very rapidly, and at Livadia, an ancient textile centre now reactivated. In addition, some thirty industrial enterprises are installed at Skimatos, on the Athens–Thessaloniki motorway.

But all this is changing the appearance of these regions very slowly and you can still see how 'these landscapes stand out with clearcut bright contours, with the light refining their beauty' (R. Clozier).

■ Brauron (Vraona)

Map of the Vicinity of Athens, p. 310.

Athens, 21.5mls (35km) – Markopoulo, 5mls (8km) – Sounion, 25mls (40km).

Among the hills carpeted with vines, on the edge of the sea, the archaeological site of Brauron, whose name is little changed in its modern equivalent, was one of the most venerable cult localities in Attica, where Iphigenia came to end her days on her return from Tauris.

ARTEMIS BRAURONIA. Brauron is one of the most ancient localities in Attica. A precinct (fortified enclosure) was discovered on the slope of a hill at the foot of which is the site dating in effect to the Middle Helladic period. The sanctuary was consecrated to Artemis Brauronia; it was created to appease the wrath of the goddess after the slaying of a bear which had killed a young girl from a village in Attica. Artemis then caused a plague and made it known through an oracle that she required the inhabitants of Attica to consecrate to her their nubile daughters, the 'little bears' or arktai who took part in the spring festivals in honour of the goddess every five years. According to a tradition mentioned in *Iphigenia in Tauris* by Euripides (v. 1464), the daughter of Agamemnon was buried at Brauron.

On the Markopoulo Road you will pass on your l., on the slope of a hill, the remains of a palaeo-Christian basilica before reaching Brauron.

Visits to the site and the museum (Tel. 0294–71 020); open weekdays in summer 08.30–15.30; in winter 09.00–14.30; Sun. 09.00–15.00 in summer and 10.00–15.30 in winter; closed Tues.; entrance fee (these hours are not guaranteed).

⁙ ARCHAEOLOGICAL SITE. While walking to the chapel which dominates the site, you will note on the l. the remains of a bridge (c. mid 5th century BC) which spanned a watercourse issuing from a sacred lake, then the ruins of a sacred portico built in the second half of the 5th century on the site of an Archaic building (7th and 6th centuries).

Below the gallery there were rooms which may have housed the 'she-bears'. They were also the depository of the luxurious garments which women about to give birth consecrated to Iphigenia.

Only the foundations of the temple of Artemis, of the Doric order, remain. It was erected in the 5th century to replace the early 6th century sanctuary destroyed by the Persians, who carried the cult statue off to Susa, according to Pausanias. Near the temple, a series of blocks probably marked off a sacred lake fed with water from a spring.

Beyond the ruins of the temple, a cutting in the rock forms a kind of corridor with a little two-roomed sanctuary built after the collapse of the rocky roof of the grotto behind it. Next comes a sanctuary with four compartments, nearly 50ft (15m) long, which was destroyed by the caving-in of the grotto where it was originally built. It is believed to be the tomb of Iphigenia. The last building at the exit from the corridor, formed as a result of the collapse of the grotto, was probably the house of the priestesses attached to the sanctuary.

Do not fail to visit the chapel of Hagios Georgios, from the 14th century, which houses some very badly damaged frescoes.

MUSEUM. Situated a few hundred yards beyond the site, it contains not only the find made at Brauron, but also vases and artifacts from the necropolis of Myrrhinous (see Vicinity of Athens), from Anavyssos and Perati. You will also notice a beautiful votive relief of the gods, from the late 5th century, which depicts Zeus (seated), Leto, Apollo and Artemis. In the second hall there are beautiful statues of children, among them the 'she-bears', the little girls consecrated to the goddess.

After visiting the museum, you can go to see a number of Mycenaean tombs by taking the first road to the l. on the main road after the fork at the museum.

4mls (7km) N of Brauron, Loutsa is a popular, very busy little beach, in the vicinity of which the remains of a temple consecrated to Artemis Tauropolos have been discovered.

Cephalonia [Island of] (Kefallinia) ***

285sq. mls (737km²) – Pop: 31,000 – admin. region of Zante.

Rich and fertile, with many pine forests covering the tawny slopes of Mt Ainos (5,315ft/1,620m), with its flowers and fruits, this island, important since the Mycenaean period, exhibits all the attractions of the most beautiful Mediterranean landscapes. Because of that and its magnificent beaches (especially in the vicinity of Lixourion), Cephalonia is today one of the new Greek tourist paradises, although not yet completely swamped by visitors. The island is also famous for its wines (Rombola and Monte Nero) and its cuisine (try the bacaliaroptia and the sweets).

IN THE WAKE OF ULYSSES. In Homer's work, the name of the Cephalonians (the people of the head, i.e. of the mountain) designates the people who took part in the Trojan war under the leadership of Ulysses, but it was later restricted to the inhabitants of the island of Cephalonia, which, in the *Odyssey*, bore the same name as its capital, Samos or Same. Archaeological exploration of Cephalonia has shown that it was prosperous in the Mycenaean period.

OFTEN INVADED, ALWAYS GREEK AT HEART. Allied to Corinth against Corcyra (Corfu), it was forced to take the side of Athens in 431 BC during the Peloponnesian war. Dominated in turn by Rome (from 189 BC), then in the Middle Ages by the Normans from Sicily, the Pisans (1099), various Italian princes, the Turks (1479), the Venetians (1500), the French (1797) and the English (1808), it finally became part of Greece, along with the other Ionian islands, in 1864.

A STRANGE TRADITION. If the inhabitants were called 'people of the head' in antiquity, nowadays they have a reputation for being a little mad, perhaps because of their proximity to the world of mystery. Apart from the natural phenomenon of the Katavothrai (see the Caves of Drougarati, below), a strange tradition has it that on 15 August the island's poisonous snakes meet and go to church to be blessed by the 'papas' or parish priest (without biting anyone).

Nestling at the end of a gulf, Sami is the busy port where you generally disembark on the W coast of the island. Opposite Ithaca, it is located near the site of ancient Same, capital of the island in antiquity (remains of the city wall, two acropolises, a bath from the early 3rd century AD and a temple on the site of the church of Hagios Georgios). 218yds (200m) from the port, remains of a Roman building with mosaics.

From Sami, the road along the gulf to the N is lined with beachside restaurants; it leads to the little harbour of Hagia Efimia.

To the S there is a road (a track, in fact, for several miles) which traverses the mountain (*views), through magnificent scenery before redescending to Poros and its very lovely beach (about 12mls/20km, but more easily accessible by a surfaced road from Argostolion).

THE CAVES OF DROUGARATI (SE of Sami) AND MELISSANI (E of Sami). They belong to a complex of caves and grottoes often containing lakes near the reappearance of the Katavothrai and are suitably equipped for visiting (*daily from 07.00 to 19.00*). The first, near the village of Haliotata, has such good acoustics that concerts are sometimes held there; at the second, near Vlahana, the lake is in the open air.

The Katavothrai are a remarkable hydrogeological phenomenon where the sea flows constantly into underground tunnels near Argostolion and goes right across the island to re-emerge at Sami on the E coast. This phenomenon has not only caused the formation of grottoes often containing lakes, but was used in the last century to work mills.

ARGOSTOLION (4mls/23km W of Sami by a little road which is winding, but has a very lovely natural setting). A small town of some 9,000 inhabitants, founded by the Venetians in 1757, is the capital of the island. The present town was rebuilt after an earthquake in 1953. Apart from its charm as a little Mediterranean seascape, it will attract lovers of archaeology by its archaeological museum containing finds made in the island, especially from the Mycenaean period: jewels, bronze weapons, etc., coming mainly from the necropolises of Metaxata and Mazaracata. You can also see a small historical and folk museum and some exquisite icons in the cathedral.

VICINITY OF ARGOSTOLION

1 THE CASTLE OF ST GEORGE AND THE PLAIN OF LIVATHO (15.5mls/25km). Leave by the Metaxata road, which crosses the plain of Krabe, one of the four towns which formed the tetrapolis of Ancient Cephalonia (together with Paleis, Pronnaioi and Same). The double acropolis of Krane dominates this plain (remains of a 13th-century fort, a little temple from the Early Classical period and a Roman portico).

3mls (5km): Kastro, a village now almost deserted, on the site of Hagios Georgios, capital of the island in the Middle Ages and under the Venetians. On the slope of the hill, the remains of the citadel with a drawbridge over the ancient moat which encircled the wall and inside the latter dilapidated buildings (churches, an English barracks). This capital which once numbered 15,000 inhabitants was destroyed by an earthquake in 1636 and abandoned for Argostolion in 1757. Near San Giorgio, visit the monastery of Hagios Andreas (frescoes of the Cretan school, icons).

5mls (8km): Necropolis of Mazacarata where Cavvadias excavated numerous Mycenaean tombs, one of them domed.

5.5mls (9km): Metaxata, where Lord Byron stayed in 1823; near the village, rich in beautiful villas and luxuriant gardens, were found three Mycenaean tombs cut out of the rock, and the ruined remains of a small apsidal temple where the cult of the dead was celebrated.

6mls (10km): Lakithra, main town of Livatho, the richest district on the island. Near the village, some Mycenaean tombs were discovered. Around them are well-shaped hollows cut out of the rock of the kind found in the Mycenaean cemeteries of Cephalonia. These were probably treasuries or silos for storing grain.

You return to Argostolion by the upper road.

2 LIXOURION. The second town on the island, Lixourion is a small port situated opposite Argostolion, on the other side of a strait (frequent boat and ferry service), but 20mls (32km) by road (to the N, then l. at Kardakata). With the exception of a folk museum, installed in an old house, there is little to hold your attention, save the ruins of Paleis, some 2mls (3km) by the Argostolion road.

3 THE CASTLE OF ASSOS AND THE N OF THE ISLAND. Running beside the Gulf of Lixourion, the road leaves Argostolion going N.

10mls (16km): Kardakata.

18mls (29km): Divarata, on a height away from the coast.

23mls (38km): road to the r. for the Venetian castle of Assos (1595) dominating the picturesque village of the same name, in the midst of vineyards, where you can enjoy lunch under the trees.

34.5mls (56km): Phiscardo, at the N tip of the island, opposite Ithaca. It is a 12th-century foundation by the Norman conqueror Guiscard, now a rather disappointing fishing port, but in a very beautiful setting.

■ Chalcidice

Route map 14.

A broad expanse of land joining the three peninsulas of Kassandra, Sithonia (Longos) and Mt Athos, where they extend into the Aegean Sea, Chalcidice is a system of orthogonal faults where deep valleys mark off plains and gulfs through the mountainous masses. The latter are still covered with dense and well-preserved vegetation, and the valleys, never thickly populated, have hardly been developed. This poor region has been isolated for a long time, without taking advantage of its maritime position and until very recently, without a decent road network.

In the N with cold winters, the poor soil permitting only scanty crops, large-scale emigration has occurred, both seasonal and permanent, to the neighbouring regions and Thessaloniki. It is only along the lower contours that subsistence agriculture is carried on. On the other hand, the coast, with a much more temperate climate and attractive beaches in a verdant setting, is the object of large-scale rapid tourist development, notably with the creation of the resort of Porto Carras (see Vicinity of Thessaloniki).

History has left few marks on Chalcidice, linked with the destiny of Macedonia, and – along with Mt Athos, of course – only the sites of Olynthus, Potidaea and Hierissos will retain the attention of lovers of archaeology.

Chios [Island of] (Hios)**

331sq. mls (858km²) – Pop: 60,000 – capital of the admin. region of Chios.

5mls (8km) off the Turkish coast, this island with its wild uneven landscape is proud of being the birthplace of Homer, a splendid title to fame, but probably not enough to attract an ever-increasing number of visitors, if it did not also offer the beauty of its scenery and its delightful beaches, especially those of Lo and Karfas. We recommend that you stay in the capital, especially if you wish to drive round the island among the olive, almond, orange and lemon trees or in Maramaro (Kardamyla) if you are drawn to the pleasures of the sea.

Of all the recommended excursions starting from Chios, you should not miss the trip to Nea Moni, but if you like the picturesque ambience of the Middle Ages, you should also go to Volissos and the region of the Mastichochoria, the mastic villages. This curious speciality of Chios is a kind of gum obtained from the resin of the lentisk tree. Mixed with certain spirits, it is used to make varnishes for oilpaints and chewing gum or is drunk with water. But Chios also produces an excellent wine and good jam.

CHIOS AND IONIA. Undoubtedly populated by emigrants of Ionian origin from Euboea, who subdued the indigenous inhabitants of the island, Chios was naturally more drawn to Asia Minor than Greece at the beginning of its history. Like all Greek cities, it was originally governed by 'kings' under whom it joined the confederacy of the 12 cities of Ionia. The dethroned kings were replaced by tyrants of the Basilids (royal) family whom the people overthrew. The Basilids were the first to engage in the slave trade. Highly developed economically, the island enjoyed a constitution from the 7th century BC. After the conquest of Asia Minor by Cyrus the Great, Chios made a treaty with the Persians, but was at their mercy after the fall of Miletus in 494, which marked the end of the revolt of the Ionian cities.

ATHENIAN IMPERIALISM After the Persian Wars, which marked the beginning of the Athenian hegemony, Chios joined the Delian League in 447, although preserving its autonomy, and remained in it until 412 BC. After the Sicilian expedition, Chios took the side of Sparta and was ravaged on several occasions by the Athenians. Later, it once again supported Athens and adhered to the Second Confederacy, formed under the aegis of Athens against whom it rebelled in 357. It recovered its independence in 355.

A FRAGILE INDEPENDENCE. In the 4th century Chios submitted to Alexander. In the 3rd century it made a pact with Aetolia, then all-powerful. Later, allied to the Romans, it fought against Antiochus, at the beginning of the 2nd century BC. Its wealth excited the greed of the legionaries and it was sacked by Verres and then by the troops of Mithridates. Lastly, retaken by Sulla, it regained its independence (86) which was respected by the Romans.

A LATIN COLONY. Another crucial period in the history of Chios began in 1172, when the Doge Vital Michieli drove the Byzantines out of the island. For nearly four centuries, but not without some interruptions, it was a Latin possession, in the hands of either the Venetians or the Genoese. In the 14th century, the Genoese formed a kind of limited company, the Maona, to exploit the island and commercialize the production of mastic, an aromatic gum much appreciated in Western Europe in the Middle Ages.

ELEGY FOR A MASSACRE. After paying tribute to the Turks for several years, the Genoese lost the island in 1566 to the Ottoman Empire. Subsequently there were various attempts at rebellion by the people, although the island lived in semi-independence. In 1821, the Samians occupied the island from which they were driven by the Turks, who for five months carried out massacres immortalized by the verses of Victor Hugo, the 'Massacre of Chios' (*Les Orientales*) and in a painting by Delacroix. The island became part of Greece in 1912.

THE BIRTHPLACE OF HOMER. This island is looked on as the birthplace of Homer (Smyrna also claims that honour), the most illustrious representative of a family of bards or aeidói. In ancient Greece, the aeidói were originally intermediaries with a religious vocation between the gods or deified heroes, who inspired them, and men. They were, then, 'possessed' creators or depositories of the hymns which were heard at religious ceremonies. Later, the function became more profane, which allowed the growth of the romantic epic, of which the *Iliad* and the *Odyssey* are the most beautiful examples.

Homer, who lived c.850 BC according to Herodotus, is the greatest Greek epic poet. However, the question of his very existence has been raised, since the 17th century. This extreme position has been abandoned today, but we will never know whether he was the sole author of the *Iliad* and the *Odyssey*.

Chios is also the birthplace of Glaucus who, in the 7th century BC, invented or introduced into Hellas the art of forging iron by hammering.

CHIOS, the capital of the island (pop. 24,000) is a very lively little town situated on the E coast, almost as far as the first slopes of Mt Aetos which forms an impressive barrier. It extends over the site of the old town, but its methodical exploration has not yet begun. The port exhibits a double aspect rather like the image of modern Greece: on the old quay lined by low houses, fishing nets dry next to caiques with peeling paintwork, while modern houses, cafés and the cosmopolitan crowds landing from the ferries give life to the modern quay. From the port, where it is pleasant to stroll when the arrival of the boat from Piraeus creates a lot of bustle, you can easily reach the centre of the town, Vounakis Square. It contains an ancient mosque which housed a museum until 1977. Since that date, the collections have been transferred to a new building where they are well displayed. Access to this new archaeological museum is by a street at right angles to the sea front, on the S side, about 330yds (300m) walk from the quay.

Open: weekdays, except Tues., 09.00–13.00 and 16.00–18.00; Sun. 10.30–14.30.

Casts of sculptures found on the island or attributed to local artists are on show in the vestibule. The main hall contains both vases and fragments of vases (numerous fragmentary but evocative examples of the polychromatic Archaic vases called 'Chian calyxes'), terracotta figurines (one Hellenistic example in a case at the end of the hall has been interpreted as a portrait of Homer), sculptures (among them two beautiful torsos of kouroi which remind us that in the 6th century BC Chios was the seat of a famous school of sculpture), various small objects and architectural elements, such as those from the sanctuary of Apollo Phanaios. Two more halls contain votive and funerary reliefs and bronze objects, on the one side, and on the other, Classical and Hellenistic vases and fragments of vases.

The kastro, visible from the port, is a 14th-century enceinte enclosing a residential quarter where the ancient Genoese houses, reoccupied by the Turks in the 14th century, decrease from year to year. In its present state, this fortress mostly dates from the Genoese and Turkish periods, but the site was fortified from the Hellenistic era.

VICINITY OF CHIOS

1 NEA MONI (New Monastery) (9mls/15km). Leave by the Avgonyma road. During the ascent of the steeply sloping sides of Mt Aetos, you will discover surprisingly beautiful panoramas before reaching this monastery church hidden in a wooded vale, in celestial calm. It was founded about 1050 by Emperor Constantine Monomachus after the miraculous discovery of an icon and shows the splendour of Macedonian Renaissance.

You will visit the 11th-century *church decorated with frescoes and *mosaics. The paintings (Last Judgement) in the exonarthex date to the early 14th century. Ask to see the refectory with its stone benches and a long table of polychrome marble.

2 THE MASTICHOCHORIA REGION (round trip 48mls/77km). Leave Chios by the Karfas road.

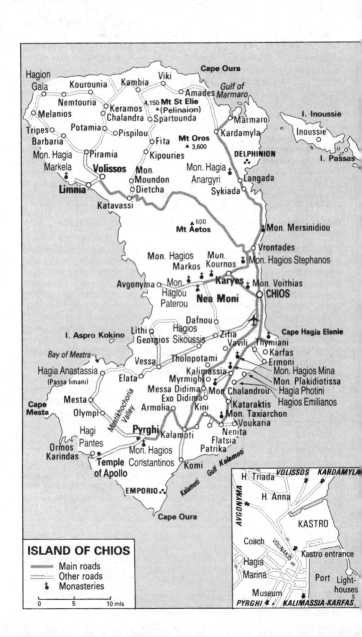

ISLAND OF CHIOS

Main roads
Other roads
♣ Monasteries

0   5   10 mls

Hagion Gala · Kourounia · **Kambia** · Viki · Cape Oura

Nemtouria · Keramos · Amades · *Gulf of Marmaro*

Melanios · Chalandra · 4,150 Mt St Elie (Pelinaion) · Spartounda

Tripes · Potamia · Pispilou · Marmaro · I. Inoussie

Barbaria · Piramia · Fita · Kardamyla · Inoussie

Mon. Hagia Markela · **Volissos** · Mt Oros ▲ 3,600 · **DELPHINION** · I. Passas

Mon. Moundon · Kipouries · Mon. Hagia Anargyri

Limnia · Dietcha · Langada

Katavassi · Sykiada

▲ 600 Mt Aetos · ♣ Mon. Mersinidiou

Vrontades

Mon. Hagios Markos · Mon. Kournos · ♣ Mon. Hagios Stephanos

Avgonyma · Mon. Hagiou Paterou · **Karyes** · Mon. Voithias

Nea Moni · **CHIOS**

Dafnou

I. Aspro Kokino · Lithi · Hagios Sikoussis · Zifia · Cape Hagia Elenie

Bay of Mestra · Georgios · Vavili · Thymiani

Vessa · Tholopotami · Karfas

Hagia Anastassia (Passa limani) · Kalimassia · Ermoni

Elata · Myrmighi · Mon. Hagios Mina

Mesta · Messa Didima · Mon. Chalandrou · Mon. Plakidiotissa

Exo Didima · Hagia Photini

Cape Mesta · Olympi · Armolia · Kini · Kataraktis · Hagios Emilianos

Hagi Pantes · **Pyrghi** · Kalamoti · Mon. Taxiarchon · Voukaria

Ormos Karindas · Nenita · Flatsia

Mon. Hagios Constantinos · Komi · Patrika · *Gulf Kalamoti*

Temple of Apollo

EMPORIO · Cape Oura

Inset map

VOLISSOS · *KARDAMYLA*

AVGONYMA · H. Triada

H. Anna

KASTRO

Coach · *VOUNAKIS* · Kastro entrance

Hagia Marina · Port · Lighthouses

Museum

PYRGHI ♣ · *KALIMASSIA-KARFAS*

5mls (7.5km): Monastery of Hagios Minas, with an ossuary containing the bones of many islanders who were victims of the 1822 massacres.

15mls (24km): Armolia, centre of the mastic region. This resin extracted from the lentisk tree (200 t. a year) is used to flavour spirits (raki and ouzo) and confectionery much appreciated by the Greeks; ruins of a 14th-century Genoan castle. Ceramic workshops.

18.7mls (30km): *Pyrghi, a medieval village with narrow, sometimes covered streets, houses adorned with xysta, strange geometric designs scratched on the walls. You will want to visit the 12th-century Hagii Apostoli Church and its frescoes.

➤ 5mls (8km) from Pyrghi, near the hamlet of Hagi Pentes, ruins of a temple of Apollo from the end of the 6th century BC, on the site of the ancient Phanai. The temple was destroyed during the erection of a small Palaeo-Christian chapel and a subsequent basilica. In 412 BC, a battle between Chios and Athens took place near Phanai, Athens being victorious.

• 6.2mls (10km) from Pyrghi, at Emporio, the British School discovered a site inhabited since the Early Bronze Age (3rd millennium). This habitat also covered a hill crowned by the remains of a Byzantine fortress destroyed c.660 AD by the Arabs during the first siege of Constantinople. Between this acropolis and the old port lie the remains of Archaic (7th and 6th century BC) and Classical (5th century BC) buildings, and also of a palaeo-Christian basilica (6th century BC), erected on the site of a 5th-century BC temple. In addition, a temple of Athena, from the 6th century BC, and a megaron, which was probably the local king's palace in the Mycenaean age, inside a fortified acropolis, were discovered on the hill of Profitis Ilias.

A little to the W of Emporio is the pleasant sandy beach of Kato Fana.

25mls (40km): Mesta, another village with narrow winding streets that has retained its medieval character, lying at the foot of a Genoan castle. Return to Chios by taking the Vavil road on leaving Kalamoti.

3 VOLISSOS (25.6mls/41km). Leaving Chios by the Kardamyla road, you will reach one of the most attractive villages on the island by a mountain road offering ***superb views. Volissos lies at the foot of another hill where a ruined Byzantine fortress seems to stand guard. Don't miss continuing to Piramia (2.8mls/4.5km), with a church housing an excellent 17th-century iconostasis and a carved wooden ornamental border, or to the monastery of Hagia Markela (3.1mls/5km) if you happen to be there on 22nd July. Then you will be able to participate in the island's most important religious festival in honour of the saint.

4 MARMARO (14.4mls/23km). Leave Chios by the Kardamyla road.

3.7mls (6km): Near the beach of Lo, the Stone of Homer or Dascalopetra is probably a very ancient holy site of the cult of Cybele (note the eroded relief of the goddess between two lions). Nearby,

Jean Psichari (d. 1929) a local writer who taught at the Sorbonne and was the son-in-law of Ernest Renan, is buried on a terrace overlooking the coast.

9.4mls (15km): Langada, near the military and naval base of Delphinion, built by the Athenians in 412 BC. The site was excavated by the British School.

15.6mls (25km): Kardamyla, from where boats leave for the bare and rocky Island of Psara (15sq. mls/41km²), to the W of Chios. Greek patriots were massacred there in 1824. It is also the birthplace of Admiral Canaris, hero of the War of Independence. Some Mycenaean tombs were uncovered at Archontiki in 1962. The island has only one village and the monastery of the Dormition of the Virgin. Lovers of solitude may also wish to visit the islet of Inousse, which has a few tavernas and unspoilt beaches.

14.4mls (23km): Marmaro, large fishing village located on a creek. Beyond Naghos, you will find some of the most beautiful beaches on the island.

■ Chora

Route map 9.

Kyparissia, 28.1mls (45km) – Pylos (Navarin), 10.6mls (17km) – Pyrgos, 68.7mls (110km).

This large town in western Messenia, located in an area especially rich in Mycenaean sites, has a museum that will interest lovers of Hellenic archaeology. Reached by the Kalamata road, the museum is devoted to regional finds. You can see there gold cups from the Peristera tholos (beehive) tombs near Kyparissia, and fragments of frescoes from the palace of Nestor at Pylos, as well as casts of Linear B tablets.

Open: weekdays, except Tues., 09.00–15.00; Sun., 10.00–15.00.

■ Christianou

Route map 9.

Kyparissia, 18.4mls (29km) – Pylos (Navarin), 38.4mls (61km) – Pyrgos, 58.7mls (94km).

Once known as Christianoupolis, now no more than a village, it was the seat of a bishopric from the early centuries of Christianity and then in the 11th century of an archbishopric as testified by an ancient Byzantine church dedicated to the Transfiguration of Our Lord. Carved fragments of an iconostasis in the interior.

The remains of a basilica with five naves from the late 5th or early 6th century have been found in the vicinity, at Hagia Kyriaki, near Filiatra. It was partially rebuilt (central nave only) before the end of the 6th century, after being destroyed by an earthquake.

Later, a small chapel was built on the ruins of this second basilica. 110yds (100m) to the S was a bath from the 4th or first half of the 5th century AD.

Corfu [Island of] (Kerkyra)***

615sq. mls (1,593km²) – Pop: 92,000 (Corfiots), 28,630 in the capital – also capital of the admin. region of the same name – Greek archbishopric – Catholic bishopric.

The island of Corfu is more of a pleasant half-way house between Italy and Greece than a genuine introduction to the Hellenic world. In addition to the gentle landscapes and lush vegetation of Italy, it preserves a style, an atmosphere bequeathed by centuries of Venetian occupation in the days when the Lion of St Mark acted as watchdog over the entrance to the Adriatic, a domain reserved for the Venetian Republic. If we add the subsequent French and British occupations, one would be entitled to ask if Corfu was really Greek at all, yet Greece is there once again at those sources where legend and history mingle, in the Phaeacia whose shores Odysseus visited. To be sure, she is not to be found in the palace-cum-mirador, the Achilleion, that debased example of Corfiot Hellenism, built by an imperial heroine straight out of a novel, the Empress Elizabeth of Austria, but rather on the carved pediment of an ancient Corcyran temple, on which a capricious goddess shows the visitors her Gorgon's smile with an ambiguity testifying to the complex origins of a civilization. She is also present in the narrow streets of the old walled city, the last urban refuge of what is genuinely Greek on an island devoted to tourism. Corfu is not Greece, but it *is* Greek, and it has enough personality of its own to attract, seduce and hold the visitor. Corfu is also an island of festivals. The Corfiots are great lovers of processions, and their numerous holidays (see Useful Information) give you a chance to hear local music influenced by Italian rather than Byzantine tradition.

A long sickle shape separated from Epirus by two straits linked by splendid maritime roads, with gentle peaks rarely topped with snow (Mt Pantokrator is only 2,965ft/904m), the island of Corfu is covered with olive, cypress, plane, orange, lemon, bay, myrtle and lentisk trees, which enjoy a climate always tempered by the sea. One hopes the tourist invasion will not spoil the charms of Corfu for a long time to come.

History of the town

A TYPICALLY BYZANTINE STORY. Although the Greek name of the island and its capital, Kerkyra, link it with Greece's glorious past, some scholars claim that Corfu is supposed to be the barely disguised corruption of a name given to the town by the local populace in the Byzantine period. *Stous Korfous* (The Breasts), an interpretation puncturing the pretensions of the official authorities who called it *Polis ton Koryfon* (the Town of Peaks) in the 14th century. These peaks, or breasts, are simply the two little hills on which the ancient citadel stood. In the Homeric period, i.e. in the *Odyssey*, it was called Scheria (The Cliff) or Land of the Phaeacians.

A DAUGHTER OF CORINTH. Corfu was founded c.734 BC, in the place known as Paleopolis, by the Corinthians, anxious to secure a port of call on the sea route to Sicily. Known as Corcyra (Korkyra or Kerkyra, the tail), she herself created colonies at Epidamnus (Durres, in Albania, and Apollonia in Epirus), but there was internecine strife everywhere and Corinth's maritime empire did not last.

THE ETERNAL CONFLICT BETWEEN THE GENERATIONS. Corcyra rapidly became a maritime power in the Ionian Sea and the Adriatic. Was Corinth an unworthy mother? Or Corcyra an ungrateful daughter? At all events, the inevitable in the Greek world of those days happened: the two clashed. The metropolis, beaten at sea in 665 BC, was forced to let its colony lead its own life.

A SACRED, BUT CALCULATED UNION. During the preparations for the second Persian campaign against Greece (480–479), Corcyra joined the sacred union, but responded to the appeal with calculated tardiness. Its fleet of 50 triremes (war galleys) emerged intact from the bloody battle of Salamis, because it arrived too late. Nevertheless, it was courted by Athens and Sparta, and even had the doubtful privilege of sparking off the cruellest conflict ever between the two main Greek powers, known as the Peloponnesian War.

AN EXPLOSIVE FAMILY QUARREL. Thus the conflicts between Corcyra and Corinth and its old colony of Epidamnus were the sparks which detonated the infernal machine. Sparta, backed by Persian gold, relied on the aristocratic party; Athens supported with its drachmas the democratic party, whose zeal was so successfully refuelled that the civil war of 427–425 ended in the extermination of the rival faction. Corcyra virtually lost its independence in playing these bloody games, being dominated first by Sparta and Athens, and then by various powers, including Rome.

THE GREAT DESPOLIATION. The entrance onto the stage of Venice, which disputed the possession of the island with the Byzantines and Normans from the end of the 11th century, inaugurated another important period in Corfu's history. The year 1204, which saw the capture of Constantinople by the Franks, was marked by a particularly black milestone in Byzantine annals. It was the signal for the great despoliation of the European territories occupied by the kings. Venice (1204), the despots of Epirus (1210) and the Angevins (1267) were successively masters of the island.

CORFU AND THE MARINE LION. At the end of the 14th century, the empire of Constantinople retained only a shadow of its former glory. The Turkish tidal wave had breached the Byzantine dyke once again and this time it surged over Europe. It encountered the Lion of St Mark on its way and Corfu's great moment had come. Becoming Venetian in 1386, Corfu was the Gibraltar of the Adriatic for more than three centuries. History has always highlighted Lepanto, and Don Juan of Austria was made to appear as the saviour of the west in the face of the Turkish peril. That is partly true, but not fair to Venice. Without the resistance of the Corfiot defence, it is possible that the Ottoman armies, effectively supported by an active fleet in the Adriatic, might have advanced as far as Venice and threatened the papacy. Two Ottoman attacks, those of 1537 and 1736, were especially violent, but Venice had the last word.

A COMIC OPERA STATE. When Venice was occupied by Napoleon, Corfu became the prey of a Russian squadron in 1799, and was then immediately promoted to the rank of capital of a republic cosseted by the Tsar and the Turks. It became French from 1807 to 1815, thanks to the resistance to the English blockade by General Danzelot. The Congress of Vienna made it a protectorate of England, who established the curious 'United States' of the Ionian islands (Corfu and six other islands), ceded in 1864 to the successful candidate for the crown of Greece, George of Denmark. (He became King George I of Greece.) These fragile and distant links have, however, due to English predilection for everything that was once under the Union Jack, made Corfu an island of opportunity for British tour operators. Ginger beer and cricket are still found here. The Club Méditerranée is popular.

Visiting Corfu

TWO DAYS ON THE ISLAND OF CORFU. On the morning of the first day you will have made a fairly rapid tour of the town and its archaeological museum in time to lunch at Paleokastritsa (Vicinity of Corfu 3). In the afternoon you can see the beautiful scenery of the NE coast and Albania (without a visa) across the straits by going to Kassiopi (Vicinity of Corfu 4).

On the second day, if you have the stamina, watch the sunrise on the islet of Pondikonissi near Kanoni (Vicinity of Corfu 1) before the tourist coaches arrive. Getting out of bed so early may be hard, but you will retain an indelible memory of this seascape, where the first rays of the sun turn the walls of the little convent of Blachernae from white to ochre, in an atmosphere of serenity.

After that, you will be ready to undertake the grand tour of the island (Vicinity of Corfu 5) passing the Achilleion (which you can visit later, if you have taken our advice to start early), the beach of Moraitika, and Hagii Deka, where you will find truly magnificent scenery. You can swim and lunch at the beaches of Hagios Gordios or Glyfada, before returning to the capital, passing the beach of Ermones.

WHERE TO PARK? Easily enough on the Esplanade (map C–2) or in its vicinity, but do not try to park in the old town.

THE TOWN ON FOOT. You will set off from the Esplanade (map C–2),

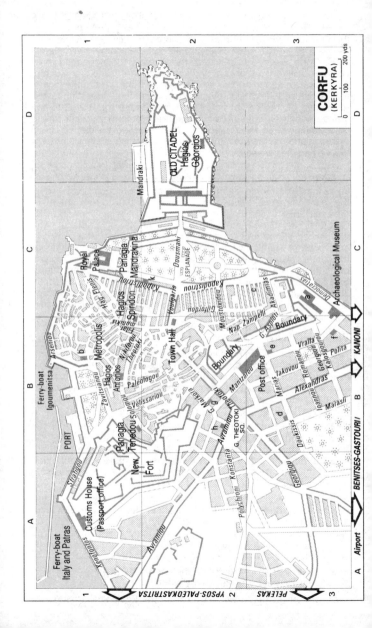

CORFU
(KERKYRA)

0   100   200 yds

Ferry-boat Italy and Patras

Ferry-boat Igoumenitsa

PORT

Xenofondos

Stratigou

Customs House (Passport office)

New Fort

Arseniou

Panagia
Tenedou Solomou

Velissariou

Paleologou

Avramiou

G. Makola

THEOTOKI

Avramiou

G. THEOTOKI SQ.

Konstanta

Polychroni

Georgiou

Doukissis

Marasli

Alexandras

Ioannou Romanou

Georgiou Kalogerou Polita

Marias Iakovou

Vraila

Post office

Boundary

Mantzarou

Nap Zampelli

G. Aspioti

Boundary

Metropolis

Hagios Antonios

Zavitsianou

Nikiforou Theotoki

Filarmonikis

Hagios Spiridon

Had Fleni

Royal Palace

Panagia Mandrakina

Kapodistriou

Moustoxidou

Vouigaris

Gilfordou

Kapodistriou

ESPLANADE

Dousmani

Akadimias

Atakimias

Dousmani

Archaeological Museum

Mandraki

OLD CITADEL
Hagios Georgios

Town Hall

YPSOS-PALEOKASTRITSA

PELEKAS

Airport

BENITSES-GASTOURII

KANONI

a b c d e f g h k

which will become your headquarters because of its cafés (it is better not to be too thirsty, for service is often slow – if you want fast service cross over to the Acteon Bar by the sea). Or perhaps you will lunch at the Aigli restaurant, and think you are in Paris. Look no further. The arcades over your table (unless you are seated beneath the acacia-trees in the square) are French, or more precisely Napoleonic, but of course the Mediterranean food will soon bring you back to reality.

Start by visiting the old citadel (map D-2), then cross the Esplanade to enter the old town by Voulgareos Street (map C-2) noting on the l. the old Venetian theatre (Town Hall; map B-2) and visiting r. the church of Hagios Spyridon (map C-1) on the edge of a working class district with narrow alleyways, which architecturally owe more to southern Italy than to continental Greece. By N. Theotoki Street (map B-1), which is a continuation of Voulgareos Street, you will reach the church of St Francis and the orthodox cathedral, easy landmarks to help you find your way to the port (map A/B-1), dominated by the New Fort (map A-1/2). You can return to the Esplanade by Arseniou Street (map B-1), then you may visit the Archaeological Museum (map C-3).

Corfu

A town of 28,630 inhabitants, Corfu suffered much damage from bombardments during World War II, yet it preserves enough character, at the foot of its fortresses, with its tall houses and narrow alleys and the animation of its streets where children play and horse-drawn cabs pass, to offer a lot of charm. And even the 19th-century architecture, with signs of French and English taste, fits easily into the unity of this Venetian city.

Between walks, you will often return to the Esplanade (map C-2), the centre of urban life, where it is pleasant to sip your ouzo. Bordered on one side by an arcaded row of houses – the Liston – built under the Empire during the French occupation (1807-14) and inspired, so it is said, by the Rue de Rivoli in Paris, it was used for manoeuvres by Venetian troops. Today, the turf at one end is used for cricket matches (in July), which remind you that the island was also occupied by the British.

OLD CITADEL (map D-2). Now a military academy, it was built in 1550 by the Venetians on a promontory dominating the access to the port. At the entrance to the bridge leading to it, note the statue of Marshal Schulenburg, who commanded the garrison which resisted the Turks in 1716.

To the S, on the side of the Bay of Garitsa, rises the old garrison chapel, now the church of Hagios Georgios, in the style of a Doric temple. To the N, now occupied by large military buildings, are some ancient Venetian barracks dominating the little harbour of Mandraki where the Venetians sheltered their warships. In antiquity there was a temple of Hera Akraia on the tip of the promontory (Cape Sidero).

On leaving the Citadel, you cross the N half of the Esplanade in the direction of the Royal Palace, passing the little chapel dedicated to Panagia Mandrakina, dating from 1700. The Esplanade is embellished with various monuments; one of them, a copy of an Ionic rotunda, was built in memory of Sir Thomas Maitland, first Lord High Commissioner (1816–24).

☐ ROYAL PALACE (map C-1). At the N end of the Esplanade, this sumptuous neo-Classical edifice with a Doric portico was built in 1816, and was the residence of the English Lord High Commissioners. In the W wing there is a collection of ancient Christian antiquities and icons. The palace also houses a collection of Far Eastern art.

Open: weekdays 09.00–15.00; Sun. from 10.00; closed Tues.; entrance fee.

You will see Chinese porcelain and pottery, among them funerary figurines of the 8th and 7th centuries BC, as well as 5th-century bronzes. Japanese art is represented by ceramics, masks, weapons and prints. These collections were formed and bequeathed to the town of Corfu by G. Manos.

Via Voulgareos Street, you will come to the Town Hall (map B-2), formerly a Venetian theatre, built in 1663–73 to serve as a meeting place for Corfiot businessmen. It faced the Catholic cathedral built in 1658, but was damaged during a bombardment in 1944. It is decorated with 17th-century Italian works of art. On the side of Nikiphorou Theotoki Street, you will see a monument erected (1691) in honour of Morosini, conqueror of the Turks in Morea.

♦ CHURCH OF HAGIOS SPYRIDON (map C-1). It was built in 1589 to house the relics of the saint, contained in a silver casket displayed in the sacristy on the r., which is full of lamps and icons. The Italianate paintings in the interior of the church were restored in 1830.

SAINT SPYRIDON. Traditionally, more than half the boys born in Corfu are christened Spyridon. This archbishop of Cyprus, martyred under Diocletian after taking part in the Council of Nicaea (325), is enormously popular in the island. His body was taken there in 1489 and is reputed to have miraculously saved Corfu from the Turks, plague and famine. This is commemorated by four solemn processions, 14th August (with candles), the first Sunday in November, Palm Sunday and Saturday in Holy Week.

🏰 NEW FORT (map A-1/2). To the E of the town, it was built by the Venetians from 1576 to 1589 after the first Turkish siege (1537), but the upper part is an English addition, after 1815. The entrance on the side of Spilia Square is surmounted by a Lion of St Mark.

▣ ARCHAEOLOGICAL MUSEUM (map C-3). By following the boundaries of the old town, where there are remnants of the old walls, you will reach the museum which is worth a visit, if only to admire one of the two pediments of the temple of Artemis. The museum comprises several halls, on the ground and first floors. There you will see a remarkable collection of sculpture and ceramics, mainly Archaic, the most flourishing period of the island in antiquity.

Open: weekdays 09.00–15.00; Sun. from 10.00; closed Tues.; entrance fee.

The west pediment of the temple of Artemis (the other has disappeared), shown in Hall 6, is the earliest large pedimental sculpture that has come down to us (it dates from the 6th century), said to have been unearthed by Kaiser Wilhelm II. It is 55ft 9in (17m) wide and more than 9ft 10in (3m) high at the centre. This pediment, although fragmentary, is very easy to interpret. In the centre is a colossal Gorgon (9ft 2in/2.79m high), flanked by Pegasus and Chrysaor, who sprang from the blood of the terrifying Gorgon when she was decapitated by Perseus. Pegasus is to the l., Chrysaor to the r. This group is framed by a pair of crouching panthers. To the r., a beardless Zeus, a fact worthy of note, is striking down a Titan. On the l., a seated female figure (?) may represent Gaia, the earth goddess, or Rhea, the wife of Cronos, threatened by her son Poseidon. Further l., at the acute angle of the pediment, a reclining figure fills the whole field. It is generally assumed to be a Titan. Another figure adorns the other acute angle of the pediment. The figures are in high relief. The presence of the Gorgon in the centre of the pediment is surprising. Although she may be identified with Artemis, as the goddess protecting animals, this anomaly undoubtedly shows the influence of local religious beliefs, which lagged behind those of other Greek cities, where the Olympian gods were ranked in a strict hierarchy.

In 1973, the l. section of another Archaic pediment was discovered, but it is more recent than that of the temple of Artemis (late 6th century BC). It is on show in the next hall (Hall 8). What is preserved shows a banquet scene, with a middle-aged man (undoubtedly Dionysus) and a naked youth lying on a bed before a decorated table, beneath which lies a lion. To the l. are a large krater and a big dog. Like the temple of Artemis pediment, this new example, which may have come from the temple of Dionysus, is of limestone.

In Hall 7, you will see an Archaic lioness of uncertain date (from 625 to 540 BC according to the experts) which may have crowned the tomb of Menecrates or another neighbouring tomb; fragments of architecture, in particular Archaic antefixae, one fragment of which (MR 730) represents a Gorgon's head (late 7th century BC) and comes from the temple on the acropolis of Corcyra, as well as two magnificent votive offerings from the 7th century BC: a bronze statuette (1602) representing a young reveller running, rhyton (drinking-cup) in hand (c.570), and the head of a small kouros (youth) in local limestone (c.530).

Showcase 19 contains 13 large terracotta statuettes (1847–59) of the goddess Artemis, usually armed with a bow and accompanied by her favourite animal, the hind (c.480–470). The last section of the hall is mainly occupied by Classical and post-Classical sculptures or by copies of such works. Note a small marble statuette (152) in the style

of the Apollo in the museum at Kassel after a bronze original by
Phidias, a portrait (133), copy of a bronze original which may have
represented the poet Menander, etc.

VICINITY OF CORFU

1 PALEOPOLIS AND KANONI (5.6mls/9km round trip). Leaving the town
proper, you will pass close to the tomb of Menecrates (see map of the
island), on the site of a necropolis of ancient Corcyra. It was a
tumulus encircled by a stone foundation and surmounted by a lioness
(on show in the museum). An early Archaic inscription in the
Corcyran alphabet says that the tomb was that of 'Menecrates, son of
Tlasias, of Oeanthe, in Locris, proxenos [consul of his city] at
Corcyra, died at sea'. A little further on are the remains of the Venetian
fort, San Salvatore.

0.6mls (1km): Shortly after leaving the sea-front road, stop briefly to
visit (take the first street to the r.) the church of SS Jason and
Sosipater (disciples of St Paul and the first apostles of Corfu), a little
12th-century gem in the Byzantine style in the middle of a garden full
of flowers, noteworthy for the simple beauty of its architecture.

0.9mls (1.5km): To the r., opposite the entrance to the Park of Monrepos, former villa of the British High Commissioners, where Prince
Philip, Duke of Edinburgh was born in 1921, you will see the ruins of
the church of Hagia Kerkyra or Paleopolis, which stands on the
remains of several buildings, the oldest of which, a temple, dates from
the 5th century BC. The site was then occupied by a public building,
an assembly (ecclesia) or senate (bouleuterium) of the 2nd or 1st
century BC, and afterwards by the church in the early 5th century.
Destroyed in the 6th century, probably during the invasion by the
Goths or Vandals, this church was rebuilt and destroyed in its turn by
the Saracens in the 11th century. The last church, ruined by
bombardments in World War II, was a modest edifice built in the 16th
century, re-using old material, which had taken the place of a 12th-
century church destroyed by the Turks in 1537. 82yds (75m) to the NE
of the church, the remains of Roman baths dating to the end of the 1st
century BC have been uncovered on the site of an Archaic ceramic
workshop and a group of Hellenistic houses. These baths were used
until the end of the 6th century. Some hypocausts, debris of mosaics
and the foundations are all that remain. A path joining the road to
Kanoni, to the r. of the church of Paleopolis, gives access to the
temple of Artemis, which is of little interest. To reach the site of the
temple, turn l. 325yds (300m) along the road to Kanoni, at the foot of
a hill. In a few minutes you come to the convent of Hagii Theodori.
Note first an Archaic triglyphic altar behind the convent and, a little
further on, the scanty remains of the temple.

A little to the W you can see traces of the walls of ancient Corcyra — a
section of the wall made of regular well-dressed stones. It is
surmounted by the remains of a Byzantine temple with two windows
with blind arcades.

1.6mls (2.5km): Take the road to the l. for Analipsis, a village on the top of the Paleopolis peninsula, site of ancient Corcyra. The ancient town was situated between two harbours: the port of Alkinoos (Garitsa bay) and the Hyllaian port (lake Khalikiopoulo). The isthmus connecting them was closed by a wall. To the NE of the site now occupied by Anemomylos were situated the agora and the rich district around the port of Alkinoos; the working-class district lay to the W around the Hyllaian port.

Near Kardaki, on the top of the hill, are the remains of a large sanctuary founded after the end of the 8th century BC, i.e. at the beginning of the Corinthian colonization. Around the main temple, probably consecrated to Hera (it was rebuilt at the end of the 7th century) were grouped other cults: those of Aphrodite, Hermes and especially Apollo. The sanctuary, burnt down towards the end of the 5th century, probably during the civil wars, was restored in the 4th century and several times after that.

2.8mls (4.5km): Kanoni, at the S tip of the Paleopolis peninsula from which you will have a charming and famous **view. In the foreground the islet with the convent of Blachernae is connected to the land by a jetty which existed at the end of the 6th century; then to the l., the islet of Pondikonissi (Mouse Island), which some scholars identify as the rock on which Odysseus was cast up by the storm or as the Phaeacian vessel turned to stone by Poseidon on the return journey after taking Odysseus to Ithaca.

2 THE ACHILLEION (a 15.6mls/25km circuit). Leave Corfu by the Benitses road (map A-3).

3.7mls (6km): Direct road to the I. for Perama (1.6mls/2.5km).

5mls (8km): Leave the road to Hagii Deka ahead of you and turn l.

6.9mls (11km): To the l., entrance to the park containing the Achilleion, a large villa built in 1890 by the Italian architect Cardita for the Empress Elizabeth of Austria (d. 1898), the famous Sisi. The villa was bought in 1907 by the German Emperor Wilhelm II, who stayed there regularly from 1908 onwards. It owes its name to the Empress of Austria's enthusiasm for Achilles, the Achaean hero who was 'honoured' by a very mediocre bronze statue standing on a hill from which you will see one of the most beautiful **panoramas in Corfu. On a nearby hill there is a French military cemetery from the 1914-18 war.

After visiting the Achilleion and especially its gardens (a folk dance group lies in wait for the arrival of tourist coaches), continue along the same road, which rejoins the E coast by a series of impressive bends.

8.1mls (13km): turn l. leaving the Benitses road to the r. (see Vicinity of Corfu 5).

10.3mls (16.5km): Perama (hotels), at the entrance to the Bay of Paleopolis (see above, **1**).

15.6mls (25km): Corfu.

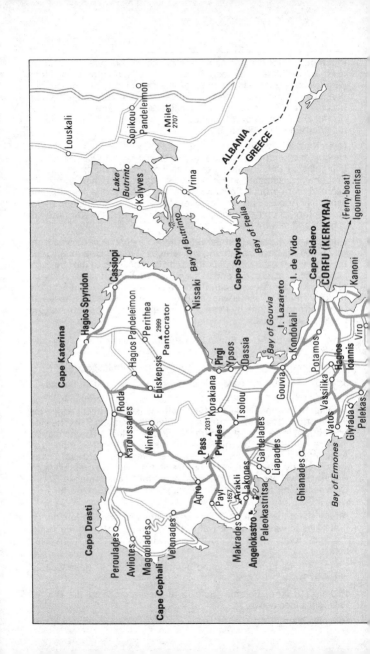

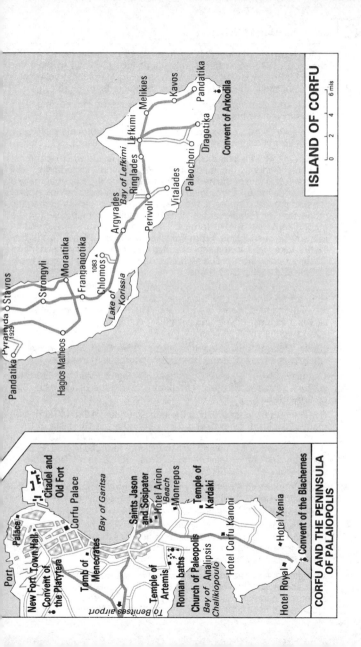

ISLAND OF CORFU

0 2 4 6 mls

Pandatika Pyramida○ ○Stavros
○Strongyli
Morattika○
Franganiotika○
1083▲
Chlomos○
Lake of
Korissia

Hagios Matheos

Argyrades○
Bay of Lefkimi
Ringlades○
Perivoli○
Vitalades○
Paleochori○
Dragotika○

Melikies○
Lefkimi○
Kavos○
Pandatika○
Convent of Arkodila ✝

**CORFU AND THE PENINSULA
OF PALAIOPOLIS**

Port
Palace ■
New Fort ■
Convent of ✝
the Platytera
Town Hall
Citadel and
Old Fort
Corfu Palace
Bay of Garitsa
Tomb of ■
Menecrates
Saints Jason
and Sosipater
Hotel Arion ■
Beach
Monrepos
Temple of ■
Kardaki
To Benitses airport ✝
Temple of
Artemis
Roman baths
Church of Paleopolis
Bay of Analipsis
Chalikiopoulo
Hotel Corfu Kanoni
Hotel Xenia ■
Hotel Royal ■
Convent of the Blachernes ✝

3 PALEOKASTRITSA (15mls/24km; map A–1/2). Leave Corfu in the direction of Gouvia. After 2.5mls (4km) take the road to the I. for Potamos from where you can visit 'The Village', a reconstruction of a Corfiot village in the Venetian period (handicrafts, restaurant).

5mls (8km): Gouvia where the Venetians stored or repaired their galleys in vaulted boathouses.

12.8mls (20.5km): to the right, 1.6mls (2.5km), Lakones, a typically Corfiot village (**panorama of the E coast of the island).

15mls (24km): Paleokastritsa in the part of the island which was most probably Scheria, the land of the Phaeacians, according to the *Odyssey*. It is one of the best known beaches on the island, actually a group of delightful coves lined with myrtles, lentisks and holm-oaks. Beyond the last restaurant, the road continues to the entrance to the monastery of Paleokastritsa, which is mainly remarkable for the magnificent view from its terrace. There are, however, some beautiful icons to be seen inside. From Paleokastritsa (or Lakones) a climb of 1½hrs takes you to the top of a high hill crowned by the ruins of Castle Angelo, most probably built in the 12th century by the despot of Epirus, Angelus Comnenus.

4 YPSOS AND KASSIOPI (8.7mls/14km and 21.9mls/35km: map A–1/2). After leaving the road to Paleokastritsa on the I. (6.25mls/10km), you travel along the E coast of the island. The very narrow winding road serves beaches, coves and villages perched on the heights, but always near a small harbour.

10mls (16km): Ypsos, fishing village. The Club Méditerranée is situated nearby, at Dasia. 11th-century church with frescoes.

11.2mls (18km): Pirghi. Churches of Hagios Merkourios, 11th-century, with frescoes, and Pantokrator, above the village, with 16th-century frescoes.

By taking the winding road to the I. to Spartylas (4.38mls/7km), with many wonderful **views, and then continuing to Strenilas (8.1mls/3km), you can climb Mt Pantokrator (2.972ft/906m; about 2hrs from Strenilas), which is crowned by a monastery founded in 1347. From it, you can see the whole island, Epirus, the lakes of Boutrinto in Albania, etc.

By taking the same road, but without passing through Strenilas, you can reach Roda, a village by an immense sandy beach with the remains of a small temple (5th century BC).

21.9mls (35km): Kassiopi, small port just W of the Corfu Channel between the island and Albania; on a hill near the port, the ruins of a large fortress built by the Angevins (1267–1386). 16th-century church with 17th-century frescoes and icons.

5 GRAND TOUR OF THE ISLAND. (71.9mls/115km). Beyond the Achilleion (see above, **2**) you leave (8.1mls/13km) on the road to the I. for Perama. Then you follow the E coast, of little interest except for the picturesque fishing village of Benitses (8.7mls/14km).

13.1mls (21km): Beach of Moraitika, with fine sandy shores.

15mls (24km): Take the road to Hagii Deka, leaving on your l. the road to the S of the island and the spacious plain of Lefkimi. Now you will see the *scenery of the interior of the island and of a basin covered with olive trees between two ranges of hills, and you will pass through charming little villages clinging to the mountain sides among luxuriant vegetation, but you will find the road very winding and narrow.

21.2mls (34km): Before you reach Hagii Deka, there is a fantastic ***panorama of the dark green foothills of the central part of the island which contrasts with the long white outline of the town of Corfu in its deep blue setting.

22.5mls (36km): Turn l. to Hagios Gordios and l. again 2.5mls (4km) further on.

28.1mls (45km): *Beach of Hagios Gordios, one of the most beautiful on the island, which you will see in all its splendour during the descent; then retrace your steps.

31.2mls (50km): Continue in the direction of Sinadares, a picturesque village with gaily painted houses.

34mls (54.4km): Turn l. to Pelekas.

35mls (56km): Pelekas, on a marvellous *site on top of a hill covered with olive trees, and with fruit trees, vines, etc., on the lower slopes. Pass through the village with its brightly coloured houses.

36.2mls (58km): Turn l. for Glyfada (*view of the coast during your descent).

37.5mls (60km): The very attractive beach of Glyfada bordered with dunes and olive groves. Retrace your steps to the fork at 36.2mls (58km) where you should take the road to the l.

40.3mls (64.5km): Continue l. to the beach of Ermones (0.9mls/1.5km) where Odysseus was supposedly cast up by the storm. There he is supposed to have met Nausicaa who was playing ball with her maidens on the banks of the river, the natural pools of which were used for washing clothes. Retrace your steps and then keep straight on for 1.6mls (2.5km) beyond the fork at 40.3mls (64.5km).

44mls (70.5km): Turn l. leaving on your r. a road to Corfu (7.5mls/12km).

50.6mls (81km): About 0.6mls (1km) beyond Liapades, turn l. on the road to Paleokastritsa, but 550yds (500m) further on, make a detour of 3.7mls (6km) there and back to the r. to climb to the village of Lakones, from which you will have a very beautiful **view of the W coast. Then return to Corfu by turning l. at the bottom of the descent from Lakones (Paleokastritsa is 2.2mls/3.5km to the r.: see Vicinity of Corfu 3). 71.8mls (115km): Corfu.

6 PAXOS AND ANTIPAXOS. 35 nautical miles from the port of Corfu and accessible by caique, this island and its islet will delight swimmers

(two beautiful beaches on Antipaxos) and enthusiasts of underwater fishing. More Greek in their scenery than Corfu, they are covered with olive trees and vines. The wine of Antipaxos is famous, but scarce. There is only one port, Gaios, with two streets, three tavernas and of course a small, blindingly white church. 1.2mls (2km) away, a new hotel has just opened and a few tavernas do take in lodgers in the villages of Lakka, on a bay in the N of the island, and Longos on the E coast. Antipaxos has nothing but a small anchorage on the E coast and a few houses scattered among the vines. From Paxos you can take a boat to some marine grottoes, including the grotto of Ypapanti in which Poseidon lived, according to Homer. With luck, you might see a few seals there.

■ Corinth (Korinthos)

Route maps 5 and 6.

Athens 54.4mls (87km) – Corinth (Ancient), 3.7mls (6km) – Epidaurus (via Loutra Elenis), 42.5mls (68km) – Epidaurus (via Nauplia), 56.2mls (90km) – Mycenae, 26.9mls (43km) – Nauplia, 37.5mls (60km) – Patras, 82.5mls (132km) – Pop: 20,892 – orthodox archbishopric – capital of the admin. region of Corinthia.

Almost completely rebuilt after an earthquake which destroyed it in 1928, the modern town is of little interest, except as a centre for visiting the Classical sites on the isthmus.

VICINITY OF CORINTH

1 CORINTH [Ancient] (3.7mls/6km).

2 CORINTH CANAL (2.5mls/4km).

3 ISTHMIA (3.1mls/5km). Leave by the road to Athens.

1.2mls (2km): Take the first road to the r. to Epidaurus (Epidavros Ancient Theatre); there is another one 1.2mls (2km) further on, just before reaching the canal.

3.1mls (5km): Vrysi. At the exit from this little village, you will pass through the site of Ancient Isthmia, containing the Sanctuary of Poseidon, god of the isthmus, where the Isthmian Festival (Isthmia) and the most famous games after those of Olympia were held in the spring every two years from 582 BC onwards. Originally these games took place, as at Delphi and Olympia, in honour of a hero and had a basically funerary character. Legend attributed the institution of the games to Poseidon or Sisyphus, in honour of a hero called Palaemon (the Wrestler).

THE ISTHMIAN GAMES. The Attic legend, recalling the time when Athens held sway over the isthmus, looked on Theseus as the founder of the Isthmian Games. The Athenian delegates or theoroi were entitled to seats of honour (proedria) whereas the Eleans (inhabitants of Elis) were excluded. The organization (agonothesia) of the festival was in the hands of Corinth after its restoration by Caesar. The Romans were allowed to compete in 228 BC. It was during the games that Alexander the Great was appointed general of all the Greeks against the Persians in 336 BC. Here, too, Flaminius, and then Nero, proclaimed the independence of Greece in 196 BC and 67 AD respectively. The competitions resembled those of Olympia and Delphi.

VISIT TO THE MUSEUM AND THE RUINS. Currently being excavated by the American School of Classical Studies and the University of California, the site of Ancient Isthmia still has a few items that may interest the non-specialist in archaeology. Some of the finds from the site and neighbouring burial grounds are excellently exhibited in a museum opened in 1978. Beyond the sanctuary, there are Roman baths against the long rampart which barred the isthmus of Corinth, then, still on the l. side of the road, a ruined theatre and the fortress built by the Emperor Justinian in the 6th century. While returning to your point of departure, you see the site of Hellenistic and Roman stadium on the other side of the road.

Open: weekdays, 09.00–15.30; Sun. 10.00–15.00; closed Tues.; entrance fee.

■ **MUSEUM OF THE ISTHMUS.** It is housed in a new building at the entrance to the site on the l. of the road. It contains finds from the isthmus and Kenchreai, one of the two ports of Corinth situated on the Saronic Gulf.

In the entrance hall, you will see some sculptures, including the funerary stele of a certain L(oukios) Komelios Korinthios (Lucius Comelius Corinthius), a flute player, proud of his victories at different games, which are recalled by inscriptions inside small crowns. You will also see a beautiful fragment of the cornice of the Classical temple of Poseidon (lion's head between palmettes).

On your l. you will enter the (only) hall which is very large and divided into two main sections: the finds from the isthmus and the finds from Kenchreai. You will note especially, besides a collection of ceramics dating from the prehistoric to the late Roman period, the material from the Archaic temple of Poseidon: plaques, ceramics, bronze and terracotta *ex votos* (including two beautiful horses' heads, a small bull and particularly four small boats, offered naturally enough to the god of the sea, a Corinthian terracotta perirrhanterion (holy water bowl) and an Archaic marble perirrhanterion, the latter resting on four caryatids alternating with rams' heads and supported by lions). Then follow objects discovered in the sanctuary of Poseidon up to the Roman period, among them an important collection of lamps.

The finds from Kenchreai comprise ceramics, 4th-century BC ivories (including two lovely plaques representing two seated men, philosophers, perhaps) and, above all, unique examples of *panels in glass of opus sectile (a kind of mosaic with varied colours) discovered in 1964 in the chests in which they were transported and which had never been opened because of an earthquake that took place shortly after their unloading in 375 AD. American archaeologists have recovered 87 panels in varying states of preservation. On those which were cleaned, treated and saved, you will note representations of floral and vegetable motifs, animals (birds, fish), maritime landscapes (view of the port of Kenchreai), and especially personages (anonymous fishermen and a portrait of Plato, contained in the same chest as that of Homer). The reproductions accompanying the originals on show in the cases give you a better idea of the subjects and colours.

SANCTUARY OF POSEIDON. This temple, now reduced to its foundations, was originally built in the 5th century BC on the site of an Archaic temple and was destroyed by fire in 475 BC. It was repaired several times during the Roman period, then demolished in the time of Justinian when its materials were used to build the rampart. The altar, reconstructed several times, was found to the E, where there are also the remains of Roman houses. The temple of Poseidon and its altar were encircled by a wall marking off the sacred area, the dimensions of which varied down the ages.

Between the temple ruins and the road, do not fail to examine the starting line of the most ancient stadium of the isthmus, which was abandoned long before the destruction of Corinth and replaced by a new stadium (on the other side).

ON YOUR MARKS. The starting line consists of a triangular flooring formerly covered with a layer of beaten clay. On this space you can make out 16 grooves fanning out from a pit that is 3ft (1m) deep. Bronze horsemen, sealed with lead, were placed at the far end of each groove. You can still see mortises cut for the insertions of small vertical poles at the ends of the grooves at the base of the triangle. This arrangement was used to regulate the start of the competitors, as described by Aristophanes (*Knights*, v. 1159). A judge, standing in the pit, could use cords to drop the barriers set up between the vertical poles and so give starting signals to the runners. The bronze horsemen were used to keep the cords in the grooves. One end of each cord was fixed to a horizontal bar. The judge held the other end in his hand. Sixteen competitors could take part in each race. About 33ft (10m) nearer the road, another starting line is simply made up of limestone foundations, formerly covered with a layer of cement.

The Palaimonion (Palaemonium) or temple of Palaemon was built during the Roman period, partly on the site of the starting line of the Greek stadium. Beneath it was a crypt where the faithful took an oath in the name of the god. A small subterranean passage has been found that undoubtedly led to the underground room mentioned by Pausanias. This temple was probably built towards the end of the 1st century BC.

ROMAN BATHS AND HEXAMILION. Behind the sanctuary, excavations have revealed different parts of Roman thermae (baths), paved with marble and mosaics (Tritons and Nereids in a seascape, with black and white motifs, remarkably well preserved) and with walls sometimes decorated with paintings. These constructions were erected on the site of a wall 25mls (40km) long, the Hexamilion, a section of which was re-used by the builders. Built between the modern town of Corinth and Kenchreai from the 13th century BC, this wall was reinforced every 110yds (100m) by towers and frequently rebuilt, the last time in the 6th century AD by Justinian.

The Theatre – Some 33yds (30m) to the NE of the sanctuary of Poseidon, it was built in the early 4th century BC, rebuilt and enlarged towards the end of the 4th century, then twice in the 1st century AD. The second Roman reconstruction may have taken place before the Isthmian Games of 66, which Nero attended in person. You can still make out several rows of seats and the stage area. The marble head of an athlete wearing the wreath of pine twigs, the 'perishable crown' quoted by St Paul in the *First Epistle to the Corinthians*, was found in the theatre.

The Fortress of Justinian – Beyond the theatre and up to the edge of the road, you will next visit this citadel built by Justinian in the 6th century with materials taken from ancient buildings to reinforce the Hexamilion.

The S gate of the Byzantine fortress between two octagonal towers is near the road. Another gate has been uncovered to the NE.

The Hellenistic and Roman Stadium – Almost opposite the S gate of the fortress of Justinian, on the other side of the road, are the ruins of the stadium which replaced the one situated near the temple of Poseidon from the 4th century BC. It was mentioned by St Paul in his *First Letter to the Corinthians* (9.24) and by Pausanias, who described it as made of marble. The starting line with 18 lanes and the double groove in which the athletes placed their feet have been discovered. The spectators stood on broad steps without seats, except on the proedria, added during the Roman period, which was found some 33yds (30m) from the starting line. A promenade, lined with stone parapets with carved mouldings, separated the part of the stadium reserved for spectators into two sections.

4 KENCHREAI AND LOUTRA ELENIS (7.5mls/12km). Road to Isthmia (see above) continued by a superb new road to Epidaurus, which has very beautiful *views of the Saronic Gulf and the island of Aegina, and passes close to the interesting monastery of Agnountos (18.7mls/30km from Loutra Elenis; see p. 651).

(5.9mls/9.5km): Beach of Kalamaki, near which the ruins of ancient Kenchreai, port of Corinth on the Saronic Gulf. Excavations by the American School, partly under water, have recovered the main parts of the ancient port and large warehouses on land. A half-submerged Roman building may have been the sanctuary consecrated to Isis and mentioned by Pausanias and Apuleius.

7.5mls (12km): Loutra Elenis, a spa with hot sea springs, is situated near the site of classical Solygeia (now Galataki), where traces of an early Archaic temple have been discovered.

5 HERAION OF PERACHORA (20mls/32km), see Vicinity of Loutraki.

Corinth [Ancient]**

Route maps 5 and 6.

Argos, 31.9mls (51km) – Athens, 58.1mls (93km) – Corinth (modern town), 3.7mls (6km) – Epidaurus (via Loutra Elenis), 46.2mls (74km) – Epidaurus (via Nauplia), 55mls (88km) – Mycenae, 25.6mls (41km) – Nauplia, 36.2mls (58km) – Patras, 80mls (128km) – admin. region of Corinthia.

Near the little village of Palea Korinthos, which for some time now has been a polyglot emporium dealing in souvenirs of all kinds, the ruins of Ancient Corinth form one of the major attractions of Greek archaeology.

The natural framework of Ancient Corinth, or at least of the lower town, does not possess the exceptional natural beauty of so many other Greek sites, although Acrocorinth, the enormous rocky peak rising in the background, is impressive without being attractive. In addition, visiting the ruins in the heat of a summer day (to be avoided as far as possible), when the sun-baked landscape acquires a lacklustre colour, will make even this terrain, once considered beautiful, look inhospitable. To erase this impression you must summon up the energy to climb to the top of Acrocorinth and only there, in addition to a fantastic panorama, will you find the reasons for this city's wealth in antiquity. For Corinth occupied a first-class strategic position close to the isthmus, a virtual bridge between the continent and the Peloponnese, and it very soon took advantage of such an exceptional situation, especially by levying heavy customs dues on merchandise in transit over the isthmus. Able to launch its fleet westwards by the Gulf of Corinth and eastwards by the Saronic Gulf, it could not fail to become a major maritime power.

FROM ITS ORIGINS TO THE ACHAEAN INVASION. Thanks to the abundance of spring water, the fertility of the littoral plain, the richness of the clay soil and its proximity to the sea, the region of Corinth has been inhabited since Neolithic times, perhaps since the 5th millennium BC. Towards 3000 BC there was a new addition to the population and the civilization of the inhabitants of the isthmus developed with the introduction of bronze weapons and tools (first Bronze Age or Early Helladic). As the probable consequence of a new migration, the villages of the Early Helladic were destroyed c.2000 BC and were nearly all abandoned during the 2nd millennium.

A BRIGAND AS FOUNDER. Around 1000 BC, after the Dorian invasion, the site of Ancient Corinth (called Ephyra) was occupied again. The legendary founder was the wily Sisyphus, who tricked Zeus and was grandfather of the hero Bellerophon. Subject to the kings of Argos, it acquired its independence thanks to the strength of the Bacchiadae who overthrew the kingdom in 747 BC and founded the colonies of Corcyra (Corfu), Syracuse and Potidaea. In 657 BC, Cypselus, a popular leader, conquered this aristocracy, set up a tyranny and devoted himself to the commercial development of his state. His son, Periander, one of the Seven Sages of Greece, reigned for 42 years (627–585 BC).

BETWEEN APHRODITE AND HERMES. After the fall of the tyranny, Corinth was governed by an oligarchy but, enriched by its trade, it became famous for its love of luxury and pleasure. Its commercial-mindedness led it to avoid war. It took hardly any part in the Persian Wars. 'In her despair, Corinth sent her courtesans to implore Aphrodite for victory and liberty' (Beulé). Its colonies despised Corinth or only called on it in case of danger. The war of Corcyra (434 BC) became one of the causes of the Peloponnesian War (431–404 BC). Corinth supported Sparta against Athens, its great maritime and commercial rival. Nevertheless, in 395 BC, it took the side of the Greek coalition against Sparta, which provoked the Corinthian War (395–387 BC). It submitted to Philip and received a Macedonian garrison (335 BC). In 224 BC, Aratus freed Corinth and made it join the Achaean League, of which it became the headquarters in 196 BC.

THE TOWN OF JULIUS CAESAR. After its wealth had excited the cupidity of the Romans, Corinth was taken and sacked by Mummius in 146 BC. Thus the visitor will see not so much a Greek town as the ruins of the Roman colony which Julius Caesar established there in 44 BC, making the town prosperous for three centuries. It was at Corinth that Nero confirmed Greek independence on 28 Nov. 67 AD (it had already been proclaimed by Flaminius at the Isthmian Games in 196 BC). Then Corinth was the seat of the proconsulate of Achaea. In 51–52 AD, the apostle St Paul came to preach Christianity to the most frivolous and dissolute society in the pagan world. Towards the end of the 2nd century, through the generosity of the Emperor Hadrian and of Herodes Atticus, Corinth became one of the most beautiful cities in Greece.

Ravaged by the Heruli in 267 AD, Corinth declined and was sacked several times in the centuries that followed. After Justinian (6th century), the medieval history of Corinth is confused with that of Acrocorinth, a fortress. The American School of Classical Studies started excavating Corinth in 1896. Since then, work has continued down to the present day.

Visiting the agora

Park your car either in the village, where you are most likely to find some shade, or near the Tourist Pavilion, so that you can enter the site of the agora near the Fountain of Glauce (see plan). In 1½ to 2hrs (including a visit to the museum), you will have gone round the excavations. Then you can inspect the ruins of the Odeon and the

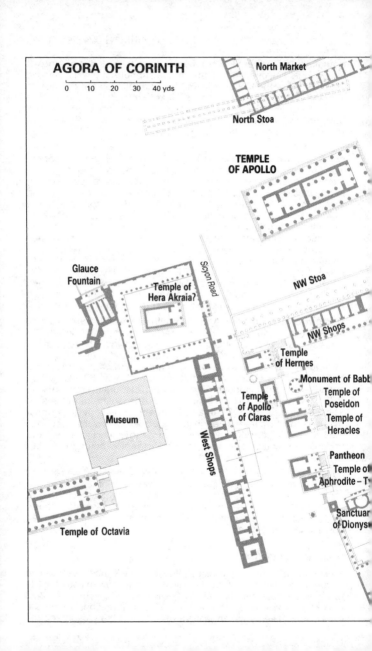

AGORA OF CORINTH

0   10   20   30   40 yds

North Market

North Stoa

TEMPLE OF APOLLO

Glauce Fountain

Temple of Hera Akraia?

Sicyon Road

NW Stoa

NW Shops

Temple of Hermes

Monument of Babb

Temple of Poseidon

Temple of Apollo of Claras

Temple of Heracles

Museum

West Shops

Pantheon

Temple of Aphrodite – T

Sanctuar of Dionys

Temple of Octavia

Semi-circular Building

Baths of Eurycles

oman rket

Lechaion Road

Greek Market

Basilica

Greek Temple of the 4th c. BC

Peribolos of Apollo

Fount of Pireus

racular nctuary

Façade of the Barbarian captives

Propylaea

Starting point of the Stadium

Julian Basilica

Triglyph Wall

Sacred Fountain Entrance to Underground Chamber

AGORA

Retaining Wall

Circular Monument

SE Building

Altar

Central Shops

Bema

SOUTH STOA

Fountain

Agonothetes (mosaics)

Senate

South Basilica

Road to Kenchreae

Shops

Theatre (15mins) before driving up to Acrocorinth (about 1hr). Devotees of archaeology will complete this programme by visiting the ruins of the palaeo-Christian basilica of Lechaion and the sanctuary of Poseidon in the vicinity of Corinth.

If you happen to be in Corinth during the grape harvest (in August), do taste the delicious grapes, which are as sweet as honey.

Lunch at the Tourist Pavilion, or better still, if you are not too tired, take the road to Argos to enjoy spit-roast lamb in a cool shady setting at Solomos or Chiliomodion (2.5mls/4km and 8.1mls/13km respectively). Swim off the beach of Kalamaki, 5.6mls (9km) on the road to Epidaurus, via Loutra Elenis.

Before you reach the entrance to the excavation site of the agora, note, almost opposite the Tourist Pavilion, the remains of the N market built during the Roman Imperial period and used until the Byzantine period (there are two entrances to the site: one opposite the Tourist Pavilion, near the museum and the temple of Apollo; the other in the continuation of the Lechaion road).

Open: daily 09.00–15.00 (15.30 in winter); Sun. 10.00–16.00 (16.30 in winter); entrance fee.

Just beyond the entrance turnstile, an enormous cube of rock is identified as the Fountain of Glauce, from the name of the daughter of King Creon, second wife of Jason, leader of the Argonauts. She is supposed to have hurled herself into the water to relieve the terrible burns caused by the poisoned robe sent to her by the enchantress Medea, Jason's first, abandoned wife. This fountain was used throughout the existence of the Greek town and was then restored by the Romans.

Museum – It houses most of the interesting pieces found while excavating the agora of Corinth and neighbouring sites, but nothing really exceptional.

Open the same hours as the site, but closed on Tues.; entrance fee (Tel. 0741–312 07).

Entrance vestibule – Above the door leading to the courtyard, a mosaic panel depicting two griffins attacking a horse, is dated to 400 BC.

Hall 1 (to the r. of the vestibule) – It contains the most remarkable antiquities (from the Archaic to the Classical period) in the museum, notably the fine black-figure pottery in the 'Orientalizing' style which was one of Corinth's main exports in the 7th and 6th centuries BC (see especially wall cases 12 and 15, which also contain Mycenaean and Geometric ceramics, and the two central cases). Case 25 contains small locally-made terracotta portable altars, one of them decorated with a lion and an extract from the legendary battle of the Pygmies and the Cranes (2nd half of the 6th century BC). You will also see fine Attic black-figure ceramics (cases 22 and 24) and red-figure pottery (case 27), as well as – something much rarer –

Corinthian red-figure ceramics of the 5th and 4th centuries BC (case 26). Case 28 has ceramics covered with black glaze from the same period.

At the end of the hall to the l., an Archaic terracotta group represents a battle scene between the Greeks and Amazons (end of 5th century BC). The head of an ephebe on show nearby is nearly contemporary (early 5th century BC). You will also see in the hall several statues of sphinxes from the 6th century BC, one of them in polychrome terracotta and another, intact, of marble. There is also a kline, i.e. a banquet bed, of limestone, found in a tomb.

Hall 2 (to the l., at the end of the vestibule) – Antiquities from the Roman, Byzantine and Frankish periods. On entering, note to the l. the group of seven statues from the Julian basilica. Most, if not all, of them were consecrated by emperors. The central statue is supposed to represent Jupiter or Julius Caesar deified.

About the middle of the l. wall, note particularly a Roman head of the Doryphorus (Spear Bearer), a copy of a famous work by the Argive sculptor Polyclitus, and next to it a 2nd-century AD mosaic of a pastoral scene (a cowherd playing the pipes near his herd of cows), thought to be a copy of a 4th-century BC painting by Pausias of Sicyon. Some more brightly coloured Roman mosaics are placed next to murals from a 1st century AD tomb (scenes round the Nile).

At the far end of the hall, colossal statues from a portico in the agora. On your way back to the entrance, note a sarcophagus with sculptures (2nd century AD) depicting the departure of the Seven against Thebes, one of the most famous epic cycles in Archaic Greece. At one end of the sarcophagus you can make out the death of Opheltes, strangled by a snake when the Seven passed through Nemea (hence the origin of the Nemean Games). Note also Roman and Byzantine ceramics and glassware.

Garden (from the vestibule) – 2nd-century AD plaques from the theatre of Corinth are situated in the gallery opposite the door. The first five represent scenes of battle between Greeks and Amazons. The four following plaques depict some of the Labours of Hercules and the last six illustrate the theme of the Battle between the Gods and Giants. This gallery houses other sculptures, including several Roman statues of Venus. At the end of the garden, to the l., a rectangular base is decorated with figures in relief, treated, in the 1st century AD, in an Archaic manner. On one side you will recognize Zeus Chthonios, holding a cornucopia in his l. hand and a phial in his r. hand, on another Demeter offering him ears of corn and poppies.

After visiting the museum, you should go to the central square of the agora, passing by a row of small rooms in ruins which formed the W shops. They remind you that the agora was the commercial as well as the civic centre of the city. These shops, some of which are comparatively well preserved, were built early in the 1st century AD. In the past they opened on to the square of the agora by a composite

Corinthian portico, on which griffins, sirens, winged lions and humans stand beside the Classical acanthus leaves of the capitals.

W side of the agora – There you will see the fountains of a series of six small Roman temples, and a monument with a circular plan, in the Corinthian order, built at the expense of a magistrate called Babbius Philinus.

IN THE FOOTSTEPS OF PAUSANIAS. The temple situated on the far r., mentioned by Pausanias, was probably consecrated to Aphrodite (Venus) in her aspect as the goddess of fortune (Eutychia). Next are the fountains of a sanctuary identified with the temple of all the gods (Pantheon). The next two temples, built in the reign of the Emperor Commodus (180–192), were undoubtedly dedicated to Heracles (Hercules), a favourite hero of the emperor's, and to Poseidon (Neptune). Pausanias, who visited Corinth before their erection, mentioned that he saw a fountain and a bronze statue of Poseidon beyond the Pantheon. Vestiges of the fountain have been found beneath the foundations of the temple of Poseidon.

The temple situated to the W. of Babbius' monument was probably consecrated to Clarian Apollo (after Claros, an oracular site in Asia Minor). It presumably housed the bronze statue of Apollo seen by Pausanias. The last edifice may have been the temple of Hermes. One of the two statues mentioned by Pausanias must have been inside the temple and the other located on the circular foundations near the cella.

*THE TEMPLE OF APOLLO. You must not miss a visit to this temple, the most venerable and most spectacular monument in Corinth. Dominating the agora, it is one of the oldest temples in Greece. It was built between 550 and 525 BC on the site of a 7th-century sanctuary. The peristyle originally comprised 38 columns, but only seven monolithic Doric columns, still with fragments of their architrave, remains standing. But the general plan of the edifice is still clear owing to cuts made in the rock to receive the foundations.

*THE LECHAION ROAD. This road, which was lined with shops below Corinthian porticoes, temples, public buildings, such as baths, and a monumental fountain, is another highlight of a visit to Corinth. It linked the agora with the port of Lechaion on the Gulf of Corinth to which it led beyond the N gate between two walls, a defensive feature like that which joined Athens to its maritime suburb of Piraeus.

Leaving the terrace of the temple of Apollo, you first cross a site occupied by the foundations of a vast Roman basilica, on the site of a Roman market, then pass a row of shops before reaching a broad paved road terminating to the r. in the agora in the propylaea which in the 1st century AD consisted of a monumental triumphal arch. It was surmounted by gilt bronze chariots, one bearing Phaethon and the other Helios.

The basilica (you will have noticed its foundations) was built of limestone, with a large colonnaded central hall, in the 1st century AD, then rebuilt on a much larger scale, perhaps in the 2nd century. The sizeable ruins of a late 5th-century BC Greek market lie beneath the remains of this edifice.

On the other side of the street, you can make out the vestiges of a 5th-or 6th-century thermal establishment on the site of a Roman bath-house possibly dating from the 1st century AD, which can definitely be identified with the baths of Eurycles, mentioned by Pausanias as being the finest in Corinth. Next come the public lavatories, then the peribolos of Apollo, consisting of a court surrounded by galleries with some of their Ionic-style columns re-erected. This building was erected in the 1st century AD, but restored later. Pausanias tells us that it contained a statue of Apollo and a painting of Odysseus killing Penelope's suitors. Recent excavations have shown that the N part of the peribolos of Apollo occupied the site of a dye works where shells of bivalves (murex) used to make the dyes have been found.

On one section of the site of the peribolos of Apollo, near the road, you will observe the well preserved foundations of a small 4th-century BC Greek temple, consisting of a vestibule and a square naos. The temple, probably consecrated to the cult of a hero, was demolished during the Hellenistic period and replaced by a baldachin supported by four square pillars, presumably with a cult statue beneath it.

THE AGORA. After viewing the propylaea, return to the agora, a vast esplanade measuring more than 218yds (200m) from E to W and with an average width of some 110yds (100m) from N to S during the Roman period, but considerably smaller in the Greek town. The Greek agora occupied a slope that rose gently from N to S, whereas the Roman agora was located on two levelled terraces. The Greek agora was paved with large pebbles, the Roman agora with marble.

Façade of the Barbarian Captives – At the exit from propylaea, in the agora, turn r. You will see on the ground several fragments of a purely decorative facade of the Corinthian order, the most striking elements of which were at least four colossal statues on the second storey. They represented barbarian captives, standing on bases decorated with reliefs symbolizing the victory of the Romans. Two bases and fragments of the statues can be seen in the museum.

The Triglyph Wall – Now look carefully and if necessary consult the plan to seek out a small wall decorated with a triglyph frieze, separated by metopes. It belonged to a particularly interesting cult which throws light on some ancient Greek religious practices, in a way that will surely surprise you!

Look closely at the triglyph wall: it is broken up by a staircase giving access to an underground room enclosed by a grating and containing a sacred spring. Originally it was in the open air and appears not to have been covered until the first half of the 5th century BC.

Water from the spring flowed from spouts (bronze lions' heads) embedded in the rear wall, opposite the staircase. The supply of water was apparently scanty and there is every indication that it dried up at the end of the 4th or the beginning of the 3rd century BC. Yet the ancient spring must still have been looked on as sacred, for it was carefully walled in. A basin, fed by springs from far outside the town, was built almost on top of it, so that the Romans, when they sacked the town in 146 BC and founded the new city, had no idea of its existence, which explains its exceptional state of preservation. The water collected in this fountain was undoubtedly reserved for religious purposes and the discovery, close to it, of the site of an oracle, seems to confirm this fact. The sanctuary was uncovered about 30ft (10m) away, below the ruins of a row of Roman shops. It was probably built in the 5th century BC around a more ancient small circular altar, near which the faithful poured libations before consulting the oracle and where they received the reply of the god (Apollo, perhaps), through a trick which deserves further explanation.

Little tricks and great mysteries – Near the altar was the mouth of a small underground channel into which libations were poured. The other end of the channel consisted of a spout embedded in a metope. The libation channel was paralleled by a tunnel just large enough for a man to crawl through. It, too, terminated in a metope, this time a moveable one, forming a kind of secret door, but indistinguishable from the other metopes. A second door, which could be locked, was a further safeguard against intrusion by the laity.

In any case the laity had no chance of approaching the wall, and even less of examining it closely, for a regulation engraved on a boundary stone (a cast of it is on show) a few metres to the r. prohibited public access on the grounds that the place was sacred.

In order to answer the questions posed by the faithful, a priest slipped into the tunnel through the secret door and crawled to the other end where he could deliver the oracles through a hole in the pavement surrounding the altar.

N-E Portico – Behind the ruins of the Roman shops, some of which are comparatively well preserved, you will note the remains of a Hellenistic portico, built in the 3rd century BC, with an external Doric colonnade and an internal Ionic colonnade. Some of the columns are still standing.

The Fountain of Peirene – Return to the propylaea, then go past them to look at the ruins of what was one of the most sumptuous monuments of the Roman town: the fountain which housed the lower Peirene spring, in use from immemorial antiquity to the end of the 19th century.

Descending into the court, a striking complex built in the 2nd century AD by that generous patron Herodes Atticus, you will find six storage basins which are connected to a large reservoir of some 523cu. yds (400 cu. m) capacity. Note the few remaining traces of Roman paintings representing fish, on the side walls of the third basin to the l.

There were two Peirene fountains, one at the top, the other at the foot, of Acrocorinth. The lower one was supposed to be the outlet for the upper one. The large reservoir, still visible, was hewn out of the rock in the Greek period. In front of the reservoir and separated from it by stone gratings, are three basins from which originally water was drawn. The rock vault was supported by pillars forming a portico. At a later date this was divided into six chambers separated by dividing walls which can still be seen. Towards the 3rd century BC, this arrangement was clad with marble. When Corinth was rebuilt by the Romans, the portico and the walls of the court in front of the fountain were refurbished in the Doric and Ionic orders, and a basin with water flowing from several spouts was placed in the centre of the court. Towards the end of the 1st century AD, the walls were faced with marble and the articulation of the main facade of the fountain modified. In the 2nd century, three massive vaulted apses were added on three sides, each of them containing three niches housing statues which were probably portraits of members of Herodes Atticus' family. The smooth-shafted columns of the projecting portico on the main façade are an early Byzantine addition.

The Julian Basilica – The ruins at the E end of the Roman agora are those of a basilica built in the age of Augustus, in which several statues of members of the Julian family or other emperors were discovered.

Greek Stadium – In front of the Julian basilica, you will observe part of the pavement of the Greek agora, about 3ft (1m) below the Roman level.

A row of limestone blocks, now known to be the starting line of a Greek stadium, has been found here. The athletes put their feet in holes in the blocks to give them extra impetus when starting. Close by, the remains of a second, differently orientated, but older starting line have been excavated. The wheel marks left on the pavement in front of the starting line suggest that the stadium was used for chariot races. We know that races forming part of a ritual of the cult of the dead took place during the Corinthian festival of Hellotia, in honour of Athena Hellotis.

A curvilinear wall supported a terrace where the judges and a few privileged spectators sat to watch the races.

Bema – The lower agora was bounded to the S by two rows of 15 shops on either side of the Bema, a monumental tribune where the Roman governor appeared before the public. This monument was compared to the Rostra, the tribunes for Roman orators, in a 2nd-century AD inscription. It is famous in the annals of Christianity for the speech made there by Paul before the Roman governor Gallio to defend himself and Christianity (*Acts*, 18).

S Portico – Corinth could boast of possessing one of the largest buildings in ancient Greece. This portico, which was built in the 4th century and restored shortly before the destruction of the city by Mummius, was a curious two-storeyed edifice with two rows of 33 shops, most of which were taverns. All but two of the front parts of the shops had wells 42ft (12m) deep supplied with water by a conduit leading to the Peirene spring. These wells were used to cool drinks and food.

This highly original building was probably conceived as a vast hotel complex for housing delegates from Greek cities when Corinth had become the headquarters of the Panhellenic Union on the initiative of Philip II of Macedon after his victory at Chaeronea in 338 BC. The storey above the taverns was probably occupied by bedrooms for those delegates.

This portico was faithfully reconstructed at the time of the Roman foundation. Then in the 1st century AD most of the shops were demolished to make way for a series of administrative buildings. The third hall from the l., where you will see some traces of a Roman mosaic pavement, was probably the meeting place of the Agonothetes or directors of the Isthmian Games. In the central panel of the mosaic you will notice a victorious athlete wearing a crown standing before Eutychia, the goddess of good fortune, apparently thanking her. Beneath a shed, you can also see the lip of a well with a Hellenistic portico. Another shed covers two mosaic pavements, one of which depicts Dionysus in a chariot drawn by two panthers and led by a satyr holding a thyrsus (staff wreathed with ivy). You can also see two centaurs carrying vases. The second mosaic shows a nereid sitting on the back of a centaur and Eros hovering in the air.

S Basilica – The first four halls opened on to a broad pavement at the end of which a marble stairway gave access to the S basilica, a vast construction with an internal court surrounded by porticoes, from which several (very mutilated) statues of emperors have been dug up.

Next you will see the ruins of a marble Roman fountain. Its floor is still covered with multi-coloured marble slabs.

Road to Kenchreai – Just in front of the Senate there was a passage joined by a road leading to Kenchreai, one of the two ports of Corinth, situated on the Saronic Gulf. A section of this road, which was faced with limestone slabs in the first half of the 1st century AD, has been uncovered.

The Senate – The main room, or council chamber, was elliptical. The walls are still preserved to a considerable height.

The upper agora was bounded to the W by a series of nine Archaic columns (6th century BC), possibly from the temple of Apollo, which were re-used by the Romans to support a conduit which supplied a rectangular basin with water. Note the remains of the basin at the N end of the colonnade.

On leaving the excavations of the agora, you then visit another site to the r. where an odeon and a theatre were discovered.

Odeon – Built in the 1st century AD, then again c.175 by Herodes Atticus, this establishment, which held 3,000 people, was devoted to cultural activities, but c.225 was transformed into an arena for fights between gladiators and animals. The stage was then destroyed.

Theatre – A paved street passing to the l. of the odeon leads to the theatre, constructed in the 5th century BC, but entirely rebuilt after the foundation of the Roman colony, and transformed in its turn into an arena for nautical spectacles (naumachiae).

Paradoxically enough, the auditorium of the Greek theatre, which could hold some 18,000 spectators, is better preserved than the Roman one. Thus the traces of seats visible on the hillside belong to the Greek theatre. You can still make out the wall, originally nearly 10ft (3m) high, which separated the auditorium from the orchestra during the Roman period, so as to protect the spectators. It was adorned with paintings of combat scenes between gladiators and wild animals. A much worn inscription, scratched in the plaster on the wall, tells us the moving story of the gladiator called Androcles, who was saved by a lion which had become his friend. This was the tale that inspired Bernard Shaw.

When the theatre was rebuilt in the 1st century BC, the seats of the Greek building were buried in the earth and the radiating containing walls were raised to support the Roman cavea. The theatre of Corinth was destroyed in 396 AD, during the sacking of the town by Alaric's troops.

Beyond the theatre, another excavation site, near the rampart, but inside the enclosure, which contains an Asclepieion (or sanctuary of Asclepius) and its annex, the Fountain of Lerna, will interest only the keen amateur archaeologist.

Some 110yds (100m) before the sanctuary of Asclepius recent excavations now mostly recovered, have revealed the existence of a long Doric portico (175yds/160m) built at the end of the 1st century AD, which probably formed part of the gymnasium mentioned by Pausanias. Digs in this sector also revealed the remains of an underground fountain and various Hellenistic installations annexed to the Roman gymnasium and then consecrated to a cult towards the end of the Roman period (end of the 4th, beginning of the 5th century). Thousands of votive lamps have been discovered here.

Asclepieion – In its final state, this temple was erected on the site of a sanctuary dating from the Archaic period (6th century BC). Like all the sanctuaries devoted to the god of medicine, that of Corinth had an abaton, a hall in which the sick spent the night in the hope that Asclepius would reveal the remedy for their ills in a dream. This hall was situated just above the E wing of the fountain of Lerna which was closely associated with the worship of Asclepius in his sanctuary.

The Fountain of Lerna – It consisted of a vast building with a central court surrounded by porticoes. Three halls opening beneath the E portico are the most remarkable feature of this complex. Situated just below the abaton of the sanctuary of Asclepius, they served as dining rooms, with stone benches on which the patients reclined in front of small tables.

VICINITY OF ANCIENT CORINTH

1 ACROCORINTH. Acrocorinth, which was the acropolis or upper town of Corinth, is like an enormous fortress on which all the occupants of the isthmus, from the Byzantines to the Turks, have left their mark. The famous temple of Aphrodite, with its hierodoulae (temple prostitutes) who men dreamt of from as far away as Rome, is now only a memory, but the unforgettable **panorama of the whole isthmus makes it a goal which we warmly recommend.

Take the road to Argos from the village of Palea Korinthos.

0.6mls (1km): Fork r. on an asphalted road which enables you to reach the site entrance near the museum.

1.1mls (1.8km): Turn l. beyond the pretty fountain of Hadji Mustapha (18th century).

1.7mls (2.8km): to the r., on the slopes of Acrocorinth, lie the remains of the sanctuary of Demeter and Kore (Persephone) which was used from the 7th century BC to the 4th century AD. It stood on terraces reached by monumental staircases intersected by landings. It comprised a small theatre (some seats cut out of the rock survive) and several buildings some of which contained a banqueting hall for ritual meals and rooms paved with mosaics.

3mls (4.8km): Entrance to Acrocorinth (open from 08.00 to 20.00).

THE GUARDIAN OF THE ISTHMUS. Acrocorinth may have been fortified under the tyranny of the Cypselids, from the 7th or 6th century BC. The remains of ancient fortifications date mainly to the 4th century BC. The ramparts were restored in the time of Justinian, shortly before the Slavic invasion of 583–586. The Acrocorinth garrison repulsed the Bulgarians in 981 and 995. Around this period, the Byzantines added new fortifications, in particular part of the second, W enclosing wall or enceinte. Admirably situated to observe both gulfs and dominate, with a strong garrison, the entrance to the Peloponnese, Acrocorinth was one of 'the shackles of Greece'. It was taken and retaken many times by everyone who aspired to dominate the Peloponnese.

A HALTED CRUSADE. The taking of Acrocorinth by the Franks was one of the results of the outrageous act of greed, whereby the Fourth Crusade renounced a return to the Holy Land in order to capture Constantinople (1204), thus temporarily breaking up of the Byzantine Empire. Nevertheless, five years of siege were needed before the Franks actually took Acrocorinth in 1210. This citadel, the fortifications of which were reinforced, then became a fief of the Villehardouins, who were succeeded by the Angevins. In 1358, the place was ceded to Niccolo Accaioli who gave it to Palaeologus of Mystra in 1394. The Knights of Rhodes held it for four years, between 1400 and 1404. Mehmet II took it from the Byzantines in 1458 after a siege lasting three months. Later it came under the domination of Venice (1687–1715), thanks to Morosini.

Approaching Acrocorinth from the W you pass through three enclosing walls. The first is preceded by a moat cut out of the rock by the Venetians, who also added parapets with embrasures for cannon on the second and third ramparts. The first gate, from the Frankish period, dates from the 14th century. The second wall is partly Byzantine, notably a two-storeyed building and the curtain wall to the r. of the second gate.

The curtain wall on the l. may have been added at the beginning of the 15th century by the Knights of Rhodes.

The third wall, strengthened by massive rectangular towers, and the gate are mainly Byzantine. Section of antique walls and a tower with fine trapezoidal masonry (4th century BC) and raised ornamental carving on this third wall.

After the third door, preferably, go l. towards a small chapel; from there you will climb up to an old mosque of which the walls and the lower part of the cupola are still well preserved. Then continue along the path which will lead you to the N face of the rampart (about 100 yds to the N. of the mosque) where there is a postern-gate; from there you will find a magnificent view over the Gulf of Corinth.

Returning to the mosque and descending again towards the S., you will reach a damaged, truncated minaret standing below the keep, before which an immense cistern has been dug (inspection ports protected by grids). From the minaret you take, to the E, a very steep slope which, leaving on the r. two ruined buildings (cistern and storehouse), will lead you to a terrace from which three paths lead off. By the one on the r. which runs along the S. face of the rampart you will quickly reach the keep, probably built by Guillaume de Villehardouin (magnificent view over the Argolid).

Retracing your steps follow the face of the rampart as far as an esplanade bordered on the l. by a ruined barracks; in front of this a modern stairway allows a descent towards the upper Peirene spring which flows into an underground chamber at the foot of an ancient stairway; the façade of this fountain is well preserved (about 6ft/2m wide by 13ft/4m high); a pilaster supports an entablature made of two blocks of an architrave and a pediment. A narrow passage opening to the l. beneath the modern staircase gives access to a room in which the vault of the fountain appears, pierced by a circular aperture. According to the legend the spring burst forth following a blow from the hoof of the winged horse Pegasus which Bellerophon later captured as it came to drink at the spring.

Returning to the terrace you will take the path on the r. which will lead you to the top of the highest mound (alt. 1900ft/574m) to see the substructure of the famous temple of Aphrodite (Venus) excavated in 1926 by the American school.

A PLEASANT ASPECT OF THE WORSHIP OF APHRODITE. According to Strabo the temple was very small and originally was only a simple tabernacle of the Syrian deity Astarte. This eastern cult was observed in the town by a community of about 1,000 priestesses devoted to hierogamy. Their financial demands inspired the proverbial line of Horace: It is not the privilege of everyone to go to Corinth (*non cuivis homini contingit adire Corinthum*).

Of the temple itself little remains but the site offers a magnificent circular panorama which stretches to the N as far as Mount Parnassus, to the E to Attica, and to the S to the mountains of the Peloponnese; quite close, to the SW, the ruins of the Frankish castle of Montesquiou (corrupted locally to Pendeskoufi) stand out on top of a rocky peak.

Near the S rampart, on the plateau, is the upper Peirene fountain which flows from a subterranean chamber.

2 LECHAION (route: 1.9mls/3km, by the Corinth road). By the sea, on the site of the ancient port of Lechaion, you will see the ruins of a 5th-century basilica which is probably one of the largest in the Greek world. It was built on a plot of ground created artificially at the beginning of the Roman period on part of the ancient port of Lechaion, destroyed by Mummius in 146 BC. To reach it, continue on the Patras road and take a road to the r. about 220yds (200m) beyond the fork.

This enormous complex of buildings was undoubtedly founded in the days of Marcian (450–457) or shortly afterwards, and later restored and enlarged on many occasions, notably in the reigns of Anastasius I (491–518), when the pavement was completed, and Justin I (518–527), when the atrium and the court were probably added. It was destroyed by the earthquake of 551.

You first enter a large court surrounded by a continuous corridor. Then you reach the atrium by a semicircular passage, the ends of which open to a portico preceding the vestibule, or narthex, of the church. To its l. are the remains of a vast baptistery, perhaps an ancient martyrium, comprising an antechamber, a vestry with four radiating apses and an octagonal building, the plan of which was complicated by alternating rectangular and semicircular niches. One of them contained one of the baptismal fonts, the other being situated in the centre. The church proper was made up of three naves demarcated by two rows of 23 columns.

■ Corinth Canal

Route maps 5 and 6.

Ancient Corinth 7.5mls (12km) - Corinth 3.7mls (6km) - Athens, 50.6mls (81km).

This channel, 6,936yds (6,343m) long and 25yds (23m) wide, which turns the Peloponnese into an island, is most impressive when seen from the bridge that spans it. The spectacle will be even more interesting if you are lucky enough to see the canal when a ship is passing through. At the end of the 19th century, the Corinth Canal put into effect an idea that was more than two and a half millennia old: that of saving ships the long detour from Piraeus to the Adriatic around Cape Matapan (185 nautical miles when sailing).

SHIPS ON WHEELS IN THE CORINTH CANAL. The idea of sparing navigators from the dangers of the capes of the Peloponnese by connecting the Ionian and Aegean Seas is very ancient. In the 7th or 6th century BC, the Corinthians built a paved slipway (diolkos) on which ships were pulled by chariots from the Saronic Gulf to the Gulf of Corinth. Periander, Demetrius Poliorcetes, Caesar, Caligula, Nero, Hadrian and Herodes Atticus all dreamt of piercing the isthmus. Caligula sent an engineer to Corinth. Nero first put the project in hand in 67 AD and inaugurated operations with a gold spade. Vespasian sent him 6,000 Jewish prisoners from Judaea to work on it. All traces of this work have disappeared since the opening of the present-day channel.

A French company began work on the canal on 1 May 1882 and a Greek company finished it in 1893.

The remains of the paved slipway built by the Corinthians in antiquity have been discovered at the point where the canal joins the Gulf of Corinth. Starting from Corinth, archaeology enthusiasts can reach it by continuing past the station. Part of it is visible between the canal and the railway line, and another section alongside the road, on the other side (ferry), between the railway bridge and the mouth of the canal on the Gulf of Corinth. The diolkos was a slipway made up of limestone slabs with two parallel grooves, 5ft (1.50m) apart. The grooves were used to guide the wheels of the chariots by which the vessels were pulled. The width of the slipway varies from 11ft 6ins (3.50m) to 16ft 6ins (5m) and reaches almost 33ft (10m) near the mouth of the canal. This esplanade, without grooves, was used for warping ships. Where the slipway curved, two low walls replaced the grooves to give the chariots more traction. According to Strabo (VIII, 380), the diolkos of Corinth started at Schionos (now Kalamaki) and ended at Poseidonia. Following the letters of the Corinthian alphabet engraved in the rock at several points on the slipway, M. Verdelis dates the diolkos to the late 7th or early 6th century BC, but it was probably rebuilt in the 5th century BC.

Cos [Island of] (Kos)

112sq. mls (290km^2) – Pop: 16,000 – admin. region of the Dodecanese.

Cos is an island whose historical memories and archaeological evidence vie with its natural attractions. This island in the Dodecanese archipelago seems to be moored to the Asian continent, from which it is separated by a strait only 3 nautical miles wide. This may be why some of its inhabitants are Muslims. It is famous mainly because of Hippocrates, the greatest physician of antiquity, who was born there c.460 BC. Yet even though Asclepius was a healer there, the island deserves to be far more than a place of pilgrimage for doctors, with its verdant plains (vines, tobacco, cereals, olive trees) and hills, the unassertive charm of its capital full of gardens and flowers, its perfect beaches, its clear sea and mild climate.

THE CHILDREN OF ASCLEPIUS. The first Greek colonists, the Achaeans, came from Thessaly or Argolis in the second half of the 14th century BC. At all events, the cult of Asclepius, the god of healing, was particularly flourishing in those two provinces of continental Greece. Asclepius was a native of Trikke (Trikkala), in Thessaly, and had his most famous sanctuary at (Ancient) Epidaurus, in Argolis. The island was originally governed by kings, two of whom marched against Troy with the Greek coalition. It was invaded by the Dorians a few centuries after the arrival of the Achaeans. In the 7th and 6th centuries Cos was a member of the Dorian hexapolis (a confederation of six Dorian cities all located in Asia Minor, except Cos), which became a pentapolis after the exclusion of Halicarnassus. In the 6th century, the island formed part of a Persian satrapy or province.

WHEN THE AEGEAN BECAME A GREEK LAKE AGAIN. Along with Rhodes, Cos rose against the Persians after the Greek naval victory at Cape Mycalae (597 BC) and paid tribute to Athens from 477 as a member of the maritime confederation against the Persians presided over by Athens.

The island wanted to withdraw from its alliance with Athens, but Alcibiades intervened in 410 BC and left an Athenian garrison there. Towards the end of the Peloponnesian War, the island supported Sparta, but was affiliated with the second Athenian Maritime League from 378–377 BC. Soon afterwards, the site of the capital was transferred to ancient Astypalaea, in the W of the island. Allied to Rhodes, Chios and Byzantium, Cos tried to free itself from Athenian vassalage in 357. It became independent in the late 4th century, forming an alliance with Ptolemaic Egypt and fighting against Antigonus in 315. The Ptolemies visited Cos frequently, attracted by its exceptional climate.

IN THE WAKE OF THE POWERFUL. After submitting to the influence of Rhodes, Cos was occupied by Philip of Macedon after the defeat of the Rhodian fleet at Lade in 201 BC. It then became a vassal of Rhodes again and, with her, took part in the war against Antiochus III, on the Roman side, in 190 BC. During the war between Rome and Mithridates, it took the side of the Romans, but was occupied by Mithridates in 88 BC and the Roman citizens who thought they had found a refuge in the Asclepieion were massacred. Cos subsequently lived on good terms with Rome. In 27–26 BC, it was ravaged by a violent earthquake, but was rebuilt due to the generosity of the

Emperor Claudius, the island's greatest benefactor. During the Roman period, it was famous for its silk fabrics which were much sought after by the women of Rome. These silks were so transparent that Seneca wrote that a woman wearing them could not say she was not naked without lying.

COS, A ROMAN OUTPOST. The island was part of the Byzantine Empire until the capture of Constantinople by the Crusaders in 1204. In the early 14th century, it was ceded to the Knights of Rhodes, but suffered many Turkish attacks, especially in 1457 and 1477, although it was finally captured by them only in 1523. The Italians took it from the Turks in 1912 and kept it until 1948 when it became Greek again.

A DAY IN COS. One day is enough to visit the most interesting sights on the island, but you may well find it so attractive that you will want to stay longer. The first thing to do is make sure of the opening hours of the castle of the Knights, the museum, the Roman house and the Asclepieion, as you will have to arrange your day to fit in with them and they can vary considerably, from year to year or season to season.

First you will probably want to visit the castle, the museum and the Roman house, and then make for (by taxi, bicycle or on foot) the Asclepieion (3.1mls/5km from Cos by a road which has a gentle gradient for the last half of the stretch). If you have a car, you can swim at Kardamena (take the Cos road from the Asclepieion and turn r. at the village of Platani so as to rejoin the main Cos-Antimacheia road, see below).

If you return to Cos during the late afternoon, you will have time to visit the town's main excavation sites, the W sector and the agora, which are not enclosed. In the evening you can take a walk by the harbour, the meeting place where everyone in the capital promenades until a late hour, and you can dine on the terrace of one of the little restaurants lining the quay.

If you stay longer in Cos, rent a car, or better still a bicycle or moped, the commonest means of transport on the island.

COS, the capital, on the site of the last ancient capital of the island, is a charming little port, with flowers everywhere and avenues sometimes lined with palm trees. In summer, it dozes during the day beside the castle of the Knights of Rhodes, but comes to life at nightfall.

The port, accessible by a narrow channel watched over for centuries by the castle of the Knights, extends into the heart of the little town. Pleasure boats and fishing caiques can tie up alongside its curved main quay, while steamers and hydrofoils moor at a mole, at the NE entrance to the channel, beyond the castle in relation to the main quay.

THE PLANE TREE OF HIPPOCRATES. By going E along the avenue beside the main quay to the far end of the port (Akti Koundouriotou), and leaving the castle to your l., you will reach a broad stepped ramp that leads you to a small garden where Corinthian capitals are exhibited.

From the end of this garden you pass into a delightful little square (Plateia Platanou), paved with cobblestones and shaded by an enormous plane tree, named after Hippocrates (although it cannot be more than 500 years old), supported by ancient columns, and a Roman altar. Its trunk is at least 40ft (12m) in circumference. On 1 September, people flock to kiss it to ensure longevity. Next to the plane tree is a Turkish fountain for ablutions and, in the S of the square, the large mosque (no longer used) of Hadji Hassan Pasha, also known as the Lontza or Loggia mosque (18th century), the minaret of which still towers up into the sky. Remains of the ancient port district and the agora, best visited in the evening (entrance free), extend below the mosque.

CASTLE OF THE KNIGHTS OF RHODES. On the side of the Plane Tree Square opposite the mosque, i.e. to the N, a bridge spanning a modern avenue built on the site of an ancient moat gives access to the castle of the Knights. The gate has a marble lintel; above it is a frieze of antique marble re-used, decorated with six masks in relief linked by a garland of flowers, foliage and fruit. A re-used antique inscription is set in the wall to the l. of the lintel and above there is a coat of arms. The castle, mainly built of re-used ancient materials, consists of two enclosures, the first of which, dating from the mid 15th century, was restored by the Grand Masters Pierre d'Aubusson (1476–1505) and Aimery d'Amboise (1505–12), as evidenced by the escutcheons embedded in the curtain wall. On the W façade, on the side next to the port, you will see, below an antique lion, the arms of Pierre d'Aubusson, surmounted by the cardinal's hat granted him in 1498. The second wall, which formed a keep reinforced with round towers, was erected in the 14th century and restored under the Grand Master Pierre d'Aubusson (escutcheons on the towers). From the top of the outer enclosure, most of which you can visit, there is a very fine view of the port and the Turkish coast, which is quite close. An open-air museum containing antique and modern marble sculpture is situated inside, below the entrance.

THE ANCIENT HARBOUR QUARTER AND THE AGORA. Returning to the Plateia Platanou, leave the great plane tree on your l. and pass in front of the old Italian palace of justice (on the wall, a Latin inscription: *legum omnes servi sumus*, 'We are all subject to the laws'). Turn your back on it and proceed to the top of the rampart laid out at the E corner of the Lontza mosque, from which you will have a sweeping view of the remains of the ancient harbour quarter and the agora.

In the foreground you can see, swamped by a number of previous walls, a row of six Corinthian columns, part of the rearrangement, around the 3rd–4th century AD, of a portico erected in the 3rd century BC. The remains of a 5th-century AD palaeo-Christian basilica lie to the r., to the W of the columns. Walking along the outside of the excavation site to the r. (SE), you will soon be able to enter and see the propylaea of the sanctuary of Aphrodite Pandemos (2nd century BC). The wall of the E precinct of the place of worship is well preserved, but the remains of the temple are reduced to the podium and a few drums of fluted Corinthian columns. A large Roman mosaic with floral, geometric and figured motifs (birds, gladiators and wild beasts) is preserved outside to the S of the temenos (place of worship) of Aphrodite. To the E of the temenos, you can see the remains of a small Hellenistic sanctuary (rebuilt in the Roman period) and of the Hellenistic temple of Heracles, with its foundations and orthostats (upright stones). To the E and SE of this monument, are two more Roman mosaics in the open, one depicting animals and people, the other birds and fishes. Beyond, to the SE, there is a section of the town's Classical or Hellenistic ramparts, some 10ft (3m) thick with a stairway leading to the curtain wall (on the S side).

To the E of the site there are three 15th-century chapels: those of Ioannes Prodromos (John the Baptist), Panagia Gorgoepikos (the Virgin Mary), where you can see some frescoes, a 17th-century iconostasis, and St George (a domed 19th-century edifice).

Returning to the sector with the ramparts, take an old road to E, leaving to your l. (i.e. S) some Roman buildings (a series of vaulted rooms). Past a cross roads (antique orthogonal roads), you will reach the site of the agora, the N portico of which is easily seen thanks to the two Doric columns, topped by their entablature, which have been re-erected (to the W are the remains of an enormous construction of Roman masonry). The centre of the agora is partly covered by the little church of Hagios Constantinos (15th century) decorated with frescoes, which the Turks whitewashed over, and a fine iconostasis (to enter the church leave the archaeological zone by a passage on the S side and take the Hippocratous Street to the r.).

MUSEUM. If you follow the above street to the W, you will pass close to one of the town's medieval gates and come to Liberty Square (Plateia Eleftherias), where the museum is located.

Open daily except Tues. in summer, from 08.30–12.30 and from 16.00 to 18.00, Sun. from 09.00–15.00; in winter, from 09.00–13.30 and 16.00–18.00, Sun. from 10.00–16.30; entrance fee.

The museum of Cos which consists of an entrance hall and three large halls arranged around a central court exhibits more than a hundred marble sculptures, mainly Hellenistic and Roman, among other discoveries made on the island.

In the first room note in particular to your left a 3rd-century BC funerary relief depicting an athlete holding his victory crown in his hands (No. 5) and several statues found at the Odeon (2nd- to 1st-century BC). These include: a beautiful male torso (No. 4), an undamaged figure of a woman (No. 6), the upper part of a portrait of a woman with a proud expression (No. 17), a portrait of a woman in the Classical style (No. 13), and one other female figure (No. 24) whose flowing garments illustrate the richness of Coan material so famous in antiquity. Note also the expressive wounded warrior (No. 14) and a huge head of Heracles (No. 21), probably a late copy of an original by Lysippus.

Note a late Hellenistic statue, copied from a Classical original, which may represent Hippocrates (No. 32). Nearby are two beautiful late Archaic reliefs (Nos. 29 and 30) showing a banquet scene and a young man holding a cockerel. In the central court, a mosaic from the 2nd or 3rd century AD shows Hippocrates seated and one of his companions welcoming Asclepius to the island of Cos. There are beautiful Roman statues in the peristyle (No. 98 represents Hygieia, daughter of Asclepius, holding a snake to which she is offering an egg).

THE ROMAN HOUSE AND THE ALTAR OF DIONYSUS. The road opening on to the far end of Liberty Square (Odhos Vassileos Pavlou, opposite the museum, leads to a charming square planted with palm trees, near which are two groups of interesting ruins. To the E, below the square, are the remains of a large Hellenistic altar of Dionysus (some 46ft/14m by 26ft/8m), which was accessible by a ramp on the W side. Further to the NE are the foundations and parts of a temple from the same period. Important Roman remains extend to the S of the square planted with palm trees on the other side of avenue Grigouriou E' (Gregory V). They include baths on the E side and to the W a 3rd-century AD patrician dwelling built on the site of a Hellenistic villa.

This vast Roman house has been partially reconstructed, with its courts and numerous rooms, to house the remarkable **mosaic pavements (one of them depicting Amphitrite on a seahorse) and the murals and coloured marble facings which have been uncovered. On the S side, a large peristyle court has been restored, with a ground floor colonnade on three sides, repeated on the first floor gallery, and a single row of large Corinthian columns to the S.

THE WESTERN EXCAVATIONS. Leaving the Roman house, you take the avenue Grigouriou E' to the l. (i.e. S) for some 330yds (300m). Just beyond the place where the avenue begins to be lined with cypresses, turn r. up some narrow steps which lead up to a small square with a modest minaret. If you then take a path to the l., you will come to the site of the antique acropolis shaded with palm trees and pines, from which you can look down on the ruins of Roman houses. Returning to the avenue, you descend to the archaeological area (entrance free) and take the ancient decumanus (main street) still with some 110yds (100m) of paving. To the N of this road, several tin roofs protect the mosaics and murals taken from the Roman houses. Take special note of the mosaic depicting gladiators fighting and the very beautiful panel of the *Abduction of Europa* (3rd century AD). She lies naked on the bull which carried her over the sea (blue, with dolphins). Some of the murals are decorated with figures.

Follow the decumanus (main street of the city) to the W and then reascend to a modern avenue. Cross it and note, just behind you, the Roman odeon, with some of its marble seats still preserved. Retracing your steps, go down to the excavations and turn l. on a section of the *cardo*, the N-S artery of the Roman city.

First, to the l., you will see the rather jumbled remains of a building entered through a lovely marble doorway giving on to a court paved in *opus sectile*. About 60ft (20m) to the W are the remains of basins and a baptistery with fonts faced with marble forming part of a palaeo-Christian baptistery situated further N. The large marble door of the baptistery has been re-erected. The ruins of large Roman baths with remnants of the heating system (hypocausts) lie beyond, on the S side. The *cardo*, on which the marks of chariot wheels are clearly visible, passes between these baths and a large square restored building (often shut). It contained the large latrines from the 3rd/4th century AD and you can see the Ionic peristyle and a court paved with mosaics (geometric motifs and dolphins) by looking through a kind of dormer window reached by going up a few steps of the stairway adjoining the building on the S side.

To the N of the baths are traces of a palaeo-Christian basilica, with its apse to the E, near the cardo.

Some 60ft (20m) to the N of the basilica, on the boundary of the area explored, a roof shelters a large *Roman mosaic with figured panels (hunting scenes in the border; the nine Muses in the company of Orpheus and the Judgement of Paris in the central panels, with, from l. to r., Paris sitting under a tree, Hermes, Aphrodite, Hera and Athena).

To the W of the baths, a row of 17 Doric columns with part of their entablature have been re-erected. They come from the ruins of a covered xystus (portico). A large Roman basin occupies the far end of the site beyond the portico to the W.

If you walk at random in the town, you will probably come upon other scattered remains, often covered with vegetation. The modern main road (avenue Tsaldari) which contains the Roman *cardo* to the N, runs alongside the site of the antique stadium (to the W of the Blvd). Beyond 25 March Street, it leads to the ruins of some Hellenistic baths near the modern port.

VICINITY OF COS

1 ASCLEPIEION (3.1mls/5km; by the Choio road, then go l. for 0.6mls/1km).

Open: weekdays in summer, from 8.00–17.00, Sun. from 09.00–17.00; in winter, from 09.00–16.000, Sun. from 10.00–16.00; entrance fee.

The Asclepieion of Cos, a famous sanctuary dedicated to Asclepius, to which patients flocked from all over Greece in search of a cure for their ills, was built in the 4th century BC and enlarged on several occasions. The sanctuary and its associated buildings occupy four terraces which dominate the plain of Cos. You start your visit with the fourth terrace.

Fourth Terrace - Note to the l. the remains of 1st-century AD baths and further l. a pool for cold baths.

Third Terrace – The largest part of the Asclepieion containing ferruginous and sulphurous springs (the island still has springs supposed to be effective in the treatment of gastro-enterological disorders) can be considered as the sacred site of the therapeutic cure as opposed to the temple zone which occupied the two upper terraces. It was reached by a ramp with a Doric propylaeum, of marble and travertine, built in the Hellenistic period. The court of the third terrace was lined on three sides by Doric porticoes on to which various rooms from the Roman period opened, as did a thermal establishment to the E. A sort of medical museum housed the *ex voto* offerings of the patients. Some underground rooms are decorated with Roman paintings.

To the r. of the stairway of the second terrace note the ruins of a small Ionic naiskos, or chapel, dedicated in the 1st century AD by Xenophon, the court doctor of Claudius I. A little further to the r. is a small fountain. To the l. of the stairway is a row of basins used for treating patients. The E sector of the terrace is occupied by the

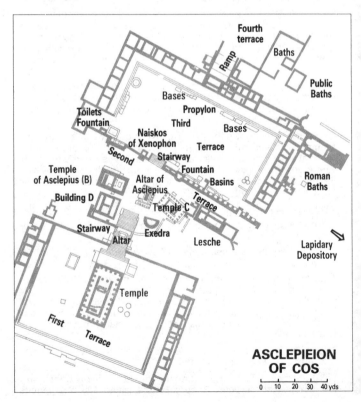

ASCLEPIEION OF COS

0   10   20   30   40 yds

remains of large baths from the time of the Roman Empire. Further on, to the E of these baths, is a storeroom of broken statues, the court of which (entrance free) contains numerous inscriptions.

Second terrace – The stairway ends opposite the monumental altar of Asclepius. To the r., two columns belong to the Ionic Temple of Asclepius (Temple B), erected between 300 and 270 BC, in which the treasures of the sanctuary were deposited. In the cella of this temple was a rectangular fosse in which pilgrims placed a votive offering (pelanos) before taking the cure. The temple was ornamented with paintings by Apelles, including *Aphrodite Rising from the Sea*, taken to Rome by Augustus.

To the l. of the altar (to the E) lie the remains of another temple (Temple C). It is a peripteral Corinthian building of white marble (seven of its columns have been re-erected) which may have been dedicated to Delian Apollo before it was consecrated to the imperial cult (2nd-3rd century AD). That would explain the different orientation of this temple in relation to the temple of Asclepius. Further E, stood a vast Hellenistic construction, undoubtedly a lesche (clubhouse). At the foot of the stairway leading to the first terrace, to the E, is a vast 3rd-century BC exedra.

First terrace – Created during an enlargement made in the first half of the 2nd century BC. In the axis of the stairway stood a large peripteral Doric temple (Temple A) of white marble, with black marble decoration. It was partially changed into a church in the 5th century, whence the presence of palaeo-Christian capitals. Various places for the cure with porticoes around them were also built on this terrace. About half an hour's walk to the S of the Asclepieion on the mountain is the oldest structure on the island consisting of a high dome approached through a 38yd-(35m) long corridor with a cantilevered covering. Nero's doctor, Andromachus of Crete, in an invocation to Asclepius mentioned a spring he called Burinna which had its source under the dome. In spite of the similarity of this domed building to Mycenaean tholos (bee hive) tombs, it is unlikely that it dates back so far.

2 KARDAMENA (19.4mls/31km by the Antimacheia road).

5.6mls (9km): Asfendiou, a village dominated by a medieval castle, in the midst of gardens, is 1.9mls (3km) on the l.

8.1mls (13km): to the l. Pyli (1.9mls/3km): a Byzantine kastro (fort) restored by the Knights of Rhodes. Several small Byzantine churches, including the Church of the Purification of the Virgin, decorated with 14th-century frescoes in the first enclosure.

15mls (24km): Antimacheia, near a triangular fortress built by the Knights of Rhodes. Visit, too, the church of Hagia Paraskevi. Airport of Cos.

3.1mls (5km): to the N, Mastichari, with a delightful sandy beach.

9.4mls (31km): Kardamena, once the prettiest village on the island but now, somewhat over-developed, beside a beach of fine sand which will entice you to swim. You reach it beyond a *panoramic view of the whole island.

Near the village are the ruins of a temple of Apollo, one of Cos's most revered deities, and a Hellenistic theatre.

3 KEFALOS (26.9mls/43km by the Antimacheia road).

25mls (40km): by the edge of the sea, in the midst of a Club Méditerranée village, is the Byzantine basilica of Hagios Stephanos.

26.9mls (43km): Kefalos, picturesquely perched on a limestone cliff, with the remains of a fortress and an actual working windmill (magnificent *panorama of Cos, Nisyros and the Turkish coast from both fortress and windmill: tip of the Cnidos peninsula). Numerous prehistoric remains have been discovered in the grotto of Aspri Petra.

1.2mls (2km) to the SW, at Palatia, the ruins of the antique Astypalaea, ancient capital of the island. Take a guide from the village to visit the remains of a Hellenistic temple, a sanctuary of Demeter and a 4th century BC theatre.

Crete [Island of] (Kriti)***

3,216.5sq. mls (8,331km²) – Pop: 456,642.

Many people would not hesitate to describe Crete as a continent, exaggerating deliberately in order to give some indication of its richness and variety. It is the fourth-largest island in the Mediterranean, 156mls (250km) long and up to 35.6mls (57km) across, with large ranges of mountains rising to over 7,875ft (2,400m); it stands at the maritime crossroads of Europe, Asia and Africa, and there is no question that the experience stored there by history has left us with a heritage we have not yet exhausted; Zeus himself was born there. But if you try to push the metaphor too far you will arouse in the Cretans a proud, untamed feeling of belonging to the Hellenic world, of being Greek: Kazantzakis and Theodorakis are Cretan names. Only recently, in 1974, the crisis in Cyprus revived this feeling of being part of the continent towards which the whole life of the island turns – an island which gave that continent its gods and its civilization. A visit to Crete will enable you to discover all this for yourself, a past where history and legend merge, and a people who are passionate, free and loyal, as many traditions still in existence bear witness.

The geography of Crete

A LAND OF MOUNTAINS. Crete is the linchpin of the archipelago formed by Kithira, Crete, Kasos, Karpathos and Rhodes which marks the boundary between the Aegean Sea and the Mediterranean. The island is largely formed of three mountain ranges, the high craggy peaks of which rise above banks of scree: the Lefka Ori (White Mountains) 8,045ft (2,452m) high, the Mt Ida chain (Psiloritis) rising to a height of 8,050ft (2,456m) and Mt Lasithiatika (Dicte), 7,047ft (2,148m) high. These limestone mountains are deeply bored through by the mole-like workings of underground water, and above ground are interspersed with enclosed depressions, the largest of which form high inland plains (the Lasithi plateau) on which there are fields and villages. The rocky S coast drops abruptly into the sea. The N coast is much more open, consisting of bays fringed by plains, and has become the site of the major ports: Chania, Rethymnon, Hagios Nicolaos and, first and foremost, Heraklion.

A MEDITERRANEAN CLIMATE. The N coast has a Mediterranean climate with rain in winter (Heraklion has an average temperature of 65.5°F/18.6°C). The inland areas have a mountain climate. But the S coast must be considered separately, as its climate is semi-arid: the total annual rainfall barely amounts to 8in (200mm), and it hardly rains at all from April to mid-October.

ECONOMY. Up until 1913 when it became part of Greece, Crete went through a long period of economic decline, as the areas of scrubland and grassland left over from the struggles against the Turks indicate. The Cretans have tried to remedy this; olive groves and vineyards have been developed on the slopes, and the large plain of Mesara is covered with huge fields of wheat, and vines and olive trees; some areas are positively luxuriant. In other parts of the island Mediterranean mixed farming is prevalent, for most of the land is divided into small farms where non-mechanized methods of work are still in use. Oil, fruit and vegetables are exported through the ports on the N coast.

As it has almost no sources of energy and no industry, Crete's only means of reactivating its economy and stemming emigration, which, although lower at present than a short time ago, is still considerable, is the tourist trade.

Crete in history

ON THE FRINGES OF MAINLAND GREECE. The excavations carried out by Sir Arthur Evans in Crete at Knossos, from 1900 on, revealed a very brilliant civilization which is known as Cretan, Aegean or Minoan. Later research has enabled us to discern the outlines of a history which is all the more appealing for standing on the fringes of that of mainland Greece and the Greek islands, which was in fact deeply affected by the influence of Crete.

BEFORE MINOS. The first human settlements in Crete date back to the Neolithic period. The population, which was still only sparse, lived in caves which are present in large numbers throughout the island and which were to have a sacred character at a later date, or in rudimentary houses built of unbaked bricks on a stone base. These people lived solely by crop cultivation and animal husbandry. Tools were made of polished stone or of bone and were extremely simple. The large number of female steatopygous idols common at that same period throughout the eastern Mediterranean, indicates the worship of a great mother goddess who dispensed fertility and fecundity; this was to remain the main divinity of the Aegean world in the subsequent age.

THE INVASION THAT LED TO MINOAN CRETE. The arrival of invaders around 2700 BC who gradually merged with the Neolithic inhabitants of the island was a crucial event in the island's history. These newcomers originated from Anatolia. We know very little about them, especially as their language is virtually unknown. The most likely hypothesis is that they were Proto-Indo-Europeans, fairly closely related to the Hittites and Luwiansns (from S. Asia Minor) and strongly influenced in Asia Minor by the primitive Mediterranean races. What is certain is that they brought with them a developed civilization. The Bronze Age, the most famous period in the island's history, began in Crete with their arrival. It is conventionally known as the Minoan period. By means of stratigraphy archaeologists have been able to distinguish three successive stages (Early, Middle and Late Minoan), each of which can be divided into three sub-periods (I, II and III). It is difficult to fix exact dates to this relative chronology, and this is done by reference to the better known civilizations of Egypt and the Middle East. Recent research, modifying Sir Arthur Evans' original datings, indicates the following timescale:

Early Minoan (EM) I to III	2800–2000 BC
Middle Minoan (MM) I to III	2000–1580 BC
Late Minoan (LM) I, II	1580–1100 BC

CRETE AND ITS PALACES. About 2000 BC the 'first palaces' appear, indicating the emergence of a strong central power on at least three sites, Knossos, Phaestos and Mallia. Somewhere around 1700 BC those palaces were destroyed in some general cataclysm, possibly an earthquake, but more probably an invasion by Greeks coming from the mainland. This disaster provided an opportunity for the palaces to be rebuilt on a larger scale and in a finer manner: this was the 'second palace' period (1700–1400 BC), during which Mallia, Phaestos (Phaestus), Kato Zakros and above all Knossos (Cnossus) were rebuilt. Soon the king of Knossos was outpacing his neighbours: he destroyed Mallia and forced the prince of Phaestos to recognize him as overlord. Knossos became supreme, and taking advantage of its central position ruled the whole of Crete and built a network of roads to reinforce its hegemony.

THE LAND OF MINOS. The existence of a strong monarchy is amply demonstrated by the size and refined luxury of the palaces. The monarchy was bureaucratic, as in the Orient. Writing was in use: Linear A, known to us through a number of tablets (which are in the process of being deciphered) and developed from a system of hieroglyphics. The power of the kings of Knossos was far-reaching. Minoan domination of the sea extended to the islands and coasts of the Aegean, and was still remembered at the time of Thucydides. Economic activity was strongly developed in every sphere. Agriculture and animal husbandry were prosperous. Craftsmanship was practised both in the palace workshops and in the towns. Trade was active not only with the islands and Greece but also with Egypt, Syria, Phoenicia and Asia Minor. Minoan vases in particular were exported throughout the eastern Mediterranean countries.

DIVINE FORCES. Religion still attached great importance to certain symbols: the sacred stone, the pillar, the double axe (or labrys), the bilobate shield, sacred trees and sacred animals still abound at the height of the Minoan period on pictures relating to worship. The crucial role was played by highly anthropomorphized goddesses, incarnating the intimate forces of life and dispensing fertility, fecundity and eternal life. The gods who were sons or lovers of the Great Mother had only a subordinate role and were still sometimes represented in the form of animals (a bull, a bird, among others).

There were no temples for these gods, only small sanctuaries which, to start with, were situated in some naturally occurring location (a cave or a mountain-top). Later, rooms in the palaces were set aside for worship: usually they had a bench running along the back where offerings were heaped. Horns of consecration were used to mark the sacredness of these places. The snake, foremost of the chthonian (earth) animals, was the object of particular veneration. But the bull was also a sacred animal, hence the countless representations of bull dancing on the large frescoes and in the lesser arts. This religion had a deep influence on Greek religion: the whole atmosphere of Aegean forms of worship was to persist in the chthonian and mystic creeds of the Hellenic world. It is their spirituality, their optimism, their preoccupation with life after death that recur in Greek beliefs.

THE SHIPWRECK OF A CIVILIZATION. Thus there was in Crete a period of extraordinary achievement. But invasion brought this to an abrupt end. In the 16th century BC the island was conquered by Achaeans, and an Achaean king followed the dynasty of Minos: part of the palace archives written in Greek in the script known as Linear B have been found. Around 1400 BC the palaces were destroyed by an earthquake and were not rebuilt, though life carried on. Crete took part in the Trojan War, contributing sizeable forces. The influence of the Cretan world on mainland Greeks was considerable: the Mycenaeans were to transmit much of the Aegean heritage to Hellenism.

A DORIAN ISLAND. The Dorian invasions took place fairly early in Crete. A line from the *Odyssey* (19, 171) refers to 'tripartite Dorians' being on the island. Social patterns very akin to those of Sparta began to be elaborated: a warrior class, representing the victorious Dorians, reduced the earlier inhabitants to bondage. Economic activity continued to flourish. Crete was a stopping place on the E-W route:

using its central position in the Mediterranean it traded with Syria, the islands, the Argolid, Egypt and Sicily. Throughout pre-Classical times Crete underwent a period of renaissance, particularly noticeable in the field of art; Cretan or Daedalic (supposed descendants of the mythical Daedalus) sculptors were behind the resurgence of great plastic art, particularly in the Peloponnese. And a new religion came into being, more mindful than others of the Minoan traditions: the Great Mother was revered everywhere while spirits of vegetation known as Curetes or Corybantes continued their ritual leaping dances. But from the beginning of the 6th century BC this renaissance suddenly ceased and no more was heard of Crete for centuries. Better-armed rivals took over Cretan markets, their art disappeared and the Cretans were unable to adapt to the new conditions of the constantly changing Hellenic world.

A LONG PERIOD OF LETHARGY. Crete then sank into a lethargy from which it was scarcely to re-emerge. During the Classical period Crete remained on the fringes of the Greek world and did not take part in the struggles, grandiose or petty, that shook it, either in the wars against the Persians or in the inter-city rivalry for hegemony. In the Hellenic period Cretan mercenaries were much sought after because of their courage.

In the 1st century BC Rome entered into the affairs of Crete. C. Metellus, who was to earn the nickname 'the Cretan', overcame resistance in the island. It was joined with Cyrenaica to form a province, the governor of which took up residence in Gortyna. This new capital was gradually enriched and embellished, and the Roman ruins there still show how striking this great administrative centre was.

MEDIEVAL AND MODERN CRETE. The history of Crete in the Middle Ages is very confused as it was much coveted because of its privileged location. It belonged to the Byzantine Empire, but in 823 AD the Arabs seized it and remained on it for more than a century until 961. The foundation of Khandak, later to become Candia, dates from this first period of Muslim rule. Recaptured by Byzantium, it was fought over after the fourth crusade by the Genoans and the Venetians. The long period of Venetian rule (1210–1669) which was at first notable for acts of extortion and violence later became milder and between the 15th and 17th century there was again a Cretan renaissance, particularly in painting (Damaskinos, and Theotokopulos, commonly known as El Greco) and in literature (Kornaros, who wrote a long romantic epic, the *Erotokritos*).

The Turks then gained control of Crete in spite of the heroic resistance put up by Candia, which lasted 23 years. The two centuries (1669–1898) during which the island was subjected to a harsh, cruel rule constitute the darkest period of Cretan history. It was at one point ceded to Mehemet Ali, but returned to Turkish hands; the Cretans tried in vain to shake off their yoke by means of several uprisings which were harshly crushed. The 1898 rebellion, supported by Britain, enabled Crete to be proclaimed an autonomous state and it became part of Greece in 1913. In 1923 the Muslims left the island and their place was taken by Greek refugees from Asia Minor. It then went through a period of rapid development, partly thanks to increased tourism, resulting from the archaeological digs organized there by foreign missions. Crete was conquered by the Germans in 1941 and became a centre of fierce resistance and suffered greatly under the Nazi occupation. It was liberated in 1944.

Minoan art

As we are virtually unable to read Cretan texts and know almost nothing of the events that make up the history of Minoan Crete, it is mainly through art that we are able to assess the very high level of Minoan civilization. There are many remains of the Neolithic civilization in Crete, mainly vases, often incised and then painted. But the most interesting documents from the artistic point of view belong to the Minoan period.

THE CRETAN LABYRINTH. The Greeks had retained a confused memory of the Minoan palaces in the legend of the labyrinth: Daedalus, King Minos' architect, had built a strange palace for his master, with thousands of rooms and corridors where the king imprisoned the Minotaur, born of the unnatural love between Queen Pasiphaë and a bull. These palaces are now fairly well known due to excavations at Phaestos, Mallia, Kato Zakros and particularly Knossos. It is true that in detail they follow an extremely complex plan (hence the meaning which the word labyrinth had already taken on in Greek), but the overall concept is simple.

THE MINOAN PALACES. At Knossos, arranged round a central courtyard, there are the reception rooms (in particular the throne room, so evocative of the past with the king's throne and benches for his advisers), the private rooms, the storehouse where great jars full of provisions stand in rows, the rooms assigned to worship and the theatre which Homer was yet to recall in the *Iliad*. The whole building is on several different levels (the E wing is on a lower level than the other wings and the courtyard), with a network of corridors, staircases and light-wells. The walls are built of small ashlars packed with earth mortar standing on a carefully laid footing. The roofs are flat, and are held up by columns which are reminiscent in shape of the original wooden pillars. The colonnades are deliberately placed on the axes, which means that the doors are to the side. Daylight is let in by a large number of windows and by small interior courtyards. It is a Mediterranean building, intended for a warm, dry climate, unlike the fortresses with which the Achaeans were to crown the citadels of Greece.

ELEGANCE AND COMFORT. In these palaces everything has been done for the convenience of those living there. For example there is a very sophisticated plumbing system. Drains carry away the water from heavy downpours of rain, and waste water; spring water is brought into the palaces for use in bathrooms and tanks. But aesthetic considerations are not sacrificed to comfort: the walls, which are constructed of fairly rough materials, are plastered with very fine stucco which lends itself to being either painted or used for painted bas-relief. And vast perspective effects are achieved at Knossos and even more so at Phaestos by the use of wide staircases, superimposed terraces and cleverly contrived vistas of the surrounding countryside.

MINOAN WALL PAINTING. A description of the architcture of the palaces gives an inadequate idea of them, for it ignores the extraordinary luxuriousness of their interior decoration. The walls were covered with large paintings, probably in fresco, sponge-printed on to the wet plaster to resemble cut stone, the colour becoming fixed when the plaster dried. The artist was forced to work fast, which produced the qualities of spontaneity and animation that are so remarkable in all these works. It is possible, particularly at Knossos, to follow the development of pictorial art. First of all we see the exuberance of a naturalism which responds to everything: plants, animals and people; there are the bundles of reeds lying on a carpet of white lilies, the dolphins swimming amidst the fish in the queen's room, or the bull with a bull dancer making a perilous leap over it before a milling, enthusiastic crowd. Then a truly classic style appears, which takes pleasure almost exclusively in representing the human figure: the finest example is the delightful 'Parisienne', with her delicate face and huge eyes, her upturned nose, her saucy mouth, long neck and carefully arranged wavy hair. And finally painting becomes stylized. It is less realistic, but still produces beautiful frescoes (separate pictures in painted frames, rather than murals) such as the formal procession of cup-bearers, and more especially the astounding composition of bull dancers: a man leaps boldly over the head and back of a raging bull at full charge towards a young woman standing with arms extended, while another has seized the bull's horns and appears to be attempting to pull herself up on them.

PAINTED RELIEF. Here we have what is in effect a mixed medium, the low relief that is produced by painting on stucco, giving us real masterpieces: the prince with the lilies, or a bull's head marvellously brought to life. Minoan painters must have obeyed strict conventions like those found in Egyptian painting: special colours are used to distinguish male from female figures, the eye looks straight out from a face shown in profile, there are no shadows and no real perspective. But one has to admire the very lively sense of colour, the skill in conveying the most fleeting of movements and the taste for the individual. What lightness and grace, what decorative richness, what ardour and love of life! These are qualities that Greece, with its greater sense of order and intellectualism, was all too often to neglect.

SCULPTURE Sculpture was developed far less than painting. Large scale statues are unknown: neither monumental sculpture nor full-sized statues have been found in Crete, only statuettes. The main materials used were steatite (soapstone), pottery, ivory, bronze and clay. The very fine ceramic snake goddess statuettes from Knossos are the most famous Cretan sculptures.

There are faience plaques in relief which probably served as decorative panels. One shows a goat suckling her kids, another a crab which is so perfect that the people involved in the excavations at Knossos at first took it for a fossil: a marvellous example of the Cretan talent for depicting animals. Three fine steatite vases from Hagia Triada are decorated in relief, one showing homage being paid to the king, another a gymnastic display and the third a countryside procession. The same naturalism is present as in the paintings (which would appear to have had a strong influence on work done in relief) and the last-mentioned vase at least shows a sense of humour and imagination that tell us a lot about the Cretan temperament.

GOLD AND SILVER WORK. The artistic genius of Crete can be seen at its best in minor arts. Crete, which the Greeks believed to be the home of the inventor Daedalus, produced masterpieces of work involving precious metals and stones. Frescoes show men and women alike always wearing jewellery. Many necklaces and pendants have been found in tombs, such as the beautiful pendant of two bees facing one another which was found in the royal burial ground of Mallia, at Chrysolakhos.

MARQUETRY AND THE ENGRAVING OF PRECIOUS STONES. Inlay techniques which originated in the East were well known in Crete. At Knossos the lapidary's workshop was uncovered as it had been left when the earthquake occurred. Some of the objects from there show what he was capable of; for example a table inlaid with 72 daisies which must have been intended for some kind of board game and in which ivory, rock crystal, gold, silver and a blue stone known as kyanos were all used.

Craftsmen in the field of glyptics produced countless seals which played an important role in administration and in private contracts. They differ from one another in shape, material and in what they depict. Their evolution can be followed through from early ideograms to decorative hieroglyphs and on to complete naturalism which delights in portraying the most varied scenes from Cretan life: landscapes, plants, animals (especially marine animals and bulls), human scenes covering all the occupations of man, and portrayals of the gods.

THE POTTER'S ART. Ceramics, the most utilitarian of the lesser arts, was developed with true artistry. From the Early Minoan period the potter's wheel was in use and potters learnt to build ovens where the temperature was high enough to give very attractive glazed effects. All decorative motifs were purely geometric (straight lines, circles and spirals). In the Middle Minoan period the invention of a slow-turning wheel enabled craftsmen to produce the 'Kamares ware' vases with sides as thin as an eggshell, a triumph of technique first found at Kamares on Mt. Ida. Rich colours came to be used. Decoration was still sometimes linear, but more often based on plants and animals. Craftsmen enjoyed combining line and colour in a stylized way that produced beautiful effects. Finally Late Minoan at first turned away from stylization in favour of naturalism: seaweeds and octopuses spiral around the sides of vases. There was then a return to a decorative style, known as the 'palace style', with craftsmen skilled in adapting the intertwining lines of the linear and plant motifs they so much liked, to the curve of the pots. There is no better illustration of the extraordinary decorative powers of the Cretans than these humble terracotta vessels.

This vital, vigorous, exuberant art had a profound influence on that of Mycenae. Except in their architecture, which remained essentially northern in tradition, the Achaeans drew their inspiration very largely from the masterpieces which they had admired in Crete and which Cretan trade had carried among them. The historical importance of Minoan artistic output can thus be seen to equal its intrinsic aesthetic value.

Sightseeing in Crete

The fact that Crete is an island, far from other Greek lands, means that it is a geographical, historical and cultural entity of such an unusual kind that it has not been possible to give descriptions of its towns and sites of interest in alphabetical order. You will therefore find them grouped in six sections:

1 – Chania (Canea) and its vicinity

2 – Rethymnon and its vicinity

3 – Heraklion and its vicinity (Mallia)

4 – Knossos

5 – Mesara (Gortyna, Phaestos, Hagia Triada)

6 – Hagios Nikolaos and its vicinity

While one of these sections is entirely devoted to the Minoan site at Knossos, the other five cover all areas of Crete working from W to E as linked on the N of the island by the road described on route map 15. Before long it will be possible to go from Rethymnon to Sitia along the S of the island via Phaestos and Ierapetra following a road which is at present under construction between Pyrgos and Pefkos.

FIVE DAYS IN CRETE. See p. 51 for the programme for the 'supplementary journey to Crete' (a sixth day would be needed to visit the eastern part of the island from Hagios Nikolaos).

IF YOU ENJOY ...

Discovering new worlds, you will be in raptures over Minoan art which grew from roots in the darkness of prehistory in Asia Minor to flower in the secret garden that is Crete. Whether your first preference is for painting, sculpture, metalwork or pottery, raised here to heights that allow it to compete on equal terms with the supposedly nobler arts, the archaeological museum at Heraklion stands at a crossing of the paths that will guide you in your search for bygone times. You will find palace architecture not only at Knossos, but also at Phaestos, Hagia Triada, Mallia and Kato Zakros. If you are seeking the mysticism, notability and rhythm expressed in Byzantine art, you will find the sources of that brilliant Cretan school which from the second half of the 15th century until the 17th stood at a point where local traditions, the strong influences of Venice and those of Constantinople merged. Here we are talking only of the inspiration and antecedents, to be found in the monasteries of Valsamenero and Vrondisi and the churches of Avdou, Bitziriano, Potamies, Kritsa, etc., for that great period of Cretan painting scattered its exponents far and wide, to Mt Athos, the Meteora, Italy, Dalmatia and even Mount Sinaï, and, above all, El Greco's Toledo; it is hardly represented in modern Crete – except by a handful of icons in the Historical and Ethnographic Museum at Heraklion.

Examples of craftsmanship worth bringing back from Crete include woven and crocheted material, woollen jackets and rugs which are always very well made, or jewellery copied from that in the Heraklion Museum; and as elsewhere in Greece ceramics and pottery and anything made of alabaster or onyx.

As for folklore and folk festivals, it is worth knowing that Crete tends more than other places to keep its traditions alive. Numerous religious festivals provide an excuse for processions and celebrations while in the tavernas there is often dancing in the evenings to the accompaniment of the 'lyra' or 'laouto'.

1   Khania and its vicinity

Khania (Canea, Hania; pop. 40,500) and Rethymnon are the two towns where it is easiest to recapture the atmosphere of the 16th and 17th century, Venetian walled city, with their old houses, ramparts and arsenals. Turkish occupation has left Khania with a slightly oriental flavour. The Khania region at the extreme W of the island, with the White mountain range as its dominant feature, is not easy to reach and is still very wild; but its sites of interest and its landscape – like the famous gorge of Samaria – should not fail to delight nature lovers.

AN ANCIENT CITY. Khania occupies the site of ancient Cydonia, which was the most powerful city in western Crete (a palace complex which was destroyed in the Late Minoan III period, then restored, is at present being excavated on Kastelli Hill). There was frequent fighting between it and its Cretan rivals, Knossos and Gortyna, particularly in 171 BC.

KHANIA AND THE LION OF SAINT MARK. The town was occupied from 1252 by the Venetians who gave it the name Canea (in Greek, Khania). After fighting between Venice and Genoa, the latter gained control of it and remained there from 1267 to 1290. In the 13th century the town consisted of an inner fortified area called Castello that contained the cathedral, the rector's palace and a few houses belonging to rich Venetians, and an outlying area which, between 1320 and 1336, was enclosed by a protective wall. In 1537 the town was devastated by the pirate Barbarossa and the following year the Venetians sent their

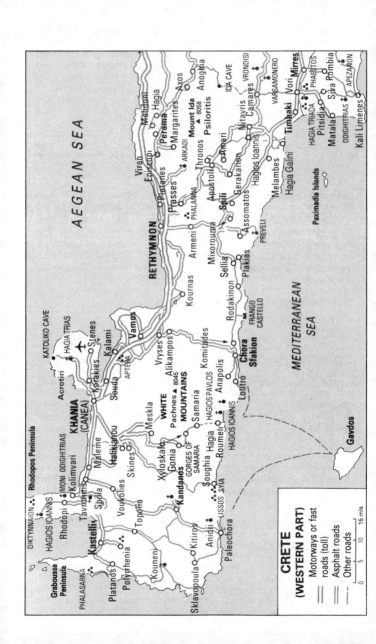

AEGEAN SEA

MEDITERRANEAN SEA

Rhodopos Peninsula

Graboussa Peninsula

DIKTYNNAION

PHALASARNA

HAGIOS IOANNIS

Platanos

Polyrhenia

Kouneni

Sklavopoula

Kitiros

Anidri

Paleochora

LISSOS SYIA

Topolia

Voukolies

Skines

Xyloskalo

Gonia

Soughia Hagia

Roumeli

GORGES OF SAMARIA

HAGIOS IOANNIS

Kandanos

HAGIOS PAVLOS

Samaria

Meskla

Halikiartou

Maleme

Kolimvari

IMONI ODIGHITRIAS

Rhodopi

Tavronitis

Spilia

Kastelli

Pachnes ▲ 8045

WHITE MOUNTAINS

Anapolis

Loutro

Chora Stakion

Komitades

Alikampos

Vryses

APTERA

Souda

Krakies

Acrotiri

KATOLIKO CAVE

HAGIA TRIAS

Stenes

Kalami

KHANIA (CANEA)

Vamos

Kournas

Rodakinon

FRANGO CASTELLO

Sellia

Plakias

PREVELI

Mixorouma

Assomatos

Armeni

Spili

PHALAMA

Apostoli

Gerakaro

Hagos Ioannis

Melambes

Hagia Galini

RETHYMNON

Prasses

Platanes

Episopi

Viran

Maltoni

Perama

Hagia

Margarites

ARKADI

Thronos

Amari

Nitavris

Psiloritis

Mount Ida ▲ 8058

IDA CAVE

Anoghia

Axos

Camares

VARSAMONERO

VRONDISI

HAGIA TRIADA

Pitsidia

Matala

ODIGHITRIAS

Kali Limenes

Timbaki

Vori

Mirres

Siva Pombia

PHAESTOS

APEZANON

Paximadia Islands

Gavdos

CRETE (WESTERN PART)

══ Motorways or fast roads (toll)

── Asphalt roads

--- Other roads

0   5   10   15 mls

famous military engineer, Sanmicheli, to fortify the town and two other sites. Despite this it was captured by Turks in 1645 after a siege lasting 55 days.

THE HARD PATH LEADING TO LIBERATION. Under the Turks Khania declined and on several occasions was subjected to reprisals following the many insurrections which shook Crete. On 15 February 1897 international forces disembarked at Khania to put an end to the struggles between the Turks and the Cretan partisan fighters. On 15 November 1898 Prince George, who had been appointed High Commissioner by the allied powers (Britain, France, Italy and Russia), made a triumphal entry into the town. After Crete became part of Greece in 1912 (the union was in fact proclaimed officially on 30 May 1913 when the treaty was signed in London). Khania remained the administrative capital of the island until 1971. The university was founded in 1978.

The old Venetian area near the harbour was heavily bombed in 1941 when the island was invaded by German troops, and as a result has lost a lot of its charm; when its narrow streets are swept by strong winds, as they quite often are, they have a desolate, abandoned air. Nonetheless it is in this area and its vicinity that the most interesting sites in Khania are to be found. Go swimming off the beach at Galatos, 3.4mls (5.5km) along the Kastelli road, where there are little restaurants that serve fresh fish.

Visiting the town

The old areas of Khania are arranged round the Venetian harbour which was built in the 13th century, whereas today it is the harbour of Souda that serves the town. On the W dock there are the terraces of a few little cafés where it is pleasant to sit in the evening, and a small naval museum. The mosque of the Janissaries, which contains the tourist information offices, is a reminder of the Turkish occupation, as is the minaret-shaped lighthouse at the end of the mole. Near the mosque at the bottom of the hill where the Castello once stood the seven large vaults of the Venetian arsenals (16th century) can be seen.

Follow the Koundouriotou quay westwards through to an old Venetian quarter where a few ancient houses still stand as a reminder of the days when the Lion of St Mark ruled supreme in the Aegean Sea. Near there by the sea, not far from the Minoa (Xenia) Hotel, there are still a few remains of the San Salvatore (or Gritti) Bastion, built between 1538 and 1540, designed by the engineer Michele Sanmicheli, and of the W section of the Venetian city walls, erected between 1540 and 1543. This wall ends to the S with the San Dimitrio bastion (1546–49) and that is almost intact.

To reach the town centre via the Halkidon road return to the mosque. In the first road r. (no. 43) there is a Venetian loggia with a coat of arms and a Latin inscription. Further along the Halkidon road on the r. the church of St Francis, a 14th-century basilica, the best preserved

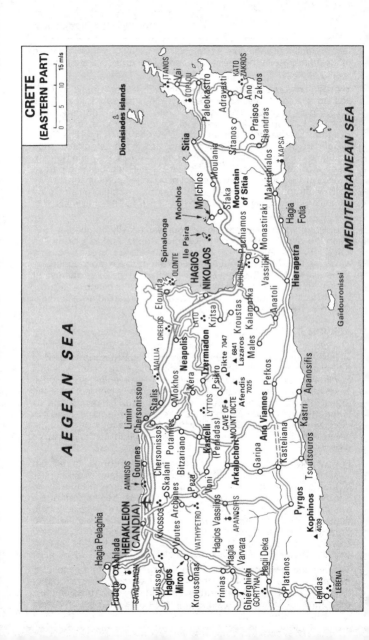

CRETE (EASTERN PART)

0   5   10   15 mls

AEGEAN SEA

MEDITERRANEAN SEA

Dionisiades Islands

Hagia Pelaghia
Fodele
Ahlada
HERAKLEION (CANDIA)
AMNISOS
Gournes
Limin
Chersonissou
Chersonissos
Stalis
MALLIA
Neapolis
Elounda
OLONTE
Spinalonga
HAGIOS NIKLAOS
Ile Psira
Mochlos
Molchlos
Sitia
TTANOS
Vai
TOPLOU
KATO ZAKROS
Paleokastro
Adravasti
Ano Zakros
Praisos
Chandras
Stanos
Sitanos
KAPSA
Moulania
Sfaka
Mountain of Sitia
Pachiamos
Monastiraki
Makinghialos
Hagia Fotia
Hierapetra
Gaïdouronissi

SAVROPETRA
KNOSSOS
Skalani
Potamies
Chersonissos
Mokhos
Kéra
Psikro
LYTTOS
Kastelli (Periadas)
CAVE OF MOUNT DICTE
DREROS
LATO
Krtsa
Krousias
Koustas
Kalamafka
Vassiliki
Anatoli
GOURNIA

Voutes
Archanes
Bitzariano
Pezé
Voni
Hagios Vassilios
Afendis 7025
Atenois 6841
Dikte 7047
Lazaros
Males
Pefkos
Ana Viannos
Kastri
Apanosifis

Tylissos
Hagios Miron
VATHYPETRO
APANOSIS
Hagia Varvara
Garipa
Kastellena
Kastelli
Tsoutsouros
Krousonas
Prinias
Ghierghien GORTYNA
Hagii Deka
Platanos
Lendas
LEBÉNA
Pyrgos
Kophinos
4039

Latin church in Khania, houses the archaeological museum beneath its triple nave.

Open summer, 08.30–12.30 and 16.00–18.00; winter, 10.00–16.30; Sun. and pub. hol., 09.00–15.00; closed Tues.; entrance fee (Tel. 0821 20334).

Items of special interest in the collection are Minoan pottery from a tomb discovered on the site of ancient Cydonia, fine painted sarcophagi from the end of the Minoan period, and an interesting collection of terracotta from the Archaic, Hellenic, Hellenistic and Roman periods. Among the statues note those from excavations at the Asclepieion at Lissos, especially that of an ephebe, and a small marble statue of Aphrodite found at Khania (Cydonia), a statue of a teacher of rhetoric from the Roman period, etc. An interesting mosaic from the Roman period shows Poseidon carrying off Amymone.

In the garden adjoining the museum a hexagonal Turkish fountain, a marble Venetian doorway and Turkish inscriptions are worth noticing.

VICINITY OF KHANIA

1 KASTELLI (26.2mls/42km) AND THE W COAST. Leave by the Maleme road.

10.6mls (17km): Maleme; 110yds (100m) to l. of road a large Mycenaean tomb with a square chamber under a pyramid-shaped roof, the only example known of this type.

15.6mls (25km): 3.7mls (6km) to r. of road near the village of Rhodopi on the E coast of the Rhodopos peninsula stands the fortified monastery of Gonia (Moni Odigitrias) founded in 1618. The present buildings date from 1662 but were restored in 1798 and further altered in 1878–84. Note the baroque-style entrance door, and especially the refectory door. There are fine 16th- and 17th-century icons; one of the Crucifixion signed by the Cretan painter Paleokapas (1st half of 17th century) is a very beautiful work. Near the monastery, modern arcaded buildings house a cultural centre for theological seminaries. Near the N headland of the Rhodopos peninsula, also on the E coast, German archaeologists in 1942 uncovered the ruins of a 2nd-century BC sanctuary dedicated to Artemis Dictynna (Diktynnaium) on the site of an earlier sanctuary dating from the Hellenistic period.

From Kolimbari the route S. towards Spilia, Dracona and Episcopi (Kissamos) is for those who like Byzantine art.

At Spilia is a small church dedicated to the Virgin (the Panagia); the frescoes are very damaged but typical of the Cretan school. Moreover, the parish priest holds the key to a little museum which houses a very old icon of the Virgin. To the r. after the village of Dracona (signpost) a path leads to a charming little church dedicated to Hagios Stephanos, dating from 900, and with some beautiful frescoes.

To the r. before the village of Episkopoi, a road leads to a church dedicated to the Archangel Michael, noteworthy for its architecture, unique in Crete. Shaped like a rotunda, its dome is rounded but in four successive stages, giving the appearance of four steps of a staircase. The date of construction is uncertain, but there is a 6th-century Christian basilica (original fragments of mosaic perfectly restored, inside the church). In the 9th-century it was enlarged (barrel naves and narthex). Formerly it had some exquisite frescoes which have almost completely disappeared. However, the beautiful head of St Michael can be made out under the cupola above the wall. Note the narthex where the original entrance to the church was; the baptismal font, a small marble basin in which were hollowed out two seats facing each other (for complete immersion, as was the custom).

26mls (42km): Kastelli, a small village fortified by the Venetians in the mid-16th century on the site of ancient Kissamos. You can still see some remains of the walls restored by the Turks and visit a small archaeological museum. Recently two fine mosaic pavements have been discovered at Kastelli, belonging to a huge group of dwellings dating from the 3rd century AD.

Of the N headland of the Gramvousa peninsula, on the little island of Gramvousa, the Venetians built a fort which they maintained until 1692. S of Kastelli lies what is believed to be the site of ancient Polyrrhenia with traces of Hellenic and Byzantine fortifications.

To the W the harbour of Phalasarna, now some distance away from the sea, has also been identified – it can be reached from Platanos. There are still remains of ramparts, rock carvings, tombs, etc.

Past Platanos, along unsurfaced roads where it is wise to have a good supply of gasoline, water and food, you can reach Amigdalokefali and then Koumeni with two Byzantine churches decorated with frescoes, or even go as far as the monastery of Chryssoskalitissa which stands isolated on a rocky islet.

2 FROM KHANIA TO PALEOCHORA (48.1mls/77km). Leave Khania on the Maleme/Kastelli road (above) and turn off r. after 11.6mls (18.5km).

36.6mls (58.5km): Kandanos, in the centre of an area rich in Byzantine chapels decorated with wall paintings (Kavalariana, Anisaraki, Kakodiki).

48.1mls (77km): Paleochora, formerly Castel Selino under the Venetians who in 1279 built a small fort here on an island linked to the mainland by a sandbank. The little castle was rebuilt in 1325, and again during the Ottoman period. There is a large, very beautiful beach here.

By hiring a motorboat from Paleochora you can reach the site of ancient Lissos in approx. 45mins and the hamlet of Soughia in approx. 1hr 10mins. In the spot known as Hagii Kyrkos are the remains of the Asclepieion of Lissos consisting of a temple with a forecourt on the W where there used to be a door leading to a wide staircase up to the sanctuary. The water from the ancient spring, the reason why the Asclepieion was built here, used to pass under the paving stones and come out at a fountain. To the N, Greek archaeologists have dug up the remains of a building dating from the later Roman period; it had three rooms, the largest of which had a bench on the S side. This must have been the house of the priests or of a *katagogeion* where sick people were lodged.

The hamlet of Soughia is situated near the site of ancient Syia, which belonged to the Confederation of the Oreioi, and in the modern church there you can see the remarkable mosaic paving of a palaeo-Christian 6th-century basilica, depicting deer, peacocks, vases wound with vine branches, etc.

The church of Anidri, lying 3.1mls (5km) E of Paleochora, has fine frescoes, as do those of Sklavopoula and Kitiros to the N.

3 OMALOS AND THE GORGE OF SAMARIA (25.6mls/41km). Leave by the Maleme road; turn l. after 0.9mls (1.5km).

8.1mls (13km) road on the r. which leads to Soughia 35mls (56km) (see above, 2). 1 ml (1km) from the charming village of Halykianou, in the direction of Koufos, you will find on the r. the Byzantine church of Hagios Kir Ioannis (14th century?). Note its beautiful architecture; a three-naved basilica designed in the form of a Greek cross, it was surmounted by a central dome supported by a circular wall, the only part no long standing today; the narthex to the W also has a dome. You may linger in the corners to the S and N, before the semi-circular arch, the columns with sculpted capitals and the exquisite fragments of frescoes.

9mls (15km): Fournes; to the l. another road goes to Meskla 3mls (5km); its chapel, Sotiros Christou, has a narthex added later. It houses beautiful frescoes dated 1303; facing the N. entrance you will admire the *Transfiguration*. Return to the main road.

Travelling through orange and olive groves you come to the plateau of Omalos (3,445ft/1,050m) and then to the village of the same name, also known as Gonia. From there you can get to the Xyloskalo (tourist pavilion) 2.5mls (4km) further on at the entrance to the **gorge of Samaria, carved out by a mountain stream between the highest summit of the White Mountains (8,340ft/2,542m) to the E and Mt Volakias (6,942ft/2,116m) to the W, which you can go through on foot (11.2mls/18km). There are places where the passage through the gorge is barely 3ft (1m) wide, and sometimes the sheer sides of the ravine rise to a height of almost 1,000ft (300m). Halfway down the gorge there is the abandoned village of Samaria. The gorge ends on the S coast of Hagia Roumeli, which can be reached by boat from Chora Sfakion. You should allow 7 to 8 hrs for the walk to Hagia Roumeli from Xyloskalo.

4 ACROTIN AND ITS MONASTERIES. (10.3mls/16.5km, leave by the elegant suburb of Chalepa and along the road to Sternes).

4mls (6km): to your l. on the hill of Profitis Ilias, tomb and monument to Venizelos by whom Crete was reunited with Greece. A fine view of Khania and the White Mountains.

✝ 10.3mls (16.5km): Hagia Triada (Moni Tzagaraliou), the largest monastery on the Akrotiri peninsula. Founded in the 17th century, it still has a Renaissance church that dates back to 1632, the entrance and campanile of which show Venetian influence. Today it is a school of theology.

By walking for 1hr N you can reach the monastery of St John the Hermit of Gouvernetou, dating back to 1548, which also reveals Venetian influence. Not far from it there are many caves which served as a refuge for hermits when pirates threatened them. Eremitism, the practice of the hermit's way of life personified by St John the Hermit, a local saint still much venerated, goes back to the 9th century on the peninsula. The hermits used to assemble on Sundays and holy days to hear the liturgy together. Gouvernete, although Orthodox by tradition, quickly became the chief monastery of the Acrotin. Providing refuge for the population rebelling against the Turkish occupation, especially during the 19th-century revolts, it was badly damaged at the time of the reprisals. Seen from the outside it is a veritable fortress, but the interior shows a strong Venetian influence. In the narthex of the church, as you enter, note a 15th-century icon of the *Raising of Lazarus* with St John the Hermit and St Anthony of Egypt, founder of eremitism. On the wall, the church's oldest icon, badly damaged, shows *Christ Enthroned*. But the most precious icon (15th century) of the Virgin and Child is hidden behind the iconostasis (N side; no women allowed in). The dome with Christ Pantocrator is the only original part of the church.

A 30 min. walk along the E. side of the ravine brings you to the grotto of Katoliko (access difficult; have a pocket torch) and the ruins of a monastery of the same name, built in the 12th century and thus the oldest on Crete. It was abandoned in the 17th century but the site is still of special interest because of its atmosphere.

Another 20 min. walk will bring you to the bottom of the gorge and the sea.

5 FROM KHANIA TO RETHYMNON (40mls/64km).

3.7mls (6km): Souda, a harbour within a well-sheltered bay, which has supplanted the too-exposed harbour at Khania since the end of the war (NATO base; no photographs allowed).

13mls (20.8km): Kalami, a hamlet near an old Venetian fort that used to defend the entrance to Suda (Souda) Bay.

On the r.-hand side of the road not far from the village of Megala Chorafia lie the ruins of ancient Aptera (remains of a Hellenic town wall, a Roman theatre, and a small Doric temple and a few traces of the Byzantine period). 8.1mls (13km): road going off r. leads to Malaxa (5mls/8km), a small town famed for its cream cheese.

20mls (32km): Vryses:

Among the orange groves outside Stylos is the beautiful Byzantine church of Panagia Serviotissa (11th–12th c.); only the centre portal is damaged. Note the harmonious proportions and the windowed cupola with its octagonal drum. In Styros there is a tomb, (Minoan with Mycenean influence), unfortunately pillaged, comparable to that of Maleme and Philaki.

Leaving Stylos on the r. there is a straight road, but with good views, for Samonas and Kiriakoselia.

Its church, dedicated to Hagios Nikolaos (11th-12th century) is one of the glories of Byzantine Crete. It has one nave surmounted by an exquisite dome placed high up on a fine drum pierced with curved windows. Well-preserved frescoes cover all the walls; they are outstanding for the quality of their execution: Christ Pantocrator in the centre of the dome, the Ascension which covers the whole of the N vault of the dome and scenes from the Life of Christ.

To the r. a road goes S towards Chora Sfakion: 25mls (40km).

From Filipa a road on the l. for Maza. In the centre of the village a small church with a single nave. Hagios Nikolaos, restored, has some beautiful frescoes signed by Pangomenos, dated 1325.

4mls (7km) a road on the l. for Alikampo; before the village on the l. below the space occupied by a fountain from the Venetian era, is the single-nave church of the Panagia (Virgin) with beautiful frescoes signed by Pangomenos, dated 1315. Note the very fine baptismal font and the Virgin Enthroned with Jesus (N side of the vault).

Chora Sfakion 25mls (40km) off to the r. (tourist pavilion) is a small seaside village; those looking for a quiet retreat to spend a holiday where the sea plays an important role will like it here.

CENTRE OF CRETAN RESISTANCE. Chora Sfakion, the main town of the Sfakia area which is protected by the natural fortress formed by the White Mountains, was always one of the most active centres of resistance against foreign occupation, particularly during the domination of Crete by the Venetians and the Turks. It was usually from here that the signal for rebellion against the Turks was given. The celebrated clan chief Daskaloyannis, immortalized in popular chronicles, who inspired the 1770 rebellion in Crete, came from this mountain district.

In 1526 the Venetians built a small fortress here which was added to by the Turks.

From Chora Sfakion you can make many boat trips along the coast, in particular to Hagia Roumeli at the bottom of the gorge of Samaria (see Vicinity of Khania, 3). A track going off to the E (6.2mls/10km) leads to Frango Castello, one of the finest Venetian fortresses, built in 1371 above a magnificent sandy beach. All along the coast are many small Byzantine churches.

26.2mls (42km): Georgioupolis, a fine beach, road goes off r. to Lake Kournas.

Kournas, a village from the Venetia era, is interesting for its architecture. The church of Hagios Ghiorgios, in stone, with a campanile with three bells, is made up of a basilica with three naves (12th c.), to which was joined, to the S, a 13th-century church. One can make out three layers of frescoes (12th, 13th and 14th centuries) some of which have been well preserved and restored.

At Philaki (E of Kournas) as at Maleme and Styla, a Minoan tomb in the same style as Mycenaean tombs was discovered. It is huge and built of large stones.

40mls (64km): turn l. for Rethymnon, 1.2mls (2km).

2 Rethymnon and its vicinity

Rethymnon, which is the third largest town in Crete with a population of over 15,000, is rather overshadowed by the fame of its two neighbours. However, this provincial capital of Venetian and Turkish times is very evocative of Crete's past and its beach, harbour and tavernas will appeal to those who like simplicity. The town still has some Venetian buildings and several churches that were used for Muslim worship during the Turkish occupation; with their minarets they give the town an Oriental flavour.

A VENETIAN HARBOUR. Rethymnon occupies the site of the ancient town of Rhithymna, the citadel of which lay S of the present built-up area. During the Venetian occupation wine known as Malvoisie from the name of the lovely nearby valley of Malevisiou was exported through the port of Rethymnon to Europe and as far away as the Portuguese trading posts in India. The town was pillaged in 1571 by Turkish pirates. The Venetians then set about building surrounding ramparts and a fortress on the headland of a small peninsula that rises to the W of the harbour. This fortress proved inadequate against assaults from the Turks who captured it in 1645.

Approaching from Khania you go past the public park on the r. and enter the old town through a gate with a minaret beside it.

A narrow lane l. after the gate leads to the mosque; a fine view from the minaret. The road leading down to the harbour goes through an area where it is still possible to see some 16th- and 17th-century Venetian doorways and some Turkish houses with wooden decorations. You then see an early 17th-century Venetian gallery which was intended for use by the merchants as an exchange and which today houses a small archaeological museum (items from the Minoan, Classical and Hellenistic periods, coins).

Open 08.30–12.30, 16.00–18.00; Sun. 09.00–15.00; Tel. 0831–299 75.

At the end of a road to the l; the Arimondi fountain dates from 1629.

The ramparts of the citadel standing on a rocky promontory are well preserved; the harbour, which is lined with the customary café terraces, has an appealing simplicity.

VICINITY OF RETHYMNON

1 MONASTERY OF PREVELI (24.4mls/39km; go out in Armeni direction).

7mls (10km): ½ml (1km) the village of Armeni is on the r. in a forest of small oaks. There is an important late Minoan necropolis; 200 tombs hollowed out of the rock have already been brought to light over a wide area. For each of them, facing E, there is a long entrance often in the form of a staircase closed by a boulder, allowing access to a funerary chamber where, in those which were not already pillaged, sarcophagi and many valuable objects (jewels, seals, tools, vases) were found. The most important of these tombs is set high up towards the NW with a central pillar and stone benches (difficult staircase).

13.1mls (21km): r. fork leads to Selia and from there an unsurfaced road goes on to Chora Sfakion (see Vicinity of Khania, 5) or the very fine beach of Plakias.

20mls (32km): Assomatos; take the first road l. on entering the village.

24.4mls (39km): Moni Preveli, superbly situated at the bottom end of the Gorge of Megapotamos.

There is a monastery dedicated to St. John the Evangelist; founded in the mid-16th century, it was rebuilt in the 17th century. It clearly shows Venetian influence. Used as a resistance post against the Turks, it was damaged many times during the reprisals. It was also a refuge for allied troops in World War II. In the centre of a vast S-facing terrace overlooking the sea, and enclosed on its other sides by monastery walls, is the church. It houses several old icons and the door of the iconostasis is from the former church. Its miraculous cross is gold and silver with a crystal stem; it contains a splinter of wood from Christ's cross and is known for its power to heal diseases of the eyes.

2 SPILI AND HAGIA GALINI (38.1mls/61km; as above for 13.1mls/21km, then l.).

18.7mls (30km): Spili, an important agricultural centre; the nearby church of Labini is decorated with fine wall paintings (Christ Pantocrator and the Virgin amidst angels).

38.1mls (61km): Hagia Galini, a busy, picturesque port from which it is possible to visit several sea caves by boat. You can go on from there to Mires and the Mesara area (see Crete, Section 5).

3 PRASSES (6.9mls/11km along the Herakleion road, 1.2mls/2km off to r.), a small village from which those interested in archaeology can set off in search of the site of ancient Phalanna at the place known as Onythe Goudelianon, and of a late 5th-century or early 6th-century palaeo-Christian basilica at the place known as Kera.

Beyond Prasses the area round Apostoli and Foufouras at the bottom of Mt Ida (8,058ft/2,456m), with Mesara (see Section 5) lying to the SE, is rich in Byzantine chapels (in particular those at Thronos and Hagia Paraskevi).

4 ARKADI MONASTERY (15.6mls/25km along the Herakleion road, 3.1mls/5km off to r.). Here was a bastion of Cretan resistance against Turkish occupation; the buildings, which dated almost entirely from the 18th century, have been restored.

At the time of the 1866 uprising this was the scene of violent fighting between local peasants who had dug in here and Turkish troops who took the monastery by assault after besieging it for two days. Many on both the attacking and defending sides died when the Abbot Gabriel set fire to some barrels of powder.

The church, which is one of the most interesting parts of the monastery, did not suffer greatly and the magnificent door dating from 1587 still offers a very fine array of paired Corinthian columns, pilasters, classical and tierce-point arches, baroque flourishes and garlands.

A small museum contains a few icons, some ecclesiastical ornaments and some mementoes of the 1866 uprising.

5 FROM RETHYMNON TO HERAKLEION (46.9mls/75km by the fast road; see route map 15).

3.1mls (5km): Road on r. for Arkadi (see above, 4).

6.2mls (10km): If you follow the old road to Herakleion you come to Viran Episkopi (3.1mls/5km) on the r., where there is an old Roman Catholic church with an early 16th-century tierce-point doorway. A small modern chapel has been built on the site of a 10th- or early 11th-century Byzantine basilica (possibly the cathedral of the medieval bishopric of Aprion). The road then goes on through Perama (2.5mls/4km), an agricultural market town, and on the l. passes the road (15mls/24km) leading to the Melidoni cave where in 1814 the Turks massacred some 500 Cretans. Taking the r. turn towards Axos (Byzantine churches, handicrafts) you reach Anoghia (21.9mls/35km) (see Vicinity of Herakleion, 1), a mountain village that was completely rebuilt after the war and which is renowned for its handicrafts. Excursions to Mt Ida and its cave (4–5hrs walking) leave from here. You then come to Herakleion via Tylissos.

10mls (16km): Panormos on l. where remains of a 10th-century Byzantine basilica have been found.

13.7mls (22km): Unsurfaced road l. leads to Bali, a small port lying in a cove.

36.9mls (59km): Fodele, supposed birthplace of Domenikos Theotokopoulos, (El Greco, c.1541); his painting was influenced by the icons of Michael Damaskinos and the Cretan school (elongation of faces and torsoes) which together with the effect on him of Venetian works of art formed his peculiar genius.

45mls (72km): l. fork for Heraklion (3.1mls/5km).

3 Herakleion (Iraklio) and its vicinity

Herakleion, pop. 77,000, also known by its Venetian name Candia (the Arab town of Khandak), is contained within strong surrounding walls built by the Venetians in the 16th and 17th century. The town itself has little of interest to offer except of course for the archaeological museum with its fabulous collections of the antiquities uncovered by excavations in Crete.

The surrounding area contains some of the best-known Minoan sites which, archaeologically speaking, have made Crete's fortune.

THE HISTORY OF THE TOWN

CREATED BY THE MOST SERENE REPUBLIC. Not much is known of the history of the town prior to Venetian occupation. Like the rest of Crete it was invaded by Arabs and then recaptured by the Byzantines in 961 – they then built fortifications and settled noble families there to strengthen their occupation. It was during the Venetian period (1204–1669) that the town really advanced. The Venetians made it into the principal fortress of the island, and under the name of Candia it became the capital of Crete. A representative appointed by the Doge with the title of Duke of Crete governed here assisted by two counsellors appointed for a two-or three-year period by the Council of the Venetian Republic. In addition Candia was the seat of a Roman Catholic archbishopric whereas the Greek Orthodox clergy were under the direct control of the Patriarch of Constantinople.

THE BELOVED CHILD OF VENICE. To ensure the development of Herakleion, Venice insisted that Venetian nobles living on the island and great Greek families must build a house in Candia and live there for part of the year. Venetian occupation before long encountered resistance from the local population and in the course of an uprising in 1274 the Duke of Crete and many Venetians were killed. After the Turks had captured Constantinople (1453) a number of Greek families settled in Crete and fomented rebellion there in 1538–60. To guard against the Turkish threat to the island, the Venetians set about strengthening the ramparts of the town after 1526, mainly under the direction of the engineer Michele Sanmicheli.

A 21-YEAR SIEGE. Candia's great moment in history was the memorable siege it faced from the Turks after the rest of Crete had already been conquered. The attackers appeared at the walls of the town on 1 May 1648, and after failing three times in their attempts to remove the ramparts, they instituted a blockade on the land side of the town. In 1660 Louis XIV and the Duke of Savoy managed to get some reinforcements through to the beleaguered citizens who were further tried by an earth tremor in 1664, while the Turkish forces were ravaged by the plague.

THE SUN KING TO THE RESCUE OF THE LION OF ST MARK. In 1667 the Venetians appointed their finest soldier, Francesco Morosini, to direct the town's defence while the Grand Vizier Ahmet Koprulu was in command of the Turkish army. In 1668 Louis XIV sent a few soldiers under the command of La Feuillade, and in 1669 another 6,000 men under the command of the Dukes of Beaufort and Navailles. After an attempt had been made to break out which ended in a bloody defeat (the Duke of Beaufort died with 500 men), the French contingent withdrew on 21 August of the same year.

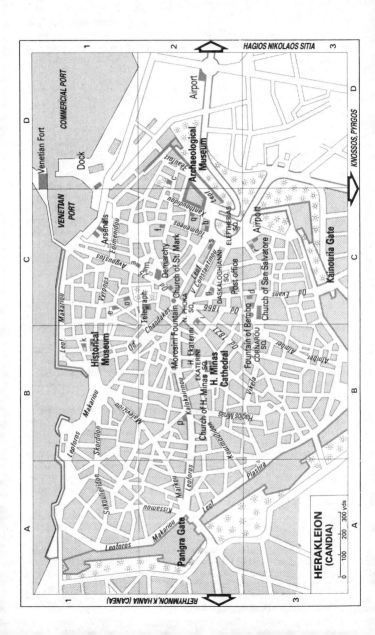

HERAKLEION (CANDIA)

0   100   200   300 yds

COMMERCIAL PORT

VENETIAN PORT

Venetian Fort

Dock

Arsenals

HAGIOS NIKOLAOS SITIA

Airport

Archaeological Museum

KNOSSOS, PYRGOS

Kainoutia Gate

Demarchy

Church of St Mark

Morosini Fountain

Telegraph

Historical Museum

H. EKATERINI
H. Ekaterini

N. PHOKA

Church of H. Minas

H. Minas Cathedral

ELEFTHERIAS SQ.

Post office

DASKALOGHIANNI SQ.

Church of San Salvatore

Airport

Fountain of Bembo

CORNAROU SQ.

Hagios Minas

Plastira

Panigra Gate

RETHYMNON, K. HANIA (CANEA)

Leoforos

Makariou

Avgoustou

A FORTRESS THAT COST DEAR. The defending forces, now down to 4,000 men, withstood the Turkish attack for another year, under constant bombardment. Morosini and his soldiers withdrew on 5 September 1669. The Venetians had lost almost 30,000 on their side while more than 100,000 Turks paid with their lives for the capture of Candia. During the Turkish occupation Candia was known as Megalo Kastro and became the main town of a pashalik. The town went into decline and Chania took advantage of this to become the most active city on the island.

Visiting the town

TWO DAYS IN HERAKLEION. The first half-day should be devoted to visiting the town and the archaeological museum. Save the museum until the end of the morning as you will be sheltered there from the heat of the sun.

Spend the first half of the morning walking through the bazaar (in the triangle formed by Constantinou Avenue, Odhos 1866 and Eleftherias Square), strolling through the area round Nikiforou Phoka Square where the Morosini fountain, a rather unexpected pearl, can be seen, and then by car follow the line of the Venetian ramparts that held the Turks at bay for more than twenty years.

You will no doubt be tempted in the course of your walk to sit down at a café terrace: the best choice is the square round the Morosini fountain where there is plenty to look at, especially if it is not yet too hot. If you feel you cannot waste a moment after visiting the museum before going for a swim, take the Hagios Nikolaos road and following the old road (you leave the new road after 5mls/8km) travel along Amnissos Beach with its fine sand; if you dislike crowds carry on a bit further and you are sure to find a deserted or near-deserted cove with a nice little restaurant nearby where they will grill fresh fish for you while you have your swim.

The second half-day should be spent visiting Knossos, 3.1mls (5km) from Herakleion (see Crete, Section 4).

On your second day set out early for Mesara (see Crete, Section 5) and in the course of the day visit Phaestos, one of the finest of Minoan sites, and the nearby villa of Hagia Triada. After Hagia Triada take the road to the neighbouring village of Dibaki, with a beach just beyond. Eat there or in the Xenia restaurant at Phaestos, then set out on the journey back to Herakleion. Return via Gortyn, and make a detour towards Zaros and the monasteries of Vrondis and Hagios Phanourios. Tackled like this the journey is just 112.5mls (180km), but it provides a very full day.

Parking – It is easy to park in the vicinity of Eleftherias Square near the archaeological museum.

IF YOU ENJOY ...

Beautiful things, allow yourself plenty of time at the archaeological museum where you can admire the Kamares (eggshell) ware vases, the snake goddesses, the acrobat, the famous 'Parisienne' and many other masterpieces of Minoan art.

Slightly old-fashioned museums, abounding in items from a past which might be just yesterday. Visit the Cretan ethnography rooms in the Historical and Ethnographic Museum of Crete.

For the subtle grace of Byzantine painting, let your inclination lead you to Hagios Minas Cathedral where four icons are attributed to the Cretan painter Michael Damaskinos who may have been El Greco's first teacher (in Greece they prefer to use El Greco's real name, Domenikos Theotokopoulos) and to the Historical and Ethnographic Museum of Crete.

Look through the second-hand shops, go to the bazaar, walk up and down Vassileos Constantinou Avenue.

Eleftherias (Liberty) Square (plan C-2) – This is one of the liveliest parts of the town; statues of Venizelos and Nikos Kazantzakis stand to the S. Leoforos Vassileos Constantinou starts halfway across the square; this main road, the busiest in town, is where antique dealers and souvenir sellers who have 'graduated' from the bazaar set up shop. Its name was changed in 1975 and it is now officially called Dikeosinis or Justice Avenue. Have a quick look at the old barracks built in the 17th century by the Venetians, and altered by the Turks who left intact the monumental door of the old structure in the middle of the central building.

✝ **Hagios Minas Cathedral** (plan B-2) – Go through the bazaar, which is worth browsing round, to get to the Hagia Ekaterini Square where Hagios Minas cathedral and a smaller, older church that is also dedicated to Hagios Minas stand side by side. This church, consecrated to St Catharine (Hagia Ekaterini), set slightly back behind the cathedral, belongs to the monastery of St. Catharine of Mount Sinai, which flourished in the 15th and 16th centuries. Now a museum, it houses some remarkable very old icons; the six most valuable (17th c.) are from the monastery at Vorondisi, and are attributed to Michael Damaskinos, a Cretan painter who also worked in the Ionian islands and Venice. Note *The Last Supper*, where Italian influence can be detected, *The Council of Nicaea*, painted in 1591, *The Adoration of the Magi, The Nativity, The Burning Bush, The Holy Trinity* and *Christ Appearing to Mary Magdalene*.

☐ **Morosini fountain** (plan C-2) – Go and enjoy this beautiful fountain, a monumental work commissioned by Francesco Morosini, the Supreme Commander of the Fleets, who inaugurated it in 1628; it is in Nikiforou Phoka Square; one of the focal points of the old town (the number of cafés and souvenir sellers here provide eloquent proof of that).

Try to forget everything around the fountain and concentrate on its detail, which is charming. The eight basins of the fountain are decorated with scenes in relief showing nymphs and Tritons astride dolphins, bulls or marine monsters. The highest basin is held up by four lions which are reminiscent of those at the Alhambra in Granada; this part which is older than the rest must date from the 14th century and must have been part of another fountain.

Odhos 25 Avgoustou (plan C-1/2) – 25 August Road, though one of the busiest shopping streets in the town, is not very remarkable in itself, but it takes you past several monuments that form part of the history of the town, while of limited intrinsic interest.

Go past Hagios Markos (St Mark) Basilica (plan C-2) on the r., formerly a Roman Catholic cathedral, which faces on to Nikiforou Phoka Square. It was built by the Venetians after the earth tremor of 1303, then turned into a mosque by the Turks. Today it is used as a lecture hall. Inside you can see the Venetian doorway of the Ittar palace and reproductions of 12th- and 14th-century Byzantine wall paintings.

A little further on, still on the r., the Dhimarkhion (plan C-2), on the site of the former early 17th-century armoury, or Armeria; it was destroyed by bombing in 1941 and has been rebuilt to house the city offices. The loggia is built on to the Armeria.

The loggia, a one-storey building adjoining the Armeria, was used as a merchants' exchange and formed the centre of public life in the city during the Venetian period; it was completely destroyed during the war and had to be rebuilt on the same site.

On the other side of 25 August Road the El Greco Park provides a pleasant stopping place. Near the Dhimarkhion on the r. in front of the Astir Hotel (plan a in C-1) stands the old church of St Titus (Hagios Titos) built in the 16th century and then altered by the Turks, who converted it into a mosque. It has been restored to Greek Orthodox worship.

■ THE HISTORICAL AND ETHNOGRAPHIC MUSEUM OF CRETE (plan B-1). This museum, which deals with the history of Crete from the Byzantine period and includes the Venetian and Turkish periods, is obviously complementary to the famous archaeological museum.

Open: daily 1 Apr.–31 Oct., 08.30–13.00 and 15.00–18.00; closed Sun. p.m.; 1 Nov.–31 Mar., Mon., Wed. and Fri., 08.30–13.00 and 15.00–17.30; entrance fee.

The collection is displayed on three floors, and is categorized both by chronology and according to theme; sculpture (and architectural fragments) ground floor; painting (frescoes and icons) first floor (along with various historical mementoes); ethnography section second floor.

Entrance hall – Note on the l. a fresco from the Venetian church of the Madonna dei Crociferi in Candia, and under the stairs a figure-head from a Venetian galley.

Go along a corridor (Room 3) where tombstones and various Venetian inscriptions in Latin and Greek are exhibited and at the end to the l. enter the room of palaeo-Christian and Byzantine antiquities.

Room 1 (early Christian and Byzantine antiquities) – Sculptures from Hagios Titos basilica in Gortyn, 6th century.

Pass under a triple-arched doorway taken from a Venetian palace in Candia, to reach Room 2.

Room 2 – Venetian antiquities: note along l. wall architectural fragments of sculpture from the loggia in Candia, built 1626–28. The double-arched doorway that follows was once part of the Candia house of a Venetian noble (c. 1600). Above this doorway is a frieze from a Venetian villa near Candia, and a coat of arms displaying a carved lion and a Hebrew inscription that belonged to a Jewish family living in Crete in the 16th century. In front of the door there is a fountain from a Venetian palace.

Room 4 – Turkish antiquities: mainly tombstones and inscriptions; also note enamelled faience tiles from an 18th-century mosque in Candia.

Go up to the first floor.

Room 5 – Various collections of bronze cult objects from the palaeo-Christian and Byzantine periods. Note also the various 14th- and 15th-century fragments of frescoes from small Cretan churches.

Room 6 – On the r. icons from the church of Gouverniotissa Pediados and the Potamies convent (late 16th, early 17th century). Facing you a painted crucifix from the church of Panagia Gouverniotissa. On the l. wall, icons dated 1655 from the Savatiana monastery (the Virgin between St Peter and St Paul); on the r. the *Deposition* and on the l. the *Virgin between two Angels*, which used to be in the Armenian church of St John.

Be sure not to miss a showcase containing 17th- and 18th-century priests' vestments from the Asomati monastery near Rethymnon, and another in which various items from the treasury of the same monastery are displayed (cross, gospels, liturgical items, etc).

After a quick glance round Room 7 (documentation on the Turkish period), go up to the second floor, calling in at Room 8 on the way if old drawings and cartography interest you, to see a display of Venetian documents relating to Crete.

Room 9 – A display devoted to the Cretan writer Nikos Kazantzakis (1885–1957), one of the originators of neo-Hellenic literature.

Room 10 – Reconstruction of a Cretan peasant home c.1900 with a loom and various everyday items.

Room 11 – Clothing and materials from the Greek islands, carved wooden items made by local craftsmen.

VENETIAN HARBOUR (plan C-1). This was defended by a small fort bearing the Lion of St Mark, mentioned in a document dated 1333 but rebuilt 1523–40; from the end of the 13th century it was protected on the E by a small breakwater. Recently the harbour has been considerably enlarged. It used to resound with the activity of the arsenals, three sections of which are still standing – they have been re-used in the customs building. The fort has recently been converted and restored: lecture rooms in the basement, an open-air theatre on the very lovely terrace.

■ ···**ARCHAEOLOGICAL MUSEUM** (plan D–2). A visit here is one of the high points of a journey to Greece and you are strongly recommended to look at the collection here before going to see the Minoan sites, if only in order to be better able to make a mental reconstruction of the splendours of Knossos, Phaestos, Hagia Triada, Mallia, Kato Zakros, etc.

The museum contains almost all the finds made in Crete by the various archaeological schools and missions (British, French and Italian), the representatives of American universities and Greek archaeologists. This museum, the only one of its kind in the world, affords the most complete perspective over the different phases of Minoan civilization, and from the first stages of Greek civilization to the Roman period.

Open: weekdays 09.00–15.00, Sun. 10.00–14.00; closed Mon. (open Mon. am in summer); entrance fee (Tel. (081) 28-23-05).

PROTECTED BY THE SULTAN'S DECREE. The origin of the museum in Herakleion is to be found in the creation of the 'Society for the Promotion of Education' in 1878 under Ottoman rule. From 1883 this society undertook the collection of any suitable item with a view to founding a Cretan archaeological museum. A decree issued by Sultan Abdul Hamid II strengthened the society's position in its dealings with the local Turkish authorities. Chance finds or those from minor digs and bequests made the creation of an embryonic museum possible and this collection was housed in a building belonging to Hagios Minas Church.

THE ERA OF LARGE-SCALE EXCAVATION. The work of Sir Arthur Evans at Knossos and that of the French and Italian Schools after the proclamation of Cretan autonomy aroused great hopes for this museum, which were not disappointed. New buildings were specially put up in 1904–07 and enlarged in 1912.

A MUSEUM WORTHY OF MINOAN CIVILIZATION. As these first buildings were inadequate to allow an integrated presentation of the collection and moreover too flimsy for a country subject to frequent earth tremors, in 1937 the decision was taken to build a new museum. It was designed to withstand earthquakes, but not the aerial bombing to which it was subjected when Crete was invaded in 1941. Fortunately the collection was unharmed. After the war the enlarged museum was reopened to the public in 1952.

ANALYSIS OF THE COLLECTION. Items in the collection come exclusively from Crete and consist only of antiquities dating from the Neolithic period (6000–5000 BC) to the end of the Roman era, (4th century AD). Where later antiquities are concerned the Historical and Ethno-graphic Museum of Crete takes up where the Archaeological

Museum leaves off, enabling one to follow the development of Crete up to the beginning of the 20th century. The sections relating to Minoan art are particularly important and enable the visitor to obtain an overall perspective of the historical development of Minoan civilization, though not so much of its geographical range. For only central and eastern Crete have so far been the object of intensive archaeological exploration: western Crete has until recent years been relatively neglected by Greek and foreign digs.

Greek art, especially sculpture, is well represented, and reflects the historical development of Crete after the Dorian invasions. While items on display are important for an appreciation of the Geometric period, the Herakleion museum's collection is crucial for the Archaic period, for Crete was at that time one of the most brilliant centres in the forging of an art that was to open a royal avenue to the Classical and Hellenistic periods. As a result of some inexplicable decline Crete, while not absent from this extraordinary flowering, did not produce anything of significance during these periods.

Museological presentation – The collection is presented in a very clear chronological and topographical order; the rooms are well filled – Crete is prodigal in its artistic production – but not to excess. Models, drawings and photographs enable one to make a graphic reconstruction both of the fragmentary items and of the overall settings useful in understanding the collection as a whole.

Itinerary – This follows the chronological layout of the collection. Begin the visit with Room I, entered by the door across the entrance hall directly opposite the way into the museum. The rooms then follow in sequence, leading one into the next, and finally to Room VI where another sequence of rooms leads to Room XIII (Minoan sarcophagi).

After that, go upstairs to the exhibition of Minoan painting (Rooms XIV–XVI) and the Giamalakis Collection housed in a special room (XVII; sculpture, ceramics, glyptics ... from the Greek period, etc.)

Then come back down to Room XIII and into the entrance hall to end the visit with the rooms devoted to Greek art (XIX and XX), entered by a door opposite the way through from Room XIII into the entrance hall.

Gallery I – In this room are mainly ceramics from the Neolithic to the Earliest Palace or Early Minoan period (2600–2000 BC), i.e. predating the construction of the great palaces which form one of the major features of Minoan civilization. There are also stone vases, figurines in marble, ivory or terracotta representing deities, worshippers, animals, etc., seals and cylinder seals, weapons, jewels, etc. Be sure to see the 'mottled' pottery known as Vasiliki pottery (cases 6 and 8); the unusual effect is produced by unequal firing of the clay – this dates from the Early Minoan period. Note also the outstanding collection of stone vases (case 7) found in tombs dating from Early Minoan II (2400–2200 BC), on the island of Mochlos in the Gulf of Mirabello in eastern Crete, and the very interesting collection of seals (case 11), mostly found in the domed tombs of Mesara (central Crete). Most of these seals were made in Crete, but some were imported from Egypt or Mesopotamia, like the cylinder seal no. 1,098 which dates from the reign of the Babylonian King Hammurabi (17th century BC).

Gallery II – This room has more marvels, including the first 'Kamares' 'egg-shell' vases; others use bright polychromy on a blackish background. There are many figurines of people at worship, sacred ships and animals, decorative compositions, weapons, seals, etc. These items from the first palaces at Knossos and Mallia and from various 'high places' in central and eastern Crete date from the New Palace period, at the start of Middle Minoan (2000–1700 BC). Look especially at the Kamares vases (cases 22 and 23) with red and white patterns on a dark background – the style is named after a cave on Mt Ida where the first known examples of this style were discovered – called 'egg-shell' (case 23) because the walls are so thin that they remind one of the shell of an egg.

Two other items are of particular interest: the three-columned sanctuary surmounted by doves that indicate the presence of the deity (case 24), and the 'town mosaic' (case 25), a decorative panel which probably formed part of a wooden box, made up of small faïence plaques showing two- and three-storey houses with latticed windows and flat roofs.

Gallery III – The *Kamares ware on display in this room includes real masterpieces which will command your attention, but take care also to examine the famous Phaestos disc, made of terracotta and covered with hieroglyphs, and the various cult objects such as rhytons or libation vessels, etc. All these items date from the proto-Palatial period, or the beginning of Middle Minoan (2000–1700 BC).

Of the Kamares vases (cases 30–37) those in case 30 do in fact come from the cave of Kamares on the southern slopes of Mt Ida. Some vases show plants or animals, especially octopuses, very beautifully portrayed. These vases must have been intended for use in the libations offered in the cave to the Great Goddess of the Minoans.

The *Phaestos disc (case 41) is covered on both faces with hieroglyphs printed on to the wet clay with seals, running from the outer edge in a spiral towards the centre (1700–1600 BC). This writing system may not have belonged to Crete. It consists of 122 hieroglyphic characters assembled in groups of between two and seven signs; each group is separated by a vertical line along with an animate figure. For a long time all attempts to decipher the disc proved unsuccessful, but a French researcher may have found its meaning; however, his interpretation is still far from being accepted as definitive in scientific circles.

Gallery IV – The crucially important items on display in this gallery come from the palaces of Knossos, Mallia and Phaestos, and date from the neo-Palatial period, or the end of Middle Minoan and the Late Minoan periods (1700–1400 BC). On display are vases including the 'Lily vases', which are regarded as being among the finest examples of the naturalist style popular in the Late Minoan period, rhytons or libation vessels, figurines made of faïence and ivory, objects relating to the worship of the sacred snake, various utensils (large saws, axes, bronze tripod cauldrons, pans and lead weights from scales, etc.), ceremonial swords, etc.

The **snake goddesses (case 50) are among the most famous of the Knossos finds. These two faïence figures probably represent the Mother Goddess and her daughter, and are decorated with the attributes of the Underworld: there are snakes round their waists and on their arms, even climbing on to the Mother Goddess's tiara, while the daughter is holding up a snake in either hand.

Study carefully the **bull's head (case 51) as well; this masterpiece dates from the 16th century BC, and is in the form of a libation vessel or rhyton. It has been carved from a block of black steatite into which have been set rock crystal, jasper and mother of pearl, to form the eyes. The horns must have been made of gilded wood, and have been reconstructed, as has the right side of the head; from the palace at Knossos.

The *royal sword (case 52) from Mallia has a grey limestone handle covered with gold, with a crystal pommel. Also in this case are a collection of intaglios and various fragments of steatite vases decorated in relief.

At the same time as the two snake goddesses were discovered in two repositories in the central sanctuary of the palace at Knossos two *faïence plaques (case 55) were found, one showing a goat suckling her young and the other a cow suckling and fondling her calf, allegorical subjects recalling two manifestations of the Minoan Mother Goddess; note too the symbol of the cross, in marble, which may represent the sun god.

The famous ivory *acrobat or bull-dancer (case 50) found at Knossos was part of a chryselephantine (gold and ivory) group; the acrobat was depicted just as he was jumping over the bull, passing between its horns – no remnants of the animal have been found.

The *royal gaming board (case 56), inlaid with precious materials, ivory, crystal, lapis lazuli, silver and gold leaf, was dug up in the ruins of the palace at Knossos.

Gallery V – All the various objects on display here, vases, silverware, figurines, lamps and seals, come from excavations at the palace of Knossos and date from the last phase of the New Palace period (1450–1400 BC).

Among the objects on display here, look closely at the archives (case 69) drawn up in Linear A and Linear B. Linear A is a system of writing that developed from the hieroglyphic method that preceded it, and it may have undergone further considerable alterations and then developed in turn from the mid-15th century BC into the system known as Linear B. Most examples of Linear A come from the royal villa of Hagia Triada, while the examples of Linear B on display in this case are mainly archival records from the palace of Knossos. Thanks to the inscriptions from Knossos and those discovered on mainland Greece at Mycenae, Thebes and especially Pylos, the English scholars Michael Ventris and John Chadwick succeeded in deciphering Linear B, which seems to be an archaic form of Greek, nowadays referred to as Mycenaean. Thus it would appear that Crete must have been subject to the Achaeans as early as the mid-15th century BC.

Gallery VI – All the items in this room have been selected from finds made in tombs in the Knossos and Mesara regions, and take us back to the final phases of the New Palace period and the early post-Palace period when invaders from mainland Greece settled in Crete (1400–1350 BC). Many items displayed were therefore thank-offerings, but some are more concerned with funeral rites such as the small-scale model of a building with two columns (case 71) representing a banquet scene.

Gallery VII – This room is one of the high points of the visit because of the exceptional quality of some of the items on display. They date from the New Palace period (1700–1400 BC) and come from villas, megara and caves used for religious purposes in central Crete. Along the r. wall note the small stone representation of double horns – a religious symbol, as was the double axe, of which there are several unusually large examples on display here from a megaron uncovered at Nirou Khani, E of Herakleion. These double axes, which were probably known in the Minoan language by the name labrys, must have stood on a base and been placed in sanctuaries as a ritual symbol. The word labyrinth no doubt comes from 'labrys' and must have meant: house of the double axes.

The **harvester's vase (case 94) which is in fact a libation vessel (rhyton) from Hagia Triada is probably the finest Minoan work of art – at least one of the most frequently reproduced. It is made of black steatite, a relatively soft stone, and shows, in relief, peasants marching in procession carrying their tools over their shoulders, preceded by a group of musicians and led by a priest. This represents a country ceremonial performed before the sowing of the seed in autumn.

The chieftain's cup (case 95) from the royal villa at Hagia Triada is another masterpiece. It is decorated with reliefs showing an officer handing over as a tribute to his chief a share of the game won from the hunting.

You will also find your eyes drawn to a large *rhyton (case 96) found in the ruins of the megaron at Hagia Triada. It is decorated with scenes in relief depicting athletic games and bull dancing (c. 1600 BC). Here too the portrayals are in no way secular, but religious and ritual in character. Note in the second row of the frieze a bull dancer performing an incredibly dangerous leap between the horns of a bull. These bull-dancing contests, which symbolized the capture of the sacred animal of the Cretans, had a religious significance not only in

Crete but in various other countries round the Mediterranean. The bulls were not killed.

As an oddity, note the copper ingots (case 99) which weigh a standard 63.8lbs (29kg) and were used as currency at the time of the Minoans. Some ingots or talents carry inscriptions in Cretan or Cypriot writing. It is probable that they originally came from Cyprus.

 Be sure not to miss a splendid *jewellery collection (case 101), a source of inspiration to the Athenian goldsmiths of our own day. Pay special attention to the necklaces with pendants shaped like bulls' heads, crouching lion cubs, and heart-shaped amulets (Hagia Triada), a pendant from Mallia decorated with two bees feeding on honey from the comb, etc.

Gallery VIII – All items on display here are from Kato Zakros on the eastern tip of the island and belong to the New Palace or Late Minoan period (1700–1400 BC). Two pieces deserve close attention: a rock *crystal vase (case 109), the neck of which is encircled by a ring made of gold bands; its handle consists of crystal beads threaded on to a bronze wire which has oxidized, giving the beads a greenish hue …

A green stone *rhyton (case 111) partly coated in gold, which has survived only on part of the surface, and decorated with scenes in low relief depicting a hill sanctuary, as indicated by the doves fluttering above, the three altars and the horns of consecration, is the second item; note too the four goats on the roof and others shown in various parts of the sanctuary.

Gallery IX – A collection of various items from the New Palace period from sites in eastern Crete: vases, statuettes of worshippers, seals (pay special attention to those in case 128), seal impressions, weapons, tools, etc.

 Look carefully at an amphora (case 121) with fine marine decoration (showing an octopus), and – another oddity – the sacred insects (case 123) which were probably the object of special veneration because they too had a horn (perhaps *Oryctex nasicornis* and *Copris hispanus* – species still found on Crete today).

Gallery X – A collection of items from the post-Palace period (post-Minoan: 1400–1100 BC), i.e. dating from the time following the destruction of the Minoan kingdom after the Achaean invasion; the Achaean civilization is more generally called Mycenaean, after the name of the most powerful Achaean principality, Mycenae.

The large number of cult figures and statuettes of worshippers and cult objects show that the preoccupation with religion was as lively as ever. Look closely at the cult figures (case 133); they are large, and stand with their hands raised, and on their heads there are various symbols.

Gallery XI – Exhibits from the sub-Minoan and Geometric periods (1100–800 BC); c.1100 BC after the Achaean invasion, Dorian warriors came and captured the island, driving the indigenous population of Minoan origin back into the mountains of eastern Crete.

The *cult figures of a goddess with raised hands (case 148) show the continued existence of the same type of large figurine as was found in the previous period; these come from Karphi, a site which was in fact situated in an area where the former population had sought refuge: Lasithi. Do not miss the rhyton symbolizing a chariot with the heads of bulls.

A few simple accessories, here brooches (case 153), the outstanding specimen of which is no. 257, indicate great changes. These brooches were in fact indispensable for holding the Doric peplos in position on the shoulders. The Minoans wore sewn garments which did not require such items.

Gallery XII – During the Geometric and Orientalizing periods (800–540 BC) Greece (and Crete) went through a kind of Dark Ages, in the course of which a new form of civilization was in preparation. The country was in no way closed to foreign influences, as the Orientalizing-style vases on display in several cases in this room attest: sphinxes, winged horses, lions and palmettes have been borrowed from Asia, probably through Phoenician art. There are few masterpieces. The only things worth special attention here are an urn (case 168) decorated with a winged figure between two sphinxes, and bronze objects (case 169) from the Geometric period, the most interesting of which are the fragments of a tripod found in the Idaean cave. These are illustrated with scenes showing a warrior dragging a woman on to a boat, chariots full of warriors, a stag-hunt, cows being milked, etc. There is also a very interesting series of bronze plaques showing peasants bearing various offerings, from the sanctuary of Hermes and Aphrodite at Symi (S of Lasithi).

Gallery XIII – This contains a collection of Minoan sarcophagi made of terracotta from various sites in Crete.

After visiting Gallery XIII, go up to the first floor to gain access to the galleries where frescoes from the palaces and rich villas of the Minoan period are on display.

Gallery XIV – Most of the frescoes on display here date from the New Palace period (1700–1400 BC) and come from central or eastern Crete; they are mostly very fragmentary and some have been very much restored, often on the basis of elements which would seem insignificant to the layman. Even so, some of these frescoes are very famous, such as:

The *Procession* fresco (34–37), only fragments of which can be seen, which adorned the entrance corridor of the palace at Knossos. All that is left of more than five hundred figures are fragments showing groups of men and women, musicians, people bearing offerings, priests and priestesses. The best preserved are those depicting two vase-bearers and the holder of a rhyton or cup. The double procession converged towards a woman, a queen or a goddess, draped in an elaborate robe (c.1400 BC).

The *Religious procession* (27) led by a man playing a seven-string lyre (royal villa of Hagia Triada).

The *Prince with the lilies* (6), Evans's 'Priest-King'; he is wearing a crown and a necklace of lilies. This fresco was found at the far N end of the long Corridor of the Procession at Knossos.

The *Charging bull* (2), a relief (c. 1600 BC) from the bastion of the N entrance to the palace of Knossos; the head is in a good state of preservation, except for the horns which have been restored.

The *Ladies in blue*, representatives of the Minoan aristocracy, elegant and full of animation (Throne Room of the palace of Knossos; c.1600 BC).

The *Bull-dancing scene*, showing an acrobat performing a double somersault over the bull's back, was in one of a suite of rooms in the eastern wing of the palace of Knossos.

The *Dolphins*, a beautiful fresco from the Queen's megaron (bed chamber) in the palace of Knossos (c. 1600 BC).

Be sure to have a very good look at the *sarcophagus from Hagia Triada in the centre of the room. It was found in a small tomb near the royal villa (c.1400 BC); it is made of stone and covered with paintings showing rites in the cult of the dead, perhaps in this case a member of the royal family; note: (1) blood sacrifice of a bull to the sound of double flutes (a procession of women) and a bloodless offering of fruit and drink; (2) offerings of drink, brought by a female relative of the dead man wearing a crown and poured out by a priestess between the double-axes to the sound of the seven-string lyre; appearance of the dead man emerging from his tomb and offerings made by priests; (3) chariot drawn by horses (of this world); (4) chariot drawn by winged griffins (from the other World).

Gallery XV – Here you will see other no less famous Minoan frescoes such as the *Tripartite sanctuary* (10), a shrine with three columns in front of which a crowd is gathered; a miniature fresco from the Palace at Knossos.

La Parisienne (12), a fragment showing a young Minoan priestess of great charm and grace christened 'la Parisienne' by Sir Arthur Evans, was part of a fresco decorating the hall with six columns in the shrine of the palace of Knossos.

Gallery XVI – Pay particular attention to these two frescoes: the *Saffron gatherer* (20), a monkey picking saffron flowers in the royal gardens of the palace of Knossos; and the *Captain of the black soldiers* (22), from the house of the frescoes at Knossos, an outstanding fresco showing a Minoan officer leading a group of black soldiers.

Gallery XVII – Minoan and Greek antiquities from the Giamalakis Collection. A remarkable collection of jewels, Minoan seals, tools, weapons, Minoan, Mycenaean and Greek pottery (Geometric period, Archaic period, etc.). Pay special attention to a bronze statuette of a man carrying a ram intended for sacrifice (Archaic period), and a *scale model of a shrine (case 181) containing a figurine shown in the attitude of the goddess with raised hands.

Gallery XVIII – A collection of objects belonging to the so-called minor arts, through it includes some true masterpieces, such as the bronze *funerary statue (near case 201) from the 1st century BC, one of the finest examples of portraiture of the Hellenistic period.

After visiting the first-floor rooms return to the entrance hall to look at the Greek and Graeco-Roman sculpture.

Gallery XIX – As already explained in the analysis of the collection, the Archaic period (700–550 BC) in Crete was of vital importance in the formation of a specifically Greek art. All the items on display in this gallery belong to this period, but we draw your attention particularly to:

A *frieze of horsemen (l.) perched on large horses and carrying lances, which used to decorate the main facade of one of the two Archaic temples in ancient Rizenia (Prinias). This work is thought to have been executed around 650 or 625 BC.

An eagle and a hawk (in the l. corner) on pedestals decorated with Ionic volutes; they were uncovered on the site of an altar to Zeus Thanatos at Amnisos. Next note a torso in the Daedalic style from Eleutherna (7th century BC), then the lower part of the statue of a seated goddess from Gortyn. The connecting doorway between Galleries XIX and XX has been built as a reconstruction of the entrance into the cella of the temple of Rizenia, with two goddesses balancing vase-shaped baskets on their heads, their hands on their laps, each sitting on a throne resting on the lintel, which is itself decorated with a frieze of animals: deer on the l., panthers, shown full-face, on the r. (c.650–625 BC).

Look too at the collection of 'sphyrelata' (case 210), or statuettes made of hammered bronze plaques riveted to a wooden core (Apollo, Artemis and Leto, from the Delphinion at Dreros), and at the splendid collection of *votive shields, bowls and cymbals made of bronze (cases 208 and 209) found in the Idaean cave. The Curetes, entrusted with the care of the infant Zeus, are said to have covered the sound of his crying by striking their shields; and here a scene depicted on a cymbal (case 209) shows Zeus on a bull tearing a lion to pieces while four Curetes, shown in the shape of winged Assyrian daemons, are striking their shields with their spears.

Gallery XX – This collection of sculptures dating from the Classical period to the end of the Graeco-Roman period (beginning of the 4th century AD) is the weak point of the museum, mainly because from the end of the Archaic period Crete went into a state of marked decline which lasted for many centuries. Most of the sculptures on display in this gallery date from the Graeco-Roman period.

Standing by the long l. wall you will see a torso of Aphrodite, probably a copy of a work by Praxiteles, a marble copy of the

Doryphorus (*Spear bearer*) by Polyclitus, and a copy of a famous work by Scopas showing Pothos, the incarnation of Desire, with his animal attribute, the goose.

Along the end wall there are: a torso of Aphrodite (159), probably a copy of a work by Praxiteles, a copy of a work by the sculptor Doidalsas showing Aphrodite in the bath (43), and a huge statue of the Pythian Apollo with a lyre found during excavations of the temple dedicated to him at Gortyn; the head is believed to be from the Hellenistic period and the body from the Roman period.

To the r. of the entrance, take more particular note of a funerary relief (378) copied from an Attic work dated 4th century BC, a metope (363) from a temple near Knossos, decorated with a relief showing one of the twelve labours of Hercules: the capture of the Erymanthian boar (late 5th century BC), a funerary relief (145), probably of Attic origin, from the first half of the 4th century BC, depicting a hunter, and finally in the centre two marble sarcophagi, one of which comes from Mallia.

The Venetian ramparts – Starting from Eleftherias Square (plan C–2) near the museum it is best to follow the line of the city walls by car.

The walls, built in their final form in the 16th and 17th century, are reinforced by seven strong bastions which are still standing, as are most of the walls and gates. St George's Gate (now destroyed) through which the soldiers of La Feuillade and then those of the Duke of Beaufort attempted a sortie against the Turks was near Eleftherias Square. The tomb of the writer and poet Nikos Kazantzakis (d. 1957) is on the NW bastion overlooking the sea.

The New Gate (formerly Gesù Gate), the finest of all the gates, has on the outside an inscription dated 1567 and on the inside another dated 1587 in the name of the governor, Mocenigo. The angle of the projection in the wall to the S beyond the New Gate was formed by a wall of exceptional strength which for 21 years resisted assaults from the Turks.

VICINITY OF HERAKLEION

1 TYLISSOS (8.7mls/14km). Leave by the Chania road.

3.1mls (5km): Take r. turning, leaving new express road and following old road.

6.9mls (11km): Turn l.

9.4mls (14km): Tylissos, a village at the foot of Mt Ida where you can visit the ruins of three Minoan villas built c.1800 BC and in use until c.1450 BC. Though they do not have as much to offer as Knossos, Phaestos, Hagia Triada, Mallia, etc., the Tylissos ruins are nonetheless worth visiting for those wishing to gain a deeper knowledge of Crete.

Contemporary with the second palaces at Knossos and Mallia, these three villas date from Middle Minoan III to Late Minoan II. They were constructed on the site of earlier buildings (Early Minoan I to Middle Minoan II) of which only a few vestiges remain as they were levelled to make way for the construction of the three villas whose remains you can see. After these had been destroyed c.1450 BC, new villas dating from the Late Minoan III period were built; their foundations were destroyed during the Hellenic period by the new occupants of the site.

Open: daily 08.30–12.30 and 16.00–18.00; Sun. 09.00–15.00; entrance fee.

The walls of Villa A have the redans characteristic of Minoan buildings.

Enter the villa through a vestibule divided in two by two pillars; a door at the end of the vestibule used to open on to stairs leading to the upper floor. A corridor paved with irregular slabs going off to the l. once led to the S wing of the villa and came out on to a little courtyard (no 1) which acted as a light-well. The magazines to the r. of the corridor still had large storage jars in them when they were excavated. At the far end of the r. (no 2) a second staircase. To the N of the villa three large storerooms.

Villa B, which lies to the W of Villa A, is far less well preserved and you may miss it in order to concentrate on Villa C, to the N of the site. Some of the floor paving in the vestibule has been preserved, and also in rooms 3, 4 and 5; the porter's lodge (no 1) lay on the r. while a corridor led to the S wing, and a staircase (no 2) went to the upper floor. There was a second staircase (no 6) to the N, not far from a large room (no 7) the floor and walls of which were covered with red stucco. A corridor led from this room to a third staircase (no 8). Room 9 was coated with white stucco. Finally the building ended with a huge room with a hypaethral courtyard (no 10); a cistern with a staircase leading to it was built subsequently against the walls of the villa. Further N are remains of a Hellenic building with an altar.

You can carry on beyond Tylissos to the village of Anogia (18.7mls/30km), 3000ft (700m) up on the N slope of Ida, a completely barren setting. Anogia has several small weaving workshops where rugs, blankets and bags are made. During World War II this village was a centre of resistance; the German General von Kreipe was taken there after his capture in Herakleion by Cretan partisans before being despatched to Egypt from the small port of Chora Sfakion. Following this abduction the village was completely destroyed as an act of reprisal.

From Anogia a beautiful road leads to (10mls/16km) the Idaean cave (Idaion Antron) across the Nidha plain (alt. 5,250ft/1,600m) which is strewn with pine woods.

The cave was excavated by Italian archaeologists in 1884, 1918, and 1956, using a sophisticated system. The huge quantity of earth already removed has revealed a small cavity to the SW and several rooms at the back. Bronze seals, gold jewellery, bronze and clay statues, three-legged stools, ivory objects, thousands of Roman oil lamps and many animal and human bones, some sacrificial, have

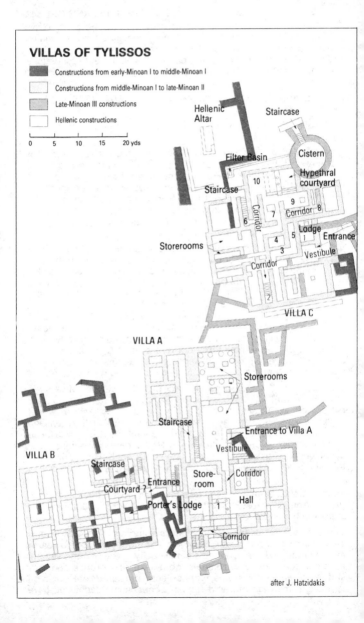

VILLAS OF TYLISSOS

■ Constructions from early-Minoan I to middle-Minoan I
□ Constructions from middle-Minoan I to late-Minoan II
▨ Late-Minoan III constructions
□ Hellenic constructions

0   5   10   15   20 yds

Hellenic Altar

Staircase

Filter Basin

Staircase

Cistern

Hypethral courtyard

10

Corridor

9

7   Corridor   8

6

5   Lodge

4   1   Entrance

3   Vestibule

Storerooms

Corridor

2

VILLA C

VILLA A

Storerooms

Staircase

Entrance to Villa A

Vestibule

VILLA B

Staircase

Store-room

Corridor

Courtyard ?

Entrance

1

Hall

Porter's Lodge

2   Corridor

after J. Hatzidakis

turned up in the sieves. At the entrance (S side of the cave) is a large boulder out of which a table for offerings has been hollowed. In front of the cave, dominating the plain, was an altar, Hellenistic and Roman, also the foundations of statues of which the shape of the feet can be discerned in the stone. The cave may have been used for religious rites in the Neolithic period, then during the Minoan, and had its period of glory in the Hellenistic and Roman eras. With the coming of Christianity it became a refuge for shepherds and lost its religious character.

The worship of Zeus – the Zeus of Mt Ida, the Cretan god who died and was reborn each year – was seemingly practised there. It is tempting to equate the written evidence evoked in mythology, taking account of the birth of the Supreme God, with archaeological reality; in that case Zeus' cave, considered for so long to be situated on Mt Dictae, would be on Mt Ida.

2 MESARA (Gortyn, Phaestos, Hagia Triada). See Crete, Section 5.

3 KNOSSOS. See Crete, Section 4.

4 ARKHANES AND PYRGOS (31.9mls/51km; exit by Knossos road; plan C/D-3).

3.1mls (5km): Knossos: See Crete, Section 4.

5.6mls (9km): Road on r. for (3.7mls/6km) Arkhanes, a large village with a pop. of 3,900 lying in the middle of a pleasant wine-producing area, where dessert grapes are also grown, with Mt Juktas (2,660ft/811m) rising above it; a road leads to the summit of the mountain.

In the village recent excavations have resulted in the discovery of a building of more than one floor in an exceptionally good state of preservation; judging from the quality of its decoration, particularly the frescoes, this could be a palace. The size of the rooms, and the frescoes and floors of red and blue flagstone, tend to confirm this judgement. All the elements of Minoan architecture are there. The excavated part in the heart of the village dates from the second Palace period (1750–1450 BC). One can see to the N—W of the field of excavation (closed to the public; visit possible on request to the guard in the village square) the remains of two rooms with magnificent floors once separated by a spiral staircase. They opened to the S onto a sort of court with an altar, a large rectangular stone to the N from which ran a channel, probably used for libations. The size and quality of the stones of the façade are exceptional for the period; one can also see traces of the foundations of three stone columns which mark out the edges of a light-well.

Near the church of Hagios Nikolaos one can see the remains of a pavement used for processions, similar to those found to the W of the palace at Knossos and at Phaestos, also used for religious processions. Comparing the plans of Minoan palaces already known and all conceived on the same plan, one notes similarities with the site of Archanaea, and the distance between the excavated parts allows easy inference of the size and importance of the site covered by the village. The presence of modern buildings on the site restricts excavation possibilities. The churches of Hagia Triada and Hagia Paraskevi are decorated with medieval frescoes and icons (both here and for the church of Assomatos, below, ask for the key at the priest's house).

The area around Arkhanes is rich in ancient remains (guides available in the main square of the village).

Approx. 1.2mls (2km) NW of the village at Fourni, a Minoan cemetery has been discovered with children's graves, a large, richly furnished burial building with an apse containing 180 graves, and a large tholos (beehive tomb). N of the tholos a Mycenaean 'circle of tombs' has been discovered, the first to be found in Crete.

To the S a very bad unsurfaced road leads to (3.1mls/5km) Vathypetro. 0.9mls (1.5km) along the way on the l. is the church of Assomatos, which has early 14th-century frescoes including an outstanding Crucifixion of great dramatic intensity. On one of the frescoes Christ is wearing Frankish armour. The ruins of a megaron have been uncovered at Vathypetro; built c.1600–1550 BC and destroyed c.1500 BC, it is one of the largest known to us. It consisted of a central courtyard, with a sanctuary, storerooms including one big hypostyle room, an oven, kitchens with two clay hearths, a press, etc.

A path leads to the N slope of Mt Juktas (fine view). To the N. of the Orthodox church a Minoan sanctuary is in the course of excavation. At the place called Anemospilia, about 1.9mls (3km) NW of Arkhanes, Professor J. Sakellarakis uncovered the remains of a building in which finds have been made that are of crucial importance for the knowledge of Minoan civilization.

HUMAN SACRIFICE IN MINOAN CRETE? The recent excavations at Anemospilia have uncovered the remains of a building consisting of three rooms of the same size adjoining one another and opening on the N on to a long vestibule; the whole structure is surrounded by a peribolus of which some sections have been discovered. This building, simple and symmetrical in plan and without known parallel in Minoan architecture, is apparently the first Minoan temple discovered. It had only one phase of use, in the first half of the 17th century BC, to judge from the large quantity of pottery collected there, and it was destroyed by an earthquake followed by a fire.

The vestibule was fitted out with wooden shelving on which ritual vases were arranged (about 150 have been recovered on the ground); in the centre the skeleton of a man was lying. The eastern room, intended for bloodless ceremonies, contained a bench with three levels on which some twenty vases were found *in situ*, some containing remains of vegetable matter. On a bench at the end of the central room were the remains of a life-size statue made of terracotta and wood.

It was in the western room that the most surprising discovery was made: in it were three human skeletons. The first two are those of a man and a woman who, like the man found in the vestibule, had been killed, according to the conclusions of anthropologists and forensic legal experts, when the roof of the building collapsed, most probably as a result of an earthquake. But the third skeleton is that of a youth who in the opinion of the experts was already dead when the catastrophe occurred, killed by a bronze dagger which was found in his chest. Unlike the three others, this last skeleton was lying not on the floor, but on a kind of rectangular altar. Everything seems to indicate that he had been sacrificed on the altar by the man found near him, identified by the director of excavations as a priest. This discovery, if it has been correctly interpreted (as seems to be the case on the basis of the information available), is therefore of crucial importance in the study of Minoan religion.

13.7mls (22km): Hagios Vassilios; in the church, 13th-century frescoes.

17.5mls (28km): An unsurfaced road on the r. leads to (2.5mls/4km) Moni Apanosifis, a monastery dating from the end of the Venetian period.

31.9mls (51km): Pyrgos, in a typically Cretan setting at the foot of Mt Kofinas (4,040ft/1,231m). The church has early 14th-century frescoes.

5 PEFKOS (47.5mls/76km; exit by Knossos road). This drive is complementary to the previous one and allows you to discover delightful villages perched on hills above huge olive groves.

23.7mls (38km): Arkalochori – if you go on a Saturday morning you will rub shoulders with the many peasants who have come to market, or you can go and see a cave used for worship from the middle of the 3rd millennium BC (it yielded rich archaeological treasures, including gold axes, about a hundred swords, etc., all dating from the middle of the 16th century BC).

41.2mls (66km): Ano Viannos, where you can visit the church of Hagia Pelagia at Plaka with its 14th-century frescoes, and the church of Hagios Georgios with wall paintings dating from 1401.

In the Ano Viannos area a Late Minoan III settlement was found at Kephala Chondrou, and at Kato Symi a shrine to Hermes and Aphrodite, on three terraces with a little temple and an altar.

44.4mls (71km): Road on r. for (3.7mls/6km) Moni Arvi, a fishing village set in a banana plantation, with a small monastery.

47.5mls (76km): Pefkos; the road continues on to Ierapetra (see Crete, Section 6, Vicinity 3).

6 FROM HERAKLEION TO HAGIOS NIKOLAOS VIA THE LASITHI PLAIN 60mls/ 96km; exit by Alikarnassos).

2.5mls (4km): Heraklion international airport.

 5mls (8km): Amnisos beach, named after the Minoan city mentioned by Homer in the *Odyssey* and which was the port for Knossos.

7.8mls (12.5km): On the r. Nirou Khani, the ruins of a Minoan building which according to Evans may have been the residence of a priest-chief and a manufacturing centre for cult objects which were despatched to mainland Greece and the Cyclades.

11.2mls (18km): Gournes; junction with fast road to (32.5mls/52km) Hagios Nikolaos (see below, 7).

15mls (24km): Take the r. turn for (1.2mls/2km) Chersonissos, a large village near a safe anchorage (Limin Chersonissou) which was the harbour for ancient Lyttos (see below, 7).

19.4mls (31km): On r. road to Bitzariano.

At Bitzariano (also known as Pighi) visit the small Byzantine church. You will recognize various ancient items which have been re-used, in particular inside the building a pillar with four Roman capitals with acanthus leaves. The early 14th-century frescoes were a popular art form. 1.2mls (2km) further on lies Kasteli, a village which is not too far away from the beaches E of Herakleion. From Kasteli follow the Apostoli road, then turn l. after 1.2mls (2km). A path on the l. shortly after the fork leads up to the hamlet of Sclaverochori, approx. 15mins. on foot, where the little church of the Presentation of the Virgin has 14th and 15th-century wall paintings devoted to the life of Christ.

1.6mls (2.5km) from Kasteli, following the road to Avdou, you can get to Xidas near the ruins of ancient Lyttos. This town makes its appearance in Cretan history in the 3rd century BC when it was destroyed by Knossos. It was still inhabited during the Byzantine period. Moreover a huge Early Christian basilica was discovered along the side of the ancient agora; it was decorated with mosaics, and was under a more recent church. But today about all Lyttos has to offer is the beauty of its position on one of the spurs of Mt Dictae.

21.2mls (34km): Potamies. In this delightful village surrounded by orchards and orange groves you come first to the monastery of Panagia Gouverniotissa, supposedly founded in the 10th century, where the church has frescoes dating from the 12th to the 15th century; pay special attention to Christ Pantocrator in the dome, from the first half of the 15th century.

23.1mls (37km): Avdou. In the church of Hagios Antonios on the vaulting of a small chamber a series of 14th-century frescoes illustrating scenes from the New Testament; in the cemetery chapel there are very faded mural paintings by Manuel and John Fokas (1445).

25.6mls (41km): Turn r. towards Kera. The road you are following keeps rising towards a pass (16.6mls/26.5km) from which you have an attractive *panoramic view over the Avdou valley, and then shortly afterwards over the strange Lasithi plain with its outcrop of windmills. This enclosed plain, varying in altitude from 2,723ft (830m) to 2,821ft

(860m), was always a place of refuge for the indigenous population at times of foreign invasion. The western part is extremely picturesque with its small fields full of cereal crops, and its windmills which ensure the irrigation of the fields in midsummer. By way of contrast with the open western side, the eastern part of the Lasithi Plain is covered with fine shrubby vegetation.

34.4mls (55km): Tzermiado, capital of the Lasithi area.

36.2mls (58km): A small asphalted road on the r. leads up to the (6.2mls/10km) Xenia Restaurant near the entrance to the Dictaean cave, passing near the (1.6mls/2.5km) monastery of Kroustallenia, founded in the mid 16th century and laid waste by the Turks in 1823.

The Dictaean cave (Diktaion antron), which nature has endowed with fine stalactites, is identified by some scholars with the sacred cave of Dictae where Zeus was born and suckled with goat's milk by the Cretan princess Amalthaea, under the protection of the Curetes. During the Minoan period and right up to the Archaic period it was used as a place of worship. The first part of the cave which was used for sacrifices contained a small shrine and an altar. Steps lead down to the second part which lies 213ft (65m) lower and is partly flooded. A good many votive offerings dating from the Minoan and Mycenaean periods have been found here.

43.7mls (70km): Exopotami, one of the prettiest villages in a valley that runs down towards the Gulf of Mirabello.

55mls (88km): Road from Herakleion to Hagios Nikolaos — turn r.

60mls (96km): Hagios Nikolaos.

7 FROM HERAKLEION TO HAGIOS NIKOLAOS VIA MALLIA (43.7mls/70km by the fast road; for first 11mls/18km, see above, 6).

16.9mls (27km): l., the anchorage at Limin Chersonissou lies on the site of the ancient port of Lyttos.

The small church of Hagios Nikolaos (17th or 18th century) stands on a small promontory on the site of a 6th-century palaeo-Christian basilica, the apse of which can still be seen. In the narthex and the central nave there are still mosaics.

Another palaeo-Christian basilica in which some of the mosaic paving has been preserved has been discovered at the place known as Kastri on another peninsula.

21.2mls (34km): Mallia, a recently developed village near the ruins of the palace (below).

22.5mls (36km): On the l., **palace of Mallia.

This palace is one of the three great Cretan palaces, along with those of Knossos and Phaestos. Although the Mallia complex does not occupy a site that can be compared with those of Knossos and, in particular, Phaestos, its harmonious proportions, the simplicity of its plan and many original details should not fail to hold your interest. All around the palace lay a Minoan town which the excavations of the French School in Athens are gradually bringing to light.

The palace of Mallia, which is contemporary with the first palaces at Knossos and Phaestos, dates from Middle Minoan I or perhaps even Early Minoan III (c.2000 BC); it was altered in Middle Minoan II (1700–1550) and was finally abandoned c.1450 BC. The first excavations were carried out by J. Hatzidakis; work was continued by the French School in Athens from 1921.

Open: daily 09.00–14.00; Sun. closed. Allow approx. 45mins for

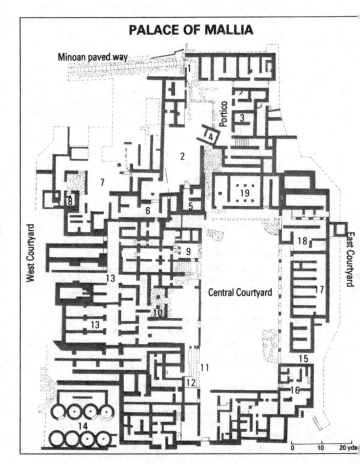

PALACE OF MALLIA

visiting the palace, or more if you plan to look at the adjoining excavations. Those interested in archaeology can also (with permission) examine the collection of the small local museum of stratigraphy.

To the r. of the road leading to the palace you see first of all some traces of houses and of a Minoan road. Further on to the l. are more remains of a Minoan building, possibly funerary, formed by an enclosing wall.

W court (see plan) – You reach the palace by crossing this vast esplanade which was covered with blue limestone flagstones and traversed by pathways paved in ammouda, a stone quarried locally.

Hypostyle crypt – Before going into the palace turn towards a modern shelter covering the remains of an underground room with columns, called the hypostyle crypt. It is believed to be a council room, a sort of prytaneum with several annexes. This crypt, which seems to have been built at the same date as the first palaces, has a different orientation from the palace as such. A square courtyard was joined on to this room, known as the orthostat courtyard, following the same orientation so as to form a group that is quite distinct from the palace.

The site of a door known as the storeroom gate leading into this courtyard has been discovered on the N of the crypt.

Orthostat courtyard – This courtyard, which is larger than the central court of the palace, measured 96ft (29.1m) across by 130ft 6in (39.8m) in length. A band of stucco about 3ft (1m) wide went all the way round it, on every side. The S half of the W side of the courtyard consisted of a portico (the foundations of the bases of four columns have been discovered) with an axial colonnade. The rest of this side was marked by a series of orthostats. This edging of white stones also occurs on the N side of the courtyard and on parts of the E and S sides. A pylon or monumental gateway used to stand at the NE corner of the courtyard, called the necropolis gate; its massive double foundation crossing a Minoan road has survived. The roadway from this gate travels towards the necropolis to the NW. This courtyard is thought to be an arena or an agora.

N sector of the palace – The main entrance (plan, 1) lay at the end of a paved roadway, which is well preserved. To the r. before entering you can see a few insignificant traces of the first palace.

The entrance vestibule opened on to a portico with three wings beside an internal courtyard (no 2) of quite large dimensions, which had to be crossed to reach the royal apartments. Under the central section of the portico there was access on the E to various storerooms (no 3). At the start of the corridor which leads to the central court, there is a small building (no 4) put up after the second palace, but at a time when it was still inhabited – possibly dedicated to the gods.

On the far side of the N courtyard (no 2) were an archives depository, a treasury, and the entrance to the royal quarters.

Royal apartments – First of all you see the ruins of the queen's chambers (megaron; no 6) which communicated with that of the king (no 7). A bathroom (no 8) lay beyond another room or vestibule. French archaeologists uncovered remains of the first palace underneath the floor of this room and found there beautiful decorated swords (in the Herakleion Museum).

Central court – You go along the corridor, partly obstructed by building 4, to reach the central court. There were originally porticoes along the N and E sides. The W side on the r. is taken up with sanctuaries or official buildings. Your eye is first caught by a small terrace (no 9) which was the royal loggia overlooking the courtyard, then by a staircase which led to the upper floor, the vestibule of the crypt with its two quadrangular pillars (no 10) a grand staircase (no 11), and finally on a platform a kernos or offering-table (no 12) with 34 small hollows in which the first fruits of the harvest, liquids or seeds, were placed. From the crypt it was possible to go to two rows of storerooms (no 13) linked by corridors. At the SE corner of the palace there was an area with circular grain silos (no 14). The portico on the E side of the court had alternating pillars and columns. At one end of the portico the E entrance to the palace (no 15) was followed by a group of rooms that made up the royal treasury (no 16). A flagstone way coming from the E ending at this entrance has been traced over a length of about 115ft (35m). It first crossed a huge esplanade with houses built around it which must have been one of the wealthiest parts of the town.

At the E entrance of the palace were storerooms (no 17) consisting of narrow cells opening on to a corridor; in each cell there are benches with storage jars on them. Notice the arrangement for allowing liquids to flow (channels leading to a collecting vessel). Next came the kitchens (no 18).

The N side of the court was marked by a portico with round columns. A staircase went up on the r. – all that is left of it are the traces of eight steps. Then it opened into a vestibule with a central pillar, the base of which is still there; this vestibule opened into a hypostyle hall (plan, 19) with two rows of three columns.

Minoan housing – Leave the palace by the N entrance and go along the Minoan road leading towards a residential area lying W of the palace. You come to a paved road with houses along it, intersected by another road. Near the crossroads to the r. one house has been restored. The door opens on to a paved vestibule leading into a corridor which divides the house into two parts; on the r. are the service rooms and the magazines; to the l. at the end of the main room is the bathroom, which is reached by a small staircase.

A little further on a recent dig has revealed the existence of a large complex dating from the Earliest Palace period (Middle Minoan II), no doubt a public building belonging to the organization of the site for palace purposes, which has architectural features anticipating buildings belonging to the following period (light-well, paved portico, megaron). The building was arranged round a large sunken lustral bath. Another building to the W has a suite of rooms that are likewise below ground level, the walls of which have been preserved up to a height of 6ft (1.80m). A dagger with a golden handle and some very delicate vases with relief work were found there (Herakleion Museum).

Chrysolakhos necropolis – If you now turn towards the coast you will pass another residential area on the l. with two paved roads, and then on the l. the site of a vast house (Villa A) which may have had an interior courtyard; it was built at the same period as the first palace (Middle Minoan I).

A little further on, 545yds (500m) N of the palace you come to the necropolis of Chrysolakhos which dates back to the first phase of the palace. Turn E along the beach path which at first runs beside modern buildings; follow the boundary fence and continue round the excavation site; then turn due N and you will quickly soon see the roof which protects a small part of the site. The necropolis is fenced off against sheep, but a gate gives access to it. This was probably a royal burial ground consisting of an enclosure with esplanades extending from each of its four sides, possibly with a portico on the E side. Internally the enclosure was divided into compartments by walls forming several chambers which probably had no doors, burials being effected from above; the upper surface probably consisted of large paving stones. In the centre there was a chamber in which a flame must have been kept burning. Inside the enclosure by the E wall were rooms devoted to the cult of the dead, and to the Great Goddess of whom there are many cult figures. In one of these rooms (in the central area) there was, according to P. Demargne, a hollow cylinder comparable to the hollow altar found by Schliemann above the fourth tomb in the royal circle at the acropolis of Mycenae, which was used for libations made in honour of the dead. It would appear that originally the Chrysolakhos necropolis consisted of adjoining chambers cut off from the outside world by the enclosing wall, surrounded by paved esplanades; these later additions date from Middle Minoan III.

The itinerary continues: 32.5mls (52km): Latsida; churches of Panagia and Hagia Paraskevi with 14th- and 15th-century frescoes.

34.4mls (55km): Neapolis, a large village of no great interest lying in the middle of a fertile plain which is famous for its almond trees and which once served the town of Dreros, now defunct and of interest only to archaeology enthusiasts (see Vicinity of Hagios Nikolaos).

38.7mls (62km): Road on l. for (5mls/8km) Hagios Nikolaos (see Crete, Section 6).

4 Knossos (Crossus)

Knossos, 3.1mls (5km) from Heraklion, is the largest and most evocative Minoan site to have been discovered in Crete, with its main

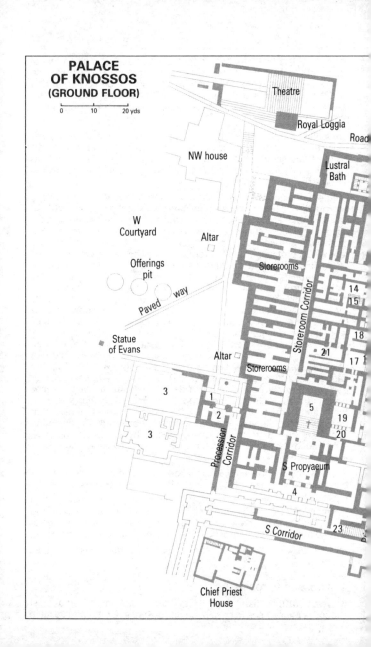

PALACE OF KNOSSOS (GROUND FLOOR)

0 10 20 yds

Theatre

Royal Loggia

Road

NW house

Lustral Bath

W Courtyard

Altar

Offerings pit

Storerooms

Paved way

Storeroom Corridor

14
15

18

Statue of Evans

Altar

21

17 1

Storerooms

3

1

2

5

19

20

3

Procession Corridor

S Propyaeum

4

S Corridor

23

Chief Priest House

ur
Hypostyle
44
room

NE house

N Passage

43

Servants'
quarters

42

22

41

40

Central

39

37

38

Courtyard

24 25

King's megaron

27
28 26
29

30

31

32

33 36

House
Sacred tribune

34

35

SE house

E Bastion

palace, its resplendent villas and its traces of paved roads. The wonderful complex was uncovered thanks to the brilliant intuition of Heinrich Schliemann who, by careful historical analysis of the stories of Homer, had just discovered the site of the city of Troy. Starting in 1900 Sir Arthur Evans, one of the pioneers of modern archaeology, devoted many years to uncovering the fabulous palace of the most powerful kings in Crete.

A LINGUISTIC ENIGMA. Despite the many brilliant discoveries made throughout Crete, the history of the island in the Minoan period is still only sketchily known. This is because we cannot read historical documents here, as we can elsewhere, either because they have disappeared or because it has not proved possible to decipher the surviving archives. It should be pointed out that only tablets written in Linear B, a system of writing that came into use c.1500 BC, have been translated or are at present being deciphered, thanks to the remarkable work of M. Ventris and J. Chadwick and the 'Mycenologists' (Linear B is 'Mycenaean Greek'). Moreover it is unlikely, judging from present discoveries, that the tablets in Linear A and other even earlier inscriptions, because they are so few in number (approx. 500), will provide an answer, though work on deciphering them is under way.

THE MYSTERIOUS KEFTIU. Thus in spite of a few brief mentions (the earliest dates back to c.2200 BC) in the annals of Mesopotamia or Egypt, where the Cretans were referred to as the Keftiu, the history of Knossos and of the entire island is based solely on the study and interpretation of such evidence as the digs have revealed. The discovery of some Minoan objects in Egypt and some Egyptian objects in Crete has enabled approximate dating of the remains dug up at Knossos and elsewhere in the island by reference to the more reliable chronology of the Pharaohs.

KNOSSOS, A MARITIME POWER. The Knossos site was inhabited from the Neolithic period, and the depth of the layer of deposits from this period – more than half the total depth – is evidence that it was quite heavily populated at that time. The first palace, however, was not built until 2000 BC, probably after a monarchy was established in Crete. That first palace, which was very spacious, indicates the power and prosperity of the King reigning at Knossos – a prosperity based on exploitation of the rich plain that surrounded the town, but also on trading links with Egypt, Phoenicia, Syria and the Mesopotamian world, through a very active fleet.

THE EMPIRE OF MINOS. Around 1750 BC it is thought that an earthquake destroyed the palaces at Knossos, Phaestos and Mallia. About 50 years later a second palace, larger and more luxurious, covered the site at Knossos and was to last, though altered a few times, for approximately three centuries. Relations with neighbouring regions were pursued more actively than ever: the Cyclades, mainland Greece, Egypt after the expulsion of the Hyksos, and the Near East were all trading posts and outlets for Cretan industry. Knossos reached its highest point of development and the town covered so large a surface area that it may well have had a population of nearly 100,000 people. Before long it had imposed its rule on its Cretan rivals and c.1500 BC King Minos or a dynasty bearing his name held sway over the island; Mallia may have been an exception, but probably had to accept the suzerainty of Minos.

CRETE-OF-A-HUNDRED-CITIES. However, Crete's period of prosperity and command of the seas was nearly at an end. This came between 1450 and 1400 BC perhaps partly as a result of attack by the Achaeans, and mainly because of an earthquake – possibly connected with the volcanic eruption on Thera (Santorini) – which led to the terrible fire in which the town and palace were destroyed. This did not lead to the site being abandoned and Achaeans took advantage of the catastrophe to come and settle at Knossos; their chiefs reigned there until the arrival of the Dorians towards the end of the 11th century BC. Moreover Crete supplied the second largest number of ships to the Achaeans after Mycenae at the time of Agamemnon's expedition against Troy. Crete is mentioned by Homer in the *Iliad* and the *Odyssey*, and the poet depicts it as a wealthy island and a front-ranking maritime power. The history of Crete-of-a-hundred-cities, to use Homer's epithet, becomes even more obscure after the Dorian invasion.

A PERIOD OF INTERNAL STRIFE. In the 4th century BC Knossos once again for a time emerged as the most important Cretan city, now in competition with Gortyn, Lyttos and Kydonia (Chania). But soon Knossos and Crete were to be a battlefield for the rival powers of mainland Greece, and even for external states such as the Egypt of the Ptolemies (which came into existence after the break-up of the empire of Alexander the Great), and Rome, from 189 BC on. These outside interventions were to have the effect of stirring up the quarrels between the bellicose Cretan cities: Knossos against Gortyn (war of Lyttos, c.220 BC) or these two cities, precariously reconciled, against Kydonia (171 BC). Rome, represented by Metellus, put an end to these conflicts by imposing its law throughout Crete in 69–67 BC. The site of the town of Knossos was still occupied during the Roman period, during which it was called Colonia Julia Nobilis, and at the beginning of the Byzantine period, so it would seem.

Open: daily 08.00 (winter 09.00)–14.00; Sun. 10.00–16.00; entrance fee. Allow approx 1½ hrs for visiting the palace. Archaeology enthusiasts may also (with permission) visit a small museum of stratigraphy.

The Palace – The various wings of the palace are grouped round a central courtyard, and the main areas open on to this; smaller, secondary courtyards and light-wells provided light to other parts of the palace. The various rooms seem to be juxtaposed without any obvious plan; corridors link one room to another as in the labyrinth of Hellenic tradition. Nearly 800 rooms have been counted, but there must have been nearly 1,300 spread over five storeys when the kings of Knossos were at their most powerful. The palace was not protected by fortified walls, but was enclosed by a thick wall with several gates in it, some of them very wide.

Sir Arthur Evans was responsible for a series of partial restorations in reinforced concrete at places where excavations provided sufficient information. These restorations, which were necessary because of the fragile state of the ruins that had been uncovered but which can at times offend aesthetic taste, were particularly useful at Knossos where remains of upper floors were found. They give visitors some concept of what the architecture of Minoan Crete looked like, and how different it is from that of the mainland. The walls were built of rubble with mud used as mortar. Large wooden beams laid horizontally or vertically were also components in the construction of Minoan houses. The poor materials used in construction were masked by coats of plaster or stucco painted with frescoes. The floors were paved with gypsum, sometimes simply covered with stucco. The columns were made of wood standing on a stone base, and broadened out as they went up; the capitals were similar in shape to flattened cakes.

W court – You reach the palace by crossing the W court (see plan) which was once traversed by several paved passages, the main one of which was linked to the road leading to the harbour.

The W court, which was probably used as an agora, was completely paved during the second-Palace period, i.e. c.1750–1450 BC. Ritual ceremonies must have taken place there, as indicated by the two altar bases with steps leading up to them which have been found there.

On the l. note three offering-wells of circular shape dating from the first-Palace period (c.2000–1750 BC) in which you can still make out remains of walls and stairs. Beyond the three wells there are some traces of Minoan houses.

Façades – The view of the palace from the W court must have been striking, looking on to a façade with recesses and protrusions that produced a play of light and shade, and storeys of differing heights built above. A plinth ran along the base of the wall of the façade forming a bench on which large gypsum flagstones were set vertically. The main entrance was at the SE of the court (r.). Passing through a single-column propylaeum (plan, 1) – the base of the column is still there – you came to a long corridor, the Corridor of the Procession as it is called, leading to the heart of the palace. On the same axis as the propylaeum there was an opening into a small square room known as the Throne Room (plan, 2). On the r. were various palace outbuildings (plan, 3) which were later converted into houses. The remains of a house (plan, 4) lie to the S.

Corridor of the Procession – This used to be decorated with frescoes showing groups of men and women, musicians, people bearing offerings, priests and priestesses – more than 800 figures in all – forming a double procession that converged towards a woman, a queen or a goddess, dressed in an elaborate robe. A few remnants of

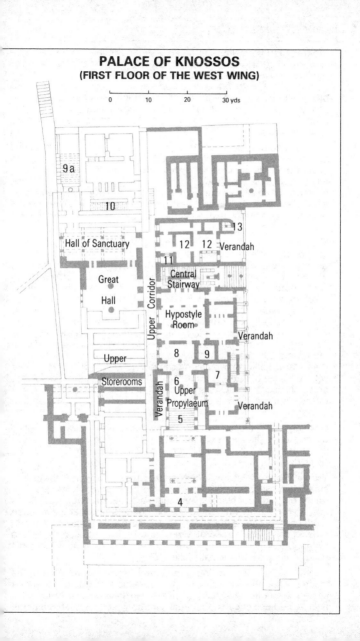

PALACE OF KNOSSOS
(FIRST FLOOR OF THE WEST WING)

0   10   20   30 yds

9a

10

Hall of Sanctuary

13

12   12   Verandah

11

Central Stairway

Great

Hall

Hypostyle Room

Verandah

Upper Corridor

8   9

7

Upper

6

Storerooms

Upper Propylaeum

Verandah

Verandah

5

4

the fresco are now kept in the Herakleion Museum. The best preserved figures are those depicting two vase-bearers and the rhyton or
cupbearer. These frescoes were made c. 1400 BC. The corridor twice
turned to the l. to come out opposite the large propylaeum (S
propylaeum) which gave access to the public part of the palace. The
southern part of the corridor is no longer there. To reach the
propylaeum you now have to turn l. (see plan) and cross three of the
subsidiary rooms.

S propylaeum – You reach this across a light-well (plan, 4) placed
between the Corridor of the Procession and the propylaeum to
ensure that this monumental gateway was well lit; it stands on four
pillars and passing through it one came to a magnificent, wide
staircase (plan, 5) leading to the first floor. The propylaeum was
decorated with frescoes (partly restored) showing bearers of
offerings, in particular vase-bearers (on the l.); note too the sacred
horns.

First floor – Next you go on up to the first floor (from this point follow
the first floor plan from staircase no. 5). This storey was restored by
Sir Arthur Evans, on the basis of those parts of the walls found in
position. First cross the upper propylaeum, then a vestibule (plan, 6)
which brings you to a corridor which was lit on the r. by a window
overlooking a light-well (plan, 7). Ahead of you another vestibule
(plan, 8) leads into a hypostyle room known as the tri-columnar
shrine; another room opening into this is called the Treasure Room
(plan, 9). A long upper corridor ran along the l. side of the hypostyle
hall and most of the rooms in the upper floor were served by this. On
the l. were a series of store-rooms, some of which can still be seen,
then a large hall with two columns followed by the room of the shrine
with two rows of three columns. The NW part of this floor, which has
now collapsed, comprised a staircase (plan, 9a) which led down into
the W Court and, it is thought, a staircase (plan, 10) going up to a
higher floor.

Now go back into the upper corridor and look down through a
window on to the kitchen (plan, 11) on the floor below. Go through a
series of rooms (plan, 12) built above the Throne Room. One contains
some copies of frescoes.

Throne Room – Pass by a terrace that formed a verandah down a
small staircase (plan, 13) to the Throne Room (plan, 14; you are back
on the ground floor plan); an anteroom with several entrances stands
in front of this, in which you should notice a basin and a wooden
model of a throne. In the Throne Room there is an alabaster seat with
a back, called the throne of Minos, and part of a fresco showing a
griffin. Steps lead down to a small room at a lower level which must
have contained a lustral bath (plan, 15).

Central court – Go out into the central court and walk along the
facade of the W wing (turn r.). It is possible that bull dancing of a
sacred description may have taken place in the great courtyard of this
palace, perhaps copying the ritual ceremony at the investiture of the

Pharaohs in honour of Apis which took place on the dromos of Egyptian temples.

W wing – After passing the large staircase which served the first floor and two storeys above it that have disappeared, you will see the façade of a small shrine known as the tripartite shrine (plan, 16) which has a colonnade along the side opening on to the courtyard. The entrance into the shrine leads into an antechamber (plan, 17), giving access to the room of the tall jars (still to be seen) and on the r. the treasury of the snake goddess (plan, 18). From there go back to the antechamber, then make a detour to the site where a Greek temple dedicated to Rhea (plan, 19) was built at a later stage, and look at a Minoan bathroom (plan, 20) beside it, where you will see a small bath, drains, etc. Go back to the antechamber of the tripartite shrine to visit two pillar crypts (plan, 21), each with a quadrangular central pillar. It appears that the double-axe symbols deeply incised on these pillars indicate the religious nature of these two crypts. You then go into the Corridor of the Storerooms linking a series of 22 storerooms where various goods, such as oil, wine and grain, were kept. It seems that these, in which the double-axe symbol can be seen engraved on the wall in several places, were adjuncts of the shrine. Moreover they were directly linked with the two crypts, and pyramidal bases were found in the corridor for holding bronze double axes. Under the corridor and store room paving stones, pits may have been used as secret hiding-places for treasure. In a few cells separated from one another by thick partition walls you can still see a good number of storage jars (pithoi).

Further on you come to the Archives Room with hieroglyphic tablets. Then return to the central court passing a group of rooms (plan, 22) on the l. which are probably traces of the first palace.

Prince with the lilies corridor – You cross the courtyard to reach the corridor of the Prince with the lilies which opened off the S side of the courtyard. There you can see a copy of the fresco of the *Prince with the lilies*; Evans called him the 'priest-king'; he is wearing a crown and necklace of lilies (the original, which is heavily restored, is in Herakleion Museum). At the end of the corridor on the r. a staircase (plan, 23) went up to the upper floor.

Grand staircase – Go back across the courtyard veering to the r. to reach the grand staircase (plan, 24) of the eastern wing of the palace that led to the royal apartments. This staircase which linked five floors consists, in the part that has been restored, of several flights lit by a light-well to which the stairs are linked by galleries with columns. Guards on sentry duty on the verandahs around the light-well watched over the comings and goings in that part of the palace. The verandahs were decorated with frescoes, some of which have been reconstituted; look at the shields fresco – the shields are shaped like the figure 8 (original in Herakleion Museum). Leave the verandah of the royal guard through the door decorated with rosettes; note the flight of stairs that led to the upper floor and a service stair (plan, 25) that served the lower floor.

Royal apartments – The corridor then bends to the r.; pass the king's Treasure Room (plan, 26) on the l. to glance into the little court of the distaffs (plan, 27) and go into the so-called 'bench' room in the area of the royal apartments (plan, 28). Then pass in front of the queen's megaron (plan, 29) on the l. above the rooms that have been built as a basement and go towards the S part of the E wing of the palace, lying at least 3ft (1m) lower, to look at a tiny child's bathroom (plan, 30) with a terracotta bathtub still in it; behind this there is a small room containing storage jars.

Shrine of the double axes – Next you come to the small shrine of the double axes (plan, 31) which dates from a later period subsequent to the destruction of the palace; cult statues, sacred horns, vases and an offering-table were found there. Beside it there is a small lustral basin (plan, 32) with steps leading to it. Further S is the SE staircase (plan, 33) one flight of which is still there, partly restored.

S of the palace the ruins of the various houses have also been uncovered, including that known as the house of the 'sacrificed oxen' (plan, 34) which stood to the W of the house of the 'fallen blocks' (plan, 35) and the house of the chancel screen which has been partly restored. This house owes its name to a platform which is reached from a side staircase and is supported by two columns (plan, 36). Further E you can see the remains of the SE house which are protected by a plastic roof. Below the Corridor of the Procession is the South house, which was that of the chief priest; in it you can see a small crypt shrine and a series of rooms on three storeys.

The queen's apartments – Retrace your steps to the service stair (plan, 25) built into part of the grand staircase that led to the royal apartments. Go down this staircase, and at the bottom on the l. there are doors opening to the lower level of the verandah of the royal guard and on the r. leading into the queen's apartments. Going r. you will see first the archives of the inscribed tablets (plan, 26) where the famous ivory acrobat was found, then the queen's boudoir (plan, 28) which is lit from the court of the distaffs. This room included plumbing with a lavatory connected to a drainage system. From there go next into the queen's megaron (plan, 29) which receives light from two light-wells and has a bathroom opening off it. Observe the copies of the dolphin fresco which was found in the megaron.

The king's megaron – Go through the door under the dolphin painting to reach the king's megaron across the hall of the double axes, lit by a light-well on the l. A throne beneath a canopy (behind a protective window) indicates that the king sometimes gave audiences in this room. Note the two large figure-of-eight shields (copies) and the double-axe symbols carved on a wall. By following the corridor on the l. of the canopy you will come back to the verandah of the royal guard and can go up to the next floor by means of the grand staircase.

The king's apartments – Almost facing but slightly to the right of the door to which the staircase leads, follow the compartmented corridor which takes you into the storeroom of the jars with medallions (plan, 37). Turn to the r. in order to visit the first floor of the king's apartments passing in front of the corridor of the draught (checker) board; take note of a staircase on the l. which you use to go down after looking at the royal apartments.

Domestic quarters – At the bottom of the staircase go l. to get to the domestic quarters which included workshops, magazines, etc. Go first to the lapidary's workshop (plan, 38) where craftsmen cut precious stones for the king; then you pass the potter's workshop (plan, 39), the court of the stone spout (plan, 40) and the storeroom of the giant jars (plan, 41) that dates back to the first-Palace period, in which you will see four large storage jars (pithoi). Go down the staircase passing in front of this storeroom to reach the east bastion which overlooks the valley. Note the arrangement for carrying water with small square filtering troughs. Go back up the stairs and turn r. after the storeroom of the giant pithoi; originally there were other storerooms there (plan, 42), but today they are in ruins.

N passage – Now proceed to the N entrance of the palace, passing by various rooms which were service apartments. The N entrance is formed by a long ramp which joined up with the road to the harbour. This sloping passage is overlooked by bastions with verandahs one of which – the one on the l. – is decorated by a relief painting of a bull (plan, 43; copy — original in Herakleion Museum). The passge ends in a hypostyle hall with 11 pillars which marked the end, by means of a propylaeum on the l. (plan, 44), of the road from the harbour which connected further to the W with the royal road.

Lustral basin – As you proceed towards the theatre pause on the l. to see a lustral basin which has been reconstituted. It is similar to the basin in the Throne Room.

The Theatre – This building, which is composed of two tiers of seats at right-angles to one another, is one of the most ancient parts of the Minoan palaces. It may be that sacred dances were performed on the esplanade enclosed by the benches, or bull-dancing displays may have been held there, such as those so brilliantly illustrated on one of the frescoes of the Palace at Knossos. In the foreground note the foundation, supposed to be that of the royal box.

A Minoan road – From the theatre a paved way links up with a Minoan road, restored by Sir Arthur Evans, and connects with the N propylaeum of the palace. It goes down into a cutting, and on the l. you can see the ruins of several houses, including the house of the frescoes. In its final state the road dates from the period of the last palace (Late Minoan II; 15th century BC), but beneath it traces of older roads have been found.

The palace vicinity – 440yds (400m) beyond the exit along the Pyrgos road (l.) you come to the ruins of a viaduct; it had a carriageway that served the S entrance of the palace, and ended in a staircase with several flights of steps. About 220yds (200m) beyond the viaduct there is a huge building known as the caravanserai; the main room was decorated with frescoes (hoopoes and partridges; originals in Herakleion Museum), and there were baths there. Travellers could stop at this building to freshen up before entering the royal palace. If you follow the path along the side of the l. bank of the ravine spanned by the viaduct you skirt the E side of the palace to reach the royal villa which lies on the r. of the path at a lower level. On the ground floor there is a large room entered from a vestibule, with a niche at the end of it for a throne. After visiting the royal villa carry on along the side of the ravine as far as the village of Makrys Teichos where you take a small asphalted road on the l. which leads back to the Herakleion-Knossos road. Turn l. here to get to the little palace on the r.-hand side of the road. It consists of a number of halls and pillared crypts; a small temple known as the fetish shrine was attached to it. It was built in the Late Minoan III (14th century BC), and is now restored. The Minoan town which extended all round the palace has not yet been fully excavated.

5 Mesara (Gortyn, Phaestos, Hagia Triada)

This trip is one of the most fascinating you can undertake from Herakleion. It takes you through the countryside towards the Minoan sites of Phaestos and Hagia Triada by way of Gortyn (see Two days in Herakleion, programme for second day).

Route: from Herakleion to Gortyn, 28.4mls (45.5km); to Phaestos, 38.1mls (61km); to Hagia Triada, 39.7mls (64km) on good roads (the return journey for visiting the three sites should be 79.5mls (128km), or 106mls (170km) if you make the recommended detour to the monasteries of Vrondisi and Valsamonero, or 120.5mls (194km) for the round trip if you go to the beach of Matala).

Exit along Chania road (Chania; map A-1/2). 1.9mls (3km): Turn l. 4.4mls (7km).

Alternative route – turn r. to Voutes, Hagios Miron and Asites. 3mls (5km) after the last village Prinias (a necropolis with cremated remains and burial places of horses); then across a mountain pass and a path on the r. takes you to the site of ancient Rizenia, near the village of Prinias. The ruins of Rizenia are at the spot known as Patela; they were explored by an Italian mission which uncovered the traces of two 7th–6th century BC temples (decorative sculpture from the oldest of the two is one of the prize items in Gallery XIX of Herakleion Museum).

A small fortress was built on the acropolis during the Hellenistic period (fine view). You rejoin the main itinerary at 17.5mls (28km).

12.5mls (20km): Venerato; an unsurfaced road (l.) leads to the (0.9mls/1.5km) convent of Paliani which until the 14th century belonged to the patriarchate of Constantinople. Embroidery and other needlework made by the nuns can be brought there.

17.5mls (28km): Hagia Varvara.

18.7mls (30km): 8.7mls (14km) away on the r. Zaros, the village from which you can reach (2.5mls/4km) the monastery of Vrondisi and (4.4mls/7km) the monastery of Hagios Phanourios of Valsamonero. (In the programme for the second day in Herakleion this visit is planned for the end of the afternoon.)

MONASTERY OF VRONDISI (turn r. 1.8mls/3km beyond Zaros). Inside the church you will see some 14th-century frescoes, but also at the entrance to the monastery there is one of the finest Venetian fountains in Crete (15th century). Monastery of Hagios Phanourios of Valsamonero (key available from the mayor's office in the village). The monastery, which must date from the 13th century, is in ruins, but the church, which remains intact, has what must be regarded as some of the finest *frescoes in Crete. The church consists of two naves which are linked on the W by a nave acting as a narthex. The nave on the l.-hand side, which is the older, dates from the 14th century, while the r.-hand one and the narthex were added between 1407 and 1431. Scenes from the life of the Virgin (14th century) are depicted on the vaulted ceiling of the l.-hand nave; other frescoes in this nave show various saints and were carried out towards the end of the 14th century or the beginning of the 15th century. The other naves are decorated with 15th-century mural paintings.

From the village of Kamares 2.5mls (4km) beyond the monastery you could go on to the famous Kamares cave 4,990ft (1,520m) up on the S slopes of Mt Ida – it is a 5-hr walk. The archaeologists who carried out excavations there, first English and then Italian, discovered some remains from the Middle Minoan period and in particular a remarkable collection of vases of a very individual style, known as 'eggshell' ware.

27.5mls (44km): Hagii Deka, on the edge of the Mesara plain which is the largest in Crete and seems to be a small corner of Africa here in the heart of the island.

From Hagii Deka to Lendas (16.9mls/27km). If you have a car in good condition and a high level of enthusiasm for archaeology, we recommend this supplementary journey to the ruins of ancient Lebena. Take the Phaestos road and turn l. towards Platanos 0.6mls (1km) from the village.

3.7mls (6km): Platanos, in the Mesara, where several beehive tombs from the pre-Palatial period were found. Now follow the road to Plora, then to Apesokarion.

6.2mls (10km): Apesokarion, where more tombs were discovered. Now follow the road to Miamou and Lendas; the road is bad, but the countryside is very beautiful.

16.9mls (27km): Lendas, near the site of ancient Lebena, by the sea, where in the 4th century BC the people of Gortyn dedicated a temple to Asclepius near thermal springs. The shrine was flourishing mainly during the Roman period. The site was explored by an Italian archaeological mission, and then by Greek scholars. You may be disappointed by the state of the ruins, but not by the beauty of the *site.

A good hundred yards from the little beach lying between two promontories are the remains of the shrine, with a temple. It stood on an artificial terrace cut out of the rock. The rear wall backing on to the hill is still quite well preserved. Beyond the temple the remains of a building of the Hellenic period were dug up, probably a treasury. The building carried on into a portico with a marble monumental staircase in front of it, on the r. Another portico was built out from the staircase, thought to be an abaton which had a nymphaeum at its E end. The spring, which is believed to have been at the origin of the shrine to Asclepius, was rediscovered E of the temple. Nearer the beach two pools with stuccoed sides had been hollowed out which may have been used for the complete immersion of the sick. Still nearer to the water's edge the ruins of some vast building were uncovered, perhaps a katagogeion or hotel for lodging the sick; part of it was a rotunda nearly 40ft (12m) in diameter which may have been a thermal establishment.

Standing at the foot of a hill, the little 11th-century church of Hagios Ioannis with 14th- or 15th-century frescoes.

28.4mls (45.5km): Gortyn, a dead town the ruins of which, scattered under magnificent olive trees, will give you some idea of what a provincial capital in Roman times could be, for there you will see most of the public and religious buildings that such a city would include. Gortyn was the Roman capital of the province of Crete and Cyrenaica.

AM AMBITIOUS CITY. There was a modest settlement on the site of the acropolis from the pre-Mycenaean period, but it became important only from the Archaic period (end of 7th century BC). Gortyn took over from Phaestos as capital of the Mesara. Its history is not really known until the 4th century BC, the period at which it was struggling with Knossos for supremacy over the island. Gortyn sought Macedonia as an ally and in the 3rd century BC was part of the Cretan *Koinon*, an association grouping together some of the main cities of the island. It took part in the Lyttos war (220 BC) against Knossos. Though later on it made overtures to Rome it offered asylum to the Carthaginian Hannibal in 189 BC.

CAPITAL AT LAST. What Gortyn was unable to achieve as an independent city was eventually granted to it under Roman dominion. After their conquest of the island (69–67 BC), the Romans turned it into the foremost city of Crete and the capital of that island and of Cyrenaica, which together formed a single province. In the 4th century AD Constantine the Great separated Cyrenaica from Crete, but Gortyn continued to be the capital of the island, and consequently from the earliest days of Christianity became a great religious centre. It no doubt went into fairly rapid decline after Arab occupation, which lasted for a period of more than 130 years (827–

961). Since 1970 Italian archaeologists have resumed excavations.

Open: daily 08.30–12.30 and 16.00–18.00; Sun. 09.00–15.00; entrance fee; allow 1hr to see the main sights. Go by car if possible.

Basilica of Hagios Titos – This church was built, according to P. Lermerie, in the 7th or 8th century, and the apse is almost all that is left standing. It combines the plan of an early Christian basilica with that of a cruciform church. The basilica stood near one of Gortyn's two agoras of which only slight traces have been found. The earliest agora dating from the 6th century BC was connected with the cult of Pythian Apollo.

The Odeon – This was built during Trajan's reign at the beginning of the 2nd century AD. It is most noted for the famous Gortyn laws engraved on slabs of stone taken from an older building. They date from the 5th century BC and are written in a Dorian dialect using a special alphabet. The laws distinguish the different categories of citizens; slaves; serfs, who are tied to their land, but are accorded the

right to own livestock and some personal property; and free men, who could be either civilians or military men. The latter were grouped into hetairiai, associations of comrades who ate together in the city's common mess or andreion – a system similar to the Spartian model and common in Cretan cities. The laws deal with rules governing the liberty of the individual, codify crimes of violence against the person, and cover the sharing of inheritances, succession, gifts, etc.

Several buildings have stood on the site of the odeon. In the Hellenistic period there was a square building in which materials from other edifices were re-used. Traces of this building, the purpose of which is not known, can still be seen between the two doors leading into the ambulacrum of the odeon, and on the r. to the W of the stage (Archaic base with two tiers). The odeon was itself built with the help of older elements from a tholos (beehive tomb), dating from the Archaic period, on which the text of the laws was engraved. It was restored in the 3rd or 4th century AD.

The Acropolis – On the other side of the ravine cut by a small stream stand the ruins of the auditorium of a theatre built on the S slope of the hill of the acropolis. On the acropolis an Italian mission found the imposing foundations of a temple that had been altered several times; in its earliest state it dated from the end of the Geometric period (7th or late 8th century BC); it was built on the site of a pre-Mycenaean settlement (c.10th century BC). In the centre of the temple there was a bothros, a sacrificial altar made of alabaster slabs. The remains of an imposing 43ft- (13m-) long sacrificial altar were also uncovered on the western slope of the acropolis hill.

A temple to Egyptian gods – About 100yds (92m) away on the other side of the road lie the remains of a temple dedicated to Isis and Serapis. It consists of a cella and annexes with a lustral basin. On the architrave, which is still in its original place, an inscription informs us that the temple was built by Flavia Philyra and her two sons.

A temple to Pythian Apollo – This shrine dedicated to Pythian Apollo (see Delphi) was founded during the Archaic period (blocks with inscriptions going back to at least the 6th century BC) on the site of a Minoan building of which there are still a very few traces, for example a wall and a few gypsum flagstones inside the Hellenistic pronaos.

Near this temple are the ruins of a little theatre built in brick which was connected with the shrine to Apollo.

In its final form the temple dates from the Hellenistic era, but it was restored during the Roman period and at that time two colonnades were added dividing the cella into three naves and an apse in which stood a statue of Apollo Citharoedus. In front of the temple there is a paved square with a pool (in front of the door) and an altar from the Roman period in a good state of preservation. Nearby are the remains of a late 3rd- or early 2nd-century BC heroön (monument to a hero).

Praetorium – This building, which was the residence of the governor of the province of Crete and Cyrenaica and the administrative centre of the province, was constructed of brick at the beginning of the 2nd century AD in Trajan's reign, then rebuilt in the 4th century, probably after the earthquake in 374 AD. The 4th-century praetorium comprised a large basilica-type hall with a monumental columned facade connected to a magnificent portico with two rows of columns that have recently been uncovered.

Beyond the praetorium are several buildings in a very damaged state: two late 2nd-century AD nymphaeums, public baths and a 2nd-century AD amphitheatre. Going from the praetorium, ignoring the not very interesting ruins lying S of it, you can proceed to a small museum built on the outer edge of the village of Hagii Deka (there is a plan to move it on to the Gortyn site). In it there are a few architectural fragments, sculptures and inscriptions. Nearby stands a Byzantine basilica with three naves and re-used columns from an earlier building and capitals with acanthus leaves. It is dedicated to the Ten Saints (Hagii Deka) who died as martyrs in 260 AD.

Do not look for the Byzantine basilica, destroyed in the 5th and 6th century, situated to the S of the road on the map. Only some broken columns remain, covered with scrub.

Italian archaeologists are now uncovering the N fortification of the Hellenistic town (3rd-2nd century BC), around which a high defensive wall (2mls/3km long, 13-16ft/4-5m thick) was built. A second, narrower wall was built in the mid-2nd century BC and is mostly outside the first. The statement of the Greek writer Strabo, from the Roman era, noting that: 'Ptolemy IV of Egypt has concluded the construction of a fortified wall at Gortyn, but he has built only eight *stadia*' (an ancient measurement) thus seems to be confirmed. Traces of an unfinished wall can be seen.

33.1mls (53km): Mires, where a road dwindling to a track goes off on the r. leading to Moni Odigitrias, a fortified monastery (fine icons). Beyond this you come to the magnificent bay of Kali Limenes, regrettably disfigured by petrol storage tanks.

The road to Messara continues for 4½mls (7km) to Timbaki close to a fine beach (on the S side). From here you can get to Rethymnon 43mls (69km) (V. section 2) on the road from Chania to Herakleion and Sitia. You may also leave the road and go to the l. towards Phaestos 1½mls (2km).

36.9mls (59km): 1.2mls (2km) to the l. ***Phaestos (Phaestum). The ruins of the palace here are among the most impressive archaeological discoveries to be seen in Greece. The palace at Phaestos was smaller than that of Knossos, but the buildings were more carefully constructed using better quality materials. They have not, moreover, been the object of considerable restoration, with the result that what remains seems more authentic.

A HOMERIC CITY. Phaestos, which was mentioned by Homer, was one of the most ancient cities of Crete. According to legend it was founded by Minos. Much later the town was destroyed by Gortyn

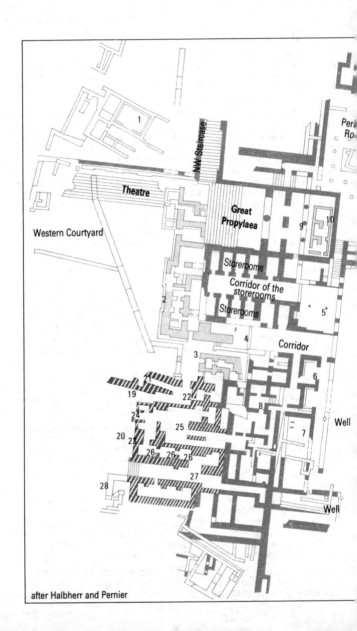

1

NW Staircase

Theatre

Great
Propylaea

Western Courtyard

Peri
Ro

9   10

Storerooms

Corridor of the
storerooms

Storerooms

5

2

4

Corridor

3

6

21

19

22

24

8

25

Well

20 23

7

26   26 26

27

Well

28

after Halbherr and Pernier

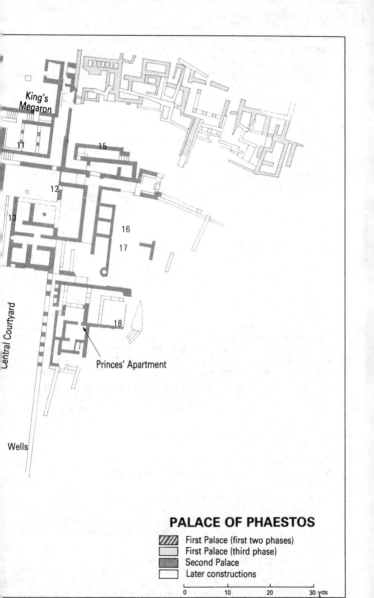

King's
Megaron

11   15

12

13   16

17

Central Courtyard

18

Princes' Apartment

Wells

PALACE OF PHAESTOS

First Palace (first two phases)
First Palace (third phase)
Second Palace
Later constructions

0   10   20   30 yds

which appropriates its territory. Strabo said that the poet Epimenides came from Phaestos.

The palace of Phaestos was built on a hilltop, on terraces at different levels linked by steps. The plan is like that at Knossos, but more regular.

Open daily 10.00–16.00; entrance fee. Allow approx. 1hr for visiting the palace. Those interested in archaeology may visit the museum of stratigraphy (with permission).

The Phaestos site was explored from 1900 on by the Italian School of Athens which uncovered the remains of two palaces, the later one built on top of the earlier one. More recent excavations have established the existence of two other earlier palaces, remains of which are particularly extensive in the SE part of the site. We will keep to the terminology of the Italian archaeologists, distinguishing between two periods of construction: the first-Palace period (Middle Minoan II–III: approx. 2000–1650 BC) and the second-Palace period (Middle Minoan III–Late Minoan II: approx. 1650–1400 BC). The ruins of the second palace are the more significant. In the first-Palace building period three phases can be identified, as recent excavations have shown. Remains from the third phase of the first palace are to be seen especially on the W façade and to the NE of the site, while remains of buildings from the first and second phases of the first palace (the oldest parts) are to be found in the SW area.

**Theatre – Approaching from the tourist pavilion you enter the palace area across an esplanade which is still cluttered with the remains of Hellenistic and Roman buildings (plan, 1). You are then confronted by the eight tiers of the theatre which was connected with the nearby palace. The W court lay in front of the theatre stretching over a vast area and serving as an arena for dancing and games.

W court – The l. side of the Court is formed by a wall with orthostats (plan, 2), limestone slabs standing upright making an external decoration at the base of the palace. Behind this wall were a shrine with a sacrificial trench and a chapel with gypsum benches on which cult objects and statuettes could be displayed. This part dates from the third phase of the first palace.

Central court – From the propylaeum you go to the central court along a corridor belonging to the second palace, built on the site of the first one.

Under the poorly preserved paved floor of the corridor the flooring of a passageway made up of beautiful alabaster slabs, corresponding to the third phase of the first palace, has recently been discovered. This passageway was divided from a series of rooms lying to the N by a wall; a remnant of this wall (plan, 4) can still be seen.

The buildings of the second palace were grouped round the huge central court which used to have porticoes with alternating round columns and square pillars forming its E, W and possibly S sides. As at Knossos the court may have been used as a setting for bull dancing displays when the spectators would have positioned themselves under the galleries behind the balustrades.

The N section of the W colonnade opened not onto a gallery but onto a megaron, the pillared hall (plan, 5). The part of the western wing lying further S is fairly dilapidated; it is possible to recognize a resting-place (plan, 6), then a crypt with two square pillars (plan, 7) with a lustral basin (plan, 8) behind it.

Storerooms – From the central court pass into the pillared hall which is lined with slabs of alabastrine gypsum and led by means of a wide corridor to a double row of storerooms. In the last storeroom on the r. you can see an ingenious arrangement for collecting oil spilt from the storage jars. From the pillared hall proceed to the site of a large state room (plan, 9), a kind of official megaron on the Cretan plan which opened on the W on to a vestibule that could be reached by means of a monumental staircase forming large propylaea. Below the western part of the megaron you can see more storerooms (plan, 10) dating from the third phase of the first palace; there are a few Middle Minoan storage jars in them.

Royal living area – From the 'official megaron' proceed to a huge state room with a peristyle in the private part of the palace where the king's and queen's apartments were situated. First visit the queen's megaron (plan, 11) which consists of a tripartite room with columns and a light-well. A staircase led up to the next floor where the queen's bedroom must have been. A small courtyard (plan, 12) to the S of the megaron could be reached by a corridor (plan, 13). There was a way from the queen's megaron into the much larger king's megaron which opened to the N on to a gallery with a colonnade. Go from the king's megaron, also lit by a light-well, to the lustral bath (plan, 14). A few traces of service quarters from the third phase of the first Palace period were discovered in the NE area. Of particular note was the famous Phaestos disc (in Herakleion Museum) dug up there from a secret hiding-place. Further S there are more remains from the second palace including a wash-house (plan, 15) and workshops (plan, 16) with a courtyard (plan, 17) to the E of them where a furnace for smelting metals was uncovered. Near the NE corner of the central court S of the workshop area were the princes' apartments (?) in which a small courtyard (plan, 18) has been distinguished with a portico on two sides.

Earliest palaces – The walls that can be seen in the SW area are the remains of the most ancient palaces in Crete. You can see the remains of a bastion (plan, 19) from the first palace to which a second defence was built during the second-Palace period. A ramp starting from the W court (plan, 20) went round the bastion and led to the high part of the palace by means of a passageway (plan, 21).

This passageway leads to a room (plan, 22) belonging to the second-Palace phase. Leave this room by the passageway with alabaster orthostats which comes out on to the W Court. On the l. of this passage note another wall (plan, 23) with slabs placed upright. A winding corridor (plan, 24) leads to a large room (plan, 25) with a series of rooms opening off the end of it.

Lying beyond this to the S were three rooms used as storerooms (plan, 26) and the second of them still has storage jars in it. From the third storeroom you go into a room (plan, 27) with benches, and linked to the W to a wide paved corridor which must have acted as an atrium or waitingroom. S of the wide staircase leading to the corridor going to room 27, observe some remains of a dwelling (plan, 28) dating from the pre-Mycenaean period.

The road carries on from Phaestos to end at Matala in the S, a little fishing harbour with cliffs riddled with small caves. Zeus is supposed to have accosted Europa here.

About 1.2mls (2km) N of Matala on the slopes of a hill overlooking the sea recent digs have uncovered the traces of a Minoan settlement in the place known as Kommos, and of a Classical-Hellenistic shrine with the remains of a temple and several altars built on to older foundations.

The itinerary continues: 38.1mls (61km): *Hagia Triada, where below a small hill rising from the Mesara you can visit a very romantic Minoan site, with roads bordered by giant reeds and its paved roads overgrown with thriving vegetation; the archaeological tour through the palace and village ruins will remain with you as one of the pleasantest memories of your journey in Crete.

It would seem probable that the palace at Hagia Triada (Holy Trinity; its original name remains unknown) which was unquestionably very grand was the residence of a vassal of the princes of Phaestos. Hagia Triada would have been a Mycenaean centre of power with several buildings, while Phaestos, at the same period, had only private dwellings. From the car park follow the path going down to the ruins; in the distance you will see the Sea of Libya and, in front of you, the palace, the plan of which you will follow from E to W. On your r., at the E end of the palace towards the N, you can make out the ruins of a village, most of the houses of which are very dilapidated and date from Late Minoan III (c. 1375-1100 BC); thus, they were built after the destruction of the palace. On the E side of the village Italian archaeologists have unearthed the walls of an agora of the same era, comprising a portico beneath which were several storerooms. To the NE of the village are a few remains of a cemetery: two tombs with a cupola and, above these, on a hillock, a small square vault which contained the famous painted sarcophagus of the Herakleion museum.

From the entrance gate you reach the palace, contemporary with the second palace of Phaestos, which was destroyed at the same time. You will then be in a courtyard of altars where a sacrificial altar was discovered near a depository for Mycenean ex-voto offerings. On the E it was bordered by a paved walk which probably linked Hagia Triada with Phaestos. On the other side of this walk is a storeroom which was part of a house of the same epoch as the palace, to the S of which lie the ruins of a temple built at the end of Middle Minoan III or the start of Late Minoan I (*c.*1550). This temple must have been burnt down at the same time as the palace, but it was rebuilt and was in use in the Late Minoan III.

On the N side of the court of altars are the fragments of a Mycenaean portico (plan, 1), built above the remains of the palace after its destruction. Slightly more to the W note a staircase (plan, 2) leading to an upper storey.

By another staircase (plan, 3) on the NE side of the court of altars you will reach the sea ramp, another paved walk, stepped, which went along the N side of the palace; you can see the redans, characteristic of Minoan architecture. At the E end is a portico (plan, 4) of the same date as the palace.

Following the sea ramp to the W you will first find on your l. a room (plan, 5) that had a window opening to the N. Then look at the imposing walls of a Mycenaean megaron built on the site of old palace storerooms (there are still storage jars in them). This building which dates from Late Minoan III (approx. 1375–1100 BC) had a small loggia (plan, 6) on the side nearest the altar court. All that remains of the loggia is its pavement, the base of a column and a bench.

A room (plan, 7) lying inside the perimeter covered by the megaron and lined with slabs of alabastrine gypsum must have been particularly splendid. A staircase near this room led to another series of store-rooms (plan, 8) built at a lower level.

The W wing of the palace lay beyond the walls of the megaron. On the side near the ramp a staircase (plan, 9), added after the palace had been completed stands against the facade. Another flight of steps (plan, 10; on the r. as you approach from the ramp) leading to a quite well-preserved door (partly restored) gave access to a small courtyard in the centre of which was a stone basin which used to have a water jet, with a tiny three-columned portico on two of its sides. From there you go into a small room once decorated with frescoes, now in the Herakleion Museum, then another larger room (plan, 11), which opens on the N on to a room with slate paving stones and an alabaster bench now almost completely in ruins. You come next to a portico (plan, 12) with two columns, also in ruins, but with the column bases still in position. This portico overlooked a light-well or a little court which also had a portico along it, and passing under this you come to a room (plan, 13), the walls of which are still partly lined with alabastrine gypsum slabs alternating so as to form a series of triglyphs and metopes. This room, which is in quite a good state of preservation, is protected by a roof. Go from there to the small adjoining room on the l. where a large slab of gypsum embedded in the ground may have served as a bed, with animal skins or blankets over it to make it more comfortable.

Beyond this group of rooms near the edge of the terrace were some service rooms (kitchens).

Before leaving the Hagia Triada site visit the small chapel of Hagios Georgios with 14th-century frescoes. (Ask the guard on the site for the key.)

Take the road to Phaestos but at the fork turn r. towards Matala. Beyond Phaestos, the road continues S. At ¾ml (a good km), at the exit from the village of Pitsidia, a track to the r. leads to a superb sandy beach, the site of Kommos, of great archaeological interest. Sir Arthur Evans guessed as much in 1924, but excavations began only in 1976, directed by the Canadian professor Joseph W. Shaw and his wife Maria. The site, protected by a wire grill fence, is not open to the public but you can walk around it and note three main centres of excavation. First at the top of a hill, then on the S flank of the same hill were discovered a series of houses of the Minoan era (respectively end of Middle Minoan and Late Minoan, 1800–1250 BC). The groups of houses were separated from one another by narrow,

PALACE OF
HAGIA TRIADA

0   10   20 yds

VILLAGE

Agora
Portico
Storerooms

PALACE

9
Sea- Ramp
1
10
Megaron
7   8   5
11
2
12   13
3
6
4
Storerooms
Paved Highway
Courtyard of the Altars
Minoan House
Hagios Georgios
Temple
Road to Phaestos

paved alleyways. This work done in these two areas has revealed certain aspects of Minoan life: the use of *pithoi* and the press (perhaps for wine) for example.

But it is to the S of these residential districts that the Minoan site takes on an unusual dimension. A wide paved road (about 6'7"/2.66m) running W–E, and therefore away from the sea, turns to the NE (at the E fence), towards the Palaces of Phaestos and Hagia Triada. This road, spectacular in itself, is bordered on the S by a long series of imposing buildings; the size of the stones making up the walls is sometimes 6'7" (2.66m) long, 3' (almost 1m) high and 8" (35cm) thick. Following on the first building to the W and partly eroded by the sea, a wall 60yds (55m) in length appears to be, for the Minoan era, a unique example in Crete of construction in perfectly cut stone. This enormous façade belonged to a building comprising several rooms, and partially closed to the S by a portico with columns (foundations of 5 columns) giving on to a large pebbled courtyard; further to the E the rooms gave on to a long corridor; these buildings may have been storehouses. Among objects discovered have been anchors and pottery from Cyprus and Italy. While a definite conclusion is not yet possible, it seems that Kommos may have been an important Minoan port, trading with other Mediterranean countries. Unlike other Minoan sites, no trace has been found of the devastating catastrophe of 1450 BC but the town was deserted c. 1250 BC.

The first digs in the S part of the site, then buried in the sand, revealed the existence of three successive temples built on the same site (above the paved road and the imposing Minoan buildings); the first small temple, which dates from c. 950 BC, gave way to a second, with signs of strong Phoenician influence and used between the 9th and 7th centuries BC. A last Greek post-Minoan sanctuary in use towards 150 BC, and comprising four rectangular altars in the centre of a courtyard surrounded by buildings, covered the earlier ruins. The present excavations should produce more decisive evidence.

44mls (70km): Matala, a fishing port with cliffs honeycombed with a multitude of caves. Zeus, it is said, accosted Europa here. It was, with Kommos, one of the ports of Phaestos in the Minoan era, then of Gortyn in the Hellenistic period. An attractive place for the beauty of the setting, the sandy beach and the limpid sea.

Beyond Hagia Triada the Mesara road carries on to (2.5mls/4km) Timbaki near a lovely sandy beach on the S coast. From there you can drive to (43mls/69km) Rethymnon (see Crete, Section 2) on the road from Khania to Herakleion and Sitia.

6 Hagios Nikolaos and its vicinity

Lying tucked into the Gulf of Mirabello, one of the finest harbours in Greece, Hagios Nikolaos is undoubtedly the most delightful little sea-front in Crete, as well as being a very pleasant and fashionable bathing resort; perhaps too much so, in the opinion of some people who regret the artificial promotion of this 'Cretan Saint-Tropez'. It is also an ideal centre for excursions in the E part of the island where the beauty – and to some extent exoticism – of the natural sites will vie for your attention with the omnipresent riches of archaeology.

Apart from a small archaeological museum and a Byzantine church, Hagios Nikolaos has only its beaches (the ones on the Elounda road are to be preferred), its little cafés and its marvellous setting to offer – a typically Mediterranean harbour setting, bustling and lively in an as yet completely unforced and unfrenzied way.

Drive along the Gulf of Mirabello to the Spinalonga peninsula for a swim, with relaxation and not archaeology in mind; and go to Kritsa and Lato – late afternoon is a specially good time for that – to see two churches decorated with frescoes and a picturesque mountain village (try the kebabs in the café in the central square: they are delicious), as well as an ancient site.

In the evening mingle with the crowd of spectators-cum-actors sitting at tables on the café and restaurant terraces, perhaps beside the lake.

Visiting the town

The town grew up last century round the *limin* (harbour), Lake Voulismeni, which was said to be bottomless (it is up to 210ft/64m deep). Since 1870 it has been linked to the sea by a narrow channel, which makes it the safest of anchorages. Two streets of shops run up from the harbour to Venizelou Square in the centre of the town.

THE ARCHAEOLOGICAL MUSEUM. *(Tel. 0841–224 62; open: summer 08.30–12.30 and 16.00–18.00; Sun. 09.00–15.00; Tues. closed)* is on the Herakleion road (Konstantin Paleologou Street) and has an interesting collection of objects from local digs (Olous, Sitia, Mochlos, Lato, and others), mainly from the Minoan and Archaic periods (terracotta figures from Lato). Several cases contain the most interesting finds made recently at Mallia, in particular a clay tablet inscribed in Linear A and an almost complete *triton made of chlorite from the Late Minoan IB period, decorated with two carapaced 'genies' making a libation. The Byzantine church of Hagios Nikolaos is to be found at the exit of Hagios Nikolaos town, to the r. of the road to Elounda, on the little peninsula of the Minos Palace Hotel. (Ask for the key at the reception desk of this hotel; your passport will be taken as a guarantee of return.)

VICINITY OF HAGIOS NIKOLAOS

1 OLOUS AND DREROS (13.7mls/22km). From the harbour follow the Elounda road, which skirts the Gulf of Mirabello over which you will have some fine *views. Approx. 3mls (5km) from the harbour you pass near the few remains of a temple in the place known as Sta Lenika; the temple was dedicated to Aphrodite and Ares and rebuilt towards the end of the 2nd century BC, and bitterly fought over by Olous and Lato, the two most important cities in the area.

5.3mls (8.5km): Spinalonga peninsula; near the pleasant Elounda Beach Hotel at the point where the peninsula joins the coast of the Gulf of Mirabello lie the Hellenic ruins of the ancient city of Olous. With a harbour protected by its roads and its islands, Olous was a lively city that had friendly links with Rhodes. An early Christian basilica with a fine mosaic floor was uncovered on the isthmus connecting the peninsula to the main coastline.

Continuing along the bay beyond the Elounda Beach Hotel you can get to (5.6mls/9km) Plaka, a hamlet across from a small island on which the Venetians built a fortress, remodelled in 1526, which was yielded to the Turks only in 1715. There remain, amid impressive ramparts, dilapidated buildings, in particular some 16th-century chapels.

The road then crosses a plateau covered with almond-trees; just after Kasteli there is a track leading to Dreros.

The site of the former Hellenic town where excavations were carried out by the French School of Athens lies on the l. of the Fourni road on top of Hagios Antonios hill where two hillocks represent two acropolises. Near the hollow between the two, the agora from the Archaic period, which like those in the palaces at Knossos and Phaestos, has stepped tiers, may have been used as a setting for displays during festivals.

S of the agora there was a temple from the Geometric period, the Delphinion, dedicated to Apollo, where the sphyrelata (statuettes in hammered bronze) in Heraklion Museum were found, and a large cistern dug out in the late 3rd or early 2nd century BC; as an inscription affirms, it was placed under the protection of Apollo of Delphi. The oldest complete constitutional law in Greece (end of 7th century BC) originated from this site. S of the Delphinion lay a building now in a very ruined condition which has been identified as a prytaneum.

2 KRITSA AND LATO (6.9mls/11km and 9.4mls/15km). Go out along the Sitia road, and turn l. at 0.9mls (1.5km).

6.6mls (10.5km): 110yds (100m) to the r. the marvellous little *church of Panagia Kera stands amid olive trees; three naves, 13th-century.

Most of the frescoes date from the first half of the 14th century. In the S nave scenes from the life of St Anne and St Joachim, and from the childhood of the Virgin; in the central nave the *Life of Christ* and the *Last Judgement*; in the N nave, *Paradise*. The ceiling frescoes show the *Ascension*.

6.9mls (11km): Kritsa, a large village with a population of approx. 2,500, and an important craft centre lying on a sloping hillside in a sea of olive trees. As you leave the village on the Kroustas road on the l. after a bridge, the church of Hagios Georgios stands, with early 14th-century frescoes. To reach the ruins of ancient Lato follow the track, not easy for cars, going off to the r. as you enter the village from Hagios Nikolaos. 2.2mls (3.5km) along this way you will see a small chapel on the r.; take a footpath on the r. that leads to the ruins in about 5mins on foot. The ruins of Lato, a town founded in the 7th century BC which was one of the most powerful cities in Crete, spread over the slopes of two acropolises from which you have a superb *view over a landscape distinguished by its grandeur and wild beauty. Lato consists of a very imposing group of ramparts, houses and shops built on terraces in a crater-shaped basin.

The site was excavated by the French School in Athens at the beginning of the 20th century, but work was resumed in 1967. Along the road that climbs towards the agora you can see on the r. workshops and houses that are oblong in shape, a type of house that appeared in the Geometric period and was in use mainly in the 7th and 6th centuries BC, especially in Crete. The houses here are much later in date, for this style of construction, where the rooms are arranged in series, remained popular throughout the town's history.

From the agora you can see, on the l. between two bastions, straight tiers overlooking the square. They must have been used as a meeting-place and led to a prytaneum (3rd century BC) lying immediately above. Other straight tiered seats at the bottom of the polygonal retaining wall of a temple (late 4th/early 3rd century BC) formed a rustic theatre; they are linked with a rectangular exedra with benches. There are also many ruins of public buildings, houses, ramparts and fortified gates rising in stages on the six terraces built into the side of the acropolis and served by a winding road.

3 GOURNIA AND IERAPETRA (22.5mls/36km; go out towards Sitia). The road begins by following the Gulf of Mirabello.

11.9mls (19km): Gournia, which from the distance seems to be no more than a heap of stones, but is of great archaeological significance: it is the only site on the island where it is possible to see a Minoan town (it must date from 1550–1450 BC) with its streets and houses (reduced to the level of foundations).

Towards the middle of the side of the hill nearest to the road climb one of the three roads (plan, 1, 2, 5) which led to the agora. They are paved, and intersected by alleys that often take the form of steps, and obviously have houses on either side. The third on the r. (plan, 3) is the best-preserved house on the site; it stood at the corner of an alleyway with steps, and one of its two entrances opened (r.) on to this. From the alleyway one went into the main room, paved and stuccoed; beside it on the l. was a store-room. A small corridor connected this group of rooms to another large room. Staircases from the corridor gave access to an upper floor. 66ft (20m) l. of the alley was a little shrine (plan, 4). Carry on along this alley and then follow a road on the l. About 33yds (30m) away from the crossroads you will see the ruins of the palace, on a much more modest scale than Knossos, Phaestos or Mallia, which was connected to the agora by means of a paved staircase (plan, 6). The palace comprised a central hall (plan, 7) with storerooms and apartments opening off it. To the E a staircase (plan, 8) went up to a higher level, the palace being built on the side of a hill.

The agora was in fact no more than a huge courtyard occupying the flattened hilltop.

13.7mls (22km): Pahia Amos where you turn r. crossing the Sitia mountains (Mt Afendis, 4,842ft/1,476m). At Episkopi I. of the road a domed Byzantine church with a fine iconostasis. At Kato Horio, a pretty Turkish fountain.

22.5mls (36km): Ierapetra, a harbour town with a pop. of approx.

GOURNIA

0   10   20 yds

5,500, is an easy place to reach on the S coast of the island which at this point may seem somewhat desolate.

A PORT THAT LOOKS TOWARDS AFRICA. Ierapetra is built on the site of the ancient port of Hierapytna which was often at variance with neighbouring towns, especially Itanos and Praesos, in the 2nd century BC. Benefiting from its position on Crete's S coast almost opposite Cyrenaica, the port of Hierapytna was at its height under Roman rule. It was occupied at the beginning of the 13th century by the Genoese who probably built the fortress that can still be seen there, and then by the Venetians.

In the harbour you can visit a little museum with a few local antiquities and a very fine standing statue of Demeter found recently in the house of a peasant of the region, and the fortress which was adapted by the Turks; there is also a Turkish fountain and a minaret, but be a little sceptical if you are shown a small house where, according to local tradition, Napoleon is supposed to have spent the night of 25 June 1798 on his way to Egypt.

From Ierapetra you could return to (26.9mls/43km) Hagios Nikolaos by way of Anatoli and Kalamafka, or further explore the S coast and its lonely beaches by driving to (40.6mls/65km) Sitia via Makrighialos (a detour to Moni Kapsa, an isolated monastery by the sea, is recommended).

Or you could drive to (62.5mls/100km) Herakleion via Ano Viannos (see Crete, Section 3, Vicinity 5); shortly before (10mls/16km) the village of Myrtos you would then pass near the site of the same name where the British School of Athens has recently uncovered a sizeable Early Minoan complex containing more than eighty rooms, with a shrine and an interesting potter's workshop. Nearby at Pyrgos a superb Late Minoan residence overlooks the area and the sea.

In the actual village of Myrtos, there are the remains of a rich Roman villa with mosaic flooring and baths.

4 SITIA (45.6mls/73km) **AND THE EASTERN PART OF THE ISLAND** (see above, up to 13.7mls/22km).

13.7mls (22km): Pahia Amos where you pass the Ierapetra road going off on the r. (see Vicinity 3). The road rises above the coast affording some of the finest *views over the Gulf of Mirabello and the Island of Psira (Minoan remains).

26.9mls (43km): Road on l. for Mokhlos. On the tiny island of the same name are the remains of Minoan houses and burial chambers.

45.6mls (73km): Sitia, reached after driving through Mouliana and the surrounding area, famed for its grapes and its wine.

Sitia, a harbour town with a pop. of 6,000 near the eastern tip of Crete (once-weekly connection with Piraeus; connections by air in season to Rhodes, Karpathos and Athens) – nowadays a depressed area, though it must once have thrived as the Minoan palace at Kato Zakros shows – is a good choice of centre for those who like to leave the beaten track.

THE TOWN OF ONE OF THE SEVEN PILLARS OF WISDOM. Sitia can be identified with ancient Eteia, the town mentioned by Stephanus of Byzantium as the native town of Myson, one of the Seven Sages of Greece. During the Venetian period it was defended by a double perimeter wall rising on the side of the hill on which the kastro stood. The defences of the square and of the kastro were strengthened in 1631, but it was not long before the town fell into the hands of the Turks who restored the fortress.

Sitia no longer has any monument from its past. But for the outstanding beauty of the countryside between Hagios Nikolaos and Sitia this part of Crete would probably attract relatively few visitors. Yet this market town is not devoid of charm, with its brightly coloured houses rising in tiers on the kastro hill.

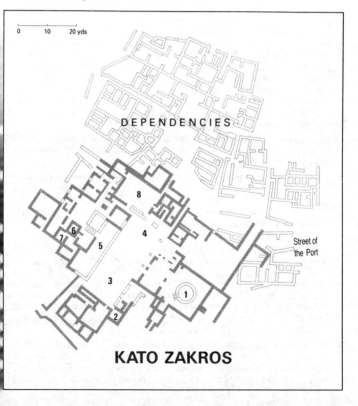

KATO ZAKROS

As you leave Sitia, take the road on the r. for (10.6mls/17km) Presos (follow signs for Chandras).

The ruins of the ancient city of Prasos, founded at the time of the Dorian invasion, cover three hills or acropolises near the modern village of Nea Presos. The British School of Athens at the beginning of this century discovered a megalithic building, the remains of a temple and tombs from the Mycenaean and Geometric periods on this site. There are also extensive indications of Minoan occupation in this area.

55mls (88km): Road on l. (1.2mls/2km) to the monastery of Toplou, which looks like a fortress in its wild, rocky setting. It is dedicated to Panagia (the Virgin) and was built at the beginning of the 17th century. An icon dated 1771 shows it as it was at that date. The church contains one of the masterpieces of Cretan art, a miniature painting of Biblical scenes (1770) by Ioannis Kornaros.

Beyond the monastery the road leads on to (3.7mls/6km) Vaï, a small hamlet, with a road leading to a (2.2mls/3.5km) beach through a palm grove, the only one in Crete. We come to the end of the road at the NE tip of Crete, at Itanos, near the modern village of Eremoupolis; this is a Hellenic site which included two acropolises and was built on a promontory. On the easternmost acropolis nearest to the sea, the French School of Athens discovered some remains indicating that the site had been occupied from the Geometric period up to the Hellenistic period. In the lower part of the town on the isthmus linking the two acropolises French archaeologists found the ruins of a Byzantine town with basilicas, baptisteries and houses.

58.7mls (94km): Paleokastro, a small hamlet near which there was a Byzantine fortress later occupied by the Venetians, for the defence of the eastern coast of the island.

1.2mls (2km) from the village the British School of Athens excavated a sizeable complex inhabited from Early Minoan to Late Minoan on a magnificent site near the sea. The remains of a temple dedicated by the town of Eleia or Heleia to Zeus of Dikti were also identified. The road then crosses an almost desert-like landscape to end at Ano Zakros. A road then leads down to the sea.

74.4mls (119km): Palace of Kato Zakros; near a delightful little beach beyond some banana plantations, the ruins of the Minoan palace of Kato Zakros, excavated since 1960 by N. Platon, form the largest ensemble discovered in eastern Crete but for Mallia. This palace and the neighbouring Minoan town were destroyed c.1450 BC by a violent earthquake, perhaps the same one that disrupted the island of Thera (Santorini), in conjunction with volcanic eruptions. Volcanic ash mixed with sulphur was in fact found in the palace.

The palace covered a surface area of 173 acres (70ha) and in addition to the royal apartments contained store-rooms and various workshops. Like Knossos, Mallia and Phaestos, the palace of Kato Zakros, although smaller, had a huge central courtyard, 100ft (30m) long by 40ft (12m) wide, around which the buildings were ranged. Enter from the E and follow a flag-stoned road named 'Street of the Port'. You will notice, to the l., the remains of a metal-smelting workroom, unique in its period, with its furnace and four air-supply ducts which opened on to an oval room with an access trap and a tap hole directed towards circular pockets constructed on the exterior. This workshop was abandoned in about 1600 BC, with the construction of the new palace on an embankment rich in artifacts, of which the most recent are not later than Middle Minoan III. Turning towards the central courtyard you will see on the r., beneath a shelter, a lustral bath with a stairway leading down to a small cult fountain. To the l. you can see the ruins of a large square room, originally covered, which held a circular pool (1), which can still be seen; a staircase went down to water level, and the water is still running today. In this well, surprisingly, olives almost 3,500 years old were found, perfectly preserved in the water, along with other vegetable matter. This room communicated to the W with the private apartments (3 and 4), now in ruins, of the king and the queen. Beyond the circular pool, a square pool (2) can be seen which could be reached by an underground corridor and a stairway with 15 steps.

Also near the car park, but on the r., you can see the central court of the palace (3); a spacious royal megaron (4) divided into two parts by an axial colonnade opened on to it. A triple-bayed door at the end of the megaron led to another fairly large room, known as the banquet hall (5), which had an 85ft (26m) long decorative band of relief spirals, no doubt running round the room below the ceiling.

The megaron also communicated with a suite of rooms on the W (you approach from the E), including a lustral bath (6) which was reached by a staircase the steps of which are still preserved, a treasury (7; SW of the lustral bath) with still surviving compartments, etc.

On the N side of the court in the western part there was a wide portico with two columns giving access to the N wing of the palace, and also on the l. to the hypostyle kitchen (8).

On the slopes of the hill there were three groups of palace outbuildings, built on terraces. This part of the palace was inhabited only during the first-Palace period, from Middle Minoan IIIB to Late Minoan IA.

A burial enclosure has recently been discovered above the valley, while new excavations have revealed an imposing building of the same date as Knossos at the E end of a little internal courtyard, which must be the first palace of Kato Zakros.

■ Cyclades [The]

The islands in the Aegean Sea today form one of the major tourist attractions of Greece, and of these islands the Cyclades are probably the most frequented. Everything tourists like is here in one place, with the much-sought-after combination of sun and sea, tempered by a gentle breeze.

The red outlines of the land barely covered with a light coat of green rise above the blue of the sea in landscapes that are generally arid; but in that heady light, the harbours, the white houses and the brightly painted caïques are astoundingly beautiful. The name of the Cyclades comes from the fact that they form a circle round the sacred island of Delos which barely shows above the water. It thus reminds us of the origins of the whole archipelago: the outcrop of an old land-mass, an underwater spine running from Greece to Asia Minor of which the islands are the highest points, the island debris of an Aegean continent. Some, like Delos, are formed of crystalline shale, others of gneiss with thick layers of marble limestone like Paros, others like Naxos, of limestone gashed with ravines, while yet others like Melos or Thera are formed of volcanic rock. The most prosperous islands (Thera, Syros, Naxos, Paros) produce and export wine, vegetables and fruit. Shipping helps the prosperity of these islands – the great Greek ship-owners came from them – but trade and fishing are far less important than they used to be.

As for the tourist trade, it benefits only a small part of the population and is still largely seasonal.

■ Cythera [Island of] (Kithira)

101sq. mls (262sq km) – Pop: 4,000 approx.

A name to dream about – and this island S of the Peloponnese doubtless has Watteau to thank for that – for as Gérard de Nerval observed, this arid, sparsely cultivated land, renowned for its honey, does not quite fit in with one's mental image of the island where Aphrodite had her temple, of which nothing remains. For a long time the island was a Venetian fief of the Venier family and paradoxically it is now part of the administrative district of Piraeus. There is a festival of St Spyridon here on 12 December.

Near the port of Hagia Pelagia you can visit the ruins of a Byzantine city (Paleokastro) at Paleopolis, which was founded shortly before the 12th century and laid waste by the pirate Barbarossa (remains of walls, houses and chapels in which some parts of ancient buildings had been reused, etc.).

Halfway between Hagia Pelagia and (17.5mls/28km) the capital of the island, Kithira (or Chora), you can see at Mylopotamos another ruined city, Byzantine and Venetian (fortifications and gate with the Lion of St Mark), and the church of Hagios Athanasios which has an iconostasis with icons showing an Ionian influence.

A 40-min walk takes you to the cave of Hagias Sofias (currently being prepared for tourists) several chambers of which had been transformed into chapels (wall paintings, mosaics) while others have small lakes in them.

The houses of Kithira are overlooked by the medieval kastro. An archaeological museum housed in an old, restored building was opened in 1981; it contains material from emergency excavations carried out on the island, and from the Anglo-American dig at Kastri (1963–65) which revealed the existence of a Minoan colony on Cythera; this latter site, abandoned in the second half of the 15th century BC, was on the SE coast of the island, not far from Kithira.

The church of Hagios Dimitrios at Pourko is made up of four little sanctuaries with wall paintings dating from the 12th century onwards.

In the church of Hagios Petros at Aresi you can see more 15th- and 16th-century frescoes, in the sanctuary.

1hr by boat from Kapsali, the tiny island of Avgou has a beautiful completely blue sea cave. Off the small island of Antikithira (7.7sq mls/20sq km), approx pop. 100; once weekly connection with Piraeus, 22hr journey; much more frequent connection by boat with Cythera), between Cythera and Crete, inhabited by a few fishermen, lies a famous wreck from ancient times which still contains about thirty marble statues in it.

Route maps 3 and 5.

Athens, 6.9mls (11km) – Corinth, 47.5mls (76km) – Eleusis, 14.4mls (23km) – admin. region of Attica.

However much of a hurry you may be in to get from Athens to Corinth do not fail to stop and visit this monastery in which the splendours of Byzantine art will be revealed in the shape of mosaics with gold backgrounds which Professor Lemerie regarded as 'the masterpiece in mosaic of the second golden age' of Byzantium.

FROM BYZANTIUM TO CITEAUX. First founded in the 5th or 6th century, the monastery of Daphni was subsequently abandoned, and then restored, perhaps around 1080, when a new church was built. It is dedicated to the Assumption of the Virgin, and the name Daphni or Daphneion was given to it because laurel trees (in Greek, *daphnai*) used to grow near it, recalling the ancient worship of Apollo whose temple, built on the same spot, was destroyed c.395 AD. In 1205 the Crusaders sacked the monastery, and then in 1211 Othon de la Roche installed Cistercians there. The Duc de la Roche and Duc Gauthier de Brienne were buried there. In 1458 when the Turks arrived the Cistercians left it. It was reoccupied in the 16th century by Greek orthodox monks who built the existing cloisters, and abandoned again during the War of Independence.

Open: daily 09.00–15.30; Sun. 10.00–15.00; entrance fee.

Part of the square enclosure from the 5th or 6th century monastery is still in existence. It was flanked by towers and arcaded buttresses, porticoes and cells.

In front of the church there is an 11th-century narthex partly rebuilt by the Cistercian monks in the 13th century. They added the tierce-point arches on the facade. On the l.-hand side of the church, notice the foundations of a large refectory built apart from the church, dating from the 11th century, and on the r. the Cistercian cloister abutting the church.

Inside the church the interior surfaces are decorated with very beautiful **mosaics with gold backgrounds dating from the end of the

CHURCH OF DAPHNI

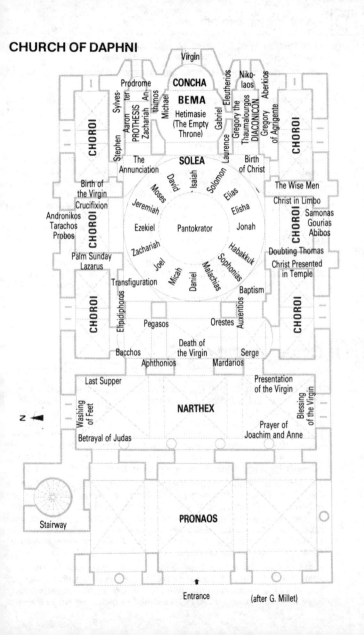

(after G. Millet)

11th century (like those in St Mark's, Venice), dominated by the superb figure of Christ Pantocrator in the dome.

With the help of the plan you can identify the various subjects and people represented.

The park near the monastery is used for a wine festival lasting for a fortnight in the autumn (in the evenings). The entrance ticket enables you to drink without further charge and in unlimited quantity (until 11 p.m.) the main Greek vintages, some of which are resin-flavoured, and to attend folklore displays.

OPENING THE CASKS. Although the festival of the Anthesteria was celebrated in honour of Dionysus, the god of wine, during the month of Anthesterion (February), the present-day wine festival is not unreminiscent of these ancient festivities in which the pithoi, large terracotta jars in which the wine had been kept since the autumn harvest, were opened. During the three days the Anthesteria lasted there was a drinking contest: at a signal given by a trumpet, mugs (*choae*) had to be emptied as quickly as possible. As this carousing was not conducive to melancholy, the second day was devoted to a kind of carnival in which a statue of the god was paraded on a boat-shaped float. But the profoundly religious nature of the Greek people regained the upper hand on the third and last day, called chytroi (cooking-pots), which was devoted to the dead and dying.

D Delos [Island of]***

This arid island in the Cyclades, tiny and parched and without obvious natural attractions, nonetheless exerts as indisputable a charm today as it did of old. For the Ancient Greeks it was a sacred ship anchored in the middle of the Aegean Sea. For the visitor today it is a mystery born of the close union between an opalescent sea wave and a small stretch of ochre-yellow earth, scattered with green, which gave sanctuary to a god, his shrine, and a town, the ruins of which possibly form the most varied archaeological ensemble in Greece.

THE APPARENT OR QUAIL ISLAND. Delos or the Apparent, also known as Ortygia or Quail Island, was already inhabited at the end of the 3rd millennium BC (remains of a very small-scale prehistoric settlement on the summit of Cynthus). Mycenaean settlement, however, was much more extensive, especially during the Late Helladic III period (1400–1200 BC), and from that time Delos was a religious centre and a frequent port of call for the island-dwellers of the Aegean.

A SEA CRADLE FOR A GOD. Like many places in ancient Greece, the Island of Delos was anthropomorphized, as were the gods, animals and plants; according to the hymn to the Delian Apollo, which may have been composed c.700 BC, Leto had to petition it when she was in search of a refuge to give birth to her son Apollo. The island gave its somewhat reluctant consent, fearing that the future god would despise it for its aridity, and thus it came about that the Titaness gave birth to Apollo and Artemis clasping a palm tree beside Mt Cynthus and the Inopos stream. At that period (the Geometric), Delos, as a place of worship, was frequented mainly by the Ionians.

THE ERA OF BITTER RIVALRIES. After the short-lived hegemony of Naxos (2nd half of 7th century BC) over the amphictyony (confederation) of the Ionians, for whom Delos was the second most important religious centre (after that at Cape Mycale in Asia Minor), Paros intervened on Delos (2nd half of the 6th century BC); but Athens made the most of its kinship with the Ionians to gain admittance into the Delian amphictyony and then assumed its leadership (purification of the shrine by Pisistratus between 540 and 528 BC). Polycrates of Samos next took Delos under his protection, chaining to it the island Rhene which he had conquered, in token of its subjection (c.525 BC).

THE POLITICO-RELIGIOUS IMPERIALISM OF THE ATHENIANS. After the Persian Wars, Athens pursued its expansionist policy in the Aegean Sea more vigorously than ever, and made the Ionian cities join in the first Attic-Ionian Maritime League, founded in 478 BC. Every one of the Ionian cities and islands had to pay a tribute intended for common defence. The money gathered in this way was placed in a federal treasury located on Delos, the religious centre of the League, but to meet her own urgent need for money Athens, under the pretext of putting the treasure in a safe place, had it transferred from Delos to Athens.

NO BIRTHS OR DEATHS ALLOWED. In 426 BC the Athenians ordered the complete purification of the island: no births or deaths were to be allowed; women in labour and the dying were removed to Rhene. To crush the resistance completely the people of Delos were deported *en masse* in 422 BC, but allowed to return to their country the following year. After the defeat of Athens at Aegospotami (404 BC) Delos appealed to Sparta and regained its autonomy (c.401 BC), but not for long: from c.394 on Athens once more controlled Delos.

THE ISLAND CONFEDERATION. About 315 BC Egypt became the most powerful influence in the Aegean Sea. Athens abandoned Delos which regained its independence (c.314 BC). The island entered the most prosperous period of its history (314–166 BC). Delos once more became the centre of an island Confederation; towards the end of the 3rd century BC this came under the control of the Ptolemies of Egypt. There was a flood of rich offerings made to the shrine; the decrees issued by the Delians granting honours to foreign benefactors of the temple and the island indicate the variety and scale of their diplomatic and trading relations. At that time Delos had a democratic constitution. The affairs of the people of Delos were managed by a local archon, a senate and assemblies of the people. Towards the middle of the 3rd century BC the Aegean area came under the hegemony of Macedonia and from that time Delos was more or less controlled by the rulers of Macedonia.

THE ERA OF THE TRADERS. In 166 BC after the defeat of Persia the Roman Senate acceded to the petitions of Roman traders living on Delos and anxious to strike a blow at Rhodes' trade by creating a free port on the island of Apollo, and handing Delos over to Athens; the entire native population was expelled. From then on the island officially became a cleruchy (a colony in which tracts of land were given to Athenians who retained their citizenship) subject to the same regime as other Athenian colonies, governed by an epimelete (civic official) who represented the parent state. In fact the Romans were the real rulers. After the fall of Corinth (146 BC) the free ports of Delos, lying near the mouth of the Mykonos Canal at the crossroads of the sea routes of the Aegean, increased enormously in importance. Although the shrine continued to attract some visitors, it was really trade that was the source of the island's power at that period; it had become a cosmopolitan warehouse for the East, Greece and Italy. Italian traders and bankers founded companies assigned to the protection of various gods (Hermes for the followers of Hermes, Apollo for the followers of Apollo, Poseidon for the followers of Poseidon). At this period Delos may have had a population of 25,000, drawn from the most varied quarters of the world. Powerful trading houses and guilds of merchants from Tyre, from Berytus (Beirut) and from Alexandria in Egypt set up there, bringing both their religions and their wealth. Monuments of every description were put up in the town.

SUNK INTO OBLIVION. But that extraordinary prosperity was not to last. In 88 BC, when Athens had declared its support for Mithridates, Delos remained loyal to Rome and broke with Athens. But in the autumn of 88 BC Archelaus and Menophanes, Mithridates' admirals, took Delos by surprise and pillaged it. It was retaken c. 87 BC by Sulla and returned to the Athenians; thanks to the efforts of the Romans it rose once again from its ruins, but proved a temptation to the pirates who controlled the Cyclades. In 69 BC Athenodorus sacked the island and reduced the Delians to slavery. From then on the decline could not be halted, for the Italian ports had forged direct links with the commercial ports of the eastern Mediterranean. Philostratus records that Athens wanted to sell it during Hadrian's reign, but could find no buyer. In the 4th century AD it was made the seat of a bishopric which included several Cycladic islands, no doubt because of its past prestige. This position lapsed in the 8th century after the island had been laid waste several times.

EXCAVATIONS. The first digs began in 1872 with the clearing of the Cynthus barracks and the summit of Mt Cynthus. Systematic exploration of the island was undertaken by the French School from 1873, and continued with some breaks up until the present day.

🛥 *Boats frequent caïque service from Mykonos; once daily in summer from Tenos.*

VISITING THE RUINS

Open: according to the official opening hours, the site is open 08.30-

14.30 in summer, 09.00–13.30 in winter, and 16.00–18.00 throughout the year; Sun. 09.00–15.00 in summer and 10.00–14.30 in winter; entrance fee. But unless you are a passenger on a cruise you have to place narrower limits on these times if you come from Mykonos as the last caïques going back there leave Delos at approx. 12.30; and you can in no way count on getting accommodation at the Tourist Pavilion. In most cases there will not be much time to see the island, but you will manage to do everything if you keep up a brisk pace from the moment you set foot ashore. It is therefore advisable to leave Mykonos by the first caïque (about 09.00). Don't forget a hat, as there is very little shade on Delos. Don't stray off the paths on to the grass for on Delos there are not only big, harmless lizards, but dangerous adders.

On the island of Delos you will visit the ancient city; it is unquestionably the best preserved and most evocative to be found in Greece. All the elements of ancient life are to be found there: namely, in the context of the Homeric *Hymn to Apollo*, a large Panhellenic shrine, a sacred cave and a sacred lake, a maritime and commercial city with its harbours, wharfs, docks, traders' shops and clubs, and, last, a town of the Hellenistic period that bears comparison with Pompeii and Timgad.

Religion was the source of Delos' good fortune. Being too small to become politically powerful, it was chosen by the Ionians in the Cyclades as the religious seat of their Confederation. The existence of a large town and a very active trading port on such a tiny island, lacking both water and a natural roadstead, may seem surprising. It can be explained by the many privileges extended to the great shrines, first among them inviolability. The traders who turned Delos into the foremost entrepôt of the eastern Mediterranean between 315 and 88 BC therefore placed themselves under Apollo's protection in order to guarantee their undertakings against pillage.

Like all great Panhellenic centres of worship Delos attracted many pilgrims and the *Deliae*, great religious festivals that took place every four years, were held in conjunction with a large fair where many business deals were transacted.

THE DELIA. The foremost Delian festival at the time of Athenian rule was the Delia, which the Athenians celebrated on Delos, once every four years, in May. They sent delegates or 'theoroi' with choirs recruited and trained in Athens by 'Deliasts', about a hundred people in all, and oxen for the hecatombs (sacrifices). The convoy was directed by a chief or 'architheoros'. Once they had disembarked on the island, the procession made its way to the temple singing the 'prosodion', a hymn telling the story of Leto's flight and the birth of Artemis and Apollo, and paeans in honour of Apollo. The procession made a solemn tour of the whole shrine. Then after the victims had been sacrificed there were gymnastic games, equestrian competitions and musical contests. There was also dancing in front of the altar of Apollo, the sacred Crane dance or geranos; and last on the programme were dramatic presentations and banqueting.

YOUR TIMETABLE. After crossing from Mykonos (35–45min depending on sea conditions), you disembark right beside the sanctuary, near the agora of the Compitaliasts (plan pp. 470-1) and by the former Sacred Port, today silted up. When there is a heavy swell, caïques put in at Gourna Bay, near the NE tip of the island; a path leads from there to the Sacred Port area across the stadium area.

After disembarking follow the itinerary in the order that it is given. You may find the first part of the tour up to the museum a bit off-putting but it will provide a lot of interesting details about the religious life of the ancient Greeks. The second part is much more eye-catching, with relatively well-preserved living areas. If you don't want to miss the caïque back, you will have to forgo a swim on the island even though the beach at Phourni, about half a mile (1km) from the landing-stage, is a very pleasant spot.

1 TOWARDS THE SANCTUARY OF APOLLO

Agora of the Compitaliasts (plan A/B-3) – Its name comes from the associations of freedmen and slaves who every year celebrated the Roman festival of the Lares Compitales (gods of the crossroads). But the agora had already been founded in the course of the 2nd century BC by other brotherhoods from Italy (the Hermaists, the Apolloniasts and the Poseidoniasts).

It was the Italian brotherhood of the Hermaists that built the Ionian naiskos which stood near the southern side of the stoa of Philip (below). The hieron of Hermes and Maia, a tetrastyle monument of the Doric order, stood to the S.

Portico of Philip (plan B-3) – Walking towards the sanctuary from the agora you take the avenue of the Processions, the third road on the l. from the landing-stage; this takes you past the ruins of the portico of Philip (on the l.), built by King Philip V of Macedon (220–178 BC) c.210 BC, and made double some thirty years later by a second portico, called the W portico, a former quay, now cemented over.

The E side of the portico of Philip opened on to a wide road linking the harbour to the S propylaea of the hieron; it had 16 Doric columns between two walls. The W portico had 26 Doric bays opening towards the harbour. A room was built on to the N of the portico of Philip which was closed on three sides and communicated with the W gallery, which had five bays and Ionic columns. The dedication made when the foundations were laid has been found: The king of the Macedonians, Philip, son of King Demetrius, dedicated this portico to Apollo.

Avenue of the Processions (plan B-3) – A 42ft (13m) wide avenue or dromos lined on either side by many bases and exedrae linked the harbour with the S propylaea (monumental gate) of the sanctuary of Apollo. Along the r. side was the S portico with small rooms opening off it which may have been used for the public weights and measures.

The S portico was erected around the middle of the 3rd century BC. On the r. at the start of the avenue you will see the base of the equestrian statue of Epigenes of Teos, a general who served Attalus I, King of Pergamum, and at the other end of the portico the foundations of an inscribed base which probably held statues of Galatians commemorating Attalus I's victory over that people.

Agora of the Delians (plan B-3) – This agora is enclosed to the N and E by a 2nd century BC angled portico, and to the S by a considerably older (3rd century BC) oblique portico, and was at one time paved; it is also called the tetragonal (quadrangular) agora.

The colonnades of the angled portico were erected between 187 and 173 BC, but the shops may be older. During the Imperial epoch baths were built on the agora, but very little remains of them. To the S and E several ruined houses mark the edge of the agora; one of them, the so-called house of Kerdon (plan, B-3) named after the stele of a shipwrecked man found inside it, is said by R. Vallois to be the only peristyle house that can be ascribed with certainty to the 3rd century BC. Near the SE corner of the agora at a triangular crossroads was the shrine of Tritopator (plan, B-3), dating back to c. 400 BC; Tritopator was a mythical ancestor of the Attic Pyrrhakides family. Nearby the ruins of a 5th-century basilica, dedicated to St Quiricus (plan, B-3), have been discovered.

2 SANCTUARY OF THE DELIAN APOLLO

At the end of the avenue of the Processions you come to a monumental propylaeum (plan 3, B-3), which gave access to the sanctuary of the Delian Apollo where the god returned in the spring of each year to spend the season. The sanctuary was developed from the 8th century BC on the site of a settlement of the Mycenaean period. In front of the monumental entrance stands a copy of a statue of Hermes Propylaeus, put up by the amphictyons in 341–340 BC (the original is kept in the museum reserve stock). On the r.-hand side of the end of the avenue of the Processions there were several votive monuments, including a little building (plan 1, B-3) associated with the Ergasteria of the Theandridae, near which a statue of a woman has been replaced on its base; also the beautiful marble exedra of Soteles (plan 2, B-3).

The oikos of the Naxians (plan 4, B-3) – On entering the sanctuary you will see on your r. the ruins of the oikos (*v.* Glossary) of the Naxians, a building dating from the beginning of the 6th century BC, which has a colonnade running down the centre and two porticoes, built on the site of an oikos dating from the Geometric period (beginning of the 7th century BC) which took its orientation from an older building of which almost nothing remains and identified by R. Vallois as the earliest known temple of the sanctuary of Apollo. This building, known as Γ, (plan 5, B-3) is believed to have been put up during the Mycenaean period.

Against the wall of the oikos of the Naxians you can see the base (plan 6, B-3) of a colossal statue of Apollo, in marble. It carries an epigram in Archaic script dating from the end of the 7th century BC saying: 'I am of the same marble, statue and pedestal'. According to

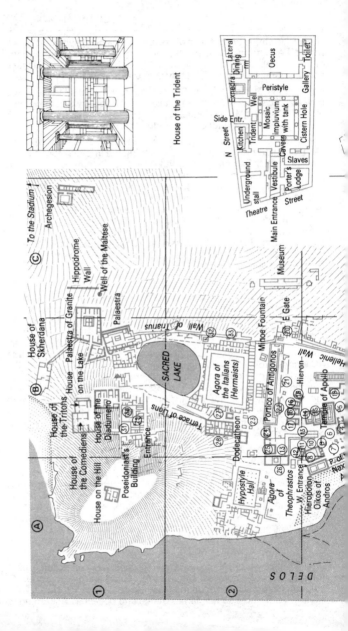

House of the Trident

House of the Trident (plan)

Underground stall · Theatre · N Street · Kitchen · Side Entr. · Well · Trident · Vestibule · Exedra · lateral · dining · Oecus · Peristyle · Mosaic impluvium with tank · Cavern with tank · Main Entrance · Porter's Lodge · Slaves · Cistern Hole · Street · Gallery · Toilet

DELOS (map)

To the Stadium
Archegesion
Hippodrome
Wall
Well of the Maltese

House of Skherdana

House of the Tritons
House of the Comedians
House on the Hill
Poseidoniast's Building
House of the Diadumeno
Palaestra of Granite
Palaestra on the Lake
Palaestra
Wall of Trianus
Mihoe Fountain
Museum
E Gate
Hellenic Wall

Terrace of Lions
SACRED LAKE
Agora of the Italians (Hermaists)
Dodecatheon
Portico of Antigonos
Hieron
Temple of Apollo
Hieron Wall

Entrance
Hypostyle Hall
Agora of Theophrastos
W. Entrance
Hierobbion
Oikos of Andros
P.oti of Nax

A · B · C
1 · 2

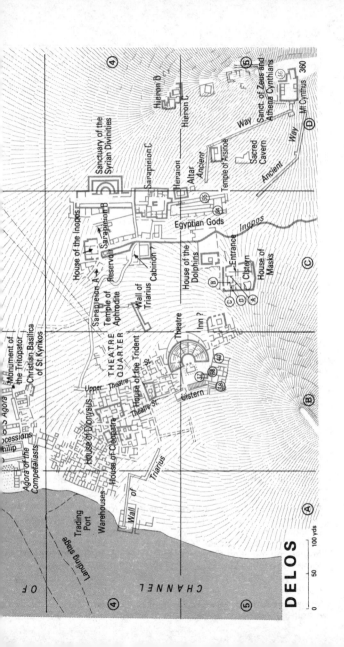

DELOS

CHANNEL

OF

Trading Port

Landing stage

Warehouses

Wall of Triarius

Agora of the Compelaliasts

ocessions

hilip

os Agora

Monument of the Tritopator

Christian Basilica of St Kyrikos

House of Dionysus

House of Cleopatra

House of the Trident

THEATRE QUARTER

Upper Theatre

Theatre St.

Theatre

Wall of Triarius

Cistern

Inn?

House of the Inopos

Sarapieion B

Sarapieion A

Reservoir

Temple of Aphrodite

Wall of Triarius

Cabirion?

House of the Dolphins

Entrance

Cistern

House of Masks

B

C

D

A

Sanctuary of the Syrian Divinities

Sarapieion C

Heraion

Altar

Ancient Way

Temple of Arsinoe

Egyptian Gods

Inopos

Hieron B

Hieron C

Way

Sacred Cavern

Ancient Way

Sanct. of Zeus and Athena Cynthians

Mt Cynthus 360

0   50   100 yds

Plutarch, the statue, which was dedicated by the Naxians, was knocked over by the fall of the bronze palm tree belonging to Nicias. There is still controversy concerning the original site of this enormous statue, two fragments of which are now kept in the temple of Artemis.

Stoa of the Naxians (plan A-3) – This angled stoa built c. 550–540 BC formed the side of a paved square. In the corner formed by its two wings the granite foundations (plan 7, B-3) with a cylindrical hole for the bronze palm tree offered by Nicias, no doubt in 417 BC, have been found; it was a memorial of the tree under which Leto had given birth to Apollo and Artemis.

On one of the fragments of the lower marble foundation that has been put back in place it is possible to read the name of Nicias, the beginning of the dedication. Near the stoa of the Naxians are the remains of two oikoi; the Hieropoion (plan A-3), the meeting-place of the hieropes who administered the sanctuary, dating from the last third of the 6th century BC; and the oikos of Andros (plan A-3) which is slightly later. Neither of these two identifications can be made with certainty.

The Keraton (plan 8, A/B-3) – You next come to the ruins of a temple built by the Athenians, which may be the Keraton, the building containing the altar constructed by Apollo, so legend has it, from the horns of his victims, in front of which the 'theores' during the festival of the Delia danced the geranos (the 'crane dance', a serpentine dance performed at night, and nothing to do with cranes). The Athenians claimed that it was first danced by Theseus after he had escaped from the labyrinth. The Keraton was built at the beginning of the second half of the 4th century BC.

Near the Athenian temple to the E you can see the remains of a building with an apse (plan 9, B-3); it was built in the 5th century BC, but altered in the second half of the 4th century BC or the 3rd century BC. Some archaeologists believe that the altar of horns (see above) was in this building. To the S of it note the pillar of Antiochus which held the statue of the Seleucid ruler (223–187 BC). Immediately N of the apsidal altar are a few traces of a temple (plan 10, B-3) called temple G; it dates from the 7th century BC, was restored during the Hellenistic period, and built on the site of a pre-Archaic, probably Mycenaean megaron.

First tomb of the Hyperborean maidens (plan 11, B-2/3) – The remains of the Sema, one of the two tombs of the Hyperborean maidens, are thought to have been recognized NW of temple G; Hyperochus and Laodice rested there in the shade of an olive tree and young men and girls came to lay locks of their hair on it. These tombs go back to Late Mycenaean II (c.1400–1300 BC) and were later used to house holy relics which were venerated in the time of Herodotus.

Temple of Artemis (plan 12, B-2) – Next proceed towards the high granite foundations of the temple of Artemis, built c.179 BC on the site of a sanctuary which may date back to the 7th century BC. Other places claimed the honour of having been the birthplace of Artemis. The hymn to Apollo simply says that the goddess was born on Ortygia, perhaps just before Apollo. The Delians concluded from this that in very ancient times their island had been called Ortygia. On the foundations of the temple lie two fragments of the colossal statue the base of which you saw near the oikos of the Naxians.

The Archaic temple must have replaced a Mycenaean building, a few granite remains from which have been found inside the cella. R. Vallois noted that the orientation of this building is in line with that of the walls of the original town which is known to have been established on this site from the Mycenaean period. The discovery near the NE corner of the temple of a collection of precious objects, ranging in date from the Mycenaean period to the 7th century BC, seems to be evidence of the continuity of some form of worship in this vicinity. The limits of the temenos of the Artemision were marked on the E and N by an angled Ionic portico (plan 13, B-2); the eastern wing is older than the N wing, which must have been added in the second half of the 2nd century BC. Beyond the portico is a pedestal made of pink stone and decorated with a Doric frieze where there are alternating rosettes and bulls' heads on the metopes. Another pedestal in bluish marble carries a metrical epigram engraved towards the end of the 3rd century BC in honour of Philetaerus (opp. Porinos Naos, see below), the first of a ruling dynasty of Pergamus.

Temples of Apollo (plan B-3) – Now turn towards the ruins of three temples facing W, which were all dedicated to Apollo. The oldest (plan 14, B-3), dating from the 6th century BC, is built of limestone with a vestibule (pronaos) and an inner sanctum (cella), and contained an Archaic statue of Apollo, the work of the Naxian sculptors Tectaeus and Angelion. It is mentioned in inscriptions by the name of Porinos Naos or Porinos Oikos. It was the repository of the federal treasure belonging to the league set up at the instigation of Athens after the Persian Wars.

The middle temple (plan 15, B-3) is in the Doric style, with six columns along its facade, built by the Athenians in Pentelic marble in the same period as the Delian temple (see below), by the Athenians between 425 and 417 BC. At the back of the inner sanctum (cella) stood seven statues. The S temple in the Doric style was begun at the time when the Attic-Delian Confederacy, in which Athens was predominant, had just been formed (477 BC). Motivated by hostility towards the people of Delos who had undertaken the building at their own expense, Athens must have delayed work on it and it was not finished until the 3rd century BC. A few marble steps that rested on a high sub-foundation of blocks of gneiss may still be made out.

Arranged in an arc behind the group of three temples, there is a series of five buildings (plan 16 and 17, B-2). By analogy with similar buildings at Olympia and Delphi they have been called treasuries, but they must in fact be oikoi. The last of the group lying to the W (plan 17, B-2) might possibly be that put up by the town of Carystus. The four others are thought to date from the second quarter of the 5th century BC.

The space enclosed between these treasuries and the western facades of the temples formed a square which was bounded on the SE by two buildings: an Archaic building (plan 18, B–3) with a central row of pillars (perhaps the bouleuterion) and the prytaneum (plan, 19, B–3) where a copy of a votive herm has been re-erected. The prytaneum was built in the first half of the 5th century, then altered at the end of the 4th century BC. S and W of the prytaneum there were several altars including that of Zeus Polieus and Athena Polias (plan E, B–3).

Monument of the Bulls (plan B–3) – This building, much longer than it is wide, owes its name to the motifs used in its decoration. Construction techniques make it possible to put its date at the beginning of the Hellenistic period, but the identity of this strange building has not been firmly established: R. Vallois thought it was the Python; in any case it had in it a boat given to Apollo as a votive offering, which can plausibly be argued to have been the ship of the king of Macedon, Antigonus Gonatas.

The gneiss and granite foundations of this monument, which is remarkable for its unusual shape, are still there. The interior was divided into three parts: the first, to the S, had a pronaos with a facade of six columns in front of which is a goddess sitting on a sea-monster and other sculpted pieces which must have been part of a long frieze; the second, in the middle, had a long gallery and a sunken central floored area with paved walkways around it; the third section on the N was a shrine containing a triangular altar of which the granite substructure remains. The gallery and the shrine had three communicating bays, and on either side of the central bay were two pilasters whose capitals were decorated with the forequarters of kneeling bulls.

The shrine of Dionysus (plan 20, B–2) – This is one of the strangest temples in the sanctuary. You can see two choragic monuments shaped like phalluses (still *in situ*). The pedestal of one (on the r.) is decorated with reliefs symbolically showing the procession of the Dionysia (l. and r. Dionysus with Silenus and a maenad; on the front the phallic bird depicts the mascot which was displayed on a float during the festivities devoted to Dionysus). This votive monument was put up c.300 BC by the choregus Carystus.

Stoa of Antigonus (plan 21, B–2) – The incomplete dedicatory inscription informs us only that it was dedicated by a king of Macedon, a son of Demetrius. This was probably Antigonus Gonatas, the son of Demetrius Poliorcetes, who must have built it between 253 and 250 BC. Two parallel lines of statue bases extended in front of the stoa one of which carried statues of Antigonus Gonatas' ancestors.

The stoa had two galleries set between two projecting wings at either end. Every second triglyph on the frieze shows a bull's head. In the E (r.) wing of the stoa a statue of C. Billienus, a Roman magistrate, has been replaced on its pedestal (late 2nd-early 1st century BC).

Second tomb of the Hyperborean virgins or **maidens** (plan 21, B-2) – A Mycenaean ossuary was found almost on the central axis of the stoa of Antigonus within a semi-circular sacred enclosure (abaton). This is probably the Theke, another tomb of the Hyperborean maidens in which Arge and Opis were buried.

The ossuary consisted of two stone-built burial chambers containing skeletons and Mycenaean and pre-Mycenaean vases. There must have been an altar built on to the sacred enclosure where the women of the island, according to Herodotus, carried out strange rites while singing a very old hymn by the Lycian, Olen, in which they invoked the maidens by their holy names. The women of Delos made the sacrifice of certain victims, the legs of which were burnt and the ashes scattered inside the abaton. Nearby you can make out the remains of the several semi-circular marble exedrae, the arms of which were decorated with dolphins. The foundations of an Archaic altar (plan 22, B-2) consisting of two parts of different ages may belong to the altar of Apollo Genetor where offerings of wheat, barley, and cakes were made.

In the road running along the outside of the stoa there is a square basin which was the Minoe fountain (plan B-2), mentioned in the inscriptions. It must have been built in the second half of the 6th century or at the beginning of the 5th century BC. The columns of the prostasis were probably put up in the course of the 5th or 4th century BC. Further along, the semi-circular precinct of an abaton (plan 23, B-2), or holy place, to which entry was forbidden, marked the site where the thunderbolt of Zeus Catabates had struck.

Leaving the sanctuary of Apollo proceed in the direction of the Sacred Lake via the agora of Theophrastus (plan A-2).

As you go along note on the r. the remains of an oikos (plan 24, B-2), thought to have been built at the end of the 4th century or the beginning of the 3rd century BC. During the Imperial Roman period baths were built on the site of this building which also extended over the W wing of the stoa of Antigonus. A little further on you pass the ruins of a building which may be the Ekkleseum (a meeting-place for a legislative assembly) (plan 25, B-2). This building passed through several stages: the early 5th-century BC building was enlarged, possibly in the 4th century, to the E and S, then the W part was added towards the middle of the 3rd century BC. There were two further alterations, at the end of the 2nd century BC and then in the Roman Imperial period. Finally you come to a 5th-century BC monument which was for a long time wrongly believed to be the Thesmophorion (a precinct for one of the great festivals of Demeter) (plan 26, A-2); this building consisted of two cellae with four columns separated by a peristyle court.

THE AREA OF THE SACRED LAKE

The agora of Theophrastus (plan A-2) – This was created by the epimelete Theophrastus in the second half of the 2nd century BC by means of embanking. The monuments (pedestals, altars, a temple with a podium) standing at the edge of the agora to the N and E are no earlier than 166 BC.

Hypostyle hall (plan A-2) – Known as the stoa of Poseidon, this building was put up in the last decade of the 3rd century BC for use as an exchange or merchants' meeting hall.

As you go towards the agora of the Hermaists (plan B-2) you will see the foundations of a Doric temple for the worship of the 12 gods, hence the name Dodekatheon (plan B-2). It was built prior to 285 BC, but the shrine was older.

Next you come to the ruins of a 6th-century BC temple identified as the Letoön (plan 27, B-2) where the mother of Apollo was worshipped. Standing across from it was a building (plan 28, B-2) of huge granite blocks which had a double courtyard and a ground floor divided into shops and workshops. The first floor must have been the meeting place of some (unknown) corporation to judge from the reliefs found nearby, dancing Lares (household gods), preparations for a libation, a sacrificial scene.

Agora of the Hermaists (plan B-2) – It was built by some private individuals and some associations (Hermaists) as a meeting place for the island's Italian peoples; so we can see how important it had become by the end of the 2nd century BC. This monument, which is the most extensive on Delos, consisted of a central courtyard bounded by four Doric porticoes with an Ionic gallery above. The inner area of the agora had cells or exedrae with votive monuments, statues and mosaics. On the W side observe the cell of L. Orbius (polychrome mosaic) and on the N that of Publius Satricanius (under a modern roof, a coloured mosaic of a bronze vase, a palm and a crown). On the E, S and W sides a row of shops opened out from the agora.

The Sacred Lake (plan B-2) – Today it is just a memory, but you can make out its elliptical shape because of the modern wall built round it. It is identified as the trochoid lake which reminded Herodotus (II, 170) of the sacred lake of Sais in Egypt. You will have to use your imagination to populate it with the swans of Apollo and the sacred geese of the sanctuary.

The marshy ground that extended to the S before the agora of the Hermaists was built probably part of Leto's domain. It is unlikely that Apollo's birth was always ascribed to the side of this lake; but from early times this stretch of water was closely associated with the legend and worship of the god.

The Lion Terrace (plan B-1/2) – If you were not particularly interested in archaeology and this return to the origins of the cult of Apollo, here you will find your first recompense. Of the nine (or 16, or maybe more) Archaic lions (they must date from the end of the 7th century BC) in Naxian marble, that stood roaring towards the lake, five can still be seen *in situ*. A sixth which was removed at the end of the 17th century has been located since then at the entrance to the Arsenal in Venice.

The institution of the Poseidoniasts (plan B-1) – This huge area was used as a meeting place by an association of ship-owners and financiers from Berytos (Beirut) and assigned to the patronage of Poseidon. It consisted of a central court (plan 29) with four chapels (one with a statue of Roma in it) opening off it under a portico, a peristyle courtyard (plan 30) and a third courtyard (plan 31) paved with mosaics. On the side of the entrance there were also reception rooms above the basement shops.

Farther W the ruins of four houses from the Hellenistic period have been uncovered. Note the apotropaic (intended to ward off ill-fortune) signs on the white marble doorframes of a house on the l. of the ancient road you have followed. The phallus, the clubs of Hercules and the caps of the Dioscuri, Castor and Polydeuces, were regarded as particularly propitious in warding off the evil eye.

Hellenistic houses – There was quite a colony of houses lying between the Sacred Lake and the shore. It is in this area that the French School has carried out its most recent digs. You can see the ruins of the hill house (plan A-1) the farthest west, with a black and white chequerboard mosaic courtyard, and then of the house of the comedians (plan B-1) which was decorated with a painted frieze of small pictures showing comic and tragic actors. It had a Doric peristyle courtyard with an Ionic attic storey. In the house of the Tritons (plan B-1) you can see a mosaic paving showing a woman with a fish's tail, probably a female Triton, holding the strings of a rudder and, above, a hovering Eros.

On your way down towards the lake go into the house of the Diadumenus (plan B-1), given this name because a replica of the famous work by Polyclitus was found in it, and then to the E of the lake house (plan B-1).

A large monument made partly with granite blocks marks the other side of the road; this is the granite palaestra, built during the Athenian period, i.e. after 166 BC, on the site of an earlier building.

Beyond that a strong granite retaining wall may mark the outer limits of the hippodrome. The well of the Maltese (plan C-1) lies between this retaining wall and the remains of a fortifying wall built by the crews of the boats placed under the orders of the Roman legate Triarius to protect Delos against pirate raids (c.69 BC).

Gymnasium by the lake (plan C-1) – The ruins of this are right beside the Sacred Lake. It was built in two phases (3rd and 2nd century BC) and destroyed in 69 BC.

At the end of the first half of your tour proceed towards the museum (plan C-2) beside which you can stop for a rest at the Tourist Pavilion before setting out on the most spectacular part of your itinerary of

Delos. Otherwise visit the area lying between the Sacred Lake, the gymnasium and the stadium (approx. 1hr).

From the lake to the stadium – From the lake proceed towards the museum following the wall of Tharius (plan B-1/2).

On the l. you pass a piece of land that stretches between the sports ground and the hippodrome (plan C-1) wall where probes have revealed a group of sacred buildings on a monumental scale consisting of a large paved courtyard containing stuccoed altars and ritual baths.

Near the wall of Triarius you can see an altar (plan 32, B-2) dedicated to Apollo Genetor and a little Archaic temple, both of which were erected in the last quarter of the 6th century BC by the inhabitants of one or several of the Cycladic islands.

Under a bastion in the wall of Triarius a little temple was discovered farther to the S, dedicated after 166 BC to a goddess who in P. Roussel's opinion must be Artemis rather than Aphrodite Soteria.

A wide avenue ran from the sanctuary to the gymnasium and stadium area (plan C-1) lying to the NE.

On the r. of the path beyond the tourist pavilion you can see traces of two unidentified temples standing about 130ft (40m) away. The largest on the r. may have been the centre of a heroic or chthonian cult. It seems to be very old, but does not go back as far as the Archaic period. Farther on, to the l., lie the ruins of a large building identified as the Archegesion (plan C-1). A row of rooms has been recognized as corresponding with the oikoi mentioned in the hieropes' accounts, particularly the central part which must be the oldest and main section of the building. The S part, which is more recent, may date from the second half of the 6th century BC. The central oikos has four chambers, the same number as that of the Ionian tribes. To the W a large paved courtyard has been uncovered may be the hieron of Archegetes, that is Anius, the mythical king of Delos. This courtyard contained a horsehoe-shaped altar, called the Escharon. Until they were evicted in 166 BC the Delians jealously guarded the hieron from access by foreigners; in fact two 4th-century BC lintels have been found with this prohibition engraved on them.

The gymnasium, put up at the time when Delos was independent and later altered by the Athenians, consisted of a huge courtyard with an Ionic peristyle with rectangular exedrae along the sides. In the 204yds (187m) long stadium the spectators sat on the slope along the W side. Running alongside the stadium on the W was a xystus (or covered track), 10yds (9m) wide and 204yds (187m) long; it was built before 200 BC, but later than the stadium and gymnasium on to which it abuts. To the E of the stadium you can visit a whole area of houses which were built along the road leading to the stadium. Notice the altar protected by a projecting roof; paintings on the actual altar which have now been destroyed used to show a sacrifice, slaves wrestling and, on the r.-hand side, Heracles with his club, a palm and an amphora. Nearby, beside the sea, are the remains of a synagogue built in the 1st century BC.

MUSEUM (plan C-2). This contains most of the antiquities discovered on the island, except for some outstanding objects which have been placed in the National Museum in Athens.

Archaic statuary, with many works in the form of Apollo and of kouroi (young men) in particular, is especially well represented. This museum also includes interesting sculpture from the Classical and Hellenistic periods.

As regards the lesser arts, you should look out for Mycenaean ivories, bronze figures from the temple of Artemis, finds made in the Heraeum including figurines, terracotta masks and vases – mainly Corinthian (fine specimens of the Orientalizing style), Attic (black-figure or red-figure) from the islands.

4 THE SHRINES ON MT CYNTHUS AND THE THEATRE AREA

Serapaeum (plan C/D-4) – A path going up from the agora of the Compitaliasts will bring you here. On the way you will see the temple of Aphrodite in grey-blue marble (plan C-4) dating from the end of the 4th century BC, and then the house of Hermes. This house, the floors which were built on a gradient of about 40ft (12m), was reached from a road which must have been the W quayside along the Inopus, an almost-always-dry mountain stream that is mentioned in the Homeric *Hymn to Apollo*. Go along a corridor (notice the latrines on the l. as you go in) to reach a paved and stuccoed courtyard that has porticoes along three sides with upper galleries (as a safety precaution, entry into the house of Hermes has been forbidden since 1984). Continue up the road until you reach one of the three temples dedicated to Serapis; the entrance is marked on the r. by a marble threshold. This sanctuary, known as Serapaeum A, had a paved courtyard with a little chapel at a raised level standing on it. As a curious inscription tells us, this temple was built by the grandson of an Egyptian of priestly caste who, when he settled on Delos, introduced the cult of his god. This sanctuary was the oldest on the island to have been dedicated to Serapis.

Next on the l. you see the ruins of the house of the Inopus; because of confined space there is a colonnade on two sides only. Beyond the house of the Inopus there are shops on the l. of the road. Between the third and fourth of these there is a passageway leading to a staircase by which you can go up to Serapaeum B, now in a very ruined condition.

Samothracaeum (plan C-4) – Farther on on the r. are the remains of a sanctuary dedicated to the Cabirai, Samothracian divinities.

It consisted of two terraces, on the higher of which was the temple – a 4th-century BC Doric building – and the lower the foundations of a monument decorated with a frieze of circular medallions showing the officers and princes who had been allies of the great Mithridates, king of Pontus. To the S there was an esplanade which had porticoes

surrounding it on three sides, perhaps belonging to a shrine of
Heracles.

Terrace of the foreign gods – The N part was devoted to Syrian gods
(plan D-4) and the S part to the sanctuary of Egyptian divinities,
which is called the Serapaeum (plan C/D-5).

In the sanctuary of the Syrian gods homage was paid to those
worshipped at Bambyke-Hierapolis, Adad, the male god, and even
more his female counterpart Atargatis, also known as Holy Aphrodite.
Settlers on Delos from Hierapolis were the first worshippers, but the
goddess from Bambyke soon attracted many adherents among the
Greek and Roman population of the island. Possibly concerned at the
orgiastic, licentious nature of this cult, Athens ensured that the high
priest was an Athenian. The sanctuary included a sacred theatre, with
a large portico running along the N, S and E sides cutting the temple
of Atargatis off from the outside world and ensuring the privacy of the
ceremonies taking place there.

Serapaeum C was by far the largest of the Egyptian sanctuaries on
the island. In the courtyard a little temple built with great care and
dating from the first half of the 2nd century BC was probably
dedicated to Serapis.

At a higher level the marble facade of the temple of Isis has been
reconstructed; it was dedicated by the people of Athens, perhaps c.
150 BC. At the end of the cella on the rocky bench that served as its
pedestal stands a statue of the goddess. The small Ionic building next
to the temple of Isis on the l. may be the temple of Serapis, Isis and
Anubis which was consecrated by the people of Athens in 135–134
BC. To the r. beyond a forecourt, an avenue lined with small sphinxes
(rectangular bases) and altars (square blocks of masonry) ran
between two porticoes.

Nearby, a small granite building with a vestibule known as temple C
(plan 34, C-5) has been identified by R. Vallois as the Metroön, or
temple of the Mother of the gods. Less than 13ft (4m) away are the
remains of an earlier establishment recognized by him as the
Escharon (plan 35, C-5).

Heraeum (plan D-4) – On a terrace overlooking Serapaeum C stood
the Heraion or temple of Hera; her cult became established on Delos
from the beginning of the 7th century BC. In earlier times the wife of
Zeus had felt hatred for the mother of Apollo, but eventually there was
a reconciliation and Hera could be worshipped on Delos.

You can see the ruins of the temple which was of marble and had a
pronaos or vestibule dating from the late 6th or early 5th century BC.
In the foundations of the cella of the temple the small rectangular
room that was Hera's inner shrine has been uncovered.

Mt Cynthus (plan D-5) – The main way leading to the summit of Mt
Cynthus starts from the Heraeum terrace.

As you go up the road you will see on your r. the ruins of a sanctuary
with a temple, oikoi, and porticoes forming two sides, which must be

the sanctuary of Agatha Tyche (Good Fortune) mentioned in Athenian inventories. It is thought to be none other than the Philadelphion of Independence, the centre of the cult of Arsinoë, sister and wife of Ptolemy II of Egypt, who was deified after her death in 270 BC under the name of Arsinoë Philadelphus.

On the r. is the sacred cave from which you can look out over Rhene to Syros. The cave itself is just a fissure in the rock made into an artificial cave by a kind of pitched roof made with ten enormous slabs of granite. Inside, a block of granite served as the pedestal of a statue.

 From the summit of Mt Cynthus (370ft/112.6m), which was arranged as a terrace on which the sanctuary of the Cynthian Zeus and Athena stood, you will be rewarded for your short climb in the bright sunshine by an excellent *view over the island, with the living quarters of the theatre at your feet, and in the distance over the Cyclades.

The NW part of the summit had houses on it from the 3rd millennium BC, but subsequently the site was abandoned and reoccupied only at the end of the Mycenaean period. The cult of Cynthian Zeus and Athena must have been practised from the 7th century BC, but the sanctuary as a building is scarcely earlier than the 3rd century BC. Work on it must have started c.281 BC and been completed in 267 BC. Against the N wall, on the town side, you can recognize a hestiatorion (an inn), later called an oikos, and an oikos which is definitely distinct from the hestiatorion (plan 36, D–5). After 166 BC the main terrace was enlarged by adding on two supplementary terraces on the E side. On one of them there is a mosaic panel with a dedicatory inscription to Cynthian Zeus and Cynthian Athena.

The remains of a small sanctuary dedicated to Zeus Hypsistus and other gods were found nearby on the S summit of Mt Cynthus. On the E slope of the hill were the hieron of the gods of Ascalon and, on a terrace which can be reached only with great difficulty, the sanctuary of Artemis Locheia, where the temple foundations still exist. To the N, an ancient road led towards other sanctuaries known as the 13 northern sanctuaries of Cynthus, which were of a Semitic type (open-air).

Return to the bottom of the Mt Cynthus stairway; leaving the Heraeum on your r. take the l. path skirting the Serapaeum terrace and leading to a small square where you can visit the house of the Dolphins and the house of the Masks.

*House of the Dolphins (plan C–5) – Both this house and the next were beside a road that linked the theatre to the sanctuaries on and near Mt Cynthus. Inside you can see mosaics, one of which is decorated with dolphins astride which are figures carrying the attributes of Greek gods (a trident, a caduceus, etc.), while the other has the sign of the 'Tanit', an apotropaic (protection from evil) motif originating from Phoenicia.

**House of the Masks (plan C–5) – As you go inside this fine 2nd-century BC house notice in the entrance the base of a domestic altar and on the l. the porter's lodge. From the entrance a corridor leads to a courtyard surrounded by a peristyle, with four columns on each side, which had an upper floor; in the courtyard there is an impluvium (rainwater cistern).

This is a good example of the Rhodian peristyle, higher on one side, mentioned by Vitruvius (*De architectura*, VI, 7, 3). The N portico, which was higher than the three others, had four granite columns.

The room to the r. of the entrance corridor (A on the plan) may have been a banqueting hall. It is decorated with a mosaic which shows Dionysus holding the thyrsus (a staff entwined with vine leaves ending in a pine-cone) and the tambourine in the central panel; here and there in this motif are lozenges with a centaur. The lower part of the wall decoration of this room has been preserved. To the N (room B on the plan) lay the oecus (formal reception room) the floor of which is also decorated with a mosaic forming a huge floor covering with *trompe-l'oeil* cubes and in some places bordered by a band, on each part of which five masks can be seen.

These masks would appear to be theatrical masks associated with the new satyr plays. By referring to the description of the 44 comic masks given by Pollux (*Onomasticon* IV, 145ff.), you can recognize, going from l. to r., in the series to the l. of the door as you go in: the braggart soldier with flowing locks; the courtesan wearing the mitra on her head; a character from satyr plays not mentioned by Pollux; the woman with a mass of frizzy hair; one of the various types of schemer.

To the r. of the door, going from l. to r.: the thin greybeard, bright-eyed but woeful; the false virgin representing the girl who has been seduced; the old man with a long flowing beard, representing the good-natured father; the procurer; the toady.

Next door there is a little room (C on the plan) worth noting for its wall decoration and mosaic flooring with a flute-player playing the aulos (double flute) and Silenus conjuring up the dances of satyr plays. The mosaic flooring in the following room (room D) is adorned with an amphora with a lid in the centre of the room (some of the mosaics were moved for restoration in 1980).

The theatre (plan B/C–4) – After passing a many-roomed building, believed to have been an inn, on the l. you next come to the theatre, finished shortly after 250 BC, and fairly dilapidated. It could hold approx. 5,500 spectators.

Some fragments of the internal tiers and of the base of the proedria (places of honour) have survived around the orchestra (dancing space). The stage stood behind the proscenium which was supported by a row of 12 engaged Doric columns on parastades (the decoration on the metopes alternates, bull's heads, tripods). Seen from the front the upper level was flanked by two parascenia each consisting of only two engaged Doric columns on a parastas, these being much higher than those of the proscenium, and on the three other sides the stage was encircled by a portico.

Nearby to the SE a large rectangular foundation was the base for an altar to Dionysus (plan 37, B–5), while a little farther on are the remains of a small temple *in antis* (plan 38, B–5) dedicated to Apollo. The base of the bench running along the back of the cella still carries the last lines of the dedication to Apollo dating from the time of the epimelete, Dionysus Nikon of Palleneus (110–109 BC). SW of this temple the ruins of a sanctuary (plan 39, B–5) possibly dedicated to Artemis-Hecate have been identified. The E temenos (plan 40, B–5), which must have been devoted to the cult of Dionysus, Hermes and Pan, is near the theatre.

House of the Trident (plan B–4) – Following the so-called road of the theatre, which is paved and lined on either side with houses, you come to the house of the Trident which has a courtyard with an impluvium, and a peristyle round it, decorated with a mosaic representing the motifs of the ribboned trident and the anchor with a dolphin attached. The water collected in the impluvium was fed into a cistern installed beneath the courtyard, an arrangement common on Delos. The room on the NE corner of the house is decorated with a mosaic featuring a Panathenaic amphora, a palm and a crown.

House of Cleopatra (plan B–4) – There, standing on a single base, you will see an Athenian statue of Cleopatra, and one of her husband, Dioscurides (2nd half of 2nd century BC).

*House of Dionysus (plan B–4) – Be sure not to miss going into this house where the impluvium in the courtyard is decorated with a mosaic showing Dionysus, holding a thyrsus, astride a panther.

5 COMMERCIAL HARBOUR DISTRICT

This area suffers by comparison with the preceding one, but will tempt bathers to the sea, at Phourni Beach, 0.6mls (1km) from the landing-stage.

When you follow the shoreline southwards from the agora of the Compitaliasts you go past a group of warehouses backing on to the theatre area and opening on to a quay which runs along one of the four docks of the commercial harbour. Carrying on in a southerly direction you soon come to a second group of warehouses.

Delos was used almost solely as a port of transit; goods from Tyre or Alexandria were soon redispatched towards Italy. The market at Delos had a plentiful supply of slaves. The storehouses form little islands of houses separated by roads running parallel or at right-angles to the shore. Inside each building was a paved courtyard surrounded by vast rooms used as warehouses.

0.6mls (1km) from the landing-stage you come to the bay of Phourni, by going round a promontory which is the site of the remains of the sanctuary of Asclepius.

Three buildings stand side by side, a Doric temple, a large granite hall with a door opening to the E, and the propylaea of the sanctuary (paved with white marble).

Behind the bay of Phourni on the lower slopes of Mt Cynthus the remains of a house on three levels have been uncovered.

About 65yds (60m) from the shore of the bay of Phourni to the SE the traces of a small sanctuary have been detected, possibly dating from the second half of the 4th century BC. It consisted of a small naiskos backing on to the rock, with a terrace in front of it. This might be the Leucothion mentioned in the Accounts during Independence.

In the Channel that separates Delos from Rhene there are two deserted reefs known as Lesser Rhevmataria to the N and Greater Rhevmataria, once the isle of Hecate. An early Christian chapel dating from the late 4th or early 5th century AD has been found on the highest point of the latter island. The Artemision en Nesoe (on the island) would appear not to have been built on Greater Rhevmataria, but more likely on Rhene.

Rhene (Rinia) or Greater Delos which is now uninhabited was used by the Delians as a necropolis and as a refuge for women soon to give birth.

Along the shore facing the channel of the Rhevmataria (islands of the current) are a series of tombs, round, funerary altars, sarcophagi with a hole allowing a stele to be inserted, and many small ruined houses, probably those used by the dying and by pregnant women (the town as such was on the other side of the island facing Syros). Across from Greater Rhevmataria on the shore below the Hagia Kyriaki chapel the necropolis, where the Athenians reburied the remains dug up on the Sacred Island of Delos after its purification in 426 BC, has been discovered.

Delphi***

Route map 4.

Athens, 101mls (162km) (via Eleusis) or 110.6mls (177km) (via motorway, toll charge) – Lamia, 55.6mls (89km) – Livadia, 30mls (48km) – Patras, 83mls (133km) – Thebes, 62.5mls (100km) – admin. region of Phocis.

A visit to this shrine of the spirit of Greece will leave you with an impression that may never be surpassed. Its religious and moral influence radiated throughout the Hellenic world, and was found even in Central Asia some 3,000mls (5,000km) away in the Graeco-Bactrian kingdom founded by Alexander the Great. It will surprise no one that from the time of Homer at least, the Greeks regarded the sanctuary at Delphi, where Zeus spoke through the voice of Apollo, as the navel of the earth. But once you have gazed at the fabulous scenery which was the setting for the sanctuary building you will think more deeply still about the astonishing destiny of the Delphic oracle. Seen from the Arachova road, the temple of Apollo, clinging to the side of Mt Parnassus, one of the most majestic mountains in Greece, is a measure both of man's weakness and of his nobility.

A place predestined for greatness, Delphi has been chosen by the Council of Europe as the site for a European Cultural Centre where conferences and seminars on philosophical and political thought can be held.

Delphi in history

BEFORE THE KILLING. Long before Apollo took the oracle for himself by force, from at least the middle of the 2nd millennium BC during the Mycenaean period, an ancient chthonian deity, Gaia, was worshipped at Delphi; Aeschylus called the goddess by the title of Protomantis. The Earth Goddess who gave oracles was associated with her daugher Themis who presided over the Delphic sanctuary after her. The springs that gush forth near the site of Delphi were the reason why this became a sacred place; it was known as Pytho, and lay on the direct route from the Gulf of Corinth to central and northern Greece. The oracle where the deity uttered prophecies through the Pythia was situated near a cave guarded by a monstrous serpent Python, the daughter of Gaia.

A YOUNG GOD'S VENGEANCE. Sometime towards the end of the 9th century BC Apollo supplanted the old goddess. The young god killed Python (who had pursued Leto, his mother) with his bow near the foot of Mt Parnassus not many days after his birth on the island of Delos. Apollo had to leave Delphi to cleanse himself from the stain of that act. He returned after a long time to take possession of the oracle. He disembarked near Krissa with people from Knossos whom he forced to be the priests of his oracle by taking the form of a fireball in order to cross over an avenue of braziers. This story is an aetiological myth of the importing to Krissa through sailors from Knossos of the cult of Apollo Delphinius, a Cretan island god worshipped in the form of a dolphin. Pytho was thenceforth known as Delphi. Legend embodied this ousting of the earth deities in the myth of Delphic Apollo's struggle against Python (6th-century BC Homeric hymn) and this was commemorated by a sacred drama enacted every eight years. The new master of the sanctuary was called Pythian Apollo and he continued to prophesy.

THE 'LIBERATION' OF THE ORACLE. Originally Krissa, a town in Phocis, was overlord of Delphi. Pilgrims landed at its port of Cirrha (modern Itea), but Krissa was too exacting an overlord and c. 600 BC the priests of Delphi instigated a coalition of Greek States with the aim of liberating the oracle. This was the First Sacred War, 600–590 BC. The history of Delphi really begins after that war, which ended in the destruction of Krissa and the consecration of its territories to Apollo.

THE ORGANIZATION OF DELPHIC POWER. After the 'liberation' the sanctuary became the centre of a religious confederacy or amphictyony involving Pylos and Delphi, made up of representatives (*hieromnemones*) from 12 Greek nations, mainly Thessalian and Dorian. Meetings were held at Thermopylae (in Anthela) and at Delphi, and the league oversaw the sanctuary and the Pythian Games, which from then on were celebrated every four years, and included new contests, in particular from 582 BC, chariot races. This was the beginning of a period of prosperity.

The temporal administration of the sanctuary was undertaken by the Amphictyonic College which assembled in Delphi in the spring and autumn, and the authorities of the town of Delphi with whom the god's fortune was lodged. The Amphictyons or Hieromnemons had the supreme power of decision. The Senate of Delphi was the executive power, acting through its financial commission, the prytaneis. For example, it is known that foreign rulers such as Gyges and Croesus (6th century BC), kings of Lydia in Asia Minor, made valuable offerings to the sanctuary.

The people in charge of the Delphian cult were two priests who held their posts for life, assisted by a neocore (sacristan), prophets, five hosioi (holy men) responsible for giving consultations, and a considerable staff of free exegetes and sacred slaves. The senior posts in the priesthood were reserved for old priestly families, often at odds with each other.

PARASITES OF APOLLO. The small town of Delphi (approx. 1,000 citizens) which lay round the sanctuary lived by exploiting the oracle and its pilgrims. The townspeople manufactured sacrificial knives, and worked as sacrificers, guides, engravers of stelae, and sellers of pious souvenirs. The people of the town were famed for their rapacity, laziness and cruel conceit: it was said that the Delphians brought about the death of Aesop who had compared them to garbage.

THE FIRST INTERNATIONAL SUBSCRIPTION. In 548 BC there was a great disaster, and the temple was destroyed by fire, but work on rebuilding it was started thanks to funds raised by an international subscription. The cost of rebuilding amounted to 300 talents, a quarter of which had to be raised by the Delphians. They made a fund-raising tour through the Greek world, but some foreign princes such as Amasis who presented 1,000 talents of alum (by weight) were anxious to show their interest in the sanctuary at Delphi. It must have been 25 years between the time when work was begun on setting the temple terrace to rights and the point at which the powerful Athenian family, the Alcmaeonids, intervened (514–513 BC).

APOLLO 'EQUIVOCATES'. When Darius and Xerxes carried out their invasions in 490 and 480 BC respectively the oracle's attitudes towards the cause of the Greeks who were threatened by the Persian and the Mede was ambiguous. There can be no doubt that, motivated by fear of pillage, it made efforts to ensure that the invaders would adopt a neutral attitude towards Delphi: so it 'equivocated'. And it was still astute enough to make the victorious Greeks forget its equivocal attitude.

In spite of its caution Delphi later became involved in rivalry between the leading Greek states (Sparta, Athens, Thebes). As a result of its readiness to take sides and accept bribes, it lost some of its standing, but still received valuable gifts.

FROM ONE SACRED WAR TO THE NEXT. Athens became seriously involved in the affairs of the Delphic sanctuary and in 448 BC Pericles gave the oracle back to the people of Phocis. The Second Sacred War enabled Delphi to regain its autonomy in the following year.

In 357 BC the Amphictyons, as a result of an accusation made by the Thebans, imposed a fine on the people of Phocis for cultivating the Sacred Plain. They resisted this, and the resulting Third Sacred War dragged on for ten years (356–346 BC). The Phocians' general, Philomelus, plundered the sacred treasury, but the exploits of Onomarchus, who succeeded him, were brought to a halt by Philip of Macedon (352 BC). Macedon replaced Phocis in the Amphictyonic Council.

The Fourth Sacred War came in 339–338 BC when the Amphissans cultivated the Sacred Plain. The Amphictyony appealed through Aeschines to Philip of Macedon who invaded Greece in 338 BC. This intervention suited Philip's plans and he took advantage of it to make Greece subject to him after his victory at Chaeronea (338 BC).

A PERIOD OF INVASION. Control of Delphi passed from the Macedonians to the Aetolians who drove back the Gauls in 279 BC.

A second wondrous tale was told, copied from the earlier one, ascribing the sanctuary's safeguarding from the barbarians to divine intervention. The Aetolians were driven out by the Romans in 191 BC. Delphi was proclaimed independent by the Senate, but in fact was under Roman protection. The very principle of its existence, the oracle, was undermined by philosophical scepticism and religious indifference. An invasion by the Gauls and Thracians was repelled in 109 BC by Minucius Rufus, and then in 91 BC the temple was burnt down by the Maedes (Thracians). A few years later in 86 BC the sanctuary was plundered by Sulla, who seized it from Mithridates.

THE DISENCHANTED ORACLE. The emperors made efforts to restore the prestige of the cult and the temple. Augustus reinstated the Amphictyony, but Nero stripped the sanctuary of 500 statues. Hadrian, Herodes Atticus and the Antonines made generous donations which engendered a renaissance of the town and the holy place. Plutarch was a priest there from 105 to 126 AD, at a time when attempts were being made to rekindle faltering religious ardour.

The oracle soon made enemies among the sceptics such as Lucian. Delphi was no longer the centre, the navel of the world. Constantine the Great embellished his new capital at the expense of the monuments and treasures of Delphi. Nonetheless a few emperors still showed interest in the famous sanctuary, in particular Julian the Apostate.

Visiting the ruins

Delphi, with Delos and Olympia, was one of the greatest Panhellenic sanctuaries. The actual site of the sanctuary endows it with a grandeur which is awesome: placed on a terrace at the foot of sheer cliffs that soar to a height of 825 or 1,000ft (250 or 300m), the famous Phaedriades rocks of the ancient Greeks, it appears perched on the side of a spur of Mt Parnassus above the deep Pleistos Gorge; sometimes an eagle, the bird of Zeus, hovers high above, and deep in the gorge the water flows green and silver down onto the Sacred Plain, which can be seen in the distance with its covering of centuries-old olive trees. The uniqueness and vigour of this splendid, varied setting 'tortured by the anger of the Earthshaker' lie in the contrast between it and the gentleness of the Sacred Plain and the luminosity of the Gulf of Itea which you can see in the distance.

A ONE-DAY VISIT TO DELPHI. The ideal way to start the day would be to have breakfast on the terrace of one of the restaurants or hotels on the edge of the Pleistos Gorge; the view from there across the Sacred Plain and the Gulf of Itea is breathtaking.

Start your tour of the sanctuary from the Arachova road, at Marmaria (see 1), which provides an especially attractive view of it. Devote the rest of the morning to the sanctuary as such (see 2), going there as early as possible, as the steepness of the gradients makes walking in the heat of the sun exhausting.

For those who like to combine the pleasures of archaeological exploration with pleasures pure and simple, it is a good idea to go for a swim in the Gulf of Itea where the water is gentle and inviting, and to lunch in a restaurant in the small port of Itea. You would then spend the hottest part of the day visiting the museum (see 3). In the late afternoon you could either make a trip to the village of Arachova or make a second visit to the sanctuary of Apollo if time permits.

Where to park – On the Arachova road near the path going down towards Marmaria, or perhaps near the Castalian spring (see plan of site), for the first section of the Delphi itinerary. There is a car park near the entrance to the sanctuary of Apollo and the museum.

1 MARMARIA, THE GYMNASIUM AND THE CASTALIAN SPRING

Marmaria – This is the name traditionally given to the sanctuary of Athena; the term in Greek simply means a place where there is marble. This shrine was dedicated during the Mycenaean period to a female deity, as indicated by the discovery of terracotta statuettes of women dating from that time (kept in the museum) in the deepest archaeological strata on the site of the altars and old temple of Athena. From the Archaic period it was dedicated to Athena, called Athena Pronaia, meaning 'she who lives before the temple' (this sanctuary was in fact encountered before that of Apollo by anyone arriving at Delphi from the E – Attica and Boeotia for example – as Pausanias did in the 2nd century AD), or Athena Pronoia, making a pun between Pronaia and Pronoia, meaning "Provident". In this sanctuary you will see the famous tholos, one of the most outstanding architectural features of the Delphic site.

At the end of the path that runs down from the Arachova road you first come to the ruins of the old temple of Athena. Looking beyond the foreground, marked by the incomparable grace of the tholos, you can see in the distance the columns and terraces of the sanctuary of Apollo at the foot of the impressive rock-face of the Phaedriades. As you climb back up towards the road you will have several glimpses of one of the most beautiful *** landscapes in the world, with the gorge of Pleistos lying open below the sanctuary of Apollo, the Sacred Plain with its carpet of olive trees, and the Gulf of Itea in the distance.

Old temple of Athena – This was built at the end of the 6th century BC on the site of an Archaic sanctuary dating from the end of the 7th century BC; notice the flattened capitals so characteristic of the Archaic period in various places inside the 6th century temple, especially on the W side.

The second temple was a peripteral Doric building which must have been put up c.510 BC. After some landslides the Delphians constructed another temple further to the W.

On the l. after you come down, on a little terrace at the bottom of a decorated retaining wall with bosses, to the NE of the temple, are the ruins of two small rectangular buildings which may have been part of the temenos dedicated to the local hero, Phylacus (the Keeper) who was said to have driven back the Persians in 480 BC with the help of Autonoös.

The first building may be the heroön of Phylacus; the second may have been devoted to the other legendary saviours of Delphi (Hyperochus, Laodocus, and Pyrrhus) who supposedly intervened to ward off the Gauls in 279 BC.

About 100ft (30m) farther E at the end of a retaining wall with regular coursework you can see the remains of a monumental doorway (a good number of slabs lying alongside the path) which was the main access into the sanctuary through the peribolus on the western side.

On the retaining wall S of the little terrace with its two rectangular buildings two inscriptions mark the positions of the altars of Hygieia (Health), and Iileithyia, the goddess of childbirth; the two altars must have backed on to the wall. A few yards to the S three upright stelae still carry their dedicatory inscriptions, in Archaic script: to Zeus Polieus (protector of the city), to Athena Zosteria (girding herself for battle), and to Athena Ergane (the toiler).

Treasuries – Between the ruins of the old temple of Athena and the rotunda are the remains of a treasury in the Doric style erected between 490 and 460 BC, and of the treasury of Massalia, an Ionic-style building constructed between 535 and 530 BC. Its decoration is similar to that of the treasury of Siphnos.

To the front of the two treasuries, two rectangular bases still stand.

The larger of the two is made of limestone and may have held the bronze trophy which, according to Diodorus Siculus, was put up by the Delphians in the sanctuary of Athena Pronaia, and dedicated to Zeus and Apollo to commemorate their miraculous intervention which put the Persians to flight near Delphi in 480 BC. The other much smaller base was a pedestal for a statue of the Emperor Hadrian which was dedicated in 125 AD, according to the inscription engraved on the front side of the base.

**Tholos – This marble rotunda, which is one of the wonders of Delphi, is a work in the Attic style dating from the first quarter of the 4th century BC. Its purpose is not known. The building was encircled by a Doric peristyle with 20 columns, three of which have been re-erected. This colonnade went round a circular cella which opened to the S. At the base of the wall round the cella on the inside there is a bench that acted as a support for ten Corinthian half-columns backing on to the wall. The two sculpted metopes of the peristyle entablature, which are badly damaged, are castings. The guttering has likewise been made up with two castings of the best fragment to have survived.

The new temple of Athena – This was built c.360 BC, a few years later than the tholos, to take the place of the old temple. The little building adjoining the W side of the temple foundations and earlier than it, might be the site workshop used during construction of the tholos.

The temple of Athena was a Doric building with a row of six columns along the front; it had a pronaos and a naos, but no opisthodomos. The dividing wall that separated the naos from the pronaos was cut through in the middle by an opening with three bays at the side of which were two Ionic half-columns set against a pilaster, and topped by capitals and an entablature of the same order. The exterior metopes of the Doric order were not decorated with sculpture. The temple was built of fine-grained limestone from Mt Parnassus on a foundation of conglomerate. External parts of the building are arranged around it; note the exquisite workmanship.

The terrace on which the sanctuary of Athena lies was protected from landslides on the N side by a big, evenly built retaining wall, which is still standing to a height of a few metres. By climbing on to the earth platform above the wall you can obtain fine downward views over the sanctuary (easily reached by several paths on the E and W). On the opposite side the S limits of the sanctuary were marked by a peribolus built of polygonally bonded masonry; a few sections of it are still standing (the outside of the peribolus can be conveniently reached by means of a little staircase opposite the treasury of Massalia).

Gymnasium – Between Marmaria and the Castalian spring, on a terrace built up near the edge of the Pleistos Gorge, stand the ruins of a gymnasium constructed in the 4th century BC (later repaired by the Romans) to replace an Archaic-period building; it can be reached from Marmaria by following a path which is level at first, then climbs for 100 to 130ft (30 or 40m). This is where athletes trained before public contests in the stadium and where the young Delphians came for exercise. On the upper terrace there was a long covered gallery, or xystus, 23ft (7m) wide, backing on to a retaining wall, and another track running parallel to it. This open-air track, or paradromus, was for outdoor running practice while the xystus could be used for training protected from the sun or the rain.

The palaestra on the lower terrace was used for wrestling, and also comprised relaxation rooms and baths with a round pool. The palaestra as such consisted of a peristyle central courtyard surrounded by the main buildings; the tufa foundations of these can be seen. In them there were changing rooms, oiling rooms and relaxation rooms, a round open-air pool, etc. Baths were added on to the outside of the building in the Roman period. A path leads directly from the gymnasium to the Castalian spring.

The Castalian spring – The famous spring stands out because of its wall hewn from the rock; it lies about 164ft (50m) above the road at the end of a ravine separating the Phaedriades. According to some versions of the legend this gorge was the lair of the serpent, Python. Be that as it may, the area was used for cult purposes; part of the base of a statue of Gaia, the Earth (a very early deity who gave oracles at Delphi well before Apollo's day) has been found in the vicinity. The Greeks spoke only of the purity of the spring's waters, which were used for purification and for washing the temple of Apollo. The Latin poets turned it into a favourite resort of Apollo and the Muses and like Hippocrene, the famous spring in the Valley of the Muses, a fount of inspiration.

The water wells up at the foot of the wall. It is first collected in a narrow reservoir between the base of the hewn rock and a wall of upright slabs which were originally 8ft (2.5m) high. There were seven spouts in the wall for the water to run out, some of which can be seen in part and which must have been fitted with ornamental bronze nozzles; it then fell into a large rectangular uncovered pool hollowed out of the rock. This was where people washed to purify themselves before entering the sanctuary.

In the course of recent investigations a huge pool dating from the Hellenic period with its paved lining still mainly intact has been uncovered lower down at the level of the present road.

Aesop's punishment – The Phaedriades rocks, and particularly the one on the r. (E), known in ancient times as Hyampeia, were where the Delphians passed the judgement of the god upon – or at least offered for divine judgement – those who had offended the deity. This was how Aesop reputedly came to be condemned to be thrown from the top of the rock of Hyampeia by the priests of Delphi.

2 THE SANCTUARY OF PYTHIAN APOLLO

Open: summer 08.00–18.45; Sun. and public holidays 09.00–16.30; winter, weekdays 09.00–15.30; Sun. and public holidays, 10.00–16.30; entrance fee.

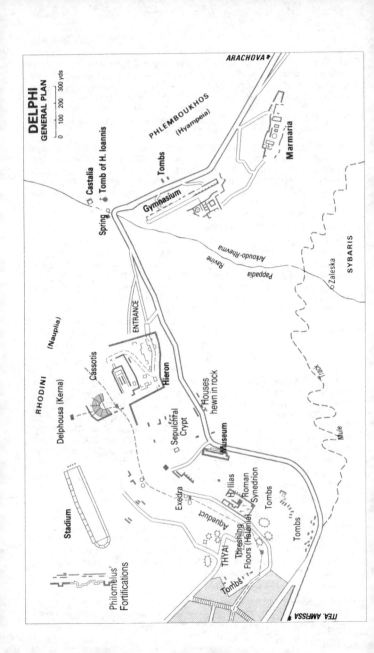

The road leading to the site of the ruins of the sanctuary of Pythian Apollo ends in an oblong paved square, which in the Roman period was edged with porticoes and shops where it is very likely that cult objects were sold.

Wall enclosing the sanctuary – As was customary the sanctuary of Pythian Apollo was encircled by an enclosing wall or peribolus with several gates in it. Some parts of the wall are built of polygonally bonded masonry from the 6th century BC, others with a pseudoregular bond, as in the S (the wall nearest the road), dating from the 4th century BC.

*The Sacred Way – From the Roman agora you enter the sanctuary by the main gate which has four steps leading up to it (so chariots were not taken inside). The Sacred Way which winds through the sanctuary begins on the other side. It is 12 to 15ft (4 to 5m) wide and still follows its original path.

On either side were a multitude of votive monuments or treasuries built by the wealthiest cities in Greece to harbour the gifts offered by their citizens or communities. These buildings tended to indicate the piety of the towns that erected them, as well as their power and wealth. The most conspicuous sites along the Sacred Way or near the temple of Apollo would appear to have been the most sought after, and they were soon taken up. Some towns such as Cyrene (in Libya), Thebes, etc., had to be content in the 4th century BC with fairly modest, poorly located sites.

It has to be admitted that the dedication of the votive monuments sometimes accompanied rather ignoble feelings which are evidence of the divisions in the Greek world. Plutarch, who was a priest of the Pythian Apollo early in the 2nd century AD, lashed out at such practices: 'These monuments which surround the god on all sides, offerings and tithes which come from massacres, wars and looting, and this temple filled with spoil and loot taken from fellow Greeks, can such things be contemplated without anger?'

Vanity Fair – This is why Syracuse chose to erect its treasury just opposite that of the Athenians after the failure of the expedition led by Alcibiades and Nicias (414–413 BC), while the Spartans, after their total victory over the Athenians at the end of the long Peloponnesian War (431–404 BC), put up a votive monument just beside one commemorating the Athenians' triumph over the Persians at Marathon, and dedicated it to the glory of their nauarchs (admirals) and generals, using the gains from their naval victory at Aegospotami, the very battle which had led to the downfall of Athens. The Arcadians in their turn, after freeing themselves from the Spartan yoke, out of sheer bravado dedicated statues of their ancestor just across from the Spartan Monument to the Nauarchs, using part of the booty taken when plundering Spartan territory.

On the r.-hand side of the Sacred Way you can see the remains of the base of the Bull of Corcyra (plan, 1) a bronze statue made c. 480 BC by Theopropus of Aegina, which was paid for by Corcyra with the profits from a good catch of tuna. Next came the offering of the Arcadians (plan, 2) consisting of a row of bronze statues of Apollo and the mythical heroes and heroines of Arcadia, then a statue (plan, 3) probably of the Arcadian general Philopoemen. Behind this there was a sizeable, very elongated terrace, the back wall of which was regularly bonded, and for a long time this was taken to be the offering of the Spartans, which was dedicated in 404 BC to commemorate their notable naval victory over the Athenians at Aegospotami. But G. Roux has shown that this terrace, which dates from the first half of the 4th century BC, actually has no connection with the Spartan offering which should be located l. of the Sacred Way across from the Offering of the Arcadians, in accordance with Pausanias's account; the most recent investigations clearly indicate that this was in fact a stoa which had a façade of 12 Doric columns. The actual offering of the Spartans consisted of 37 statues: in the foreground the Dioscuri, Zeus, Apollo, Artemis, Poseidon crowning Lysander, Agia the soothsayer, and the pilot Hermon; the other 28 statues portrayed Sparta's and her allies' generals and admirals, who had collaborated with Lysander, hence the name Monument of the Nauarchs, given to it in Plutarch's time. The inscriptions designating Lysander and the Dioscuri were written in verse by Ion of Samos.

On the l.-hand side of the Sacred Way beyond the Spartans' offering was the offering of the Athenians, now completely ruined, which was built in 460 BC with booty taken at Marathon 30 years earlier, in honour of Miltiades, who was commander of the Greek contingent, and a little higher up came the Dourian horse (plan, 5), reminiscent of the famous Trojan horse, which the Argives offered in commemoration of a victory over the Spartans. The offering of the Athenians, none of which remains *in situ*, consisted of 16 statues (Athena, Apollo, Miltiades, kings and heroes of Athens), the oldest of which were attributed to Phidias, according to Pausanias. The remains of the dedication relating to the Dourian horse can be seen on the substructure of the monument.

Proceeding along the Sacred Way you will next observe two semi-circular foundations which held two Argive monuments. That on the r., known as the Kings of Argos monument, was erected by the Argives shortly after 369 BC when Messene was founded, to outshine the Monument of the Nauarchs. The paved exedra (interior diameter 40ft/12m) held, grouped in the W half of the hemicycle, ten statues of the early kings and queens of Argos, each named in an inscription: Danaus, Hypermnestra, Lynceus, Abas, Acrisius, Danaë, Perseus, Alectryon, Alcmene, Heracles (names written from r. to l. on the vertical faces of the slabs); under the names of Danaë and Perseus the signature of the sculptor, Antiphanes of Argos, can also be read.

As for the other circular foundation on the l. of the Sacred Way, according to an inscription recently deciphered by C. Vatin, it used to bear the statues of the 'Seven Against Thebes' of the legendary expedition, standing on its l.-hand side, while on the r.-hand side were those of their successors, the Seven Epigoni; the chariot of

Amphiaraus, the seer, must have stood at the back of the hemicycle between the two groups. According to Pausanias, some of these statues were the work of Hypatodorus, while others were by Aristogiton, and they had been dedicated by the Argives following their victory over the Spartans at Oinoe in Argolis c.456 BC; the inscription, which has been deciphered, states that Hypatodorus sculpted the statues of the 'Seven Against Thebes' while Aristogiton was responsible for those of the Epigoni.

The niches which follow on the right-hand side of the Sacred Way have not been identified with certainty. The first one (plan, 6), which is square, is covered with decrees in honour of a wide variety of people. On a terrace behind them lie the jumbled remains of foundations belonging to an anonymous Aeolic treasury (plan, 7).

To the l. of the Sacred Way there was the Offering of the Tarentines (plan, 8) which commemorated a victory (subsequent to 473 BC) over the Messapii. It consisted of bronze statues of horses and captive Messapian women, and was the work of Agelades of Argos. Four pedestals are still standing, three of which carry inscriptions.

You next come to the foundations of the treasury of Sicyon, built towards the end of the 6th century re-using parts of two buildings put up by Cleisthenes, who was tyrant of Sicyon at the beginning of the 6th century BC. One of these was a tholos and the other a monopteros which was decorated with 14 small metopes, four of which are still in a good state of preservation (in the museum).

Next came the treasury of Siphnos built c.525 BC from the proceeds of gold mines developed on that small island. It had a decorative sculpted frieze which is now in the museum.

A little terrace (plan, 9) with statues from Cnidus standing on it, lay between the treasuries of Sicyon and Siphnos. Opposite the treasury of Siphnos to the r. of the Sacred Way can be seen a limestone retaining wall in front of the remains of an anonymous treasury (plan, 10) built of tufa, with several decrees engraved on it in honour of citizens of Megara.

Just as the Sacred Way curves round for the first time there are a few traces of the sub-foundations of a treasury known as that of the Boeotians (plan, 12) and in the SW corner of the sanctuary, remains of the treasury of the Thebans, built after the Battle of Leuctra (371 BC); an omphalos has been placed in front of it. Nearby on the W side are either the remains of a small building, or the blue limestone bases of some statues dedicated by the Liparians after winning a naval battle against the Tyrrhenians, by Pausanias' account (plan, 13).

Enthusiasts can also go to see the ruins of three Archaic treasuries, the first of which is believed to be that of the Potidaeans (plan, 14), and the second and third probably those of the Athenians and the Etruscans respectively.

A small shrine to Asclepius was built on the ruins of this last treasury, and from it you will mainly notice the small, well-preserved fountain.

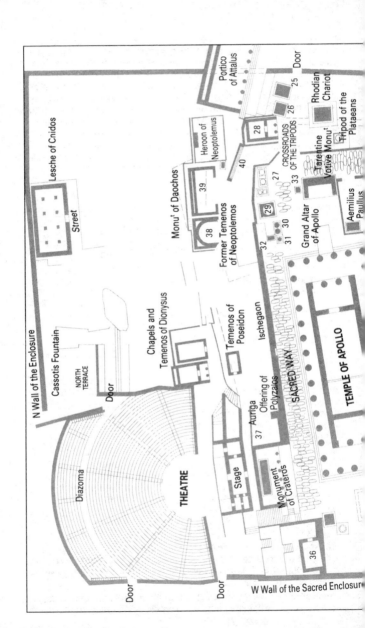

N Wall of the Enclosure

Lesche of Cnidos

Street

Portico of Attalus

Door

Cassotis Fountain

NORTH TERRACE

Door

Chapels and Temenos of Dionysus

Temenos of Poseidon

Heron of Neoptolemus

Monu' of Daochos

Former Temenos of Neoptolemos

38 39 40

28

26 25

Rhodian Chariot

Tripod of the Plataeans

Tarentine Votive Monu'

CROSSROADS OF THE TRIPODS

29 27 33

31 30

32

Grand Altar of Apollo

Aemilius Paullus

Ischegaon

Offering of Polyzalos

Auriga

37

SACRED WAY

Monument of Crateros

Stage

THEATRE

Diazoma

Door

TEMPLE OF APOLLO

36

Door

W Wall of the Sacred Enclosure

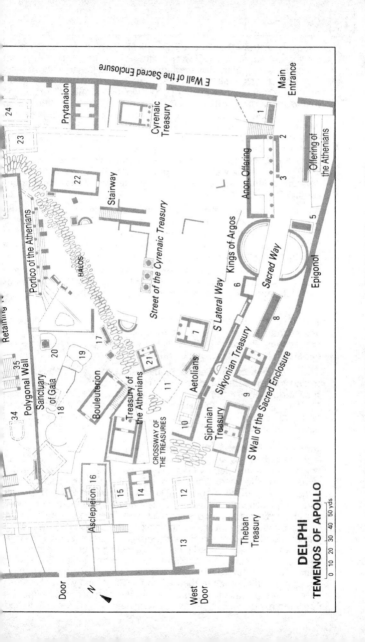

DELPHI
TEMENOS OF APOLLO

0 10 20 30 40 50 yds

Main Entrance

E Wall of the Sacred Enclosure

Prytanaion

Cyrenaic Treasury

Anon. Offering

Offering of the Athenians

Street of the Cyrenaic Treasury

Kings of Argos

S Lateral Way

Sacred Way

Epigonoi

Stairway

Portico of the Athenians

HALOS

Retaining

Polygonal Wall

Sanctuary of Gaia

Bouleuterion

Treasury of the Athenians

CROSSWAY OF THE TREASURIES

Aetolians

Sikyonian Treasury

Siphnian Treasury

S Wall of the Sacred Enclosure

Asclepieion

Theban Treasury

West Door

Door

N

*Treasury of the Athenians – This building, which was constructed between 490 and 485 BC with a tithe levied on the loot taken at Marathon, is one of the few monuments in the sanctuary to have been restored. It was built of marble from Paros and decorated with sculptures (kept in the museum) depicting the exploits of Heracles as well as those of the Athenian hero, Theseus, and, well positioned on the main facade, a series of scenes from the Greeks' war against the Amazons, symbolizing the Athenians successful struggle against the Persians under Darius. As well as the inscription: 'The Athenians to Apollo, after their victory over the Persians, an offering commemorative of the Battle of Marathon' which is engraved on a base for statues in front of the S wall, many other inscriptions, mostly decrees honouring Athenians, were cut into the treasury walls from the 3rd century BC on.

Among the inscriptions on the treasury, many of which are decorated with crowns, there are decrees relating to the Athenian *theoria* or Pythiad (a special embassy), two hymns to Apollo with musical notation (kept in the museum), a *senatus consultum*, and decrees relating to Dionysiac artists.

The building was constructed on the site of an earlier one, a few traces of which still survive in a pit inside the treasury; W.B. Dinsmoor suggests that the foundations should be dated c.580 BC, after the first Sacred War.

The site of the treasury of Syracuse (plan, 11) must have been located across from the treasury of the Athenians on the other side of the Sacred Way; Pausanias tells us that it was put up after the Athenian disaster in Sicily, that is, at the end of the 5th century BC.

The bouleuterion or Senate House of Delphi stood beside the treasury of the Athenians on the l. of the Sacred Way. Opposite it lie the foundations of the treasury of the Cnidians (plan, 21) built in Parian marble before Cnidus fell to the Persians (544 BC). A side road ended near the treasury of Cyrene, which was built between 350 and 325 BC according to very elaborate specifications.

Sanctuary of Mother-Earth – The sanctuary of Mother-Earth lay at the foot of a retaining wall on the l., and this is where the original Gaia-Themis oracle guarded by Gaia's snake-daughter Python is believed to have been located. But it is possible that the goddess Gaia in conjunction with her daughter Themis was worshipped in several different places under different names, and some scholars consider that the main place of worship must have been near the Castalian spring. Behind a few bases standing along the Sacred Way, including that of the offering of the Boeotians (plan, 17), lies a circle of large blocks of stone surrounded by a small uneven peribolus marking the limits of the temenos of the Earth-Mother, which included a spring (plan, 18). An outcrop of rock (plan, 19) with a crevice running through it corresponds to the rock of the Sibyl who was believed to have uttered prophecies long before Apollo, and perhaps before the Earth-Mother goddess. There was a rock nearby from which Leto had called out to her son, Apollo, to kill Python and seize the oracle for himself. The column of the Naxians (plan, 20), 32ft (10m) high, stood on another rock, with a sphinx perching on the Ionic capital of the column (the sphinx and the capital are on display in the museum). This offering, made of Naxian marble, was dedicated c.580 BC. An inscription engraved on its base in 328 BC serves as a reminder that the Naxians had been granted the right of Promanteia (first consultation with the oracle).

The threshing floor – About 55yds (50m) from the treasury of the Athenians the Sacred Way crossed a circular open space, the threshing floor; it is about 50ft (16m) in diameter, and once had benches and seats around it; it was here that the sacred drama showing the killing of the snake-monster Python by Apollo was celebrated during the Pythian Festival. This is where P. Amandry in 1939 discovered in two pits concealed under the Sacred Way a rich store of Archaic votive objects discarded in the 5th century BC (see in the museum, Room 4).

Stoa of the Athenians – Near the threshing floor on the l. of the Sacred Way there stood the stoa of the Athenians which seems to have been built after 478 BC as a shelter for the trophies taken from the Persians. The inscription engraved in large 5th-century BC lettering on the third step indicates that this was booty taken in a maritime expedition. P. Amandry believes that the portico would have housed the cables of the pontoon bridge built by Xerxes to enable his army to cross the Hellespont, and various figureheads from the prows of enemy ships captured after the siege of Sestos in the spring of 478 BC. Loot taken after other victories was subsequently put on display here.

The stoa stood on a base with three steps which held eight Ionic columns made of Pentelic marble (the bases and capitals were in Parian marble), three of which have been partly re-erected. Public writs were engraved on the wall at the back.

The site of the treasury of the Corinthians (plan, 22) is opposite the portico on the r.-hand side of the Sacred Way; Herodotus attributed it to the tyrant Cypselus (657–627 BC), and it was the earliest building of this description. It contained a bronze palm tree which rose above a floor covered in snakes and frogs. Nearby are the remains of two destroyed treasuries (plan, 23 and 24). On the r. near the treasury of Cyrene was the prytaneum.

*Retaining wall of the temple of Apollo – Before continuing your ascent towards the temple of Apollo, look closely at the retaining wall for the temple terrace, which is a marvel of precise workmanship; it was built in the 6th century BC with irregularly shaped, interlocking blocks, a style known as 'polygonal'. The ancient Delphians engraved more than 800 official notices, mainly to do with the freeing of slaves, on this wall (between 200 BC and 100 AD).

Tripod of Plataea – After curving round for a second time the Sacred Way, which is paved with large flagstones, climbs towards the temple entrance, lined to the r. by the ruins of votive monuments, including the offering of Plataea, a gold tripod standing on a column which rose from a circular pedestal consisting of a double course of masonry. It was dedicated by the Greeks with the tithe on the booty taken from the Persians after the battle of Plataea (479 BC).

The tripod rested on a bronze column in the shape of a coil formed by the regular intertwining of three snakes on which the names of the Greek towns participating in the victory over Xerxes at the battles of Salamis and Plataea were engraved. The tripod was removed by the Phocians between 356 and 346 BC and the Emperor Constantine had the column transported to his capital, Constantinople, to the Hippodrome, where a few remains of it can still be seen.

Near the tripod of Plataea were the votive offering of the Rhodians with a chariot of the Sun, and further on the statues (plan, 25 and 26) of two kings of Pergamum, Eumenes II and Attalus I.

Crossroads of the tripods – The Sacred Way ends at the crossroads of the tripods originally surrounded by several rows of offerings which have disappeared. The most notable must have been those of the two tyrants of Syracuse, Gelon and Hiero, and of their brothers, and the acanthus column or column of the Thyiades, now in the museum. It is known that Gelon's offering (plan, 27), made after his victory at Himera (481 BC) over the Carthaginians, consisted of four monuments supporting gold tripods and Victories which weighed at least 50 talents (approx. 4,080lb/1,855kg of gold).

On the r. of the base dedicated by Gelon is an offering in the name of his brother Hiero and on the l. two other smaller ones, without inscriptions, identified as being the offerings of their brothers Polyzelus and Thrasybulus.

Further to the r. are fragments of the treasury of Brasidas and the Acanthians of Chalcidice (plan, 28). Near the tripod of Plataea there is a small plinth pierced by numerous square holes in which were placed the golden swords sent by the citizens of Apollonia.

On the little esplanade in front of the temple, at the foot of the retaining wall known as Ischegaon, other votive monuments used to stand: a big square base (plan, 29) which may be that of Apollo Sitalcas, a pedestal for the offering of Aristaenetus (plan, 30), then the base of the palm tree of Eurymedon (plan, 31). On top of this bronze palm tree there was a statue of Athena; it was dedicated by the Athenians after their victory over the Persians near the mouth of the Eurymedon (Asia Minor) in 468 BC. The pillar of Prusias II, king of Bithynia (182–149 BC), rises behind, resting on the base of the palm tree, and has been completely restored (plan, 32). A dedicatory inscription engraved high up on the S face of the pedestal gives the information that an equestrian statue of the king, a votive offering from the Aetolians, stood on top of the pillar.

Great altar of Apollo – At the entrance to the temple of Apollo you can see the remains of this altar built in the 5th century BC by the people of the island of Chios, according to the dedication engraved on the cornice. It had three steps made of grey limestone and the main part was built of dark blue marble from Chios, framed by two courses of white marble.

It is not known when the altar was dedicated, only that it was put up by Chios in gratitude for its liberation either when the Ionian cities rebelled against the Persians (499–494 BC) or after the Battle of Mycale (479 BC). The altar is placed in the axis of the temple, but at a slight angle, no doubt because it was erected on the site of the altar that stood there prior to the fire of 548 BC. In the 2nd century BC a high pillar (plan, 33) was erected beside the altar on which stood the golden statue of Eumenes II, king of Pergamum, a gift from the Aetolians.

*Temple of Apollo – You have now arrived in front of the building which harboured the omphalos, the navel of the world for the Ancient Greeks, a point from which a religious and moral influence, of which the oracular pronouncements of the Pythia represented only a very specialized aspect, radiated out over all Hellas and over some foreign countries too. It was in the vestibule of this temple that the mottoes 'Know thyself' and 'Nothing to excess', were engraved, extolling a prudent, pragmatic morality.

The ruins you now see are those of a temple built between 370 and 330 BC. It replaced the famous temple of the Alcmaeonids, built between 514–513 BC and 506–505 BC with the proceeds of an international collection after an enormous amount of terracing work had been undertaken requiring approx. 7,850 cu. yds (6,000 cu. m) of filling material. The temple built by the Alcmaeonids, which was destroyed by an earthquake in 373 BC, had itself replaced an earlier sanctuary, destroyed by fire in 548 BC, the building of which was ascribed to two mythical architects, Agamedes and Trophonius (a son of Apollo). The Pythia officiated inside the building in a special room, where she could lean over the omphalos and, so it was believed, breathe in fumes which caused her to go into a trance.

The 4th-century temple was a Doric peripter, with six columns made of stuccoed tufa at the back and front, 15 columns on either side, as well as two columns between the antae of the pronaos and the opisthodomos.

Earthquakes and systematic destruction by the Christians have seriously damaged the temple; but it is possible to recreate the main divisions, thanks to ancient texts and some architectural remains. It opened towards the crossroads of the tripods with a vestibule or pronaos which contained a statue of Homer. Above the door leading from the pronaos into the cella the letter 'epsilon' was fixed, lying on its side, first in bronze, and later in gold (a gift from Livia, wife of the Emperor Augustus).

In the cella there was an altar dedicated to Poseidon, statues of two of the three Moirai (Fates; the third was replaced by a statue of Zeus), of Apollo Moiragetes, the iron seat of Pindar and the hearth on which

Apollo's priest had killed Neoptolemus (one of the many versions of his death).

The temple also comprised an adyton, an underground room which contained the omphalos and the prophetic props, the oikos, the writing-room for those wishing to consult the oracle, adjacent to the adyton, and finally the opisthodomos, which corresponded to the pronaos.

AN ABSORBING PROFESSION. The Greek author Lucian (noted for his irony), speaking in the person of Zeus, informs us that 'Apollo, with the absorbing profession he has chosen for himself, is all but deafened by importunate people coming to ask him for oracles'. At first the god gave audience only once a year, on the seventh day of Bysios, the eighth month of the Delphian year (Feb.-Mar.), then later at any time; in the 2nd century once a month. In emergencies (threat of war, an influx of visitors) the oracle could be consulted at any time except in winter, when Apollo was absent.

THE ORACLE AND THE RITES OF CONSULTATION. Any man wishing to consult the oracle (women were not admitted) had to pay a tax called the pelanos, which gave the suppliant the right to go to the great altar of Apollo to carry out the sacrifice required before entry into the temple was permitted. Generally the sacrificial animal was a goat. Scrutiny of the victim was the basis for a decision whether or not the consultation was approved. Thus the priests watched for a tremor in all the limbs of the sacrificed animal when water was sprinkled over it. If there was no tremor, the consultation was put off until another time.

The petitioners passed into the waiting-room next to the underground chamber where the Pythia officiated; lots were drawn to decide who would go first. Those to whom the Delphians had granted the privilege of Promanteia, priority in consulting the oracle, went in first.

The Pythia, after purifying herself with water from the Castalian spring, went into the temple and fumigated it with laurel leaves and ground barley over the cella hearth, possibly in the presence of the priests and perhaps also of the petitioners. Then the Pythia went down the stairs leading to the manteion (where the oracles were pronounced) and to the prophetic place.

THE OMPHALOS AND THE TRIPOD. The manteion contained the gold statue of Apollo, the tomb of Dionysus, the tripod on which the Pythia sat to prophesy and the omphalos. The omphalos was a stone believed to have fallen from heaven. A later explanation was that it symbolized the meeting point of two eagles released by Zeus, one from where the sun rises and the other from where the sun sets, and it thus marked the centre or navel of the earth. The tripod, which was endlessly reproduced on vases and bas-reliefs, is the accessory that characterizes Delphic prophecy. It consisted of a metal cauldron set on three legs with a covering lid that transformed it into the seat on which the Pythia had to take her place in order to prophesy. The tripod recalled a funeral rite associated with the death of Dionysus, as the Bacchantes of Mt Parnassus had in fact gathered up the young god's limbs in a cauldron.

THE PYTHIA'S STATE OF 'RAPTURE'. After performing a preliminary rite over the hearth, the Pythia drew some water from the Kassotis spring, then mounted the tripod, drank the water and chewed laurel leaves (Apollo's sacred tree). In this way she fell into a state of rapture, or divine possession, which people took to be a state of delirium but which was simply a very profound meditation, Apollonian and not Dionysian in character, though many ancient commentators allowed their imaginations to lead them to a false conclusion concerning this.

APOLLO THE OBLIQUE. Inspired in her ecstasy by Apollo the Oblique (as his nickname Loxias meant), the Pythia did no more than choose between answers (positive, negative, ambiguous) prepared by the priests and placed in a bowl. The petitioners were not seeking to fathom the mystery of their future, which would have displeased Zeus, the master of their fate; rather they asked very precise questions, for example concerning the suitability of undertaking a journey or an expedition to found a colony, or the likelihood of success in war, marriage, a trading venture, etc.

APOLLO'S HANDMAIDENS. To begin with, Pythiae were chosen from among the young women of Delphi, and then, so as to be more certain of their virtue, women over 50 years of age were chosen, at least at some epochs. There were up to three of them when Delphi was at its height, but only one during the Roman period.

Between the foundations of the temple and the big polygonal wall there are also the ruins of a small building (plan, 34) and at the foot of a stairway a fountain which was the famous Kassotis Spring, at least as it was in the 6th century BC (plan, 35). The offering of the Messenians to Naupactus (location not known) also stood on this esplanade, put up by the Messenians after their success alongside the Athenians fighting the Spartans at Sphacteria and Pylos in 425 BC. S of the ramp and lower down was the pillar of Aemilius Paullus commemorating his victory over the last king of Macedon, Perseus, at Pydna in 168 BC.

To the rear of the temple there are the remains of several buildings, including a treasury (plan, 36).

Outside the sanctuary precinct there are some surviving remnants of a long portico more or less identical in orientation to the temple. This monument, traditionally known as the W portico because of its position in relation to the sanctuary, had two rows of columns: one on the axis of the building was of the Ionic order, and the other which formed the façade, was of the Doric order. A large, recently discovered inscription engraved on to the W side of the back wall of the portico says that it was built by the Aetolians with proceeds from booty taken at a victory over the Galatians in the first half of the 3rd century BC. The eastern part of the portico was transformed into baths around the 4th century AD.

Ischegaon – To the N of the temple of Apollo, the Sacred Way was protected on the sloping side by a retaining wall known as the Ischegaon, which was built in the 4th century BC.

Under the steps leading to the theatre, recent excavations have uncovered the presence of an earlier stairway of great age, which was never finished; its function remains a mystery.

On the r. there was a road ending at the stairway skirting the stage buildings of the theatre and overlooking a huge rectangular exedra, identified by means of a rhyming epigram engraved on the back wall (second course up) as the monument dedicated after 320 BC by the son of Craterus, one of Alexander the Great's lieutenants, who saved his king during a lion-hunt near Susa. A bronze group by Lysippus and Leochares showed Alexander wrestling with a wild animal and Craterus hurrying to his rescue.

The famous bronze auriga (plan, 37) from the offering of Polyzelus, what are thought to be the foundations of a small sanctuary of Poseidon, and two treasuries built of tufa and thought to have been dedicated to Dionysus have been found nearby.

Further on are the ruins of an exedra for statues (plan, 38 and beside them those of the monument of the Thessalonians (plan, 39), built thanks to the generosity of Daochus II who represented Thessaly from 336 to 332 BC at the council of the Amphictyons. He had made and offered to Apollo a series of nine statues representing his ancestors; one of the most powerful families in Pharsalus (the inscribed base and the statues are on display in the museum).

Beside the monument of the Thessalians is the temenos of Neopotolemus, the son of Achilles who was killed and buried at Delphi, to whom the Thessalians dedicated an open-air sanctuary surrounded by a polygonal-style peribolus on the site of a Mycenaean place of worship near a village also of the Mycenaean period. Near the temenos of Neoptolemus is the base of the monument of the Corcyreans (plan, 40), and between the two the base of the acanthus column which held a group of Bacchae (now exhibited in the museum).

Running across the precinct wall of the sanctuary was a terrace installed by King Attalus I of Pergamum to commemorate his victory over the Galatians in Asia Minor at the end of the 3rd century BC. A portico decorated with paintings, copying the stoa poikile of the agora in Athens, ran along the N side of the terrace. In front of the portico a large base extended (the largest in Delphi: it was up to 90ft/27m wide) with larger-than-lifesize statues on it, probably evoking the battles between the Pergamenes and the Galatians. A small building standing at the E end may have sheltered an altar. On the terrace alongside the road leading to the sanctuary there was a vaulted exedra equipped with benches where pilgrims could rest; this is the first known example in Greek architecture of ribbed vaulting.

*Theatre – This building, which was built in the 4th century BC and restored at the expense of Eumenes II, king of Pergamum, in 159 BC, then again in the Roman period, is a place conducive to daydreams, as you look out from the tiers of the theatre across the marvellous ***panorama unfolding before you; the tiers are made of grey stone from Parnassus. The 5,000 or so spectators that the theatre could accommodate came to attend Delphic festivals, in particular those given to celebrate Apollo's victory over the monstrous snake Python, or the Pythian Games.

THE PYTHIAN GAMES. At first, they took place every eight years, then from 590 BC every four years, and again every eight years during the Roman Imperial era; they were held at the beginning of September under the superintendence of the Amphictyons. The festival consisted of sacrifices, a sacred drama enacting the god's struggle against Python, then music (cithara, flute, singing) and cantata (paean) competitions – the paeans were in honour of Apollo and were performed in the theatre (later on tragedies and comedies were also performed); of gymnastic contests held in the stadium; and finally of chariot races held in the hippodrome on the plain. The prizes were laurel wreaths. In addition to the Pythian Games, the Athenians sent a special embassy or Pythiad to Delphi and celebrated a separate festival with games and drama.

To the E of the theatre by the N wall of the sanctuary's peribolus are the remains of the Lesche of the Cnidians which was decorated with paintings by the famous painter Polygnotus of Thasos. It was built as a meeting-place by the Cnidians in the first half of the 5th century BC.

According to Pausanias' account, the frescoes decorating the four walls of the hall represented the Iliupersis (the sacking of Troy by the victorious Greeks) and the Nekyia (Odysseus' evocation of the dead, as described in Book XI of the *Odyssey*).

Until recently it was possible to see an ancient spring, known by the modern name of Kerna, as you went along the path leading to the stadium above the theatre; unfortunately it was completely destroyed and buried by falling rocks early in 1980. Though it is hoped that it will be restored, this may prove to be a long and difficult task.

Stadium (can also be reached by car from the W of the town) – The 3rd-century BC stadium, later altered by the Romans, lies on a small artificial plateau in the middle of a pine wood, and was able to hold approx. 7,000 spectators. In front of the entrance you can see the pillars of a Roman triumphal arch; the athletes paraded from this gate of honour.

The track, which is from 82ft 10ins (25.25m) to 84ft 2ins (25.65m) wide at the two ends and 93ft 6ins (28.5m) wide in the middle and 582ft 6ins (177.5m) in length (a Pythian stadium of six plethra), lies between the starting line (aphesis) and the finishing line (terma), both made of marble slabs with grooves hollowed out as supports for the runners' feet, and square holes which held the stakes separating the runners (there were 17 to 18 lanes). Herodes Atticus undertook the expense of building the tiers in limestone; previously they had been made of earth, as at Olympia. The reinforcements for the bank as it goes downhill, now largely collapsed, date from the 3rd century. An Archaic-looking inscription engraved on a long stone on the outer face (3rd course down, 49ft/15m from the entrance) prohibits the removal from the stadium of the new wine poured as a libation to certain deities, on pain of a fine of 5 drachmas. This inscription must come from the original stadium which must have been on the plain, like the hippodrome.

A rectangular tribune, its benches with back-supports, was the proedria where those presiding over the games sat. In the NW corner of the stadium before the sphendone (semi-circular end of the stadium) the remains of a drainage system can be seen (mouth of a flanged drain at the top of the tiers).

■ 3 THE ***MUSEUM

The exhibits are exclusively from Delphi, yet this local museum is one of the four greatest museums in Greece. Because of its role as a Panhellenic religious centre Delphi was richly endowed with works of art, some of which, such as the sculpted friezes of the treasury of Siphnos and of course the famous auriga (charioteer), one of the leading works of Greek art, are vitally important.

Open: summer, weekdays 08.00–18.00 and Sun. 10.00–16.30; winter, 09.00–15.30; closed Tues.; entrance fee (Tel. 0265–823 13).

From the entrance hall take the stair on the r. At the top of the staircase you enter the room of the omphalos.

Room of the omphalos – This contains the most important cult object to have been found at Delphi: an omphalos (8194), or sacred stone, which belonged in the manteion (the place where oracles were given).

THE LEGENDARY TOMB OF THE SON OF THE EARTH-MOTHER AND THE NAVEL OF THE WORLD. The omphalos, which is made of marble and gives the appearance of being covered with a net made of tufts of wool, is in fact a copy made in the Roman period, but it must be very similar to the original. According to unsupported legends which are at variance with the geology of the place, it is supposed to have been placed over a crevice from which noxious gases escaped, long regarded as responsible for the prophetic delirium of the Pythia. These gases were supposedly produced by the body of the snake Python, the Earth-Mother's daughter, whom Apollo had killed to gain possession of the oracle; the omphalos was supposed to have been her memorial stone.

According to another very widespread legend, the omphalos was said to have marked the centre, or navel (the word's primary meaning in Greek) of the world: after Zeus released two eagles from the two opposite ends of the earth, the two birds flew towards one another and their meeting-point was at Delphi, which was therefore regarded as the centre of the world.

On the wall to the l. of the omphalos the upper part of a stele (2707) made of Pentelic marble has as its uppermost part a small sculpted tableau which actually depicts the Delphic omphalos between Apollo and Athena (c.330 BC). In the corner of the room there is a tripod made of iron rods (9467), the bronze feet of which are shaped like the hooves of a bull; it acts as a support for a large bronze *lebes* (cauldron) (1146); both objects, which are typical of the kind of offering which was very much used in the sanctuary during the Archaic period, date from the 7th century BC.

Also note the frieze from the theatre proscenium along the l. wall (1st century AD) illustrating the Labours of Heracles.

From the hall of the omphalos go past the reliefs of the Labours of Heracles into a newly arranged room (unfortunately often closed) in which small items mainly from the Archaic period are exhibited.

Room of small items – There are two showcases on the walls in which bronze jewellery (fibulae, bracelets) found at Amfissa (8th–7th century BC), Geometric-style vases found at Delphi (900–700 BC), and Proto-Corinthian and Corinthian vases (7th–6th century BC) from Delphi or Amfissa are displayed, and five central showcases containing small bronze objects, displayed chronologically starting from the back of the room and working towards the door.

As you go along you will notice small Geometric-style bronzes of men and animals (900–700 BC), fragments of bronze tripods (8th century BC), then some very fine **reliefs (especially griffins and sirens) taken from cauldrons or other utensils (7th–6th century BC), next Archaic and Classical items (including two reliefs, one of which shows Odysseus underneath the ram escaping from Polyphemus' cave, while the other shows a group with Heracles carrying the Erymanthian boar on his shoulders and King Eurystheus hiding in terror in his storage jar), fragments of bronze vases and utensils from a number of periods, and finally weapons (four helmets and two shield armbands with relief decoration) and other bronze votive objects found in the sanctuary of Apollo.

A final showcase (l. of entrance) contains terracotta vases and figurines from a sanctuary in Cirrha (6th–4th century BC); an Attic red-figure drinking vessel with a lid (5th century BC) and a group of miniature Corinthian vases are noteworthy.

From this room return to the hall of the omphalos and go l. into the hall of the bronze shields.

Hall of the bronze shields – Here there are some fine specimens of the skill for which Greek bronzesmiths from the Archaic period onwards became renowned, well beyond the Hellenic world. As well as three shields (7226, 7227 and 7127) dating from the first half of the 7th century BC (the last two have a central decoration known as a protome, that is, the forequarters of a lioness surrounded by incised animal figures: lions, deer, rams), there are two **protomes of griffins, one in hammered bronze (7739), the other cast (8396), which were meant to be fixed as ornamental handles on to the bowl of a large bronze cauldron (7th century BC). Dating from the same period there is a very fine bronze statuette of a kouros (2527), with a typically Daedalic head-dress, a kind of pyramid-shaped wig of superimposed layers.

Look finally at a marble perirrhanterion (5733), finished with plaster, on the r. as you go in; the basin is held by three female statuettes (korai) positioned symmetrically round a slender central column (first quarter of 6th century BC). Vessels such as this, which were used for the ritual washing of hands, have been found in several Greek sanctuaries.

Go through the door between the shields into the hall of the treasury of Siphnos.

 Hall of the treasury of Siphnos – Here you will see some of the greatest masterpieces of Archaic sculpture: the **reliefs from the treasury of Siphnos, which was built c.525 BC.

The E pediment to the l. of the door shows the dispute between Apollo (l.) and Heracles (r.) over the Delphic tripod.

Furious that the Pythia has refused to give him an answer, claiming that he had not purified himself after killing Iphitus in a fit of madness, Heracles tries to carry off the prophetic tripod on his back, intending to go and found an oracle of his own. Apollo is attempting to hold on to the sacred tripod and has grasped the end of its feet. Behind him a female figure who must be his sister, Artemis, appears to be advising moderation and is holding Apollo by the arm. Between the two contenders is someone who is trying to separate them, traditionally believed to be Athena; it has recently been suggested that it is more likely to be a god, Zeus or perhaps Hermes.

Below the pediment is the **E frieze which is divided into two complementary parts: on the r. fighting among hoplites between two chariots during the Trojan War; on the l. a gathering of the gods of Olympus watching the fight and making an impassioned commentary on it. The gods are divided into two groups. On the l.-hand side these are generally accepted as being from, l. to r., Ares, Aphrodite, Artemis and Apollo, who support Troy; and they are separated by Zeus, seated on a throne with Thetis prostrate in supplication before him (the figure has disappeared), from the supporters of the Greeks on the r.-hand side, who are, from l. to r., Athena, Hera and probably Demeter.

Those taking part in the fight are the Trojans, Aeneas and Hector, who have come down from the chariot, against Menelaus, king of Sparta, carrying a shield decorated with a Gorgon, and (perhaps) Ajax; they are fighting to gain possession of the body of a dead warrior, probably Sarpedon, a son of Zeus. At the far r. prudent Nestor is making exhortatory gestures towards the combatants.

Along the side wall on the l. the **N frieze depicts the Battle of the Gods and Giants (gigantomachy).

The protagonists are grouped round three chariots which give the composition its balance. On the l. Hephaestus is working his bellows to loose the winds against the giants, then there are two goddesses fighting two giants dressed as hoplites. Behind this Heracles is wrestling with a giant; the goddess Cybele goes in front of him in a chariot drawn by lions, one of which is devouring a giant; next come two gods dressed for battle: Artemis and Apollo drawing his bow, and a routed giant wearing a helmet with a cantharus-shaped crest; a line of three giants is facing them (the artist's signature is on one of the shields). The corpse of the giant Ephialtes is lying between the two groups. Then, there is a rearing team of horses pulling a second divine chariot (Zeus). In the foreground Hera is spearing a toppled giant. Athena, who can be recognized by her aegis, is engaged in combat with two opponents. Then come four similar groups, with a god dressed as a hoplite wrestling against two giants: first there is a bearded god, Ares, stepping over a prone giant, a god wearing a pointed head-dress (Hermes) and holding a large sword, then Poseidon (very fragmentary) in front of the remains of a third team, and last, an unidentified deity before two adversaries, one of whom has fallen to his knees.

On the wall opposite the entrance, the W frieze (on the l.), very incomplete, depicts the Judgement of Paris, and the S frieze (on the r.), also very fragmentary, perhaps represents the Dioscuri abducting Leucippus' daughters as well as a procession of chariots and horsemen with superb *horses.

The Judgement of Paris almost certainly consisted of three groups, of which only the first two have survived: on the l. Hermes comes before the winged chariot of Athena who is about to depart in a fit of rage; on the r. Aphrodite, whom Paris had chosen as the most beautiful of the three goddesses, is getting out of her chariot and at the same time placing a necklace round her neck; nothing remains of the group with Hera.

There are also some architectural fragments from the treasury of Siphnos on display in this room; these are in marble. The door casing (1184) with its rich decoration of palmettes, lotuses and rosettes and a bell capital with an ornamental relief showing two lions devouring a stag are particularly noteworthy. This capital was positioned above one of the two caryatids which acted as columns *in antis* at the entrance into the main room of the treasury and supported the entablature. One of these two caryatids, which has been partly preserved, stands in front of the capital: it has the appearance of a young woman (a kore) dressed in a tunic and a short cloak, wearing on her head a headdress shaped like a basket decorated with relief pictures of Sileni and Maenads. To the r. of the capital another kore is exhibited; very mutilated it is also thought to be a caryatid which must have come from another Archaic treasury. As for the second caryatid from the treasury of Siphos, the very fine head in Parian marble (1203), might have belonged to it. The head has a basket-shaped headdress with a little frieze showing Apollo with his cithara followed by four nymphs and preceded by the three Graces together with Hermes playing the syrinx.

In this room you can see some other finely-worked specimens of Archaic architecture (two small Doric columns in Parian marble dating from the 2nd half of the 6th century BC, and the 'Aeolic' palm capital from the treasury of Massalia, c.530 BC) and be sure not to miss the Ionic capital and the **winged Sphinx which stood at a height of more than 32ft (10m) on top of the column of the Naxians (c.560 BC).

Veering to the r., go diagonally across the room of the bronze shields.

Room of the kouroi – Look first at a kouros statuette in bronze (perhaps Apollo – c.530 BC) on the r. as you enter, and then on your l. at five of the metopes from the Doric Monopteros of Sicyon (c.560 BC) which probably had 14 of them; these had been reused in the foundations of the treasury of Sicyon, which accounts for their damaged condition. Nonetheless it is possible to recognize, from l. to r., an episode from the expedition by the Argonauts (the prow of the ship Argo between two horsemen, the Dioscuri); Europa being abducted by Zeus, who has taken on the appearance of a bull; the return of a cattle raid led by the Dioscuri (Castor and Polydeuces) and their cousins, Aphareus' sons (only one of which has been preserved); the Calydonian boar-hunt; and Phrixus on the back of the ram with the Golden Fleece.

At the back of the room stand two large kouroi in Parian marble (first quarter of 6th century BC), traditionally believed to be Kleobis and Biton, twin brothers from Argos who, according to the legend recorded by Herodotus, fell into an eternal sleep in the peace of the sanctuary of Hera near Argos, this being the goddess's reward for an act of uncommon piety: as there was no team of horses available, they had harnessed themselves to the chariot of their mother, one of Hera's priestesses, and drawn it from Argos to the Heraion, a distance of approx. 4.4mls (7km). C. Vatin has in fact proved that this identification was based on a questionable reading of the very worn remains of the inscription engraved on one of the bases; all that can be established with certainty from the inscription is that one of the statues (and most probably both) was the work of the sculptor Polymedes of Argos. As to the identity of the two young men, they should either be regarded as anonymous or tentatively identified as the Dioscuri, as was suggested when they were first discovered.

Room of the bull – After the room of the kouroi an outstandingly well-presented little room, with a lot of information, contains the material found in the two pits under the Sacred Way opposite the stoa of the Athenians.

It was in fact common practice in ancient times to bury discarded offerings inside the sanctuaries. These two pits were part of the sacred ground belonging to the temple of Apollo, but the Sacred Way did not go over them in the Classical period, and the paving of the Sacred Way, which consists of slabs from various monuments in the sanctuary, goes no further back than the 5th century AD. The oldest items found in the pits go back to the 7th century BC and the most recent to the end of the 5th century BC.

There is a reconstituted *statue of a bull made of partly gilded silver sheets nailed on to a wooden core (6th century BC); the fragments of three life-size *chryselephantine statues of human figures (the heads, hands and feet are made of ivory, the hair and dress of gold and the rest of the bodies of wood); three gold plaques mounted on bronze (a griffin and a Gorgon) and gold rosettes and palmettes which may come from the throne of one of the statues; bronze and ivory statuettes; and small ivory reliefs depicting scenes from mythology (9944; the Harpies being pursued by the sons of Boreas) and epic poetry (battle, warriors setting out, etc.). There is also a magnificent **bronze perfume jar (7723) in this room, made of three parts: a female figure, wearing a peplos, supports on her head and hands a hemispherical bowl made of hammered sheet-metal which was covered by an openwork lid (c.450 BC).

Go back through the room of the kouroi and the room of the bronze shields, then turn r.

Room of the Athenian treasury – The reliefs which decorated the pediments and the metopes from that small Doric-order building erected after the Battle of Marathon (490 BC) are displayed here, with scenes illustrating the battle of the Amazons on one side, and on the other, the exploits of Heracles and Theseus.

Of the 24 metopes exhibited (there were thirty in all) the best preserved are: 1st l., Heracles and Cycnus; 1st r., Heracles leaping to capture the Cerynitian hind with the golden antlers; 2nd r., Heracles seizing the Nemean lion; opposite the entrance the three metopes on the l.: Theseus and the Minotaur, Theseus and Antiope, and Theseus and the bull of Marathon; and the 1st metope on the r.: Theseus and Athena – the style of this last metope which is already pre-Classical is in contrast with the distinctly Archaic influence evident in several others.

Rooms relating to the temple of Apollo – In the first of these two rooms on the l. are sculptures from the W pediment of the so-called temple of the Alcmaeonids, built in the second half of the 6th century BC in place of an earlier temple destroyed by fire in 548 BC. This pediment dealt with the Battle of the Gods and the Giants; the goddess Athena and a giant can be identified. These sculptures are attributed to the Athenian artist, Antenor (c.510 BC).

Near the pediments you will see a small headless marble kouros wearing a garment, which is quite unusual (late 6th, early 5th century BC). The female figure wearing a peplos to the r. must have stood on a plinth at one end of a pediment in the Doric treasury of the sanctuary of Athena Pronaia (c.470 BC). On the opposite wall you can see an example of ancient musical notation: two hymns to Apollo, the text of which is accompanied by musical symbols engraved on the stone coursework of the S wall of the treasury of the Athenians (c.138–128 BC).

At the back of the second room are the remains of sculptures from the E pediment of the Alcmaeonids' temple; the theme here was the epiphany of Apollo, i.e. his triumphal arrival at Delphi on a quadriga (chariot) accompanied by his mother Leto and his sister Artemis, watched by a variety of people and animals.

Along with the pedimental sculptures various items that belonged to the same temple are on display: figures from acroteria (including Nike or the Winged Victory in marble, exhibited on the r.) and beside them fragments from the guttering with a gargoyle in the shape of a lion's head. The other lion's head (8198) displayed on the opposite wall comes from the guttering of the 4th century BC temple; observe the differences in style. To the l. of the second lion's head there is the torso of a kouros in Parian marble (c.530 BC) and a bronze statuette of a cow (early 5th century BC); opposite it are another torso of a kouros, slightly earlier, and a statue pedestal with an inscription telling us that this was an offering made by the sons of Charopinus of Paros who had also dedicated a small marble column (mid-6th century BC). Two of the four inscribed plaques (4th century BC) on either side of the door contain the accounts of the city of Delphi relating to the rebuilding of the temple between 388 and 310 BC. The plaque above the door, in Latin, is a reminder of the temple repairs financed by the Emperor Domitian in 84 AD.

Go back into the first temple of Apollo room and turn to the r.

Room of the funeral stelae – The first part of this room contains items connected with burial: glass-plate and terracotta vases (especially lekythoi from the Classical period), the upper half of female figures (protomes) in terracotta, small ivory pyxides (boxes), two bronze cinerary hydriae (opposite the entrance), and – of special note – three marble stelae, including one of a young athlete scraping oil from his skin with a strigil, accompanied by his small servant boy (c.460 BC). In the corner of the second half of the room there is a round altar from the sanctuary of Athena Pronaia, decorated with reliefs showing a graceful frieze of girls tying bands on to a garland of leaves (1st century BC); there are also some incomplete statues, including an Apollo with a cithara (1876) of a very well known type (3rd century BC).

Room of the tholos – This is devoted to architectural fragments and pieces of sculpture from the famous tholos (beehive shaped tomb) of the sanctuary of Athena Pronaia (c.380 BC).

Opposite the entrance, part of the external Doric entablature has been reconstituted, with the frieze (including four metopes), the dripstone and the guttering. To the l. of the door there is a Doric capital from the exterior colonnade and on the r. a section of the external Doric entablature and a Corinthian half-column with its capital, from the interior order of the tholos. Going from r. to l. many fragments are on display from the sculpture on the metopes, which was in high relief. Some of the metopes on the outside of the building illustrated the battle between the Centaurs and the Amazons; but there were also smaller metopes from inside the building which belonged to a frieze that ran round the top of the outer face of the circular wall of the cella; they probably depicted the labours of Heracles and the exploits of Theseus.

Room of the dancing girls – One of the museum's masterpieces is on display here: the **group of Thyiades (priestesses of Dionysus) which stood on top of the approx. 36ft/11m-high acanthus column. This group of women dancing, which dates from the 4th century BC, perhaps c.330–325, is one of the most beautiful examples of Classical art, and inspired Debussy to compose the 'Danseuses de Delphes'.

Behind the dancing girls stand the statues from the offering of Daochus II (c.335 BC), a prominent citizen of Thessaly (which he represented from 336 to 332 BC in the Delphian amphictyony) who wished to honour his ancestors and the famous members of his family by erecting their statues in the sanctuary. The statues have recently been replaced on their inscribed bases, which have been moved from the site to the museum.

Going from r. to l. you will see Acnonius, forefather of the family and tetrarch (governor) of Thessaly at the beginning of the 5th century BC, shown wearing a chlamys (cloak); his sons **Agias, a famous athlete who was several times champion pancratiast (boxer and wrestler at the Olympic, Nemean, Isthmian and Pythian Games in the second half of the 5th century, whose statue – the best preserved of the group – seems to be copied from a bronze statue by Lysippus dated 340 BC, and Agelaus, a running champion at the Pythian Games, both nude as befitted athletes; Daochus I, Agias's son and Daochus II's grandfather, also a tetrarch of Thessaly, draped in a heavy chlamys; his son, Sisyphus I, wearing a tunic; Daochus II himself, who dedicated the offering, Sisyphus I's son – only his feet have survived; and lastly his son, Sisyphus II, nude with his chlamys over his shoulder and his l. arm resting on a hermaean stele. The only statues missing are that of Apollo which was in front, before that of Acnonius, and that of Telemachus, who was Agias' and Agelaus' brother, an athlete like them; his statue stood between those of his brothers. Note how the artist has striven to avoid monotony by varying and alternating the stance and clothing of the figures, but without disrupting the unity of the group. R. of the door leading into this room there is a beautiful athlete's torso with striking musculature, dating from the 4th century BC, and on the l. a **Dionysus (2380), recently reconstructed, which was the central figure on the W pediment of the 4th-century temple of Apollo, and is attributed to the Athenian sculptor Androsthenes (c.340–330 BC); according to Pausanias, the pediment showed the god surrounded by his usual companions, the Maenads (there is another school of thought according to which the statue is more likely of Apollo himself).

Before leaving the room look at the marble statue of an old man (1819), who may have been a philosopher or a priest, wrapped in a cloak (himation) that leaves the upper part of his chest and his right shoulder uncovered (c.280 BC).

Room of the auriga (charioteer) — The opportunity to see the famous

***statue of the auriga of Delphi is one of the highlights of a visit to this museum. This statue formed part of a bronze quadriga commemorating a win by Polyzelus, the Greek prince of Sicily, in a chariot race at the Pythian Games in 478 or 474 BC.

The auriga, or charioteer, stands upright during the parade (the victorious prince is thought to have been beside him) with his reins in his r. hand (his l. hand must have been in a similar position) and on his head he wears a narrow band; the eyes are made of coloured stones. There is still something reminiscent of the Archaic style in his stance, but it is elegant and noble. This statue must have been cast shortly after 474 BC, and the sculptor's identity is not known. There are some other fragments from the same group in the room: horse's legs, a tail, reins and the l. arm of a secondary figure, that of a child who was holding the horses by their bits. A block from the base that held the group still has on it a fragment of the inscribed dedication. Do not miss a **small Attic vessel in a wall showcase (8190); it is from the same period as the auriga. The background colour is white, with a medallion showing Apollo sitting crowned with myrtle holding the seven-string lyre in his left hand, and in his right, a phial from which he is pouring a libation; in front of him is a black bird which may be a crow – the Greek word for crow is similar to Coronis, the name of a young woman beloved of the god, and mother of Asclepius.

Room of Graeco-Roman antiquities – The first item to strike you will be the excellent marble *statue of Antinous (117–138 AD), the favourite of the Emperor Hadrian who came from Bithynia in Asia Minor, dating from the 2nd century AD, and opposite it the marble bust of a philosopher (same period).

Near Antinous are marble statues of a child holding a goose (late 3rd century BC) and of a little girl smiling (early 3rd century BC), both common subjects from the Hellenistic period on. Then there is a hermaic pillar jointly erected by the people of Chaeronea and the Delphians, according to the inscription, in honour of the writer Plutarch (46–120 AD), who was born in Chaeronea and served for a long time as a priest of Apollo at Delphi. Beyond that is a fine marble head (1706) dating from the early 2nd century BC identified as the portrait of the Roman general and consul Titus Q. Flamininus who proclaimed the freedom of Greece and the independence of its cities from the suzerainty of Macedon in 196 BC.

There are two showcases with vases from the Early and Late Helladic period (3rd and 2nd millennium BC) and ten or so terracotta figurines from the Mycenaean period mainly from the sanctuary of Athena Pronaia, indicating the existence there of a place of worship, probably in honour of a female deity, from the 2nd millennium BC. The showcase beside the windows has a display of devotional objects found in the Corycian cave on the slopes of Mt Parnassus which was dedicated to Pan and the nymphs: figurines, terracotta vases and plaques, knuckle-bones, small bronzes (including a little Geometric-style horse).

VICINITY OF DELPHI

If you succumb to the charm of the village built near the sanctuary, you could stay on at Delphi for a day or two and visit one of the most beautiful monasteries in Greece, Hosios Loukas, and the outstanding scenery around Mt Parnassus, etc. Unless you are a seasoned climber, don't attempt to climb the famous mountain (although you would be rewarded by a superb panoramic view); instead you can take a road from Arachova to Kalivia and even right up to the Corycian cave, which can easily be negotiated by car.

1 THE SYBARIS CAVE AND THE PLEISTUS GORGE (3–4hrs on foot). The path leaves the road to the r. as you leave the village in the direction of the sanctuary. After a winding descent it reaches the bottom of the ravine, then passes several small caves, crosses the stream and comes to (1hr) the side of a very deep chasm, the spring of Sybaris, named after the monster which used to live in the cave lying opposite. First follow the stream, then (l. for 164yds/150m) an irrigation ditch, and you will come to (l. for 65yds/60m) a path leading to the monastery of the Panagia and the Pleistus, and from there a path goes back to rejoin the road E of Marmaria.

2 ITEA. (see under Itea; 10.6mls/17km; follow Amfissa road, turn l. after 8.7mls/14km). For those who like swimming in the sea.

3 AMFISSA. (see under Amfissa; 14.4mls/23km). A picturesque little town overlooked by an old Frankish castle, reached after crossing a huge olive plantation, growing on the famous Sacred Plain.

4 ˮHOSIOS LOUKAS. (see under Hosios Loukas; 24.4mls/39km; follow Livadia road and turn r. after 16.2mls/26km). A monastery whose church has outstanding mosaics with gold backgrounds, among the finest to be seen in Greece.

5 CORYCIAN CAVE. This cave lies near Mt Parnassus, and can be reached in 2½hrs on foot from Delphi, but it can now also be reached by car. As you leave Arachova to the W take the Parnassus road which will take you over a pass to a huge plateau (cultivated fields and a summer village on the l. of the road) and after approx. 6.6mls (10.5km) you take the l. fork on to an unmade-up road which goes on for approx. 1.6mls (2.5km), climbing steeply, and ends below the entrance to the cave, which is nowadays called Saranda-Vli (the forty rooms).

The cave of Pan – The Corycian cave, or 'double-bag' cave, which Pausanias described admiringly, was sacred to Pan and the nymphs. On the r. of the entrance there is a dedication to these deities by Eustratus of Ambrysus (a Phocian city on the site of modern Distomon); above it is a partly indecipherable inscription mentioning Pan, the nymphs and the Thyiades. It was on the nearby plateau that the Thyiades or Bacchantes, women from Delphi, every five years celebrated Bacchic orgies and nocturnal races and dances, dressed in animal skins and bearing thyrsi and torches (Aeschylus, *Eumenides*, 22).

The cave, which consists of a big chamber 197ft (60m) long and 98ft (30m) across at its widest point and another much smaller one, was identified more than 200 years ago by Eustratus's dedication and excavated in 1970 and 1971 by the French School. As well as a layer from the Neolithic period and remains from the Mycenaean period, the dig was found to contain a huge variety of archaeological material (samples of it are exhibited in a showcase in the museum at Delphi): dedications on stone and on earthenware, sculptures in the round (a fine statue of a satyr among them) several thousand terracotta figurines, painted earthenware, objects made of metal (gold, bronze and silver), coins, and knuckle-bones (more than 20,000 have been counted; some have been engraved with signs). Most of the offerings date from the 6th, 5th and 4th centuries BC, a few go back to the 7th century, and others belong to the Hellenistic period. Like the Delphic sanctuary of which the cave became a kind of annex, it was at its most prosperous from the 4th to the 3rd century BC.

 6 CLIMBING MT PARNASSUS. Climbing to the summit of Mt Parnassus on foot, which is best done in July and August, is today easier and shorter (it can be done in one day, unless you want to see sunrise) following the road which goes to the recently built ski resort (ask for information at Arachova and take a guide). To get to the ski resort follow the route for the Corycian cave, but instead of taking the l. fork on the plateau carry on a bit further and turn r.

From the main summit of Parnassus (Liakoura), at an altitude of 8,061ft (2,457m), about 8½hrs walking distance from Delphi (5hrs from Kalivia), you can identify with the help of a compass some of the farthest distant details of the map of Greece. To the NW, Timfristos and the Pindus; to the N beyond Callidromus, Oeta, Othrys, Pelion, Ossa and snow-capped Olympus.

To the NE the grey mass of Athos rises sheer from the sea. In the distance the Sporades are silhouetted; nearer at hand, the gulfs of Lamia and Volos, and the channel and island of Euboea. To the SE, Helicon, Attica and the Cyclades; to the S, the gulf of Corinth, from the isthmus and promontory of Perachora to Naupactus (Lepanto); the mountains of the Peloponnese (Killini, Mainalon, Aroania, Erymanthus and Panakhaikon), and Taygetus behind. To the W beyond the valley of Amphissa the view is restricted by the mountains of Locris and Doris (ancient Corax), with the peaks of Ghiona (8,235ft/2,510m) and Vardousia (7,995ft/2,437m).

■ Diakopton

Route map 5.

Patras, 29.4mls (47km) – Corinth, 53mls (85km).

This popular bathing resort on the shores of the Gulf of Corinth is the starting point for the railway (partly a rack-railway) and the road that leads to the monastery of Megaspilaion and to Kalavryta through a striking landscape (see under these names). The narrow-gauge

(29.5in/75cm) railway climbs 2,175ft (700m) in 13.7mls (22km); it crosses a good many bridges, goes through a good many tunnels, and travels through the **gorges of the Vouraikos which the road rejoins shortly before (8mls/13km) Kato Zaklorou.

■ Dodecanese [The]

The island province of the Dodecanese which is made up of the islands of Rhodes, Cos, Calymna, Leros, Patmos, Carpathus, etc. has become a magnet for the tourist industry due to the construction of a large number of hotels in Rhodes and the establishment of regular sea and air links from Piraeus and Hellenikon (Athens airport) and now from Mykonos and Herakleion in Crete. The main attraction of some of the islands, such as Astypalea, Calymna, Carpathus, Cos (or Kos), Nisyrus and Rhodes, is their scenic beauty, while others have a lot to offer architecturally, with monuments from ancient times, as well as Byzantine and even Frankish buildings, such as Rhodes, Patmos and Cos.

The Dodecanese is the most Asiatic part of Greece; while historically its ties are clearly Hellenic, geographically it is a dependency of Asia Minor. The northern islands, starting with Calymna, are fragments like the Cyclades of the ancient rock-bed of deeply folded gneiss and limestone, where the contours depend on which of these two constituent elements is predominant. Further S, from Cos to Rhodes, the islands belong to the relief system of the Taurus mountains, with crystalline schists and marbles which produce sharp, pointed reliefs. Rhodes, which has a wet, warm climate (more than 39ins/1m of rainfall) should be considered separately because of the luxuriance of its vegetation, which contrasts with the aridity of the Cyclades and most other islands in the Dodecanese.

■ Dodona*

Route map 10.

Arta, 52.5mls (84km) – Igoumenitsa, 79.4mls (127km) – Ioannina, 13mls (21km).

Lying in the heart of the harsh mountains of Epirus, Dodona is the earliest oracular sanctuary at which the Greeks communicated with Zeus. A group of buildings still remind us of the past, and are quite well preserved, in particular the theatre which is used as the setting for an annual festival (mid-August).

A FLUENT GOD. Although the oracle at Dodona never rivalled the Delphic Oracle, it is probably the oldest on mainland Greece. The deity presiding over the sanctuary was Zeus 'who rules Dodona with its two winters'. The voice of Zeus could be heard in the leaves of the sacred oak tree and significance was also given to the flight of the doves and the sound made by a brass cauldron given by the people of Corcyra, above which stood the statuette of a child holding a thonged whip which the wind blew against the sides of the vessel. The will of the gods was also revealed in the fall of the dice and the murmur of the miraculous spring. Zeus's prophets, the Selloi, slept on the ground and walked barefoot as the earth gave off inspirational exhalations.

A SANCTUARY THAT WAS SOMETIMES ECLIPSED. While the oracle at Dodona seems to have gone through a period of eclipse around the 5th century BC, it flourished anew in the Macedonian period. The temple which had been destroyed during the wars of the Aetolian and Achaean Leagues (219 BC) was rebuilt, then burnt down again by the Romans in 168-167 BC. It is mentioned by Pausanias in the 2nd century but was not known to Livy or Plutarch. Later, Dodona became the seat of a bishopric, and bishops from Dodona attended the councils held in the 5th and 6th centuries. The site of Dodona was not really established until excavations undertaken by Karapanos in 1873. Digging has been resumed by the archaeological society and finds have been lodged in the Ioannina museum.

Open: summer, 09.00-13.00 and 16.00-18.00; winter, 10.00-16.30; Sun. and public holidays, 10.30-14.30; closed, Tues; entrance fee.

Theatre – This building, which is the best preserved (it has been restored), was built early in the 3rd century BC at the time of Pyrrhus (292-272 BC), laid waste by the Aetolians in 219 BC, then rebuilt by the people of Epirus and Philip V (220-178 BC) at the end of the 3rd century BC. It was then that the wooden stage structure was replaced by one in stone and that the doors of the lateral access corridors were built. It was subsequently transformed into an arena intended for gladiator fights and displays simulating the hunting of wild animals.

In front of the retaining wall, which is strengthened by a tower-shaped bastion on an artificial embankment, there are several rows of tiered seating which must have belonged to the stadium where gymnastic contests were held during the festival of the Naïads.

Sanctuary of the oracle – This consisted of a consecrated house where oracles were delivered, and of several temples, little treasuries and votive monuments. Just beyond the theatre you find on your l. the ruins of a huge hypostyle hall with three rows of columns and tiered seating: this was the bouleuterion (Senate House).

Next you come to the remains of several little buildings which were treasuries and votive monuments, and of a Hellenistic temple, and finally those of the sacred house, a large building which has been altered several times and which was used for ceremonies connected with the oracle and with worship.

The earliest building dates back to the 4th century BC, but it was built on the site of a small naiskos. The 4th-century BC building, made of large isodomic blocks (i.e. laid in staggered courses) on orthostats, was probably destroyed by the Aetolian general, Dorimachus, in 219 BC. It was rebuilt from its ruins, and it may be that the propylaeum was added at that time (late 2nd century BC). It was destroyed by

Aemilius Paullus in 168–167 BC and once again rebuilt, and the rectangular building to the N was added. At a later date the N propylaeum was built at the northernmost end of that building matching the S propylaeum.

Further on remains of the old and new temple of Dione can still be seen, dedicated to an earth-goddess and consort of Zeus, and last of all the ruins of a late 6th-century basilica with three apses, standing on top of the remains of another church with a single apse which was built in the 5th century, partly on the foundations of the temple of Heracles dating from the late 2nd century.

◼ Drama

Route map 14

Kavalla, 21.9mls (35km) – Serres, 43.7mls (70km) – Thessaloniki, 98.7mls (158km) – Pop. 29.690.

Drama lies not far from the Greek-Bulgarian frontier on the edge of a large cultivated plain (tobacco crops); known in ancient times as Drabescus, the town has no trace left of its past. It is a commercial centre, and for the tourist will serve only as a stopping point near Philippi.

Thucydides and Pausanias mention the town under the name of Drabescus. The Athenians were defeated there in the 5th century BC by the king of Macedon. The exact date when the Turks occupied the area is not certain, but it must have been c.1371. In the early 17th century it was joined together with the metropolitan See of Philippi. In 1912 the town was occupied by the Greeks, in 1917 by the Bulgarians, and it reverted to Greece in 1918.

■ Edessa

Route map 13.

Florina, 45mls (72km) – Kastoria, 85mls (136km) – Thessaloniki, 55.6mls (89km) – Pop. 14,960 – archbishopric – district capital of the admin. region of Pella.

Edessa, a former capital of Macedon, now derives its main income from spinning, and offers a water festival for everyone who arrives on a hot summer's day, for there are countless streams running through it which join to form waterfalls, providing irrigation for the very attractive orchards on the plain.

A MACEDONIAN STRONGHOLD. For a long time it was thought that Edessa must be the same place as ancient Aegae which at one time was the capital city of Macedon, before Pella; but it is now believed that it is Vergina that can rightfully lay claim to that distinction. Be that as it may, the town was officially named Edessa during the Roman period. The perimeter wall round the lower town, which is at present being uncovered by Greek archaeologists, seems to date from the 4th century BC, but it was often restored both by the Romans and the Byzantines. Pyrrhus had his general headquarters there when he was fighting against King Demetrius after Macedon had been partitioned between Lysimachus and himself. Throughout antiquity the town remained one of the main fortresses of western Macedon. It was captured by the Bulgarians, then reconquered by Basil II 'Bulgaroctonus', (1013–27). The Greek army gained control of it in October 1912.

Edessa suffered cruelly during the German occupation, when most of its churches were burnt down, and has consequently lost a lot of its appeal.

 In the area around the archbishop's palace near the edge of the plateau (go r. once in the town if coming from Thessaloniki) you can visit the church of the Kimissis tis Panagias (Dormition of the Virgin) to the l. of the archbishop's palace, where there is a fine iconostasis carved in wood, and a few remains from ancient buildings, incorporated in the architecture. Near the archbishop's palace there is a fine *view over the waterfalls and the monastery of Kaisariani.

■ To get to the museum (of limited interest) follow the Thessaloniki road to Florina and turn l. shortly after passing a school on the r. The museum is housed in a former mosque and the collection mainly consists of funerary sculptures, stelae, and various architectural fragments from the area.

Not far from Edessa at the place known as Loggos the remains of three early Christian basilicas have been found, evidence albeit sparse, of the town's importance at that period. In one of them there are mosaic floors and marble chancel screens.

Eleusis (Elefsis)*

Route map 5.

Athens, 14.4mls (23km) – Corinth, 40mls (64km) – Daphni, 7.5mls (12km) – Thebes, 26.2mls (42km) – Pop. 18,535 – admin. region of Attica.

This industrial town (steelworks, cement works and petrochemical works) which now languishes beyond the dreary suburbs of Athens, was one of the most illustrious cities of ancient Greece. Its priest-governed state, which had its origin in the legend of the king-priest Eumolpus ('sweet singer'), for a long time rivalled Athens. Its name was thought to mean 'the arrival'. And it was here, according to tradition, that Demeter (Ceres) had been offered hospitality by King Celeus when she was looking for her daughter Kore (Persephone or Proserpina), abducted by Hades (Pluto). To show her gratitude the goddess gave Triptolemus, the king's son, the first grain of wheat and taught him to cultivate the land. The famous Eleusinian Mysteries, which Eumolpus founded at Demeter's command, were intended to perpetuate the remembrance of the benefit thus accorded. The cult of the Great Goddesses (Demeter and Kore) was the basis of the renown of Eleusis until the end of the 4th century AD.

Another mystery is the rapture inspired in some visitors by the ruins of Eleusis which lie in such confusion that only the trained eye of the professional can make out any detail.

Eleusis in history

A PRE-ACHAEAN CITY. The acropolis, which towers above the Thriasian Plain behind the bay of Eleusis, was occupied well before the Achaean migration.

The original settlement was protected within a perimeter wall quite distinct from the ramparts that went round the summit of the hill, and together with the king's palace formed the acropolis. Tradition, preserved by Homer in his hymn to Demeter, placed the palace of King Celeus at a point overlooking the sanctuary.

At the beginning of the 1st millennium BC, during the Geometric

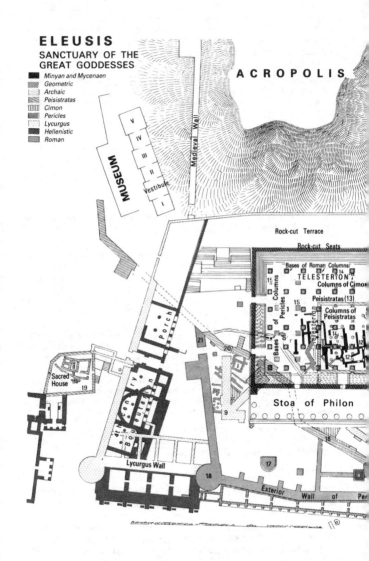

ELEUSIS
SANCTUARY OF THE GREAT GODDESSES

- Minyan and Mycenaen
- Geometric
- Archaic
- Peisistratos
- Cimon
- Pericles
- Lycurgus
- Hellenistic
- Roman

ACROPOLIS

MUSEUM

V
IV
III
II
I
Vestibule

Medieval Wall

Rock-cut Terrace

Rock-cut Seats

Bases of Roman Columns
TELESTERION
Columns of Cimon
Peisistratos (13)
Columns of Peisistratos

Porch

Sacred House
19

Bouleuterion

Lycurgus Wall

21
20

Bases of Columns of Pericles

Parastenion

9

Stoa of Philon

18
17
16

Exterior Wall of Per

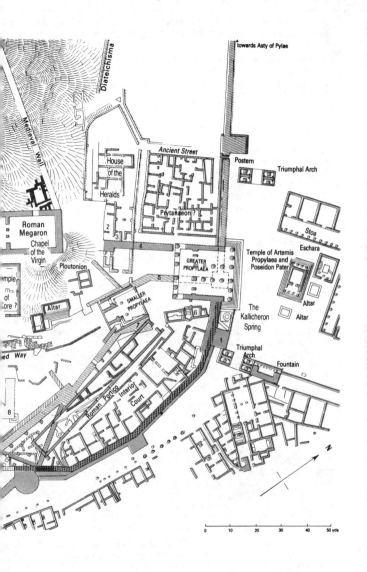

towards Asty of Pylae

Diateichisma

Medieval Wall

Ancient Street

House of the Heralds

Postern

Triumphal Arch

Roman Megaron

Chapel of the Virgin

Prytanaeon ?

Ploutonion

2
3

Stoa

Eschara

emple

of
Kore ?

Altar

GREATER
PROPYLAEA

Temple of Artemis
Propylaea and
Poseidon Pater

SMALLER
PROPYLAEA

5

6

The
Kallicheron
Spring

Altar

Altar

ed Way

Roman Portico

Interior
Court

1

Triumphal
Arch

Fountain

8

N

0   10   20   30   40   50 yds

period, this settlement also extended on to the N slope, while at the same time the private dwellings built on the E slope began to disappear.

ATHENA'S TRIUMPH. Rivalry between Athens and Eleusis was symbolized by the quarrel between Athena and Poseidon for possession of Attica. Though it was conquered and annexed by the State of Athens during the 7th century BC, Eleusis retained certain privileges, in particular the right to control the Mysteries. Twice a year the festivals of the Great Goddesses were held at the Lesser Eleusinia (Anthesterion; Feb.-Mar.) and the Greater Eleusinia (Boedromion: Sept.-Oct.). When the latter festival was held, Athenians and Greeks of every nationality came to celebrate the Mysteries and to be initiated. After a period of brilliant prosperity under Hadrian and Antoninus Pius, Eleusis was sacked in 395 AD by Alaric. The Mysteries were banned at the end of the 4th century AD in the reign of Theodosius. There have been recent excavations of the site conducted by the American School and the Greek Archaeological Service.

VISITING THE RUINS

Open: weekdays, 09.00–15.00 (18.00–16.00 in winter); Sun. and public holidays, 10.00–15.00; entrance fee.

•⁰• **The sanctuary of Demeter and Kore** – The uninitiated were forbidden entry into the sanctuary on pain of death. It was surrounded by a high fortified wall, which was doubled on the side of the entrance. Outside the town gates lay the Rharian Plain, the sacred ground where the first grain given by Demeter had been sown; Triptolemus's threshing-floor and altar were there. The Sacred Way went across the plain, linking the sanctuary with Athens. Near the entrance you can still see a stretch of the road, about 44yds (40m) long, which was recently discovered; it dates back to the Hellenistic period, and has been frequently repaired, remaining in use until the 6th century AD.

The temple of Artemis Propylaea and Poseidon Pater – Shortly after entering the excavation area you come to a huge paved esplanade dating from the 2nd century AD, scattered with the ruins of the buildings that used to stand round it. On the r. you first see the foundations of the two altars that stood next to the temple of Artemis Propylaea and Poseidon Pater. These came from the Doric temple dedicated to these two gods, which was built during the Roman period, partly covering the site of an earlier Geometric-period sanctuary (8th century BC). On the r. of the temple are the foundations of a rectangular structure inside which you can see a pit or eschara from the Roman period, a hollow altar where the victims sacrificed to the chthonian, or earthly, deities were burnt.

The arc-shaped part of a wall between the temple and the wall surrounding the eschara was part of a west-facing apsidal building which was used between the Geometric period and the 7th century BC. This seems to have been a sanctuary. Beyond that are the ruins of a portico. The large paved Roman esplanade built in the Imperial period was surrounded on three sides by galleries.

The greater propylaea – This monumental entrance was built from Pentelic marble in the reign of Antoninus Pius (138–161 AD) on the model of the propylaea of the acropolis in Athens. It followed the Doric order; the outer façade consisted of a six-column portico, pieces of which are lying on the esplanade. The greater propylaea form a break in the outer perimeter wall which was built early in the 5th century BC and restored by the Romans. They must occupy the same position as an earlier gate. On the l. it is possible to recognize the ruins of a rectangular tower (plan, 1) which strengthened the outer perimeter wall.

The Kallichoron spring – To the l. of the great propylaea at a lower level than the esplanade you can see the mouth of the Kallichoron spring mentioned in the Homeric hymn to Demeter as well as by Euripides and Pausanias. It was round this spring that the women of Eleusis first danced and sang in honour of Demeter. It was in existence before the greater propylaea were built, and the bottom step of the propylaea is indented so as not to cover the spring. Note behind it the well-laid polygonal masonry of the lower courses of the perimeter wall (built by Cimon, 5th century BC).

The triumphal arch – Further l. you can see the remains of one of the two triumphal arches in the Corinthian order dedicated by the Panhellenes to the Great Goddesses and the Emperor Hadrian, the second of which is at the other end of the paved esplanade.

Lesser propylaea – After passing through the great propylaea you come out into a large interior area contained between two perimeter walls where the candidates for initiation were assembled and probably checked before they entered the sanctuary through the lesser propylaea. This area is now littered with the ruins of Roman houses, stores and various ramparts. To the r. of the path, in a pit, notice a section of Peisistratos's wall (6th century BC – plan, 5). On the l. is a Roman cistern (plan, 6).

The lesser propylaea, the remains of which are still visible, were built on the site of a fortified gate (plan, 7) in the 6th century BC perimeter wall (contemporary with Peisistratos) c.54 BC by the proconsul Appius Claudius Pulcher, a friend of Cicero.

On the l. of the Sacred Way there is a wide, deep trench where the remains of buildings and ramparts that were built in succession on this part of the site from the Geometric to the Roman periods lie hopelessly jumbled together.

Sheltered under a zinc roof are the remains of the wall of unbaked bricks put up by Peisistratos (6th century BC), foundations (plan, 8 and 9) dating from the 4th century BC, several square pillars from a larger storehouse and the ruins of a gate put in when Cimon's ramparts were built which was guarded by a tower (plan, 10) in the wall built by Peisistratos. A large pile of unbaked bricks is still standing from the tower, with a protecting shed over it. The large, quite well-preserved wall beyond the tower dates from the time of Pericles.

The Telesterion or sanctuary of the Mysteries – This hall of initiation was the most important of the sacred buildings in Eleusis. The Telesterion, as you can see it, is the combined result of all the buildings that followed one another on this site from the time of Peisistratos up to the Imperial Roman period. The plan followed by the Telesterion in its final state in the Roman era is admittedly the most apparent, but archaeologists have attempted to replace any parts they could find of the buildings that stood on this site from the time of Peisistratos up to the Roman era. In the trenches you can even see a few traces of the Mycenaean megaron, a very early temple which lay in the shadow of King Celeus' palace according to the Homeric hymn to Demeter, as well as the remains of the sanctuary from the Geometric period. This results in an extraordinary mixture of walls, which do, however, enable the visitor to follow the entire historical development of the building.

A WELL-KEPT SECRET. The secret of the Eleusinian Mysteries has been well kept, but the general meaning of the legend of Demeter is quite clear. Her despair after the abduction of her daughter by the god of the underworld and the annual reappearance of Kore after spending six months with Hades symbolize the mourning of nature when the plants and leaves have died, the travail of the seed entrusted to the earth, and the reappearance of the plant reborn from its death. The Mysteries must have included a moral, cosmogonic doctrine and speculations as to the links between human fate and these natural phenomena, and the problem of life and death. Those initiated received not only truth but happiness and hope as well. 'Blessed is he among those dwelling on earth', the Homeric hymn to Demeter says, 'who has gazed on these great sights! But he who is not initiated is forever deprived of such happiness even when death has led him down into the realms of darkness.'

A PRACTICAL GUIDE TO THE WORLD BEYOND. It is thought that the Mysteries consisted of a sacred drama in which the legend of Kore and the union of Zeus and Demeter were enacted. Then 'candidates for initiation were shown the soul's journey in the underworld and they were taught how to bring it to a successful conclusion'. The hierophant gave them practical information about the topography of Hades, with its obstacles and monsters, and formulae for getting the better of them, and of the Elysian Fields, with mystic formulas which were supposed to gain them access there. After the sacred play had been enacted, the candidates were led by the hierophant and *dadouchos* (torch-bearer) on a torch-lit tour of the hall of initiation, the different parts of which reproduced, according to convention, details of the topography of Hades. Next the sacred objects (hiera) were revealed to them. The ceremony must have been completed by visits to the temples of Demeter, Kore and Pluto.

THE ROUTE FOLLOWED BY THE MYSTAI. All Athenians had to go through at least the first stage of initiation (*as mystai*). The second stage was gone through a year later (*as epoptai*). The Eleusinian festival lasted ten days from 13–23 Boedromion (Sept.-Oct.). On the 13th the ephebes went from Athens to Eleusis. On the 14th the sacred objects (hiera) were covered over and transferred with great ceremony from Eleusis to the Eleusinion in Athens on the slopes of the acropolis. On that day the procession stopped near a bridge over the Cephisus on the edge of the Sacred Fig Tree area, about 3.7mls (6km) from the acropolis where the gephyrisms, or bridge farces, took place. The people of Athens were waiting there for the procession to greet it with catcalls and insults in memory of the jokes old Baubo had used against Demeter to ridicule her.

On the 15th the mystai gathered at the Stoa Poikile (Painted Portico) where the exclusion of unpurified murderers and of those who did not speak with an intelligible voice was pronounced, meaning no doubt those who could not speak Greek.

On the 16th the candidates made their way to Phaleron Bay, where at the prompting of the priests ('Mystai to the sea') they rushed into the water dragging with them a piglet destined to be sacrificed. On the 17th and 18th the mystai went into retreat, fasting and purifying themselves. On the 19th a solemn procession escorted the sacred objects back to Eleusis, along with the statue of Iacchus, and the 20th was spent making sacrifices and fasting.

On the 21st, 22nd and 23rd the Mysteries were celebrated and at night the initiations took place under the seal of greatest secrecy, which those initiated were bound to preserve on pain of death. The general return to Athens took place on the afternoon of the 23rd.

The Telesterion's maximum measurements were 177ft 8ins (54.15m) by 169ft 11ins (51.8m); it was a covered building backing on to the acropolis and built on an esplanade carved out of the rock and covering an artificial earth platform.

On each of the three accessible sides there were two doors. The floor, which now consists of rock or beaten earth, may have been covered with paving stones of tufa. Six rows of seven columns held up the wooden first-storey floor 20ft (6m) above; all that remains of them are round bases in blue stone. Eight rows of tiered seating were arranged on each of the four sides, cut out of the rock or built in stone, with breaks opposite the doors, providing accommodation for 3,000 people. The large portico known as the Stoa of Philon, after its builder, runs along one side of the building; it was started c.350 BC and completed between 317 and 307 BC.

The appearance of the Telesterion on that façade was of a large low temple. There was no crypt but there was an upper storey on the same level as the terrace behind, which could be reached by side staircases. This was the megaron or anactoron where the sacred objects were kept and revealed during the ceremony; there was a lantern (opaion) on the roof over the megaron. The mystai set out from the ground floor and ended their round in the megaron.

To try to bring order into the confusion of these ruins, some architectural facts should be made clear, such as the existence of traces of a Mycenaean megaron (plan, 12) which would certainly have had an opening above the hearth. This megaron must be regarded as the original temple, which was rebuilt several times on the same site, in particular during the Geometric, and then the Archaic, period before the Telesterion of Peisistratos (plan, 13), the plan of which is much more apparent, was built. It consisted of a square hall with a side measurement of 88ft 7in (27m), with five rows of five columns each and a portico standing before it (there are remains of the paving).

After the fire of 480–479 BC, Cimon rebuilt the hall as an oblong (89ft by 144ft/27m by 44m approx.), i.e. half the width of the present square, with seven rows of three columns (plan, 14), which necessitated cutting out the first tiers at the back and on the NE side. Pericles made the whole into a square by cutting out and building beside Cimon's hall a room of the same size, but with just four rows of two columns (plan, 15). It is not known whether the two rooms were made into one or whether they were still separated by a wall, with one being used by the mystai and the other by the epoptai. The following century the stoa of Philon was added. And finally the emperors unified the whole interior colonnade and added the tiered seating at the back of the Telesterion.

In a pit in front of the stoa of Philon you can see a section of Peisistratos' wall with its capping of unbaked bricks. To allow for the enlargement of the Telesterion, Pericles had the perimeter wall moved farther SE. Farther on there is a base (plan, 17) from a monument of the Roman period. If you follow the ramparts along you come to a round tower (plan, 18) on which you can see where Pericles's wall was pulled down when the wall of Lycurgus was built in the second half of the 4th century BC. On this part of the site you can see the ruins of storerooms and of the bouleuterion from the 4th century BC.

Near the door on the outside you can see an enclosure carefully built in polygonal masonry which has been pinpointed as the site of a sanctuary in use from the Geometric period. This little temple, sometimes known as 'the sacred house', appears to have been built as part of a former dwelling house of the Geometric period (8th century BC). Later on when the house was demolished worship continued on the same site and a little temple was built nearby. The peribolus was constructed in Peisistratos' time and a small building which may have been a chapel was erected on the ruins of the former house.

A little further on in a pit you can see part of Peisistratos' wall (plan, 20) and of Pericles' wall (plan, 21) and a substantial mass of foundations (plan, 9) which must have been meant to support a gallery.

■ **Museum** – A wide staircase cut out of the rock, which now leads to the museum, used to lead to a rock terrace on the same level as the upper storey of the Telesterion.

Open: same times as the site, but closed Tues. (Tel. 554-60-19).

The museum's collection is mainly derived from the sanctuary and its vicinity, but the best sculptures are in the National Museum in Athens. They are however shown in the form of castings, such as the famous relief depicting Demeter offering Triptolemus the first grain of wheat.

Even so, some of the originals are well worth seeing, for example the statue of Demeter in the entrance hall, which is attributed to Agoracritus, a pupil of Phidias, who is believed to have sculpted it c.420 BC, or again the statue of an ephebe (Room II) credited to Lysippus beside an Archaic kore dating from the 6th century BC. Among the vases, whole or in pieces, pay special attention to a large Proto-Attic amphora in the middle of Room I (mid 7th century BC) on which Odysseus can be seen blinding the cyclops Polyphemus, and Perseus killing Medusa (Athena is depicted between the hero and the Gorgons). The model of the site at different periods is extremely useful in helping you to understand the remains.

Visiting the acropolis and the excavation site W of the great propylaea (see plan: Prytaneum and house of the Heralds) is unlikely to be of interest to anyone who is not a keen archaeologist.

Acropolis – A staircase from the rock terrace at the foot of the acropolis leads to an esplanade where the chapel of the Panagia stands on the site of a Roman megaron. On the l. of the bell-tower you can see the ruins of a Mycenaean building which could not be identified as the palace of Celeus for lack of evidence. Beyond that this small excavation site is confined by medieval ramparts which guarded the summit of the acropolis.

Prytaneum and the House of the Heralds – To look at this part of the sanctuary go out through the great propylaea and turn l. Near the remains of a 2nd century AD triumphal arch there is a stretch of Peisistratos' ramparts built with characteristic polygonal masonry. Guarded by a tower that reinforced the wall there was a postern-gate which marked the end of an ancient road, in use from the Mycenaean period, that led to the acropolis. Another gate a little further on in Peisistratos' wall is named in inscriptions as the 'Gate leading to the town'.

Go through the first gate and follow the road which skirts a building which has been identified as the prytaneum and the place (pompeion) where the sacred chariots, which carried the sacred objects of Demeter and the statue of Iacchus when the Greater Eleusinia took place, were dismissed.

A little further on the ancient road bends to the r. An intersecting road on the l. runs alongside the House of the Heralds, which was part of the sanctuary outbuildings. Where you see no. 2 on the plan some remains of paintings from the Roman period can be seen and at no. 3

a large half-buried storage jar. Follow the line of a large wall (plan, 4) and you come to the great propylaea; this wall was built during the reign of the Emperor Valerian (253–260 AD) and linked the great propylaea to the acropolis rock.

In the opposite direction, the modern path round the side of the hill just at the bottom of the acropolis escarpment skirts a section of wall identified as the diateichisma, mentioned in an inscription dated 329–328 BC which separated the sanctuary from the town.

VICINITY OF ELEUSIS – ROMAN BRIDGE AT KATO PIGADI (1.2mls/2km along Athens road). On the r. of the road there are the remains of a large Roman bridge with four arches. It was probably constructed in 124 AD by Hadrian when he was initiated into the Eleusinian Mysteries.

■ Eleutherae [Fortress of]

Route map 3.

Athens, 31.8mls (51km) – Eleusis, 17.5mls (28km) – Thebes, 10.6mls (17km).

 Standing at one end of the Kaza pass, the fortress of Eleutherae held a strategic position on the direct road from Athens to Thebes. Its ruins are among the most intact to be found in Greece.

The perimeter wall, which is strengthened with towers, dates from the 4th century BC. Near the citadel the remains of a temple have been uncovered as well as those of two three-naved basilicas dating from the 5th or 6th century, which must have been built on the site of ancient Eleutherae.

E Epidaurus (Epidavros)***

NB: the archaeological site of Epidaurus should not be confused with the two villages which bear the same name: it is 10.6mls (17km) from Nea Epidavros and 13.7mls (22km) from Palea Epidavros.

Route map 6.

Argos, 26.2mls (42km) – Athens (via Loutra Elenis), 96mls (153km) – Athens (via Nauplia), 111mls (177km) – Corinth (via Loutra Elenis), 42.5mls (68km) – Corinth (via Nauplia), 56.2mls (90km) – Mycenae, 34.4mls (55km) – Nauplia, 18.7mls (30km) – admin. region of Argolis.

The sanctuary of Asclepius at Epidaurus is one of the most visited sites in Greece. This fascination is justified not only by the exceptional interest of the theatre, which is the best preserved and most perfect building of its type, but also by the charm of the surrounding countryside; its gentle appeal must have been a factor in the cure which most visitors coming here in ancient times were seeking.

The sanctuary of Asclepius, the most famous place of worship devoted to the god of healing – Asclepius was said to have been born on a nearby mountain – enjoyed a period of extraordinary popularity in the 4th century BC, and it was during that period that most of the buildings whose ruins can be visited and the theatre now used as a setting for the festival of Epidaurus, were built.

Epidaurus in history

A GOD TO CURE THE SICK. Excavations have shown that the site was consecrated from a very early date, during the Early Helladic period, but the cult of Asclepius, or Aesculapius in Latin, which had originated in Tricca in Thessaly, was not introduced here until the 6th century BC.

Pausanias (II, 26) records several versions of how the cult came to be established here. According to the best known of these. Phlegyas, king of Orchomenus in Boeotia, had come to Epidaurus with the intention of conquering the country. His daughter Coronis who came with him had allowed Apollo to seduce her and secretly gave birth to Asclepius on Mt Tithion. Coronis died in childbirth and Asclepius was suckled by a goat. Apollo entrusted Chiron the Centaur with the upbringing of his child, and Chiron disclosed to him the secret properties of wild plants. A shepherd who found the young child was astonished to see a bright halo shining round his forehead, and soon the legend spread that a god had been born who would cure illnesses and even bring the dead back to life; this aroused Zeus' anger against him.

A sanatorium and a spa were built alongside the sanctuary which belonged to the town of Epidaurus. Every four years, nine days after the Isthmian Games, a festival of gymnastics and drama in honour of Asclepius was held here, with a competition for rhapsodes who recited poetry, particularly Homer's works, without musical accompaniment but with free use of mime. (Plato, *Ion*, 530).

Visiting the ruins

Open daily, summer, 10.00–16.00; winter, 10.00–16.30; entrance fee.

• ***THEATRE.** Vaunted as the wonder of Epidaurus, the theatre is unquestionably one of the finest in Greece. It was built in the 4th century BC by an Argive architect and sculptor, Polyclitus, known as the 'Younger', to distinguish him from his namesake, an extremely famous sculptor who lived in the 5th century BC. For the festival of Epidaurus a light stage is put up for the productions. The orchestra where the chorus danced consists of a circle of beaten earth, as in theatres of the Greek period. The auditorium, the l. wing of which has been restored, can hold approx. 14,000 spectators. The acoustics of this theatre are exceptional and local guides – to prove how well sounds can be heard in the most distant rows – are sure to conduct little experiments, which you may enjoy repeating, standing in the centre of the orchestra, where the altar used to be. A whisper or the rustling of paper travels with remarkable distinctness.

TEMPLE OF APOLLO MALEATAS. Follow the fence behind the theatre and 15 mins walk through scrub brings you up to the middle summit of Mt Kynortion. Archaeology enthusiasts can study the meagre remains of the temple of Apollo Maleatas there where supplicants at the sanctuary of Asclepius offered their first sacrifice. The temple must have been built in the 4th century BC beside a pre-Hellenic altar; we know of its existence through literary tradition and the discovery of ashes from the sacrifices. You can still see a strong retaining wall which had a portico backing on to it, and the remains of several 2nd-century AD Roman buildings, in particular those of the houses where the priests of Apollo lived. The view over the theatre is superb

MUSEUM. It is mainly devoted to antiquities found during digs carried out at the sanctuary of Asclepius.

Open: same times as the site, but closed Tues.; entrance fee (Tel 0753–220 09).

Items of interest include sculpture (the finest examples are in the National Museum in Athens), particularly several statues of Asclepius and Hygieia, some very evocative architectural fragments from the tholos (rotunda), one of the most remarkable buildings in the sanctuary of Asclepius (external Doric columns, entablature guttering pieces from a carved, panelled ceiling, a door, interior order), and (at the l. end of the third room) a Corinthian capital, also from the tholos, ascribed to Polyclitus the Younger; if not executed by him, at least made from his design.

A collection of surgical instruments from the Roman period on display in the first room is also of interest: it is a reminder that the sanctuary of Asclepius was also a centre of healing and as such attracted a sizeable clientèle. In the same room there are several plans and graphic reconstructions which will help you to imagine the sanctuary as it was at the height of its glory.

GYMNASIUM. After a quick look at the remains of a large square building which has been identified as a katagogeion (hotel) built in the Hellenistic period, and of Greek baths where there must have been a place of worship dedicated to Asclepius and Hygieia, you come to the gymnasium, which is similar in plan to the palaestra at Olympia, with its large inner peristyle courtyard.

In the Roman period the gymnasium was turned into an odeon and its monumental entrance (propylaeum) became a place of worship dedicated to Hygieia with a statue, the base of which can still be seen

Beyond that are the ruins of the portico of Cotys and a small palaestra which was rebuilt in the 2nd century AD by the senator Antoninus

THE SANCTUARY. The sanctuary (hieron) proper began immediately after the palaestra with sacred buildings encircled by a peribolus wall it was made into a fortress by the Byzantines.

You first come to the remains of the foundations of the temple of Themis built in the Hellenistic period, then to the unimportant ruins of a little Roman building and finally to the remains of the temple of Artemis, built in the 4th century BC.

AN EARLY ABATON. Just beside the temple stood a building (E on the plan) which some archaeologists think must be an earlier abaton, a dormitory where the sick waited for the god (who was to bring about their cure) to appear. Another abaton was built in the 4th century BC and replaced this building.

Amidst the sacred snakes – The abaton was the most ancient part of an asclepiaeum, which figured as both a temple and a hospital. After going through various ritual tests, such as fasting, a purifying bath, etc. and offering a sacrifice, the person having the consultation started on the most critical sequence in his treatment, incubation. He spent the night in the abaton and waited for the god of healing to appear to him in his sleep. Naturally the sick person was not able to interpret what he had seen in his dreams and the priest-doctors belonging to the sanctuary, the asclepiads, explained the meaning of the dreams and gave prescriptions.

TEMPLE OF ASCLEPIUS. Only the foundations and the fragments exhibited in the museum remain of this temple, built by the architect Theodotus, probably c.380 BC.

It was a peripter in the Doric order, and except for the sculpture, the gutter and the door ornaments, built entirely of Corinthian tufa. A pit 8ft 10ins (2.7m) long by 5ft 9ins (1.75m) wide running along the l. wall of the cella may have served to display to best advantage the chryselephantine statue of Asclepius by the sculptor Thrasymedes of Paros, which Pausanias tells us stood in a well. According to R. Martin this kind of pit may well have been a common feature in sanctuaries devoted to healing and oracular cults, serving as an indispensable part of the rites of consultation. These pits may have been used as treasuries where petitioners laid their offerings before sacrifices were made, or even, in the case of the earliest sanctuaries, they could have been used in consultation rites requiring the faithful to go down into a pit. Gradually this custom would appear to have fallen into disuse and as the rites disappeared the pits were done away with; the pit at the temple of Asclepius in Epidaurus was therefore filled at a late date.

THE THOLOS. This rotunda is one of the most outstanding works created by 4th-century BC Greek architecture. It was built in the second half of that century to plans by Polyclitus the Younger who supervised at least the first stage of the building work. This monument, which is referred to in the description of the building as a thymele, or altar, is one whose purpose has aroused as much debate as any in Greece.

A mysterious labyrinth – Only the foundations are left, but you are immediately aware of a curious feature: the foundations consist of six concentric circular walls. The three walls that are furthest from the

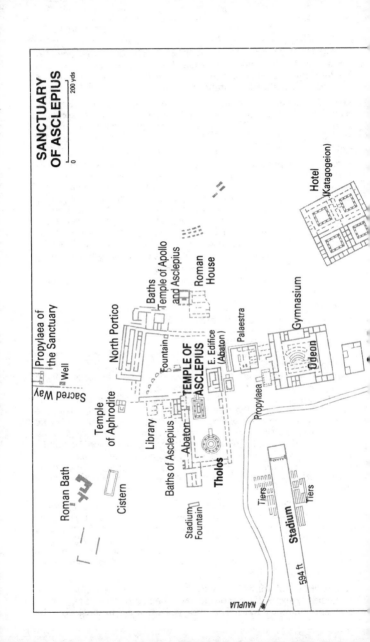

SANCTUARY OF ASCLEPIUS

0 ─── 200 yds

Roman Bath

Cistern

Temple of Aphrodite

Propylaea of the Sanctuary

Well

Sacred Way

North Portico

Baths

Temple of Apollo and Asclepius

Roman House

Library

Fountain

TEMPLE OF ASCLEPIUS

E. Edifice (Abaton)

Palaestra

Baths of Asclepius

Abaton

Tholos

Propylaea

Oertdeon

Gymnasium

Hotel (Katagogeion)

Stadium Fountain

Tiers

Tiers

Stadium

594 ft

NAUPLIA

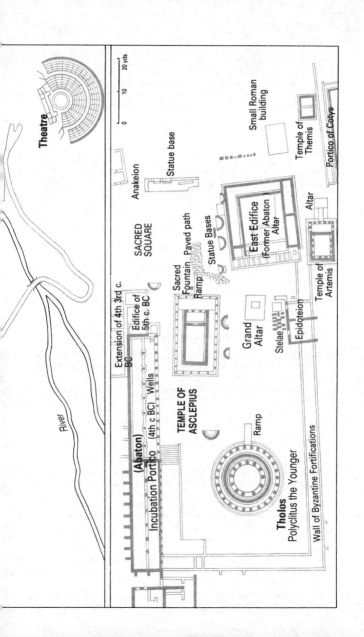

Theatre

River

0   10   20 yds

SACRED SQUARE

Extension of 4th 3rd c. BC

Edifice of 5th c. BC

Anakeion

Statue base

(Abaton)

Incubation Portico   (4th c BC)   Wells

TEMPLE OF ASCLEPIUS

Sacred Fountain   Paved path

Ramp

Statue Bases

Small Roman building

East Edifice (Former Abaton)

Altar

Grand Altar

Ramp

Tholos

Polyclitus the Younger

Wall of Byzantine Fortifications

Stelae

Epidoteion

Altar

Temple of Artemis

Temple of Themis

Portico of Cotys

centre were continuous, but another strange feature is that the three inner walls had doors in them and partition walls running across the gap between them. The doors and the partition walls were so arranged that to get from one corridor to the next and so reach the centre you had to go almost the whole way round the corridor you wanted to leave. Thus, to reach the centre, you had to go round an almost full circle no fewer than three times. How you got into this labyrinth from the outside remains a mystery.

A snake pit – This layout has given rise to many hypotheses, one of the most arresting being that the labyrinth was where the sacred snakes belonging to the sanctuary were kept. However, it would seem most likely that whatever rites this building was intended for would have been enacted at its centre. The very name by which the building is described – thymele or altar – seems to indicate that whatever took place there was religious in nature and that the role of the tholos was at least partly as a place of sacrifice.

Beginning with the outside, the first wall held an outer colonnade, the second a full wall broken on the E by a door with an access ramp leading to it, and the third supported the inner colonnade. The other three walls, as well as serving whatever religious function their layout may imply, supported the flooring of the tholos. The outer range was made up of 26 Doric columns and the inner of 14 Corinthian columns, some parts of which have been reconstructed in the last room in the museum. Pausanias tells us that inside the building there were paintings by Pausias depicting Love and Intoxication.

THE NEW ABATON. Beyond the tholos there was a portico with an internal partition or cross wall running along the middle of it and dividing it into two; in the inscriptions it is referred to as the Enkoimeterion (portico of incubation) or abaton (secret portico); when it was built in the 4th century BC it is thought to have replaced, or performed the same function as, an earlier building (plan, E) which some archaeologists believe fulfilled the same purpose.

BATHS OF ASCLEPIUS. These were built in the 2nd century AD by a senator called Antoninus, partly over a 5th-century BC building.

This earlier building consisted of a large chamber divided into three parts by two transversal walls. At a later stage in the 4th-3rd century BC it was enlarged by the addition of two suites of rooms to the N. It had all been reduced to its foundations by the time the Roman buildings were erected. But it seems as if the 5th-century BC building was placed on a site that was already used for worship. Traces of a previous building have been found, mainly round a well at the E end of the abaton. When the 5th-century BC chamber was built at a slightly higher level, the well was in fact given a new curb-stone. This was not disturbed when the Ionic portico was built and was incorporated into it. The well, which may date from the 6th century BC, offers evidence that this was one of the oldest places of worship in the sanctuary of Asclepius. It seems to have gone out of use from the time when the 4th century BC buildings were put up, but was piously preserved out of respect for Archaic places of worship.

PROPYLAEA. On the way to the propylaea you cross the Sacred Square where you can see several bases and the remains of exedrae, and then the ruins of a group of Roman buildings, including baths and temples (to Apollo and Asclepius). You then reach the propylaea, and can look at their remains, which were built of tufa in the 4th century BC, and formed a monumental gate on the road from Epidaurus into the sanctuary. Along this road to the r., a hundred yards from the propylaea, the necropolis begins.

STADIUM. This was installed in the 5th century BC in the hollow of a natural ravine. The tiered seating, some of which has been preserved, was partly cut out of the rock and partly constructed in masonry. There was a vaulted passageway in the bank near the road. Just across from there a rectangular area built among the tiered seating was the tribune of the judges who announced the winners. The starting and finishing lines, marked by two rows of grooved paving stones, are still there.

VICINITY OF EPIDAURUS-OLD EPIDAURUS (Palea Epidavros; 13.7mls/22km via Ligourio). Near this little port on a peninsula is the site of the ancient city of which the sanctuary of Asclepius was a dependency. Those interested in antiquities can see the core of the capitals of many Doric columns re-used in a later building, the theatre now uncovered on the side of a hill and, on its summit, the remains of an early Christian church. What is more, investigation by aerial photography has revealed significant submerged remains of the ancient harbour. Recent excavations have uncovered a huge necropolis.

Epirus

Route maps 10 and 11.

Epirus, stretching from the Albanian frontier to the Ambracian Gulf, from the Ionian Sea to the Pindus mountains, is a very mountainous area where the preponderance of limestone rock provides favourable conditions for the subterranean movement of water and is the cause of the development of broad enclosed depressions, such as the Ioannina basin with a lake at its centre; water is absorbed by the depressions in the basin during the summer and flows back during the winter.

The Pindus mountains to the E separating Epirus from Thessaly are a massive range, rising to their highest point at Mt Smolikas, which is 8,815ft (2,687m) high; the mountain slopes are covered with forests of conifers and beech trees.

Some parts of the coastline are rocky, as between Igoumenitsa and Parga, while towards the Ambracian Gulf the coast is low and sandy. In this coastal area the climate is of a damp Mediterranean type, but in the interior the mountains are responsible for a very harsh continenta climate (winter temperatures are -16° to -20°F/-9° to -12°C), with temperature variations of more than 68°F (20°C) between summer and winter.

Epirus, which was an Albanian province united with Greece in 1922 has a population of 310,000, making it one of the least populous regions in Greece, and its empty, limestone uplands are left to wandering flocks. Only the fertile Ioannina basin, with vineyards fields of cereals and the lushest meadows in the land, and the Ambracian Plain, with huge irrigated fields and orchards of citrus fruit, offer a semblance of prosperity.

■ Eratini

Route map 4.

Naupaktos, 30.6mls (49km) – Delphi, 33mls (53km).

Lying on the new coast that links Naupaktos and Itea, Eratini is a newish bathing resort near Vidavi, where ancient Tolophon stood From it you can visit a quite well-preserved ancient fortress at the place known as Marmara, 30mins walk away.

E | Euboea [Island of] (Evia or Evvia)*

1,457 sq. mls (3,775 km²) — Pop: 163,000.

Euboea hardly seems like an island, so easy is it to travel between there and the mainland; however the famous Euripos channel does nonetheless separate it from the mainland, and is crossed by a bridge some 44yds (40m) long, which takes you to Chalcis, the island's capital, an active, rapidly developing centre. The bathing resort and spa of Loutra Aedipsos and the ruins of the city of Eretria are other places to visit or stay, though the rest of the island should not be neglected. Its terrain is mountainous, a continuation of central Greece, and Euboea shares with that a mosaic of different landscapes, but its climate is similar to that of neighbouring Attica There are three main areas:

The N part from Chalcis to Loutra Aedipsos is made up of high forested hills – one of the most appealing areas in Greece unfortunately ravaged by forest fires in 1977 – dotted with basin forming little plateaux where a clay soil favours Mediterranean mixed farming.

In the centre there are arid limestone masses rising to culminate in Mt Dirphys (5,718ft/1,743m), which stands pyramid-like above forests of chestnut trees, lime trees and conifers. Steep narrow creeks cut into the coastline, except on the W where the rivers spread out as they reach the sea creating the alluvial plain of Chalcis; the flourishing vineyards, olive groves and fields of cereals scattered with fig and walnut trees are evidence of its fertility.

The S part of the island is a fragment of an ancient mountain mass, a detached pillar of Attica. It consists of a block of marmorean limestone rising to a height of 4,586ft (1,398m) at Mt Okhi. The area is cut through by ravines, and the steep coastline is notched by narrow bays. The people mainly live by animal husbandry.

Euboea in history

A COLONY THAT GOES ON TO HAVE COLONIES OF ITS OWN. Euboea was first populated by colonial settlers, Thessalians in the N, Thracians in the centre and Dryopes in the S. At the time of the Dorian invasion some Ionians took refuge in Euboea, thus beginning a long period of emigration to the island, so that from the 7th–6th century BC the country could be regarded as being Ionian. The island was divided into independent states, the two most important of which in the 8th century BC were Eretria and Chalcis; their wealth and power was based on trade and they founded colonies in Macedon (the name Chalcidice is still evidence of this), Sicily and Italy. Chalcis formed an alliance with the Boeotians against the Athenians, but in 506 BC Athens seized its territory.

ATHENIAN HEGEMONY. Athens needed wheat and cattle from Euboea, and so began to interfere in the affairs of the island after the fall of the Pisistratids in 506 BC and to establish settlers (cleruchs) there. The island's fate for about 150 years depended on the reverses and successes of the Athenians: Pericles gave it to the Athenians in 446 BC, but they lost it towards the end of the Peloponnesian War, regaining it from 378 BC when most of the island's towns were enlisted in their maritime confederacy. Then after the Battle of Leuctra (371 BC) Thebes gained control of it. Macedon settled the quarrel between Boeotia and Athens (350–349 BC) to its own advantage and Euboea was a Macedonian dependency until 196 BC when the island, like the rest of Greece, was proclaimed free by the Romans, who had conquered the Macedonians.

NEGROPONTE. Frankish domination lasted from 1205 to 1470, with Euboea being divided into three feudal baronies owing fealty to the king of Salonika and occupied by the Carceri of Verona, who subsequently adopted the title of Lords of Negroponte. The Venetians were in control of the ports while a large number of small Frankish principalities took over in the interior, building a multiplicity of watch-towers and keeps on their domains. In 1336 the Venetians gained control of almost the whole island; the name Negroponte (black bridge) comes from that period, first applied to the Euripus, making a pun with the popular form of its name, Egripo (instead of Evripo), and then extending to the whole of Euboea.

In 1470 the island came under Turkish control, and in 1830 became part of Greece.

I – Chalcis (Khalkis) and the N of Euboea

The town of Chalcis, with a pop. of 36,300, capital of Euboea and principal town of the Northern Sporades, is an important economic centre, thanks to the bridge linking it with the mainland; but for the visitor it appears first and foremost as an attractive bathing resort, much frequented by the Greeks who appreciate its relative coolness at the height of summer.

The town in history

THE KEY-TOWN OF THERMOPYLAE BY THE SEA. Livy nicknamed Chalcis, with its two harbours on the Euripus, Thermopylae by the sea; it was one of the most active cities in ancient Greece. It had a strong navy and from the 8th century BC formed colonies in the Sporades, in Thracia and even as far away as Sicily and Italy. Its metal-workers were famed for their manufacture of weapons, vases and tripods, which were used as offerings at sanctuaries or as rewards for the victors in the various famous games that took place in Greece. Its name Khalkis (bronze) indicates the prominence of this industry which was so highly prized in Hellas.

INDEPENDENCE BRINGS PROSPERITY. Situated on the maritime trading route linking Thessaly, which exported horses and cereals, Thrace, Macedon (gold from Thasos and then from Mt Pangaeus, wood, wheat), Attica and central Greece, Chalcis, with its own production of wheat and horses, was a very prosperous city before Athens gained control in the 5th century BC. It had many colonies, particularly in Macedon – Strabo claims that Chalcidice owes its name to Chalcis. It seems that Chalcis got the better of its rival Eretria in the 7th century BC, but the last king of Chalcis, Amphidamas, who was contemporary with Hesiod, died in one of the battles between the two cities and power passed into the hands of the hippobotes (horse-breeders), who formed the aristocracy, until they were overthrown by the Athenians in 506 BC.

FROM LATIN TO TURK. After falling into the power of a Latin race in 1205 when it was granted in fief to Jacques d'Avesnes, who died in the siege of Acrocorinth (1205–10), Chalcis and then Euboea came under the control of Venice until 1470, when the Turks arrived. They kept the island for three and a half centuries despite the efforts of Morosini (1688).

Visiting the town

IF YOU ENJOY …

Archaic sculpture, don't fail to visit the local museum where the group statue with Theseus and Antiope awaits you.

And if you like swimming, fresh fish and shellfish and ouzo, go to the little beach on the Euripus channel (the water is particularly inviting there) and the little restaurants on the mainland bank opposite the Hotel Lucy. In the evening take an aperitif, preferably an ouzo, and nibble some pistachio nuts as you observe the perpetual motion of an especially lively crowd from the terrace of a café beside the Hotel Lucy.

The town has lost a lot of its charm since the Venetian city walls were destroyed and new residential areas developed. The sole surviving testimony of the duel between Venice and the Ottoman Empire is the Turkish fort of Karababa on the other side of the Euripus; it was built in 1686 at the time of Morosini's offensive on Morea. But the Euripus channel, though not particularly spectacular in itself, is nonetheless worth thinking about: it gives you a chance to try to solve an enigma of nature. There is no need, however, to go to the same lengths of a legendary man by the name of Aristotle who is said to have thrown himself into the channel because his lack of comprehension caused him to despair.

A CHANNEL WITH AN ALTERNATING CURRENT. The Euripus – the name means fast current – is actually famous because of the curious phenomenon that it has alternating currents which change direction six to seven times a day, and at certain periods even as often as 14 times. The flow in either direction lasts on average for three hours, and the water travels at speeds of up to 3.7mls (6km) an hour. It seems that the Euripus is a threshold or lock between the two reaches of the Euboean channel.

A BRIDGE IN MANY GUISES. In 441 BC the Chalcidians and the Boeotians, despite opposition from an Athenian fleet, blocked the Euripus with a dyke defended by towers, leaving only a narrow passage through which one boat could pass. A wooden bridge spanned this passage. This meant that communications between Euboea and the mainland were no longer at the mercy of Athenian fleets, and Chalcis was in command of the sea route to the N. In Justinian's reign the fixed bridge was replaced by a movable one. The Turks put up a wooden bridge which was eventually fixed. In 1856 a wooden swing bridge about 33ft (10m) long was put in its place. In 1896 a Belgian company widened the channel, dismantled the Venetian fort and built the existing bridge.

From the bridge follow the esplanade along the Euripus on the same side as the Hotel Lucy, then go back up the avenue that comes out near the landing-stage. This brings you to the archaeological museum.

Open: in summer, 09.00–13.00 and 16.00–18.00; in winter, 10.00–16.30; Sun., 10.30–14.30; closed Tues.; entrance fee.

This small provincial museum's prize possession can be seen at the back of the main room: this is the **group with Theseus and Antiope or Hippolyta, sculpted in marble, which decorated the central part of the W pediment of the temple of Apollo Daphnephorus at Eretria. The sculpture depicts an abduction and carries the hallmark of the Archaic period in the faint smile on the hero's face known as the 'Archaic smile'. It dates from c.500 BC.

In the same room note a votive relief portraying a sacrificial scene (mid 5th century BC) from Larymna and an Archaic-period bust of Athena, with a gorgon's head on her breast.

In the room to the l. of the entrance hall on the r. there is a statue of Antinous in the character of Dionysus, and a statue of Hermes, probably the one mentioned by Pausanias as being in the gymnasium at Chalcis (X, 39, 6), etc.

The truly dedicated could also visit the church of Hagia Paraskevi in the old town, a former Byzantine basilica altered by the Franks in the 13th and 14th century (the chevet or eastern end, is in the style typical of Champagne). To get to the church, follow the Euripus towards the bridge, and turn l. into Tsavara road (2nd after the bridge).

VICINITY

1 TEMPLE OF ARTEMIS AULIDEIA (5.3mls/8.5km along Thebes road, but turn off towards Aulis after 2.5mls/4km). Only the foundations of this 5th-century BC temple are left; it was altered in the Hellenistic period, then by the Romans, but this is the traditional location for the ritual murder of Iphigenia, sacrificed by Agamemnon to the goddess Artemis so that she might grant favourable winds to the Greek fleet gathered in the bay at Aulis before they set sail for Troy. Beside the first column in the l.-hand row of columns there is a base which supposedly acted as a support for the thousand-year-old plane tree mentioned by Pausanias (IX, 19, 7).

2 FROM CHALCIS TO LOUTRA AEDIPSOS (95mls/152km). This **road, which winds for most of its length through an area which has as yet attracted relatively few visitors, is one of the pleasantest and most picturesque to be found in Greece. It is a source of constantly renewed delight, with its pine forests, its shady vaults formed by magnificent plane trees, its wide views over mountainous landscapes, or on the N coast of Euboea with the deep blue sea water lapping against it, and where, on a clear day you can see across to the island of Skopelos.

Take the Limni road out of Chalcis.

5mls (8km): Artaki; road on r. leads to Steni, the starting point for climbing Mt Dirphys (5,725ft/1,745m), a 2½-hr walk (Alpine Club hut).

10mls (16km): Psachna; Byzantine church of Hagia Trias Krietsoti. 25mls (4km) away, convent of Makrimalli, where you can buy woven work made by the nuns. The Venetian castle of Kastri is an hour's walk to the N. The road climbs to an alt. of 1,968ft (600m) – Hagios Georgios pass; restaurant – then drops again through superb *wooded landscape, affording views of Skiathos and Skopelos. In a gorge, the church of Hagios Gregorios.

32.5mls (52km): Prokopion; health centre and model farm.

35mls (56km): Mandoudi, a large industrial village (harbour on the E coast).

41.2mls (66km): Strofylia: road on l. for (10.6mls/17km) Limni, a pleasant little fishing port in the midst of pine trees, with the ruins of an early Christian building. 1.6mls (2.5km) N (Rovies road), a lovely beach fringed with olive trees.

The road crosses a huge pine forest, damaged by fire in 1979.

68mls (109km): On a promontory 1.2mls (2km) away the remains of the Artemision or temple of Artemis Proseoa (eastward-looking) were discovered. If you make this detour it will give you an opportunity of obtaining a panoramic view of the N coast of Euboea.

80mls (128km): Istiea, located as if in an amphitheatre overlooking the N plain of the island.

85.6mls (137km): Orei, an unassuming port on the site of ancient Histiaea-Oreos, a Thessalian colony which Homer described as 'polystaphylos' (rich in vines). According to Titus Livius, Oreos had two acropolises; one now has a Venetian kastro on top of it, built on the site of a Hellenic perimeter wall. A marble bull dating from the Hellenistic period which was found in the sea stands in a public square.

88.7mls (142km): 1ml (1.5km) away on the r., Hagios Kambos; a ferry-boat leaves from there for Glifas (see route map 2) seven times daily; a beach and some very rustic little restaurants, which do however serve fresh fish.

95mls (152km): Loutra Aedipsos, a fair-sized spa and bathing resort on the Gulf of Euboea, across from Arkitsa (boats and ferries). The sulphur springs come up near the sea at the foot of Cape Therma; their beneficial effects were known in ancient times, and Sulla came here for a cure. Near the Hagiou Anargyrou spring there are the remains of Roman baths.

II – The South of Euboea

In Eretria the ruins of the second largest city of Euboea can be seen, second only to Chalcis, which a Swiss archaeological team is at present engaged in excavating. Darius ordered its capture in 490 BC because it had taken part in the rebellion of the Ionian cities of Asia Minor in 499 BC; it was taken just before the Battle of Marathon and partly destroyed, but soon rebuilt. The modern village is much liked by artists and writers.

Leave Chalcis in a SE direction, crossing through industrial suburbs.

6.2mls (10km): Vassiliko, with a Frankish tower. 1.2mls (2km) S the site of Lefkandi was investigated by the British School of Archaeology.

13.7mls (22km): Eretria, a modern town founded in the last century by refugees from the island of Psara on the remains of the ancient city.

To get to the main excavation site (*08.30–12.30 and 16.00–18.00; Sun.: 09.00–15.00*), leave the main street in a NW direction. A metalled road leads up to the little museum of sculpture, ceramics and various objects from ancient Eretria.

THEATRE. This is the best preserved of the ancient buildings and can be used as a point of reference. You can see the passageway with ribbed vaulting going under the orchestra (dancing space) which communicated by means of staircases with the area under the stage (the hyposcenion) and the centre of the orchestra; characters from the underworld made their entrance from this. Like the gymnasium, remains of which can be seen 164yds (150m) to the E, the theatre dates from the end of the Classical period, with alterations from later times.

AREA NEAR THE W GATE. There is a new dig which will be of special interest to archeologists 220yds (200m) to the r. (with your back turned to the hemicycle formed by the theatre); it is near the ramparts of the city walls. You first come to the foundations of the temple of Dionysus quite near the theatre, following the Doric order and dating from the end of the Classical period, then to the imposing remains of a city gate in quite a good state of preservation, built at several different periods, and of a strong bastion which was put up to reinforce the gate there in the Classical period; it is a characteristic example of the Hellenistic art of fortification.

To the r. of the gate the high wall of polygonally bonded masonry which dates in part from the 7th century BC served to channel the course of a stream. There was a necropolis in this area with large terraced tombs, dating from the 4th century BC. To the l. of the gate (the S) beyond the ruins of an 8th-century BC heroön covered over shortly after 700 BC by a cult precinct made of stone slabs arranged to form an equilateral triangle, and beyond a long 7th-century BC building consisting of five rooms, possibly a place of worship used by a noble fraternity, you can see the remains of one of the dwelling houses uncovered in this area. It was built during the first half of the 4th century BC, and is evidence of Eretria's prosperity at that time. In the following centuries the house was altered several times.

A little further on still beside the ramparts are the ruins of a second building consisting of a series of five rooms, one of which was intended for banquets. Then there is a second house from the same period as the first, built even more generously, which was, like it, destroyed in 198 BC by the Romans, and partly lived in later.

The second house was larger than the first and had a large central courtyard; it was conceived on a grand scale which you will not find at Olynthus. Opposite this house on the other side of the road another building has been uncovered, but its purpose is not yet known.

TEMPLE OF APOLLO DAPHNEPHORUS. You can reach the site of this temple by taking Leoforos Isidos from the museum, which leads to a square in the modern village where you turn r. The temple is of the Doric order, peripteral and dates from the end of the Archaic period; it had carved pediments depicting the battle between Theseus and the Amazons (group with Theseus and Antiope in the Chalcis museum).

It was built to replace an Ionic peripteral temple (with a wooden colonnade) similar in plan to the temple of Hera on Samos.

The cult of Apollo on this site goes back to the Geometric period. Recent investigations have resulted in the discovery in the area of several buildings the remains of which were buried when terracing was built in the first half of the 7th century BC: a long apsidal building and a small building, also apsidal, which has been tentatively identified as a sort of offering, copying the mythical laurel hut which legend tells us was Apollo's first temple at Delphi; its roof was supported by a double colonnade running round the periphery with three central columns, all made of wood. This is one of the earliest known Greek temples.

From the temple of Apollo proceed towards the acropolis which can be seen in the distance. At the bottom of the mound look at the 'house of mosaics', uncovered between 1972 and 1978. It is a fine house dating from the 4th century BC, with its rooms arranged round a central courtyard, and was destroyed early in the 3rd century BC by fire. The furniture has been preserved in the debris, as have four exceptional pebble mosaics from the beginning of the 4th century BC, showing mythological scenes (a Nereid astride a seahorse, a fight between griffins and Arimaspians), sphinxes, panthers and leaf and flower decorations. The quadrangular enclosure and the sarcophagi which can be seen in the NW corner of the house belong to a 1st century BC tomb.

19.4mls (31km): Amarinthos, a bathing resort with a sandy beach and two Byzantine churches.

29.4mls (47km): Aliveri, not far from a fair-sized lignite mine; near the shore, a medieval fortress.

33mls (53km): road on r. for Dystos (2.5mls/4km), on the banks of a sometimes dry lake; the village is near the site of ancient Dystus, which was on a lonely rock now topped by a Venetian kastro. The polygonally bonded town walls (5th century BC) with 11 reinforcing towers curve round a cliff. The agora and 5th-century BC houses were built on terraces.

35mls (56km): on the l., a road leading to (21.8mls/35km N) Kymi, a pretty little market town on the E coast across from the island of Scyros, nicknamed 'balcony of the Aegean'. 0.6ml (1km) from the town are the thermal springs of Honeutikon, whose waters are bottled and distributed throughout Greece – their therapeutic effect on kidney ailments are widely recognized. The site of ancient Cyme is thought to lie an hour's walk from the present village, where the monastery of the Saviour now stands, near a small Venetian fortress. As it travels S the road takes you through some very lovely *scenery in the heart of the S peninsula of Euboea.

60.6mls (97km): Styra – a tower from the acropolis of the ancient town of Styra to the W of the village of (3.1mls/5km) Nea Styra near the coast. 50mins away to the NE at Spitia tou Drakou (the houses of the

dragons), there are ancient cipolin quarries (see below) with three quarrymen's houses built of schist slabs standing on a terrace.

80.6mls (129km): Karystos, a pretty little town at the foot of Mt Okhi, 1.9mls (3km) from the port (ferries to Rafina in Attica and the island of Andros). The ancient city of Carystus, the town of the Dryopes, was famous for its asbestos and for its white and green marble, (also called 'cipolin' from the word for onion), much admired by the Romans.

The ancient acropolis was on the site of the Venetian kastro, known as Castel Rosso because of its reddish colour, and of the town of Paleo Choro where there are the remains of a bridge, a few inscriptions and the Metropolitan church.

■ Evzoni

Route map 2.

Lamia, 212mls (339km) – Larisa, 123mls (197km) – Thessaloniki, 47mls (75km).

Evzoni is the main frontier post between Greece and Yugoslavia, and considerable road traffic passes through it.

■ Farsala (Pharsalus)

Route map 1.

Lamia, 39.4mls (63km) – Larisa, 30mls (48km) – Pop: 6,500 approx.

 This little town, on a site which has been inhabited continuously since the Neolithic era, owes its rise from obscurity to a battle. It was near Pharsalus on 29 June or 9 August (Julian and Gregorian dates respectively) 48 BC that Caesar won one of his most famous battles, inflicting a crushing defeat on Pompey's troops.

VICINITY OF FARSALA

PALEOKASTRO (8.1mls/13km; along the Larisa road, then r. after 1.9mls/3km). Paleokastro near the village of Ano Derengli is the site of a town identified as Paleopharsalus, occupied from the early Helladic period (c.2,500 BC) until the 6th century BC. There are other sites in the vicinity, in particular those of the Thetidaeum, a sanctuary of Thetis and Peleus (near Bekides); and of Skotoussa (near Soupli), where the oracle of Zeus Phegonaeus was located, said to be a forerunner of the Dodona oracle, captured in 367 BC by Alexander of Pherai and in 191 BC by Antiochus, then by the Romans.

To the N rises the mountain of Karadag (2,382ft/726m) known in ancient times as Cynocephalae (dogs' heads). The two battles of Cynocephalae (the first in 364 BC between Alexander of Pherai and Pelopidas who met his death there, the second between Flamininus, with 26,000 men and some elephants, and Philip V of Macedon in 197 BC) were fought W of Skotoussa.

■ Florina

Route maps 1, 13 and 15.

Edessa, 51.2mls (82km) – Kastoria, 66.2mls (106km) – Niki, 9.4mls (15km) – Thessaloniki, 102.5mls (164km) – Pop: 12,300 – alt. 2,231ft (680m) – district capital of admin. region.

Set in the heart of the country, Florina has little of interest to offer, but it is a pleasant place to stop.

In the town near the station there is a little museum with funerary stelae, some sculpture, including a statuette of Artemis and a marble

statue of an ephebe, a Roman copy of a 5th-century BC prototype. The museum's collection also includes some Byzantine sculpture and post-Byzantine icons.

VICINITY OF FLORINA

MEGALI PRESPA AND MIKRI PRESPA LAKES. These two lakes, Great and Lesser Prespa, lie in a superb setting on the border between Greece, Albania and Yugoslavia. Though access to them is restricted, you can admire them from the village of Hagios Germanos (31.2mls/50km W of Florina); the view from there is magnificent.

■ Folegandros [Island of]

14sq. mls (36 km²) — Pop: 650.

The bare, rocky island of Folegandros is one of the smallest in the Cyclades archipelago, and on several occasions served the sad function of a place of political exile. The few boats serving the island (Piraeus-Santorini line, thrice weekly, and in the summer the Piraeus-Rhodes ferry) call in at Karavostassi, which is no more than some small inlets with a few houses on their shores. From there a wild pass leads through to the main village of Folegandros (2.5mls/4km) which suddenly appears with dazzling whiteness, its houses with their outside stairs close-packed within the walls of a medieval fortress. The light floods down, playing with the volumes and colours, and the domes of little churches break the pattern; two or three squares, about the same number of tavernas: the true magic of the Greek islands. Just for pleasure visit the church of the Panagia and the Chrissopilia cave, and go swimming from the very lovely beach of Angali. Apano Meria, the island's third village, lies NW of Folegandros.

■ Gastouni

Route map 9.

Patras, 41.2mls (66km) – Pyrgos, 16.9mls (27km) – Pop: 5,000 approx.

This large village, once the residence of the Frankish princes of Achaea, when it was known as La Gastogne, is the starting-point for a visit to the site of ancient Elis, part of which is fated to disappear under the waters of a reservoir.

VICINITY OF GASTOUNI

ELIS. (7.5mls/12km along the Nea Ilis road). Between the villages of Paleopolis and Bouchioti a few remains of the agora and the gymnasia where athletes trained before taking part in the Olympic Games, and of a theatre have been identified on the site of the ancient town of Elis. The theatre dates back to the Hellenistic period and was altered during the Roman period. It is the only monument of Elis easily reached from the museum.

The area N of the theatre is littered with tombs and the remains of relatively late buildings, among them an early Christian basilica with mosaic flooring.

Since 1980 one of the rooms and the patio of the depository of antiquities have been arranged as a museum (open daily, 09.00–13.00). Fragments of architecture and funerary stelae (of the Hellenistic period) are displayed in the patio, while in the room mainly small objects are exhibited, from a wide range of periods (from the 2nd millennium BC to the Roman period): jewellery, weapons, tools, figurines, vases (bronze and especially pottery), and coins.

■ Gherolimin

Route map 6.

Areopolis, 15.6mls (25km) – Kalamata, 64.4mls (103km) – Sparta, 60.6mls (97km).

 Gherolimin is a harbour at what feels like the edge of the world, in the wild Mani region, near small Byzantine churches with marble iconostases (Bourlariori, Hagia Pelagia), and it is the starting point for an excursion to Cape Matapan, or at least to the very picturesque old village of Vathia about 5ml (8km) away (see itinerary dep. Areopolis); perched on a rocky peak and partly abandoned, this village, bristling with towers, is one of the most typical of Mani: from on top a magnificent view over the sea and towards Cape Matapan.

It will take you approx. 5hrs on foot (you may prefer to go by caïque) to reach Cape Matapan, known in ancient times as Taenarum. The cape, which is often lashed by storms, was the centre of the Free-Laconian confederation, an association of coastal towns which was formed during the Roman period. The temple of Poseidon there was also the seat of an oracle, and on occasion the area was used as a safe hiding place by pirates. A few vestiges of it can be found in the walls of the chapel *ton Assomaton* (of the Spirits), near the bay of the Kisternaes, at a place which has been identified as the site of the ancient port of Psamathos. The cave from which Heracles reputedly emerged dragging Cerberus from the Underworld lay to the W.

The Bay of Porto Cayo beyond the Cape is overlooked by a hill on which stand the scant remains of the Frankish fortress of Maina, referred to in the chronicles as the Grande Maigne, built in 1250 by Guillaume de Villehardouin and surrendered to the Byzantines in 1263.

Off the Cape lies the Inousses chasm, the deepest abyss in the Mediterranean (15,026ft/4,580m).

■ Gythion

Route map 6.

Areopolis, 16.2mls (26km) – Sparta, 28.7mls (46km).

Founded by the Phoenicians and at one time the harbour and arsenal of Sparta, Gythion today is a sleepy little town with a none too attractive pebble beach.

A small museum on the ground floor of the town hall (in a little road at right-angles to the seafront) has some stone-carved inscriptions (some from the Archaic period), pottery and a few pieces of sculpture from the Roman period.

MYTH AND HISTORY. The town lies at the foot of Mt Koumaro, in ancient times called Larysium, across from the tiny island of Marathonisi which is linked to the mainland by a causeway and has been identified as Kranaë, where the Phoenicians called to trade in purple dye and which was also famous as a place of asylum. Paris is supposed to have taken refuge there after abducting Helen. Opposite the island in the Migonion, an open market with Oriental traders in what was a suburb of the ancient town, there was a sanctuary of Aphrodite Migonitis, founded by the Phoenicians (it may have stood on the site of the Metropolitan church of Hagios Georgios).

At the summit of Mt Larysium, which was dedicated to Dionysus and the Praxidicae, are the ruins of a kastro. At the foot of the hill on the l. of the Sparta road there is a recess with a cube-shaped altar cut out of the rock (now called Pelekito), which is thought to have been part of the sanctuary of Zeus Terastios. This has often been identified as the altar stone of Zeus Kappotas where Orestes sat and was cured of his madness.

- The ancient town was 275yds (250m) away, beyond the Selenitsa stream. The triangular hill of the acropolis rises on the l. and on it there are the remains of some walls. The theatre was hollowed out at the bottom of the hill. There are other remains which are partly buried.

5.6mls (9km) away to the N of the Areopolis road are the ruins of the Castle of Passava, built in 1254 by Jean de Neuilly, Marshal of Morea, restored by the Turks, and then dismantled by the Venetians. The site has been identified as that of Homer's Las.

Gla [Island of]

Route map 3.

Athens, 76mls (121km) – Chalcis, 45mls (72km) – Lamia, 65.6mls (105km) – Thebes, 20mls (32km).

This was an island in Lake Copaïs now drained and dry as it was between 2000 and 1300 BC. Now it is just a hill, but on it there are the ruins of a royal residence, built around the 16th century BC in the middle of a Minyan city. These constitute the largest known site of the Mycenaean period. The track leading to the bottom of the acropolis goes right round it.

The length of the *perimeter wall is 1.9mls (3km); it encircled the whole island. These impressive walls are 17ft 9in–19ft thick (5.4–5.8m) and as at Mycenae and Tiryns are of cyclopean construction.

The main gate to the S was reached by a road which has been uncovered for a length of 104yds (95m). This gate was set over an oblique passageway, and on either side of it there were two long towers.

At the highest point you can see the ruins of the palace, in as bad a state of preservation as those at Mycenae or Tiryns; only the foundations remain. The building was L-shaped, with an enclosed courtyard before it. One wing was built on the ramparts and the other on a terrace. Both wings had reception rooms at one end (a large megaron and its vestibule approached by a broad external corridor) and private apartments towards the middle, carefully isolated and served by internal corridors. The palace must have had two floors, the second being built of baked bricks.

- An agora surrounded by ramparts lay at the middle of the island, communicating with the palace by means of a gate. This great courtyard with two groups of buildings standing on it was connected to the main gate through the city walls by a road running from a gate with a square tower on either side.

THE KATAVOTHRAE OF LAKE COPAÏS. From the village of Kastro you can walk to these famous natural curiosities in the hollow formed by the former lake.

LAKE COPAÏS. This lake was said to be the largest in Greece and its eels were famed throughout the ancient world; Strabo tells us that its perimeter measurement was 44mls (70km). In dry weather it shrank greatly in size, but when it rained heavily it overflowed its banks, in spite of the natural outlets formed by the katavothrae or swallow-holes, subterranean caves, abysses and channels; it was drained between 2000 and 1300 BC, and the dried-out bed of the lake produced excellent crops.

By the time historical records were kept the lake had filled again, and once more there were schemes to control it (outlet channels built by Crates, see below). A major scheme was undertaken at the end of the 19th century, with the construction of various channels diverting water from the rivers to the sea (the Gulf of Euboea) and eastwards to Lake Iliki.

In 1311 a violent battle known as the Battle of Lake Copaïs was fought not far from Orchomenos, NW of the lake, between a Catalan army and the Frankish knights of Greece, with the armies of the latter being almost annihilated.

It takes 1½hrs to reach the Spitia katavothra and 220yds (200m) S of it the remains of a Minyan acropolis have been discovered on what used to be a peninsula; another peninsula to the W of the first also had an acropolis on the crest of it, with a dyke running between the two. Beyond them are the katavothrae of Sitia and (2hrs) Vynia at the entrance to the Kephalari gorge where Crates, an engineer of the time of Alexander the Great, undertook the boring of a subterranean outlet channel 2,625yds (2,400m) long between the lake and Kephalari valley. 2¼hrs: Megali-Katavothra, where the River Melas tumbles in a spray of foam to the bottom of an 82ft — (25m)-high cave.

Hagii Theodori

Route map 5.

Athens, 41.8mls (67km) – Corinth, 12.5mls (20km).

Hagii Theodori lies on the Corinth side of the road past the Scironian Rocks, a high cliff from the top of which the evil Sciron threw travellers down into the sea until Theseus did the same to him; and occupies the site of what must have been the ancient port of Crommyon. It has a long sandy beach with a few little hotels and restaurants. It is safe to bathe there, and the water of the Saronic Gulf is especially warm. Wicked Sciron is only a memory now, killed by Theseus on his way from Troezen to Athens, as was the sow of Crommyon which fed on human flesh.

Hagios Constantinos

Route map 3.

Athens, 110mls (175km) – Lamia, 29.4mls (47km).

N of the modern church of this little port baths have been found that were part of a much larger development; they were in use in the early Christian era and at the beginning of the Byzantine period.

Hosios Loukas [Monastery of]*

Route map 4.

Athens, 94.4mls (151km) – Delphi, 23mls (37km) – Livadia, 23mls (37km) – Thebes, 51.2mls (82km).

A visit to the churches of the monastery of St Luke in Phocis, set in a calm landscape of olive trees and with some outstanding mosaics of the second golden era of Byzantine art, would prove a judicious complement to a visit to Delphi, enabling you to discover the beauty and interest of Byzantine Greece after sampling those of Ancient Greece.

THE TOMB OF ST LUKE STIRIS. This monastery is not dedicated to St Luke the Evangelist, but to a local saint, the hermit Luke Stiris – the word *hosios* is used to describe a hermit saint – who died in 946 or 949. The church he had built subsequently became a place of pilgrimage.

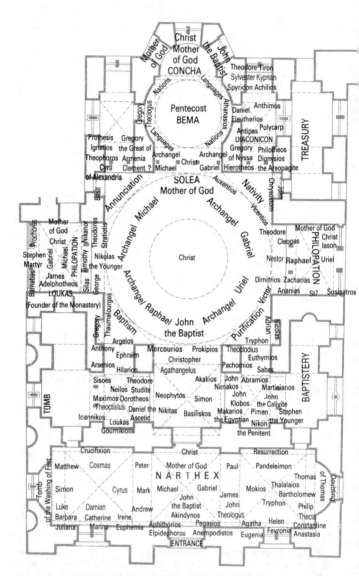

CHURCH OF HOSIOS LOUKAS

✝ The monastery of Hosios Loukas consists of a group of monastic buildings, to which staircases and vaulted passageways lend a great deal of charm, and in the midst of these are three churches, one of which now serves as the crypt of the main church. Be sure to look at the chevets of the two others which clearly demonstrate the difference in the building dates.

Open: 08.30–12.30 and 16.00–18.00; Sun., 09.00–15.00 Possibility of accommodation at the monastery.

The main church or Katholikon, a massive building constructed in 1011 (or 142 in E Stikas' estimation), is dedicated to St Luke (Hosios Loukas). It is on the walls of this church that the famous **mosaics can be seen, while the polychrome marble claddings and flooring also warrant admiration. The adjoining plan shows where and what the main mosaics are; those lost as a result of damage caused to the church by an earthquake in 1659 were replaced in the 17th century by paintings. Note too the marble iconostasis and four icons dated 1570, painted by the Cretan artist, Damaskinos.

On the l. the smallest church, built c.950, is dedicated to the Virgin Theotokos (Mother of God), and is also decorated with frescoes, some old, and ornamental ceramics and sculpture. In the crypt, which was the original church of St Barbara, there are some 11th-century frescoes that have recently been cleaned; as well as five tombs including that of Hosios Loukas, reconstructed a short time ago in marble.

■ Hydra [Island of]

21.2sq. mls (55km²) – Pop: 2,530.

There is something surprising about the fate of this island lying at the mouth of the Saronic Gulf, with its strong naval tradition; it was at one time a haunt of pirates – barely a century ago – but now the upsurge in tourism has turned it into a fashionable holiday resort, a meeting place of painters, artists and writers, even though it has hardly any beaches. While its port is a delightful and typically Mediterranean little sea-front, something peculiar to Hydra are the tall, distinguished houses perched on its slopes: though they all cast the same magic spell, the Greek islands can be varied.

A SANCTUARY FOR THE ORTHODOX. The island of Hydra, which is 11.2mls (18km) long and 2.5–3mls (4–5km) across, acquired most of its population from the 15th century on, at which time it became a place of refuge for Orthodox Christians and Albanian soldiers escaping from the tyranny of Mystra, or victims of Turkish persecution. After 1770 when the Morea rebelled against Ottoman rule, a new wave of refugees settled on Hydra, which became the main port of rebel Greece. As the island was too poor to provide food for all these people (there was a population of up to 20,000 compared with slightly fewer than 4,000 at present), the Hydriots turned to piracy and looked

to the sea to provide them with the means of existence which the land would not give.

Hydra's sea power in the 19th century led to its being nicknamed 'Little England'. When the War of Independence began in 1821 the great families of the island, particularly the Coundouriotis, sacrificed their wealth to fit out fleets. The naval tradition is upheld today by a training school for officers of the Merchant Navy.

Near the harbour, you can visit some old houses dating from the late 18th century, often Italian in inspiration, which were built for wealthy shipping families: these include the house of Boulgaris, the house of Tombazis (adapted by the Athens Fine Art School as a hostel for its students), the Boudouris house with its private chapel, and, above all the Coundouriotis house. A small museum contains documents relating to the War of Independence. You can divide your time between swimming, strolling around the harbour or the art galleries, waiting at the harbour where the arrival of the boat from Piraeus always causes a great deal of bustle, and taking trips around the island. One of the most interesting of these, and also the shortest, is a climb up to Kalo Pigadi where you can see some old 17th-century houses and a few tiny chapels.

It takes about 1½hrs to walk to Mandraki Bay, which used to be guarded by two small forts.

Or you can walk up to the monastery of Profitis Ilias, at an altitude of 1,640ft (500m), in 1 hr. The monastery lies in pine woods and was found in the early 19th century. The view is very beautiful.

The monastery of Zourvas stands isolated on the eastern tip of the island, and it takes 3hrs to walk there.

An outing to the western side of the island would take you near the hamlet of Episkopi, leaving the town of Hydra through the smart Kaminia district. On your way you pass an old humpbacked bridge, then through the hamlet of Vlicho with its chapel planted on a red reef with waves breaking against it. Before you reach Molo cove you pass the Hagios Kyprianos chapel, and after Molo you climb up along a wide pine-clad valley towards Episkopi. From there make your way back towards Hydra via the Hagia Marina chapel, its whiteness accentuated by the pine trees, and the ruins of the abandoned monastery of Hagia Irini.

■ Icaria [Island of]

103sq. mls (267km²) – Pop: 9,500.

This mountainous, wooded island in the Aegean, 145 nautical miles from Piraeus on the way to Samos, naturally evokes memories of Icarus and his fall, which supposedly occurred not far from the coasts of the island. Nowadays it is a good port of call for all who love nature in its untamed state, though there are some fertile areas on the island which are farmed. The island's produce includes fruit, heather honey and arbutus honey and a renowned 'raki', a strong drink based on the arbutus berry.

Hagios Kyrikos, built on a hillside, is a very unassuming capital (a small archaeological museum) for this island, but it boasts Therma (1.2mls/2km NE), with its radioactive springs, the beneficial qualities of which were recognized from ancient times (ruins of Roman baths).

Not far from Therma the acropolis of Kataphygion can be found on the summit of a mountain known as Kastro, overlooking the coast and the sea. 5.6mls (9km) from Hagios Kyrikos at the place known as Na near Perdiki, there are the remains of a temple identified as that of Artemis Tauropole.

Past Kataphygion the island's main road goes back down towards Miliopion on the N coast, an early Christian fortress, then on towards Karavostamos (a beach) and finally Evdilos (15mls/24km from Hagios Kyrikos; beach); if you go a bit further along the coastline (on a track), you come to a superb *beach 1.9mls (3km) long at Yaliskari.

The whole W side of the island can be explored on foot; in the hills there are the pretty villages of Christo, Lapsachades, and Hagios Polykarpas.

You can hire a caïque to take you to the beaches on the W coast (Xylosirti) or to Phanari, on the N tip of the island. And finally you can go to the tiny islands of Fourni and Themena, inhabited by only a few fishermen.

■ Igoumenitsa

Route maps 10 and 11.

Athens, 303mls (485km) – Ioannina, 68.7mls (110km) – Kalambaka

(Meteora), 142mls (228km) – district capital of admin. region of Thesprotia.

This Ionian port of entry into mainland Greece, about 80 nautical miles from the heel of the boot of Italy, sometimes takes people by surprise, for in spite of its very beautiful setting it is not at all what people imagine Greece to be like. Bide your time, and enjoy the scenery, which is in fact typically Balkan, while it is before you.

While you are waiting for a boat to Corfu or Italy you may feel tempted to go for a swim (go to Drepanos Beach which has fine sand – 3.4mls/5.5km along the Ioannina road, turn l. for 0.9mls/1.5km), or to explore the vicinity a little: visit Parga, for instance, though you need to allow 3hrs for that.

VICINITY

1 FILIATES (13.1mls/21km; follow Ioannina road for 6.2mls/10km, then l.). This lush green village lies in the very beautiful area to the N of the Ioannina road, and near it is the monastery of Giremeri, the catholicon of which dates from 1568 (18th-century paintings). Further N, is Kamitsani, a former convent, the church of which is decorated with 18th-century frescoes.

2 PARGA (30.6mls/49km; see under Parga).

■ Ioannina (Jannina)*

Route maps 11 and 15.

Arta, 45.6mls (73km) – Igoumenitsa, 68.7mls (110km) – Kalambaka (Meteors), 78.7mls (126km) – Pop: 40,000 – district capital of admin. region – university.

Ioannina, with its bazaar with its eastern atmosphere and its citadel under the shadow of a slim-minareted mosque, is a reminder of the Turkish occupation of the Balkans. Be sure to visit the monasteries built on an island on the romantic lake, one bank of which is filled with picturesque old parts of the town, and in the vicinity, the caves at Perama and the ruins of Dodona.

THE SHORT-LIVED CAPITAL OF A DESPOT. It is not known when Ioannina was founded. The year 700 is often suggested, but with no certainty. History becomes more precise in the 11th century when the town was captured by Bohemond, Robert Guiscard's bastard son, who fortified the acropolis. In 1204 when Epirus became an independent entity under the rule of a despot, Ioannina became the country's capital, which it remained for ten years until the first despot, Michael Angelus Comnenus, was assassinated.

In 1345 it was captured by the Serb Stefan Dusan and, with the rest of Epirus, annexed into the kingdom of Serbia, then at the height of its power.

THE SAD DESTINY OF A PASHA. After being captured by the army of Sultan Murad II in 1431 Ioannina became the capital of one of the three pashas who shared the sovereignty of Epirus among them. But it was only with the accession of Ali Pasha of Tepelini that Ioannina became famous. Born in Tepelini (in Albania), Ali Pasha was forty when he took over his first public office; he then became pasha of Trikkala, and exchanged that position for the pashalik of Ioannina. It then had a population of 25,000, making it the most populous town in Albania and Epirus, and it was a centre of Hellenism and an important commercial centre. Ali continually added to his domain and in 1805, only nominally answerable to the Sublime Porte, Ioannina was in fact the capital of a State encompassing part of present-day Albania and the major part of Greece. Lord Byron stayed there in 1807. But Ali's power worried the Porte and in 1820 he was declared guilty of rebellion. After a siege lasting more than 15 months Ali had lost control of all but the kastro. He agreed to parley with the commander of the besieging army in the monastery of Hagios Panteleimon, on the island, and was conveyed to it along with his wife and 12 of his supporters. But in the afternoon of 22 February 1822 an Ottoman troop arrived at the monastery. A fight began and Ali was shot, beheaded and his head exhibited at Ioannina and then at Constantinople.

◼ After having felt the town's heartbeat in Pirrou or Kentriki Square, at the foot of the clock-tower, wander through the maze of bazaar stalls, dusty but full of character and almost Oriental in atmosphere. Behind the army headquarters go up and look at what remains of the kastro, dismantled by Ali Pasha, where you are rewarded with a very attractive view of the town, the citadel, the lake and its island.

Coming back down towards the gardens which cover the major part of the former kastro, you can visit the new museum (Municipal Park, Averof Street).

Open: in summer, 09.00 (Sun. 10.00)–13.00 and 16.00–18.00; winter, 10.00 (Sun. 10.30)–16.30 (Sun. 14.30); closed Tues.; entrance fee.

As well as a gallery of modern painting and sculpture and a small collection of 18th- and 19th-century Greek jewellery, this museum has an excellent archaeology section: Palaeolithic tools, pottery from the Agrinion area, finds from the necropolises at Vitsa, Nekromanteion and above all Dodona (votive statues, vases and oracular plaques of lead). Note too a sarcophagus decorated with a Dionysiac procession, Ionic capitals from Cassope and some Byzantine sculpture (a fine capital with two eagles confronting one another from the basilica of Glykis in Thesprotia).

⬛⬛ Follow Averof Street northwards until you come to the walls of the citadel, or Frourion, restored by Ali Pasha in 1815 and used by him as his headquarters. There are still several Byzantine buildings within the walls: among them a Turkish library, recently restored. In the NE corner a second wall runs round what was the pashas' residence now partly in ruins and occupied by the army; but the mosque is in a good state of preservation, and in it there is an old-fashioned, picturesque, museum of history and popular art. Just beside it is the tomb of Ali Pasha.

Below the citadel and the kastro there are shady promenades and squares along the banks of the lake, with cafes and restaurants that are very pleasant in fine weather. This is where you can get a motor boat to take you out (a trip worth making) on to the lake of Ioannina and across to the island to visit the island monasteries, founded around the 13th century.

In the church of the monastery of the Prodromos there are 18th-century frescoes retouched in the 19th century. The nearby monastery of Panteleimon was the scene of Ali Pasha's murder. The catholicon (church) dates from the early 16th century. The monastery of Hagios Nikolaos Spanos, built in the 16th century, stands on a hill. In the church there are frescoes dated 1660, and in a corner of the narthex you can see, from l. to r. Plato, Apollonius, Solon, Aristotle, Plutarch, Thucydides and Chiron.

The monastery of Hagios Nikolaos Dilios, the oldest here, was founded in the 11th century. There are frescoes (restored in the 16th century) in the catholicon: Judas handing back the money received for betraying Jesus. In the narthex there are the lives of the Mother of God and St Nicholas (the Last Judgement; 16th century).

In the monastery of Hagios Nikolaos ton Ghioumaton, 18th-century frescoes: the Last Judgement.

VICINITY OF IOANNINA

1 *PERAMA CAVES (3.1mls/5km along Trikkala road). To see chambers full of stalactites and stalagmites formed one and a half million years ago by an underground river involves walking 875yds (800m) from start to finish (open 08.00–19.00; guides available).

2 *MOUZAKAIVI AND VRELLIS MUSEUM (5mls/8km SE of Ioannina along a small direct road which forks off the Arta road). This is a local Madame Tussaud's which brings back to life the history of Epirus in the 17th and 18th centuries by means of a great number of waxwork figures skilfully modelled by the sculptor Pavlos Vrellis; at that period this area was a particularly important centre of Hellenism during Ottoman rule.

3 *DODONA (see under Dodona; 13mls/21km along Arta road, turn r. after 4.4mls/7km).

4 *MONODENDRI AND THE VICOS GORGE (30mls/48km; follow Konitsa road and turn r. after 15.6mls/25km, shortly after Asfaka). See under Monodendri.

■ Ios [Island of]

40.5sq. mls (105km²) – Pop: 1,250.

Boats bound for Santorini usually call in at Ios and for some years past it has experienced a tourist boom. Yet this little island in the Cyclades where legend has it that Homer died is bare, dry and rocky; but perhaps, with the white houses and the windmills of its unassuming capital, its hidden beaches accessible only by sea, and with its fashionable nightclubs and souvenir shops, it is the incarnation of the Cyclades people dream of in this age of mass tourism in Greece.

You land in a well-sheltered bay with the Hagia Irina chapel, lovely in the simplicity of its outlines, acting as its beacon. Unless you stop at Milopita Beach (the one at Yalos is less well known and more attractive), proceed to the main village (approx 40 mins walk), Ios (Chora), above the harbour, which is sparkling white in the midst of arid countryside, with scant cultivation on terraced slopes and a few windmills.

Though there are said to be more than 400 churches or chapels, there is not a lot of variety in the excursions you can make on the island (hire a guide from the village); the convent of Pyrgos and - 3hrs round trip on foot from the village - the ruins of the castle of the Crispo family (15th century) are worth mentioning. Apart from Yalos, there are fine beaches at Koumbaros, Manganari and Psathi.

From Ios you can go by caïque to Sikinos, a small island with few visitors, one of the driest in the Cyclades. You land at Alapronia and from there you climb on foot or by mule to the village of Chorio, overlooked by the ruins of a monastery. An hour's walk away the little chapel of the Panagia stands on the site of a temple of Pythian Apollo dating from the 2nd century BC.

Itea

Route map 4.

Amfissa, 9.4mls (15km) - Delphi, 11.8mls (19km) - Levadia, 44.4mls (71km) - Naupaktos, 56.9mls (91km).

This little port of call lying on the edge of the Sacred Plain below Delphi, which was used as a harbour by the pilgrims to Pythian Apollo, is a perfect place to relax between two visits to the famous sanctuary, with its beach where the water is warmer than anywhere else in Greece, and its little restaurants.

Itea is near the site of the ancient sacred port of the Delphians, Cirrha, which was situated near the hamlet of Magoula, where excavations by the French School of Athens have revealed the existence of a settlement inhabited from the early Helladic period.

Ithaca [Island of] (Ithaki)*

39.8sq. mls (103km^2) - Pop: 5,000.

Ithaca forms part of the Ionian archipelago and is separated from Cephalonia by a channel 1-2.5mls (2-4km) wide. It consists of two mountain ranges encompassing the gulf of Molo, and is, par excellence, the island of legend. For it was over this unyielding land that Odysseus is supposed to have reigned. In spite of such fame, visiting Ithaca is still something of an adventure, away from the beaten tracks of mass tourism; admittedly the island, though it is ideal for diving, has nothing much except its delightful seascapes to offer to visitors, who as often as not go there to pay their respects to Homer. Rather than foreign crowds, the islanders are used to welcoming large numbers of Greeks, coming to attend the several drama and music festivals, while the mayors of most of the villages are endeavouring to preserve traditional local festivals.

AN ISLAND FIT FOR GOATS. Homer tells us that in the archipelago lying at the mouth of the gulf of Corinth there was a very active maritime power with piratical and trading interests, which acted as a staging post between the coasts of Elis and Triphylia (Nestor's kingdom), the coast of Thesprotia (Epirus), the island of Corcyra (home of the Phaeacians), southern Italy and Sicily. Odysseus, as king of Ithaca, is the epic personification of this world of the sea. According to the *Odyssey*, his kingdom consisted of islets and four islands; Ithaca, Dulichium, Same and Zacynthus; Ithaca is low, and farthest towards the Zophos (NW); the others stand apart, towards the dawn and the sun. 'In Ithaca there are no wide tracks and no meadows ... It is a steep island, not suited to horses, yet not too poor despite its small size. It is suitable for goats ...' (*Odyssey*, IV, 605; XIII, 242).

VATHAY (Ithaca), the capital and main port of the island, its white houses built like an amphitheatre at the end of a very deep bay, is the ideal place to start a journey in the footsteps of Odysseus in search of Homeric sites. It has been identified as the ancient port of Phorkys where Odysseus was put ashore by the Phaeacians at the Nymphs' grotto (*Odyssey*, III, 96), now known as Marmarospilia. Odysseus is supposed to have hidden his treasures there on Athena's advice. There you can visit a little museum (if it is open, which is seldom) of antiquities (Mycenaean, proto-Geometric, Geometric and Archaic vases; Hellenistic funerary stelae).

EXCURSIONS ON ITHACA

1 NYMPHS' GROTTO (Marmarospilia; 33mls/53km). Leave Vathy along the Stavros road, then follow a track on the l. after 0.6mls (1km). About 10yds from the end of the track in a rockface is the mouth of the Nymphs' grotto – it corresponds reasonably well to the description in the *Odyssey* (XIII, 105), but is further from the harbour than seems to be indicated by Homer.

2 THE FOUNTAIN OF ARETHUSA, RAVEN'S ROCK AND EUMAEUS' PIGSTIES (2½hrs there and back). Take the road going away from the harbour at the end of the bay. After walking for one hour you come to a plateau, and shortly after that the track turns in a hairpin bend; 110yds (100m) after the bend a path going off on the l. leads in 20 mins to the fountain of Arethusa (now called Perapigadi), overlooked by a rockface 130ft (40m) high which has been identified as Homer's Raven's Rock. The Marathia plateau, which is thought to be the site of Eumaeus' pigsties, (*Odyssey*, XIV, 6 and 533) lies beyond where the path to the fountain forks off, at the most southerly point of the island (*Odyssey*, XXIV,

150), a long way from Odysseus' capital (XVII, 25) about 12.5mls (20km) from Port Polis, so that it would have taken Eumeaus a whole day to go there and back. From the Marathia plateau it takes 40 mins to get to the bay of Port Andreas where Telemachus supposedly landed on his return from Pylos to avoid Penelope's suitors, who were lying in ambush, on the little island of Asteris (*Odyssey*, XV, 36). From there he followed the only path which took him up to Eumaeus' sites.

3 **THE CAPITAL OF ODYSSEUS** (from Vathy to Stavros; 12mls/19km; bus). 3.7mls (6km): You pass below Mt Aetus; on its summit are the ruins of ancient Alalcomenae, wrongly identified by Schliemann as the capital alluded to by Homer. There are remains of a polygonally bonded perimeter wall dating from the 7th century BC and some traces of the lower town.

10mls (16km): Anoghi; church of the Dormition of the Virgin (badly restored 18th-century frescoes).

12mls (19km): Stavros; from there you can go into the surrounding countryside in search of ancient sites or attractive scenery. For example, it takes 20 mins to go down to the bay of Port Polis, the name of which is reminiscent of that of Homer's capital; from there, near the coast of Cephalonia, you can see the little island of Daskalio, thought to be the islet of Asteris where the suitors lay in wait for Telemachus on his return, meaning to murder him (*Odyssey*, VI, 846).

Less than 0.6ml (1km) N of Stavros at the place known as Pelikata the British School uncovered the remains (not easily discernible) of a small town founded c.2200 BC and occupied up until the Mycenaean period. Lying between the bays of Port Polis and Port Phrikes, this would seem to be the most likely candidate for identification as the acropolis of Odysseus. The beaches on the N of the island are the most pleasant: Frikes and Kioni (10mls/16km and 12.5mls/20km from Vathy, beyond Stavros).

■ Kalamata (Kalamai)

Route map 8.

Areopolis, 48.7mls (78km) – Pylos, 32.5mls (52km) – Sparta, 37.5mls (60km) – Tripolis, 58mls (93km) – Pop: 39,462 – district capital of admin. region of Messenia.

Kalamata would like to be both an industrial town and a bathing resort. This confusion of aims does not augur well, but there are a good beach and a few sites of interest in the vicinity, as well as some pleasant specialities in the food line: the local olives, which are much sought after, figs that are exported dried, and bananas.

ONCE HELD BY MENELAUS. It is probable that Kalamata occupies the site of Homer's Pherae, which must have belonged to Menelaus, for it is given as one of the seven towns promised by Agamemnon to Achilles to assuage his anger. Recent excavations at Akovitika, 2.5mls (4km) W of the town, prove that the area where the plain of Messenia opens on to the sea has been inhabited since the early Helladic period (remains of a megaron).

THE STRANGE CONSEQUENCES OF A CRUSADE. In 1206, two years after the capture of Constantinople by the Fourth Crusade, the area was won from the Byzantines by Guillaume de Champlitte, the first prince of the Morea, and his lieutenant, Geoffroy I de Villehardouin whom he appointed Lord of Kalamata in 1208. About 1425 it passed into the hands of the Despot of Mistra. It was subsequently captured by the Turks and remained in their hands until 1685, when it came under Venetian control, falling to the Turks again in 1715; but the town prides itself on having been the first in Greece to rise against them in 1821 in a prelude to the liberation of the country.

In the bazaar, the part of the market near Martiou Square, N of the modern town, visit the Hagii Apostoli church, built in the Italian style (1626) with a 10th-century Byzantine church incorporated as its choir. Nearby the houses of the Benaki and Kyriakou families are used as an archaeological and historical museum (Roman mosaics, icons, mementoes of the War of Independence).

The kastro or castle of the Villehardouins was built in 1208 by the Franks on the site of the acropolis of ancient Pherae where the

Byzantines had built a fortress and a monastery. It consists of a keep, an internal redoubt and an external perimeter wall.

VICINITY

1 KORONI (32.5mls/52km following Pylos road, bear l. at 13mls/21km). This peaceful little port has houses stacked one above the other on a promontory topped by an imposing Venetian and Turkish citadel, well preserved, which bears witness to the rivalries that bedevilled Greece in the Middle Ages and up until the 18th century. As you walk up to the citadel you can see the romantic ruins of several little churches surrounded by lush vegetation.

MUSICAL CHAIRS. Koroni is on the site of ancient Asine. In 1205 it was taken by Guillaume de Champlitte and Geoffroy de Villehardouin, but a year later the Venetians dislodged them. In 1500 the inhabitants rebelled against the Venetians and handed back the port to the Turks. The Genoan Andrea Doria raided it in 1532, but the Turks, regained possession a year later. In 1662 it fell into the hands of the Spanish, then of the Venetians and finally of the Turks who repelled a Russian attack in 1770.

2 FROM KALAMATA TO AREOPOLIS. See Vicinity of Areopolis.

3 FROM KALAMATA TO SPARTA. See Vicinity of Sparta, 7, reversing directions.

■ Kalambaka

Route maps 11 and 12.

Ioannina, 79mls (126km) – Larisa, 57.2mls (82km) – Thessaloniki, 163mls (261km).

This little town which was mentioned by Caesar and Livy under the name of Aeginium is the starting-point for an excursion to the ***Meteora, that extraordinary group of rocks which was the setting for one of the strangest expressions of eastern asceticism.

Visit the Metropolitan church (in the upper part of the town); it was rebuilt in 1309 on the foundations of an earlier church (mosaic floor in the apse). The paintings date from 1573 when the church was partly rebuilt; they are the work of the Cretan monk Neophytos, son of the painter Theophanes Batha. Note the unusual marble ambo, possibly from an earlier building, and some 12th-century frescoes which have been preserved on a wall beside the choir.

■ Kalavryta

Route map 5.

Aegion, 31.2mls (50km) – Corinth, 79mls (126km) – Patras, 51.8mls (83km) – Pop: 2,000.

This town, which lies at an altitude of 2,296ft (700m), would make an excellent overnight stop off the main Athens-Patras axis if you have been feeling the heat during your travels, especially as the road leading to it from the coast, and the narrow-gauge railway, is worth making a detour for because it takes you through such beautiful scenery (see Diakopton).

Kalavryta has been identified with ancient Cynaetha, an Arcadian town two stadia away from the Alyssus spring (said to cure rabies), now known as Kalavrytini. The people of Cynaetha were noted for their wild, independent nature and their godlessness. The town was destroyed by the Aetolians in 220 BC, but regained its prosperity in Hadrian's reign.

In 1209 the fief of Kolovrata (Kalavryta) was granted to Othon de Tournay, and later (1301) passed into the possession of the barons of Chalandritsa, the de la Trémoille family. The town suffered greatly during the Resistance in 1943.

VICINITY

1 MONASTERY OF HAGIA LAVRA (4.4mls/7km; follow Tripolis road). The monastery was founded in 961 and burnt down in 1943 by the Germans because of its role in the Resistance. It has been rebuilt, but has lost almost all its interesting features, though students can visit a small historical museum with 11th- and 12th-century manuscripts.

2 MONASTERY OF MEGASPILAION (see under Megaspilaion; 6.8mls/11km along Athens road). Carry on until you reach (22.5mls/36km) Diakopton; the beautiful **panorama over the gulf of Corinth as the road drops back down cannot fail to delight you.

3 LEONTION (23mls/37km along Patras road). This site, to which only those with a recognized interest in archaeology are admitted, comprises a poorly preserved 4th-century theatre.

■ Kalymnos [Island of]*

42sq. mls (109km²) – Pop: 12,000 approx.

The fame of this island of the Dodecanese which is off the main tourist circuits is due to sponge diving; the divers set out as they have for centuries between Easter and the beginning of May and keep working until autumn.

Though the island is mountainous and stony, it does have a small plain which is covered with gardens and orchards or olive groves; it is noted for its honey and its mandarins. There are many little sanctuaries, monasteries or chapels scattered around the island.

The port of Kalymnos with its lively narrow streets and its colourful market is the unpretentious and attractive capital of the island. Its houses are decorated with blue and white paint – Greece's national colours – supposedly as a means of flouting the Italian occupying authorities during World War II. The church of the Saviour is worth a visit, as is a little museum with a collection of the finds made in caves (Neolithic objects) or on the site of a sanctuary of the Delian Apollo.

Near Pothia to the N of the capital is the cave of the Seven Virgins (Hepta Partheni) where niches for offerings and various inscriptions can be seen. There is a road from Kalymnos to the port of Vathy (3.7mls/6km), with a superb beach, on the E coast, and from there you can go on to the village of Damos (5.6mls/9km), where a Mycenaean necropolis has been discovered. Leaving Kalymnos by a different road (8mls/13km) you can go to Linaria (Myrtes) on the W coast and on to Emporio on the N tip of the island where a Mycenaean tholos (beehive) tomb has been uncovered. From Linaria you can get a boat to the island of Telendos (nude sun-bathing permitted) with the ruins of the monastery of Hagios Vasileios, a medieval fortress and Hellenic and Roman buildings, or to the tiny island of Pserimos.

■ Kamena Vourla

Route map 3.

Athens, 114mls (182km) – Chalcis, 83mls (133km) – Lamia, 25mls (40km) – Thebes, 54.4mls (87km) – Pop: 2,130.

Greeks come to this spa town to take the waters, but the beach is also very pleasant.

VICINITY

MENDENITSA (14.4mls/23km along Lamia road, turn l. after 6.2mls/ 10km). Near this village, in ancient times known as Pharigai, you can visit the castle of Bodonitsa which was the seat of a marquis during the Frankish period, for more than two centuries from 1205 to 1410. The fortress was enclosed by two perimeter walls, the first of which was built on ancient ramparts.

■ Karditsa

Route map 1.

Lamia, 54.4mls (87km) – Larisa, 60mls (96km) – Trikkala, 16.2mls (26km) – Pop: 23,708.

Karditsa is a small market town in Thessaly with nothing to make you stop unless you find it is a convenient place to break a journey into the heart of central Greece.

VICINITY

MITROPOLIS 6.8mls (11km) to the W, was occupied by Caesar before the Battle of Pharsalus, and there are a few remains of the acropolis; nearby are the remains of two small fortresses at Vounesi and Portitsa. The sizeable reservoir of Megdova (Tavropos) lies 12.5mls (20km) to the W, with a road enabling you to drive right round it (25mls/40km). Loutra Smokoyon, 23.7mls (38km) to the S near a hill with the remains of an ancient fortress on top of it, is a spa where rheumatic and respiratory complaints are treated.

■ Karpathos [Island of]

108sq. mls (280km²) – Pop: 3,000 approx.

This long, narrow island, 280 nautical miles from Piraeus between Crete and Rhodes, one of the largest in the Dodecanese, is wild, mountainous and one of the most remote islands in the group. It is probably because of this that traditions have been kept alive (the women still sometimes wear traditional dress), and a dialect which is close to Doric can still sometimes be heard. Those seeking quiet and who like walking will be delighted with it as there are almost no roads.

The boat from Piraeus calls in at Pigadia on the E coast, near the ancient capital of the island, a few traces of which can still be seen.

About 6mls (10km) from Pigadia on the W coast at Arkassa (a pretty beach) you can see the remains of a Byzantine church which was decorated with mosaics. Walking in the interior of the island you can visit delightful villages, where the men are often absent looking for work on mainland Greece or in the States; they return for the holidays and sometimes build rather undistinguished houses for themselves. Messochori, Olympus and Kilion Aperi are among the most attractive villages. At the N tip of Karpathos the island of Saria is nicknamed Goat Island as wild goats live there.

Karytaina

■ *Route map 7.*

Andritsena, 17.5mls (28km) – Olympia, 67mls (107km) – Pyrgos, 58mls (93km) – Tripolis, 32.5mls (52km).

This must be one of the most picturesque villages in Arcadia with its cascade of houses tumbling down the hillside from a Frankish castle above. Karytaina is built on the edge of a gap with the river Alpheus running along its bed, and is certainly worth a short stop during which you can visit the church of the Panagia, explore the narrow streets so evocative of its medieval past, and go up to the castle.

A FRANKISH BARONY. Karytaina stands on the site of ancient Brenthe. In 1209 the Franks made it the capital of a large barony granted to Hugues de Bruyères who was responsible for building the castle. In 1320 Karytaina was bought back by the Emperor Andronicus II Paleologus.

✝ The 11th-century church of the Panagia is in the lower part of the village (a Frankish bell-tower, early paintings, and the coat of arms of the Albamonte family).

▆▆ It takes about 10 mins following a path from the village to reach the only entrance to the castle, an imposing example of medieval fortification built in 1254 within a triangular perimeter wall. *Fine view.

VICINITY

1 DIMITSANA (16.8mls/27km). Leaving the Tripolis-Andritsena road, take the paved road that forks off near the Karytaina railway crossing. As you go along you will see some of the most beautiful **scenery in the Peloponnese. Dimitsana, in ancient times Teuthis, is a mountain village overhanging the ravine formed by the Lusius (medieval remains).

2 GORTYS IN ARCADIA (can be reached from Karytaina following the Dimitsana road). After following the paved road for 4.6mls (7km) turn l. in the hamlet of Helleniko on to a track which can be negotiated by car; after 3.7mls (5km) go l. again (the r.-hand track would take you after 1.9mls/3km to a little chapel perched dizzily on a projecting rock from which you can walk down to the monastery of St John the Baptist, see below; from the chapel you can then carry on along the track by which you came and after 5 very winding miles (8km) uphill you rejoin the paved Karytaina-Dimitsana road; superb view of the Lusius gorge). This trip is of particular interest to archaeologists as it affords a view of the ruins of two sanctuaries of Asclepius which have been excavated by the French School of Athens.

The Asclepiaeum on the banks of the river Gortynios was begun around the middle of the 4th century BC but never completed. The baths were built near the end of the 4th century, then altered in the middle of the 3rd century BC. There were some Hellenistic and Roman houses nearby (to the SE). The Asclepieion lying SW of the acropolis is very dilapidated. It was built towards the end of the 5th or beginning of the 4th century BC. The building known as the Baths of Asclepius stood close by, built towards the end of the 3rd century BC; it backed on to a portico which is considered to have been the abaton. The wall round the acropolis, interrupted by three gates, is the best preserved of the buildings here. The S fortress beside it was much smaller in perimeter. The remains of the ramparts are still visible.

If you go back up the Gortynios gorge on foot you come in about ½hr along a sometimes rather steep path to a picturesque monastery perched on the side of the gorge amidst wild, but beautiful scenery. It is also possible to reach this monastery (Hagios Ioannis Prodromos, or St John the Baptist) by a steep winding track from the road that goes from Karytaina to Dimitsana (see above).

■ Kasos [Island of]

24sq. mls (62km²) – Pop: 1,000 approx.

Kasos is one of the hardest islands in the Dodecanese to get to, and the simple life you will lead here (staying with the islanders) will not be without charm if you can make do with minimal comfort.

You land at Emborio and then proceed to Fry, the main town of the island. There you can visit the monastery of Hagios Mamas and a small museum of popular art as well as the cave of Sellai with its stalactites and the cave of Hellenikomara which has around it walls built with Pelasgic bonding. There is a fine beach on the islet of Armathia which can be reached by caïque as can many other equally isolated tiny islands.

■ Kastania

Route map 5.

Corinth, 40mls (64km) – Patras, 94.4mls (151km) – Xylokastron, 31.2mls (50km).

A peaceful holiday centre in the mountains overlooking the gulf of Corinth.

VICINITY

FENEOS (16.8mls/27km). At the place known as Pyrgos are the ruins of ancient Pheneos or Phenea; part of the perimeter wall, constructed in polygonal masonry, has been excavated, as have the ruins of an Asclepieion.

■ Kastoria*

Route maps 13 and 15.

Florina (via Aetos), 66.2mls (106km) – Kalambaka, 93.7mls (150km) – Thessaloniki, 133.7mls (214km) –Pop: 15,407 – archbishopric – district capital of admin. region of Kastoria.

Kastoria was without question the most beautiful little town in the Balkans with its old wooden houses and its churches and chapels with their frescoes – until around 1970, when the charm of this typically Balkan town was destroyed, victim to a measure of prosperity brought about by the fur trade; this led to many of the distinguished old houses being demolished to make way for ugly concrete buildings. Kastoria still has its churches, mostly in the form of basilicas, and its outstanding setting, but a definite shadow has been cast over its future as a tourist centre.

Kastoria has been identified as ancient Celethron, mentioned by Livy. According to Procopius (*De aedificiis*, IV, 3) the town was at one time known by the name Diocletianopolis. Since around the early 19th century Kastoria has been an important centre for the fur trade and has links with the main markets in Europe and the United States.

There are no fewer than 72 churches or chapels in Kastoria; of these you should visit the chapel of the Taxiarkhis, built between the 11th and 13th centuries, and the delightful church of the Panagia Koubelidiki, late 11th century (13th- and 16th-century frescoes on the facade and inside the building) which can be reached along Mitropoleos Road. Further on to the S, on Omonia Square, Hagios Nikolaos tou Kasnitzi still has its 11th-century frescoes.

Still further on, near the (modern) cathedral, on Pavlou Mela Square visit the church of Hagios Athanasios, 1384–85, with its 14th-century frescoes, and the church of the Taxiarkhis, late 11th century, with frescoes both outside (15th century) and inside (14th century).

Go back to the church of Hagios Nikolaos and turn r. along the Valala road where you can see the chapel of St Peter and St Paul (remains of paintings on the façade and inside the building). The Hagiou Mina road on the r. leads to the chapel of Hagiou Mina; just before that the Vitsiou road on the l. takes you to the church of Hagios Stephanos, an 11th – century building decorated with frescoes (Archaic-style Crucifixion; 13th–14th century carved wood iconostasis).

The Vitsiou road leads straight to the church of Hagii Anargyri, built in the 10th century and restored in the 11th, with wall paintings depicting on the l., the Deisis and on the r., the Virgin praying between two angels. Return to the town centre along the Hagion Anargyron road, then the Athanasiou road.

Go for a stroll by the *lakeside – Kastoria still has two magnificent frontages; and from one bank or the other you are still able to see a few old wooden houses which have been spared by the mania for modernism.

Excavations carried out on the S shore of the lake have uncovered a few remains from a prehistoric village built on piles dating from c.2000 BC.

7.5mls (12km) from Kastoria on the direct road to Florina there is a superb *panoramic view over the lake. You could always go back to Florina along an unpaved road which takes you through marvellous scenery. You would simply have to pass through a military police checkpoint (this should be a mere formality) as the road, which runs near the border with Albania, is under police supervision.

■ Katerini

Route map 2.

Larisa, 52.5mls (84km) – Thessaloniki, 55mls (88km) – district capital of admin. district.

From this town with its big agricultural market a road (towards Elasson) will take you across the Olympus range.

Not far from Katerini at Kitros (see route map 2) there is the site of ancient Pydna where Aemilius Paullus beat Perseus in 168 BC, and by annexing Macedon opened up Greece to Romanization.

VICINITY

DION (8mls/13km), following a paved road from the town centre going directly to (3.7mls/6km) Nea Ephesos and then (7.5mls/12km) Karitsa.

Excavations undertaken since 1973 by the University of Thessaloniki under the direction of Professor D. Pandermalis are revealing the ruins of the ancient Macedonian city of Dion where Alexander the

Great came to offer a sacrifice before setting out (334 BC) on his great campaign against the Persians which was to take him to the heart of Asia.

About 880yds (800m) after leaving Karitsa on the l. of the road near a modern bridge you can see a small section of the town ramparts with a tower. The city of Dion was in fact surrounded by ramparts which were very regular in shape, forming a rectangle, with a perimeter measurement of approx. 2.5mls (4km). Note the masonry of the lower part of the wall which shows the original blocks of whitish limestone laid in isodomic fashion (in staggered courses), dating back to the Classical period, and the later alterations (for example a stele has been reused in the tower).

About 220yds (200m) further on, and some 55yds (50m) from the road, you can see a late 4th- or early 3rd-century BC vaulted Macedonian tomb with a dromos as an entrance and a façade with a Doric entablature (at present the inside of the tomb is not open to visitors; it consists of an ante-chamber and a chamber; the door linking the two rooms is set between two engaged Ionic half-columns in the chamber a marble bed was found and there were two painted friezes depicting lions).

The Dion necropolis has so far produced three other smaller Macedonian tombs, each with just one chamber.

If you carry on towards the centre of the village, you come to a crossroads; go l. on to a track which cars can go along, which soon skirts the city ramparts on your l., for a stretch of approx. 330yds (300m). 550yds (500m) from the crossroads you come to the entrance into the archaeological site.

Open: 08.30–13.00 and 16.00–18.00; Sun. 10.00–16.00.

The area which can be visited corresponds to the town within the walls, laid out essentially as it was in the Imperial Roman period. You can see several paved streets with drainage gutters, inter-secting one another at right-angles, following lines which were already those of the Hellenistic town and marking the limits of the blocks (insulae) of buildings. The wide N–S road which you first go along on the same axis as the entrance has on its l.-hand side about 110yds (100m) from the entrance the ruins of a large building dating from the middle of the Hellenistic period (late 3rd, early 2nd century BC), the facade of which is decorated with limestone plaques which were once stuccoed and decorated alternately with breast-plates and shields.

Along the street near this building there are shops, workshops and latrines. Behind them there is a group of very large public buildings: baths from the Imperial Roman period (2nd century AD) with mosaic floors, rooms for warm baths (which can be recognized by their hypocausts – the little stacks of bricks from them are still partly in position) and latrines; an open paved area which must have been the forum; an odeon which may also have been used for political meetings. You can go right round these buildings by taking a road on the l. at right-angles to the main street and turning again at right-angles to the l. into another street.

In other *insulae*, houses have been uncovered, sometimes with the remains of a polychrome wall coating. It has been established that the early Christian basilica went through two superimposed forms, one 4th-century, the other 5th-century AD.

One remarkable peculiarity of the city of Dion is that some important buildings were erected outside the walls. Among these were several sanctuaries and the town's two theatres.

If you go back out of the supervised archaeological area, in the middle of the fields on the other side of the track you can see the ruins – reduced to mere foundations – of the sanctuaries of Demeter, Asclepius and Dionysus. The first of these is especially interesting as votive offerings (including terracotta objects) going back to the early 5th century BC were found there; the megaron built on to the temple is the earliest building of this kind that has been found in Macedon to date. Further S among some trees there are the ruins of a Roman theatre.

If you carry on another 275yds (250m) along the track leading to the entrance of the supervised site, on the r. just after a bridge beside a small river, you can see the remains of a composite sanctuary (being restored) surrounded by a peribolus wall; a long central corridor led to an altar and to a flight of seven steps in the centre of a space in which three naiskoi have been identified, corresponding with the temples of Artemis (4th century BC), Isis Lochia (Imperial Roman period) and, just to the S, Isis Tyche (Hellenistic period). The last of these three, a triple conch in plan, still had its cult statue, found still standing on its base inside the monument; an altar stood in front of the entrance with the name of the goddess inscribed on it. The identification of Isis Lochia is confirmed by inscriptions engraved on the steps of the monumental staircase that led to the temple.

Below the modern bridge the river covers over and crosses a stretch of the ramparts that have been excavated recently; here it is easy to distinguish between the building of the lower part dating from the Hellenic period, in big, well-laid blocks, and the upper part dating from the Roman period, made of stone and brick rubble; a little statue and a marble head are embedded in the masonry. Turning your back to the sanctuary of Isis and Artemis, you can follow the outline of the ancient ramparts N of the modern track through fields for 30 or 40 yds. They have been excavated to reveal their total thickness (3–5ft/1–1.5m) and part of their height; at this point the outline is quite complicated, with towers, a doorway and recess, and the method of construction shows a mixture of techniques.

Returning to the front of the entrance into the supervised area, you can take a path that goes off at on oblique angle to the l., in a SW direction. After about 275yds (250m) you will see on the l. the site of a theatre from the Hellenistic period the special feature of which is the tiered seating, constructed of bricks and not in stone (unfortunately it is in a rather poor state of preservation).

Continue along the same track and you will soon come to the paved road that goes through the village; cross it and carry on until you reach the museum about 110yds (100m) further on. to the l. The main exhibits are marble sculpture from the Hellenistic and Roman periods, in particular about 15 statues from the sanctuary of Artemis and Isis and a group formed in the baths, with Asclepius, the god of healing, with his family (including his daughter Hygieia, goddess of health; late 2nd-century AD).

After visiting Dion you can rejoin the main Thessaloniki-Larissa road (4.3mls; 7km). When you leave Dion, take the asphalt road to the right all the way to Karitsa. In about 0.62 mls (1km) you will reach the village of Platanakia; take the asphalt road to the left to reach the highway, about 0.62mls (1km) to the N. of the intersection of the roads from Olympia and Litochoron.

If you are approaching from Larisa and want to continue travelling in a northerly direction, it would obviously be better to make the whole visit in the opposite direction.

■ Kavalla

Route map 14

Alexandroupolis 108.7mls (174km) – Thessaloniki, 102.5mls (164km) – Pop: 46,834 – district capital of admin. region.

Of all Greek towns Kavalla is the one that best evokes the Orient, especially in its old Muslim quarter with the 'Imaret', the convent built by Mehmet Ali, pasha of Egypt, who was born here. The town is built in an amphitheatre of hills with the harbour forming the 'stage' (the tobacco produced in great abundance in the area is exported through Kavalla) which provides a rich variety of picturesque scenes, and a superb Roman aqueduct acting as the 'balcony'; the whole is dominated by a Byzantine fortress.

AT ONE TIME A STAGE FOR POST HORSES. Kavalla stands on the site of ancient Neapolis. It is thought to have been a colony of Thasos, Athens or Eretria. Later on the town was called Christopolis (the Franks' version was Christople). Its present name, according to Heuzey, may be a reminder of the important stage for post horses that was once established in the town. The town remained under Turkish control until 1912. It became Greek again on 9 June 1913, during the second Balkan War.

■ At the western end of the harbour on the seafront between the new Olympic swimming pool and the Thessaloniki road there is an archaeological museum with a good selection of antiquities found in Kavalla itself and the surrounding area.

Open: summer 09.00–13.00 and 16.00–18.00; winter, 10.00–16.30; Sun. 10.30–14.30; closed Tues.; entrance fee.

Go through the entrance hall into a corridor where, after an archaeological wall map of the area, there are stone and terracotta objects (figurines, vases and shards) from the Neolithic period and the Bronze Age found in eastern Macedon and in Thrace (particularly at Dikili Tach and Sitargi).

On the l. there is a first courtyard with a collection of parts of sculptures and inscriptions. Beyond that there is the Neapolis room (the ancient name for Kavalla). At the back you can see architectural fragments from the temple of Athena Parthenos (which was built on top of the hill where the Byzantine fortress now stands), in particular two superb early 5th-century BC Ionic capitals. There are also two showcases with terracotta figurines (Archaic and Classical), one showcase with coins and several showcases of black-figure Archaic vases (of Attic, Corinthian, Ionian or Thasian manufacture, as Neapolis was founded by Thasos; among the Thasian vases, note a fragmentary dish in from the late 7th century BC depicting Apollo and Artemis drawing their bows against a giant). Four large vases, broken but nonetheless very interesting, are exhibited outside showcases: a 'Melian' (i.e. Parian, no doubt) amphora from the 2nd half of the 7th century BC, with a picture of the abduction of Thetis by Peleus on its neck; an early 6th-century BC krater depicting the famous hunt of the Calydonian boar and bearing an inscribed dedication; the upper part of an Attic black-figure krater (c.530–520) with a battle scene and decorations on the rim and flat parts of the handles (Heracles and the lion); the mouth of an Attic red-figure krater (late 5th century BC) with a Dionysiac assembly.

A second courtyard has a few pieces of sculpture, reliefs, some with inscriptions, and architectural remains. At the end of the corridor a (damaged) metope from the late 5th century BC shows two hoplites fighting, the statue of a woman (headless) from the 1st century BC, and a Roman mosaic depicting the abduction of Europa (2nd century AD) are exhibited. The Amphipolis room is on the l. with the main finds from the Amphipolis site: funerary stelae (including one from the 2nd half of the 3rd century BC which still has its three painted figures), reliefs, terracotta figurines (some very fine 4th-century BC protomes), vases, jewellery, items of personal adornment (including gold crowns and diadems), and glass objects from the Classical and Hellenistic periods. At the back of the room on the r. the funeral chamber of a Macedonian tomb, with paintings, from around 250 BC has been partly reconstructed.

Upstairs a large number of showcases provide an overall view of the finds made on the various sites in Thrace, especially in the necropolises of Galepsos, Oisyme and Abdera; the exhibits are mainly vases, terracotta figurines and jewels from the Archaic, Classical and Hellenistic periods.

If you take the Alexandroupolis road beyond the central square (Eleftherias Square, at the heart of the modern town), you come to the *Roman aqueduct (Nikotsara Square). Go r. and you come to the old Muslim quarter. Right on the southernmost point of the promontory, well beyond the Byzantine citadel and not far from a belvedere on its E shore, is the house where Mehmet Ali was born (*open 08.00–20.00*), built in 1720. In this part of the town you can see remains of ramparts from the Byzantine period, altered in the 14th century. On the other side of the promontory coming back towards the modern town you can see a curious maret, a kind of hospice with several domes, which was capable of accommodating 300 guests or students.

VICINITY

1 DIKILI TACH (9.4mls/15km via the Philippi road, turn r. after 8.2mls 13km) is a very important prehistoric site excavated jointly by the Greek Archaeological Service and the French School in Athens; it has yielded a large quantity of material (pottery, statuettes) from the Neolithic period. Across from it is a Roman monument erected by the officer C. Vibius.

2 LOUTRA ELEFTHERON (25mls/40km). What makes this excursion noteworthy is the fine new coast road which goes W from Kavalla to Amphipolis offering some beautiful views of the sea. Loutra Eleftheron is a small spa town (for rheumatic complaints) which in view of its location should have a promising future.

■ Kea [Island of] (Tzia)

39.7sq. mls (103km²) – Pop: 1,650.

This island in the Cyclades, which is still sometimes referred to as Keos, lies at the far end of Attica and will be prized by those who would like to leave the beaten track, through tourism is gradually gaining ground there. However, you will still find the local colour of the town of Kea appealing; the island is intersected by two valleys covered with vineyards and orchards.

There are some nice beaches on the island, at Koundourou, Pisses (to the SW) and best of all at Vourkari and Livadi; Livadi (Korissia) is the main port on the NW coast, the ancient town of Koressia. From either of these two places you can get up to the town of Kea (1½hrs approx. from Livadi), which is built on the site of ancient Ioulis, a few remains of which have survived in the kastro. A recently opened archaeological museum exhibits finds from Hagia Irini (see below). 0.6ml (1km) to the NE on the r. after the cemetery you can see a big lion, 10ft (3m) high, carved in the rock in the Archaic period. According to legend, it is there on Zeus' orders to protect the islanders from the Nereids.

NW of Livadi on the peninsula of Hagia Irini, across from the village of Vourkari, you can visit the ruins of a sizeable fortified town inhabited from the early Bronze Age (3rd millennium BC), but particularly flourishing in the Minoan period. Later on during the late Bronze Age there was closer contact with the mainland, that is, with the Mycenaean world.

You can explore the SE part of the island from the main town in approx. 6–8 hrs. going through (1hr 20mins) Astra, a hamlet overlooked by an old church with frescoes then (2hrs) Hellenika (a little church decorated with paintings) and (approx. 3hrs) the site of ancient Carthaea, which is on a dry stony plateau. There were three white marble Doric temples on the acropolis, dating from the first half of the 5th century BC. Lastly look at the ruins of the monastery of Hagia Marina standing isolated in the middle of the island, which enclose one of the finest Hellenic towers in Greece with outstanding coursework (hire a guide from Kea).

Kineta Beach

Route map 5.

Athens, 36.2mls (58km) – Corinth, 18mls (29km).

A bathing resort between Athens and Corinth, lying at the foot of the Scironian Rocks from which the bandit Sciron cast travellers into the sea.

Komotini

Route map 14.

Alexandroupolis, 40mls (64km) – Kavalla, 68.7mls (110km) – Pop: 28,000 – district capital of admin. region of Rhodope.

This is a little town with a pronounced oriental atmosphere, set amidst luxuriant vegetation about 12.5mls (20km) from Bulgaria. (Note that you cannot cross the border here.)

Present-day Komotini is based on an early Christian settlement on the Via Egnatia; part of the defensive perimeter wall with round and square towers has been located in the centre of the modern town. A small colony known as Koumoutsena was founded in and around this settlement in the early Christian and Byzantine periods.

You can enjoy sauntering through the old town where there are still several mosques and many shops with a look of the East; Komotini can also offer the archaeological enthusiast a fascinating museum, exceptionally well presented in a new building beside the Alexandroupolis road (A. Simeonidi Boulevard) opposite a well-shaded park.

Open: summer, 09.00–17.00; winter, 10.00–16.30; Sun. 10.30–14.30; closed Tues.; entrance fee.

In its three rooms the museum has a remarkable selection of objects found on sites in the region (you can locate these by glancing at a large wall map near the entrance) dating from prehistoric times (vases, fragments of vases, stone and bone tools) up until the Roman period. Finds from the Greek and Roman periods come mainly from Abdera, Maronea and Mesembria.

On display there are pottery (vases and figurines, including a very graceful group of seven dancers), coins, jewellery, various bronze objects (among them a greave, a helmet and, of special note, about twenty fibulae from the Archaic period), inscribed stelae (with a very interesting hymn in praise of Isis from the Hellenistic period), and several fine pieces of marble or limestone sculpture. the torso of a kouros and a little Archaic-period lion from Mesembria; the upper part of a funerary stele with the head of a girl (final quarter of 6th century BC); the funerary stele of a young man carved on both faces, late 6th century (the original of the upper part is in Athens' National Museum); a headless statue of a young girl wearing a peplos (2nd quarter of 5th century BC); a broken funerary stele with a young man playing a lyre (mid-5th century BC); and an amusing altar in the form of a large phallus with the inscription 'altar of all gods'. There is also a 'Clazomenaean' painted sarcophagus from Abdera (late 6th–early 5th century BC). The most unusual collection of items in the museum is a group of about 50 little gold and silver votive plaques which were found in the sanctuary of Demeter at Mesembria in 1973; some of them have reliefs which seem to be connected with worship practised on the neighbouring island of Samothrace. But for many visitors the main treasure of the museum will be the very well-preserved, pure gold bust of the philosopher–Emperor, Marcus Aurelius (161–180 AD).

VICINITY

1 **MAXIMIANOUPOLIS-MOSSYNOPOLIS** (3.7mls/5km W along the old Xanthi road, near the village of Mischos, below Mt Papikion) was a Roman and early Christian town under the first name, then from the 9th–10th century a Byzantine town known by the second name; it was prosperous and visited by the Emperors until its downfall in the 13th century. You can see the remains of part of the perimeter wall with round and square towers.

2 **MARONEA** (18.7mls/30km via a good direct road which first travels across the plain, then over hillier ground which affords fine views of Mt Ismaros) is interesting in three different ways: there is an old village (Maronia) with fine old houses and a Balkan-style church; an extensive archaeological site (between the village and the sea, for about 1.2mls/2km: remains of ramparts, of houses with mosaics, a monumental gate, a theatre or odeon, etc.); and a beach with fine sand at the bottom of picturesque red ochre cliffs.

Maronea was founded in the 7th century BC on the SW slopes of Mt Ismaros by settlers from the island of Chios, and because of its climate and geographical location it quickly became a centre for agriculture and animal husbandry and a very active commercial port.

In the 5th century BC Maronea, Abdera and Aenas were among the richest cities in Thrace; Maronea was a member of the first Athenian Confederacy. In the 4th century BC fortified walls with towers were built round the city, with a total perimeter measurement of more than 6.2mls (10km), and an artificial harbour was made to protect warships and merchant ships. In 350 BC the town was occupied by Philip II of Macedon. During the Hellenistic period it often changed masters and went into relative decline, but in the Roman period it was it was again important as a trading and economic centre. In the early Christian and Byzantine periods too it was an important centre and a bishopric.

Konitsa

Route maps 11 and 15.

Igoumenitsa, 96.2mls (154km) – Ioannina, 40mls (64km).

This Balkan market town lies in the heart of an area full of decorated churches, but because the Greek-Albanian frontier is so near it is not possible to explore it fully.

Near Konitsa (along the Ioannina road) the church of the Kokkini Panagia (Moni Vellas) is decorated with frescoes from the time of the Paleologus dynasty.

Kozani

Route maps 1 and 12.

Florina, 51.2mls (82km) – Larisa, 88.7mls (142km) – Thessaloniki, 86.8mls (139km) – Pop: 23,240 – district capital of admin. region of Kozani.

Kozani is a convenient stopping-place on the Haliacmon plain, and a hunting centre in season, but is not likely to arrest the attention of those passing through; yet it has several old houses and its two museums, both in the town centre in Ionos Dragoumi Street, are worth visiting. The little archaeological museum, on the ground floor of a block of flats, has several bronze and pottery vases and marble reliefs. The regional ethnographical museum in a large building nearby is on a grander scale. The church of Hagios Nikolaos is decorated with frescoes and in it there is a fine iconostasis made of carved wood. The town library, with more than 50,000 rare manuscripts, is second only to the Athens library in the whole of Greece.

VICINITY

1 AIANI (12.5mls/20km). Here you should visit the church of the Taxiarkhis and the church of the Panagia, both decorated with 16th-century paintings. In Aiani the Hagios Dimitrios basilica, which has three naves, is decorated with 15th-century frescoes painted over 11th-century paintings which show through in places. Near Aiani on a mountain overlooking the l. bank of the river Haliacmon stands the monastery of Zavorda, founded in the 16th-century.

The paved road takes you across the Haliacmon dam towards

(17.5mls/28km) Rimnio and alongside the dam in a NE direction to Aules, then (27.5mls/44km) to Servia, a name indicating the town's Serbian origin, where a 13th-century Byzantine fortress guards a pass. If you travel back to Kozani via Vathilacos you go back across the Haliacmon dam over the longest road bridge in Greece.

2 SIATISTA (14.4mls/23km to the W). This was once an important centre for trade, with grand houses which are gradually disappearing. There is a small collection of objects found at local digs at the municipal library.

■ Kyllini

Route map 9.

Loutra Kyllini, 9.4mls (15km) – Patras, 42.3mls (68km) – Pyrgos, 65.6mls (105km).

While you are waiting for the ferry-boat to Zante (thrice-daily service), you will find little to distract you in this peaceful little port other than a mediocre beach and the odd reminder of its past.

THE CAPITAL OF A FRANKISH PRINCE. Kyllini is the same place as ancient Cyllene, the naval base for Elis. During the Peloponnesian war the port was used by Spartan ships. In the Middle Ages the fortified town of Clarentza (called Clair-Mont by the Franks) was situated on what is taken to be the site of the ancient town and it was the usual residence of the Villehardouins, Princes of Achaea, then of the Angevins. It was captured in 1430 by the despot Constantine Dragatzes.

Not much remains of the medieval city which spread over the plateau near the harbour. You can see bits of the perimeter wall, the gates and the towers.

The most remarkable ruins are those of a big church built to the same plan and dimensions as St Sophia in Andravida.

■ Kyparissia

Route map 9.

Pylos (Navarino), 38.7mls (62km) – Pyrgos, 35.6mls (57km) – Tripolis, 62.5mls (100km) – Pop: 4,506.

Kyparissia on the W coast of the Peloponnese was Arkadia in the Middle Ages, and is now an unassuming little town below a Frankish castle in an area where sites from the Mycenaean period abound.

A FRANKISH BARONY. Ancient Cyparissia was brought to prominence by Epaminondas who turned it into the port for Messene. In the Middle Ages it took the name of Arkadia. It was captured in 1205 by Guilaume de Champlitte who granted it to Geoffroy de Villehardouin in fief. In 1391 it became the property of the Genoan family, the Zaccarias, then in 1460 it passed into Turkish hands.

Near a tower where you can see ancient blocks of masonry reused, you can visit the castle built by the Franks, with two perimeter walls, and a tower from the Byzantine period, on top of the hill.

Between the town and the sea, in the place known as Kalamia, there are traces of a temple of Apollo, and a few remains of the city walls and of Roman houses.

SW of the harbour there is the Hagia Lougoudis spring, encircled by ancient stones, which corresponds to the ancient Dionysias which Dionysus supposedly caused to gush forth.

VICINITY

1 AMPHIGENEIA (5.6mls/9km to the E). Near the village of Mouriatada, which is thought to be on the site of Nestor's ancient town of Amphigeneia, cyclopean buildings have been uncovered, and on the top of the hill a small palace with a megaron. 220yds (200m) N there is a tholos (beehive) tomb.

2 PERISTERIA (6.2mls/10km; follow the Pyrgos road, turn r. after 2.5mls/4km). The Peristeria site was one of the main centres of Mycenaean civilization in this part of the Peloponnese.

Three tholos tombs were discovered here, one well preserved. On the l. of the door two signs of Minoan origin depict a double axe and a palm. This 16th-century BC Mycenaean tomb was in use until the Hellenistic period.

3 CHRISTIANOU (15.6mls/25km via Filiatra and a road on the l. as you leave the village). Here you can visit the Metropolitan church of ancient Christianoupolis, built in the 11th century (finely sculptured fragments from the iconostasis).

Kythnos [Island of]

33.2sq. mls (86km²) – Pop: 1,500.

Kythnos is sometimes also called Thermia because of the springs at Loutra; it lies on the sea route from Piraeus to Melas and is one of the Cyclades that is becoming ever more popular with tourists. You will still get a warm welcome and simple accommodation, but the beaches will be increasingly crowded.

The boat calls in at the bay of Hagia Irini near the small spa of Loutra (radioactive waters); it takes 2hrs approx. to get from there to the castle of Orias, once a pirates' hide-out, standing on a cliff overlooking the N coast of the island (ruins of several chapels, houses and cisterns). From Hagia Irini a road leads to the main town of the island (3.7mls/5km), Kythnos or Chora; with its white and blue houses lying beneath windmills, it is very typical of the Cyclades. In the town you can visit St Saba's church, built in 1613. There are two other religious buildings on the island for you to see – the monasteries of the Panagia tou Nikous and the Panagia tis Kanalos (hire a guide).

Lamia

Route maps 1, 2 and 3.

Athens, 141mls (226km) – Delphi, 55.6mls (89km) – Larisa (via Farsala), 69.4mls (111km) – Larisa (by motorway), 88.7mls (142km) – Volo, 69.4mls (111km) – Pop: 27,800 approx. – district capital of admin. region of Phthiotis.

Lamia lies at an important road intersection, overlooked by a hill with the ruins of a Frankish and Catalan fortress at its summit, built on the site of the ancient acropolis.

THE WAR THAT FAILED TO FREE ATHENS OF THE MACEDONIAN YOKE. This former capital of Malis is known historically mainly through episodes in the Lamian war (323–322 BC). On the death of Alexander the Great the Athenians and Aetolians wanted to free themselves of the Macedonian yoke and get rid of the viceroy, Antipater. The Athenian general Leosthenes gained control of Thermopylae, then shut Antipater up inside Lamia, but he was killed on a raid (323 BC); the Greek army was then crushed (332 BC) at Cranon (in Thessaly). During the Frankish period Lamia belonged to the Dukes of Athens who called it Gipton, then to the Catalans whose name for it was El Cito.

 From the citadel or kastro you have a very extensive view over the Spercheios valley and Mt Oeta, and of the town which has little to offer by way of sightseeing.

VICINITY

 1 HERAKLEIA (6.8mls/11km along Amfissa road). Between the junction with a secondary road towards Thermopylae and the foot of Mt Oeta – the Amfissa road drops down – you go in through the site of ancient Herakleia, a town founded in 426 BC by the Spartans who established a colony there.

Some rock tombs have been carved out of the mountainside. The city was encircled by a rampart built out from the side of the mountain. According to Yves Bequignon, the citadel of Herakleia was the same place as the acropolis of ancient Trachis, which was abandoned when the Spartans founded Herakleia, 6 stadia away from it. Trachis is claimed to have been founded by Heracles, who was believed to have stayed there before going to his funeral pyre on Mount Oeta in Thessaly.

2 THERMOPYLAE (see under Thermopylae; 9.7mls/15.5km along Athens motorway).

3 LAMIA TO KARPENISION AND AGRINION (48.7 and 118.7mls/78 and 190km). This road is difficult and taxing, unpaved for about 25mls (40km), and not conducive to fast driving (allow at least 6hrs driving to reach Agrinion). Your slow travelling will be rewarded by some of the loveliest scenery you can find in Greece.

Allow for at least one break in the journey to unwind: there is a little café 46.8mls (75km) from Agrinion, near the little church of Hagios Sotiras, pleasantly shaded, which would make a perfect stopping-place.

Go back up the Spercheios valley, where antiquity has left fortresses such as (20.6mls/33km) Makrakomi (at the place known as Kastri, mentioned by Livy as Macra Come, or (24.3mls/39km) Vitoli (ancient Spercheia, on Kastrorachi hill). At Makrakomi a road branches off on the l. to (3.7mls/5km) Platystomon, a little thermal establishment.

40.6mls (65km): Pass below the main peak of Mt Velouchi.

48.7mls (78km): Karpenision, a large mountain village on the slopes of Mt Velouchi, ancient Tymphrestus, with unexpectedly Alpine scenery. A road goes off on the r. from the village which has been built to serve a winter sports centre quite high up on the slopes of Mt Velouchi. Carry straight on for Agrinion.

To begin with, the road is paved for about 12.5mls (20km). It then takes you from crest to crest and from one rough patch to another to the other side of the Tymphrestus mountains, passing through the village of Frangista (73.7mls/118km). Soon you can see the Achelous reservoir (83.7mls/133km), the biggest artificial lake in Greece, which you cross (84mls/135km) after a steep descent, only to climb back up again on the other bank. From 87.5mls (140km – a promontory with a little chapel and the tomb of a local pope nearby) to 93.7mls (150km – the village of Karamaneika) you are constantly confronted by a marvellous ***panorama over the huge lake set amidst crystalline mountains.

103.7mls (165km): Potamoula – 117mls (188km): road on l. for Thermos (see Vicinity of Agrinion) – 118mls (190km): Agrinion.

Langadia

Route map 7.

Olympia, 36mls (58km) – Pyrgos, 48.7mls (78km) – Tripolis, 45mls (72km) – Pop: 17,000 approx.

This village, perched on steep valley slopes, is a must for those nostalgic for the romantic Greece depicted in 19th-century lithographs, for Langadia has hardly changed since then. It still has the peaceful atmosphere of the mountain villages with peasants who keep up their traditions, passing through; the market affords an opportunity of looking at these shepherds and farmers who still wear the fustanella (the short skirt of the Greek national costume) though the rustic simplicity of its appearance here is in sharp contrast with the stylish fustanellas worn by the *evzones* in the Guards.

VICINITY

1 **VITINA** (15mls/24km E), on the lovely Tripolis road which goes through wooded countryside (School of Forestry, forestry work), is a pleasant place to stay in summer near the finest inland scenery in the Peloponnese.

2 *LADONOS DAM (8.7mls/14km W, on the Olympia road as far as Stavrodhromi; then r. towards Tropaia). 4.4mls (7km) from Tropaia (track; 0.9mls/1.5km E, remains of a Frankish castle) the dam has been built across the river Ladon, forming a long reservoir lake in a superb, lonely site. A hydroelectric station is 3.7mls (5km) further on, fed from the dam by underground pressurized piping.

■ Larisa

Route maps 1, 2 and 11.

Athens (via Farsala), 208mls (333km) – Athens (by motorway), 227mls (364km) – Evzoni, 123mls (197km – by motorway) – Kalambaka (Meteora), 51mls (82km) – Lamia (via Farsala), 69.4mls (111km) – Lamia (by motorway), 88.7mls (142km) – Thessaloniki, 107.5mls (172km) – Volos (by motorway), 34mls (55km) – Pop: 72,700 – district capital of admin. region of Larisa.

The capital of Thessaly, and one of the hottest places in Greece, Larisa is a good overnight stop at an intersection of main roads, but offers little else as far as tourists are concerned, though the archaeological museum is worth a visit, and the ouzo and ice cream are good.

THESSALY, AND ITS CHANGING FACES. The Thessalian plain with Larisa as its centre has always had a peculiar attraction, and from the most distant times was repeatedly invaded by different races. In the course of the 2nd millennium BC it was occupied by the Pelasgi, and Larisa (a Pelasgian name meaning a citadel) was supposedly founded at the same time by the legendary Acrisius. Other invaders followed in their wake. After the Trojan war the province was invaded by Dorians from Thesprotia in Epirus; they reduced the earlier inhabitants to servitude or forced them to emigrate while they formed the landed and military aristocracy of the area. Dynastic principalities were established in Larisa (the Aleuades), Krannon (the Scopades) and at Pharsalus (the Echecratides family), and joined together in the 6th century BC. The Aleuades attracted writers, scholars and artists to their court, such as Pindar and Hippocrates (460–370 BC) – the latter lived in Larisa for a long time and died there.

A PACT WITH THE DEVIL. In 480 BC Larisa did not join with the other Greek cities which had been invaded by Xerxes, but made a pact with him. In 476 BC Sparta launched an unsuccessful punitive expedition against Larisa. Thebes reorganized the Thessalian Confederacy in 364 BC, but shortly after Theban protection was lost the last of the Aleuades had to ask for Philip of Macedon's help in overturning the power of the Pherai. Larisa and Thessaly passed under the control of Macedon in 334 BC. In 196 BC the Romans made Larisa the capital of a new Thessalian confederacy.

GREATER WALLACHIA. In the Middle Ages, after being invaded by the Goths, the Huns and the Bulgars, Thessaly became the centre of a Bulgar-Wallach kingdom in the 12th century, known as Greater Wallachia.

Larisa was subsequently occupied by the Franks, the despots of Epirus and, in 1989, by the Turks who stayed in control until 1881.

THE ARCHAEOLOGICAL MUSEUM is housed in a former Turkish mosque in the centre of the town on a big square beside the modern market, at the E end of Venizelos Avenue. Viewing its collection will help you to appreciate how far back the inhabitation of this province goes (the valley of the Peneus river was occupied at least from the Palaeolithic age), and the importance of the civilizations that flourished there in the Neolithic period (Gremmos Magoula, Sesklo, Dimini, etc.). There is a collection of sculpture with exhibits from the Archaic period (6th century BC) up to early Christian times.

Open: summer, 09.00–13.00 and 16.00–18.00; winter, 10.00–16.30; Sun., 10.30–14.30; closed Tues.; entrance fee.

There are interesting fragments of a Hellenistic sarcophagus from Cranon, decorated with painting showing the influence of the Archaic period. A collection of stelae from the Late Empire (2nd–4th century AD) is of special interest as it enables us to perceive the antecedents of a theme which was to be popular in Byzantine art: the hero on horseback (the Dioscuri for the Romans, and for the Byzantines, St George).

Venizelos Avenue as it goes towards the river Peneus, passes the ancient acropolis on the r. (with the clock tower, and traces of a Byzantine citadel), and on the l. the living heart of the modern town (see Sofias Avenue). Sample borings in this part of town have established the position of the town's Hellenistic theatre, unfortunately buried beneath modern buildings. Five rows of tiered seating made of marble have been located, and the W end of the stage building, decorated on the facade with Doric half-columns. A proposal for compulsory purchase and systematic excavation is being studied. On the l. bank of the Peneus, it is pleasant to walk in the Alcazar Park.

VICINITY

1 MAGOULA OF GREMMOS (6.8mls/11km following the Kozani road l. after 4.7mls/7.5km). Excavations have established that here and to the N were the remains of a large town identified as ancient Argoula (Homer's Argissa), occupied from the Neolithic until the Imperial Roman periods.

2 GOUNITSA. At the end of the Kalamaki pass on the Kozani road, the church belonging to Gounitsa cemetery is built of reused ancient blocks of masonry, and decorated with medieval frescoes.

3 HAGIA AND MT OSSA (20.6mls/33km; leave by the Volo road, turn l. after 3.1mls/5km). Hagia is the capital town of the province of Hagia, and has a little museum; there is also the church Hagii Apostoli to visit. The main attraction for enthusiasts however is that it is the departure point for climbing Mt Ossa (6,490ft/1,978m; 10hrs to the top and back; hire a guide in Hagia).

■ Lemnos [Island of] (Limnos)*

184sq. mls (447m²) – Pop: 17,000.

Halfway between Mt Athos and Asia Minor, Hephaestus island of Lemnos – Hephaestus (Vulcan), the crippled son of Zeus and Hera, had his forges here – has become one of the tourist paradises of the Aegean Sea, without yet being overcrowded. This was brought about simply by building a first-class hotel on a very attractive beach near Myrina (or Kastron), the island's capital, on the site of the ancient town of the same name, overlooked by an impressive Venetian fortress.

THE ISLAND WITH NO MEN. The island's history is enhanced by many legends which are proof of the manifold links between Lemnos and the mainland from earliest known times. It is said that Hephaestus, driven out by Zeus and Hera because of his lameness, set up his forges there and married Aphrodite. He asked the women of Lemnos to bear witness to his marital wrongs, and they censured the goddess, who avenged herself by making them all stink, which kept their husbands away from them. The women of Lemnos retaliated and killed all their husbands. King Thaos alone was saved by his daughter Hypsipyle, who became queen. When the Argonauts called in at the island, they were kept there for a while and the island's population was regenerated.

THE ISLAND OF THE PELASGI. The first known inhabitants of the island are thought to have been the Pelasgi, the same race as the Tyrrheni, and there is an inscription written in an as yet undeciphered language thought to be theirs. Shortly before the Persian wars, Miltiades, the victor of Marathon, dislodged them and installed Athenian settlers in their place. The island had several different masters, and was subject to Macedon and then to Rome. Later, it was part of the Byzantine Empire until 1204. The Genoese and the Venetians fought over it, and in 1478 it was surrendered to the Turks in whose hands it remained until 1918.

You land on the island of Lemnos at the port of Myrina, the main town of the island, with its old houses with their wooden balconies, and there you can visit an archaeological museum (finds from Hephaestia and Poliochni, see below). But you may be more tempted by the nearby *Hagia Varvara beach.

To explore the island set off along the road to Moudros; as you leave Myrina you will see old Turkish baths.

Moudros (Mudros, 15.6mls/25km from Myrina) has always been considered one of the best anchorages in the Aegean. During World War I the bay on which the town lies was used for the embarkation of the Franco-British expeditionary corps to the Dardanelles; this memory is preserved by cemeteries and commemorative monuments, as is the Turkish surrender of 1918.

A track takes you to the NE of the island, enabling you to reach the shores of the gulf of Pournias. There at Paleopolis are the remains of ancient Hephaestia, situated on a rocky promontory (hire a guide from Kondoupoli).

Italian archaeologists uncovered a 5th- or 6th-century BC theatre which had been altered during the Roman period. At the place known as Chloi, on a promontory overlooking the entrance to the harbour, the remains of a sanctuary of the Cabiri were discovered; it may have been built by Seleucus during the Hellenistic period to outshine another famous Cabirium, that on Samothrace. Excavations have revealed a paved area, a portico and part of a temple. Nearby there are the ruins of a basilica with three naves and tribunes dating from the end of the Roman period.

Also on the Gulf of Pournias there is the medieval castle of Kokkino; not far from it at Mosychlos, one day each year, siliceous earth with healing properties was extracted with great religious ceremony, and this custom was kept alive from ancient times until the 19th c. On the E coast of the island at Poliochni there is a Neolithic site, and the modest remains of a Bronze Age city, with some traces of a perimeter wall.

Finally, to the S, towards the monastery of Hagios Sozon, there is a strange sandy landscape nicknamed the 'Lemnos Sahara'.

About 18mls (32km) S of Lemnos, the island of Hagios Evstratios stands aloof from the Aegean traffic routes. It covers an area of 8sq. mls (43km^2), and its few inhabitants live off fishing and fruit crops.

Lerna

Route maps 6 and 7.

Argos, 6mls (10km) – Tripolis, 30.6mls (49km) – Leonidion, 31.8mls (51km).

Lerna is just beyond Myli if you come from Argos, and is famous in mythology as the setting of Heracles' fight against the Hydra, a water-serpent with a hound's body and many heads estimated at from five to 100, that lived in a swamp.

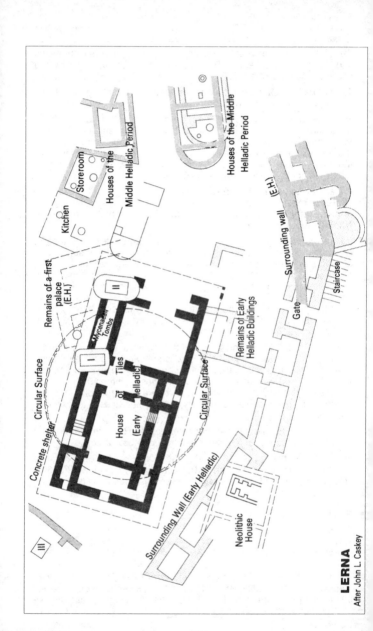

LERNA
After John L. Caskey

Houses of the Middle Helladic Period

Houses of the Middle Helladic Period

Storeroom

Kitchen

Remains of a first palace (E.H.)

Circular Surface

Concrete shelter

Mycenaean Tombs

House of Tiles (Early Helladic)

Circular Surface

Remains of Early Helladic Buildings

Surrounding Wall (Early Helladic)

Surrounding wall (E.H.)

Gate

Staircase

Neolithic House

THE PROBLEMS OF DRAINAGE. It is generally accepted that the story of the Hydra is an aetiological myth that explains the obstacles encountered by ancient peoples when they tried to drain the disease-harbouring swamps of this area by digging ditches; this work was continually threatened by water welling up from several springs, and constantly had to be undertaken afresh (the Hydra's heads which grew again after they had been cut off).

THE OLDEST KNOWN SITE IN THE ARGOLID. The plentiful water supply was conducive to settlement, and the site was in fact occupied from the Neolithic period (4th–3rd millenium BC) up until the beginning of the Mycenaean period (1580–1200 BC). Excavations undertaken by an American mission under the direction of John L. Caskey resulted in the discovery of this settlement, which was at its most active during the early Helladic period (beginning of the 3rd millennium BC).

Open: summer, 09.00–13.00 and 16.00–18.00; winter, 10.00–16.30; Sun. 10.30–14.30; closed Tues.

Though only the foundations remain, archaeological enthusiasts should visit the ruins of Lerna because they are so well presented.

Before entering the building on the l. which protects the most interesting remains, look first at remnants of an outer wall, fortified with towers, dating from the early Helladic period, and altered several times during it. Next, in a pit, you can make out some traces of a Neolithic house.

Further on there are more remains of early Helladic fortifications; note some remains of a staircase, of two towers that were built at different times, during the Helladic period, and, under a modern roof, a stretch of wall made of unbaked bricks which formed part of the outer wall.

Beyond these near the end of the rampart are the foundations of two apsidal-style houses built almost on top of one another, from the middle Helladic period (c.2000–1580 BC).

As you make your way towards the concrete shelter, note a few traces of the walls of a huge building which may have been the first palace, before the House of the Tiles, the remains of which are protected under a modern building.

This palace was built with great care during the early Helladic period, and had an upper floor. It was devastated by fire during the same period and the rubble from it was used in part to construct a huge circular space edged with boulders (still visible in places) in which bothroi, hollow altars for making sacrifices, were sunk.

Several tombs were dug on the site in the middle Helladic period (plan II and III) and at the beginning of the Mycenaean period (plan I).

VICINITY

LEONIDION (33.1mls/53km; follow the Tripolis road, turn l. after 1.2mls/2km).

1.2mls (2km): Kiveri – after this village the road follows the sea.

11.8mls (19km): Paralia Astros, fine beach.

14.4mls (23km): Astros (work in progress on an archaeological museum); from here it would be possible to go to Hagios Petros (17th-century tower) and rejoin the Tripolis-Sparta road near Teghea (temple and museum, see Vicinity of Tripolis).

33.1mls (53km): After passing a succession of creeks and olive-fringed beaches the road reaches Leonidion, standing back from the sea at the foot of Mt Parnon (6,037ft/1,840m). From there it is possible to get back to Sparta along a very bad mountain track via Kosmas and the Geraki vicinity (see Vicinity of Sparta).

■ Leros [Island of]

24.7sq. mls (64km²) – Pop: 8,000 approx.

This fertile island with its forests and mountains, made up of three peninsulas and penetrated by deep bays, is one of the most peaceful in the Dodecanese. A large part of the population lives off sponge diving. It will please those who want to live simply during their holiday: the accommodation is rustic and the meals as frugal as you could wish for, but the islanders will welcome you generously and the island with its orchards and vineyards will appeal to you. The tradition of the carnival has been kept up, and the local craftsmanship is attractive.

A PORT OF CALL FOR RHODES. Leros is mentioned by Herodotus and Thucydides. Its original population, who were Carians, were driven out by Cretans, and then Ionians colonized the island when it passed into Miletus' hands. Later, it was a haunt of pirates. The Byzantines and the Knights of St John from Rhodes, fought over it, but in 1319 a fleet which had set out from Rhodes to the assistance of the Genoese in Chios seized it. In modern times the island has been used on several occasions to house deportees.

The boat calls in at Lakki, a little harbour sheltered in a deep bay. A road goes from there towards the main village, Platanos, built on the side of a hill with a Byzantine fortress on top of it that has been restored by the Knights of St John. As you enter the village, you pass the church of the Panagia.

From Lakki it is possible to reach (1.8mls/3km) Hagia Marina and (7.5mls/12km) Partheni by road, or the village of (2.5mls/4km) Xerocampos on the strait separating Leros from Kalymnos.

■ Levkas [Island of]*

Route map 10

Agrinion, 61.4mls (99km) – Arta, 44.6mls (72km) – Preveza, 13mls (21km). 125.5sq. mls (325km²) – Pop: 24,500.

This corner of Greek soil is still relatively free of visitors despite its attractive and varied scenery and the appeal of its rugged coastline, sometimes dotted with marine grottoes (W coast). As the island is hilly and fertile, a very pleasant wine is produced from its vineyards, the Santa Mavra, and you can savour it in the quiet of the main town where life seems to flow along at the gentlest of paces. You reach Levkas after crossing the lagoon which lies between the mainland and the 'island' (whether or not Levkas is an island is a matter of opinion), and taking the ferry across a narrow channel (uninterrupted service from sunrise to sunset).

A HOMERIC PUZZLE. There are still some who adhere to the theory that Levkas (ancient Leucadia) is Homer's Ithaca, but though a Mycenaean principality did exist here, and at Cephalonia, modern-day Ithaca fits Homer's descriptions better.

THE PULL OF THE MAINLAND. About 640 BC, more than a century after Corcyra had been colonized, the Corinthians settled on Levkas and built a canal across the isthmus, which must have silted up, for in 425 BC the Peloponnesian fleet coming from Corcyra had to be carried across the isthmus. Augustus had the canal dug out again, and linked the town to the mainland by a bridge which is now submerged owing to subsidence.

The island was too near to the mainland to escape prolonged occupation by the Turks, as the other Ionian islands did; in 1467 they took over from the Franks and Venetians as rulers of the island. However, the Republic of Venice regained a toehold there in 1684 and from then on Levkas shared the same history as the other Ionian islands.

Whether you intend to stay on the island or merely make a quick tour of it, you have to enter and leave at Levkas, a little town with a population of 6,500, almost at sea level, and facing the Frankish and Venetian castle of Santa Maura (14th century, with later alterations). While there, visit Hagios Dimitrius church in which there are four paintings attributed to Panaghiotis Doxaras (d. 1729), and Hagios Minas church, the ceiling of which is decorated with paintings by Nicolas Doxaras (d. 1761).

In the archaeological museum at 21 Phaneromenis Road there are finds from early excavations (directed by Dörpfeld 1906–12) and more recent ones on the island. As well as pottery (vases and terracotta items) and objects in stone ranging from the Bronze Age to the Roman period, items exhibited include Hellenistic funerary stelae, stone cinerary urns, and a sundial from the Roman period carved out of a block of limestone.

If you are looking for a pleasant, almost deserted beach go about 3mls (5km) W of the town, between Tsoukalades and Hagios Nikitas, to Vai.

 TOUR ROUND THE ISLAND (54.4mls/87km, excluding a 32.5mls/52km detour to Hagios Nikolaos and the Leucadian Leap and back). You are almost sure to respond to the beauty of the *scenery that unfolds as you go round the island, though the roads are unfortunately none too good; you can call in at country churches, many of them decorated with frescoes of the Ionian school, mainly from the 17th and 18th centuries. Leave Levkas on the Nydri road.

1.8mls (3km): Ruins of ancient Levkas, not very interesting; remains of the perimeter wall of the lower town, in polygonal masonry, of the theatre, and of the acropolis rampart, in cyclopean masonry.

11.2mls (18km): Nydri, in a superb *setting (tavernas). You can cross by boat in a few minutes to the other side of the bay where the romantic little house in which the German archaeologist Dörpfeld (d. 1940) stayed when he was conducting excavations on Levkas has been transformed into a museum; he wanted to prove that Levkas was in fact the Ithaca described by Homer.

Across the Nydri on the tiny, green island of Madouri is the house where the poet Valaoritis was born, while the islet of Scorpio was one of the favourite residences of the shipping magnate, Aristotle Onassis.

16.2mls (26km): Fterno; in the church of the Panagia of Fao there are 18th-century frescoes.

At Poros, 1.8mls (3km) away to the l., is the church of the Analipsis (Assumption), decorated with paintings including one of the Virgin dating from the 17th century.

17.5mls (28km): 1.8mls (3km) away on the r. is the church of the Panagia tis Skalas, near the convent of Haghios Ioannis sto Rodaki, the church of which is decorated with frescoes (1st half of 17th century for the Ascension above the apse; the hierarchs date from the early 18th century).

20.6mls (33km): Marandochori; in the church of Hagios Georgios of Bisa the frescoes date from the late 15th or early 16th century

25mls (40km): Vassiliki; a little beach tucked well into the bay of Vassiliki (connecting service with Ithaca and Cephalonia). The road is not paved from this point.

29.4mls (47km): Hagios Petros. Track on the mountainside.

36.2mls (58km): To the l. 13.1mls (21km) along a fairly good road, Hagios Nikolaos; from there a footpath leads to (3.1mls/5km) the *Leucadian Leap, a high cliff known in ancient times as Leucatas (White Cape), which the Venetians by a play on words turned into Ducato. It announced entry into the western world and the country of the dead, not far from Acheron. There was a temple of Apollo (a few remains near the lighthouse) on top of the cliff.

The katapontismos, or leap into the sea, took place from the W cliff standing 236ft (72m) above the sea; it was thought to be some sort of Judgement of God to which some accused people were subjected, and could also be undertaken to curb love-sickness. Sappho is supposed to have died in the attempt for love of Phaon; in Strabo's and Cicero's day the leap was often made successfully. The risk was reduced by attaching feathers to the sufferer to break their fall and placing boats and nets to catch them. The priests of Apollo were able to make the dive without injury.

47.5mls (76km): A road on the r. leads to (2.5mls/4km) Karia, the most typical village on the island, with criss-crossing roads and blooming gardens. From there it is possible to take various walks into the centre of the island.

54.4mls (87km): Back in Levkas.

■ Lidhoriki

Route map 4.

Andirrhion, 59.4mls (95km) – Delphi, 40mls (64km).

A rough mountain village which is full of character; it is difficult to reach because of having to go round the Mornos reservoir.

VICINITY

KALLION. 3.1mls (5km) as the crow flies from Lidhoriki in the direction of Naupaktos the acropolis of Kallion stands surrounded by a perimeter wall with fine Hellenic coursework. The site, which will be partly submerged under the water behind the dam which is being built across the Mornos, has been identified, thanks to recently discovered inscriptions, as ancient Callipolis, which was destroyed by the Gauls in 279 BC. The new road giving access to what remains of the site will mean a considerable detour.

■ Litochoron

Route map 2.

Larisa, 42.5mls (68km) – Thessaloniki, 65mls (104km).

This large village on the E slope of Mt Olympus is generally chosen as the startling base for excursions and walks in this range of mountains; but if you so wish, it should be a pleasant place to stay, near the huge beaches of the Thermaic gulf. To climb Mt Olympus (see under Olympus), for which training is necessary, get in touch with the Greek Alpine Club in Athens or Thessaloniki; it will make guides and equipment available, and allow you to use the shelters.

If you are not intending to climb Olympus but just to walk on its slopes, you can follow a track going W from Litochoron extending for about 5mls (8km), then a path with markers, and you will come to the ruins of the monastery of Hagios Dionissios, on the side of Mavrolongos valley. It was established in the 16th century, destroyed by the Turks in 1828, rebuilt, then destroyed again in 1943 by the German army. Beyond that a large part of the mountain is protected as a nature park.

Route map 4.

Delphi, 30mls (48km) – Lamia, 60mls (96km) – Thebes, 30mls (48km) – Pop: 16,200 – district capital of admin. region of Boeotia.

This town lying between two hills one of which has a Frankish castle on it was famous in ancient times because of its oracle of Trophonius (the foster father), an early deity of the underworld assimilated to Zeus. Two springs played an important part in the consultation rites: Mnemosyne, the spring of Memory, and Lethe, the spring of Forgetfulness. The second must have flowed more freely than the first for there is virtually nothing left to recall that era.

A TOWN AT THE GATES OF HELL. Throughout the Classical period Livadia (Lebadaea) was an unimportant little town. Such notoriety and prosperity as it had were due to the infernal gorge of the Hercyna and the oracle of Trophonius. By Pausanias' time it had become the most prosperous town in Boeotia. In the Middle Ages its strategic position at the intersection of passes through the Parnassus range attracted a lot of people. In the 13th century it became the property of the Dukes of Athens, then in 1311 the Catalans gained control of it, and built the fortress which the Navarrese took by storm in 1380. The Turks captured it in 1460, and the town suffered greatly during the War of Independence.

Today the oracle is silent, but those who enjoy history can, by examining the lie of the land, find where petitioners anxious to know the fate of their enterprises came to consult the oracle. It takes about two hours of patient search without much reward. On the other hand, those who like good food may well prefer to savour the delicious lamb kebabs or cherry jam for which the town is noted: these can be sampled in one of Livadia's many cafés, giving you time to convince yourself that it is worth making a detour to visit Orchomenus, one of the oldest and wealthiest cities of heroic Greece; the *Iliad* extolled its treasures.

IN SEARCH OF MEMORY AND OBLIVION. The ancient town lay to the S of the present town, on the r. bank of the Hercyna, which runs through a gorge formed by Mt Hagios Ilias with the medieval fortress on its summit to the W and Mt Laphystion. An old Turkish bridge spans the river just below the springs of Trophonius. On the l. bank of the stream as you go down the gorge the Kria spring (cold), water from which is collected in a reservoir, is believed to be Mnemosyne, the spring of Memory or Remembrance, alluded to by Pausanias.

The rockface near the spring has votive niches and a room with benches hollowed out of it; the room may be the sanctuary of the Good Genius and Good Fortune. Another spring that gushes forth not far from there was Lethe, the spring of Forgetfulness or Oblivion.

The sanctuary of Zeus and the oracle of Trophonius were situated on Mt Hagios Ilias. Only a few foundations of the former have survived on the summit of the mountain. Scant remains of an underground building that housed the oracle, dating from the 3rd century BC, are all that have been found of the latter.

A PETITIONER BY THE NAME OF PAUSANIAS. The oracle of Trophonius, famous as early as the 6th century BC – it was said to have been consulted by Croesus, the wealthy king of Lydia – attracted many pilgrims. In the 2nd century AD, Pausanias, the most famous traveller of the time, consulted the oracle and recorded its rites. After spending several days in the sanctuary of the Good Genius and Good Fortune feeding on flesh from sacrifices, the petitioner drank water from Lethe to forget the past, and from Mnemosyne so that he would remember what he was going to see and hear. Then during the night, after being anointed with oil, he was taken on to the mountain towards the mouth of the prophetic cave, carved out of the rock. He went down a ladder to get into it. At the bottom of this narrow shaft was a hole of the same dimensions as the human body. The petitioner lay down, with a honey cake in each hand, and pushed his legs into this. He then slid through into the sacred cave or adyton where the revelation took place. He was then taken back up the same way, feet first, thoroughly stupefied. The priests placed him on a chair of Mnemosyne, and questioned him about what he had seen, and recorded what he said on a tablet.

Your pursuit of the oracle has thus taken you on to the hill where the Frankish fortress stands, with three perimeter walls surrounding it, rising in tiers on a slope of Mt Hagios Ilias. The first wall was defended by a big external bastion which must be a later addition to the original fortress.

On the side of the gorge the first wall ends in a huge tower, and at the other end in a big square tower. The second perimeter is fortified with three towers and like the previous one had a defensive tower through which the gate giving access to the redoubt was built.

VICINITY

1 ORCHOMENUS (9.7mls/13km; leave by Lamia road, turn r. after 3.7mls/6km). Before going to the site of ancient Orchomenus, visit the convent of the Assumption of the Virgin, the church of which was built in 874 on the site of the temple of the Graces. Its style is in transition between the basilica and the cruciform shape with a dome, following a Bulgarian tradition of which this is the only example in Greece.

Opposite the church on the other side of the road there is a small ancient theatre which was discovered recently and excavated by the Greek Archaeological Service. Near the end of a concrete road that climbs up behind the theatre, and about 440yds (400m) from it, are the scant remains of a temple of Asclepius. In the distance on the rocky heights are a few remains of the perimeter wall that surrounded the upper town of the Macedonian period (4th–3rd century BC).

Below in a modern enclosure just W of the theatre is the monument which Pausanias described as the treasury of Minyas, from the name of the legendary ancestor of the Minyans: it consists of a domed tomb or tholos from the Mycenaean period, and a rectangular vault carved out of the rock; inside there is an altar from the Greek period.

A HOMERIC CITY. This last monument will help you to appreciate how far back in time the origins of this city lie; it was the capital of the Minyans, a people native to the Thessalian seaboard. Orchomenus was in fact the seat of a brilliant civilization whose industriousness is attested to by the legends concerning the builders Agamedes and Trophonius and the first scheme to drain lake Copais. Its power extended as far as Larymna, possibly over Thebes which Heracles supposedly subjugated. In the Archaic period it was a member of the Boeotian confederacy from the early 7th century BC, and sided with the Persians during the Persian Wars.

BOEOTIAN QUARRELS WITH BOEOTIAN. The aristocracy of Orchomenus was on good terms with that of Thebes, but at the end of the Peloponnesian war the democratic revolution in Thebes turned the two cities against one another. Orchomenus gave its support to Sparta against Thebes in 395 and 394 BC. The Thebans had to recognize its independence and after the Battle of Leuctra (371 BC) spared Orchomenus only at the instance of Epaminondas. But in 364 BC they destroyed it giving no quarter. It was rebuilt by the Phocians in 353 BC, but destroyed for a second time by the Thebans in 349, then rebuilt by Philip and Alexander.

Excavations conducted at various points on the site in the course of the last ten years have led to the discovery of some remains of the Mycenaean palace, with a lot of pottery and fragments of mural paintings, as well as buildings from the Archaic, Classical and Hellenistic periods, but almost none of these remains can be seen at present.

2 CHAERONEA (8.75mls/14km along Lamia road). The village of this name is near the battlefield where Philip of Macedon in 338 BC defeated a coalition of Greek city states; this victory in which his son Alexander took an active part enabled Macedon to conquer the whole of Greece. On the l. of the road as you enter the village there is the big marble lion which stood over the collective tomb (polyandreion) in which the Thebans placed the bones of the warriors of the Sacred Band who had died during the battle.

Near the lion there is a little museum with a collection of antiquities from various sites in the region, especially prehistoric sites such as Hagia Marina, Drachmani (Elateia), Orchomenus, etc.

Open: 09.00–12.30 and 16.00–18.00; Sun. 09.00–15.00; closed Tues.; entrance fee.

In the garden there is a collection of funerary stelae. In the entrance hall, there is a piece worth noting: a headless Archaic marble kouros, from Orchomenus (mid-6th century BC). The exhibits in the room on the l. are mainly prehistoric pottery. In the room on the r. they are more varied: many vases, terracotta figurines (men and animals), jewellery, lamps (mainly Roman and early Christian), bronze coins from various periods; note specially, in the first two showcases on the r., Mycenaean vases found at Andicyra and Orchomenus, then fragments of frescoes from Orchomenus, Archaic vases (Corinthian, Attic and Boeotian) and Classical vases (red-figure Attic) from the Abai necropolis in Locris, Geometric-style vases, Boeotian vases with floral decoration (at the back of the room on the r.) and lastly Classical black-glazed vases (including a good many Boeotian canthari) and Hellenistic vases.

On the l. of the road as you leave the village you can see a few remains (in particular a theatre carved out of the rock) of the ancient town of Chaeronea where Plutarch (46–120 AD) was born and died; there is a statue in the village square in his honour.

On the slopes of the acropolis, there were walls, encircling the two peaks of Mt Petrachus. The entrance was at the top of a ramp cut out between the rocks. The wall on this side is built with Hellenic masonry; on the other slope the original perimeter wall is in cyclopean masonry.

3 PANOPEUS (11.2mls/18km along the Lamia road, turning l. after 10mls/16km on to road to village of Hagios Vlassios). The modern village lies at the foot of the acropolis of Panopeus; its perimeter wall, built with fine Hellenic masonry in the 4th century BC, and its towers are, in places, among the best preserved in Greece.

This legendary Phocian city, believed to be the native place of Epeius who built the Trojan horse, was destroyed on several occasions: in 480 BC by Xerxes, in 340 BC by Philip of Macedon, in 198 BC by Flaminius and in 86 BC by Sulla. In the 2nd century AD Pausanias was astonished to find only a poverty-stricken village.

To reach the ancient town and its ramparts, which can hardly be seen from below, you have to allow for a good half hour's walk up quite steep slopes, but you will have very happy memories of a walk which takes you off the beaten track.

From the village you have to head first towards the l. (i.e. the E) in order to climb as far as a pass from which you can see a first tower belonging to the perimeter wall. From there on you can follow this along its S face; it has been well preserved for a length of several hundred yards. It is also worthwhile to go into the town where there are many remains, not easy to identify (there have been very few excavations of the site), and a little church; there are excellent views in every direction, particularly looking towards Parnassus.

On the way down, to get a broad view of the site, first climb a little hill to the S from which you have an impressive overall view of the S face of the perimeter wall. From there it is easy to rejoin the pass at which you arrived, and you can go back down to the village through the undergrowth.

4 DAVLIA (17.8mls/28.5km; follow the Lamia road, turn l. after 12.5mls/20km). Davlia is a little town at the foot of Mt Parnassus near the acropolis of ancient Daulis, which was reoccupied by the Catalans in the Middle Ages; they built a fortress there with a perimeter wall standing on the remains of ancient ramparts. The acropolis is situated on top of a spur between two steep gorges, overlooked by the white mass of the convent of Jerusalem (1hr distant) and the broad slopes of Mt Parnassus. The walls and their square towers are well preserved; the masonry is partly polygonal and partly quadrangular.

The myth of Tereus, who was given his son Itys to eat by his wife Procne, after he had raped and cut out the tongue of her sister Philomela, took place at Daulis. The city was destroyed in 480 BC by Xerxes and wiped out in 346 BC by Philip.

5 ELATIA (23.1mls/37km; follow the Lamia road, then after 12.5mls/20km the Atalandi road, and l. after 16.8mls/27km). Elatia is a village near the site of ancient Elatia, a small town that commanded the road between southern and northern Greece. Athens' sense of stupefaction when Elatia was captured by Philip in 339 BC is described in a famous passage by Demosthenes (*Discourse on the Crown*).

Only scant remains of the acropolis of the ancient town are visible; but if you have plenty of energy we recommend that you climb up (on foot or by mule) to the sanctuary of Athena Cranaia (allow 3hrs; take a guide) where you can see a fine perimeter wall and the foundations of a Doric temple (capitals, drums of columns) and enjoy an astounding view towards Mt Parnassus and the valley of the Cephisus. Excavations at the sanctuary where copies of the official documents of the Phocian confederacy were kept have produced a valuable collection of epigraphic documentation.

■ Loutra Kaiafa

Route map 9.

Olympia, 27.5mls (44km) – Pylos (Navarino), 59.4mls (95km) – Pyrgos, 15mls (24km).

This little bathing resort and spa situated between two long, cultivated coastal plains uses the sulphur springs that rise on an island on lake Kaiafa at the bottom of two caves, which had been used in ancient times.

VICINITY

SAMIKON (1.25mls/2km along Pyrgos road). Archaeological enthusiasts can set out from this little bathing resort in search of the acropolis of ancient Samicum, or Macistos, which has a fine polygonal perimeter wall dating from the 6th century BC and altered in the 5th century BC. The town was famous for its temple of Samian

Poseidon, on which the amphictyony of the six Minyan towns of Triphylia was based; it must have stood on one of the three mounds near the lagoon crossing, which used to be protected by a wall.

■ Loutra Kyllini

Route map 9.

Olympia, 37.5mls (60km) - Patras, 45.6mls (73km) - Pyrgos, 25mls (40km).

A spa (respiratory and skin complaints) and a bathing resort, Loutra Kyllini with its *Golden Beach stretching for several miles, appeals to people who prefer not to travel around but to establish themselves for the duration of their holiday in a place which is neither too busy nor too deserted.

VICINITY

KASTRON (3.7mls/6km). In this superbly isolated village on top of a high hill you can visit the castle of Chlemoutsi, built by Geoffroy de Villehardouin and named Clairemont by him. c.1220-23. Constantine Paleologus conquered it in 1427 and dismantled it in 1430.

Its crenellated walls, its keep, its high towers and vaulted galleries make it one of the most imposing medieval buildings in the Morea. The round tower in the middle of the curtain wall through which the entrance gate passes, and the bastion on top of the ramparts, are from the Turkish period.

■ Loutra Ypati

Route map 3.

Lamia, 11.2mls (18km) - Volo, 86.8mls (139km).

This quiet spa (skin ailments) below Mt Oeta, where Heracles met his end by climbing on to his own funeral pyre, is a good choice for an overnight stop for those who prefer not to spend the night in Lamia, which is hot in summer.

VICINITY

YPATI (3.7mls/6km). This village on the site of ancient Hypata (an acropolis with a few ramparts of ancient and medieval walls) is the starting point for climbing (6hrs) the main summit of Mt Oeta (7,106ft/2,166m). Hire a guide at Ypati. You will come back down the E face, passing near the site of the funeral pyre of Heracles where a German mission found the remains of a Doric temple.

■ Loutraki

Route map 5.

Athens, 56.8mls (91km) - Corinth, 7.5mls (12km).

This is by far the most popular of Greek spas, and comes to life only in the summer months. The waters (85°F/29.5°C) are recommended for rheumatic complaints. Loutraki is also a bathing resort, and lies amid woods on the gulf of Corinth.

VICINITY

HERAEUM OF PERACHORA (12.5mls/20km). There you can see the rather unspectacular ruins of a sanctuary dedicated to Hera, but we recommend a visit for from both the approach road and the actual site you can see rural, pastoral *scenery of great beauty. You may well be tempted to have a swim in the creek which used to be the harbour for the sanctuary.

The almost entirely paved road that leads to the archaeological site leads town to the N, along the coast. 3.8ml (6km) after a zig-zag climb (fine views over the Gulf of Corinth) take the road to the l. (5ml/8km) to Perachora 5.6ml (9km); turn l., then l. twice more to Lake Vouliagmeni (9.4ml/15km), going along the N. shore. 10.6ml (17km) beach at the NW extremity of the lake.

11.9ml (19km) road ends; parking. A few yds to the S you will find an almost aerial panoramic view of the sanctuary and its little port, dominated by a modern chapel, towards which you descend.

To the l. the vestiges of a large oblong cistern can be seen, apsidal at each end, below a rectangular esplanade which consisted of two square rooms partly bordered by seats.

The port was flanked to the E. and N. by an L-shaped portico of the Doric order (remains of two columns of stuccoed limestone and parts of the entablature). Next in the middle of a paved area may be seen the remains of an altar decorated with a frieze of triglyphs and metopes. On the site the foundations of an apsidal building from the Geometric period have been dug out, thought to be the first temple of Hera Acraea. Further on are the ruins of the temple which replaced it in the third quarter of the 6th century BC. The esplanade, which has been partly cut out of the rock near there was laid out in the 5th century BC as the agora (however, the polygonally constructed walls near the sea date from the 6th century BC).

Still further on you come to the site of the temple of Hera Limenia of which virtually only the foundations remain. The rectangular peribolus has survived in part. Almost at the centre of the temple there was a sacrificial pit edged with stone slabs, three carrying votive inscriptions from the late 7th century BC. These dedications refer to Hera Leukolenos, the only evidence we have of the use of this term.

A sacred pool to the W of the temenos of the temple of Hera Limenia may have been the prophetic shrine of the Heraeum of Perachora; according to a classical source, oracles were given there.

■ Macedonia

Route maps 1, 2, 12, 13 and 14.

Macedonia, which includes the administrative regions of Chalcidice, Drama, Ematheia, Florina, Kastoria, Kavalla, Kozani, Mt Athos, Pella, Pieria, Serres and Thessaloniki, and has a population of almost 2,000,000 is a huge region whose history and geography and unusual in the context of the Hellenic world. Macedonia, Epirus and Thrace together form a transition zone between the Balkans to which they are attached geographically and Mediterranean Greece. Those keen on archaeology will find sites there to visit, particularly from the Hellenistic and Roman periods, and admirers of Byzantine art will find churches, particularly in Thessaloniki and Kastoria, which will remind them that Macedonia was one of the main provinces of Byzantine Greece. Those who are drawn by beautiful scenery should not neglect Macedonia either, with its splendid rural landscapes around Kastoria, and grand mountain panoramas near Mt Athos and in the Kozani area.

BALKAN GREECE. Along with Thessaly and Thrace, Macedonia constitutes a continental frontier of Greece, and has certain of the characteristics of eastern Europe: the partitioned patchwork prevalent in the peninsula gives way to wider groupings, where steppe-like plains spread out on a broad scale between old, flat-topped mountain ranges; the climate is continental and the landscape is enlivened by running water. Thus northern Greece presents a rather different image from that of classical Hellas; it is less richly endowed with remains of the past; Turkish occupation went deeper here; and the area was revitalized when Greek refugees from Ionia settled here after the Turkish invasion led by Kemal Ataturk (1923).

A FOUNDATION OF BROKEN-UP ROCK. The geological structure is of the same tectonic type in Macedonia as in Thessaly, with a subfoundation of ancient rocks broken up and distorted into a series of raised masses and collapsed basins. The raised masses are great high areas, often ending in steep faults; they can be as high as 6,500ft (2,000m), or more.

FLUVIAL CORRIDORS. The basins are wide corridors with rivers running through them, such as the Serres basin with the Strymon, the Kastoria basin with the Haliacmon, and the plain of Thessaloniki with the Axius (Vardar). A characteristic feature of these basins is the presence of lakes (Kastoria, Vegorritis, Volvi, etc.); some of these are poljes (hollows which become lakes after heavy rain), such as Lake Vegorritis, but most are in rift valleys which have not been completely filled by the alluvial deposits of the rivers. The rivers, after moving across the plains at a leisurely pace, often run through gorges cutting deep into the ancient bedrock.

The coast is generally flat and not deeply indented by the sea, except for the peninsula of Chalcidice which divides into three smaller peninsulas, the most famous of which is that of Mt Athos (6,670ft/2,033m).

A CONTINENTAL CLIMATE. The typical climate pattern is for warm summers (average temperature 73° F/23° C) and severe winters with temperatures sometimes falling to -4°F (-20°C); it often rains, and there is a lot of snow (above 6,500ft/2,000m there is snow from October to May). The plains are green and muddy in the rainy season, but in summer the sun scorches them and they are covered by clouds of dust stirred up by the slightest breeze.

A CEREAL AND TOBACCO AREA. The plains have been transformed by agricultural improvement schemes, and are developing towards intensive farming with cereal crops predominating.

Thessaloniki is the region's principal town, with its harbour in a remarkable location at the mouth of the Morava-Axius (Vardar) valley; its main industrial activity centres round textiles and tobacco.

■ Malandrinon

Route map 4.

Eratini, 13mls (21km) – Itea, 29.4mls (47km) – Lidorikion, 5mls (8km).

You can see the ruins of ancient Physkeis near this village. Look first of all at the Hagi Apostoli chapel near the lower rampart, which is in a very poor condition; the chapel seems to have been built on the site of an ancient building, possibly a temple.

Inside the acropolis, surrounded by a defensive perimeter wall, are the chapel of Hagios Nikolaos and foundations of ancient buildings reduced to the level of the rocky ground.

Below the acropolis are the ruins of a Byzantine church, on the site of a temple dedicated to Zeus Melichios. Beyond the village are the remains of a 5th- or 4th-century BC base which may have stood in the sanctuary of Athena Ilias.

■ Marathon

Map of the Vicinity of Athens, p. 310.

Athens, 24.4mls (39km).

The modern village of Marathon (which means 'field of fennel') is less interesting than the plain lying to its S, on which the famous battle was fought. On it there are several necropolises and a new museum with a collection of the finds made in the area.

THE BATTLE. The Battle of Marathon was fought in 490 BC (probably on 10 August, or possibly 12 September). The Persian fleet under the command of Datis and Artaphernes first took Eretria in Euboea, then, acting on the advice of Peisistratos' son Hippias, cast anchor in the bay of Marathon on the shingle between Soros (a tumulus) and the great marsh to the N to disembark an army corps that was to march on Athens. Herodotus assessed the army as having 100,000 infantrymen and 10,000 cavalry. These wildly exaggerated figures have been reduced by some modern critics to about 6,000 infantrymen (mostly archers) and 800 cavalry (excluding non-combatants). The Athenians hastened to the scene, probably via Kifissia and Vrana. Tradition puts their numbers at 9,000 hoplites, who were soon reinforced by 1,000 Plataeans, all under the command of the polemarch, Callimachus, and of the ten generals, including Miltiades and Aristides. Miltiades' colleagues conferred upon him the rank of supreme commander. They took up position on a slope of Mt Agriliki commanding the road on to the plain from Athens.

THE COURSE OF THE CONFLICT. After waiting for a week, Datis, fearing that Spartan reinforcements would arrive, decided to attack. The Greeks' line of battle, or phalanx, extended from the church of Hagios Dimitrios (the l. wing, with the Plataeans) to the Vrexisa marsh (the r. wing, under the polemarch Callimachus), not far from the modern road. They were thus protected from flanking movements by the Persian cavalry which could not take part. Miltiades had concentrated his forces on the flanks, leaving only a thin line of troops in the centre to draw the enemy on. The Persian forces advanced opposite Soros tumulus parallel to the Greek line, in a column of the same length. What happened was very simple: Miltiades led his phalanx into the plain and as soon as he was within range of the Persians ordered his men to charge. The decisive fighting took place near Soros. In Herodotus' words: 'In the centre, held by the Persians themselves and the Sacae, the advantage was with the foreigners, who were so far successful as to break the Greek line and pursue the fugitives inland from the sea; but the Athenians on one wing and the Plataeans on the other were both victorious. Having got the upper hand, they left the defeated Persians to make their escape, and then, drawing the two wings together into a single unit, they turned their attention to the Persians who had broken through into the centre. Here again they were triumphant, chasing the routed enemy, and cutting them down as they ran right to the edge of the sea.' (Herodotus VI, 113).

THE RACE. Legend has it that a soldier ran to give the Athenians news of the victory which they may hardly have dared to hope for. He died on arriving there, but the message concerning the victory was given. The marathon, a long-distance race (26.37mls/42.195km) run on the road, was dreamt up by a French philologist, Michel Bréal (1832–1915). It was run for the first time in 1896 during the first Olympic

Games of modern times, and won by the Greek, Spiridon Louys, in 2hrs 58mins 35secs, with another Greek in second place. There is a statue in honour of the winner at Marathon.

The village of Marathon, on land that is one of the oldest demes in Attica, is in the heartland of the area where the first Ionians settled. Theseus here captured the wild bull which was laying waste the plain.

THE TUMULUS OF THE PLATAEANS (3.7mls/6km from the village along the Rafina road, turning r. after 2.2mls/3.5km). After leaving the main road you pass a shed on the r. that protects a group of early Helladic graves, then 1.5mls (2.4km) from the fork, you can see the tumulus on the l. The soldiers sent by Plataea to Marathon as reinforcements for the Athenians were buried in this tumulus; but to the r. of the museum approx. 110yds (100m) further on there is also a necropolis with four tumuli which is much older, going back to the middle Helladic period (2000–1500 BC) and the Mycenaean period (1580–1100 BC).

This necropolis, which is now protected by a huge building to the r. of the museum, consists of four circles (one is outside the building, and another is merely suggested by the alignment of some stones). The tumulus nearest to the entrance contains the tomb of a horse, the skeleton of which is in a perfect state of preservation. Further l. there is a smaller circle with a single tomb, oblong in shape, like a corridor.

■ THE MUSEUM. This is a collection of the discoveries made on the plain of Marathon and its vicinity; the large number of graves found here means that virtually the whole area was a necropolis.

Open: summer, 08.30–12.30 and 16.00–18.00, Sun. 09.00–15.00; winter, 09.00–12.30 and 16.00–18.00, Sun. 10.00–15.30; closed Tues.; entrance fee.

Displayed in the entrance hall are the casting of a statue found in the sea off Marathon and that of a fine eastern-style helmet. In the first room there is Neolithic pottery, particularly from the cave of Pan, W of the modern village of Marathon; in the second room, earthenware, from early Helladic to the Geometric period (necropolis at Tsepi); in the next room finds from the two main tumuli (tumulus of the Athenians or Marathon, and tumulus of the Plataeans), with black-figure pottery. The fourth room has a display of earthenware and objects mainly from Nea Makri, and some marble reliefs from the Classical period. The last room has a collection of various reliefs and funerary statues from the Hellenistic, Roman and Byzantine periods, and some glassware and lamps. Under the peristyle surrounding the little garden, there are some pieces of sculpture and architecture (Ionic capitals). A path on the l. of the museum leads to several Mycenaean tombs.

TUMULUS OF THE ATHENIANS (or of Marathon; 3.7mls/6km from the village along the Rafina road, turning l. after 3mls/5km). This was raised after the battle in 490 BC as a receptacle for the ashes of the 192 Athenians who met their deaths in the fighting and were incinerated where they had fallen.

Excavations undertaken in 1890 by the Greek Archaeological Society resulted in finding charred bones of men and animals sacrificed in the tumulus as well as shards of early 5th-century BC vases. On the surface flint arrow points were found that belonged to the Ethiopian archers (Herodotus, VII, 69). Marble stelae placed on the tumulus commemorated the names of the 192 Athenian dead, listed by their tribes.

VICINITY OF MARATHON

1 **MARATHON LAKE** (5mls/8km W). This was originally a natural lake fed by streams running down from Mt Parnes or from the nearby wooded hills; since a dam was built to enlarge its capacity at the beginning of the century, it has contributed to Athens' water supply. The dam is believed to be the only one in the world to be lined with marble. The entrance into the underground galleries is in fact a replica of the treasury of the Athenians at Delphi.

The road going up to the top of the dam passes below the site of ancient Oinoe where the cave of Pan and the Nymphs described by Pausanias has been discovered.

2 **RHAMNIUS** (8.1mls/13km; see Vicinity of Athens).

■ Megalopolis

Route maps 7 and 8.

Kalamata, 36.2mls (58km) – Tripolis, 21.8mls (35km).

The Great City and its theatre which was, needless to say, the biggest in Greece, with seating for 20,000 people, have been reduced to the status of mere curiosities in the smoke of a large thermal power station. But a visit to the ruins will give you some idea of the huge scale of an attempt at town planning that failed.

THE GREAT CITY OR THE GREAT SOLITUDE? Megalopolis was built by Epaminondas in four years, 371–368 BC, to be the capital of a united Arcadia; it was intended to complete the string of strongholds, the others being Messene and Mantinea, which its founder thought should keep Sparta contained in Laconia. The new town was populated by shifting people from forty Arcadian villages and towns. After the death of Epaminondas in 362 BC, quarrelling soon broke out and undermined the enterprise; the peasants transported into Megalopolis were homesick. It was besieged and damaged several times, and the Great City, which a comic poet described as the Great Solitude, was just a pile of ruins in Pausanias' day. In the time of the last emperors it was a bishopric, and was still being mentioned in the 7th century, but disappeared at the time of the Slav Invasion.

The ruins are 0.9ml (1.5km) away from the modern town along the Pyrgos road.

THEATRE. To get to the theatre go l. just before the bridge over the Elisson. It was built on a grand scale to accommodate approx. 20,000 spectators. To the W (r. as you face the tiered seating) the parados was taken up by a long building which was a storeroom for props. In the 4th century BC the stage was made of wood and could be dismantled; between productions the equipment was kept in this building, the skenotheke. In the Roman period there was a stone stage with a proscenium wall with round columns. At the back of the stage there was a projecting portico.

THE THERSILION. This huge building, which is now barely a memory, was on a scale worthy of Persian palaces; it was where meetings of the federal Assembly of the Ten Thousand were held. It communicated with the portico of the theatre. The inside of this great hall, which is arranged in a way reminiscent of the Telesterion at Eleusis, and where 6,000 people could be accommodated sitting, or 10,000 standing, was planned like an odeon. The roof was supported by lines of pillars that formed rectangles round an almost central square, taking the place of the orchestra, on which there was a platform. The ordinary members of the Assembly sat on the tiered seating that circled the hall.

On the other side of Elisson was the municipal city, or Megalopolis proper, as opposed to the federal city, or Orestia; it is the principal ruins of the latter that have just been described (there was also a stadium beyond the theatre, and on the near side on the l. of the bridge there was a sanctuary of Asclepius).

THE MUNICIPAL CITY. This centred on the agora, on the l. of the road to Pyrgos, approx. 220yds (200m) after the bridge. First there was the Perfume Market (Myropolion), a portico which is today intersected by the road, built c.250 BC by the tyrant, Aristodemus, then the sanctuary of Zeus Soter, built on the river bank. On the other side, on the l. of a line of subfoundations which the road cuts across, possibly the Archeia or administrative buildings, there was a portico with a triple colonnade, 170yds (156m) long, recognized as the portico of Philip.

VICINITY

1 **LEONDARION** (7.5mls/12km from the central square of the modern town). The church of the Holy Apostles in this village lying at the N tip of the Taygetus mountains was built in the 10th or 11th century. The Frankish castle which overlooked and controlled a way through to Laconia and Messenia is now just ruined ramparts, towers and churches.

2 **LYCOSURA** (7.5mls/12km, 4.4/7 along an unpaved road; leave on the Kalamata road, turn r. after 2.5mls/4km just after the bridge over the Alpheios in the direction of Issaris, then r. again 1.2mls/3km further on). In a lonely, rustic site, inhabited only by pine trees, are the remains of the temple of Despoina (a small museum, frequently closed). The 4th-century BC temple consisted of a pronaos and a cella most of which was occupied by a pedestal that held the cult statue. You can still see the foundations of a Doric portico in front of which stood three altars dedicated to Demeter, Despoina and the

Great Mother. The bodies of the huge 3rd-century BC cult statues are in the museum: Despoina, Demeter, Artemis and the giant Anytus, by the Messenian sculptor Damophon (the heads of three of the statues are in the National Museum in Athens).

■ Megara

Route map 5.

Athens, 28.1mls (45km) – Eleusis, 13.7mls (22km) – Corinth, 26.2mls (42km).

Megara was one of the most influential cities in ancient Greece, with fearless sailors going out to found rich colonies, such as Megara Hyblaia, Selinus in Sicily, and Byzantium at the mouth of the Bosporus; but now it has only the phantoms of its past glory to hold our attention for a few minutes.

A BUFFER STATE. Megara was occupied by the Cretans in the 18th century BC, then by the Dorians when they invaded Greece. It became independent in the 8th century BC, and from that period it began to found colonies both in the East and the West. Theagenes, a popular leader who became a tyrant from 640 to 600 BC, embellished the town, in particular building the aqueduct, remains of which are still visible. Megara was often in dispute with Athens, especially between 570 and 565 BC, mainly over Salamis. A quarrel with Corinth made Megara decide to accept an Athenian garrison: it was then (459 BC) that the Long Walls connecting the town to its port of Nisaea were built. Ten years later the Megarans with the help of the Peloponnesians drove the Athenians out; but during the Peloponnesian War the area was laid waste every year, and its harbour was blockaded. The town fell into decay in the 5th century AD. Megara is the native town of the elegiac poet, Theognis (c.570–485 BC) and of the sophist, Euclides (450–380 BC), a disciple of Socrates, who was head of the Megaran School, famous in particular for the study of dialectics.

The main square is probably located on the site of the agora. The most interesting ancient remains are those of the aqueduct and the fountain of Theagenes, as described by Pausanias (I, 40, 1); the fountain was in fact built, according to archaeological evidence, towards the beginning of the 5th century BC.

■ Megaspilaion

Route map 5.

Corinth, 69.4mls (111km) – Diakopton, 16.8mls (27km) – Kalavryta, 6.2mls (10km) – Patras, 46.2mls (74km).

This monastery is one of the oldest in Greece, but it is not as interesting as it once was since it was rebuilt after being burned by the Germans in 1943. Nonetheless, a journey to the monastery of the Great Grotto (megaspilaion; see route leaving from Diakopton) is still one of the high spots of visiting the Peloponnese mainly because of the fantastic beauty of the **scenery of the gulf of Corinth that unfolds as you come down the road from Kalavryta to Diakopton (obviously the scenery can be seen better in all its splendour when travelling in that direction, providing the air is really clear).

A NOBLE SHEPHERDESS AND A MIRACULOUS ICON. The monks tell us that a shepherdess with royal blood called Euphrosyne found an image of the Virgin in a cave in the 8th century, and it was immediately credited with miraculous properties. The monastery, which is dedicated to the Assumption, was finished by Constantine Paleologus. As a result of legacies and gifts, and also thanks to the work of the monks who cleared a lot of land, the monastery acquired huge estates in Achaea and Elis. It caught fire on several occasions, but the church, which was rebuilt in 1641 and decorated with frescoes in 1653, was spared.

In the grotto, you can visit the church, dedicated to the Panagia Chrysospiliotissa; with its votive offerings and its relics, including the famous waxwork miraculous icon, it has the inimitable appearance unique to Greek Orthodox sanctuaries. The clumsy 8th- or 9th-century icon representing the Virgin and Child was, according to legend, found in the cave by Euphrosyne and attributed to St Luke the evangelist.

Be sure to visit the lower cavern as well, in which there are huge vats (the biggest, which are almost 200 years old, hold 15,000 okes, or approx. 4,400 gallons/20,000 litres of wine), and the refectory, the bakery, the maze of cells opening beneath the galleries on the facade, and the library, nowadays very impoverished.

EXCURSION TO THE WATERFALL OF THE STYX (6½hrs walk across the mountains to get there; hire a guide at Kalavryta). In 4hrs you reach the village of Solos and from there you can attempt the ascent of the Aroania peaks. From Solos you go up along the r. side of the mountain stream also known as Solos running between high banks formed of black, green and purple schist, apparently issuing forth from some dark, mysterious region. The waterfall of the Styx (Mavronero) is formed by two streams that come down from two firns (fields of granular snow) on top of the twin summits of the mountain. Latin poets refer to the Styx as a murky river, whereas all Greek writers speak of it as a pure, limpid stream.

■ Messene [Ancient]*

Route map 8.

Kalamata, 18.1mls (29km) – Pylos (Navarino), 39.4mls (63km) – Tripolis, 50.6mls (81km).

This is one of the most unusual sites in Greece: in the heart of a harsh, mountainous area, at the foot of Mt Ithome, a small, unsophisticated farming village, Mavromati (the Black Eye), stands almost at the centre of an ancient city, still surrounded by walls that are accepted as being the supreme achievement of the 4th-century BC military fortification.

Modest little houses, fields, orchards and remains from antiquity stand next to one another, as on romantic 19th-century prints, but the civic centre of this ancient capital of Messenia, which is quite well preserved, adds to the evocativeness of this collection of ruins in which life still goes on.

FORWARD INTO THIS LAND WHICH IS OURS TO TAKE. This was the cynical message proclaimed by Polydorus, king of Sparta, inviting his subjects to seize Messenia and share it out among themselves. It resulted in the First Messenian War, around the end of the 8th century BC, which was followed by two others, in 645–628 BC and 459–450 BC, when the Messenians tried to free themselves from Spartan rule.

BACK TO THE LAND OF THEIR FATHERS. After Sparta's defeat at Leuctra in 371 BC, Epaminondas summoned the Messenians back to their country and built a new capital city, Messene, which with Megalopolis, Mantinea and Argos formed a strategic barrier intended to keep Sparta at bay. Messene was beseiged (214 BC) by one of Philip V's generals, Demetrius of Pharos, and he died beneath its wall, then in 202 BC by Nabis who was forced to withdraw by the Achaean general, Philopoemen.

When you reach the foot of Mt Ithome, go through the village of Mavromati; approx. 220yds (200m) before the museum (at present closed to the public; in it are some pieces of sculpture, small bronze objects and a model of the Asclepieion), turn l. onto a track negotiable by car, that goes down to the village cemetery (approx. 330yds/300m from the road); from there a path takes you to the central area of the ancient town in a few minutes.

*Agora – In the SE near the cemetery are the remains of a small, half-buried theatre, barely recognizable. A little further on, a huge terrace bears the ruins of a big temple, perhaps the Hierothysion, where there were statues of all the gods recognized by the Greeks, and a bronze statue of Epaminondas.

The civic centre or agora, still further on, was an enormous esplanade, with a double portico, dating from the end of the Hellenistic period or the beginning of the Roman period surrounding it. There is a drainage gutter, still well preserved, running along the bottom of the portico. In the central area you can make out the foundations of a peripteral temple from the Hellenistic period, dedicated to Asclepius and Hygieia, and in front of its E side (beside a small theatre) there is a wide altar. There are also remains of smaller monuments, in particular several exedrae.

Some large buildings stood along the eastern side of the agora, including a small theatre to the N (on the l.) with its orchestra paved with coloured marble (the tiered seating, divided into three sections by two staircases, has been restored), a monumental entrance with four pilasters leading on to a street, and finally on the r. a building identified as the Synedrion (where the Messenian Assembly met in restricted session; the bench that ran round the base of the three main walls is well preserved); when there was a full assembly, meetings must have been held in the nearby theatre.

Starting from the theatre and going anti-clockwise round the agora, you will observe a small room with an entrance porch with two pillars (at the back, there is the lower part of a pedestal where a huge statue from the Roman period used to stand), then a small staircase. A little further on, a monumental staircase led to a building which may have been the Sebasteion, devoted to the worship of the Roman emperors.

On the next (W) side of the agora there was a chapel of Artemis, a tripartite sanctuary; in the central chamber there was a cult statue (probably a group) on a base which is still there, and around it a semi-circle of statues of priestesses (six of them, dating from the end

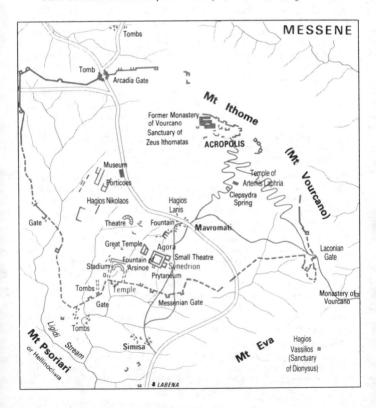

of the Hellenistic period, are in the museum). The two side rooms of the sanctuary contained benches with lions' feet. Beyond the chapel of Artemis several other rooms have also been excavated as far as the SW corner of the agora.

On the S side the remains of a building with an interior court edged by porticoes have been uncovered, which may have been the prytaneum, and those of a heroön. A little below the level of the agora was the stadium which is now in very poor condition.

·ARCADIAN GATE. Go back to the village and continue along the road (to the l.) for about 0.6ml (1km) to the Arcadian (or Megalopolis) gate, one of the best preserved and most representative examples of 4th-century BC Greek fortification, perfected to a far higher level than that of earlier centuries, in line with the progress made in poliorcetics, i.e. the art of taking and defending cities.

A paved way (traces of chariot wheels) led to the gate which consisted of two entrances with a round, open-air court between them contained within a block built with Hellenistic bonding, in which no mortar was used, remarkable for the perfection of its masonry with almost invisible joints, standing on a foundation with two courses of huge blocks. The outer entrance had two big square towers on either side of it, of which only the foundations remain. From the gate the walls went up the slopes of Mt Ithome. The escarpments almost all along its length, which made it impossible to bring battle equipment near, served to supplement the relatively low rampart (15ft/4.57m); it was nonetheless high enough to enable the defending forces armed with the long Dorian lance or launching projectiles to keep the attackers at a distance. There are towers along the rampart, square or in some cases round on one side, built astride the curtain walls to separate them from one another.

From the Arcadian gate go W along the paved road that follows the rampart inside the city (i.e. on the S); after about 0.6ml (1km) you come to the W front of the rampart along which several towers are still standing; from there you have a good view of Mt Ithome to the E.

·MT ITHOME (approx. 2hrs). From the village a steep climb taking about 40 mins brings you to the summit of Mt Ithome, with the old convent of Vourkano, built prior to the 16th century, on top. It stands on the site of the sanctuary of Zeus Ithomatas, a simple altar where human sacrifice was sometimes practised (Aristodemus sacrificed his daughter there). The sanctuary was an asylum for slaves to whom the priest could grant freedom. On the summit of Mt Ithome (the Steep) around the sanctuary there is also the ancient fortress used as a refuge by the Messenians during the second two Messenian Wars. From the summit you can look round at Mt Taygetus, the two Messenian plains, Mt Hellenitsa, Mt Lycaeus, Mt Erymanthus, the coast of Elis and the island of Zante.

Following a path going off on the l. of the way you came, about 330yds (300m) from the edge of the acropolis, you come to the Laconian gate in about 30mins; it was built on a pass separating Mt

Ithome from Mt Eva, which was dedicated to Dionysus and the Evades (Bacchantes). Near the summit you can see the remains of a gate forming part of a perimeter wall.

It is also possible to reach the Laconian gate from the centre of the village along a track that is first paved, then cobbled (for about 0.6ml/1km); from the pass on which the gate stands there is a good view of the Taygetos mountains to the SE. The track carries on down towards the modern monastery of Vourcano, about 0.6ml (1km) away.

VICINITY

ANDROUSSA (11.2mls/18km; to the r. on the road to modern Messini after the village of Eva). This little village, called Druges in the Chronicle of Morea, and Corinth were the joint seats of a Frankish administrative division. You can still see the ruins of a Frankish castle and to the N on the other side of the ravine there is the old Hagios Georgios church. 3.1mls (5km) from Androussa at Elinoklissia there is the lovely 14th-century church of the Zoödochos Pigi, with three apses and a dome supported on ancient columns; remains of mosaics and frescoes.

M Meteora [The] (Meteora)**

Route maps 11 and 12.

Ioannina, 82.5mls (132km) – Kalambaka, 5mls (8km) – Larisa, 56.2mls (90km) – admin. region of Trikkala.

Near Kalambaka in a surrealist mountain setting reminiscent of the fantastic universe of Hieronymus Bosch, the 'meteora monastiria', the monasteries in the air, are among the most outstanding sights in Greece, particularly because of their location, perched on top of high gritstone and conglomerate rocks formed by the erosion of the dried-out sea bedrock; they stand like menhirs of cyclopean stature. 'Seeing them hovering in the air, you are half tempted to believe the legend that God built these natural columns especially for the monks, with the aim of propagating one of the strangest manifestations of eastern asceticism and giving the world the chance of seeing communities of stylites.' (Heuzey).

A NEW THEBAID. The origins of the Meteora go back to the 14th century and the troubled period of wars between the Serbian emperor and the emperor of Byzantium. Brigandry led to the development of little hermitages in inaccessible retreats that were used as refuges. The oldest of these was that of the Panagia Doupiani, whose superiors held the title of regional Superiors of the Ascetics of Stagoi. One of them, Kyr Nilos, in 1367 founded four other communities on nearby rocks. Between 1356 and 1372 the coenobite Athanasius founded the

Meteoron with nine brethren, bound by a very strict rule. In 1388 his disciple, the hermit King Joasaph, son of King Symeon Ourosh of Serbia, enlarged the monastery. In the 16th century the communities quarrelled bitterly over the arable plots of land. The monasteries went into decline, falling in number from 24 to 4. Most of them are uninhabitated. Only a few very old monks still live in the monasteries of the Great Meteoron, Varlaam, Hagia Trias, and Hagios Stephanos.

Open: the monasteries are all so similar that it is not necessary to visit more than two or three (perhaps Hagios Stephanos, Varlaam and Meteoron), but it is interesting to drive round the whole group. Suitable clothing: the wearing of shorts is not permitted, women should wear long sleeves, and a skirt below the knees, not trousers. There are first-class roads from Kalambaka enabling you to reach the monasteries easily; the return journey including visits to the three main monasteries is about 13mls (21km).

The Meteora are built on top of sheer rocks, with no continuous paths leading up to them. In former times hinged ladders 65–130ft (20–40m) long were used which could be withdrawn in emergencies.

The other means of access which is certainly original was a load-carrying net, but that is now used only to take provisions up. Stairs have been installed for all the monasteries.

The monasteries are generally closed in the middle of the day, and one day a week in rotation.

As you leave Kalambaka by the Ioannina road, take the road on the r. before the Xenia Hotel. On the r. there is Kastraki Hill, the ancient acropolis of Aeginion, which overlooks Kalambaka.

1.6mls (2.5km): On the l. below a rock called the column of Doupiani, a chapel probably founded in the 12th century, which was the church of the first hermitage of Stagoi. The present chapel is pre-16th century. On top of the column there are the remains of two monasteries (Pantokrator and Doupiani), but they are very hard to reach.

1.8mls (3km): On the l. the monastery of Hagios Nikolaos Anapausas, founded c.1388 and enlarged in 1628, is decorated with frescoes by the monk Theophanes, painted in 1527 (*Last Judgement; Paradise*). A little further on, still on the l., the ruins of the monastery of Hagia Moni, founded in 1315, hard to reach.

2.2mls (3.5km): You pass below the monastery of Hagia Rossanou, founded as a hermitage in 1388 and changed into a convent in 1639.

3.7mls (6km): 1.6mls (2.5km) off the road on the r., the monastery of Hagia Trias, founded in 1438 (a stair goes up through a tunnel; 1476 church with a 1684 narthex; pretty garden), and 1.8mls (3km) from the main road the monastery of Hagios Stephanos; near Hagia Trias a new road forks off allowing you to go back down towards (approx. 5mls/8km) Kalambaka on another face of the mountain.

Hagios Stephanos (*open: 08.00–12.00 and 15.00–18.00; closed Mon.*), originally a hermitage, was founded in 1312 and turned into a monastery by the Emperor Andronicus III Paleologus (1328–41) about 20 years later. In it you can visit the Hagios Charalambos church, with a carved iconostasis, the Hagios Stephanos chapel, built in 1798 (frescoes), and the refectory.

4mls (6.5km): 220yds (200m) to the l. the monastery of Varlaam (*open: 09.00–13.30 and 15.30–18.00*) was founded in 1517 based on the former hermitage of a 14th-century anchorite called Varlaam.

The main areas of interest here are All Saints' Church (frescoes painted by Frangos Castellanos and Georgios of Thebes in 1565 in the narthex, restored in 1870), the refectory (now a museum), the library, the remarkable guests' room, the fortified garden, and the winch which the monks used to use.

4.7mls (7.5km): end of the road usable by cars, near the Meteoron, or the Great Meteoron (*open: 09.00–13.30 and 16.00–17.00; closed*

Tues.), built by Athanasius and Joasaph at a height of 1,752ft (534m).

In the beautiful *church of the Metamorphosis (Transfiguration) you can see late 15th-century frescoes: the *Nativity*, the *Transfiguration*, the *Crucifixion*, and the *Resurrection*. In the apse (the original chapel), built in 1387–88 by Joasaph, there is a portrait of the founder Athanasius in the garb of a western monk. A series of icons and devotional objects from the 14th century has recently been unearthed by the Yugoslav Byzantinist, Gojko Subotic, who has also put forward new dating (14th century) for the frescoes in the nave. The domed refectory dates from 1557 and the chapel of the Prodomos (St John the Baptist) and Hagios Constantinos from the 17th century. N of the Great Meteoron, approx. 30mins walk away, the ruined monastery of Hypapanti still has some remains of frescoes and of its iconostasis.

■ Methoni

Route maps 8 and 9.

Kalamata, 36.2mls (58km) – Pylos (Navarino), 6.2mls (10km) – Pyrgos, 80.6mls (129km).

This little town whose origins go back to ancient times stands on a promontory which has on its tip a Venetian fortress which is truly impressive both for its state of preservation and its size. There is a delightful harbour and a beautiful, big beach.

A VENETIAN LOCK ON THE ENTRANCE TO THE ADRIATIC. We can pass rapidly over the Greek past of this ancient Messenian city, known as Methone or Mothone, which the Spartans granted to the Nauplians, and concentrate on its history from the Middle Ages on. Its position at the entrance to the Ionian Sea, i.e. the Adriatic, did not pass unnoticed by the Venetians.

The doge Domenico Micheli first had the Byzantine fortress that stood there in 1125 razed to the ground, and then a Venetian fleet took possession in 1206. From that time the town was known as Modon. In 1500 Bajazet II surrounded the 7,000 men defending the fortress with an army said to number 100,000 men, with 500 siege cannons. The fortress capitulated on 9 August 1500. The Knights of St John tried in 1531, and Don Juan of Austria in 1572, to recapture it, but in vain. Morosini gained control of it on 10 July 1686, and the Venetians managed to hold it until 1715.

The fortress is cut off from the town by a curved moat across the promontory. The wall around the moat consisted of a protected walkway and an open slope which is no longer there. The present bridge giving access to the fortress was built in 1828 by French soldiers under the command of Marshal Maison.

Most of the moat dates from the 15th century as do the false openings and the central part of the wall and the embankment. The rampart on this side runs between the 15th-century Bembo bastion on the r.

and the 1714 Loredan bastion on the l.; these were intended for artillery.

After passing through the first gate you turn l. and go through a second gate, and then a third, described on Venetian plans as Porta di Terra Firma, before coming inside the fortress. Then follow the E rampart (on the l.), fortified with towers and firing emplacements for guns and cannons, installed by the Turks. One of these towers has on its outer face the Lion of St Mark between two blazons of the Foscarini family, above the Michieli escutcheon.

The firing step ends by a square tower in a very dilapidated condition, which may date back to Roman times or the early Byzantine period. At the tip of the promontory there is a high tower near the sea gate, rebuilt by the Turks with old masonry, including a block with the Lion of St Mark and the blazon of the Foscolo carved on it. A bridge used to connect this entrance to the Bourzi tower, standing isolated on a rock, which was built by the Turks in the 16th century.

The W rampart, which runs along a cliff top, is fortified with five towers. It must have been part of the first programme of fortifications undertaken by the Venetians. After that you come to a transverse wall round a sort of redoubt. The gate leads into the central court, and there are four other similar structures reinforcing this wall put up by the Turks in the early 16th century. Next visit the huge Bembo bastion, built in 1480 but altered to some extent by the Turks. It overlooks another older bastion which it is possible to visit by going along the passage which comes out on the r. after the first gate through the N rampart. From the bastion, observe the redoubt built at one end of the wall. The Lion of St Mark carved on its N side indicates that it also was built by the Venetians.

1.2mls (2km) away along the Pylos road, on the l., there is the early Christian cemetery of St Onuphre in a grotto-shaped depression; it was used as a hermitage in the Byzantine era.

Off Methoni the little islands of Sapientza and Schiza will delight keen fishermen (but be aware of dangerous currents).

■ Metsovo

Route map 11.

Ioannina, 37.5mls (60km) – Kalambaka (Meteors), 43.7mls (70km) – Larisa, 95mls (152km).

This is a place where you can set out in search of the past. It is a large village, and tourism has started to undermine its authenticity; it is in a superb site on the side of a mountain in the heart of the well-wooded Pindos range. But its narrow, winding streets, rich in the smells and sounds of a bygone era, with a diminishing number of old, typically Balkan wooden houses, may soon cease to be redolent of the past which you hope to find. If you are lucky, you may be there on a day when a country wedding is taking place, when you can admire the proud bearing of the mountain-dwellers who are descended from the klephts, brigands with a keen sense of honour who were the heart and soul of Greek resistance to all repressive regimes.

A recently installed chair-lift makes snow skiing possible.

A TOWN OF REFUGE. When the cruel regime of Ali Pasha was in force in Ioannina, rich Christian families (the Tositsas and the Averoffs) sought refuge in Metsovo, and they were responsible for building the fine houses found in the village. The village itself was treated leniently by the Turks in return for the fact that a vizier in disgrace with his sultan had been granted asylum here a few years previously. Thus Metsovo was able to enjoy the peace and relative independence which led to its prosperity.

Visit the church of Hagios Dimitrios belonging to the monastery of Hagios Nikolaos, with its Byzantine frescoes dating from 1702, the little monastery of the Panagia below the village near the ravine, and especially the Tositsa house which has been turned into a museum, with a reconstitution of a traditional interior of the Pindus region.

■ Milos [Island of] (Melos)*

62sq. mls (161km²) – Pop: 4,500.

This island, where the famous Venus de Milo was found, lying 44 nautical miles from Piraeus, is one of the most picturesque in the Cyclades archipelago, but also one of the least visited. The whole island is a volcanic mass, and the roadstead, which is one of the finest and safest in the Aegean, is probably an old crater, breached on one side. The island had a period of relative prosperity in the 3rd and 2nd centuries BC, probably thanks to trade in obsidian; now it keeps neighbouring islands supplied in fruit.

Most people stay in Adamas, a typically Mediterranean little port (fine beach); boats from Piraeus call in there, and the churches of Hagia Triada and the Dormition of the Virgin are worth visiting (in the latter, note the fine icon of the beheading of St John the Baptist, c.1639, the work of the priest, Emmanuel Scordili).

From Adamas you can travel into the island to (2.5mls/4km) Milos or Plaka, the island's main town (a small archaeological museum), partly built on the site of ancient Melos. The new town is not particularly interesting, so go straight up to the site of the ancient theatre, making for Mt Prophitis Ilias, with a little chapel standing on top of it overlooking ancient Melos (remains of ancient walls).

THEY SURRENDERED UNCONDITIONALLY TO THE ATHENIANS. Ancient Melos extended from Mt Prophitis Ilias to the sea. The town was founded c.700 BC, taking over from Phylacopi (below), after a hiatus of nearly four centuries. Melos did not take part in the Persian Wars except for the Battle of Salamis (480 BC) to which just two vessels were sent, and the Battle of Plataea (479 BC). In the wars between Athens and Sparta, the city wanted to remain neutral, which displeased the

Athenians, who besieged it in 416 BC. The outcome was tragic according to Thucydides, 'the inhabitants surrendered unconditionally to the Athenians. They killed all men old enough to bear arms, and sold the women and children into slavery'. The city was repopulated with Athenian settlers, but no longer played an important role and was abandoned in the 5th century AD.

Open: weekdays, 08.30–12.30 (summer). 09.00–13.30 (winter), and 16.00–18.00; Sun. 09.00–15.00 (summer) and 10.00–16.30 (winter); charge for admission into the catacombs.

Part of the marble tiered seating of the theatre from the Roman period has survived, and nearby are the remains of other buildings, including ramparts, temples, etc. From the theatre go to the catacombs, the work of the first Christian communities on the island, dating from the 2nd century AD and later. The main entrance is low and narrow (take torches).

The site of Phylacopi (a 30-min walk from Voudia, 8.1mls/13km from Adamas), where the British School uncovered the remains of the first city to flourish on the island, is not particularly interesting now that the dig has finished.

The earliest town goes back to the Early Minoan period (2600–2000 BC approx.); this trading port was used by Phoenician sailors who were exporting obsidian, which was used for knife blades, arrow points, etc. The second town dates from the Middle Minoan period (2000–1700 BC approx.) and the Late Minoan I and II periods (1600–1500 BC), and was destroyed by fire. The third town (1500–1100 BC), mainly from the Mycenaean period, was the zenith of Cycladic civilization on Milos.

You can hire a caïque to take you to the pleasant beaches on the SW coast: Emborio, Rivari, Hagios Dimitrios, Moudrakia, Chivadolimni.

VICINITY

ISLANDS OF KIMOLOS AND ANTIMILOS (get there by the Piraeus or Santorini lines). Kimolos (20.5sq. mls/53km^2; 8½ hrs from Piraeus), lying on the other side of the fairway overlooked by the Phylacopi acropolis, is a little island with a population of about 1,000, on which you can see the ruins of a medieval fortress at Paleokastro. In the village of Kimolos there is a 17th-century church, and in Adamanta church there is a fine iconostasis made of carved and gilded wood. W of Kimolos are the volcanic islets of the Glaronissia (sea cave), and to its E the islet of Poliegos; Antimilos, still further W, is uninhabited.

■ Missolonghi

Route map 10.

Agrinion, 21.8mls (35km) – Delphi, 109.4mls (175km) – Patras, 30mls (48km) – Pop: 6,000.

One of the symbols of the Greeks' spirit of resistance, Missolonghi is the port where Lord Byron died, who had championed Greek independence, and where one of the cruellest tragedies of the War of Independence occurred.

The Greek rebels, who were besieged by the Turks in 1822, 1825 and 1826, withstood the attack of an enemy better armed and more numerous than themselves. When they had completely run out of supplies they decided to make a mass break-out on 12 April 1826 at night. A mere 1,800 men succeeded in breaking their way through the Turkish lines and reaching the mountains while Christos Kapsalis set fire to the powder-magazine which exploded, finally destroying the heroic city.

To the r. of the main gate of the Venetian ramparts, which was rebuilt by King Otto, there is a monument commemorating the various sieges of the city, and the burial of the heroes of the independence, and a monument to Lord Byron. Those stirred by the Romantic period will want to see the museum (in the town hall, Botsaris Square) which is devoted to the War of Independence. On the W side of the town a garden of remembrance is on the site of the house where Byron died.

VICINITY

1 CALYDON (6.2mls/10km along the Andirrhion road). This town, with a name than recalls Meleager's feat when he killed the Calydonian boar hereabouts, is now little more than a memory in spite of excavations carried out on the site by Danish archaeologists.

On the l. of the turning for Andirrhion are the remains of a sanctuary of Artemis Laphria. The most recent temple, now reduced to just its foundations, dates from the 4th century BC, but it had replaced a 6th-century BC (570) temple which had itself replaced another 7th-century (620) BC temple. The temple of Apollo, dedicated in the 6th century, was on a nearby terrace.

2 PLEURON (6.2mls/10km; follow the Arta road, turn r. after 3.1mls/5km). Go through a village, then follow the road at the foot of the mountain along a canal; start your climb (approx. 45 mins) from a hamlet near the canal. In the lower town there are the remains of a little theatre that abuts on to the rampart and a tower; the agora, now an esplanade strewn with ruins, is near the E wall; the acropolis with square towers stands on a mound. The kastro Kyra Irini, a 50-min walk away to the N, is the site of New Pleuron (a perimeter wall 1.2mls/2km long with 31 towers, built of Hellenic masonry).

Mistra***

Route map 6.

Kalamata, 40.6mls (65km) – Sparta, 3.1mls (5km) – Tripolis, 42.5mls (68km) – admin. region of Laconia.

A ghost town that was the capital of Byzantine, Turkish and Venetian Morea, Mistra is a striking evocation of a Byzantine city of the 14th and 15th centuries, in which the grace of the churches (often decorated with fine paintings) is in sharp contrast with the ruggedness of the houses and palaces ranged in tiers on a steep slope, and even sharper contrast with the harshness of the medieval fortifications – the oldest of these were built by the Franks – which so well reflect the political uncertainty experienced by Greece at the end of the Middle Ages. You will find that this high hill with its monasteries and churches, its ghostly houses, and winding roads which smell so deliciously of fig trees will remain as one of your clearest impressions of travelling in Greece.

A FICKLE MISTRESS. In 1249, after Guillaume de Villehardouin had captured Monemvasia, looking for a favourable place to build a fortress that would contain the 'Sclavonians' of the Taygetus, he decided on a height known as Mezithra or Myzithra (cheese) by the Greeks. On its summit he built an impregnable fortress; the Franks changed its name to Mistra, which is supposed to have meant 'Mistress' in French patois. But the castle did not stay in French hands for long. After being taken prisoner by Michael Paleologus in 1259, Guillaume gave it along with Monemvasia and Maina, to ransom himself (1263). The Byzantines were finally beaten in 1265. When the victor, Guillaume, wanted to spend the winter in Lacedemonia, he found the town abandoned; its inhabitants had settled on the hill below Mistra, under the protection of the fortress that had been ceded to the Emperor.

THE WONDER OF THE MOREA. After 50 years of fighting against the Frankish barons, the Byzantines reconquered most of the Morea. From 1349 these lands formed a dependent territory governed by the sons or the brothers of the emperor, who held the personal title of Despot. In the 15th century the famous philosopher Gemistus Plethon lived in Mistra and attracted many men of letters to it. The silk industry was flourishing. The town went to the Turks in 1460, then to the Venetians from 1687 to 1715; at that time it had a population of 42,000, and was still the wonder of the Morea. In its second period of Turkish rule it went into decline; the old town was set on fire in 1770 by the Albanians at the time of the Maina rebellion, and from then on people gradually moved away.

ROUTE TO FOLLOW. It will take approx. 3–3½ hrs to see the whole town, and another hr for the castle; by way of reward you will be able to gaze at a panorama embracing the town at your feet and at Mt Taygetus which is perhaps the most beautiful mountain in Greece. In summer, make an early start on your tour round this sleeping city, as otherwise the heat will spoil your enjoyment of it. Make your visit with the help of the plan which is marked with arrows.

Open: weekdays, 08.00–17.00 (winter, 16.00); Sun., 09.00–17.00 (winter, 16.30); from 10.00 for the monastery of Peribleptos; entrance fee.

After going through the vaulted passageway of the main entrance, follow the path l. towards the chapel of St Christopher. You pass the Marmara fountain on your l.

CHAPEL OF ST GEORGE – This is one of the most elegant examples of the little funerary chapels built by the aristocratic families of Mistra.

 MONASTERY OF THE PERIBLEPTOS – This monastery was built around the middle of the 14th century, and the church, built against a rockface and disguised by prolific vegetation, is the main survivor; the beauty of its position, its architectural lines and its **frescoes are sure to delight you. Note also the strong crenellated tower, a reminder of Italian architecture, that rises above the refectory.

The paintings which date from the reign of Manuel Cantacuzene (1340–80) are the finest you will see in Mistra, with their rich tones, elegant draughtsmanship and skilfully rhythmic composition. Above the entrance door, note the excellent composition of 'The Dormition', the best of a series of scenes devoted to the life of the Virgin that run almost all round the church.

To the l. of the door, in the prothesis, a little apsidal chapel to the l. of the central apse, there is a picture of the Divine Liturgy, i.e. the communion procession celebrated by Christ and angels who look as if they are running quite quickly. In the central sanctuary the Virgin is depicted on the half dome of the niche, the Ascension on the vault, and the Communion, the Sacrifice of Issac and the Three Hebrews in the Fiery Furnace on the side walls.

In the diaconicon (sacristy, on the l.), we see Christ sleeping, in the conch, St Peter's Denial (l. vault) and the Ascent to Calvary and the Crucifixion (r. vault). In the centre of the calotte dome, a large Christ in majesty (Pantocrator) sits enthroned; below are the twelve apostles and the Virgin, then the prophets. In the vaulting framing the bay containing the dome, there are scenes from the life of Christ; Nativity, Baptism, Transfiguration, the Last Supper, the Entrance into Jerusalem, Pentecost, and the Doubt of St Thomas. On the wall facing the sanctuary there is a painting depicting the two donors holding a model of the church, and above them a scene showing the Descent into Hell.

 *CONVENT OF THE PANTANASSA – Notice, as you pass, the facade of the House of Frangopoulos, 15th-century, before coming to the convent where a few nuns are in attendance who are unlikely to disturb you as long as you behave correctly. This monastery was dedicated to the queen of the world (Pantanassa) in 1428 by John Frangopoulos, a minister of the despot Constantine Dragases (1443–48).

The outside of the church is interesting with its bell tower showing Gothic influences, and its apse. It is built on the same plan as the Brontochion, but with slenderer proportions. The gallery running along the E side affords delightful views across the plain of Sparta.

Inside the building the lower paintings are more recent than the date of construction of the church, except for the very fine portrait of

MISTRA

0   50m

Episcopal Palace

Cathedral (Museum)

Entrance

Vaulted passage

Saint Theodor

1.226

Evanghelistria

400 Church

Afendiko Church

1.286

400

Refectory

Monastery of the Brontochion

1.312

Gothic Arcade

Monemvasia Gate

1.472

Nauplia Gate

Palace of the Despot (Grand Palace)

Mosque

St Nicholas

Turkish Baths

1.536

Small Palace

UPPER TOWN

St Sophia

1.965

Secondary entrance

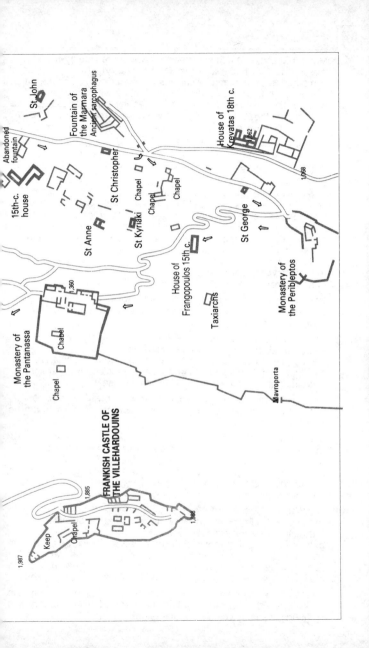

FRANKISH CASTLE OF
THE VILLEHARDOUINS

Keep

Chapel

1,987

1,885

1,886

Monastery of
the Pantanassa

Chapel

Chapel

1,360

Chapel

House of
Frangopoulos 15th c.

Taxiarchs

Monastery of
the Peribleptos

Mavroporta

St George

Chapel

Chapel

Chapel

St Kyriaki

St Anne

St Christopher

15th-c.
house

Abandoned
fountain

Fountain of
the Marmara

Ancient sarcophagus

St John

House of
Krevatas 18th c.

1,062

1,068

Manuel Chatzikis (1445) in the narthex. Go up into the tribune to look closely at the fine paintings (15th century). Note the happy combination of architectural line, painted ornament and statue. Other paintings worth singling out are *Palm Sunday*, with a host of children playing, the *Annunciation*, the *Presentation at the Temple*, *Lazarus Rising from the Dead*, *the Transfiguration*, and the *Translators of the Septuagint*. In the aisles, note the *Acathist Hymn*.

MONEMVASIA GATE – This gate opened into the second perimeter wall, which dates from the 13th century and leads into the upper town where the houses of the aristocracy crowded round the despot's palace.

DESPOT'S PALACE – This is now a huge ruin, fantastic yet forbidding in appearance, with its great rubble-stone walls with gaping holes where the windows were. It position on the edge of a terrace overlooking the Euratos valley is really outstanding, but that nowadays is the palace's only point of interest; it was probably begun by Guillaume de Villehardouin (the main building has tierce-point windows, r. from the main square) and enlarged by Manuel Cantacuzene (1340–80; wing to l. of previous building) and by the Paleologi (1338–1460; wing at right-angles).

Behind the palace the Nauplia gate with a tower on either side of it is one of the most impressive works of military architecture in the lower town.

ST SOPHIA CHURCH – Perhaps built for use as a burial place for the first despot of Mistra, Manuel Cantacuzene, in 1350, this church (which has been restored) still has some wall paintings, particularly in two small chapels (the first opens off to the l. of the entrance portico, the second on the r. of the triple apse inside the naos).

The paintings that have been preserved show *Christ in Majesty* (Pantocrator) in the conch of the apse, and the *Ascension* on the sanctuary vault.

In the first chapel you will see the *Annunciation*, the *Passion of Christ*, the *Dormition of the Virgin* and the *Resurrection* on the walls, while on the semi-circular dome there is *Christ Surrounded by the Heavenly Powers*. In the chapel, frescoes depicting the Virgin at prayer, the figure of Christ and the Nativity were discovered under a coat of whitewash.

THE FRANKISH CASTLE – After a steep climb taking 30 mins you come to this impressive Frankish fortress, built by Guillaume de Villehardouin, but restored by the despots of Mistra and the Turks. The entrance gate is under a high tower; both gate and tower were built by the Byzantines. The outer perimeter wall ends in a platform installed above a cistern and a circular bastion. The redoubt is overlooked by a big keep, now almost a ruin, which the Franks put up over a cistern.

CHURCH OF ST NICHOLAS – This spacious building dates from the Turkish period (17th century); it is decorated with 18th-century wall paintings in a fairly coarse, popular idiom.

CHURCH OF THE EVANGHELISTRIA – After going back through the Monemvasia gate you come to this beautiful late 14th-century church which still has some of its original frescoes.

CHURCH OF THE SAINTS THEODORE – This was built before 1296 to the same plan as the basilica at Daphni, but on a smaller scale, and has in it very faded mural paintings; note the *Angel of the Annunciation*, to the l. of the entrance into the sanctuary. In the chapel on the l., the Emperor Manuel Paleologus is shown kneeling before the Theotokos. In the chapel on the r. there are scenes from the life of the Virgin.

'MONASTERY OF THE BRONTOCHION – The church belonging to the monastery, known as Afendiko or Odhigitria, was put up shortly before 1311. Inside the church one is struck by the classical proportions, the purity of architectural line, the carved decoration, and above all the mural paintings.

Narthex – on the r., *Miracles of Christ*; chapels at r. end of the narthex: portraits of Theodorus I Paleologus as a despot and a monk, group of saints; l. end: rooms with chrysobuls painted on their walls; in the vaulting, an angel bearing a medallion of Christ; l. side of the church: chapel with tombs. Fresco of the *Dormition of the Virgin*, recently discovered. In the central nave, the nuns of the Pantanassa have discovered several frescoes.

'METROPOLITAN CHURCH – Inscriptions tell us that this cathedral church dedicated to St Demetrius was built in 1309 by the Metropolitan Nicephorus Moschopoulos, but it seems in fact to have been built by the end of the 12th or the early 13th century. It originally followed the plan of a basilica, but in the 15th century another floor was added. This resulted in partial damage to the paintings in the main nave. A lot of pieces of carved marble dating from the 9th–11th century have been incorporated into the masonry.

The earliest and most interesting paintings are in the aisles: to the N (l. aisle), *Torment and Burial of St Demetrius*, who suffered from dropsy and leprosy; to the S (r. aisle), near the sanctuary, the *Adolescence of the Virgin*, *Christ's Miracles in Galilee*, etc.; these paintings are imbued with a sober, vigorous realism that can be dated to the 14th century. In the narthex there is the *Last Judgement* (early 14th century). While there you can also visit a small museum (same opening times as the site, but closed Tues.): fragments of decoration that have been gathered among the ruins, fragments of a lintel with the monogram and coat of arms of Isabelle de Lusignan, frescoes, icons, vases, inscriptions, etc. In the courtyard there is a marble sarcophagus from the Roman period, decorated with sphinxes, griffins and a Dionysiac scene.

As you make your way back towards Marmara gate, you pass the church of St John (15th-century paintings including a *Crucifixion*) and the church of St Christopher, which is decorated with 15th-century frescoes.

■ Molyvdoskepastos

Route map 15.

Ioannina, 49.4mls (79km) – Konitsa, 16.8mls (27km).

3.1mls (5km) beyond Melissopetra and 13.7mls (22km) from Konitsa by the Bridge of Mertzani road which crosses the Sarandapotamos, a river which at this point serves as the frontier between Greece and Albania, a path going off on the l. leads to (3.1mls/5km) Molyvdoskepastos, a village which is likewise on the Greek-Albanian frontier (ask in Konitsa whether it is possible to get there).

In this village which at one time was the seat of the archbishopric of Pogoniani is the monastery of the Dormition of the Virgin, now deconsecrated, believed to have been founded in the 7th century by the Emperor Constantine IV (668–685). Its church seems to date from the late 13th or early 14th century, a period at which the archbishopric of Pogoniani experienced revived prosperity. The catholicon, which is very dark, was decorated with frescoes of which a few fragments (16th century) have survived; the narthex also dates from the 16th century.

In the village you can also see the church of Hagios Dimitrios, from the 11th century, which is quite dilapidated, and, even better, Hagii Apostoli church, the former cathedral of Pogoniani thought to have been built in the 13th or 14th century (inside, well-preserved 18th-century frescoes).

■ Monemvasia*

Route map 6.

Ghythion, 59.4mls (95km) – Sparta, 60.6mls (97km).

Although as you might not think it, the name of this village where the poet Yannis Ritsos was born, which lies in a picturesque setting on a promontory that has been turned into a little island, could be the title of a drinking song. The Duke of Clarence, if he could still speak, might have a lot to say about it, and would tell you that this place-name was associated in a corrupted form with one of the most famous wines of the Middle Ages – malmsey. But don't go there today to drink with your friends, for the famous vineyards have disappeared; go instead to explore one of the least well known yet most delightful corners of Greece.

FROM MINOS TO THE GRAND TURK. The former peninsula on which the village lies used to be called Minoa, a name which seems to indicate that it was once a naval station of the Minoans. After the Slav invasion it was used as a refuge by the Greeks of Laconia and became a fortress and a port. In 1147 Monemvasia repelled an attack by the Normans from Sicily, but in 1249 Guillaume de Villehardouin wore it down by famine after a three-year siege; he had to relinquish it to the Emperor of Byzantium to ransom himself in 1263. It then passed into the hands of the Pope (1460–64), the Venetians (1464–1540 and 1690–1715) and the Turks, until 1823.

The town is guarded by a rampart running from the bottom of the promontory to the shore. This rampart is thought to have been built by the Turks in the 16th century, probably following the line of the Byzantine walls.

In the lower town the main places of interest are the cathedral (13th century; portal rebuilt in the 17th century), the former church of Hagios Pavlos (St. Paul) opposite (10th century, altered by the Turks, deconsecrated), Hagios Stephanos of Crete (16th century) in a mixture of Italian and Byzantine styles (note the icon of Christ Elkomenos, meaning literally 'dragged on the Cross'), Hagia Anna, a 14th-century basilica restored by the Venetians in 1697, and many old houses. From the upper part of the town a path leads to the citadel which was built on the summit of the promontory, overlooking the town. There be sure to see the *church of Hagia Sophia, founded by Andronicus II (1287–1328) and based on the plan of the Daphni basilica (frescoes depicting the martyr saints); the narthex is a Venetian addition.

VICINITY

NEAPOLIS (38mls/61km). This little village almost on the SE tip of the Peloponnese is on the site of ancient Boae. A small archaeological collection is on show in the town hall.

Off the coast, the island of Elafonissos (9sq. mls/23km^2 – Pop. 500 approx.) closes the side of the gulf of Neapolis across from Cythera.

Monodendri*

Route map 15.

Ioannina, 30mls (48km) – Konitsa, 42.5mls (68km).

You climb the western face of the Pindus chain along a picturesque little mountain road to reach this village which has lost none of its authenticity; the houses are covered with grey stones. From the village square, go towards Vicos. The road comes to an end at the entrance to a monastery. Go across the courtyard to a platform, and from there you will have a magnificent view over the gorges of the Vicos.

Mycenae (Mykinai)***

Route map 6.

Argos, 8.1mls (13km) – Athens, 56.2mls (90km) – Corinth 26.8mls (43km) – Nauplia, 15.6mls (25km) – admin. region of Argolis.

This is one of the few sites in the world where the least well-informed visitor will still feel a sense of recognition, where things and especially people will trigger a flood of far-off memories. You need look no further, you are at the nerve-centre of heroic Greece, from which so many dramatists have drawn their inspiration. The focal point of this great epic is there before you in the shape of a rugged hill on which the Acropolis stood, haunted by sinister memories of the family of the Atreids 'whose crimes have provided the subject matter for two thousand years of tragedy' (E. About). As well as the memories attached to Agamemnon, the head of the Achaean coalition that fought Troy, to his wife Clytemnestra who had him murdered by her lover, Aegisthus, and to the crime perpetrated by Orestes against his own mother to avenge his honour, there are several monuments of exceptional interest which have stood there for three thousand years and are among the greatest architectural or achaeological wonders of the world: the Lion Gate, the Treasury of Atreus, and the Cyclopean perimeter wall.

BEFORE THE ACHAEAN INVASION. As is the case with most of the other cities of heroic Greece, the most distant past of Mycenae is bathed in an aura of magic and myth. According to tradition, the Pelasgi, regarded as the aboriginal inhabitants of the area, were first subdued by Danaus, believed to have come from Egypt. Danaus' kingdom was shared out among his descendants: Acrisius was established in Argos, his brother Proetus founded Tiryns with the help of the Cyclopes, while Perseus, Acrisius' grandson who had been cast into the sea, returned home after far-flung travels through Asia, and founded Mycenae. The Perseid dynasty disappeared when the Achaeans under the Pelopids came from Elis and settled in the Peloponnese. Though it is not possible to throw light on all these legendary details, archaeological research has confirmed that the hill on which the Acropolis stands was occupied from the early Bronze Age, c.3000–2800 BC.

THE CITY THAT HAS GIVEN ITS NAME TO CIVILIZATION. Archaeological evidence places the arrival of the Achaeans at about 2000 BC, the start of the middle Bronze Age which lasted until 1600 BC. From that period Mycenae became the capital of a powerful kingdom whose princes were related to other rulers in Phthiotis and Laconia, and in giving its name to the civilization that flourished over a good part of mainland Greece in the 2nd millennium BC, archaeologists were recognizing its primacy.

'POLYCHRYSOS' MYCENAE. As the large number of precious objects found in the shaft tombs of the two royal grave circles indicates, Mycenae must have been a very prosperous city as early as the end of the middle Bronze Age (approx. 1600 BC), justifying Homer's use to describe it of the epithet *polychrysos* (rich in gold). There were close links with Crete, and Cretan influence is evident in the finds made in the tombs. Shortly after the middle of the 14th century BC, the citadel was enlarged and a protective wall of cyclopean masonry was built round it. Mycenae was the most powerful of the Achaean

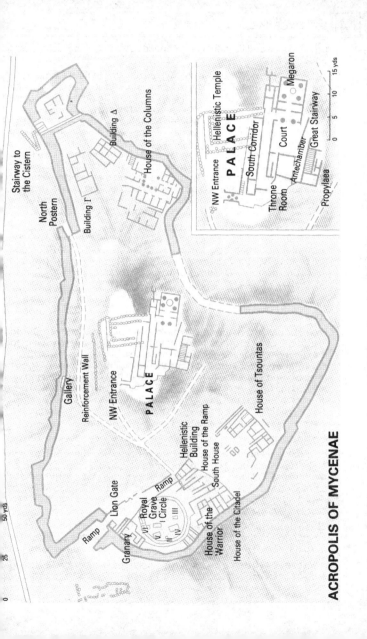

ACROPOLIS OF MYCENAE

Stairway to
the Cistern

North
Postern

Building Γ

Building Δ

House of the Columns

Gallery

Reinforcement Wall

NW Entrance

PALACE

House of Tsountas

Lion Gate

Ramp

Hellenistic Building

House of the Ramp

South House

House of the Warrior

House of the Citadel

Ramp

Granary

Royal Grave Circle

VI V I
II III
IV

0   25   50 yds

PALACE

NW Entrance

Hellenistic Temple

South Corridor

Throne Room

Court

Megaron

Antechamber

Great Stairway

Propylaea

0   5   10   15 yds

principalities and its influence extended as far as Syria, Palestine and Egypt.

THE HOMERIC CITY. The power of Mycenae seems to have increased in the 13th century BC. King Agamemnon of Mycenae was the undisputed leader of the Achaean coalition against Troy. Homer tells us that he reigned over Argolis and many islands. During Agamemnon's absence and after his return crimes and disorders brought blood on the house of the Atreids. Aegisthus and Clytemnestra murdered Agamemnon. Orestes killed his mother and had to leave the kingdom of his father. At about this period the lower town was set on fire, probably during a civil war or dynastic crisis, for the royal town, protected by its strong cyclopean walls seems to have suffered no damage during these troubles. The Dorian invasion signalled the end for the kingdom of Mycenae, around the end of the 12th century BC, and the citadel and town were set on fire.

In the period covered by recorded history, Mycenae and its neighbour Tiryns were just villages. When Mycenae opposed the suzerainty of Argos, the Argives destroyed the town c.468 BC. In the 3rd century BC, the Argives founded a small fortified town there, and in the 2nd century AD Pausanias saw only the ruins of it.

Open: 08.00–18.00 weekdays; 10.00–18.00 Sun. and public holidays; entrance fee.

YOUR ROUTE

From the car park at the end of the road bringing you to Mycenae, go first to the acropolis (see plan), then back through the Lion Gate to the second royal grave circle and the tomb of Clytemnestra. Go back down the road by which you reached the acropolis, observing the ruins of various houses in the lower town on the l., before coming on the r. to the treasury of Atreus, 550yds (500m) from the car park. Then go back up to the car park. This takes in the main areas of interest. You will find a flashlight very useful for visiting the underground cistern in the acropolis and the Treasury of Atreus.

THE ACROPOLIS

 ˙˙LION GATE – This famous gate opens between two powerful bastions at the top of a ramp, marking the entrance into the bloody palace of the Atreids. The lintel is formed by a huge single slab of stone and in its relieving triangle you can see a carved emblem, Cretan in origin, depicting two animals confronting one another on either side of a sacred pillar that stands on an altar.

The gate opening, which widens at the bottom, is framed by four monoliths. On the threshold of the gate, note a square cavity which must have been used to secure the two sides of the gate in position.

˙CYCLOPEAN PERIMETER WALLS – This gate goes through a strong rampart, varying in thickness from 10–26ft (3–8m), built from 1350–1330 BC. It is in fact possible to distinguish three different types of masonry; the oldest consists of huge blocks of limestone which have been roughly squared with small stones and clay wedged between them. The Lion Gate and the postern gate to the N were built later using carefully dressed big blocks laid in more or less regular courses.

A few sections were rebuilt in the 3rd century BC with very compact polygonal masonry, for example at the acute angle to the l. of the Lion Gate and in the middle of the SW side (near Tsountas' house) where the wall is up to 56ft (17m) high.

ROYAL GRAVE CIRCLE ON THE ACROPOLIS – Once through the Lion Gate you go along a passageway that must have had a roof and a door at the other end, now gone. On the l. there is a tiny niche which was the porter's lodge. On the r. there were buildings, a granary and, of greatest interest, royal tombs contained within a circular precinct 87ft (26.5m) across, which is still well preserved. The precinct was formed by two rows of slabs approx. 5ft (1.5m) high standing upright and sunk into the earth. The enclosure, which is not as old as the six tombs contained within it, was probably built when the old royal graveyard was incorporated inside the fortified perimeter when the Lion Gate was built.

The six royal tombs which Schliemann excavated in 1876 held 19 skeletons and the treasures which had been laid in them as offerings to the dead. These graves had been dug (approx. 1600–1500 BC, in A.J.B. Wace's opinion) in a huge cemetery, traces of which have been found outside the walls near the Lion Gate. For more than 100 years the kings of Mycenae and their families were buried in them.

Unless you are a very keen archaeologist, you will find the residential area beyond the grave circle very puzzling because of the complexity of its levels and tangle of walls. We know that there was a prehistoric cemetery there and Mycenaean houses (Ramp House, House of the Warrior Vase, Tsountas' House), rebuilt or restored on several occasions, some with an upper floor, which were occupied up to the time of the Dorian invasion at the end of the period known as late Helladic III C (c.1100 BC). In Citadel House, recent excavations have actually revealed the existence of two buildings, one with a room which is still partly decorated with a fresco, while the other was a temple extending into a chamber of strange terracotta statues of a type hitherto unknown on the mainland (given to Nauplia museum). At the end of the 3rd century BC the Argives added still further to the complexity of this group of buildings by putting up various new ones.

PALACE OF THE ATREIDS – Opposite the Lion Gate a wide ramp, built at the same time as the cyclopean wall constructed after the gate to support the terrace on the l., was used for the way leading to the main staircase up to the palace of the Atreids. At the top of the staircase a gently sloping ramp went on to the NW entrance of the palace, which was built on a series of terraces on the highest part of the acropolis. All that can be seen now of this palace, which was built in the 14th century BC, is the overall plan.

First go into a big cobbled court; the NW gate used to open off on the r., consisting a long time ago of a propylaeum with a double portico, each portico having one column. Beyond the gate was a rectangular court which used to be covered with a coat of cement, from which the corridor leading to the central court went off on the l., with the main rooms ranged along it. There was a monumental staircase of which one flight still exists, the throne room and a portico with the vestibule to the megaron opening off underneath it. The floor of the courtyard is covered with a cement surface which was later covered by a layer of painted stucco. Some traces of the fire that destroyed the palace can be seen and at the base of the walls there are remains of the painted stucco.

The throne room where the kings of Mycenae gave official audiences was preceded by a vestibule with a door on to the upper landing (now gone) of the grand staircase. It seems that this part of the palace, dating from the 14th century BC, was destroyed by fire and had to be rebuilt.

The portico of the megaron was paved with slabs of gypsum, probably imported from Crete. You can still see two circular bases that held columns, probably wooden. At either end of the portico on the same alignment as the bases of the columns you can see the foundations of a stone pillar.

Between the column and the pillar on the r., there was a decorated base which probably held a large tripod, an altar or a table for offerings, probably made of bronze. Just beside this base on the r. there was a shallow bowl hollowed out in a gypsum slab where libations must have been poured.

From the porch you went into the vestibule by a door the threshold of which is still in place. The floor was covered by a layer of painted stucco, with a surround of gypsum slabs at the base of the walls. The fire that destroyed the vestibule and the megaron has made it impossible to find the slightest trace of the painted decoration of the stucco. In the centre of the megaron, the floor of which is covered with stucco with a gypsum surround, there was a raised circular hearth, framed by four wooden columns, the stone bases of which have survived. The walls were also decorated with frescoes of which a few remains have been collected.

A door from the porch gave access to a vestibule in which fragments of carbonized wood from a staircase that led to a room about 5ft (1.5m) higher in level were found. This vestibule also gave access to a large back room. There must have been a staircase at the far end of that room leading to a terrace and perhaps to the upper floor of the megaron.

THE PALACE TEMPLE – On the acropolis summit there are the foundations of a 6th-century BC Doric temple built on the site of the Mycenaean temple belonging to the palace. Between the 10th century BC and the Roman period several temples succeeded one another on this site. Excavations have shown that the terrace was enlarged at least twice towards the N, which would correspond to two successive extensions of the temple, which was probably dedicated to Athena.

UNDERGROUND CISTERN – Proceed towards the redoubt at the easternmost end of the acropolis (see plan), crossing an excavation site on which there are the shapeless remains of several Mycenaean buildings the largest of which is the House of Columns. This is in fact the central part of the E wing of the palace, surrounded by storerooms, workshops, etc. Further on you cross the foundation line of a retaining wall which was the outer wall of the citadel in the 14th century BC before a salient wall was built (13th century BC) encompassing the entrance into an underground passage on the l. with a staircase leading down to it (quite hard to climb down, harder still to climb back up; flashlight essential). The underground passage with corbelled vaulting passes below the N face of the rampart, following a natural fissure in the rock, before coming to a secret cistern, supplied by the Perseia spring, at a depth of 39ft (12m). This tremendous undertaking which was carried out in the 13th century BC was intended to ensure the citadel's water supply in the event of a siege. A narrow postern gate was built into the wall of the redoubt near the entrance to the underground cistern. Nearby, in the ruins of the storehouses you will see several pithoi (protected by a shelter), their necks decorated with linear motifs.

Once you are back in the fresh air retrace your steps as far as the Lion Gate, passing the NW part of the acropolis (on the r.), which is littered with the ruins of the Hellenistic village.

THE TOMBS AND THE LOWER TOWN

*CLYTEMNESTRA'S TOMB – Ignoring the Lion tomb on the r. after the ramp leading to the acropolis, built between 1460 and 1400 BC and poorly preserved, proceed towards what is known as Clytemnestra's tomb, on the l. before you reach the road. It was built c.1300 BC to shelter the mortal remains of one or several members of the royal family. First there is a corridor, then the entrance door with three enormous lintels across it. The funeral chamber which is 42ft 6ins (12.95m) high from the floor to the keystone, is in very good condition, after restoration work. A tomb in which a woman had been buried was located in the corridor.

Nearby, but nearer to the road, there are the remains of the second royal grave circle (17th century BC), partly destroyed when Clytemnestra's tomb was built. The circle enclosed eight shaft tombs of the same type as those in the acropolis grave circle, and a considerable quantity of funerary embellishments were dug out from them.

The side of the hill on which Clytemnestra's tomb is situated has been cut into to form a line of tiered seating for the Hellenistic theatre. Several tiers can be seen cutting across the corridor. A few yards away in the direction of the acropolis, there is another domed tomb called the tomb of Aegisthus, built between about 1510 and 1460 BC, but not as well preserved as the previous one.

As you go back up towards the road leading to the entrance into the acropolis there are the remains of a fountain which must be identified as the fountain of Perseia mentioned by Pausanias. It consisted of two basins backing on to a wall that dates from the early Classical period.

THE LOWER TOWN – Go along the road towards the village and on the l., shortly after the second royal circle, there are the remains of Mycenaean houses, of which only the foundations have survived.

There is the House of Shields (much decoration based on the shape of the bilobate shield was found in it), the House of the Oil Merchant, a huge 13th-century BC building on a Cyclopean terrace (a storeroom contained thirty pithoi, many of which still had their stamped clay stoppers), and the House of Sphinxes, also dating from the 13th century BC (very lovely ivory figurines were found there, including a plaque depicting two sphinxes facing one another, and a collection of 72 Mycenaean small columns in ivory, scale models of the goddess column of the Lion Gate). The presence of these three houses outside the citadel indicates that in the 13th century BC Mycenae was not afraid of invasion. Their destruction may have occurred during a civil war, well before the Dorians annihilated Mycenae.

**TREASURY OF ATREUS – About 550yds (500m) from the acropolis is the most splendid of the Mycenaean tombs, known either as the Treasury of Atreus or the Tomb of Agamemnon, which lies a few yards to the r. of the road.

The Treasury of Atreus is one of the most outstanding Bronze Age monuments on mainland Greece, and the finest example of Mycenaean architecture. It was built c.1330 BC on the site of an earlier building. It comprises a huge corridor, cut out of the rock, leading to a monumental door topped by a lintel made up of two enormous blocks, the lower of which weighs at least 120t.

The threshold of the door, which is made of red conglomerate, is still *in situ*. Homer's descriptions of Mycenaean dwellings would lead us to suppose that it was covered by a wooden or bronze sill. A wooden door frame, held in position by bronze nails that have left marks on the door jambs, enclosed the opening. You enter a circular, beehive-shaped room (tholos), 43ft 4ins (13.2m) high and 47ft 7ins (14.5m) in diameter. The dome is made up of 33 courses of masonry, each circular, but not all of the same height; the courses are corbelled, then dressed using a bronze chisel to follow a parabolic curve. The top is closed with a round slab fulfilling the role of a keystone. The upper part of the dome is coated on the outside with a layer of clay to make the tomb watertight.

On the r. a passage with a supporting triangle above it leads to a side chamber which once had a door where a pit has been dug out of the rock. As well as the tholos tombs described above there are five other graves in the immediate vicinity of the acropolis. About 275 yds

(250m) beyond the Treasury of Atreus is the so-called Panagia tomb, which was built between 1460 and 1400 BC. A little further W is the very dilapidated Epano Phournos tomb, built betwen 1510 and 1460 BC. A footpath takes you from Epano Phournos to Epano Pigadi to the SW, and from there a second footpath heading N leads to three other tholos tombs. The first, which seems also to be the oldest, is called the Cyclopean tomb. The facade is constructed of limestone and conglomerate blocks in cyclopean fashion, as is the tholos. The lintel is very short, and has no supporting triangle above it.

To the r. of the path the very well preserved tomb of the Genii was built c.1400 BC. And a little further on is the last tomb, Kato Phournos, built between 1460 and 1400 BC.

We should also mention the recent discovery 0.6ml (1km) N of the acropolis of the foundations of a small temple of Enyalius at the place known as Aspra Chomata. It was rebuilt in the 3rd century BC by the Argives, but it may go back to the beginning of the 16th century BC.

Mykonos [Island of]***

29sq. mls (75km²) – Pop: 3,500 – Cyclades admin. region.

Though it is small, arid, made of granite and sparsely populated, Mykonos has become the star attraction among the Cyclades islands, and its mere name embodies all the charm of the Greek islands. No doubt this is partly because of the proximity of Delos, the archaeological pearl of the Aegean; but to see this as the only reason for its enormous popularity would be to underestimate its own assets and its unusual beauty. With its unparalleled azure-tinged golden light enhancing the immaculate brilliance of the houses, whitewashed so often that their outlines have been strangely softened, its labyrinth of impeccably clean little streets in which every single object, the fishermen's little houses, the countless humble chapels, the cypresses, the olive trees, the nooks and crannies, the arches and the windmills, owes its place and form to year upon year of popular imagination. Mykonos is the most perfect example of those islands in which everything conspires to make a break from humdrum everyday existence. It has to be admitted that this break produces surprising behaviour in the case of some visitors to the island, and Mykonos's detractors don't fail to stress this; but is that not one of the conditions attached to a non-stop party, which is what a successful holiday should be?

A MISSILE IN THE WAR BETWEEN THE GODS AND THE GIANTS. According to legend, Mykonos is the piece of rock hurled by Poseidon against the giants. The Ionians settled here around the beginning of the 1st millennium BC. In the Frankish period, it belonged to the dukes of Naxos, and was then linked to the Venetian monastery on Teinos. In

1821 at the beginning of the War of Independence against the Turks, the Mykonians who are excellent sailors were prominent in the fleet commanded by Tombasis. In 1822 the heroine Manto Mavrochenous and the Mykonians repelled an attack by the Turks.

If you want a quiet stay on Mykonos take rooms with an islander in the higher part of the town or away from the coast in the island's interior: at night noise and music are widespread near the harbour and in the area round Paraportiani church.

Don't go to the beaches near the Xenia Hotel, the Megali Amnos or the Paradisos (nudism); (1.2mls/2km) the Bay of Ornos, (1.8mls/3km) Hagios Stephanos beach (the best sand), (1.8mls/3km) the little beach of Platy Ghialos (or Xylokeratia), (6.2mls/10km) Psirou beach, or lastly Elia or Kalafati beaches, which are much quieter, are to be preferred; the first two can be reached by boat, the others by bus or taxi (leaving from near the harbour); nudism is accepted on some of these beaches.

In and around the village there are a great many chapels (there are said to be more than 365), most of them built by sailors from the island with the profits from their fishing catches or their pirate enterprises, to gain protection from the perils of the sea. Visit the Paraportiani church; it is made up of four chapels lying at different levels and orientated according to the four cardinal points, and forms an interesting architectural volume. Near the church there is a small ethnographical museum. In the same area you can see some old houses, one of which, Captain Malouchos', dates from the 17th

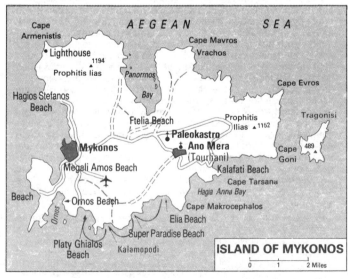

century. At the foot of Kato Myli hill, with picturesque windmills on the top, you can visit several churches, including the Metropolitan church and the Catholic church, which has the arms of the Ghizzi family above its door.

■ The museum of antiquities is near the Leto Hotel, and contains mainly objects found in the course of excavating the necropolis on Rheneia or Greater Delos to which the Athenians transferred the remains of those who had been buried on the sacred island (Delos) prior to its purification in 426 BC. Note a large 7th-century BC amphora, decorated with reliefs; on its neck is the famous Trojan horse, and on its sides are scenes based on the sack of Troy, each shown on a rectangular panel forming a metope.

You can hire a taxi (the fare tariffs are posted up in the car park near the Delos Hotel), and go to the monastery of Paleokastro, near the Venetian castle of Darga, or to the very lovely *Kalafati beach, and then by motorboat to the islet of Tragonissi, a sanctuary for seals; but of course you must set aside a whole morning to visit Delos.

■ Mytilene [Island of] (Mytilini or Lesbos)

623sq. mls (1,614km²) – Pop: 62,000 – district capital of admin. region of Lesbos.

This is mountainous country, with two very deep gulfs – two magnificent stretches of water – cutting into the coastline; the island of Mytilene, formerly Lesbos, is the largest in the northern Aegean. It is still not attracting as many tourists as the beauty of its coast and its sites, such as Molyvos, warrants, though its size (it is the third largest Greek island after Crete and Euboea) and the variety of its scenery, pine-covered mountains, or valleys carpeted with olive groves, a superb coastline, are a guarantee against the monotony that can be experienced on an island. Remember that the ouzo is known as the best in Greece; drink it with sardines.

SAPPHO'S ISLAND. The history of the island is bound up with that of its capital. Mytilene, ancient Lesbos, was one of the areas where the Aeolians were concentrated; around the 10th century BC they spread on to the coast of Asia Minor across from the island. In the 6th century BC when the Tyrant Pittacus, who was also one of the Seven Sages of Greece, ruled, two of the greatest poets of the Archaic period, Alcaeus and Sappho, lived there. Sappho was admired almost as much as Homer, but she had an erotic spiritual ascendancy of a very special kind over the girls whose education was entrusted to her. In a world in which homosexuality was almost exclusively a masculine affair, this may have caused a scandal, but there is no evidence that Sappho was a Lesbian in the sense in which the word is understood today.

The island was under Persian rule, and then freed; in the 5th century BC it joined the maritime confederacy presided over by Athens, but tried in 428 BC and in 412 to leave it and was severely punished.

In the 4th century BC it came under Macedonian control. From 88–79 BC it was occupied by Mithridates, and soon became part of the Roman province of Asia. Under the Byzantine Empire, the island's history was disturbed by Arab, Turkish, Venetian and Genoese invasions: the rivalry between Venice and Genoa led to a proliferation of fortresses on the island. At the end of the 15th century it fell into Ottoman hands, and was not delivered from them until 1912.

Mytilene, which is the main town, stands on the site of the ancient city, at the foot of the hills on an isthmus linking it to the Genoese kastro, built by the Gateluzzi family in 1373 on the site of a Byzantine castle, and altered by the Turks. The archaeological museum, near the port, houses a selection of antique objects found on the island.

Open daily except Tues., summer 07.00–19.00, winter 09.00–15.00; Sun., summer 09.00–17.00, winter 09.00–14.00.

First, you will see in the garden, two fine Archaic capitals in the Aeolian style. In the first room on the l., note in particular the mosaics (end of the 3rd c. AD) from a Roman villa in Mytilene, itself excavated in 1961–62 (see plan on wall of room). These exceptional mosaics,

besides the portrait* of Menander (at the end of the room in the centre on the wall, there is an inscription in Greek: MENANDROS), illustrate scenes from several of his comedies. Plokion or 'The Necklace' (on the wall, l. of Menander) shows three characters in a scene from Act II: the young Moschion, the old Laches and his wife Krobyle (indicated by inscriptions; the letters ME B after the name of the play are abbreviations for *meros B*, i.e., Act II); *Samia* or 'The Samian Woman' (on the wall to the r. of Menander) of which the illustration is from Act III (*meros Γ*), shows Demeas, in the presence of the cook (Mageiros) throwing out his mistress Chrysis, whom he suspects of infidelity (she is clutching to her breast a baby she adopted in Demeas' absence, but which he believes to have been born of her by another man); *Kybernetai* or 'The Steersmen' (in the floor in line with the mosaic of *Plokion*) three unidentified characters from Act III; 'The Leucadian Woman' (in the floor, next) three unidentified characters; *Misoumenos* ('The Man who was Hated') in the floor to the side, three unnamed characters from Act V (*meros E*); *Phasma* or 'The Ghost' (in the floor by the entrance) three more anonymous characters; a girl appears in the doorway, facing two men, one young (to the r.), the other old, in a scene from Act II (*meros B*).

Other panels illustrate five more Menander comedies: *Synaristosae* ('Ladies at Breakfast') in a scene with four players from Act I (three characters, named Philaenis, Plangon and Pythias, with a little slave); *Epitrepontes* or 'The Litigants' with three men (the old Smicrines, between the shepherd Syros, a slave to the l., and Anthraceus the charcoal-burner to the r.) accompanied by a small female character carrying a swaddled baby, from Act II; *Theophoroumene* ('The Inspired Woman') with three men and a child (Act II); *Encheiridion* ('The Dagger') with, from Act IV, two old men, Stratus and Dersippus on either side of the slave Cerdon; finally *The Messenian Woman* with the young Chareinus flanked by two slaves, Syrus and Tibius, from Act V. The name of each play is given in the genitive since it complements the noun *meros*; that of each character is in the nominative.

From the same place are the murals depicting Socrates with his two Theban disciples Simmias and Cebes (with reference to the Platonic dialogue *Phaedo* which brings together these three interlocutors), the large mosaic (floor) with Orpheus charming the animals with his lyre, and three panels (floor) with theatrical masks.

Having returned to the museum entrance hall you will be able to see also, in two further rooms, antique objects of different periods from various sites on the island (vases, terracotta figurines, coins, bronze weapons and buckles); also some sculpted wooden coffers from modern times.

In Arionos Street in front of the church of Hagios Therapon (very close to the port, on the N side), there is a small museum of Byzantine art (icons, pottery etc.), open daily except Sun: 09.00–13 00.

Of the antique theatre brought to light on the side of the hill overlooking the town to the E, there survives part of the tiers of seats and the sparse remains of the stage building. The view of the kastro is superb.

2.5ml (4km) to the S of Mytilene by the airport and Cape Malea road, a road branches off at Varia to (1ml/1.6km) Akrotiri, where there are two small museums of modern art: one is devoted to the naive painter Theophilus Hadjimichalis (1868–1934), probably the most famous of modern Greek painters (open daily except Mon. 09.00–13.00 and 17.00–19.00; entrance fee); the other, founded by the publisher and collector Teriades, contains lithographs by Picasso, Matisse, Miró, Chagall, Giacometti and others (open daily except Mon., 09.00–14.00 and 17.00–20.00; entrance fee).

VICINITY

1 MYTILENE – MOLYVOS – MYTILENE VIA THE GULF OF YERA (89.4mls/143km; 25mls/40km of the route is along unpaved roads, very poor indeed between Mandamados and Molyvos). From Mytilene, take the Pamphyla road.

2.5mls (4km): Road on l. for (1.2mls/2km) Moria; to the W of this small village you should not miss going to see the grand ruins of a Roman aqueduct that spans a delightful valley, carpeted with greenery and oleanders. The many arches of the upper level still rise high into the sky and both in its scale and state of preservation it can bear comparison with the Pont du Gard near Nîmes. If you carry on along the track leading to the aqueduct, which can be driven along, you could rejoin (approx. 1.9mls/3km) the road from Mytilene to Kaloni.

 7.5mls (12km): Thermi, a thermal establishment (saline and chalybeate springs) on the eastern coast of the island, is near a prehistoric site excavated by the British School of Athens. It is a favourite meeting-place of the young, and one of the liveliest spots on the island.

This spa seems to have been occupied from the beginning of the Bronze Age until a period which can be equated with Troy II, i.e. from 3400 to 2000 BC. The site was colonized by peoples from Asia Minor at a period when Asia Minor was occupied by an apparently homogeneous race judging from the kind of black pottery which has been found in various sites in Anatolia. This people is believed to have founded the first city of Troy (c.2750 BC). However, the settlement founded near Thermi was subject to influences from the Cyclades which must have been much stronger than those from Asia Minor. The only real fortifications to be discovered belong to the fifth and last city (2400–2000 BC approx.). At a later date, around 1400 BC, Thermi was occupied again. This settlement was probably destroyed at the period when Troy was laid waste.

 23mls (37km): Mandamados; 880yds (800m) to the N the church of the Taxiarkhi has a very fine carved icon of St Michael.

38mls (61km): Molyvos, ancient Methymna, the town of Daphnis and Chloë, is a charming village full of colour (square painted houses), very much in fashion, situated near a magnificent, long beach and a little harbour below a hill with a Genoese kastro on top of it (view). As evidence of its Hellenistic and Roman past, there are a few pieces of sculpture in a little museum. The village itself, built in tiers coming down from the kastro, is extremely picturesque.

42.5mls (68km): Petra, a fishing hamlet at the foot of a rock with the church of the Panagia Glykofiloussa on top of it. As at Molyvos, a few of the more aristocratic houses still have beautiful painted interiors. The church of Hagios Nikolaos (16th century) is adorned with icons and frescoes.

51.8mls (83km): Kaloni, a large village 1.2mls (2km) from its harbour (Skala); 3mls (5km) along the road to Filia you can visit the monastery of Limonos, dedicated to St Ignatius of Antioch (church gold and silver, icons, old manuscripts, etc.).

55mls (88km): road on the l. for (2.5mls/4km) Hagia Paraskevi.

THE BULL FESTIVAL. Every year on the last Sunday of May or first in June this festival celebrates the local saint, St Charalambos, by recalling the memory of a legend that dates from the Turkish occupation; but there is no question that its true origin should be sought in much older pagan rites.

According to the legend, a peasant who had set out to look for a straying bull was attacked by a Turkish bandit and was protected only by the miraculous intervention of the saint. For good measure the saint also converted the Turk who brought the peasant back his bull and advised him to burn a candle in front of the icon of St Charalambos .

The festival lasts three days. On the first day, Friday, the bull, which is a gift from a rich villager (often an expatriate home for the occasion) is decked with flowers and its horns are gilded. A band goes in front, and the bull is led through the village streets, followed by a large crowd. On Saturday the bull is sacrificed, dismembered, and cooked in big pots with wheat; the resulting dish is called 'kiskek'. Throughout the night there is eating, singing and music. On Sunday morning there is a solemn religious ceremony, with a procession to the icon of St Charalambos; in the afternoon the young villagers take part in horse races. The festival continues throughout the night, with the young men courting the girls and offering them red carnations while the devout lay offerings before the icon of the saint.

62mls (100km): 8mls (13km) away to the r., Hagiassos on the side of Mt Olympus is one of the prettiest inland villages on the island, and is famous for its pottery. From the village you have superb views over the gulf of Yera. In it you can see the church of the Panagia where there are a lot of icons (its treasure, one of the richest on the island, includes gold and silver plate, some illuminated manuscripts, etc.).

71mls (115km): Turn r. on to the Plomari road (Plomari is the second most important town on the island, famous for its ouzo), then l. towards Perama 8mls (13km) further on.

83mls (133km): Perama, a hamlet at the entrance of the narrows linking the gulf of Yera to the sea; passage across the narrows. On the other side, Yera beach. On the l., church of the Panagia Kondozodia.

89.4mls (143km): Mytilene.

2 EXCURSION TO SYGARI AND ERESSOS (125.6mls/201km, or 93mls/149km if you leave from Molyvos). Leave Mytilene along the Kaloni road.

23.7mls (38km): Kaloni (see above at 51.8mls/83km), where you follow signposts for Molyvos (Methymna), then go l. towards Antissa shortly afterwards.

41.2mls (66km): Antissa; the monastery of Hagios Ioannis Theologos has a collection of icons (in the sacristy), embroidery, gold and silver plate, etc.

Approx. 4.4mls (7km) NE of the village, the acropolis of the ancient town of Antissa or Artissa stands near a medieval fortress built by the Genoese. The castle stands on a rocky promontory cut off from the island by a moat which was also made by the Genoese.

50.6mls (81km): Sygri is a small village from which you can walk (2–2.5mls/3–4km) to the petrified forest, a collection of tree trunks that were buried millions of years ago under volcanic ash; rainwater uncovered these plant fossils which are thought to be oak, cedar and plane trees.

41.2mls (66km): Eressos, where a basilica dedicated to Hagios Dimitrios, built in the 6th century, and a second basilica dating from the 5th century, referred to as Hagios Andreas, Syriac in style, have been discovered.

Skala Eressou, 1.8mls (3km) away on the S coast of the island, is a small bathing resort (restaurants) with a sandy beach. A little museum (same opening hours as Mytilene museum) has a collection of Hellenistic, Roman and early Christian sculpture, and mosaic flooring from Eressos.

From Eressos it is best to come back to (102mls/163km) Katoni by the Agra road which gives you the best views over the Gulf of Kaloni.

131mls (210km): Mytilene.

■ Naupaktos (Nafpaktos)

Route map 4.

Delphi, 62.5mls (100km) via coast road or 81mls (130km) via Lidorikion – Missolonghi, 30mls (48km) – Patras, 14.4mls (23km) – Pop: 8,400.

Behind the name (which means 'the arsenal') of this little town at the entrance to the gulf of Corinth lies hidden another name, Lepanto, one of those battles which are said to have changed the world. The town is dominated by an imposing Venetian citadel, whose ramparts descend as far as the sea and enclose a little harbour which is full of charm.

A PAWN ON THE CHESSBOARD OF THE PELOPONNESIAN WAR. Naupaktos, situated in a strategic position at the entrance to the gulf of Corinth, was the town of the Ozolian Locrians. In 455 BC the Athenians conquered Naupaktos, where they settled the Messenians, who had been expelled from their own country by the Spartans. Naupaktos played a role of foremost importance during the Peloponnesian War, especially during the expedition to Sicily by the Athenians. At the end of the Peloponnesian War the town was given back to the Locrians and the Messenians were expelled. In 1407 it was occupied by the Venetians; in 1499 it was taken by the Turks but came under the control of Venice again between 1687 and 1700.

BATTLE OF LEPANTO, WHERE THE CREATOR OF DON QUIXOTE DE LA MANCHA WAS WOUNDED. It was at the celebrated Battle of Lepanto, which took place on 7 October 1571, that the fleet of the Holy League, commanded by Don Juan of Austria, annihilated a Turkish fleet of 200 galleys. The Holy League fleet consisted of galleys belonging to the pope, Venice, Spain, Genoa, Savoy and the Knights of Malta. It was at the same battle that Cervantes lost the use of his left hand. The battle itself took place much further W, at the entrance to the gulf of Patras, under the isle of Oxia. Lepanto was the port from which the Turkish admiral had set sail for battle. Crillon (the 'brave Crillon' of Henry IV) took part on one of the Maltese galleys.

Today Naupaktos is just a seaside resort, with a mediocre pebble beach, where one can spend a few quiet hours. One can take a pleasant walk through the pine woods and visit the citadel, where the remains of ramparts of earlier times lie around. This evokes memories of the past whilst allowing one, at the same time, to view the gulf of Corinth and the Peloponnesian mountains.

VICINITY

1 **HELLENIKO DE VELVINA** (5.3mls/8.5km; after 3.7mls/6km on the road to Agrinion, turn r.). Near the village of Velvina, there are ruins of an ancient acropolis with the site of a temple on the top terrace. Towards the E, on another terrace, there are remains of a temple and a Hellenistic portico.

2 **PARALIA SERGOULA** (14.4mls/23km; take the road to Delphi, then at 3.7mls/6km turn r. towards Monastirakion). Paralia Segoula is a peaceful fishing hamlet on the gulf of Corinth. Near here (40 mins.' walk) you can reach the so-called Glypha, where you will find ruins of an ancient town, scattered on a promontory overlooking two small bays. The lower surrounding wall, which is poorly preserved, may have existed since antiquity. The higher surrounding wall is better preserved and was carefully constructed in polygonal form.

3 **ANDIRRHION** (6.2mls/10km W). Ferry boat every 15 mins for Rhion and the Peloponnese.

N | Nauplia (Nafplion)*

Route maps 6 and 7.

Argos, 7.5mls (12km) – Corinth (via Argos), 37.5mls (60km) – Corinth (via Loutra Elenis), 50mls (80km) – Epidaurus, 18.7mls (30km) – Mycenae, 15.6mls (25km) – Tiryns, 3mls (5km) – Tripolis, 45.6mls (73km) – Pop: 9,300 – chief town in the admin. region of Argolis.

Beautifully situated at the foot of a rocky spur, crowned with an impressive Venetian citadel, at the head of the gulf of Argolis, Nauplia is one of the most attractive little towns in Greece. The charm of the old quarter, its tiny streets and its harbour, the quality of its hotels and the closeness of sites like Epidaurus or Mycenae make it an ideal place to stay. Although Nauplia is not really a seaside resort, the superb beach, which has recently been developed at Karathona, is an added attraction, for it is one of these privileged localities which have been created solely for holiday pleasure.

THE TROJAN WAR: COULD IT HAVE TAKEN PLACE WITHOUT PALAMEDES? Nauplia, whose name means Naval Station, without doubt was a port of call, founded by navigators from the E. They were represented in legend by Palamedes. In order to amuse the Achaeans during the siege of Troy, Palamedes is said to have introduced them to the games of dice and chess. At first Nauplia was independent and affiliated to an Amphictyony of Calauria, then around 628 BC it fell under the control of Argos, which made it into the maritime port and arsenal. By the time of Strabo and Pausanias it had been abandoned.

THIS OTHER NAPLES. Nauplia stayed under the domination of the Byzantines until 1210, when the Franks took it along with Argos in 1212. It became a fief of Otto de la Roche. In 1377 its last Frankish lords placed it under the protection of the Venetians, who called it Napoli de Romanie, and fortified it so well that the Turks were unable to take it in either 1500 or 1537. Finally the town was handed over to them in 1540, when the sultan and Venice signed a peace treaty. During the 16th century and 17th century under Turkish rule Nauplia was the capital of the Morea. Morosini deprived them of it in 1686 and the Venetian garrison was maintained there until 1715.

THE FIRST CAPITAL OF MODERN GREECE. At the beginning of the War of Independence, Greek insurgents succeeded in taking it from the Turks. While it was the capital of liberated Greece, from 1829, Nauplia welcomed Prince Otto of Bavaria on 5 February 1833. He was crowned king of Greece and left the town for Athens in 1834.

Nauplia owes a great deal to the proximity of famous sites, such as Tiryns, Mycenae and Epidaurus, but it should also be appreciated for itself, as a little port full of Mediterranean charm. Within a little over an hour you will have exhausted the buildings of interest in Nauplia, particularly the Palamedes citadel. So you will have time to saunter along the picturesque alleyways and then sit at a table on a café terrace. If the sea attracts you, take the Palamedes citadel road and head for the splendid, well-kept beach of Karathona, 2.5mls (4km) from town.

CITADEL OF ACRONAUPLIA. From whichever direction you arrive, you will enter the old quarter by passing through Nikitara Square, a sort of huge present-day caravanserai for buses, from where you will discover the citadel of Acronauplia. This fortress was established at the foot of the Palamedes citadel, on the end of the promontory, which cuts through the waters of the gulf of Argolis like the prow of a trireme.

You will see first the bastion of Grimani, built by the Venetians in 1706 and dominated by a mighty structure with two towers, which were erected at the end of the 15th and the beginning of the 16th century. This work is part of a surrounding wall erected by the Venetians on the E side, and of another erected by the Franks during the siege of 1205–10. At the end of the promontory are the remains of another surrounding wall, constructed by the Byzantines before the Frankish conquest, directly on the foundations of fortifications dating from the Classical era. Under the government of Daniel Dolfin (1701–04) a half-bastion was built, which reinforced the defences of the N face of the Byzantine castle. The monumental entrance, put up against this half-bastion, was added by the Venetians in 1713.

One can reach the citadel by car, by following first the paved road which goes to the Hotel Xenia, then an ancient cobbled road which ends at a car park with fine views.

OLD TOWN AND MUSEUM. By penetrating the old town, and following

Vasileos Constantinou Street, you will arrive at the archaeological museum, situated on the first floor of a Venetian barracks.

Open: summer, 09.00–15.30; winter, 09.00–15.00; Sun. 10.00–15.00 in summer and 10.00–16.00 in winter; closed Tues.; entrance fee.

In the large room of this museum are assembled finds made in the whole of the Argolid. You will see Neolithic pottery from Asine and Berbati, ceramics from both ancient and recent Helladic periods, as well as Mycenaean jewellery and fragments of frescoes. Among the Mycenaean pottery, you will note, besides several vases with floral and leaf motifs, a very fine vase decorated in the 'marine' style with octopods, their tentacles spreading untrammelled (at the end of the room on the r.), and two other vases, one with animals, the other with people in a chariot.

 The set of terracotta *cult figures coming from Mycenae will attract your attention: they are strange statues or anthropomorphic vases discovered in a house in the citadel, and of a type until now unknown on the mainland. Then at the end of the room you will be able to admire *the oldest cuirass known, from the 15th century BC, found at Dendra (see Vicinity of Argos). It is made of bands of bronze placed on top of each other. Above it has been placed a helmet, made from wild boars' tusks of the same period, of a type described by Homer in the *Odyssey*. A cabinet contains a number of tablets inscribed in Linear B.

In the corridor leading to the staircase to the second floor, are carved flints from the Neolithic Age.

The entrance hall on the second floor contains two large pithoi, an Archaic Doric capital, and a number of sculptures. In the gallery numerous terracotta objects are displayed (vases and figurines) from the Geometric, Archaic and Classical eras; there are also a few jewels. Among the black-figure vases a Panathenaic amphora (on a pedestal) shows on one side the goddess Athena, and on the other a young, triumphant horseman. Argive potteries are represented (Geometric period), Attic, Corinthian and Boetian (Archaic period).

The most curious objects (towards the end of the room) are masks from the 8th c. and two small votive shields (in terracotta) from the beginning of the 7th c. BC from Tiryns; the larger of the two shows on its slightly concave interior a centaur accompanied by wild animals and, on the outside, a combat between a tall warrior (Achilles? Heracles?) and an Amazon, in the presence of two other warriors (one standing in action, the other lying dead) and another Amazon. Warriors and animals appear on the other shield also. Finally, note a small terracotta bath.

In a corner of the Syntagama Square, where the museum is situated, you will also find the ancient Vouleftiko mosque, which housed the first assembly of liberated Greece. To the l. of the museum are little alleyways, generally finishing with steps, which lead to the foot of the Acronauplia citadel. On your r., other alleyways lead to the harbour, from where you can see Bourzi island with its old Venetian fortress (15th century). On the quayside you will see a monument to General Favier, Admiral Rigny and the French who fell during the War of Independence. In a little street which leads on to the Bouboulinas quay, there is an interesting Museum of Popular Art (*open every day from 09.00–13.00 and 17.00–20.00*).

*PALAMEDES CITADEL. If you want to reach this citadel by a formidable set of 857 steps, you can do so by leaving from Nikitara Square (the entrance is on the l., a little way along the road leading to the Hotel Xenia). You will climb in this way for 710ft (216m) and discover, as you go, the sumptuous marine decorations which surround Nauplia. You may, however, prefer to follow the road which, 110yds (100m) before the fork leading to Epidaurus, goes off to the r. and leads to the citadel 1.9mls (3km).

The road to the fortress of Palamedes goes first of all through the suburb of Pronia, where you can see the church of Evangelistria, perched on a rock amongst the cypress trees. In the square at Pronia, the Assembly met in 1832 to confirm the election of Prince Otto to the title of King of the Hellenes. Near there, on orders from King Ludwig I of Bavaria, Siegal sculpted a colossal lion, in homage to the Bavarian soldiers who died in Greece 1833–34.

The Palamedes Citadel was erected by the Venetians, 1711–14, under the direction of the French Colonel La Salle, when Augustino Sagredo was governor. It used to be linked with the citadel of Acronauplia by a secret passage. It consists of seven isolated forts which bear, for the most part, the names of ancient warriors (Themistocles, Miltiades, Achilles, Phocion, Epaminondas, Leonidas).

Open daily 10.00–16.00 (16.30 in winter); entrance fee.

VICINITY OF NAUPLIA

1 HAGIA MONI (2.2mls/3.5km; follow the Epidaurus road, at 1ml/1.5km turn r.). This little convent, haven of peace in the heart of exquisite Mediterranean landscape, was founded in 1144. Its church (1149), typically Byzantine, is situated near a spring identified with Canathus, a sacred spring where, by virtue of a strange privilege, each year the goddess Hera took a bath which restored her virginity.

2 ***TIRYNS (3.1mls/5km) and *ARGOS (7.5mls/12km), see under Tiryns and Argos.

3 TOLON (7.5mls/12km; follow the Epidaurus road, and 2.5mls/4km after the village of Aria turn r.). A modest seaside resort, with small restaurants, where you can have a meal of freshly caught fish at a table overlooking the sea.

About half a mile (1km) before reaching Tolon, a little road to the l. will lead lovers of ancient sites to the acropolis of Asine, which crowned a promontory overlooking the sea. Of the ancient Asine, mentioned by Homer in the *Iliad* (II, 560), and excavated by a Swedish group, there remain only a few fragments of the imposing surrounding wall of the acropolis. The wall was built in polygonal form. A Mycenaean necropolis, with corridor-like tombs cut into the rock, was discovered on a hill facing the acropolis. Asine inspired a beautiful poem by Seferis, Greece's great poet.

4 CIRCULAR TOUR IN THE PENINSULA OF ARGOLIS. (128mls/205km by mostly asphalted roads, with the exception of a section of about 12.5mls/20km between Galatas and Thermissia, which is mediocre and very dusty, and also a very difficult stretch after Kosta before rejoining Drepanon; one may prefer to use the inland road again for the return.)

This excursion from Nauplia, which takes a good day, will appeal particularly to those who seek out paths untrodden by the mass of tourists. In addition to visiting ancient sites of the first order, such as Epidaurus, you will have the opportunity, in the course of this excursion, to discover remarkable seascapes made even more attractive by vast tracts of pine forests and picturesque little fishing villages.

Leave Nauplia by the road to Epidaurus.

9mls (14.5km): a little after the signpost indicating the entrance to the village of Arkadicon, and about 55yds (50m) before crossing a ravine by a modern bridge, you will notice on the l. a Mycenaean bridge, in pseudo-cyclopean form. The road which crossed this stream at this point led to the acropolis of Kasarmi, on the l. In 15 mins. by foot you can climb as far as the main gateway of the surrounding wall, preceded by a ramp and defended by a round tower. The wall, of polygonal form, from the 5th century BC, was reinforced by round towers. On the foundations of some of them, bastions were erected during the Frankish period. The Argives built the fortress in the 5th century BC to guard the Epidaurus road. On the slope facing the road, a little to the l., was an ancient town, sometimes considered to be the city of Lissa, mentioned by Pausanias (II, 25, 10). However, the presence of a tholos tomb from the 15th century BC, near the acropolis, shows that the site was already inhabited as early as the Mycenaean era.

10mls (16km): on the r., the butte of Kastraki is crowned by the ruins of another acropolis. You will reach the summit in about 15 mins by taking the path on the r. (facing E), where you will rejoin the ancient road which ends at the main gateway. The walls have been executed in beautiful polygonal form reinforced by round or square towers. This fortress, whose name is unknown, is contemporary with that of Kasarmi.

15.3mls (24.5km): on the l. is the church of Hagia Marina where you can recognize fragments of an Ionic building: it was erected on the site of a temple dedicated to Athena. Near the church there are remains of a pyramid, probably constructed in the 4th century BC, which may have been a small fort, restored several times, and which stayed in use until the 5th century AD.

15.6mls (25km): Ligourio, a large village (with many taverns). Keep r. here. You will pass, on the l., a picturesque road to Corinth (40.6mls/65km). 12.5mls (20km) along the road there is the *fortified monastery of Agnountos or Agnounta.

This monastery, founded in the 9th century, preserves within its church some frescoes of the 13th century (the Last Judgement, scenes from the Life of Christ and his Apostles) as well as an iconostasis. The latter dates from the 16th century and is carved in wood, partly gilded, with two painted panels representing the Annunciation. On the W facade of the church are remains which have doubtless come from Epidaurus: a fragment of a gutter with the head of a lion and foliated scrolls from the 4th century BC, and above, a cross with the inscription in Greek 'Jesus Christ is Conqueror' sculpted in relief.

Along this same road towards Corinth, you will see, (18.7mls/30km), a pretty little Byzantine church (at the l. of the road in a clump of trees); and a few miles before reaching Loutra Elenis (31.2mls/50km), you will have a very good view over the gulf of Saronika.

17.5mls (28km): on the l., in 1.2mls (2km), is Epidaurus.

27.5mls (44km): keep l. Pass, on the r., the road to Kranidion.

45.6mls (73km): The road on the l. leads to Methana. At 7.5mls (12km) along this road, which is one of the *most beautiful in the whole excursion, you will reach the peaceful little port and seaside resort of Methana. Near the harbour (port of call for certain Piraeus-Hydra-Spetsae boats) there are remains of a Hellenic fortress, constructed in a trapezoidal and polygonal form during the 4th century BC.

47.5mls (76km): the road on the r. leads to Trizin (1.9mls/3km), a picturesque little village situated on the mountainside, probably on the site of ancient Troezene.

Troezene was a very ancient Ionian colony, linked so closely to Athens that the cultures and traditions of the two towns converged. It was at Troezene that Theseus was born and where the legend of Phaedra and Hippolytus originated. At the time of the Persian invasion, 480–479 BC, Troezene gave refuge to the women and children of Athens, but later it grew closer to Sparta out of hatred for Argos. Under the Franks, it was the seat of the barony of Troezene or Damalet.

In the centre of the village you will find a pathway on the r. which leads, in 20–25 mins, to the site of the sanctuary of Hippolytus. After 10 mins walking you will pass on the r. a pathway, and then 220yds (200m) farther you will come to the remains of a town wall with a rectangular Hellenic tower. The smaller shape of the higher layers reveals a Frankish restoration.

From there you can climb, in 15 mins, to the Devil's bridge, (Gephyra tou Diavolou), a natural bridge which crosses the deep ravine of the Gephyraeon river.

Also from the tower, you can climb in approx. 30 mins by a path which leads to the terrace of the sanctuary of Pan, cited by Pausanias (II, 32). The temple of Athena Steniades used to be on the very small plateau that you will find at the top of the acropolis.

Farther down from the tower, on the r. of the path, in a field, are some fairly considerable, though dilapidated and incomplete, foundations of a temple and also a large bathing pool of the Byzantine period.

After the tower, ford the Gephyraeon river, the ancient Chrysoroas. A little further, you will pass near a farm, called the Kokkinia, which was built on the site (controversial) of the temple of Aphrodite Kataskpia, from where Phaedra watched Hippolytus exercising. The depression on the side of the plateau where the farm is situated would correspond to the location of the stadium.

You will finally reach a field full of ruins, where there are the remains of a building, 101ft (31m) square, identified as a monastery refectory, dating probably from 250–200 BC.

Farther along, the remains of a Byzantine church called Episkopia, from the 12th century, which had replaced a smaller 9th-century church, would have marked the true position of the temple of Aphrodite Kataskopia. At the foot of the hills which mark the boundary of the terrace where the church is situated, lie the chalky foundations of a temple, 67ft 6in (20.60m) by 31ft 6in (9.60m), which may have been dedicated to Hippolytus.

Near the church lie foundations which Philip Legrand has identified with the tomb of Phaedra or the monument of Hippolytus. The tomb of Hippolytus, which comprised a mound, was situated close to the tomb of Phaedra and a myrtle bush, with its leaves perforated. This was located near the temple of Aphrodite Kataskopia.

52mls (83km): Galatas, mainland suburb of *the island of Poros. Poros is situated on the other side of an isthmus, at the far side of the straits, its shoreline is bordered with pines. It lies in a setting of great natural beauty.

 64mls (102km): Thermissia, which you reach after you have skirted Hydra beach, opposite the island of Hydra. Thermissia is one of the quietest beaches of the mainland which, because of its hotel facilities, merits more than a fleeting visit.

71mls (114km): Ermioni, a peaceful fishing village and seaside resort, on the site of a small ancient town.

In front of the school, a vast complex from the palaeo-Christian era (6th century) was discovered. It consisted of a large basilica with three naves, a group of buildings erected against the N side of the basilica, a large hall with an apse at the end that could be identified as a baptistry, a room used possibly for exorcisms, another for the holy oil, etc., and several rooms which were probably the bishop's residence.

77mls (123km): Kranidion.

≋ 4.4mls (7km) from Kranidion is Porto Chelli (or Porto Helli) and at 7.5mls (12km) is Kosta. These two seaside resorts facing the island of Spetsae are very popular from the beginning of June.

The excavations opposite the harbour of Porto Chelli have shown that the site, identified with the ancient Halieis, was in fact inhabited from the Neolithic period to the end of the ancient Helladic II (the acropolis). The oldest remains of buildings from the 7th century BC confirm that the site was inhabited again from the Archaic period until the destruction of the town in the last quarter of the 4th century BC. At the summit of the acropolis a sanctuary, probably dedicated to Hera, and the foundations of a tower from the 5th century BC, restored following a circular plan in the 4th century BC, have been uncovered.

On a side of the hill, the University of Pennsylvania has brought to light, on the inside of the surrounding wall, an industrial quarter with a factory for making purple dye. Lower down, near the E rampart, the remains of a rectangular building were discovered, perhaps the bouleuterion or senate, and other buildings. On the W side of the town, near the coast, are remains of houses bordering a street, now partly submerged in the sea. Also submerged are the important remains of a temple of Apollo.

Not far from Porto Chelli, at the edge of the sea, is the Franchti cave, an important prehistoric site explored by the University of Indiana, which was used as a place of worship until the 2nd century AD.

88mls (141km): Didyma. You can see on the l. of the road, at the foot of the mountain, a deep circular depression (impact of a meteorite?); another crater of the same kind can be seen on the plain, close to the first, after about a quarter of a mile (0.5km) on the l. of the road; both can be reached by an earth track. A chapel has been built inside the hole.

94mls (150km): a col with very beautiful views in all directions.

99mls (159km): if a few miles of rough road do not bother you, turn l. towards Karnezeika (10.6mls/17km), where you will meet a paved road which will allow you to rejoin, after about 16mls (25km), the road going from Tolon to Nauplia (see above, 3); you will pass by Drepanon (beach, little Venetian fort). If you prefer, do not turn l. to Karnezeika, but continue straight ahead to rejoin, after 1 mile (1.5km), the outward route.

100mls (160.5km): take the road to the l. towards Ligourio and Nauplia (and follow the outward journey in reverse).

124mls (199km): on the l. is the beach of Tolon (see above, 3).

128mls (205km): Nauplia.

■ Naxos [Island of]*

170sq. mls (442km²) – Pop: 14,000.

Naxos, the largest of the Cyclades, is a surprising island where you can forget the sea, so fertile and smiling are the valleys in the interior, landscapes which are rare in the Aegean archipelago. This isle of Ariadne, which enchanted Byron, will be a source of happiness to those who enjoy both the sea and the country, dotted around with little Byzantine churches, decorated with frescoes, and old towers. The island produces an excellent white wine and a lemon liqueur.

Unfortunately, a growing influx of tourists, noticeable from spring onwards, makes a stay at the height of the season (15 July to 15 August) difficult.

'ARIANE, MA SOEUR! DE QUEL AMOUR BLESSÉE VOUS MOURÛTES AUX BORDS OU VOUS FÛTES LAISSÉE!' This line of Racine, translated roughly as 'Ariadne, my sister, wounded with such love You died on the shore where you were deserted' will recall for you, without doubt, the unfortunate fate of Ariadne, abandoned by Theseus on a Naxian beach, when he was returning from Crete. He had gone there to release Athens from the tribute paid to the Minotaur.

THE ISLE OF DIONYSUS. The modern town of Naxos does not extend very far, perhaps no further than the original site of a Mycenaean city. Known for its fertility from the most ancient times, Naxos was called Dionysia because it produced an abundance of excellent wines. Under Athenian control, it received numerous settlers from Attica. After Byzantium was taken by the Franks in 1204, Naxos and the Cyclades came under the rule of Venice, which sent Marc Sanudo to conquer the island in 1220. The Turks occupied Naxos in 1566 but, like the majority of the other islands of the Cyclades, it was allowed some self-government.

NAXOS. The capital is a picturesque little maritime town, where Venice has stamped its mark. You will have noticed, on arriving at the harbour, the little chapel of Myrtidiotissa, standing solitary on its island. On an island quite close to the harbour, you will see the ruins of a temple, certainly built in the 6th century BC under the tyrant Lygdamis, and which may have been dedicated to Apollo, although by its tradition it is called the temple of Dionysus.

In the town you can climb through little alleyways to the top of the hill, once crowned with a Venetian castle. On the way you will notice the remains of some Venetian nobles' homes, decorated with sculpted coats of arms. In the ancient French college, founded in 1637 to receive Orthodox and Catholic alike, there is an archaeological museum exhibiting discoveries made on the island. In particular, you will see there little marble figurines. Cycladic cult figures of the Bronze Age, a period when the island was flourishing. On the outside of the museum there is a Hellenistic mosaic.

The main tower of the Venetian castle is still wedged inside the very dilapidated Barozzi palace. On a square is the Latin cathedral, dedicated to the Virgin, founded in the 13th century. At the harbour, near the waterside, there is the little church of St Antony the Hermit, which was built by the Knights of Rhodes who had special military privileges on the island in the 15th century.

Not far to the S of the town is the long sandy beach of Hagia Anna.

EXCURSION FROM NAXOS TO APOLLONA (30mls/48km by bus). This is the most interesting excursion you can make in one day on the island of Naxos, with magnificent scenery all around.

On the Chalcis road you will pass near the Hagios Mamas church, one of the oldest on the island, built in the 9th century, with a cupola and vaulted narthex. About 1ml (2km) further on, you pass on the l. the villages of Kato Sangri (Venetian tower) and Ano Sangri (ancient convent of the Taxiarchs).

9.4mls (15km): to the N of the road lies Chalcis, a strange little village where several towers, in which the inhabitants took refuge at the time of raids by Saracen pirates, rise up. See also the church of Hagii Apostoli, of the post-Byzantine period.

3.1mls (5km) along the Chalcis to Moni road there is the church of the Panagia Damiotissa, decorated with two layers of murals, one on top of the other, of which the older dates from the 12th century. Beyond Moni you can reach on foot Melanes, situated in a green valley and dominated by a tower. Lying not far away, unfinished, is the kouros of Flerio (a second one can be found a little farther).

Chalcis is also the point of departure for a visit to the castle of Apano Kastro, built by Marc Sanudo II (1244-63), which you can reach in about an hour. You will pass by the chapel of Hagios Georgios Diossoritis and the chapel of Hagios Stephanos, both with frescoes. Around the castle, which has three surrounding walls reinforced with towers, you will be able to distinguish various types of houses and churches.

11.9mls (19km): Filoti, situated at the end of the vast olive grove of the Tragea, is a village from where you can undertake the ascent of Mt Ozia, highest point in the island (3,290ft/1,003m) and the whole of the Cyclades.

16.2mls (26km): Apeiranthos, which was the most important village in the interior of the island. Near at hand is the Byzantine church of Hagios Ioannis Theologos, decorated with murals, of which the most recent dates from 1309. The village is well known for its woven goods.

30mls (48km): Apollona, a small fishing village on the N coast, on the site of an ancient city, where there was a temple to Apollo. From the village there is a magnificent view over the coast, with its over-hanging coloured cliffs. Within a few mins. walk, in a marble quarry, you can see a colossal statue, rough-hewn and measuring more than 32ft (10m) long.

From Apollana you can return to Naxos via a poor road, which hugs the NW coast, passing the fortified monastery of Hagios Pyrgos on the way.

You can be sure that the rest of the island, covered in groves of lemons, oranges, olives and figs, does not lack interest; but it is reserved, for the most part, for good walkers, since even tracks are rare in the S. Beaches, as numerous as they are beautiful, espcially along the SW coast, are for the most part isolated though accessible by boat; they complete the attributes of the island. One road, however, leading to the SW, gives access to the beach of Mikri Vigla or Kastraki, beyond the village of Aliko (about 9mls/15km from Naxos).

On leaving Naxos, you can take a caïque and see a string of little islands still unknown on the tourist circuit: Iraklia, Schinoussa, Koufonissia and Donoussa. Lodging is in private houses, and usually the donkey is the only form of transport; the beaches are still sometimes deserted.

■ Nekromanteion*

Route map 10.

Arta, 45.6mls (73km) – Igoumenitsa, 36.9mls (59km) – Preveza, 33.1mls (53km).

This name, charged with mystery, is that of a famous sanctuary where oracles were delivered. According to the ancients, the sanctuary was placed at the entrance to the Underworld, or Hades, on the banks of the Acheron.

From the village of Mesopotamos, which occupies the site of the ancient Ephyrus of Thesprotia, mentioned in the *Odyssey*, you can see the dark and imposing walls of this sanctuary, built at the beginning of the 3rd century BC on a place of worship dating perhaps from the Mycenaean period and destroyed in 168 or 167 BC.

Open: summer, 09.00–13.00 and 16.00–18.00; winter, 10.00–16.30; Sun. 10.30–14.30; closed Tues.; entrance fee.

After passing through the access gate to the site, you will walk along a passage, bordered on the l. by three rooms with hearths, where a special diet was imposed on the pilgrims before they were allowed to enter the sanctuary. They ate the flesh of sacrificed animals (goats, calves, pigs) and wild boar, as well as green beans and shellfish. They were probably also subjected to drugs, which put them in a suitable state to pass through the most sacred parts of the sanctuary. A bath served for the purification of the body and the soul.

At the end of the passage note, on the l. a large lebes or vase on feet, on the r. a heap of stones in a corner; these were thrown there by the pilgrims, before they went into the Nekromanteion, in order to ward off evil spirits. Do not renew this ancient custom, but go into a second passage where the flesh of sacrificed animals was burned in the little hearths. Soon this passage is cut by dividing walls, broken by doorways with semi-circular vaults, and it will seem like a harmless little labyrinth. This tortuous way, however, symbolized the wanderings of the soul in Erebus before the kingdom of the dead was reached.

After the turning and another doorway you at last enter the sanctuary where the oracles were delivered. It is a construction with three bays and impressive walls, which today are overlooked by a chapel. You enter first into the central bay, situated above a low, dark crypt, hewn out of the rock, which was supposedly the home of Persephone and Hades, rulers of the Underworld.

This central bay has preserved its paving of slabs of limestone, lying on the 15 arches of the room below. Libations to Persephone and Hades were poured there, while offerings to the souls of the dead were deposited in the side rooms. At the end of and to the r. of the central bay there was a staircase which led to the upper floor where, doubtless, you could find machines intended to make the 'idols of the dead' descend to the underworld when the pilgrimages took place.

In the side room are the pithoi and amphorae which contained the offerings, mainly drinks and cereals.

■ Nemea

Route map 6.

Argos, 15mls (24km) – Corinth, 22.5mls (36km) – Mycenae, 11.9mls (19km) – Nauplia, 22.5mls (36km).

Nemea recalls the time when the forest of Greece were still filled with fallow deer (certainly up until the Archaic period). It has remained famous in the annals of mythology because of the victory of Heracles in one of his famous labours over a lion that was spreading terror in the region. Every two years, under the presidency of Cleonae and then Argos, the Nemean Games, which were one of the four great Panhellenic festivals, used to be celebrated here.

THE GAMES BORN OF TRAGIC NEGLIGENCE. According to tradition, it was on the advice of the soothsayer Amphiaraus that the Nemean Games were founded in 1251 BC. They were instituted to commemorate the death of young Opheltes, son of King Lycurgus, who was strangled by a serpent while his nurse Hypsipyle had left him for a moment in order to lead the renowned Seven, who were marching against Thebes, towards a spring where they could quench their thirst. Thus the legend pointed towards the funereal character of the games. After a period of decline, they were restored in 573 BC, and their victors were extolled by Pindar. During the first half of the 4th century, the Nemean Games were transferred to Argos and the place became completely deserted. But then prosperity came back with the return of the games in about 350 BC and Nemea remained important for several centuries. Today the University of California is excavating the sanctuary and surrounding area.

Arriving via the Corinth–Argos road and discovering the remains of the temple of Zeus at the bottom of the valley, you will stop first at the stadium, situated below a hill, to the l. of the modern road. Its running track, made of beaten earth, has been uncovered for a length of about 110yds (100m).

At the foot of the embankment, where the spectators thronged, the track is edged with a gutter-stone. In the direction of the sphendone, (i.e. the end curve of the stadium, to the S) this gutter is supplied, along the axis of the stadium, with two decanting basins at the place where the water, coming from a spring on the slope of the hill to the E, reaches it. (Broken pieces of terracotta for a canalization system have been found). Subtending the arc of the sphendone the S starting line is entirely preserved; there were 13 running lanes. The original construction of the stadium dates back (according to the latest estimate by American archaeologists) to the last third of the 4th century BC.

Along the W side of the track is a vaulted gallery, discovered in 1977 and now entirely cleared away; it is 6ft 10½in (2.10m) wide, 8ft 1½in (2.48m) high at its centre, and 119ft 3in (36.35m) long. Its construction was contemporary with the construction of the stadium, about 320 BC. The lower stones are covered with graffiti: about 50 of them acclaim the beauty of this or that young man (beginning of the Hellenistic period). This gallery constituted the entrance to the stadium for the competitors and the officials present, and one can almost certainly surmise that it was connected to the sanctuary of Zeus by a sacred way.

At the beginning of the 1st century, then again during the second half of the 6th century AD, the gallery served as a shelter, as finds of bronze coins from these two periods have shown.

After the visit to the stadium, follow again the paved road, and the first road on the r. will lead you to the sanctuary of Zeus, passing en route near to the museum. Opened in 1984 this exhibits antiquities from Nemea itself, and from the vicinity.

Open daily except Tues., 09.00–15.30. Sun. 10.00–15.00.

In the entrance hall a display of photographs shows the original plan of the temple of Zeus, and earlier reconstructions (drawings of the 18th and 19th centuries). In front of the entry is a peristyle garden where, beneath the galleries, are gathered architectural fragments (one from the cyma of the 4th-century temple with foliated scrolls and lion-gargoyles in marble).

To the l. of the entrance you enter a very large room (the only one open at present) where, beside many photographs of digs, can be seen vases, coins (mostly silver), terracottas, bronzes (including a fine hydria decorated in relief with the head of a woman where the vertical handle is attached), all from Nemea; two models reconstitute, with copious explanations, the stadium in its ancient form and the temple of Zeus. A cabinet contains palaeo-Christian objects from the basilica. At the end of the room are assembled objects found in the vicinity of Nemea, notably prehistoric vases, Mycenaean vases and jewels.

Continuing on to the sanctuary of Zeus (opening hours as for the museum) you first see, to the l., remains of public baths (thermae), dating probably from the Hellenistic period (the ruins are enclosed in a modern building which, before the museum opened, served as a storage house for stones).

In 1979, to the W of these thermal baths, the corner of a huge building became visible. It was erected on a much older building, dating from the end of the 4th century BC or beginning of the 3rd century BC (perhaps a palaestra). Immediately to the E of the thermal baths stretched a long building of the Classical period which was without doubt an inn rather than a gymnasium, used particularly at the time of the Nemean Games. On one part of this building a Christian basilica, containing three naves, narthex and baptistery, was constructed in the 5th century AD.

Between the inn (?) and the temple, there was an esplanade planted with cypress trees, according to Pausanias. On its S side, recent excavations have shown nine small rectangular buildings, all facing N (i.e. towards the temple) and constructed in the 1st quarter of the 5th century BC. These were probably treasuries or oikoi for offerings, as were found in other large sanctuaries (for example at Delos or Olympia). Stone inscriptions confirm that one of these oikoi was built by the people of Rhodes, another by the inhabitants of Epidaurus.

The temple, which has three columns re-erected and the drums of several others lying side by side, just as they fell, dates from the third quarter of the 4th century BC. This is a peripteral building, six columns by twelve columns, in the Doric order, erected on the ruins of an earlier temple built at the beginning of the 6th century BC and destroyed towards the end of the 5th century BC. The inside of the temple consists of two parts: a pronaos, at the entrance of which are two Doric columns *in antis* which have been re-erected; and a fairly long cella, whose central nave was edged by colonnaded floors. The lower Corinthian columns were surmounted by Ionic half-columns bracketed on to quadrangular pilasters. At the far end of the cella, a staircase led to a little underground adyton or priests' room.

About 16yds (15m) to the E of the eastern facade of the temple there was a large altar, stretching for about 44yds (40m), constructed at the beginning of the Classical era but altered in the 2nd century AD. On the W side the remains of a long wall aligned N–S have been located. Its construction was improvised and older than the temple, which corresponds perhaps to a piece of the stone enclosing wall which, according to Pausanias, surrounded the tomb of Opheltes. In actual fact, a discovery was made in 1979, to the W of the oikoi, of the sub-foundation of a circular building, 16ft 6in (5m) in diameter, erected during the second quarter of the 5th century BC with blocks which came from a round and more ancient monument, perhaps the tomb of Opheltes.

1.2mls (2km) S of the present-day village of Nemea, you will find the Byzantine hermitage of Polyphengos, decorated with frescoes of the 12th century.

VICINITY OF NEMEA

Philonte (about 2.5mls/4km by a direct road from the village of Nemea). On the r. of the road you will notice the acropolis of the original Philonte which had a surrounding wall in polygonal form. A badly preserved theatre has been uncovered there. On returning to Nemea, if you do not mind rough roads, you can take on the r. a mountain road which is asphalted at first. Afterwards it rises in a passable state as far as a high pass, then descends (in about 15mls/25km to Stymfalia (see under Stymfalia). Along the road there are magnificent views over impressive countryside.

■ Nicopolis*

Route map 10.

Arta, 26.9mls (43km) – Igoumenitsa, 55mls (88km) – Preveza, 5mls (8km).

In 31 BC Octavian (soon to be named Caesar Augustus) vanquished Antony in a naval battle just off Actium and later on, he founded a new town to commemorate the success. You can visit the scattered ruins of this Roman, then Byzantine, town.

Approaching from Arta, you will notice first on the r. an imposing theatre built of brick. The tiers have disappeared but the concrete foundations on which they rested still remain.

Having left the Igoumenitsa road on the r., you will go through the rampart of the Byzantine town, still fairly well preserved. A little further on the l. is the palaeo-Christian basilica of Alkyson, a huge church from the begining of the 6th century, which was probably the metropolis.

Farther still, to the r. of the Preveza road, you will notice a large ruined fountain situated near a second palaeo-Christian basilica, dating from the second half of the 5th century, called the basilica of Doumetios: the name derives from two bishops. Doumetios I and II, who contributed to its construction. You will see some very interesting mosaics from the 5th century. A little museum which displays local finds, especially sculptures, has been built not far from the basilica.

Beyond the basilica have been discovered the remains of a Roman building which has been given the name 'bishop's palace'. It consists of a porticoed courtyard decorated with mosaic pavements some of which date from the 5th or 6th century. Nicopolis has at least two other basilicas: the one to the N dates from the end of the 6th century or beginning of the 7th century, the other to the S dates from the end of the 5th century or beginning of the 6th century (mosaics).

A little nearer the centre of the Roman town lay the remains of an odeon.

VICINITY

1 PREVEZA (4.4mls/7km, see under Preveza).

2 KASSOPE (13mls/21km, follow road to Igoumenitsa for 9.4mls/15km and then turn r. towards Zalongen). Founded at the beginning of the 4th century BC, the town is built on a hippodamean plan and has a polygonal surrounding wall. It was destroyed by the Romans probably in 167 BC, but survived to the end of the 1st century BC, when the inhabitants were compelled to settle in the newly founded city of Nicopolis.

Previous excavations have uncovered, in the centre of the complex, several buildings laid out round an agora. To the E, there is a little theatre; to the W, a Doric portico from the 3rd century BC; to the N, another similar portico; and behind that a building, probably a katagogeion or public hostel, 100ft (30m) square, which was erected (according to latest estimates) in the second half of the 3rd century BC, on top of the ruins of an even older building (perhaps previously a public building, of the 4th century BC). Stone slabs have been found amongst all the fragments excavated, and among some of these are hearths which belong to the second building.

In 1977 excavations were begun in the section situated immediately to the N of the katagogeion. Beyond the alley with flagstones can be seen the remains of a large house which occupied half the island site where it stood. The sub-foundation of the walls, preserved to a maximum height of 5ft 7in (1.7m), is in polygonal blocks of limestone precisely laid, while the higher parts are in brick. The clearing of other houses is in progress.

■ Nisyros [Island of]

16.5sq. mls (43km^2) – Pop: 1,500 approx.

Nisyros, an almost round island in the Dodecanese, is hardly the place to attract the ordinary tourist. In Nisyros you will find real solitude. The land is volcanic but still green, although there are no springs other than sulphurous ones. (There is a small desalination plant). It was during the famous Battle between the Gods and the Giants (gigantomachy) that Poseidon took part of the island of Cos, hurled it at Polybotes to crush him, and thus formed this island. In its centre, the slopes of a crater, 2.5mls (4km) in diameter, are no longer well cultivated, though the island still has a reputation for growing figs and almonds: old customs live on.

The main centre on the island is Mandraki, which has buildings like white or grey cubes resting on black basalt. It is on the site of ancient Nisyrus and has ruins of a medieval castle surrounding the monastery of the Panagia Spiliani (feast day, 15 August). Two other villages are Emborio and Nikia, the latter clinging to the side of the crater (very good view; monastery of St John). There is a fine beach near the unpretentious fishing village of Pali. At the so-called Stephanos (crown), volcanic phenomena can be observed on the surface of a mud lake. On the island of Yali, N of Nisyros, pumice stone is quarried.

Olympia (Olymbia)***

Route maps 7 and 9.

Athens, 201mls (324km) – Patras, 70mls (113km) – Pylos (Navarino), 86mls (139km) – Pyrgos, 12mls (20km) – Sparta, 120mls (193km) – Tripolis, 81mls (130km) – admin. region of Elida.

One of the most prestigious historic sites of ancient Greece is situated amidst a landscape contrasting sharply with the originality of the site of Delphi. The atmosphere is warm, the valley where the river Alpheus sparkles is restful and the whole setting is bathed in light, reflecting the delicate hues of its hillsides and wooded valleys. This peaceful spot, whose tranquility was said to encourage reconciliation among the Greek states, encircles the great Panhellenic sanctuary in a harmonious embrace.

This sanctuary, whose evocative remains you will visit, provided the setting for the Olympic games. The importance of this festival was such, in the eyes of the Greeks, that the interval of four years, known as the Olympiad, was recognized throughout Greece as the only valid time scale after 776 BC, when the games were officially instituted.

The History of Olympia

THE LABORIOUS ESTABLISHMENT OF THE PANTHEON OF OLYMPIA. The tribes which followed one another in Altis brought their gods with them, and all left their stamp on the legend. The worship of Zeus, which was the dominant one at Olympia from the Classical period onwards, seems to have been preceded by that of a female divinity, called Gaia (Ge, the Earth). Other goddesses of chthonic origin were also worshipped. Mt Cronium itself, as its name implies, was dedicated to a god of Cretan origin. Under the Achaeans, Zeus succeeded Cronos and Hera was substituted for the Minoan mother goddess. It was then that the oriental Pelops appeared, the one who defeated the Aetolian Oenomaus.

ELIS, SOVEREIGN OF OLYMPIA. According to one legend, Pisa took over the administration of the temples and presided over the games, representing the confederation of the 16 towns of the Elid. But Elis, which was jealous of this predominance, is said to have contested it and won a decisive victory over her rival in 576 BC. From 471 BC, Elis, as head of the confederation, is said to have been recognized as sovereign of Olympia under the protection of Sparta, despite the jealousy of the Arcadians. However, wrangles between Elis and her neighbours, and even Sparta, during the 5th and 4th centuries BC, did not prevent the regular celebration of the festivals under the Elean administration. In 364 BC, the Arcadians invaded. They sacked the Altis and presided over the games, but in 360 BC the Eleans once again became masters of Olympia.

OLYMPIA, THE MUSEUM OF THE GREEK WORLD. The holy city gradually established itself, thanks to the generosity of its patron towns and princes, and to the ability of its administrators. Because of the frequent festivals which accompanied the celebration of worship, Olympia became a meeting place for the whole of the Greek world. There, in the name of the sacred truce, the different tribes of the Greek nation could forget for a moment their discord, and Hellenism became conscious of its unity. Enriched by the devotion of its worshippers and the glory of its champions, the sanctuary of Olympia became a true museum, where each Greek state could find the reminders and records of its past. It even became a diplomatic centre for the handling of both private and state affairs. The fame of the contests in the stadium and the solemnity of the festivals held around the temples, kept up the tradition of a pilgrimage to Olympia until the decline of the pagan world, and made it a cosmopolitan assembly of both the devout and the inquisitive.

THE WORSHIP OF ZEUS BECOMES IRREGULAR. In the 2nd century BC the Romans appeared. At that time the decline of Olympia was undeniable but prosperity returned with the Caesars. After Hadrian, in the 3rd and 4th centuries AD, Olympia no longer had either a political or a religious role to play. The crowds which flocked to the festivals were curious, but sceptical and disrespectful. As Lucian rhetorically exclaimed to Zeus: 'Sacrifices are no longer made to thee and thy statues are no longer wreathed with flowers except by chance.' However, the five-yearly festival was celebrated until 393 AD. At that time the life of the sanctuary, which had long been in decline, was shaken by the edict of Theodosius I forbidding pagan festivals. In 426 AD, Theodosius II ordered the destruction of the temples and the temple of Zeus was not spared. A Byzantine town grew up on the ruins of Altis, and then a hamlet of shepherds spread its huts between the temple of Zeus and the stadium.

EXCAVATION. From 1723 onwards, Montfaucon, a French scholar, and Cardinal Guirini, the Archbishop of Corfu, then later Winckelmann and Richard Chandler, became interested in investigating Olympia. The latter even made a few explanatory probes. The first excavations were made in May 1829 by two members of the Morean Commission, Blouet and Dubois. In Germany, the historian Ernst Curtius took up the idea of more extensive excavation and won over to his cause his pupil, the Crown Prince Frederick (Emperor Frederick III) as well as the Emperor William I. In 1875 a treaty, ratified by the Greek Chamber, authorized Germany to incur the excavation expenses, and work continued until 1881. There were further periods of work from 1936 to 1941 and from 1952 onwards.

Visiting the ruins

HALF-DAY AT OLYMPIA. Save the visit to the museum for the hottest part of the day. When in need of rest, you can go up to the SPAP Hotel near the former museum; from its flower-bedecked terrace you can admire the gentle Olympian countryside, while taking some refreshment. For lunch (or dinner, if you are not committed to half-board), there is no shortage of eating places in the village.

FULL DAY AT OLYMPIA. Visit the Olympic sanctuary early in the morning, followed by the museum. Then take the road to the sea, preferably to Katakolon (22mls/36km away, via Pyrgos), where you will find a fine long sandy beach. Lunch on fresh fish available on the spot, and then, if your timetable allows, return to Olympia to visit once more the sanctuary of Altis, without your guide book, for the sheer beauty of the site.

The sanctuary of Olympia

The group of buildings situated in this corner of ancient Pisatia, at the foot of Mt Cronum, and described under the general name of Olympia, did not constitute a town. It was a huge sanctuary, where the temples and altars of various deities were united under the spiritual sovereignty of Zeus and under the temporal sovereignty of towns, Pisa first, and Elis after 471 BC. Of the sanctuary of Olympia there remains only a motley collection of ruins of various periods, which can sometimes be a little disappointing, but its natural setting, shaded by pine trees, lends it a very real charm.

THE CITY OF THE GODS. The sanctuary of Altis was reserved exclusively for the gods. Priests and other officials had their quarters outside the sacred precinct. 'In theory, the monuments, ex-voto offerings and the treasures of Olympia belonged to Zeus, lord of Altis. In practice, the Eleans, fellow countrymen of the god and his heirs here on earth, had all the wealth, which was enclosed in the precinct, at their disposal, but they could only use it for the embellishment of the sanctuary.' (Monceaux).

REVENUES THE MANAGEMENT OF ZEUS'. This was the responsibility of the Olympic senate, who sat in the bouleuterion and whose members came from the Elean aristocracy. The senate administered the sanctuaries with the assistance of a boulograph, or secretary of the senate, and had jurisdiction over all the Olympic officials.

THE STAFF OF THE ALTIS. The magistrates and priests were recruited from the Elean aristocracy and were elected for an Olympiad (four years). Each sanctuary had its own special staff but there was a hierarchy. At the top, three theokoles or high priests of the Olympiad conducted the main sacrifices. Then there were three spondophores, who travelled abroad to announce the dates of the festivals, and the manteis or soothsayers who were descended from two old Elean families, the Lamides and Clytiades. The latter pronounced the oracles and held a particularly powerful position in the Greek world. The inscriptions refer to a daily sacrificer, flute players, dancers, exegetes who were both masters of ceremonies and interpreters of the legends, an architect, a doctor, a chef, and a xyleus (woodcutter) who provided wood for the sacrifices, etc.

THE FESTIVALS OF ALTIS. The monotony of liturgical life was broken by the festivals of Cronos, Gaia, Pelops and Hippodamia. There were also the festivals of Sosipolis, the divine child who became a serpent, when women were admitted as an exception, and Hera, when women only participated, while doing exercises in the stadium. But the most important ceremony of all was the five-yearly festival of Zeus, which was further enhanced by the great Olympic contests.

THE FIVE-YEARLY FESTIVALS. These were held every four years or every fifth year, counting as the Greeks did the year of the festival twice. They took place at the full moon between the end of June and the beginning of September. The spondophores and the sacred envoys, the theores, set off in all directions to announce the exact date and proclaim the start of the sacred truce (from the 4th century BC). They forbade armed forces from entering the Elid and proclaimed the inviolability of the pilgrims. The festivals lasted for five days, from the 12th to the 16th of the month. The official deputies from the towns and states were the public guests of Olympia. There were also special delegations, or *theoroi* whose expenses were paid by the towns, and simple pilgrims who camped outside Altis.

THE RITUAL OF THE FESTIVAL. The first day was dedicated to sacrifices to Zeus Olympia, to Zeus the banisher of flies, and to Hestia at the tomb of Pelops. From the second to the fourth day the games and contests took place, starting with a procession. On the third day, a sacrifice was made to Zeus, followed by a procession in front of his statue, and then the wrestling began. The festival closed on the fifth day with a procession of the champions followed by a banquet at the prytaneum. The Eleans have presided over the games (agonothesia) since 572 BC.

THE OLYMPIC GAMES. Ten months before the festival began, the magistrates of Elis would appoint a jury of ten members, or Hellanodices, from the residents of Elis, who could get to know the competitors and teach them the rules of the games. The competitors had to be Hellenes and freemen; slaves were excluded but Romans were not. Participants could only compete after a long training period at the gymnasium of Elis and they brought their trainers (aliptas) with them. They would swear on the altar of Zeus Horkios at the bouleuterion to comply faithfully with the rules of the games – an oath which bound the competitor's family and even his native town.

THE OLYMPIC EVENTS. The competitions varied in number and kind; they were made up of thirteen or fifteen events according to the period. Pindar links their origins to the funeral games held near the tomb of

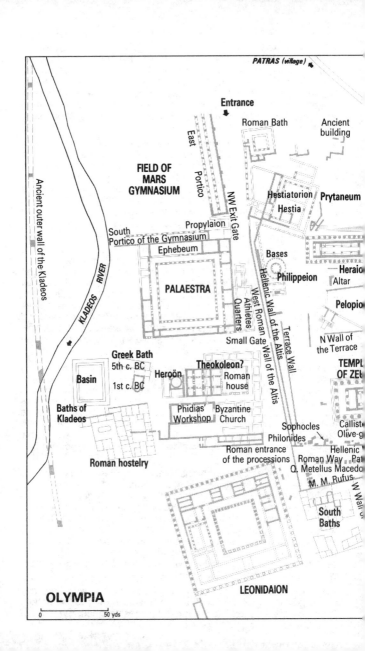

PATRAS (village)

Entrance

Roman Bath

Ancient building

FIELD OF
MARS
GYMNASIUM

East

Portico

NW Exit Gate

Hestiatorion

Prytaneum

Hestia

Propylaion

South
Portico of the Gymnasium

Ephebeum

Bases

Philippeion

Heraio

Altar

PALAESTRA

Athletes'
Quarters

West Roman Wall of the Altis

Hellenic Wall of the Altis

Terrace Wall

Pelopio

N Wall of
the Terrace

Small Gate

TEMPL
OF ZEU

Greek Bath

5th c. BC

Heroön

Theokoleon?

1st c. BC

Roman house

Basin

Phidias'
Workshop

Byzantine
Church

Baths of
Kladeos

Sophocles

Philonides

Callist
Olive-g

Roman entrance
of the processions

Hellenic
Roman Way Pa
Q. Metellus Macedo

M. M. Rufus

Roman hostelry

South
Baths

KLADEOS RIVER

Ancient outer wall of the Kladeos

OLYMPIA

0   50 yds

LEONIDAION

W Wall o

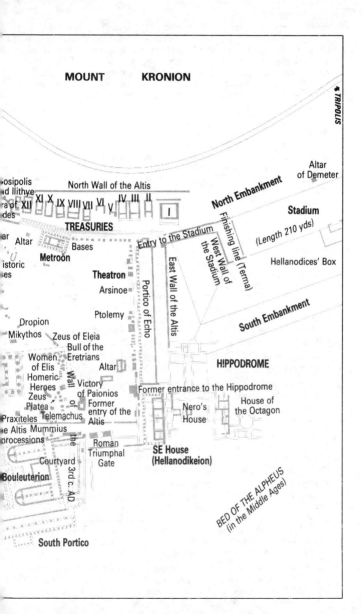

MOUNT KRONION

osipolis
d Ilithye
ra of XII XI X IX VIII VII VI V IV III II
des

TREASURIES

North Wall of the Altis

Altar
of Demeter

North Embankment

Stadium
(Length 210 yds)

Hellanodices' Box

ar Altar
istoric
ses

Bases

Metroön

Entry to the Stadium

West Wall of
the Stadium

Finishing line (Terma)

East Wall of the Altis

Theatron

Arsinoe

Ptolemy

Portico of Echo

South Embankment

Dropion

Mikythos Zeus of Eleia
Bull of the
Women Eretrians
of Elis
Homeric Altar
Heroes
Zeus Victory
Platea of Paionios
Praxiteles Telemachus Former
e Altis Mummius entry of the
processions Altis

HIPPODROME

Former entrance to the Hippodrome

Nero's
House

House of
the Octagon

Courtyard

Roman
Triumphal
Gate

SE House
(Hellanodikeion)

Bouleuterion

South Portico

BED OF THE ALPHEUS
(in the Middle Ages)

Pelops. Usually they began at sunrise with foot racing, for a distance of one (dromos), two (dolichos) or six lengths of the stadium. Towards the end, races under arms (hoplitodromos), i.e. in full battle order, were discontinued. They continued with wrestling using the flat of the hand, boxing, pancration (combined wrestling and boxing), and the pentathalon, which included discus, javelin, sprinting, jumping and wrestling.

The hippodrome was the scene of the four-horse chariot or quadrigas races, the oldest type of chariot racing, the two-horse chariot or bigas races, and races for mounted horses and mules. Distinctions were made between adult and adolescent races. To entertain the crowds, there were music, readings, recitations and orations held in various places. Herodotus read excerpts from his *Histories* at Olympia; sophists, rhetors and scholars of greater or lesser renown gave lectures; artists exhibited their work; Nero introduced competitions for music, poetry and drama (67 AD).

THE OLYMPIC CHAMPIONS. After each event, the herald would announce the victor (known as the Olympionikos) and the Hellanodikai would present him with a palm. On the last day, all the champions received a crown made with an olive branch (kallistephanos), and perhaps some valuables or cash prizes. Then the festival would finish with the procession and banquet for the champions. They would then return in triumph to their native region and attend a state banquet where they would listen to a musical cantata composed in their honour by a well-known lyric poet. Their fame became supreme when sung of by a Pindar or a Simonides, and their glory extended to their families and native towns, who would then dedicate statues to them in the Altis.

Open: weekdays 07.00–18.00 or 19.00 (summer); 07.00–16.30 (winter); Sun. 10.00–18.00 (summer); 10.00–16.30 (winter); entrance fee.

PORTICOES OF THE GYMNASIUM. Soon after entering the site, on your r. you will walk alongside the ruined portico (or xystus) of a gymnasium of the Hellenic period. It consisted of two long colonnades bordering a huge square or 'champ de Mars' (parade ground).

The E portico was used for running practice in bad weather and consists of a double gallery, with a median colonnade and a lateral colonnade, both in the Doric order. It covered a track 630ft (192.27m) long, the exact size of an Olympic stadium.

The S portico was a simple gallery with one Doric colonnade. At one end of the portico, note an oven of the 3rd century AD covered by a roof. Where the two porticoes meet, a propylaeum gave access from the road to the exercise area. It was constructed in the 2nd or 1st century BC and is an example of fine workmanship. The gymnasium contained the official list of Olympionikoi (Olympic champions) and the Olympiads, and numerous statues of athletes.

PALAESTRA. This building, constructed at the end of the 3rd century BC, was the part of the gymnasium used for wrestling practice. It was equipped with special rooms where the athletes could cover themselves with oil and bathe. The gymnasium proper consisted of large galleries (xysti) and tracks (dromoi) for foot races, with a large court for the games. In the paleastra and gymnasium of Olympia, the wrestlers and runners would spend the last month of their statutory period of training and initiation into the rules under the scrutiny of the Hellanodikai. The first nine months could be spent in the gymnasium of Elis, or the whole ten months at Olympia.

The palaestra of Olympia corresponds exactly to the palaestra described by Vitruvius, and no doubt served as his model. It consisted of a central court surrounded by a quadruple portico of Doric columns. This court was used for practice in wrestling, boxing and jumping. On the N side was an area paved with ribbed bricks, 80ft (24.20m) long by 18ft (5.44m) wide, probably intended to stop the boxers' bare feet from slipping. It may also have served as the run-up track for the jumping.

Leading off the galleries of the peristyle were private rooms or open rooms (exedras), some of which were fitted with benches and led on to the portico through Ionic colonnades with various types of capital.

In the central exedra of the N wing, you will see the ephebium of Vitruvius, adjoining on the l. the elaeothesium (unction room) and on the r. the conisterium (where the athletes rubbed themselves with sand). The private room in the E corner with its basin served as the frigida lavatio or cold bath, as did that in the W corner. The changing-room or apodyterium must be the private room situated next to the SW entrance. The other open rooms were used for training under cover, as shelters for the idle or for spectators, and as meeting rooms.

THEOKOLEON. This building, constructed in the 4th century BC, housed the priests, theokoles (high priests) and soothsayers. During the Roman period, a house with a central court was erected here.

HEROÖN. Just next to the theokoleon were discovered the ruins of a building of the 6th century BC, which is described in dedications as a heroön, or chapel of a dead hero. Part of a small terracotta altar, mixed with ashes, charcoal and charred bones from sacrifices, was unearthed in one room.

Near the river Cladeus (see plan) are the remains of several public baths, dating from the Classical period (5th century BC) to the Roman period. The oldest part of the first baths dates from the 5th century BC but this building was altered in the 1st century BC. The baths of the Cladeus, erected during the Roman period, included a large swimming pool, some remnants of which can be seen. To the S of this group, German archaeologists uncovered the remains of a large building, dating from the 2nd century AD, which must have been a hostel similar to the Leonidaeum (see below).

THE WORKSHOP OF PHIDIAS. This Athenian sculptor of genius received from Olympia an order for a chryselephantine (gold and ivory) statue for the cella of the temple of Zeus. Consequently this building, whose ruins you can see, was constructed in the 5th century BC as an exact full-sized replica of the cella, to enable the sculptor to assess the effect of his work viewed from the ground and from the side galleries. The Byzantines destroyed the layout by building a church on the same site.

Close to this workshop were other premises where the artists and craftsmen who assisted the master made parts of the statue. Later the workshop must have been used as a storeroom (pompeion), where costumes, urns, oil, incense, etc., were kept, and as premises for the phaedryntes (the officials responsible for maintaining the statue) and for priests.

LEONIDAEUM. This immense building, of which only the foundations remain, was constructed towards the end of the 4th century BC by Leonidas of Naxos, and was used as a hostel for distinguished guests. It was enlarged twice during the Roman period (around 174 BC and in the 3rd century AD).

In the centre there was an atrium with an impluvium (water tank) and lawns, surrounded by a Doric peristyle of 44 columns. Around this were the apartments, rooms which were either enclosed or entered through colonnades. Finally there was a ring of outer galleries surrounded by four lines of 138 Ionic columns. This promenade gave direct access to the outside and was a grandiose piece of ornamental architecture.

SOUTH PUBLIC BATHS. This set of buildings, dating from the 3rd century AD, is very poorly preserved, since it is situated in an area disrupted by the construction of a defensive wall of the same period. Hence there is a section of wall made of limestone dating from the 5th century BC, several courses of which remain, and which leans outwards to the S. This was probably a retaining wall marking the boundary of an irregularly shaped mound, which was perhaps the hippodameion.

BOULEUTERION. This structure, completed at different times (from the 6th to the 2nd century BC), was the palace of the Olympic senate. Here the competitors vowed to observe the rules of the contests in front of the Hellanodikai or members of the jury.

It consisted of a large Ionic portico as a facade to the E, and a square central area flanked with two long wings terminating in apses. The square area, which was in the centre of the building and open to the sky, was the precinct of Zeus Horkios whose statue stood in the centre. The N wing (6th century BC) is less well preserved than the S wing, which was built one century later. The two wings opened on to the front portico (built 3rd or 2nd century BC). In the post-Roman period, a trapezoidal court with a crude Doric peristyle was added to the front portico. The altar situated in the middle of the E gallery of this courtyard could be that of Zeus Agoraios. The S portico, dating from the 4th century BC and altered in the Roman period, extends beyond the bouleuterion.

The bouleuterion is built along the Roman wall of the Altis, which at that period marked the boundary of the sanctuary area. The enclosing wall or peribolos of the Hellenic period was smaller (see plan). On this side, in the section between the Roman and Hellenic walls, the Roman processional way is marked out with bases of stelae, among which is that of the consul Q. Caecilius Metellus Macedonicus, consecrated around 143 BC, and the equestrian statue of Mummius with the ten Roman legates (146 BC), in front of the triumphal arch built by Nero in 67 AD.

TEMPLE OF ZEUS. The abode of the sovereign god of Olympia is now no more than an immense confusion of huge blocks and column drums of colossal size, which cover the vast sub-foundation of the building. Such today is the condition of this Doric temple which was once the richest and largest in the Altis.

It was erected between 468 and 457 BC by the architect, Libon of Elis, with the booty taken from the Pisates by the Eleans in 468 BC, but it may have been altered soon afterwards for the installation of the colossal statue of worship executed by Phidias towards the middle of the 4th century BC (337 BC ?).

The temple was surrounded by a gallery of thirteen lateral columns and six frontal columns. The capitals and the drums are made of shell-based stone faced with fine white stucco made of marble dust. Note the huge abacus of the scattered capitals. The pediments were filled with great pieces of sculpture, which have miraculously been preserved (they are now in the museum). By way of a central plinth the E pediment carried a gilded Victory, to the base of which was fixed a golden shield, presented in 456 BC by the Spartans to commemorate their victory at Tanagra. Gilded bowls on tripods formed the acroters at the corners. The acroters of the W pediment must have been similar, since they were all created by Paeonius.

Between the columns were bronze statues and ex-votos whose fastening holes are still visible.

Leaving the peristyle, you enter the vestibule or pronaos. Here stood various ex-votos (traces of the bases), including Cynisca's horses and the group of Iphitus, organizer of the sacred truce, with Ecechiria, his wife, on top. The pebble mosaic, the remains of which still adorn the ground, is not earlier than the 4th or 3rd century BC.

Only one entrance, with a bronze double door, led into the holy place or cella. There in the central nave, beyond the fifth set of columns, rose the renowned gold and ivory statue of the god. Sunk in the floor in front of it was a square basin lined with blue marble tiles and edged with a Pentelic marble border. According to Pausanias, this would have held the oil with which the statue was anointed.

THE MASTER OF THE ALTIS. The statue of Zeus, which was executed by Phidias and his colleagues, Panaenus the painter, and Colotes the chiseller, was 40–43ft (12–13m) high. The god was seated, holding a chryselephantine Victory in his r. hand and a sceptre surmounted by an eagle in his l. hand. The ebony and bronze throne had ivory and gold plate on top, and was decorated with precious stones and paintings.

The naked parts, that is the feet, abdomen, and torso as well as the head, were made of ivory. The himation hanging from one shoulder, falling on to the thighs and covering the legs, was studded with jewels, as were the beard and hair. The statue, which was probably later than the statue of Athena in the Parthenon, was no doubt created by Phidias between 438 and 430 BC. Special officials, known as phaedryntes were responsible for anointing the colossus with oil. The statue was removed under Theodosius II and taken to Constantinople where it was destroyed in a fire in 475 AD.

In front of the steps at the temple entrance many statues were erected, and you can still see some of their bases. They include the triangular pedestal of the Victory by Paeonius. Because of the quality and variety of the works assembled here, this little corner of the Altis resembled an open-air museum. Here were to be found the creations of famous artists, such as Paeonius, Calamis (chariot of Hiero), Glaucias of Aegina (chariot of Gelon), Onatas of Aegina (chariot of Hieron, in collaboration with Calamis, and the Homeric heroes), Dionysus of Argos (group of Micythus), etc.

HELLANODIKEION. The general layout of this monument, the substructure of which is partially covered by the house of Nero, was similar to the Leonidaeum but on a smaller scale. It must have been an official residence, possibly for the Hellanodikai (presidents of the festivals).

Beyond the remains of the huge villa, which Nero had built for his own use during his visits to Olympia, lie the ruins of the House of the Octagon, a Roman construction of the Antonine period (2nd century AD) near a place of worship dedicated to Artemis, from the middle of the 5th century BC.

HIPPODROME. On the E side (near an altar of Zeus Moeragetas?) was the entrance to the hippodrome, swept away when the river Alpheus flooded.

A manuscript from Constantinople tells us that it was 754yds (690m) long by 350yds (320m) wide. Behind Nero's house was an ingenious arrangement of gated stalls where the chariots took up their positions before getting into line. At the furthest point, where the teams of horses turned round, was the haunted monument, Taraxippus (horse-scare) which was intended to frighten them back. It was at this spot also that the horses belonging to Oenomaus, king of Pisa, bolted.

ECHO COLONNADE. The Echo colonnade, or Poecilia, which faced directly on to the Altis, extended from the entrance to the hippodrome as far as the entrance to the stadium. The name 'Echo colonnade' refers to the fact that a spoken word would echo seven times there, while the second name 'Poecilia' refers to the paintings which decorated the rear wall. It was built in the second half of the 4th century BC, and lay partly on the finishing line of the stadium of the ancient Classical period (around 450 BC). The stadium thus opened on to the sanctuary and jutted quite a long way into it, confirming the close relationship which existed at that time between the Olympic games and religion.

STADIUM. You will enter the stadium where the Olympic games were held, through the passageway used by the competitors and members of the jury. It was converted into a vaulted tunnel in the 1st century AD. The entire track has been uncovered: you can see the finishing line (terma), and the starting line (aphesis) at the opposite end. The stadium could hold around 20,000 spectators. Throughout ancient times, the track was surrounded only by an embankment where the public sat. At the end of the Roman period, the S bank (on the r.) was rebuilt in tiers. At the time of the excavations, German archaeologists unearthed the foundations of a wooden tribune, opposite the altar of Demeter Chamynae, no doubt the tribune (apse) of the Hellanodikai.

During the stratigraphic excavations, five periods in the development of the stadium were identified, from the Archaic period up to the end of Roman times. The track of the ancient Classical period (around 450 BC) was more to the S and at a higher level, and stretched further W towards the sanctuary.

The starting line was marked by a white limestone strip, 18in (0.48m) wide, with square holes cut in it to hold the posts between which the twenty runners lined up. To start themselves off, the runners wedged their feet in triangular grooves hollowed out in the ground. The finishing line was of a similar layout and thus could also serve as a starting point, for the double and sextuple races for example. The distance between the two lines is 630ft (192.27m), the length of the Olympic stadium. According to legend, this distance was set by Heracles when he marked out the side of the Altis by placing one foot in front of the other six hundred times.

TREASURIES. On a terrace at the foot of Mt Cronium were the treasuries which were like small chapels, consecrated in the 6th and 5th centuries BC by various Greek cities. In a row, below the terrace, stand the bases of the Zanes, or bronze statues of Zeus, which the Eleans had erected with the proceeds from the fines imposed by the Hellanodikai. On the first base, on the r. as you come out of the stadium, you can see the signature of the Sicyonian sculptor Daedalus, son of Patrocles (early 4th century BC.)

OFFENCES AGAINST THE OLYMPIC IDEAL. According to Pausanias, the first six Zanes must have been paid for by Eupolus, the Thessalian, who had bribed his fellow competitors in the boxing (98th Olympiad, 388 BC). Two others had been erected with the proceeds of a heavy fine imposed on the Athenians, held responsible for cheating one of their compatriots, Callipus (342 BC).

THE TREASURIES. Only their foundations remain today, but most of them have been identified (the Roman numbers below refer to the plan).

I. Treasury of Gela, built shortly before 600 BC, the oldest of all, and enlarged by a Doric peristyle around 491 BC.

II. Treasury of Megara, which must have been the richest because of its external decoration and its magnificent ex-votos (2nd half of the 6th century BC).

III. Treasury of Metapontum, from which some attractive decorative fragments made of terracotta have been found.

IV. Treasury of Selinus, earlier than the year 409 BC but later (2nd half of 6th century BC) than its two neighbours. It recalls the style of the temples of Selinus.

V. This construction has been identified by Dorpfeld, with some credibility, as the altar of Ge (Gaia).

VI. Treasury of Cyrene (around 550 BC).

VII. Treasury of Sybaris.

VIII. Treasury of Byzantium.

IX. Treasury of Epidamnus, with its unusual type of Doric column.

X and XI. These two buildings had disappeared in the Roman period.

XII. Treasury of Sicyon, the inscription of which has been discovered, built between 480 BC and 470 BC. It contained, between bronze shrines consecrated by Myron after his victory in the chariot race, the sword of Pelops, etc.

At the foot of the terrace of the Treasuries, stood the Metroön (temple of the Mother of the Gods or Rhea-Cybele). It was converted into a temple of Augustus and the Roman emperors, whose statues were discovered in the cella.

Beyond the Metroön, Dorpfeld discovered six houses of prehistoric construction each terminating in an apse. Traces of two of these are still to be seen opposite the ruins of the exedra of Herodes Atticus, the rich Athenian citizen who was also a benefactor of the Altis. This exedra, built between 157 and 160 AD, consisted of a large rectangular basin flanked with small rotundas. Each rotunda enclosed a shallow bowl, one of which has survived. Fifteen round or square recesses contained statues, including imperial effigies, consecrated by Herodes Atticus, and fifteen statues of Herodes and members of his family, consecrated by the Eleans. Judging from its dimensions, the exedra must have been the highest monument of the Altis after the temple of Zeus.

HERAION. This temple of Hera, one of the oldest known Doric temples, was built by the inhabitants of Scillus at the end of the 7th or beginning of the 6th century BC. In the cella were found the base and a copy (or the original – a much debated question) of the Hermes of Praxiteles, now exhibited in the museum.

Three temples in succession have been built on this site. The earliest was the size of the cella of the present temple. It was replaced by another larger temple with wooden columns. Finally the present building was constructed. Pausanias refers to the existence of several primitive columns made of oak, which were replaced at various times by stone columns with no regard for symmetry or uniformity. Moreover a variety of styles was used for the capitals, from the Archaic flat capital of the 7th and 6th centuries BC to the straight-shafted Roman capital, passing through the gentle curves of the 5th-century BC capitals.

The altar of Hera (Gaia) should not be identified with the remains of the great rectangular altar to the S, but with the foundations of the conglomerate situated in front of the exedra of Herodus Atticus; it would have been contemporary with the second temple.

PELOPION. Here you will see the remains of a wall surrounding a small mound, but this enclosure, dedicated by the Acheans of Pisa to Pelops, was one of the most revered and ancient monuments in the Altis. In the centre was the altar dedicated to the hero, his statue and a pit where black rams were sacrificed.

Near the Pelopium was probably situated the altar of Zeus, where human victims were slaughtered. It would have been circular and surrounded by a stone wall. The platform of the altar supported a kind of terrace formed by the accumulated ashes of the victims, which were kneaded together once a year with water from the Alpheus.

PHILIPPEION. This building, of which only the foundations remain, had an Ionic peristyle and a circular layout and was started on the instructions of Philip II of Macedon, shortly after the Battle of Chaeronea (338 BC). It was no doubt completed by Alexander the Great. In the centre of the cella was a large base on which stood five gold and ivory statues carved by Leochares, of Philip, his father Amyntas, his mother Eurydice, his son Alexander and his wife Olympias.

PRYTANEUM. Before leaving the archaeological site, you will see the ruins of this edifice of the 5th century BC, which was altered several times and which was the political centre for the whole sanctuary as well as the meeting place of the Eleans. It contained the chapel of Hestia, with its public meeting place where the fire burned day and night, and the Hestiatorion, the huge refectory where the public guests and the Olympic victors were fed during the festivals and where the priests and officials took their meals at ordinary times.

The ***Museum

■ The new museum of Olympia is a modern building of vast proportions, a short distance from the road to Tripolis and not visible from the Altis. Here you can see displayed practically all the treasures found on the site. The collections are presented in a very clear way, without overcrowding, in chronological order.

Open: weekdays 07.00–18.00 or 19.00; Tues. 11.00–17.00; Sun. 08.00–18.00.

Start with the gallery at the l. of the entrance hall. The galleries are not clearly numbered but their arrangement is quite straightforward; they follow one another round a large central hall where the pediments from the temple of Zeus are on show.

Entrance hall. Here you will see some inscribed bases, which once carried statues of the victors of the Olympic games, and some photographs on the walls, depicting athletic scenes, taken from painted vases of the 6th and 5th centuries BC. In particular you will see a *model of the sanctuary, which will give you a better understanding of its topography, and so conclude your visit to the site.

1st gallery. In the centre of the gallery is a bronze horse belonging to the Geometric period. The other exhibits date mainly from the Mycenaean period (note a strange helmet made of boars' tusks, just as it was described by Homer) and the Geometric period (9th and 8th centuries BC). You should note especially the foot of a bronze tripod with a scene depicting Apollo and Heracles fighting over the prophetic tripod (late 8th century BC), figurines in terracotta and bronze and, in a small wall cabinet, three Cycladic cult statues (3rd millenium BC).

2nd gallery. This gallery contains a very rich *collection of bronzes from the end of the Geometric period (8th century BC) and from the Archaic period (7th–6th centuries BC). It includes parts of cauldrons, metope decorations (late 7th century BC) consisting of a bronze leaf decorated with a female griffin suckling her offspring, the upper part of a *hammered bronze statue from the early 6th century BC representing a winged figure with chubby face, lit by a gentle 'Archaic' smile, and inlaid eyes (one of the rare examples of the Archaic technique of hammered bronze which has survived to this day). There are also *plaques decorated with strongly defined reliefs, depicting scenes inspired by the heroic legends. On one, from around 630 BC, two Centaurs are struggling to force Caeneus, a chief of the Lapiths, into the ground, for he could only be killed by being buried alive. On another, from around 590 BC, a warrior, while climbing on to his chariot, turns towards a woman carrying a child on her shoulders: this is probably the departure of the hero Amphiaraus. On a third plaque, from around 570 BC, the scenes are arranged on three levels on top of each other, probably showing in the centre Orestes, piercing his mother Clytemnestra with his sword.

The largest collection is of pieces of armour which were given as votive offerings to the sanctuary. There are helmets, whose development can be traced through the centuries. As well as Greek examples, there is a fine Illyrian specimen, from around 530 BC, decorated with figures worked in silver, with a boar between two lions on the front and a horseman on each cheek plate. You can see shinguards, or greaves, and *cuirasses. These latter include a splendid specimen of a backplate from the mid-7th century BC, decorated with engravings. On the lower part Apollo, playing the lyre, is followed by the two Hyperborean maidens; opposite him must be Zeus with two young men; at the top are lions, bulls, a sphinx and panthers. This exhibit was found in Olympia in the 19th century and has only recently been recovered by the museum after disappearing for more than half a century. There are also shields, one of which is decorated with a winged Gorgon, another shows a monster with a Gorgon's head, deer's feet and a sea-monster's hindquarters; both date from the 6th century BC.

In the last wall cabinet on the r. you will notice three small bronze figures of satyrs feasting (cauldron decorations).

Opposite on the l. side of the gallery, is a lion made of tufa from the 7th century BC, which was used as the waterspout of a fountain. The coarse limestone head near the back of the gallery on the r. no doubt belonged to the devotional statue of the Archaic Heraeum (early 6th century BC). Placed next to it is the reconstruction of the great central acroterium in terracotta from the same monument (restoration plan on the left-hand wall). At the end of the gallery is the headless kouros of Phigalia, from around 570 BC.

3rd gallery. This gallery is dominated by the partial reconstruction on the l. of the pediment of the treasury of Gela, in coloured terracotta, to its original condition (c. 560 BC), and, at the end, the reconstruction of the limestone pediment of the treasury of Megara (c. 510 BC), whose theme is the Gigantomachy (the fabulous Battle between the Giants and the Gods). This gallery also contains painted urns (Attic, Corinthian and Laconian), including an interesting Attic black-figure skyphos attributed to the painter of Theseus and apparently unfinished. Two terracotta exhibits will also attract your attention: a bowl from the late 7th century BC with a stand decorated in relief with superimposed layers (horsemen, rosettes), and a *female head which has retained its black and white colours (around 520 BC). Note also, at the end of the room on the r., the bronze lower part, decorated on each side with rams' heads, of one of those war machines which were in fact called battering rams (mid-5th c. BC).

4th gallery. This contains several remarkable specimens of terracotta statues, belonging to a genre which was quite widespread in antiquity but few examples of which have survived to the present day. In the cabinet on the r. there is a fine *head of Athena with curly hair wearing a crown of painted flowers (around 490 BC), and heads of a satyr and a young woman who formed part of the same group (c. 500 BC). On the l. is one of the greatest masterpieces of the severe style: the group of **Zeus abducting Ganymede (around 470 BC), which has retained some of its paint (note, for instance, the painted Pegasi which adorn the lower edge of the god's cloak). The lord of Olympus, whose sceptre here resembles a traveller's staff, is holding tightly against himself the young and handsome Trojan, to whom he has offered a cockerel as a love token, as he carries him away towards his palace where he will make him his cupbearer; this group was either part of a plinth or an independent offering. The sleeping lion (2nd half of the 5th century BC), which comes just after, also shows traces of colour. Towards the end of the gallery, on the l., is the terracotta torso of a warrior in the Severe style (around 490 BC), unfortunately headless. Displayed in a cabinet on the r. are some finds made during the excavation of the workshop of Phidias, moving reminders of the time when the artist was working on the creation of the huge chryselephantine statue of Zeus, designed for the cella of the temple.

They consist of fragments of Attic red-figure vases, black varnished ceramics (including a goblet bearing the inscription 'I belong to Phidias' on the outside of the base), terracotta lamps, tools, fragments of ivory, and terracotta moulds used to fashion the folds of the golden cloak of the god.

Finally, the gallery contains, besides three marble statues (including a fine Classical torso), an elegant small bronze horse (obviously an Argive work from the years 470–460 BC) and some helmets from the 5th century BC. There is one item of particular interest: a bronze helmet consecrated by Miltiades (inscription), the victor of Marathon, probably in the decade which followed his victory over the Persians (490 BC). Also note a gilded helmet from Media, part of the booty amassed at the expense of the Persians during the Persian wars, and dedicated to Zeus by the Athenians, and two bronze helmets, one Corinthian and the other Etruscan, dedicated to Zeus by Hiero, tyrant of Syracuse, after his victory over the Etruscans in 474 BC.

This is also the gallery where the Victory of Paeonius is shortly to be exhibited.

 STATUE OF VICTORY. Raised up high on a triangular pedestal stands this Victory, which was a votive offering, dedicated to Zeus Olympius – as the inscription tells us – by the Messenians and the Naupactians with the tithe from the plunder taken during operations against the Spartans, in Laconia, after their defeat by the Athenians on the island of Sphacteria in 425 BC. This masterly work was the creation of Paeonius of Mendae (in Thrace), and the inscription tells us that the sculptor won the competition introduced for designing acroteria for the temple, i.e. for the Nike and the tripods which surmounted the apex and the corners of the E pediment.

In the middle of the 4th gallery is the doorway leading to the large central hall where the pediments, metopes and four gargoyles from the temple of Zeus (c. 460 BC) are exhibited in a new arrangement.

Hall of the temple of Zeus. The length of this hall is equal to the width of the temple of Zeus. The two complete pediments of the temple have been placed against the side walls. When the opportunity arose to transfer the statues from the old museum, the arrangement of the groups within each pediment was changed, to reflect the result of detailed studies made over the past few years.

 ***East pediment. (On the r., i.e. on the W wall of the hall.) This monumental collection of sculpture shows the preparations for a chariot race between Pelops and Oenomaus. It is the portrayal in stone of a local legend, enacted under the patronage of Zeus, who occupies the centre position in the pediment.

A LEGEND WHICH GIVES THE FIRST PERVERSION TO THE OLYMPIC IDEAL.
Oenomaus, the Aetolian king of Pisa, learned from an oracle that he would be killed by his son-in-law. So he subjected all the suitors of his daughter Hippodamia to a dreadful test. He challenged them to a chariot race with himself, for which the penalty for losing would be death. But he always chased the suitors and speared them in the back. Thirteen suitors had already paid for their boldness with their lives, when Pelops, leader of the Achaeans, came forward. He bribed Myrtilus, the king's charioteer, to arrange for a wheel of his master's chariot to come off the hub during the race. According to another legend he put a curse on the horses of Oenomaus and they bolted into a ravine. Pelops, the winner, killed the Aetolian king with his spear and won both Hippodamia and the kingdom of Pisa at the same time.

The way the figures have been arranged on this pediment has given rise to several hypotheses. In the centre is Zeus, with naked torso, his himation falling from his hips and covering his legs. On his l. (or r. for the viewer), in the new arrangement, stands a helmeted man with a clean-shaven face and naked body, except for his chest which must have been covered with a bronze cuirass: this is the young Pelops. By his side is a woman dressed in a full-length chiton (tunic) folded over her chest, no doubt Hippodamia. Then there is a servant woman kneeling in front of the horses of the quadriga. Beside them is seated an old man, possibly a soothsayer; next comes a young man crouching, possibly a stablehand, lastly is the allegorical figure of the river Cladeus reclining, in sharp profile.

On the r. of Zeus (l. for the viewer) stands Oenomaus, recognizable by his bearded face and broad chest, indicating a man in his prime of life. Next comes a woman dressed in a full-length peplos (mantle), her arms folded, in pensive mood, no doubt his mother Sterope. Beside them are a servant squatting in front of the horses of the quadriga, followed by possibly Myrtilus, the charioteer of Oenomaus (?) and a soothsayer (?). Finally, in the corner, is the reclining figure of the river Alpheus.

***West pediment. (On the l., i.e. on the E wall of the hall.) In striking contrast to its counterpart, this pediment, which portrays the combat between the Lapiths and the Centaurs at the marriage feast of Pirithous (another legend), is a scene of movement and fury observed by the god Apollo, with a gaze of Olympian serenity.

The marriage feast of Pirithous was a legend of the Thessalian invaders of Elida. Pirithous, the friend of Theseus, married Hippodamia, daughter of Butes, king of the Lapiths. The Centaurs were invited to the marriage feast as friends of the Lapiths (both races claimed a common ancestor, Apollo) and became violently drunk. Their leader wanted to abduct the women and young boys. A terrible battle ensued and, thanks to the help of Theseus and Caeneus, many of the trouble makers were killed and driven out of Thessaly.

The arrangement of the figures in this pediment is just as

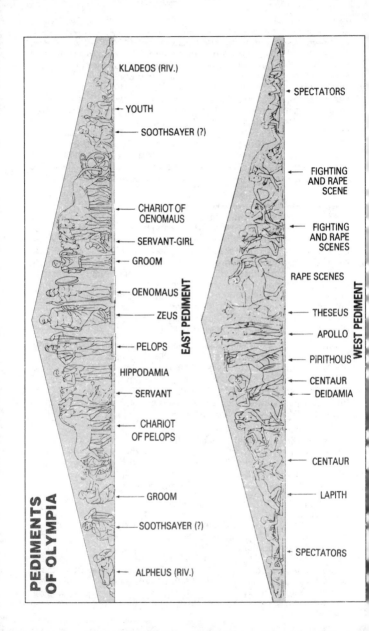

PEDIMENTS OF OLYMPIA

EAST PEDIMENT

KLADEOS (RIV.)
YOUTH
SOOTHSAYER (?)
CHARIOT OF OENOMAUS
SERVANT-GIRL
GROOM
OENOMAUS
ZEUS
PELOPS
HIPPODAMIA
SERVANT
CHARIOT OF PELOPS
GROOM
SOOTHSAYER (?)
ALPHEUS (RIV.)

WEST PEDIMENT

SPECTATORS
FIGHTING AND RAPE SCENE
FIGHTING AND RAPE SCENES
RAPE SCENES
THESEUS
APOLLO
PIRITHOUS
CENTAUR
DEIDAMIA
CENTAUR
LAPITH
SPECTATORS

controversial as that of the East pediment. On the l., in an abduction scene, the Centaur Eurytion, while clutching Hippodamia, is also struggling with Pirthious (insignificant remains), who was about to strike him with his sword. Further on the l., a badly damaged group supposedly represented a young boy struggling in the grip of a Centaur who is bending over to knock him down. This is followed by a young Lapith woman on her knees, her hair grasped by a Centaur, whilst a Lapith man presses down with all his strength on the head of the ravisher. Lastly are two reclining women, one an old woman dressed like a slave, possibly Hippodamia's nurse, rising up from her banqueting couch with a terrified look. Behind her, a nymph stretches out her rounded breasts; this must have been a river goddess, indicating the scene was set in Thessaly.

The right-hand side is symmetrical with the one just described. To the l. of Apollo (i.e. the r. for the viewer) is an abduction scene, with a Centaur seizing the girdle of a young Lapith woman, a friend of Hippodamia. One character, of which only a few fragments remain, must have been Theseus dealing axe blows with both hands, as the skull of the Centaur is already cracked. This is followed by a Centaur, who has been forced to bend his forelegs under the grip of a young Lapith whose arm he is biting. Then a Lapith woman with a torn tunic, kneeling, is trying to free herself from a Centaur brought down by a Lapith on his knees who has pierced the Centaur with his sword. An old slave woman, leaning over a cushion, watches the scene with eager interest, as does a Thessalian nymph stretched out in the corner.

This provincial sculpture was a great surprise to archaeologists. Some see in it the work of a Peloponnesian school, a manifestation of the Dorian spirit; others recognize in it an Attico-Ionian influence. A date of between 470 and 450 BC has been suggested.

The various scenes are full of movement and tumult. Displaying savage anger, the characters are contorted and entwined in unnatural positions, and yet their distress is shown only by a few furrows on their brows. The search for variety within symmetry has still not prevented the intrusion of certain blemishes, inexactitude, and apparent negligence, in the execution of some of the details, such as the folds of the clothing; and yet other parts are modelled superbly and the faces especially must be admired for their purity or their lively vigour. There is a close relationship between the virile, bold style and the rough, hasty execution of the two pediments, sculpted more in high relief than in the round. It is thought today that the W pediment is earlier than the E pediment. It seems that one artist was the originator of the composition, and he was inspired by an Attic painting, but the sculptures themselves are supposedly the work of five different artists. In actual fact, the creator of these pediments is still unknown. Pausanias suggests two names: Paeonius for the E pediment and Alcamenes for the W, but this is implausible.

This hall also contains the interior metopes of the temple of Zeus. These are displayed in four groups of three, against the N and S walls of the hall, on both sides of the two entrance doors. We shall describe them in the order in which they are placed.

These twelve sculpted metopes were placed above the entrance to the pronaos and the opisthodomos of the temple (six on each side; the external metopes were not sculpted). They depict the labours of Heracles in their legendary order. Uneven in their execution, they may be the work of the same sculptors who created the pediments and, with their generally restrained and harmonious design, illustrate a very mature Archaism already resembling Classical art.

If you wish to follow the approximate order of the legendary labours of Heracles as recounted to us by the writers of the ancient myths (for example, Pseudo-Apollodorus, around the 1st century AD), begin with the metopes which were placed to the W, above the entrance to the opisthodomos (enclosed section) of the temple; then go towards the NW corner of the hall (on the r. if you enter by the door from gallery 4) and you will see the four groups in succession.

Heracles and the Nemean Lion. (Original in the Louvre in Paris.) The lion is on the ground. In his l. hand the hero is holding the club, the instrument which helped the hero to kill the lion.

Heracles and the Hydra of Lerna. The hero is struggling to cut off the ever-reproducing heads of the monster with his sword.

Heracles bringing the Stymphalian birds to Athena. (Athena and the head and r. arm of Heracles are in the Louvre in Paris). The goddess, recognizable by her shield, is seated to the l. on a rock; she is turning towards the hero who is offering his protectress a tithe from his hunt.

On the other side of the doorway is the next group.

Heracles and the Cretan bull. (The original is in the Louvre, except for the head and hind feet.) The hero is pulling with all his strength, his r. arm on one end of a rope, the other end of the rope passed round the bull's foot, while with his l. hand he tries to grasp the beast's nostrils.

Heracles and the Cerynitian hind. (This is a badly damaged metope.) The hero is springing to the l., to overcome the powerful animal.

Heracles and the Amazon Hippolyta. The hero fells, with a blow from his club, the Amazon queen whose girdle he must win.

Go to the opposite wall where you will see the next group (from l. to r.).

Heracles bringing the boar of Erymanthus to Eurystheus. The hero is bringing Eurystheus the live boar over his l. shoulder. Eurystheus, terror-struck, has taken refuge in his large bronze jar partly buried in the ground. Only his head, arms and shoulders protrude from the hiding-place.

Heracles mastering one of the mares of Diomedes, (king of the Bistonians), who fed on human flesh.

Heracles killing Geryon, a triple-bodied ogre, one of whose heads has already been cut off.

On the other side of the doorway is the last group.

Heracles receiving the golden apples of the Hesperides. In the centre is Heracles, holding the celestial globe on a cushion on his shoulders and steadying it with his sinewy arms. Behind him is Athena helping to carry his burden. In front of the hero the wily Atlas lays out the six golden apples which he has gone to fetch, but Heracles, supporting the sky, still cannot grasp them.

Heracles and Cerberus. On the r., one of the three heads of the monster dog is emerging from an opening, the entrance to Hades. Heracles, who has tied a rope round the animal's neck, is pulling at it to bring it out into the open.

Heracles cleaning the stables of Augeas. On the l. the hero is breaking down the door, probably with an iron bar, while Athena, wearing a helmet and full-length tunic and with her l. hand on the edge of her shield, gives him directions with her r. hand, which must have held a spear.

Lastly you will see in this hall four large lions' heads which served as side drainage spouts on the temple of Zeus.

You can then go back into the 4th gallery and turn to the r.

5th gallery. This contains some sculptures from the end of the Classical period and the Hellenic period (including a young man's head in bronze along with its modern copy), as well as some terracotta and ceramic exhibits from the 4th and 3rd centuries BC.

At the end of this gallery is a doorway leading to the Hermes room, while the main route continues to the r.

THE HERMES ROOM. In the centre of this room stands the famous statue of the ***Hermes attributed to Praxiteles, in Parian marble, discovered in the cella of the temple of Hera. Although the statue has been attributed to the great sculptor, this is disputed by some authorities who regard it, perhaps rightly, as a copy made during the Roman period.

The name of the artist is only revealed to us in a cursory reference by Pausanias, the historian and geographer of the 2nd century AD: 'In the Heraeum, amongst other ex-votos, there is a marble Hermes carrying the child Dionysus: it is the work of Praxiteles.' This statue could symbolize a treaty of alliance between Arcadia (Hermes) and Elis (Dionysus), but this is by no means certain.

The group can be explained as follows. Hermes, the messenger of the gods, was commissioned by Zeus to protect the young Dionysus, born of the love of Zeus and Semele, from Hera's jealousy. He was to take him to the nymphs who were to rear him in secret. Hermes stopped on the way, near a tree, and is holding the child on his arm, amusing him with a bunch of grapes.

The marble has retained its patina, speckled with just a little brownish incrustation. Hermes is a robust ephebe who has trained in the Argive palaestrae. He looks almost humiliated by the role of nursemaid imposed on him by the gods. 'He is looking absent-mindedly at the road in the distance; his protruding lower lip suggests a slight disdain; his haughty eyes smile wistfully . . ., the lower eyelid is smoothed over, almost obliterated; the rather veiled expression of his gaze increases the air of mystery.' (Ch. Picard).

This work was not original in either its theme or its treatment, nor do the ancients seem to have paid any particular attention to it. Its execution is faultless and one could even say that the marble has been worked too much. If the little Dionysus is wanting – for artists were not yet interested in childhood – this is compensated for by the detailed treatment of the back and the carefully studied folds of the cloak which conceals the support.

You will note traces of polychrome on the lips and hair. Surprising as this might seem to us, it must be remembered that Praxiteles preferred those of his works which the painter Nicias had coloured.

6th gallery. This contains ceramics and sculptures from the Hellenic and Roman periods, in particular a fine marble head of Antinous the well-known favourite of Hadrian, and two statues of Roman emperors. In the second half of the hall the statues from the nymph's grotto of Herodes Atticus (2nd century AD) are grouped together.

7th gallery. Here you will see some inscribed Archaic bases, a cabinet of small bronzes and some Archaic terracottas, and last, some accessories relating to ancient Olympic games: stone weights, which the jumpers used to propel themselves forwards, and bronze strigils for cleaning the skin of oil.

Close to the new museum on the hill, a Mycenaean acropolis has been uncovered with chamber tombs and Roman and palaeo-Christian burial places.

In the modern village of Olympia you can visit a museum of the Olympic games set up by the International Olympic Committee. It traces the history of the modern Olympic games since their reintroduction in Greece in 1894, with medals, photographs, stamps and various souvenirs.

Open: weekdays 08.00–19.30 (summer); 08.00–15.45 (winter); Sun. 09.00–18.00 or 09.00–16.45. entrance fee.

VICINITY OF OLYMPIA

Krestaena (7mls/12km) and Platania (18½mls/30km). To the S of Olympia (but the road starts off to the W), the outskirts of Krestaena have revealed several archaeological sites of lesser importance. At 1¼mls (2km) along the Pyrgos road is a track on the r. leading to Makrysia, possibly situated near ancient Scillonte, where the remains of a large peripteral Doric temple were discovered on top of a terrace. On the plateau of Babes, Yalouris has also discovered another small Doric temple of the 5th century BC on the hill of Arnokatarachon. Below this temple the remains of houses confirm the existence of a town of unknown name, whose origin dates back to the Geometric period.

At Platania, 11mls (18km) further on, the village is dominated by the remains of the walls of ancient Typaneia; traces of a theatre, reservoirs, and the ruins of two churches can be seen. Not far away to the E are the medieval ruins of Paleokombo, a Frankish castle built in 1364 by Marie de Bourbon.

About 1¼mls (2km) beyond Platania a track to the l. (going N) leads to the ruins of the Gothic monastery of Our Lady of Issova, built by the Franks and burned down by the Byzantines in 1264.

Olympus [Mt]**

Route maps 1 and 2.

Olympus is the sacred mountain where the gods dwelt and Zeus ruled, lying between the earth and Uranus, the heavenly vault which formed the upper boundary of the Greek universe. It is part of the highest mountain range in Greece, reaching 9,470ft (2,917m).

Mountain excursions in this range usually leave from Litochoron (see under Litochoron). The best time of year is during the month of July.

The main summits from S to N are as follows. In the S are Serai (8,871ft/2,704m), Kalogheros (8,861ft/2,701m) and Palimanastri (9,235ft/2,815m); the central group is made up of Skolion (9,470ft/2,917m), Skala (9,403ft/2,866m) and Olympus or Throne of Zeus (9,470ft/2,917m); then, to the N, divided from the central group by the high pass known as Porta, there are Toumba (9,137ft/2,785m) and Prophitis Ilias (9,140ft/2,786m), from which the ridge called Petrostrounga descends steadily into the valley of Varkos.

Besides the excursions from Litochoron, there is a mountain road, not asphalted but suitable for motor vehicles in fine weather, which leaves from Leptokarya (see route map 2) and joins the Niki-Larisa road at Elasson (35mls/57km) (see route map 1), passing through Karya (15½mls/25km), a village in the midst of forests of oak and pine at an altitude of 2,789ft (850m). The monastery of Hagia Triada (wall paintings) is a 2hr walk, and the plateau of Bara, at about 7,710ft (2,350m) is a 3hr walk, the starting point for the main sumit of Olympus (9,470ft/2,917m). The ascent usually leaves from the mountain hut belonging to the Hellenic Alpine Club (information from the Club's head office in Athens, 7 Karageorgi Servias St; Tel. 23-18-67). The hut is situated at an altitude of 7,218ft (2,200m) and can be reached by a newly constructed road.

Another road goes from Katerini (see route map 2) and also leads to Elasson (40mls/65km) via the N part of the range.

■ Parga

Route map 10.

Arta, 56.9mls (91km) – Igoumenitsa, 30.6mls (49km) – Preveza, 35.6mls (57km).

As you approach Parga by road, you will appreciate the wonderful beauty of the coast where it is situated. It is a large fishing village, nestling under the bluff of a hill crowned by the ruins of a Venetian fortress (1572). The Club Méditerranée, which initiated the tourist development of the area, has taken full advantage of this little paradise. But the charm of Parga still remains. Having been in the hands of the Franks, the Venetians, the Turks, the French, the Russians, the English, the Turks again, and finally the Greeks, Parga is able to receive the cosmopolitan summer crowds without being spoilt. Admiral Kanaris, hero of the Greek War of Independence, was born here in 1790.

■ Paros [Island of]*

75sq. mls (195km²) – Pop: 6,500.

This island, which has some of the finest marble in the world, is one of the most attractive in the Cyclades. Its main centre, Paros or Parikia, is an important and charming little market town. Its smart white houses, often decorated with flowers, are situated in the most imaginative way along twisting streets. A large influx of tourists, especially Germans and British, is the price of beauty.

A DAY ON PAROS. If you have the wanderlust, you will perhaps succeed in tearing yourself away for a day, to appreciate the subtle charm of the island. You can visit its little capital, or bathe off the beach of Krias. (Go to Krias by boat since it is on the other side of the bay.) You can have a meal in a little restaurant near the harbour, or go round the island by bus, departing from the Mill. You can go as far as the valley of Petaloudes or take a tour of the whole island. (There are beautiful beaches at Drios, Pisso Livadi, Alikes and Santa Maria, where nudists are allowed.)

Near the harbour, with its flower-bedecked white houses, visit the venerable church of the Panagia Hekaton-dapyliani (Katopoliani;

collection of religious artifacts). It has a holy tower with a hundred doors, which is dominated by the cupola. It was built as early as the 6th century, testified to by the façade, but it owes much to a restoration in the 10th century (frescoes, icons).

In the little museum attached to the church, you will find an inscription reminding you of the lyric and satirical poet Archilochus. In the 7th century BC he delighted his contemporaries with his bitter-sweet poems, full of lyrical irony, his hymns and his elegies. Poet, but also adventurer, he was a mercenary. He died, at Paros, in some minor fight with the people of Naxos.

The marble of Paros, also in the museum, is another curiosity. It is a fragment of stone containing a chronological table, giving us the unauthenticated date of Homer's birth. This chronology covers a period of 1,318 years, from Cecrops to 263 BC. Another fragment is preserved in Oxford.

If you follow the main street, running parallel to the sea front, you will discover the remains of an old Frankish kastro, built partly of ancient blocks from a temple to Hera. Continue as far as the Hotel Xenia, from where you will see a few windmills, obviously less famous than those of Mykonos, but just as elegant. On the other side of the town there is the fine beach of Krias.

On Mt Koumados, to the N of the town, the very dilapidated remains of a sanctuary of Aphrodite have been uncovered. Near there you will also find the remains of a sanctuary of Apollo (Delian), bounded by a peribolus wall from the Archaic period and including a temple to Artemis. To the S of the town there are remains of an Asclepiaeum and a Pythion.

VICINITY

1 **VALLEY OF PETALOUDES** (about 3½hrs walking there and back). In order to reach this valley, haunted in summer by a myriad of butterflies, leave the coast road and take a mule track, on the l. near the Hotel Xenia. Follow a small and very green valley, and in 1½hrs you will arrive at the convent of Christos tou Dassous. 20 mins. after that you will be in the valley of Petaloudes, planted with arbutus, walnut and various fruit trees.

2 **TOUR OF THE ISLAND** (about 31mls/50km). This will be, in practice, a journey across the N part of the island which you can make by taxi, taking 2½-3hrs. You will pass by the ancient marble quarries, where a little sculpture, consecrated to the nymphs, marks the entrance to the cave made by the quarrymen.

In the centre of the island is Lefkes (8.7mls/14km from Paros), without doubt the most beautiful village, situated on an amphitheatre of hills, cut into terraces. On the E coast you will then see (11.9mls/19km) Marpissa, well-known for its fish and its fine beach of Pisso Livadi. Further on (21.9mls/35km) is Naoussa, a charming little fishing village, where a collection of icons has been preserved. Near the harbour basin is a round tower, the last vestige of a Venetian ducal castle, an outpost of Naxos. Opposite Naoussa is Kolimbithres, sited at the end of the beautiful sandy bay.

About 1hr's walking distance from Naoussa is the monastery of the Zoodochos Pighi, also called Moni Laggovarda, founded in the 17th century. The church dates from 1657 (frescoes) but the monastery was restored towards the middle of the 19th century.

 3 ANTIPAROS (13½sq. mls/35km² – Pop. 530). To the W of Paros, this little island, accessible by caïque, is particularly noted for its cave, an immense underground room 230ft (70m) deep (visiting in mornings), and for its deserted beaches. On the small island of Saliagos, between Paros and Antiparos, the remains of an important Neolithic camp have been uncovered. Only rabbits and wild pigeons live on the numerous surrounding tiny islands.

■ Patmos [Island of]**

13sq. mls (33.6km²) – Pop: 2,400.

This little piece of earth in the Dodecanese archipelago, sparsely inhabited, arid and almost without resources, is nevertheless one of the most famous in the world. It is the land of the Apocalypse, the place of retreat of St John the Evangelist, where he wrote his prophetic work. It is also a place of pilgrimage, not only for Christians who will visit the venerable Byzantine monastery and the cave of the Apocalypse, but also for those who love beauty. To be convinced that the island really is beautiful, you will need the courage to climb Mt Profitis Ilias, immediately to the S of the monastery. The sunsets are marvellous.

A LAND OF EXILE. Patmos was mentioned as early as the 5th century BC by Thucydides. There are still a few remains of the 6th century to 4th century BC fortifications of the ancient capital, which was situated near Skala, on the top of the Kastelli hill. Very poor, it served mainly as a detention camp for political prisoners during the Roman period. That is the reason for the apostle's deportation there, some time between AD 81 and 95, until AD 96. His stay gave rise to legends: for example, it was there that he was said to have turned the magician Kynops to stone.

UNDER THE PROTECTION OF THE PAPACY. In 1088 the Emperor Alexius Comnenus gave the island as a gift to St Christodulos. St Christodulos founded a monastery, named after Hagios Ioannis Theologos, on the site of an altar dedicated to Artemis. In 1207 the Venetians snatched Patmos from the control of the Byzantines. In 1461, after the fall of Constantinople, Pope Pius II took the island and the monastery under his protection. Those who might have been tempted to pillage it were threatened with excommunication. The Turks had no obligation to take the papal threats seriously; but even so they did respect the monastery. The island even achieved a certain prosperity, thanks to enterprising donors who filled the holy monastery with sumptuous gifts.

You may have plenty of spare time on the island of Patmos, or you may be restricted, depending on whether you take the regular boats or a package cruise. In either case you will visit the celebrated monastery. In the former case only will you have the chance to bathe (choice between the beaches of Grikou at 3mls/5km from Skala, Miloi, Netia, Diakopti, or Psli Ammos where nudists are allowed). You will also have the chance to patronize the little quayside restaurants (for example under the plane trees overhanging the terrace of the Unica) and to visit the taverns.

From Skala, the little port where you will disembark, you will take a taxi or bus and climb as far as the monastery of Hagios Ioannis Theologos (2.5mls/4km), and to the market town of Chora. This is one of the strangest settlements in the Greek islands, with its somewhat medieval charm, dominated by the monastery. It has some attractive patrician houses rising in tiers along narrow paved streets.

On the way, you will pass near (1.2mls/2km) the grotto of Hagia Anna, where St John lived. This cave is built inside a little monastery which protects it. The place where the apostle laid his head to sleep can be seen, marked with a metal ring. On the r. is the rock, shaped like a desk, where St John's 'disciple', Prochorus, is said to have written under his master's instructions.

MONASTERY OF HAGIOS IOANNIS THEOLOGOS. The monastery overlooks Chora, and has retained the appearance of a medieval fortress, in spite of restorations. A school of theology still exists there.

Open: summer, 08.30–12.00 and 14.00–16.00, Fri. and Sat. 08.30–12.00, and Sun. 09.00–15.00; winter, 09.00–13.00 and 14.00–16.00, Sun. 10.00–16.00; entrance fee.

You will visit there the catholicon, preceded by a narthex decorated with frescoes (story of the Evangelists and the Last Judgement). The church itself is decorated with frescoes, on a gilded ground, illustrating the life of St John. On the r. is the chapel of the Panaghia, with frescoes from 1745 and an iconostasis from the beginning of the 17th century. On the l. is the treasury.

You will see the quest room, the refectory decorated with frescoes (14th century?) and in particular the rooms set out as a museum. As well as objects of worship, canonical vestments, icons, frescoes and various documents, you will be able to admire some of the treasures from the monastery library. The library contains several hundred manuscripts from the Byzantine, Frankish and Turkish periods, as well as numerous printed works.

From the terrace there is **a superb view.

Off Patmos, to the E, is the island of Lipsi (6.5sq. mls/17km^2 – Pop: 500), surrounded by numerous islets. It provides a home for a few fishermen, produces a little wine, and has lovely deserted beaches.

■ Patras (Patrai)

Route maps 4, 5, 9 and 10.

Athens, 136.8mls (219km) – Corinth, 82.5mls (132km) – Delphi, 76.4mls (123km) – Igoumenitsa, 178.7mls (286km) – Olympia, 70.6mls (113km) – Pylos (Navarino), 132.5mls (212km) – Pop. 120,000 – bishopric – chief town of the admin. region of Achaea.

This important port, which is starting to overtake Piraeus in its passenger traffic because of the development of maritime connections with the Italian Adriatic ports, is a town of only moderate interest to the tourist. It will hardly be a stopping-off place; this no doubt explains the mediocrity of its hotel resources.

ANOTHER TRIPOLIS. Patrai (Patras, the English name, is the accusative case) was formed by the merger of three rural settlements: Aroe ('the farm'), Antheia ('the blossom') and Mesatis ('the town in the middle'). Aroe was the home of the native King Eumelus (the richest in cattle) and was inhabited from earliest antiquity by an Ionian colony under Triptolemus. After the Dorian invasion, an Achaean colony from Laconia came to settle there, and Patras drew closer to Athens and Argos. Augustus founded a military colony, called Aroe Patrensis, which became very prosperous through commerce and a byssus (precious linen) textile industry. St Andrew preached Christianity and, according to legend, is said to have been crucified and buried there.

Under the Byzantines, from the 8th to the 10th century, it was populated by refugees from the mainland who had been pushed out by the Slavonic invasion. In the 13th century, after the Frankish conquest, Patras became the fief of Guillaume Aleman, a knight from Provence, and also the seat of a Latin archbishopric. The Venetians seized it in 1408 and kept it until 1430. In 1460 it was taken by the Turks. Venice controlled it again between 1687 and 1715.

Archaeological enthusiasts will visit (in 2hrs) the archaeological museum, a Roman odeon and the kastro. Before embarking, you can stroll round the harbour area, particularly busy in summer, where the café terraces seem very inviting. But to refresh yourself more comfortably, take the Olympia road which is lined with little taverns.

The centre of the town is Trion Simmachon Square, in front of the station and the port. From here Hagios Nikolaos Avenue goes S.

■ ARCHAEOLOGICAL MUSEUM. Hagios Nikolaos Avenue will lead you to the museum, at 550yds (500m), if you are careful to take the second turning on the l. (Maizonos Street), along by the Gardens of Queen Olga.

Open: 09.00–15.30; Sun., 10.00–15.00; closed Tues.; entrance fee.

This museum contains Mycenaean artifacts, some sculptures, notably fragments from a gigantomachy (Battle between the Gods and the Giants) from the temple of Mazi (perhaps dedicated to Athena Skillountia), a head of a kore from the Archaic period (6th century BC), some Roman sculptures found at Patras, some mosaics, etc.

KASTRO. Take Hagios Nikolaos Street again, go S, and climb to the kastro, which consists of an exterior surrounding wall and a keep.

The main gateway opens on to a large tower of the Turkish period. In the N curtain wall (on the l.) there are still some remains of the Byzantine era, prior to the conquest and perhaps even to the siege which the citadel withstood in 805 against the Slavs. This defensive wall contains numerous fragments of ancient stone already used before, as do some parts of the keep. The keep, at the summit of the ancient acropolis (Aroe), was reinforced by the Paleologus dynasty (1430–60), which built a bastion on its projecting corner. A large bastion, with sloping sides, was erected by the Venetians at the beginning of the 15th century or perhaps by the Turks, soon after they had taken the town in 1460.

ROMAN ODEON. To reach the kastro, you would have left behind, at the end of Hagios Nikolaos Street, a street on the r. called Hagios Georgios Street. Follow this, and then at 330yds (300m) you will reach the site of the odeon, at one time situated near the agora (Square of 25 March 1821). It was built during the Roman period and destroyed in the 3rd century AD. The stage wall has been restored to its original state, with recesses, doors and tiered seats.

Open daily 09.00–15.30. Sun. 10.00–15.30. Entrance fee.

Alongside the odeon recent excavations have uncovered the remains of earlier buildings and basket tombs of a more recent period. Mosaics from the Roman and palaeo-Christian eras, found in town, have been placed there. Beyond the odeon, in Psila Alonia Square, also recently dug, the existence of an important collection of Roman buildings has been revealed. One of them must have been the villa of a well-known rich citizen: there were also workshops and other buildings.

VICINITY OF PATRAS

1 RHION (6mls/10km along the road to Corinth). Near the landing-stage are the ruins of the castle of Morea, a fortress built by Sultan Bajazet II before his campaign in the Morea in 1499, at the entrance to the gulf of Corinth. The gulf of Corinth is 1.2mls (2km) wide here.

2 WALL OF THE DYMEANS (20.6mls/33km; follow the road to Olympia, then turn r. towards Araxos, at 12.5mls/20km enter Kato Achaea). Kato Achaea, main settlement of the deme of Dyme, was founded by the Aegeans and afterwards made the seat of an important Roman settlement under Augustus. From Kato Achaea the road to Araxos crosses a marshy area formed from the alluvium of the Larisus.

Near Araxos is the prehistoric acropolis of Kastro tis Kalourias, which had been occupied since Neolithic times. Fortifications identified with *'teichos ton Dymaion'*, the wall of the Dymeans, described by the Greek historian Polybius, have been uncovered there. According to

Polybius the wall was more than 39ft (12m) high. On the sides not protected by the sea there was a strong rampart, in the cyclopean style and 16ft 6in (5m) thick, built in a period still not determined, but restored some time in antiquity. The main gate opened up under a protective tower. A secondary entrance was built in the middle of the longer side; this gateway, blocked during the Byzantine period, was probably covered by an archway cut out from the corbel.

■ Pella*

Route map 13.

Edessa, 30.6mls (49km) – Thessaloniki, 25mls (40km) – Verria, 33.7mls (54km).

Very close to the Thessaloniki road you will see the ruins of buildings which belonged to the ancient Pella. They are more impressive for the size and precision of their layout than for their state of preservation. The museum housing the finds has some remarkable mosaics from the Hellenistic period.

AN ANCIENT CAPITAL OF MACEDON. During the Classical period the name of Pella was barely mentioned, by Herodotus (VII, 123) and Thucydides (II, 99, 4 and 100, 4). Pella became the capital of Macedon towards the end of the 5th century BC, when King Archelaus, abandoning Aegae (Edessa or Vergina?), had a palace built where he attracted some of the most famous authors and artists of the time. They included Euripides (480–406/5 BC), who spent the last years of his life there, and the painter Zeuxis (464–398 BC). At the time of Xenophon, Pella was said to be the largest town in Macedon. However, it was hardly mentioned in the literature, even when Macedon was at the height of its power under Philip II (360–336 BC), Alexander the Great (336–323 BC), Demetrius Poliorcetes (295–283 BC) and Antigonus Gonatas (278–240 BC).

THE DESCRIPTION FROM LIVY. According to the historian Livy, the town consisted of a centre protected by a surrounding wall and a fortress, built on the island of Phacos. Phacos was a natural prominence overlooking the marshes which surrounded Pella and where the Macedonian kings stored their treasure. Excavations corroborate in part the information from this Roman historian concerning the island of Phacos, where Greek archaeologists have uncovered fragments of massive walls from the Classical and Hellenistic periods. It seems that Pella had two acropolises. One of them is identified with the present-day Palea Pella; the other is situated a little to the W where the Greek Archaeological Service has opened up another site for excavation. The remains of buildings already uncovered, near the road from Thessaloniki to Edessa, were probably in the central part of the town.

Open daily, summer, 08.30–12.30 and 16.00–18.00, Sun, 09.00–15.00; winter, 09.00–13.30 and 16.00–18.00, Sun. 10.00–16.30; entrance fee; museum closed Tues. (Tel. (0382) 312–78).

You will see the foundations of a building constructed around 300 BC, no doubt for housing the State departments. It is surrounded by streets crossing at right-angles: Pella thus appears to be a town constructed on a hippodamean plan (from the name of the architect Hippodamos of Miletus who, in the 5th century BC, recommended the first such town plan in grid form for new cities).

In its central part this building consists of a large courtyard lined with porticoes, several columns of which remain, having been re-erected. The main rooms had the floor decorated with mosaics, some geometric (visible *in situ*), others decorated with figures (on view in the museum). Several yards to the W, you will be able to see another building whose beautiful mosaic pavements (3rd century BC) have been replaced. It is a large composition which includes the abduction of the ten-year-old Helen by Theseus (the names are inscribed), stag hunting (signed by Gnosis), and a combat between Greeks and Amazons.

On the l. of the road, you will visit the museum housing the finds, where you will notice in particular the *mosaic pavements made of variously coloured stones, from the main Hellenistic period.

You will see a griffin devouring a deer, a pair of centaurs and, in particular, two compositions representing Dionysus seated on a panther, and one scene of a lion hunt (Craterus saving Alexander the Great during a lion hunt near Susa?). There are also various sculptures, including a marble dog (Hellenistic period), a bronze statuette of Poseidon, which is a Hellenistic replica in the style of the Lateran (of Lysippus) type of Poseidon, etc.

On the l. of the road there are other ruins: a Hellenistic house fronting a wide street, a small tholos, decorated with a mosaic floor (griffin) at the time of discovery, a large building in circular plan, etc.

By the road to Palea Pella, archaeological enthusiasts will find other excavation sites, notably that where archaeologists Ch. Makaronas and Ph. Petsas uncovered an orthostat wall. Its thickness and careful construction indicate that it may have been a royal building, perhaps the palace. (In the village follow the signposts leading to the 'acropolis').

Peloponnese [The]

Route maps 5, 6, 7, 8 and 9.

The physical diversity of this peninsula, with its small plains sheltered in the folds of a particularly contorted mountain system, partly accounts for the unique character which each of the city-states of ancient Greece claimed for itself when opposing the others. What common denominator could exist between the austere Laconia, with its impressive natural fortress where Sparta forged its power, and the rich Argolid, cradle of the first Greek civilization, centred in Mycenae, the source of modern archaeology? Or again, what common denominator could exist between the green areas of Triphylia, Pisatis and Elis, and 'envious' Arcadia, with its brigands in the harsh mountains of Andritsena and Mt Erymanthus, curiously linked to 'happy' Arcadia, with its poets who would have lived in the plain of Tegea (today Tripolis)? Each valley, each mountain, each promontory conceals its own microclimate and history. Such is the land which has made the greatest contribution, along with Athens, to what might be called the glory that was Greece.

THE ISLAND OF PELOPS. The Peloponnese (literally the island of Pelops) is one peninsula connected to another, the Balkan peninsula, by the isthmus of Megaris, which narrows to a width of 3.7mls (6km) near Corinth. It is this narrowing which has allowed the Corinth canal to be built. The waters of the gulfs of Corinth, Nauplia, Laconia and Messenia have moulded the shape of this peninsula into that of a plane tree leaf.

GREECE IN MINIATURE. The relief is a smaller version of that of the whole of Greece. The W, with Messenia and Elis, has the geomorphological form of Epirus, Achaea, Arcadia, eastern Messenia, Laconia and Argolis have the structure and broken relief of central and northern Greece. The whole area is formed of a series of limestone masses separated by lowlands, orientated N-S.

A VARIED CLIMATE. The climate is Mediterranean, but it has its peculiarities. In the interior it manifests a certain harshness which prevents the cultivation of the olive. In the E, Argolis has the same weather as Attica. In the S, the plains of Messenia and Laconia are sufficiently warm and humid for bananas to ripen. The W seaboard is swept by wet westerly winds.

ECONOMIC PROBLEMS. Arcadia, sheltered by a labyrinth of mountains giving long winters, is an economically backward region, where the walnut has replaced the olive and maize is grown on reclaimed marshland. Argolis grows many Mediterranean crops, such as cereals, tobacco, the grape, the olive and market garden vegetables. Messenia and Laconia have an abundance of olives, lemons, oranges, vines, wheat and maize. The western seaboard, which is the most densely populated area in the Peloponnese, is also the richest, with modern irrigation (and crops such as grapes, cereals, olives). It also has a large port, Patras, the third most important Greek town. But the Peloponnese has not escaped depopulation, which began with the exodus from the rural mountain regions and today has reached the valleys. The tourist trade, which is too localized and seasonal, cannot replace the older economy, and industry lacks incentive to establish itself there, except around the town and port of Patras.

■ Philippi (Filippi)**

Route map 14.

Alexandroupolis, 118mls (189km) – Kavalla, 9.4mls (15km) – Thessaloniki, 105.6mls (169km).

This town is best known for the battle in 42 BC between two Roman armies; one side was led by Brutus and Cassius, the assassins of Julius Caesar, while the other side was led by Octavius and Antony, the victors. This encounter decided the fate of the Roman Republic. The vanquished committed suicide, whilst the victors contributed to the fortune of the town by sending important civil and military colonies to Philippi. It was at Philippi that the Apostle Paul gave his first sermon on European soil (*Acts* XVI, 9-40).

A CITY OF FARMING SOLDIERS. Under the leadership of the banished Athenian Callistratus, the inhabitants of Thasos founded, under the name of Crenides, the first settlement, a short while before Philip II (356–336 BC) arrived. In 356 BC the town received its name from Philip II, king of Macedon. This region was very rich owing to the presence of the gold mines of Pangea. According to a tradition, quoted by Pliny, this is where the king Cadmus, founder of Thebes, is said to have discovered and smelted the precious metal for the first time. During the Roman period the town was the centre of a mainly agricultural and military colony, created to settle the veterans of Antony's army after the battle of 42 BC, which had taken place on the plain between the marshes and the escarpment of the mountains. Philippi had new settlers.

After St Paul had passed through and certainly after the arrival of Constantine, Christianity grew rapidly in this town; it had an important basilica by the 5th century. In the 10th century, under Leo the Wise, it was the seat of a Byzantine metropolis. Philippi was mentioned by the Arabian geographer Idrisi around the middle of the 12th century, but it declined during the following century with the arrival of the Franks. The French School of Athens, as well as the Greek Archaeological Service, opened up various sites and excavation work has been revived in recent years.

In about 1hr you will be able to visit the rather impressive ruins of a Roman and Byzantine city, which was of average size, though it did have a vast forum and a theatre, setting for the festival of Philippi and Thasos, 15 July to end of August. Philippi derived its importance from the Via Egnatia, an artery more than 1,000 Roman miles (about 937mls/1,500km) long, which joined Dyrrachium (today's Durazzo or Durres in Albania) to Byzantium. Parking place near the theatre.

Open: daily, summer, 08.00–19.00, Sun., 09.00–15.00; winter, 09.00–13.30 and 16.00–18.00, Sun. 10.00–16.30; entrance fee; museum closed Tues. (Tel. (051) 51–62–51).

THEATRE. The theatre, positioned right against the slope of the acropolis and the ramparts, dates back to the 4th century BC. Nothing remains of this era for the building was greatly altered during the Roman period. During the 3rd century AD it was altered to allow gladiatorial combats and also fights with wild animals. From this period date three bas-reliefs (plan, 8) showing Nemesis, protective goddess of arena games, Ares and Nike, the goddess of Victory.

The rampart, which abuts the theatre and climbs to the top of the

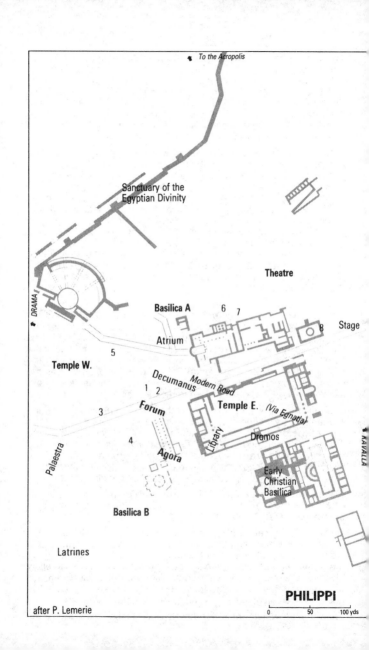

To the Acropolis

Sanctuary of the
Egyptian Divinity

Theatre

DRAMA

Basilica A   6 7

Atrium

5   8   Stage

Temple W.

Decumanus   Modern Road

1 2

Forum   Temple E.   (Via Egnatia)

3

4   Library   Dromos

Agora

Early
Christian
Basilica

Basilica B

KAVALLA

Latrines

Palaestra

PHILIPPI

after P. Lemerie

0   50   100 yds

acropolis, was built by the Byzantines in the 10th century, frequently on the foundations of the wall constructed by Philip II in 356 BC. One of the main gateways to the town, cut through this rampart, is visible near the theatre, below the level of the other side of the main road. The keep, at the top of the acropolis near the middle of the redoubt, was built by the Byzantines in the 10th century.

During the Hellenistic period, the Macedonian rampart was reinforced by square towers, which jutted out at roughly regular intervals, and was castellated. The rampart came down the S side of the acropolis and surrounded the town. Its position can be traced for its full length across the plain, showing up as cart tracks.

From the theatre in the E, you can take a path W leading to the Basilica A.

BASILICA A. It dates from the end of the 5th century AD and is situated on a terrace overlooking the modern road.

It was approached from the W through an atrium, from which one passed into the narthex, which was connected to a vestibule and the baptistry. In the naos a staircase led to the repository of relics under the altar. To the W of Basilica A, near the museum, is another palaeo-Christian church, also from the end of the 5th century AD, which also had three naves.

Near the SW corner of the atrium of Basilica A, a dog-legged passageway led to a Roman cistern (plan, 5). According to local tradition, this marked the place where St Paul was imprisoned. At the top of the staircase, notice on the l. the remains of a Macedonian building, no doubt a heroön, which the Byzantines turned into a cistern.

SANCTUARIES CUT INTO THE ROCK. If you climb the mound overlooking Basilica A, you will see a series of small sanctuaries cut into the rock at its base. Three large recesses (plan, 6) and a bench from one still exist. On the r., several Latin inscriptions (plan, 7) are scratched on the rock. Executed during the 2nd and 3rd centuries AD, they give a list of the members of a religious foundation, in tombstone fashion, and also the list of subscribers who contributed to the construction and ornamentation of the temple of this foundation, dedicated to Silvanus.

ROCK CARVINGS. The 180 or so reliefs and inscriptions cut on the S and SW sides of the rock of the acropolis at Philippi are certainly one of the notable features of the site. A large number are grouped above the theatre, outside the boundary fence of the site, and also above the museum, along the path which leads to the top of the acropolis. This path goes close by the sanctuary of Egyptian deities. They can also be seen above the monastery of St Lydia, which is half a mile (1km) further on at the extreme W of the town. More than half the reliefs represent Diana, Goddess of the Hunt, with a dog. She has her bow in her hand, ready to hunt a stag or hind. The goddess often has a short spear in her right hand and a branch in her left hand. The numerous offerings to the huntress bear witness to the ancient veneration which the goddess enjoyed in this region and which continued into the Imperial era. It is thought, in fact, that the majority of carved rock reliefs date from the 2nd or the 3rd century AD. Alongside the representations of Diana, there is often the figure of a woman wearing a long garment, perhaps a goddess, a priestess or just a worshipper. Among the other deities whose pictures have been carved on the rocks, mention should be made of the Horseman-Hero, a god of Thracian origin, Jupiter, Minerva, Cybele, etc. Recently, several drawings (boat, chariot), no doubt going back to the middle of the first millennium BC, have been discovered at the summit of the acropolis, about 22yds (20m) S of the lower bastion of the Byzantine fortress.

·FORUM. Situated on the other side (i.e. to the S) of the main road from Basilica A, this large complex, consisting of a huge square paved in marble and lined on three sides with porticoes, was probably built under Marcus Aurelius (AD 161–180) and altered in the palaeo-Christian era. Located in the centre of the town, it was bordered by the symmetrical facades of two temples.

Before reaching the square, notice the ruts left by the wheels of the chariots in the surface of the decumanus (main street), which was the stretch of the Via Egnatia which went through the town.

The decumanus has been uncovered for about 110yds (100m), along the N side of the forum. As it left the forum on the W side it passed through a monumental gateway, the pillars of which still stand.

Going along the decumanus towards the forum, you will see the remains of the speakers' tribune (plan, 1) and an Ionic building (plan, 2). There are numerous fragments of the W temple scattered on the ground. Near the SW corner there is a measuring table in marble, with five cupules hollowed out (plan, 3). Not far away you will see little holes dug out of the stylobate of the S portico, by idlers who wanted to play marbles; and elsewhere you will notice circles for playing dice on the paving slabs of the square.

Numerous pieces from the E temple have been laid out neatly. Not far away are the fragments of an entablature of a library which looked on to the E portico. The S side of the forum was lined by little shops which opened at a lower level on to a street. Beyond this street was the market, partly covered over by Basilica B. You can get there along a path leading out from the middle of the S side of the forum.

On the floor of the market hall, you will notice that several games have been etched on the slabs; for example, circles (plan, 4) divided into four equal quarters, and used for the game of hopscotch, as mentioned by Ovid in his *The Art of Love* (III, 365–366).

BASILICA B. This building, which attracts attention by its high columns, was built in the 6th century. After the collapse of the cupola, it seems it was not finished. In 827 the Bulgarians had an inscription (now kept in the museum) engraved in Greek in this church. It tells of an expedition against the Smolians, a Slav tribe who occupied the region between Strymon and Nestros.

This basilica consisted of a narthex, which opened on to a space on the W which was probably the atrium, and a naos. The naos had three naves and was flanked on the E side by two small constructions with apses. The one to the N consisted of a baptistry and a chrismarion, where the bishop's throne was located; this was used for the preparation and for the ceremony of baptism. The two rooms to the S no doubt formed the diaconicon, where the offerings of the faithful were kept. They were given to the deacons for the benefit of the community or for the celebration of the eucharist. After the collapse of the cupola, the narthex was flanked on the E by a small secondary choir which encroached on to the central nave, unused from that time onwards.

PALAESTRA. Built in the 2nd century AD, it was razed to the ground and partly built over during the construction of the basilica. Note, in particular, the remains of a small odeon with tiers, intended for public lectures. Near there, to the S., are large latrines, exceptionally well preserved.

PALAEO-CHRISTIAN BASILICA. Before reaching the forum you will see, from the road, the remains of one of the four large palaeo-Christian basilicas uncovered at Philippi. It could be reached by following a porticoed way which opened on to the Via Egnatia by a propylaeum with three bays. On the l. are the not very interesting remains of a small bath, or loutron, which formed an annex to the church.

Before reaching the courtyard in front of the basilica, a rectangular room was crossed, forming a sort of propylaeum. On the l. there is a collection of rooms, the first being a monumental fountain (phiale) open to the sky, the centre of which was occupied by a basin. Near the phiale was the baptistry, which had a floor paved with marble slabs, and the baptismal fonts, in the shape of a Maltese cross, also in marble. Beyond the fountain stretches the basilica.It consisted of a narthex and the naos proper, asymmetrical in shape, so as to retain on the outside of the sanctuary a circular building of unknown usage, which was at some time covered with a cupola. The church had an apse at each corner and a central octagon surrounded by a tiered portico, except on the E side where the choir was situated. During the 6th century the building was altered and the synthronon, or benches reserved for the clergy, was added. On the site of the octagon, a mosaic belonging to an older basilica with three naves has been uncovered.

Outside the octagon, on the side of the baptistry, a Macedonian tomb of the 3rd century BC has been discovered. Beyond the basilica, towards the l., are the remains of an episcopal palace, twenty or so rooms of which have so far been uncovered.

The University of Thessaloniki work each year on the excavations in this section.

MUSEUM. (Reached from the road to Drama by taking a dirt track to the r. about 330yds (300m) beyond the site. Car park at the end of the track.) It houses most of the finds made on the archaeological site (Hellenistic, Roman and palaeo-Christian), and also Neolithic pots and artifacts from Dikili-Tach and Sitagri. The antiquities displayed outside the building (inscriptions and fragments of architecture) are from the region.

Open: summer, 09.00–13.00 and 16.00–18.00; winter, 10.00–16.30; Sun. 10.30–14.30; closed Tues; entrance fee. Entrance on the r. side of the building in the 1st floor.

VICINITY

1 KRENIDES (0.6ml/1km before Philippi when coming from Kavalla). Towards the middle of the village, about 110yds (100m) from the main road (on the l. when coming from Philippi), along the Street of 28 October, one can see the remains of a fairly large palaeo-Christian church.

2 DIKILI TACH (0.6ml/1km to the E of Krenides; see Vicinity of Kavalla, 1).

Piraeus (Pireefs or Piraias)*

Route maps 3 and 5.

Athens, 6mls (10km) – Corinth, 54mls (87km) – Patras, 136mls (219km) – Thessaloniki, 337mls (542km) – Pop: 190,000 – admin. region of Attica.

The most important port in Greece, Piraeus gives an insight into a typically Mediterranean civilization, seen much less frequently on other seaboards: the town looks generously on to both its port and the sea. This double aspect produces happy results, of which cosmopolitanism is one of the most attractive, for Piraeus is such a bustling port. The explosion of Greece into innumerable islands in part explains it, the industrialization of the Athens-Piraeus-Eleusis triangle and the size of the Greek merchant marine (sometimes under flags of convenience) make up the rest. For those who are looking for local colour, Piraeus will provide a unique theatre for observation.

CAN ANYONE MAKE AS MUCH MONEY AS AN ATHENIAN? The creator of the ports of Piraeus and the Athenian navy was Themistocles. His work was completed, under Cimon and Pericles, by the construction of the Long Walls which joined Athens to its port, and by the building of the town to the plans of Hippodamus of Miletus. The key to the economic activity of Athens, which had a hegemonic character in the 5th and 4th centuries BC, was in the hands of the emporoi or merchants of Piraeus. The port of Athens enjoyed, at this period, an extraordinary prosperity, which allowed Xenophon to ask if there existed in the whole of Greece and among the Barbarians a people more gifted than the Athenians in the art of making money.

WITHOUT PIRAEUS, ATHENS WOULD BE SUFFOCATED. The possession of Piraeus assured the future of Athens. That is why Lysander had the surrounding wall of Piraeus and a part of the Long Walls demolished in 404 BC; and why the aristocratic government of the Thirty surrendered to Sparta, for 30 talents, the harbour rights for vessels (they had cost them 1,000 talents). Conon, victor over the Spartan fleet at Cnidos in 394 BC, restored the ramparts and arsenals of Piraeus. Lycurgus completed this work by finishing a skeuotheke (arsenal for ships' gear), built by the architect Philon 346–329 BC and situated near the port of Zea (Pacha Limani). Under Macedonian control, the fortress of Munychia was occupied by Alexander's successors 322–229 BC. In 86 BC, Sulla destroyed Piraeus; Strabo described it as a little village of no importance. It stayed like that till 1835.

THE PORT. It has undergone a tremendous expansion, especially since the end of World War II. Without including the extensions at the port of Herakes (unloading coal and merchandise for the interior, loading of minerals) and several other harbours towards Eleusis, used by the Athens-Piraeus-Eleusis industrial area (shipbuilding, metallurgy, chemical works, glassworks, spinning factories, distilleries, flour mills, soapworks, etc.), the main port of Piraeus can be divided into three parts, namely the Limin Alon, the grand harbour and the outer harbour.

The Limin Alon, the ancient Kophos Limin, is an inner basin where the boats carrying cargo for the interior drop anchor and are unloaded.

The grand harbour, the Kantharos of the Ancients and Porto Leone or Draco of the Middle Ages, has quays which are in part occupied by coasters and, near the customs house, by liners. The east quay corresponds to the emporium of the ancient port.

Finally, the outer harbour contains the naval dockyards, the dry docks and the installations of the Greek navy.

To the E, Pacha Limani is a pleasure harbour, recently enlarged by the Zea marina (embarkation point for hydrofoils crossing to the islands in the Saronic gulf), and this includes the little bay of Microlimano.

Consider Piraeus for what it really is: a suburb of Athens. You would probably not stay there, but you would certainly be tempted to go there several times. A half-day is sufficient for a visit to Piraeus. A morning would be particularly good, because you could then lunch, probably on fish, at Pacha Limani or Microlimano.

WHERE TO PARK?

This is not easy, unless you arrive early in the morning, and then you may be able to park along the side of Pacha Limani (map C-2) or in the Akti area.

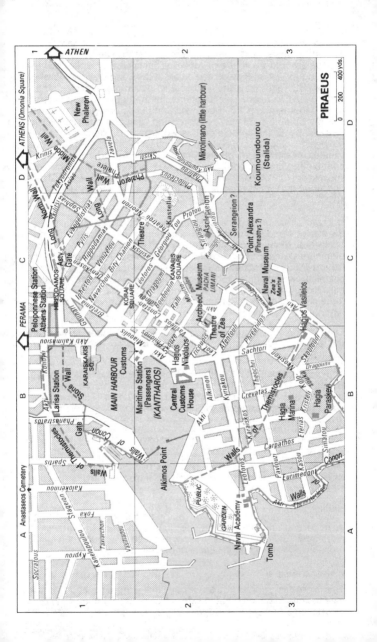

THE TOWN ON FOOT

See map for references. First, use your car to make a tour of the Akti, the centre of which is the working-class quarter of Peraiki (map B-3), and then go to Pacha Limani (map C-2). From Pacha Limani, walk along Tricoupi Street (map B-2) to reach the grand harbour area. If you are fond of archaeology, make a little detour to Karaiskakis Square (map B-1) and the Asty Gate (map C-1), then return to Pacha Limani by Ralli Street (map C-2). From here, complete your tour of the town by visiting Microlimano (map D-2), which is overlooked by the working-class quarter of Kastella (map C-2).

AKTI. A walk round the circumference of this peninsula allows you to discover *some beautiful views over the port and the coast, as well as the ruins of the surrounding wall of Conon, built between 394 and 391 BC. The wall attributed to Themistocles used to cut transversely across the peninsula, following the high ground (see map).

ZEA MARINA AND PACHA LIMANI (map C-2, C-3). This yachting marina occupies the site of the ancient port of Zea, where the Athenians kept a large part of their naval fleet.

This port of Zea, mentioned in the inventories of the Athenian navy, was the most important of three ports for triremes, of which it could hold 196 in covered berths, the ruins of which have been partly uncovered.

The skeuotheke of Philon was in the NE corner of the basin, where Kanaris Square is now situated.

Alexander's point (map C-3), which forms the E boundary of Pacha Limani, may have been the Phreattys. This is where a criminal court gave judgement on murderers who had crossed the frontier: the accused was on a boat while the tribunal sat on shore.

NAVAL MUSEUM (map C-3). Located at the far end of the Zea marina, below the Themistocles quay, it is dedicated to the history of the Greek navy from antiquity to the present day.

Open: daily, except Mon. 09.00–12.00; Sun. 10.00–13.00 and 17.00–20.00; entrance fee; Tel. 451-68-22.

ARCHAEOLOGICAL MUSEUM (Map B-2, C-2). Situated on Charilaou Tricoupi Street, it has just been reorganized and reopened to the public after having been closed for several years. Since then it has contained the four large bronze statues which, though discovered on Piraeus, were kept until 1983 in the National Museum in Athens.

Open: daily, except Tues., 09.00–15.30; Sun. 09.00–14.00.

From the entrance hall, where there is a marble statue of a naked man, dating from the 2nd century AD, pass through to the first room, which specializes in reliefs. Among these is a series of marble slabs from the 2nd century AD, found at Piraeus in 1930–31, showing scenes of the Amazonomachy (Battle of the Amazons) which Phidias had sculpted on the shield of the Parthenon's Athena. There are also a few other subjects inspired by mythology, such as a disputation between Apollo and Heracles seated on three-legged tripods from Delphi, the Three Graces, a group of Nymphs, Nysa receiving the child Dionysus. On the l. is a large funereal lion (4th century BC), to its l. a relief (no: 2120) shows Heracles in his chariot, abducting Iole.

To the r., pass into a second room which is rich in funeral stelae from the 4th century BC among which are the fine stele (no: 429), a leave-taking scene, with three figures, *c*. 330, and in marble statues from the Roman period. They include portraits of the emperors Claudius (AD 41–54) and Trajan (AD 98–117), a colossal head of Hadrian (117–138), a full-length statue of the emperor Balbinus (238), head of an old man (3rd century AD). You will notice two small unfinished statues of Artemis and Athena, attributed to a local craftsman of the 2nd century AD.

Third room (opposite the museum entrance). It contains the remains of a *monumental tombstone in marble from the second half of the 4th century BC, found at Kallithea (between Athens and Piraeus) in 1967. This monument, commemorating a certain Niceratus of Istria and his son Polyxenus, was about 16ft (5m) high. It consisted of a base with three steps, then orthostatic blocks and three rows of isodomic blocks, followed by a sculpted frieze of an Amazonian battle (variously coloured remains). Above that came a cornice, itself surmounted by three steps with yet another sculpted frieze (animals fighting).This served as a base for a naiskos which had two Ionic columns framing three life-size marble statues in the background at the end of the naiskos (father, son and obviously one of their servants). The monument was crowned with an Ionic entablature. The extravagance of such a memorial sculpture explains the law forbidding it, which was promulgated at the end of the 4th century BC by Demetrius of Phaleron.

At the end of the room is a statue of the goddess Cybele seated.

Take the staircase leading to the upper floor.

In the entrance hall (in the course of being arranged) are displayed a few reliefs of the Classical period, also two Hermes and a small female statue in marble.

The two following rooms house the *four large bronze statues, discovered by chance. According to a recent theory, they could have originated from Delos, the intention being to take them off to Rome or the south of Italy, like many large Greek statues, no doubt at the time of Sulla (beginning of the 1st century BC). But they must have been stored at Piraeus, where they then remained owing to some accident or unforeseen event.

***Statue of Apollo, of the kouros type, probably the work of a Peloponnesian bronze worker at the end of the 6th century BC. The god must have held a bow in his left hand and an unknown object (perhaps a phial) in his right hand. This statue, the oldest known kouros in bronze, has another peculiarity: the right leg is forward, not the left leg as in most other kouroi.

**Statue of Athena. Standing 7ft (2.35m) high, Athena, with a crested helmet, is armed, one hand held out supporting a Victory or a phial, the other hand holding a spear, now disappeared, and her aegis, a sort of marvellous cuirass covered with the skin of the goat Amalthea and the hideous mask of the Gorgon. By using this cuirass to protect her breast, the goddess contrived to put fear into the hearts of her enemies. This wonderful work, from the second classical period, dates from around 375 BC. It may have originated from Cephisodotus, perhaps the father of Praxiteles. In this room there are also *two statues of Artemis, dating from the middle of the 4th century BC.

The large room on the first floor (on the l. at the top of the staircase) houses a fine collection of *marbles. The first statue on the r. (2530) is an Archaic kore of Samian type (around 580 BC). Most of the other exhibits are Attic stelae or funeral vases from the end of the 5th century BC or the beginning of the 4th century BC. Note, in particular, the following numbered items. There is a fragmentary stele (3580) of the first quarter of the 4th century, especially interesting for the inscription engraved on the face, in Phoenician script, attesting the presence of a Phoenician colony in Piraeus at that time. There is a fragmentary stele (1703) from the beginning of the 4th century, representing a girl holding a doll in her hand. From the first half of the 4th century is a funerary lekythos (1700), decorated with a sculpture in low-relief. Also exhibited is a stele, crowned with a sphinx, which has one woman seated at its foot between two other standing women. A magnificent *stele (2555) from the second quarter of the 4th century, shows, in very high relief, a woman standing on the r., richly robed and accompanied by her servant; notice the exquisite hands, originally adorned with a painted bracelet, and the suppleness of her posture. A stele (386) from the beginning of the 4th century, shows a beautiful scene of dexiosis (greeting) between the young Hippomachus and probably his father Callias. There is a small stele (1161) of the Athenian Andron, dating from the 2nd quarter of the 4th century. One stele (46), from the end of the 5th century, represents a middle-aged man, tall and upright, holding the hand of a young man. The *stele of two hoplites Clairedemos and Lyleas (about 420), shows one of them nude and the other clothed in a chlamys, each one carrying a lance and a buckler.

THEATRE OF ZEA (map B-2, C-2). There are only scanty remains of this construction of the Hellenistic period (2nd century BC), situated next to the archaeological museum and a short distance from the ancient port of Zea.

KARAISKAKI SQUARE (map B-1). This is located between the inner basin (Limin Alon) and the Kantharos (meaning goblet, because of its shape). It lies on the site of an ancient breakwater, the Choma, where the Council of Five Hundred met on the eve of naval expeditions.

ASTY GATE (map C-1). Leave Hippodamos Square and follow Skylitsi Street to reach this gate. Its two towers stood at the end of the road from Athens. It was built by Themistocles, then restored by Conon in 394 BC and by Lycurgus in 337 BC.

Beyond the gate was the beginning of the Northern Long Wall, running along the top of a rocky spur. It is overlooked by the remains of an ancient sanctuary and another gate, partly visible, with an interior courtyard, to which the road between the two walls (Northern Wall and Middle Wall) led.

Other remains of ramparts can be seen at the foot of the hill of Munychia, which the city wall scaled so as to follow the ridge. You can reach them by following Pylis Street (map C–1), which passes in front of Asty gate before coming to Kodrou Street (foundations of walls and towers).

SERANGEION. If you make your way from Pacha Limani to Microlimano, you will have to climb up a cliff hollowed out with deep cavities, thought to be the Serangeion (map C–2). The hollows where the ruins of thermal baths were discovered are called Zenon's cave (Spilia Zinonos).

MICROLIMANO (map D–2). This marina, too, occupies the site of an ancient harbour. It is one of the most picturesque corners of Piraeus, congested with pleasure craft and fishing boats. In the 4th century BC it was surrounded by a line of sheds for 82 triremes, traces of some of them still being visible to the S and N when the water is calm.

From there, climb the hill of Munychia (today Kastella, map C–2) a working-class area, where you will capture scenes of daily life. The climb may seem a little arduous, but you will be well rewarded with a *panoramic view over Piraeus and the Saronic Gulf.

The remains of a theatre, discovered in 1880, have been buried under various constructions and piles of earth. There is therefore no chance of confusing it with the large theatre seating 2,000 people, called the Skylitsion, built by the city council and modelled on ancient theatres.

■ Platamon

Route map 2.

Larisa, 30mls (48km) – Katerini, 22mls (36km).

This is a small seaside resort lying at the foot of the Mt Olympus range, near a medieval fortress. This *Platamon castle, erected by the crusaders at the beginning of the 13th century to control the entrance to the Thermaic Gulf, still stands proudly behind the beautiful long beaches. Other beaches follow on to the N, often partly given over to camping sites, and made accessible by the fast Larisa-Thessaloniki road.

■ Poros [Island of]

13sq. mls (33km²) – Pop: 4,500.

On a map, this island seems to be simply an extension of Argolis, so narrow are the straits that separate it from the mainland. Of volcanic origin, the island is attached by an isthmus to Calavria (Caularie), an ancient islet with a much richer vegetation. Poros, so close to Athens, is above all a very pleasant place for an out-of-town stay; but the crowds making bathing almost impossible from the beginning of June onwards. Archaeological enthusiasts, however, can satisfy their interests by visiting on the island the sanctuary of Poseidon, and on the mainland the site of ancient Troezene (see Vicinity of Nauplia).

The little town of Poros lies gently terraced above the harbour where the ancient battleship *Averoff* passes its last days (visits possible). With its white houses with blue shutters floating between the sea and sky, it offers little to the visitor except its charm, but that is sufficient to justify staying awhile. The buildings of the first arsenal of independent Greece today house a naval school.

VICINITY

SANCTUARY OF POSEIDON (3mls/5km, passing by the monastery of the Zoodochos Pighi, accessible by taxi). From this monastery (see the gilded wood iconostasis in Italianate style), set in a delightful spot near a spring, you will climb up a newly built road through pine woods to the site of the sanctuary of Poseidon. It was the headquarters for a maritime Amphictyonic council (Hermione, Epidavros, Nauplia, Prasiai, Aegina, Athens, Orchomenus) and a home for the shipwrecked and those needing shelter. Demosthenes, pursued by Antipater's soldiers, poisoned himself there in 322 BC. The temple, quite dilapidated, is from the 6th century BC. The view from this site is extremely good.

Neorion, accessible by boat or on foot, is close to numerous coves and some most attractive beaches.

By boat from Poros, you can reach Lemonodassos, at the end of the Argolis peninsula, where there is a marvellous plantation of 30,000 lemon trees whose perfume pervades the air.

■ Porto Ghermeno

Athens, 43mls (70km) – Thebes, 27.5mls (43km).

Porto Ghermeno recalls the legend of Oedipus being abandoned by his father Laius, after the oracle at Delphi had revealed to Laius that his own son, born of his union with Jocasta, would kill him. This little harbour, hidden at the head of an inlet in the gulf of Corinth, and at the foot of Mt Citheron, could be the object of a walk for those who like to get off the beaten track. You will see there the ruins of the fortified acropolis of Aegosthena, on the l. of the road, which leads off the main road inland, before you reach Porto Ghermeno. The remains of the town wall and the acropolis of the ancient town, from the 4th century BC, are remarkably well preserved, and in particular there are several towers, about 33ft (10m) high, which are still standing.

■ Preveza

Route map 10.

Agrinion, 61.5mls (99km) – Arta, 31.5mls (51km) – Igoumenitsa, 59.5mls (96km) – Nicopolis, 5mls (8km) – Pop: 11,500.

This small port, guardian of the entrance to the gulf of Arta, as witness its Venetian fortress, sees its serenity jeopardized today by the construction of new roads linking Igoumenitsa and Amphilokhia directly.

But Preveza, the ancient Berenicia, is accustomed to turmoil, having witnessed the Battle of Actium.

IN HOMAGE TO BERENICE. Pyrrhus, king of Epirus, the famous 'winner of a Pyrrhic victory', built this town around 290 BC in honour of his mother-in-law, Berenice, wife of Ptolemy, king of Egypt. Occupied by the Venetians in 1499, it was lost and retaken by them several times before coming under the control of the French, at the same time as the Ionian Islands, under the terms of the Treaty of Campo Formio (1797). It was then seized by the notorious Ali Pasha, followed by the Turks, until 1912.

You can climb on to the main bastion of the Venetian fort, near the landing stage of the ferry which provides a service across the mouth of the gulf of Arta. From there, while looking out over the Gulf and the hinterland, you can relive some of the actions of the famous Battle of Actium which, in 31 BC, was the finale to the civil war between Octavian and Antony. Actium was a port situated not far from the small Venetian fort which you can see on the other side of the strait, near the temple of Apollo Actios. It has been decided that work should start on refloating of the ships which took part in the battle, some of them perfectly preserved.

THE ADVERSARIES MOVE THEIR PAWNS. Antony, who had his headquarters at Patras in the autumn of 32 BC, sent his fleet to Actium. Agrippa, who had prepared the crossing of Octavian from Brindisi, ordered his troops to move to Corcyra, then he sent them to the gulf of Ambracia from the N. They took up a position at Michalitsi, to the N of Nicopolis; the fleet dropped anchor in the bay of Gomaros to the W. Antony hastened from Patras and placed his army in the neighbourhood of the temple of Apollo; from there he set up camp, with his troops, to the NW of Preveza, and tried unsuccessfully to draw Agrippa into battle. His cavalry, which he had sent all the way round the gulf of Ambracia, was routed by Octavian near the river Louros. Antony's men, in a marshy area, were suffering from fever when, in an audacious raid, Agrippa seized Leucas, pushing a column as far forward as Corinth.

CHECK AND CHECKMATE. Antony's position was becoming critical and he thought of retreating. Withdrawing his camp near Actium, he had the idea of returning to Athens. As his fleet was stationed at the entrance to the gulf, he kept it close to land, hoping to lure his opponent towards the heavy ships which he was using, and then to encircle them with his own more manoeuvrable ones. Agrippa, who saw through the ruse, kept at a distance. After a long wait, Antony took to open water where Octavian's fleet, having withdrawn still further, outflanked Antony by virtue of its superiority in lighter ships. During the battle Cleopatra escaped and Antony followed her, while the remainder of his fleet was annihilated.

■ Ptolemais

Route map 1.

Florina, 49.5mls (80km) – Kozani, 17mls (28km).

To the S of a beautiful region of lakes (Petra, Vegorritis, Chimaditis) and near an important electrical power station, Ptolemais is a small ancient city on the outskirts of which several prehistoric habitations have been discovered.

■ Pylos (Navarino)*

Route maps 8 and 9.

Kalamata, 32mls (52km) – Patras, 131.5mls (212km) – Pyrgos, 74mls (119km) – Tripolis, 85mls (137km) – Pop: 3,000.

This pleasant little town, its streets bordered with arcades, is situated on one of the most beautiful bays in Greece, that of Navarino. As a coastal town it is one of the finest in the Peloponnese, where, away from the main tourist traffic, you will find the atmosphere of the Greek family beach.

THE CASTLE OF THE AVARS. The name of Navarino, given to the European navies by the Venetians, and today fallen into disuse locally, is derived from Ton Avarinon (castle of the Avars), which is the name the Byzantines gave to the acropolis of Pylos after the Slav invasion. In 1573 some Turks built a citadel there and called it Neo Kastro (new castle) to distinguish it from the old castle of Pylos. In 1686 the Venetians captured it from them and kept it until 1715. In 1825 Ibrahim Pasha encamped there with his Turko-Egyptian troops. His excesses provoked the intervention of the European powers and the famous Battle of Navarino.

THE BATTLE OF NAVARINO: A DEPLORABLE EVENT. As a result of the Convention of London (June 1827), France, England and Russia decided to establish official relations with insurgent Greece and to impose an armistice on the belligerents. Turkey rejected it. The allied squadrons, commanded by Admirals Codrington, de Rigny and von Heyden, entered the bay of Navarino on 20 October 1827 where they found a Turko-Egyptian fleet. The admirals proposed, 'without hostilities or bloodshed', to intimidate Ibrahim, force him to remove his fleet and cease ravaging Messenia. A few shots fired by the Turks provoked a full battle. By nightfall the Ottoman fleet, reduced to 29 small vessels, had lost 6,000 men. This unexpected victory was badly received in Anglo-Russian diplomatic circles and was considered as a deplorable event by the king of England. Greece, from then onwards, was free. It was the French who rebuilt the town in 1829.

Pylos-Navarino does not offer any ancient monuments, but it could be considered a good centre for excursions to the palace of Nestor (at Pylos), the Venetian castle of Methona, or the bay of Navarino (see below). Near the harbour, in the cool shade of the main square, there are pleasant little cafés and restaurants to welcome you.

From Neo Kastro, near the harbour, you will be able to see over the bay of Navarino. The fortress was built by the Turks in 1573 and rebuilt by the French in 1829; its mosque has been converted into a church. In the town centre you will find a little museum exhibiting French lithographs and items from the celebrated Battle of Navarino.

*EXCURSION IN THE BAY OF NAVARINO. From the harbour, embark on a caïque or motor boat for a trip (4–5hrs) round the bay of Navarino, one of the finest anchorages in the world.

On the side of the open sea the bay is closed by the island of Sphacteria (Sfaktiria), a long natural breakwater which has attractive cliffs on its landward face.

On this island are the tombs of Major Maillet, a French officer killed in a duel at Navarino in 1833, and Prince Paul-Marie Bonaparte, killed on board the frigate *Hellas* in 1827 near Spetsae (the urn containing his ashes is in Athens), a monument to Russian sailors, etc.

Near the N point of the island are the remains of a small ancient fort, on Mt Hagios Ilias, remains which still bear witness to a tragic episode in the Peloponnesian war. 420 Spartans, surrounded by the Athenians in 425 BC, resisted for 72 days near two wells of salty water. After a desperate resistance, 292 survivors surrendered.

On the other side of the channel of Sykia, which separates the N point of Sphacteria from the mainland, is a promontory which is crowned with the remains of the acropolis of Pylos. It is a little coastal site which gained its importance only at the time of the Peloponnesian War, and because of the ruins of a Frankish castle, built in 1278, and occasionally given the name Paleo-Kastro.

From the water's edge, you can climb in about 30 mins to the entrance of the castle, whose crenellated walls are well preserved. They are flanked by both round and square towers, and in places are resting on foundations, built in trapezoidal form, of the ancient acropolis, whose walls were rebuilt by Epaminondas.

Near the castle you can explore Nestor's cave, which is linked, through a hole overhead, to the kastro. The large chamber is full of stalactites shaped like animal hides hung out to cure, from where we get the legend that Neleus and Nestor shut their herds of cattle in here. It may also have been the Pylian cavern of the Homeric hymn, where Hermes is said to have hidden the cattle, which he had stolen from Apollo, and hung up their skins after slaughtering them.

Returning to the harbour, you will pass near the islet of Chelonaki (the turtle) or Marathonisi, where there are graves of English seamen.

■ Pylos [Palace of Nestor]

Route map 9.

Kalamata, 37mls (60km) – Kyparissia, 30mls (48km) – Pylos (Navarino), 11mls (18km).

Although it is more or less reduced to its foundations, the palace of Nestor takes its place amongst the important archaeological curiosities of Mycenaean Greece. It certainly cannot rival Mycenae or Tiryns, for it does not have their impressive cyclopean ramparts. However, the University of Cincinnati's work here has shown that the neatness of the plan of the buildings, which were constructed between 1300 and 1200 BC, and the various reminders of King Nestor, who took part in the Trojan war with 90 vessels, are worthy of a visit.

NESTOR'S KINGDOM. According to tradition, western Messenia, during the Mycenaean period, was ruled by the Neleids, a family which came from Iolkos, near present-day Volos. Neleus' successor, Nestor, made Pylos one of the richest cities in the Mycenaean world. After the capture of Troy, Nestor returned to Pylos, where he continued to reign for a few more years. After his death, his descendants governed for two generations, before Pylos was suddenly destroyed by the Dorians (between 1200 and 1190 BC?).

MYCENAEAN, PRECURSOR OF THE GREEK LANGUAGE. The discovery, among the ruins of the palace of Nestor, of numerous tablets with inscriptions (in Linear B) which complete the epigraphic material uncovered at Knossos and more recently at Mycenae, have made it possible for M. Ventris and J. Chadwick to decipher this language, which appears to be the direct precursor of Greek.

Open: weekdays 09.00–15.30; Sun. 10.00–15.00; entrance fee; allow about 30 mins.

MAIN PALACE (see plan of palace of Pylos for references given in brackets). You will enter the palace by a propylon (1) with an axial column. On the l. are two archive storerooms (2) where 600 tablets inscribed in Linear B were found. To the r. is a room (3) which was probably the guard-room. At the end of the courtyard (4) is a portico (5), extending into a vestibule (6), which leads to the large megaron (7) or reception hall. To the r. of the courtyard there is another suite of rooms; note in particular a portico (8) with two pillars, leading into a long corridor (9). To the r. is a stair well (10) serving the upper floor or the flat roof.

The corner of the palace facing E was probably for the queen's apartments with a large room (11) with circular hearth, a bathroom (12) and a lavatory (13). From the large room it was possible to go out into an enclosed courtyard (14) probably reserved for the queen's use.

If you follow the long corridor (9), the first door that you meet gives access to a suite of chambers (15) which must have been waiting rooms, where those who were to be received at the palace could refresh themselves. In one of these rooms were found two benches covered with painted stucco, and in another room was a large quantity of cups. Opposite these rooms was a bathroom (16) with tub. Just at the side was another closed courtyard (17).

Farther along the corridor you will pass, on the r., a staircase (18), which still has eight steps, which led to the upper floor. Then you will come to a range of store-rooms (19). In the other wing of the palace, kitchen quarters (20) have been uncovered, one room of which had in it the fragments of more than 3,000 cups.

SECOND PALACE. To the SW of the main palace one can visit the ruins of another palace (Recent Helladic IIIA), older than the preceding one (Recent Helladic IIIB), from which it was separated, after the erection of this latter one, by a courtyard (21). The courtyard was at one time paved with large stone slabs and then with stucco. Farther to the E of the courtyard is a ramp (22), built between the archives room (2) and servants' quarters (23) where a large quantity of tableware was found.

This second palace consisted of two main halls, one of which (24) was approached through a portico with two fluted columns. The walls of this room, called the 'State room', were covered with painted stucco. A painting from this room, or from a room above, represented a scene of carnage where the defeated were thrown from the ramparts of a citadel or a town that had been stormed.

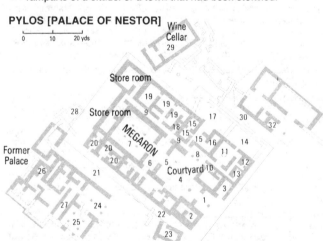

PYLOS [PALACE OF NESTOR]

From this room one can pass into a large square hall (25) where the throne may have been placed. Farther to the W are various annexes, servants' quarters, bathrooms (26) and a staircase (27) leading to the upper floor.

ANNEXES OF THE MAIN PALACE. From here, turn l. and go round the outside of the main palace. On the way, notice the remains of a house or warehouse (28), contemporary with the last stage of building, and the remains of a vast store-room (29), approached through a vestibule. A large quantity of earthenware jars were discovered there standing in holes dug in the ground. This building probably had another floor above where the caretaker may have lived. Farther to the E was a huge building accessible by a ramp (30). It may have been the administrative offices or the barracks for the palace guards. It consisted of a courtyard (31) with an altar positioned opposite a small sanctuary (32). In a room to the N (33), 50 or so inscribed tablets were uncovered. All round the palace numerous tombs with cupolas have also been unearthed. The nearest is situated 73yds (80m) to the NE of the palace. It belongs to the type known at Mycenae.

The principal finds made during the excavations of the palace and the tombs are exhibited in the Chora Museum (2mls/3km) along the road to Kyparissia (see Chora).

■ Pyrgos

Route maps 7 and 9.

Olympia, 12.5mls (20km) – Patras, 57.5mls (93km) – Pylos (Navarino), 74mls (119km) – Pop: 20,000.

This large market town, uninteresting and rather grim in appearance, is identified with the ancient Letrini (or Ledrinoi, as on a dedication at Olympia). It originated on the Holy Way of Elis at Olympia.

VICINITY

1 EPITALION (4mls/7km by the Kyparissia road). This town is sometimes identified with the Homeric Thryoessa, which became the ancient Epitalion, mentioned by Xenophon. Just before entering the town, lovers of archaeology will notice, near the bridge over the Alpheus, the ruins of a Roman bath of the 2nd century AD which was altered in the 4th century.

2 PHEIA. At Katakolon (8mls/13km; beach) the submerged remains of the ancient port of Pheia have been located. Pheia was at the foot of Pondiko Kastro, the ancient Beauvoir of the Villehardouins, whose foundations are those of its acropolis. This was the only harbour on the coast of Elis and the only access by sea to the sanctuary of Olympia. It is mentioned in the *Iliad* and in the *Odyssey*.

Rhodes [Island of] (Rhodos)***

579sq. mls (1,500km²) – Pop: 72,000 – capital of the admin. region of the Dodecanese.

This pearl of the Dodecanese has, since the 1960s, become a paradise for tourists in the eastern Mediterranean with the beauty of its monuments, its balmy climate, its typically Levantine appearance. At the height of summer, the capital of this island, once praised in song by Pindar, becomes a Tower of Babel where the islanders themselves are clearly in the minority, engulfed by the hordes of tourists from all over the world. Even then, the island is still full of flowers, the buildings of the Knights of Rhodes are still as impressive, the countryside and the beaches still as attractive as ever.

Rhodes town, which boasts almost all the hotel capacity on the island, has more than 42,000 inhabitants. It consists of two distinct parts: the new town built since 1912 outside the city walls, and the medieval city enclosed within the ramparts built by the Knights of St John. The very busy central harbour, hemmed in by high walls, like gigantic pincers, seems like the old city extended out to the sea. The Mediterranean vegetation, which blooms with wild exuberance in the ancient moats and various corners of the town outside the walls, is one of the enchantments of Rhodes.

Within its stonework, the old walled city retains a little of the epic spirit of the Crusades. Its Street of the Knights, in the most venerable part of the city, the Collachium or Knights' quarter, is a remarkable example of Gothic splendour, though much restored. It is from the sea that you should discover the old town, bristling with towers, turrets and tapering minarets rising above the powerful battlements of the surrounding walls. If you arrive by air, we recommend that you see this spectacle, by taking a boat in Mandraki harbour.

Rhodes in history

THE ISLAND BORN FROM THE LOVE OF HELIOS AND A NYMPH. In antiquity, the island bore different names. The name of Rhodes is of uncertain etymology, but probably does not come from the Greek word rhodon, meaning rose; it may derive from the Phoenician rodos, meaning snake. In one of his odes, Pindar sang of the birth of Rhodes, the result of the love between Helios, the Sun, and the nymph Rhoda.

In prehistoric times the island was inhabited by emigrants from Crete and the mainland. Proof of this comes in particular from the necropolises exposed at Ialysos and Camiros, where ceramics discovered show a Creto-Mycenaean influence. Before the Trojan War, it was invaded by colonists from Attica and the Peloponnese.

A DORIAN ISLAND. A little later, around 1100 BC, the Dorians settled there and founded the three towns of Ialysos, Lindos and Camiros on which Zeus poured immense riches (Homer, *Iliad*, II, 670). These three cities probably became part of the Dorian Hexapolis, which also included the cities of Halicarnassus (Bodrum) and Cnidos, from Asia Minor, and Cos. The three cities achieved great prosperity, thanks to commerce, and founded colonies both on the neighbouring islands and on the coasts of Asia and Europe.

WHEN THE TYRANTS WERE WISE MEN. In the 6th century BC they were governed by 'Tyrants', of whom the most famous was Cleobulus, tyrant of Lindos, one of the Seven Sages of Greece. Then, until the beginning of the 5th century BC, they were under Persian rule. In 477 BC, the Rhodians took part in the first confederation formed by Athens.

ONE ISLAND, ONE TOWN. In 408 BC, the three cities in the island decided to create, in the extreme NE, a new political, religious and commercial centre: the town of Rhodes. It was laid out according to the principles of Hippodamus of Miletus, the most famous architect of the period. Because of its location, the new city soon flourished and became involved in all the events of the time.

PENDULUM POLITICS. Endowed first with an oligarchy, it came under the influence of Sparta until 396 BC. Then it had a democratic constitution and turned towards Athens whom it helped, with the assistance of the Persian fleet, to defeat Sparta's fleet in the waters of Cnidos (394 BC). In 377 BC it joined the second confederation of the islands, set up by Athens, but it withdrew in 356 BC, at the instigation of Mausolus, satrap of Caria, who installed a garrison there. Allies of the Persians, the Rhodians took part in the defence of Tyre when it was besieged by Alexander the Great, and in 332 BC they were forced to accept a Macedonian garrison. After the death of the great conqueror and the splitting up of his empire, the Rhodians, because of their commercial interests, took the side of the Ptolemies of Egypt against Antigonus, whose son Demetrius Poliorcetes besieged them by land and sea (305 BC). The siege lasted a year and Demetrius was forced to withdraw.

THE TIME OF THE COLOSSUS OF RHODES. This success increased the prestige of Rhodes considerably, and it was from this period that the first relations with Rome began. Rhodes now reached the height of her splendour: her port was the centre of commercial transactions between Italy, Greece, Macedon, Asia, Africa; her power extended across a part of the Aegean Sea; her money was accepted everywhere; her commercial law was everyone's law, so just, that it was adopted three centuries later by Augustus for the whole of the Roman Empire. With 60,000 to 80,000 inhabitants, the city expanded, adorning itself with temples, schools, theatres, statues. Among these were the Chariot of the Sun sculpted by Lysippus and the famous Colossus of Rhodes, one of the Seven Wonders of the Ancient World, erected by Chares of Lindos. In the 1st century AD when the town had already been stripped in large part of its treasures, Pliny still counted 2,000 statues, 100 of which were colossi. At the same time, the people enthusiastically practised athletics, music, oratory; Aeschines founded a School of Rhetoric which was later attended by Cato, Cicero, Caesar, Cassius, Marcus Brutus and Lucretius.

THE MOMENT OF DECISION. At the time of Macedonian expansion under Philip V, Rhodes took the side of Rome and Pergamum. When Rome entered into conflict with Antiochus in 191-190 BC, Rhodes once more took the side of the Romans and received a part of Lycia and a part of Caria as a reward for its assistance. This policy was not all that successful, for it was not long before Rhodes fell out with Rome and looked for alliances with, or at the very least offered its friendship to, the king of Macedon, Perseus. But his fall in 168 BC was to have dire consequences for Rhodes. The Romans did not forget this affront and, by favouring the free port of Delos, struck a severe blow to the economy of Rhodes. Nevertheless, the island became faithful to Rome once more during the war against Mithridates, when it was closely besieged, and, at the peace of Dardana, Sulla gave it back its Asian territories which it had lost. Finally, Rhodes took the side of Pompey, then of Antony, and Crassus finally became its ruler.

Augustus confirmed its title of 'allied city' and Vespasian incorporated it into the Roman Empire. Belonging to the Province of Asia, it became the capital of the Province of the Islands under Diocletian. St Paul visited it during his second or third journey and, very soon, it became the seat of a bishop.

When the Roman Empire broke up in AD 395, Rhodes naturally became a part of the Eastern Empire, to whose destiny it was henceforth linked. From 653 onwards, it was sacked several times by the Arabs, particularly in 654 and in 807, yet it never ceased to belong to the Byzantine emperors.

RHODES AT THE TIME OF THE CRUSADES. During the time of the Crusades, ships belonging to the Christians called in at the harbours around the island of Rhodes several times. Finally, when the leaders of the Fourth Crusade had founded (1204) the Latin Empire of Constantinople, the Greek governor of Rhodes, Leon Gabalas, declared independence. In 1248 the Genoese became masters of the island, to which they invited the Knights of St John of Jerusalem around 1306. The Knights quickly asked the emperor to cede Rhodes to them as a feudal benefice, but when their request was rejected, they seized it in 1309 and retained it for more than two centuries.

THE KNIGHTS OF ST JOHN. The Order of the Knights of St John had been founded in Jerusalem in the 11th century by the merchants of Amalfi.

At first it was a military and religious order founded to care for sick or poor pilgrims; but at the time of the Crusades the Knights set up a military organization, for the defence of the Holy Land. In 1291, compelled to withdraw from St Jean d'Acre, they took refuge on Cyprus, and then Rhodes. They were divided into three classes: the military knights, the lay brothers and the chaplains. There were also seven groups or 'langues': Provence, Auvergne, France, Italy, Spain (sub-divided later into Aragon and Castille), England and Germany. Each 'langue' had at its head a bailiff. Under the presidency of the grand master, elected for life by the Knights, the bailiffs formed the Chapter of the Order. The most famous of the grand masters were Foulques de Villaret, who settled the Order in Rhodes, Pierre d'Aubusson, who successfully defended the town when it was besieged by Mohammed II and was then made a cardinal by Innocent VIII, and Villiers de l'Isle-Adam, who had to give up the island to the Turks and withdraw to Italy.

A THORN IN THE SIDE OF THE OTTOMAN EMPIRE. Having become masters of Rhodes, the Knights of St John organized a large fleet and encouraged trade. Soon afterwards, Clement V assigned to them some of the possessions of the Order of the Knights Templars, which had been dissolved in 1312. For two centuries they had to resist the Turks. They helped in the capture, and then the defence, of Smyrna and they survived two important sieges: one in 1444 by the Sultan of Egypt and the other in 1480 by Mohammed II. Finally, in 1522, Suleiman II resolved to take over Rhodes. He came to lay siege to the town with an army reported to be 100,000 strong. There were only 650 Knights, helped by 200 Genoese sailors, 50 Venetians, 400 Candiots (from Crete) and 6,000 local inhabitants. Pope Adrian VI vainly implored the Christian princes to go to the help of the besieged, but after six months they were forced to capitulate. On 1 January 1523, Villiers de l'Isle-Adam embarked with the 180 Knights who had survived and left the island.

A FALSE LIBERATION. In 1912 Italy took the island from the Turks. The inhabitants of Rhodes and the whole of the Dodecanese saw in this event the beginning of their liberation. They resisted the Italian occupation with all their strength when it seemed to be taking root permanently on the island. Rhodes finally returned to Greece in 1948.

TWO DAYS ON RHODES

Two days is definitely the minimum needed to see Rhodes; but it is a safe bet that many visitors will be tempted to stay longer on this island.

First day – If you do not delay too long as you cross the neo-Gothic part of the new town close by Mandraki harbour, you can devote half a day to walking round the medieval town (see under 1 – The medieval city, pp. 745–754). (At nightfall you should watch, from the Palace Avenue gardens (map II, B-1, C-1) a performance of *Son et Lumière*. This spectacle lends enchantment, by its prepared lighting, to the marvellous setting of this part of the city walls.) During the

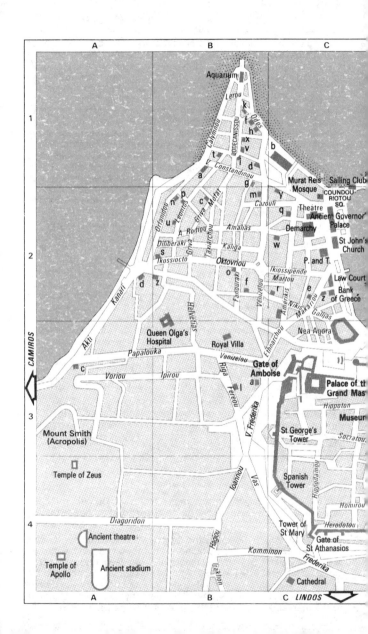

CAMIROS

LINDOS

Aquarium
Lerou
k
f
h
x
Odos
v
b
t
a V. Constandinou
DODECANISSOU
Kalymnou
d
g
n p
c
Ortandou
Leonida
Diva Moral
m
Murat Reis
Mosque
Sailing Club
COUNDOU-
RIOTOU SQ.
Cazouli
y
q
Theatre
Ancient Governor'
Palace
u
A. Romiou
Taxiarchou
Amalias
Demarchy
St John's
Church
Diliberaki
Kaliga
w
s
Ikossiocto
Oktovriou
o
f
P. and T.
Ikossipende
Martou
Law Court
d z
Fanourak
Venizelou
r
e
Amerikis
z
Bank
of Greece
Makariou
Gallias
Kanari
Helvetias
Queen Olga's
Hospital
Royal Villa
Nea Agora
Akti
Papalouka
Venizelou
Voriou
Ipirou
Riga
Fereou
Gate of
Amboise
a
E.Eftharchou
Palace of th
Grand Mas
c
Hippoton
Museum
V. Frederika
Mount Smith
(Acropolis)
St George's
Tower
Socratou
Temple of Zeus
Ioannou
Spanish
Tower
Hipppdamou
Homirou
Vas.
Diagoridon
Herodotou
Ancient theatre
Hagou
Komminon
Tower of
St Mary
Gate of
St Athanasios
Temple of
Apollo
Iraklion
Frederika
Cathedral

A   B   C

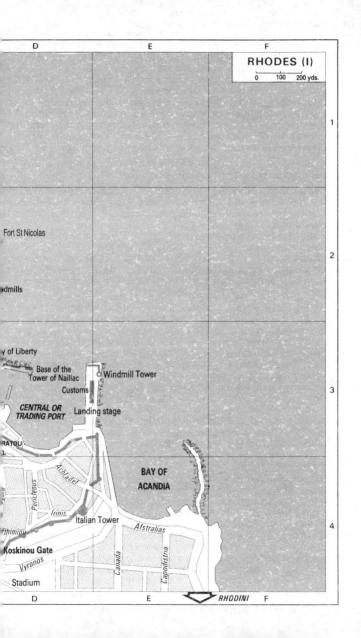

D   E   F

RHODES (I)

0   100   200 yds.

1

Fort St Nicolas

2

dmills

y of Liberty

Base of the
Tower of Naillac   ○ Windmill Tower

Customs

*CENTRAL OR
TRADING PORT*   Landing stage

3

RATOU

Achladet

Pericleous

**BAY OF
ACANDIA**

Irinis

Italian Tower   *Afstralias*

4

Koskinou Gate

Vyronos

Canada

Capodistria

Stadium

D   E   ⬇ *RHODINI* F

afternoon (Thursday or Saturday), take a walk round the ramparts (see under 2 – The medieval city walls, pp. 754–756), by going to the court of the Palace of the Grand Masters (map II, B–1) a little before 17.00 (check the time). If this is not possible, take an excursion to Mt Philerimos and the valley of Petaloudes (return journey about 3hrs.) which is swarming (from June to September only) with thousands of red and gold butterflies, seen only if you encourage them to take flight by make a noise. Then, at the end of the afternoon, visit the ancient city (2.5mls/4km there and back) and watch the sunset from Mt Smith (see under 3 – The ancient city and Mt Smith, pp. 756–758).

In the evening, possibly after the *Son et Lumière* spectacle, dine in the courtyard of a taverna, fragrant with jasmine.

Second day – Leave very early (about 07.00) in order to explore two of the main ancient sites on the island outside the capital: Camiros and Lindos. Between Camiros and Lindos you will cross the wooded slopes of Mt Prophitis Ilias (2,618ft/798m), from where you will see some of the most attractive scenery on the island. Fairly soon you will reach the Rhodes-Lindos road that you will join. Having arrived at Lindos, you will discover the advantage of the early morning departure, for you will be able to bathe off the beach of the Grand Harbour, before having lunch (on the beach), though probably quite late.

During the afternoon, wander quietly round the acropolis and take a stroll through the village of Lindos. Here the architecture from the time of the Knights of St John, mixed with Byzantine elements, and a touch of Arab influence, has inspired the master masons of later centuries. Before returning to Rhodes, let yourself be tempted by some pottery from Lindos (but it is at Rhodes, in the antiquarian shops of Socratous Street – map II, C–2 – that enlightened enthusiasts will ferret out ancient specimens). On the way back, stop at Archangelos, where you will find the shoemakers who make those brightly coloured boots that you might have noticed some of the peasant women wearing in the market at Rhodes. This circuit of 103.7mls (166km) will take you all day; a more ambitious programme, to the southern half of the island, will require two days.

IN THE TOWN, ON FOOT

Assemble at the Nea Agora (map. I, C–3), the New Market, the former Foro Italico, the meeting-place for citizens, tourists and villagers from the surrounding areas, which has not only its cafés and little restaurants (Astoria, Ivireus), but also its street stalls. There, you will be very close to Mandraki harbour (map I, C–2), an excellent place for excursions out to sea. According to your tastes and your means, you can hire a boat by the hour, by the day, or by the week, to go round the neighbouring islands or to cruise farther afield all round the island of Rhodes or along the coast of Turkey. You can dine by the harbour on the Kon-Tiki, listening to bouzouki music or dreaming of the Colossus of Rhodes.

You can enter the walled city by the gate of Liberty (map I, D–3 and map II, D-1) and, within a few paces, you will jump back several centuries in time to an heroic past. It is the period of the Knights of St John, restored by the Italians during their occupation of the island, and improved on by numerous sellers of souvenirs and duty-free goods. (The Dodecanese benefit from tax allowances and reduced duties on goods imported directly from abroad.) You will soon discover that not all the shops have the elegance of the Lalaounis store. After visiting the archaeological museum, you will then find yourself in the marvellous Street of the Knights (map II, C-2), or Odos Hippoton whose beautiful façades shelter the archaeological services of the Dodecanese. After visiting the imposing palace of the Grand Masters (map II, B-1), find your way past Suleyman Square (map II, B-2) and Socratous Street (map II, C-2) towards the port, where you will join the 'commercial round' again. The Marina gate (map II, D-2) will lead you to the central harbour, hemmed in by high walls like gigantic pincers. Turn l. and walk alongside the commercial port to reach the Nea Agora again.

1 - The medieval city

More or less restored, if not sometimes completely rebuilt, the buildings of the medieval city of Rhodes will plunge you back into the Middle Ages, when Christianity was pushing forward the frontiers of the Western world, marking its military advances with its crusader architecture. But the collections in the archaeological museum will remind you that you are in Greece, by recalling the island's ancient past. The mosques of the old town bear Turkish names, but are almost all ancient Byzantine churches reconverted, progressively retrieving their old identities or, simply, being rebaptized in cases where their names have passed out of ordinary speech.

MANDRAKI HARBOUR (map, I, C-2). Very picturesque, with its multicoloured boats and its windmills, it has existed since antiquity. The tower of St Nicolas, an outwork which constituted the key to the N defences of the city of the Knights, was situated at the end of the mole, where there are now attractive windmills.

It was certainly not on this mole, at the entrance to the harbour, that the Colossus of Rhodes, the gigantic statue dedicated to the sun-god Helios, once stood. It is known that this bronze statue, 70 cubits (about 100ft/31m) high, and renowned in ancient times as one of the Seven Wonders of the World, was the work of Chares of Lindos, a disciple of Lysippus, and his metal workers, and made between 304 and 292 BC.

Its construction was financed by the sale of equipment that Demetrius Poliorcetes had brought to Rhodes for the siege in 305 BC. The Colossus collapsed during an earthquake in 227 BC and, on the advice of the oracle at Delphi, was not re-erected. During the Arab invasion of AD 654, the remains were sold to a Jew from Emesa in Syria, who needed nine hundred camels to transport all the pieces.

The part of the town at the entrance to Mandraki harbour is the result of Fascist megalomania during the Italian occupation of Rhodes. Of huge proportions, certainly overdone, for it always appears a little empty, it consists of St John's church (map I, C-2), rebuilt in 1925 to designs by Rottiers and Flandin, the Governor's palace, whose appearance resembles somewhat the Doges' palace in Venice, etc.

A little further on the small Murat Reis mosque (map I, C-1, C-2), in a Turkish cemetery full of romantic charm, occupies the site of St Antony's church, destroyed by the Turks during the siege of 1480.

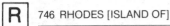 **GATE OF LIBERTY** (map I, D-3 and map II, D-1). Built into the medieval wall by the Italians in 1924, this gate leads to the Collachium, the quarter where the Knights lived. Situated there were the palace of the Grand Masters, St Mary's cathedral, the 'Inns' or residences for each 'langue' which were mostly strung out along the street called the Street of the Knights.

On Symi Square, just after coming in through the gate, you will notice a few remains of the temple of Aphrodite (map II, D-1), from the 3rd century BC.

PALACE OF ARMERIA (see Infirmary on map II, C-1). Bearing the coat of arms of Roger de Pins, one of the first grand masters (1355-65), it housed the first hospital in Rhodes. The fountain, on the little square at the corner of this palace, is a former Christian baptistry from a village on the island, placed there by the Italians. In the building of the Ionian Bank, you will find a gallery of modern art containing work by local artists.

Open weekdays, except Mon., 09.00-13.00, 16.00-19.00

■ **MUSEUM OF DECORATIVE ARTS** (map II, D-1). Established in what was probably an arsenal belonging to the Knights of St John, it has assembled a beautiful collections of furniture, costumes and Rhodian ceramics (originating from Lindos).

Open: Mon., Wed., Fri., 09.00-13.00; entrance fee.

☐ **INN OF THE AUVERGNE 'LANGUE'** (map II, D-1). On the other side of Symi Square is the inn's covered gallery with an outside staircase. An arched passage under the inn itself leads to Alexandron Square, on to which faces the S façade of the inn in which there is a Gothic door with, above it, an inscription by Guy de Blanchefort (1512-13).

On the l. of the square (to the E.) opposite the Commercial Bank of Greece building, is the church of St Mary. The Knights consecrated the church for Latin worship in the 15th century and made it their cathedral; then it was converted into a mosque by the Turks (the Red mosque, commemorating the massacres perpetrated against the Christians).

■ **HOSPITAL OF THE KNIGHTS, ARCHAEOLOGICAL MUSEUM.** (map II, C-2). The construction of this beautiful and imposing building was undertaken in accordance with the wishes of the grand master Antonio Fluvian (1421-37), in 1440, three years after his death. It was not completed until 1489, under the government of the grand master Pierre d'Aubusson (1476-1506). Above the entrance, notice a bas-relief of two angels supporting the shield of the Order and, projecting slightly, the apse of the hospital chapel.

Open: weekdays 08.30–12.30, 16.00–18.00; Sun. 09.00–15.00; closed Tues.; entrance fee.

First you will enter a courtyard surrounded by a portico, which has above it a gallery with ogival vaults. The ground floor was occupied by storerooms. In the courtyard are displayed a marble lion and a palaeo-Christian mosaic (birds and fishes), beside piles of stone cannon balls; beneath the porticoes are carved inscriptions from various periods. A passage opening to the S (at the foot of the big staircase) leads to a second courtyard with wall mosaics. A staircase leads to an upper floor, where the hospital departments administered by the bailiff of the French 'langue' were situated. In the middle of the gallery on the l., at the top of the staircase, is the hospital's main hall, which could hold about a hundred beds. It is divided into two naves by a line of octagonal pillars, whose capitals are decorated with the arms of the grand master Pierre d'Aubusson. Opposite the entrance, note the delicately sculpted head arch of the little chapel projecting outwards, above the porch. Various tombstones of the Knights have been placed in the main hall, most decorated with coats of arms or relief sculptures with Latin inscriptions. You will see there a marble sarcophagus from the Classical period, which served as the tomb for the grand master Pierre de Corneillan (1354–55).

The most interesting collections of the archaeological museum are set out in the other rooms on the upper floor. One of these is a refectory, a huge room whose vault is supported by two arches.

The museum's possessions have come entirely from ancient remains found in the Dodecanese, in particular from the necropolis at Ialysos (8th to 4th centuries BC). The refectory, entered by a small door, either from the gallery or from the main hall, contains reliefs and stelae of the Hellenistic and Roman periods. The small room divided into two parts, adjoining to the NW (on the gallery side), is more interesting; it is devoted to Archaic and Classical sculptures. Some pieces will especially draw your attention. There is a perirrhanterion (vase for lustral water) (end of 7th century BC), where three priestesses, standing on a lion, hold the cistern, two fragmentary kouroi from the third quarter of the 6th century BC, two kouroi heads from the middle of the 6th century, the beautiful funeral stele of Krito and Timarista, a Classical work from the end of the 5th century BC and the slightly later work by Calliarista, dedicated by Damocles, the deceased's husband (inscription carved on the epistyle). Three small rooms, of which two open on to the garden near the refectory, contain important marble statues of the Hellenistic period, typical of the Rhodian school which was then flourishing.

Aphrodite is particularly well represented, with the renowned Aphrodite Pudica, a life-size work in marble from the 3rd century BC, the Aphrodite (?) with one foot resting on a rock, which may date from the end of the 2nd century BC, and the Aphrodite of Rhodes,

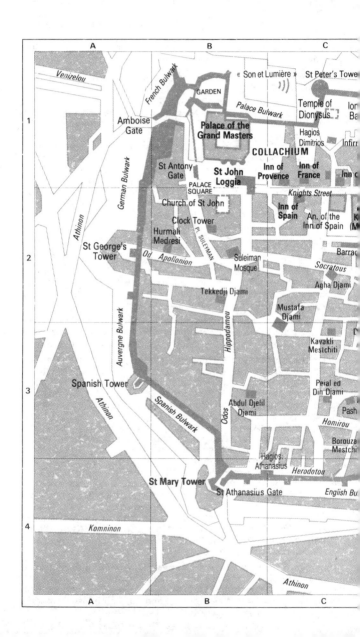

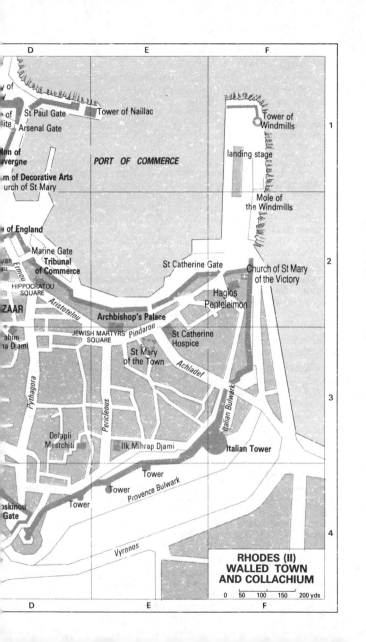

**RHODES (II)
WALLED TOWN
AND COLLACHIUM**

0 50 100 150 200 yds

D   E   F

of
y

of   St Paul Gate   Tower of Naillac
ite   Arsenal Gate

Inn of
uvergne

m of Decorative Arts
urch of St Mary

of England

Marine Gate
Tribunal
of Commerce
van
n

HIPPOCRATOU
SQUARE

ZAAR

Aristotelou

ahim
na Djami

Archbishop's Palace

JEWISH MARTYRS'   Pindarou
SQUARE

St Mary
of the Town

Pythagora

Pericleous

Dolaplí
Mestchiti

Ilk Mihrap Djami

Tower

Tower

Tower   Provence Bulwark

oskinou
Gate

Vyronos

Tower of
Windmills

landing stage

Mole of
the Windmills

St Catherine Gate

Church of St Mary
of the Victory

Hagios
Penteleimon

St Catherine
Hospice

Achiadef

Italian Bulwark

Italian Tower

PORT OF COMMERCE

1

2

3

4

combing her hair with one knee on the ground, a work from the beginning of the 1st century BC.

You will also note, near the Aphrodite of the Rock, an impressive head of Helios, tutelary god of Rhodes (1st. half of the 2nd century BC). Several statues repeat the type of Artemis-Hecate and that of the nymph seated on a rock. Two statuettes of the 3rd century BC represent Asclepius and his daughter Hygieia, both with a serpent. In the third room, the most notable piece is a marble head, taken to be a Roman copy of a portrait of Menander.

Returning to the upper gallery around the main courtyard you will be able to visit several rooms displaying many terracotta vases found in the burial grounds and decorated in the Geometric and Archaic styles (8th–6th century BC). In the first of these (near the staircase) are Geometric vases and some in the Orientalizing style (mainly Corinthian, including a finely modelled vase in the form of a female head, no. 11543); in the second room are Corinthian, Attic, Laconian and Rhodian ceramics of the 6th century; many pieces are greyish in colour because they were burnt at the time of the funeral; the third room contains mostly Attic black-figure pottery (6th–5th century BC).

In the four rooms opening on to the gallery opposite (N side) are more vases in the Geometric style (8th century), the Orientalizing style (7th century) and Archaic black-figure (6th century), notably some pieces in the style called *Fikellura* which are no doubt local (nos 12394, 12396, 13235, 13330, 13481).

On the gallery itself are displayed altars and funerary stelae of the Hellenistic and Roman periods.

▫ ****STREET OF THE KNIGHTS** ('Odos Ippoton' – map II, C-2). This cobbled street, which was a main thoroughfare in the 15th century, epitomizes the architectural style of the period, and constitutes one of the main places of interest in Rhodes.

Running in a straight line, it probably follows the course of a road in the ancient town, of which many traces have been found. Lined by some of the finest secular buildings of the Collachium – mostly inns – the Street of the Knights, situated in the middle of the eastern Mediterranean, has a most astonishing collection of buildings in the Gothic style at its most pure.

You will notice first, on the r., the Inn of the Italian Langue (map II, C-1), then the Inn of the French Langue (map II, C-1). It is the largest and most beautiful of these inns, where the knights of the country which had built them used to live. Above the gate is an inscription dated 1492, which bears the name of the grand prior Aimery d'Amboise, who was probably grand master of the Order 1505–12.

Further along, on the r., you will pass in front of the chapel of the French Langue, decorated with a canopied niche (Virgin and Child). Among the shields which decorate the facade is that of the grand master Raymond Beranger (1365–74), who probably built the chapel. Then you will come to the house belonging to the chaplain of the

French Langue. After that, on the l., is the Inn of the Spanish Langue (map II, C-2), linked by an archway to the Inn of Provence.

At the end of the Street of the Knights you will reach the residence of St John (map II, B-1), a portico with two wings, the longer of which, running out across the end of the street, served as some sort of monumental entrance to the palace of the Grand Masters. This residence, for the most part rebuilt, would probably have had an upper floor, judging from the drawings of Rottiers and Flandin.

⌐ PALACE OF THE GRAND MASTERS (map II, B-1). Almost completely destroyed by the explosion of a powder-magazine in 1856, this imposing construction, which was both a fortress and a palace at the same time, was rebuilt by the Italians before World War II in the style of the late 14th century. It therefore appears quite new, and even Hollywoodian in certain parts of the interior, probably because it was rebuilt to serve, if necessary, as a residence for King Victor-Emmanuel III and Mussolini.

While it would be unwise to include this palace for discussion in a thesis on military architecture at the end of the Middle Ages, it is certainly worth a visit, if only to see the interesting Roman and palaeo-Christian mosaic floors, mostly brought from Cos and distributed amongst the rooms.

Open: weekdays, except Tues., 08.00–18.00; Sun. 09.00–18.00; entrance fee.

Passing through a majestic entrance flanked by two crenellated towers, you enter a large hall, then go into an arcaded courtyard, paved with marble. Under this were ten grain silos which could provide food for the defenders in time of siege. Under the palace there were also three levels of storerooms for other supplies and munitions.

From the main hall a staircase leads to the upper floor, where you will see a series of large rooms. The one with two pillars may have been used as a meeting room for the Council of the Order. Among the many mosaics, for the most part from the Island of Cos, and reused for the paving of the rooms, note especially those depicting a nymph astride a hippocampus (sea-monster), a deer hunt, and the Nine Muses (in medallions). In the second room is a casting of the famous Laocoon (marble original in Rome, Vatican Museum).

You can also visit a very fine exhibition on the antique and medieval town (entry to the r. of the staircase leaving the main hall): 12.30–14.30 except Tues. and Sun. Here are presented the plans of Hippodamus, the Pirean architect, the remains of two Byzantine frescoes of the 13th century from Thari, as well as Franco-Byzantine icons and numerous photographs.

SOCRATOUS STREET (map II, C-2). First, look at the heavy clock tower (map II, B-2), built, after the earthquake of 1851, on the site of the guard tower which strengthened the SW corner of the city walls of the Collachium. Then walk along Socratous Street, which probably

corresponds to a street of the ancient town. Running from west to east, it separated the Collachium to the N from the SW district, inhabited at the time of the Knights by the Greeks; but from 1522 the Turks settled there. The Jewish quarter has remained to the SE of the old town.

On the l., at the entrance to this street, is Suleiman's mosque (map II, B-2), founded a little after the siege of 1522, perhaps on the site of the church of the Holy Apostles, and reconstructed in the 19th century. Further along, the Agha Djami (map II, C-2), the mosque of the Agha (garrison commander), interrupts the line of souvenir shops.

At the far end of Socratous Street are the Courts of Commerce (map II, D-2), a beautiful 16th-century building. On the ground floor, to the r. of a wide staircase, under the gallery is a loggia with ribbed vaults. On the facade, notice the arms of Pierre d'Aubusson and those of the Order joined together on the same shield (dated 1507), supported by two beasts. There is also a marble mullioned window, decorated with fleurs-de-lys. Above the entrance doorway, on the marble lintel, an angel is holding on the l., the shield of the Order and on the r., the shield of Aimery d'Amboise (1505–12).

THE TURKISH QUARTER (B-3; C-3; D-3). From Socratous Street, plunge into the labyrinth of paved alleys of the Turkish quarter with its many minarets. You will pass beneath arches formed by houses spanning the streets; note the doors and windows with their fine four-centred arches.

In Apollonian Street is the Byzantine church of Hagios Georgios (St George) with four apses surmounted by a drum dome on pendentives (14th and 15th century); this was once perhaps the church of St Mark and is thought to have belonged to a Frankish convent. In the Turkish period it was turned into the Hurmali Medresesi mosque, attached to the nearby Koranic school. In Hippodamon Street is the Byzantine church of Hagia Paraskevi (15th century) built in the form of a cross with a dome; this became the Tekkedji Djami mosque (pl. 11, B-2) From this street go down the pretty Platia Arionos Square, shaded by plane trees, bordered to the NE by the Mustafa Djami mosque (pl. 11, C-2), and to the SE by the Turkish baths, still in use (open daily 05.00–19.00; closed Sun.; reduced prices Tues. and Sat.). The interior is worthy of a quick look. From the square rejoin Hagios Fanourios Street, pass the open-air theatre where the Traditional Greek Dance Centre presents an agreeable display of Greek folk dancing which combines a high quality of choreography with the sparkling colours of the costumes and sets (21.15 each evening, 1 Mar.–31 Oct. except Sat., entrance fee).

At the end of Hagios Fanourios Street you will see, on the l., at the end of the entrance alley, the Radjep Pasha Djami mosque (late 16th century; pl. 11, C-3), one of the town's old Turkish monuments: note, on the square, the fountain where believers came to be purified. In a courtyard giving on to Hagios Fanourios Street just before Homirou Street, the little Byzantine Church dedicated to Hagios Fanourios

(13th century), in the form of a Latin cross, is decorated with frescoes dating from three periods. Those in the dome showing Christ Pantocrator are in good condition; note also one dated 1335-36 (at the entrance to the r.) depicting the donors of the church; one is offering a model of the building to God. When it was turned into a mosque it took the name of Peial ed Din Djami (pl, 11, C-3). Next, turn l. into Homirou Street. To your r. and slightly set back is the single-nave church of Hagia Kiriaki (15th century); it was converted into a mosque under the name of Borouzan Meschiti (pl. 11, C-3). The minaret is an addition; the first floor of this church is still in use.

From the middle of Socratous Street turn S (to the r. if you are going downhill) into the street opposite Apellou Street (which leads to the Hospital of the Knights); you will arrive at a large open space at the back of which, to the r., among dilapidated houses, stands the church of St Spyridion. This Byzantine church, backing on to a house to the SW and flanked by a minaret to the SE, was built around 1300 on the remains of an older church; it later underwent several modifications and was converted after 1522 into the Kavakli Mestchiti mosque (Pl, 11. C-3). It is now the subject of excavations; substantial foundations, earlier in date than the church, have been uncovered; in particular the archaeologists have discovered, intact, a subterranean tomb; on a marble plaque with Renaissance decorative details, is the date 1508. On the E wall of the funerary chamber a perfectly preserved fresco, dated 1510, depicts the Crucifixion with the Virgin and St John; at the base of the fresco are two Greek nobles, richly attired, with the coat of arms of an inn, a detail giving insight into the relations maintained by the Knights with the Greeks of the town.

Before heading for the harbour, those interested in an oriental atmosphere and Gothic architecture would be well advised to follow Aristotelou Street (map II, D-2), a bustling street lined with metal-workers' stalls. To the l., on the Square of the Jewish Martyrs (map II, E-3), there is a beautiful 15th-century building, the Archbishop's palace, where the Roman archbishop or Greek Metropolitan probably lived. The present-day name of the square is in memory of the community of 2,000 Jews deported from Rhodes.

From this square you can return S to Leonidou Ridiou Square on which stands the large church of Hagia Triada (Holy Trinity); its architecture is interesting. The original part, in the form of a Latin cross surmounted by a beautiful cupola, is Byzantine, possibly 15th century. In a later period a chapel with an octagonal cupola was added to the N branch of the cross, and the S branch was extended, bringing the whole into balance. The interior was covered with frescoes of which traces remain in the central and S naves (the three Fathers of the church are recognizable: Basil, Gregory and John Chrysostom). Finally converted to a mosque, Dolaphi Mestchiti (Pl. 11, D-3), it had a high minaret, the upper part of which collapsed during an earthquake. On the S side of the square, embedded between two houses, hides Ekaterina Church, dedicated to St Catherine (14th century); it comprises three naves of unequal size;

only the central nave has an apse. The frescoes of the S and central naves are badly damaged, but in the N you will recognize, to the l. on entering, St George and in the arch, to the l., St John nave, and to the r. St. Andrew.

Follow Pindarou Street and you will reach the apse of the church of St Mary of the Bourg (map II, E-3), built at the beginning of the 15th century, and the ruins of the hospice of St Catherine (map II, E-3), founded towards the end of the 14th century by Admiral Domenico d'Allemagna, bailiff of the Italian Langue, and rebuilt in 1516. Visitors to the Order used to lodge there during their stay. Nearby are the Byzantine church of Hagio Panteleimon (map II, F-2) and the ruins of the church of St Mary of the Victory (map II, F-2), built a little after the siege of 1480 to commemorate the resistance of the garrison against the Turkish assaults. Not far from this church is St Catherine's gate (map II, E-2, F-2), which you will pass through to reach the commercial harbour, immediately opposite the mole of the Windmills which rests on medieval and ancient foundations. All the windmills except one have disappeared. From there, by walking round the harbour, you will come to the Harbour gate (see below), but this part of the walk is not very pleasant because of all the motor traffic.

☐ HARBOUR GATE (map II, D-2). Constructed by Pierre d'Aubusson in 1478, the Harbour gate is flanked by two fine crenellated and machicolated towers. Above the gate notice a canopied bas-relief, which represents the Virgin and Child, with St Peter on the l. and St John the Baptist on the r. Above the bas-relief, between the shield of the Order and that of Pierre d'Aubusson, was emblazoned the crowned coat of arms of France.

ST PAUL'S GATE (map II, D-1). Walking alongside the city walls facing the central harbour, also called Commercial harbour, you will notice St Paul's tower, the former tower of Trebuc, which changed name about 1477, when it was restored by the grand master Pierre d'Aubusson.

At the end of the mole on the l. was the Naillac tower, still called the tower of the Arabs because, according to Biliotti, the Knights employed many Arabs to help them in its construction. It fell during the earthquake of 1863. On each of its faces a shield belonging to the grand master Philibert de Naillac (1396-1421) could be seen; these have now been placed in the museum.

2 – The medieval city walls***

This walk round the walls of the old city of the Knights of St John may remind you of the city of York, but you will be delighted by many Eastern touches and by the almost tropical exuberance of the vegetation which decorates the ancient moats with bright colours.

Open: Mon. and Sat. 16.00–18.00 (from 16th March to 15th October) or 15.00–17.00 (from 16th October to 15th March), but confirm these times. Meet a little before the starting time, in the court of the palace of the Grand Masters (map II, B-1), for a guided tour of some of the walls; payment required.

The outer city walls of Rhodes are about 2.5mls (4km) in circumference. They replaced the Byzantine walls and were constructed at the beginning of the 14th century and constantly altered until just before the siege of 1522. Originally the fortifications consisted of a rampart 6ft 10½ins (2.10m) thick with a parapet 1ft 6ins (45cm) thick on top. Along part of the German bulwark and as far as the Italian bulwark, a false wall was built at the foot of the rampart. The rectangular or circular towers were then separated from the main wall and reinforced the false wall. At the foot of either the main or the false wall was a moat, with scarp and counterscarp walls, which held up a sloping embankment. Later these original fortifications were to be strengthened extensively. Under the grand master, Orsini (1467–76), the towers on the W and S facing sides were reconnected to the main walls, as were the terrepleins protecting their base. The terrepleins or platforms also had parapets and gun emplacements to give protection to the moats. Pierre d'Aubusson, who became grand master of the Order in 1476, was notable in particular for consolidating and reinforcing the walls, and more than fifty shields set in the outer face of the rampart attest to his activities. He did even more work after the siege of 1480 and the earthquake in 1481: he had the thickness of the rampart increased from 6ft 10½ins (2.10m) to 17ft 4ins (5.28m), and set up artillery gun-platforms. They were placed in front of the curtain wall along the W and S facing sides which were more likely to be threatened. All this work had the effect of creating a second moat along certain lengths of the fortified perimeter, especially along the Spanish, English and Italian bulwarks. The first moat was also widened, sometimes up to 65ft (20m). Finally, the number of gates was reduced and access to them made more difficult for the enemy. Work continued under the grand masters Aimery d'Amboise and Fabrizio del Carretto, so that at the beginning of the 16th century the walls were 39ft 4ins (12m) thick, and had a 13ft (4m) wide parapet with embrasures, allowing artillery to be fired at different angles. The gate of Amboise, the most imposing of all the gates, was erected in 1512 when Aimery d'Amboise was grandmaster.

From the palace of the Grand Masters, you will reach the gate of St Anthony (map II, B-1), surmounted by two turrets. Before the gate of Amboise was erected, it was one of the gates leading out of the city. Climb on to the first terreplein, through which the gate of Amboise (map II, A-1), the most impressive of all the town gates, has been cut; it was built in 1512. It is flanked by two towers propped up against the scarp wall. On the outer side of the walls are shields of the Order and of Aimery d'Amboise. Note also, on a five-sided bastion reinforcing the defences on the palace side, the arms of the grand master Fabrizio del Carretto (1513–21).

Between the gate of Amboise and the tower of St George (map II, A-2), stretched the defence line of the German Langue. A little beyond the gate of Amboise, note the false wall overlooking the moat.

The tower of St George was reinforced with a spurred bastion in which munition storerooms were built. You will see a bas-relief of St George slaying the dragon, and below that, the arms of the grand master Antonio Fluvian (1421–37) framing those of Pope Martin V and the Order.

THE TOWER OF SPAIN (map II, A-3). Of circular plan, this tower is surrounded by a polygonal terreplein with low gun-holes for firing along the moat. The Spanish bulwark finished at the circular tower called the tower of St Mary (map II, B-4), dating from 1441. This tower is reinforced with a polygonal bastion with embrasures for artillery fire. The capture of the Spanish bulwark, one of the weaker places around the walls, brought on the defeat of the Knights in the siege of 1522. Between the tower of St Mary and the gate of Koskinou stretched the English bulwark.

Protected by the tower of St Mary was the gate of St Athanasius, decorated with the coat of arms of the grand master d'Aubusson.

THE GATE OF KOSKINOU (map II, D-4). This is also called the gate of St John because it is decorated with a relief representing St John the Baptist. Above the gate, notice the arms of Pierre d'Aubusson, placed there before he became a cardinal, that is, some time between the siege of 1480 and 1489. Beside the arms of the grand master are those of the Order.

Between the gate of Koskinou and the tower of Italy used to stretch the Provence bulwark. This part of the walls is reinforced by a series of unnamed towers. On these towers, as well as on the counterscarp, you will notice the arms of the grand master Pierre d'Aubusson, while those of Jean de Lastic (1437–54) and Jacques de Milly (1454–61) appear on the false and the main walls. The tower of Italy (see map II, F-3) was protected by an enormous circular terreplein 49ft (15m) in diameter, which acted as a formidable defence point with embrasures for artillery fire. Gun-holes were built into the base to allow the defenders to protect the moats. You will see the arms of Fabrizio del Carretto on the terreplein, and cannon-balls in the tower and main walls, no doubt embedded there during the Turkish siege of 1522. Protected by the tower was the entrance to the gate of Italy, walled up after the siege of 1480. The Italian bulwark stretched from the tower of Italy, ran a short way along the bay of Ancandia, and finished a little farther N.

3 – The ancient town and Mt Smith

Take this walk, which is 2.5mls (4km) there and back, just before sunset. The visit to the ancient site will be a little disappointing, because the remains are either very dilapidated or much restored.

∴ The ancient town, constructed from 408 BC onwards, extended from the top of the acropolis (Mt Smith) (map I, A-3) to the N point of the island and eastwards, as far as the site later occupied by the walled town of the Knights.

Open: weekdays, 08.30–12.30 and 16.00–18.00; Sun. 09.00–15.00.

THEATRE (map I, A-4). Entirely rebuilt by the Italians before World War II it acted in some way as a second theatre for the much larger one, which, according to Diodorus Siculus, was situated near the harbour, perhaps on the site of Symi Square.

STADIUM (map I, A-4). It was built in the 2nd century BC and restored by the Italians. The steps of the sphendono (semicircular part) are ancient, the others are modern.

TEMPLE OF APOLLO (map I, A-4). Accessible by a wide flight of steps, this temple, dedicated to Pythian Apollo, was erected in Doric style,

ISLAND OF RHODES

Asphalt roads
Other roads
Tracks
Ancient ruins

0   5   10   15 mls

RHODES

Kremasti
Trianda Ixos
Paradissi
906
Mt. Philerimos
IALYSOS
Rodini
Hagia
Marina
Dhamatria
Theologos
Pastida
Koskinou
Thermae
of Kallithea
Soronio
Fanes
Kalamon
Maritsa
1365
Cumuli
Eleoussa
Monastery
Kalavarda
Petaloudes
(Valley of Butterflies)
Kallithea
Cape
Ladiko
CAMIROS
1572
Psinthos
Afandou
Mandrikon
Salakos
Koskinistis
Potamoulias
Archipolis
Sperioti
Mt. Prophitis
Ilias
1828 7 Sources
Cape Vaghia
Alimia
Kastelos
Moni
Cariona
Apollona
Platania
Mt. Tsambika
Moni Tsambikas
Alimia
Kritinia
Emborias
Castle of Faraclos
Archanghelos
3986
Moni
Atramitis
Moni
Camirou
Malona
Cape
Archanghelos
Mt. Atabyros
Masari
Mt. Acramytis
Hagios Isidoros
Ghadhoura
Cape
Armenisti
Siana
Mt. Kariona
1791
Laerma
Mt. Kalathos
Monolithos
Istrios
Ingo
1276
Kalathos
Cape Hagios Milianos
Profilia
Lardos
Marmari
1503
Lindos
Apollakia
Arnitha
Vati
Asclipio
Pefkas
Gulf of
Apollakia
Cape Mirtias
Moni Skiadi
Ghenadion
Mt. Skiadi
Messanagros
MEDITERRANEAN
SEA
Katavia
Moni H. Georgios
Lachania
Hagios
Pavlo
Plimiri
Vroulia
Cape Viglos
Cape Prassonisssi

but only a few columns remain. The view that you will obtain over the modern town and the walled city will reward you for your efforts, though you may well prefer the panorama from Mt Smith.

MT SMITH (map I, A–3). Believed to be the ancient acropolis, it owes its name to the English admiral, Smith, who set up his headquarters in Rhodes in 1802, while the English fleet was guarding the approaches to the sea of Marmara.

On the acropolis were the temples of Zeus and Athena Polias, some remains of which were uncovered in 1927 and 1929.

From the summit, there is a first-class *view over the town and the wooded hills on the N side of the island: and to see the setting sun over a shimmering sea is a fine spectacle.

THE ISLAND OF RHODES

Even during a short stay on Rhodes, you cannot neglect the excursions inland. Certainly the most typical villages, the most characteristic landscapes, the ancient sites and the Byzantine chapels do not lack attraction or charm; but above all the discovery of the island, particularly towards the S, allows you to get away from the tourist crowds and to see the authentic country. It is one of the most beautiful of the Greek islands.

1 PARK OF RHODINI AND KALLITHEA (6.2mls/10km; leave by Afstralias Road). The park of Rhodini, at the gates of the town, is a pleasant place to walk and relax. There are always flowers in bloom and it has a small zoo. From there you can visit the so-called tomb of the Ptolemies, dating from the Hellenistic period. You can also see the cemeteries of Rhodes which are behind the walls of the old town and are of great historical interest; they are presently being excavated and the archaeologists have discovered hundreds of tombs and, especially in those of the Hellenistic period, objects of immense value which are shortly to be exhibited in a new museum. Finally, the former cemetery, situated in the present one, contains tombs of all nationalities, but mainly Greek Orthodox, Jewish and Turkish.

6.2mls (10km): Kallithea, a spa town (for digestive problems), built during the Italian occupation, is set in an attractive position.

2 MT PHILERIMOS AND THE VALLEY OF THE PETALOUDES (return journey 37.5mls/60km). Leave by the Camiros road (map I, A–3).

5mls (8km): Trianda. Turn l. towards Philerimos (Filerimos).

9.4mls (15km): summit of Mt Philerimos, site of the acropolis of the ancient Ialysus, one of the three Dorian cities, which claimed as founder a mythical person, from whom the town took its name. Excavations in the plain below the village of Trianda have uncovered some remains of the Neolithic era, and of the beginning of the Bronze Age, but more importantly, the ruins of a large Minoan town, the ancient Achaea, without doubt the most significant outside Crete. This may have been a Cretan colony. At all events, the influence of Crete was predominant there. The town flourished for some years around 1500 BC and was influenced by Mycenean culture, then, like all the buildings in Crete, was destroyed by a natural catastrophe, possibly caused by the eruption of the volcano of Santorini. Abandoned after 1400 BC, it was rebuilt at the foot of Mt Philerimos.

After the Dorian invasion of the 10th century BC it was known by the name of Ialysos; the town was moved nearer the coast, towards the village of Kremasti. It declined considerably from 408 BC onwards, with the founding of the town of Rhodes to which it must have supplied most of the inhabitants.

Passing by the remains of an 11th century Byzantine church, to the r. of the car park at the end of the road, and then passing, also on the r., the way of Calvary, built by the Italians before the last war, you will come to the flight of steps leading to the top of the acropolis.

Open: 09.00–15.30; Sun. 10.00–15.00.

At the top, on the l., lie the foundations of the temple of Athena and Zeus Polieus, built in Doric style in the 4th century BC, on the site of a sanctuary.

On the l., the underground chapel of Hagios Georgios is decorated with mural paintings from the 14th and 15th centuries AD, retouched before the last war.

On the r., notice a palaeo-Christian baptistry, then go into the church of Our Lady of Philerimos, built on a site dedicated for worship from the 2nd millennium BC. This church formed part of a monastery, founded by the Knights of St John, a cloister of which still exists. Take the path on the l. at the bottom of the steps from the car park, and you will come to a Doric fountain, from the 4th century BC, which you can only just see behind the railings. There is fine scenery all around. At the same time you will appreciate the strategic importance of Mt Philerimos, recognized by the Byzantines who entrenched themselves here when the Genoese raided the island in 1248, and again during the invasion of Rhodes by the Knights of St John. The Sultan Suleiman the Magnificent set up camp here to lead the siege of Rhodes in 1522.

13.7mls (22km): Return to Trianda. Turn l.

17.2mls (27.5km): Koufa. In the chapel of Hagios Ioannis, on the l., are medieval wall paintings (obtain the key from the café near the road).

18.8mls (30km): Paradissi, airport for Rhodes. In the chapel of Hagios Markos, on the l., is a fresco of St George, in typically Byzantine style. In the village, take the road on the l. towards Kalamon.

22.5mls (36km): Valley of the Petaloudes. From the tourist office, continue on foot into the green, wooded area where thousands of butterflies have chosen to settle (June to mid-September) – hence the name 'valley of the Butterflies'. But you will only see them if you disturb their peace a little; whistle or clap your hands, and you will see them fly off from the shrubs and bushes or boulders where they are hidden. The place still does not lack charm, even outside the season when these graceful creatures appear.

37.5mls (60km): return to Rhodes.

3 CAMIROS AND LINDOS (excursion of 104mls/166km with stretches of very bad road in the centre of the island).

This long excursion, across the green countryside of the northern half of the island, will lead you to discover the two main archaeological sites on Rhodes, Camiros and Lindos, as well as the marvellous forest scenery of Mt Prophitis Ilias. Such a programme demands an early morning start (around 07.00; see 'Two days on Rhodes – Second day, page 744), unless you prefer to split up this one-day excursion into two days (visit Camiros and Mt Prophitis Ilias one day; visit Lindos the second day). This would be necessary, in any case, if you could not get hold of a sturdy car, or if you are inclined to wander off the main excursion route, particularly in the southern part of the island, going from Camiros to Lindos via Katavia and Messanagros. In this second case (taking two days), you would follow the main excursion route in reverse on the second day, from Rhodes to Lindos.

Leave the town of Rhodes by the road to Camiros. See Excursion 2 above, and follow this as far as Paradissi, omitting the detour to Philerimos.

10mls (16km): Paradissi.

 15mls (24km): Soroni. On 30 July a large Festival of Praise takes place. (This religious festival is held in honour of the local saint, Hagios Soulas, but there are some secular events, such as the races for donkeys and horses.)

18.7mls (30km): Kalavarda. Pass, on the l., the road to Salakas, which you will take later for Mt Prophitis Ilias.

21.2mls (34km): Camiros. You will see, in a valley, the ruins of a part of the old city, dating from the Hellenistic period, one of the three ancient towns of the island, which united towards the end of the 5th century BC to form a new capital, Rhodes. There is no acropolis overlooking the fields of ruins, which confirms the accounts of ancient writers who said that Camiros was not a fortified town. However, Italian archaeologists, in their excavations, have discovered its temples and houses.

Open: weekdays 09.00–15.30; Sun. 10.00–15.00; entrance fee.

About a hundred yards from the end of the road, there is a vast temenos, enclosing a sacred area where a Doric temple of the 3rd century BC stood, a few columns of which still exist. Lower down, on the coastal side, you will notice the remains of a semicircular exedra and a sacrificial area, with a large altar and nine smaller ones. From there, a set of steps leads to a street crossing a huge area of private houses.

As you climb the street, you will see on the l. several re-erected columns, indicating a peristyle house of the Hellenistic period. Then you will reach a long Doric portico of the 3rd century BC, built alongside the agora, above a cistern of the 6th or 5th century BC. Six columns have been re-erected with their entablature. Beyond this there are a few remains of the temple of Athenia Camiria, from the 6th or 5th century BC, which was restored during the Hellenistic period.

If you wish to go directly from Camiros to Lindos without seeing the southern part of the island, omit this next excursion section and go to the section headed 'Continuation of main 104mls (166km) excursion route from Camiros to Lindos'.

Camiros to Lindos via Katavia and Messanagros. This excursion of 85mls (135km-5-6hrs.) in the southern part of the island will take you off the beaten track, on roads which are not paved, and sometimes difficult as between Katavia and Messanagros, but which will allow you to discover some of the hidden delights of Rhodes, such as the castle of Monolithos and some fine views between Katavia and Messanagros.

Beyond Camiros, keep on the same road towards Mandrikon.

8.4mls (13.5km): Camiros Skala. This is the ancient port of Kritinia, founded by Cretan sailors during the Minoan period, today simply a fishing hamlet, but one of the rare places on the island where you can enjoy freshly-caught fish in one of the two tavernas. From the port small boats cross to the island of Halki (crossing 1½hrs).

9.4mls (15km): Castello de Camiros. This castle was rebuilt at the beginning of the 16th century by the Knights of St John on a rocky bluff, and commands a fine view along the coast. Very dilapidated, this castle still sports the coats of arms of the grand masters Aimery d'Amboise and Fabrizo del Carretto.

11.2mls (18km): Kritinia, from where access is direct to Siana and Monolithors.

16.2mls (26km): Embona. This is a really picturesque Rhodian village, situated on an escarpment. You can leave from here (but not without a local guide) to climb Mt Atabyros (3,986ft/1,215m), the highest summit on the island, where the ancients dedicated a temple to Zeus during the Hellenistic period. (Allow at least 6hrs. to get there and back.)

26.2mls (42km): Hagios Isidoros. A little before reaching this village, there is a road to the l. which leads to Laerma (6.9mls/11km), Lardos (14.4mls/23km) and Lindos (18.7mls/30km). If you have already had second thoughts about making this excursion into the southern part of the island, now is your opportunity to turn off for Lindos via Laerma. If you do this, you can console yourself by visiting the monastery of Thari, near Laerma. Take the Profilia road out of Laerma, then at 1.2mls (2km), turn l. on to a rough track, which is only 1.2mls (2km) long, and it will lead you to this monastery, nestling in the hollow of a valley, probably since the 9th century. The church, with a cupola, will interest you especially because of its *wall paintings in the nave, apse and cupola. Some of the murals are four layers thick, the oldest dating from the 11th century. The frescoes in the nave and transept were painted in the 17th century, those on the cupola in the 13th and 16th centuries (these 16th century ones are to be removed to uncover the earlier ones), while the three layers of frescoes in the apse were painted in the 11th, 13th and 16th centuries.

30.6ml (49km): You rejoin the road leading directly from Kaitinia, 31.3ml (50km), Siana, a village in whose necropolis have been found Archaic vases, notably some Attic black-figure cups of the 2nd quarter of the 6th c. BC, which by convention, are now called 'Siana cups'.

 34.4mls (55km): Monolithos. This is a little village perched high on the sides of Mt Acramytis, from where a road leads to the 15th century castle of Monolithos (1.2mls/2km), a little lower down the slopes of the mountain. The castle is located on a **marvellous site, on the top of a scarp face, a veritable eagle's nest, from where its defenders, the Knights of St John, could look down over the sea. The track continues down to the shore (approx 2¼ml/4km).

41.9mls (67km): Apollakia. From here you take the coast road to Katavia. A road to the l. leads directly to Genadio (10.6ml/17km) on the E coast.

46.2mls (74km): a road to the l. leads (4.4mls/7km) to the monastery of Skiadi, now deconsecrated. It was founded during the Byzantine period and restored in the 18th century. The church, which is dilipidated, still preserves a few frescoes, especially on the cupola. A local couple, who look after this monastery while it awaits restoration, will be pleased to offer you a night's lodging in these peaceful and pastoral surroundings.

 52mls (83km): Katavia, a village renowned for its weaving. Turn l. towards Messanagros and take a very winding, narrow road which follows a ridge over Mt Skiadi (2,175ft/663m). From here you will have **superb views over the whole of the southern part of the island.

 60mls (96km): Messanagros.

66.2mls (106km): Lachania. This village is situated on the eastern coastal plain of the island, which you will be following from now on.

75.6ml (121km): road to the l. for 2¼ml (4km) to Asklipio, a peaceful village perched high, interesting for its site, its houses, its fortress and especially its Byzantine church of the Dormition of the Virgin, with fine frescoes.

80mls (128km): Lardos. On the l., at the entrance to the village, is the road for (3.1mls/5km) the monastery of Ipseni, gleaming white in the hollow of a valley; to the r., a small road leading directly to Lindos via Pefki: very fine views.

82.5mls (132km): meet the main Rhodes-Lindos road, turn r.

84.4mls (135km): Lindos. For description of Lindos, see below, at 69.4mls (111km): *Lindos.

Continuation of main 104mls (166km) excursion route from Camiros to Lindos. From Camiros (at 21.2mls/34km) return to Kalavarda (at

23.7mls/38km – also at 18.7mls/30km), then turn r. towards Salakos (28.7mls/46km).

33mls (53km): turn l. towards Prophitis Ilias. The road continues to climb towards the summit (36.2mls/58km) of Mt Prophitis Ilias (2,618ft/798m), through pine forests, a region clearly considered to be a little Switzerland in Rhodes, judging by the chalets built on its slopes.

A track leads you to (40ml/64km) Foundoukli, a pretty site affording a panoramic view; the church of Hagios Nikolaos to the r. is unusual in its architecture; this has the form of a Greek cross with four apses; the cupola is characterized by a ten-sided drum embellished on the outside with blind niches, the sides of which are emphasized with colonettes with capitals. It is decorated with several layers of frescoes (10th and 11th century), repainted later by the Italians; note the figures drawn on the same model.

41.9mls (67km): Eleoussa.

51.2mls (82km): meet Rhodes–Lindos road, turn r.

55.6mls (89km): Archanghelos. This is a pretty little village of 2,500 inhabitants, with cube-shaped houses and overlooked by a castle built by the Knights of Rhodes.

59.4mls (95km): round to the r. to (1¼ml/2km) Malona and on the l. (1¼mi/2km) to the castle of Faracilos, one of the most formidable ever built by the Knights of St John.

69.4mls (111km): *Lindos. This pretty little township occupies the site of one of the three ancient Dorian towns on the island. It is overlooked by the scarp face of the acropolis, with two little bays, one either side, which used to have their own sheltered harbours.

The history of Lindos is indissociable from that of its rock, which, from early Antiquity, was a place of worship. Traces are to be found there of all the cultures which succeeded one another in Rhodes, whether Hellenistic, Byzantine or from the time of the Knights and of the Turks.

In the Middle Ages, Lindos was built as a castellany by the Knights and provided with a strong castle where twelve Knights and a Greek garrison were stationed. The town had famous potteries, the dishes from which were held in high esteem in western Europe.

The village, with its narrow streets climbing up the hillside, is picturesque: many of the 15th century houses are still almost intact with their Gothic decoration. Having passed through the village, climb up to the castle. A double lunette protects the approaches; a long flight of steps leads to the main gate; on the l., a second parallel flight of steps led directly to an upper doorway. Below the large set of steps, the rock face has been cut out to form an exedra; on the r., a large relief shows the stern of a boat with its side rudder and the pilot's seat; the bridge, jutting out 3ft (1m), served as a base for the statue of a priest of Neptune, called Hegesander, son of Micion. To the r. of the relief there still exist a few steps from the ancient staircase to the acropolis. At the top of the steps you will see the ruins of the castle of the Knights, littered with materials from other ancient and medieval constructions. Then you will be able to make out the ruins of the Byzantine Church of St John, which was next to the castle.

THE SANCTUARY OF ATHENA LINDIA. Dating from the middle of the 4th century BC (excavated by a Danish team and partially restored by Italian archaeologists) this sanctuary occupies most of the flat top of the acropolis. It was reached by a monumental propylaeum, with a central flight of steps and portico with two reversed wings, some columns of which have been re-erected. This portico, in Doric style, was built around 200 BC. The Doric temple of Athena, tetrastyle and amphiprostyle, stands at the top of the terrace (magnificent view over the sea).

Open: daily 08.30–12.30 and 16.00–18.00; Sun. 09.00–15.00.

Mt Krana, which is opposite the castle, has been cut into for tombs. One is like a facade of a Doric temple with twelve columns, preceded by four monumental columns, (cippi) in fact altars, which were at this level, decorated with bucranes (sculpted ox-heads) and garlands, and with a wide inscribed base. From the partially-shaded terrace that precedes all this a ***magnificent view of the village, the acropolis, the theatre and the two ports; access is easy from the SE via a narrow street in the village, then by a path.

(Another tomb, shaped like a stone tumulus, called the tomb of Cleobulus, is built on the cape of Hagios Milianos, 15 mins to the N of Lindos; a corridor leads to the sepulchral chamber.)

From the main square of the village, you can reach the theatre by first going towards the late Byzantine church of the Panagia (inside are frescoes from 1779, and icons), and then taking a narrow street on the r. Set underneath the acropolis, the theatre is quite well preserved.

If you wish to go from Lindos to Camiros via Messanagros and Katavia see page 762 section headed 'Southern extension to the 104mls (166km) excursion from Camiros to Lindos via Katavia and Messanagros'. Start at '84.4mls (135km)' and make the journey in the reverse direction.

Continuation of the main 104mls (166km) excursion route, from Lindos to Rhodes: From Lindos, which you reached in 69.4mls (111km), now turn back and retrace your route to the junction at 51.2mls (82km), where you joined the main Rhodes-Lindos road.

87.5mls (140km): just after Kolymbia, the road on the l. leads to Mt Prophitis Ilias and Camiros.

95mls (152km): the road on the r. leads in 0.6mls (1km), to the beach of Faliraki (fine sand; small cafés on the beach, very popular).

100mls (160km): the road to the r. leads to Koskinou (1.2mls/2km), a pleasant village with flowers everywhere, and Kallithea (4mls/6.5km) – see Excursion 1 on page 758.

104mls (166km): Rhodes (see map I, C–4).

4 ISLAND OF CASTELLORIZO or **MEGISTI** (connections by boat with Piraeus or Rhodes once a week). The most easterly of the Greek islands, well to the E of Rhodes, this little island is situated 1.5mls (2.4km) from the Turkish coast, facing the port of Kas. The island is, in fact, an enormous rock, dominated by a medieval castle constructed by the Rhodian Nicagoras and restored by the Knights of Rhodes.

The island was occupied as far back as the Prehistoric era; there was also a Mycenaean settlement, several tombs from which have been excavated. It was then colonized by the Dorians who venerated the Lycian Apollo (the temple was on the mainland). After having joined the States of the Knights of Rhodes, the island was subjected to Turkish occupation and finally took part in the War of Independence.

The little fortified harbour and its citadel of the Knights of Rhodes are interesting to visit. In Castellorizo, an old house of the Turkish period (18th c.), also called *Koukai* – The house of the rich Turk – has just been converted into a museum (09.00–14.00 except Tues.); in it you will see pieces from the Hellenistic, Roman and Byzantine periods (plates, remains of frescoes, icons); a small part is set aside for local traditions. The ruined citadel of Paleokastro was erected on the site of an ancient acropolis.

■ Salamis [Island of]

36sq. mls (93.2km²) – Pop: 20,000.

You could say of Salamis, now almost part of the suburbs of Piraeus, that here is an island which, with the township of Marathon, is a symbol of heroic Greece, the Greece of the Persian wars. Today part of the Piraeus-Eleusis-Athens industrial triangle and suffering from heavy water and air pollution, Salamis' single tourist attraction is the memory of this glorious feat of arms. The ferry, between Perama on the mainland and Paloukia on the east coast of the island, crosses the strait where the famous battle took place in 480 BC.

THE ISLAND OF AJAX. Salamis may have been a Phoenician trading station. Much later it became a dependency of its neighbour, Aegina, but took part in the Trojan war under an autonomous king, Ajax, son of Telamon. In 632 BC Megara and Athens fought for its control, but in 612 BC it was finally captured by Solon, for Athens, and considered to be a 'cleruchia' (colony) of that city. From 318 BC it came under Macedonian rule. It was only in 229 BC that Aratos gave it back to the Athenians, who drove out the Salaminians and settled new colonists there.

During the crossing (20 mins.) from Perama (shipyards) to Paloukia, you will have extensive views over the coastline of Attica and, on the l., the valleys and shores of the bay of Ambelaki, on the island of Salamis. At the same time, while going over the waters where the Battle of Salamis took place, you may have some thoughts for those men who confronted each other more than 2,500 years ago in this strait. One side was trained by a king, a god to his people and the ruler of an immense empire, to avenge the unbelievable accident of Marathon. The other side was fighting for its freedom. You might also have time to reflect that, without Marathon and Salamis (victories made complete by the Battle of Plataea), there would never have been the miracle of Greece.

THE TRAGEDY OF SALAMIS AS SEEN BY A DRAMATIST. The story of the battle has been told by Aeschylus, an eyewitness, in his tragedy of *Persians*, performed in March 472 BC, and by Herodotus, who gives a confused version from both Ionian and Athenian sides. Taking account also of the version of Diodorus Siculus, it seems the battle can be reconstructed as follows.

WHEN PERSIA CAMPED ON THE ACROPOLIS. The Persians had occupied Attica, Athens and the Acropolis. Their fleet, estimated by Aeschylus and Herodotus at 1,207 ships (a number that should be reduced by at least half), was anchored in the bay of Phaleron. The Greek fleet, with a strength of 378 triremes of which 200 were Athenian, was stationed at the head of the bay of Ambelaki.

SNARED IN A TRAP. After a lively debate, Eurybiades and the Peloponnesian chiefs, implored by Themistocles, resigned themselves to stay and fight. Xerxes, on his part, had decided to take the offensive. At nightfall on the eve of battle, the Persian fleet executed its first manoeuvre: it left the bay of Phaleron and deployed itself opposite the bay of Salamis, along that part of the coast of Attica which his land forces were occupying. But, during the night, Xerxes made his fleet execute a second manoeuvre: the most heavily armed boats closed the N exit from the strait while the slower boats formed a blockade to the S, between Cape Varvari, the island of Psittalia and the citadel of Piraeus, with the intention of cutting off the escape route of the Greek fleet.

WEEP, PERSIANS, WHEN YOU LEARN OF THIS MISFORTUNE. The next morning, the Greeks, aware that their fleet had been surrounded, launched their ships and deployed them in line opposite the N blockade, consisting of the more powerful ships of the Persian fleet. At the end of this manoeuvre the Athenian fleet was stationed close to the coast of Salamis. The Peloponnesians, who formed the right flank, were opposite the Ionians; the Athenians, on the left flank, to the W, had the Phoenicians opposite them. The Persian line attacked the Greeks while they were forming up and at first made them fall back. But the Greeks returned to the attack. The Athenians drove back the Phoenicians on the Attic coast near Xerxes, and by a turning movement, managed to outflank the Ionians, whom they pushed back in front of them. The collapse of the Persian N line led to the collapse of the S blockade. By evening, the remainder of the Persian fleet, reduced to 300 ships, assembled at Phaleron; the Greeks returned to Salamis. The 600 noble Persian warriors, abandoned at Psittalia, were massacred by the hoplites of Aristides.

THE FLIGHT AT THE MERCY OF THE WIND. Xerxes, having decided to flee, diverted the attention of the Greeks the following day by pretending to build a bridge of boats between Cape Amphialae, the tiny island of Hagios Georgios and Salamis. This allowed his fleet at Phaleron to escape on the following night. The king returned to Asia by land with his army, leaving Mardonius in Greece with 300,000 men. Imagine for a moment the joy of Sophocles, an adolescent about 15 years old, with lyre in hand, conducting a children's choir and singing a paean of victory.

Return now to dry land, by disembarking at Paloukia (to the N, important naval base), at the northern entrance to the bay of Ambelaki, and set off from there to explore this island.

Those interested in archaeological sites can turn to the l. or to the r.

To the l. at 0.9ml (1.5km) is Kamatero, situated at the foot of the acropolis of Salamis, the second capital of the island at the time of Athenian control (remains of harbour construction seen underwater, near the chapel of Hagios Dimitrios). To the r., at about 1.6mls (2.5km), beyond the arsenal, are two ancient terraces with walls in polygonal form, that could perhaps be the sanctuary of Athena Skiras and Enyalios, founded by Solon.

Going straight ahead, those interested in post-Byzantine religious art will reach Salamis at 2.2mls (3.5km). The church of the Panagia tou Katharou has icons by Georgios Markou on the iconostasis, and in a chapel close by is an icon by Poulakis, of the 17th century Cretan school. 3.7mls (6km) further on is the monastery of Phaneromeni (*Apparition of the Virgin*), built in 1661, whose church contains frescoes (*Last Judgement*) painted in 1735 by Georgios of Argos, his pupils Venizelos and Kypriotos and his brother Antony.

To the S of the monastery are remains of an ancient wall more than 1,640yds (1,500m) long, a section of the surrounding wall of Boudoron, an Athenian outpost during the Peloponnesian war. At 0.9ml (1.5km) from the monastery there is a ferry to take you back to the mainland, about 4.7mls (7.5km) from Megara.

■ Samos [Island of]

189.6sq. mls (491km²) – Pop: 35,00 approx.

Samos, the Greek island nearest to the Asiatic coast – barely more than 1.2mls (2km) – deserves to take back its original name of Stephanea, because of the abundance of its flowers and vegetation. Away from the well-trodden tourist tracks, this island, famous for its sweet (*moschato*) and dry wines, should be a favourite for those attracted to long deserted beaches, extensive hills and woods, and villages which have preserved the stamp of ancient times.

A LAND OF THE IONIAN DIASPORA. The island seems to have been inhabited by the Pelasgians who introduced the worship of Hera. Leading the Ionians, Procles settled himself there around the 9th century BC. His descendants retained power until about 680 BC. After the death of Amphicrates, the last of Procles' descendants. Samos declared independence and created a democratic regime. Under the tyrant (i.e., ruler) Polycrates, Samos was one of the principal cities in Ionia. Allied with Corinth, it founded colonies, especially in the Propontis (the Sea of Marmara). The Samians were renowned during the Archaic period as metalworkers and goldsmiths (hollow bronze castings), as engineers and architects (Rhoecus and Theodorus), and their school of sculpture was famous. The most illustrious of Samos' children, however, was Pythagoras, a philosopher of the 6th century BC, who was also a great mathematician, as witnessed by his famous theorem for calculating the length of the hypotenuse of a right-angled triangle, and the multiplication table, another of his inventions.

A TYRANT WITH INSOLENT GOOD LUCK. Samos attained its greatest prosperity under the Tyrant Polycrates. According to Glotz, he was 'a brilliant statesman and a wanton ruffian', 'famous for his insolent good luck and fabulous wealth', who is thought to have come to power around 532 BC. But autocratic government could perhaps have been set up at Samos as early as 560 BC by Ajax, the father of Polycrates. A familiar story is told by Herodotus (III, 41), of the gold ring set with emeralds which Polycrates, uneasy at his growing prosperity, threw into the sea to tempt fate, and which was served up at table inside a fish. Allied to Amasis, the king of Egypt, Polycrates dominated the Aegean region. He held a sumptuous court with his favourite poets (including Anacreon of Teos). At the head of a fleet of one hundred vessels, he annexed several neighbouring islands and defeated the Lesbians and their allies the Milesians. But, in 522 BC, drawn into a trap by the satrap Oroetes, he was taken prisoner and, after he had been flayed alive, was crucified.

BETWEEN ATHENS AND SPARTA. Conquered by the Persians, Samos took part in the revolt of the Ionian cities and became part of the Attico-Delian League. After another revolt it was besieged and taken by the Athenians (439 BC), who set up a democratic government there. At the end of the Peloponnesian war, it came under the influence of Sparta, but was retaken by Athens who sent colonists there in 366 BC.

BETWEEN THE ROMAN CARROT AND STICK. Independent from 322 to 205 BC, but subject to the influence of Alexander the Great's successors (in particular, the Ptolemies), Samos was conquered by Philip V of Macedon, then given by the Romans to the kings of Pergamum, and finally joined to the Roman province of Asia in 129 BC. Plundered in 92 BC by Licinius Verres, its prosperity was restored during the Asian propraetorship of Quintus Cicero (62 BC). It was pillaged again in 39 BC by Mark Antony. Augustus gave it back its freedom, which was later restricted by Vespasian.

GO TO SAMOS OR GO TO YOUR DEATH. Samos declined during the Byzantine period and, invaded by the Turks in 1453, it became depopulated, but underwent a rebirth in the 17th century. In 1821, there was an uprising and the Samians rose triumphant against the Turks for whom the saying 'Go to Samos' had become a proverb meaning 'Go to your death'. A remarkable run of successes allowed Samos, in 1832, to obtain a special form of government, with a prince chosen by the Sublime Porte from amongst the Christians on the island, and a Chamber. In 1912, the Turkish fleet was driven away after a harmless bombardment by two Italian warships, and the reunion with Greece was proclaimed.

YOUR STAY ON SAMOS. You will probably not go to Samos just for one day, but that is all you need to make a tour of the island and to see the most important sights. You will probably stay at Vathy or, preferably, Pythagorion (formerly Tigani), on the site of the ancient capital, still rich in remains, of which one, the tunnel of Eupilanos, is of exceptional interest; you will be close to the Heraeum (approx. 4mls/6km), and to some fine beaches.

The restrictions of opening hours may oblige you to visit the Heraeum, the Pythagorion museum and the tunnel of Eupilanos in the morning; the other sites, which are not enclosed, are freely accessible.

To tour the island after visiting the important Vathy museum, take the picturesque coastal road towards Karlovassi, then follow the road to Marathokambos, the prettiest village on the island. From there, continue as far as Marathokambos beach. If you like huge deserted beaches (there are two other fine beaches at Tsamadou and Kokkari), then pick up the circular route again and dine at Pythagorion harbour.

If you split the sightseeing into two less demanding days, visit Pythagorion and the Heraeum on the first day, and make the tour of the island the second day, with a long pause at Vathy. If you have the opportunity, do not miss a trip to Kusadasi (pronounced 'Kooshadaser'), a little Turkish port 10.6mls (17km) from the ruins of ancient Ephesus (boat Vathy-Kusadasi; the return journey is possible in one day).

You may disembark at Vathy-Samos or Karlovassi (N coast) or even Pythagorion (S coast).

8.7mls (14km) **VATHY**, the capital of the island, is a pleasant little township, its green hills enclosing a deep bay, with a port which wakens from its slumbers when the boats arrive from Piraeus. Since it is forbidden to use the beach near the harbour (polluted water), you will bathe 0.6ml (1km) beyond the harbour, on the road to the lighthouse (maintained beach, bar-restaurant). Behind the Hotel Xenia, next to the post office, the archaeological museum (in the course of reorganization with the transfer of part of the collections to a new, neighbouring building (reopening expected imminently), contains antiquities of the Archaic period, notably sculptures in marble (e.g. the group by Genelaos *c.* 560; a fragmentary but colossal kouros – more than 16ft/5m high – the face of which was discovered in 1984, or the statue found in the same year at the Heraeum, which was an offering by Cheramyes, like the Hera of Samos, now in the Louvre). There are also figurines in bronze (including several cauldron decorations) and in ivory (notice especially a little relief from the 7th century BC of Perseus slaying Medusa). The vases and fragments of painted terracotta vases are numerous.

VICINITY OF VATHY

1 **MONASTERY OF ZOÖDOCHOS PIGI** (5.6mls/9km along the Kamara road). From this monastery, at the top of a hill, you will have a wonderful view over the strait of Samos, Cape Mycale and the Turkish coast.

Leaving Vathy, take the road to Karlovassi along the N coast of the island, frequently running through pine woods. The road is quite winding along the edge of the sea; it passes the little harbour of Kokkari where caïques are made.

28.7mls (46km) from Vathy: Karlovassi, a small port of about 5,000 inhabitants, regularly served by the boats making the crossing between Piraeus and Vathy-Samos. The hinterland of Karlovassi is covered with the vineyards which make Samos famous throughout the world. 1.2mls (2km) NW of Karlovassi there is a fine beach at Potami.

33.7mls (54km) from Vathy: Hagios Theodoros.

Turn r. here, and in 3.7mls (6km) you will find Marathokambos, a charming, brightly coloured village, in a *marvellous location, like a balcony overlooking the S coast of the island, with a long beach 2.5mls (4km) away. You could take a boat to the tiny island of Samiopoula, also having a superb sandy beach.

Between Hagios Theodoros and Pirgos (at 43.7mls/70km), the road through the pine forests is one of the most attractive on the island, especially in the early morning light.

A SANCTUARY WHICH WAS AN OPEN AIR MUSEUM. A centre for sacrifices, which has been dated from the 2nd millennium BC, grew up on the site of the Heraeum from the prehistoric period onwards. This settlement flourished particularly during the Mycenaean period. Hardly anything is left except the foundations of the monuments which, starting mainly from the Archaic period, crowded into the sanctuary in large numbers. Many offerings, dedicated to the goddess by sailors made rich during their far-off journeys, also accumulated there. In becoming a veritable art museum, the Heraeum encouraged the blossoming of a wealth of artistic talent which gave Samian art its special character.

You will first come to the great temple, probably founded around the middle of the 6th century BC by Rhoecus, one of the most famous of Samian artists, though some authors suggest that the architect Theodorus may also have been involved. This temple was conceived on a grandiose scale, certainly in keeping with the personalities of the Samian Tyrants Ajax and Polycrates. It was destroyed by a fire shortly after being completed, probably during the invasion of the island by the Spartans in 525–524 BC, and then rebuilt on an even larger scale (it was a dipteral temple of the Ionic order measuring 182½ft x 356 ft (55.16 x 108.63m) at the stylobate). The column bases of the old temple were used again in the foundations of this new temple, probably before the death of Polycrates in 522 BC. Work was interrupted again by political troubles which flared up on Samos after the Tyrant's agonizing death, and was not completed until the Hellenistic and Roman periods. Of this great temple there survive the impressive substructure, rising from the luxuriant vegetation, and several parts of columns; one of these has been reassembled upright, its many drums stacked one on top of another.

In front of the temple you will see, on the l., the remains of small baths and a Roman temple from the 2nd century AD, and on the r., the remains of a later construction and a peripteral temple from the Roman period. Immediately beyond are the remains of the great altar, said to be by Rhoecus, and rebuilt in the Roman period. It was erected on the site of a place of worship of the 2nd millennium BC where sacrifices were made, and above a more recent altar restored in the Geometric period.

Near the l. corner of the altar, note a small apse from a palaeo-Christian basilica and, at the side, a large round base.

On the part of the site to the l. of this collection of ruins note, beyond the great temple, the foundations of a small temple of Aphrodite, a temple with podium (late period) and a temple of Hermes. Further to the l. still a Roman house is in process of being uncovered. Nearer the great temple, a few yards from the long r. side (nearest the site entrance), are the remains of a Hellenistic portico, in the extension of an Archaic portico under which have been found various parts of the great temple which were buried after the sanctuary was burned down. So the portico would probably date from the end of the Archaic period. Various remains from the prehistoric period have been uncovered between the temple and the portico, including four megarons, one of which had a paved courtyard in front, with store-rooms opening on to it.

44.4mls (71km) from Vathy: you will pass over the original Samos, of which the village of Pythagorion occupies only a part. You could now undertake the visit to the archaeological area, leaving from the car park on the l. of the road, or alternatively from the village, as described immediately below.

Pythagorion (formerly Tigani), a pleasant little harbour squatting in a corner of the ancient island capital. The fishing habour is protected by a breakwater resting on foundations dating from the time of Polycrates.

■ In a small shady square about 100yd behind the central part of the port you will be able to visit the small archaeological museum, where some of the finds from ancient Samos and the Heraeum are on display.

Open: weekdays except Tues. 08.00–15.00 in summer, 09.00–14.30 in winter; Sun. 10.30–14.30; closed Tues.; entrance fee.

You will notice three Archaic statues from the middle of the 6th century BC, belonging to the group by the sculptor Genelaus (inscription), found while excavating the Heraeum, and also statues of women from the Hellenistic period. It is from ancient Samos that the statue of Ajax and numerous fragments of sculpture and architecture of the Roman period originate.

Retracing your steps a little to go along the r.-hand side of the harbour basin, you will see, at about 330yds (300m), the castle of the Logothetes, or kastro, built at the beginning of the 19th century on a hill which might have been the oldest acropolis of Samos, occupied since the prehistoric period. In the castle courtyard are two porticoes of a Roman building from Imperial times and the remains of palaeo-Christian churches.

To visit the ancient site, follow the Vathay road for 330yds (300m) from the main crossroads in the village, then turn l. on to the track leading to the chapel of the Panagia Spiliani, built inside a cave and to the tunnel of Eupalinus. On the way you will notice some remains of the old walls (to the r.) and of a villa of the Hellenistic period.

Turning r. will take you up to the little monastery and chapel of the Panagia Spiliani (about 330yds/300m); continuing straight ahead will bring you to the entrance to the tunnel of Eupalinus (275yds/250m), excavated under the direction of Eupalinus of Megara, when Polycrates was tyrant in the 6th century BC. According to one present-day estimate the work would have taken about 15 years; it was probably started by Ajax, Polycrates' father, and completed by the famous tyrant before the Spartan siege of 525–524 BC. This tunnel was intended to provide the town with a water supply and an emergency escape route, for it is known that Maeandrius used it when Darius occupied Samos.

Within the tunnel, on the l., is a narrow walkway, and running parallel, on the r., is a cut-out section containing the water supply system. About 15 mins walk from the entrance, you will see the ruins of a Byzantine chapel amongst the stalactites. A little further, the ceiling becomes progressively lower. After recent work undertaken by the German Institute of Athens, it is possible to go through the whole length of the tunnel, but the unlit part is closed to the public.

About 110yds (100m) past the entrance to the tunnel you will reach a section of the old walls. From there, go down towards the road leading to Karlovassi, which you will reach (crossing an ancient necropolis on the way) close by the hotel mentioned below (54.7mls/87.5km). Turn l. towards Pythagorion, 1ml (1.5km) distant. On the way, notice on the r. some thermal baths with a portico, from the late Imperial Roman period, uncovered by the German Institute along with a sanctuary of Artemis.

51.2mls (82km) from Vathy: The road to the r. leads to the deserted shingle beach of Aliki (3.7mls/6km).

53.7mls (86km): Return to Vathy.

To the SW, between Samos and Icaria, are the neighbouring islands of Fourni, which has a very indented coastline, and Thimena, which is even smaller; you can reach them by caïque.

To the SE, 51 nautical miles from Samos, about 150 people live on the tiny island of Agathonissi.

Samothrace [Island of] **(Samothraki)** *

69.5sq. mls (180km²) – Pop: 3,500 approx. – admin. region of Evros.

This island, lying about 25mls (40km) off Alexandroupolis and without any natural harbour, is known today mainly thanks to the celebrated Winged Victory which now greets visitors to the Louvre in Paris. Samothrace was renowned in antiquity for its sanctuary of the Cabiri, a place of mysterious cults. It is necessary to look into a past enriched with legends for the origins of the sanctuary of the Great Gods. In the Hellenistic period it would have been one of the largest Panhellenic centres where the Greek peoples, forgetting their differences, came to sacrifice to their gods and their heroes. At Samothrace, as at Eleusis, the secret of the Mysteries has been well guarded. The ancient texts give us just about enough information to get a vague idea of the ceremonial which took place at the initiation of the Elect. The excavations undertaken by New York University, under the auspices of the American School of Classical Studies, while giving us useful and precise information on the topography of the holy places, have rekindled the long held interest in the sanctuary of the Cabiri. Thanks to these excavations, the ruins of the sanctuary, although very dilapidated, will awaken many memories of a past which has been dead for more than 15 centuries.

TO THE SOURCES OF THE LEGEND. Some mythical accounts, brought to us by ancient authors, told of the wonderful adventure of Dardanus who left Samothrace on a raft, which took him to Asia where he founded the kingdom of Troy. Dardanus' brother, Iasion, was considered to be the originator of the Mysteries of Samothrace, after Zeus had revealed to him the mystic rites, which became the heart of further developments there. Iasion, like Celeus, king of Eleusis, had been clever enough to win the esteem of Demeter, who gave him the gift of an ear of wheat.

According to another legend, the Phoenician Cadmus, who set off to look for his sister Europa, had met Harmonia there during his initiation into the Mysteries. The couple fell in love and the abduction of Harmonia, followed by their mystical marriage, was similar to that of Persephone by Hades at Eleusis.

A RELIGIOUS MELTING POT. The Samothracian pantheon was very complex and varied through the ages, particularly after Greek colonies were established around 700 BC. Excavations have confirmed the distant pre-Hellenistic roots of the Mysteries, roots already glimpsed through the legends. It seems that originally there was a Great Mother goddess, Axierus. The discovery of altars carved into the rock, comparable to those in Phrygia, makes one think that this divinity was probably the local incarnation of Cybele, the Phrygian mother goddess, sometimes identified with Rhea. According to some sources, the Cabiri were the Corybantes (male followers) of Cybele or the Curetes of Rhea, or even the two Samothracian heroes Dardanus and Iasion. The pantheon included two other chthonic divinities, Axiouerscs and Axiocersa, who were probably worshipped according to separate rites.

THE MYSTERIES OF SAMOTHRACE. According to Plutarch, we can believe that the festivals of the Great Gods were celebrated every year at the end of July or the beginning of August. Literary references concerning the rites of initiation into the mysteries are scant and controversial. After gathering information from several excavation projects, it seems that, from the Archaic period, two sets of religious ceremonies became dominant. They were the Anactoron, where the Elect probably received their first initiation, and the ceremonies given the name 'New Temple', where the mystes (those already initiated to the first degree) could become epoptes (initiated to the second degree).

PROSPERITY AND OBLIVION. The sanctuary of the Great Gods seems to have achieved great prosperity during the Hellenistic period. Most of the places for worship were restored by the kings of Macedon and the Ptolemies of Egypt, and they stayed in use in Roman times. After paganism was proscribed, however, at the end of the 4th century AD, the island fell into oblivion and its temples were destroyed by earthquakes a few centuries later.

THE EXCAVATIONS. Excavations were started by the French expedition of Deville and Coquart in 1856. This expedition was followed by Champoiseau who discovered, in 1863, the famous Winged Victory now in the Louvre. Then came two Austrian expeditions, in 1873 and 1875 (Conze). After them investigations were carried out by the French School at Athens in collaboration with the University of Prague. In 1938 systematic exploration was begun by New York University. Excavation work resumed after World War II.

The excursion to Samothrace is a 'serious' one; it will only be interesting to those who have the gift of bringing the ruins alive again and imagining their lost splendour. You should allow about 5hrs to go from Kamariotissa to the sanctuary, look around it, and return. But if you like wild and wooded locations, you will no doubt let yourself be tempted to wander around the ruins for several hours surrounded by attractive Mediterranean vegetation. You can then stay the night at the Hotel Xenia, or with a local inhabitant in one of the rustic houses in the little village.

From Kamariotissa harbour, at the head of the only sheltered bay on the island, by going E along the coast, you will reach, in 3.1mls (5km), Paleopolis, close to the ruins of the sanctuary of the Great Gods.

Open: weekdays, 08.00–17.00 in summer, 09.00–15.30 in winter; Sun. 10.00–16.30; entrance fee.

Leaving from the Hotel Xenia, you will come first of all, at about 110yds (100m), to the museum, a visit to which you should save for the hottest part of the day. To the E of the museum is a winding path which will lead you, in about 110yds (100m), to the entrance to the archaeological zone. The path continues inside this zone as far as the heart of the sanctuary, but you should first go up a small path leading off to the r. This leads to the W part of the site.

MILESIAN BUILDING AND RUINENVIERECK. Go up on to a terrace facing that of the Arsinöeion, and near a Byzantine fortification called Ruinenviereck ('Crossroads of the Ruins'). Here you will find a building uncovered by a Franco-Czechoslavakian team in 1923 and called the building of the Milesian, after the dedication to a Milesian (woman of Miletus, in Asia Minor) discovered among the ruins. It dates from the second half of the 3rd century BC, and was preceded by a massive rectangular structure, no doubt a monumental altar.

To the W of the Milesian building, under the ruins of the fortification, have been uncovered the foundations of another building of large proportions (116ft 11½ x 80ft 8½ins/35.64m x 24.60m), a sanctuary or place of initiation, dating from the middle of the 3rd century BC, according to F. Chapouthier. Under the further part of the Ruinenviereck were discovered the foundations of three small treasuries, facing towards a road, dating from the Hellenistic period.

PORTICO AND NICHE OF THE VICTORY. If you walk in a southerly direction up the zigzag path, you will reach the ruins of a long portico with outer Doric colonnade and inner Ionic colonnade, erected towards the end of the Hellenistic period. Finally you will come to the remnants of the niche which held the Victory, now in the Louvre, an ex voto of Demetrius I Poliorcetes after his naval victory at Salamis. It was made towards the end of the 3rd century or the beginning of the 2nd century BC. The famous statue was set up in a basin on a base shaped like the prow of a ship. On the hillside down below was the theatre.

THEATRE – Erected in the 2nd century BC, it was used for performances of sacred dramas; perhaps the mystical marriage between Cadmus and Harmonia could have been staged here.

All that remains are a few sections of the tiers buried in the undergrowth. It seems there was never a permanent building for the stage, but rather wooden constructions set up for each festival.

NEW TEMPLE (OR HIERON). On the other side of the valley are the remains of several buildings. They include a courtyard called the Altar Court, given by Arrhidaeus, dedicated to the Great Gods (between 340 and 330 BC), a Hall of Votive Gifts, where the offerings presented to the Great Gods were displayed, and a worship area given the name of New Temple.

The building called Altar Court, of which some foundations and various blocks of the superstructure still exist, faced towards the valley. According to K. Lehmann, it is possible that the courtyard at

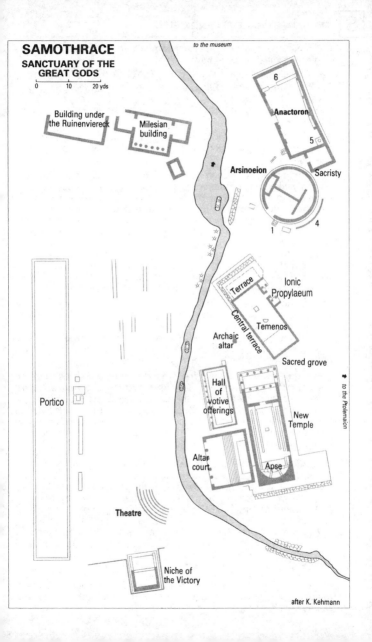

SAMOTHRACE

SANCTUARY OF THE GREAT GODS

0   10   20 yds

to the museum

Building under the Ruinenviereck

Milesian building

Anactoron

6

5

Sacristy

Arsinoeion

1   4

to the Ptolemaion

Ionic Propylaeum

Terrace

Central terrace

Temenos

Archaic altar

Sacred grove

Portico

Hall of votive offerings

New Temple

Altar court

Apse

Theatre

Niche of the Victory

after K. Kehmann

one time served as the stage for theatrical performances which were part of the initiation ceremony.

The foundations of the Hall of Votive Gifts are quite well preserved. The hall was probably built in the 6th century BC, then later altered several times, notably in the 5th century BC, and during the Hellenistic and Roman periods. It stayed in use until the end of the pagan era.

The New Temple was not a proper temple, but a place of worship where the Elect probably received the second degree of initiation (epoptia).

According to a text of sacred law discovered during the excavations, only mystes (those initiated to the first degree) or epoptes were permitted to enter the New Temple. Inside this complex building were two sacrificial pits (escharai), and a bothros, that is a hollow altar into which the priests poured libations, surrounded by an apse. The spectators probably sat on benches placed parallel to the longer walls of the cella. The building, whose foundations and a few courses of marble stone can still be seen, as well as several sections of the superstructure, was constructed around 320 BC, on the site of older places of worship. Five columns of the Doric order and one block of the architrave have been reinstated in the NE corner.

Excavations carried out in the Hellenistic apse have revealed the existence of a sanctuary from the end of the Archaic period, erected about 500 BC, and rebuilt around the year 400 BC, thus just a little less than a century before the Hellenistic building whose ruins you have just seen. The New Temple was itself restored several times, particularly during the Imperial Roman period.

All around the New Temple the ground is littered with debris from ancient buildings, altars, etc. Consequently American archaeologists have unearthed, to the N of the cella, outside the foundations, a curious collection of stones, consisting of two sacred stones flanking a torch, which must have been placed in the square slot of a limestone block. This device, altered several times, no doubt played a part in the initiation ritual.

PTOLEMAEUM. To the E, beyond a hillock where one of the necropolises was situated, and beyond a second valley, you will recognize the massive foundations of the Ptolemaion, made from blocks of well-dressed poros. This building, erected by Ptolemy Philadelphus around 280 BC, has the base of its foundations crossed at an angle by a vaulted tunnel, completely preserved, which would have given a channel for the water from the neighbouring stream in time of flood. The Ptolemaeum served as propylaea to the sanctuary. Materials for its construction came from a building of the 6th or 5th century BC.

Ramparts – Beyond the Ptolemaeum to the E, you quickly reach the rampart walls, flanked with square towers. The wall runs up the steep slopes until it reaches a ridge of jagged rock.

Circular building – To the W of the Ptolemaeum, a low round terrace includes a saucer-shaped paved area, at one time accessible by five marble steps (three are in place), also circular. In the centre there was probably an altar, perhaps the round altar seen in the entrance hall of the museum. This perplexing building probably dates from the end of the 5th century BC or the beginning of the 4th century BC. However, it was altered several times, particuarly when extra steps were added on behind the original ones, and in the 4th century BC when a building was erected which was itself replaced by a Doric one named after Philip III Arrhidaeus and Alexander IV (between 323 and 316 BC). You can still see solid foundations of this last building, which would have formed an annex.

Central terrace – This area between the New Temple and the Arsinöeion (see plan) seems also to have played an important role in Samothracian worship. Most of the ruins visible today belong to an enclosure (temenos), surrounded by walls and furnished with a propylaeum in Ionic style, which was decorated with a frieze representing girls dancing (now in the museum – see heading 'Museum' on page 781). This collection of buildings, all included under the name central terrace, was probably erected around the year 340 BC. The N part of the terrace is supported by very strong foundations made from large regular blocks of limestone.

We know that sacrifices were held there, hence the buildings for receiving them, dating from the 8th century BC onwards. These were rebuilt several times, the Hellenistic enclosure being the most recent.

The enclosure entrance (propylaeum), parts of whose foundations still exist, faced the Arsinöeion. The frieze of the girls dancing was placed under the propylaeum portico. Inside, the enclosure would have been partially paved in marble. It contained an eschara, the group of Aphrodite and Pothus sculpted by Scopas, and perhaps also a bothros.

THE MYSTERIES OF SAMOTHRACE. According to K. Lehmann, it is possible that the temenos served as the site for the public festival, when the search for Harmonia in the underworld and her sacred marriage with Cadmus were performed. If ancient authors are to be believed on this subject, a chorus of dancing girls would have been present at this evocation of the past, which symbolized nature in mourning during the winter season, the task of germination entrusted to the soil, and, through the mystical marriage of Harmonia and Cadmus, the opportunity for vegetation to come alive again in the spring. Now we know for certain that the propylaeum of the temenos was decorated with a frieze showing a chorus of girls dancing. The Archaic treatment of these reliefs, surprising for the period, probably reflected the ancient origin of the ritual conducted within these walls. At the time of Alexander the Great, the ceremony would have begun with sacrifices on the terrace adjoining the temenos, then continued inside the enclosure with offerings on the sacred hearth, probably in front of statues of Aphrodite and Pothus; these, according to Pliny, were held in special veneration during the festival of the Great Gods. The dances of the female chorus to the sounds of drums, flutes, lyres and other instruments, must have taken place in this enclosure, at the same time as the rituals were being performed around the altars and hearths.

ARSINŐEION. This vast rotunda (more than 22yds/20m in diameter) lay on impressive foundations consisting of blocks of poros, extremely well dressed and perfectly preserved. It was decorated with ox skulls and rosettes and dates from the 2nd decade of the 3rd century BC. It was erected by Arsinoe Philadelphus on the site of ancient places of worship, of pre-Hellenic origin, some remains of which you can still distinguish in the interior and around the foundations.

There is no doubt that the Arsinoeion played an important role in the development of worship here. The discovery of a sacrificial pit (plan, 1) to the r. of the entrance to the Arsinoeion, with which it is contemporary, tends to prove that this building was only the successor of more ancient establishments, but of a type more monumental than its predecessors. According to Lehmann, one can therefore summarize the evolution of religious establishments on the site as follows. Towards the end of the Bronze Age or the beginning of the Iron Age, on the site of the future Arsinoeion, a terrace was constructed, supported by a cyclopean wall still preserved for a length of about 32ft (10m). During the 7th century BC a double set of walls, whose religious significance is apparent, was built. The N wall, which enclosed an old pre-Hellenic carved rock altar, was in some way the adyton of this open-air sanctuary. The S wall must also have been reserved for worship, for a sacrificial pit, dating from the 7th century BC, was found there. It would have been dedicated to the chthonic divinities Axiocersos and Axiocersa. This double set of walls was replaced in the 6th century BC by another structure which lasted two or three centuries. In the 3rd century BC, at the time when the Arsinoeion was erected, the 6th century BC places of worship were buried in the rubble which formed the foundation for the rotunda. Borings made in 1974 place in doubt the very ancient character of the installations earlier than the Arsinoeion which, according to J. MacCredie, probably only date from the 4th century BC.

ANACTORON. This probably acted as the hall of initiation to the first degree for the uninitiated. In the 'sacristy' several inscriptions, dating from the 1st century BC to the 3rd century AD, have been uncovered, listing those initiated to the first degree (mystes). Moreover, the ruins visible today belong to buildings from the Hellenistic period or the Roman period, which replaced yet older buildings.

Excavations carried out on the side of the 'sacristy', which was thought for a long time to have belonged to the Hellenistic period but which in fact belonged to the 1st century AD, have confirmed the existence of older buildings, the oldest of which would be of the Geometric period, before the arrival of the Greek colonies on the island. This first building was destroyed by a fire and replaced, in the 8th or 7th century BC, perhaps at the time of the Greek immigration, by another structure. This latter was probably substituted by yet another one at the beginning of the Archaic period. Finally, one finds a new establishment, dating from about the 3rd century BC, called the proto-Anactoron, several parts of which remain, in particular a piece of wall in polygonal form. The building of the 1st century AD stayed in use until the end of the pagan era, but was restored at a much late period (4th century AD).

The Anactoron, mentioned by St Hippolytus, where two famous statues of the Cabiri were situated, consisted of a central hall and two raised parts. The Elect probably sat on this platform so that they could follow the sacrificial acts of the initiation ritual. During the Hellenistic period a sacrificial pit (plan 5) was placed in the S part.

While excavating the central hall of the Anacoron, American archaeologists uncovered traces of a circular platform, which, while burning, broke up the stones acting as the sub-foundations. We know, according to an account of initiation into the Egyptian Mysteries, that the mystes were presented to the public, just after their initiation, on a circular wooden platform, placed in the centre of the hall. We could, therefore, consider the podium, which on burning left behind its mark in the hall of the Anacoron, as a replica of the platform used in the Egyptian Mysteries to present the new mystes. The N platform no doubt acted as the adyton (plan 6), or holy of holies, where the initiation of the mystes probably finished with the presentation of some sacred objects. An inscription of the 2nd or 3rd century AD confirms that this part of the Anacoron was strictly forbidden to those who were refused the revelation of the Mysteries.

■ **MUSEUM** (*same visiting hours as for the site*). Situated about 110yds (100m) from the sanctuary of the Great Gods, on the site of a church dating from the time of Heraclius in the 7th century, the museum houses finds made during the excavations. It includes partial reconstructions of various buildings, notably the New Temple, the Arsinoeion, the Anacoron, some inscriptions, sculptures, ceramics, etc. in four rooms.

You will notice in particular two sculptures in Thasian marble (Room B), probably executed by a Thasian artist around 460–450 BC. One of them represents the blind soothsayer Tiresias emerging from the underworld (the eyes were re-cut in the 19th century). For a long time this statue was considered to be the portrait of Aristotle, and sculptures of the same type served as models for Renaissance sculptors. The other sculpture represents Persephone, clothed in a peplos.

On either side of the doorway leading into Room C look at the frieze of girls dancing (about 340 BC); notice the girls playing the zither, drum and flute.

In Room C there is a statue of Victory which served as an acroter (around 130 BC).

Beyond the Ptolemaeum there exist sections of the high defensive wall of the ancient town (4th or 3rd century BC), built with polygonal blocks. Higher up are the ruins of the castle of the Gateluzi, built in 1431–34.

Further still are the remains of a Roman aqueduct. Beyond some medieval ruins you will see vestiges of a 5th century church destroyed during the Byzantine period, and then some remnants of a Roman fountain.

VICINITY OF SAMOTHRACE

From the village of Paleopolis, the ascent of the peak of Samothrace (Phengari, 5,249ft/1,600m) requires 5–6hrs. According to the *Iliad*, this is where Poseidon climbed to watch the battles taking place under the walls of Troy. In clear weather you will have a wonderful view over the Thracian coast, the Dardanelles, the islands of Thasos and Lemnos, Mt Athos and Trojan Ida.

In a day you can take a boat tour round the island, stopping at the beach of Ammos and, on the S coast, in front of a waterfall cascading straight into the sea.

■ Serifos [Island of]

27sq. mls (70km²) – Pop: 1,500.

This precipitous little island in the Cyclades archipelago, whose name means 'barren', has for a long time been considered a good place to get away from it all. With its hill-top villages, steep paths and two fertile little valleys in surroundings which can hardly be called that, it was indeed an ideal place to which people who felt at odds with society could retreat. But the island is being visited more and more; you will have to hurry to take advantage of its somewhat relative peace. Several rocks, sometimes taking on human shapes, seem to want to keep alive the memory of Medusa, the terrifying Gorgon, whose look turned people to stone and who frequented these parts.

7.5mls (12km) from the landing place of Mega Livadi (fine beach) is Chora or Serifos, the main village of the island. It is an unassuming place, cowering under a rocky peak once protected by a Venetian kastro. A 20 mins' walk NE takes you to the beach at Paili Ammos. In the same direction, but about 2hrs' walking distance away you can visit the monastery of the Taxiarchs (Archangels), built around 1600. Its catholicon is decorated with badly faded frescoes, painted early in the 18th century (Byzantine manuscripts in the library).

In the hamlet of Panagia is a 10th century Byzantine church. There is a good beach at Koutalas.

■ Serres (Sere or Serrai)

Route map 14.

Kavalla, 65.6mls (105km) – Thessaloniki, 55mls (88km) – Pop: 39,890.

This Macedonian town, an old Byzantine stronghold, was too badly damaged during the Balkan wars at the turn of the century, and again more recently, to have preserved anything of interest for tourists. It is only a stopping place on the road from Thessaloniki to Sofia.

THE PLAINS OF THE SUN CHARIOT'S MARES. Serres is a town which originated in pre-Hellenic times: 'Xerxes, on his march against Greece, left the sacred mares of the Sun Chariot on the plain of Siris, guarded by the Siropaiones.' In the 10th century, after the Bulgarians had conquered a large part of the Balkan peninsula to the N of it, Serres acted as a transit fortress for the Byzantine emperors. The outcome of the struggle between the Emperor Basil II and Tsar Samuel was decided in the Serres region, in the Strymon gorge. The town was occupied by the Turks in 1368 and remained in their hands until 1913, when the Bulgarians entered it and burned it down. Serres became part of Greece under the Treaty of Bucharest (10 August 1913) at the end of the second Balkan war.

Near the town centre the metropolis (11th century) features, behind the apse, a synthronon with three steps, as in palaeo-Christian churches. Nothing remains of the decorations except a few sparse fragments of frescoes. Some of the mosaics disappeared when the basilica was set on fire by the Bulgarians.

Lovers of archaeology can visit a small museum set up in an old domed Turkish building on the edge of the central square. It displays ancient artifacts found in the area, such as sculptures and ceramics. In the old Turkish quarter two picturesque mosques are still standing.

You can obtain a good view over the town by climbing up to the completely ruined kastro dating from the 14th century (1.6mls/2.5km). To get there take the road to Drama, turn l. towards Chrysophi just before a bridge, and then l. again after 0.9ml (1.5km).

VICINITY

NIGRITA. A spa town 13.7mls (22km) S of Serres, known for treating illnesses of the digestive system, Nigrita lies in the middle of an area rich in mineral springs.

■ Sicyon (Sikion)

Route map 5.

Corinth, 20.6mls (33km) – Kiaton, 3.7mls (6km) – Patras, 69.4mls (111km).

The Town of Cucumbers, for such was the name of this city, was founded in the 2nd millennium BC by the Ionians, and later conquered by the Dorians in the 12th century BC. It had some fame in Greece during the Archaic period, thanks to a school of painting and sculpture. The small museum that you can visit unfortunately contains nothing of this heritage but the location, overlooking the blue sheet of the Corinthian Gulf, has some interest.

AN ENLIGHTENED TYRANNY. Under the peaceful tyranny of the Orthagorides, from Orthagoras to Cleisthenes, Sicyon shone brilliantly in the world of the arts, because of its school of wax painting (Eupompus, Pamphilus, Pausias) and school of sculpture (Aristocles, Cleoitas, Canachus). After Cleisthenes, the struggles between the aristocracy and democratic forces engulfed the city in blood, with the result that it played only a very small part in the Persian wars. Conquered by Epaminondas in 368 BC and destroyed by Demetrius Poliorcetes in 303 BC, it was rebuilt with the name of Demetrias. Aratos, born at Sicyon, brought about a revival of the city by having it join the Achaean League (251 BC). Although it was at first favoured by the Romans in preference to Corinth, a steady decline ensued and an earthquake completed its ruin in AD 23.

After having passed through the village of Vessiliko (beautiful church in the square: turn r., at the exit of the village, go l. and continue for 0.6ml/1km) which you will reach easily only from Kiaron (a small coastal town on the old Corinth–Patras road) go towards 'ancient Sicyon' – 3.1mls/5km. You should first visit the museum set up in the partly rebuilt Roman baths. It contains vases from as far back as the 7th century BC, mosaic pavements from the 4th century BC, figure of a naked Ethiopian, real and imaginary animals, terracotta figurines (from the Archaic to the Roman periods), and various sculptures including a marble head of Apollo (in a glass case on the first floor), executed using a technique of Praxiteles and a statue of Pan, showing beautiful workmanship (11th century AD), as well as a head, perhaps of Demetrius Poliorcetes (beginning of the Hellenistic era), both in the same room.

Open: weekdays except Tues. 09.00–13.00 and 16.00–18.00 in summer, 10.00–16.30 in winter; Sun. 10.30–14.30; closed Tues.; entrance fee.

Opposite the museum, on the other side of the road, lie the remains of the temple of Artemis dating from the Hellenistic period. It has the elongated layout of an Archaic temple, which makes one think that it was a second construction with the same plan as an older temple situated on the acropolis.

Beyond the temple are the remains of the senate house dating from the Hellenistic period and turned into baths in the Roman period, and also the remains of a long portico.

About 220yds (200m) from the museum on the l. of the road which goes up the hill, you can visit the remains of the gymnasium. It extended across two terraces, both with thick retaining walls. The oldest part, on the lower terrace, dates from the Hellenistic period. Notice especially, on either side of a staircase, two fountains with partly preserved basins, close to the retaining wall of the upper terrace.

The upper part of the gymnasium was built in the 3rd century AD and was connected to the Hellenistic gymnasium by three sets of steps.

Go back to the road and cross it to visit the remains of the theatre, built into the side of the hill, below the acropolis of the Hellenistic town. In the middle of the skene was a staircase leading to an underground passage, which came out in the middle of the orchestra and was used by infernal apparitions. The skene building, the proedria seats and a section of the tiers have all been cleared.

Close to the theatre to the NW in a ravine stood the stadium, whose embankments terminated in two walls constructed in the polygonal method.

■ Siphnos [Island of]

28.6sq. mls (74km²) – Pop: 2,000.

This island in the Cyclades archipelago was rich enough in antiquity to dedicate a magnificent treasury to the temple of Apollo at Delphi, with some of the yield of its gold mines. If this exceptional prosperity is nothing but a memory today, the island is still just as pleasant, covered with olive groves, and boasting at Plastis Yalos one of the finest beaches in the archipelago. So it ought not to disappoint those who like to witness the dawn of tourist development. Here you can buy anaphia, woollen blankets beaten in the sea to give them a fluffy feel, embroidery and pottery. At Vathy, a charming bay in the SW of the island and accessible by caïque, the potters work on the beach.

Boats drop passengers at Kamares, a small collection of houses having the characteristic architecture of the islands. Apollonia, 3.7mls (6km) away (bus, taxis), is the island capital. Here you can visit the Hagios Soter (Holy Saviour) church with its frescoes and a fine iconostasis, as well as a small folk museum in the square. (*Open: 18.00–21.00 in summer.*) The houses in the village reveal the architectural style of the Cyclades at its purest.

A walk of 1½hrs along the E coast takes you to Kastro, the former capital of the island, with its houses spread out below an old Venetian castle. On the NW slope of the hill there have been uncovered remains of a 4th century BC marble wall, which protected the ancient acropolis, as well as ruined houses of the Geometric period. At the top of the hill, the chapel of Panagia Geraniofora is built on the ruins of a temple dating perhaps from the 7th century BC. Artemon, 1.2mls (2km) from Apollonia, is a charming hamlet surrounded by windmills. All around the island there are numerous ancient towers and several ruined Byzantine monasteries perched on hill tops. The monastery of Chryssopigi, sitting on a peninsula jutting out from the SE coast, completely white and dating from 1650, is one of the most enchanting. Nearby there is a fine sandy beach. A 20 mins' walk to the N leads to the little harbour of Pharos.

■ Skiathos [Island of]***

23.5sq. mls (61km²) – Pop: 3,500.

Green and wooded, this little island in the Northern Sporades has just recently become very fashionable both with Greeks and foreigners. It is said that the finest beach in the whole country is that at Koukounaries. Whether it is or not, you will find many others, less crowded and sometimes even deserted. But it has to be admitted that this beach with its sand, speckled with gold, and its luxuriant pine wood is extremely attractive; the island, even though overcrowded in high summer, is also one of the most pleasant, with its gentle hills covered in a vegetation of pines, plane trees, cork oaks and arbutus.

Skiathos was not made for lovers of archaeological sites but rather for those who enjoy a holiday close to the sea, sitting on sunny beaches, taking part in water sports and leading a peaceful life, the most important elements of which are walking and drinking an ouzo in the evening on a café terrace by the harbour. For those on a touring holiday Skiathos could make a restful stopping place.

SKIATHOS, the small capital of the island, has much charm with its white houses, its pink-tiled roofs, its maze of alleyways and steps and its harbour, where little by little yachts are taking over from caïques.

Near the harbour you can visit the house of Alexander Papadiamantis (1815–1912), one of the best known of Greek novelists, who in his works brings to life his island's past both before and after 1825. The house is one of the oldest on the island and is built in peasant style with large wooden balconies enclosed by trellis-work, also in wood. Alexis Moraitides (1851–1929) was also born at Skiathos.

The main road on the island, connecting Skiathos with Koukounaries, is only 8.1mls (13km) long and gives access to numerous coves and beaches strung along the S coast.

In 1½hrs by boat (or 2½hrs on foot) you can reach the kastro, the location of the former town until 1825, a truly medieval fortress sitting on a promontory. Today it is just a heap of stones, out of which can be distinguished the bastioned gate, some ancient Turkish baths, ruined house walls and a few churches (there were said to have been 22), the best preserved of which is the church of Christ (frescoes on the walls representing martyrs, saints, etc.; chandelier with icons of the prophets and apostles).

≈ You must not miss the trip to **Koukounaries beach (15 mins by taxi or by bus leaving from the harbour or, better still, 1hr by boat; when going by road stop off at the monasteries of Kerias and Kounistria). The beach is 0.6ml (1km) long, bordered by a superb and justly famous pine wood, and close to a small lake. On the way to it and also served by the bus, are smaller but quite pleasant beaches at Troulos, Platania, Kanaritsa and Akhladia. The beaches of Hagios Elenis, Mandraki and Gournes are much quieter and easily accessible on foot from Koukounaries. The beach at Lalaria, though shingle, is likewise very attractive with its strange rock of Tripia Petra, and can be reached by boat. Another excursion by caïque could take you to the verdant islet of Tsougria, where there are also good sandy beaches.

■ Skopelos [Island of]*

37sq. mls (96km²) – Pop: 4,500.

Close to Skiathos, this island is one of the most interesting in the

Northern Sporades, mainly because of the singular appearance of its
largest settlement, Skopelos, a picturesque collection of small houses
and white chapels, where the women still sometimes wear their
traditional costume. The island has nearly 360 little chapels, most of
which are buried in the middle of a countryside consisting of olive,
plane, pine, almond, and plum trees. The plums of Skopelos,
moreover, are considered to be the best in the world. Lovers of fishing
will be attracted to the island.

SKOPELOS town, or Chora, with its gently sloping roofs of tile or flat
stone, and spread out above the harbour, is one of the pleasantest
seaports in the Aegean Sea. More than 132 chapels and 12
monasteries from the 17th and 18th centuries have apparently been
counted there. You should certainly see the church of the Zoödochos,
whose miraculous icon is said to have been painted by St Luke, and
the church of St Michael, built to a unique design.

A road 21.8mls (35km) long crosses the island through superb
scenery and connects the capital with the harbour of Loutraki,
situated on the NW coast. Skopelos is probably the only one of the
Sporades to possess some remains from the past. In 1927
archaeologists uncovered, in the cove which today bears his name,
the tomb of King Staphylus, the founder of the ancient Cretan colony
here (the artefacts unearthed are kept in the museum at Volos).

Some of the monasteries can be visited: those of the Metamorphosis,
Prodomos, Hagios Varvara, and Evangelistria are easily accessible on
foot from Skopelos. There is a succession of beaches and coves,
often backed by pine woods, extending mainly along the S and W
coasts, and they are served by a very irregular bus service from
Loutraki (leaving from the harbour). You can also reach them by boat.
From Skopelos, Staphylos and Velanio are 3.1mls (5km) away,
Agnodas 5mls (8km), Panormos 10mls (16km), and Milia, the finest
and most surprising, is 11.8mls (19km) away. Mention should also be
made of the beach at Sares, accessible only by boat, taking 7 mins
from the harbour.

In the NW of the island is the pretty village of Glossa, made up of two
clusters of houses. It is said to have been an ancient Cretan harbour
and is notable for its Macedonian architecture (houses with upper
floors and wooden balconies).

■ Skyros [Island of]*

81sq. mls (210km²) – Pop: 2,500.

Skyros, 23 nautical miles from Kymi in Euboea, and the largest of the
Northern Sporades, is still little affected by the development of
tourism in the Greek islands, though many Athenians visit it. Without
any important archaeological remains, it preserves a natural charm
which it offers to those who wish to devote their holidays to the sea.

A REFUGE AND A TOMB FOR TWO HEROES. On Skyros two mythological heroes found opposite fates. Achilles as a child found refuge and protection here with the daughters of the king of the island, on the insistence of his mother; but Theseus, king of Athens, was murdered here by the same island king, Lycomedes. In 470 BC Cimon, who had conquered the island and enslaved the inhabitants, was able to send back to Athens the bones of the famous hero.

Skyros is justly famed for its loyalty to popular traditions and for its arts and crafts. You will discover this while walking through the narrow streets of its little capital and going into some of the houses, which zealously retain furniture with wooden panels carved with designs showing Byzantine influence. Besides furniture, embroidery, pottery and basket-work are the main crafts on the island. You should not miss tasting the crabs and crayfish. The old shepherds still wear the Turkish baggy trousers and the traditional waistcoat and cap, and they still keep up the ancient Byzantine art of recitative.

You will get off the boat at Linaria on the W coast of the island, situated at the head of a narrow bay enclosed by the islet of Valaksa. A road (bus, taxis) goes along the E coast to Aspos and Skyros (6.8mls/11km), the main town on the island.

SKYROS, the capital, is built in an amphitheatre at the foot of an acropolis (kastro) from which it can be seen with its cascades of little houses, like whitewashed cubes, the terraced roofs forming an astonishing mosaic.

Walk in any direction you fancy among the narrow, hilly, twisting streets of the village, and don't be afraid of appealing to the kindness of the people who live there and asking permission to look inside the houses. It will be worth while: you will find large chests, low tables and small wooden chairs with simple but highly-skilled decoration: often a loom is still standing on the loggia. Some houses possess beautiful sets of old plates and everyday pottery from Skyros and Rhodes.

Archaeological enthusiasts may go to the museum (in the town hall), where they may find collections of local ceramics, carvings and crafts, while lovers of post-Byzantine frescoes will visit the church of Panagia Kitsou.

On the kastro you will see remains of ancient ramparts in the foundations of the Venetian surrounding wall. Notice the lion of St Mark above the entrance gate.

Hire a motor launch or sailing boat for trips out to sea or along the coast (ask at the Hotel Xenia). The main excursions are: the cliffs of Diatrypiti, Pentakali cave, the blue grottoes of Limmionari and the bays of Tris Boukes (tomb of the poet Rupert Brooke, 1887–1915) and Achilli.

Olympiani monastery at the foot of Mt Olympus (1,214ft/370m high and about 5mls/8km from Skyros) also makes a good excursion.

S | Sparta (Sparti)

Route map 6.

Athens, 162mls (259km) – Corinth, 107.5mls (172km) – Kalamata, 37.5mls (60km) – Nauplia, 85mls (136km) – Mistra, 3.1mls (5km) – Olympia, 120.6mls (193km) – Tripolis, 39.4mls (63km) – Pop: 11,900 – capital of the admin. region of Laconia.

Sparta is a modern collection of buildings devoid of any character. A visit to the ancient town is just as disappointing, because from the 6th century BC onwards Sparta lived under a regime of absolute austerity, not troubling to erect the grandiose religious and civil monuments which contributed to the prestige of the city states everywhere else in Greece. In fact most of the remains date mainly from the Hellenistic and Roman periods. It is impossible to forget the prediction of the Athenian historian Thucydides: 'If Lacedaemon were one day laid waste, and there only remained the temples and foundations of public buildings, posterity in some distant future would have difficulty in believing that its power had corresponded to its renown.'

LACEDAEMON, THE ABSOLUTE TOTALITARIAN STATE. Totalitarianism was the exact opposite of the idealized picture of the Greek cities. However, Athens itself could not escape from it entirely, since according to Aristotle the city justified slavery as an economic necessity and it condemned Socrates to drink hemlock. Lacedaemon was the scene of one of the strangest political experiments in antiquity, an experiment which must have contributed to making Hellenic unity impossible. It started in the 9th century BC, some time after the Dorian conquest, with the merger (synoecism) of the populations of four villages. It gained momentum after the half-historical, half-legendary legislator Lycurgus (end of 9th century BC?) had laid down the basis of a military oligarchic state, which was to last without change for centuries, until it became an anachronism towards the end of its existence.

In time of war the state was run by two kings for life, one of whom apparently came from an old Achaean family which had succeeded in foisting itself on the Dorian conquerors. In peacetime power was exercised by an aristocratic senate (gerousia) consisting of 28 members and, from about 756 BC, an executive body of five magistrates or ephors.

THE EATERS OF GRUEL. Spartan society was divided into three classes. At the top were the Spartiates, descendants of the Dorian conquerors, citizens having full rights and a hereditary life-interest in an untransferable piece of public land situated on the outskirts of Sparta. They lived on their property without having to cultivate it themselves. From a tender age they received a strict military education and were subjected to a harsh discipline. For that reason they had to eat a communal meal (syssitia) every day where the commonest dish was the notorious black gruel, a stew made with pork, blood, vinegar and salt.

THE CRYPTAEA AND MAN-HUNTS. At the bottom of the Lacedaemonian social ladder were the Helots, the old Achaean inhabitants reduced to slavery by the conquest and without any civil rights. They cultivated the land held by the Spartiates and by law they had to pay them a rent. They were held in a perpetual state of servitude and terror, continually maintained by the crypaea (secret police) with secret massacres which served as ritual tests for the young Spartiates.

THE MIDDLE CLASS. Because the Spartiates had to devote themselves solely to the profession of arms or service to the State and because the Helots were tied to the soil, a third class, the Perioeci, who were the original non-Dorian inhabitants or fallen Dorians, could take up the indispensable activities of skilled crafts and commerce. As citizens who remained free men, they were, however, allowed into the army but not the assembly.

THE ENEMY OF THE DEMOCRACIES. This rugged constitution made Sparta the premier aristocratic and military state in Greece, the master of the Peloponnese and the enemy of the democracies. At the time of the Persian wars, she dominated the whole of the Peloponnese, except Argos, but her selfishness rendered her role less brilliant than that of Athens. The Peloponnesian war (431–404 BC) set the two rivals against each other. After its victory the austere city of Lycurgus allowed itself to be corrupted by Lysander's booty and Persian gold. The pride of Agesilaus and the excesses of a brutal political system caused an uprising against her by the rest of Greece and freedom was finally achieved by the victory of Thebes at Leuctra (371 BC). Epaminondas of Thebes laid waste to Laconia (369 BC), gave the Spartan women their first sight of the smoke of an enemy camp and methodically organized Sparta's isolation. The Achaean League continued Thebes' work. Cleomenes III (235–219 BC) tried in vain to restore the laws of Lycurgus and the lost hegemony. Crushed at Sellasia (221 BC) by Aratus and Antigonus Doson, Sparta was deprived of its outer provinces. After its subjection to Macedon there was a brief independence under the tyrants Machanidas (207 BC) and Nabis (195–192 BC). The Romans took it over in 146 BC and granted it autonomy only as part of the Eleuthero-Laconian confederation of coastal towns.

BARONS AND DESPOTS. Captured and destroyed by Alaric in AD 396, Sparta was subjected to Slav raids in the 9th century and as a result its population emigrated to the Mani. The Byzantines repopulated it and gave it the name Lakedaimonia. In 1248 the Franks under Guillaume II de Villehardouin took it, only to abandon it in favour of Mistra. In 1261 Guillaume II had to surrender it to Michael Paleologus, together with Monemvasia and the Mani, by way of ransom. For two centuries the region was governed by despots of the Paleologus family. In 1460 it fell under the control of Mohammed II. Then the Venetians took it in 1669, but it was recaptured by the Turks in 1715.

But for the presence of Mistra nearby it is probable that Sparta would be little visited. But the **scenery has much grandeur, especially Mt Taygetus with its serrated peaks, cut by gorges and ravines, and flanked by steep impressive bluffs and rocky heights. On top of one of these is the Frankish castle of the Villehardouins and the ruins of ancient Mistra. In Sparta you can visit the museum and the ruins of the ancient city. They hardly evoke the past; rather does their modest quantity and quality teach how relative is glory in history. However, they will be of interest to lovers of archaeological sites and can be covered in about 1hr.

MUSEUM. The main street, which is a continuation of the Tripolis road, crosses Eurotas (pronounced Evrotas) Street more or less at the town centre. 110yds (100m) to the l. of this junction stands the archaeological museum, in a charming garden. It is especially interesting for its collection of artefacts from the Archaic period, such as sculptures, ceramics, and bronze, lead and terracotta figurines.

Open: weekdays except Tues. 09.00–15.00 in summer, 09.00–14.30 in winter; Sun. 10.00–15.00 in summer and 10.00–15.30 in winter; entrance fee.

In the entrance hall you can see some strange votive stelae, decorated with an iron sickle, which were dedicated to Artemis Orthia.

In the first gallery on the r. you will notice a curious stele in the shape of a pyramid, from the Archaic period, on which you can see Agamemnon and Clytemnestra. Menelaus and Helen, and snakes, symbols of the Dioscuri. You will see two Archaic earth deities, seated (behind the seat a serpent rises), holding a cantharus and receiving homage from bringers of offerings, carved on a much smaller scale than the gods. The glass case on the r. contains Mycenaean vases, that opposite has terracotta vases from the sanctuary of Amyclae (see page 794). The second room houses architectonic pieces from the Archaic era, notably a marble block carved with a gorgon from the edge of a roof, which had concealed the tiles (above the door), three very flattened Doric capitals, and three strange capitals from the Amyclaeum, mixing the Doric with the Ionic order (end of the 6th century BC). You will also see other Archaic reliefs, one of which shows the Dioscuri holding a lance, both sides of two large amphorae and several Archaic sculptures in the round, among them an amazing representation of Ilithyia, the goddess of childbirth, kneeling naked between two male figures. In the third gallery is the torso supposedly of Leonidas, a work in the Severe style (5th century BC) which formed part of a group. There are also two pieces of a shield belonging to the warrior who was fighting Leonidas. Look out for a small relief in the Severe style (circa 460 BC) showing a young person with bent head, seated on a rock leaning on his l. hand. Another relief, Attic, from the early 4th century BC, show Apollo and Artemis pouring a libation over an omphalus, encircled by two eagles, which evoke Delphi. The colossal head of Heracles on a wall bracket is a Hellenistic copy of the original by Lysippus. At the end of the room are the remains of a basin used for lustral water from the 2nd half of the 7th century BC and, in two large glass show-cases, Mycenaean vases, figurines and jewellery; a small show-case contains a Panathenaic amphora from the sanctuary of Athena of the Bronze House (incised horizontally around the lower part of the belly the upper part of the letters of the dedication can be read: AθANAIA).

In the first gallery on the l., in a cabinet on the r., there are some lead figurines and terracotta votive masks from the Archaic period found in the sanctuary of Artemis Orthia. Notice especially, in a cabinet on the l., some bronze figurines from the Archaic period, masterpieces of the Laconian bronzeworkers' art. They include a kouros and a hoplite doryphorus (lance-bearer). You will also see limestone votive plaques decorated with reliefs of people, horses, etc. (end 8th-beginning 6th century BC) still with their painted decoration, and fragments of two terracotta metopes (warriors). Pottery is represented by several vases or Archaic fragments with relief decoration, and by pieces of painted vases (especially Laconian cups and kraters).

In the last gallery you can see several votive reliefs and a mosaic (Triton and dolphins) from the Hellenistic era, some mosaics from the Roman period, including a fine portrait of Alcibiades and one of the poetess Sappho. A separate case contains a terracotta model of a Roman galley (1st century BC–1st century AD).

∴ ANCIENT CITY. To visit the ruins of ancient Sparta, leave the town by the Tripolis road and carry straight on to the point where the road veers to the r.; 3 30yds (300m) on the l. from this point is the supposed tomb of Leonidas (plan A3). Actually it is a small Hellenistic temple with a pronaos and cella, and the real tomb stands opposite the theatre. Retracing your steps to near the modern sports stadium, you will find a road through an olive grove leading to the S gate of the acropolis.

The acropolis formed an irregular plateau which was surrounded by a protective wall in AD 268 and AD 386 after the Herulian and Gothic invasions. The wall was finished, notably on the E, after the Slav invasion in the 9th century.

Beyond the ruins of the S gate you will see the remains of a Roman portico, whose rear wall has 25 alcoves for exedrae each with a niche. By following a road to the l. you will find a semi-circular retaining wall from the 5th century BC, forming a podium. On it stood a sacrificial well, or bothros, dedicated probably to some earth god.

Near this wall are the ruins of a 10th century Byzantine church, which was enlarged in the 11th century. The building in front of the church entrance is an 11th-century chapel which contained the tomb of St Nicon and the myrotheca (see Glossary).

To reach the site of the theatre, continue past the semi-circular wall and follow the ramparts for a distance. The theatre dates from the 2nd or 1st century BC and is built into the side of the acropolis hill facing towards the modern town. It has lost its white marble tiers which were used in the construction of Mistra. What you see is a motley collection: remains from the Augustan period, a Roman proscenium, part of the skene (back wall of the stage) turned into an independent block in the 4th century AD, and the Byzantine fortress.

Behind the theatre lie the remains of the temple of Athena Chalcioekos (of the house of bronze). Its walls were covered with bronze shields by the Lacedaemonian Gitiadas. King Pausanias, convinced that treason was afoot, took refuge there in 477 BC. He was walled up and when brought out was almost dead from starvation.

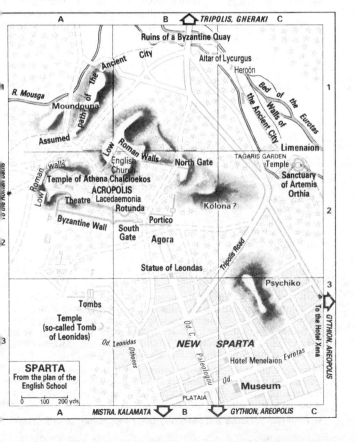

About 0.6ml (1km) from the acropolis, and 110yds (100m) downstream from the bridge used by the Tripolis road to cross the river Eurotas, are the ruins of a triple-arched Byzantine bridge. This bridge is at the same location as the ancient bridge called Babyka, used by the road to Tegea.

By walking downstream along the r. bank of the river Eurotas you will come across a section of the town wall. This is followed by the remains of a large altar and of a heroön. Finally, about 770yds (700m) from the bridge is the site of ancient Limnaion, the sanctuary of Artemis Orthia.

It consisted of a small temple of the 2nd century BC, built on top of an Archaic temple (6th century BC), whose *ex votos* filled the lower layers of the excavation. There was also a horseshoe-shaped Roman amphitheatre which surrounded half of the temple like a stadium. Originally a ceremony of ritual flagellation was celebrated here, which the Spartiates later turned into a trial of endurance for adolescents. Dances were also performed here, with masks, which were offered to the goddess Artemis.

VICINITY OF SPARTA

Apart from a visit to ***Mistra, the immediate vicinity of Sparta offers excursions to archaeological sites of interest only to specialists (see below, excursions 1 and 2). Some longer excursions, such as to Chrysapha and Gheraki, are recommended for those interested in Byzantine and post-Byzantine art.

1 THE MENELAEUM. (3.1mls/5km. Leave by the Tripolis road and then at 1.2mls/2km turn r. on to the Gheraki road. After another 1.6mls/2.5km turn l. on to a track and follow this for 550yds/500m.) Here you will find the chapel of Hagios Ilias. By following the track to the r. of the chapel, 20 mins. walk will take you to the Menelaeum. The remains of the Menelaeum or heroön of the deified Menelaus and Helen have been located at the top of the hill.

On a platform was a small temple which must have been built there in the 5th century BC. But this edifice was preceded by another one. Excavations by the British School at Athens have recently started again.

2 AMYCLAE AND THE AMYCLAEION (4mls/6.5km. Follow the Gythion road for 2.8mls/4.5km and then turn l. Keep on this road for 1.2mls/2km.) Near the hamlet of Tsaousi is the site of ancient Amyclae, the capital of the Achaeans living in Laconia (Menelaus and Helen), which, independently of the Heraclides in Sparta, continued as the seat of an Achaean dynasty until the first Messenian war (743–724 BC).

The sanctuary of Zeus-Agamemnon and Alexandra-Cassandra, mentioned by Pausanias, was perhaps situated where the Hagia Paraskevi church now stands. Excavations carried out in 1961 did not produce any results.

On the hill of Hagia Kyriaki stood the Amyclaeion or sanctuary of

Apollo Amyclae. It was the tomb of Hyacinthus, the son of Amyclas. Above the tomb was an Archaic statue of Apollo, 30 cubits (42–46ft/13–14m) high, with the god seated on a monumental gold and ivory throne, decorated with bas-reliefs by Bathycles of Magnesia.

3 CHRYSAPHA. (12.5mls/20km. Take the Tripolis road, at 1.2mls (2km) turn r. on to the Gheraki road, and turn l. immediately afterwards. Follow this for 11.2mls/18km.) You can visit the church of the Chrysaphiotissa (AD 1290), decorated with frescoes. All Saints' church (1367–68), with frescoes of the Transfiguration, the church of the Dormition (17th century) and St Demetrius church (1641).

4 ROAD FROM SPARTA TO KALAMATA. At 3.4mls (5.5km) from Sparta there is a good view over Mistra on the l. At 5.6mls (9km) notice, also on the l., a rocky hillock thought to be the Caiadas, from which the Spartiates threw their deformed children. At 5.9mls (9.5km) is the village of Trypi, where the road enters the Langadas gorge. At 17.5mls (28km) on the l. is the small village of Ghiannitsa with a church possessing a beautiful iconostasis dating from 1767. Above the village and around the chapel of Hagios Taxiarchis an acropolis with cyclopean walls has been located, thought by some to be the Homeric Ira. The road then climbs over the Langadas pass (4,429ft/1,350m) before dropping down into Kalamata after 38.1mls (61km) (see under Kalamata).

5 LONGANIKOS. (23.1mls/37km NW.) This village, at the foot of Mt Kelmos, is dominated by the Pelasgic ruins of ancient Aegis, and Kelmos castle, built by the Franks.

6 GHERAKI. (25.6mls/41km. Take the Tripolis road. At 1.2mls/2km turn r. and follow the l. bank of the river Eurotas. Fork E. at Skoura.) This large village, the ancient Geronthrae, sits on a high hill. You can see the ruins of a Frankish castle, built in 1254 by Guy de Nevelet, Baron of Tsaconia, and several medieval churches. In the village itself you may visit the church of the Evangelist with its somewhat faded frescoes.

To reach the Frankish castle, follow the road to Hagios Dimitrios, pass the cemetery church (frescoes) on the l., and 550yds (500m) further turn l. into a road not suitable for cars. After 45 mins walking you will reach the castle. First there is a small chapel with some frescoes, then the church of Hagia Paraskevi (12th century), and further on another small chapel also decorated with frescoes. Just below the entrance to the fortress is a single-naved church with a narthex added later (a few paintings).

Inside the walls of the fortress the best preserved church is that of Hagios Georgios. It is built on the plan of a basilica with three naves, and dates from the 13th century. It contains some frescoes and an iconostasis with an icon of St George.

On a projection of the rocky spur are three more churches. The most southerly of them probably dates from the first half of the 14th century and is decorated with frescoes (Joshua attacking an Amorite city, probably dating from the 14th century).

■ Spetsai [Island of]*

8.5sq. mls (22km²) – Pop: 3,500.

Well patronized by Greek, and especially Athenian, high society and by a few foreign tourists, this pretty island at the mouth of the gulf of Argolis is the Pityusa (planted with pines) of the ancients. It claims to hold its vistors with its Aegean charm, consisting of beaches, the aromatic perfume of pines, a colourful harbour, tavernas and guitar music, rather than with archaeological sites. You can hire horse-drawn carriages, mopeds or bicycles to travel about the island. On the weekend nearest to 8 September there is the nautical festival of the Panagia Aramata, in the evening, to commemorate a victory over the Turks, with mock battles, fireworks, etc.

☐ In the 19th century several Spetsiot ship-owning families achieved a certain degree of wealth, as is witnessed by some old houses with carved wood ceilings. One of these, the Mexis House, has been turned into a museum. You should make a point of visiting the church of Hagia Triada at the top of the town; built in 1793, it contains a carved wood iconostasis. Also to be seen is the birthplace of Bouboulina, a famous heroine of the struggles for independence, who died in 1821.

Spetsai is quite peaceful and the horse-drawn carriage dominates everything. You should take advantage of this to discover some of the more beautiful places on the island. On the road to Hagia Marina, attractive with its open-air tavernas and cafés, you should stop awhile near the lighthouse to visit the little chapel of the Virgin of Armata. It was built to commemorate a victory achieved by the Spetsiots, Hydriots and Psariots in a naval battle against the Turks on 8 September 1822. Inside, an immense canvas painted by Coutzis recalls the events of this battle.

 On the road to Brelou you will pass the area of Paradissos – an evocative name. The scenery becomes impressive near Brelou, and from the corniche road a wide *panorama over the N coast of the island and the strait which separates it from the mainland will be revealed. Beyond Brelou there are some delightful coves with beautifully clear water.

Off the SE coast of the island, the islet of Spetsopoula is owned by the Niarchos family.

■ Stratos

Route map 10.

Agrinion, 6.2mls (10km) – Arta, 46.2mls (74km) – Preveza, 55.6mls (89km).

Well-preserved ramparts of the 5th century BC, in front of which the Spartans suffered a setback during the Peloponnesian war in 429 BC, are what you will discover on a visit to this archaeological site, situated on the r. bank of the Achelous, a sacred river against which Heracles struggled.

SIEGE-PROOF WALLS. Stratos became important only in the 5th century BC at the time when the walls were built. Three years after Cnemus the Spartan was defeated (429 BC). Euryclochus passed below the walls without daring to attack. Agesilaus, in 391 BC, made several fruitless attempts. Stratos was taken over by the Aetolians in 263 BC. Later the Romans defended it against the expeditions of the son of Philip V of Macedon. Sacked in 57–56 BC by the Dolopes, the town ceased to have any further importance.

The site has been explored by the French School of Athens in 1892, 1910–11 and 1924.

The defences of the town take advantage of four hills which are connected together by walls of pseudo-isodomic construction. The main entrance was on the S, a short distance from the present road and about 220yds (200m) beyond the tourist pavilion (coming from Agrinion). Still quite well preserved, it contained an inner court clearly intended for defensive purposes.

Near the village on the l. you can see a few sparse remains of the agora. On the other side, beyond a wall of pseudo-isodomic construction which split the town into two halves, is the theatre dating from the Macedonian period. It is still buried but its cavea is visible.

THE TEMPLE OF ZEUS is the best known monument of this city. It occupied a terrace supported by retaining walls to the W of the town. A strange feature is that it was built on the very line of the walls. An inscription from the 2nd century BC, which allowed the temple to be identified, concerns deed of emancipation of slaves in the form of consecration to a god. There are a few surviving vestiges of this Doric peripteral temple, built of local limestone (second half of the 4th century BC).

■ Stymfalia

Route map 5

Corinth, 31.2mls (50km) – Kiaton, 15.6mls (25km).

This village, today quite unpretentious, was only really well known, through mythology, as Stymphalus. In antiquity the lake of the same name was the scene of one of the 12 labours of Heracles. From Kiaton the approach road (through the villages of Souli, Kephalari and Kaliani) passes through magnificent hilly countryside and then goes past the foot of grandiose cliffs.

Leaving the village by the road to Kastania, you will see on the l. the remains of a Frankish church, probably dating from the 13th century, which was once part of the old Cistercian abbey of Zaraka; Gothic in style.

On the very shores of Lake Stymphalus stretched an ancient city, founded according to legend by Stymphalus, son of Elatus and grandson of Arcas. It is principally known for the legendary birds of which Heracles rid the valley and whose pictures Pausanias saw in carved wood on the ceiling of the temple of Artemis Stymphalia. This story of Heracles seems to have its origins in the noxious gases which desolated this swampy region before the construction of dykes and canals.

The ancient city had an acropolis on a low hill which jutted out like a promontory into the frequently flooded plain. A temple dedicated to Athena Polias, a palaestra, etc. have been discovered there.

■ Symi [Island of]

41.8sq. mls (67km²) – Pop: 3,000.

This small, arid, sun-baked piece of earth in the Dodecanese (a solar distillation plant has been built there), formerly known for its shipyards (you can still see caïques being built at Aegialo), whose inhabitants devoted themselves until quite recently to fishing and underwater sponge collection, will guarantee you a holiday out of the ordinary. The island still has a wild beauty, greenest on the S coast (pines, arbutus, fruit trees).

✝ SYMI. The main town of the island is spread out at the foot of an old castle of the Knights of Rhodes, where you can visit the church of the Panagia which preserves a few painted murals and a few remains of a temple of Athena. The upper quarter, Chora, partly occupies the site of an ancient acropolis from the time when Symi played a small role in the Dorian hexapolis. Its multi-coloured houses with triangular pediments show an Italian influence; as elsewhere on the island, they sometimes possess beautiful painted ceilings.

Bathe at Emborio (1.2mls/2km W of the capital), where the remains of a Byzantine basilica have been discovered, or bathe in the bay of Pedhi (another 1.2mls/2km) which has a fine sandy beach.

By hiring a mule and obtaining the services of a guide you can reach (in 4hrs) the bay of Panormitis (small restaurants), where you will see the monastery of St Michael founded in the 18th century (frescoes, icons, ex votos, fine iconostasis: pilgrimage, 8 November).

By boat, you can go to the bays of Nanou or Morathounda, or go and explore the deserted islets of Nimo (to the N) or Seski (to the S).

■ Syros [Island of]

33.2sq. mls (86km²) – Pop: 30,000 – capital of the admin. region of the Cyclades – Greek Orthodox archbishopric – Roman Catholic bishopric.

This Roman Catholic island in the Cyclades owes its importance to its port, Syros or Ermoupolis, which is also the capital. It is an important town (pop. 13,000), with its white houses and public buildings dating from the 19th century, spread out on two levels. In the evening they shine with a thousand lights. Covered with orchards and vineyards, the island has some fine beaches but is still not much visited by tourists.

The town occupies the site of the ancient city of which nothing remains. The High Town (Ano Syros) was founded in the 13th century by the Venetians and still constitutes the Catholic quarter. It is where the Capuchins settled under Louis XIII, who had brought the island under his protection. Later the Jesuits settled under Louis XV and finally the Lazarists arrived. In 1821 the inhabitants of Psara and Chios were expelled from their islands by the Turks and took refuge on Syros, where they founded the seaport town (Ermoupolis) and the Vrontado quarter. Dating from this period it became the main port for distribution in the Cyclades archipelago.

Syros is the turntable for ships plying between Piraeus and the Cyclades and so you may have the opportunity to visit it during the course of a journey between two other islands. If so, join the bustling crowds of Syriots taking their evening stroll in Miaoulis Square in the Ermoupolis quarter. You will find both there and on the harbour numerous small cafés and restaurants where you can buy turkish delight and other local delicacies. There is a fine beach at Galissos (nudists allowed).

From the quayside with its continual hubbub (fish market to the W). Venizelou (or Ermou) Street leads to the arcades of Miaoulis Square, the main square of the town, which is flanked by the Palace of Justice and the town hall. On the l. is a small museum of local antiquities.

You are also recommended to stroll through the alleyways of Vrontado, the Greek Orthodox quarter, and those of Ano Syros, the Roman Catholic quarter, sitting on a hill crowned by the cathedral of St George (superb view); the houses, quite different from those of Ermoupolis, form a simple rectangle. Like steps, one above the other with tiny little gardens, they display a whole spectrum of colour. You can reach it in about an hour by the somewhat difficult climb up through the stepped streets, but the best course is to take a taxi up and to walk back down.

 By taxi you can reach the fine beach of Kini (4.4mls/7km), passing through Episkopion (3.7mls/6km), or the beach of Finikias (8.7mls/14km) at the head of a bay. There is also Poseidonia (Della Grazia) with a wide, well-frequented, fashionable beach, where you can lunch in some pleasant little tavernas.

At the S tip of the island is Megas Yalos, a small township in pretty green surroundings.

■ Tanagra

Route map 3.

Thebes, 15mls (24km) – Chalcis, 18mls (29km) – Athens, 42.5mls (68km).

A place, but mostly a name (sometimes incorrectly) linked with terracotta objects, whether they be Greek or not. Although the remains of the ancient town are unimportant, the finds from the Mycenaean necropolis (in the museum of Thebes) are exceptional. The necropolis is situated to the E of the modern village. It consists of chamber tombs cut out of the rock which yielded some 30 terracotta *sarcophagi, mostly decorated with scenes of processions of women. Late Helladic ceramics, bronze weapons and utensils have also been found.

■ Tempe [Vale of] (Tembi)*

Route map 2.

Katerini, 29.4mls (47km) – Larisa, 16.8mls (27km) – Thessaloniki, 84.4mls (135km).

This narrow transverse valley, 6.2mls (10km) long, between Ossa and Olympus, through which the Peneus flows over the Thessalian plain to the sea, was famous in antiquity for its natural beauty and cool shade. Its formation was attributed either to Poseidon Petraeus (i.e. 'of the rock'), who is supposed to have split the mountain, or to an earthquake.

You can follow the tracks of processions which, every eight days, came to gather laurels near the sanctuary of Apollo, where the god was purified after slaying Python, guardian of the Delphic oracle.

AN ENTRANCE TO GREECE. Geologists explain this gorge as a fracture ravine, completed during the Quaternary era by the effects of a torrent from Pelion which gradually rose to the level of the ancient Larisan lake and swallowed it. The waters of the lake and then those of the Peneus completed the gorge's formation. Arriving from Larisa, the village of Tembi marks one of the entrances to this gorge. To the l., near a small Turkish funerary monument, a road leads to Goni (3.7mls/6km), on the site of the ancient Greek Gonnos, known by

Herodotus, which dominated the Macedonian pass and played an important part in the Persian war (471 BC). It preserves part of the 4th-century rampart built by Philip II of Macedon (on a hill to the r. of the road, about half a mile/1km before reaching the village).

If you do not have to worry about transport, continue from Tembi up to Ambelakia (3.1mls/5km), a pretty town, which enjoyed some prosperity in the 17th century owing to its production of cotton and silk. Some lovely restored patrician houses are a reminder of that period; one, the house of the Schwarz brothers, called the Arkontikon, is open to the public: outstanding woodwork, painted murals, ornamental and with landscapes, furniture, fireplaces (a porter will show you round); at the end of the village, St. John's church has some interesting frescoes and an iconostasis. You will also enjoy a beautiful panorama over the vale of Tempe from the slope of Ambelakia. 2.8mls (4.5km) from Tembi in the direction of Thessaloniki, you will see the cool shady spot marking the spring of Aphrodite (or Venus, as a sign rejecting the Greek origin of this kindly goddess tells us). 5mls (8km) from Tembi, an inset in the rock to the r. has a Latin inscription, now illegible, reminding us that Cassius, Caesar's proconsul and legate, fortified the gorge of Tempe.

The spring of Daphne (or Apollo), 5.6mls (9km) from Tembi, flows from the coolest and shadiest site in the gorge, near the exit to Thessaloniki.

Thasos [Island of]*

153sq. mls (398km²) – Pop: 12,000 – admin. region of Kavalla.

Lying off Thrace, but almost moored to the continent, the island of Thasos, a marble-and-schist massif with a crown of small plains covered with pines and crops, was a kind of outpost of Hellenistic civilization on the borders of the Barbarian world. From the 6th century to the middle of the 4th century BC, it enjoyed a prosperity and a political regime rare in this part of Greece. You will find evidence of this in the ruins of the ancient city, which reflect this prosperity, based mainly on exports of wine and marble. Perhaps it would be exaggerating to thank this distant past for the delightful Aegean ambience pervading the island, but you will find there a peacefulness which is not paralleled on the Thracian coast; perhaps this is due to the island way of life.

THE GOLD RUSH. Probably attracted by the rich gold and silver deposits of Mt Pangaeus, the Parians settled on the island, which became the centre of their expeditions to the continent in the first half of the 7th century. Herodotus claims to have seen gold mines on the island and this is apparently confirmed by recent finds. However that may be, the agricultural (oil and wine) and mineral wealth of Thasos and the fruitful relations which the Thasian sailors formed with the coastal barbarians, Egypt and Phoenicia, rapidly brought into being a flourishing island civilization.

THE THASIAN PENDULUM BETWEEN ATHENS AND SPARTA. In the 6th century, the prosperity of the town of Thasos was such that it tempted the adventurer Histaeus of Miletus, in Asia Minor, in the early 5th century. His attack failed. About 494, the Thasians built their fine marble rampart to guard against any future eventualities, but the Persians occupied the island in 491 BC and Darius had it destroyed. Athens tried to impose its hegemony over the island after the Median wars. In 465 Thasos tried to withdraw from the Delian League and was only conquered by the fleet of Cimon in 463. Then Thasos suffered the vicissitudes of the struggle between Athens and Sparta, passing from one side to the other at least six times.

A WINE CELLAR FOR THE ROMANS. It avoided Macedonian sovereignty in the 3rd century BC, no doubt because it was sacked by Philip. After his victory, Rome favoured Thasos, which had adopted a hostile attitude to Macedon. The island continued to support the Romans in the war against Mithridates. The State of Thasos was reconstituted and, being more important now, spread as far as the Sporades. None of these crises appears to have affected the prosperity of the island, whose traders were the main intermediaries between Thrace and the Greek world in the 2nd and 1st centuries BC. Thasian products, especially wine and marble, had a tremendous reputation under the Empire.

THE NORIA OF THE OCCUPYING POWERS. Prosperous under the Byzantine Empire, it was then subject to various Frankish principalities. In the 15th century it became a fief of the Gattilusi, Genoese princes of Ainos and Samothrace, and then passed to the Turks. In 1813, it was given to the house of Mehemet Ali, a native of Kavalla, which held it until the end of the Turkish occupation. The site of the antique town has been excavated by the French School since 1911.

A DAY ON THASOS. One day is enough to visit the site of the ancient town and make the tour of the island, but much too short really to savour the pleasant way of life offered by the island to anyone making a longer stay.

Assuming that you arrive by one of the early morning boats, you will visit the antique town (especially the agora, the museum, the gates of Silenus, Zeus and Hera, and the theatre), so that you can reach the beach of Makry Ammos around noon. Then return to lunch at Thasos in one of the little harbour restaurants, before making the round-the-island excursion.

1 THE MONUMENTS OF THE LOWER TOWN

NAVAL PORT (see map). The modern fishing port occupies the ancient Thasian naval port. Only a few remains are left, such as the foundations of a large round tower visible in the water (map, 1).

CHARIOT GATE (see map). The town gates were decorated with reliefs contemporary with the wall, something unique in Greece. Thus, on this gate, you will recognize a goddess (Artemis?) in her chariot, the horses of which are held by Hermes (?).

GATE OF THE DIVINE PROCESSION (see map). The gate is decorated with a mutilated group of four figures (divine procession in which only Hermes is identifiable). Directly behind this gate, inside a rampart, lie the remains of a housing district divided by two streets into four irregular housing blocks occupied at least from the 6th century BC to the 4th century AD. Some beautiful walls of polygonal masonry date to the first period. This gate opened on to the Commercial harbour, sheltered by the promontory of Evraio-kastro (see map), and defended by a bastion (two columns belong to a palaeo-Christian basilica on the site of a sanctuary which has yielded numerous figurines.). A modern chapel has partially covered the antique basilica).

THE SANCTUARY OF POSEIDON (see map). Its ruins are worth only a brief stop. Near the gate of the sanctuary (map, 2) are two bases with 4th-century BC inscriptions and, a little in front of them, an altar consecrated to Hera Epilimenia (protectress of harbours) on which was engraved a sacred law forbidding the sacrifice of goats.

THE SANCTUARY OF DIONYSUS (see map). You will find the remains of this sanctuary, mentioned in the late 5th century BC by Hippocrates in his *On Epidemics*. The dedication of a sanctuary of Dionysus, who along with Heracles was the guardian of the Thasian city, goes back to the early days of the Parian colonization. Among the edifices on the sanctuary there are two exedral monuments one of which – the one still visible – was a 4th-century BC choregic monument on which were engraved the names of the victors in a drama competition, each name appearing below the statue representing the literary category in which its bearer had triumphed.

AGORA (see map). Although it is badly ruined, this enormous public square, once the site of all types of monument, will be one of the best moments of your visit, especially if you take a keen interest in archaeology. The main entrance is just next to the museum.

From the top of the ramparts by the modern street there is a beautiful overall view of the agora (especially in the afternoon). You are in a broad street ending to the SE in a propylaeum (plan of agora) which has preserved part of its paving. To the r. of the road, you can see the confused remains of buildings, what is left of a palaeo-Christian site built on top of a Roman shop. In the axis of the propylaeum extend the ruins of the Doric SE portico (plan of agora) with 33 columns. It was probably built in the 1st century AD through the generosity of two Thasian notables, who may have been rich ship-owners.

This gallery was mainly a thoroughfare, as is shown by the many openings communicating with the exterior. Towards the E end of the portico, roughly in the axis of the great altar (see below) was a monumental passage opening on to the agora by a bay with two Ionic columns between pilasters, and on the opposite side by a gate (plan of agora), which still retains its two monolithic engaged piers.

In front of the SE portico extended a kind of avenue lined by five exedrae (plan of agora), which were probably adorned with statues.

Behind the exedrae, you will see the large bases of two altars. The first (plan of agora, 2) was probably orientated to the E. The second (plan of agora, 3) was undoubtedly a low, probably Roman altar. Between these two altars, small walls mark off two adjoining enclosures, the purpose of which is uncertain. One of them (plan of agora, 4) surrounded a court paved with gneiss. A few bases lie near the enclosures (plan of agora, 5).

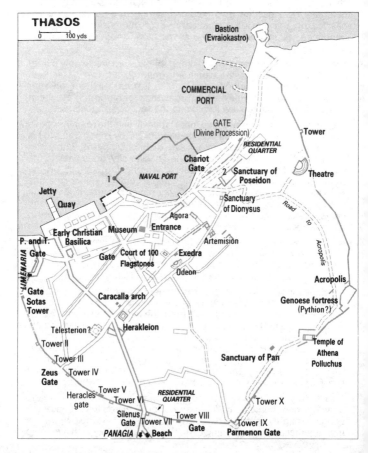

THASOS

0   100 yds

A large marble altar (see plan of agora), now badly ruined, was erected at the E end of the avenue with the exedrae, undoubtedly in the 3rd century BC. The passage which connected the agora with the districts extending to the S (see above) emerged opposite, below the portico.

To the E of the monumental entrance (see plan of agora) was an apsidal hall, probably devoted to the imperial cult. In fact, a statue of the Emperor Hadrian in Thasian marble was found there. It may have been erected c.124–125 when he visited Thrace and the N islands of the Aegean, leaving from the Troad or the Hellespont (in the museum).

Next you proceed along the ruins of the SE portico, a vast gallery with 31 Doric columns, some of which have been re-erected. In front of this portico, possibly built in the 1st century AD, note a marble conduit, with decantation basins, which must be older than the gallery. The SE portico was duplicated by a gallery, the ceiling of which was supported by a colonnade with 16 pillars (hypostyle gallery). Behind, a group of ruined houses was bordered by a road with an underground drain.

This road is the continuation of the paved Roman road excavated near the 'Court of the Hundred Flagstones' (see map) and continued in the direction of the arch of Caracalla (see map). At the other end, this road went by the passage of the Theoria (plan of agora). The continuation of this road has been confirmed on the first slopes leading to the acropolis.

At the end of the hypostyle gallery is the base of the monument of Glaucus (plan of agora, 9), general and companion of the poet Archilochus, which was erected towards the end of the 7th century BC. It is the most ancient find from the agora. A painted statue or stele, before which the rites of a heroic cult were celebrated by placing offerings, must have stood on this base.

The N end of the SE portico joins another edifice, known as the oblique or NE portico (plan of agora), in the Doric style and undoubtedly from the 2nd century BC. It was built against an older edifice, probably constructed during several periods; it contained shops. Note, in front of the portico, another marble conduit, nearly all of which is visible, and a base shaped like a ship's prow (plan of agora, 10) in the centre of a large rectangular exedra.

The building with the shops has two rows of shops in the W part. A first series of six rooms opened beneath the portico and a second series of five shops gave on to the ancient road, more or less parallel with the portico. These 11 shops apparently date from the 4th century BC.

In the W corner of the agora, at the E end of the NE portico, a wall, pierced by two gates (plan of agora, 11), was erected in the 1st century AD (note the threshold of one of the gates, still in place). It separated the agora from a court lined by a paved way near the passage of the Theoria.

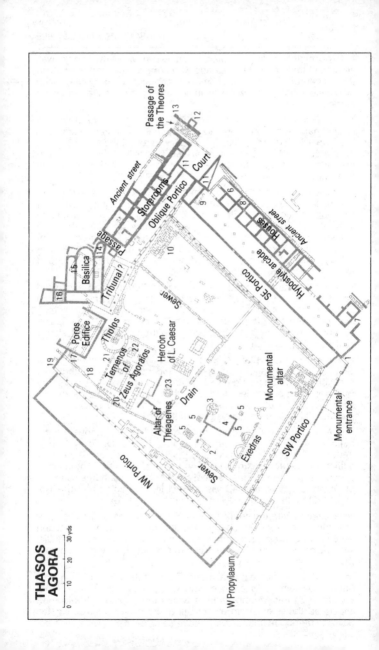

THASOS
AGORA

0 10 20 30 yds

W Propylaeum

NW Portico

Sewer

Altar of
Theagenes

Temenos of
Zeus Agoraios

Tholos

Poros
Edifice

Basilica

Tribunal?

Passage

Passage of
the Theores

Ancient street

Storerooms

Oblique Portico

Court

Heroön
of L. Caesar

Sewer

SE Portico

Hyposyle arcade

Houses

Ancient street

Drain

Exedras

Monumental
altar

SW Portico

Monumental
entrance

19 17 18 20 21 22 23 16 15 14 13 12 11 10 9 8 6 7

3 4 5 2 1

The monumental passage of the Theoria was marked off by two marble walls on either side of a paved way. Two large reliefs from the 2nd quarter of the 5th century BC, which were taken to the Louvre in 1863, were found there, as were numerous inscriptions, mostly lists of theoria (magistrates sent as ambassadors to represent a Greek state at the great Panhellenic Games, or to consult an oracle, or to place offerings in sanctuaries). This passage, contemporary with the reliefs, was therefore a sort of monumental propylon, which must have been consecrated, as evidenced by the little altar exhumed in a niche in the E wall.

The relief of the Three Graces, taken to Paris by Miller, was probably situated to the l. of the niche (plan of agora, 12) and the relief of Hermes and a female personage on the r. As for the relief of Apollo and the nymphs, it must have been opposite the niche on the W wall (to the l.). These reliefs date from 470 to 460 BC. A catalogue listing the Thasian theoria was not engraved on the walls of the passage until a century later. The plaque of the relief of Hermes was engraved with a sacred law stipulating the sacrifices that could be offered: 'To the Graces, neither goats nor pigs'. Another, inscribed on the relief of Apollo, states 'To the nymphs and Apollo Nymphagetes, neither goats nor pigs; the paean must not be sung'.

Beyond the passage of the Theoria, the road broadens into a small square as yet not completely excavated. On the E side, there is a large rectangular public well, several feet deep and divided into four compartments by three large gneiss beams forming transoms about half way up the wall.

Above this sector is the temenos of Artemis Polo, or Artemision (see map, p. 804), mentioned in the 5th century BC by Hippocrates, where the cult of the goddess was celebrated from the founding of the colony.

In the present state of the excavations, resumed in 1975, one can make out a lower terrace, still being explored, and an upper terrace surrounded by a wall, mainly visible on the NE side and bordered by a portico on the SE side (towards the acropolis). Very few architectural remains have been found, but numerous votive objects have been revealed (mostly terracotta figurines and vases; a selection of them is on show in the museum). In 1977, the remains of a monumental altar (nearly 33ft/10m long), dating to the early 5th century BC, was uncovered on the lower terrace, near the N corner of the upper terrace. The extension of excavations to the NW of the altar has made possible the partial clearing of two streets, one of which, well paved, went down to the square with the rectangular well. To the N of this street and encroaching slightly on it was a building – undoubtedly a villa – from the early Roman period, destroyed at the beginning of the 7th century AD during the Slavic invasions.

Returning to the small square, you will see a large stairway with several steps, discovered in 1979, which undoubtedly formed one means of access to the lower terrace of the Artemision. Some 50ft (15m) to the NW of this stairway, the remains were uncovered in 1982 of a large circular wall, of unusual construction and several metres deep, which had been installed towards the end of the 5th century BC and abandoned near the end of the 4th century BC, at which time it was covered over by a small, rectangular monument (temple?), unfortunately completely ruined. Three wells had therefore been sunk in the square, which shows that there was an important centre of supply there for a whole district of the city.

Return towards the NE sector of the agora. Near the oblique portico, you find a public building, perhaps a tribunal (plan of agora), which was built about the middle of the 4th century BC on the site of older edifices. Behind these ruins are the remains of a palaeo-Christian basilica on the site of another structure with a peristyle court.

Bases which supported offerings or honorific statues were aligned in front of the tribunal. A well (plan of agora, 15), which was undoubtedly installed at the same time as the antique building below, was uncovered on the l. nave of the palaeo-Christian basilica. A hypogaeum with three vaults was found beneath an annexe to the narthex (plan of agora, 16) of the church. The centre vault contained an inscription in honour of Acacius, martyr. This Acacius may have been a Cappadocian soldier, beheaded at Byzantium in 303.

Disregard the ruinous buildings which formed the NW angle of the agora and note, in the square itself, the remains of the temenos of Zeus Agoraios (plan of agora) which consisted of a small temple, an altar and various cult installations for libations. A small sanctuary was erected in this part of the agora in the Archaic period. This installation was restored around the beginning of the 4th century BC. The majority of the ruins now visible date to this period, with the exception of the tholos, or circular building with an altar, which was built towards the end of the 3rd or the beginning of the 2nd century BC. It has been suggested that this circular building was a heroön of Telesicles, the founder of the Parian colony of Thasos, but this identification is by no means certain.

This building, known as the Poros Edifice (plan of agora), dating to the 3rd or 2nd century BC, probably housed some of the town's administrative services. It was superimposed on an older construction. To the SE of the temenos of Zeus Agoraios, you will see the rectangular foundation of two bases of an altar dedicated to Caius and Lucius Caesar (plan of agora), adoptive sons of Augustus, one of whom died in AD 2, the other in AD 4. To the SE of the temenos, you will see a circular base with marble steps (plan of agora, 23), on which the flesh of animals offered to the gods was burnt. On this altar, a few blocks of which remain, note an iron ring to which the victims were tied.

One of the most famous Thasians of all time, the athlete Theagenes, was honoured there. The monument (plan of agora) was identified with the help of a cylindrical collection box for offerings which bore a 2nd century BC inscription. These foundations apparently date to the end of the 4th or the beginning of the 3rd century BC.

OFFERINGS WITH A SCALE OF FEES. This inscription mentioned among other things the amount of the miniumum offering (one obol) which the faithful had to put in the collection box for sacrifices in honour of Theagenes.

Another inscription advised the faithful desirous of obtaining a favour for their wives or children to make an offering to the hero. It seems that the faithful came to the altar to seek a remedy against or protection from the fevers which were endemic on the island, according to Hippocrates in his *On Epidemics*.

THE EXEMPLARY CAREER OF AN OLYMPIC LAUREATE. The personality of Theagenes is rather curious and the history of the cult rendered to him at Thasos is eloquent testimony to the immense prestige enjoyed in the Greek cities by athletes victorious in the great Panhellenic competitions. Theagenes was an athlete who won many victories in the Olympic and Pythian (Delphic) Games, especially in 480 and 476 BC. Shortly after his exploits, the Thasians must have decided to erect a monument to him in their agora, for one of Theagenes' old rivals was, so it is said, crushed by the statue he had come to insult when it fell on him. This was seen as a clear manifestation of the athlete's power.

THE 'BEATIFICATION' OF THE OLYMPIC HERO. Later, in order to justify the cult of Theagenes, a legend was put about attempting to prove his supernatural powers. There was a story that when his statue was thrown into the sea, an epidemic struck Thasos. To avert their fate, the Thasians decided to send an embassy to Delphi (on two occasions) to consult the Pythia. In execution of the oracle the statue of Theagenes was restored to its base in the agora after its miraculous recovery from the sea. From then on, the epidemic ceased to ravage the island, which regained its former prosperity. Thus Pausanias could write in the 2nd century AD that Theagenes was looked on as the town's heroic benefactor.

TAKING LIBERTIES WITH HISTORY. The Thasians went so far that for a time they worshipped him as founder of the colony, which was actually established by Telesicles in the 7th century BC. They also sought to identify him with the Thasian Heracles in order to render him the honours reserved for heroes, even though he had not been given burial honours. Therefore he was raised to the dignity of son of Thasian Heracles. You will note that the name of the hero on the inscription is twice followed by a gap showing traces of a word that has been chiselled out. Perhaps this word was an epithet attributing to him the founding; of the colony of Thasos and was later removed when the islanders restored to Telesicles the honours due to him. The long Doric NW portico (plan of agora) with 35 columns was built in the 3rd century BC on the site of an older Archaic building. A series of honorific bases have been dug up in front of the central sector of the portico. Thus, at least 13 bases, the alignment of which is not exactly the same as that of the portico, are consecrated along a length of some 100ft (30m).

Recent excavations have uncovered the area behind the portico. A semicircular exedra backs on to its NW wall. Flanked by two podiums, one of which supported five bases, this exedra opens on to a small square still partly paved and bordered by a peristyle on three sides. The complex dates to the 1st century AD. A section of the 14th-century Byzantine enceinte, as well as traces of a palaeo-Christian building, have been revealed in the NW of the square, beyond a moat. After leaving the agora, to the r. of the entrance to the museum, on either side of the road coming from the village, you will observe the well-preserved ruins of a section of the 4th-century BC rampart, which formed part of the original defences. At the end of the road linking the agora with the sea, a postern situated below the modern street was preceded by a paved esplanade. To the S of it, the rampart was reinforced by two casemates, windowless on the ground floor, and a bastion with two loopholes which controlled the S and W approaches. A marble stairway led to the storey where the catapults were ranged. To the N of the street another stairway, this time of gneiss, led to the curtain wall which dominated the port, closed by two fortified breakwaters.

MUSEUM (see map). Situated outside the agora, it contains collections of sculptures after the Archaic period, Archaic stelae, terracotta objects in relief or painted, ceramics, etc., from excavations on Thasos.

Open: summer, 09.00–13.00 and 16.00–18.00; winter 10.00–16.30; Sun., 10.30–14.30; closed Tues. entrance fee.

Note especially the kouros carrying a ram (hall 1), a colossal Archaic statue discovered in a retaining wall of the acropolis where it was reused as building material. The statue is unfinished, no doubt because of a crack which formed in the marble. The god's face is merely adumbrated, but his hair is finished. He is naked, clutching a sacrificial ram to his chest. The work probably dates from the end of the 7th century BC.

In the same hall, a sculpture representing the forequarters of Pegasus (late 6th or early 5th century BC), the famous winged horse born of the blood of Medusa when Perseus cut her head off, a fine horse's head in marble, a male torso of the first half of the 5th century BC, an expressive bust of Silenus (end of the 6th century BC) and decorative architectural terracotta elements (540–525 BC) from the sanctuary of Heracles will also attract your attention. Opposite there is an important collection of lamps from various periods. Do not fail to turn aside to the hall on the r., which contains a rich group of sculptures in Thasian marble from the Classical to the Roman period. Note especially a very beautiful head of Dionysus dating to the middle of the 4th century BC. Antiquities discovered during the excavation of the Artemision and the sanctuary of Athena Poliouchos are the main exhibits in the hall at the end.

You will see small ivory lions' heads (probably executed in Phoenicia or N Syria, during the second quarter of the 7th century BC) and a magnificent bronze mirror holder, in the form of a female statuette with a narrow skirt and arms raised (of Peloponnesian origin), as well as terracotta ceramics and figurines (from the 7th to the 2nd century BC). Also from the excavations of the Artemision should be mentioned fragments of Archaic terracotta korai, which are very interesting. One of them, larger than lifesize and unfortunately far from complete, probably dates to the 7th century BC and is one of the most ancient works of Hellenic sculpture (these very mutilated statues are not yet on show).

Between the museum and the gate of Silenus (see map), you will cross an excavation site which will interest only lovers of archaeology, for whom the following details are intended. A street, 18ft (5.50m) to 18ft 8¼in (5.70m) wide, paved with large marble blocks from the Roman period, starts from the S corner of the agora (see map). Alongside it the French School of Athens uncovered the ruins of the Exedra of Limendas (see map) to the l., and to the r. the court of a Hundred Flagstones (see map) and a building from the age of Hadrian, to the N. Next note the remains of an odeon (see map) beyond the exedra. The remains of the arch of Caracalla (see map) lie a good deal further to the SW. This street led to the Herakleion (see plan) or sanctuary of Heracles, founded in the 6th century BC. About all you can still see of the ancient cult installations are the foundations, some traces of an altar beyond a court paved with gneiss, the remains of a staircase etc., to the l. of the road and the ruins of an Archaic edifice to the r.

THE GARDEN OF HERACLES. An inscription dealing with the lease of several plots, one of which is the garden of Heracles, has been found on a block on the façade of a building, probably a club. These properties were situated near the gate of Heracles and Dionysus, where another inscription has been found. It tells us that the priest of Asclepius was responsible for the maintenance of the sacred garden of Heracles. From the inscription we know that the garden was planted with ten fig trees, ten myrtles and several hazelnut trees. It is supposed to be the garden of the Blessed, where Heracles presided over banquets, after laying down his arms.

GATE OF SILENUS (see map). Set in the town walls and built of marble blocks c.500-490 BC, this gate is decorated to the l. with a colossal late 6th century BC bas-relief of a naked ithyphallic Silenus, holding a cantharus (cup). It was defended by a tower built on to the wall in the Hellenistic period and provided with two embrasures for military engines.

Behind the gate recent excavations have revealed a sizeable living district where you can see, on either side of the road, a complex exhibiting several successive stages of construction between the 6th and 4th centuries BC. Fortunately, the Greek levels here have not been disturbed by any subsequent building.

Going back up to the acropolis, you can see another gate with its lintel still preserved, then past a bend, a large block of the enceinte wall signed by the workman who dressed it *c*.500 BC: 'Parmenon made me'.

From the gate of Silenus and following the rampart to the W, you will observe the wall's imposing mass and fine masonry (uncovered on various levels in 1978). You will see the ruins of another tower with embrasures, then a gate formerly adorned with two bas-reliefs, one depicting Dionysus (lost) and the other Heracles (in the Istanbul Museum). According to a 5th century BC verse inscription still in place on the l. slope of the passage (looking towards the outside of the town), these two divinities were the town's special protectors.

GATE OF ZEUS AND HERA (see map). Probably erected before the Persian invasion and destroyed during the expedition of Xerxes *c*.480 BC (then rebuilt shortly afterwards), this gate is decorated with a bas-relief in the Archaic manner, apparently executed in the last quarter of the 5th century BC. This almost obliterated sculpture represented the goddess Hera, and Iris, the messenger of the gods.

During the second half of the 5th century BC, the layout of this gate was changed and the carved pillars were probably added at the same time. The bastion which preceded the gate proper was erected in the first half of the 4th century BC, under the archonate of Pythippus. Beyond the gate of Zeus and Hera, the rampart rejoins the port, running alongside the seashore, but at a distance. In the vicinity of the gate of Zeus and Hera there was a walk lined with large Roman sarcophagi, only one of which remains. This cemetery took the place of an older acropolis which contained a heroön.

On the way to the port, you will pass close to the ruins of a palaeo-Christian basilica (see map), presumed to date to the 6th century BC. Diggings near there have revealed the presence of an important architectural complex, the main part of which dated to the 4th or 5th century AD: a paved court surrounded by porticoes and a mosaic with cupids fighting (in the museum).

2 THE ACROPOLIS

THEATRE (see map). From the modern jetty, go past the fishing port, cross a square and leaving the site of the agora on the r. take the road to the acropolis, which ascends in a series of bends. After a few minutes' walk, take a path to the l. to reach the Hellenic theatre (the seats and remains of the stage have been uncovered). During the Roman period, the orchestra was altered so that fights between gladiators and wild animal hunts could be held. During the excavations, some blocks attributed to the 3rd century BC stage building have been found. From the end of the 7th or beginning of the 6th century BC, the slopes below the theatre were occupied by a residential quarter which was destroyed *c*.500 BC.

ACROPOLIS (see plan). In 20 mins you will climb to the top of the acropolis now occupied by a medieval fortress built by the Genoese partly from re-used ancient materials. The panorama of the town, the port and the strait is well worth the climb.

Beyond the acropolis, the rampart continues to the SE as far as a high terrace, with the foundations of a temple of Athena Poliouchos (see map). The terrace and temple were built in the 5th century BC on the site of an Archaic chapel elevated on a platform. A propylaeum situated on the terrace presumably connected the temple of Athena and the sanctuary of Pythian Apollo, to be found on the site of the Genoese fortress.

The path then descends to a small col on which lie the ruins of a sanctuary of Pan (see map), with a rock bas-relief of the god playing the syrinx to his goats. By following the rampart and then entering the enceinte at the gate of Parmenon, you can redescend either to the odeon or the gate of Silenus.

3 ROUND THE ISLAND

An excellent asphalt road mostly running close to the shore will enable you to see the delightful wooded countryside, where the pine is the king of trees and sometimes grows right down to the sea.

Leave by the Prinos and Limenaria road (see map).

1.9mls (3km): Glyfada; beach and hotel.

2.5mls (4km): Papalimani; beach and restaurant.

6.9mls (11km): Rachoni; camping.

8.7mls (14km): Skala de Prinos; ferry-boat to Kavalla.

9.4mls (15km): Prinos. A forest track which branches l. in the village leads through forest and mountain to Maries (some 12.5mls/20km) passing the picturesque old village of Kazaviti.

21.8mls (35km): Skala de Maries, small port from which an asphalt road leads to Maries (5mls/8km), a large peaceful village, abounding in flowers.

26.2mls (42km): Limenaria, a busy port in a pleasant setting; fine beaches nearby.

29.4mls (47km): Potos. Leave an asphalt road to the l. for Theologos (5mls/8km), a large village with houses straggling along the only street.

32.5mls (52km): Aliki peninsula, where a double sanctuary was undoubtedly dedicated to the Dioscuri from the 7th century BC. This sanctuary, in use until the end of the Imperial Roman period, stood on a terrace accessible by two porticoes, one Ionic, from the end of the 6th century BC, the other Doric, from the first half of the 5th century BC.

Above the isthmus, you will see the ruins of two palaeo-Christian basilicas built side by side. They were altered on various occasions until the end of the 5th century. The smaller N basilica opened on to a court or atrium where numerous tombs have been found. In 1976, the apse and SE corner of a previous chapel were discovered beneath the basilica. The larger S basilica was fitted with tribunes in its final state.

The baptismal liturgy may explain the presence of two fonts used in succession.

Part of the peninsula has been much exploited as a marble quarry. Extraction, encouraged by the ease of removal and the special qualities of the material, lasted from the Archaic period to the end of the 6th century AD. The SW tip has entirely disappeared beneath the quarryman's pickaxe, but you can still see sizeable walls of shining marble overhanging the sea and showing the marks of tools. Fragments of columns and several roughed-out blocks are visible on the side of the quarries in a dazzling white setting.

43.7mls (70km): Kinyra, a hamlet overhanging the sea, opposite a small island.

 48.7mls (78km): Skala de Potamia: a few houses and restaurants at the S end of a magnificent sandy beach (Chryssi Ammoudia) 2.5mls (4km) long.

50mls (80km): fork l. for Potamia (1.2mls/2km); beautiful view from the village of a valley open to the sea. Near the church on the square in the upper part of the village an interesting old house serves as a small museum of modern art. It contains paintings and sculptures of a native of the island, Polygnotos Vagis (1894–1965), who made his career in the USA.

Open: June–Sep. only, daily except Tues. 08.00–12.00 and 17.30–21.00; Sun. 08.30–15.30; entrance free.

50.9mls (81.5km): second fork on the l. to (0.6mls/1km) Potamia.

52.5mls (84km): Panagia, former capital of the island, with handsome houses in the Macedonian style. At the exit from the village, take the road to the r. for Avlakia (3.7mls/6km), at the N end of the beach of Chryssi Ammoudia.

57.5mls (92km): at the entrance to Limenas, a road to the r. to Makry Ammos (0.6mls/1km; hotel and private beach).

58mls (93km): Limenas or Thasos.

Thebes (Thive)

Route maps 3 and 4.

Athens (via Eleusis), 43.1mls (69km) - Athens (by the motorway), 52.5mls (84km) - Chalcis, 21.9mls (35km) - Delphi, 58.1mls (93km) - Lamia (via Livadia), 101mls (162km) - Lamia (via the motorway and Thermopylae), 83mls (133km) - Livadia, 28.1mls (45km) - Pop: 15,970 - admin. region of Boeotia.

From the heroic times which followed its foundation, Thebes was the scene of countless dramatic legends, the contents of which inspired some of the most famous Greek tragic authors, such as Aeschylus (*Seven against Thebes*), Sophocles (*Oedipus Rex, Antigone*) and Euripides (*Phoenician Women*). This town at the source of Greek tragedy also had a brilliant history, no trade of which remains except in its museum, for after the ephemeral Theban hegemony over Greece, the city was mostly famous for its misfortunes.

THE MURDER OF OEDIPUS. Thebes, founded by the legendary Cadmus, a Phoenician king, was first governed by the Labdacidae, descendants of Cadmus, but misfortune soon befell it. Laius, the son and successor of Labdacus, was killed by his son Oedipus, who did not know who he was. Soon a cruel sphinx, who devoured the passers-by unable to solve the riddles it asked them, appeared at the gates of Thebes. Creon, Laius' successor, then promised the hand of his sister Jocasta, the mother of Oedipus, to the man who would rid the country of this scourge. Thus Oedipus became, without his knowing it, his mother's husband, which drew the wrath of the gods down on Thebes with fresh disasters.

SEVEN AGAINST THEBES. Polynices and Eteocles joined in a fratricidal struggle for the heritage of Oedipus, their father. The siege of Thebes, the town with seven gates, by the Seven Chiefs of Argos, who supported the cause of Polynices, is placed in this period (13th century BC?). The sons of the Seven Chiefs succeeded where their fathers had failed, by destroying the unfortunate city which, however, became the capital of Boeotia 60 years after the Trojan War.

THEBES, ALLY OF THE PERSIANS. In the 7th century, it was the capital of a confederation of important villages, links between which were always weak. It became the rival of its neighbour Orchomenus, but could not unite Boeotia. Out of hatred for Athens, Thebes was an ally of the Persians during the Persian wars and shared their defeat at the Battle of Plataea in 479 BC. Thebes beat the Athenians at Tanagra in 457 with the help of Sparta, and then alone at Chaeronea in 447. Haughty Sparta, after its hard-won victory over Athens, wanted to impose its domination on the whole of Greece, and by treason Phoebidas occupied the acropolis of Thebes in 382 BC.

THE BRIEF THEBAN HEGEMONY. Epaminondas and Pelopidas were quick to cast off the Spartan yoke and chase the aristocratic government which supported Sparta from Cadmaea. Between them, they were to effect the unity of Boeotia and snatch the supremacy from Sparta for some years, owing to the victory of Leuctra (371), with the 'sacred band' as spearhead, an elite troop of 300 hoplites, many of them homosexuals, who, it seems, fought even more heroically because of their emotional attachment.

Epaminondas invaded the Peloponnese, rushing to the aid of Arcadia and Messenia, but he died during a second expedition near Mantinea in 362 and the Theban hegemony ended.

THE HEAVY HAND OF ALEXANDER. On the death of Philip II of Macedon (336), Thebes tried to recover its independence, hoping no doubt to exploit the inexperience of his successor, the young Alexander, who was not yet the Great. It was an unfortunate mistake, for Alexander reoccupied Cadmaea and carried out terrible reprisals against Thebes.

The town was destroyed and only the house of Pindar was spared. 6,000 inhabitants were massacred and more than 30,000 enslaved, and the Theban territory was split up between other cities. Twenty years later, Thebes was restored by Cassander. In 293 and 290, Cadmaea was taken by Demitrius Poliorcetes, then Mummius, Mithridates and Sulla completed its ruin.

In the Middle Ages, Thebes was repopulated and its silk and dyeing industries restored its prosperity. Taken in 1205 by Boniface III of Montferrat, it was allotted to Otho de la Roche, at the same time as Attica. Thebes, promoted to the rank of capital of the Duchy of Athens, then passed by marriage to the family of St Omer. Nicolas II of St Omer (1258–94) built the castle of Cadmaea (one large tower remains). Under the Turkish domination, Thebes was no more than a miserable village.

■ Leaving the town by the road to Livadia, near a Frankish tower built in the 13th century by Nicolas II of St Omer, which formed part of a fortress destroyed by the Catalans in 1311, you will visit the archaeological museum which contains the antiquities rescued from the ravaged town or found in Boeotia.

Open: summer, 08.30–12.30 and 16.00, Sun. from 09.00–15.00; winter, from 09.00–13.00 and from 16.00–18.00, Sun. 10.00–16.30; closed Tues; entrance fee.

Among the collections, Archaic sculpture is particularly well represented, notably by typically Boeotian works from the sanctuary of Ptoion in the vicinity of Thebes. You will note the 6th-century BC statue of a kouros (no. 3) in the centre of the first hall. In the second hall, you should not miss a collection, unique in Greece, of lapis lazuli cylinder seals, of eastern origin. Their presence at Thebes is unexplained. You will also see numerous Attic and Boeotian vases, mostly black-figure, from the necropolis of Rhitsona (the ancient Mycalessus, between Thebes and the Euripos). Some of them date to the 2nd half of the 6th century and others to the 1st half of the 5th century BC. In the third hall you will note a series of classical stelae from Thespia and Tanagra which cannot be classified as sculptures, because they are decorated with incised figures. They are black stone funerary stelae representing Boeotian warriors, mentioned by name, among them a certain Saugenes (stele no. 56), killed in the Battle of Tanagra in 424 BC. We also recommend that you examine the very **rich collection of painted Mycenaean sarcophagi from the 13th century BC, unique in continental Greece. They depict funerary themes with scenes of lamentation, in which weeping women make the ritual gestures of mourning, and the laying out of corpses, etc. They come from a necropolis near Tanagra. The museum also exhibits some fragments of architecture and sculpture, some ceramics, terracotta figurines and, in the court, mosaics.

A visit to the town, where elements of medieval architecture exist side by side with antique remains, which will give you some idea of the topography of ancient Thebes, will be of interest only to specialists. On the town's highest point which formed the acropolis (the Cadmaea), was the palace of Cadmus. Some remains of the megaron and its annexes were discovered right in the centre of Thebes, near Pindarou Street. This edifice, dated from upper Helladic II (1450–1350 BC), was burnt down during upper Helladic III (1350–1150 BC). The direct road from Athens to Thebes enters the town near the site of the ancient port of Onca (or Hypsistai), close to which stood the sanctuary of Athena Onca, where Cadmus, conqueror of the dragon, had sacrificed a cow to Athena. On the l. of the road ran an arcaded aqueduct built by the Franks. The primitive aqueduct was attributed to Cadmus. It brought to the town the waters of three springs fed by a river, the Plakiotissa, the ancient Dirce, 'the most nourishing of the springs made to flow by Poseidon who girdles the earth and the children of Tethys'. One of the springs gushed forth at the spot where the torture of Dirce ended. (She was tied to the horns of a bull by Amphion and Zethus, sons of Antiope, thus avenging their mother for whom she had planned this same fate.) The river passes close to the Paraporti spring, the ancient spring of Ares or Areios, also called the spring of Dirce. It gushed from a little grotto and flowed into a stone basin through eight spouts. According to tradition, this grotto was the lair of the dragon of Ares killed by Cadmus. Amphion threw Dirce's ashes into this spring and into it King Menoeceus leapt from the top of the acropolis, as an expiatory victim to appease the wrath of Ares, who encouraged the siege of Thebes after his dragon was killed (Euripides, *The Phoenician Women* 931 *et seq.*).

The road to Lefktra (Leuctra), via Ambelosialesi, leaves the enceinte near the place where the ruins of the ancient port are located. Another road leaving by the Neistaean gate then crossed the district where Eteocles and Polynices killed each other and a necropolis where Antigone placed the body of Polynices on the funeral pyre prepared for Eteocles. Dirkis Street (Dirce) leads to the vale of the ancient Ismenus with the scanty remains of the Electran gate, to the r. It was flanked by two circular towers (the foundations of one of them still visible). The road which left by this gate crossed a large suburb containing the vast Heracleum, marked by the chapel of Hagios Nikolaos (Byzantine lintel in the interior) and near which were situated the house of Amphitryon and the Heroön of Alcmene. Near there, you are shown the field where Cadmus sowed the dragon's teeth on the advice of Athena.

Beyond the gate in the direction of the cemetery, to the l., lie the scanty remains of the Ismenion or temple of Apollo Ismenius, where the festival of the Daphnephoria was celebrated. The oracle of the Ismenion, mentioned by Herodotus (VII, 133–5), was consulted by Mardonius through the intermediary of a Theban during the winter of 480–479 BC.

To the r. of the road to Chalcis, just beyond a Frankish tower, was the

Proetidean gate, near which some remains of the ancient Cadmean
wall with polygonal masonry have been found.

The temple of Dionysus and the house of Lycus stood near to this
gate. A little further on, to the r. of the road to Chalcis, gushed the
spring of Hagi Theodori, the ancient spring of Oedipodeia, where
Oedipus washed off his father's blood. To the l. of the Livadia road,
just beyond the museum, a mound marks the site of the tomb of
Amphion.

VICINITY

1 PLATAIAI (PLATAEA) (10.6mls/17km by the direct road to Athens, then
r. for 7.5mls/12km.) This Boeotian village is mainly famous for being
the site of the last great battle on Greek soil during the Persian wars in
479 BC. The defeat of the Persians, commanded by General
Mardonius, by the Greek allies (minus the Boeotians, Thessalonians,
Locrians and Malians, who fought alongside the invaders) marked the
final check to Xerxes' campaign against Hellas. The 'eleutheria'
which were celebrated every fourth year in Plataea were instituted in
memory of this battle.

All that remains of the ancient Plataea on a spur of Mt Citheron are
traces of the fortified enceinte, the foundations of a temple, perhaps
the Heraeum, and those of a vast construction which may be the hotel
or katagogeion built by the Thebans to house visitors to the temple
after the destruction of the town.

2 LEUCTRA (Lefktra; 11.2mls/18km by the direct road to Athens and to
the r. at 1.2mls/2km.) You will find there the reconstruction of the
trophy erected by the Thebans to commemorate the victory of
Epaminondas over the Spartans in 371 BC, thus giving Thebes
hegemony over Greece. About 1.8mls (3km) before reaching Lefktra,
you will pass close to the ruins of a 550yds (500m) enceinte of
polygonal masonry, which is without doubt the Homeric Eutresis, the
town founded by Amphion and Zethus. The site was inhabited from
the 2nd millennium BC onwards.

3 THE CABIRIUM (5.3mls/8.5km) **AND THE VALLEY OF THE MUSES** (19.4mls/
31km). Leave Thebes by the Livadia road.

2.8mls (4.5km): leave to your l. a road to Leondarion and Prodromos,
which you can take on the return journey if you are coming back to
Thebes.

4.4mls (7km): take a road passable by car to the l. 0.3mls (0.5km) from
the crossroads, turn l. 220yds (200m) further on, then go straight
ahead along a track which gently ascends the hill. About 1ml (1.5km)
from the main road, you reach on the r. the ruins of Cabirium or
sanctuary of the Cabiri, a cult site where oracles were delivered. A
Hellenistic and Roman temple have been discovered in front of the
temple which to some extent occupies the position of the stage, and
the remains of a 44yds (40m) long portico. Beyond the Cabirium, the
track continues to the S; after reaching the top of the hill, you can
make the descent to rejoin the asphalted road from Thebes to

Prodromos (see below). But it is preferable to return by the Thebes-Livadia road.

7.5mls (12km): road to the l. for Vagia (1.9mls/3km), Louterion (4.4mls/7km) and Thespiai (5mls/8km). The road climbs in the midst of hills, offering beautiful views.

12.5mls (20km): go straight through the village of Thespiai, taking the road to the l. at the exit. This village is near the site of the ancient Thespia which lay in the plain. Nothing is left of the temple of the Muses mentioned by Pausanias.

13.1mls (21km): at the bottom of a steep descent, turn r. to Panaghia.

14.4mls (23km): turn r. leaving on your l. the road to Neochorin (660yds/600m further on).

15.5mls (25km): Panaghia. Leave the asphalted road and take, in the village, a track passable by car which branches off just to the l. of the church.

16.2mls (26km): follow the track straight ahead.

16.9mls (27km): crossroads where you turn l., leaving on the hill to the r. a tower known as Paleo Pyrgos (acropolis of Keressos). About 0.6ml (1km) further W, you will find the acropolis of Ascra, home of the poet Hesiod (7th century BC) and according to him 'an accursed village, vile in winter, atrocious in summer, never pleasant'. This high pyramidal acropolis, easily visible from the road, is crowned by a small tower. 550yds (500m) further on, turn l. by passing over a bridge

18.1mls (29km): take the track to the l.

18.7mls (30km): to the r., on a height, a modern church.

19.4mls (31km): after a steep climb, the track fords a stream, the ancient Permessus. You have reached the valley of Muses, now unfortunately deforested, but once, with its woods and springs, consecrated to the Muses who had their sanctuary (*Mouseion*) there in the middle of a sacred wood (*alsos*).

A CRADLE OF POETRY. The cult of Muses, originally divinities of the mountains and mountain springs, is of pastoral origin. It was born in Pieria, in the Thracian region of Olympus, of the River Helicon, Mt Pierus and the Libethra spring, where legend located the cradle of the poets Linus, Orpheus, Musaeus, Thamyris, Olen, etc. A Thracian colony settled at Ascra and adapted the cult and names of its own country to the neighbouring mountains. The Boeotian sanctuary of Helicon also became a focus of poetic inspiration, made famous by Hesiod. The Musean games, held every four years in the sacred wood, consisted of competitions in the fields of music, song, lyric poetry and drama.

THE OLDEST MUSEUM IN THE WORLD. Groups of statues by the Muses by Cephisodotes, Strongylion and Olympiosthenes, of Dionysus by Miron, of great lyric poets by Lysippus, and *ex votos* turned the sanctuary into a veritable art museum. It was looted by Constantine.

You reach the archaeological site by taking a path downstream on the r. bank of the Permessos. In about 10 mins. you come to a kind of grassy esplanade where you will see a monumental altar dating to the 3rd century BC. Upstream, the sanctuary also included a vast Ionic portico, 317ft 4in (96.70m) long and 32ft 9½in (10m) deep, as well as a theatre where Musean concerts were given. Unfortunately there are no visible traces of these two monuments, which are buried in the ground and the undergrowth.

The fountain of Aganippe, dedicated to the Muses, is to be sought in the ravine of another stream, a tributary of the Permessos, further S. As for the famous Hippocrene (spring of the Horse) of the poets, it is generally identified with the spring of Krio Pigadi (the Cold Well) 2½hrs' walk from Hagios Nikolaos in the direction of the summit of Mt Helicon. Beyond the stream where you have stopped, the track climbs steeply to a high point on the slopes of Mt Helicon, with magnificent views of the valley of the Muses, the acropolises of Ascra and Keressos and the surrounding mountains. To return to Thebes, take the same road to mile 13.1 (km 21) (crossroads to Panaghia). Turn r. there. 550yds (500m) further on you rejoin the asphalted road from Thebes to Prodromos.

If you wish to return to Thebes (17.5mls/28km), you will take this road to the l., which later rejoins the Livadia-Thebes main road. If you would like to explore some more Boeotian roads which are very picturesque and have little traffic, turn r. to Korini and Prodromos where you can see some antique remains (traces of walls) and even reach the sea on the gulf of Corinth after a drive of about 18.7mls (30km).

4 THE PTOION (19.4mls/31km by the motorway to Lamia and to the r. to Akreinion, 16.2mls/26km). To the r., the motorway passes lake Iliki (motel), partly fed by the waters of the ancient lake Copais and Lake Paralimni, to the NE between Iliki and the Euboean canal. Beyond Akrefnion, a small village on the site of the ancient Acraephlia (remains of 4th-century BC rampart; church of Hagios Georgios, 14th century), you follow the track from Kokkino to the fountain of Perdiko Vrysi, at the foot of Mt Pelaghia, the ancient Ptoon, site of the Ptoion or sanctuary of Ptoan Apollo.

The Ptoion was the seat of an ancient 'infallible' oracle, which prophesied in the name of the local god of the mountain, who was soon identified with Apollo. The excavations were carried out by the French School of Athens as from 1855.

The spring was the birthplace of the oracle. It is situated at the very top of the sanctuary and should not be confused with the lower fountain now dried up. The ruins of the ancient sanctuary cover three terraces from the fountain to the spring. On the lower terrace a vast cistern collected the waters of the upper spring and in its turn supplied the establishment where the oracles were delivered.

The middle terrace, occupied by two long porticoes separated by a paved way, was situated on top of the cistern.

The topmost terrace bore the sacred edifices: a Doric temple, rebuilt in the 3rd century BC on the ruins of a 7th century temple, and a cavern with a spring, cut out of the rock, which was undoubtedly the sacred spring and seat of the primitive oracle, and an esplanade with altars and bases.

The foundations of a temple have been uncovered on the height of Kastraki, near the village of Akrefnion. It was probably consecrated to a courotrophic goddess (one carrying a child), mother of the hero Ptoios, who, according to P. Guillon, could be Gaia-Demeter or Gaia-Europa. At the foot of this sanctuary was an esplanade to the hero Ptoios, whose cult seems to have taken root here at the beginning of the 6th or the end of the 7th century BC, under the protection of Acraephia. Digs have revealed the remains of two altars from different periods and the foundations of two edifices, one of which was built of ancient polygonal masonry. 28 bases of tripods arranged in two rows were also found. These offerings were probably made between the middle of the 6th and the end of the third quarter of the 5th century BC, i.e. during the two periods when Acraephia enjoyed relative autonomy (c.550–480 and 456–446).

14mls (23km) NE of Akrefnion (25mls/40km from Thebes), Larymna is a charming village at the land end of a bay on the gulf of Euboea; remains of a partly submerged 4th-century BC port. Nearby, a nickel mine unique in Europe.

T | # Thera [Island of] (Santorini)**

29.3sq. mls (76km²) – Pop: 10,000 approx.

The recent uncovering of a town contemporary with the palaces of Crete has turned Thera into the 'star' of the Cyclades. There were already good reasons for visiting this strange island, but now there are even more. Thera is the product of a cosmic tragedy which the discovery of this town buried beneath masses of volcanic ash enables us to place about the end of the 16th century BC. This tragedy was a terrifying explosion which fractured and broke up the island, by causing waves estimated by some authorities as more than 650ft (200m) high.

The well-protected harbour, with tremendous depths (1,280ft/ 390m), where your ship will dock, covers the pulverized land. Therasia and the other islets which surround it are fragments that escaped the cataclysm, for this fantastic archipelago of scoria, lava, sulphur and red and white cliffs surmounted by the immaculate silhouettes of its villages was originally all one island, or rather volcano, of marble and schist, the crater of which was roughly in the centre of the present-day harbour.

Seen from the harbour, Thera offers the unforgettable image of a long precipitous cliff from 197 ft (60m) to 394ft (120m) high, a geological section with layers of scoria, black and red ash, lava and pumice, cut into by vertical chimneys. Below, lies the ancient harbour, and on top the town now reached by a cable-car rather than on foot or mule-back.

THE EARTH'S FURY. Naturally we have no written reference to the catastrophe which shook this island known in legend as Calliste (Most Beautiful) or Strongyle (the Round), but we do have archaeological references, both to Thera itself and to Crete, where the Minoan palaces of Knossos, Mallia, Kato Zakros, etc. suffered the backlash of this cataclysm. Towards the end of the 16th century BC, the volcano which formed the single island erupted, resulting in a gigantic circular crater some 7.5mls (12km) in diameter where the sea poured in at the SW. On this side, the little island of Aspronissi constitutes a fragment of the ancient littoral. In 236 BC, another earthquake fractured the N part of the island, forming Therasia, which ships from the N leave to the r. on entering the harbour. In 196 BC the islet of Hiera emerged, then Thea appeared in AD 46, but disappeared later. In 1570, the S shore of the large island (Thera), with the port of Eleusis, disappeared beneath the sea. Three years later Mikra Kaimeni surfaced, as did New or Great Kaimeni in 1711-12. A new eruption, studied on the spot by the geologist Fouqué, which lasted two years, began in January 1866. It gave birth to new craters (the volcano Georgos) and the islet of Aphroessa, soon joined to Great Kaimeni. New eruptions took place in 1925-26 and in 1928, while an earthquake ravaged the islands in 1956.

THE ISLAND MYSTERY. Human existence on such an unstable island seems to depend on a series of miracles or a permanent challenge. We know virtually nothing about the peoples who occupied the island towards the beginning of the 2nd millennium BC. It is assumed that they were visited by Phoenician sailors, but links with Minoan Crete must have been quite close, to judge by the frescoes and all the archaeological material found near Akrotiri, Perhaps completely abandoned when the volcano began to vomit forth enormous quantities of ash before the final explosion, Thera was populated by Dorians towards the end of the 2nd millennium BC. In the historic period, the island took the side of Sparta, but it became temporarily tributary to Athens. The Ptolemies made it into a naval base in the Aegean sea. The Byzantine period ended in 1204, when the island was ceded to the Venetians, who added it to the possessions of the Dukes of Naxos. It was taken by the Turks in 1537.

A DAY ON THERA. You should not leave the Cyclades, or even Greece, without visiting this island which has an ambience and scenery perhaps unique in the world, even though it has no good beaches you should swim preferably on the beaches of Perissa or Kamari on the E coast) and the vegetation (mostly vines, tomatoes and broad beans) is sparse.

During the morning, you can visit the capital Thera (or Phira) and its archaeological museum, and then the site of Akrotiri. In the afternoon, make an excursion to the Kaimeni islands, or, if you are interested in archaeology, to the ruins of ancient Thera. The agencies near the bus station organize one-day trips by caïque: a complete tour of the bay combined with the ascent of the volcano of Nea Kaimeni, bathing in the hot springs of Palea Kaimeni and stops on Therasia and Ia. Don't fail to taste the wine of Santorini, preferably the dry variety. The best wine is reminiscent of sherry.

Until recently boats moored about 110yds (100m) from the narrow but very sheltered harbour, with a few houses, some cafés and a chapel nestling between the sea and the foot of the cliff. You climb to the village, a line of houses perched on the cliff top, by a precipitous path. But today the arrival by regular ships is less picturesque. They dock at a harbour recently constructed some miles to the S, from which you reach the main village by taxi or bus.

THERA (Phira). Capital of the island, Thera is a little village of about 1,500 inhabitants, with very picturesque alleyways broken up by arcades and stairways sometimes opening up vistas of the harbour and the sea (the **view from the terrace of the Hotel Atlantis is very beautiful).

You will visit the archaeological museum which houses the prehistoric ceramics found at Akrotiri; Mycenaean, Geometric and Archaic ceramics from various places on the island, in particular from ancient Thera and the necropolis of Sellada; and sculpture from the Archaic to the Roman period. The collection of Archaic ceramics (7th–6th century BC) is particularly comprehensive.

Open: summer 09.00–15.30; Sun. from 10.00–13.00; winter from 09.00–13.30; Sun. from 10.00–13.30; closed Tues.; entrance fee.

A second museum is planned to house the finds from Akrotiri, now mostly on show in Athens (National Museum).

In the Metropolitikon Megaron, beside the modern cathedral, there is a small collection of religious art (icons, goldsmiths' work and a carved wooden cross). Dating to the 18th century and recently restored, the Ghyzi palace, near the Catholic cathedral, contains the Dimitiri Tsitouras collection (engravings from the 15th to the 19th century representing Santorini as seen by European travellers; and 19th century paintings from the L. and K. Pintos donation).

Open: summer 09.30–13.00 and 17.30–02.00; closed Wed.

From the upper station of the cable-car, you can walk along the corniche track with splendid *views, pretty houses (rooms for rent) and some very simple restaurants.

VICINITY

1 PYRGOS (3.7mls/6km). Here you can see some old dwellings from the 18th and 19th centuries, and the monastery of the Prophet Elijah (45 mins. walk), founded in 1711 on the summit of the tip of the island (1,916ft/584m), where the sacristy of the church contains a small

museum (post-Byzantine icons, carved crosses, sacerdotal vestments, etc.). You will also see an interesting reconstruction of the old monastic handicrafts (cooking, weaving, embroidery, basketwork, bookbinding, etc.).

2 EXCAVATIONS OF AKROTIRI (9.7mls/15.5km). 5mls (8km) from Thera, leave on your r. a road which descends to the small port of Athinios.

8.7mls (14km): village of Akrotiri, with the ruins of a Venetian fort. The view of the S coast of the island and particularly of the roadstead is most impressive.

9.7mls (15.5km): the excavation site. You will visit a 16th-century BC town, with houses of two or three storeys, which after being shaken and mostly destroyed by an earthquake was buried under a thick layer of volcanic ash. The heat was so intense that the stones were calcinated, but the town was deserted just before the catastrophe (yet some houses were reoccupied very shortly afterwards, a few days or weeks before everything was engulfed).

Open: daily in summer 09.00–15.00, Sun. from 10.00–15.00; in winter, from 09.00–13.30, Sun. from 10.00–15.30; entrance fee.

The site, the existence of which was known for more than a century, was excavated by S . Marinatos from 1967 until his accidental death on the site in 1974. The majority of the finds have been left in place so as to form an archaeological park. They are protected by plastic roofs of unpleasing appearance. There have already been surprising finds, notably of mural paintings, mostly on show – temporarily – in the National Museum in Athens (see p. 304). Storehouses have been found full of pithoi, those large terracotta vessels, still *in situ*, used to preserve foodstuffs (some of them still contained fossilized food). Even if the complex of excavated buildings is confusing to the layman, you will observe several rooms with the window and door frames still in place, as well as sections of the paved road. Although the visit need not take long (an hour is enough), you will be as impressed as you might be after seeing Pompeii.

3 ANCIENT THERA (10mls/16km to the beach of Perissa, then about 40 mins. on foot; allow about 1½hrs for a visit to the site, which can also be reached from the N and the beach of Kamari). You pass the chapel of Hagios Nikolaos Marmaritis (7.5mls/12km), built with marble from an antique temple, then drive by the village of Emporion (8.1mls/13km) with some remains of a Venetian fortress.

10mls (16km): Perissa (impressive modern church of Stavros; beach). The remains of the military and religious city of ancient Thera extend over a length of some 880yds (800m) and a width of 165yds (150m) on a rocky ridge at a height of 1,115 to 1,210ft (340 to 369m).

Open: daily 09.00–15.30; Sun. 10.00–15.00. Entrance fee.

Archaic tombs and inscriptions on this site show that the capital of the Dorian colonists was located here from the 9th century BC onwards. The Ptolemies installed a large garrison here to guard the archipelago. The ruins, mostly from the Ptolemaic (300–145 BC) and

Byzantine periods, were explored by the German archaeologist Hiller von Gärtringen from 1895 to 1903.

The main street, intersected by side streets, traversed the whole length of the town. It began near the chapel of Hagios Stephanos built on the remains of a basilica dedicated to the Archangel Michael in the 4th or 5th century. Following a path to the l., note first the temenos of Artemidorus of Perge, admiral of the Ptolemies. Cut out of the rock, it consisted of an altar of Concord, the eagle of Zeus, the lion of Apollo Stephanephoros and the dolphin of Poseidon. A little farther on you will pass in front of the remains of a temple of Dionysus, to the r., just before the agora, which was lined by the royal portico with an internal colonnade and exedra. One of the Hellenistic houses behind the portico contains phalli and an inscription 'to the friends' carved in a cartouche. Beyond the agora you come to a square bordered on the l. by the Sacred Way. To the r., you will note the remains of the sanctuary of the Egyptian Gods, carved in the rock. It was consecrated to Isis, Anubis and Serapis.

The theatre (stage refurbished in the Roman period) is located to the l., near the square. A little further on are the remains of baths and nearby is the chapel of the Evangelismos, close to the remains of an antique heroön and rotunda.

The small sanctuary of Ptolemy III was to the r. of the Sacred Way. Nearby stood the column of Artemis, half embedded in the rock, and a heroön possibly dedicated to Thera, the founder of the colony; the foundations of very ancient masonry still exist. To the l. of the Sacred Way, in front of the terrace of the Festivals, note the remains of the temple of Apollo Carneus, founded in the 6th century BC. The terrace of the Festivals was laid out with retaining walls (the E one dates to the 6th century BC). This terrace was the religious centre of the most ancient Dorian cults of Thera. On it were celebrated festivals, especially the Gymnopaedeia, solemn dances by nude youths in honour of the Dorian god, Apollo Carneus.

On the rocks, the names of the gods engraved by the faithful are mingled with the names of beautiful dancers, accompanied by amorous epithets. Some of these graffiti go back to the 7th century BC. Beyond it stood some Roman baths, an annexe of the gymnasium of the Epheboi, the ruins of which occupy the S end of the site. The gymnasium consisted of a large court on to which opened a grotto of Hermes and Heracles, gods of the Epheboi, a rotunda and a series of rooms.

Returning towards the chapel of Hagios Stephanos, at the entry to the site, turn l. some 33yds (30m) beyond the agora. You will pass the governor's palace, near the garrison gymnasium (to the l.) and the grotto of Christos (to the r.), a small rock cavern, 10ft (3m) long, converted into a chapel. 33yds (30m) further on is the votive niche of Demeter and Kore, with a throne carved out of the rock at the entrance to a cave.

4 IA, OR APANOMERIA (6.9mls/11km) **AND THE ISLAND OF THERASIA.** Ia, a large very picturesque village, situated like Thera on the edge of a cliff, was badly damaged by the 1956 earthquake. The Byzantines or Venetians built a fortress on the top of the promontory.

From the port of Ia, near the reef of Hagios Nikolaos, with a chapel, it is 15 mins by boat to the island of Therasia, which is also worth a visit. From Manolas, the main village, you can reach the convent of Panagia Kimissis (about 2.5mls/4km), which was built on the Trypiti promontory. Some 0.9mls (1.5km), from Manolas is the troglodytic hamlet of Potamos, an oasis shaded by palm trees in a rocky setting.

ISLAND OF THERA
(SANTORINI)
Asphalt roads
Other roads
Tracks
0   1   2   3 mls

5 THE KAIMENI ISLES (2 to 3 hrs by boat). By hiring a motorboat at the port of Thera, you will arrive in 40 mins at the N tip of Little Kaimeni, a volcanic island which appeared in 1573 and from that time was attached to Great Kaimeni, which emerged in 1711-12. About 30 mins walk from the N tip of Little Kaimeni (Mikra Kaimeni) is the edge of the crater which formed in 1925. Mofettes and smoke-holes emit fumes through the burning sulphurous crust.

From the bay you can also take a boat to the sulphur spring at the point of Aphroessa (emerged in 1966 to the SE of Great Kaimeni) and the two bays on the W coast. A round trip of the Kaimeni islands is also highly recommended, especially at sunset.

6 ANAFI (to the E of Thera; twice weekly boats from Piraeus). Anafi is a small island (14.7sq mls/38km²; pop: 350). It is the most southerly of the Cyclades and Apollo is supposed to have made it rise from the sea to shelter the Argonauts when they were surprised by the storm. Chora, the only village on the island, is 15 mins' walk from the anchorage of Hagios Nikolaos. There are very few antique remains on the island; most of them are near the monastery of Kalamiotissa (remains of a temple of Apollo). The island was a place of deportation.

■ Thermopylae

Route map 3.

Athens, 130mls (208km) – Lamis, 11.2mls (18km) – Thebes, 70.6mls (113km) – admin. region of Phthiotis.

This pass, cramped between the sea and Mt Zastini, the ancient Callidromus, considerably enlarged since antiquity, is one of the heroic sites of Greece. In 480 BC, Leonidas, king of Sparta, and his long-haired soldiers, engaged in a hopeless combat with the Persian avalanche. A modern monument has been erected in memory of this king who deliberately sacrificed his own life because he was jealous of the laurels won 10 years earlier by the Athenians at Marathon.

Passing through the pass, which is 3.1mls (5km) long (the monument of Leonidas is roughly in the middle), you will recognize the main positions accurately described by the historian Herodotus, in spite of the changes which have taken place since antiquity. On the side nearer the mountains, the modern road has only cut into the foothills, but on the side next to the sea, the shore has retreated several miles to the N. The alluvium of the Sperchius and mineral deposits have enlarged the pass and changed the river beds. The Asopus, the Dyras and the Melas, tributaries of the Sperchius, once flowed directly into the gulf of Malis.

Herodotus distinguishes three passes or gates: the W and E entrances (towards Lamia and Athens respectively), reduced to a road width for one car only and commanded by the vanished fortresses of Anthela (1.2mls/2km from the monument of Leonidas towards Athens) and Alpenus (2.2mls/3.5km from the monument of

Leonidas towards Athens), and, in the centre, the pass of Thermopylae proper situated near hot springs (present-day Loutra, a spa); it was barred by a very ancient wall, with a gate, which the Phocians erected in the 6th century to halt the incursions of the Thessalians. This wall, situated at the height of the monument of Leonidas, was discovered in 1939 by S. Marinatos.

A VAST HORDE OF MEN. Determined to avenge the humiliation of his father at the Battle of Marathon in 490 BC, Xerxes, master of an empire stretching from the shores of Asia Minor (present-day Turkey) and Egypt to the heart of Asia, invaded Greece in 480 at the head of an imposing army backed up by a fleet of many hundred vessels. This army crossed the Hellespont (the Dardanelles) on a bridge of boats and, escorted by the fleet, marched along the Aegean coast, passing through Thrace, Chalcidice, Macedon and the Vale of Tempe, which marked the entrance to Greece proper at the time. At the end of this long march, the Persian army camped near the W entrance to Thermopylae, in front of the fortress of Anthela. A troop of 7,300 Greeks, under the orders of Leonidas, encamped in the middle of the defile behind a line of fortifications, barred his way.

HERE 4,000 MEN FROM THE PELOPONNESE FOUGHT 300 MYRIADS. After several unsuccessful attacks on the rampart held by the forces of Leonidas, Xerxes despaired of forcing the pass, when the Malian Ephialtes suggested taking a new position by a path he knew, the Anopaca, which led through the wooded heights of Mt Phrikion. On his arrival, Leonidas had learnt of the existence of this path and posted 1,000 Phocians to guard it. Hydarnes, head of the royal guard, left in the evening, led by Ephialtes, with 2,000 men. He met and dispersed the Phocians, and came out of the defile to the E the next morning to take the defenders from the rear. This was the time fixed for Xerxes to attack the position from the W. Informed of the movement of Hydarnes and foreseeing that he would be crushed between the two attacks, Leonidas, according to Herodotus, ordered most of the Greeks to withdraw. He retained only 300 Spartans and 700 Thespians to make the heroic sacrifice, plus 300 Thebans kept as hostages.

THE HEROIC DEATH OF A KING OF SPARTA. Xerxes was the first to attack, about ten in the morning. Battle was joined to the W in front of the rampart in the place where the pass broadened out. 'Now that the fray was joined over a vast space, the Barbarians swarmed in, behind them officers, whip, in hand, driving them on with blows. A great number fell into the sea and drowned; even more were trampled underfoot by those who came on. The Greeks, knowing that they were going to perish by the swords of those who turned the mountain, used the greatest vigour against the barbarians, despising danger and risking their lives. Most of them soon had their javelins broken and struck with swords. Leonidas fell in this conflict ...' Two brothers of Xerxes fell while fighting over the body of Leonidas which Persians and Spartans disputed bitterly. The Greeks carried it away four times by driving the enemy back.

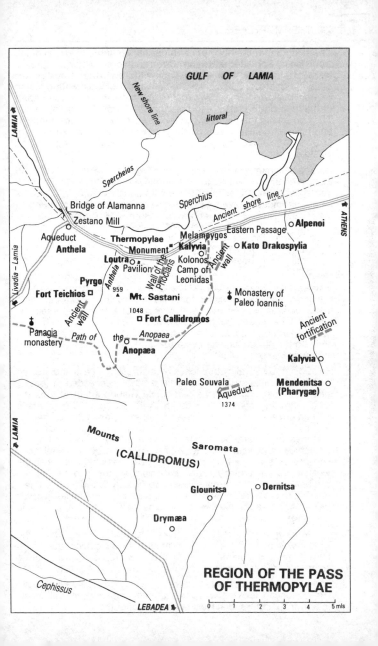

GULF OF LAMIA

New shore line

littoral

LAMIA

Sperchios

Bridge of Alamanna

Zestano Mill

Sperchius

Ancient shore line

ATHENS

Aqueduct

Anthela

Thermopylae Monument

Melampygos

Eastern Passage

o **Alpenoi**

Kalyvia

o **Kato Drakospylia**

Loutra

Anthela

Pavilion

Kolonos
Camp of
Leonidas

Ancient wall

Livadia – Lamia

Pyrgo

Fort Teichios □

959
▲

Mt. Sastani

Monastery of
Paleo Ioannis

Ancient
wall

1048

□ **Fort Callidromos**

Panagia
monastery

Ancient wall

Path of   the   *Anopaea*

o
Anopaea

Ancient
fortification

Kalyvia o

LAMIA

Paleo Souvala

Aqueduct

1374

Mendenitsa o
(Pharygæ)

Mounts

Saromata

(CALLIDROMUS)

o **Dernitsa**

Glounitsa
o

Drymæa
o

Cephissus

LEBADEA

REGION OF THE PASS
OF THERMOPYLAE

0 1 2 3 4 5 mls

The struggle for the body of Leonidas lasted until the arrival of the troop led by Ephialtes (between eleven and noon). When the Greeks learnt of this, the battle changed. They withdrew to the narrowest part of the pass, crossed back over the wall and took up position on the mound, in a serried mass, except for the Thebans, making a rampart of the their bodies, clad in red (so that the blood would not show). They defended themselves with their swords, their hands and their teeth. Nevertheless, the barbarians crushed them with showers of arrows, some attacking from the front, others surrounding them on all sides at once.

THE AGE OF EPITAPHS. The setback of the Persians at Salamis (480) and Plataea (479) and their return to Asia allowed the Greeks to give their heroes a decent burial. Over those who perished early in the battle before Leonidas had sent the allies away, this epigraph covering all the Greek troops was engraved: 'Here 4,000 men from the Peloponnese fought against 300 myriads', while the special inscription for the Spartiates read as follows:

Go tell the Spartans, thou who passest by,

That here, obedient to their laws, we lie' (Herodotus, VII, 223–228).

OTHER BATTLES AT THERMOPYLAE. The tactics of Xerxes were constantly re-used by those who wished to force the pass. In 279, Brennus, with a band of Gauls, held up by the troops of Callippus, turned the position by Anopaea, but the Greeks had time to flee to their ships. In 191, the king of Syria, Antiochus III, with 10,000 men, tried to bar the defile to the 40,000 legionaries of the consul M. Acilius Glabrio and his legate M. Porcius Cato.

He had a double wall with ditches built across the pass and erected forts on the slopes of Mt Callidromus. Cato succeeded in forcing them and attacking from the rear, while Glabrio attacked from the front. The king managed to escape with 500 men. Lastly, Alaric entered Greece through the pass of Thermopylae in 395. In the 6th century Justinian removed the fortifications. After the lapse of centuries, the visit (about 1hr) to the places where the heroic tragedy of Leonidas and his warriors took place cannot leave unmoved those who love the search for 'time past'. The fortresses which defended the two exits from Thermopylae are now only a memory and the Phocian wall before which the armies fought so fiercely is reduced to a few remains, but the site does not fail to impress, no doubt because it was the scene of a drama which has become symbolic of heroic resistance.

THE PHOCIAN WALL. Some remains of the wall behind which the Spartiates withstood the first Persian assaults have been found on a hill near the monument of Leonidas. It was built in a zigzag with a square tower at its W end, separated from the wall by a gate.

Originally (6th century), the wall was built of large blocks which gave it a cyclopean look. It was subsequently repaired several times, notably in 480 BC, and at least once more after that.

KOLONOS. This hill, about 33ft (10m) high, where the last Spartiates perished and where the lion stood consecrated to the memory of the heroes of the battle in 480 BC is situated 0.6mls (1km) from the monument of Leonidas, to the r. of the road in the direction of Athens. Excavations have yielded numerous iron and bronze arrowheads of various types, but all common in the 5th century BC if we compare them with those found at Marathon and on the Acropolis at Athens in 5th-century layers.

THE WALL OF ANTIOCHUS AND THE PATH OF ANOPAEA. 1ml (1.8km) from the monument of Leonidas in the direction of Athens are some sections of an antique wall about 1,970yds (1,800m) long, which must have been erected in the period when the battle between Antiochus and the Romans took place in 191 BC. It was rebuilt by Justinian in the 6th century BC. This wall barred the ravine down which the path of Anopaea led. It started to the W of the gorge of the Asopus, passed below the convent of the Panagia, followed a ravine (barred by the remains of walls at the place called Pyrgos), then climbed again between the twin peaks of Lithidza (ancient Mt Anopaea) and Zastani (3,438ft/1,048m) and emerged to the E near the narrowest part of the pass between Alpenoi and the rock of Melampyges (the Black Buttock), the name given to Heracles by the mother of the Cercopes, two knavish dwarfs, when she was warning them about him. Heracles once caught them and tied them to a pole slung over his shoulder, so that they had a view of his buttocks covered in black hair. Their ribaldry amused him so he released them. (Later, Zeus turned them into monkeys.)

FORTRESS OF ANTHELA. The fortress of Anthela, which guarded the W pass of Thermopylae, was on a height to the l., 1.2mls (2km) from the monument of Leonidas by the Lamia road. The modern road follows the line taken by the ancient one. In the 5th century BC, the sea came almost to the foot of the hills, leaving only a narrow pass about 770yds (700m) long, just wide enough for a road.

At the W exit from the pass, about 550yds (500m) further on, was the sanctuary of Demeter Amphictyonis and the hero Amphictyon, where the Amphictyonic meetings of Anthela were held in the spring and autumn.

Thessaloniki**

Route maps 2, 12, 13 and 14.

Athens, 332mls (532km) – Edessa, 55.6mls (89km) – Florina, 109mls (175km) – Igoumenitsa, 293mls (469km) – Istanbul, 395mls (633km) – Kastoria, 134mls (214km) – Kavalla, 102mls (164km) – Larisa (by the motorway), 107mls (172km) – Skopje, 149mls (239km) – Verria, 49mls

(78km) – Pop: 345,800 (560,000 in the metropolitan area – capital of the admin. region – archbishopric – university.

Second biggest metropolitan area in Greece and second port after Piraeus, headquarters of the Government of Northern Greece, Thessaloniki is both a large industrial and commercial city (important annual fair) and a city of artistic interest which can almost match Constantinople or Ravenna for the beauty and interest of its Byzantine churches.

The typically Mediterranean lower town extends on either side of the Via Egnatia, the main artery, towards the sea and Mt Chortiatis, crowned with impressive fortifications. Cassandrou Street is a frontier between the modern city and the old Turkish town, the houses of which cover the ancient acropolis, but the transition between the two is eased by a quarter forming the middle town, which has partly preserved its network of narrow streets in the Turkish style. The upper town, which only a few years ago looked like an oriental city, with its maze of tortuous alleyways squeezed between crumbling wooden houses, is losing more and more of its local colour. Thessaloniki puts forth long tentacles along the roads to Athens and Kavalla, but also towards the beaches of the gulf of Therma and the peninsula of Chalcidice, scene of the latest influx of tourism.

The town in history

A TOWN WITH A WOMAN'S NAME. Thessaloniki is near the ancient Therma, founded in 316–315 by Cassander, who named it after his wife, Thessaloniki, the half-sister of Alexander the Great. Its maritime situation and the Via Egnatia, the vital artery linking Italy with Constantinople, guaranteed it great prosperity.

A CHURCH OF ST PAUL. Once Macedonia was captured by the Romans in 168 BC, Thessaloniki became the capital of one of the four provinces formed by the Romans out of the possessions of Perseus. A few years later in 146, it was promoted to the rank of metropolis of a much enlarged province. It was also an intellectual centre, and Cicero lived here in exile (58 BC.) During the winter of AD 49–50, St Paul preached here. He founded a church to which he was strongly committed (Epistles to the Thessalonians) and returned there in 56.

AN IMPERIAL TOWN. The Emperor Galerius settled here *c.*300. Theodosius published the famous edict which gave an official character to the creed worked out at Nicaea, but he became infamous for the massacre of 392 in which 7,000 inhabitants perished. During the centuries that followed, Thessaloniki, became an important town thanks to Justinian; then it suffered attacks by the Goths, Avars and Slavs (6th and 7th centuries). Still later, the Saracens sacked it in 904 and the Normans in 1185.

CAPITAL OF THE LATIN STATE. After the Fourth Crusade, it became (1205–23) the capital of a Latin kingdom founded by Count Boniface of Montferrat, but it became part of the despotate of Epirus (1224–46).

THE RETURN OF BYZANTIUM. Recaptured by Byzantium in 1246, it fell under the influence of the Genoese in the 13th and 14th centuries, and then of the Venetians on whom Michael Paleologus VIII conferred important privileges. The 14th century was marked by a violent religious struggle (the quarrel of the hesychasts: contemplative monks) and by the revolution of the zealots (friends of the people) in 1342–49, who massacred the nobles in 1345.

THANKS TO THE CATHOLIC KINGS. A period of anarchy followed, then the Turks settled here for several centuries, from 1430. The population, then very small, increased suddenly at the end of the 15th century with the immigration of 20,000 Jews banished from Spain by the Edict of the Alhambra. Their community formed the larger part of the population and a small autonomous state. It ensured the town's prosperity and some of its members distinguished themselves as savants, Benjamin Halevy Eskenazi, Ashkenazy Moses Almohino. The Greeks returned towards the end of the 15th century and played their part in the economic revival. This prosperity was followed by poverty during the decline of Venice at the end of the 17th century.

THE END OF A TURKISH BASTION. At the beginning of the 20th century, the atrocities of the Red Sultan (Abdul Hamid II) in Macedonia made themselves felt in Thessaloniki, which became a centre of intrigue. It was from there, at the instigation of the Central Committeee of Union and Progress, that the rising of 23 July 1908 began and led to the deposition of the Sultan. During the first Balkan war, the Greek army made a triumphant entry on 8 November 1912 and the town was ceded to the kingdom of Greece by the Treaty of Bucharest.

TWO WORLD WARS. During World War I, a French expeditionary force landed at Thessaloniki (15 October 1915) and Venizelos, faithful to the Entente, set up a Government of National Defence opposed to the king. Occupied for four years during World War II, it lost nearly all its Jewish population, victims of Nazi barbarism.

A DAY IN THESSALONIKI

In the morning you may visit (in about 3½hrs) most of the interesting churches. They bear witness to the wealth of the lower town in the Byzantine period. Before visiting the church of the Holy Apostles (Hagii Apostoli), you cross the picturesque central market. For lunch, return to the cool of the sea front, beside the White Tower (map D–4), for example. Then you will be fortified to tackle your afternoon programme, beginning with a visit to the archaeological museum. After that you can visit the upper town where you will see some Byzantine churches, especially Hosios David (magnificent mosaic), the ramparts and the citadel of ancient Thessaloniki, going through districts with a pronounced oriental character. In summer enjoy the freshness of the late evening, like many Thessalonikians, on the sea front, between Aristotelous Square and the White Tower.

HALF A DAY IN THESSALONIKI

Begin by visiting the church of St George after passing the arch of

Galerius, then walk to the church of St Sophia and take a taxi from there to the churches of St Dimitrios and Hosios David. Lastly drive to the archaeological museum.

WHERE TO PARK. This is not easy in the central districts on weekdays, but there is plenty of room in the vicinity of the White Tower and the archaeological museum. Parking lots are still quite rare. The one situated near Egnatia Street, behind Panagia Chalkeon (map C–2) may solve your problems.

THE TOWN ON FOOT

Thessaloniki is a very big town, which is why we sometimes suggest using your car, or better still taking a taxi (cheap), to save you the trouble of parking.

For your visit to the lower town, leave the beach of Hagia Sophia (map C/D–3) and from the church of St Sophia, follow Patriarchou Ioakim Street and Egnatia Street on foot to the arch of Galerius (map D–3). Beyond the church of St George (map E–3), return to Egnatia Street (where you will turn r.) passing the church of Hagios Panteleimon (map D–3).

Via Platonos (map D–2) and Philippou Streets, you will reach the agora (map C–2) near the church of St Dimitrios. Then retrace your steps to make for the church of Panagia Chalkeon (map C–2) on the edge of Egnatia Street. Cross this road, very busy in this district, especially in the direction of Axiou Square (map B–1), where popular restaurants attract customers with their famous doner kebabs ('turning roast' in Turkish). Via Komninon Street, opposite Panagia Chalkeon, you will cross the picturesque central market, where business is still organized in the old style of the oriental bazaar. If necessary, return to collect your car in Hagia Sophia Square by following Emou Street (map C–2/3), then make for the Church of Hagii Apostoli (map B–1) by Egnatia Street and return to the lower town by Anapafseos Street (map E–2) where you will find a taxi more easily.

IF YOU LIKE ...

Byzantine mosaics, you will be seduced by the imperial splendour of those covering part of the interior of the church of St George, should you miss the mosaics in the churches of St Sophia, St Dimitrios and Hosios David.

Byzantine painting; the churches of Panagia Chalkeon and Hagii Apostoli will hold your attention with their 14th-century frescoes.

1 – The lower town

 CHURCH OF HOLY WISDOM (Hagia Sophia; map D–3). Built in the 8th century, this church, one of the most interesting in Thessaloniki, is consecrated to Holy Wisdom (Hagia Sophia). It is the result of a combination of the basilica with three naves and the domed church built on a Greek-cross plan. From the first, it borrows the lateral wings and the galleries above the side aisles (the gallery above the entrance dates from the end of the Byzantine period). To the Greek-cross plan it owes its overall squared arrangement, its domes with pendentives and lastly the barrel vault above the choir.

In the interior, you will note the capitals with acanthus leaves turned back as if by a gust of wind, a rather rare architectural ornament which come from an older, probably 5th-century building. The mosaics on the dome (end of 9th century) represent the Ascension. The Virgin in a violet robe, and the Apostles in greyish draperies are beautifully executed and form a harmonious whole. You will observe 'the face, thin and sad, the straight dark hair and the short dark beard' of Christ Pantocrator (C. Diehl). Lastly, in the apse, note a Virgin and Child enthroned on a gold ground. This mosaic has replaced a more ancient figure (a cross from the Iconoclastic period?) with some traces still remaining. Restoration apparently dates from the time of the mosaics in the dome. Near the S side of St Sophia (to the r. opposite the church), there are some remains of a Nymphaeum, possibly used as a baptistery.

ARCH OF GALERIUS (map D-3). Built in AD 303, it commemorates the victories of the Emperor Galerius over the Persians in Mesopotamia and Armenia. This imposing monument, decorated with reliefs illustrating the emperor's valour, stood at the crossing of an important path traced in the same direction as present-day Egnatia Street and another that led to the rotunda which today forms the church of St George. In fact, a second similar arch stood in parallel a little further E. A dome supported by four central pillars covered the crossroads on to which opened the monumental vestibule leading to the area of the palace and hippodrome, on the other side of Egnatia Street.

On the pillar nearest the road, observe on the lower part, bas-reliefs representing a battle scene outside a town (note the elephants). Higher up, there is a sacrifice above an altar (Zeus is on the l., Heracles on the r.); Diocletian, who still ruled over the eastern provinces of the empire with the title of Augustus, is on the l., while his son-in-law Galerius, who bore the title of Caesar, is on the r. The third part shows us the triumph of Galerius before kneeling oriental warriors, and on the fourth, Galerius addresses his soldiers.

The other reliefs also recount Galerius' successes: Mesopotamia and Armenia, personified by two women, offer their submission. In the third area Galerius is fighting, and the same personage, in a chariot, in the fourth section, receives a delegation from a town which is opening its gates to him.

THE PALACE OF GALERIUS. Situated alongside the hippodrome, this palace was on the other side of Egnatia Street (which did not cross the town in those days), in the axis of the street which now descends to the sea. At the entrance to this street, you will note the church of the Transfiguration of our Saviour (map D-3), which may date from the 14th century. Further S, you will see the remains of a portico and also of a circular building before reaching Navarinou Square, the site of the actual palace. The main edifice is arranged around a rectangular court lined with porticoes. To the SE a broad corridor has preserved its mosaic pavement with geometric design. In the SW corner are the remains of a vast octagonal building, perhaps the throne room or a mausoleum, known as the Octagon, which may have been subsequently transformed into a church (addition of baptistry).

■ CHURCH OF ST GEORGE (Hagios Georgios; map E–3). It forms a vast rotunda which was apparently built to serve as the mausoleum of the Emperor Galerius. At the beginning of the 5th or 6th century, it was consecrated to the Christian religion and underwent considerable changes. The minaret you will see to the r. of the entrance shows that it was briefly transformed into a mosque (during the 16th century). Today it is a museum.

The main changes effected around 400 or 500 consisted in enlarging the rotunda with a deep apse and raising a wall covering the original construction, while the rear wall of each of the eight niches in the mausoleum was knocked down to form an edifice on a circular plan with three naves, more than 177ft (54m) in diameter. As for the main entrance, it was left to the S, i.e. connecting with the path with porticoes which led to the palace, but a second entrance was created to the W, which is the one by which you enter.

 At the time of the transformation into a church, the niches and dome were decorated with **mosaics on a gold ground. On the dome, you will see eight panels on which, against an elaborate architectural background borrowed from Hellenistic architecture, saints at prayer treated with wholly oriental realism stand out in the foreground. Above are the vestiges of a second part comprising a dozen personages (apostles) with only their feet surviving, and beneath the keystone of the dome, the remains of a large figure of Christ, but all you can see are the halo, the fingers of the l. hand, and the cross of a sceptre, as well as the faces of three of the four angels who completed the composition, probably supporting the mandorla surrounding the standing Christ.

Three of the eight niches have partially preserved their mosaic patterns of plant and geometric motifs. Towards the 10th century, the apse was ornamented with frescoes of which a few traces remain (Christ between two angels, Virgin flanked by two angels and the twelve apostles). This church fulfils its new function as a museum by housing sculptures and fragments of architecture from churches in the region. To the l. of the apse a mosaic panel on a gold ground (St Andrew) comes from the metropolis of Serres.

CHURCH OF HAGIOS PANTELEIMON (map D–3). Probably built in the 13th century, its 14th-century frescoes (in the small rooms on either side of the apse) will interest lovers of detail.

CHURCH OF ACHEIROPOIETOS (Hagia Paraskevi; map D–2). After undergoing numerous restorations, this 5th-century basilica, possibly built in honour of the Virgin towards the end of the century, is of limited interest. But you may note the mosaics (5th century) to be found under the arcades of the tribunes and the ground floor, as well as the fine capitals. This church stands on the site of a Roman villa. A fragment of a mosaic pavement from it is visible at the end of the l. side-aisle (below a wooden panel). The name of Acheiropoietos ('not made by the hand of man') comes from a miraculous icon which was preserved there.

AGORA (map C–2). This is a recent discovery right in the heart of the town. You will see the remains of a Hellenistic and Roman square, notably a double portico, one element of which, on the Philippou Street side, was laid out above an underground gallery. From the road which climbs to the r. alongside the excavation site you will see the rather better preserved remains of a small odeon. All these structures date from the 1st century AD.

*CHURCH OF ST DEMETRIUS (Hagios Dimitrius: map D–2). Although recently reconstructed after a fire, this church is a monument of exceptional interest for its frescoes and above all its mosaics. According to legend, the church stands on the actual site of the martyrdom of St Demetrius, the town's patron saint. Originally there were a small sanctuary and martyrion consecrated to St Demetrius, killed in 303, under Diocletian and Galerius, in a Roman bath. These edifices were destroyed towards the middle of the 5th century to make way for a vast basilica with five naves and a transept, the plan of which is echoed in the present-day church, in spite of two

CHURCH OF SAINT DEMETRIUS

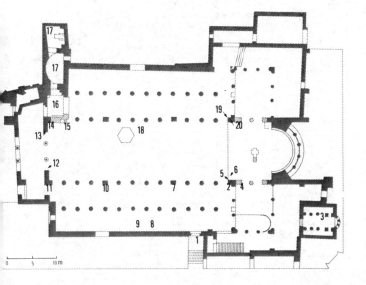

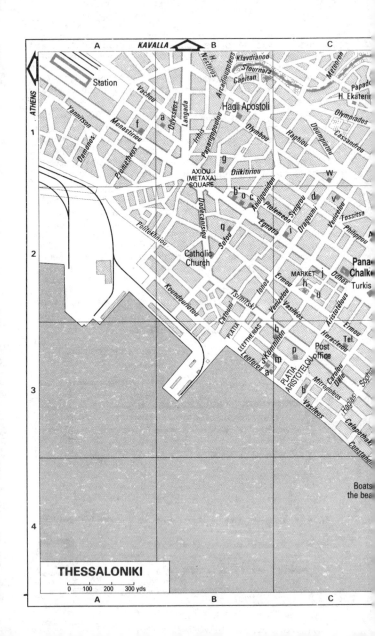

THESSALONIKI

0   100   200   300 yds

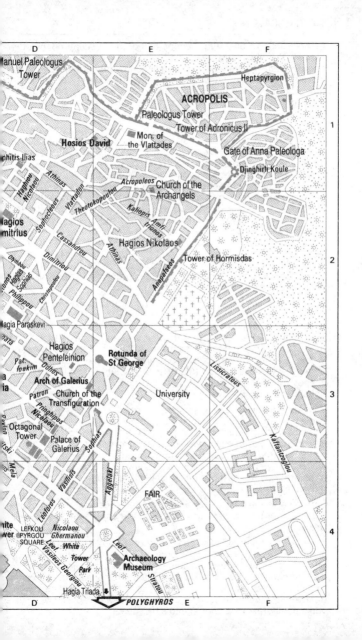

D   E   F

Manuel Paleologus Tower

Heptapyrgion

ACROPOLIS

Paleologus Tower

Tower of Adronicus II

Hosios David

Mon. of the Vlattades

Gate of Anna Paleologa

Djinghirli Koule

phitis Ilias

Haghios Nicolaou

Athinas

Viattadon

Acropoleos   Church of the Archangels

lagios mitrius

Sophocleus

Theotokopoulou

Kalopis

Amfi Trionos

Cassandrou

Dimitriou

Athinas

Hagios Nikolaos

Olympiou

Hagia Sophias

Christopatrov

Anaplaseos

Tower of Hormisdas

Philippou

lagia Paraskevi

Hagios Penteleinion

Rotunda of St George

Pat. Ioakim

Dulos

Lissicratous

Arch of Galerius

Patron

Church of the Transfiguration

Panaghios Nicolaou

University

Octagonal Tower

pavlion

Palace of Galerius

Sophias

Kalianroglou

Vrastisfis

Mela

Aggelaki

Leoforos

FAIR

ite wer

LEFKOU PYRGOU SQUARE

Nicolaou Ghermanou

Leof. Vasileos Georgiou

White Tower

Park

Archaeology Museum

Leof. Stratou

Hagia Triada

POLYGHYROS

D'   E   F

1

2

3

4

reconstructions, one in the second half of the 7th century, the other after the fire which destroyed it in 1917. On this occasion, most of the original elements were used, which accounts for certain polychrome marble facings, the ancient capitals and the majority of the white, green and red marble columns from the 7th-century basilica. The varying heights of these columns show that they came from older buildings.

 In the interior, take special note of the **mosaics on a gold ground visible on the pillars, on both sides of the entrance to the apse. Most of them date from the 7th century. On the pillar to the r. you will see on three panels, St Demetrius and a bishop (plan, 4). St Sergius (plan, 5) and St Demetrius between two personages (plan, 6). The one on the r. is probably the prefect Leontius who built the 5th-century church and the one on the l. the bishop who rebuilt it in the 7th century. The mosaic of St Sergius, martyred in Rome in 296, is magnificent. He is clad in a white tunic embroidered with gold and green at wrists and neck; his short white cloak with red circles on which are flowers, has a broad red band; he wears a gold collar and his very finely modelled head is crowned with curling blond hair. On the pillar to the l. the mosaic of St Demetrius accompanied by two children (plan, 19) also dates from the 7th century, but that of the Virgin (and a saint; plan, 20) cannot be earlier than the 11th or 12th century.

You will also see various murals in the double side-aisle to the l. A curious calendar painted for the years 1474 to 1493 (plan, 13), indicating the dates of movable feasts, is on an engaged pier on the door of the narthex; nearby, to the l. of the central nave you will find (plan, 15) a Florentine sarcophagus from the end of the 15th century. Before entering a small chapel opening on to the first l. side-aisle, note a fragment of mosaic (plan, 16; St Demetrius and angels). The chapel (plan, 17) decorated with frescoes, is supposed to have housed the tomb of St Demetrius.

You descend a staircase (plan, 2) to the crypt which was originally at street level, not underground. In the central niche you will see the end of a pipe through which holy oil, poured from the choir of the basilica, flowed into a basin, and a large circular pool. We know that a sacred oil considered as a sovereign remedy against disease and as a talisman flowed from the tomb of St Demetrius. Today this crypt is transformed into a museum (architectural fragments, ceramics, mosaic fragments).

Returning to the basilica, observe frescoes executed in 1303 above 12th-century paintings in the chapel at the end of the r. side-aisle (plan, 3).

CHURCH OF PROPHITIS ILIAS (The Prophet Elijah) (map, D–1). This church belongs to a monastery founded in the 14th century, perhaps on the site of a Byzantine palace. Its trifoliate plan is reminiscent of the churches on Mt Athos. Externally, the three apses are decorated with two rows of very elegant blind arcades. Paintings were discovered in the narthex under a coat of whitewash applied when the Turks transformed the church into a mosque.

CHURCH OF PANAGIA CHALKEON (map C–2). This sanctuary, consecrated to Our Lady of the Coppersmiths, which can be dated to 1028 by an inscription, constitutes an excellent example of the type of church in the form of a Greek cross which reached perfection in the 10th century and which was to become the model for Byzantine sanctuaries for hundred of years.

In the narthex and the sanctuary you will see beautiful frescoes contemporary with the monuments, with the exception of the paintings above the main door and below the fillet, which date from the 14th century.

CHURCH OF THE HOLY APOSTLES (Hagii Apostoli; map B–1). This very pretty little church in the form of a Greek cross was built entirely of brick at the beginning of the 14th century (1312–15) by the Patriarch of Constantinople, Niphon I. The outside walls, especially the east end with three apses, exhibit remarkable brick decoration in a wide variety of patterns. Inside, the dome and the four vaults of the crossing are adorned with mosaics and the lower parts with 14th-century frescoes. Beneath the coating which covered the dome, another 14th-century mosaic was discovered. It represented a bust of Christ Pantocrator, the head of which is missing, and the figures of ten prophets. The capitals of the four columns supporting the dome undoubtedly come from a more ancient church.

CHURCH OF HAGIA EKATERINI (map C–1). This charming little church, apparently dating from the 13th century, resembles the church of the Holy Apostles in plan. Inside, it is decorated with frescoes showing scenes from the Gospel and figures of saints, while the two domes of the l. aisle are decorated with 13th-century mosaics (Christ seated, surrounded by the mandorla supported by angels, and Jesus Emmanuel which fills the whole vault of the dome).

2 – The upper town

CHURCH OF HOSIOS DAVID (map D/E–1). Founded towards the end of the 5th or beginning of the 6th century, it formed part of a monastery and contains a *mosaic of the Vision of the Prophet Ezekiel contemporary with the construction of the edifice. A beardless Christ sits in a luminous cloud surrounded by the four symbols of the Evangelists. You see the prophets Ezekiel, to his r., and Habakkuk to his l. At his feet flow the Four Rivers of Paradise, on which the Jordan is superimposed.

MONASTERY OF VLATTADES (map E–1). Situated near the foot of the rampart, it includes the little church of the Transfiguration of our Lord, dating from the 14th century. To the r. of the choir, remains of 14th-century frescoes.

THE RAMPARTS. The oldest part of the enceinte of Thessaloniki dates from the middle of the 5th century AD, but was partially built over 3rd-century fortifications with some Hellenistic traces. This enceinte was altered in the Byzantine period and later by the Turks. It is reinforced by towers projecting at irregular intervals and was pierced by gates which were gradually destroyed to improve the flow of traffic (several have been preserved on the N front).

Proceeding alongside the rampart to the W, lovers of detail can still see some courses of re-used blocks from the Roman wall between the gate of Eski Delik (5th century) and the 14th-century tower of Manuel Paleologus (map D–1), with a verse inscription giving the names of the two founders. By following the foot of the rampart, you will pass in front of the tower of Paleologus (map E–1), and then the 14th-century tower of Andronicus II (plan, E–1) before reaching the gate of Anna Paleologa (map F–1), dating from 1355, which gives access to the acropolis.

THE DJINGHIRLI KOULE OR CHAIN TOWER (map F–1). This is a veritable dungeon built by the Turks shortly after the conquest of the town (1430) or by the Venetians who occupied Thessaloniki from 1423 to 1430. Roughly half way between this tower and Egnatia Street is the tower of Hormisdas (map E–2), built in the middle of the 5th century by a Persian called Hormisdas, as an inscription in brick, 29ft 6in (9m) long, bears witness. From there lovers of Byzantine art can visit the lovely church of Nikolaos Orphanos (map E–2); temporary exhibitions (Tel. 27–15–55), erected in the 14th century and entirely decorated with contemporary frescoes, and the church of the Taxiarchs (map E–1/2), built in the 14th century over a crypt with three naves used for burying the monks from the monastery to which this sanctuary was attached. Inside, the triangular spaces at the base of the roof were decorated with paintings representing the Crucifixion on the narthex side and the Ascension on the choir side.

3 – THE WHITE TOWER AND THE ARCHAEOLOGICAL MUSEUM

THE WHITE TOWER (map D–4). Built by the Venetians in the service of the Turks at the beginning of the 15th century, it served as a prison for the Janissaries in the 18th century. After the massacre of the Janissaries on the orders of Sultan Mahmoud, it was briefly nicknamed the Bloody Tower. It reinforced the defences of the sea wall demolished in 1866.

ARCHAEOLOGICAL MUSEUM (map E–4). Situated near the park of the Fair of Thessaloniki, it contains antiquities from Macedonia.

Owing to competition from other museums in the province, the permanent exhibition was in danger, until recently, of not coming up to the visitor's expectations with regard to the number of works on show, especially in view of the town's importance (to get a broader view of ancient art in Macedonia, you must visit the museums of Pella and Verria). But since August 1978, the museum has been enriched by prestigious finds from the Great Tomb (Philip II's) of Vergina shown in two successive exhibitions (1978–79 and 1980). In addition, sumptuous funerary artefacts (vases, jewellery made with precious metals) were acquired by the museum in the summer of 1980 from tombs discovered by chance a few miles to the W of the town in the necropolis of Sindos. These last finds have been presented, since October 1982, in a special exhibition.

Open: daily, except Tues., summer from 08.30–19.00, Sun. from 10.00–17.00; winter from 09.00–15.30, Sun. from 10.00–16.30; entrance fee (Tel. 83–05–38).

The museum is currently being reorganized. Two new halls which were opened in 1980 in the S part of the museum to house an exhibition devoted to Alexander the Great and which contained most of the rich material shown since 1978 (the finds from Vergina in a special exhibition particular) seem very likely to continue to house these treasures of Classical and Hellenistic Macedon. Unfortunately it is impossible to say at present what the definitive arrangements will be, especially as certain pieces lent to exhibitions abroad were absent in 1984. The halls on the ground floor contain the exhibition devoted to the finds from Sindos. It is probable that these finds will be on show for some time. In view of all this uncertainty, it is impossible to describe the whole museum systematically at the time of writing. Nevertheless it seems likely that some halls will remain unchanged, so we shall begin with them.

Halls open in 1985. The exhibition begins in the entrance halls where you will see, to the l., fragments of architecture (including three beautiful capitals) of an Ionic temple from Thessaloniki dating originally from the end of the 6th century BC and rebuilt towards the end of the Hellenistic period, and to the r. a beautiful marble arch with delicately carved decoration from the palace of Galerius (early 4th century BC).

A room opening to the l. houses prehistoric pottery from old and recent excavations (like those at Castara near Kilkis, and from Assiro near Langadas in northern Macedonia). It also has vases and small bronze pieces (pins, brooches, bracelets, small vases, etc.) from the Bronze Age and the beginning of the Iron Age. After viewing this room, return to the hall.

Go up a few steps to the l. and you will reach the five rooms devoted to sculpture. Works are arranged in chronological order from the Archaic period to the 4th century AD. In the first room, in addition to a headless kouros and kore from the late Archaic period and some Classical funerary reliefs, you will note a Roman copy (832) of a statue by Phidias known as Artemis Aricia, fragments of a colossal statue of Athena of the Medicis type (2nd-century AD Roman work after an original attributed to Phidias), a charming Roman copy (831) of Aphrodite of the 'Fréjus' type, the prototype of which dates back to the end of the 5th century BC, as well as a head of Serapis (897), a Roman copy of a famous work by Bryaxis (4th century BC). In the second room, a funerary relief from the first half of the 1st century BC bears the signature of the sculptor Evandrus, son of Evandrus of Verria. The third room contains several pretty Roman *mosaics, including one from a Thessalonikian house made up of three panels with mythological scenes: Dionysus finding Ariadne, Zeus (in the form of an eagle) carrying off Ganymede, Apollo pursuing Daphne (?; 1st half of the 3rd century AD). The fourth and fifth rooms mainly house portrait statues, including one in marble of the Emperor

Augustus (27 BC–AD 14), and a fine bronze head of the Emperor Alexander Severus (AD 222–235).

The ***treasures of ancient Macedon*. At the time of writing, it is impossible to say exactly how and where the museum will exhibit the magnificent group it now possesses of objects discovered in Macedonia and dating mostly from the 4th century BC or the Hellenistic period, especially the rich finds discovered in 1977 in the 'royal tombs' of Vergina (see p. 862) and those found at Derveni a little earlier. Until it is possible to give an accurate description of how the exhibits are arranged, we shall confine ourselves to a brief account of the most remarkable pieces, now regrouped in a large room in the S wing of the museum. This recent rearrangement is reached by a corridor leading from the hall with Roman portraits.

From the tumulus of Vergina, excavated by Professor M. Andronikos, the most important are the magnificent finds from the 'Royal Tomb' and its antechamber: gold **larnax (chest: weight 3lb 2oz/8.240kg), its lid ornamented with a 12-pointed star, and the sides with rosettes which contained the bones of the personage buried in the sarcophagus from the antechamber of the tomb; a gold diadem which accompanied it; magnificent ***gold plaques decorated in relief (mainly battle scenes, undoubtedly the sack of Troy) and used to adorn a quiver; a gold necklace and a pair of gilded bronze greaves; a crown of leaves and myrtle flowers and various ornaments (three of them stamped with a star, the emblem of the sovereigns of Macedon), also discovered in the vestibule of the tomb; objects from the actual tomb: a breastplate of articulated iron plates, with gold appliqué ornaments of palmettes and lotus blossoms; an iron sword with a hilt inlaid with gold and ivory, and the neck piece of the breastplate; exceptional group of *silver vases and a curious polychrome pottery vase; a sumptuous *larnax of solid gold (weight 4lb 14½oz/10.800kg) ornamented with a 16-pointed star on the sides with rosettes and lavish floral designs (this chest contained calcined and purple-dyed bones), and a ***gold crown of oak leaves and acorns of great delicacy; vases, arms and a bronze tripod; pottery vases valuable for dating the tomb: a gilded silver diadem and five small **ivory portrait heads, carved with great attention to detail, which Professor Andronikos presumes to be of members of the Macedonian royal family, including Philip II, bearded, his son Alexander and his wife Olympias; several ivory reliefs: Muse (seated at l., holding a lyre); Dionysus, seated, leaning towards the l. and a bearded Silenus facing him, seated symmetrically; small hermaic stele (case 16); dionysiac group (a silenus playing a flute, Dionysus holding a torch and leaning against Ariadne); bearded figure in a long robe, facing front, arms opened wide (case 9); a *parade shield (diameter 2ft 10in/0.86m) whose scrupulous restoration was finished only in 1982: inside, a brassard decorated with figures in relief (Victory, lions facing each other); on the outside, inlaid geometric pattern (gold, glass, ivory) around the central motif: a man and a woman in high relief in ivory on a gold ground. The treasure from Vergina Tomb III is not quite so rich. Nevertheless it comprises two gold crowns, several silver vases, a pair of greaves, bronze strigils and lance tips. Lastly the tumulus of Vergina yielded many 4th-century painted funerary stelae. You can also admire the splendid collection of objects which were the museum's pride until 1978: bronze and silver vases, gold jewels, terracotta objects discovered at Derveni to the N of Thessaloniki in tombs from the second half of the 4th century BC.

You will notice in particular a large gilded bronze **krater with silver inlays, ornamented and even overloaded with repoussé motifs, in addition to appliqué figures on the shoulder.

Exhibition devoted to the finds at Lindos. It was displayed in October 1982 in the halls surrounding the central court of the museum on the ground floor. The material comes from tombs dating from the late Archaic to the early Classical period (between 550 and 480 BC); the artefacts are exhibited with scrupulous regard to the way in which they were found in the tomb. You will see vases (lekythoi, skyphoi, cups, phiales), mostly Attic black-figure, but also red-figure, jewellery (silver and bronze fibulae, pins, bracelets, rings, earrings, gold pendants), weapons (swords, lance heads, knives, helmets) and terracotta objects. Among the isolated finds, you will notice two soldiers' funerary masks in gold, an iron box for unguents and several small models including a four-wheeled chariot, a three-legged table and a bed.

Other objects (pottery in particular). It is probable that the museum will put back on show the numerous prehistoric, Archaic and Classical vases (especially those found at Olynthos) which were exhibited in the ground-floor rooms surrounding the central court before the 1978 exhibition. The room which opens to the entrance hall to the l. will house the collection of prehistoric ceramics from old or recent excavations (for example, those from the tumuli of Castana, near Kilkis, and Assiro, near Langada, in northern Macedonia).

In the early evening, you can take a pleasant walk from the White Tower along the sea front by following Vasileos Constantinou Avenue to Eleftherias Square (map B-3), which has yielded the remains of a small Roman odeon probably erected in the age of the Tetrarchy (the Roman Empire was governed by two Augustuses and two Caesars at the time), i.e. at the end of the 3rd or beginning of the 4th century.

In the modern quarter of the E town, at the corner of Vasilisis Olgas Avenue (no. 68) and Anaktoron Street (off the map), you may wish to visit an interesting folk museum with a most attractive collection of Macedonian costumes and jewellery.

Open: daily except Tues. from 09.30–14.00; entrance free (Tel. 83–05–91).

VICINITY OF THESSALONIKI

1 PANORAMA (5.6mls/9km). Leave by the road to Polyghyros (map E-4).

2.5mls (4km): Turn l. at 25 (Ikossipende) Martious Street, 3.1mls

(5km): fork r. in Anatolikis Thrakis Street, then l. (opposite a Shell service station).

5.6mls (9km): Panorama, a residential suburb of Thessaloniki on the slopes of Mt Chortiatis 3,940ft (1,201m); the ascent takes about 2hrs from Panorama (alt. 1,148ft/350m).

2 ROUND TRIP IN CHALCIDICE, the peninsula of Cassandra (177.5mls/ 284km). This one-day drive will enable you to make the tour of the peninsula of Cassandra and take you to beaches and spas forming some of tourism's most recent conquests in Greece. Apart from the ruins of Olynthus, which will mainly interest lovers of archaeology, this circuit has little to offer except the scenery of the peninsula, almost virgin territory only a few years ago, but now rather spoilt by some small resort towns for tourists. The coast is quite beautiful and the landscape of the peninsula is made up of foothills covered with wheat fields, olive groves and, at its tip, pine forests.

Leave Thessaloniki by the road to the airport (map E–4).

7.5mls (12km): leave the road to Polygyros and Hagion Oros (Mt Athos) to your l. and the airport road to your r.

10mls (16km): turn l. towards Cassandra.

The road leads straight on to Epanomi and the beach of Hagia Trias (4.4mls/7km) at the entrance to the Thermaic gulf (for the beach, do not forget to leave the Epanomi road and turn r. just beyond the fork at 10.9mls/17.5km).

22.5mls (36km): to the r., road to the beach of Nea Kalikratia (2.5mls/4km).

25.6mls (41km): Nea Silata; to the r., track to the coast where there is a succession of beaches.

29.4mls (47km): Eleochoria; a skeleton from the middle Palaeolithic (Neanderthal) was discovered in a cavern.

32.5mls (52km): Nea Triglia, road to the r. to the sea.

40mls (64km): to the r., Nea Moudania, a very popular beach, in a somewhat unattractive location (tourist police; Tel. 21–370).

40.6mls (65km): Leave the Polygyros road to your l., unless you want to go straight to the site of Olynthus (see below, 117.5mls/188km).

47.5mls (76km); bridge over the Potidaean canal cut through the isthmus of the Cassandra peninsula (ancient Pallene peninsula); the village of Nea Potidea partially occupies the site of ancient Potidaea, a town founded towards the end of the 6th century by Corinth – only a few sections of the ramparts remain.

During the Persian Wars, Potidaea was ravaged by Xerxes, then became a tributary of Athens, but rebelled against her during the Peloponnesian war. A long siege from 432 to 429 put an end to the resistance of the inhabitants, who were replaced by Athenian colonists. This was the cause of numerous quarrels with the neighbouring town of Olynthus, which occupied it in 382, but was driven out by Athens in 364; Potidaea was finally ceded to Olynthus again by Philip II of Macedon in 356. But the town was destroyed and rebuilt by Cassander, who called it Cassandreia. It then became very prosperous and was able to repulse a Roman fleet during the war with Persia. It was entirely destroyed by the Huns.

50.3mls (80.5km): to the r., pleasant beach of Sani (5.6mls/9km).

≋ 55.6mls (89km): Kallithea, a spa of some extent between a beach and pine woods. At Kallithea, leave to the r. a road to Cassandra and Possidion, which you will pass after going round the loop at the end of the peninsula, unless you want to go straight to Kalandra (see below, in the opposite direction, as from 102.5mls/164km). Then you will follow the N coast of the peninsula.

58.7mls (94km): Kryopigi; 65mls (104km): Haniotis; 67mls (107km): Kapsochora, near the site of ancient Aigai.

73.7mls (118km): Paliori, one of the few villages on the Cassandra peninsula.

77.5mls (124km): Hagia Paraskevi.

83mls (133km): Nea Skioni, near the site of antique Skioni.

90.6mls (145km): Kalandra, a still rather modest spa near the site of antique Mende.

≋ 93mls (149km): beach of Fourka.

99.4mls (159km): Cassandra.

102.5mls (164km): return to Kallithea (58.7mls/94km, above).

117.5mls (188km): return to the fork at 40.6mls (65km); drive towards Polyghyros.

121mls (193.5km): to the l. (1.9mls/3km), Nea Olynthos, near the site of ancient Olynthus, where an American archaeological expedition revealed some traces of an enclosing wall and several districts of the ancient town situated on a long spur dominating the plain.

Olynthus was a town which first belonged to the Boeotians, but during the Persian Wars it was ravaged by the Persians and abandoned to the Chalcidians. It was populated in 423 by Athenian colonists from Chalcidice on the authorization of the king of Macedon, Perdiccas II. It quarrelled with Athens, was besieged by the Spartiates in 383–379 BC, then Demosthenes reconciled it with Athens, who sent troops to help in the town's defence against Philip II of Macedon, but he destroyed it in 348. It was never rebuilt. The main purpose of the excavations carried out in 1928–38 was to tell us about Greek domestic architecture in a period predating the remains at Delos, but today it is difficult even to recognize the layout of the streets.

126.2mls (202km): beach of Gerakini. Take the Polygyros road to the l. (to the N).

134.4mls (215km): Polygyros, capital of the admin. region of

Chalcidice, a modest village, but with character; small archaeological museum (head of Dionysus; cult figures found at Olynthus).

141.3mls (226km): road to the r. for Hierissos (see Vicinity of Thessaloniki, 4, at 36.2mls/58km).

170mls (272km): return to the fork at 7.5mls (12km).

177.5mls (284km): Thessaloniki.

3 ROUND TRIP TO CHALCIDICE: The Sithonia peninsula (180.6/289 or 192.5mls/308km). From Thessaloniki to the fork at 40.6mls (65km), see above, Vicinity 2.

43.4mls (69.5km): to the l. at 1.9mls (3km), Nea Olynthos, see Vicinity 2, at 121mls (193.5km).

48.7mls (78km): Gerakini. Follow the coast road.

59.4mls (95km): Metamorphossi; 64.4mls (103km): a fork, where you will take the S road which runs round the Sithonia peninsula on mountain slopes and often through woods. Many deserted creeks allow you to keep away from tourist regions in the course of development.

75mls (120km): Neos Marmaras which is still a pleasant fishing village. Beyond it lies the estate of the ship-owner J. C. Carras, with a model farm (vines).

78.1mls (125km): to the r., a road descending to Porto Carras, a new village and leisure port built entirely in the Mediterranean style, with numerous sporting and cultural facilities and pleasant beaches.

89.4mls (143km): to the r., Toroni; beach.

90.6mls (145km): Porto Koufas, fishing port to the S of which stood the ancient Torone, remarkably situated on a promontory dominating the sea and girdled by a rampart mentioned several times by Thucydides. Excavations carried out in 1975 have enabled scholars to establish that the site, partially occupied from the 3rd millennium BC, was fortified by Chalcidian colonists in the 8th or 7th century, and that the first enceinte was extended to the E and S in the Classical period. The road leaves the sea and climbs back to the N, cutting across the peninsula of Cape Drepanon protruding into the sea. Passing Kalamitsa, it drops back to the coast which it joins at the little port of Sarti (108mls/173km). The corniche road faces of Mt Athos on the other side of the gulf.

Beyond Vourvouras and Ormos Panagias, you will rediscover, at 132.5mls (212km), the fork from 64.4mls (103km); you can return to Thessaloniki either via Polygyros (60mls/96km, see Vicinity 2), or by your outward itinerary, but going in the opposite direction (48.1mls/77km).

4 FROM THESSALONIKI TO OURANOPOLIS (towards Mt Athos, 98mls/ 157km). Leave by the road to Polygyros.

7.5mls (12km): leave the road to Cassandra to your r. (see Vicinity of Thessaloniki, 2, at mile 7.5/km 12). You will drive through Chalcidice by a very winding but picturesque road which passes by Mt Cholomon.

36.2mls (58km): road to the r. for Polygyros (see Vicinity of Thessaloniki, 2). Running through magnificent scenery, the road climbs into the Cholomon area, then redescends to the charming village of Arnea (53.7mls/86km), famous for its fruit and wine.

56.9mls (91km): Paleochori; to the r., road to Megali Panagia, in a lovely setting. The road then passes through the village of Stagira, birthplace of the philosopher Aristotle (small modern monument to the r. of the road), remains of a fortress and a Byzantine church.

71.9mls (115km): Stratonion, by the sea (track to the l. along the coast, for Stavros at 20.6mls/33km), near the road from Thessaloniki to Kavalla. A beautiful drive along the gulf of Hierissos.

88.7mls (142km): Hierissos, the ancient Acanthus, small port where there are still some remains of the antique town walls and re-used blocks in the small Byzantine chapel of the medieval kastro.

98mls (157km): Ouranopolis, port where one normally embarks for Daphni, the point of access to ***Mt Athos.

5 LANGADAS (13.1mls/21km; leave by the Serres road). Large village situated near warm springs, where you can watch an extraordinary spectacle on 21st May (feast of Saints Constantine and Helen): the villagers, according to a very ancient custom, dance barefoot on burning coals, holding very old icons. A bull is sacrificed during the same ceremony. The origin of this custom goes back to 1250 when the church of the little village of Kosti (now in Bulgaria) whence many of the inhabitants of Langadas came) was destroyed by fire and the icons were saved by villagers who plunged into the flames to rescue them.

■ Thessaly

Route maps 1, 2, 10, 11 and 12.

Situated on the border of Greek civilization until the classical period, Thessaly was a region which played a marginal role in the history of the Hellenes, even though it was, together with Iolcus, near present-day Volos, a centre of civilization in the Mycenaean period. Thus its archaeological sites are not as interesting as those of the Peloponnese and of course of Attica, but it does possess the famous group of monasteries of the Meteora, and the fabulous scenery of Pelion, in addition to Olympus.

A PLAIN BETWEEN ANCIENT MOUNTAINS. Thessaly as a whole consists of a vast plain eaten into in the SE by the gulf of Volos and framed by mountains: to the E, Ossa 6,490ft (1,978m) and Pelion on the edge of the Aegean sea; to the N, Olympus 9,570ft (2,917m), the highest summit in Greece; to the W, Pindus, line of demarcation with Epirus; to the S, Othrys 5,662ft (1,726m), the last evidence of the ancient shield which forms the foundations of the whole of Thessaly. This plain is a vast zone of subsidence. As far as the eye can see, the low spurs of the hills unfold, hollowed out by two huge basins, those of Trikkala and Larisa, drained by the Peneus. In the upper basin of this river, erosion, biting into thick layers of sandstone and conglomerates, has formed the blackish pillars, sometimes surmounted by hermitages, called the Meteora.

ANCIENT MOUNTAINS BOUNDED BY FAULTS. Olympus, the sacred mountain where the Aeropagus of the gods presided over by Zeus was situated, is a wide dome veiled in mist until the middle of the summer. The peaks are hollowed out by glacial cirques. The E slope is cut into the Vale of Tempe, a long band of greenery between sheer limestone walls. Ossa rises like a pyramid above a pedestal of plains, Pelion forms a sheer cliff on the sea side, but to the W has slopes comparable to the Vosges. Othrys, whose massive ridges are sometimes intersected by escarpments, forms a climatic boundary, with the forests of the N side contrasting with the Mediterranean maquis on the southern slopes.

A CONTINENTAL CLIMATE. The climate is characterized by the sharp difference between winter and summer. The summers are scorching, even stifling in the interior basins, which become arid dusty steppes. But there is sufficient humidity everywhere for agriculture, which is mainly based on wheat. The mountains, with more extreme weather conditions, are snow-clad throughout the winter.

AN ECONOMY BASED ON AGRICULTURE. In the plain, the population lives in miserable villages without orchards or gardens, in houses of sunbaked brick. The towns, where some textile industries are situated, are primarily country markets, for example Trikkala, with its big cattle fairs, and Larisa, an important crossroads in the midst of fertile, highly cultivated countryside. Volos, Thessaly's only port, exports fruit, wheat and tobacco.

■ Thrace

Route map 14.

Divided between Greece and Turkey, Thrace (pop: 360,000) extends over the SE slopes of the Rhodope mountains and a region of arid hills interspersed with plains, marshy at times (vicinity of Porto Largo), and forms the administrative region of Rhodope, Xanthi and Evros. Off its coasts, Thasos and Samothrace, the highest of the Aegean islands (5,203ft/1,586m), are two insular fragments of the continental shield.

The Thracian steppes, which for centuries have been crossed in winter by seasonally migrating flocks and herds, are mainly devoted to agriculture, owing to the persevering work of refugees from Asia Minor and eastern Thrace.

Thasos, celebrated in antiquity for its gold mines, marble and wine, is considered to be the most fertile of the Aegean islands, with its olive groves, gardens and forests, mainly pine, which supply large amounts of wood for heating and building.

There is evidence of human occupation of Thrace from the Palaeolithic period (traces in the regions of the Hebros or Evros, a river now separating Greece from Turkey) and above all from the Neolithic period (4500–3000 BC), when humans began to live on permanent sites, to cultivate the land and domesticate animals. Several finds tell us about the way of life, the habitat, tools and utensils used by the Thracians of those days (tumuli of Paradimi and Lafrouda, caverns of Maronia, Strymi, Makri and Hagii Theodori). The transition to the Bronze Age (3000–1000 BC) and then to the Iron Age brought Thrace to a new cultural stage, in close liaison with the Balkan peninsula and Asia Minor. Remains from the 13th century BC show the existence in that period of groups of circular or rectangular houses, surrounded by fortifications, and from the beginning of the 1st millennium Thrace played an important part in the growth of Greek mythology, especially in the fields of poetry and music. Eumolpus sought refuge there and Orpheus was a native of Thrace.

In the 7th century BC, colonists from Central Greece and the Aegean islands founded several towns at Thasos and along the Thracian littoral. These rapidly became powerful independent states, which had close commercial and cultural relations with the indigenous inhabitants, but were often at loggerheads with them. These relations were kept up until Roman conquest suppressed the independent states and managed to impose Greek civilization throughout the territory. Thrace was a geographically and historically unifrom region during the palaeo-Christian period (4th–6th centuries AD). Owing to its location between Constantinople, the capital, and Thessaloniki, the second town of the Byzantine Empire, it played a very important part in the development of that empire. A series of Byzantine towns situated either along the coast or on the central artery of the period, the Via Egnatia, which connected the Adriatic sea with Constantinople, were the administrative, financial and cultural centres of the region, able to extend Byzantine civilization into the very heart of the Balkan peninsula. The region of Evros, in particular, under the immediate influence of Constantinople, is the only part of Greek territory which possesses monuments of really pure Constantinopolitan art.

■ Tilos [Island of]

22.8sq. mls (59km²) – Pop: 1,000.

Very few boats serve this Dodecanese island, which means that it is unspoilt, having escaped the worst excesses of modern tourism. It is a very peaceful little island dotted with modest Byzantine churches, where ancient traditions are still very much alive. Thus you might see women wearing local costume with rich embroidery (especially on 27 July, at the convent of Hagios Panteleimon to the E of the island). Mountainous and lacking proper roads, Tilos is green and fertile thanks to large numbers of water-courses. It is best to stay in private houses. You land at Livadia on the E coast or Megalochoria on the N coast. The two villages are linked by a track 6.9mls (11km) long (taxis). The second one occupies the site of ancient Telos and its church is built on the remains of a temple, while a ruined Venetian castle dominates the whole. To swim, have yourself driven to the beaches of Livadia, Hagios Antonios or Plaka, or to the innumerable deserted creeks, with sand or pebble beaches, which surround the island.

■ Tinos [Island of]*

75.3sq. mls (195km²) – Pop: 10,000.

The holy island of Greek Orthodoxy, and at the same time the most Catholic of the Cyclades, Tinos attracts crowds during the countless feasts of the Virgin celebrated here. At these times and the weekends, it is one vast centre of pilgrimage and it is difficult to find anywhere to stay. Rather unfairly, Tinos is otherwise somewhat neglected by foreigners, for the peaceful beauty of its countryside, and its coasts are worth more than a brief look from the deck of a ship making for Mykonos, its neighbour.

The island is also celebrated for its marble, the Venetian dovecotes which abound and its artistic tradition. Many painters and sculptors were born here and many more come to visit.

THE MOST CATHOLIC OF THE CYCLADES. This island colonized by Ionians from the 10th century BC possessed a famous sanctuary consecrated to Poseidon and Amphitrite. Conquered in 1207 by Andrea Ghizzi, it remained in the power of Venice for more than five centuries. This lengthy domination made it into the most Catholic of the Cyclades. The Turks occupied it from 1714 until the rebellion of 1821. The Catholics, who did not take part in the War of Independence, withdrew to Xynara, where they still have their own churches, convents and schools. The discovery of an icon of the Virgin in 1822 by Sister Pelagius turned Tinos into a place of Orthodox pilgrimage famous throughout Greece.

The capital, Tinos, is a pretty town with streets paved with marble and dazzling white houses, dominated by the convent and church of Panagia Evangelistria (the Annunciation), a centre of pilgrimage on 25 March and 15 August. The white marble building includes re-used antique material from the temple of Apollo at Delos. Beyond a large court lined with arcades, a staircase leads to the church. Its interior exhibits the traditional aspect of Orthodox sanctuaries, with a profusion of gilding, ornaments, *ex votos*, etc., which give it a lot of charm; it contains the miraculous icon found in 1822. In town you will visit a small museum, enriched by finds made during the excavation of the sanctuary of Poseidon and Amphitrite, and ancient Tenus.

In 1973 the French School of Athens resumed the excavation of the sanctuary of Poseidon and Amphitrite, at Kiona 1.6mls (2.5km) from the present-day port, by the sea. In this sanctuary, founded at the end of the 4th century BC, you can see the remains of a temple, a monumental altar and a fountain-cum-exedra. By the shore, a double portico 186yds (170m) long served as a refuge for pilgrims. A restaurant and kitchens were installed in front of the portico. These buildings were divided between two large-scale construction programmes, the first in the 3rd century BC, the second in the middle of the 2nd century. Destroyed by pirates, like Delos, in the middle of the 1st century BC, the sanctuary was reoccupied by the Romans who built baths there in the 2nd century AD. The island of Tinos contains nearly sixty villages, mostly situated in the interior in delightful surroundings on the mountains (taxis, bus).

To the NE in the direction of Falatados, you can reach (5.6mls/9km from Tinos) the monastery of Kekrovounion, founded in the 12th century and still in use. In it you can see the cell of St Pelagius, much honoured in the island, and the remains of ancient churches, while enjoying a magnificent panorama from an exceptionally peaceful setting. To the N of the town of Tinos, the town's main road leaves to the r. a track to the hill of Xombourgo crowned by a Venetian fortress (1½hrs' climb from Xynara, residence of the Catholic bishop). The remains of the island's antique capital, a 7th-century BC sanctuary and enceinte, have been revealed on this hillside. Further along the main road, another fork to the r. leads to Loutra, a verdant well-situated village, with an old Jesuit convent and a French college run by Ursuline nuns; further on, Komi (8mls/13km from Tinos) and Kalloni (9.4mls/15km).

Following the summits of the island to the NE, the main road leads to Kardiani (8.7mls/14km), crossing a vale dotted with dovecotes; beautiful view.

13mls (21km): Ystierna, with beautiful gardens and a church with domes faced with faience; beach of Ormos, 1.2mls (2km).

14.4mls (23km): Pyrgos, big village with a strong artistic tradition where craftsmen still work marble. You can see the house where the painter Yannoulis Healpas was born and work by pupils of the School of Fine Arts. The fountains are ornamented with marble, which is also used to pave the streets.

15.6mls (25km): Panormos, port of Pyrgos, where marble is loaded, very beautiful * beach. The quarries are still worked (green marble); they are sited further N., near Marias.

T | Tiryns**

Route maps 6 and 7.

Argos, 4.4mls (7km) – Mycenae, 12.5mls (20km) – Nauplia, 3.1mls (5km).

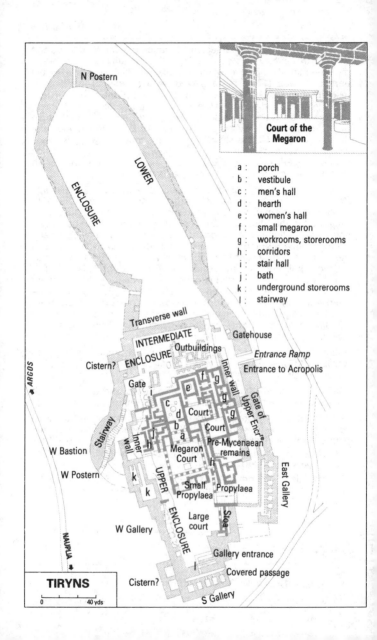

Court of the Megaron

a : porch
b : vestibule
c : men's hall
d : hearth
e : women's hall
f : small megaron
g : workrooms, storerooms
h : corridors
i : stair hall
j : bath
k : underground storerooms
l : stairway

N Postern

LOWER

ENCLOSURE

ARGOS

Transverse wall

INTERMEDIATE

Cistern?   ENCLOSURE   Outbuildings

Gatehouse

Entrance Ramp

Entrance to Acropolis

Gate

Inner wall

Gate of Upper Encre

Court

Court

W Bastion

Stairway

Inner wall

Megaron Court

Pre-Mycenaean remains

W Postern

East Gallery

Propylaea

UPPER

Small Propylaea

W Gallery

ENCLOSURE

Large court

Stoa

NAUPLIA

Gallery entrance

Covered passage

Cistern?

S Gallery

TIRYNS

0   40 yds

Undoubtedly because visitors do not see them until they have reached their foot, the walls of Tiryns, although in a less exceptional setting, are an even more astonishing sight than are those at Mycenae. Pausanias, the 2nd-century AD geographer, attributed their construction to the Cyclopes, thus enshrining them in legend. This impressive masterpiece of military architecture, is still being excavated.

A CYCLOPEAN LABOUR. There was something prodigious about such an accumulation of enormous blocks and legend was inevitably called on to explain it. Thus Tiryns is supposed to have been founded by Proetus, twin brother of Acrisius, king of Argos, with the help of Lycian Cyclopes who were very strong, and possessed only one eye.

THE LABOURS OF HERACLES. The successors of Proetus were Perseus, Amphitryon and a certain Eurystheus who was the instigator of some other labours – those of Heracles. We know that this hero, after killing the children he had by Megara, had to serve Eurystheus for 12 years in order to purify himself.

Hoping to be rid of this over-valorous servant, Eurystheus thought up 12 labours which he believed were impossible. However, Heracles acquired a reputation as a redresser of wrongs by triumphing in all these tests.

ANOTHER OF SCHLIEMANN'S DISCOVERIES. Archaeology also contributed to the knowledge of the site. Schliemann, covered in glory after his prodigious discovery of Mycenae, previously believed to be mythical or the product of Homer's imagination, carried out the first excavations there in 1884, in the company of Dorpfeld. Resumed in 1926–27 and more recently, they have made it possible to establish the chronology of the site. It was inhabited from the lower Helladic (3rd millenium BC) and already comprised a palace with a circular plan 92ft (28m) in diameter. The circumference of the mound was fortified during the middle Helladic (2000–1600 BC) and the housing quarter overflowed on to the plain to the S. The fortifications were altered in the 16th century. There was undoubtedly a palace, but subsequent changes removed it, except for a few stucco remains.

THE CYCLOPES AT WORK. Lastly, c.1400 BC, the ramparts you see today were built, if not by the Lycian Cyclopes of legend, by anonymous workmen, no doubt slaves or subjects of the kings of Tiryns. This was certainly a long-term project and changes were made, notably on the E and S façades between 1350 and 1250. The extraordinary casemates lodged in the walls, the great gate and the lower enceinte date from this period. The palace was not neglected and c.1200, i.e. just before the Dorian invasion destroyed the Mycenaean civilization, it was rebuilt or altered to the form you see today.

After the destruction of the palace, Tiryns still had the rather modest historical role of rival to Argos. It took part in the Battle of Plataea in 479, in spite of the hostility of its neighbour, which finally conquered it in 468 BC.

Open: daily, summer 08.00–18.00 or 19.00, Sun. 09.00–18.00; winter, 09.00–16.00, Sun. 10.00–16.30; entrance fee.

THE ACROPOLIS. Access is by a ramp which is 15ft (4.60m) wide and so could be used by chariots. At the top, you reach the main entrance dominated by two reinforcements of the rampart which, at this point is no less than 24ft 6in (7.50m) thick.

**Enceinte – It rests on the crest of a rocky hummock which descends from the S (where the palace is) to the N. The walls are built of cyclopean masonry with the help of irregular blocks (the largest weigh some 13t.), partly hammer-dressed. Other sections, to the W, exhibit less crude masonry with more regular courses, tighter joints and an external facing. The thickness of the walls varies between 23 and 33ft (7 and 10m). It is broken by salients, half moons and bastions with casemates, the thickness of which attains 57ft 5ins (17.5m) in the S. The crest, undoubtedly crenellated, was of sun-dried brick.

Gate of the upper enceinte – In the passage running to the l., between the external rampart and the enceinte of the palace, there is a gate like the Lion Gate at Mycenae, and with very similar dimensions. In the monolithic threshold, note the holes for the pivots of folding doors and the holes in the gateposts made to receive the cross-bar lodged in the left-hand wall.

Great Propylaea – You cross a terrace, once lined with a kind of wooden loggia, above casemates (vaulted rooms) which served as shops in time of peace and as shelters in time of war. The external facing of the rampart has collapsed, leaving the six casemates bare, but they were built into the mass of the wall. The great propylaea, the threshold of which consists of a blue flagstone, formed the entrance of honour into the palace. A corridor to the r. led to the gynaeceum (women's quarters).

Great court – It was surrounded by the rampart on three sides and by the palace to the r. To the l., at the S end, five casemates are built into the thickness of the wall; they were served by a gallery, the floor of which is 23ft (7m) below the court.

Palace – Nothing much is left except the foundations. It was reached by a small propylaeum which led to a small inside court, the ground of which is still covered with cement. To the r. of the entrance a square mass of masonry represents the royal altar with its sacrificial pit. To the r. and l. of the court are two porticoes and some halls reserved for visitors and servants. The palace proper opened opposite. Its main room or megaron was preceded by a small portico and a vestibule. In the centre was the massive round hearth, 10ft 9½ins (3.3m) in diameter, inside four wooden columns on a stone base which supported the ceiling. The palace also had a bathroom (plan, j). The women's quarters or gynaeceum also comprised a megaron (plan, e) opening on to an internal court.

W postern – A secret passage, one of the most striking features of the acropolis, gave access to it by a well-preserved staircase inside the thickness of the wall. Note the corbelled vault of the postern.

Near the NW corner of the acropolis, two galleries have been found; after traversing the wall of the enceinte, they lead to an artificial cavity forming a reservoir with two springs which obviously supplied the acropolis in times of siege. Here again, the two galleries are built of cyclopean masonry and have corbelled vaulting.

The ground is covered with large flagstones, except at some points where there must have been wooden staircases. These galleries may be the 'tombs' of the two daughters of Proteus, Lysippe and Iphianassa, mentioned by Pausanias (II, 25, 8–9).

Various buildings isolated from the lower enceinte by a transverse wall stood on the terrace beyond the palace. Excavations carried out in recent years by the German Archaeological School have already shown that this lower part of the enceinte was successively, in the 2nd millennium BC, a necropolis and a residential area; several Mycenaean houses have been uncovered. The excavations continue.

Trikkala

Route map 11.

Kalambaka, 13.1mls (21km) – Karditsa, 16.2mls (26km) – Larisa, 38.1mls (61km) – Pop: 34,974.

In the heart of the Thessalian plain whose horses were once famous throughout Greece, Trikkala could be considered as a place of pilgrimage for doctors, like the sanctuary of Cos. The recent resumption of excavations in the town has in fact stimulated interest in the oldest and most celebrated Asclepieion in the antique world. It was sited in this very city of Tricca which is reputed to have had the doctor – god Asclepius as king.

Trikkala, its eastern character debased by the recent introduction of some sham modernism, has not much to attract the visitor. We might just mention the excavation site of what was probably the famous Asclepieion between the main square and the church of Hagios Nikolaos, to the r. of the road to Kalambaka (Odhos Vassileos Constantinou). With a little imagination you can conjure up the vanished splendour of this large Roman building from the 2nd century AD, but founded as early as the Hellenistic period, containing mosaic pavements such as the panel of the legend of Lycurgus and Ambrosia, from the 2nd century AD. Opposite the church of Phaneromeni, some hundred yards to the W of the Asclepieion, a small archaeological collection (in an ancient Balkan house; no admission fee). At the exit from the town in the direction of Karditsa, the sizeable remains of an ancient mosque with a truncated minaret built in 1550 by Sinan Pasha, later the church of Hagios Constantinos (16th century). The hill dominating the town is crowned by the remains of a Byzantine fortress (Frourion) erected on Hellenistic remains.

CHURCH OF PORTA PANAGIA

(73.1mls/21km). Take the Pili road to the SW.

7.5mls (12km): to the l., the road for Gomfi (0.9mls/1.5km), the ancient Gomphi, which controlled the pass from Thessaly into Epirus. The place was fortified by Philip II. The Byzantines established the town of Epitopia there.

11.9mls (19km): Pili, at the entrance to the Pass of Portaes. About 1 mile (1.5km) upstream, on the other bank, the basilica of Porta Panagia was founded in 1283; it preserves mosaics from that period and frescoes from the first half of the 15th century.

3.1mls (5km) from Pili, perched above the village, is the very large monastery of Dousiko (16th century) with no fewer than 336 cells and a large 18th-century church.

The road continues through superb scenery to Elati (16.2mls/26km), at the foot of Mt Kerketion (6,234ft/1,900m), then to Pertouli (23.7mls/38km), at an altitude of 3,937ft (1,200m) (end of asphalted road).

■ Tripolis

Route maps 6, 7 and 8.

Andritsena, 50mls (80km) – Argos 36.9mls (59km) – Kalamata, 58.1mls (93km) – Nauplia, 44.4mls (71km) – Olympia 81.2mls (130km) – Pylos (Navarino), 85.6mls (137km) – Pop: 18,500 – capital of the admin. region of Arcadia.

Tripolis, founded in the Middle Ages to replace the three derelict ancient cities of the plain, is an important crossroads in the centre of a plateau, where a very animated bazaar will make you feel that you are in the Orient.

1 TEGEA (5.6mls/9km; by the road to Sparta and to the left at 2.5mls/4km).

To reach Tegea directly from Argos, you can turn l. at Steno (a few miles before you get to Tripolis) on to an asphalted road which will take you there (3.7mls/6km), passing Lithovounia (1.2mls/2km) and Stadio (2.5mls/4km), which you traverse going almost straight ahead. If you come from Sparta, you can also make directly for Tegea by turning r. a few miles before Tripolis.

4.4mls (7km): Palea Episkopi; in the park in front of a modern basilica, a mosaic (now under a concrete shelter) from a palaeo-Christian church from the 1st half of the 5th century, depicts sea creatures, busts of people and the Four Rivers of Paradise at the corners (Geon, Phison, Tigris and Euphrates) separated by allegories of the months, grouped in pairs. The modern basilica is on the site of a theatre erected at Tegea by Antiochus IV Epiphanes (175–164 BC).

5.6mls (9km): Tegea (or Alea), modern village near the ruins of Tegea's most famous sanctuary, the temple of Athena Alea, whose cult was introduced in the 9th century BC by King Aleus and which was a celebrated place of asylum (Orestes and Pausanias, the king of Sparta, found refuge there). A very ancient town, formed by the uniting of nine rural demes, Tegea fought for the independence of Arcadia against Sparta, whose hegemony she accepted c.550 BC. After the victory of Leuctra, Thebes restored her autonomy.

Under the Frankish domination, Tegea was one of the most powerful cities in Morea and seat of a barony until 1296.

The Archaic temple, burnt down in 395–394, was rebuilt and decorated by the sculptor Scopas, probably about 360, to house the old ivory statue of Athena, the work of Endoeus, and the corpse of the Calydonian wild boar, a memento of the heroic hunt by Atlanta and Meleager, a hunt which supplied the theme for the sculptural decoration on the pediment. All you can now see of the temple and the altar are the foundations and the lower courses.

220yds (200m) in front of the temple, you can visit a small museum which contains a few carved fragments of the temple, and some originals and casts of sculptures in the manner of Scopas (notably the torso of the nymph Hagno), of the federal altar of Tegea, of bronzes, ceramics, etc.

Open: summer, 09.00–15.00; winter 10.00–14.30; Sun. 10.00–15.00; closed Tues.; entrance fee.

In particular you will note, in the hall to the r., a Roman sarcophagus decorated with a relief inspired by the *Iliad*: Achilles, standing in his chariot, drags Hector's body round the ruins of Troy in the dust. In the next hall, you will see small geometric bronzes, vases and terracotta objects from various periods (from the Neolithic to the 3rd century BC) and some funerary stelae.

2 MANTINEA AND ORCHOMENUS (8.7mls/14km and 20.5mls/33km; by the direct road from Olympia, turning r. at 5.3mls/8.5km for the first site, and at 15.6mls/25km for the second). These two sites were once important Arcadian towns, a fact worth mentioning as they are of no interest today. The first was defended by an oval enceinte of 4,311yds (3,942m), built in 370 BC. Now only the jumbled remains of a temple, the agora and several theatres lie there. The second contained a sanctuary of Artemis Mesopolitis, excavated by the French School of Athens, and, in the upper city, a 6th-century Doric temple consecrated to Apollo or Aphrodite.

3 PALANTIUM AND ASEA (5.6mls/9km and 10.6mls/17km by the Kalamata road: the first site is to the l. at 5.6mls/9km, the second to the r. near the road). These are two more sites mentioned for the sake of their historical attractions. The first, excavated by an Italian team, has revealed the remains of a megaron, a 5th-century BC temple and,

0.9mls (1.5km) to the S of the acropolis, an Archaic temple consecrated to Poseidon and Athena Soteira. The second site, an acropolis excavated by Swedish archaeologists, has revealed continuous occupation from the Neolithic to the middle Helladic (2000–1600 BC), as well as the remains of Hellenistic fortifications.

4 KARYE (26.9mls/43km; by the Sparta road and l. at 21.2mls/34km). You can see a mural dated to 1638 in the monastery of Karye.

Veria (Verria)

Route map 12.

Edessa, 30.6mls (49km) – Kozani, 38mls (61km) – Thessaloniki, 48.7mls (78km) – Pop: 30,425 – capital of the admin. region of Ematheia.

An animated, typically Balkan town, Veria will hold the attention of lovers of Byzantine painting, with its churches scattered in a labyrinth of alleyways redolent of the Orient. But you should not neglect its vicinity. Recent excavations at Vergina, some 9.4mls (15km) away, have yielded treasures (on show in the museum of Thessaloniki) and are a must on any Greek archaeological circuit.

IN THE STEPS OF ST PAUL. Veria, the ancient Beroea, appeared in history in the late 5th or early 4th century BC. This was the first Macedonian city to surrender to the Romans (in 168) who made it the capital of a 'Republic'. Pompey spent the winter of 49–48 BC there before being beaten by Caesar at Pharsalia (Farsala). Around 54, St Paul came to preach the new faith to the town's large Jewish community. When the administration of the empire was reorganized, Diocletian made it one of the capitals of Macedonia. It was occupied by the Serbs in the 14th century, and then the Turks established a military colony there.

Near the fork of the Thessaloniki and Edessa roads, you can still see some remains of the rampart which encircled the ancient city, with a town gate and two towers, one Hellenistic, the other with a square plan, from the 3rd century AD. In the lower town you can visit several churches, often hard to find. Following a practice intended to fool the watchful Turks, they were built at the far end of courtyards and there is often nothing outside to show that they exist. We recommend that you engage a guide rather than waste time looking for them on your own. Ask to see the church of Hagios Ioannis Theologos, decorated with murals, the church of Hagios Christos (key in the archaeological museum), one of the most interesting with its painted decorations (c.1315), the church of Hagia Potini, also with frescoes, as well as the churches of Hagios Georgios, Hagios Nikolaos, etc. On the edge of the plateau on which the town lies, you will visit an archaeological museum with rich finds from a necropolis and Roman baths, from an Iron Age cemetery at Vergina (weapons and jewellery) and from various sites in the province (sculptures, architectural fragments), as well as a collection of Byzantine icons. You can also see painted panels from houses of the Turkish period.

1 **VERGINA** (just before reaching Palatitsia; 9.4mls/15km). Vergina has long been known for a Macedonian tomb and Hellenistic palace, as well as a vast older necropolis, made up of small tumuli. Scholars also knew of the existence, in the middle of the village, of an enormous artificial tumulus 130yds (120m) in diameter and 33ft (10m) high, known as the great tomb. This was virtually untouched by modest digs until Professor M. Andronikos of the University of Thessaloniki undertook its systematic excavation using modern mechanical equipment. During the summer of 1977, the patient researches of Professor Andronikos were crowned with success: at a level sometimes 33ft (10m) below the primitive surface of the tumulus three adjoining monuments were discovered. The first, reduced to its foundations 31ft 6in by 26ft 3in (9.6 by 8m) and a few collapsed blocks of the upper courses, was built on the ancient ground level. Its purpose is not clear, but it might have been a heroön rather than a tomb. Construction seems to date to the 2nd half of the 4th century BC. The other two monuments, which were covered by a tumulus of red earth about 100ft (30m) in diameter and 13ft (4m) high, are tombs. The first, of the 'cist' type, is a parallelepiped, the internal dimensions of which are 11ft 6ins by 6ft 10¼ins by 9ft 10ins (3.5 by 2.09 by 3m). Completely looted, it contained no objects, but the walls are decorated with magnificent frescoes. The second, of a monumental type with a semi-Doric, semi-Ionic façade, comprises a chamber, 14ft 7½ins (4.46m) square and 17ft 4½ins (5.3m) high and an antechamber or vestibule of 12ft by 14ft 7½ins (3.66 by 4.46m) communicating with the main chamber by a marble door with two wings. The two rooms were discovered intact. They contained exceptionally rich material (temporarily exhibited in the museum of Thessaloniki). The façade still bears a fairly well preserved painted frieze, 18ft 3ins (5.56m) long by 3ft 9½ins (1.16m) high. In 1978 Professor Andronikos discovered another tomb comparable to the preceding one. Unfortunately, the painted façade is badly damaged, but the artefacts inside, which included numerous silver vases, two gold crowns and various bronze objects (a pair of greaves, strigils, lance heads, etc.) are intact.

The monumental character of these two tombs, as well as the richness of the grave goods and the quality of the decoration, clearly indicate that the dead were of high social rank. The presence in the two-chambered tomb of two massive chests made of gold, containing bones dyed purple or wrapped in purple and gold cloth, as well as a diadem and two ivory portraits of Philip II and Alexander, shows that this is a royal tomb – perhaps that of Philip II, the father of Alexander (d. 336 BC), if the material actually dates, as it seems to, from the 3rd quarter of the 4th century BC. Therefore, the site of Vergina is definitely that of ancient Aegae, the capital of Macedonia, where the royal necropolis was located according to ancient evidence, although most scholars had located it at Edessa until now. According to Plutarch, this necropolis was looted by the Galatians in the 3rd century BC, but it is not impossible that the looting was only partial and that certain tombs, including the monumental tombs (more difficult to violate), escaped it.

In 1979, the removal of the upper layers of the tumulus in the N and NE sectors led to the discovery of two brick tombs with rather ordinary artefacts and no connection with the royal tombs. During the digs, more than 70 funerary stelae datable between 400 and 280 BC were collected, the majority of them painted and inscribed. The names of the dead are purely Greek (for example, Alcetas, Hermon, Theocritus, Theodocus, Theophanes, Xenocrates, etc.), which is of the greatest interest for the study of the population of Macedon in the 4th century BC. The digs of 1980 saw the discovery of a new tomb to the W of the others. In a very ruinous state and completely looted, it has the peculiarity, so far unique in Macedonian tombs, of being preceded by a prostoön with four free-standing Doric columns in front of the façade, instead of being attached to it.

Coming from Veria, you reach Vergina by leaving on your r. the direct Palatitsia road, a road which enables you to rejoin, some 12.5mls (20km) beyond Vergina, the main Eizoni-Katerini axis, passing the villages of Palatitsia (1.2mls/2km), Meliti (5mls/8km), Hagia Triada (8.1mls/13km), Trilophia (10mls/16km), Angathia (10.6mls/17km) and Kypseli (12.5mls/20km); in this way, you arrive about 3.7mls (6km) to the N of the little town of Aiginion and 1.2mls (2km) to the N of the hamlet of Megali Gephira.

0.9mls (1.5km) from the crossroads, take a road to the r. after traversing most of the village. 550yds (500m) from the fork, about 50yds (50m) to the l. of the road, you will see a very beautiful Macedonian tomb from the middle of the 3rd century BC, with an Ionic façade (four engaged half-columns). You will note the wings of the marble gate and in the funerary chamber a marble throne (traces of encaustic painting), as well as a table or banquet couch.

0.6mls (1km) from the fork, you will come, by the same road, to the entrance to the site of the palace of Palatitsia (*open in summer daily from 09.00–18.30; 10.30 to 16.00, Sun. and holidays*), built in the Hellenistic period, probably in the reign of Antigonus Gonatas (278–240 BC) and enlarged at the end of the 3rd or beginning of the 2nd century BC. The palace, now reduced to its foundations, consisted of a vast central court surrounded by porticoes with Doric columns. Some halls were adorned with mosaic pavements. One very large one has been put back in place in a hall, access to which is by a beautiful marble threshold. Around a central rosette, there is rich floral decoration in a circle inscribed in a square; there are female figures at the corners of the square. The site of the palace is very pleasant; on a fine day, there is a very extensive view to the NNE.

Excavation carried out in the summer of 1982 resulted in the discovery of several buildings in the fields which extend between the

3rd century tomb and the palace, and in particular of the city's theatre, just below the palace. As of October 1982, only the orchestra had been partially uncovered.

Returning to the fork, take the road to the r. which descends towards the road to Palatitsia. About 110yds (100m) on the l., you will see the site of the large tumulus excavated by Professor M. Andronikos. In view of the continuing excavation and the many problems of preservation and arrangement which arise, admission will certainly not be authorized for several years. Nevertheless, we give a brief summary of the monuments uncovered by the end of the summer of 1984.

Below the ruined building which may have been a heroön (see above), there is a 'cist' or prehistoric sepulchral tomb, decorated inside with **frescoes, genuine masterpieces, with delicate and varied colours (mainly blue, violet, ochre, and yellow). On the long N side there is a representation of Hermes, running ahead of a chariot on which Hades is carrying off Persephone; behind the chariot is a female personage surely to be identified as Cyane, the friend of Persephone, trying in vain to stop her abduction. On the shorter E side there is one single personage: an unidentified seated female figure, perhaps the dead nymph, if it was a woman's tomb, or the goddess Demeter. On the long S side the painting is less well preserved, but you can make out three feminine silhouettes, possibly the Moerae. The W wall has no figured decoration, but a band with griffins facing each other alternating with palmettes runs below the main scenes of the three other sides. This decoration, reminiscent of that on lekythoi with a white ground from the 2nd half of the 5th century, must date from the 4th century BC. According to Professor M. Andronikos, it could be the work of the great painter of the middle of that century, Nicomachus.

A short distance to the NE, roughly in the centre of the primitive tumulus, is the great tomb, the **façade of which is a masterpiece of architecture and painting. The lower part, completely uncovered, has a large door with two wings (height about 11ft 6ins/3.5m; of the greyish-blue marble) flanked by two engaged Doric half columns. Above is a Doric entablature with well-preserved polychrome decoration (red, white and blue). This entablature with its architrave and frieze with metopes and triglyphs was protected by a (partly damaged) cornice, above which unfolds, following a very elegant and symmetrical composition, the great **'Ionic' painted frieze, depicting an extraordinary hunting scene in which ten characters take part (seven on foot and three on horseback), as well as dogs confronting wild beasts (deer, wild boar, lion) set in a forest near a mountain. Although the colours have partly worn off you can still clearly distinguish the yellows, violets, pinks and coffee-coloured browns. The document, which probably dates from the 3rd quarter of the 4th century, is of major importance for the study of great Classical Greek painting. Another cornice decorated with polychrome mouldings sits above this frieze.

A few yards to the NE of the monumental tomb is the façade of another smaller tomb of the same type (the one which was discovered in 1978). There was a painted frieze here, too, but it was unfortunately executed on a perishable material (wood or leather) stuck to the stone and so has been lost for ever. The façade does not have a colonnade attached, but it is adorned with two large shields in relief (one to the l., the other to the r. of the door). The interior of the tomb still has its painted decoration. It consists of a bigae race (chariots drawn by two horses) which unfolds in a narrow frieze along the walls of the ante-chamber. The horses stand out in white against a dark blue ground; each chariot is seen from a slightly different angle. As for the tomb discovered in 1980, it is situated to the W of the preceding tombs, but it is in a very dilapidated state.

In 1981, a group of three very interesting new Macedonian tombs was discovered about half a mile (1km) from the village, to the r. of the road to Palatitsia (access road just beyond a modern bridge may be closed to the public). They probably date from the 3rd century BC. The largest, preceded by an entrance corridor or dromos, consists of two rooms: the rectangular antechamber (about 10ft by 4ft/3m by 1.2m) with a ceiling with consoles, and the chamber proper, which is roughly square (sides about 10ft/3m). It is vaulted, with a large stone kline (bed) in the corner in relation to the left of the carved door, which is both richly painted and (legs in relief with floral motifs, painted bands: little Dionysus playing with a panther, seated man and griffin). The *façade, about 16ft 6ins (5m) high, is pierced by a gate with two studded halves (about 8ft/2.5m high and 4ft/1.2m wide), framed by four engaged Doric half columns. The Doric entablature is complete. The other two more modest tombs have only one room. The largest (about 13ft by 10ft/4m by 3m) contains in the axis of the door a well-preserved stone throne with a *trompe-l'oeil* footstool and chairback in a checkerboard pattern.

But it is mainly remarkable for its *façade. In the free space (some 11ft 6ins/3.5m wide by 4ft 7ins/1.4m high) above the gate are painted three well-spaced figures: to the l., a young man, showing his r. profile, wearing a violet himation, seated beside a shield placed vertically; in the centre, a young man standing, face front, in a very supple pose, his r. hand raised to lean on a lance held vertically (quite complicated polychrome clothing); to the r., holding out a crown to a young man, a standing woman, showing her l. profile with bare arms, clad in a long chiton treated in a rich range of colours; the elongated figures stand out against a white ground.

The third, smaller tomb (about 10ft by 10ft/3m by 3m) contains a stone sarcophagus; a pediment projects above the door. No funerary material has been found in any of the three tombs, which were looted in antiquity.

2 LEFCADIA NAOUISSIS (11.2mls/18km by the Edessa road). 7.5mls (12km) from Veria you leave on your l. the road to Naoussa, centre of a region producing a celebrated red wine, and Seli, a winter sports resort (alt. 4,659ft/1,420m) on the wooded slopes of Mt Vermion,

2.2mls (3.5km) beyond this fork, about 660yds (600m) to the r. of the road (take a track just beyond the bridge and cross a railway line), you can visit a splendid Macedonian *hypogeum from the early 3rd century BC, with a façade (Doric below, Ionic above) decorated with well-preserved paintings. You will note those on the lower zone depicting from l. to r. a warrior carrying a lance and a sword (probably the dead man), the god Hermes as Psychopompos 'leader of souls', then beyond the door, two of the three judges of the Tribunal of the Underworld, Aeacus and Rhadamanthus. Above the first order you can distinguish a row of triglyphs and metopes with paintings depicting a centauromachy (a battle between Greeks and centaurs) and still higher, above a small painted cornice, a stucco frieze painted with scenes of combat between Greek cavalry and infantry, and barbarians, probably Persians. 165yds (150m) further on, to the l. of the same track, you reach another tomb, accessible by a dromos some 33ft (10m) wide (not open to the public at present). Two more tombs are visible. One is accessible by a track to the r. before you reach the bridge; and the other is in an orchard on the other side of the road just before the bridge. This, like the preceding one, is a Macedonian tomb, known as the tomb of Lyson Callicles, decorated with paintings in good condition (ask a guardian of the great tomb to accompany you).

 # Volos (Volo)

Route maps 2 and 11.

Athens, 147mls (235km) – Kalambaka (Meteora), 85.6mls (137km) – Lamia, 69.4mls (111km) – Larisa 34.4mls (55km) – Thessaloniki, 142mls (227km) – Pop: 51,290 – capital of the admin. region of Magnesia – archbishopric.

The third largest port of Greece, Volos is situated on the edge of the Gulf of Volos and at the foot of Mt Pelion. The establishment of maritime links with Syria, realizing Greece's desire for an opening to the Near East, resulted in the town's financial and industrial development. No fewer than five large towns preceded Volos – from the Neolithic age onwards. First there were the Neolithic cities of Sesklo and Dimini (the remains still exist in the vicinity), and then Iolcus, the capital of Mycenaean Thessaly. Long before the Trojan war, a king of Iolcus, Pelias, incited Jason to set off to capture the Golden Fleece in his famous ship, the Argo. In the historical period, the ports of Pagasae and Demetrias, of which Volos is the heir, bear witness to the vitality of the region and the need for Thessaly to possess a large port on the Pagasitic gulf (gulf of Volos). From Volos, a modern town of limited interest, you can set out to visit all these sites and especially the green peak of Pelion, also legendary because the famous centaur Chiron, who taught illustrious pupils such as Jason and Achilles, lived there in a cave. If you wish to avoid staying in Volos in the full heat of summer, there is no need for you, too, to become a troglodyte. Since Chiron's day there has been a good deal of building on Pelion, which now has some excellent hotels.

The town consists of a modern district by the sea (promenade where you can enjoy the cool of the evening, Argonafton Street) and old quarters where the houses rise in layers on abrupt slopes to a height of 2,625ft (800m). Between the two, but very near the port, is the bazaar, the axis of which is formed by Ermou Street, where you will make astonishing discoveries such as the shoe shops which resemble grottoes covered with glittering gilt, with walls and ceilings entirely covered with shoes and slippers. The site of the ancient Iolcos, marked by a tumulus, is at the exit from the town by road to Larisa, to the r., between the railway lines and a river, frequently dry, which may be the ancient Anaurus.

Excavations carried out here have brought to light the remains of two Mycenaean palaces, the older of which was built c.1425 BC. It may have been the palace of Pelias, Jason's uncle who had usurped the throne of his brother Aeson. We know that Jason's mother, fearing for her son, had him taken to the centaur Chiron on Pelion. During his stay, an oracle revealed to Pelias that a man would arrive at his palace, wearing only one sandal, and that he would steal his throne. On his return to Iolcus, Jason lost a sandal in the Anaurus. To get rid of this trouble-maker, Pelias sent him to distant Colchis in search of the Golden Fleece. Thanks to the sorceress Medea, Jason and the Argonauts were able to overcome all the dangers they found in their path. On their return, Medea killed Pelias and fled to Corinth with Jason.

The second, slightly more recent palace, which was destroyed by fire c.1200 BC, may have belonged to Eumelus.

THE ARCHAEOLOGICAL MUSEUM (1.2mls/2km from the centre, near the sea, to the r. of the Tsangarada road) houses the most important collection of Greek painting (more than 200 Hellenistic painted stelae from Demetrias), collections of Archaic stelae from Phalanna (to the N of Larisa) and stelae found at Pherae (3rd century BC to the Roman period), as well as sculptures, finds from the Neolithic sites of Sesklo, Dimini, Pyrassus, and Iolcus, Mycenaean objects from Thessaly, Geometric and Archaic bronzes and vases found at Pherae, etc. Two large halls are arranged in a way that is both instructive and attractive. Hall 3 is entirely devoted to Neolithic Thessaly and the hall at the end, to the l., to burial artefacts from all periods, with reconstructions of tombs.

Open daily, summer 09.00–14.00, Sun. 09.00–13.00; winter, 09.00–13.30 and 16.00–18.00, Sun. 10.00–16.30; entrance fee; closed Tues.

In the medieval suburb of Ano Volos, 1.2mls (2km) from the town centre, a house of Anakassia, with a fresco by Theophilos, has become a museum devoted to this primitive painter from the beginning of the century (*open 10.00–13.00 and 17.00–20.00*).

VICINITY OF VOLOS

1 GORITSA (0.9mls/1.5km beyond the museum). The road runs between the sea and a rocky mound, long regarded as the site of the Acropolis of Demetrias. In fact, recent excavations have shown that the enceinte sheltered a vast military camp with geometrically aligned barracks and capable of housing 20,000 men. It was undoubtedly established when Demetrias was founded.

2 PAGASAE AND DEMETRIAS (2.5mls/4km and 3.1mls/5km; ruins mainly interesting to the visitor with a keen interest in archaeology). Leave by the road to Lamia and Athens.

1.9mls (3km): You pass the foot of a hill where the N rampart of Demetrias stood: it extended along the ridge to the acropolis. In the vicinity was a temple consecrated to Hera. Take a road to the l. for Pefkakia (0.6mls/1km). Pagasae was the port of Iolcus (2.2mls/3.5km) and then of Pherae (8.7mls/14km). According to one version of the legend of Jason, it was there that the leader of the Argonauts built the Argo and embarked for Colchis. The town gave its name to the Pagasitic gulf; it was the home of a famous oracle. Flourishing in the 4th century under the domination of Pherae, it was taken in the 4th century by Philip II of Macedon, who annexed it to Magnesia. After the foundation of Demetrias, it came under the domination of that city, which incorporated part of Pagasae in its enceinte.

Demetrias, together with Pella, was the favourite city of the Antigoni, and their main port. Flaminius took it in 196 BC and its fortifications were partly dismantled on the orders of the Roman Senate in 167.

The enceinte of Demetrias has a perimeter of 4.9mls (7.8km) and comprises 87 towers, without counting those on the acropolis. The painted stelae now on show in the museum of Volo were discovered in the enormous towers of the SE and SW salients, hastily enlarged c.50 BC. Only the remains of the rampart standing on the hill to the r. of the road are still visible. The others, between the road and the sea, are barely discernible.

Many remains of the town, which was very large, have been or are still being uncovered, notably the remains of a palace arranged around a central peristyle above the agora where there was a temple of Artemis. You can reach the palace from the Pefkakia road. 820yds (750m) from the fork from the main road, take the mediocre road to the r. which climbs to a plateau (about 1,312ft/400m) with a football field; from there you ascend on foot to the SW and reach the palace hill in a few minutes. Some 330ft (100m) below the palace, near the shore, are the ruins of Basilica A, from the 4th and 5th centuries, with well-preserved mosaics, unfortunately covered over. 220yds (200m) to the W of the basilica, a large building with three rooms and an apse also has sumptuous mosaics with geometric designs (undoubtedly from the 4th century; they, too, are covered). Excavations at Pefkakia have shown that the site was occupied from the beginning of the Bronze Age (c.2500 BC) and during the Mycenaean period.

2.5mls (4km): to the r, is the theatre of Demetrias, which was the theatre of Pagasae before the foundation of this town by Demetrius Poliorcetes in 294 BC. It is hollowed out at one end of a rocky hillock on which stood the royal palace of Demetrius, perhaps on the site of the ancient residence of the tyrants of Pherae.

A little beyond the theatre, the road intersects a ruined aqueduct, built in the Roman period to supply Demetrias.

2.9mls (4.6km): the road winds between two hills, through which the rampart of Demetrias passed. The circuit wall of Pagasae was also traced along the flanks of the hill to the l.

3.1mls (5km): to the r., a high hill with some remains of ramparts corresponds to the site of ancient Pagasae. The rampart was undoubtedly built in the 4th century BC, for in 353 Philip II of Macedon had to besiege the town in order to capture it.

3 DIMINI (4mls/6.5km: by the Larisa road and to the l. at 1.9mls/3km from the centre, i.e. 880yds/800m from the Larisa-Lamia crossroads). This site, mainly interesting to lovers of archaeology, has revealed the existence of a Neolithic city from the 4th millennium BC (ruins of a palace, houses and an enceinte, all reduced to their foundations), as well as Mycenaean tholos tombs. To reach it, turn r. twice (signs) in the village of Dimini (*open, summer 09.00–16.00, except Fri.*).

4 SESKLO (9.4mls/15km; by the Larisa road and l. at 6.6mls/10.5km). Lovers of archaeology will see the remains of a large palace and a palaeokastro, possibly Aesonia, the town of Aeson, Jason's father, on a prehistoric acropolis (Neolithic period) in a magnificent setting (*open, summer 09.00–13.00 and 16.00–18.00, except Thurs.*).

Recent excavations (especially in the sector to the r. of the road, about 220yds (200m) in front of the perimeter) have established the existence around the acropolis of a Neolithic site founded during the pre-ceramic period which reached its apogee in the middle Neolithic before it was destroyed, perhaps by fire, and abandoned c.4300 BC.

5 PHERAE (13.1mls/21km by the Larisa road). The modern village of Velestinon occupies the site of ancient Pherae, legendary residence of King Admetus, husband of Alcestis, whose sacrifice inspired a famous tragedy by Euripides and an opera by Gluck. Pherae was a particularly flourishing town in the 4th century BC under the tyrants Jason and Alexander, but only scanty vestiges remain today, notably an early 4th century BC rampart and the temple of Zeus Thaulios, founded in the 6th century BC and rebuilt in the 4th century. Recent researches have located the town's acropolis to the SE of the church of Panagia. A start has been made on uncovering the walls, which are quite well preserved.

11.9mls (19km) from Velestinon, in the direction of Larisa (turn r. at 8mls/3km), Petra, possibly the ancient Cercinium is an antique site on three hills dominating the shore of lake Viviis (ancient Boibeis), with the remains of a cyclopean enceinte with a perimeter of 5mls (8km), which probably makes it the largest Mycenaean fortress in Greece.

6 NEA ANCHIALOS (11.2mls/18km by the road to Lamia). This village occupies the site of the ancient Thessalian Thebes (Phthiotic Thebes) at the foot of the acropolis of ancient Pyrasus. The ruins of four palaeo-Christian churches uncovered by the Archaeological Society can be seen in an archaeological park, which is charmingly arranged.

Open: daily, summer 08.30–12.30 and 16.00–18.00, Sun. 09.00–15.00; winter 09.00–13.30 and 16.00–18.00, Sun. 10.00–16.30; entrance fee.

Beginning your visit on the outskirts of the village coming from Volos, you will see the ruins of the 5th century. Basilica A (St Demetrios), with three naves, near which a house with a paved court and a bath were uncovered. Further on are the remains of a vast porticoed court laid out on the site of an older building in the 3rd or 4th century AD and the ruins of the 5th-century Basilica B, where you will note the synthronon, a series of seats where the clergy sat on either side of the bishop's throne. Lastly, at the foot of a hill which was the acropolis of ancient Pyrasus, a palaeo-Christian building has been found. There are many older architectural elements in its foundations. The very old sanctuary of Demeter and Kore, mentioned in the poems of Homer, might have been situated in these parts.

Basilica C (of Archbishop Peter) from the late 4th or early 5th century, discovered on the Zorba terrain, was preceded by an atrium with a porticoed fountain originally reserved for scholastic use; it was altered in the age of Justinian, perhaps to serve as a religious school.

At the exit from Nea Anchialos by the Lamia road, some 330yds (300m) to the r. by the Evloghimenou road, a fourth basilica from the middle of the 7th century (Basilica D) has been uncovered. Its three naves were decorated with rather simple mosaics with geometric designs and birds. Recent digs have raised the number of basilicas so far found at Nea Anchialos to seven. The name of the donor of the last one, discovered in 1978, is given on an inscription engraved on a large stone block. He was a certain Martyrios.

At Nea Anchialos you can visit a small museum, with various architectural remains, inscriptions, mosaics, etc., from ancient Pyrasus and especially Christian Thebes.

7 ···**PELION** (circuit of 126mls/202km). Pelion is a mountainous mass formed of Achaean rocks and schists with a climate humid enough to produce a lush vegetation which is exceptional in Greece. The charm of its old houses (especially at Tsangarada and Zagora) and its churches, of a rather special type, add to the interest of this region, which was a refuge for Hellenic culture during the dark days of the Turkish domination. All the roads through this sometimes domesticated, sometimes wild Garden of Eden are tortuous (you will rarely average more than 15 or 18mls/25 or 30km per hour), but always charming amid the broom, ferns and heather, and the strident call of the cicadas. All the villages are surrounded by orchards with luxuriant vegetation. You will traverse the Aegean slope, domain of the (sometimes monumental) chestnut tree, the walnut, the hazelnut or, lower down, the olive tree, and the Pagasitic slope, domain of the

deliciously scented maquis, with pines, larches and heather on the heights, or the forest of olive trees dotted with isolated farms near the coast.

On the Aegean slope with its deep valleys, you will take an astonishing corniche road cut out of cliff sides which dominate the sea from a dizzy height. Sometimes it winds to the end of gorges, bare and gaping near the sea, above emerald creeks, leafy and mysterious near the mountain. Finally during the descent to Volos, your drive will become a panorama opening up incredibly broad horizons between earth and sky. Leave Volos by the Tsangarada road.

2.2mls (3.5km): Acropolis of Goritsa (see Vicinity of Volos, 1).

4.7mls (7km): Agria, on the edge of the gulf of Volos, with some attractive tavernas where seafood is served.

10mls (16km): Kato Gazea, where you leave a road to Milies on your l.

11.9mls (19km): Kala Nera, where you leave a road to Milies on your l.

16.9mls (27km): Afete, village with cubic houses on a series of terraces; *view of the gulf of Volos.

19.4mls (31km): leave to the l. the road to Tsangarada, which you will take a little later (see below, mile 58.1/km 93).

24.4mls (39km): Argalasti, with a pleasant little restaurant in a cool and shaded setting.

26.2mls (42km): leave a road for Chorton and Milina to your r. (see below). Shortly afterwards you will pass through Metochi, one of the villages of Pelion which has best preserved their old rustic character, in a splendid location.

30.3mls (48.5km): Lafkos. Another road to the r. for Milina (see below, mile 43.1/km 69).

32.8mls (52.5km): the road to Promiri continues straight ahead, but the little road to Platanaia to the r. is better.

36.6mls (58.5km): Platanaia, hamlet at the end of the world, anachronistic but indeed real, full of charm with its two large and quiet beaches.

 43.1mls (69km): return to Lafkos; go in the direction of Mina, a beach you will reach by a hairpin road offering superb *views of the gulf of Volos.

 46.9mls (75km): Milina, a quite modest seaside resort, but very pleasantly situated on the gulf of Volos; it is better to swim at Chorton, a small beach with warm calm water 1.9mls (3km) further on.

51.2mls (82km): return to the fork at mile 26.2 (km 42), near Metochi, where you turn l. to drive back to the fork of the Tsangarada road 58.1ms (93km), which you follow to the r. (see above, mile 19.4/km 31).

 62.8mls (100.5km): go l. to Milies (3.7ml/6km), small village where you can visit the church of Hagios and its library, as well as the church of the Taxiarchs (Archangels) Athanosios carved wooden iconostasis. Then return to the Tsangarada road.

80mls (128km): Tsangarada, village clinging to the slopes of a steep mountain, plunging down to the sea, which you can reach by a road to Mylopotamos (4.7mls/7.5km), a magnificent beach with limpid water and a little restaurant.

87.5mls (140km): to the r., 3.7mls (6km), Hagios Ioannis is a small resort nestling at the end of a creek.

93.7mls (150km): turn r. to Zagora (3.7mls/6km), a very pretty village with an extremely mild climate, surrounded by olive groves and chestnut groves, where you can visit the churches of Hagia Kyriaki and Hagios Georgios. A road from the village leads down to the charming beach of Horefto (3.1mls/5km).

101.2mls (162km): once back at the fork (mile 93.7/km 150), continue straight on to Volos on a road which rises on the slopes of Mt Pelion to cross the col of Khania (109.4mls/175km: skiing resort) at an alt. of 3,937ft (1,200m), from where you descend to the Pagasitic slope.

117.5mls (188km): Portaria, village at an alt. of 1,968ft (600m), a haven of cool in the height of summer, where you will see tall narrow old houses with wrought iron balconies full of flowers, the chapel of Hagii Anargyri (SS. Cosmas and Damian) and the monastery of Theotokos Portares (13th century).

At 1.9mls (3km), Makrinitsa is a pretty village clinging to a rocky ridge covered with cypresses and olive trees. You can visit the church of the Panagia, dated to 1272; old houses in the local style adapted as tourist lodgings by the GNTO. Beautiful view of the gulf of Volos from the central square, which is paved with marble.

126.2mls (202km): Volos.

■ Vytina

Route map 7.

Olympia, 53.1mls (85km) – Tripolis, 28mls (45km).

A mountain village at a height of 3,380ft (1,030m) surrounded by forests of fir trees.

■ Xanthi

Route map 14.

*Alexandroupolis, 73.7mls (118km) – Kavalla, 35mls (56km) –
Thessaloniki, 137.5mls (220km) – Pop: 24,867 – capital of an admin.
region.*

A small town, but a large agricultural market, on the site of the ancient
and medieval Xantheia. You can still see fortifications of the Byzantine
citadel (13th century) with its square and round towers and its big
walls on the heights near the monastery of the Taxiarchs. You can visit
a charming Museum of Popular Arts and Traditions installed in two
neo-Classical houses from the part of the old town that was preserved
(19–21, Antika Street, near the Metropolis).

Open: daily except Tues., 17.00–20.00; Sun. from 10.00–13.00.

You will see costumes, fabrics, wooden and copper furniture, tools
and jewellery made and used in Thrace.

VICINITY

1 TOXOTES (ancient Topirus-Poroi; 7.5mls/12km by the Kavala road).
At the mouth of the gorges of the River Nestos (which forms the
present-day boundary between Macedonia and Thrace) beyond the
bridge on the Macedonian side of the river, you see the remains of a
town identified with ancient Topirus and the Byzantine town of Poroi;
ruins of the town's Roman and Byzantine fortifications; ruins of
palaeo-Christian edifices (5th–6th centuries) outside the enceinte
near the village of Paradissos, and on the summit of a nearby rocky
hill. On the slopes of this hill you can find out inscriptions carved in
the rock and Roman tombs.

2 ABDERA (17.5mls/28km; by the Alexandroupolis road and r. at
5mls/8km). Beyond Abdira (13.1mls/21km), take an asphalted road to
the r. which leads to the ruins of ancient Abdera, of very limited
interest, where digs have exposed Hellenistic enceintes and the
remains of several buildings: workshops for producing terracotta
objects and 3rd century BC shops, Roman baths, traces of a
sanctuary consecrated to Cybele, of a villa decorated with a mosaic of
dolphins, etc. Near the entrance to the site, a vast Byzantine
necropolis (9th–11th centuries). Abdera was an important Ionian
colony, celebrated in the history of philosophy for the great school

which Leucippus founded there towards the middle of the 5th century BC. Democritus, looked on as the father of atomic theory, was an illustrious pupil. The Sophist Protagoras, mocked by Plato, was also a native of Abdera.

3 **PORTO LAGO** (15mls/24km by the Alexandroupolis road). You will see a region at sea level between sea and lake, a sort of Holland with its ponds and marshes, but also the ruins of a Byzantine church and a little monastery dedicated to St Nicholas on an islet. About 1.2mls (2km) to the SE by the sea, vestiges of antique Dikaia, founded at the beginning of the 6th century BC (remains of a 4th-century BC rampart, Hellenistic houses and the necropolis).

4 **ANASTASIOUPOLIS - PERITHEORION** (some 12.5mls/20km to the E, at Kaledes, to the S of the village of Amaxades, by the old Komotini road which passes to the N of the lagoon of Porto Lago and r. at 5mls/8km). The town of Anastasioupolis, later rechristened Peri-theorion, was an important stage on the Via Egnatia in the Roman and Byzantine periods, in the centre of a fertile, pleasant region where the horses of Diomede pastured, according to Homeric tradition. You will want to visit the impressive ruins of Byzantine walls, with square and round towers; the perimeter is polygonal. On the S side are the remains of a tall vaulted gate which led to the town's port; a plaque embedded at this point has the engraved monogram of the Paleologus family. Other monograms were formed by the bricks on some of the fortified towers. The repair of the town walls and the construction of a long defence wall which served both as aqueduct and fortification is attributed to the Emperor Justinian (527–565). Staying on the Komotini road, about 6.2mls (10km) further on, you reach the river Kompsatos; 1.2mls (2km) upstream from the modern bridge, there is a very beautiful bridge with rounded arches.

■ Xylokastron

Route map 5.

Corinth, 25mls (40km) – Kastania, 31.2mls (50km) – Patras, 57.5mls (92km) – Pop: 4,900.

Situated near the ancient port of Aristonautae and the fortress of Oluros, this seaside resort extends along the S shore of the gulf of Corinth, in a verdant setting formed by olive groves and luxuriant orchards.

Zante [Island of] (Zakinthos)*

155sq. mls (401km²) – Pop: 30,000; 9,000 in the capital – capital of an admin. region.

The Venetians called it 'fior di Levante', this island in the Ionian sea which rivals Corfu for its pleasant climate, the fertility of its vineyards and the beauty of its olive trees. Zante the green, more and more visited by foreign tourists, has everything necessary to please those who dream more of sun, flowers, fruit and perfumes, beaches and swimming than of archaeology and history. This island has a past to be sure, but much of it was effaced, especially its Venetian legacy, by an earthquake in 1953; nevertheless the reconstructions have preserved all the island's charm.

THE EMERALD OF THE MARITIME KINGDOM OF ULYSSES. Zante (the ancient Zacynthus), which was originally populated by the Achaeans, was part of the kingdom of Odysseus and formed the first port of call for Greek navigation on the maritime route to the W. It was thus a very important naval station for guarding the coast of the Peloponnese, and as such excited a great deal of envy on the part of Athens, which imposed an alliance on it (455) and that of Sparta, whose attempt at invasion failed (430).

In the Middle Ages, it was ravaged by the Vandals, the Saracens and the Normans, conquered by the Counts of Tocchi (14th century), and depopulated by the Turks (1479); it belonged to Venice from 1485 to 1797, thus sharing the lot of the island of Corfu, until its adherence to Greece in 1864.

THEY WERE BORN AT ZANTE. At the end of the 18th and beginning of the 19th century, Zante was a very lively literary and musical centre, which may have encouraged the talents of three poets who were born there: Ugo Foscolo (1778–1827), who by his political commitment to Italy was in some ways the Gabriele D'Annunzio of his day, and had an influence on the flowering of Italian romantic literature; Dionysios Solomos (1798–1857), author of the Greek National Anthem, who wrote in Italian and Greek and was the first poet of modern Greece; and Andreas Calvos (1792–1867), author of two collections of poetry exalting Greek patriotism on the eve of independence.

ZANTE. The capital is a charming little town at the foot of a high green hill, crowned by a Venetian citadel (*view), which is unfortunately the only evidence now visible of the architectural activity of the Republic of Venice since the earthquake in 1953. A few steps from the port's main jetty at the far end of Solomon Square, an arcaded building houses the museum of Zante, which contains post-Byzantine murals from the 17th and 18th centuries, and icons from the 16th to the 19th centuries, some by minor masters such as Damaskinos, Tzanes, Kallerghis, Doxaras, etc., as well as superb sculptures from the island's churches, plus a few Hellenistic and Byzantine sculptures.

Further into the town, the Solomos Museum (Hagios Moikos Square) recalls the memory of the poets Solomos and Calvos. Another literary souvenir is a monument to Ugo Foscolo in a garden on the site of his house.

As for the churches, mostly destroyed in 1953, they have been reconstructed, but are of little interest, including the church of Hagios Dionysos, in the neo-Byzantine style located at the end of the promenade by the port in the direction of the beach of Argassi (1.9mls/3km). There is another very pleasant long sandy beach at Lagana (5mls/8km). The tour of the island (41.2mls/66km), of limited interest, will take you, if you begin in the direction of Lagana, past Macheradi (icon and beautiful carved iconostasis in the church of Hagios Mavra) at 8.4mls (13.5km), Hagios Nikolaos (16.9mls/27km), near the W coast, where you will find a landscape of plateaus covered with scrub, and then Anafonitria (23.7mls/38km) and the E coast, the most beautiful because of the *views of the island of Cephalonia.

 The island possesses two curious grottoes, one beyond Anafonitria on the W coast, the grotto of Xyngia, in which gushes a sulphurous spring that colours the sea; the other, at the northern tip of the island, the Blue Grotto, accessible by boat.

To the S of Zante, the islet of Stophades is occupied by a fortified monastery of Byzantine origin.

A Guide to Greek Mythology

Achilles: son of Thetis and Peleus (king of the Myrmidons of Thessaly) is one of the most famous Greek heroes of the *Iliad*. He killed Hector beneath the walls of Troy but was mortally wounded in the heel by a poisonous arrow shot by Paris.

Actaeon: the hunter who accidentally stumbled upon Artemis (Diana) while she was bathing. The goddess changed him into a stag and he was eaten by his own hounds.

Aeacus: one of the 3 judges of the dead appointed by Zeus.

Aegeus: king of Athens and father of Theseus, he leapt from the heights of the Acropolis to his death, believing (wrongly) that his son had been eaten by the Minotaur.

Aeneas: the son of Anchises and Aphrodite. One of the most valiant Trojan warriors. After the war he led the survivors of the massacre to Latium, where they settled.

Agamemnon: king of Mycenae who led the Greeks in the siege of Troy. He sacrificed his daughter Iphigenia to the goddess Artemis. On his return he was murdered by his wife Clytemnestra and her lover Aegisthus.

Aglaurus: the wife of Cecrops; one of Athena's priestesses, she was turned to stone.

Ajax: son of Telamon and a famous Greek warrior. He and Odysseus protected Achilles' dead body during the siege of Troy. He then wanted the dead hero's arms as a reward for his valour, and when Odysseus was given them instead, he went mad and killed himself.

Amazons: warrior-women who lived near the Euxine (Black Sea). Theseus abducted their queen's sister, Antiope, and her fellow Amazons invaded Greece.

Amphiaraus: one of the Seven Chiefs against Thebes and a famous seer. Zeus made the earth open to swallow him.

Amphitrite: wife of Poseidon and queen of the seas.

Amymone: daughter of Danaus, king of Argos. A satyr attacked her after she accidentally struck him with her spear, and Poseidon rescued her. In her honour he created the spring of Lerna with his trident.

Anchises: a Trojan prince who was saved by his son Aeneas when Troy fell. He died in Sicily while travelling with Aeneas to the land of their ancestors.

Andromache: Hector's wife. After the fall of Troy she became the slave of Achilles' son Neoptolemus (Pyrrhus), who married her.

Antaeus: son of Poseidon and Gaia. He was a cruel giant who terrorized Libya and was squeezed to death by Heracles.

Antiope: daughter of Nycteus, regent of Thebes. Zeus took the form of a satyr and seduced her.

Antiope: sister of Hippolyta, queen of the Amazons. She married Theseus, and they had a son Hippolytus (see Hippolytus).

Aphrodite (Venus): goddess of love and mother of Eros. She is also goddess of fertility and giver of beauty, originally worshipped in Cyprus.

Apollo (Phoebus): son of Zeus and Leto, one of the greatest gods, he was born on the island of Delos. He killed the snake Python, and presided over the oracle at Delphi.

Ares (Mars): only son of Zeus and his consort Hera, and god of war. One of the 12 major gods of Olympus.

Ariadne: daughter of Minos. She helped Theseus to find his way out of the labyrinth. She was abandoned on the island of Naxos by Theseus, and then rescued by Dionysus who married her.

Artemis (Diana): daughter of Zeus and Leto, and twin to Apollo. According to Homer, she was born on Delos. She is best known as the goddess of hunting. She avoided marriage, sometimes by killing her suitors, but paradoxically is also worshipped as a goddess of fertility. To the people of the Aegean she is known as Potnia Theron, the tamer of wild animals.

Asclepius: son of Apollo. Some say he was born near Epidaurus. He is the great doctor god of healing reared by Chiron.

Atalanta: daughter of a hero (perhaps named Melanion) from Boeotia or Arcadia. Hippomenes won her hand in marriage by beating her in a footrace. This he did by means of a trick: Aphrodite had given him three golden apples, which he dropped, one by one during the race, so that each time the young girl would stop to pick them up.

Athena (Minerva): daughter of Zeus. She was born, fully armed, from her father's head. She was worshipped as the goddess of beauty, of the arts, and of warlike wisdom. Protectress of Athens, her symbol is the owl.

Atlas: the legendary king of Mauretania, said to bear the vault of the sky on his shoulders.

Autonoe: daughter of Cadmus and mother of the unfortunate Actaeon (see Actaeon).

Bellerophon: son of Glaucus. He was a hero of Corinth who rode the winged horse Pegasus and killed the Chimaera.

Boreas: god of the North Wind.

Cassandra: daughter of Priam, king of Troy. Agamemnon carried her back to Mycenae as his concubine, where she was killed by his wife Clytemnestra.

Cecrops: a snake-man sprung

from the earth, he married Aglaurus and inherited Acte (Attica). He became king and called it Cecropia.

Celeus: a legendary king of Eleusis. Demeter stayed with him during her search for Kore Persophone, her daughter, who had been carried off by Hades.

Centaurs: Creatures half man, half horse, who fought the Lapiths. They lived in Thessaly, between Mt Pelion.

Cephalus: son of Hermes, a young hunter whom Eos (Aurora) loved and abducted against his will.

Cercyon: a king of Eleusis. He was killed by Theseus near Megara.

Cerynitian (Hind): the third of Heracles' Labours was to capture this animal, a beast sacred to Artemis.

Charites (Graces): generally considered to be the daughters of Zeus. They personified charm and beauty combined.

Charon: the boatman of Hades, who ferried the souls of the dead across the river Styx, the fare being one obol.

Chimaera: a fabulous monster, with the forequarters of a lion, the body of a goat and the tail of a snake, who laid Lycia waste. It was killed by Bellerophon, mounted on Pegasus.

Chiron: the wise, kind Centaur to whom the education of Achilles and many other heroes was entrusted.

Clytemnestra (Clytaemnestra): wife of Agamemnon, king of Mycenae. Helped by her lover Aegisthus, she murdered Agamemnon on his return from the Trojan War.

Corybantes: the male followers of Rhea, mother of Zeus. When the god-child Zeus was born, they danced round him, clashing their shields against their swords to drown the sound of his cries. This saved him from the fury of his father, Cronos, who wanted to eat him.

Creusa: daughter of Priam and Hecuba, and Aeneas' first wife. She disappeared during the night of the fall of Troy.

Curetes: see Corybantes.

Cybele: a Phrygian goddess whom the Greeks called Rhea. She embodied the strength of everything that grows.

Daedalus: artist, inventor and sculptor. He built the labyrinth where the Minotaur was kept. He is said to have been the first to create a statue and bring it to life, and he thus represents the beginning of the plastic arts.

Demeter (Ceres): the great Earth-goddess of the Eleusinian Mysteries, whose daughter, Persephone (Kore), represents the annual growth of vegetation.

Diomedes: son of Ares. He fed shipwrecked strangers to his four mares to which, in turn, Heracles fed him, and they became tame.

Dionysus (Bacchus): the most popular tradition says that he was the son of Zeus and Semele, and the god of wine and ecstasy.

Dioscuri (Zeus' boys): Castor and Polydeuces (Pollux): sons of Zeus and Leda, or of Tyndareus and Leda. They were worshipped as warrior gods, often shown on horseback, or as gods of the seas.

Electra: daughter of Agamemnon and Clytemnestra. She and her brother Orestes avenged their father's murder.

Elysian Fields: also known as the Happy Islands. This was where the souls of the brave and good lived in the afterlife.

Erechtheus: Athenian hero, son of Pandion. He vanquished Eleusis and imposed Athenian rule on it.

Erichthonius: son of Hephaestus and of Earth. He was protected by Athena, and is normally seen as the grandfather of Erechtheus.

Erinyes: daughters of the Earth. They hunted criminals to bring them before the judgment of Hades. Euphemistically, they were called the Eumenides (Kindly Ones) and Semnai (Venerable Ones). Roman name: Furies.

Eros: most sources say he was the son of Aphrodite. He was chiefly worshipped as the god of love.

Erymanthus (Boar of): this monster spread terror throughout Arcadia, and Heracles' fourth task was to capture it alive.

Eurystheus: king of Tiryns. He imposed the 12 labours on Hercules.

Eurytion: a Centaur. He tried to carry off the wife of the king of the Lapiths while attending the wedding of Pirithous. This led to the battle between the Lapiths and the Centaurs.

Eurytus: a famous archer, king of Oechalia. He taught Heracles how to handle a bow and was later outdone by his pupil.

Gaia (Ge, Ga): goddess of the Earth, often associated with her daughter Themis for the giving of oracles. She gave birth to Cronos, the father of Zeus.

Ganymede: a Trojan prince. Zeus took the form of an eagle and carried him off to Olympus. He became cup-bearer to the gods, and attained immortality by eating nectar and ambrosia.

Gorgons: three sisters, Euryale, Medusa and Stheno, who had the power to turn all those who looked at them to stone. Perseus cut off Medusa's head.

Hades (Pluto): this son of Rhea and Cronos was given the world beneath the earth as his share. He was god of the nether world, and wore a helmet which made him invisible.

Hebe: daughter of Zeus and Hera, and the personification of eternal youth.

Hecate: a goddess of magic, who watched over cities, houses and crossroads. She was also a chthonian deity and the guardian of the dog Cerberus.

Hector: bravest of the Trojan chiefs, and the son of the king of Troy, Priam. He was the husband of Andromache, and was killed by Achilles.

Hecuba: wife of Priam, mother (of Paris, Hector and Cassandra).

Helen: wife of Menelaus. She was seduced by Paris who took her to Troy. To avenge this insult the Greek princes joined forces and besieged Troy.

Helios: the sun-god. He is sometimes taken to be the same as Apollo, but it seems that he was in fact a separate deity.

Hephaestus (Vulcan): son of Zeus and Hera, god of fire and of metalwork. His mother banished him from Olympus being ashamed of having given birth to a lame child, but he returned later and built himself a sparkling house of bronze. Husband of Aphrodite.

Hera (Juno): wife of Zeus, goddess of wedlock, queen of Heaven.

Heracles (Hercules): son of Zeus and Alcmene, known for his great size and strength. Following the murder of his own children, he was obliged to place himself in the service of King Eurystheus of Tiryns. He became famous for carrying out the 12 legendary labours.

Hermes (Mercury): one of the 12 major gods of Olympus. He was credited with many qualities, notably being god of commerce and of thieves, god of eloquence, messenger of the gods, guide to the souls of the dead.

Hesperides (The): daughters of Atlas. They were in charge of a garden whose trees bore golden apples. In order to obtain these apples (his eleventh labour), Heracles had to kill the serpent with a hundred heads who guarded the garden.

Hestia (Vesta): goddess of the hearth, whose task was to ensure that women maintained the family virtues.

Hippolyta: queen of the Amazons, Hercules fought and killed her, and took her belt (his ninth labour).

Hippolytus: son of Theseus and the Amazon Antiope, born at Troezene. His stepmother, Phaedra, fell in love with him, and when he turned down her advances, she accused him of having made approaches to her. Theseus then cursed his own son and had him killed by Poseidon.

Hygieia: the daughter of Asclepius and goddess of health.

Hypnos: son of Erebus and Nyx (Night) the god of sleep and brother of Death.

Iacchus: one of the gods of Eleusis, usually identified with Dionysus, but otherwise said to be either the son of Demeter, or of Persephone, or the husband of either one.

Icarus: son of Daedalus (see Daedalus). He and his father escaped from the Labyrinth by fixing feathered wings to their shoulders with wax. Icarus flew too near to the sun, the wax melted and his wings fell off. He drowned in what has since been known as the Icarian sea.

Iole: daughter of the famous archer Eurytus, king of Oechalia. Heracles won her as his prize but Eurytus would not let her go.

Ion: son of Xuthus and legendary ancestor of the Ionians.

Iphigenia: daughter of Agamemnon and Clytemnestra. Her father, who was the leader of the coalition of Achaean princes against Troy, sacrificed her to the goddess Artemis so that the Greek fleet might be allowed to set sail from Aulis where it was hampered by lack of wind.

Iris: goddess of the rainbow, and messenger of the gods of Olympus.

Kore (Persephone): daughter of Demeter. Hades carried her off to his kingdom of darkness, where she took the name Persephone. Her reappearance on the earth each spring symbolized the renewal of life.

Lapithae: the people of Thessaly whose king Pirithous became a friend of Theseus (see Centaurs).

Lerna (Hydra of): a many-headed water-serpent with a hound's body that lived in the Lerna marsh in the Argolid. For his third labour Heracles killed it.

Maenads (Bacchae): frenzied female followers of Dionysus.

Marsyas: a satyr who picked up a flute that Athena had thrown away as playing it distorted her face. He claimed that his flute playing outdid Apollo, the god of the lyre. After the contest the Muses judged Apollo the winner, and the god tied Marsyas to a tree and flayed him alive. His blood formed the river Marsyas.

Medea: a sorceress, daughter of King Aeetes of Colchis. She ran away with Jason, leader of the Argonauts, when he stole the Golden Fleece. When Jason left her for another woman, she murdered their children to get revenge.

Medusa: one of the three Gorgons, she was killed by Perseus.

Memnon: king of Ethiopia and son of Eos. He came to help the Trojans when they were besieged by the Greeks; he was

killed by Achilles; Zeus made him immortal

Menelaus: king of Sparta and brother of Agamemnon. His wife the beautiful Helen was carried off by Paris. To avenge this insult, Menelaus, together with Agamemnon, Achilles and the other Achaean princes, made war on the Trojans.

Minos: legendary king of Crete, father of Phaedra and Ariadne. With Aeacus and Rhadamanthus he was one of the three judges in Hades.

Minotaur: a fabulous monster, with a bull's head and a man's body, the offspring of Pasiphae, wife of King Minos. To free Athens from having to pay a tribute in human lives exacted by Minos, Theseus killed the Minotaur.

Mnemosyne: a Titaness born of the union between Uranus and Ge (Gaia) she embodied Memory which ensures the victory of mind over matter. Zeus and Mnemosyne were the parents of the nine Muses.

Muses: daughters of Zeus and Mnemosyne. According to the ancient Greeks these nine goddesses presided over the liberal arts.

Nemesis: goddess of justice and of vengeance, daughter of Nyx.

Oedipus: the tragic hero of Theban legend. After it was prophesied that he would murder his father and marry his mother, brought up by Polybus, the king of Corinth. He met his father on the road from Thebes to Delphi, and killed him, not knowing who he was. When he later rid Boeotia of the Sphinx, he won Queen Jocasta's hand as a prize, and unaware that she was his mother, married her. When he learned the truth he was so struck with horror that he blinded himself and went to Colonus, near Athens, where he wandered for many years and became a cult hero upon his death. Only Theseus knew the whereabouts of his tomb.

Orpheus: son of Oeagrus and the Muse Calliope. He came back to his native Thrace from the Argonaut expedition, and married a Naiad, Eurydice. She died soon after, and Orpheus went down to the Underworld hoping to move the shades by his entrancing songs and the sweet sound of his lyre. Hades relented and allowed Orpheus to take Eurydice back on condition that he should not look back until he had reached the upper air again. He did however look back, and Eurydice turned into mist and went back to the House of Hades. For seven months he played heartbreaking sounds on his lyre, and wild animals fell under his spell. Finally he was torn to pieces by the Thracian Maenads who lusted after him.

Pallas: see Athena.

Pan: son of Hermes and a daughter of Dryops. He was born with horns, and the feet and tail of a goat, and was the favourite companion of Dionysus. He was a rusty mustic god and played the pan-pipes which he made from the reeds into which Syrinx, the nymph, had been turned to save her from Pan's lust.

Pandion: son of Cecrops, a mythical king of Athens.

Pandora: the first woman, created by Hephaestus on Zeus' orders, as a pest for mankind.

Paris: son of King Priam of Troy. He seduced and carried off Helen, the wife of the king of Sparta, Menelaus, which caused the Archaeans to make war on Troy.

Patroclus: companion to Achilles. Hector killed him, and this prompted Achilles to leave his tent and rejoin the battle against the Trojans.

Pegasus: the winged horse which was born of Medusa's blood when Perseus cut off her head. Bellerophon tamed Pegasus, and rode him when he went to kill the Chimaera.

Peleus: husband of Thetis and father of Achilles.

Persephone: see Kore.

Perseus: son of Zeus and Danae. He was thrown into the sea in a box when a baby, and brought up by the king of the island of Seriphus. He is famous for having killed Medusa, the most terrible of the three Gorgons.

Phaedra: daughter of Minos, wife of Theseus, stepmother of Hippolytus (see Hippolytus).

Phaethon: son of Helios, the sun and of the Oceanid, Clymene. He persuaded his father to let him drive his chariot for one day, but having little experience he nearly set the world on fire. Zeus, furious, struck him down with a bolt of lightning and he fell to his death in the river Eridanus.

Pirithous: king of the Lapiths. After he fought Theseus in single combat, the two men became friends, and Theseus helped him in his war against the Centaurs.

Pluto: see Hades.

Polyphemus: the best-known of the Cyclopes who lived near Etna. Odysseus put out the Cyclops' only eye, and then escaped from the monster's cave with his companions by clinging to the underbellies of Polyphemus, sheep.

Poseidon: son of Cronos. He and his brothers Zeus and Hades divided up the world between them, and Poseidon became king of the sea. He was also patron of Eleusis, and he and Athena argued over the ownership of Attica. He was called Earth-Shaker, the one who makes continents tremble (i.e. the sender of earthquakes). It seems that his worship began in Thessaly.

Potnia: see Artemis.

Priam: king of Troy. He died during the fall of Troy.

Procrustes: a bandit who robbed travellers between Athens and Megara after killing them on a bed which was too long or too short. He was killed by Theseus.

Prometheus: Bestower of fire (and symbolically civilization) to humanity.

Rhadamanthus: one of the three judges of the dead.

Styx: river of the Underworld. From Arcadia to Hades.

Talus: he was killed by his uncle, Daedalus, who was jealous of his talent for sculpture, his invention of the saw and the potter's wheel.

Themis: the goddess of eternal justice. She was Zeus' counsellor, and brought about peace in Olympus and in the Universe.

Theseus: Athens' greatest hero, in the style of Heracles. Like his model, he accomplished tasks which give him the reputation of a redresser of wrongs. He is credited with having brought about *synoikismos*, the union of the city states of Attica.

Thetis: a Nereid, wife of Peleus and mother of Achilles. In order to make her son invincible, she held him by the heel and dipped him in the Styx, and induced Hephaestus to make his weaponry.

Triptolemus: son of Celeus, king of Eleusis. Demeter gave him the very first grain of wheat and introduced him to the art of cultivating the soil.

Triton: son of Poseidon and Amphitrite, and his parents' messenger and servant. He held the power of water and fathered a horde of monsters.

Zeus (Jupiter): supreme ruler of the gods of Olympus; son of Cronos and Rhea. He reigned over the earth and sky.

Glossary

Abaton: place too holy to enter; the priest's room.

Acroterion: plinth at the ends and apex of a pediment on which statues or ornaments stand; the ornament itself.

Adytum: the inner sanctum of a temple where only priests are allowed.

Aegis: shield with Gorgon's head forged by Hephaestus for Zeus and then given to Athena.

Alabastron: a small flask or vase (e.g. for scent), made of alabaster.

Amphictyony: gathering of several states for mutual protection and the worship of a common deity.

Anta: a pilaster at the end of the walls and of a temple or treasury cella, the base and capital of which do not conform with the order used on the building.

Antefixae: ornamental blocks to hide the ends of roof tiles.

Aphesis: starting line on a stadium track.

Apobates: athlete who did mounted gymnastics at public games, especially during chariot races.

Architrave: lowest part of the entablature above the capitals of the columns; moulded door frame.

Archon: magistrate with the highest public office in a Greek city.

Archonship: period of office of an archon.

Arrehephore: young Athenian girl of noble birth who took part in making the sacred peplos offered to Athena during the Panathenaea.

Atrium: inner courtyard of a house, open to the sky.

Aula: courtyard.

Auriga: charioteer.

Bard: epic poet who recited or sang of the exploits of the gods and of heroes accompanying himself on a lyre.

Basilius (pl. *basileis*): in ancient times an especially powerful ruler; from the time of Heraclius (630) title given to Byzantine rulers.

Bema: platform or pulpit from which orators spoke.

Bothros: hollow altar where sacrifices were laid.

Bouleuterion: meeting place of the Boule (senate).

Canephora: young girl who carried a basket in certain ceremonies.

Catholicon: church of a monastery or convent.

Cavea: all the tiers in a theatre.

Cella: sacred room of a temple, chamber of the divinity.

Chiton: long tunic.

Chlamys: short mantle for men held together by a brooch on the right shoulder or in front of the chest.

Choregic: (of a monument) dedicated by a choregus whose chorus has been successful in a competition of drama or music.

Choregus: patron who recruited, fitted out and arranged rehearsals for a chorus which would represent the city in drama or music competitions.

Chryselephantine: made of gold and ivory. flesh of colossal statues was made of ivory and the drapery of gold sheeting.

Chrysobull: diploma sealed with a seal of gold.

Chthonian: adjective used to describe Earth gods.

Cleruch: settler who retained the citizenship of his native country.

Cleruchy: settlement of cleruchs.

Cosmetes: master responsible for the education of the ephebes.

Cottabus: game of skill where the player had to throw the last drops from his cup onto a target chosen in advance by his fellow guests.

Cuneus (pl. *cunei*): section of the tiers in a theatre.

Cyma: double curved coping, either c. recta or c. reversa.

Deme: administrative division, borough.

Diazoma: concentric promenade in a theatre.

Dromos: corridor into a tomb, avenue.

Entablature: upper part of an order formed by the architrave, the frieze and the cornice rising above the columns and other supports.

Ephebe: adolescent youth.

Epimeletes: high official whose job it was to supervise a wide variety of offices.

Epistyle: the architrave or crossbeam placed on the top of the column.

Eschara: altar on which burnt offerings were made to heroes.

Exedra: alcove or recess for conversation, provided with seats.

Exonarthex: outer vestibule of a Greek Byzantine church.

Gigantomachy: Battle between the Gods and Giants.

Gorgoneion: head of the Gorgon.

Greave: piece of leg armour.

Herm: column holding the head of Hermes or of another god, used to mark boundaries.

Heroön: sanctuary where a hero was worshipped.

Hexastyle: temple with six frontal columns.

Hieron: sanctuary or sacred place.

Hoplite: heavily armed infantryman.

Hydria: large vase for carrying water.

Hypaethral: describing a building open to sky.

Hypocaust: underground room with system of pipes for heating baths.

Hypostyle: used to describe a hall, the roof of which is supported by rows of columns.

Iconostasis: screen in Greek churches which separates nave from the sanctuary reserved for priests and on which icons are hung.

Impluvium: basin for collecting rainwater in the centre of an atrium.

In antis: having a façade with an anta at each end, as distinct from Prostyle.

Kantharos: deep bowl with two handles that stand out a long way from the belly of the vase.

Kore: statue of a woman from the archaic period (pl. *korai*).

Kouros: statue of a naked man from the archaic period (pl. *kouroi*).

Krater: jar used for mixing wine and water.

Krepis: masonry foundation.

Kylix: drinking vessel with horizontal handles.

Lampadaodromy: torchlight race.

Lekythos: vase for oil.

Lesche: public place for conversation.

Logeion: raised part of the stage where the actors perform.

Loutrophoros: water jar for marriage bath or to put on tombs of unmarried persons.

Megaron: reception room in a Mycenaean palace.

Metope: stone plaque, blank or carved, that alternated with the triglyphs in a Doric frieze.

Mutulus: projecting square block under the corona and above the triglyph of a Doric order.

Naiskos: chapel, small temple.

Naos: see Cella.

Narthex: transverse vestibule of a Byzantine church.

Nome: administrative division in modern Greece corresponding to a county.

Nymphaeum: a Roman pleasure-house containing fountains and statues. (Literally: temple of the nymphs.)

Oinochoe: vase for pouring wine into drinking vessels.

Oikos: (pl. *oikoi*): building used for leaving offerings, such as a meeting-place for a religious fraternity; sometimes ritual banquets were held there.

Opaion: opening made in a roof.

Opisthodomos: near vestibule of a temple, sometimes a treasury.

Orchestra: circular area in a Greek theatre in which the chorus sings and dances.

Orthostates: any of a number of slabs facing the lower part of the cella.

Paean: song celebrating the victory of Apollo over Python; any song or thanksgiving or praise.

Paidotribes: teacher of gymnastics.

Palaestra: building in which athletics and wrestling were practised.

Paradromis: open-air gymnasium track.

Parascenium: either of projecting two wings of a theatre stage.

Parodos: side entrance of a theatre.

Pentelic: used to describe marble from the quarries on Mount Pentelicon.

Peplos: mantle worn by women over their tunic.

Peribolus: wall enclosing a temenus or other sacred enclosure.

Peripteral: building with a single external colonnade.

Perirrhanterion: basin for lustral water.

Peristasis: external peristyle of a peripteral temple.

Peristyle: gallery of free-standing columns round a courtyard or building.

Petasus: wide-brimmed hat.

Phial: shallow vase or drinking vessel having no handles.

Phylarch: chief officer of a tribe; magistrate.

Plectrum: quill used to pluck the strings of a lyre.

Poros: tufa, soft rock.

Proedria: official platform for the presidents of assemblies or games; right to reserved theatre seats granted to magistrates, priests, etc.

Pronaos: front vestibule of a temple with a range of columns in front.

Propylaeum: monumental entrance.

Proscenium: front of logeion facing tiers.

Prostasis: projecting portico.

Prytaneum: town hall of the prytaneis or magistrates, centre of city affairs.

Pyrgos: tower, bastion.

Pyrrhic: warriors' dance.

Pyxis: small casket.

Redan: a small ravelin (military architecture); an outwork with two embankments raised before the counterscarp.

Refend: chiselling outlining the joints of an embossed stone.

Rhyton: drinking cup shaped like a horn or an animal's head.

Sekos: part of a temple that is enclosed by walls; the cella.

Skene: the wall at the back of a Greek stage.

Soffit: the underside of any architectural element; stair, archway, etc.

Sphendono: rounded end of a stadium.

Stereobate: solid mass of masonry work that forms a foundation for a wall, row of columns, etc.

Stoa: covered portico, gallery.

Strategos: Athenian army general.

Stylobate: substructure on which the colonnade stands; the top step of the structure forming the crepidoma.

Synthronon: benches reserved for the clergy in the apse of a Byzantine or early Christian church.

Syrinx: Pan-pipes.

Talent: unit of weight (varying from one city to another).

Tambour: the core of a Corinthian or composite column.

Temenus: sacred enclosure.

Terma: finishing line on the track of a stadium or palaestra.

Thallophorus: old man who carried olive branches in the Panathenaea processions.

Thesmothete: one of the six junior archons responsible for preparing or presenting changes in the law.

Thiasus: a band of revellers in honour of Dionysus.

Tholos: beehive shaped building.

Thymele: theatre altar in the centre of the orchestra.

Thyrsus: staff entwined with ivy and vine leaves.

Triglyph: blocks on a Doric frieze alternating with the metopes; each one has three grooves or glyphs.

Trireme: galley with three banks of oars one above the other used in battles.

Xystus: A long portico for athletic contests; in Roman architecture, a long, colonnaded walk, sometimes covered.

Useful Information
Index

Key

rms:	rooms	com.:	communal
Tel.:	telephone	conf. rms:	conference rooms
V:	see	fest.:	festival

Tourist and hotel symbols

This list of accepted symbols for tourist and hotel information is common to all the *Guides Bleus*; all the symbols do not, therefore, necessarily appear in this volume.

⒤	Tourist office, information	A/c	Air conditioning
✈	Airports, airlines	🛗	Lift Elevator
⚓	Boat services	🚿	Bathroom or shower
🚄	Stations, reservations, information	☏	Telephone in rooms
🚋	Trams, streetcars, trolleybuses	🚌	Private bus service
		❀	Garden
🚍	Buses	♣	Park
🚗	Motoring information: Car hire, taxis, garages	🏊	Swimming pool
✉	Postal services, post codes	⚓	Private or public beach
△	Camping	♂	Tennis
	Hotel classification	⌿/9	Golf – 9 holes
*****	Deluxe	⌿/18	Golf – 18 holes
****	Very good		
***	Average	🐴	Riding
**	Simple		
*	Modest	🅿	Hotel Parking
⅋	Restaurant	P	Parking
*	Exceptional cooking	□	Special events
▥	Central heating	᪶	Handicrafts

Please note that the information in this section is subject to change.

A

ACTION (Preveza; central Greece), Tel. 0682

Air services: 4 times a week to and from Athens.

AEGINA [Island] (Saronic gulf), Tel. 0297

Tourist police: od. Paraliaki (Tel. 22-391).

Hotels:

In the town:
- ** *Danae* (Tel. 22-424) 52 rms ¶ ⅢⅢ A/c ᗰ ☎ ▦ **P**
- ** *Nausica* 55, leof. N. Kazantzaki (Tel. 22-333) 34 rms ¶ ᗰ ☎ **P**; open April-Oct.
- * *Brown*, 4, Toti Chatzi (Tel. 22-271) 26 rms ¶ ⅢⅢ ᗰ ▦ **P**
- * *Faros*, od. Paralia (Tel. 22-218) 46 rms ¶ ⅢⅢ ᗰ ᔆ **P**

At Moondy Beach (3.75mls/6km):
- ** *Moondy Bay* (Tel. 25-146) 72 rms ¶ ⅢⅢ ᗰ ☎ ▦ ᔆ ⚲ **P**; open April-Oct.

At Hagia Marina:
- ** *Apollo* (Tel. 32-271) 107 rms ¶ ⅢⅢ ᗰ ☎ ▦ ᔆ ⚲ **P**; open April-Oct.
- * *Argo* (Tel. 32-266) 60 rms ¶ ⅢⅢ A/c ᗰ ☎ ᔆ ⚲ **P**; open April-Oct.
- * *Galini* (Tel. 32-203) 35 rms ¶ ⅢⅢ ᗰ ᔆ **P**; open April-Oct.

- * *Kyriakakis* (Tel. 32-222) 30 rms ¶ ⅢⅢ ᗰ ᔆ **P**
- * *Oasis* (Tel. 32-204) 19 rms ¶ ⅢⅢ ᗰ ᔆ **P**; open March-Oct.

At Perdica:
- ** *Aegina Maris* (Tel. 25-130) 165 rms or bungalows ¶ ⅢⅢ ᗰ ☎ ✻ ᔆ ⚲ **P** night-club; open April-Oct.

At Souvala:
- * *Elphi* (Tel. 52-045) 32 rms ¶ ⅢⅢ ᗰ **P**; open May-Oct.

△ **Campsite:**
Moni, on the island of Moni (20 mins from Aegina; Tel. 61-242); reservations at the Touring Club of Greece, in Athens (Tel. 524-86-00); ᔆ 120 persons, hydroplane connections, water sports; open May-Sept.

Holiday Club:
Angistiri, island of Angistiri (to the W of Aegina); reservations in Athens: STS Ltd, 1, od. Philellinon (Tel. 322-79-93); open April-Oct.

⚓ **Boats:** linked by a large number of daily sailings from Piraeus and for Poros, Hydra and Spetsae; possibility of a day-long minicruise to Aegina and around the other islands of the Saronic gulf (information at Piraeus and at travel agencies). Hydroplane connections in summer.

AEGION (Peloponnese),
Tel. 0691

Hotels:
* ** *Galini*, 35 Vas. Georgiou
(Tel. 26-150) 31 rms ▥ ⌂ P
* ** *Long Beach*, 8.1mls/13km
NW, at Longos (Tel. 31-256)
111 rms ⑪ ▥ ⌂ P ; open
April-Oct.
* ** *Poseidon Beach*, 3.8mls/6km
SE, at Nikoleika (Tel. 81-400)
90 rms ⑪ ▥ A/c ⌂ ☎ ✳ ▨
≈ ⚲ P
* ** *Rodia*, 4.4mls/7km SE, at
Paralia (Tel. 81-195) 26 rms
⑪ ▥ ⌂ ≈ ▣ P ; open
July-Sept.
* * *Eliki*, 3.4mls/5.5km SE, at
Valimilika (Tel. 91-301) 144
rms ⑪ ▥ ⌂ ▨ ≈ ▣ P
night-club.

Holiday Club:
Club Méditerranée,
8.1mls/13km NW, at Lambiri.
(Reservations in Athens,
Manostravel System, 39, odos
Panepsistimiou Tel. 325-07
11); open May-Oct.

△ **Campsites:**
Acoli Beach, in Rododafni
(Tel. 71-317); 25 sites; open
April-Oct. ≈
Corali Beach, in Rododafni
(Tel. 71-546); 50 sites;
open April-Oct. ≈

🚍 **Trains and buses** to and from
Athens several times a day.

AFYSSOS (Pelion), Tel. 0423

Hotels:
* ** *Alexandros*, 7 Pighis
(Tel. 33-246) 9 rms A/c ⌂ P ;
open April-Sept.
* ** *Galini* (Tel. 33-214) 29 rms ▥
⌂ P
* * *Faros* (Tel. 33-293) 11 rms ⑪
▥ ⌂ P ; open April-Sept.

AGRIA (Thessaly),
Tel. 0421

Hotel:
Barbara (Tel. 92-367) 9 rms.
▥ ⌂ P

AGRINION (central Greece),
Tel. 0641

ⓘ **Tourist police:** 29, odos
Papaskota (Tel 23-381).
🏛 *ELPA:* 79, odos H. Tricoupi
(Tel. 20-293).

Hotels:
* ** *Esperia*, 31, Trikoupi
(Tel. 23-033) 26 rms ⑪ ▥ ⌂
P
* ** *Galaxy*, 19, Kazatzi
(Tel. 23-551) 36 rms ▥ A/c
⌂ P
* ** *Motel Soumelis*, on Athens
road, at Arta (Tel. 23-473) 20
rms ⑪ ▥ ⌂ ☎ P
* * *Acropole*, 1 Elia Heliou
(Tel. 22-231) 26 rms ⑪ ▥ ⌂
P *Aliki*, 2, Papastratou
(Tel. 23-056) 34 rms P
* * *Leto*, Platia Democratias
(Tel. 23-043) 36 rms P
* * *Tourist*, 51, Papastratou
(Tel. 26-665) 44 rms P

🚍 **Bus** to and from Athens
several times a day.

⚒ **Handicrafts:** exhibition,
Bellou Square (Tel. 28-043).

ALAGONIA (Peloponnese),
Tel. 0721

Hotel:
* ** *Taygete* (Tel. 76-236) 14 rms
⑪ ▥

ALEXANDRIA (Macedonia),
Tel. 0333

Hotel:
Manthos, 36 leof. Venizelou
(Tel. 24-400) 42 rms ▥ ⌂ P

ALEXANDROUPOLIS
(Thrace), Tel. 0551

⊡ **Tourist police:** 6, od. Karaikaki
(Tel. 26–211).

Hotels:

** *Motel Astir*, 280, Komotinis
(Tel. 26–448) 53 rms ¶ ▥ ⌂
☎ ❀ ▨ ⇌ P

** *Motel Egnatia*, leof. Makris,
(Tel. 28–661) 96 rms ¶ ▥ ⌂
☎

* *Alex*, 294 Vassileos Georgiou
B (Tel. 26–302) 28 rms ▥ ⌂
☎

* *Galaxias*, 150 Vassileos
Georgiou B (Tel. 28–112) 28
rms ▥ ⌂ ☎ P

△ **Campsite:**
Akti Alexandroupoleos, odos
Makris (Tel. 28–735); 218
sites; water sports; open
May-Oct.

▤ **Train and bus services** to
◈ and from Athens several
times a day.

✦ **Air services:** 3 daily (except
Sat.) flights to and from
Athens.

▟ **Boats:** car ferry for Samothrace 5 times a week.

↳ **Handicrafts:** Showroom, 406,
leof. Vas. Georgiou
(Tel. 27–067).

ALONISSOS [Island]
(Sporades), Tel. 0424

Hotels:

** *Alkyon*, Alonissos
(Tel. 65–450) 11 rms ▥ ⌂;
open May-Oct.

* *Galaxy*, Patitiri (Tel. 65–251)
37 rms ¶ ▥ ⌂ P ; open
May-Oct.

* *Marpounta*, Marpounta
(Tel. 65–219) 104 rms
(bungalows) ¶ ⌂ ❀ ▨ ⇌ ⚲;
open May-Sept.

▟ **Car ferries** to and from
Hagios Konstantinos 3 time
a week, via Skiathos and
Skopelos, taking 6 hours; to
and from Kimi (Euboea), 4
times a week, taking 2h.45;
once a week to and from
Volos, taking 5h.

AMPHILOKHIA (central
Greece), Tel. 0642

Hotels:

* *Amvrakia* (Tel. 22–845) 39 rms
¶ ▥ ⌂ ⇌ P

* *Mistral* (Tel. 22–287) 40 rms
¶ ▥ ⌂ ⇌ P

△ **Campsite:**
Stratis Beach Park, Kata-
phourko (Tel. 51–123) 31
sites; open April-Sept.

↳ **Handicrafts:** 38, od. N.
Stratou (Tel. 22–598).

AMFIPOLIS or Amphipolis
(Macedonia), Tel. 0322

△ **Campsite:**
Loghari, Nea Kerdilia
(Tel. 32–302) 35 sites; open
May-Sept.

AMORGOS [Island]
(Cyclades), Tel. 0285

Hotel:

* *Mike*, Aighiali (Tel. 71–247) 10
rms ¶ ▥ ⌂ ⇌; open
July-Sept.

▟ **Boats:** in summer, 4 sailings
each week for Piraeus, taking
about 12h; one can reach
here by caique from Naxos.

ANAVYSSOS (Attica),
Tel. 0299

Hotels:

*** *Alexander Beach*
(Tel. 53–461) 105 rms ¶ ▥
▦ ⌂ ☎ ▨ ⇌ P night-club;
open April-Oct.

*** Saronic Gate (Tel. 53–711)
105 rms ¶ ▥ A/c ⌂ ☎ ▦ ≋
⚲ P ; open April-Oct.
** Akti Apollon, by the beach
(Tel. 36–493) 91 rms ¶ ▥ A/c
🛎 ⌂ ☎ ≋ P night-club;
open April-Oct.
** Motel Calypso (Tel. 52–274)
47 rms ¶ ▥ ⌂ ☎ ✳ ≋ P
night-club.
** Eden Beach (Tel. 52–761) 286
rms ¶ ▥ ⌂ ☎ ✳ ▦ ≋ ⚲ 🏊/9
P night-club; open April-Oct.
* Silver Beach (Tel. 36–203) 28
rms ¶ ▥ ⌂ ≋ P ; open
April-Oct.

Ancient Epidaurus or Palea
Epidavros, *see Epidaurus.*

ANDIKYRA or Antikyra
(central Greece), Tel. 0267

Hotels:
** Avra, 13, Vas. Aspris (Tel.
42–045) 15 rms ¶ ▥ ⌂ ≋
Aktaeon (Tel. 41–280) 13 rms
▥ ⌂ ≋

ANDIRRHION or Antirrion
(central Greece), Tel. 0634

△ **Campsite:**
Antirrion Camping
(Tel. 28–860) 37 sites; open
May-Oct.

🛥 **Ferry services** to Rhion all
year round.

ANDRITSENA
(Peloponnese), Tel. 0626

Hotel:
** Theoxenia (Tel. 22–219) 17
rms ¶ ▥ ⌂ ☎ P ; open
March-Oct.

🚌 **Buses** daily to and from
Athens.

ANDROS [Island] (Cyclades),
Tel. 0282

Hotels:
At Andros:
** Paradissos (Tel. 22–187); in

Athens (Tel. 801–27 22) 41
rms ¶ ▥ ⌂ ☎ ≋ ▣ P ; open
April-Oct.
** Xenia (Tel. 22–270) 26 rms ¶
▥ ⌂ ☎ ≋ P ; open April-Oct.
* Aegli (Tel. 22–303) 14 rms ¶
⌂ ≋

In Apikia:
* Helena B (Tel. 22–281) 13 rms
⌂; open July-Aug.

At Batsi:
** Lykion (Tel. 41–214) 14 rms ⌂
☎ ≋ P ; open April-Oct.
* Chryssi Akti (Tel. 41–236) 61
rms ¶ ▥ ≋ P open
April-Oct.
* Skouna (Tel. 41–315) 20 rms
¶ ▥ ⌂ ≋ P ; open May-Oct.

At Gavrion:
** Aphrodite (Tel. 71–209) 23
rms ¶ ▥ ☎ ≋ ▣ P
* Gavrion Beach (Tel. 71–209)
21 rms; open April-Sept.

At Korthion:
** Korthion (Tel. 61–218) 15 rms
¶ ▥ ≋ P ; open April-Oct.

🛥 **Car ferries** from Rafina, twice
a day, taking 3h.

Angistri [Island]: *see Aegina*

ANIXI or Boghiati (Attica),
Tel. 01

Hotel:
** Motel Ouranio Toxo, 5, H.
Athanassiou (Tel. 81–32–180)
38 rms ¶ ▥ ⌂ P

ANO VOULA (Attica)

Hotels:
*** Aphrodite (Tel. 89–54–158) 12
rms ▥ ⌂ ☎ open May-Oct.
** Actaeon, 49 leof. Alkyonidon
(Tel. 89–58–555) 16 rms ¶ ▥
⌂ ≋ P
** Galini, 95 leof. Alkyonidon
(Tel. 89–59–093) 20 rms ¶ ▥
⌂ ≋ ⚲ P

ARACHOVA (central Greece),
Tel. 0267

Hotels:
** *Anemolia* (Tel. 31–640) 42 rms
📶 🍴 A/c 🛁 ☎ P night-club.
** *Xenia* (Tel. 31–230) 43 rms 🍴
📶 🛁 ☎ P

Archanes (Crete): *see
Herakleion.*

AREOPOLIS (Peloponnese),
Tel. 0733

Hotels:
*** *Pyrgos Kapetanakou*
(Tel. 51–233) 6 rms 📶 🛁 P in
traditional house furnished by
the GNTO.
Mani (Tel. 51–269) 16 rms 🍴
📶 📺

ARGOS (Peloponnese),
Tel. 0751

Hotels:
* *Mycenae*, 12, Platia Haghiou
Petrou (Tel. 28–569) 24 rms 📶
🛁 ☎ P
* *Telessila*, 2 od. Danaou
(Tel. 28–351) 32 rms 📶 🛁 P

🚍 **Trains and buses** several
🚌 times a day to and from
Athens, taking about 3h.
Argotolion (Cephalonia): *see
Cephalonia.*

ARKITSA (central Greece).

Hotels:
** *Faros* (Tel. 91–230) 6 rms 📶
🛁
** *Kalypso Club* (Tel. 91–392; at
Athens Tel. 981-27-31) 250
rms 🍴 A/c 📶 🛁 ☎ 🛁 🏊
🏊 🍸 💧/⁹ P night-club; open
April–Oct.
* *Helena* (Tel. 91–343) 34 rms
🍴 📶 🛁
* *Panorama* (Tel. 91–237) 12 rms
📶 🛁 🏊 P ; open May–Oct.

△ **Campsite:**
Côte d'Azur, 3.8mls/6km S at

Livanates; 40 sites 🏊

⚓ **Car Ferries** to Loutra
Aedipsos (Euboea), 7 times a
day.

ARTA (Epirus),
Tel. 0681.

ℹ️ **Tourist police:** 66, od. V. Pirou
(Tel. 27–580).

Hotels:
** *Xenia*, within Citadel
(Tel. 27–413) 22 rms 🍴 📶 🛁
☎ 🍸 P
* *Amvrakia*, 13, Priovoulou
(Tel. 28–311) 60 rms 📶 🏓 🛁
☎
* *Cronos*, Platia Kilkis (Tel 22-
21-1) 55 rms 🍴 📶 🛁 P
night-club.

🚌 **Bus** to and from Athens,
several times a day, taking 6h.

ASPROVALTA (Macedonia),
Tel. 0397

△ **Campsites:**
Asprovalta (Tel. 31–249) 624
sites; water sports 🏊 🍸
Europe (Tel. 31–319) 91
sites; open May–Oct. 🏊

ASTPALEA [Island]
(Dodecanese), Tel. 0242

Hotels:
Astynaea (Tel. 61–209) 20 rms
🍴 📶 🏊
Paradissos (Tel. 61–224) 🍴
🏊; open June–Sept.

⚓ **Boats** operate twice weekly
sailings to and from Piraeus,
taking 13h, and to and from
Rhodes in 10h. 30.

ATHENS (Attica), Tel. 01

ℹ️ **Tourist police:** Tel. 171, or
else 7, leof. Syngrou
(Tel. 9239–224); Larisa station
(Tel. 8213–574); Hellenikon
Airport (Tel. 9819–730).

GNTO (Central office, 2 odos Amerikis (Tel. 3223–111); Platie Syndagma and 2, odos Stadiou (pl. II, E–1; Tel. 3222–545, inside the National Bank of Greece); Hellenikon Airport (Tel. 9799–500).

🚗 *Automobile and Touring Club of Greece (ELPA)*: 2, od. Messoghion (Tel. 7791–615). 6, od. Amerikis (Tel. 3638–632).

Useful telephone nos:
Emergency aid for Athens 166

Police assistance 100

Police assistance (suburbs) 109

Fire brigade 199

Breakdown service 104

Tourist information 174

Hotel information 323–69–62

Foreign visitor service 362–83–01

Tourist police 171

Hotels:
If you are only staying a short time or if you have no car at your disposal, it is a good idea to put up at a hotel in the capital, but book your accommodation well in advance, especially if you are hoping for a high or medium class establishment in a central part of the city.

For a longer stay, 4 or 5 days for instance, and if you have a car, do not neglect the possibility of staying at a hotel on the outskirts. In summer, optimists and those who have failed to plan ahead stand a fair chance of being forced to stay there, for many Athenian hotels are fully booked; if such is the case, go to the Hotel Bureau in Karageorgi Servias Street (inside the National Bank of Greece) or at Hellenikon Airport.

Does the sea attract you? Then choose a beach on the Apollo coast from Kavouri onwards (see Vicinity of Athens, 6). You will thus be less or not at all disturbed by the air traffic of Hellenikon Airport, which can make a stay at Glyfada sheer hell.

Does being cool attract you even more? Do you want to do without air conditioning, which is so desirable in Athens in the height of summer? Then choose one of the following hotels: *Mount Parnis* (see Vicinity of Athens, 5), *Amaroussion, Kifissia, Variboli, Ekali* (see Vicinity of Athens, 7). Although they are of an equal standard, their tariffs are cheaper by 20 to 30% (with the exception of *Mount Parnis Hotel*).

Platia Syndagma (Square) area:

***** *Inter Continental*, 89–93 leof. Syngrou (off pl. 1, in the direction of B–4; Tel. 922–59–50) 605 bedrooms 3 ❚❙ A/c 🛏 🔲 ☎ TV 🚌 ❋ 🖾 P; shopping arcade; gymnasium, etc. a city within the city, the last word in Athenian luxury.

***** *Grande Bretagne* (pl. II, a in F–1). Platia Syndagma (Tel. 323–02–51) 394 rms ❚❙ ▥ A/c 🛏 🔲 ☎ 🖳. Renovated in 1981, a traditional grand hotel.

** *N.J.V. Meridien* (pl. II, c in F-1), Platia Syndagma (Tel. 325–53–00) 183 rms ¶ A/c ♨ ⌂ ☎ TV shopping arcade.

** *Athenee Palace* (pl. II, b in E-1), 1, Kolokotroni Platia (Tel. 323–07–91) 109 rms ¶ ▥ A/c ♨ ⌂ ☎ TV. Modern comforts and efficient service in a traditional setting.

** *King George* (pl. II, b in F-1), Platia Syndagma (Tel. 323–06–51) 140 rms ¶ ▥ A/c ♨ ⌂ ☎ TV

** *Royal Olympic* (pl. II, a in E-4), 28, od. Diakou (Tel. 922–64–11) 297 rms ¶ ▥ A/c ♨ ⌂ ☎ TV ▨ ▨ night-club; peaceful and luxurious; excellent view of the Acropolis.

** *St Georges Lycabettos* (pl. II in D-2), 2, od. Kleomenous (Tel. 729–07–11) 150 rms ¶ ▥ A/c ♨ ⌂ ☎ TV ▨ nightclub; peaceful, comfortable, superb view.

** *Amalia* (pl. II, a in F-2), 10, leof. Amalias (Tel. 323–73–01) 97 rms ¶ ▥ A/c ♨ ⌂ ☎ TV P

** *Astor* (pl. II, c in E-1), 26, od. Karageorgi Servias (Tel. 325–55–55) 133 rms ¶ ▥ A/c ♨ ⌂ ☎ P in the busiest district of the capital; garden terrace open all year.

** *Attica Palace* (pl. II, d in E-1), 6, od. Karageorgi Servias (Tel. 322–30–06) 78 rms ¶ ▥ A/c ♨ ⌂ ☎

** *Athens Chandris* (off the plan, by pl. I, B-4), 385, leof. Syngrou (Tel. 941–48–24) 380 rms ¶ A/c ♨ ⌂ ☎ ▨ ▨ P One of Athens' newest hotels. Good value for money.

** *Divani-Zafolia Palace* (pl. I, B-4), 19, od. Parthenonos (Tel. 922–96–50) 193 rms ¶

A/c ♨ ⌂ ☎ ▨ ▨ P

*** *Electra* (pl. II, a in E-2), 5, od. Ermou (Tel. 322–32–22) 110 rms ¶ ▥ A/c ♨ ⌂ ☎

*** *Electra Palace* (pl. II, in C-3), 18, od. Nikodimou (Tel. 324–14–01) 106 rms ¶ ▥ A/c ♨ ⌂ ☎

*** *Esperia Palace* (pl. II, e in E-1), 22, od. Stadiou (Tel. 323–80–00) 122 rms ¶ ▥ A/c ♨ ▨ ☎ ▨

*** *Herodion* (pl. I in B-4), 4, od. Rovertou Galli (Tel. 923–68–32) 90 rms ¶ ▥ A/c ♨ ⌂ ☎ Moderate prices for the location and superb facilities – a bargain.

*** *Olympic Palace* (pl. II, b in E-3), 16, od. Philhellinon (Tel. 323–76–11) 90 rms ¶ ▥ A/c ♨ ⌂ ☎ P night-club.

*** *Parthenon* (pl. II in D-4), 6, od. Makri (Tel. 923–45–94) 79 rms ¶ A/c ♨ ⌂ ☎

** *Acadimos* (pl. III in E-4), 58, Akademias (Tel. 362–92–20) 116 rms ¶ ▥ ⌂ ☎

** *Adrian* (pl. I in B-3), 74, od. Adrianou (Tel. 325–04–54) 22 rms ▥ ♨ ⌂ ☎ P

** *Athens Gate* (pl. I in B-4), 10, leof. Syngrou (Tel. 923–83–02) 106 rms ¶ ▥ A/c ♨ ⌂ ☎

* *Christina* (pl. I in C-4), 15, od. Petmeza (Tel. 921–53–53) 93 rms ▥ ♨ ⌂ ☎ ▨

** *Damon* (pl. I in B-4), 142, leof. Syngrou (Tel. 923–21–71) 97 rms ¶ ▥ A/c ♨ ⌂ ☎ ▨

** *Galaxy* (pl. III in D-3), 22, Akademias (Tel. 363–28–31) 102 rms ¶ ▥ A/c ♨ ⌂ ☎

** *Minerva* (pl. II, f in E-1), 3, od. Stadiou (Tel. 323–09–15) 47 rms ▥ A/c ♨ ⌂ ☎

** *Omiros* (pl. II in D-2), 15, od. Apollonos (Tel. 323–54–86) 37 rms ¶ ▥ A/c ♨ ⌂ ☎

** *Pan* (pl. II, b in E-2), 11. od. Mitropoleos (Tel. 323–78–16)

48 rms ▥ A/c ♨ ☏ P
** *Plaka* (pl. II, a in D-2), 7, od. Kaprikareas (Tel. 322-20-96) 67 rms ❙❙ ▥ A/c ♨ ☏
* *Attalos* (pl. II, a in C-1), 29, od. Athinas (Tel. 321-28-01) 80 rms ❙❙ ▥ ♨ ☏
* *Hermes* (pl. II in D-2), 19, od. Apollonos (Tel. 323-55-14) 45 rms ❙❙ ▥ A/c ♨ ☏
* *Imperial* (pl. II, in D-2), 46, od. Mitropoleos (Tel. 322-76-17) 21 rms ▥ ♨ ☏
* *Royal* (pl. II, c in D-2), 44, od. Mitropoleos (Tel. 323-42-20) 20 rms ▥ ☏ P
* *Tony's* (pl. I in A/B-4), 26, od. Zaharitsa (Tel. 923-63-70) 13 rms ☏ small pleasant guesthouse.

Omonia Square area:
**** *Acropolis Palace* (pl. III, a in C/D-1), 51, leof. 28 Octovriou (Tel. 522-38-51) 107 rms ❙❙ ▥ A/c ♨ ☏ night-club; peaceful and well-situated.
*** *Divani-Zafolia Alexandras* (pl. I in D-1), 87, leof. Alexandras (Tel. 692-51-11) 191 rms ❙❙ A/c ♨ ☏ P
*** *King Minos* (pl. III, b in B-3), 1, od. Piraeus (Tel. 523-11-11) 168 rms ❙❙ ▥ A/c ♨ ☏
** *Alfa* (pl. III, a in C-2), 17, od. Chalcocondili (Tel. 522-12-53) 88 rms ❙❙ ▥ ♨ ☏ P
** *Anastasia* (pl. I in A-2), 7, Platia Victoria (Tel. 883-45-11) 61 rms ❙❙ ▥ A/c ♨ ☏
** *Athens Center* (pl. III in B-4), 26, od. Sophocleous (Tel. 524-85-11) 136 rms ❙❙ A/c ♨ ☏ P
** *Atlantic* (pl. III, b in C-1), 60, od. Solomou (Tel. 523-53-61) 158 rms ❙❙ ▥ A/c ♨ ☏
** *New Cairo City* (pl. III, c in B-2), 42, od. Marni (Tel. 523-33-61) 86 rms ❙❙

A/c ▥ ♨ ☏ night-club.
** *Candia* (pl. I in A-1), 40, od. Deligianni (Tel. 524-61-17) 142 rms ❙❙ ▥ A/c ♨ ☏ P
** *Dorian Inn* (pl. III in A-4), 15, od. Piraeus (Tel. 523-97-82) 146 rms ❙❙ ▥ A/c ♨ ☏ P. Terrace with 2 swimming pools, overlooking Acropolis.
** *El Greco* (pl. III, a in C-3), 65, od. Athinas (Tel. 324-45-53) 92 rms ❙❙ ▥ A/c ♨ ☏
** *Eretria* (pl. III, c in D-2), 12, od. Chalcocondili (Tel. 363-53-11) 63 rms ❙❙ ▥ A/c ♨ ☏ P
** *Grand Hotel* (pl. I in C-1), 19, od. Patission (Tel. 524-31-56) 99 rms ❙❙ ▥ A/c ♨ ☏ P
** *Ionis* (pl. III in C-2), 41, od. Chalcocondili (Tel. 523-23-11) 102 rms A/c ♨ ☏ Unexpected comfort in unpretentious building.
** *Lycabettos* (pl. I in C-2), 6, od. Valaoritou (Tel. 363-35-14) 39 rms ❙❙ ▥ A/c ♨ ☏
** *Marathon* (pl. III in A-2), 23, od. Carolou (Tel. 523-18-65) 93 rms A/c ♨ ☏
** *Marmara* (pl. III, d in C-2), 14, od. Chalcocondili (Tel. 362-63-62) 140 rms ❙❙ ▥ ♨ ☏. The place for devotees of the Archaeological Museum, right next door.
** *Minoa* (pl. III, a in A-2), 12, od. Carolou (Tel. 523-46-22) 42 rms ❙❙ A/c ♨ ☏ P
** *Oscar* (pl. I in B-1), at the intersection of Samou and Filadelfias Streets (Tel. 883-42-15) 124 rms ❙❙ A/c ♨ ☏ P night-club.
** *Palladion* (pl. III, a in D-3), 54, Panepistimiou (Tel. 362-32-91) 58 rms ▥ ♨ ☏
** *Plaza* (pl. I in B-1), 78, od.

Acharnon (Tel. 822-51-11)
126 rms ¶ ▥ A/c ♨ ⌂ ☎ P

** *Stanley* (pl. I in A-2), 1, od.
Odysseos (Tel. 522-00-11)
395 rms ¶ ▥ A/c ♨ ⌂ ☎ ⌣
▣ pleasant and cheap.

** *Titania* (pl. III in D-3), 52,
leof. Panepistimiou
(Tel. 360-96-11), 398 rms ¶
▥ A/c ♨ ⌂ ☎ ▣ P beautiful
view of the Acropolis.

** *Xenophon* (pl. I in B-1), 340,
od. Acharnon (Tel. 202-03-
10) 186 rms ¶ ▥ A/c ♨ ⌂
☎ ▣ P

* *Achillion*, 32, od. H. Constandinou (Tel. 523-09-71) 56 rms
▥ ♨ ⌂ ☎

* *Alma* (pl. III, e in C-2), 5, od.
Dorou (Tel. 522-28-33) 64
rms ▥ ♨ ⌂ ☎

* *Amaryllis* (pl. III, f in B-2), 45,
od. Veranzerou (Tel. 523-87-
38) 57 rms ▥ ♨ ⌂ ☎ P

* *Artemission* (pl. III, h in C-2),
20, od. Veranzerou (Tel. 523-
05-24) 43 rms ▥ ♨ ⌂ ☎

* *Banghion* (pl. III, g in C-3), 18,
Platia Omonia (Tel. 324-23-
09) 54 rms ¶ ▥ ⌂ ☎

* *Delta* (pl. I in A-2), 27, od.
Kerameon (Tel. 524-75-22) 31
rms ▥ ⌂ ☎ P

* *Epidaurus* (pl. III, n in B-3),
14, od. Koumoundourou
(Tel. 523-04-21) 50 rms ▥

* *Iniohos* (pl. I in B-1), 26, od.
Veranzerou (Tel. 523-08-11)
134 rms A/c ♨ ⌂ ☎

* *King Jason* (pl. I in A-1), 26,
od. Kolonou (Tel. 523-47-21)
114 rms ¶ ♨ ⌂ ☎ P

* *Nestor* (pl. III, c in A-2), 58,
od. Hagiou Constandinou
(Tel. 523-55-76) 50 rms ¶ ▥
♨ ⌂ ☎

Omonia (pl. III, p in C-2), 4
Platia Omonia (Tel. 523-72-
10) 260 rms ¶ ▥ ♨ ⌂ ☎

* *Paris* (pl. III, s in B-3), 49, od.

Gheraniou (Tel. 523-99-55)
57 rms

*Ilissia and Ambelokipi
districts:*

***** *Hilton* (pl. I, a in E-3), 46,
leoforos Vasilisis Sophias
(Tel. 722-02-01) 480 rms ¶
▥ A/c ♨ ⌂ ☎ ▣ P
night-club; luxurious – and
expensive – Greek marble
palace, near Acropolis,
greatly favoured for its
nightlife – bars, taverns and
restaurant.

**** *Caravel* (pl. I in E-3), 2,
Vassileos Alexandrou
(Tel. 729-07-21) 471 rms ¶
▥ A/c ♨ ⌂ ☎ ⌣ ▣ P

**** *Park* (pl. I in F-1), 10, leof.
Alexandras (Tel. 883-27-11)
146 rms ¶ ▥ A/c ♨ ⌂ ☎ ⌣
P opposite largest park in
Athens – intimate and cosy.

*** *Delice* (pl. I, b in E-3), 3,
Vasileos Alexandrou
(Tel. 723-83-11) 46 furnished
apartments ▥ A/c ♨ ⌂ ☎

*** *Embassy* (pl. I, a in F-2), 15,
od. Timoleontos Vassou
(Tel. 642-11-52) 22 furnished
apartments ▥ A/c ⌂ ☎

*** *Golden Age* (pl. I in F-2), 57,
od. Mihalakopoulou
(Tel. 724-08-61) 122 rms ¶
▥ A/c ♨ ⌂ ☎ P night-club.

*** *Holiday Inn* (pl. I in F-2), 50,
od. Mihalakopoulou
(Tel. 724-83-22) 200 rms ¶
A/c ♨ ⌂ ☎ ▣ P American-
style comfort.

*** *President* (off plan, by pl. I in
F-1), 43, leof. Kifissias
(Tel. 692-46-00) 513 rms ¶
A/c ♨ ⌂ ☎ ▣ P night-club.

** *Alexandros* (pl. I in F-2), 8,
od. Timoleontos Vassou
(Tel. 643-04-64) 96 rms ▥
A/c ♨ ⌂ ☎ ▣ P

** *Ilissia* (pl. I in E-3), 25,
od. Mihalakopoulou

(Tel. 724–40–51) 69 rms ⑪ ▥
A/c ♨ 🛁 ☎

** *Stadion* (pl. I in D-3), 38,
Vassileos Constandinou
(Tel. 722–60–54) 70 rms ⑪ ▥
A/c ♨ 🛁 ☎ **P**

Youth hostels: 1, od. Drossi
(Tel. 646–36–69); 87, leof.
Alexandras (Tel. 642–65–69);
20, od. Kallipoleos
(Tel. 766–48–89); 57, od.
Kypseli (Tel. 822–58–60); 3,
od. Hamilton (Tel. 822–64–25).
YMCA, 28, od. Omirou
(Tel. 3626–970).
YWCA, 11, od. Amerikis
(Tel. 3624–294).
Maison d'accueil Cleo, 3, od.
Patrou and 18, od. Apollonos,
at Plaka (Tel. 323–56–40).
Maison Cristal, 28, od. Nikis
(Tel. 325–47–20).

Δ **Campsites:**
Athens Campsite, 198, leof.
Athens, Peristeri (road to
Daphni; Tel. 581–41–13); 55
sites; open April-Oct.
Acropolis Campsite,
9.4mls/15km from Athens on
the main road to Lamia, at
Nea Kifissia (Tel. 808–31–04);
150 sites ⑪ 🏖 ♨ ♒; open
May-Sept.
Dafni Campsite, 6.3mls/10km
from Athens on the Corinth
road (Tel. 590–95–27); 300
sites ⑪ shops.

Restaurants:
**** *Galaxias* (pl. I, a in E-3), 46,
leoforos Vasilisis Sophias
(Tel. 722–02–01) A/c **P** on
the roof of the Hilton Hotel:
breathtaking view, at night, of
lit-up town and Acropolis.
*** *Dionyssos* (pl. II in A-4), 43,
od. Rovertou Gali, opposite
the Acropolis, at the foot of
the hill of the Muses
(Tel. 923–31–82) A/c **P** Greek

and Continental cuisine.
*** *Dionysos* (pl. I in D-2), at the
summit of Lycabettos (access
by cable car; Tel. 722–63–74).
*** *Le Grand Balcon* (pl. II in
D-2), 2, od. Kleomenous
(Tel. 729–07–11) A/c (Saint-
George-Lycabettos hotel).
*** *Brasserie des Arts* (Hotel
Meridien; (pl. II, c in F-1),
Platia Syndagma
(Tel. 325–53–01) A/c. French
'Nouvelle cuisine'.
*** *Ta Nissia* (pl. I, a in E-3), 46,
leoforos Vasilisis Sophias
(Tel. 722–02–01) A/c **P**
(Hilton hotel; tavern style.)
Authentic Greek cuisine.
*** *Tower Suite* (pl. I in F-2), top
floor of the Athens Tower
leof. Vasilisis Sofias and od.
Messogion (Tel. 706–111) A/c
*** *Tudor Hall* (pl. II, d in E-1),
Syndagma Square
(Tel. 323–06–51) A/c terraced
(King George hotel); English
Manor in style – a fine view of
Acropolis.
*** *Abreuvoir* (pl. I, e in E-2), 51,
od. Xenocratous
(Tel. 722–91–06); good French
cuisine; alfresco in summer.
*** *Da Walter* (pl. I in D-3), od.
Evzonon (Tel. 724–87–26);
Italian specialities.
** *Balthazar* (pl. I in F-2), 27, od.
Vournazou (Tel. 644–12–15);
evenings only; French
cuisine.
** *Le Calvados* (pl. I in F-2) 3,
od. Alkmanos (Tel. 726–291);
near the Hilton Hotel; French
cuisine.
** *Bagatelle* (pl. I in E-3), 9, od.
Ventiri (Tel. 730–349); known
for its cuisine.
** *Athenian Bistro* (Meridien
Hotel; pl. II, c in F-1), A/c
Platia Syndagma
(Tel. 325–53–01)

** *GB Corner (Great Britain Hotel*, pl. II, a in F-1), Platia Syndagma (Tel. 323-02-51) A/c Excellent European cuisine.

** *Byzantine Coffee Shop* (pl. I, a in E-3), 46, Vasilisis Sophias (Tel. 722-02-01) A/c **P** (Hilton Hotel).

** *Floca* (pl. II, n in F-1), 9, leoforos Venizelou (Tel. 323-40-64) A/c

** *Kapolos* (pl. I in E-4), 102, od. Formionos (Tel. 766-99-05); closed in summer.

** *Kastalia* (pl. I in C-2), 6, od. Valaroitou (Tel. 363-35-17) A/c

** *Michiko* (pl. II in D-3), 27, od. Kidathineon (Tel. 322-09-80); Japanese specialties.

** *La Maison du Steack* and annex, 6, od. Aigihitou (Tel. 721-74-45) A/c

** *Gerofinikas* (pl. II in F-1), 10, od. Pindarou (Tel. 363-67-10); one of the best restaurants serving authentic Greek cuisine.

* *Vladimiros* (pl. I in D-2), 12, od. Aristidemou (Tel. 721-74-07); in summer the shaded garden is very pleasant.

* *Corfou* (pl. II, s in F-1), 6, od. Kriezotou (Tel. 361-30-11) A/c a few specialties from Corfu.

* *Delphi* (pl. II in F-1), 3, od. Nikis (Tel. 3234-869) A/c pleasant and cheap.

* *Fatsios* (pl. I in E-3), 5, od. Efroniou (Tel. 717-421).

* *Hellenikon* (pl. III in C-3), 1, od. Satovriandou (Tel. 522-756).

* *Kentrikon* (pl. II in E-1), Platia Kolokotroni (Tel. 323-56-23).

* *Kostoyiannis* (pl. III in E-1), 37, od. Zaimi (Tel. 822-06-24).

Tavernas:
Plaka, at the foot of the Acropolis, nowadays a tourist trap displaying a distorted view of Greek folklore, is riddled with tavernas. You will certainly no longer be able to find traces of that authenticity now hiding in remote parts of the city. Reputations are made and lost overnight; prices are becoming prohibitive. The tavernas are only open in the evenings.

At Plaka:
Adam, 8, od. Makriyanni (Tel. 910-795).
Erotokritos, 16, od. Lyssiou (Tel. 322-22-52).
Mostrou, 22, od. Minisikleous (Tel. 322-53-37); view over the town.
Platanos, 4, od. Diogenes (Tel. 322-06-66).
Xinos, 4, od. Angheiou Gheronda (Tel. 322-10-65). Mainly frequented by Greeks, this taverna is one of the pleasantest in Plaka; guitarists, garden filled with gardenias – or you may prefer the interior decorated with scenes of Greek daily life, painted by penniless artists in exchange for a meal.
Yero Tou Moria, 27, od. Minisikleous (Tel. 3221-753), very lively.
Zafiris, 4, od. Thespidos (Tel. 322-39-01).

Outside Plaka:
Andronatos (pl. I in E-3), od. Eratosthenous (Tel. 7191-149).
Costoyannis (pl. I in C-1), 37, od. Zaimi, in a student quarter (Tel. 822-06-24).
Myrtia (pl. I in C/D-4), 35, od. Marcou Moussourou (Tel. 701-22-76); one of the best tavernas in Athens, behind the stadium.

Rodhia (pl. I in D-2), 44, od. Aristipou, at the foot of Lycabettus (Tel. 722–98–83).
Pitsios, 3, od. Paviou Mela at Terma Karea, on the slopes of Mt Hymettus (Tel. 7640–240), a real country taverna, close to the centre although very difficult to find.
Steki tou Yanni, 1, od, Trias (Tel. 821–29–53), also one of the best.
Rouga (pl. I in D-2) od. Kapsali (Tel. 722–79–34).

Cafés, ouzo-bars and pastry-shops:
Besides the pavement cafés of Platia Syndagma where you will find it very pleasant to stop for a while now and then (ices, pastries and sandwiches are served there; the coffee is outstanding at the *Café do Brasil; Phivos* serves excellent pastries), do not hesitate to join in Athenian life in places where tourists do not often go. Try Platia Kolonaki (pl. I D-3), odos Phokionos Negri (*The Oriental Café*), off pl. I in the direction of C-1, or Kapnikarea Square in Plaka (pl. II D-3). The ouzo bars are often very simple places and are found more or less everywhere: near Syndagma, *Apotsos* and *Orfanides* (7 and 10 Panepistimiou) are typical ones, as is *Athinaikon*, behind Omonia. You cannot really claim to know Athens if you have not been to *Zonar* and *Flocas*, each a great café and pastry shop on leoforos Panepistimiou (the former has a restaurant); you should go there also for the quality of the drinks served there as much for the pleasure of watching the spectacle of Greek social life.

Banks: *American Express* Platia Syndagma (Tel. 324–49–75).
Bank of Attica, 19, od. Panepistimiou (Tel. 324–74–15).
National Bank of Greece, 2, od. Karageorgi Servias (Tel. 323–64–81) and 86, od. Eolou (Tel. 321–05–01).
Credit Bank, 10, od. Pesmatzoglou (Tel. 328–06–31) and 9, leoforos Venizelou (Tel. 323–42–84).
First National City Bank, 8, od. Othonos (Tel. 322–7471).
General Bank of Greece, 4, od. Stadiou (Tel. 322–53–38).
Société Générale, 3, od. Korai (Tel. 325–50–01).

✉ **Post Office:**
Main post office and Post restante 100, od. Eolou (Tel. 321–60–23) (pl. III in C-4); other offices, 4, od. Stadiou (pl. II in F-1); Platia Syndagma (pl. II in E-2); also Poste restante telegraph (pl. III in C-4), od. Athinas; Tel. (pl. II in E-1), od. Stadiou.

✈ **Airport:** Hellenikon, 7mls (11.5km) (for the airport used by foreign airlines, proceed via odos Vouliagmenis, pl. I in C-4; for the airport used by Olympic Airways, take the road for Sounion, pl. I in B-4). Buses from opposite the National Park and Olympic Airways coaches from the air terminal. NB: there is no left luggage check at the airport used by internal flights.

Air terminal: *Olympic Airways*, 96, leof. Syngrou (Tel. 923–23–23).

Air lines: *British Airways,* 10, od. Othonos (Tel. 322–25–21); *Olympic Airways,* 6, od. Othonos (Platia Syndagma: Tel. 929–25–55), Terminal 96, leof. Syngrou (pl. I, B-4; Tel. 929–22–51); *T.W.A.,* 8, od. Xenofontos and od. Filellinon (Tel. 323–68–31).

🏛 **Shipping companies:** see Piraeus.

🚂 **Rail services:** Larissa Station (pl. I A/B-1) for the lines to Chalcis, Thessaloniki and Northern Greece; Peloponnese Station (pl. I A-1) for the lines to Patras and Kalamata. Information: 1, odos Karolou (Tel. 522–24–91).

Underground: line from Piraeus via Thesion, Platia Monastiraki, Platia Omonia, Platia Victoria, Patissia and Kifissia.

🚌 **City bus and trolleybus services:**
Due to recent changes in the numbering of the routes, you will find it useful to get a bus-route map from one of the tourist bureaus or principal bus stations (Syndagma, Omonia). The city is well-served by its bus network, which is a very practical way of getting about. All the same, because the buses may well be overcrowded, you are sure to want to make use of the taxis although they are hard to find at peak periods.

Buses out to the suburbs:
They leave from Platia Kanigos (pl. I C-2) for Kifissia, Amaroussion, Varibobi and Chalandri; from the leoforos Olgas (pl. I C-4) for Glyfada, Vougliameni, Varkiza; from Platia Elepherias (pl. III A-4) for Eleusis, Perama and Salamis, Daphni; from Platia Omonia (pl. I B-2) for Piraeus; from Platia Syndagma for Piraeus and New Phalere.

Buses for Hellenikon Airport:
As well as the Olympic Airways coaches (from terminal 96, leof. Syngrou) which run a service to the airport used by this company, (western air terminal), route 184 goes to the eastern air terminal from leof. Olgas (opposite the National Park).

🚌 **Buses serving routes in Attica:**
From the Parade Ground (pl. I C-1; Platia Egyptou) for Marathon, Rafina, etc., and, from the other side of the square, for Anavyssos and the Sounion headland.
From odos Ermou (near odos Hagiou Assomaton, pl. 1 A-3): for Hagii Theodori (road to Corinth), Porto Ghermeno, etc.

🚌 **Coaches for the provinces:**
Coach station, 260, od. Liossion (pl. I B-1), which can be reached by buses nos. 24 and 63, coaches for Chalcis, Delphi, Lamia, Larisa, Thebes, Thessaloniki, Solos etc.
Coach station, 100, od. Kifissiou, which can be reached by buses no 51 and 62, coaches for Cephalonia, Corfu, Corinth, Igoumenitsa, Ioannina, Kalamata, Kavalia, Nauplia, Olympia, Patras, Sparta, Zante, etc.
Coach station, 18, Hagiou

Constandinou (pl. I B-2), for Patras, Thessaloniki, Zante, etc.

Guided tours and excursions: all the Athens travel agents offer tours of the city and of Attica, as well as visits to the major archaeological sites in Greece, of one or more days in length. Among the agents are: *American Express*, Syndagma (Tel. 324-49-75); *Chat Tours*, 4, od. Stadiou (Tel. 322-31-37); *Key Tours*, 2, od. Hermou (Tel. 323-25-20).

Taxis: they have set charges, controlled by meter. Main taxi-rank in Platia Syndagma (Tel. 323-79-42). You should however allow for the fact that they will often all be engaged.

🚗 **Car rentals:** *Autorent*, 118, leof. Syngrou (Tel. 923-84-38); *Avis*, 48, leof. Amalias (Tel. 322-49-51), at the Hilton and the airports; *Budget*, 90, leof. Syngrou (Tel. 921-95-55); *Hellascars*, 7 od. Stadiou (Tel. 923-53-52); *Hertz*, 12, leof. Syngrou and at the Hilton (Tel. 922-01-02) and at the airports.

🚗 **Garages:**
Talbot, 100, leof. Syngrou (Tel. 923-60-65).
Citroën, 51, Plateon (Tel. 346-31-93).
Fiat, 73, leof. Syngrou (Tel. 921-47-71).
Ford, 165, od. Piraeus (Tel. 361-225).
Peugeot, 97, leoforos Syngrou (Tel. 921-94-11).
Renault, MAVA, S.A. Service, Terma, Kolokynthous (Tel. 512-81-05).

Embassies:
UK: 1, od. Ploutarchiou, Athens 139 (Tel. 7236-211).
US: 91, leof. Vasilissis Sophias, NY 09253 (Tel. 721-2957).

Antiques: You will find a choice of antiques and tasteful souvenirs at Antika, 4, leoforos Amalias, and at the Antiqua Gallery in the Athens Tower, 2, odos Messogion, as well as at Haritakis, 7, Valaoritou, or at Zoumboulakis Tassos, 7, odos Kriezotou. At Mintzas, 22, odos Pindarou, there are some fine icons, some ancient ex-votos and some small original pieces of furniture to be had. The small shops and stalls in the quarter of the city at the foot of the Acropolis are like a real oriental bazaar (particularly odos Ermou, near Platia Monastiraki, and in the neighbouring streets), where the most dreadful objects rub shoulders with some that are occasionally acceptable: copper articles, necklaces and belts that are usually poor imitations of ancient designs. You may come across an interesting icon or antique (but watch out, as you will be checked by the Customs if it is an item of value), old jewellery, silverware. Have a look, too, in the Monastiraki quarter at Martinos and Zarakovitis, in odos Pandrossou.

Handicrafts: National Society for Greek Handicrafts, 9, odos

Mitropoleos (Tel. 322-10-17), has a wide selection of bedcovers in long-haired wool (flokati) from Arachova, filigree silver from Macedonia, silver and gold ornaments from Rhodes, woodcarvings from Metsovon and Vytina, embroidery from Mykonos, etc. For long-haired rugs and bedcovers, have a look in no. 91, leoforos Alexandras or in the Trikkala House, 31, odos Voulis. There is a good selection too at the Co-operative of Greek Craft Workshops, 56, leoforos Amalias (Tel. 323-34-58), but they do not sell direct to the public. At Rossopoulos, 18, leoforos Venizelou, you will find some lovely rugs woven in Macedonia. Their simple designs have cheerful bright colours. Anna Anghelou Sikelianou, 1, Panou Aravantinou, and Maria Alkeou, 11, odos Vrassida (behind the Hilton Hotel), also both feature most attractive weaving and embroidery. In addition visit Elokati, 47, odos Adrianou; Kori, 13, odos Mitropoleos, for popular art; Tanagrea, 15, odos Mitropoleos, for pottery. Finally, at the Greek Women's Institute, 13, odos Voukourestiou, you will find a choice of pretty delicately embroidered tablecloths in linen, or other fabrics.

Jewellery: Ilias Lalaounis, 6, leoforos Venizelou (in Athens, there are branches at 4, odos Stadiou, at the Hilton and Grande Bretagne hotels). Former artistic designer for Zolotas, Ilias Lalounis, can offer those with enough money modern jewellery unusual both in conception and in craftsmanship, in which there are showy combinations of precious stones and gold. In the Chryssotheque, 10, leoforos Venizelou, Zolotas has on view jewellery inspired by antiquity or the Byzantine period, which is more conventional, but the craftsmanship is very fine. You should also go to Fanourakis, 2, odos Evangelistrias, who creates jewellery inspired by antiquity. Also worth a mention is Frangoulis, 7, odos Amerikis, for his reproductions of ancient and classical jewellery; Vourakis, 8, odos Voukourestiou, for his beautiful stones; Tzorbazis and Taznika, 12-14, odos Karageorgi Servias, for their reproductions of ancient jewellery and their very fine modern jewellery, attractively priced; Athiniotakis, 20, odos Voukourestiou, for his collection of ancient and modern jewellery, including Greek crosses, with beautiful stones. Mati, odos Voukourestiou, offers for sale jewellery and other objects that are Greek in character and elegant. Maroulina, 19, odos Solomou (Tel. 362-60-34) sells jewellery and objects of modern art that incorporate old pieces. In the shopping arcade of the Hilton, at Cleo's you will find a wide choice of silver and gold jewellery, as well as at the Emerald, especially guilloche-patterned (interlace) gold jewellery; Alexis Efstathiadis displays and sells here in this arcade his modern cameos and intaglio work.

To round off your shopping: For a tunic-dress, or a gathered and embroidered blouse, try the shops selling chlamydes in odos Ermou, near Platia Monastiraki, or, if you have more expensive tastes, in the boutiques in leoforos Venizelou, without having to go far from Platia Syndagma, in the Kolonaki district and in the Athens Tower about a mile from the Hilton Hotel along the Kifissia road. Are you aware that Kastoria in Macedonia is one of the world capitals of the fur trade? It is unnecessary to go there unless you happen to be interested in medieval paintings: you can find furs from there in the shops in odos Mitropoleos and odos Philhellinon, in particular at Voula Mitsakou, 7, odos Mitropoleos, at Sistovari, 14, odos Voulis and 4, odos Ermou, which is the most famous (mink, ocelot, astrakhan, beaver, etc.).

Bookshops (selling foreign books): Eleftheroudakis, 4, odos Nikis (pl. II in E-2); Kauffman, 28, odos Stadiou (pl. I in C/2-3); Pandelides, 11, odos Amerikis (pl. II in E-1). All the foreign newspapers can be found at the kiosques in Platia Syndagma.

Special events: in July and August, there is always something interesting happening in the Athens Festival, in the Odeon of Herodes Atticus (information GNTO, Festival Bureau, under Spyrou Milliou Arcade, 4 od. Stadiou; Tel. 322–14–59). This festival, which was boycotted by foreign companies during the previous regime, has regained its pre-1967 sparkle. In spite of or because of its extreme eclecticism, it is unquestionably one of the most dazzling festivals in Greece, with performances of Greek theatre, but also appearances by foreign companies of the very highest standard, with concerts, operas and ballets. In summer, folk dancing is regularly performed at the Dora Stratou Theatre (Philopappos Hill; Tel. 322–48–61). In addition, the Daphni wine festival (8mls/11km from Athens) which takes place from mid-July to the beginning of Sept. will allow you to try all the Greek wines in the joyful atmosphere of a local fête.

Son et lumière: from 1 April to 31 October, viewed from the Pnyx (you will be facing the Acropolis), every evening except those of full moon, at 9 pm in English; Tuesdays and Fridays at 10 pm in German; the other days at 10 pm in French (tickets from 4, odos Stadiou and at the entrance).

Night-clubs: dining and dancing from 22h to midnight, with band, also Greek (bouzouki) music and with currently fashionable singers: Athinia, the Old Phaleron hippodrome (from May to October; Tel.

942-21-58) or 6, leoforos Venizelou (in winter; Tel. 362-07-77); Dilina, 2, odos Vasileos Georgiou, in Glyfada (Tel. 894-73-21); Neraida, 11, Vasileos Georgiou, in Kalamaki (Tel. 981-20-04). Only couples are admitted.

 Beaches: they are a good distance away; on the Apollo coast (see Vicinity of Athens, 6). We recommend those at Vouliagmeni and Varkiza (the beaches between Eleusis and Glyfada can be the source of minor medical upsets, such as ear infections and tracheitis); on the east coast of Attica, the beach at Schinias (see Vicinity of Athens, 7) is the most pleasant.

B

BRAURON or Vraona (Attica), Tel. 0294

Hotel:
*** *Vraona Beach* (Tel. 862-57-92) 352 rms (or bungalows) ¶ ▦ A/c ⚒ ⌂ ☎ ❋ ▨ ⇌ ⌇ ♪/9 **P** night-club.

C

CASTELLORIZO [Island] (Dodecanese), Tel. 0241

 Boats: 2 weekly links from Rhodes.

CEPHALONIA [Island], or Kefallinia (Ionian Islands), Tel. 0671 (Argostolion, Lassi, Lixourion, Platis Yalos), 0674 (Phiscardo, Poros, Sami).

ℹ **Tourist police:** at Argostolion in summer only, od. Metaza (Tel. 22-200).

ℹ *GNTO*, at Argostolion, od. Metaxa (Tel. 22-847).

Hotels:
At Argostolion:
** *Xenia*, Platia Rizospaston (Tel. 22-233) 24 rms ¶ ⌂ ☎ **P**
* *Armonia*, 1, od. Geroulanou (Tel. 22-566) 13 rms
* *Phocas*, 3, od. Geroulanou (Tel. 281-00) 18 rms
* *Tourist*, 94, od. J. Metaxa (Tel. 22-510) 21 rms

At Lassi (1.2mls/2km from Argostolion):
*** *Méditerranée* (Tel. 28-760; at Athens, Tel. 722-29-15) 277 rms ¶ A/c ⚒ ⌂ ☎ ▨ ⇌ ♀ **P** night-club; open April-Oct.
* *Lassi* (Tel. 23-126) 20 rms ▦ ⌂ ⇌ **P**

At Platys Yalos (1.9mls/3km from Argostolion):
**** *P.L.M. White Rocks* (Tel. 28-332) 155 rms ¶ A/c ⌂ ☎ ▨ ⇌ **P** night-club; half-board only; open April-Oct.

At Poros (1.6mls/2.6km from Sami):
* *Iraklis* (Tel. 52-351) 5 rms ¶ ⇌ **P** full board; open April-Oct.

* *At Sami:*
Ionion, 5 Horofylakis (Tel. 22-035) 16 rms ▦ ⇌ **P**

At Svoronata (6.9mls/11km from Argostolion):
*** *Irinna*, Hagia Pelaghia (Tel. 41-285; at Athens Tel. 361-83-83) 168 rms ¶ ▦ ⚒ ⌂ ☎ 🚍 ▨ ⇌ **P**; open April-Oct.

△ **Campsite:** *Karavomilos Beach*, at Sami (Tel. 21-680), 300 sites ¶ ⇌ shaded.

The GNTO has converted some traditional houses at

Phiscardo; 51 rms in all; information from GNTO and (Tel. 39–718).

✈ **Air services:** 1 flight per day to and from Athens in summer, taking 45 min *(Olympic Airways,* od. Vergoti, Argostolion 28–808).

🚢 **Boats and car-ferries:** every day to Patras, taking 3h.30; several weekly sailings for Ithaca.

🚌 **Buses:** to and from Athens, three times a day, taking 8h.

🚗 **Car hire:** *Budget,* 5, od. Rogou Vergoti (Tel. 23–125).

CHALANDRI, or Halandri (Attica), Tel. 01

Hotels:
** *Barbagalos,* 5, od. Pendelis (Tel. 681-54-15) 32 rms ▥ 🏛 ☎ P
** *Olympic,* 1, od. Souri (Tel. 681-34-30) 22 rms ▥ 🏛 ☎ ❋ P
* *Egyptos,* 6, od. Ghini (Tel. 682-93-00) 31 rms ¶¶ ▥ 🏛 ☎ P

Restaurants:
** *Kalamia,* 15, od. Messo-longhiou (Tel. 68-05-29) P
* *O Costas,* 340, leof. Vassileos Georgiou (Tel. 683-340) ❋ P

CHALCIS or Halkis (Euboea), Tel. 0221

ℹ️ **Tourist police:** 32, od. El. Venizelou (Tel. 24-662).

Hotels:
At Chalcis:
*** *Lucy,* 10. L. Voudouri (Tel. 23-831) 92 rms ¶¶ ▥ A/c 🏛 🏛 ☎ ≈ P night-club.
*** *Saint Minas Beach,* at Hagios Minas (2.5mls/4km on road to Thebes and turn r. after bridge on the Euripe; Tel. 82-

411) 70 rms ¶¶ A/c 🏛 ☎ ≈ ❝ P ; open April-Oct.
** *Hilda,* at the intersection of od. Favierou and od. Goviou (Tel. 28-111) 122 rms ¶¶ ▥ A/c 🏛 🏛 ☎ P
** *John's,* 9, Angheli Goviou (Tel. 24-996) 57 rms ¶¶ ▥ A/c 🏛 🏛 ☎ ≈ ▣ P
** *Paliria,* leof. Venizelos (Tel. 28-001; at Athens Tel. 361-86-79) 118 rms A/c 🏛 🏛 ☎
* *Hara,* 21, L. Karoni (Tel. 25-541) 51 rms P
* *Kentrikon,* 5, Angheli Goviou (Tel. 22-375) 20 rms P

At Nea Artaki (5mls/8km):
* *Bel Air* (Motel: Tel. 42-263) 44 rms ¶¶ ▥ A/c 🏛 ☎ ❋ ≈ ≈ P

🚆 **Trains:** 19 services to and from Athens daily, taking 1h.40.

🚌 **Bus service:** bus service to and from Athens every half hour from 6am to 9pm, then every hour until midnight, taking 1h.30.

CHERSONISSOS (Crete), Tel. 0897

Hotels:
**** *Creta Maris* (Tel. 22-115) 516 rms, 229 bungalows ¶¶ ▥ A/c 🏛 ☎ ≈ ≈ 🛥 night-club, bowling, sauna, shopping arcade, open-air cinema, etc.; open April-Oct.
*** *Belvedere* (Tel. 22-371) 226 rms ¶¶ 🏛 ≈ ≈ ❝ P night-club; open March-Oct.
*** *King Minos Palace* (Tel. 22-781) 143 rms ¶¶ A/c 🏛 ≈ ❝ ⚲/9 P ; open April-Oct.
*** *Lyttos,* od. Agissaras (Tel. 22-575) 325 rms ¶¶ A/c 🏛 ≈ ❝ ⚲/9 P night-club;

open April-Oct.
** *Heronissos* (Tel. 22-501) 89 rms ¶ 🛏 🖼 ≈ P ; open April-Oct.
** *Maragakis* (Tel. 22-405) 49 rms ¶ 🛏 ≈ P Surfing School; open April-Oct.
** *Nora* (Tel. 22-271) 181 rms ¶ 🛏 🖼 ≈ P night-club, sauna; half-board only; open March-Oct.
** *Villes Esperides* (Tel. 22-322) 27 rms ¶ 🛏 🖼; open April-Oct.

△ **Campsite:**
Caravan, on the beach at Plakias (Tel. 22-025) 36 sites, bungalows, ≈ open April-Oct.

🚗 **Car hire:** *Budget,* od. Venizelos (Tel. 22-194); *Hertz:* Creta Maris Hotel (Tel. 22-115).

CHIOS, or Hios [**Island**], (Aegea), Tel. 0271 (Chios), 0272 (Kardamyla).

[i] **Tourist police:** 35, od. Neoriou (Tel. 265-55).

Hotels:
At Chios (town):
** *Chandris* (Tel. 257-61) 156 rms ¶ ▥ A/c 🛏 🖼 ≈ P night-club.
** *Xenia* (Tel. 235-07) 28 rms ¶ 🛏 ☎ P open April-Oct.; half-board only.
* *Kyma* (Tel. 225-51) 59 rms P

At Marmaro (Kardamyla):
** *Kardamyla* (Tel. 213-78) 32 rms ¶ A/c 🛏 ☎ ≈ ⚲ P night-club; open May-Oct.

The GNTO has converted some traditional houses in Metsa: 33 bedrooms in all; information from GNTO (Tel. 27-908).

✈ **Air services:** at least one daily

flight to and from Athens, taking 1h *(Olympic Airways,* Prokymaia, Tel. 224-14).

⚓ **Car-ferries:** 4 times a week to and from Piraeus, taking between 8h.30 and 10h; 3 times a week to Mytilene taking between 3h.30 and 4h; twice a week to Rafina taking 7h; daily, though not guaranteed, service to Cesme (Turkey) in summer, taking 1h.

CORFU, [**Island**] or Kerkyra (Ionian Islands) Tel. 0661 (Corfu Town) 0663 (Nissaki, Paleokastritsa, Roda).

[i] **Tourist police:** 31, od. Arseniou (Tel. 30-265).
GNTO: Governor's Palace (Tel. 30-360).

🚗 *ELPA:* od. Patr. Athinagora (Tel. 39-504).

Hotels:
At Corfu Town:
**** *Corfou Palace* (Pl. a, C-3), od. Democratias (Tel. 394-85) 106 rms ¶ ▥ A/c 🛏 🖼 ☎ 🚗 ※ 🖼 ⚲ P ; open April-Oct.
*** *Cavalieri* (Pl. c, C-3), 4, od. Capodistriou (Tel. 390-41) 48 rms ¶ ▥ 🛏 🖼 ☎ ※ ⚲ P ; open March-Oct.
** *Astron* (Tel. 39-505) 33 rms ¶ ▥ 🛏 🖼 ☎ ⚲ P
** *King Alkinoos* (Pl. d, B-3), 29 od. Zafiropoulou (Tel. 393-00) 61 rms ¶ ▥ 🛏 🖼 ☎ P
** *Olympic* (Pl. e, B-3), 4, od. Doukisis Marias (Tel. 305-32) 50 rms ¶ ▥ 🛏 🖼 ☎ ⚲ P
* *Arkadion*, 44, od. Capodistriou (Tel. 376-71) 55 rms ¶ ▥ 🖼 ☎ P
* *Calypso* (Pl. f, B-3), 4, od. Vraila (Tel. 307-23) 19 rms ▥ 🖼 ☎ ⚲ P

* *Hermes* (Pl. g, B-2), 14, od. Markora (Tel. 392-68) 33 rms ▦ ᵅ ☎ P

* *Ionion*, 46, od. Stratigou (Tel. 399-15) 81 rms ❰❰ ▦ ⛨ ᵅ ☎ P; open April-Oct.

At Anemomylos:
** *Arion* (Tel. 379-50) 105 rms ❰❰ ▦ ⛨ ᵅ ☎ ✳ ▱ ≈ P night-club; open March-Oct.
** *Marina* (Tel. 327-83) 102 rms ❰❰ ▦ A/c ⛨ ᵅ ☎ ✳ ▱ P open April-Oct.

At Alykes (1.9mls/3km):
*** *Kerkyra Golf* (Tel. 317-85) 240 rms ❰❰ ▦ A/c ᵅ ☎ ☎ ✳ ▱ ⚲ P night-club; open April-Nov.

At Benitses (8.1mls/13km via Perama or 8.8mls/14km via the Achilleion road):
*** *San Stefano* (Tel. 92-292) 250 rms ❰❰ ▦ A/c ⛨ ᵅ ☎ 🚌 ▱ ≈ ⚲ P; open April-Oct.
** *Achilleus* (Tel. 92-425) 74 rms ❰❰ ▦ ⛨ ᵅ ☎ P; open April-Oct.
** *Potamaki* (Tel. 308-89) 149 rms ❰❰ ▦ ᵅ ☎ ✳ ▱ ≈ P night-club; open April-Oct.

At Dafnila (6.3mls/10km):
**** *Eva Palace* (Tel. 912-86) 174 rms ❰❰ ▦ A/c ⛨ ᵅ ☎ ✳ ▱ ≈ ⚲ P night-club; open April-Oct.
*** *Robinson Club Hotel* (Tel. 35-836) 260 rms ❰❰ A/c ᵅ ☎ ✳ ▱ ≈ ⚲ P night-club; open April-Oct.

At Dassia (7.8mls/12.5km by the Ypsos road):
**** *Castello* (Tel. 301-84) 74 rms ❰❰ ▦ ᵅ ☎ 🚌 ♦ ⚲ P; open April-Oct.; we recommend it if you are not so keen on living on the beach.
**** *Corfu Chandris* (Tel. 338-71) 301 rms (28 bungalows and 12 villas) ❰❰ ▦ A/c ⛨ ᵅ ☎ 🚌 ✳ ▱ ≈ ⚲ P night-club; open April-Oct.
**** *Dassia Chandris* (Tel. 338-71) 251 rms ❰❰ ▦ A/c ⛨ ᵅ ☎ 🚌 ✳ ▱ ≈ ⚲ P; open April-Oct.
*** *Elaea Beach* (Tel. 93-490) 198 rms ❰❰ ▦ A/c ⛨ ᵅ ☎ ▱ ≈ P; open April-Oct.
* *Dassia Beach* (Tel. 932-24) 54 rms ❰❰ ▦ ᵅ ☎ ≈ P; open April-Oct.

At Ermones (10.3mls/6.5km):
**** *Ermones Beach* (Tel. 942-41 or 22-26-94 in Athens) 272 bungalows ❰❰ ▦ A/c ᵅ ☎ ✳ ▱ ≈ ⚲ P; open May-Oct.

At Gastouri (6.6mls/10.5km by the Achilleion road):
* *Achilleion* (Tel. 305-31) 15 rms ▦ ᵅ ☎ P; open April-Sept.

At Glyfada (8.8mls/14km via Pelekas):
**** *Grand Hotel Glyfada Beach* (Tel. 942-01) 242 rms ❰❰ ▦ A/c ⛨ ᵅ ☎ 🚌 ✳ ▱ ≈ ⚲ ▱ P night-club; open April-Oct.; in a secluded position on the edge of one of the finest beaches on the island.
** *Glyfada Beach* (Tel. 94-257) 35 rms ❰❰ ▦ ᵅ ☎ P open April-Oct.

At Gouvia (5mls/8km by the Ypsos road):
**** *Astir Palace* (Tel. 914-81) 308 rms or bungalows ❰❰ A/c ⛨ ᵅ ☎ ✳ ▱ ≈ ⚲ ᵥ/18 P; open April-Oct.
**** *Corcyra Beach* (Tel. 307-70) 242 bungalows ❰❰ ▦ A/c ᵅ ☎ 🚌 ✳ ▱ ≈ ⚲ P night-club; open April-Oct.
*** *Radovas* (Tel. 91-218) 64 rms, 52 bungalows ❰❰ A/c ⛨ ᵅ ☎ ▱ P; open April-Oct.

* *Galaxias* (Tel. 921-20) 35 rms ⅢⅢ ☎ P open April-Oct.

At Hagios Gordios (9.4mls/15km W):

*** *Hagios Gordios* (Tel. 36-723) 209 rms ⑪ ⅢⅢ A/c ⌂ ☎ ☐ ☀ ▦ ☎ ♀ night-club; open April-Oct.

** *Alonakia* (Tel. 30-407) 15 rms ⅢⅢ ⌂ ☎ open April-Oct.

At Kanoni (2.8mls/4.5km; Pl. B/C-3):

*** *Corfu Hilton* (Tel. 356-40) 236 rms, 38 bungalows ⑪ ⅢⅢ A/c ⚑ ⌂ ☎ ☐ ☀ ▦ ♀ P night-club; open April-Oct.

*** *Ariti* (Tel. 38-885) 174 rms ⑪ ⅢⅢ A/c ⚑ ⌂ ☎ ☀ ▦ P; open April-Oct.

*** *Corfu Divani Palace* (Tel. 38-996) 165 rms ⑪ ⅢⅢ A/c ⚑ ⌂ ☎ ☀ ▦ P night-club; open April-Oct.

* *Royal* (Tel. 35-343) 114 rms ⑪ ⅢⅢ ⌂ ☎ ☀ ▦ P night-club.

At Kontokali (3.8mls/6km by the Ypsos road):

**** *Kontokali Palace* (Tel. 38-736) 238 rms ⑪ ⅢⅢ A/c ⚑ ⌂ ☎ ☐ ☀ ▦ ☎ ♀ P night-club; open April-Oct.

At Moraitika (13mls/21km: v. vicinity of Corfu 5):

**** *Miramare Beach* (Tel. 30-183) 149 bungalows ⑪ ⅢⅢ ⌂ ☎ ☐ ☀ ▦ ♀ ♪/9 P; open April-Oct; near one of the finest beaches on the island, pleasantly secluded, with a wonderful lawn.

*** *Motel Delfin* (Tel. 30-318) 83 rms ⑪ ⅢⅢ ⌂ ☎ ☀ ▦ P night-club; open April-Oct.; on the edge of an olive grove, beside the beach at Moraitika.

** *Messonghi Beach* (Tel. 38-684) 796 rms ⑪ ⅢⅢ

⚑ ⌂ ☎ TV ☐ ☀ ▦ ☎ ♀ ♪/9 P night-club; open April-Oct.

At Nissaki (15.6mls/25km by the Ypsos and Kassiopi roads):

**** *Nissaki Beach* (Tel. 91-232) 239 rms ⑪ ⅢⅢ A/c ⚑ ⌂ ☎ ☐ ☀ ▦ ☎ ♀ ♪/9 P night-club; open April-Oct.; in a lovely secluded spot by the seashore.

At Paleokastritsa (15mls/24km):

**** *Akrotiri Beach* (Tel. 41-275) 128 rms ⑪ ⅢⅢ A/c ⚑ ⌂ ☎ ☀ ▦ P; open April-Oct.

** *Paleokastritsa* (Tel. 41-207) 163 rms ⑪ ⅢⅢ ⌂ ☎ ☀ ▦ ☎ P night-club; open April-Oct.

At Perama (5.3mls/8.5km by the road to the airport):

*** *Alexandros* (Tel. 36-855) 75 rms ⑪ A/c ⚑ ⌂ ☎ ☀ ▦ P; open April-Oct.

*** *Eolos Beach* (Tel. 33-132) 324 rms (bungalows) ⑪ ⅢⅢ ⚑ ⌂ ☎ ☀ ▦ ♪/9 P; open April-Oct.

** *Motel Akti* (Tel. 39-445) 55 rms ⑪ ⅢⅢ ⌂ ☎ ☀ ▦ ☎ P; open April-Nov.

** *Oasis* (Tel. 38-190) 66 rms ⑪ ⅢⅢ A/c ⌂ ☎ ☀ ▦ ☎ P; open April-Oct.

* *Aegli* (Tel. 39-812) 37 rms ⑪ ⅢⅢ ⌂ ☎ ☎ P; open April-Oct.

At Pyrghi (9.4mls/15km by the Ypsos road):

* *Emerald* (Tel. 93-209) 58 rms ⑪ ⅢⅢ A/c ⌂ ☎ ☀ ☎ P night-club; open April-Oct.

At Roda (25.7mls/41km; v. vicinity of Corfu 4):

** *Roda Beach* (Tel. 31-225) 360 rms ⑪ A/c ⅢⅢ ⌂ ☎ ☀ ▦ ☎ ♀ ♪/9 P night-club; open April-Oct.

At Sinarades (5.6mls/9km W.):
**** *Yaliskari Palace* (Tel. 31–400) 227 rms ❙❙ A/c 🛏 🏦 ☎ ☀ 🖼 ♋ ♪/⁹ **P** ; open April-Oct.

At Tsaki (Benitses, 8.8mls/14km):
*** *Regency* (Tel. 92–305) 185 rms ❙❙ A/c 🛏 🏦 ☎ 🚌 🖼 ♋ **P** night-club; open April-Oct.

At Ypsos (8.8mls/14km; Pl. A-2):
** *Ypsos Beach* (Tel. 93–232) 60 rms ❙❙ ▥ 🏦 ☎ 🖼 ♋ **P** ; open April-Oct.
** *Sunrise* (Tel. 93–414) 36 rms ❙❙ ▥ 🛏 🏦 ☎
* *Mega* (Tel. 93–208) 33 rms ❙❙ 🏦 ♋ **P** ; open April-Oct.

Youth Hostels: at Hagios Ioannis (5mls/8km from the town), Platia Georgiou Theotoki (Tel. 284–08); at Kontakoli (4.4mls/7km; Tel. 91–102).

Holiday Club:
Club Mediterranée-Ypsos and *Club Mediterranée-Helios.* Reservations at Athens, Minostravel system, 39, od. Panepistimiou (Tel. 325-07-11); open May-Sept.

Restaurants:
None of the restaurants in Corfu Town is particularly outstanding; one of the most agreeable is perhaps the *Aigli* in Platia Esplandade (Tel. 308–41). The *Rex* (od. Kapodistriou, Tel. 296–48) offers local specialities, simply served. Numerous tavernas in od. Dona. In the town centre, the *Akteon's* mediocre cooking is made up for by a wonderful view. As for the

island itself, *Tripa* (at Kinopiastes, 9.4mls/15km) from the town centre, (Tel. 307–91) offers some of the best cooking on Corfu in a very pleasant setting (reservation necessary); *Yannis*, at Garitsa (Tel. 310-66) offers local cooking. At Paleokastritsa (and to a lesser extent at Glyfada), you will be able to enjoy crayfish, shellfish and fresh fish, perhaps trying them at *Akti Glyfada*, at the end of the beach, or at Kassiopi.

△ **Campsites** (open April-Oct.): *Dionysos*, on the beach at Dafnila (Tel. 91–417) 88 sites. ♋
Karoussades Camping, at Karoussades (Tel. 712–11) 65 sites. ♋
Kerkyra Camping, at Ypsos (Tel. 93–246) 100 sites.
Kondokali Beach International, in Kondokali (Tel. 91–202) 93 sites.
Kormarie Camping, at Dassia (Tel. 93–587) 100 sites. ♋
Paradise Camping, at Pyrgi (Tel. 93–282) 110 sites. *Roda-Beach Campsite*, in Roda (Tel. 31–120) 80 sites. ♋
Sea-Horse Campsite, at Messoghi (Tel. 92–364) 70 sites.

🚌 **Buses:** to Kanoni, leave from Esplanade Sq. (Pl. C-2); to Ypsos and N of the island, at the port (Pl. B-1); for the S, Platia Theotoki (Pl. B-2).

🚗 **Car hire:** *Autorent*. Nisi Kondokali (Tel. 31–504); *Avis*, 31, leof. Alexandras (Tel. 38–820), at the airport and at the Hilton Hotel;

Budget, 406, leof. Alexandras (Tel. 39–217); *Europcar*, 76, od. Capodistriou (Tel. 31–497) 18, od. Capodistriou (Tel. 31–497); *Hertz*, 38, od. X. Stratigou (Tel. 38–388) and at the airport.

Boats: only weekly ferries to Patras, about ten a day to Igoumenitsa; at least once a day for Paxi.

Shipping companies: all the companies (*Fragline, Hellenic Mediterranean Lines. Mediterranean Sun Lines*) have their agencies at the port (Pl. A-1), near the New Fort for boats operating services for Italy (or Igoumenitsa and Patras), but for the Igoumenitsa ferry-boat you should go to the old port (Pl. B-1); no later than the eve of your departure, you should book your car space by getting your name put on the embarkation list (you will pick up your tickets shortly before your departure); several services a day to Igoumenitsa taking 1h.30 to 2h according to the conditions at sea.

Air services: several flights a day to and from Athens, taking 50 min; airport 7.5mls (12km) taxis and buses; *Olympic Airways*, 20, od. Capodistriou (Tel. 38–694).

Shopping: nothing very outstanding except perhaps the jewellery from Lalounis, 29, od. Voulgareos, and Zolotas, 5, od. Capodistriou, but the choice available is far inferior to what is available at the branches in Athens and Rhodes. It is in the old town, particularly in od. Voulgareos

and od. Capodistrious, that you will come across chlamydes (short cloaks) on sale and other souvenirs that are often mediocre. Craft Shop, 32 b, od. X. Stratigou (Tel. 32–167).

✝ **Special events:** 21 May, feast celebrating the uniting of the Ionian Isles with Greece; in July, the Corfu Festival, at Gastouni; from 1 August to 15 September, Kerkyraikon Chorodrama, popular folk dances; 6 August, procession of boats leaves the old port for Pondikonissi; 11 August, Feast of St Spyridon in Corfu Town.

Son et lumière: from the beginning of April to the end of October, at 9.30pm in the old citadel; in French on Thursdays, Italian on Mondays, Greek on Sundays, English other days.

Casino: at the Achilleion (6.9mls/11km; see vicinity of Corfu 2) where, in the sumptuous Italian-style residence built by Sisi, you can play roulette and baccarat (minimum stake 20 drachmas).

�▵ **Beaches:** those around Corfu Town are very poor; the finest are at Ypsos, Ermones, Glyfada, Hagios Gordios (perhaps the best), Moraitika, but there are many little coves, as at Paleokastritsa.

Sports: Nautical Club (Pl. C-3), Platia Esplanade; Tennis Club (Pl. B-3), od. Georgiou Kalosgourou; Golf course (18 holes) at Livadi Ropa, near the Bay of Ermones (Corfu Golf and Country Club);

sailing and motor boat hire at Corfu, Gouvia and Paleokastritsa.

CORINTH, or Korinthos (Peloponnese), Tel. 0741

[i] **Tourist police:** 33, od. Koliatsou (Tel. 232–83).

Hotels:
** *Belle Vue*, 41, od. Damaskinou (Tel. 22–088) 19 rms ▥ ▥ ☎ **P**
** *Kypselos*, 41, od. G. Theotoki (Tel. 22–451) 18 rms ¶ ▥ ☎ **P**
* *Ephira*, 52, od. Vassileos Constantinou (Tel. 24–021) 45 rms ▥ ▥ ☎ **P**

At Kalamaki (6mls/9.5km: v. vicinity 4).
** *Kakamaki Beach* (Tel. 37–331) 74 rms ¶ ▥ ▥ ☎ ▥ **P**

△ **Campsites:**
Blue Dolphin, at Hagios Gerassimos (Tel. 25–766) 150 sites; open May–Oct. ▥
Corinth Beach, at Diavatika (Tel. 279–67) 150 sites; open April–Oct.
Diminio at Kato Diminio (Tel. 28–770) 80 sites.

🚋 **Trains and buses:** run very
🚌 regularly to and from Athens, and to the Peloponnese, taking about 1h.30.

CORINTH [ANCIENT], or Palea Korinthos, Tel. 0741

Hotel:
** *Xenia* (Tel. 31–208) 3 rms ¶ ▥ ▥ ※ **P**

CORINTH [Canal], Tel. 0741

Hotels:
*** *King Saron* (Tel. 25–301) 152 rms ¶ ▥ A/c ▥ ▥ ☎ ▥ ◁ **P**; open April–Oct.
** *Isthmia* (Tel. 23–454) 78 rms ¶ ▥ ▥ ☎ **P**

COS [Island] or Kos (Dodecanese), Tel. 0242

[i] **Tourist police:** 9, od. Koundouriotou (Tel. 28–227).

ONTO: on the quayside (Tel. 28–724).

Hotels:
**** *Atlantis* (Tel. 28–731) 223 rms, 74 bungalows ¶ ▥ ▥ ▥ ☎ ※ ▥ ▥ ◁ **P**; open April–Oct.
**** *PLM Dimitra Beach* (Tel. 28–581) 47 rms and 89 bungalows ¶ ▥ ▥ ☎ ※ ▥ ▥ ◁ ⊿/9 **P**; open April–Oct.
*** *Caravia* (Tel. 41–291) 214 rms and 83 bungalows ¶ ▥ A/c ▥ ☎ ▥ ▥ ◁ ⊿/9 **P**; open April–Oct.
*** *Continental Palace*, at Psalidi (Tel. 22–737) 180 rms ¶ ▥ ▥ ▥ ☎ ※ ▥ ▥ ◁ **P** April–Oct.
*** *Hippocrates Palace*, 2½mls/4km from Kos (Tel. 28–755) 155 rms ¶ ▥ A/c ▥ ☎ ▥ ▥ ◁ **P** night-club.
*** *Kos*, 31 Vassileos Georgiou; (Tel. 22–480) 137 rms ¶ ▥ ▥ ☎ ▥ **P** April–Oct.
*** *Ramira Beach*, at Psalidi (Tel. 28–489) 262 rms ¶ ▥ A/c ▥ ▥ ☎ ※ ▥ ▥ ◁ **P** April–Oct.
*** *Tigaki Beach*, at Tigaki (Tel. 29–446) 170 rms ¶ A/c ▥ ☎ ▥ ▥ **P**
** *Carda Beach*, at Kardamena (Tel. 51–332) 67 rms in bungalows ¶ ▥ ▥ ▥ ☎ ※ ▥ ◁ **P** April–Oct.
** *Alexandra*, od. 25 March (Tel. 28–301) 79 rms ¶ ▥ ▥ ☎ ▥ **P** April–Oct.
* *Christina*, 3, Charmilou (Tel. 22–466) 21 rms ¶ **P** May–Oct.

* *Oscar*, 59, od. Venizelou
  (Tel. 28-090) 193 rms ⑪ ▥
  🛏 🛀 ☎ 🖭 P April-Oct.
* *Eli*, 10 Themistocleous
  (Tel. 28-401) 78 rms ▥ 🛀 ☎
  P April-Oct.

△ **Campsite:**
  Kos Camping, in Psalidi
  (1½mls/2.5km from Cos;
  Tel. 23-275) 72 sites; May-
  Oct. ⚓

✈ **Air services:** to and from
  Athens and Rhodes (taking
  50 and 45 min) twice a day
  (*Olympic Airways*, Vas.
  Pavlou Tel. 28-331).

🚢 **Car ferries:** frequent services
  between Piraeus and Rhodes
  taking at least 12h.30; links
  with Turkey (Bodrum) though
  not guaranteed.

🚗 **Car hire:** *National Rent a Car*,
  3, od. Antinav Ioannidi
  (Tel. 28-828).

  Crete [Island] or Kriti, see
  *Khania, Rethymnon,
  Herakleion.*

  CYTHERA [Island] or Kythira
  (Laconia), Tel. 0733

  Hotel:
  Cythera, at Hagia Pelagia
  (Tel. 33-321) 10 rms ▥ 🛀 ⚓
  P full board.

🚢 **Car ferries:** 3 times a week to
  and from Piraeus, taking 12h,
  via Monemvassia and
  Neapolis, and to Kapsali,
  taking 13h.50; the route
  continues to Anticythera and
  Castelli (Crete).

✈ **Air services:** 1 flight daily for
  Athens in summer taking 1h.
  Olympic Airways, Potamos
  Kythiron, Tel. 33-201).

DAPHNI [Monastery] (Attica),
Tel. 01

△ **Campsite:**
  Daphni Camping
  (Tel. 590-95-27) 300 sites.

🛉 **Special event:** in late August-
  early September, Wine
  Festival in the park adjoining
  the monastery; all the Greek
  wines you could wish for.

  DELOS [Island] (Cyclades),
  Tel. 0284

  Hotel:
** *Xenia* (Tel. 22-259) 4 rms
  usually reserved for
  archaeologists.

🚢 **Boats:** you can sail here by
  caique from Mykonos (be
  warned, last boats back
  around 12.30), and in
  summer, boats to Tinos.

  DELPHI (Central Greece),
  Tel. 0265

ⓘ **Tourist police:** 27, od.
  Friderikis (Tel. 82-220).

  Hotels:
*** *Amalia*, Apollonos
  (Tel. 82-101) 185 rms ⑪ ▥
  A/c 🛏 🛀 ☎ P
*** *Vouzas*, 1, Pavlou and
  Friderikis (Tel. 82-232) 60 rms
  ⑪ ▥ 🛏 🛀 ☎ P
** *King Iniohos* (Tel. 82-701) 40
  rms ⑪ A/c 🛏 🛀 ☎ ❀ 🖭 P
** *Xenia* (Tel. 82-151) 44 rms ⑪
  ▥ 🛀 ☎ P
** *Europe* (Tel. 82-353; Athens
  Tel. 23-18-59) 46 rms ⑪ ▥ 🛀
  ☎ P
** *Kastalia* (Tel. 82-205) 21 rms
  ⑪ ▥ 🛀 ☎ P open
  March-Oct.
* *Greca* (Tel. 82-321) 23 rms.
  P ; open April-Oct.

* *Hermes* (Tel. 83–318) 24 rms
🛏 **P** ; open March-Oct.
* *Parnassos* (Tel. 82–321) 23
rms ⫠ 🛏 **P** ; open
March-Oct.
* *Pythia* (Tel. 82–328) 27 rms ⫠
P
* *Zeus*, 10, od. D. Fragou
(Tel. 82–691) 28 rms ⫠ ▥ 🛏
☎ **P**
Leto, 25, od. Apollonos
(Tel. 82–302) 22 rms ⫠ A/c
P
Kastri, 1, od. Sygrou
(Tel. 82–322) 24 rms **P**
Phoebos (Tel. 82–319) 20 rms
⫠ **P**

Youth Hostel: 31, od.
Apollonos (Tel. 82–268).

△ **Campsites:**
Apollo (Tel. 82–380) 1ml
(1.5km) from the village on
the Itea road; 96 sites; open
April-Oct. Beautiful site.
Chrissa Camping
(3.75mls/6km; Tel. 82–050) 55
sites.
Delphi Camping, on the Itea
road (Tel. 28–944) 48 sites;
open April-Oct.

🚌 **Buses:** to and from Athens 5
times a day, taking 3h.30; day
excursions from Athens.

DIAKOPTON (Peloponnese),
Tel. 0691

Hotel:
* *Panorea* (Tel. 41–216) 7 rms
▥ 🛏

Holiday Clubs:
Calogria: booking in Athens:
K. Arvanitis, 36, od. Voulis
(Tel. 322–67–47); open May 15
– Oct. 30.
Engali-Z. Plage; information
and booking in Athens, 6, od.
Ag. Constantinou (Tel. 361–
99–03); open June-Sept.

△ **Campsites:**
Kryoneri Camping, at Kration
(Tel. (0696) 31–405) 50 sites;
Open April-Oct.
Lemon Beach, at Silaveniotika
(Tel. (0696) 31–639) 80 sites;
open April-Oct. ⚓

🚆 **Trains:** to and from Athens,
on the Patras line, taking
3h.20.

DIDIMOTIKON (Thrace),
Tel. 0553

Hotel:
** *Plotini*, 1, Hag. Paraskevi
(Tel. 23–400) 67 rms ⫠ ▥ ♨
🛏 ☎ 🖵 night-club.

🚆 **Trains:** on the Thessaloniki-
Istanbul line, taking about 1h
from Thessaloniki and 2h.40
from Alexandroupolis.

DIROU [Caves of] (Laconia),
Tel. 0733

ℹ **Tourist police:** (Tel. 52–200).

DRAMA (Macedonia),
Tel. 0521

Hotels:
** *Xenia*, 10, od. Eth. Amynis
(Tel. 23–195) 48 rms ⫠ ▥ A/c
🛏 ☎ **P** night-club.
* *Apollo*, 20, od. Lambrianidou
(Tel. 25–551) 40 rms ▥ 🛏 ☎
P
* *Emborikon*, 8, od. Eth.
Amynis (Tel. 22–044) 48 rms
▥ 🛏 ☎ **P**

🚆 **Train:** to and from Athens,
taking 11h.30, via
Thessaloniki (3h.30).

🚌 **Buses:** twice a day to and
from Athens, taking 10h.

DREPANON (Peloponnese),
Tel. 0752

Hotel:
* *Plaka* (Tel. 59–420) 120 rms

🍴 🍺 🛏 🛁 🖃 ⚓ **P** ; open
March-Oct.

Δ **Campsites:**
Alkyon Beach, at Plaka
Drepanon (Tel. 92–336) 108
sites; open May-Oct. ⚓
Argolis Beach, at Plaka
Drepanon (Tel. 92–376) 44
sites; open March-Sept. ⚓
Blue Beach, at Candia
(Tel. (0753) 91–353) 45 sites
open May-Sept. ⚓
Iria Beach, at Paralia Iria
(Tel. (0753) 91–253) 44 sites;
open April-Oct. ⚓
Old Assini Beach, at Plaka
Drepanon (Tel. 92–396) 43
sites; open April-Oct. ⚓
Plaka Beach, at Plaka
Drepanon (Tel. 92–294) 36
sites. ⚓
Poseidon Camping, at Iria
(Tel. (0753) 91–341) 38 sites;
open May-Oct. ⚓

E

EDESSA (Macedonia),
Tel. 0381

🛈 **Tourist police** (from June to
Oct.) 31, od. Philippou
(Tel. 23–355).

Hotels:
** *Katarraktea,* 4, od. Karanou
(Tel. 22–300) 44 rms 🍴 🍺 A/c
🛏 🏦 ☎ **P**
** *Xenia,* 41, od. Philippou
(Tel. 22–995) 20 rms 🍴 🏦 ☎
P
* *Olympion,* 1, od. Vassileos
Georgiou (Tel. 23–485) 34 rms
P

�)🚃 **Trains:** to and from Florina
and Kozanti, and connections
for Athens and Thessaloniki.

🚌 **Buses:** twice a day to and
from Athens, taking 9h.25.

EKALI (Attica), Tel. 01

Hotels:
** *Ariadne,* 1, Platia Ariadnis
(Tel. 803–11–41) 9 rms 🍴 🍺
🏦 ☎ **P** open May-Sept.
* *Neon Aridne,* 3, od. Fassideri
(Tel. 803-12-02) 18 rms 🍴 🍺
🏦 **P**

ELEUSIS or Elefsis (Attica),
Tel. 01

Hotel:
* *Melissa,* 13, od. Persephonis
(Tel. 554-65-47) 17 rms 🍴 🍺
🏦 **P**

Elounda (Crete): *see Hagios
Nikolaos*

EPANOMI (Macedonia),
Tel. 0392

Δ **Campsite:**
Epanomi Camping
(Tel. 413-78) 560 pitches;
open April-Oct. ⚓

EPIDAURUS, or Epidavros
(Peloponnese), Tel. 0753

Hotels:
** *Xenia II* (Tel. 22-005) 24 rms
🍴 🍺 🏦 ☎ ♣ 🖃 open
April-Oct.

*At Nea Epidaurus
(10.6mls/17km):*
Epidauros (Tel. 31-209) 7 rms
🏦 **P**

*At Palea Epidaurus
(13.75mls/22km):*
** *Stratos* (Tel. 41-535) 12 rms
open June-Sept.
Maronika (Tel. 41-391) 10 rms
🏦 **P**
Koronis (Tel. 41-209) 7 rms 🏦
P
Aktis (Tel. 41-407) 8 rms 🏦 **P**

Restaurant:
At Palea Epidaurus:
Douce France (Tel. 41-219).

Δ **Campsites:**
Bekas, at Palea Epidaurus, on the beach (Tel. 41–394) 43 sites; open April-Oct.
Nicolas, at Palea Epidaurus (Tel. 41–297) 28 sites.
Verdellis, at Palea Epidaurus on the beach at Galiassi (Tel. 41–425) 36 sites; open April-Oct.

� **Special event:** from 23 June to 9 Sept. Epidaurus Festival, performances of the ancient tragedies (information GNTO Festivals Office, under the Spyrou Miliou Arcade, 4, od. Stadiou, Athens. Tel. 322-14-59; at Epidaurus Tel. 21–005 and at travel agencies).

ERATINI (central Greece), Tel. 0266

Hotel:
** *Delphi Beach* (Tel. 31–237) 177 rms ¶¶ ▥ A/c ♨ 🅐 ☎ ☀ 🖼 ≈ ℚ P

Δ **Campsite:**
Doric, Hagios Nikolaos Beach, 70 sites; open April-Oct.

ERETRIA (Euboea), Tel. 0221

Hotels:
*** *Chryssi Akti* (Tel. 61–012) 100 rms ¶¶ A/c ♨ 🅐 ☎ ☀ 🖼 ≈ ℚ P ; open April-Oct.
*** *Holiday Club Olympia,* at Malakonta (Tel. 62–411) 234 rms ¶¶ ▥ A/c ♨ 🅐 ☎ 🖼 ≈ ℚ P night-club; open March-Oct.
** *Perighiali Eretrias* (Tel. 62–439) 42 rms ¶¶ ▥ ♨ 🅐 ☎ open April-Oct; bed and breakfast only.
** *Karystos Beach* (Tel. 23–141) 85 rms ¶¶ ▥ ♨ 🅐 ☎ 🖼 ℚ P ; open April-Oct.
** *Holidays in Evia*, at Magoula (Tel. 62–612) 324 rms ¶¶ ▥

♨ 🅐 ☎ 🖼 ≈ P night-club.
** *Malaconta Beach,* at Malakonta (Tel. 62–511) 155 rms ¶¶ ▥ A/c 🅐 ☎ 🖼 ≈ ℚ P night-club.

At Amarinthos (5mls/8km):
** *Blue Beach* (Tel. 72–305) 210 rms ¶¶ ▥ A/c 🅐 ☎ 🖼 ≈ ℚ ♪/9 P ; open April-Oct.
** *Stephania* (Tel. 72–485) 80 rms ¶¶ A/c ♨ 🅐 ☎ ≈ P night-club.

At Karystos (6.6mls/10.6km):
** *Apollon Resort*, Psyli Amnos Beach (Tel. 22–045) 79 rms ¶¶ ▥ ♨ 🅐 ☎ ☀ ≈ P ; open April-Sept.

Holiday Club:
*** *Dream's Island* (Tel. 62–209) information and booking in Athens, 51, od. Stadiou (Tel. 321-48-28) 98 bungalows ¶¶ 🅐 ☎ 🖼 ≈ ℚ ♪/9

⚓ **Car ferries:** run frequently to Skala Oropos, taking 25 min.

ERMIONI (Peloponnese), Tel. 0754

Hotels:
*** *Porto Hydra*, in Plepi (Tel. 41–270) 271 rms or bungalows ¶¶ A/c ♨ 🅐 ☎ TV ☀ 🖼 ≈ ℚ ♪/9 P night-club.
*** *Hydra-Beach Kappa Club,* in Plepi (6.3mls/10km; Tel. 41–206) 272 rms or bungalows ¶¶ ▥ A/c 🅐 🅐 🚌 ♦ 🖼 ≈ ℚ P night-club; open April-Oct.
** *Costa Perla* (Tel. 31–111) 190 bungalows; information in Athens, 11, od. Voukourestiou (Tel. 324-10-07) ¶¶ ▥ 🅐 ☎ 🚌 ☀ 🖼 ≈ ℚ ♪/9 P ; open April-Oct.
** *Lena-Mary Beach* (Tel. 31–451) 120 rms ¶¶ ▥ A/c ♨ 🅐 ☀ ≈ ℚ ♪/9 P ;

open April-Oct.
** *Aquarius*, at Petrothalassa
(2½mls/4km; Tel. 31–430) 210
rms and 212 bungalows ¶ ▦
A/c 🛁 🏠 ☎ 🚌 ☀ 🔲 ⚓ ⚲ ⚲/9
P night-club; open April-Oct.

Euboea [Island], or Evia: *see
Chalcis, Eretria, Hagios
Nikolaos, Loutra Aedipsos
and Kymi.*

EVZONI (Macedonia),
Tel. 0343

 GNTO: frontier post
(Tel. 512-08).

F

FLORINA (Macedonia),
Tel. 0385

Hotels:
** *King Alexander,* 68, leof. Nikis
(Tel. 23–501) 38 rms ¶ ▦ 🛁
🏠 ☎ P
** *Lyngos,* 3 Tagmatarchou
Naoum (Tel. 28–322) 40 rms
¶ ▦ 🏠 ☎ P
** *Tottis* (Tel. 22–645) 32 rms ¶
▦ 🏠 ☎ P
* *Antigone,* 1, od. Arianou
(Tel. 23–180) 80 rms ¶ ▦ 🛁
🏠 ☎ P

G

Galaxidi: *see Itea*

GASTOUNI (Peloponnese),
Tel. 0623

Hotel:
Odysseus, 4, Platia
Eleftherias, 10 rms

△ **Campsites:**
Amaliada Camping, at
Kourouta (Tel. (0622) 28-543)
166 sites; open April-Oct. ⚓
Kourouta Camping (Touring

Club of Greece), at Kourouta
(Tel. (0622) 22–901) 130
sites; open March-Oct. ⚓
Paradise Car Camping, at
Palouki (Tel. (0622) 22-721)
300 sites; open April-Oct. ⚓

Gavrion (Andros): *see Andros.*

GHERAKINI (Macedonia),
Tel. 0371

Hotel:
*** *Gerakina Beach* (Tel. 51-118)
503 rms ¶ ▦ 🛁 🏠 ☎ ☀ 🔲
⚓ ⚲ ⚲/9 P night-club; open
April-Oct.

△ **Campsite:**
Aphroditi (Tel. 51-444) 100
sites; open May-Sept.

GHYTHION (Peloponnese),
Tel. 0733

Hotels:
** *Belle Hélène,* at Vathy
Ageranou (Tel. 22-867) 98
rms ¶ ▦ 🏠 ☎ ☀ ⚓ ⚲ P;
open April-Oct.
** *Lakonis* (Tel. 22-667) 74 rms
¶ 🏠 ☎ ⚓ 🔲 P

△ **Campsites:**
Ghythion Beach, on the
beach at Agadeika, 2mls
(3km) from Ghythion on the
Aeropolis road (Tel. 22-770)
71 sites ⚓ open April-Oct.
Mani Beach, at Mavrovounion
(Tel. 23-450) 238 sites; open
April-Sept.

🚌 **Buses:** to and from Athens, 4
times a day, taking 6h.30.

GLYFADA (Attica), Tel. 01

 Tourist police: 1, od. Alsou
(Tel. 894-65-55).

Hotels:
**** *Astir,* 58, Vassileos Georgiou
(Tel. 8946-461) 128
bungalows ¶ ▦ A/c 🏠 ☎ ☀
🔲 ⚓ ⚲ P night-club; open
April-Oct.

*** *Atrium,* 10, Vassileos Georgiou (Tel. 8940–971) 56 rms ¶¶ ▥ A/c ♨ ⌂ ☎ ≈ ♪/9 ▣ P

*** *Congo Palace,* Vassileos Georgiou (Tel. 8946–711) 93 rms ¶¶ ▥ A/c ♨ ⌂ ☎ P night-club; open April-Oct.

*** *Emmantina,* 33, Vas. Georgiou B (Tel. 893-21-11) 80 rms ¶¶ A/c ♨ ⌂ ☎ ▤ ▣ P

*** *Florida,* 33, od. Metaxa (Tel. 894-7215) 86 rms ¶¶ ▥ A/c ♨ ⌂ ☎ ▤ P night-club.

*** *Golden Sun,* 72, od. Metaxa (Tel. 895-52-18) ¶¶ A/c ♨ ⌂ ☎ ▤ P

*** *Oasis,* 26, Vas. Georgiou B (Tel. 894-16-62) 70 apartments A/c ♨ ⌂ ☎ TV ☀ ▤ ♀ ▣ P

*** *Palace,* 4, Vassileos Georgiou (Tel. 894-16-11) 79 rms ¶¶ ▥ A/c ♨ ⌂ ☎ ▤ P

*** *Palmyra Beach,* 70, Vassileos Georgiou (Tel. 894-58-08) 49 rms ¶¶ ▥ A/c ♨ ⌂ ☎ ≈ P

** *Antonopoulos,* 1, Vas. Friderikis (Tel. 894-62-42) 44 rms ¶¶ ▥ A/c ♨ ⌂ ☎ ♪/9 P

** *Delfini,* 5, od. Xanthou (Tel. 895-30-40) 39 rms ¶¶ A/c ▥ ♨ ⌂ ☎ ≈ P

** *Fenix,* 1, od. Artemidos (Tel. 894-72-29) 139 rms ¶¶ ▥ A/c ♨ ⌂ ☎ ▤ ≈ P night-club.

** *Four Seasons,* 79, Vassileos Georgiou (Tel. 894-22-11) 78 rms ▥ A/c ♨ ⌂ ☎ P

** *Gripsholm,* 4, od. Karapanou (Tel. 894-49-11) 67 rms ¶¶ ▥ A/c ♨ ⌂ ☎ P

** *Ideal,* 47, Vas. Constantinou (Tel. 894-49-37) 40 rms ▥ ⌂ ☎ P

** *John's,* 3 Pandors Vas. Konstantinous (Tel. 895-17-73) 68 rms ¶¶ A/c ♨ ⌂ ☎ P

** *London,* 38, Vas. Georgiou (Tel. 894-5634) 75 rms ¶¶ ▥ A/c ♨ ⌂ ☎ ▣ P

** *Niki,* 47, od. Diadochou Pavlou (Tel. 894-62-31) 61 rms ¶¶ ▥ A/c ♨ ⌂ ☎ ☀ ≈ P

** *Regina Maris,* 11, od. Diadochou Pavlou (Tel. 895-51-18) 71 rms ¶¶ ▥ A/c ♨ ⌂ ☎

** *Riviera,* 2, od. Fivis (Tel. 895-20-11) 81 rms ¶¶ A/c ▥ ♨ ⌂ ☎ ≈ P

** *Sea View,* 4, od. Xanthou (Tel. 895-13-11) 74 rms ¶¶ A/c ♨ ⌂ ☎ ▤ ♀ P night-club.

** *Stergios,* 31 Ilias, at Ano Glyfada (Tel. 894-37-23) 44 rms ¶¶ ▥ ♨ ⌂ ☎ P

* *Beau Rivage,* 87, Vas. Georgiou B (Tel. 894-92-92) 82 rms ¶¶ A/c ♨ ⌂ ☎ ♀ ♪/9 P

* *Glyfada,* 40, Vassileos Georgiou (Tel. 894-68-33) 52 rms ▥ ♨ ⌂ ☎ ☀ ≈ ♀ P

* *Oceanis,* 23, od. Vasilisis Friderikis (Tel. 894-40-38) 74 rms ¶¶ ▥ ♨ ⌂ ☎ ▤ P

* *Perla,* 7, od. Chryssilidos (Tel. 894-42-12) 58 rms ¶¶ ▥ ♨ ⌂ ☎ ☀ ≈ P night-club.

Restaurants:

** *Psaropoulos,* sea front (Tel. 894-56-03) P popular but quite expensive.

** *Asteria,* sea front (Tel. 894-56-75) P taverna-cabaret.

* *Antonopoulos,* by the sea (Tel. 894-56-36).

* *Water-Wheel,* 71, Vas. Georgiou (Tel. 893-21-19).

Tavernas:

Kyra Antigoni, 54, od. Pandoras (Tel. 895-24-11), pleasant garden.

Night-Club:
**** *Dilina*, 2, Vassileos Georgiou (Tel. 894-73-21) **P** dinner from 10p.m. to midnight, with band and dance floor, then Greek bouzouki music.

HAGIA PARASKEVI (Macedonia), Tel. 0374

Hotel:
** *Aphrodite*, at Loutra (Tel. 71-228) 24 rms ¶ ▥ ⌂ ☎ **P**; open April-Sept.

HAGIA TRIAS (Macedonia), Tel. 0392

Hotels:
*** *Sun Beach* (Tel. 51-221) 120 ¶ A/c ♨ ⌂ ☎ ▱ ≈ ⚲ ⚱/⁹ **P**; open May-Oct.
* *Galaxy* (Tel. 22-291) 80 rms ¶ ▥ A/c ♨ ⌂ ☎ ≈ **P**

Δ **Campsite:**
Akti Thermaikon (Tel. 51-360) 440 sites ≈ ⚲

HAGI APOSTOLI (Attica), Tel. 0295

Hotels:
*** *Calamos Beach* (Tel. 81-465) 277 rms ¶ ▥ ♨ ☎ ※ ▱ ≈ ⚲ **P** night-club.
* *Delphinia* (Tel. 81-202) 138 rms ¶ ▥ ♨ ☎ ※ ▱ **P**

HAGII THEODORI (Attica), Tel. 0741

Hotels:
** *Hanikian* (Tel. 67-151) 271 rms ¶ ▥ A/c ♨ ⌂ ☎ ※ ≈ ⚲ ⚱/⁹ **P**; open April-Oct.
** *Margarita* (Tel. 67-434) 12 rms ¶ ⌂ ☎ ≈ **P**; open April-Sept.
** *Siagas Beach* (Tel. 67-501) 101 rms ¶ ▥ ⌂ ☎ ≈ ⚱/⁹ **P** night-club.

HAGIO KAMBOS (Euboea).

⚓ **Car ferries:** 5 times a day to Glyfa, taking 30 min.

HAGIOS AVGOSTINOS (Peloponnese), Tel. 0722

Hotel:
*** *San Agostinon Beach* (Tel. 22-150) 330 rms and bungalows ¶ ▥ ♨ ⌂ ☎ ※ ▱ ⚲ ⚱/⁹ **P** night-club.

Δ **Campsites:**
Eros Beach, at Petaloudi (Tel. 31-208) 70 sites; open April-Oct. ≈
Zervas Beach, at Petalidi (Tel. 31-009) 44 sites; open April-Oct. ≈

HAGIOS CONSTANTINOS (Central Greece), Tel. 0235

Hotels:
*** *Leventi* (Motel; Tel. 31-806) 28 rms ¶ ▥ ⌂ ☎ ≈ **P**
* *Acrogiali* (Tel. 31-656) 15 rms ⌂ ☎ ≈ **P**; open June-Sept.

⚓ **Car-ferries:** have frequent sailings for Loutra Aedipsos (Eubea); services to Skiathos, Glossa, Skopelos, Alonissos, Lemnos, Kavalia, Samothrace and Alexandroupolis.

HAGIOS IOANNIS (Thessaly), Tel. 0426

Hotels:
** *Aloe* (Tel. 31-241) 44 rms ¶ ▥ ♨ ⌂ ☎ **P**
* *Mars* (Tel. 31-477) 47 rms ▥ ⌂ ☎ open March-Dec.
Aegeon (Tel. 31-240) 22 rms ¶ ▥ ⌂ ☎ **P**; open April-Oct.

HAGIOS NIKOLAOS (Crete), Tel. 0842

Tourist police: 7, od. Ormirou (Tel. 22-321).

Hotels:

**** *Minos Beach*, Akti Ilia Sotirchou (Tel. 22–345) 125 bungalows ⫪ ▤ ⌂ ☎ ☀ ▨ ⇌ **P**

**** *Mirabello Village* (Tel. 28–401) 131 rms and bungalows ⫪ A/c ⌂ ☎ ▨ ⇌ ⚲ **P** night-club; open March-Nov.

**** *Minos Palace* (Tel. 23–800) 148 rms ⫪ A/c ⛴ ⌂ ☎ TV ▨ ⇌ ⚲ ⚮/9 ▣ **P** night-club.

*** *Hermes*, Akti Koundourou (Tel. 28–253) 204 rms ⫪ ▤ ⌂ ☎ ▨ ⚮/9 **P**; open April-Oct.

** *Ariadne Beach*, Gargadoros (Tel. 22–741) 76 rms ⫪ ⌂ ☎ ⇌ **P**; open March-Oct.

** *Corali*, Akti Koundourou (Tel. 28–363) 170 rms ⫪ ⌂ ☎ ▨ **P**

** *Domenico*, 5 Argyropoulon (Tel. 22–845) 25 rms ⫪ ⌂ ⇌ **P**; open March-Oct.

** *El Greco* (Tel. 28–894) 38 rms ⫪ ▤ ⌂ ☎ ⇌ **P**; open March-Oct.

** *Rea* (Tel. 28–321) 113 rms ⫪ ▤ ⛴ ⌂ ☎ ☀ ⇌ **P**

* *Akratos*, 19, 28 Octovriou (Tel. 22–721) 31 rms ⫪ ⌂ **P**

* *Alcestis*, 30, Akti Koundourou (Tel. 22–454) 24 rms ⫪ **P**

* *Du Lac*, 17, 28 Octovriou (Tel. 22–712) 40 rms **P**

At Kalo Horio (8.1mls/13km, E. Tel. 0841):

**** *Istron Bay*, Pilos (Tel. 22–850) 106 rms ⫪ ▤ A/c ⌂ ☎ ▨ ⇌ ⚲ **P** night-club; open April-Oct.

At Elounda (7.5mls/12km E. Tel. 0841):

***** *Astir Palace Elounda Bay* (Tel. 41–580) 297 rms and bungalows ⫪ A/c ⛴ ⌂ ☎ 🚌 ☀ ▨ ⇌ ⚲ **P** March-Oct.

**** *Elounda Beach* (Tel. 41–412) 156 rms and 140 bungalows ⫪ ▤ A/c ⌂ ☎ ☀ ▨ ⇌ ⚲ **P**

**** *Elounda Mare* (Tel. 41–512) 50 rms and 30 bungalows, 18 of which have a private swimming pool ⫪ ▤ A/c ⌂ ☎ ☀ ▨ ⇌ ▣ **P**; open March-Oct.

** *Elounda Marmin* (Tel. 41–535) 108 rms and bungalows ⫪ ▤ A/c ⌂ ☎ ▨ ⇌ ⚲ open March-Oct.

** *Driros Beach* (Tel. 41–283) 16 rms, open April-Oct.

* *Aristea* at Shisma (Tel. 41–300) 37 rms ⫪ ⌂ ⇌ ⚲ ⚮/9 **P**

At Hierapetra (22.5mls/36km; vicin. 3; Tel. 0842):

*** *Ferma Beach* (Tel. 28–418) 89 rms and bungalows ⫪ A/c ⌂ ☎ ☀ ▨ ⚲ **P**; open March-Nov.

*** *Petra Mare* (Tel. 22–412) 221 rms ⫪ A/c ⛴ ⌂ ☎ ☀ ▨ ⇌ ⚲ **P**; open April-Oct.

* *Coriva Vaillage*, 5mls (8km) from Ierapetra (Tel. 61–263) 40 rms and bungalows ⫪ ⌂ ☎ ▨ ⇌ open April-Oct.

* *Kyrva*, 45, od. Emm. Lambraki: (Tel. 22–594), 16 rms ⌂

* *Atlantis*, in Hagios Andreas (Tel. 28–555) 69 rms ⫪ A/c ⌂ ⇌ **P**

At Sitia (42mls/66km; vicin. 4; Tel. 0843):

*** *Sitian Beach Kappa Club* (Tel. 28–821) 162 rms ⫪ A/c ⌂ ☎ ☀ ▨ ⇌ ⚲ **P**; open April-Oct.

** *Maresol* (Tel. 28–933) 27 bungalows ⫪ ⌂ ☎ ▨ ⇌ ⚲ **P**; open April-Oct.

* *Crystal*, 19, od. Kapetan Sifi (Tel. 22–284) 41 rms ▤ ⇌ **P**

At Zakros (67.5mls/108km: vicin. 4; Tel. 0843):

* *Itanos* (Tel. 22–146) 72 rms ⫪ A/c ⛴ ⌂ ☎ **P**

* *Zakros* (Tel. 28-479) 15 rms 🏛 P

Youth Hostels: at *Hagios Nikolaos*, 3, od. S. Koraka (Tel. 28-121); at *Hierapetra*, 32, od. S. Samouil (Tel. 22-463); at *Sitia*, 24, od. Angelaki (Tel. 22-693).

Δ **Campsite:**
Hierapetra Camping, at Hierapetra (see Vicin. 3; Tel. 22-739); 45 sites; open May-Oct.

Restaurants and tavernas: there are numerous tavernas at the port and by the lakeside (*Poseidon, Zorba, Dolfin, Dilina*), as at Sitia or Hierapetra.

🚗 **Car hire:** *Avis,* Akti Koundourou (Tel. 28-497); *Budget*, 36, Akti Koundourou (Tel. 22-800); *Hertz*, 17, Platia Koundourou (Tel. 28-311). At Hierapetra: *Avis*. 1, od. Kothri (Tel. 28-673). At Sitia: *Budget,* 2, od. Demokritos (Tel. 28-446).

HANIOTIS (Macedonia), Tel. 0374

Hotels:
** *Dionysos* (Tel. 51-402) 32rms ▥ 🍴 🏛 ☎ P ; open April-Oct.
** *Soussouras* (Tel. 51-251) 17 rms 🍴 A/c 🍴 🏛 ☎ 🛏 ≈ ⚲ P ; open April-Oct.
* *Strand* (Tel. 51-261) 45 rms 🍴 A/c 🍴 🏛 ≈ P night-club; open April-Oct.

HERAKLEION (Crete), Tel. 081

ℹ️ **Tourist police:** od. Dikaiossinis (Tel. 283-190).

GNTO: 1, od. Xanthoudidou (Tel. 282-096).

ELPA: leof. Knossou and G. Papandreou (Tel. 28-94-40).

Hotels:
*** *Astoria* (Pl. b, C-2), Platia Eleftherias (Tel. 28-64-64) 145 rms 🍴 ▥ A/c 🍴 🏛 ☎ 🛏 ⚲ P night-club.
*** *Atlantis* (Pl. c, D-2), Meramvelou and Hygias Streets (Tel. 28-82-41) 164 rms 🍴 ▥ A/c 🏛 ☎ 🛏 ⚲ P
*** *Galaxy*, 67, leof. Demokratias (Tel. 236-421) 148 rms 🍴 A/c 🍴 🏛 ☎ ✳ 🛏 P
*** *Xenia* (Pl. k, B-1), od. Venizelou (Tel. 28-40-00) 84 rms 🍴 ▥ 🏛 ☎ 🛏 P
** *Cosmopolite* (Pl. d, C-3), 44, od. Evans (Tel. 28-33-13) 36 rms ▥ 🏛 ☎ P
** *Castro* (Pl. e, C-1), 20, od. Theotokopoulou (Tel. 28-50-20) 38 rms ▥ 🏛 ☎ P
** *Esperia* (Pl. f, C-2), 20, od. Idomeneus (Tel. 28-82-11) 52 rms 🏛 ☎ P
** *Mediterranean* (Pl. g, C-2), Platia Daskaloyanni (Tel. 28-93-31) 55 rms 🍴 ▥ A/c 🏛 ☎ P
** *Petra,* 55, Dikeossinis (Tel. 28-00-33) 30 rms ▥ 🏛 P
* *Daedalos,* 15, od. Dedalou (Tel. 22-43-91) 60 rms A/c P
* *El Greco* (Pl. i, C-2), 4, od. Chilia Oktakossia Ikossi (Tel. 28-10-71) 82 rms P
* *Herakleion* (Pl. p, B-2), od. Kalokairinou (Tel. 28-18-81) 41 rms P
* *Knossos* (Pl. m, C-2), 37, od. 25 Avgoustos (Tel. 28-32-47) 18 rms P
* *Lato,* 15 Epimedinou (Tel. 22-50-01) 54 rms
* *Marin,* 12, od. Beaufort (Tel. 28-85-82) 48 rms P
* *Olympic* (Pl. n, C-3), Platia

Korrou (Tel. 28–88–61) 53 rms **P**

* *Park* (Pl. o, C-1), 5, od. Koroneou (Tel. 28–39–34) 27 rms **P**

Vicinity of Herakleion:
*** *Agapi Beach*, at Amourada (3.1mls/5km Tel. 22–55–01) 203 rms ¶¶ ▥ ⌂ ☎ ▭ ☞ **P**; open April-Oct.

*** *Akti Zeus*, at Linoperamata (5mls/8km Tel. 82–15–03) 400 rms ¶¶ ▥ A/c ♨ ⌂ ☎ ▭ ☞ ९ ₊/⁹ **P**; open April-Oct.

*** *Apollonia Beach*, at Linoperamata (5mls/8km; Tel. 22–37–66) 237 rms or bungalows ¶¶ ▥ ♨ ⌂ ☎ ❋ ▭ ☞ **P** night-club; open April-Oct.

*** *Arina Sand*, at Hani Kokkini (7.5mls/12km; Tel. 76–11–13) 233 rms or bungalows ¶¶ A/c ♨ ⌂ ☎ ❋ ☞ ९ **P**; open April-Oct.

*** *Candia Beach*, at Gouves 12.5mls (20km) on the Hagios Nikolaos road (Tel. 41–241) 217 rms ¶¶ ▥ A/c ⌂ ☎ ▭ ☞ ९ **P**; open March-Nov.

*** *Creta Beach*, in Amoudara (3.1mls/5km; Tel. 28–63–01) 160 Bungalows ¶¶ ▥ ⌂ ☎ ❋ ▭ ☞ ; open March-Oct.

*** *Dolphin Bay*, at Amoudara (Tel. 82–12–76) 141 rms ¶¶ ▥ ♨ ⌂ ☎ TV ▭ ☞ ९ **P**; open April-Oct.

*** *Knossos Beach*, at 7.5mls (12km) on the road to Hagios Nikolaos (Tel. 28–84–50) 106 rms and bungalows ¶¶ ▥ ⌂ ☞ **P**; open April-Oct.

*** *Marina*, at Gouves (Tel. 41–361) 250 rms ¶¶ A/c ♨ ⌂ ☎ ▭ ☞ ९ **P**; open March-Nov.

*** *Minoa Palace*, at 4.4mls (7km)

on the Hagios Nikolaos road (Tel. 22–53–33) 124 rms ¶¶ A/c ♨ ⌂ ☎ TV ❋ ▭ ☞ **P**; open April-Oct.

*** *Themis Beach*, at Hani Kokkini (Tel. 76–13–74) 124 rms ¶¶ ▥ A/c ⌂ ☎ ▭ ☞ ₊/⁹ **P**; open April-Oct.

** *Xenia*, at 4.4mls (7km) on the Hagios Nikolaos road (Tel. 28–18–41) 41 rms ¶¶ ▥ ⌂ ☎ ☞ **P**; open May-Oct.

** *America* (Tel. 76–231) 48 rms ¶¶ ▥ ⌂ ☎ ☞ **P**

** *Amnissos (Motel)*, at 4.4mls/7km on the Hagios Nikolaos road (Tel. 28–13–32) 54 rms ¶¶ ▥ ⌂ ☎ ▭ **P**; open March-Nov.

** *Aphrodite*, at Gouves (Tel. 41–271) 234 rms ¶¶ A/c ♨ ⌂ ☎ ▭ ☞ **P**

** *Karteros*, at 4.4mls (7km) on the Hagios Nikolaos road (Tel. 225–231) 54 rms ▥ ♨ ⌂ ☎ **P**; open April-Oct.

At Hagia Pelaghia (15mls/24km NW):
*** *Capsis Beach* (Tel. 23–33–95) 554 rms and bungalows ¶¶ A/c ⌂ ☎ ▭ ☞ ९ ₊/⁹ **P**; open March-Oct.

** *Panorama* (Tel. 28–94–01) 56 rms ¶¶ ⌂ ☎ ☞ ▭ ९ open April-Oct.

At Archanes (9.3mls/15km; vicin. 4):
** *Dias* (Tel. 75–810) 31 rms ▥ ⌂ ☎ open April-Oct.

At Limin Chersonissou (15mls/24km: vicin. 7; Tel. 0897):
**** *Creta Maris* (Tel. 22–115) 516 rms and 229 bungalows ¶¶ ▥ A/c ♨ ⌂ ☎ ▯ ▭ ☞ ९ **P** night-club; open April-Oct.

*** *Belvedere* (Tel. 22–010) 320 rms ¶¶ ▥ ♨ ⌂ ☎ ❋ ▭ **P**; open March-Oct.

** *King Minos Palace*
(Tel. 22-781) 143 rms ⵏ A/c
🏠 ☎ 🖼 ≈ ⵊ ⌇/9 **P**; open
April-Oct.
** *Lyttos*, Agissanas (Tel. 22-575)
325 rms ⵏ A/c 🏠 ☎ 🖼 ≈ ⵊ
⌇/9 **P** night-club; open
April-Oct.
** *Glaros*, 5, od. Bouboulina
(Tel. 22-106) 141 rms ⵏ 🏠 ☎
≈ **P**; open April-Oct.
** *Heronissos*, od. Zotour
(Tel. 22-501) 89 rms ⵏ 🏠 ☎
🖼 ≈ **P**; open April-Oct.
** *Maragakis*, ⵏ ⅏ 🏠 ☎ 🖼 **P**;
open April-Oct.
** *Nora* (Tel. 22-271) 181 rms ⵏ
⅏ 🍴 🏠 ☎ 🖼 ≈ **P** night-
club; open April-Oct.
** *Sergios*, od. E. Venelou
(Tel. 22-583) 97 rms ⵏ ⅏ 🏠
☎ ≈ **P**; open April-Oct..
** *Villes Esperides* (Tel. 22-322)
27 rms ⵏ 🏠 🖼 ≈ **P**; open
April-Oct.

*At Mallia (22mls/35km; vicin.
7; Tel 0897):*
** *Ikaros Village* (Tel. 31-267)
172 rms and 92 bungalows ⵏ
⅏ 🍴 🏠 ☎ 🚌 ❊ 🖼 ≈ **P**
** *Kernos Beach* (Tel. 31-421)
246 rms ⵏ ⅏ A/c 🍴 🏠 ☎ ❊
🖼 ≈ **P**
** *Siren's Beach* (Tel. 31-321)
220 rms ⵏ ⅏ A/c 🍴 🏠 ☎ ❊
🖼 ≈ **P**; open April-Oct.
** *Grammatikaki* (Tel. 31-366)
50 rms ⵏ ⅏ 🍴 🏠 ☎ 🖼 **P**;
open March-Nov.
** *Mallia Beach* (Tel. 31-210) 52
rms ⵏ ⅏ 🍴 🏠 ☎ ≈ **P**;
open April-Oct.
** *Phaedra Beach* (Tel. 31-560)
71 rms ⵏ 🏠 ≈ **P**; open
April-Oct.

*At Stalis (17.5mls/28km;
vicin. 6):*
** *Anthoussa Beach* (Tel. 31-
380) 167 rms ⵏ ⅏ A/c 🍴 🏠

☎ 🖼 ≈ **P**; open April-Oct.
** *Blue Sea* (Tel. 31-371) 190
bungalows ⵏ ⅏ A/c 🍴 🏠 ☎
❊ 🖼 ≈ **P**; open March-Nov.
** *Palm Beach* (Tel. 31-375) 22
rms ⵏ ⅏ 🏠 ≈ **P**; open
April-Oct.

Youth Hostel: at *Herakleion*,
24, od. Handakos
(Tel. 28-62-81) and *Mallia*
(Tel. 31-355) given the state
of building, a small, cheap
hotel would be
preferable.

Δ **Campsites:**
Caravan, at Limin
Chersonissou (Tel. 21-025) 36
sites, 14 bungalows; open
April-Oct. ≈
Creta, at Gouves (Tel. (0897)
41-400) 90 sites; open April-
Oct. ≈
Herakleion, at Amoudara
(Tel. (081) 28-63-80) 283
sites; open April-Oct. ≈
Mallia Camping (Tel. 31-460)
158 sites, 17 bungalows; open
April-Oct. ≈

Restaurants:
Caprice, od. Venizelou
(Tel. 283-675).
New Ionia, 5, od. Evans
(Tel. 283-213).
Knossos, Platia Venizelou
(Tel. 282-848).

Tavernas: there are numerous
tavernas in the town, both
with and without music, for
example, on the road to
Knossos. Od. Daedalou:
Kostos, Klimataria, Minos; in
the El Greco Park: *Maxim;* od
25 Avgoustos: *Psaria:* and at
the port. *Ligeros:* near Platia
Eleftherias Square: *Kalithea*,
etc.

Post Office:
Main Post Office (Pl. C-2), od.

Zografou; *telegraph and telephone* (Pl. C-2).

✈ **Airport:** 2.5mls (4km) along the Hagios Nikolaos road; 5 to 8 daily flights to Athens, taking 45 min; daily flights to Rhodes, taking 40 min; 3 flights a week to Mykonos; 3 to 4 flights a week to Santorini (Thera).

Airlines:
Olympic Airways (Pl. C-3), airport, Platia Ethnikis Anastasseos (Tel. 28-88-66). Air France, od. 25 Avgoustos (Tel. 22-59-44).

⚓ **Boats:** at least 2 daily direct car-ferry links with Piraeus, taking 11h, and 2 sailings a week via Santorini and Paros.

Shipping companies:
Efthimiadis (ferry boats *Knossos, Minos* and *Sophia*) od. 25 Avgoustos; a daily service to Piraeus, taking 11h or 12h.30.

🚌 **Buses:** at the port to Rethymnon, Chania and Hagios Nikolaos, Knossos Archanes, Mallia; take the Chania bus for the W. and SW of the region; take the Kenouria bus for the SE of the region.

🚗 **Car hire:** *Autorent,* 17, Platia Venizelou (Tel. 282-933); *Avis,* 58, od. 25 Avgoustos (Tel. 282-9631), and at the airport; *Budget,* 34, od. 25 Avgoustos (Tel. 221-315); *Hellas-cars,* Platia Mag. Dimitrios (Tel. 235-596); *Hertz,* 44, od. 25 Avgoustos (Tel. 225-371), and at the airport. *At Mallia; Avis,* 94, Venizelou (Tel. 31-238); *Budget,* 3, leof. Venizelou (Tel. 31-339).

Shopping: beautiful copies of ancient jewellery and attractive modern designs at Fountoulakis, 4, Platia Eleftherias; a wide choice of souvenirs of all kinds at the Knossos Palace, 51, leof. Constantinou. Cretan embroidery and weaving at Kastrinogiannaki, opposite the Archaeological Museum. *Handicraft Exhibition,* Zografou and Houdrou (Tel. 28-02-25).

Hierapetra (Crete): *see Hagios Nikolaos.*

HIERISSOS (Macedonia), Tel. 0377.

Hotel:
** *Mt Athos* (Tel. 22-225) 45 rms ¶ A/c 🛏 🛁 ☎ ⚓ ♀ P open April-Oct.

Hios [Island] or Chios (Cyclades), *v. Chios.*

HOSIOS LOUKAS [Monastery]

🚌 **Bus:** to and from Athens, once a day, taking 4h.

HYDRA [Island] (Saronic gulf), Tel. 0298

ℹ **Tourist police:** od. Navarchou N. Votsi (Tel. 52-205).

Hotels:
*** *Miramare* (Tel. 52-300; Athens Tel. 62-00-97) 28 rms ¶ 🛁 ☎ ⚓ boarding house, open April-Oct.
*** *Miranda* (Tel. 52-230; Athens Tel. 52-29-686) 16 rms ¶ 🛁 ☎ P pension.
** *Amaryllis* (Tel. 52-249) 10 rms ⚓ boarding house.
** *Hydroussa* (Tel. 52-400) 36 rms ¶ ⾨ 🛁 ☎ ⚓ open all year.

* *Leto* (Tel. 52–280); Athens Tel. 971-17-95) 39 rms ⁉️

🔱 **Car ferries and boats:** very frequent services to and from Piraeus, taking 2 to 3 hours; in summer hydroplane service taking 1h.50.

I

ICARIA [Island] (Aegean Sea), Tel. 0275

ℹ️ **Tourist police:** in summer (Tel. 21–222).

Hotels:
** *Toula*, on the beach at Hagios Kyrikos (Tel. 22–298) 246 rms ⁉️ ▦ ♨ ☎ ❋ ≈; open April-Oct.
* *Apollo* (Tel. 22–477) 39 rms ≈ P ; open June-Oct.
* *Ikarion* (Tel. 22–481) 32 rms ≈ P ; open May-Oct.

🔱 **Boats and car ferries:** 6 to 8 times a week to and from Piraeus, taking 8 to 12h.

IGOUMENITSA (Epirus), Tel. 0665

ℹ️ **Tourist police:** 17, od. Hagios Apostolos (Tel. 22–302)

GNTO: on the quayside (Tel. 22–227).

Hotels:
** *Motel Xenia*, 2, od. Vas. Pavlou (Tel. 22–282) 36 rms ⁉️ A/c ♨ ⅏ ☎ ▦
* *Astoria*, 147, Hagios Apostolos (Tel. 22–704) 14 rms ⁉️ ▥ ⅏ P
* *Jolly*, 20, Vas. Pavlou (Tel. 23–970) 27 rms ▥ ⅏ ▦
* *Tourist*, 22, Vas. Pavlou (Tel. 22–406) 24 rms ▥ ⅏ P

△ **Campsites:**
Kalami beach, at Plataria (Tel. 71–245) 67 sites; open Feb-Oct. ≈
Sole Mare, at Ladochorion (Tel. 22–105) 35 sites. ≈

🔱 **Car ferries:** frequent service to Corfu (1h.45), Patras and Italy.

🚌 **Bus:** to and from Athens, taking 8h.30.

🚗 **Car hire:** *Budget*, 60, od. Vas. Pavlou (Tel. 33–901).

ILIKI [Lake], Tel. 0262

Hotel:
Motel Iliki, on the road from Athens to Lamia (Tel. 22–466) 8 rms ⁉️ ▥ ⅏ P

IOANNINA, or Jannina (Epirus), Tel. 0651

ℹ️ **Tourist police:** 5, od. 28th October (Tel. 25–673).

GNTO: 2, od. Napoleoutos Zerva (Tel. 25–086).

ELPA: 2, Platia Omirou (Tel. 20–695).

Hotels:
** *Palladion*, 1, od. P. Scoumbourdi (Tel. 25–856) 136 rms ⁉️ ▥ ⅏ P
** *Xenia*, 33, od. Vassileos Georgiou (Tel. 25–087) 60 rms ⁉️ ▥ ⅏ ☎ P in an exceptional site dominating the whole town.
* *Acropole*, 3, od. Vassileos Georgiou A (Tel. 26–560) 33 rms ⁉️ ▥ ⅏ ☎ P
* *Alexios*, 14, od. Poukevil (Tel. 24–003) 88 rms ▥ ♨ ⅏ ☎
* *Egnatia*, 2, Dagli and Avrantinou Streets (Tel. 25–667) 52 rms ▥ P
* *Esperia*, 3, od. Kaplani (Tel. 27–682) 35 rms P

* *Olympic,* 2, od. Melanidi (Tel. 25-888) 44 rms ▥ **P**

✈ **Air service:** to and from Athens daily, taking 50 min; to and from Thessaloniki twice a week, taking 40 min. *Olympic Airways,* 1, od. Angelou (Tel. 26-518)

🚌 **Buses:** to and from Athens 9 times a day, taking 7h.30; some lines go via Patras.

🚗 **Car hire:** *Budget,* 5, od. Mich. Angelou (Tel. 25-102) and at the airport.

Handicrafts: 9, od. M. Tricoup (Tel. 25-654).

IOS [Island] (Cyclades), Tel. 0286

Hotels:
** *Chryssi Akti* (Tel. 91-255) 10 rms ¶¶ ▥ ☎ ﹋ **P**; open May-Oct.
** *Manganari* (Tel. 91-215) at Manganari (access via caique) 41 rms ¶¶
* *Sea Breeze* (Tel. 91-285) 14 rms ▥ ▥ ☎ ﹋; open April-Oct.
* *Armadoros* (Tel. 91-201) 27 rms ¶¶ **P**
* *Corali* (Tel. 91-272) 12 rms ¶¶ ▥ ▥ ☎ **P**; open March-Oct.
* *Deifini,* at Mylopatas (Tel. 91-341) 16 rms ¶¶ ▥ ▥; open April-Oct.

△ **Campsites:**
Ios Camping, Hagia Irina beach (Tel. 91-329), 96 sites. ﹋
Souli Camping, Mylopotas beach (Tel. in Athens 894-06-57) 90 sites. ﹋

🛥 **Car ferries and boats:** 12 sailings a week to and from Piraeus, taking 9 to 12h, on the routes serving Syros, Paros, Naxos and Thera.

ITEA (central Greece), Tel. 0265

ℹ **Tourist police:** in summer, 56, od. Karaiskaki (Tel. 32-222).

Hotels:
** *Galini,* 57, Akti Possidonos (Tel. 32-278) 30 rms ¶¶ ▥ ▥ ☎ **P**
** *Kalafati,* Paralia (Tel. 32-294) 37 rms ▥ ▥ ☎ ﹋ **P**
** *Motel Xenia* (Tel. 32-262) 18 rms ¶¶ ▥ ▥ ☎ ﹋ **P** night-club.
* *Akti,* 81, Akti Possidonos (Tel. 32-257) 22 rms ¶¶ ▥ ▥ ☎ **P**
Nafsika, leof. Iroon (Tel. 33-300) 77 rms ¶¶ ▥ ▥ **P**

△ **Campsites:**
Agiannis, at Thesis Skliri, on the road to Delphi (Tel. 32-555) 330 sites; open March-Oct.
Beach Camp, on the Kirka Fokidos beach (Tel. 32-305) 62 sites.
Kaparelis Camping, at Kirka Fokodis (Tel. 32-990) 108 sites. ﹋
Galaxidi Camping, in Galaxidi, 9mls (15km) S. (Tel. 41-530); open April-Oct. 200 sites. ﹋

ITHACA [Island] or Ithaki (Ionian Islands), Tel. 0674

Hotels:
** *Mendor* (Tel. 32-433) 36 rms ¶¶ ▥ ▥ ☎ **P** open May-Oct.
* *Odysseus* (Tel. 32-381) 10 rms ¶¶ ▥ ▥ ☎ **P** boarding house; open April-Oct.

🛥 **Car ferries:** daily services to and from Patras via Sami (Cephalonia).

KALAMAKI (Attica), Tel. 01

Hotels:

*** *Marina Alymos,* 15, Vas. Georgiou and 1, od. Davaki (Tel. 982-89-11) 47 apartments A/c 🛏 🏠 ☎ TV ☀ P

*** *Saronis,* 13, Vas. Georgiou (Tel. 981-03-65) 38 rms ¶ ▥ A/c 🛏 🏠 ☎ ☀ P

** *Albatros,* 77, Vas. Georgiou (Tel. 982-49-81) 80 rms ¶ A/c 🛏 🏠 ☎ ☀ ≈ P

** *Rex,* 40, Vas. Georgiou (Tel. 981-07-62) 34 rms ¶ ▥ A/c 🛏 🏠 ☎ ☀ P

** *Venus,* 9, Meghistis (Tel. 981-08-06) 28 rms ¶ ▥ A/c 🛏 🏠 ☎ ☀ P

* *Attica,* 18, Platia Tsaldari (Tel. 981-05-76) 32 rms ¶ A/c 🛏 🏠 ☎ ☀ P

* *Blue Sea,* 49, Themistocleous (Tel. 981-57-07) 73 rms ¶ ▥ 🛏 🏠 ☎ ☀ ≈ P

* *Galaxy,* 39, Vas. Georgiou (Tel. 981-86-03) 44 rms ¶ A/c 🛏 🏠 ☎ ☀ ≈ P

* *Hellenikon,* 76, Vas. Georgiou (Tel. 981-72-27) 52 rms ¶ ▥ A/c 🛏 🏠 ☎ ☀ ≈ 🕵 P

* *Nefeli,* 5, Fan Vaik and Vas. Georgiou (Tel. 982-70-49) 39 rms ¶ A/c 🏠 ☎ ☀ ≈ P

* *Tropical,* 74, Vas. Georgiou (Tel. 981-39-93) 46 rms ¶ ▥ 🛏 🏠 ☎ ☀ P

Restaurants:

** *Saronis,* sea front (Tel. 981-03-66) P

** *Marida,* sea front (Tel. 981-02-84) P

Night-club:

**** *Neriada,* Vassileos Georgiou (Tel. 981-20-04) dinner from 22h to midnight, band and dance floor, also Greek bouzouki music.

KALAMAKI [Beach] (Peloponnese), Tel. 0741

Hotel:

** *Kalamaki Beach* (Tel. 37-331) 74 rms ¶ A/c 🛏 🏠 ☎ ☀ ≈ P

KALAMATA, or Kalamai (Peloponnese), Tel. 0721

🛈 **Tourist police:** 46, od. Aristomenous (Tel. 23-187).

🚗 *ELPA:* 131, od. Aristomenous (Tel. 21-166).

Hotels:

*** *Rex,* 26, Aristomenous (Tel. 22-334) 51 rms ¶ ▥ 🏠 ☎ P

** *Elite* (Tel. 22-434) 49 rms ¶ 🏠 ☎ ≈ 🕹 P

** *Filoxenia,* on the beach (Tel. 23-166) 155 rms ¶ ▥ 🛏 🏠 ☎ ☀ ≈ ⚲ P night-club.

** *Messinian Bay,* Almyros beach (Tel. 41-251) 45 rms ¶ ▥ 🏠 ☎ ≈ 🕹/9 P

* *Achillion,* 6, Kapeton Crompa (Tel. 22-348) 14 rms ▥ 🏠 ☎

* *America,* at Paralia (Tel. 22-719) 22 rms ▥ 🏠 ☎ P

Alexandrion, at Paralia (Tel. 26-821) 6 rms ¶ 🏠

Δ **Campsites:**
Hagia Sion, at Verga; 50 sites; open May-Oct.
Elite Camping. od. Navorinou (Tel. 22-015) 37 sites; open May-Oct.
Fare Camping, at Verga (Tel. 29-520) 28 sites; open May-Oct.
Kalogria, at Stoupa Messinia (Tel. 54-319) 105 sites; open April-Oct.
Patista Camping, E. coast of the gulf (Tel. 29-525) 70 sites.

Sea and Sun, at Haghia Sion, Verga (Tel. 41–314) 35 sites.

🚌🚆 **Trains and buses:** to and from Athens several times a day, in 10h and 7h.30 respectively.

KALAMBAKA (Thessaly), Tel. 0432

ℹ️ **Tourist police:** 1, od. Rammidi (Tel. 22–813).

Hotels:
** *Divani* (Motel; Tel. 23–330) 165 rms ⫪ ▥ A/c ▦ ☎ ▨ P
** *Xenia* (Motel; Tel. 22–327) 22 rms ⫪ ▥ A/c ▦ ☎ P open April-Oct.
* *Aeokikos Astir* (Tel. 22–325) 16 rms ▥ ▦ P
* *Odyssion* (Tel. 22–320) 21 rms P ; open April-Oct.

△ **Campsites:**
Cave, at Kastraki (Tel. 22–289) 28 sites; open Feb.-Nov.
International Meteora Rizos (Tel. 22–954) 84 sites ▨
Kalambaka Camping (Tel. 22–309) 86 sites ▨
Meteora Garden, (Tel. 22–727) 60 sites ▨
Theopetra (Tel. 81–405) 100 sites ▨ open April-Nov.

🚆 **Trains:** 3 times a day to and from Athens, taking 6h.30.

KALAMITSA (Macedonia), Tel. 051

Hotel:
** *Lucy* (Tel. 83–26-00) 217 rms ⫪ A/c ▦ ▦ ☎ ❋ ▨ ≈ P

KALAMOS (Attica), Tel. 0295

Hotel:
** *Kalamos Beach,* at Hagii Apostoli (Tel. 81–465) 181 rms ⫪ ▥ A/c ▦ ▦ ☎ ❋ ▨ ≈ ⫯ ⫯/9 P

KALANDRA (Macedonia), Tel. 0374

Hotel:
*** *Mendi* (Tel. 41–323) 172 rms ⫪ A/c ▦ ▦ ☎ ❋ ▨ ≈ ⫯ ⫯/9 P night-club; open April-Oct.

△ **Campsite:**
Kalandra – GNTO at Possidi (Tel. 41–345) 170 sites; open May-Oct. ▨

KALA NERA (Thessaly), Tel. 0423

Hotels:
** *Alcyon* (Tel. 22–364) 11 rms ▥ ▦ P boarding house.
* *Izela* (Tel. 22–379) 31 rms ▥ ▦ P; open May-Oct.
* *Roumeli* (Tel. 22–217) 14 rms ⫪ ▥ ▦ P

KALAVRYTA (Peloponnese), Tel. 0692

Hotels:
** *Chelmos,* Platia Eleftherias (Tel. 22–217) 27 rms ▥ ▦ ☎ P ; open June-Oct.
* *Maria,* 2, od. Sygrou (Tel. 22–296) 14 rms ▥ ▦

🚌 **Trains and buses:** to and from Athens several times a day, in 3h.45 and 5 to 6h respectively.

KALLITHEA (Macedonia), Tel. 0374

Hotels:
*** *Athos Palace* (Tel. 22–100) 600 rms and bungalows ⫪ ▥ A/c ▦ ▦ ☎ ❋ ▨ ≈ ⫯ ⫯/9 P night-club.
*** *Pallini Beach,* 1.6mls/2.5km towards Paliouri (Tel. 22–480; 324–80-31 at Athens) 495 rms and bungalows ⫪ ▥ A/c ▦ ▦ ☎ ❋ ▨ ≈ ⫯ ⫯/9 ▣ P night-club, yachting and harbour, open May-Oct.
** *Ammon Zeus* (Tel. 22–356)

112 rms �4 ▥ A/c 🛁 🏠 ☎ ≈
P night-club; open May-Oct.

KALYMNOS [Island]
(Dodecanese), Tel. 0243

Hotels:
** *Armeos Beach,* at Massouri
(Tel. 47-488) 34 rms �4 ▥ 🛁
🏠 ☎ ❋ 🖾 ℚ **P**; open April-
Oct.
** *Themis,* at Myrties
(Tel. 47-230) 9 rms �4 ▥ 🏠 ☎
≈ **P**; open April-Oct.
* *Drosos,* at Panormos
(Tel. 28-918) 52 rms �4 ▥ 🏠
☎ ❋
* *Olympic* (Tel. 28-801) 42 rms
�4 ▥ 🏠 ☎
* *Plaza,* at Panormos
(Tel. 28-907) 12 rms 🖾 **P**;
open April-Oct.
* *Thermae* (Tel. 29-425) 15 rms
�4 ▥ 🏠 **P** night-club.

⚓ **Boats:** Six weekly sailings to
and from Piraeus, with
continuation to Rhodes, 2 of
which are car-ferries, taking
11-15h.

KAMENA VOURLA (central
Greece), Tel. 0235

ℹ️ **Tourist police:** 1, od. 25
Martiou (Tel. 22-425).

Hotels:
** *Galini* (Tel. 22-327) 131 rms
�4 ▥ 🏠 ♣ 🖾 ≈ ℚ **P** thermal
baths.
** *Leto* (Tel. 22-517) 25 rms ▥
🏠 ☎ ≈ **P**
** *Pantheon* (Tel. 22-351) 29
rms �4 ▥ 🛁 🏠 ☎ **P**; open
July-Sept.
** *Posseidon* (Tel. 22-721) 93
rms �4 ▥ 🛁 🏠 ☎ ❋ 🖾 ≈
P; open April-Oct.
** *Rhadion* (Tel. 22-310) 62 rms
🏠 ☎ ≈ **P** thermal baths;
open May-Oct.
** *Sissi* (Tel. 22-277) 102 rms �4

▥ 🏠 ☎ 🖾 ≈ **P** thermal
baths, night-club; open
March-Oct.
** *Sonia* (Tel. 22-361) 20 rms �4
▥ 🏠 ☎ ≈ **P**; open
March-Oct.
** *Thronion* (Tel. 22-325) 44 rms
🏠 ☎ ≈ ℚ **P**; open July-Sept.
* *Acti,* G. Vassiliadou
(Tel. 22-211) 19 rms ≈ **P**;
open April-Oct.
* *Asteria,* 71, G. Vassiliadou
(Tel. 22-278) 14 rms �4 🖾 **P**
* *Delfini* (Tel. 22-321) 22 rms
�4 ▥ 🛁 🏠 ☎ **P**
* *Pringipikon* (Tel. 22-516) 28
rms ▥ ≈ **P**

△ **Campsites:**
Apollon (Tel. 22-486) 60 sites;
open April-Oct. ≈
Copellia (Tel. 22-000) 41 sites;
open April-Sept. ≈
Kamena Vourla (Tel. 22-053)
252 sites and 50 bungalows
≈
Leonidas, in Lithini
(Tel. 31-449) 97 sites; open
May-Sept. ≈

🚌 **Buses:** to and from Athens
every hour between 5h and
19h.30, taking 3h.

KAPANDRITI (Attica),
Tel. 0295

Hotel:
** *Golden House,* 18.8mls
(30km) from the Athens-
Lamia motorway (Tel. 52-455)
15 rms �4 ▥ 🛁 🏠 ☎ 🖾 **P**

KARDAMYLI (Peloponnese),
Tel. 0721

△ **Campsite:**
Kalogria, 3mls (5km) S.
(Tel. 94-319) 102 sites; open
April-Oct. ≈

KARDITSA (Thessaly),
Tel. 0441

Hotels:
* *Arni*, 4, Karaiskaki
  (Tel. 22–161) 38 rms 🏠 **P**
* *Astron*, 97, Iezekiil
  (Tel. 23–551) 47 rms 🏠 **P**
* *Avra*, 42, Karaiskaki
  (Tel. 21–523) 21 rms 🏠 **P**

🚌🚆 **Trains and buses:** several
times a day to and from
Athens, taking 4h.30 and
5h.30 respectively.

KARPATHOS [Island]
(Dodecanese), Tel. 0245

Hotels:
** *Romantica* (Tel. 22–460) 20
rms 🍴 🏠 🕿 ⚓ ⚓/9 **P**; open
April-Oct.
* *Porphyris* (Tel. 22–294) 21
rms 🍴 🍴 🏠 🕿 ⚓ ⚓/9 **P**;
open April-Oct.

✈ **Air services:** 1 or 2 daily
flights to and from Rhodes,
taking 40 min; 2 flights a
week to and from Kassos; 3
flights a week to and from
Sitia in Crete, taking 30 min.
Olympic Airways, Paralia
Karpathou (Tel. 25–291).

⚓ **Car ferries:** once a week to
and from Piraeus via Rhodes,
taking 26h.

KARPENISSION (central
Greece), Tel. 0237

Hotels:
** *Lecadin* (Tel. 22–131) 104 rms
🍴 🍴 🏠 🕿 **P**
** *Mont-Blanc*, Vas. Pavlou and
2, Friderikis (Tel. 22–322) 37
rms 🍴 🍴 🏠 🕿 **P**
* *Helvetia*, 32, Zinepomou
(Tel. 22–465) 71 rms 🍴 **P**

🚌 **Buses:** to and from Athens
twice a day, taking 6h.

KASSOS [Island]
(Dodecanese), Tel. 0245

Hotel:
* *Anagenissis* (Tel. 41–323) 10
  rms 🍴 🏠
* *Anessis*, 9, od. G. Mavribaki
  (Tel. 41–201) 7 rms 🍴 🏠 ⚓

✈ **Air services:** 4 flights a week
to and from Rhodes, taking
50 min.

⚓ **Boats:** one weekly sailing for
Piraeus. Caiques link Kassos
and Karpathos.

KASTANIA (Peloponnese),
Tel. 0747

Hotel:
** *Xenia* (Tel. 31–283) 17 rms 🍴
🍴 🏠 🕿 **P**

KASTORIA (Macedonia),
Tel. 0467

ℹ **Tourist police:** 25, od.
Grammou (Tel. 22–696).

Hotels:
*** *Xenia of the Lake*, Platia
Dexamenis (Tel. 22–565) 26
rms 🍴 🍴 🏠 🕿 **P**
** *Maria* (Motel; Tel. 74–696) 47
rms 🍴 🍴 A/c 🏠 🕿 **P**
** *Tsamis*, 1.9mls (3km)
(Tel. 43–334) 81 rms 🍴 🍴 🏠
🏠 🕿 ⚓ **P**
* *Europa* (Tel. 23–826) 34 rms
🍴 🏠
* *Orestion*, 1, Platia Davaki
(Tel. 22–257) 20 rms 🍴 🏠 **P**

✈ **Air services:** to and from
Athens 4 times a week, taking
1h.25. *Olympic Airways*, 7,
od. 11 Nouvembrios
(Tel. 22–275).

🚌 **Buses:** daily service to and
from Athens, taking 11h.

KASTRAKI (Thessaly),
Tel. 0432

Δ **Campsites:**
Vrachos Kastraki, od.

Meteorou (Tel. 22–293) 150 sites.

KASTRI (Attica), Tel. 01

Hotel:
*** *Kastri* (The American Club; Tel. 801–39–71) 63 rms ¶ ≡ 🛏 🛎 🕾 ☀ 🏊 **P**

KATERINI (Macedonia), Tel. 0351

ℹ **Tourist police:** 92, od. Alexander the Great (Tel. 23–440).

🚗 *ELPA*: road to Larisa (Tel. 27–515).

Hotel:
* *Olympion*, 15, Vas. Georgiou B. (Tel. 29–892) 56 rms ¶ ≡ 🛎 🕾 **P**

△ **Campsites:**
Agiannis, at Methoni (Tel. (353) 51–323) 160 sites; open April–Oct. 🏊
Gritsa, at Gritsa (Tel. (0352) 82–296) 110 sites; open May–Sept. 🏊
Kalypso, at Litochoron (Tel. (0352) 81–270) 250 sites 🏊
Mytikas, at Gritsa (Tel. (0352) 82–276) 80 sites; open May–Sept. 🏊
Olympus Beach, at Paralia Skatinas (Tel. (0352) 41–487) 300 sites; open April–Oct. 🏊 Q

🚆🚌 **Trains and buses:** to and from Athens several times a day, taking 6h.15 and 6h.30, respectively.

KATO ACHAIA (Peloponnese), Tel. 0693

Hotels:
**** *Stamac*, at Lakopetra (Tel. 22–845) 199 rms ¶ A/c 🛎 🕾 ☀ 🏊 **P** open May–Oct.

** *Alexander Beach*, at Arachovitika (Tel. (061) 93–12–62) 144 rms and bungalows ¶ ≡ 🛎 🕾 ☀ 🏊 **P** night-club; open April–Oct.

△ **Campsites:**
Aliki, at Aliki (Tel. 22–730) 62 sites; open May–Oct. 🏊
Demiris Camping, at Kato Alissos (Tel. 71–248) 60 sites; open April–Oct. 🏊
Golden Sunset, at Kato, Alissos (Tel. 71–276) 150 sites; open May–Oct. 🏊 Q
Kato Achaia Camping, road to Araxos (Tel. 22–400) 30 sites; open April–Oct. 🏊
Niforeika Beach, at Niforeika (Tel. 22–539) 60 sites; open April–Oct. 🏊

KATO GAZEA (Thessaly), Tel. 0423

△ **Campsites:**
Hellas (Tel. 22–267) 100 sites 🏊
Marina (Tel. 22–277) 200 sites; open May–Oct. 🏊
Sykia (Tel. 22–279) 100 sites 🏊

KAVALLA (Macedonia), Tel. 051

ℹ **Tourist police:** 9, od. Erythrou Stayrou (Tel. 22–29–05).

GNTO: 2, od. Phillelinon (Tel. 27–86–21).

🚗 *ELPA:* 109, od. Evdomis Merarchias (Tel. 22–97–78).

Hotels:
*** *Tosca Beach* (Tel. 22–48–66) 100 bungalows ¶ 🛎 🕾 🏊 🏊 **P**; open May–Sept.
** *Egnatia*, 139, od. 7 Merarchias (Tel. 83–58–41) 38 rms ¶ ≡ 🛎 🕾 🔲 **P**
** *Galaxy*, 51, od. Venizelou

(Tel. 22-45-21) 150 rms ¶¶ ▥ A/c ⌂ ☎ **P**

** *Oceanis,* 32, leof. Stavrou (Tel. 22-19-80) 168 rms ¶¶ ▥ A/c ♨ ⌂ ☎ ▨ **P** night-club.

** *Philippi,* 3, od. Venizelou (Tel. 22-28-56) 42 rms ¶¶ ▥ ⌂ ☎ **P**

* *Esperia,* 42, od. Erythrou Stavrou (Tel. 22-96-21) 100 rms ¶¶ A/c ♨ ☎ ◵ **P**

* *Nefeli,* 50, od. Erythrou Stavrou (Tel. 22-74-41) 94 rms ¶¶ ▥ ♨ ⌂ ☎ ≈ ◵ **P**

* *Panorama,* 32, od. Venizelou (Tel. 22-42-05) 52 rms ¶¶ ▥ ⌂ ☎ ≈ **P**

Δ **Campsites:**
Akti Kavalla Beach, GNTO (Tel. 22-71-51) 152 sites ≈
Alexandros, at Nea Karvali (Tel. 31-62-40) 85 sites ≈
Estella, at Iraklitsa (Tel. (0592) 71-465) 92 sites ≈
Irene Camping, at Perigiali (Tel. 22-97-85) 110 sites ≈
Keramoti, at Keramoti (Tel. (0591) 51-279) 200 sites; open May-Sept. ≈

✈ **Air services:** daily flight to and from Athens, taking 1h.
Olympic Airways, leof. Paraliaki (Tel. 22-36-22).

⚓ **Car-ferry:** daily service to and from Thasos in 1h (Prinos) and 1h.30 (Limin).

🚌 **Buses:** to and from Athens, twice a day, taking 11h, via Thessaloniki.

🚗 **Car hire:** *Budget,* 34, od. Venizelos (Tel. 228-785).

KAVOURI (Attica), Tel. 01

Hotels:
**** *Apollon Palace,* od. Hagios Nikolaos (Tel. 895-14-01) 286 rms ¶¶ ▥ A/c ♨ ⌂ ☎ ▨ ≈ ◵ **P**

*** *Kavouri,* od. Iliou and 7, od. Terpsichoris (Tel. 895-84-61) 114 rms ¶¶ ▥ A/c ♨ ⌂ ☎ ❈ ▨ ≈ ▣ **P** night-club; open April-Oct.

** *Castello Beach,* od. Kerkyros and 4, od. Aktis (Tel. 895-95-33) 32 rms ¶¶ ▥ ⌂ ☎ ≈

** *Pine Hill* (Tel. 896-08-71) 52 rms ¶¶ A/c ▥ ♨ ⌂ ☎ ❈ ▨ ≈ ◵ **P**

KEA, or Tzia [**Island**] (Cyclades), Tel. 0288

ⓘ **Tourist police:** in summer, at Ioulis (Tel. 31-300).

Hotels:
** *I Tzia Mas* (Motel; Tel. 31-305) 24 rms ¶¶ ⌂ ☎ ≈ **P**; open April-Oct.

** *Kea Beach* (Tel. 22-144; Athens Tel. 921-77-26) 80 rms ¶¶ ⌂ ☎ ≈ **P** night-club; open May-Oct.

* *Carthea* (Tel. 31-222) 35 rms ¶¶ ▥ ⌂ ≈ **P**

KHANIA, or Chania Canea (Crete), Tel. 0821

ⓘ **Tourist police:** 42, od. Karaiskaki (Tel. 24-477).

ⓘ *GNTO:* 6, Tombazi quay (Tel. 26-059).

🚗 *ELPA:* 1, od. R Pacha (Tel. 26-059)

Hotels:
*** *Kidon,* Platia Agoras (Tel. 26-190) 113 rms ¶¶ ▥ A/c ♨ ⌂ ☎ **P** night-club.

** *Doma,* 124, od. Venizelou (Tel. 21-772) 29 rms ▥ ⌂ ☎

** *Lissos,* 68, od. Democratias (Tel. 24-671) 41 rms ▥ ⌂ ☎ **P**

** *Samatia,* Kydanas and Zimrokakidon Streets

(Tel. 51–551) 58 rms A/c 👯 🏠 ☎ 𝒶 **P**

* *Xenia*, od. Theotokopolou
(Tel. 24–562) 44 rms ⫪ ▥ 🏠 ☎ 𝒶 **P**

* *Aptera Beach,* Paralia Hagion Apostolon (Tel. 22–636) 45 rms ⫪ ▥ 🏠 𝒶 **P**

* *Astor*, 2, Verovos Passo
(Tel. 55–557) 36 rms ▥ 🏠 𝒶 **P**

* *Canea*, 18, Platia 1866
(Tel. 24–673) 50 rms ▥ 🏠 ☎ **P**

* *Criti,* Nikiforou Foka and Kyprou (Tel. 21–881) 91 rms ⫪ ▥ A/c 🏠 ☎ **P**

* *Diktyna*, 1, od. Belollo
(Tel. 21–101) 35 rms ▥ 🏠 𝒶 **P**

* *Lucia*, Akti Kountourioti
(Tel. 21–821) 39 rms ▥ 🏠 𝒶 **P**

* *Omalos*, 71 leof. Kydonias
(Tel. 57–171) 31 rms A/c 🏠

At the port:
** *Porto Venetsano* (Tel. 29–311)
63 rms ⫪ ▥ A/c 👯 🏠 ☎

At Galatas (2.5mls/4km):
** *Panorama* (Tel. 54–200) 167 rms ⫪ A/c 🏠 ☎ ▦ 𝒶 𝒬 ⌁/⁹ **P**; open April–Oct.

At Hagia Marina (5mls/8km):
** *Santa Marina*
(Tel. 48–460) 146 rms ⫪ ▥ 🏠 ☎ **P**; open March–Oct.

At Kastelli (24mls/39km; vicin. 1):
* *Castle* (Tel. 22–140) 11 rms ⫪ ▥ 🏠 **P**

*At Chora Sfakion
(45mls/72km; vicin. 5):*
* *Xenia* (Tel. 91–202) 12 rms ⫪ ▥ 🏠 𝒶 **P**

At Maleme (10.6mls/17km; vicin. 1):
** *Crete Chandris* (Tel. 91–221)
400 rms and bungalows ⫪ ▥

A/c 👯 🏠 ☎ ❀ ▦ 𝒶 𝒬 **P**
open April–Oct.

At Omalos (27.5mls/44km: vicin. 3):
** *Xenia* (Tel. 93–237) 3 rms ⫪ ▥ 🏠 ❀ **P**; open April–Oct.

At Platanias (5.6mls/9km):
** *Filoxenia* (Tel. 48–502) ⫪ ▥ 🏠 ☎ 𝒶 **P**; open April–Dec.

△ **Campsite:**
Hagia Marina, at Hagia Marina (Tel. 48–555), 80 sites; open April–Oct.

Youth hostel: Papaioannou school, od. Khatzidaki.

✈ **Air services:** 4 to 5 daily links with Athens, taking 45 min. Airport 10mls (16km) E. *Olympic Airways*, 88 Stratigou Tzanakaki (Tel. 27–701).

🚗 **Car hire:** *Avis*, 58, od. Tzanakaki (Tel. 50–510); *Budget*, 46, od. Karaiskaki (Tel. 52–778); *Hertz*, 21, od. Tzanakaki (Tel. 29–019).

⚒ **Handicrafts:** 6, od. Tombrazi (Tel. 22–568).

KIFISSIA (Attica), Tel. 01

Hotels:
**** *Pentelikon,* 66, od. Delighiani Kefalari (Tel. 801-28-37) 63 rms ⫪ ▥ 👯 🏠 ☎ ♠ **P**
*** *Aperghi*, 59, od. Delighiani Kefalari (Tel. 801-35-37) 99 rms ⫪ ▥ 🏠 ☎ ❀ **P**
*** *Cecil*, 7, od. Xenias Kefalari (Tel. 801-38-36) 84 rms ⫪ ▥ 👯 🏠 ☎ ❀ **P**
*** *Costis Dimitracopoulos,* 65, od. Delighiani Kefalari (Tel. 801-25-46) 27 rms ⫪ ▥ 👯 🏠 ☎ ❀ **P**
*** *Grand Chalet*, 38, od. Kokkinara (Tel. 801-48-88) 20 rms ⫪ ▥ 👯 🏠 ☎ ❀ **P**

*** *Semiramis,* 36, od. Charilaou
Tricoupi Kefalari
(Tel. 801-25-87) 42 rms ⸾⸾ ▥
🛏 🕋 ☎ ✳ 🖼 **P** night-club.

*** *Theoxenia,* 2, od.
Philadelpheos Kefalari
(Tel. 801-27-51) 64 rms ⸾⸾ ▥
🛏 ☎ ✳ **P**

** *Nafsika,* 6, od. Pellis
(Tel. 801-32-55) 17 rms ⸾⸾
A/c ▥ 🕋 ☎ **P**

* *Aegli,* Platia Platanou
(Tel. 801-25-91) 25 rms ▥ 🕋
☎

Restaurants and tavernas:
*** *Blue Pine Farm,* od. Venizelou
and Tsaldari (Tel. 801-29-69)
✳ **P**

** *Bokaris,* od. Socratous and
Acharnor (Tel. 801-25-89) ✳
P

* *Grigoris,* 8, od. Argyropoulou
(Tel. 801-46-32) ✳

* *O Takis Salmatani,* od.
Trifonos and Syngrou
(Tel. 801-53-94) ✳ **P**

* *O Nikos,* 5, od. Skopelou
(Tel. 801-55-37).

△ **Campsites:**
Akropolis, at Nea Kiffissia
(Tel. 808-83-10) 150 sites;
open May-Sept. 🖼 ⸛ ⚲
Dionissiotis Camping, at Nea
Kifissia (Tel. 807-14-94) 300
sites.
Nea Kifissia (Tel. 801-64-35)
80 sites.
Nea Europaikon
(Tel. 801-54-02) 100 sites.
Patritsia Camping, at Kato
Kifissia (Tel. 801-19-00) 160
sites; open June-Oct.

KINETA BEACH (Attica),
Tel. 0296

Hotels:
*** *Kineta Beach* (Tel. 62-512)
181 rms and bungalows ⸾⸾
A/c 🕋 ☎ ✳ 🖼 ⸛ ⚲ **P**

** *Sun* (Tel. 62-243) 51 rms ⸾⸾
▥ 🛏 🕋 ☎ 🖼 **P**

* *Hotel 50* (Tel. 62-444) 20 rms
⸾⸾ ▥ 🛏 🕋 ☎ ⸛ **P**

KOMOTINI (Thrace),
Tel. 0531

Hotels:
** *Xenia,* 43, od. Sismanoglou
(Tel. 22-139) 26 rms ⸾⸾ ▥ 🕋
☎ ⚲ **P**

** *Orfeus,* 48, Platia Vas.
Constantinou (Tel. 26-701) 79
rms ⸾⸾ ▥ A/c 🛏 🕋 ☎ 🖼 **P**
night-club.

* *Astoria,* 28, Platia Vassileos
Constantinou (Tel. 22-707) 16
rms ▥ 🕋 ☎ **P**

△ **Campsite:**
Fanarion (Tel. 31-270) 200
sites.

🚂 **Trains:** to Athens several
times a day, via Thessaloniki,
taking 17h.

Buses: to and from Athens,
once a day, taking 12h.

Handicrafts: 15, od. Vas.
Georgiou A (Tel. 24-745).

KOZANI (Macedonia),
Tel. 0461

Hotels:
** *Xenia,* 1, od. Aetorahis
(Tel. 30-886) 30 rms ⸾⸾ ▥ 🕋
☎ **P** night-club.

* *Aliakmon,* 38, od. El.
Venizelou (Tel. 36-015) 85
rms ▥ 🕋 ☎ **P**

* *Metropolis,* 16, od. Diadochou
Konstantinou (Tel. 22-998) 51
rms ⸾⸾ ▥ 🛏 🕋 ☎ **P**
night-club.

✈ **Air services:** to and from
Athens, 3 times a week,
taking 1h.30. *Olympic
Airways,* 6, od. Paviou Mela
(Tel. 22-187).

🚂 **Trains and buses:** run several

times a day to and from Athens taking 12h and 8h.30, respectively.

KRYOPIGI (Macedonia), Tel. 0374

Hotels:
** *Kassandra Palace* (Tel. 51–471) 192 rms ¶¶ A/c 🛎 🏦 ☎ TV ❊ 🖼 ≈ ♀ 🖼 **P** night-club; open April-Oct.
** *Alexander Beach* (Tel. 22–433) 129 rms ¶¶ ⅢⅢ 🛎 🏦 ☎ ❊ ≈ ♀ **P**; open April-Oct.

Δ **Campsite:**
Kryopigi Camping (Tel. 22–321) 125 sites; open May-Oct. ≈

KYLLINI (Peloponnese), Tel. 0622

Hotel:
* *Ionion* (Tel. 92–318) 22 rms ⅢⅢ 🏦 ≈ **P** thermal baths.

KYPARISSIA (Peloponnese), Tel. 0761

Hotels:
* *Artemis*, 6, od. Doula Paralia (Tel. 22–145) ⅢⅢ 🏦 ≈ **P**
* *Ionion*, 1, od. Kalantzakou (Tel. 22–511) 33 rms ⅢⅢ 🛎 🏦 ☎ **P**
* *Vassilikon*, 7, od. Alexopoulou (Tel. 22–655) 20 rms ¶¶ ⅢⅢ 🛎 🏦 ☎ **P**

Δ **Campsite:**
Hani Plaz, at Kampos (Tel. 23–330) 132 sites; ≈

🚂 **Trains** to and from Athens several times a day, taking 8h.

KYTHNOS [Island] (Cyclades), Tel. 0281

[i] **Tourist police:** in summer, at Loutra (Tel. 31–201).

Hotels:
* *Xenia*, at Loutra (Tel. 31–217)

46 rms ¶¶ ☎ ≈ **P** thermal baths; open June-Oct.
* *Poseidonion,* at Mericha (Tel. 31–244) 83 rms.

🏛 **Car-ferries and boats:** 5 weekly links to and from Piraeus, taking 4h.

LAGONISSI (Attica), Tel. 0299

Hotels:
**** *Xenia Lagonissi* (Tel. 83–911) 357 rms and bungalows ¶¶ A/c ⅢⅢ 🏦 ☎ ❊ ≈ ♀ **P** night-club, cinema, yachting, sports ground; open April-Oct.
** *Var* (Tel. 83–512) 22 bungalows ¶¶ ⅢⅢ 🏦 ☎ ❊ 🖼 **P**; open May-Oct.

LAMIA (central Greece), Tel. 0231

[i] **Tourist police:** 13, od. Patrokiou (Tel. 23–281).

🚗 *ELPA:* 9, od. Miaouli (Tel. 26–883).

Hotels:
* *Apollonion*, Platia Parkou (Tel. 22–668) 35 rms ⅢⅢ A/c 🏦 **P**
* *Helena*, 4, od. Thermopylon (Tel. 25–025) 51 rms. ⅢⅢ 🏦 **P**
* *Leonideon*, 8, Eleftherias Sq. (Tel. 22–822) 31 rms ⅢⅢ 🏦 **P**
* *Sonia*, 10, od. Eslin (Tel. 23–136) 24 rms **P**

Δ **Campsite:**
International Beach, at Melissia (9.4mls/15km; Tel. 22–214) 100 sites; open June-Oct. ≈

🚌 **Buses:** to and from Athens, every hour, taking 3h.15.

LANGADIA (Peloponnese), Tel. 0795

Hotel:

★ *Langadia* (Tel. 43-202) 20 rms 🍴 ▥ 🚿 ☎ **P**

△ **Campsite:**
Mitropoulos (Tel. 21-393), 150 sites; open April-Oct.

LARISSA (Thessaly), Tel. 041

ℹ **Tourist police:** od. Vas. Sofias (Tel. 227-900).

GNTO: 18, od. Koumoundourou (Tel. 25-09-19).

🚗 *ELPA:* road to Athens (Tel. 22-86-60).

Hotels:

★★★ *Divani Palace,* 19, leof. Vas. Sofias (Tel. 25-27-91) 77 rms 🍴 ▥ A/c 🛗 🚿 ☎ **P**

★★ *Astoria,* 4, od. Protopapadaki (Tel. 25-29-41) 84 rms 🍴 ▥ A/c 🛗 🚿 ☎ 📺 **P**

★★ *Grand Hotel,* 16, od. Papakyriazi (Tel. 25-77-11) 91 rms ▥ A/c 🛗 🚿 ☎ **P**

★★ *Metropole,* 8, od. Roosevelt (Tel. 229-911) 96 rms 🍴 ▥ A/c 🚿 ☎ 📺 **P**

★★ *Xenia* (Motel Tel. 22-70-02) 30 rms 🍴 ▥ A/c 🚿 ☎ **P**

★ *Ambassadors,* 67, od. Papakyriazi (Tel. 25-48-25) 89 rms 🍴 A/c 🛗 🚿 ☎ **P**

★ *Achillion,* 10, od. Kentavron (Tel. 22-98-01) 45 rms ▥ A/c 🚿 ☎ **P**

★ *Anessis,* 25, od. Megalou Alexandrou (Tel. 22-72-10) 56 rms ▥ 🚿 **P**

★ *Dionyssos,* 30, od. Vas. Georgiou (Tel. 23-01-01) 84 rms A/c 🛗 🚿 ☎ **P**

★ *El Greco,* 37 leof. Megalou Alexandrou (Tel. 25-24-11) 90 rms 🍴 A/c 🛗 🚿 ☎ **P**

★ *Esperia,* 4, od. Amalias (Tel. 22-25-95) 20 rms ▥ 🚿 **P**

★★ *Melathron,* 20, od. Kouma (Tel. 226-021) 45 rms ▥ 🚿 ☎ **P**

★ *Olympion,* 1, od. Megalou Alexandrou (Tel. 22-60-41) 29 rms ▥ 🚿 **P**

✈ **Air services:** to and from Athens 3 times a week, taking 1h.15.

🚆 **Trains:** 7 times a week to and from Athens, taking 5h.30.

🚌 **Buses:** to and from Athens, 7 times a day, taking 5h.

🚗 **Car hire:** *Budget* (Tel. 229-029)

LEGRENA (Attica), Tel. 0292

Hotels:

★★ *Amphitrite* (Motel Tel. 39-154) 32 rms 🍴 ▥ 🚿 ☎ ❀ 🏊 **P**

★★ *Minos* (Tel. 39-321) 38 rms 🍴 ▥ 🚿 ☎ **P**; open April-Oct.

LEMNOS [**Island**], or Limnos, Tel. 0276

Hotels:

★★★★ *Akti Myrina* (Tel. 22-681; Athens Tel. 323-02-49) 125 bungalows 🍴 ▥ 🚿 ☎ 📺 🏊 🎾 ⛳/9 **P**; open May-Oct.

★★ *Kastro Beach* (Tel. 22-772) 🍴 ▥ 🚿 ☎ 🏊 **P**. Situated by a superb beach.

★ *Lemnos* (Tel. 22-153) 29 rms 🚿 **P**

★ *Sevdalis* (Tel. 22-691) 36 rms 🚿 **P**

✈ **Air services:** 3 times a day to and from Athens, taking 45min; a daily flight to and from Thessaloniki, taking 1h.10.

⛴ **Car-ferries:** to and from Hagios Konstantinos once a week, taking 10h.30; and to

and from Kovalia 3 times a
week ing 5h.

LEPTOKARIA (Macedonia),
Tel. 0352

Hotels:
- ** *Olympian Bay* (Tel. 31-311)
228 rms and bungalows ¶ ▥
A/c ⛺ ⌂ ☎ ☀ ≈ ⏌/⁹ P ;
open March-Oct.
- * *Galaxy* (Tel. 31-224) 26 rms
¶ ▥ ⛺ ⌂ P

LERNA (Peloponnese),
Tel. 0751

Δ **Campsite:**
Lerna, Myli beach
(Tel. 47-520) 47 sites; open
May-Oct. ≈

LEROS [Island]
(Dodecanese), Tel. 0247

Hotels:
- ** *Xenon Angelou*, at Laki
boarding house (Tel. 22-514)
7 rms ¶ ⌂; open April-Oct.
- * *Alinda* (Tel. 23-266) 24 rms ¶
⌂ P ; open May-Oct.
- * *Artemis*, at Laki (Tel. 22-416)
8 rms ⌂ P
- * *Leros*, at Laki (Tel. 22-940) 19
rms ¶ ▥ ⌂ P
- * *Maleas Beach* (Tel. 23-306)
47 rms ¶ ⌂ P ; open
April-Sept.
- * *Panteli* (Tel. 22-152) 28 rms
¶ ⌂ P

Δ **Campsite:**
Leros camping, Xirocambos
beach, (Tel. 23-372) 30 sites;
open May-Sept.

⚓ **Car-ferries:** to and from
Piraeus 4 times a week,
taking 10h. via Mykonos,
Kalymnos and Cos.

LEVCAS, [Island] or Levcadia
(Ionian Islands), Tel. 0645.

ⓘ **Tourist police:** in summer, at
Nydri (Tel. 95-207).

Hotels:
- ** *Lefkas*, 2, od. Panagou
(Tel. 23-916) 93 rms ¶ ▥ ⛺
⌂ ☎ P
- * *Niricos*, Hagia Mayra
(Tel. 24-132) 36 rms ¶ ⛺ ⌂
☎ P

Δ **Campsites:**
Dessimi Beach, 11mls (18km)
from Leucadia (Tel. 95-225)
42 sites; open May-Oct. ≈
Episkopos Beach, 5mls (8km)
from Leucadia (Tel. 71-388)
45 sites; open June-Sept. ≈
Kariotes Beach, 1.9mls (3km)
from Leucadia (Tel. 23-594)
34 sites; open May 15th-Oct.
1. ≈
Poros Beach, at Poros
(Tel. 95-298) 90 sites; open
June-Sept. ≈

🚌 **Buses:** to and from Athens 3
times a day, taking 7h.

LITOCHORON (Macedonia),
Tel. 0352

Hotel:
- * *Aphroditi*, Platia Eleftherias
(Tel. 21-868) 24 rms ▥ ⛺ ⌂
☎ P

Δ **Campsites** (along the coast,
about 6mls/10km):
Apollon, at Plaka (Tel: 22-
109) 170 sites; open May-
Sept. ≈
Calypso Camping, at Gritsa
(Tel. 81-270) 200 sites ≈
Dolfin, at Plaka (Tel. 22-128)
80 sites; open July-Sept. ≈
Evridiki, at Gritsa (Tel. 82-398)
150 sites ≈
Gritsa 66, at Gritsa
(Tel. 82-296) 110 sites; open
May-Sept. ≈
Helena, at Plaka (Tel. 22-146)
146 sites; open April-Oct. ≈
⚲
Minerva, at Haskara
(Tel. 22-178) 150 sites; open

April 15-Oct. 15 ≈
Mytikas camping, at Gritsa, 52 sites; open April-Sept. ≈
Olympios Zeus, at Plaka (Tel. 22-115) 100 sites and 100 bungalows; open April 15-Oct. ♀
Olympios Beach Plaka, at Plaka (Tel. 22-112) 110 sites; open March 15-Oct. ≈

LIVADIA (central Greece)
Tel. 0261

Hotels:
** *Levadia,* 4, Platia Katsoni (Tel. 23-611) 51 rms ▥ A/c ▥ ☎
* *Helikon,* Platia Georgiou (Tel. 23-911) 22 rms ⫪ ▥ ☎ P
* *Midia,* 5, od. Kontsopetalou (Tel. 28-215) 14 rms ▥ ▥ ☎ P

🚌 **Buses:** to and from Athens every hour, taking 2h. 10.

LOUTRA AEDIPSOS
(Euboea), Tel. 0226

🛈 **Tourist police:** in summer, 3, od. Oceanidou (Tel. 22-456).

Hotels:
*** *Aegli,* 18, od. 25 Martiou (Tel. 22-216) 78 rms ⫪ ▥ ▥ ☎ P thermal baths
*** *Avra,* 16, od. 25 Martiou (Tel. 22-226) 72 rms ⫪ ▥ ▥ ☎ ✳ ≈ P thermal baths
** *Herakleon,* 7 od. Remvis (Tel. 22-245) 35 rms ⫪ ▥ ▥ ☎ P; open May-Oct; thermal baths.
** *Hermes,* 12, od. Ermou (Tel. 22-233) 45 rms ⫪ ▥ ▥ ☎ P thermal baths
** *Kentrikon,* 14, od. 25 Martiou (Tel. 22-302) 30 rms ▥ ▥ ☎ P; open June-Oct.; thermal baths.
* *Anessis,* 7, od. Philellinon

(Tel. 22-248) 55 rms ▥ ≈ P; open May-Oct.; thermal baths.
* *Capri,* 45, od. 25 Martiou (Tel. 22-496) 45 rms ⫪ ▥ ≈ thermal baths; open June-Oct.
* *Galini,* od. Hagiou Nicolaou (Tel. 22-448) 36 rms ▥ ≈ P
* *Ilion,* 37, od. Philellinon (Tel. 22-390) 20 rms ▥ ≈ P thermal baths.
* *Mitho,* od. Thermopigon (Tel. 22-780) ⫪ ▥ ≈ P thermal baths.

At Lichas (16mls/25km from Loutra Aedipsos):
***** *Gregolimano* (Club Méditerranée; Tel. 33-230) 330 rms ⫪ ▥ A/c ♨ ▥ ☎ 🚌 ✳ 🎱 ≈ ♀ P; open April-Oct.

⚓ **Car-ferries:** to Arkitsa 7 times a day, taking 50 min.

🚌 **Buses:** to and from Athens, via Chalcis, 4 times a day, taking 3h.30.

LOUTRA ELENIS
(Peloponnese), Tel. 0741

Hotels:
*** *Politis* (Tel. 332-50) 28 rms ⫪ ▥ A/c ▥ ☎ P
** *Alymri Beach* (Tel. 333-01) 50 rms ⫪ ▥ ♨ ▥ ☎ ♀ P; open April-Oct.
** *Orea Heleni* (Tel. 33-231) 22 rms ⫪ ▥ ▥ ☎ ≈ P
△ **Campsites:**
Biarritz, at Laka (Tel. 33-441) 32 sites ≈
Poseidon Camping, in Almyri (Tel. 33-302) 81 sites ≈

LOUTRA KAIAFA
(Peloponnese), Tel. 0625

🛈 **Tourist police** (Tel. 31-201).

Hotel:
* *Geranion* (Tel. 31-707) 46 rms

¶ ⫿⫿⫿ ⌂ ☎ P ; open May-Oct.

LOUTRAKI (Attica), Tel. 0741

ⓘ **Tourist police:** 7, od. El Venizelou (Tel 42-258).

Hotels:
*** *Achillion,* 12, od. Venizelou (Tel. 42-271) 61 rms ¶ ⫿⫿⫿ A/c ⌂ ☎ ⇌ P ; open April-Oct.
*** *Akti,* 5, od. Lekka (Tel. 42-338) 38 rms ¶ ⫿⫿⫿ ⌕ ⌂ ☎ P thermal baths.
*** *Karellion,* 23, od. Lekka (Tel. 42-347) 39 rms ¶ ⫿⫿⫿ ⌕ ⌂ ☎ P
*** *Pallas,* 19, od. Lekka (Tel. 42-343) 56 rms ¶ ⫿⫿⫿ ⌕ ⌂ ☎ ⇌ P
*** *Paolo,* 16, od. Korinthou (Tel. 48-742) 80 rms ¶ ⫿⫿⫿ A/c ⌂ ☎ P
*** *Park,* 8, od. Lekka (Tel. 42-270) 64 rms ¶ ⫿⫿⫿ A/c ⌂ ☎ P
*** *Pefkaki* (Tel. 42-426) 38 rms ¶ ⫿⫿⫿ ⌕ ⌂ ☎
*** *Petit Palais,* 48, od. Lekka (Tel. 42-267) 43 rms ¶ ⫿⫿⫿ ⌂ ☎ ⇌ P ; open April-Oct.
*** *Theoxenia,* 17, od. Lekka (Tel. 48-166) 26 rms ⫿⫿⫿ ⌕ ⌂ ☎ ⇌
** *Beau Rivage,* 1, od. Poseidonos (Tel. 42-323) 42 rms ⌂ ☎ ⇌ P ; open April-Oct.
** *Excelsior,* 30, Platia 25 Martiou (Tel. 42-254) 33 rms ⫿⫿⫿ ⌕ ⌂ ☎ ⇌
** *Grand Hotel,* 14, od. Venizelou (Tel. 42-348) 32 rms ⌂ ☎ ⇌ P thermal baths.
** *Marinos,* 1, od. Damaskinou (Tel. 42-575) 51 rms ¶ ⫿⫿⫿ A/c ⌂ ☎ ⛱ ⇌ P night-club.
** *Pappas,* Pefkaki beach (Tel. 48-103) 84 rms ¶ ⫿⫿⫿ ⌕ ⌂ ☎ ✳ ⇌ P night-club.
* *Alkyonis,* 11, od. Damaskinou (Tel. 48-173) 27 rms ⫿⫿⫿ ⌂ ⇌

P open April-Oct.
* *Galaxy,* od. Neraida (Tel. 48-282) 39 rms ¶ ⫿⫿⫿ A/c ⌂ ☎ ⇌ P ; open April-Oct.
* *Mitzithra,* 25, od. Venizelou (Tel. 42-316) 43 rms ¶ ⫿⫿⫿ A/c ⌂ ☎ ⇌ P night-club.

Holiday Club:
**** *Holidays Club Poseidon* (Tel. 42-498) ¶ ⫿⫿⫿ ⛱ ⇌ many water sports and other activities; night-clubs; open April-Oct.

Δ **Campsite:**
Hellenic Touring Club, at Limni Hierou (Tel. 25-670) 70 sites; open May-Oct.

🚌 **Buses:** run very frequently to and from Athens, taking 1h.30.

🚗 **Car hire:** *Loutraki Tours,* 49, leof. Venizelos (Tel. 43-063).

LOUTRA KYLLINI (Peloponnese), Tel. 0623

ⓘ **Tourist police:** in season (Tel. 92-202).

Hotels:
*** *Killini Golden Beach,* 3.75 mls (6km) from Loutra Kylini and 2.5 mls (4km) from Kastron (Tel. 95-205; Athens Tel. 322-38-88) 346 rms ¶ ⫿⫿⫿ A/c ⛱ ⌂ ☎ ⛱ ⇌ � 🎾 𝄞/9 P thermal baths; night-clubs; open April-Oct.
* *Glarentza* (Tel. 92-397) 30 rms ¶ ⫿⫿⫿ ⌂ ☎ ⇌ P
* *Xenia* (Tel. 96-275) 75 rms ¶ ⫿⫿⫿ ⛱ ⌂ ☎ 🎾 P ; open April-Oct.

Δ **Campsites:**
Aginara Beach, at Ligia (Tel. 96-211) 78 sites ⇌
Kyllini Camping, at Vartholomio (Tel. 96-270) 120 sites, 41 bungalows ⇌

⚓ **Car-ferries:** to Zante and Cephalonia.

LOUTRA YPATI (central Greece), Tel. 0231

Hoteis:
- *** *Xenia* (Tel. 59–510) 81 rms ¶ ▦ ⌂ ☎ **P** ; open April-Oct.
- ** *Oete* (Tel. 59–525) 38 rms ¶ ⌂ ☎ **P** ; open May-Oct.
- ** *Pigae* (Tel. 59–524) 33 rms ¶ ⌂ ☎ **P** ; open June-Sept.
- * *Alfa* (Tel. 59–507) 27 rms ⌂ **P** ; open April-Oct.
- * *Alexakis* (Tel. 59–372) 27 rms ⌂ **P**
- * *Astron* (Tel. 59–595) 27 rms ⌂ **P** ; open March-Oct.
- * *Galaxias* (Tel. 59–506) 25 rms ⌂ **P** ; open March-Oct.
- * *Martini* (Tel. 59–300) 41 rms ¶ ⌂ **P**

M

MAKRINITSA (Thessaly), Tel. 0421

Hotels:
- *** *Archontikon Mousli, Archontikon Sissilianou, Archontikon Xiradakis* (ancient restored houses; Tel. 99–228, 99–556, 99–250) 22 rms. Information from *GNTO* (in Volos, Platia Riga Ferraeou Tel. 23–500).

Mallia (Crete): *see Herakleion.*

MARATHON (Attica), Tel. 0294

Hotels:
- ** *Golden Coast,* on the beach near Nea Makri (Tel. 92–102) 242 rms ¶ ▦ A/c ⌂ ☎ ❋ ▨ ⌖ ⌣/9 **P** night-club; open April-Oct.

* *Marathon* (Tel. 55–122), by the sea, 24 rms ¶ ⌂ **P**

△ **Campsites:**
Marathon (Tel. 55–577) 100 sites ⌖.
Papa Camping, at Zorgianni, on the Athens-Lamia road (Tel. (01) 814–14–46) 121 sites; open June-Oct.
Ramnous, on the beach at Rizari (Tel. 55–855) 100 sites; open March-Nov.

🚌 **Buses:** to and from Athens every half hour taking 1hr, leaving from the Tumulus of Marathon; and twice a day taking 1h.20, leaving from Lake Marathon.

MATI (Attica), Tel. 0294

Hotels:
- *** *Costa Rica* (Tel. 71–103) 60 rms ¶ ▦ ⌘ ⌂ ☎ ❋ ▨ ⌖ **P** ; open April-Oct.
- *** *Mati,* 33, od. Possidonos (Tel. 71–511) 70 rms ¶ ▦ ⌘ ⌂ ☎ ❋ ▨ ⌖ **P** night-club.
- ** *Attika Beach,* 32, od. Possidonos (Tel. 71–711) 94 rms ¶ ▦ ⌘ ⌂ ☎ ❋ ▨ ⌖ **P** ; open April-Oct.
- * *Myrto,* 34, leof. Marathonos (Tel. 71–4321) 31 rms ¶ ▦ ⌂ **P**

MEGALOPOLIS (Peloponnese), Tel. 0791

Hotels:
Achillion, 61, od. Sambakataki (Tel. 23–276) 18 rms ▦ ⌂
Pan, 7, od. Papanastasiou (Tel. 22–270) 17 rms ▦ ⌂

🚌 **Buses:** to and from Athens
🚆 several times a day, taking 5h; **night train** to and from Athens, taking 5h.30

METAMORPHOSSI (Macedonia), Tel. 0375

Hotel:
** *Haus Danai* (Tel. 22-310) 15 rms ▥ ⌂

△ **Campsites:**
Mylos, at Nikiti (Tel. 22-041) 120 sites; open May-Sept.
Stamatis, at Nikiti, 126 sites ≈
Sithou, on the beach at Metamorphossi (Tel. 22-414) 150 sites; open May-Sept.
Sylva, 1.3mls (2km) from Nikiti (Tel. 21-496) 91 sites; open May-Sept. ≈

METHANA (Peloponnese), Tel. 0298

ⓘ **Tourist police:** in summer, 34, leof. Vas. Konstantinou (Tel. 92-463).

Hotels:
** *Avra* (Tel. 92-382) 55 rms ⫙ A/c ⚇ ⌂ ☎ ✳ ≈ P
** *Pigae* (Tel. 92-258) 27 rms ⫙ ▥ A/c ⌂ ☎ ≈ P thermal baths; open June-Oct.
* *American* (Tel. 92-285) 31 rms ⌂ ☎ ≈ P; open May-Oct.
* *Gionis* (Tel. 92-321) 52 rms ⫙ ▥ ⌂ ☎ P; open June-Oct.
* *Methanion* (Tel. 92-22) 30 rms ▥ ⌂ P

METHONI (Peloponnese), Tel. 0723

Hotels:
** *Methoni Beach* (boarding house, Tel. 31-455) 12 rms ⫙ ▥ ⌂ ☎ ≈ P night-club.
* *Alex* (Tel. 31-219) 20 rms ⫙ ▥ A/c ⌂ ☎ ≈ P

METHONI (Macedonia), Tel. 0353

Hotels:
* *Arion* (Tel. 41-214) 39 rms ⫙ ▥ ⚇ ☎ ≈ P; open April-Oct.

* *Ayannis* (Tel. 451-216) 28 rms ⫙ ▥ ⌂ ☎ P open May-Oct.

△ **Campsite:**
Ayannis (Tel. 51-323) 27 sites; open April-Oct.

METOCHI (Peloponnese), Tel. 0693

Hotel:
** *Kalogria Beach* (Tel. 31-276) 96 rms and 253 bungalows ⫙ ▥ ⚇ ⌂ ☎ ✳ ≈ ⚲ ♪/9 P night-club; open May-Oct.

METSOVON (Epirus), Tel. 0656

Hotels:
*** *Diasselo,* Platia Kentriki (Tel. 41-719) 22 rms ⫙ ▥ ⌂ ☎ P
** *Victoria* (Tel. 41-771) 30 rms ⫙ ▥ ⌂ ☎ P night-club.
* *Enatia,* od. Tossitsa (Tel. 41-263) 36 rms ▥ ⌂ P winter sports area 1.3mls (2km) away.
* *Galaxy* (Tel. 41-202) ⫙ ▥ ⌂ ☎ P
* *Olympic* (Tel. 41-337) ⫙ ▥ ⌂ P

MILINA (Thessaly), Tel. 0423

△ **Campsite:**
Olyzon (Tel. 65-236) 100 sites; open May-Sept.

MILOS [Island] (Cyclades), Tel. 0287

Hotels:
** *Adamas* (boarding house, Tel. 41-844) 10 rms ⫙ ▥ ⌂ ☎ ≈ P
** *Venus Village* (Tel. 41-770) 91 rms and bungalows ⫙ A/c ⌂ ☎ ⌸ ≈ ⚲ ♪/9 night-club; open April-Oct.
* *Chronis* (Tel. 41-625) bungalows 16 rms ⌂ ≈
* *Gorali* (Tel. 41-625) 16 rms ⌂ ≈
* *Milos* (Tel. 41-837) 19 rms ⌂

⚓ open April-Oct.

✈ **Air services:** 2 daily flights in summer (4 a week in winter) to and from Athens, taking 55 min; *Olympic Airways,* Adamas (Tel. 41-880).

⚓ **Car-ferries and boats:** at least once a day to and from Piraeus, taking 10h. via Senilos, Siphnos and Kimolos.

MISSOLONGHI (central Greece), Tel. 0631

ℹ **Tourist police:** 11, od. Damaskinou (Tel. 22-555).

Hotels:
** *Liberty,* 41, Heron Polytechniou (Tel. 280-50) 60 rms ⟨⟩ ⟨⟩ ⟨⟩ ☎ P
** *Theoxenia,* Limin (Tel. 224-93) 80 rms ⟨⟩ ⟨⟩ ⟨⟩ ☎ ⚓ P

🚌 **Buses:** to and from Athens every hour, taking 4h.

Handicrafts: 1, od. Avgostos Favros (Tel. 22-751).

MISTRA (Peloponnese), Tel. 0731

Hotel:
** *Vyzantion,* Vassilissis Sophias (Tel. 93-309) 22 rms ⟨⟩ ⟨⟩ ⟨⟩ ☎ P

△ **Campsite:**
Mystras, at Slaviki (Tel. 22-724) 37 sites.

MONEMVASSIA (Peloponnese), Tel. 0732

Hotels:
*** *Castro,* Gefyza (boarding house Tel. 614-13) 12 rms ⟨⟩ ☎ ⚓ P ; open April-Oct.
** *Monemvassia* (Tel. 61-381) 9 rms ⟨⟩ ⟨⟩ ⟨⟩ ☎ P
** *Malvasia* (boarding house Tel. 61-323) 6 rms ⟨⟩ A/c ⟨⟩ ☎ P

⚓ **Car ferries:** links with Piraeus 3 times a week.

MONI [Island]: *see Aegina.*

MYCENAE, or Mikinai (Peloponnese), Tel. 0751

Hotels:
* *Agamemnon* (Tel. 66-222) 8 rms ⟨⟩ ⟨⟩ P
* *Little Planet* (Tel. 66-240) 13 rms ⟨⟩ ⟨⟩ ⟨⟩ ☎ ❀ P

△ **Campsites:**
Atreus (Tel. (0752) 66-221) 44 sites; open April-Oct.
Mycenae Camping (Tel. 66-247) 25 sites; open April-Oct.

🚌 **Buses:** to and from Athens every hour, taking 2h.

MYKONOS [Island] (Cyclades), Tel. 0289

ℹ **Tourist police:** Platia Apovathros (Tel. 22-482).

Hotels:
*** *Ano Mera,* at Ano Mera (Tel. 71-215) 67 rms ⟨⟩ A/c ⟨⟩ ☎ ⚓ P night-club; open April-Oct.
*** *Leto* (Tel. 22-207) 25 rms ⟨⟩ ⟨⟩ ⟨⟩ ⚓ P
** *Alkistis,* Hagios Stephanos beach, 1.9mls (3km) away. (Tel. 22-332) 102 rms ⟨⟩ ⟨⟩ ⟨⟩ ☎ ⚓ P ; open April-Oct.
** *Aphrodite,* Kalafati beach, 7.5mls (12km) away (Tel. 71-367) 95 bungalows ⟨⟩ ⟨⟩ ⟨⟩ ☎ ⚓ ⚓ ⚿ P night-club; open April-Oct.
** *Despotika* (Tel. 22-009) 21 rms A/c ⟨⟩ ☎; open April-Oct.
** *Rohari* (Tel. 23-107) 53 rms ⟨⟩ ⟨⟩ ☎; open April-Oct.
** *Kouneni* (Tel. 22-301) 19 rms ⟨⟩ ⟨⟩ ☎; open April-Oct.
** *Rhenia* at Tourlos (Tel. 22-300) 37 bungalows ⟨⟩ ☎ P ; open April-Oct.

** *Theoxenia* (Tel. 22–230) 57 rms ¶ ▥ ᜟ ☎ open April-Oct.
** *Ornos Beach*, at Ornos (Tel. 22–243) 24 rms ▥ ᜟ ☎ open April-Oct.
** *Konhyli*, at Vrysses (Tel. 22–107) 29 rms ▥ ☎ open April-Oct.
* *Manto* (Tel. 22–330) 15 rms ▥ ᜟ ≈ P
* *Mykonos Beach*, Megali Amnos beach (Tel. 22–572) 27 bungalows ¶ ▥ ᜟ ☎ ≈ night-club; open April-Oct.

Accommodation: in the homes of local people is easy to arrange: contact the tourist police.

△ **Campsite:** *Paradise*, 3.8mls (6km) from the town (Tel. 22–129) 76 sites; open April-Oct.

✈ **Air service:** 2 daily flights to and from Athens in summer, taking 50 min.

⚓ **Car-ferries and boats:** to and from Piraeus, taking 5h.30.

MYTILENE [Island] or Lesbos (Aegean Sea), Tel. 0251

ℹ **Tourist police:** Platia Customs (Tel. 22–776).

Hotels:
** *Blue Sea*, 1, Platia Kountourioti (Tel. 28–383) 61 rms ¶ ▥ ᜟ ☎ P night-club.
** *Lesviou*, 27 od. P. Kountourioti (Tel. 22–038) 38 rms ¶ ▥ ᜟ ☎ P
** *Xenia*, 1.3mls (2km) away (Tel. 22–713) 74 rms ¶ ▥ A/c ᜟ ☎ ≈ ≈ ₊/9 P night-club.
* *Rex*, 3, Katsakouli Kioski (Tel. 28–523) 16 rms ▥ ᜟ P
* *Sappho*, Prokymea (Tel. 28–415) 31 rms ▥ ᜟ P

At Kratigos:
** *Katia* (Tel. 61–403) 38 bungalows ¶ ▥ ᜟ ☎ ❋ ▦ ≈ ◖ P thermal baths; open April-Oct.

At Mithymna-Molyvos, (Tel. 0253):
*** *Molyvos* (boarding house; Tel. 71–386) 30 rms ¶ ▥ ᜟ ᜟ ☎ P ; open March-Oct.
** *Delfinia,* by the beach (Tel. 22–627) 68 rms ¶ ▥ ᜟ ☎ ▦ ≈ ◖ P

At Neapolis:
** *Lesvos Beach* (furnished apartments Tel. 27–531) 39 rms ¶ ▥ ᜟ ᜟ ☎ open March-Oct.

At Thermi:
** *Blue Beach* (Tel. 21–290) 6 bungalows ▥ ᜟ ☎ ❋ ≈ P ; open June-Sept.
** *Votsala*, by the beach (Tel. 71–231) 47 rms ¶ ▥ ᜟ ☎ ≈ ◖ ₊/9 P ; open May-Oct.

✈ **Air services:** 5 times a week to and from Athens, taking 45 min; *Olympic Airways*, 13, od. Smyrnis (Tel. 22–820).

⚓ **Car-ferries:** to and from Piraeus 5 times a week, taking 13h.30; connections for Thessaloniki, Kavalla and, though services not guaranteed, Turkey.

🚗 **Car hire:** *Lesbos cars*, 59, od. Prokymaia (Tel. 23–072).

N

NAUPAKTOS (central Greece), Tel. 0634

Hotels:
** *Amaryllis,* 3, Platia Limenos

(Tel. 27–237) 18 rms ⅋ ▥ ⌂
☎ P
** *Lido* (Tel. 22–501) 15 rms ⅋
A/c 苗 ⌂ ☎ ⇌ P night-club.
** *Xenia* (Tel. 22–301) 48 rms ⅋
▥ ⌂
* *Akti* (Tel. 28–464) 57 rms ▥ ⌂
P
* *Nea Hellas* (Tel. 27–400) 11
rms ⌂ ⇌

🚌 **Buses:** twice a day to and
from Athens, taking 4h.

NAUPLIA, or Nafplion
(Peloponnese), Tel. 0752

ℹ️ **Tourist police:** Platia
Ethnosinelefseos
(Tel. 27–776).

Hotels:
**** *Xenia Palace*, Acronauplia
(Tel. 28–981) 51 rms and 54
bungalows ⅋ ▥ A/c 苗 ⌂ ☎
❋ ▱ ⇌ P
*** *Amalia*, 1.9mls (3km) from
Nauplia (Tel. 24–401) 171 rms
⅋ A/c ⌂ ☎ ⇌ P
*** *Amphitryon*, Akti Miaouli
(Tel. 27–366) 48 rms ⅋ ▥ ⌂
☎ ▱ P
*** *Xenia*, Acronauplia
(Tel. 28–991) 58 rms ⅋ ▥ 苗
⌂ ☎ ⇌ P
** *Agamemnon*, 3, Akti Mialouli
(Tel. 28–021) 40 rms ⅋ ▥ ⌂
☎ ▱ ⇌ P
* *Alkyon*, 43, leof. d'Argos
(Tel. 27–714) 18 rms ⅋ ▥ ⌂
☎ ⇌ P
* *Diozkouri*, od. Zigomala
(Tel. 28–644) 51 rms ⅋ ▥ ⌂
☎
* *Nafplia*, 11, od. Navarinou
(Tel. 28–167) 56 rms ▥ ⌂ ☎
P
* *Rex*, 17, od. Bouboulinas
(Tel. 28–094) 51 rms ⅋ ▥ ⌂
☎ P
* *Victoria*, 3, od. Spiliadou
(Tel. 27–420) 36 rms ⅋ ▥ A/c
⌂ ☎ P

Youth hostel: 15, Argaunauton,
Neou Vyzantiou district (Tel.
27–754).

Restaurant:
Savouras, 5, od. Bouboulinas;
pleasant little taverna.

△ **Campsites:**
Candia Beach, in Iria
(Tel. 91–351) 60 sites; open
May-Sept.
Nafplion, road to Argos
(Tel. 280–30) 70 sites; open
April-Sept. ⇌
Lefka Beach, on the beach at
Lefka, near Vivari
(Tel. 92–334) 70 sites; open
April-Oct. ⇌
Sunset, at Tolo (Tel. 59–566)
120 sites; open March-Oct. ⇌
ℚ
Xeni Beach Tolo, ¼mls
(800m) from the beach at Tolo.

🚌 **Buses:** to and from Athens
every hour, taking 3h.

🚗 **Car hire:** *Avis*, 2, Platia
Bouboulinas (Tel. 23–629);
Staikos Tours, 18, Platia
Bouboulinas (Tel. 27–950).

NAXOS [Island] (Cyclades),
Tel. 0285
Hotels:
** *Ariadne* (Tel. 22–452) 24 rms
⅋ ⌂ ☎ ⇌ P ; open
May-Sept.
* *Apollo* (Tel. 22–468) 19 rms ⌂
P
* *Coronis* (Tel. 22–297) 32 rms
⅋ ▥ ⌂ ☎ P
* *Hermes* (Tel. 22–220) 20 rms
▥ ⌂ ☎ P

⚓ **Car-ferries and boats:** 11
services a week to and from
Piraeus, taking 8h, on the
route serving Syros, Paros,
Ios and Thera.

NEA CHALKIDON
(Macedonia), Tel. 0393

Hotel:
- ** *Philippos* (Tel. 22–125) 32 rms ¶ ▥ ▦ ⌂ ☎ P night-club.

NEA MAKRI (Attica), Tel. 0294

Hotels:
- ** *Marathon Beach* (Tel. 91–255) 166 rms ¶ ▥ ▦ ⌂ ☎ ※ ▱ ≈ ♨/9 P night-club.
- ** *Thomas Beach* (Tel. 92–790) 30 rms ¶ ▥ ⌂ ☎ ※ ≈ P
- ** *Zouberi* (Tel. 71–920) 128 rms ¶ ▥ ▦ ⌂ ☎ ※ ▱ P night-club; open April–Oct.

Δ **Campsite:**
Nea Makri, 156 leof. Marathonos (Tel. 92–719) 78 sites; open April–Oct.

🚌 **Buses:** every half hour to and from Athens, taking 45 mins.

NEA MOUDIANA (Macedonia), Tel. 0373

[i] **Tourist police:** 31, od. 28th October, (Tel. 21–370).

Hotel:
- * *Kouvraki* (Tel. 21–292) 21 rms ▥ ▦ ⌂ ☎ ≈ P

NEA PAGASAE (Thessaly), Tel. 0421

Hotels:
- ** *Adonis* (Tel. 98–015) 20 rms ▥ ▦ ⌂ ☎ ≈
- * *Filoxenia* (Tel. 98–336) 17 rms ▥ ⌂ ☎ ≈ P

NEAPOLIS (Peloponnese), Tel. 0732

Hotel:
- ** *Aivali* (Tel. 41–561) 26 rms ▥ ⌂ ☎ P

NEOS MARMARAS (Macedonia), Tel. 0375

Hotels:
- **** *Meliton Beach,* at Porto Carras (Tel. 71–380) 446 rms ¶ A/c ▦ ⌂ ☎ TV 🛏 ※ ▱ ≈

♀ ♨/18 ▣ P; open April–Oct.
- *** *Sithonia Beach,* at Porto Carras (Tel. 71–381) 468 rms ¶ A/c ▦ ⌂ ☎ TV 🛏 ※ ▱ ≈ ♀ P; open April–Oct.

Δ **Campsites:**
Areti, at Katsivelia (Tel. 71–253) 80 sites ≈ ♀ open June–Sept.
Europa, at Hagios Kyriaki (Tel. 71–078) 250 sites ≈ ♀ open May–Sept.
Marmaras (Tel. 71–246) 150 sites; open June–Sept. ≈

NEW PHALERON or Neon Faliron (Attica), Tel. 01

Hotels:
- ** *Bianca Beach* (Tel. 482–30–65) 67 rms ¶ A/c ▦ ⌂ ☎ P
- * *Carol* (Tel. 412–29–33) 35 rms ▥ A/c ▦ ⌂ ☎ ≈ P
- * *Hermion* (Tel. 481–29–19) 42 rms ▥ ▦ ⌂ ☎ ≈ P
- * *Olympic* (Tel. 482–08–00) 100 rms ¶ ▥ ▦ ⌂ ☎ P

NISYROS [Island]

⚓ **Boats:** 2 weekly links with Piraeus (19h) via Astypalea and Kalymnos, and with Rhodes via Tilos and Symi.

O

OLYMPIADAS (Macedonia), Tel. 0376.

Δ **Campsite:**
Olympias Camping (Tel. 51–295), 147 sites; April–Sept. ≈

OLYMPIA, or Olympia (Peloponnese), Tel. 0624

[i] **Tourist police:** 13, od. Douma (Tel. 22–550).

Hotels:
- *** *Amalia* (Tel. 22–190) 147 rms

   ¶¶ A/c 🛗 🏛 ☎ 🖼 P
*** *Antonios* (Tel. 22–348) 65 rms
   ¶¶ ▥ A/c 🏛 ☎ ❄ P
** *SPAP* (Tel. 22–514) 51 rms ¶¶
   ▥ 🏛 ☎ ❄ P
** *Apollo* (Tel. 22–522) 86 rms
   ¶¶ 🏛 ☎ P
** *Neda* (Tel. 22–563) 43 rms ¶¶
   ▥ 🏛 ☎ P night-club.
** *Neon Olympia* (Tel. 22–547)
   31 rms ¶¶ ▥ 🏛 ☎
** *Olympic Village* (Tel. 22–211)
   51 rms ¶¶ A/c 🛗 🏛 ☎ P
   night-club.
** *Xenia* (Tel. 22–510) 36 rms ¶¶
   ▥ 🏛 ☎ 🖼 P
** *Xenios Zeus* (Motel;
   Tel. 22–551) 36 rms ¶¶ ▥ 🏛
   ☎ P
* *Ilis* (Tel. 22–547) 57 rms ¶¶ ▥
   🏛 ☎ P
* *Kronion* (Tel. 22–502) 23 rms
   ¶¶ ▥ 🏛 P
* *Olympic Torch* (Tel. 22–668)
   18 rms ¶¶ ▥ 🏛 P

△ **Campsites:**
   Diana (Tel. 22–314) 42 sites;
   open Feb.-Oct.
   Olympia Camping
   (Tel. 22–745) 73 sites.

   Youth hostel: 18, od.
   Praxitelous (Tel. 21–580).

🚌 **Buses:** once a day to Athens
   and 3 times daily from
   Athens, taking 6h; approx.
   hourly service for Pyrgos
   (connecting with the
   Peloponnesian Railways),
   taking 45 min.

   ORMYLIA (Macedonia),
   Tel. 0371

   Hotel:
* *Sermili* (Tel. 51–308) 123 rms
   ¶¶ ▥ 🛗 🏛 ☎ ❄ ～ P ; open
   April-Oct.

   OURANOPOLIS
   (Macedonia), Tel. 0377

   Hotels:
*** *Eagles Palace* (Tel. 71–250; at
   Athens, 3, od. Alckimachou,
   Tel. 21–92–16) 162 rms and
   bungalows ¶¶ ▥ A/c 🛗 🏛 ☎
   ❄ ～ P night-club; open
   April-Oct.
** *Xenia* (Tel. 71–202) 42 rms
   and bungalows ¶¶ A/c 🏛 ☎
   ❄ ～ Q P ; open May-Sept.

P

   Palea Epidavros, or Ancient
   Epidaurus: *see Epidaurus.*

   PALEON FALIRON, or Old
   Phaleron, Tel. 01

   Hotels:
**** *Athens Chandris,* 385, leof.
   Syngrou (Tel. 941–48–24) 386
   rms ¶¶ A/c 🛗 🏛 ☎ 📺 ❄ ～
   P
** *Coral,* 35, od. *Possidonos*
   (Tel. 981–64–41) 89 rms ¶¶ ▥
   A/c 🛗 🏛 ☎ 🖼 ～ ♪/9 P
** *Possidon,* 72, leof.
   Possidonos, (Tel. 982–20–86)
   90 rms ¶¶ ▥ A/c 🛗 🏛 ☎ 🖼
   ～ P

   PALIOURI (Macedonia),
   Tel. 0374

   Hotel:
** *Xenia* (Tel. 92–277) 72 rms ¶¶
   ▥ 🛗 🏛 ☎ ～ P night-club;
   open May-Sept.

△ **Campsite:**
   Paliouri (Tel. 92–206) 450
   sites; open April-Oct. ～ Q

   PANORAMA (Macedonia),
   Tel. 031

   Hotels:
*** *Nepheli* (Tel. 94–20–02) 70
   rms ¶¶ ▥ A/c 🛗 🏛 ☎ P
   night-club.

*** *Panorama* (Tel. 94–11–23) 50 rms ¶ ▥ 苗 🏠 ☎ P
* *Pefka* (Tel. 94–11–53) 50 rms ¶ ▥ 苗 🏠 ☎ P

PARALIA KATERINI (Macedonia), Tel. 0351

Hotels:
** *Alcyon* (Tel. 61–613) 34 rms ¶ ▥ 苗 🏠 ☎ ≈ P
** *Alcyonis* (Tel. 61–679) 20 rms ¶ ▥ 🏠 ☎ P
* *Akteon* (Tel. 61–424) 36 rms ¶ ▥ 🏠 ☎ ≈
* *Avra* (Tel. 61–213) 15 rms ¶ ▥ 🏠 ☎
* *Konstantinos* (Tel. 61–561) 28 rms ¶ ▥ 苗 🏠 ☎
* *Muse's Beach* (Tel. 61–212) 60 rms ¶ ▥ 苗 🏠 ☎ P

PARGA (Epirus) Tel. 0684

[i] **Tourist police:** in summer (Tel. 31–222).

Hotels:
** *Hellas* (Tel. 31–255) 10 rms ▥ 🏠 ☎ P; open June-Oct.
** *Parga Beach* (Tel. 31–293) 80 rms and bungalows ¶ ▥ 苗 🏠 ☎ ⚓/9 P; open April-Oct.
* *Avra* (Tel. 31–205) 18 rms ¶ ▥ 🏠 ☎ P; open April-Oct.
* *Calypso* (Tel. 31–316) 23 rms ¶ ▥ 🏠 ☎ ≈ P; open April-Dec.

Δ **Campsites:**
Elea Camping (Tel. 31–130) 65 sites; open April-Oct. ≈
Lichnos Camping (Tel. 31–371) 150 sites; open April-Oct. ≈
Parga Camping (Tel. 31–161) 120 sites; open April-Oct. ≈
Valtos Camping (Tel. 31–287) 92 sites; open April-Sept. ≈

PARNIS [Mt] (Attica), Tel. 01

Hotels:
**** *Hotel-casino Mt Parnis*

(Tel. 246–91–11, or in Athens, Tel. 322–94–12) 106 rms ¶ ▥ A/c 苗 🏠 ☎ ❋ ▦ ९ P
** *Xenia* (Tel. 246–91–01) 161 rms ¶ ▥ 苗 🏠 ☎ P; open June-Sept.
* *Kyklamina* (Tel. 246–92–40) 15 rms ¶ ▥ 🏠 ☎ P

PAROS [Island] (Cyclades), Tel. 0284

[i] **Tourist police:** in summer, at Apovathra (Tel. 21–673).

Hotels:
** *Aegeon* (Tel. 22–153) 24 rms ▥ 苗 🏠 ☎
** *Xenia* (Tel. 21–394) 23 rms ¶ ▥ 🏠 ☎ ≈ P; open April-Oct.
* *Nicolas* (Tel. 22–251) 43 rms ¶ ▥ 🏠 ☎ ≈ P
* *Paros* (Tel. 21–319) 12 rms ▥ 🏠 ☎ ≈ P; open April-Oct.

At Marpissa:
** *Xenon Marpissis* (Tel. 41–288) 110 rms ¶ ▥ 🏠 ☎ ≈ P; open June-Sept.
* *Vicky* (Tel. 41–333) 13 rms ¶ ▥ 🏠 ☎ open April-Oct.

At Naoussa:
** *Hippocampus* (Tel. 51–223) 49 rms ¶ ▥ 🏠 ☎ ≈ P; open April-Oct.
** *Naoussa* (Tel. 51–207) 10 rms ¶ ▥ 🏠 ☎ ≈ P; open April-Oct.
* *Minoa* (Tel. 51–309) 26 rms ¶ ▥ 🏠 open April-Oct.
* *Piperi* (Tel. 51–295) 8 bungalows ¶ ≈ P

At Aliki:
** *Afroditi* (Tel. 21–489) 20 rms ▥ 🏠 ☎ ≈ open June-Sept.

Δ **Campsite:**
Koula Camping (Tel. 22–081) 71 sites ≈

✈ **Air services:** several daily flights to and from Athens, taking 45 min; 3 flights a week to and from Herakleion (Crete); 4 flights a week to and from Rhodes; *Olympic Airways*, Parikia Parou (Tel. 22–015).

🏛 **Car-ferries:** frequent services to and from Piraeus, taking 7h, via Syros, and towards Thera and Crete.

PATMOS [Island]
(Dodecanese), Tel. 0247

Hotels:
** *Patmion* (Tel. 31–313) 21 rms ¶¶ ▥ ⌂ ☎ ⚓ **P**; open April–Oct.
** *Grikos* (Tel. 31–167) 17 rms ¶¶ ⌂ **P**
** *Xenia* (Tel. 31–219) 35 rms ¶¶ ▥ ⌂ ☎ ⚓ **P**; open April–Oct.
* *Astoria* (Tel. 31–205) 14 rms

🏛 **Car-ferries and boats:** daily service to and from Piraeus, taking 6h.30 in 8h, via Syros, and towards Thera and Crete.

PATRAS (Peloponnese), Tel. 061

ℹ **Tourist police:** 40, od. Othonos and Amalias (Tel. 22–09–02) and, for the region (Tel. 32–55–61).

GNTO: at Glyfada (Tel. 42–03–04).

🚗 *ELPA*: od. Astingos and 127, od. Kozinthou (Tel. 42–54–11).

Hotels:
*** *Acropole*, 32, Hagiou Andreou (Tel. 27–98–09) 33 rms ¶¶ ▥ 🛗 ⌂ ☎
*** *Astir*, 16, od. Hagiou Andreou (Tel. 27–63–11) 120 rms ¶¶ ▥ A/c 🛗 ⌂ ☎ ▦ **P**
*** *Moreas* (Tel. 42–54–94) 105 rms ¶¶ ▥ ⌂ ☎ **P**
** *Achaea Beach*, 1.9mls (3km) away, in Paralia Proastiou

(Tel. 99–18–01) 87 rms ¶¶ ▥ A/c ⌂ ☎ ▦ ⚓ � **P** night-club.
** *Florida*, 5mls (8km) away, at Psathopyrgos (Tel. 93–12–79) 82 rms ¶¶ ▥ 🛗 ⌂ ☎ ▦ **P**; open March–Oct.
** *Galaxy*, 9, od. Hagios Nikolaos (Tel. 27–88–15) 55 rms ▥ ⌂ ☎ **P**
** *Majestic*, 67, od. Hagiou Andreou (Tel. 27–20–24) 73 rms ¶¶ ▥ ⌂ ☎ **P**
** *Tzaki*, in Bozaitika, 1.9mls (3km) (Tel. 42–83–03) 38 rms ¶¶ ▥ A/c 🛗 ⌂ ☎ **P**
* *Delphini*, 102, Heroön Polytechniou-Terpsithea (Tel. 42–10–01) 71 rms ¶¶ ▥ ⌂ ☎ ▦ **P**
* *Méditerranée*, 18, od. Hagios Nikolaos (Tel. 27–96–02) 93 rms ¶¶ ▥ ⌂ **P**

At Rhion (10.6mls/17km E):
*** *Averof Grand Hotel* (Tel. 99–21–02) 267 rms ¶¶ A/c 🛗 ⌂ ☎ ❄ ▦ ♀ **P** night-club.

Restaurants:
Apostolis, on the corner of od. Londou and od. Roufou (Tel. 27–34–44).
Daphnes, at Bozaitika (about 2.5mls/4km from Patras; Tel. 42–10–08), near the sea, set in a pretty garden; good cooking and reasonable prices.
Eva, 2.5mls (4km) from Patras on the Pyrgos road (Tel. 32–93–97); seafood and fish.
Evanghelatos, Hagiou, Nikolaos (Tel. 27–77–72); one of the oldest and best known restaurants in Patras.
Koukos, at Koukouli, about 1.25mls (2km) from the town centre (Tel. 32–50–77).

△ **Campsites:**
Patron Camping, at Hagia Patron (Tel. 42–413) 178 sites 🏕

Rhion Camping, at Rhion (Tel. 99–15–85) 26 sites; open May-Oct.
Rio Castle Camping, in Rhion (10.6mls/17km E.; Tel. 99–13–23) 26 sites.
Rio Mare Camping, at Rhion; 50 sites.

✈ **Air services:** *Olympic Airways,* 16, od. H. Andrea and Aratou (Tel. 22–29–01).

⚓ **Car-ferries:** sail regularly for Italy, some via Corfu. Daily links with Cephalonia; 3 times a week with Ithaca; once with Paxos. Ferry between Rhion and Andirrhion.

🚂 **Trains:** numerous services to and from Athens, taking 3 to 4h.

🚌 **Buses:** every hour to and from Athens, taking 3h.30; to Ioannina twice a day, taking 4h; to Thessaloniki 4 times a day, taking 9h.30; to Zante 3 times a day, taking 2h.30.

🚗 **Car hire:** *Avis,* 11, leof. Othonos and Amalias (Tel. 275–547); *Hertz,* 5, od. Kolokotroni (Tel. 220–990).

👜 **Handicrafts:** Exhibition, 40, Platia Georgiou A (Tel. 57–27–73).

🎭 **Special events:** carnival, 3 weeks before the start of the Orthodox Lent; the town is extraordinarily lively at this time.

PAXOS [Island] (Ionian Islands), Tel. 0662

Hotel:
** *Paxos Beach* (Tel. 31–211) 40 rms 🍴 🍺 🛏 🛁 ☎ ☀ 🏊 **P** ;

open April-Oct.

⚓ **Car-ferries:** 5 times a week to and from Corfu, taking 3h.

PIRAEUS (Attica), Tel. 01

ℹ️ **Tourist police:** 43, Akti Miaouli *GNTO* (Tel. 452–36–70). Diikitirio Marina Zea (Tel. 413–57–16).

Hotels:
** *Cavo d'Oro,* Vasileos Pavlou Kastella (Tel. 411–37–42) 74 rms 🍴 🍺 A/c 🛏 🛁 ☎ night-club.
** *Diogenis,* 27, leof. Vas. Georgiou (Tel. 412–54–71) 78 rms 🍴 🍺 A/c 🛏 🛁 ☎ 🖼 night-club.
** *Estai Naftikon,* od. Bizaniou and Skylitsi (Tel. 417–52–37) 174 rms 🍴 🍺 🛏 🛁 ☎ **P**
** *Homiridion,* 32, od. Charilaou Tricoupi (Tel. 451–98–11) 59 rms 🍴 🍺 A/c 🛏 🛁 ☎ **P** night-club.
** *Noufara,* 45, od. Vasileos Constantinou (Tel. 411–55–41) 48 rms 🍴 🍺 A/c 🛏 🛁 ☎
** *Park,* 103, Kolokotroni and Gladstonos (Tel. 452–46–11) 80 rms 🍴 A/c 🛏 🛁 ☎ **P** night-club.
** *Savoy,* 93, Vas. Konstantinou (Tel. 413–11–02) 71 rms 🍴 A/c 🛏 🛁 ☎
** *Triton,* 8, od. Tsamadou (Tel. 417–34–57) 56 rms 🍺 🛁 ☎
* *Anemoni,* 65, od. Evripidiou (Tel. 411–17–68) 45 rms 🍺 🛏 🛁 ☎
* *Atlantis,* 138, od. Notara (Tel. 452–68–71) 54 rms 🍴 🛁 **P**
* *Capitol,* od. Charilaou Tricoupi (Tel. 452–49–11) 56 rms 🍺 🛁 ☎
* *Scorpios,* 156, Akti Themistocleous (Tel. 451–21–72) 🍺 🛁

Restaurants and tavernas:

** *Freattys*, Zea Marina (Tel. 451–95–12), opposite yacht harbour.

* *Pantheon*, 149, od. Koundouriotou (Tel. 417–77–68).

Vasilenas, 72, od. Vitolion Aitolikou (Tel. 461–24–57); evenings only.

At Microlimano:

** *Aglamair* (Tel. 411–55–14); modern, very elegant.

** *Kanaris* (Tel. 417–51–90); this is the king of the fish restaurants; do not fail to try the prawns.

** *Papakia*, 8, od. Karageorgi Servias (Tel. 417–25–86); luxurious surroundings, Greek and French cooking. For fish and seafood, go to Koumoundourou Quay: *Kuyu*, Prosina Trehandiria, Zephyros, Zorba.

At Kastella:

* Panorama; good cooking but above all a splendid view across the bay.

✉ **Main Post Office:** od. Tsamadou.

✈ **Airlines:** *Olympic Airways*, 27, Akti Miaouli (Tel. 452–09–68).

⚓ **Shipping companies:** *Adriatica*, 97, Akti Miaouli (Tel. 418–19–01); *Blue Aegean Sea Lines* and *D.F.D.S. Seaways*, 14, od. Xenofontos, Athens (Tel. 323–42–92); *Ceres Flying Hydroways*, 8, Akti Themistokleous (Tel. 453–17–16); *Ceres Hydrofoils*, 69, Akti Miaouli (Tel. 452–36–12); *Chandris Lines*, 95, Akti Miaouli (Tel. 412–09–32); *Nouvelle Compagnie de Paquebots-Compagnie Française de Navigation*, 39, Akti Miaouli (Tel. 452–01–26); *Türkiye Denizcillik Bankasi*, 17, Akti Miaouli (Tel. 417–81–17); *Epirotiki*, 87, Akti Miaouli (Tel. 452–66–41); *Fragline*, 5, od. Rethymnon, Athens (Tel. 822–12–85); *Helit*, 10, Akti Kondili (Tel. 412–52–71); *Hellenic Mediterranean Lines*, electric railway station (Tel. 417–43–41); *Karageorgis Lines*, 10, Akti Kondili (Tel. 417–30–01); *"K" Lines*, 33, Akti Miaouli (Tel. 452–20–11); *Med. Sun Lines*, 5, od. Sachtouri (Tel. 452–47–28); *Townsend Thoresen*, 1, od. Novarinou (Tel. 412–21–71); *Trans Tirreno Express*, 71, Akti Miaouli (Tel. 451–21–09).

🚂 **Rail services:** (Pl. B-1) for northern Greece, od. Phanostratos; for the Peloponnese, Akti Kalimassiou.

Underground: line serving Piraeus, Athens, Kifissia, Akti Kondili.

🚌 **Buses:** two routes into Athens (Platia Syndagma or Platia Omonia); for the Apollo coast, departures from od. Klissovis and od. Hatzikiriakou; for the northern and eastern suburbs of Athens, buses leave from od. G., Theotoki.

🚗 **Car hire:** *Avis*, 71, Akti Miaouli (Tel. 452–06–39); *Hertz*, 9, od. Hagios Nikolaos (Tel. 452–66–00).

PLATAMON (Macedonia), Tel. 0352

Hotels:

** *Maxim* (Tel. 41–305) 73 rms
🍴 ▥ 🛁 ☎ ⚓ P

** *Platamon Beach* (Tel. 41-212) 170 rms ⅋ ▥ A/c ♨ ⌂ ☎ ☀ ⌨ ⚭ ♻ P

** *Xenia* (Motel; Tel. 41-204) 4 rms ⅋ ▥ ⌂ ☎ ☀ P

* *Alkionis* (Tel. 41-416) 32 rms ⅋ ▥ ♨ ⌂ ☎ P

* *Dias* (Tel. 41-267) 24 rms ⅋ ▥ ⌂ ☎

△ **Campsites:**
Arion, Panteleimon beach (Tel. 41-115) 80 sites; open April-Sept. ⚭

Castle Camping, in N. Panteleimouas, (Tel. 41-252) 350 sites; open April-Oct. ⚭ ♻

Hellas Camping, in Skotina (Tel. 41-490) 260 sites; open May-Oct. ⚭

Kalamaki Camping, Xirokampi beach (Tel. 41-676) 350 sites; open May-Sept. ⚭

Orfeas, Mati beach (Tel. 41-702) 40 sites ⚭

Platamon Camping (Tel. 41-301) 140 sites; open May-Oct. ⚭

Poseidon Beach, in Hagios Panteleimon (Tel. 41-654) 350 sites; open March-Oct. ⚭

POLYDENDRI (Attica), Tel. 0295

Hotel:
*** *Golden Horse* (Tel. 52-455) 15 rms ⅋ ▥ ♨ ⌂ ☎ ⌨ ♻ P

POROS [Island] (Saronic Gulf), Tel. 0298

🛈 **Tourist police:** in summer, 37, od. Dimosthenon (Tel. 22-462).

Hotels:
** *Epta Adelfia* (Tel. 23-412) 16 rms ⅋ ▥ ⌂ ☎; open April-Oct.

** *Latsi* (Tel. 22-392) 39 rms ⅋ ▥ ⌂ ☎ P

** *Neon Aegli,* at Askeli (Tel. 22-372) 72 rms ⅋ ▥ ⌂ ☎ ☀ ⚭ P

** *Pavlou* (Tel. 22-734) 36 rms ▥ A/c ♨ ⌂ ☎ P night-club.

** *Poros,* Neorion beach (Tel. 222-16) 91 rms ⅋ ▥ ⌂ ☎ ☀ P night-club.

** *Sirene* (Tel. 22-741) 120 rms ⅋ ▥ ♨ ⌂ ☎ ☀ ⚭ P night-club; open April-Oct.

** *Stella Maris,* Galatas beach (Tel. 22-562) 93 rms and 35 bungalows ⅋ ▥ ⌂ ☎ ⌨ ⚭ P; open April-Oct.

* *Angyra* (Tel. 22-432) 53 rms ⅋ ▥ ♨ ⌂ ☎ ⚭ P

* *Chryssi Avgi* (Tel. 22-277) 77 rms ⅋ ▥ ⌂ ☎ ⚭ P

* *Galatia,* at Galatas (Tel. 22-227) 30 rms ⅋ ▥ ⌂ P

⚓ **Car-ferries and boats:** run regularly to and from Piraeus (3h.40); in summer, hydroplane services

PORTARIA (Thessaly), Tel. 0421

Hotels:
** *Xenia* (Tel. 25-922) 76 rms ⅋ ▥ ♨ ⌂ ☎ P

* *Alkistis* (Tel. 99-290) 47 rms ▥ ♨ ⌂ ☎

Porto Carras: *see Neos Marmaras.*

PORTO GHERMENO (Attica), Tel 0263

Hotels:
** *Akteon,* at Villia (10.6mls/17km; Tel. 22-560) 26 rms ⅋ ▥ ⌂ ☎ P; open April-Oct.

* *Aegosthenion* (Tel. 41-226) 80 rms ⅋ ▥ ⌂ ☎ P; open April-Oct.

PORTO HELI (Peloponnese), Tel. 0754

Hotels:

*** *Hinitsa Beach* (Tel. 51-401) 206 rms ¶¶ A/c 🛗 🍸 ☎ 🚌 🔲 ≈ **P**

*** *Kosmos* (Tel. 51-327) 151 rms ¶¶ A/c 🛗 🍸 TV 🚌 ❋ 🔲 ≈ ᪖ **P** ; open April-Oct.

*** *Porto Heli* (PLM) (Tel. 51-490) 218 rms ¶¶ ⅢⅢ A/c 🛗 🍸 ❋ 🔲 ≈ ᪖ **P** night-club; open April-Oct.

** *Apollo Beach* (Tel. 51-431) 151 rms ¶¶ A/c ⅢⅢ 🛗 🍸 ❋ 🔲 ≈ ᪖ **P** night-club; open April-Oct.

** *Galaxy,* at Tzemi (Tel. 51-271) 171 rms ¶¶ ⅢⅢ A/c 🍸 ☎ ≈ ᪖ **P** ; open April-Oct.

** *Giouli* (Tel. 51-217) 163 rms ¶¶ ⅢⅢ A/c 🛗 🍸 ☎ ❋ 🔲 ≈ ᪖ **P** ; open April-Sept.

** *Saladi Beach,* at Saladi (15.6mls/25km; Tel. 21-601) 328 rms and 76 bungalows ¶¶ ⅢⅢ A/c 🛗 🍸 ☎ 🚌 ❋ 🔲 ≈ ᪖ **P** ; open April-Oct.

** *La Cité* (Tel. 51-265) 88 rms ¶¶ ⅢⅢ A/c 🍸 ☎ **P** ; open March-Oct.

** *Ververoda* (Tel. 51-343) 244 rms ¶¶ ⅢⅢ A/c 🛗 🍸 ☎ ❋ 🔲 **P** ; open April-Oct.

* *Alcyon* (Tel. 51-479) ¶¶ ⅢⅢ A/c 🍸 ☎ ≈ **P** night-club.

At Kosta:

** *Cap d'Or* (Tel. 51-360) 107 rms ¶¶ ⅢⅢ A/c 🍸 ☎ 🔲 ≈ ᪖ **P** night-club; open April-Oct.

** *Lido* (Tel. 51-395) 40 rms ¶¶ ⅢⅢ 🍸 ☎ **P**

△ **Campsites:**
Costa Camping, at Kosta (Tel. 51-571) 100 sites; open May-Oct. ≈

🛩 In summer, hydroplane service from Piraeus, on the route serving Hydra, Poros, Spetsae.

🚗 **Car hire:** *Staikos Tours,* on the quay (Tel. 51-316).

PORTO KOUFAS (Macedonia), Tel. 0375

△ **Campsite:**
Porto Koufo (Tel. 41-488) 100 sites 🔲 ≈ ᪖

PORTO RAFTI (Attica), Tel. 0299

Hotels:

*** *Artemis* (Tel. 72-000) 32 rms A/c 🛗 🍸 ☎ 🔲 **P**

* *Korali* (Tel. 72-602) 16 rms ¶¶ ⅢⅢ 🍸 ☎ ≈ **P**

* *Kyani Akti* (Tel. 72-241) 25 rms ¶¶ ⅢⅢ 🍸 ☎ 🔲 **P**

PREVEZA (Epirus), Tel. 0682

ℹ **Tourist police:** in summer (Tel. 22-225).

Hotels:

** *Preveza Beach,* at Kastrossykia (Tel. 51-483) 264 rms ¶¶ A/c 🛗 🍸 ❋ 🔲 ≈ ᪖ **P** night-club; open April-Oct.

** *Margarona Royal* (Tel. 24-361) 17 rms ¶¶ ⅢⅢ A/c 🛗 🍸 ☎ 🔲 ≈ **P** night-club.

* *Aktaeon,* 1, od. Kolovou (Tel. 22-258) 17 rms ⅢⅢ 🍸 ≈ **P**

* *Metropolis,* 1, od. Parthenagogiou (Tel. 22-235) 16 rms ⅢⅢ 🍸 ≈ **P**

△ **Campsites:**
Bel Mare, at Kyani Akti (Tel. 22-192) 90 sites; open May-Oct. ≈
Indian Village (Tel. 27-185) 40 sites; open May-Oct. ᪖
Kalamatsi Beach (Tel. 23-268) 135 sites ᪖
Nicopolis Beach, at Monolith (Tel. 23-109) 84 sites; open April-Sept. ᪖

🛩 **Ferry:** for Aktion every half-hour.

Buses: 3 times a day to and from Athens, taking 7h.

Handicrafts: municipal library, on the sea front (Tel. 23–108).

PTOLEMAIS (Macedonia), Tel. 0463

Hotel:
* *Costis* (Tel. 26–661) 27 rms ¶¶ ⅢⅢ 𝄞 P
* *George* (Tel. 24–845) 26 rms ⅢⅢ 𝄞 ☎

PYLOS (Peloponnese), Tel. 0723

Hotels:
** *Kastro* (Tel. 22–264) 10 rms ¶¶ ⅢⅢ 𝄞 ☎ P
** *Nestor* (Tel. 22–226) 16 rms ¶¶ ⅢⅢ 𝄞 ☎ ☞ P
* *Galaxy* (Tel. 22–780) 34 rms ¶¶ ⅢⅢ 舊 𝄞 ☎ P

Buses: twice a day to and from Athens, taking 6h.30.

PYRGOS (Peloponnese), Tel. 0621

Tourist police: 4, od. Karkavitsa (Tel. 23–685).

Hotels:
* *Alkistis* (Tel. 23–661) 30 rms ⅢⅢ 𝄞 P
* *Letrina* (Tel. 23–644) 68 rms ¶¶ ⅢⅢ 𝄞 P
* *Olympos* (Tel. 23–650) 37 rms ⅢⅢ 𝄞 P

At Skafidia:
*** *Miramare Olympia Beach* (Tel. 94–363) 354 rms and bungalows ¶¶ ⅢⅢ 𝄞 ☎ ☞ ☞ 𝑄 P night-club; open April-Oct.

Train: to and from Athens 6 times a day, taking 6h.30.

Buses: to and from Athens 9 times a day, taking 5h.

R

RAFINA (Attica), Tel. 0294

Hotels:
* *Avra* (Tel. 22–781) 96 rms ¶¶ ⅢⅢ 舊 𝄞 ☎ P night-club; open April-Nov.
* *Bravo* (Tel. 26–489) 18 rms ¶¶ ⅢⅢ 𝄞 ☞ P night-club.
* *Ina Marina* (Tel. 22–215) 79 rms ¶¶ ⅢⅢ 𝄞 ☀ ☞ P

△ **Campsites:**
Cococamp (Tel. 23–775) 95 sites ☞
Kokkino Limanaki (Tel. 26–601) 65 sites ☞
Polycamp (Tel. 23–808) 150 sites ☞
Rafina Camping (Tel. 23–118) 200 sites; open March-Oct. ☞

Buses: run very regularly to Athens (1h) and Attica.

RETHYMNON (Crete), Tel. 0831

Tourist police: 264, od. Ariadiou (Tel. 28–156).

Hotels:
** *Brascos,* od. Daskali (Tel. 23–721) 78 rms ¶¶ ⅢⅢ 舊 𝄞 ☎ P night-club.
** *Edaeon,* 9, Platia Plastirai (Tel. 28–667) 71 rms ¶¶ ⅢⅢ 𝄞 ☎ ☞ P
** *Joan,* 6, od. Dimitrakaki (Tel. 24–241) 50 rms A/c 舊 𝄞 ☎ P
** *Olympic,* od. Moatsou (Tel. 24–761) 59 rms A/c 舊 𝄞 ☎ P
** *Orion,* Kambos Adele (Tel. 71–471) 73 rms ¶¶ ⅢⅢ A/c 舊 𝄞 ☎ ☞ ☞ P ; open April-Oct.
** *Xenia,* N. Psarou (Tel. 29–111) 25 rms ¶¶ ⅢⅢ 𝄞 ☎ ☞ P

* *Astali* (Tel. 24–721) 36 rms ❚❚ ⅢⅢ ≈ P

* *Golden Beach*, at Adele (Tel. 71–012) 72 rms ❚❚ ⅢⅢ ⓕ 🖼 ≈ ९ ⌁/9

* *Park*, 6, od. Igoumenou Gavriel (Tel. 29–958) ⅢⅢ ⓕ ≈ P

* *Valari*, 78, Koundourioti quay (Tel. 22–236) 29 rms ⅢⅢ ⓕ ≈ P

On the road to Herakleion:

*** *Rithymna Beach* (at Adele, 3.8mls/6km away; Tel. 29–491) 556 rms and bungalows ❚❚ ⅢⅢ A/c 🛏 ⓕ ☎ 🚌 ☀ 🖼 ≈ ९ P night-club; open April-Oct.

*** *El Greco* (5mls/8km; Tel. 71–102) 307 rms, parties catered for ❚❚ ⅢⅢ A/c 🛏 ⓕ ☎ ☀ 🖼 ≈ P night-club.

** *Adele Beach* (Tel. 71–047) 50 rms ❚❚ ⓕ ☎ ☀ 🖼 ≈ ९ P

At Panormos (10.6mls/17km; vicin. 4):

** *Lauris Bungalows* (Tel. 51–226) 28 bungalows ❚❚ ⅢⅢ A/c 🛏 ⓕ ☎ ☀ 🖼 ≈ ९ P ; open April-Oct.

△ **Campsites:**
Arcadia (Tel. 28–825) 28 sites.
Elisabeth (Tel. 28–694) 164 sites; open April-Oct.

🚗 **Car hire:** *Avis,* 116, od. Arkadiou (Tel. 23–146); *Hertz,* 1, od. Hortatzi (Tel. 23–404); *Budget,* 83, od. Koundouriotou (Tel. 24–386).

⌂ **Handicrafts:** 8, od. Igoumenou Gavriil (Tel. 29–362).

† **Special events:** Wine Festival in the public park, at the end of July; information 10, od. Koundouriotou (Tel. 29–148).

Rhion: *see Patras.*

RHODES [Island], Tel. 0241

ⅰ **Tourist police:** 31, od. Papagou (Tel. 27–423).

GNTO: od. Makariou (Tel. 23–655; Pl. I z, in C-2).

Tourist office of Rhodes town: Platia Son et Lumière, opposite Mandraki port; at the airport; at the central port (mornings only).

🚗 *ELPA:* 16, od. Gallias (Tel. 24–377).

Hotels:

**** *Grand Hotel Astir Palace* (Pl. I, a, B-1), Akti Miaouli (Tel. 26–284) 378 rms ❚❚ ⅢⅢ A/c 🛏 ⓕ ☎ 🖼 ≈ ९ P night-club.

**** *Miramare Beach*, at Ixia, 3.8mls/6km on the road to Camiros (Tel. 24–251) 179 rms ❚❚ ⅢⅢ 🛏 ⓕ ☎ 🖼 ≈ ९ night-club; open March-Nov.

**** *Olympic Palace*, Ixia, 2.2mls/3km on the road to Camiros (Tel. 28–775) 333 rms ❚❚ A/c ⓕ ☎ 🚌 ☀ 🖼 ≈ ९ P night-club; open March-Nov.

**** *Rodos Palace*, at Ixia (1.9mls/3km on the road to Camiros; Tel. 25–222) 610 rms ❚❚ ⅢⅢ A/c 🛏 ⓕ ☎ 🚌 🖼 ≈ ९ P

*** *Apollo Beach*, at Faliraki, 8 mls/13km (Tel. 85–251) 293 rms ❚❚ A/c 🛏 ⓕ ☎ 📺 🚌 ☀ 🖼 ≈ open April-Oct.

*** *Blue Sea*, at Faliraki (Tel. 29–271) 296 rms ❚❚ A/c 🛏 ⓕ ☎ 📺 🚌 ☀ 🖼 ≈ P ; open April-Oct.

*** *Colossos Beach*, in Faliraki (Tel. 85–458) 516 rms ❚❚ A/c 🛏 ⓕ ☎ 📺 🚌 🖼 ≈ P ; open April-Oct.

*** *Esperides*, at Faliraki (Tel. 85–503) 550 rms ❚❚ A/c

open April-Oct.

*** *Avra Beach*, at Ixia (1.9mls/3km on the road to Camiros; Tel. 25-284) 125 rms and 61 bungalows. A/c P; open April-Oct.

*** *Bel Air*, at Ixia (2.5mls/4km on the road to Camiros; Tel. 23-711) 186 rms P; open April-Oct.

*** *Belvedere* (Pl. I, c, A-3), Akti Kanari (Tel. 24-471) 212 rms P; open March-Nov.

*** *Blue Bay*, at Ixia (Tel. 92-352) 359 rms and apartments A/c P; open April-Oct.

*** *Blue Sky* (Pl. I, d, A-2), Platia Psaropoulas (Tel. 24-091) 182 rms A/c P night-club; open March-Nov.

*** *Cairo Palace* (Pl. I, e, C-2), 28, od. Makariou (Tel. 27-600) 111 rms open April-Oct.

*** *Chevaliers Palace*, 3, od. Griva (Tel. 22-781) 188 rms A/c P night-club.

*** *Dionysos*, at Faneromeni (Tel. 23-021) 281 rms A/c P night-club; open March-Nov.

*** *Doretta Beach*, 11.3mls (18km) from the town (Tel. 41-441) 295 rms A/c P night-club; open April-Oct.

*** *Eden Roc*, 3.8mls (6km) on the road to Rhodini (Tel. 23-851) 374 rms and bungalows A/c P night-club; open April-Oct.

*** *Elafos Elafina*, at Profitis Ilias (Tel. (0246) 22-225) 68 rms

P; open April-Oct.

*** *Electra Palace*, Trianta beach, 5.6mls (9km) away (Tel. 92-521) 220 rms A/c P; open March-Nov.

*** *Elina*, in Ixia, 3.8mls (6km) away (Tel. 92-466) 150 rms A/c P; open April-Oct.

*** *Elisabeth*, at Ixia (furnished apartments; Tel. 92-656) 95 rms A/c P; open April-Oct.

*** *Faliraki Beach*, Faliraki beach, 7.5mls (12km) from the town (Tel. 26-511) 310 rms and apartments A/c P night-club; open April-Oct.

*** *Golden Beach*, 5mls (8km) on the road to Camiros (Tel. 92-411) 225 rms A/c P night-club; open March-Oct.

*** *Ibiscus*, 17, od. Nissyrou (Tel. 24-421) 205 rms P

*** *Ialyssos Bay*, at Ialyssos (Tel. 91-841) 153 rms A/c P; open April-Oct.

*** *Imperial* (Pl. I, g, B-1), 23, od. Vasileos Constantinou (Tel. 22-431) 81 rms open March-Oct.

*** *Lindos Bay*, Vlyha Beach, at Lindos (Tel. 42-210) 192 rms A/c P; open March-Oct.

*** *Mediterranean* (Pl. I, h, B-1), 35, od. Cos (Tel. 24-661) 154 rms

*** *Metropolitan Capsis*, 2.5mls (4km) on the road to Camiros (Tel. 25-015) 692 rms A/c P night-club.

*** *Oceanis*, 2.5mls (4km) on the

road to Camiros (Tel. 24–881)
240 rms ¶ A/c ▥ ▤ ▥ ☎ ▦
⚓ ♀ P night-club; open
March-Nov.

*** *Paradise*, od. Reni Kaskinou
(Tel. 29–220) 495 rms ¶ A/c
▤ ▥ ☎ ▦ P; open
March-Oct.

*** *Park* (Pl. I, i, B-3), 12, od.
Riga Fereou (Tel. 24–611) 84
rms ¶ ▥ ▤ ▥ ☎ ※ ▦ P
night-club.

*** *Regina* (Pl. I, e, C-2), 20, od.
Makariou (Tel. 22–171) 82 rms
¶ A/c ▥ ▤ ▥ ☎ ※ P

*** *Riviera*, 2, Akti Hiaouli
(Tel. 22–581) 62 rms ¶ ▥ ▤
☎ ⚓ open April-Oct.

*** *Rodos Bay*, 3mls (5km) on
the road to Camiros
(Tel. 23–662) 330 rms and
bungalows ¶ ▥ A/c ▤ ▥ ☎
※ ▦ ⚓ P night-club; open
April-Oct.

*** *Siravast* (Pl. I, k, B-1;
Tel. 23–551) 92 rms ¶ ▥ A/c
▤ ▥ ☎ ⚓ P; open
March-Nov.

*** *Sunwing*, in Kallithea
(Tel. 28–600) 389 rms ¶ ▥
▤ ▥ ☎ ▦ P night-club;
open April-Oct.

** *Acandia* (Pl. I, m, B-2), 16,
od. Heroön Polytechniou
(Tel. 22–251) 82 rms ¶ ▥ ▤
▥ ☎ ※; open April-Oct.

** *Aglaia*, 35, od. Apollonos and
od. Amerikis (Tel. 22–061) 110
rms ¶ ▥ ▤ ▥ ☎ ▦ open
March-Nov.

** *Alexia* (Pl. I, n, B-2), 54, od.
Orfanidou (Tel. 24–061) 135
rms ¶ ▥ ▤ ▥ ☎; open
March-Nov.

** *Amphitryon*, 10, od. A.
Diakou (Tel. 26–880) 101 rms
¶ ▥ ▤ ▥ ☎ night-club;
open April-Oct.

** *Angela* (Pl. I, o, B-2), 7, od. 28
Octovriou (Tel. 24–014) 64
rms ▥ ▥ ☎ ※ open
March-Oct.

** *Athina*, at Neockorion
(Tel. 22–631) 142 rms ¶ ▥
▤ ▥ ☎ ※ ⚓ P

** *Cactus*, 14, od. Cos
(Tel. 26–100) 177 rms ¶ ▥
▤ ▥

** *Constantinos* (Pl. I, q, C-2),
65, od. Amerikis (Tel. 22–971)
133 rms ▥ ▤ ▥ ☎ P

** *Corali*, 28, Vas. Constantinou
(Tel. 24–911) 115 rms ¶ ▥
▤ ▥ ☎

** *Delfini*, 45, od. Ethnarhou
Makariou (Tel. 24–691) 70 rms
¶ A/c ▤ ▥ ☎

** *Despo* (Pl. I, r, C-2), 40, od.
Vasilisis Sophias (Tel. 22–571)
64 rms ¶ ▥ ▤ ▥ ☎ ※

** *Europa* (Pl. I, s, B-2), 94, od.
28 Octovriou (Tel. 22–711) 80
rms ¶ ▥ ▤ ▥ ☎ open
March-Oct.

** *Lito*, at Trianta (Tel. 23–511)
97 rms ¶ ▤ ▥ ☎ ※ ▦ P;
open April-Oct.

** *Manoussos*, 25, od. Leon (Pl.
I, u, B-2; Tel. 22–741) 124 rms
¶ ▥ ▤ ▥ ☎ ⚓

** *Olympic* (Pl. I, v, B-1), 12,
Platia Vasileos Pavlou
(Tel. 24–531) 46 rms ¶ ▥ ▤
▥ ☎ ⚓ P

** *Plaza* (Pl. I, w, C-2), 1 od.
Lochou (Tel. 22–501) 128 rms
¶ A/c ▥ ▤ ▥ ☎ ▦ P

** *Solemar*, 3.8mls (6km) on the
road to Camiros (Tel. 22–941)
102 rms ¶ ▥ ▥ ☎ ▦ P;
open April-Oct.

** *Xenia*, at Afandou
(Tel. 51–121) 26 rms ¶ ▥ ☎
▦ ⚓/18

* *Achileion* (Pl. I, x, B-1), 14,
Platia Vasileos Pavlou
(Tel. 24–604) 48 rms ▥ ▥ ☎
※ open March-Oct.

* *Adonis* (Pl. I, y, C-2), 7, od.
Vasileos Constantinou

(Tel. 27–791) 15 rms ▦ ⌂ ☎
❀ **P**; open March-Nov.
* *Africa* (Pl. I, z, B-2), 63, od.
Diakou (Tel. 24–979) 75 rms
❙❙ ▦ 🛁 ⌂ ☎ open April-Oct.
* *Als* (Pl. I, i, B-1), Platia
Vasileos Pavlou (Tel. 22–481)
52 rms ▦ ⌂ ☎ ⏝; open
March-Oct.
* *Carina* (Pl, I, c, B-2), 12, od.
Griva (Tel. 22–381) 59 rms ▦
⌂ ☎ open March-Oct.
* *Isabella* (Pl. I, t, B-2), 12, od.
Amochostou (Tel. 22–651) 42
rms ▦ ⌂ ☎ **P**; open
March-Oct.
* *Marie* (Pl. I, d, B-1), 7, od.
Kastelorizou (Tel. 30–577) 122
rms ▦ ⌂ ☎; open March-Nov.
* *Soleil* (Pl. I, a, B-3), 2,
od. Vasilisis Frederikis
(Tel. 24–190) 90 rms ❙❙ ▦ 🛁
⌂ ☎ ⚲ **P**; open June-Sept.

Restaurants and tavernas:
*** *Kon-tiki*, a raft moored in the
Mandraki port (Pl. I, C-2);
Tel. 22–411; bouzouki,
evenings only.
*** *Piccolo*, 9, od. Kastellorizo
(Tel. 20–374); Greek and
international cooking, live
music in the evenings.
** *Maison Fleurie,* odos Riga
Fereou (Tel. 25–340); garden,
pianist in the evenings.
** *Casa Castellana,* od.
Aristotelou (Tel. 28–803); in
the old town, garden
enclosed by the ramparts.
** *Loukoulos,* 13, od. Amerikis; a
truly Greek restaurant.
* *Alexis,* od. Socrates; fish.
* *Anexi,* at Trianta
(3.8mls/6km); Greek clientele.
* *Fotis,* in the old town, behind
od. Socrates.
* *Manolis,* in the old town, od.
Socrates.
* *Pythagoras,* in the street of
same name.

* *Roumelli,* its roast meats are
particularly good value.

At Treis (6.3mls/10km) along
the Camiros road, then left
and after another 4.4mls
(7km):
* *Recep.,* taverna, only open
evenings.

At Lindos (35mls/56km):
* *Triton,* on the beach.
* *Lindos Beach.*

Banks: National Bank of
Greece, at Mandraki and
Platia Cyprus; Credit Bank,
Platia Cyprus.

✉ **Post Office:** Central post
office, Platia Eleftheria (Pl. I,
C-2), at Mandraki;
telephones, corner of od.
Amerikis and od. 25 Martiou.

✈ **Airport:** at Paradisi, 12mls
(18km) on the Camiros road;
numerous internal flights to
Athens, Herakleion and Sitia
(Crete) and, in summer, Cos
and Karpathos.

Airlines: *BEA* and *Cyprus
Airways,* Platia Kyprou;
Olympic Airways, odos Ierou
Lochou (Tel. 24–571).

⚓ **Boats:** daily departures from
Piraeus, taking between 11h
and 24h depending on the
boats and the ports of call
(Astypalea, Patmos, Leros,
Kalymnos, Tilos, Cos, Symi,
etc.). Once a week route is
continued to Castellorizo.

Shipping companies:
Epirotiki, 41, od. Vasilisis
Sophias; *Kavounides,* od. 25
Martiou; *Nomikos,* Platia
Kyprou; *Panormitis,* od.
Kirmichalis; *Typaldos,* od.
Ethelondon.

🚍 **Buses:** *K.T.E.L.* (serving E,
coast areas) and *R.O.D.A.*

(serving W. coast areas), od. Averoff, near the Nea Agora (Pl. I, C-3).

🚗 **Car hire:** *Autorent,* 26, od. E. Dodekanission (Tel. 24–008); *Avis,* 9, od. Gallia (Tel. 24–990) and at the airport; *Budget,* leof. Talissou (Tel. 22–508); *Hellascars (Europcar),* od. E. Dodekonission (Tel. 22–816); *Hertz,* 10, od. Griva (Grand Hotel; Tel. 21–819) and at the airport.

Shopping: Lalaounis, Gate of Liberty (Pl. II, D-1), in medieval surroundings, has a rather limited choice of the work of this master goldsmith, but the quality is extremely fine (mostly modern jewellery and some that draws inspiration from antiquity); numerous furriers in the modern town; silverware, copper, pewter, ceramics (not always old) to be found at the antique shops in od. Socrates (Pl. II, C-2); goods imported from abroad, but without going through Piraeus, are duty free; alcohol is particularly good value.

⚴ **Handicrafts:** 33, od. Ipoton (Tel. 20–050).

✝ **Special events:** Son et lumière, April-Oct., in English, French, German, Greek, at the foot of the ramparts, in the direction of the Palace of the Grand Masters (Plan ii, B/C-1). Folk dancing in the theatre of the old town every evening from 20h.15 except Sat. (21h.15) from May to Oct. (gardens behind the Turkish bath). Wine Festival in July and August, Rodini Park: wine tasting, music, dancing. Numerous religious festivals throughout the island according to the liturgical calendar.

⚓ **Beaches:** *Nautical Club* (Pl. I, C-1); *Akti Kanari* (Pl. I, A-2/3); between Rhodes and Trianda (on the Camiros road); *Faliraki,* 9.4mls (15km) on the Lindos road; at *Lindos,* 34.4mls (55km) from Rhodes Town; in general, the beaches of the W. coast are windswept and shingly; those on the E. coast are much more attractive, as they are sandy, quieter and the sea is calmer.

Boat trips: ask at the port of Mandraki (Pl. I, C-2).

S

SALAMIS [Island] (Saronic Gulf), Tel. 01.

ℹ️ **Tourist police:** leof. Salaminos and Thermoplion (Tel. 465–11–00)

⚓ **Car-ferries:** frequent from Perama (12mls/18km from Athens) and frequent boats to and from Piraeus (40 min).

SAMOS [Island] (Aegean Sea), Tel. 0273

ℹ️ **Tourist police:** in summer, 89, od. Sofouli (Tel. 274–04).

Hotels:
At Vathy:
** *Aeolis,* 33, od. Themistokli Sofouli (Tel. 28–904) 51 rms A/c 🛏 🛁 ☎ P ; open April-Oct.
** *Xenia,* 23, od. Themistokli Sofouli (Tel. 27–463) 31 rms 🍴 ▥ A/c 🛁 ☎ P

* *Samos*, 6, od. Themistokli Sofouli (Tel. 28-377) 83 rms ¶ ▦ A/c ⌖ ⌂ ☎ ≈ P

At Karlovassi:
** *Merope* (Tel. 32-650) 80 rms ¶ ▦ ⌂ ☎ P

At Pythagorion:
** *Dorissa Bay* (Tel. 61-360) 176 rms ¶ A/c ⌖ ⌂ ☎ ✳ ▣ ≈ ⚲ ♪/9; open April-Oct.
** *Phito* (Tel. 61-314) 75 bungalows ¶ ▦ ⌂ ☎ ✳ ▣ P; open April-Oct.

Youth hostel: at Vathy (Tel. 27-751).

✈ **Air services:** at least 1 daily flight to and from Athens, taking 1h; *Olympic Airways*, 23, od. Thermistokli Sofouli (Tel. 27-237).

⚓ **Car-ferries:** 6 times a week to Karlovassi (taking 10 to 14h) via Icaria; connection for Turkey, though services not guaranteed.

🚗 **Car hire:** *Budget,* od. Sofouli (Tel. 27-146).

SAMOTHRACE [Island] or Samothraki (Thrace), Tel. 0551

Hotels:
* *Xenia*, at Paleopolis (Tel. 41-230) 7 rms ¶ ▦ ⌂ ☎; open March-Oct.

⚓ **Car-ferries:** to and from Alexandroupolis 5 times a week, and daily in summer, taking 2h.30; sea links with Kavalla.

SANI (Macedonia), Tel. 0374

Hotel:
*** *Robinson Club Phocea* (Tel. 31-221) 218 bungalows ¶ ▦ ⌂ ☎ 🚌 ✳ ▣ ≈ ⚲ ♪/9 P night-club; open May-Oct.

△ **Campsite:** *Sani Camping* (Tel. 31-224) 400 sites and 26 bungalows; open May-Sept. ≈

SARONIS (Attica), Tel. 0299

Hotel:
** *Delfinia* (Tel. 52-449) 18 rms ▦ ⌖ ⌂ ☎

SERIFOS [Island] (Cyclades), Tel. 0281

Hotels:
** *Perseus*, at Livadi Paralia (Tel. 51-273) 10 rms ¶ ▦ ⌂ ☎ ▣ open April-Oct.
* *Serifos Beach*, at Livadi Paralia (Tel. 51-209) 33 rms ¶ ▦ ⌂ ☎ ▣ P

⚓ **Car-ferries and boats:** 10 services a week to and from Piraeus, taking 5 to 6h.

SERRES, or Serraï (Macedonia), Tel. 0321

ℹ **Tourist police:** 9, od. Christoforou (Tel. 22-001).

Hotels:
** *Xenia*, od. H. Sophias (Tel. 29-561) 55 rms ¶ ▦ A/c ⌂ ☎ P
* *Galaxy*, 24, od. Merarchias (Tel. 23-289) 49 rms ▦ ⌂ ☎ P
* *Park*, Platia Eleftherias (Tel. 22-133) 64 rms ▦ ⌂ ☎ P

🚍 **Trains and buses:** to and from Athens 2 or 3 times a day, taking 9 or 10h, via Thessaloniki.

Handicrafts: exhibition, 9, od. Vas. Konstantinou (Tel. 24-979)

SIPHNOS [Island] (Cyclades), Tel. 0284

Hotels:
At Apollonia:

** *Apollonia* (Tel. 31–490) 9 rms ▥ ⌂ ☎ **P**

At Artemon:

* *Artemon* (Tel. 31–303) 28 rms ❙❙ ⌂ ☎ **P**; open April-Oct.

At Piatis Yalos:

** *Platis Yalos* (Tel. 31–224) 22 rms ❙❙ ▥ ⌂ ☎ ≈ open June-Sept.

At Kamares:

** *Kamari* (Tel. 31–641) 18 rms ▥ ⌂ ☎ **P**; open May-Sept.

⚓ **Car-ferries:** run very regularly to and from Piraeus, taking 6 to 7h.30 some via Serifos.

SITHONIA (Macedonia), Tel. 0375

△ **Campsite:**
Kalamitsi (Tel. 41–410) 450 sites; open May-Sept. ≈ ⚲

Sitia (Crete): *see Hagios Nikolaos.*

SKALA OROPOS (Attica), Tel. 0295

Hotels:
* *Alcyonis* (Tel. 32–490) 91 rms ❙❙ ▥ ⌂ ☎ ≈ **P**
* *Flisvos* (Tel. 32–480) 60 rms ❙❙ ▥ ⌂ ☎ ≈ ▣ **P** night-club.

⚓ **Car-ferries:** run very frequently to and from Eretria (Euboea).

SKIATHOS [Island] (Sporades), Tel. 0424

Hotels:
**** *Skiathos Palace,* at Koukounaries (Tel. 42–242) 200 rms ❙❙ ▥ A/c ♨ ⌂ ☎ ➡ ⌷ ≈ ⚲ **P** night-club.
*** *Esperides,* at Akladia (Tel. 42–700) 162 rms ❙❙ ▥ A/c ♨ ⌂ ☎ ⌷ ≈ **P** night-club; open April-Oct.
*** *Nostos,* at Tzaneria (Tel. 42–420) 104 rms ❙❙ ▥

A/c ⌂ ☎ ❄ ≈ ⚲ **P**; open May-Oct.
** *Alkyon,* at Ammoudia (Tel. 429–81) 80 rms ❙❙ ▥ ☎ ❄ night-club.
** *Xenia,* at Koukounaries (Tel. 420–41) 32 rms ❙❙ ⌂ ☎ ≈ **P**; open May-Oct.
* *Akti* (Tel. 420–24) 11 rms ▥ ⌂ ☎ ≈ **P**
* *Koukounaries* (Tel. 420–48; Athens Tel. 324-59-63) 18 rms ▥ ⌂ ☎ ≈ **P**; open April-Oct.

△ **Campsites:**
Skiathos Camping, Kolios beach (Tel. 42–668), 35 sites; open May-Sept.

🚗 **Car hire:** *Budget* (Tel. 42–593).

✈ **Air services:** 1 daily flight in summer to and from Athens, taking 35 min; *Olympic Airways,* od. Papadiamanti (Tel. 42–200).

⚓ **Car-ferries and boats:** daily to and from Volos (3h) and Hagios Constantinos.

SKOPELOS [Island] (Sporades), Tel. 0424

Hotels:
** *Amalia* (Tel. 226–88) 50 rms ❙❙ ▥ ♨ ⌂ ☎ ➡
* *Aelos* (Tel. 222–33) 41 rms ⌂ ☎ ➡ ≈ **P**
** *Rigas* (Tel. 22–618) 32 rms ❙❙ ▥ ♨ ⌂ ☎ **P**
** *Xenia* (Tel. 22–232) 4 rms ❙❙ ▥ ⌂ ≈ **P**
* *Avra,* at Loutraki (Tel. 42–341) 11 rms ❙❙ ▥ ⌂ ☎ ≈ **P**
* *Denise* (Tel. 226–78) 22 rms ❙❙ ▥ ♨ ⌂ ☎ **P**

⚓ **Car-ferries and boats:** run regularly to and from Volos (4h.30), Hagios Constantinos, Skiathos, Skiros, Alonissos.

SKYROS [Island] (Sporades), Tel. 0222

Hotel:
- ** *Xenia* (Tel. 91–209) 22 rms ❙❙ ▥ ♨ ▥ ☎ ☂ P; open April–Oct.

✈ **Air services:** 1 flight daily to and from Athens.

⚓ **Car-ferries:** at least 3 times a week to and from Kymi (Euboea), taking 2h.

SOUNION [Cape] (Attica), Tel. 0292

Hotels:
- *** *Belvedere Park* (Tel. 391–02) 90 rms and bungalows ❙❙ ▥ ▥ ☎ ❊ ▥ ♀ P night-club.
- *** *Cape Sounion Beach* (Tel. 39–391) 152 rms and bungalows ❙❙ ▥ A/c ▥ ☎ ❊ ▥ ♀ P; open April–Oct.
- *** *Egeon* (Tel. 392–00) 44 rms ❙❙ ▥ ▥ ☎ ☂ P
- ** *Surf Beach Club* (Tel. 22–363) 266 rms and bungalows ❙❙ ▥ A/c ♨ ▥ ☎ ▥ ♀ P night-club; open April–Oct.
- ** *Triton* (Tel. 391–03) 41 rms ❙❙ ▥ ▥ ☎ ❊ ☂ P
- * *Saron* (Tel. 391–44) 28 rms ❙❙ ▥ ▥ ☎ P

△ **Campsites:**
Sounion camping (Tel. 239–358) 210 sites
Vakcos (Tel. 39–262) 35 sites; open June–Sept.

⚌ **Buses:** run regularly to and from Athens, taking 1h.30 via the Apollo coast and 2h via Markopoulo and Laurion.

SPARTA, or Sparti (Peloponnese), Tel. 0731

ⓘ **Tourist police:** 8, od. Hilonos (Tel. 28–701).

Hotels:
- *** *Xenia* (Tel. 265–24) 33 rms ❙❙

- ** *Lida*, od. Ananiou (Tel. 236–01) 40 rms ▥ ▥ ☎
- ** *Menelaion*, 65, od. C. Paleologou (Tel. 221–61) 48 rms ❙❙ ▥ ▥ P
- * *Apollo*, 14, od. Thermopylon (Tel. 224–91) 44 rms ▥ ▥ ☎ P
- * *Dioscouri*, 96, od. Lykourgou (Tel. 284–84) 33 rms ❙❙ ▥ ▥ ☎ P
- * *Lakonia*, 61, od. C. Paleologou (Tel. 289–51) 33 rms ▥ A/c ▥ ☎ P

⚌ **Buses:** to and from Athens 7 times a day, taking 6h.

SPETSAE [Island] (Saronic Gulf), Tel. 0298

ⓘ **Tourist police:** in summer, Platia Dapias (Tel. 73–100).

Hotels:
- *** *Kastelli* (Tel. 721–61) 72 rms and bungalows ❙❙ ▥ A/c ♨ ▥ ☎ ☂ P
- *** *Poseidonion* (Tel. 722–08) 55 rms ❙❙ ▥ ♨ ▥ ☎ P
- *** *Spetses* (Tel. 726–02) 77 rms ❙❙ ▥ A/c ♨ ▥ ☎ ❊ ☂ P
- ** *Roumanis* (Tel. 722–44) 35 rms ❙❙ ▥ ▥ ☎ ☂ P
- * *Ilios* (Tel. 724–88) 27 rms ❙❙ ▥ A/cl ▥ ☎ ☂ ▣
- * *Myrtoön* (Tel. 72–555) 39 rms ❙❙ ▥ ▥ ☎ ☂ P; open March–Oct.
- * *Star* (Tel. 722–14) 37 rms ▥ ▥ P

⚓ **Car-ferries:** daily to and from Piraeus; in summer, hydroplane services. Regular links with Kosta, on the mainland.

STRATONION (Macedonia), Tel. 0376

△ **Campsite:**
Olympias Camping, by the

Olympia beach (Tel. 51–295)
180 sites; open April-Sept.

SYMI [Island] (Dodecanese),
Tel. 0241

Hotels:
- *** *Aliki* (Tel. 71–665) 15 rms ▥
  A/c ᐠ ☏ ⚓ open April-Oct.
- ** *Nireus* (Tel. 71–386) 6 rms ¶
  ▥ ᐠ ☏ ⚓ P ; open April-Oct.

⚓ **Car-ferries:** or boats at least
twice a week to and from
Piraeus, taking a day; to and
from Rhodes, taking 2h.

SYROS [Island] (Cyclades),
Tel. 0281

Hotels:
- ** *Hermes,* Platia Kanari
  (Tel. 230–11) 28 rms ¶ ▥ ᐠ
  ☏ P
- * *Europe,* 74, od. Proeou
  (Tel. 287–71) 28 rms ▥ ᐠ P
- * *Nissaki,* od. Papadam
  (Tel. 282–00) 42 rms ▥ ᐠ P
- * *Domenica,* at Vari
  (Tel. 612–16/612–89) 22 rms
  ¶ ᐠ ⚓
- * *Olympia* (Tel. 42–212) 40 rms
  ¶ ▥ A/c ᐠ ☏ ⚓ P
- * *Finikas* (Tel. 42–111) 13 rms
  ¶ ᐠ ☏ ⚓ P

🚗 **Car hire:** *Budget,* 12, od. P.
Ralli (Tel. 22–866).

T

THASOS [Island]
(Macedonia), Tel. 0593

ⅰ **Tourist police:** in summer
(Tel. 22–500).

Hotels:
At Limenas:
- ** *Timoleon* (Tel. 22–177) 30 rms
  ¶ ▥ ᐠ ☏ ⚓ P open
  March-Nov.

- ** *Xenia* (Tel. 22–105) 27 rms ¶
  ▥ ᐠ ☏ ⚓ P open April-Oct.
- * *Angelika* (Tel. 223–87) 26 rms
  ▥ ᐠ ☏ ⚓ P
- * *Glyfada* (1.8mls/3km W.;
  Tel. 22–164) 54 rms ¶ ▥ ᐠ
  ☏ P open April-Oct.
- * *Lido* (Tel. 22–929) 18 rms ▥
  ᐠ ☏ ⚓ P

  *At Makryammos
  (1.3mls/2km E):*
- *** *Makriammos Thassou*
  (Tel. 221–01; Athens
  Tel. 216–429) 206 rms and
  bungalows ¶ ᐠ ☏ ⚓ P
  night-club; open April-Oct.

  At Prinos:
- ** *Electra* (Tel. 71–374) 18 rms
  ¶ ▥ ᐠ ☏ P

△ **Campsites:**
Pefkari (Tel. 51–595) 101 sites;
open April-Oct.
Ioannides Camping, at
Rahoni (Tel. 71–377) 200
sites; open May-Oct. ⚓

⚓ **Car-ferries:** run regularly to
and from Keramoti (45 min),
Kavalla (1h.30).

✝ **Special events:** Thasos and
Philippi Festival, from July
15th to the end of August;
information from the GNTO
(at Kavalla, Tel. (051)
27-86-21).

THEBES, or Thive (Central
Greece), Tel. 0262

Hotels:
- ** *Dionyssion Melathron*
  (Tel. 27–855) 30 rms ▥ ᐠ ☏
  P
- * *Meletiou* (Tel. 27–333) 34 rms
  ▥ ᐠ ☏ P

🚌 **Buses:** run very frequently to
and from Athens, taking
1h.30.

THEOLOGOS (Malessina)
(Central Greece), Tel. 0233

Hotels:

*** *Economos Silver Bay*
(Tel. 51–491) 196 rms ¶ A/c
🛗 🛏 ☎ ❄ 🏊 ⚓ ⚲ P night-
club; open April-Oct.

* *Nafsika* (Tel. 51–004) 8 rms ¶
🎽 🛏 ☎ ⚓ P

THERA [Island] or Santorini
(Cyclades), Tel. 0286

Hotels:

*** *Atlantis* (Tel. 22–232) 25 rms
¶ 🎽 🛗 🛏 ☎ P ; open
April-Oct.

** *Arvanitis,* at Akrotiri
(Tel. 31–295) 18 rms 🎽 🛏 ☎
open April-Oct.

* *Kavalari* (Tel. 22–455) 20 rms
🎽 🛏 ☎ open April-Oct.

* *Panorama* (Tel. 22–481) 20
rms ¶ 🎽 🛗 🛏 ☎ P

* *Kamari,* at Kamari
(Tel. 31–243) 55 rms ¶ 🎽 🛗
🛏 ☎ 🏊 ⚲ P ; open April-Oct.

Youth hostel: in Kontochori
(2.2mls/3.5km from Thera;
Tel. 21–267). At Ia, the GNTO
has converted some
traditional houses: 45 beds in
all (Tel. 71–234).

✈ **Air services:** 2 flights a day
link Thera with Athens in
summer, taking 45 min;
Olympic Airways
(Tel. 22–493).

⚓ **Car-ferries and boats:** several
daily services to and from
Piraeus, taking 10 to 12h.
Caique trips (tour of the
island calling in at Therasia
and Ia) ask at the agencies
near the bus station.

THERMOPYLAE (Central
Greece) Tel. 0231

Hotel:

* *Aegli* (Tel. 93–304) 45 rms ¶
🛏 ☎ P ; open June-Oct.

THESSALONIKI, or Salonica
(Macedonia), Tel. 031

ℹ **Tourist police:** 10, od. Egnatia
(Tel. 52–25–89).

🚗 *GNTO:* 34, od. Mitropoleos
(Tel. 27–18–88).
ELPA: 288, od. Vas. Olgas
(Tel. 42–63–19).

Hotels:

**** *Macedonia Palace,* leof.
Megali Alexandrous
(1.3mls/2km from the centre
on the Polyghyros road; Pl. E-
4; Tel. 837–520) 287 rms ¶ 🎽
A/c 🎽 🛏 ☎ ❄ 🏊 🖥 P

*** *Capitol* (Pl. a, B-1), 8, od.
Monastiriou (Tel. 516–221)
194 rms ¶ 🎽 A/c 🎽 🛏 ☎ 🖥
P

*** *Electra Palace* (Pl. p, C-3),
5, Platia Aristotelous
(Tel. 232–221) 131 rms ¶ 🎽
A/c 🎽 🛏 ☎ P

** *Astor,* 20, leof. Tsimitski
(Tel. 527–121) 88 rms ¶ 🎽
🎽 🛏 ☎ P

* *Capsis* (Pl. I, A-1), 28, Platia
Monastiriou (Tel. 521–421)
428 rms ¶ 🎽 A/c 🎽 🛏 ☎ 🏊
P night-club, sauna.

** *City* (Pl. b, C-3), 11, od.
Komninon (Tel. 269–421) 104
rms ¶ A/c 🎽 🎽 🛏 ☎ P

** *Egnatia* (Pl. q, B-2), 11, od.
Leontos Sofou (Tel. 536–321)
142 rms ¶ A/c 🎽 🛏 ☎

** *El Greco* (Pl. o, B-2), 23, od.
Egnatia (Tel. 520–620) 90 rms
¶ 🎽 A/c 🎽 🛏 ☎

** *Metropolitan,* 65, Vas. Olga
(Tel. 82–42–21) 118 rms ¶ 🎽
A/c 🎽 🛏 ☎ P

** *Olympia,* 65, od. Olympia
(Tel. 23–54–21) 111 rms ¶
A/c 🎽 🛏 ☎ P

** *Olympic* (Pl. c, B-2), 25,
Egnatia Odhos (Tel. 522–131)
52 rms 🎽 🎽 🛏 ☎

** *Palace,* 12, od. Tsimitski

(Tel. 270–505) 58 rms ▦ ♨ ⌂ ☎

** *Philippion,* at Asvestochorion (3mls/5km from the centre; Tel. 203–320) 96 rms ⑪ ▦ ♨ ⌂ ☎

** *Queen Olga,* 44, Vassilissis Olga (1.6mls/2.5km from the centre on the Polyghyros road; Pl. E-4; Tel. 824–621) 148 rms ⑪ ▦ A/c ♨ ⌂ ☎ ▣ P

** *Rotunda,* 91, od. Monastiriou (Tel. 517–121) 79 rms ⑪ ▦ A/c ⌂ ☎

** *Victoria,* 13, od. Langada (Tel. 522–421) 68 rms ⑪ A/c ▦ ♨ ⌂ ☎ P

* *A.B.C.* (Pl. t, E-3), 41, Platia Angeloki (Tel. 265–421) 112 rms ⑪ ▦ ♨ ⌂ ☎

* *Amalia* (Pl. u, C-2), 33, od. Ermou (Tel. 268–321) 66 rms ▦ A/c ♨ ⌂ ☎

* *Ariston* (Pl. g, B-1), 5, od. Dikitiriou (Tel. 519–630) 35 rms ▦ ⌂ ☎ P

* *Delta,* 13 via Egnatia (Tel. 51-63-21) 113 rms ⑪ A/c ♨ ⌂ ☎ ▭ P

* *Emborikon* (Pl. i, C-2), 14, od. Syngrou (Tel. 525–560) 39 rms ▦ ⌂ ☎

* *Esperia* (Pl. v. C-2), 58, od. Olympou (Tel. 269–321) 70 rms ⑪ ▦ A/c ♨ ⌂ ☎

* *Park* (Pl. w, C-1), 81, od. Ionos Dragoumi (Tel. 524–121) 56 rms ⑪ ▦ A/c ♨ ⌂ ☎

* *Pella* (Pl. d, C-2), 65, od. Ionos Dragoumi (Tel. 524–221) 79 rms ▦ A/c ♨ ⌂ ☎

* *Thessalikon* (Pl. j, C-2), 60, Egnatia Odhos (Tel. 223–805) 29 rms ▦ ⌂ ☎

* *Vergina,* 10, od. Monastiriou (Tel. 52-74-00) 133 rms ⑪ ▦ ♨ ⌂ ☎ P

Youth hostel: 42, od. Prinkipos Nicolaou (Tel. 22-59-46); *YMCA,* Platia HANTH (Tel. 27-40-00); *YWCA,* 11, od. Hagios Sofias (Tel. 27-61-14).

△ **Campsites:** (on the coast to the S, quite far from the town). *Akti Thermaikou,* on the Hagia Trias beach (15.6mls/25km Tel. (0392) 51–352) 440 sites ⚓ � *Epanomi,* on the Epanomi Beach (18.8mls/30km Tel. (0392) 41–378) 650 sites ⚓ ✗

Restaurants and tavernas:
** *Electra* (Pl. p, C-3), 5, Platia Aristotelous (Tel. 516–121) A/c

** *Kaïron,* 54, leof. Megalou Alexandrou.

** *Kritelas,* 284, leof. Vas. Olga (Tel. 411–289).

** *Olympus Naoussa* (Pl. B-3), 5, leof. Constantinou; an institution; good cooking.

** *Krikelas,* 284, Vas. Olga (Tel. 411–289). Marvellous hors d'oeuvre, kokoretsi and roast lamb.

** *Remvi,* Nea Krini (Tel. 411–233); one of the best restaurants in the town; specialities fish and seafood; garden.

* *Psarotavernes,* 5, od. Votsis; popular tavern.

* *Ragotis,* 8, od. Venizelou (Tel. 277–694).

* *Tottis,* Platia Aristotelous and leof. Constantinou, the terrace is a pleasant place to take a break.

Banks:
Commercial Bank of Greece, 1, od. Tsimiki and od. Kalouri (Tel. 532–221); *National Bank*

of Greece, corner of od. Mitropoleos and od. Dragoumi (Tel. 538–621), 160, od. Egnatia (Tel. 232–937); *Chase Manhattan Bank*, 26, od. Komninon (Tel. 23–62–21).

✉ **Post Office:** Central office (Pl. C-3), 28, leof. Tsimitski; *Telegraph and telephone* (Pl. C-3), 55, od. Vas Heracleiou.

✈ **Airport:** at Mikra 9.7mls (15.5km) on the Polyghyros road (Pl. E-4); numerous daily flights to Athens and Limnos.

Airlines: *Olympic Airways*, 2, od. Komninon (Tel. 26–01–21).

⚓ **Boats:** 1 direct weekly link with Piraeus, taking 7h (from Piraeus, via Chios and Mytilene); 1 weekly service to Skiathos, Skopelos, Limnos, Mytilene, Chios, Samos, Patmos, Leros, Kalymnos, Cos, Rhodes.

🚂 **Trains:** *Station* (Pl. A-1), od. Monastiriou (to Athens, 7h.50; Alexandroupolis 8h.20); booking at the station (Tel. 51–75–10) or 49, od. Egnatia (Tel. 27–54–12).

🚌 **Buses:** *SEK*, 1, od. Venizelou (to Athens); 3, od. Platonos (to Hierissos; to Mt. Athos); 1, od. Enotikon (to Ioannina); 23, od. Antigonidon (to Kastoria); 61, od. Ionos Dragoumi (to Kavalia); 5, od. Odysses (to Pella). International lines to Sofia and Paris.

🚗 **Car hire:** *Avis*, 3, leof. Vas. Constantinou (Tel. 22–71–26) *Autorent*, 7, od. Neas Paralias (Tel. 81–12–69); *Budget*, 15, od. Angelaki (Tel. 22–95–19); at the airport (Tel. 49–14–91);

Hellascars (Europcar), 8, od. Venizelou (Tel. 23–39–27); *Hertz*, 4, od. Venizelou (Tel. 22–49–06).

Shopping: you will find the greatest choice of souvenirs and antiques, etc., within the rectangle formed by Platia Aristotelous, leof. Vasileos Constantinou, leof. Megali Alexandrou and od. Pavlou Mela.

♿ **Handicrafts:** exhibition; 90, Megali Alexandrou (Tel. 26–98–11).

✝ **Special events:** besides the secular and religious festivals celebrated all over Greece, at the Thessaloniki International Fair, in September, there is a festival of cinema and song, and especially of the Dimitria, which goes on into October (theatre, dance, operas, concerts) information from the GNTO or from 27–55–72.

≈ **Beaches:** the nearest are on the Gulf of Thermai (see Vicinity of Thessaloniki, 2).

TILOS [Island] (Dodecanese) Tel. 0241

Hotel:
Livadia (Tel. 53–202) 20 rms; open March-Oct. Mediocre hotel – accom. with local family preferable.

⚓ **Car ferries or boats:** twice a week on the Piraeus – Rhodes route via Patmos, Leros, Kalymnos, Cos and Nisyros, taking 24h from Piraeus.

TINOS [Island] (Cyclades), Tel. 0283

ℹ **Tourist police:** in summer, Platia Eleftherias (Tel. 22–255).

Hotels:

*** *Tinos Beach* (Tel. 226-26) 180 rms and bungalows ¶ A/c ▥ ⌂ ☎ ☒ ≈ ⚲ ⚲/9 P night-club, sauna; open April-Oct.

** *Aeolos Bay* (Tel. 23-339) ¶ ⌂ ☎ P

** *Theoxenia* (Tel. 222-74) 31 rms ¶ ▥ ⌂ ☎ P; open March-Oct.

** *Tinion* (Tel. 222-61) 24 rms ▥ ⌂ ☎ P; open April-Oct.

* *Argo* (Tel. 22-588) 12 rms ¶ ▥ ⌂ ☎ ☒ P; open March-Oct.

* *Asteria* (Tel. 22-132) 48 rms ▥ A/c ⌂ ☎ P; open March-Oct.

* *Delfinia* (Tel. 222-89) 38 rms ¶ ⌂ P

* *Meltemi* (Tel. 228-81) 43 rms ⌂ ☎

* *Oceanis* (Tel. 22-452) 47 rms ¶ ▥ ⌀ ⌂ ☎ P

⚓ **Car-ferries and boats:** several times a day to and from Piraeus, taking 4h.45.

TOLO (Peloponnese), Tel. 0752

Hotels:

** *Dolfin* (Tel. 59-192) 22 rms ¶ ▥ ⌂ ☎ ≈; open March-Oct.

** *Solon* (Tel. 59-204) 28 rms ¶ ▥ ⌂ ☎ ≈; open March-Oct.

** *Sophia* (Tel. 59-567) 52 rms ¶ ▥ ⌀ ⌂ ☎ ≈ P; open March-Nov.

* *Aris* (Tel. 59-231) 30 rms ¶ ▥ ⌀ ⌂ ☎ ≈ P; open March-Oct.

* *Epidavria* (Tel. 59-219) 39 rms ¶ ▥ ⌂ ☎ ≈ P; open March-Oct.

* *Flisvos* (Tel. 59-223) 28 rms ¶ ▥ ⌀ ⌂ ☎ ≈ P; open March-Dec.

* *Minoa* (Tel. 59-207) 44 rms ¶ ▥ ⌂ ☎

* *Possidonion* (Tel. 59-345) 36 rms ¶ ▥ ⌀ ⌂ ☎ P

* *Tolo* (Tel. 59-248) 39 rms ¶ ▥ ⌀ ⌂ ☎ ☒ ⚲ P; open Feb.- Nov.

△ **Campsites:**

Avra (Tel. 59-085) 50 sites; open May-Oct. ≈

Kastraki Camping, Asini Beach (Tel. 59-386) 160 sites; open April-Oct. ≈

Lido (Tel. 59-489) 40 sites; open March-Nov. ≈

Lido II, at Sfakes (Tel. 59-396) 200 sites; open May-Oct. ≈

Stars (Tel. 59-226) 95 sites ≈

Sunset (Tel. 59-566) 120 sites; open April-Oct. ≈

Tolo Beach (Tel. 59-133) 12 sites; open April-Oct. ≈

Xeni, at Kastiraki (Tel. 59-338) 70 sites ≈

TRIKKALA (Thessaly), Tel. 0431

Hotels:

** *Achillion*, 1, Platia Vasileos Georgiou (Tel. 28-291) 73 rms ¶ ▥ ⌂ ☎ P

** *Divani*, 13, od. Dionyssiou (Tel. 27-286) 66 rms ¶ A/c ▥ ⌂ ☎ P

* *Rex*, 1, od. Apollonos (Tel. 28-375) 58 rms ▥ ⌂ P

🚃 **Trains:** 5 times a day to and from Athens, taking 6h;

🚌 **buses:** 7 times a day, taking 5h.15.

TRIPOLIS (Peloponnese), Tel. 071

ℹ **Tourist police:** 7, Platia Georgiou (Tel. 22-30-39).

Hotels:

*** *Menalon*, Platia Areos (Tel. 22-24-50) 36 rms ¶ ▥ ⌀ ⌂ ☎ P

** *Arcadia*, Platia Kolokotroni (Tel. 22-55-51) 45 rms ¶ ▥ ⌀

* *Artemis,* 1,
  od. Dimitrakopoulou
  (Tel. 22-52-21) 69 rms ▥ 🛏
  🛆 ☎

* *Galaxy,* Platia Georgiou B
  (Tel. 22-51-95) 80 rms ▥ 🛏
  🛆 ☎ P

△ **Campsite:**
  Milia Tripoleos, in Milia
  (Tel. 22-24-24) 180 sites.

🚆 **Trains:** 5 times a day to and
  from Athens, via Corinth,
  taking 3h.45; **buses:** 10
  services within 4h.

⚐ **Handicrafts:** 2, od. Hag.
  Constantinou (Tel. 22-66-24).

  TSANGARADA (Thessaly),
  Tel. 0423

  Hotels:
** *Kentavros* (Tel. 49-233) 24
  rms ❙❙ ▥ 🛆 ☎ P
** *Xenia* (Tel. 49-205) 46 rms
  A/c ❙❙ 🛆 ☎ P; open
  April-Sept.
* *San Stefano* (Tel. 49-213) 37
  rms ❙❙ ▥ 🛆 ☎ P

V

VARIBOBI (Attica), Tel. 01

Hotels:
**** *Auberge Tatoï*
  (Tel. 801-45-37) 9 rms ❙❙ ▥
  🛆 ☎ ✳ ⚲ P
** *Varibobi* (Tel. 801-63-05) 29
  rms ❙❙ ▥ 🛏 🛆 ☎ ✳ ⚲ P

VARKIZA (Attica), Tel. 01

Hotels:
*** *Glaros* (Tel. 897-12-17) 48
  rms ❙❙ ▥ 🛏 🛆 ☎ 🌊 P;
  open May-Oct.
** *Varkiza* (Tel. 897-09-27) 30
  rms ❙❙ ▥ 🛏 🛆 ☎ P; open
  April-Oct.

* *Holidays* (Tel. 897-09-15) 34
  rms ❙❙ ▥ 🛏 🛆 ☎ P; open
  April-Oct.

  Restaurant:
** *Pamela's,* by the sea
  (Tel. 895-21-05).

△ **Campsite:**
  Varkisa Beach
  (Tel. 897-00-12) 200 sites ⚓

  VERRIA (Macedonia),
  Tel. 0331

  Hotels:
* *Polytimi,* 35, od. Megalou
  Alexandrou (Tel. 23-007) 32
  rms ▥ A/c 🛆 P
* *Villa Elia,* 16, od. Elias
  (Tel. 26-800) 37 rms ❙❙ ▥ 🛆
  ☎ P

🚆 **Trains:** to and from
  Thessaloniki; **buses:** to and
  from Athens and
  Thessaloniki.

  VOLOS (Volo) (Thessaly),
  Tel. 0421

ℹ **Tourist police:** 87, od.
  Hatziargyri (Tel. 27-094).

  GNTO: od. Riga Ferraerou
  Square (Tel. 23-500).

🚗 *ELPA:* 2, od. Aiolidos
  (Tel. 25-001).

  Hotels:
*** *Pallas,* 14, od. Iassonos
  (Tel. 23-510) 50 rms ▥ 🛏 🛆
  ☎ P
** *Alexandros,* 3, od. Topali
  (Tel. 31-221) 78 rms ❙❙ ▥ A/c
  🛏 🛆 ☎ P
** *Argo,* 135, od. Vasileos
  Constantinou (Dimitriados;
  Tel. 25-372) 21 rms ▥ 🛆 ☎
** *Aegli,* 17, od. Argonafton
  (Tel. 25-691) 40 rms ▥ 🛏 🛆
  ☎ P
** *Nefeli,* 6, od. Koumoundourou
  (Tel. 30-211) 53 rms ▥ A/c 🛆
  ☎ P

** *Park,* 2, od. Deligiorgi
(Tel. 36-511) 119 rms ¶ A/c
🛄 🛏 🏠 ☎ P

** *Xenia,* 2, od. Plastira
(Tel. 24-825) 48 rms ¶ ▥ 🛏
🏠 ☎ ☀ ⚓ P

* *Galaxy,* 3, od. Hagiou
Nicolaou (Tel. 20-750) 54 rms
▥ 🛏 🏠 ☎ P

Restaurants and tavernas:
Several small tavernas along
the sea front, (od Argonafton).

△ **Campsite:**
Pefkafia (Tel. 38-257) 300
sites. ⚓

⚓ **Car-ferries:** daily to Skiathos,
Skopelos, Alonissos; weekly
to Symi and Skyros.

🚆 **Trains:** to and from Athens
(6h), Lamia, Larisa,
Thessaloniki.

🚌 **Buses:** to and from Athens
(5h).

🚗 **Car hire:** *Budget,* 137, od.
Jason (Tel. 32-360).

Handicrafts: 12, od.
Dimitriados and Glavani
Streets (Tel. 237-88).

VOULA (Attica), Tel. 01
Hotels:
*** *Voula Beach,* 103, od.
Alkyonidon (Tel. 895-88-36)
54 rms ¶ A/c ▥ 🏠 ⚓ ☎ P
night-club.

** *Castello Beach,* 8, Kerkyras
and Aktis Streets
(Tel. 895-89-85) 34 rms ¶ ▥
🛏 🏠 ☎ 🖼 P

** *Plaza,* 17, od. Alkyonidon
(Tel. 895-34-80) 18 rms ▥ 🏠
☎

* *Noufara,* 2, od. Metaxa and
od. Vassileos Georgiou
(Tel. 895-34-50) 22 rms ¶ ▥
🏠 ☎ ⚓ P

* *Orion,* 4, od. Metaxa

(Tel. 895-29-50) 26 rms ▥ 🏠
☎ ⚓ P

* *Palmal,* 7, od. Alkyonidon
(Tel. 895-10-20) 34 rms ¶ ▥
🏠 ☎ ⚓ P

△ **Campsite:**
Voula Camping
(Tel. 895-27-12) 101 sites; ⚓;
open March-Nov.

VOULIAGMENI (Attica),
Tel. 01

Hotels:
**** *Astir Palace* (Tel. 896-06-02)
239 rms and bungalows ¶ ▥
A/c 🛏 🏠 ☎ 🚗 ☀ 🖼 ⚓ ⚲ ♨/9
P night-club.

**** *Nafsika Astir Palace*
(Tel. 896-02-11) ¶ ▥ A/c 🛏
🏠 ☎ ☀ 🖼 P

*** *Elektra* (Tel. 896-05-37) April-
Oct.; 16 furnished apartments
▥ 🏠 ☎ ⚲ ♨/9 P

*** *Greek Coast* (Tel. 896-04-01)
55 rms ¶ ▥ 🛏 🏠 ☎ ☀ ⚓ P;
open April-Oct.

*** *Margi House* (Tel. 896-20-61)
95 rms ¶ ▥ A/c 🛏 🏠 ☎ ☀
🖼 ⚓ P night-club.

* *Blue Spell* (Tel. 896-06-76) 38
rms ¶ ▥ A/c 🏠 ☎ ☀ ⚓ ⚲
P; open April-Nov.

** *Hera* (Tel. 896-03-21) 38 rms
¶ ▥ 🛏 🏠 🖼 ⚓ P; open
March-Oct.

** *Strand* (Tel. 896-07-05) 72
rms ¶ ▥ A/c 🏠 ☎ ☀ ⚲ ♨/9
P night-club; open April-Oct.

Restaurants:
** *Blue Spell* (Tel. 804-06-76) P
** *Club House* (Tel. 804-06-42).
** *Moorings,* at the pleasure-
boat port (Tel. 896-13-10).
* *Lambros,* opposite the lake
(Tel. 804-02-50); taverna.
* *Leonidas,* od. Eolou
(Tel. 896-01-10) P
particularly pleasant in the
evenings for dining on the

terrace; the proprietor, named Leonidas, serves taverna cooking of rare quality; beautifully prepared fresh fish will delight you.

VOURVOURAS Tel. 0375

Δ **Campsite:**
Lacara, Koutloumoussi Beach (Tel. 21–215) 200 sites; open May–Sept. ⚓

VYTINA (Peloponnese), Tel. 0795

Hotels:
** *Villa Valos* (Tel. 21–210) 51 rms ⅋ ⃞ ⛉ ⏏ ☎ P
** *Xenia* (Tel. 21–218) 20 rms ⅋ ⃞ ⛉ ⏏ ☎ P
* *Aegli* (Tel. 21–316) 11 rms ⅋ ⃞ ⏏ ☎

XANTHI (Thrace), Tel. 0541
Hotels:
** *Nestos* (Tel. 27–531) 74 rms ⅋ A/c ⛉ ⏏ ☎ P
** *Xenia* (Tel. 24–135) 24 rms ⅋ ⃞ ⛉ ⏏ ☎ P
* *Dimokritas* (Tel. 25–111) 40 rms ⃞ ⛉ ⏏ ☎ P night-club.

XYLOKASTRON (Peloponnese), Tel. 0743

ⓘ **Tourist police:** 1, od. Frantzi (Tel. 22–331).

Hotels:
*** *Arion* (Tel. 22–230) 64 rms ⅋ ⃞ ⏏ ☎ ⚓ P
** *Apollo* (Tel. 22–239) 27 rms ⅋ A/c ⃞ ⏏ ☎ ⚓ P
** *Miramare* (Tel. 223–75) 24 rms ⅋ ⃞ ⏏ ☎ ⚓ P

** *Rallis* (Tel. 22–219) 74 rms ⅋ ⃞ ⏏ ☎ ⚓ P

Z

Zakros (Crete): *see Hagios Nikolaos.*

ZAKINTHOS [Island] or Zante (Ionian Islands), Tel. 0695

ⓘ **Tourist police:** 2, od. Lomvardou (Tel. 22–550).

Hotels:
In town:
** *Strada Marina*, 16, od. Lomvardou (Tel. 22–761) 112 rms ⅋ ⃞ ⏏ ☎ ✳ P
** *Xenia*, 66, od. D. Roma (Tel. 22–232) 39 rms ⅋ ⃞ ⏏ ☎ ⚓ P
* *Phoenix*, 2, Platia Solomou (Tel. 22–419) 38 rms ⃞ ⏏ P

On the Argassion Beach (1.9mls/3km):
** *Chryssi Akti* (Tel. 28–022) 81 rms ⅋ ⃞ ⏏ ☎ ⚓ ९ P
** *Mimosa Beach* (Tel. 22–588) 44 rms and bungalows ⅋ ⃞ ⏏ ☎ ⚓ P; open April–Oct.

On the Lagana Beach (5mls/8km):
** *Galaxy* (Tel. 72–271) 80 rms ⅋ ⃞ ⏏ ☎ ⚓ P
** *Zante Beach* (Tel. 72–230) 252 rms ⅋ ⃞ ⏏ ☎ ⌨ ⚓ ९ P

✈ **Air services:** 4 weekly flights to and from Athens, taking 1h; *Olympic Airways*, 3, od. Vas Georgiou B (Tel. 28–611).

⚓ **Car-ferries:** leave from Loutra Kyllini 3 times a day, taking 2h.

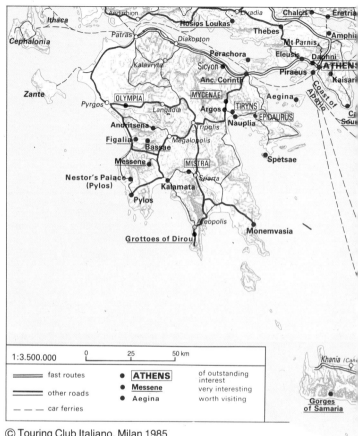

1:3.500.000

| | 0 | 25 | 50 km |

═══ fast routes
═══ other roads
– – – car ferries

● **ATHENS**   of outstanding interest
● **Messene**   very interesting
● Aegina   worth visiting

© Touring Club Italiano, Milan 1985

What to see in Southern Greece

***
Athens
Delos (Island of)
Epidaurus
Herakleion
Knossos
Mistra
Mycenae
Olympia
Phaestos
Rhodes (Islands of)
Tiryns

**
Ancient Corinth
Astypalea (Island of)
Bassae
Cape Sounion
Chalcis
Chios (Island of)
Coast of Apollo
Daphni
Dirou (Grottoes of)
Hosios Loukas
Mallia

**
Figalia
Messene
Mykonos (Island of)
Parnis (Mt)
Patmos (Island of)
Samaria (Gorges of)
Thera (Island of)
Zakros

*
Aegina
Amphia
Andrits
Andros
Argos
Cephal
Cos (Is
Coast o
Eleusis
Eretria
Gortyn